Planning Academic and Research Library Buildings

Panels 22, 23, and 24 from the ambitious mural *The Epic of American Civilization,* painted in striking color by the Mexican artist José Clemente Orozco between 1932 and 1934 in the reserve corridor of Baker Library.

Offering a complex and compelling narrative that covers the history of the Americas from the migration of the Aztecs into central Mexico to the development of our modern industrialized society, the mural is composed of twenty-four individual panels, or "scenes," and covers approximately 3,200 square feet.

One of Orozco's greatest works, *The Epic of American Civilization* must also be counted among the finest examples of mural painting in this country and is one of the greatest treasures of the Dartmouth College collection. (Commissioned by the Trustees of Dartmouth College, Hanover, New Hampshire. Used with permission)

Planning Academic and Research Library Buildings

THIRD EDITION

Philip D. Leighton

David C. Weber

FIRST EDITION BY
Keyes D. Metcalf

All architecture proposes an effect on the human mind, not merely a service to the human frame.

—John Ruskin

American Library Association
Chicago and London   1999

Composition by the dotted i in Stempel Schneidler and Optima using QuarkXpress 4.04

Printed on 50-pound natural offset, a pH-neutral stock, and bound in Roxite B cloth by MacNaughton & Gunn

The paper used in this publication meets the minimum requirements of American National Standard for Information Sciences—Permanence of Paper for Printed Library Materials, ANSI Z39.48-1992. ∞

Library of Congress Cataloging-in-Publication Data

Leighton, Philip D.
    Planning academic and research library buildings /
Philip D. Leighton, David C. Weber. — 3rd ed.
      p.   cm.
    Includes bibliographical references and index.
    ISBN 0-8389-0747-4
    1. Library architecture—United States. 2. Academic libraries—United States. 3. Research libraries—United States. I. Weber, David C., 1924. II. Title.
Z679.5.L45   2000
022'.317—dc21   98-46757

Printed in the United States of America.

04 03 02 01 00   5 4 3 2 1

To E.E.W., J.F.C., and E.G.M.,

> who each in a different way made a major contribution toward the transformation of this volume from a dream to a reality.   —1964

To K.D.M.,

> the librarian par excellence who shared his extraordinary knowledge.   —1985

And to Joan and Natalie,

> who brighten our lives, tolerate our foibles, and give us comfort and strength—as should any good library building. And, with deep affection, to our children in the hope and expectation that they also shall love books and libraries and the fruits to be gained from a lifetime of learning therein.   —2000

Contents

5   General Programming   **107**

11   Master Planning and Siting   389

12   Schematic Considerations   418

13   Design Development   487

14   Construction Documents   568

15 Bidding, Business Concerns, and Construction 599

16 Activation 634

APPENDIXES

Preface

For I owe great gratitude to all those who . . . gathered from all time, each in his department provided stores from which we, like those who draw water from a spring and use it for their own purposes, have gained the means of writing with more eloquence and readiness; and trusting in such authorities we venture to put together a new manual of architecture.

—Marcus Vitruvius Pollio,
On Architecture; Book VII, ca. 25 B.C.

Several challenging facts faced by research organizations, colleges, and universities require a comprehensive volume dealing with the problems involved in the planning and construction of academic library buildings:

1. Planning an academic or research library building is an important and complex undertaking.
2. The building design must be done exceptionally well because it can be altered later only with considerable difficulty and expense.
3. A building is a costly undertaking, and the raising of funds may be very difficult, particularly so for very large buildings.
4. The need for library space confronts every academic institution sooner or later, and often with great frequency.
5. The planning and design process often is the responsibility of persons who have little or no experience in this field.

This book does not attempt to provide answers to all the problems that may arise, but it does try to identify the more important issues and problems, break them down into the component parts, and indicate the factors that ought to be taken into account in arriving at solutions. No building is perfect. Yet the most serious mistakes are likely to be those made when one does not realize that a problem exists. This volume, then, is intended to provide a substitute for much of the understanding gained from firsthand experience.

Every college and university and independent research library will sooner or later need to plan for a library addition, a major renovation, or an entirely new wing or separate building. Whether enrollments are being held steady, are decreasing, or are growing, the library will change because the collections will have a net increase in size, the types and quantity of materials in other than book format will increase, and computer-based technological changes will prompt alterations, if not major changes, in a library building.

Keyes D. Metcalf wrote the first edition of this book in the early 1960s. Sponsored by the Association of Research Libraries and the Association of College and Research Libraries, it was the product of Metcalf's 60 years of experience in planning library space and hundreds of building projects. This experience began in 1905–1908 during the planning of a new building for the Oberlin College Library; the result proved to be one of the best college libraries constructed up to that time. His own work on space planning, at the New York Public Library and then at Harvard, contributed to his education. One exceptional product was the New England Deposit Library, a building designed as a book warehouse or auxiliary facility to be as simple, inexpensive, and functional as possible. A second was the Houghton Library for rare books and manuscripts, with a great deal of highly specialized space, and a third was the Lamont Library for undergraduates.

As Metcalf wrote in the first edition of this book: "Since Harvard had more than 80 special and departmental libraries, I had many occasions during my eighteen years as director to deal with alterations, additions, rehabilitation, and repair. Moreover, because the Lamont Library was well received, invitations to serve as a consultant for building problems elsewhere began to come to me in increasing numbers. Indeed, since my retirement from Harvard in 1955, I have served as the building consultant to more than 250 libraries on six continents and have spent some fifteen months studying library problems in countries other than the United States." It was not realized in 1965 that Metcalf would thereafter serve as a consultant on at least another 250 projects.

Clearly, the Metcalf product was a very specialized volume, a tour de force containing a good deal of his library philosophy. It will rest as a classic, the product of an extraordinary librarian who for over three-quarters of a century worked in and for libraries. Keyes Metcalf's father was a prominent railroad engineer who retired in 1855. No doubt some of the organizational and analytic skills that Keyes later applied to building planning were inherited from this engineer whose work from New England to Minnesota required precise measurement and exceptional planning.

The present authors were mindful in writing the second edition that any revision of Metcalf's work would lose some of the flavor of his creation. Although this text retains all of Metcalf's principles, it is hoped that the many changes, deletions, and additions in this edition will serve the current need of architects, librarians, and others involved in the planning process without obscuring his wise guidance. The authors are grateful to Keyes Metcalf for his trust in putting the continued life of his product in their hands. It is intended for the same audience and to provide the same practical help that made the first volume so universally acclaimed.

Most dimensional statements and plans are presented in both the metric and customary, or imperial, scales. Although dimensional metric conversions have been made in most cases, it should be stressed that they are directly obtained from conversion of the customary foot/inch system. Actual practice in countries using equipment designed and constructed in the metric system will likely result in some variation of these data. In this case, the reader should use the text merely as a guide, and, where accurate measurements are required, individual calculations based on actual conditions should be undertaken.

Any cost estimate in this book should be considered to be for illustrative purposes only. The estimates are at best rough, they are certain to change, and in all cases costs should be obtained locally.

Major additions in this third edition have come in the treatment of the very wide-ranging influence of information technologies and automated services and modern telecommunications. A host of other technical issues have been included. Access for the physically limited is emphasized. More examples of library concerns and solutions are referenced to libraries throughout North America and in a variety of other countries. Value engineering is developed as a concept for cost and project benefit. The treatment of preservation-based environment is revised and expanded.

However, computers and their technological siblings have most dramatically affected libraries, and especially so during the 1990s. The evidence is everywhere—card catalogs gone, teaching styles sharply altered, full books and articles in digital form, multimedia products with sound and motion pictures, abundant hookups for PCs and laptops, and the World Wide Web providing us hypertext links to open a universe of instant information. As we embark on a discussion of planning academic and research library buildings, we offer you a provocative quotation from Professor Richard A. Lanham of UCLA, who speaks with a somewhat deconstructivist view of this systemic change:

> What of the whole architectural plan of a university, based as it is on *substance,* the book, the embodied teacher, the chairs we rent out to our students? And what of the only center the multiversity has left, the library? The library world feels *depaysé* today, and rightly so. Both the physical entities, the buildings and the books they contain, can no longer form the basis for planning. And the curatorial function has metamorphosed, if I may borrow a phrase from an archivist acquaintance, "from curatorial to interpretive." Librarians of electronic information find their job now a radically rhetorical one—they must consciously construct human attention-structures rather than assemble a collection of books according to commonly accepted rules. They have, perhaps unwillingly, found themselves transported from the ancillary margin of the human sciences to their center. If this be so—and I don't see how it can be doubted—how should we train librarians, much less plan the building where they will work?[1]

---

[1]Richard A. Lanham, "Electronic Texts and University Structures," in *Scholars and Research Libraries in the 21st Century,* ACLS Occasional Paper, No. 14 (New York: American Council of Learned Societies, 1990), pp. 41–42.

Acknowledgments

Keyes D. Metcalf deserves the gratitude of all concerned with the planning of research and academic library buildings, as also with many of their administrative issues. He was a giant in the field for many decades, and the reflection and echoes of his professional contributions continue to benefit us worldwide.

As an advisory committee gave value-added to the first edition, and as a different and equally talented advisory committee critiqued and contributed very significantly to the preparation of the second edition, so this third edition much revised has benefited materially and widely from the comments, critiques, and contributions of ideas and experience from members of various professional disciplines from several countries. Also, if we were to list the libraries from Asia to Europe that have provided new perspectives and solutions, many dozen additional institutions and their officers would deserve our gratitude.

Appreciation is also expressed to authors and publishers who gave permission to include statements or quotations in this volume. Gratitude is expressed to librarians and to libraries approving the use of excerpts from building programs or planning documents, material used as illustrations, and texts of celebratory or dedication programs. Because passages from the first and second editions have been retained, we underscore our appreciation to authors and publishers who gave these permissions.

Despite the many changes and additions in this edition, it rests on the original to such an extent that we again thank the Council on Library Resources for financial support and appreciate the sponsorship of the Association of Research Libraries and the Association of College and Research Libraries, a division of the American Library Association. Contributions to the original publication by James Ford Clapp, Jr., and Edwin E. Williams were exceptional. For this edition, we express our gratitude to Carolyn Crabtree for her skillful copy editing. We also acknowledge the editorial and publishing guidance of Mary Huchting, Dianne Rooney, and Connie Richardson, which has made the latter stages of this publication a special pleasure for the authors.

Special help with respect to appendix D was provided by William P. Lull. Appendix C comes from the American Library Association, LAMA. Exceptional personal service was given by officers of the following libraries: California State University, Bakersfield; Columbia University; Princeton

University; Stanford University; University of British Columbia; University of California, Los Angeles; University of North Carolina, Charlotte; University of Michigan; University of Toronto; U.S. Library of Congress; and the U.S. National Archives and Records Service. Further, the authors have visited, called upon, or consulted for dozens of libraries and archives in the United States and Canada as well as some in Europe and Asia, to each of which we are deeply grateful for help and pleased if in some small way we could be of service to them. May this volume be of service to libraries and archives worldwide, as we have benefited from the work of so many.

Permissions to Quote or Illustrate

The following permissions are gratefully acknowledged, for their materials assist substantially in describing, explaining, and illustrating the building planning process and the results:

American Association for State and Local History
American Council of Learned Societies
The American Institute of Architects
Archetype, Architects
Architectura, Inc.
Architectural Forum
Asbury Theological Seminary Library
Association of College and Research Libraries
Association of Governing Boards of Universities and Colleges
The Association of Research Libraries
Bowdoin College Library
Brigham Young University Libraries
Butler University
California State University, Bakersfield, Library
California State University, Sacramento, Library
California State University, San Jose, Library
David G. Cogan
Colby College
Columbia University Libraries
Cornell University Library
Dartmouth College
Davis Brody Bond, LLP
Delaware Public Archives
Educational Facilities Laboratories
Ekstrom & Associates, Architects
Ralph E. Ellsworth
Fields & Devereaux, Architects
Fordham University Library
Genentech Corp., Library
Gerald R. Ford Presidential Library
Godfrey Memorial Library, in memory of Mr. A. Fremont Rider
Harvard University Library
Harvard University Press
Helmuth Obata & Kassabaum, Architects
Humanité Services Planning
Ingraham Planning Associates, Inc.
Interior Design

Professor David Kaser
Lake Forest College Donnelley Library
Louisiana State University Library
William P. Lull, Garrison/Lull
MBT Architecture
Stephen A. McCarthy
McLellan & Copenhagen, Inc.
Phyllis Martin-Vegue, Simon Martin-Vegue Winkelstein & Morris
Massachusetts Institute of Technology Press
Microcard Editions Books
Mission College, Santa Clara, California
Moeckel Carbonell Associates, Inc.
Mohawk Midland Mfg.
National Center for Higher Education Management Systems
New York Public Library
Gloria Novak
Planning for Higher Education, Society for College and University Planning
Princeton Theological Seminary Library
Princeton University Library
Process Four Design, Ltd.
Pruett Press
Reed College
Rice University
Roanoke College Library
Scarecrow Press
Shepley Bulfinch Richardson and Abbott
Simon Fraser University
Society for College and University Planning
Society of the Cincinnati
Standing Conference of National and University Libraries (SCONUL)
Stanford University Facilities and Services
Stanford University Libraries
Thomas Miller & Partners
Tilburg University
Tufts University Library
U.S. Library of Congress
U.S. National Archives and Records Service
U.S. National Library of Medicine
University of British Columbia
University of California
University of California, Irvine
University of California, Los Angeles
University of California Northern Regional Library Facility
University of California, San Diego
University of California, Santa Cruz, Library
University of Central Florida Libraries
University of Chicago Libraries
University of Chicago Press
University of Delaware Libraries
University of Illinois Graduate School of Library Science
University of Illinois Library
University of Maryland, Baltimore County
University of Michigan Media Union

University of North Carolina, Chapel Hill, Library
University of North Carolina, Charlotte, Library
University of Southern California Libraries
University of Texas, Austin, Libraries
University of Toronto Library
University of Toronto Press
University of Wisconsin, Milwaukee, Library
Vanderbilt University Library
Washington and Lee University Library
Washington University Library
Western Washington University
Zimmer Gunsul Frasca Partnership, Architects

Trademarks

We make note of the fact that some names used in the text are registered trademarks, each owned by a company or organization. The authors and publisher are referring to these trademarks with no intent to infringe, but to provide information and be entirely beneficial to the trademark owners. Any trademark name mentioned but not here listed is purely the authors' unintentional oversight. The trademarks are the following:

Ariel	Celotex	Compo
Dempster Dumpster	Ellison	Fadex Firecycle
FE-36	Gemtrac	Gortex
Halon	I-Beam joinery	Kenway Mini-Load
Lally	Lexan	Marvelseal
Masonite	Nixalite	Plexiglas
Q-deck	Saflex	Seismoguard
Store-Mor	Suprema	Telautograph
Teletype	Thermopane	Transite
Twindow	Tygon	U-Matic
Verd-a-ray Fadex	Vikane	Visqueen
Von Duprin	Walkerduct	Watt Mizer

Introduction

This is not the Yale library. That is inside.

> —Andrew Keogh, Yale Librarian,
> playfully suggesting this as a motto
> above the main portal, stated before the
> opening of the Sterling Memorial Library

The client asks for areas, the architect must give him spaces.

> —Louis Kahn

Each library building is unique, just as is each academic and each research institution. A library building for a college or university should reflect the needs of scholarship, the teaching program, the relative emphasis on different subjects, and the special character and style of the institution. Furthermore, the building reflects the individual philosophy and practice of library service at the time that the building is programmed and designed. It is conditioned by its particular site and neighboring buildings. Finally, each library reflects some of the architectural concepts and construction practices of its particular design team and era. These differences serve to fashion the interesting variety of physical settings in which scholarship and higher education are served.

An addition to an older structure has its own kind of constraints, as does a major renovation project. Every entirely new building offers appreciably greater freedom of design. To help guide the best appropriate design for each particular library, this book provides general principles because local circumstances differ and the attitudes in architecture and librarianship as well as academic administration will change over the years to come. It also provides a variety of detailed information to help in applying the principles. Selected library examples are used to illustrate points and clarify solutions.

What specifically does this volume try to achieve? In 16 chapters it presents the planning, programming, design, construction, and occupation processes from beginning to end. These are arranged in the general chronological order in which most projects proceed, though there will be some variations from institution to institution, and several phases may overlap and a few may in special cases be omitted. The several appendixes contain important planning information gathered to illustrate or explain.

For whom is this book intended? This book is designed for practitioners in the field. It is intended to help novices in planning library buildings, whether they be librarians, planners, architects, consultants, or academic administrators. At the same time, the book is not intended as a primer, and it makes the assumption that those undertaking a major remodeling project, an addition, or a new separate facility have some understanding of the processes of analyzing an institution's mission and objectives, can determine the nature of space that should be provided, will be familiar with the appropriate local channels for obtaining academic and business support for the project, and have a rudimentary understanding of architecture, interior designing, construction, and finance. To the extent that the reader seeks some detailed background in these aspects of a building project, the Bibliography may provide some assistance. The Glossary included in this volume is designed to clarify terminology used in this book where uncertainty of usage in the United States or abroad may exist and where architects, librarians, and others may not know some terms common to others.

This volume is addressed to at least six different groups: presidents, governing boards, and administrative officers; library building planning committees; librarians and their staffs; library schools, library school students, and other librarians interested in administration; the library building planning team; and architects, engineers, and consultants. Each group is interested primarily in different aspects of planning library buildings, although the objectives of all should be in harmony. Each group wants a good-looking, functional library that will attract intended users, will suitably house and safeguard the collections, will not cost too much to erect or for the library staff to operate, and will at the same time be economical of annual plant operating maintenance costs. Each group will have particular interests in different factors, and a better building should result if each group has some understanding of the interests and concerns of the other groups.

In a large project, well over a hundred individuals may play a significant role in decisions or approvals at one or another stage. Often few, if any, will have previously dealt with a library building project. Thus, it is hoped that this volume is a practical guide. Clearly, not everyone will need to be familiar with everything in a volume of this scope; therefore, it will be used more as a reference work or a handbook than a volume to be read from cover to cover.

Because financial conditions are so extremely important to educational institutions and to independent research libraries, an overall goal of this volume is to assist those concerned with short-term and long-term costs of libraries in capital construction as well as ongoing operating expenses. This book attempts to show how a maximum of utility in library buildings can be achieved with the funds available, while at the same time assuring attractiveness and considerable flexibility for the years to come. Academic buildings are generally intended to last for a great many years. For a major building, a useful life of 50 years may be so short as to be a great disappointment to an institution; utility over 100 or more years is feasible and will be more common in the future. On the other hand, a warehouse or auxiliary facility may have a fairly short life span. Those involved in a project have the problem of how best to arrange the space and how best to use available funds. Is a handsome library building needed? Is the layout to emphasize the collections or reading spaces? Might the building later be converted to some other use? Will an addition be required within the next half-century? Is the library to be an educational symbol for the institution? These and many other questions with financial implications must be answered, at least tacitly.

What are the deliberate limits of the book? Persons responsible for building projects will have to rely heavily on standards, guides, and documents issued by the system headquarters of a college or university and by professional associations and governmental agencies with authority over various parts of the project, as well as on publications from the fields of architecture, interior design, engineering, and academic finance, and by other professionals who play some role in the total effort. These guides and documents may be brought in by administrative officers at one or another stage in the process. Some will be binding and others will be advisory. Again, each institution is unique and each library building project will be unique, and so the total array of documents pertinent to a particular project will need to be assembled. This is certainly the case where local, state, or federal governments bear major administrative and financial responsibility. Academic institutions in foreign countries will, of course, apply the local standards, guides, and planning documents.

Although this volume is concerned with the planning of academic libraries, there are many similarities with the planning of research library buildings that are not part of academic institutions, such as those of historical societies, museums, county law libraries, governmental or special archives, commercial research and development firms, and state and national libraries that support professional studies. The principles of design for such libraries are similar as long as the planner has clear recognition of the particular characteristics and goals of that individual organization, the requirements of its clientele, the standards and expectations of management in designing for that particular type of library, and the specific accommodations appropriate for the mix of book and nonbook materials and online informational resources that are required for such a library.

Several points at which this volume may be useful for other types of libraries may be noted:

1. Much library planning involves an understanding of the special nature of an individual institution—its organization, objectives, and dynamics as well as the community it serves. Those responsible for planning any library building must realize that this is a matter of first importance. So all libraries face similar basic planning issues and must ask the same fundamental questions in determining the direction in which to take a library.

2. Any building to be reasonably successful must have an architect to prepare the construction plans and specifications. The judgments involved in the selection of the architect are similar in whatever type of library is to be designed.

3. All libraries face financial problems involved in building planning. These may differ as much from one academic library to another as from an academic library building to some other type. The concerns are very similar regardless of the type of library.

4. The preparation of a program statement for a library building is generally, if not always, the most important single contribution by the

institution's representatives. The accommodations and relationships for book storage, seating, furniture and specialized equipment, and aesthetics must be dealt with in any type of library. The general principles are the same, although details will, of course, differ.

5. Many of the physical considerations involving module size, structure, environmental control, durability, rearrangements and remodeling, and aspects of activation will have common applications in a vast majority of libraries.

The Inexorable Constant: Change in Academic and Scholarly Libraries

One condition of overriding importance in the planning of academic library buildings deserves emphasis. Libraries have particular pressures for continuing growth and change. The constant publication of new works and the major application of information technology to library work and services are paramount. Library buildings, therefore, must be able to accommodate change more readily than other types of academic buildings. Even assuming no growth in student enrollment, the library building is the one facility that may need expansion, primarily to accommodate growth in the book and other collections. This is particularly true for a research institution.

Although the growth of physical collections to support teaching and research is documented over many years, the most striking change in the character of the library over the past few decades has been the result of computer systems, the Internet, the World Wide Web (WWW), the personal computer, the laptop computer, e-mail, CD-ROM databases, OPACs, multimedia—terms that immediately bring to mind the quite phenomenal growth and presence on college and university campuses of the technology supporting the Information Age. The resulting impact on library services, on management of library collections, on access to online data, and, in fact, on every single aspect of the library has been equally dramatic. The 1960s saw the beginnings; the 1990s are experiencing this tidal wave in full force, and the tapering off of this sweeping change is nowhere yet in sight. These developments influence the library building in tremendous fashion, in major and minor ways, nationally and globally, as can be seen in a reading of this volume.

The other major dimension is the collections of books, journals, documents, manuscripts, and other scholarly materials. If the library planning team can accurately forecast rates of growth for a 20-year period, and if the corresponding building plan can be financed, then it should be 15 years before plans for further expansion may need to be undertaken. If a library could be planned for 30 years, then an institution may have 20 or even 25 years before it needs to again consider library expansion. This constant growth has continued for many decades. Nevertheless, in some cases, techniques are now available for ameliorating this inexorable demand for new library space on campus, and these will be dealt with in Chapters 1, 2, and 10.

Academic library collections have tended for decades to grow at the rate of 4 to 5 percent a year until they become what may be called "mature." This growth, which means doubling the collection size in perhaps 16 or 17 years, has been true in this country for at least two centuries. In due course, libraries become increasingly "mature," and the growth rate slackens to a rate of 2 to 3 percent a year—doubling in 25 to 40 years instead of half that time. This slackening in the growth rate generally does not occur until the library is so large that even 2 percent is a serious increment. For example, at Harvard, 2 percent now amounts to 200,000 or more volumes a year, requiring in traditional shelving some 14,000 square feet (about 1,300 square meters) of floor space for additions to the book collection alone. Such growth must slow on a percentage basis, though perhaps not in the number of volumes added per year.

New technology, such as microreproduction and electronic transference of information, has so far seemed to have little effect on growth rates of library collections, although it has increased total resources. The rates of collection space growth will necessarily have to slow down in the years ahead for obvious fiscal reasons. The slowing process will be conditioned by development of different interinstitutional dependencies, auxiliary facilities, optical disk technology with electronic networks, and the various services that can be provided by multi-institutional programs, federal libraries, or consortia. Even with the above forces at play, libraries should expect space demands for collections to increase so that a new building should be planned, wherever possible, to house further growth.

However, the effects of the Information Age and the continuing growth of book collections needed for higher education are not the only current constants. There also is bound to be considerable change in architectural and construction practice. One need only look back 20 to 50 years to see the contrasts in buildings designed and constructed by different generations. Just as there are today certain conditions of aesthetic taste, financing, construction techniques, sociological expectations, and management practices, so it is predictable that in another one or two decades many of these will again change. Academic institutions are very strongly affected by shifts in national and world economics and by birthrates. They are affected to some extent by governmental policies, for example, in accommodating the needs of physically limited or disabled persons. The ability of both publicly and privately supported institutions to obtain major construction funds varies from decade to decade.

It is then necessary to establish general planning principles and practices that have long-term applicability, although the specific examples provided in this volume will change with the passage of time. One of the great dangers in planning library buildings is that, in searching for planning formulas and rules, the planning team may make the mistake of adopting blindly what has been used by others. This tendency, perhaps, is the reason why, all too often, one may find a college library equipped with tables whose dimensions are entirely suitable for public or school libraries but which do not provide sufficient reading surface so that an undergraduate can use materials effectively, and thus all seats at a table may never be filled. Similar problems arise in other areas of planning. This volume tries to bring out points of this kind in the hope that they may help people plan academic and research library buildings that will be effective, efficient, and flexible for educational and scholarly purposes for many decades to come.

Keyes D. Metcalf wrote in the introduction to the first edition of this book:

> The writer is a librarian, not an architect or an engineer, and it is only fair to admit that he was attracted to this phase of library work not because of any special interest or talent in architecture or engineering, but because he was looking for ways to stretch the library dollar so that more of it would be left over and

made available for book acquisition and service. He will not attempt to tell the architect and engineer about their professions, but will try to explain to them the architectural and engineering features that help to make a building a functional library. . . .

The author has studied library building problems for many different types of libraries in many countries, in the belief that he would learn about possible solutions and would be enabled to broaden his background and outlook and obtain a better perspective. As a result, he hopes that this volume will be useful throughout the world. It is written from the American point of view, but it has tried to avoid a dogmatism that would limit its usefulness. No two libraries are alike, but they have much in common whatever their type, clientele, and nationality.

Library Requirements and the Planning Process

For planning of any sort, our knowledge must go beyond the state of affairs that actually prevails. To plan, we must know what has gone on in the past and feel what is coming in the future.
—Sigfried Giedion, *Space, Time and Architecture*

The emphasis in this text is on the libraries that support higher education and scholarship. Thus, this book covers planning library buildings for all sizes and locations of colleges and universities. The process, concepts, and concerns are also covered for libraries of community colleges, technical (or polytechnic) schools, and specialized professional schools or institutes in such fields as art or music or psychiatry. Independent research libraries are also covered because they have collections and services that are very similar to if not identical with elements of a large university library. However, the philosophy of purpose and function of the university library is given some emphasis to provide a theoretical basis on which any academic and research library can be planned. Furthermore, this book assumes the reality of library planning in North America in the 1990s, with attention to current trends and what seem to be well-considered forecasts.

Higher education includes the provision of basic and advanced training in a wide variety of disciplines, the provision of new knowledge and social and aesthetic criticism, the sorting of human talent into useful career paths, and the preparation of unformed minds for the changes and the challenges of a lifetime. Research, on the other hand, is the process of using the resources of a laboratory or library to piece together new understanding and knowledge, frequently resulting in a publication that is added to the corpus of information available to others.

The activities of higher education divide into academic programs at the undergraduate, graduate, and professional levels designed to convey the principles, practices, methodology, content, and evolution of information about nature, society, and human beings. The programs are intended to teach the ability of clear expression, the basis of scientific method and discipline, an understanding of intellectual processes and values, and critical thinking. They are designed to yield a capacity for judgment, discrimination, interpretation, and synthesis, a tolerance for and understanding of new ideas and concepts, and intellectual honesty. The academic institution is deeply concerned with the advancement and promulgation of knowledge—which amounts to the support of research.

The library is much more than a book repository. It provides study places in an environment conducive to serious thought and learning. It is a social instrument, encouraging the student co-hort to use this tool of education both individually and with friends or classmates. It is symbolic of the process of higher education in this last stage of formal education. And the form of an academic library can today go beyond its traditional physical concept, for libraries involve television, audio resources, motion picture film, and a great range of informational technologies utilizing computers and advanced telecommunications. Yet, even beyond that, the library building is often now conceived of as a facility supporting an increased or broadened role in instruction and learning, with classrooms, meeting rooms, auditoria, and computer labs. As will be evident in Section 11.5 describing the George Mason University Johnson Learning Center and the University of Michigan Media Union, there are today intriguing collegiate examples of the merger of libraries with related learning circumstances—what might be called a meta-library, a library building going well beyond the traditional in concept and educational function.

A library plays a key role in these processes in community colleges, liberal arts colleges, technical colleges, universities, and other research organizations. The library is a major academic resource complementing and supplementing lectures, laboratories, and the critiques and counseling of the faculty.

1.1
Purposes of the Library Building

The library building serves the following 10 purposes in furtherance of these academic objectives:

Protecting books and collections in other formats from the elements, poor environment, and mishandling

Housing books and other materials in a variety of accommodations for ease of access

Housing catalogs and related bibliographic tools, including their electronic equivalents, which enable the reader to find relevant materials in the local collections and supplementary material and information in other institutions

Accommodating study, research, and writing activities of students, faculty, and visiting scholars

Housing staff who select, acquire, organize, care for, and service the collections, and who aid readers in their informational needs

Quartering ancillary functions, such as photocopy services, bibliographic instruction, audiovisual materials preparation, computer support facilities, and so on

Housing library administrative and business offices

Providing space for publicizing resources or services through exhibits, lectures, publications, and so on

Memorializing an individual (rarely more than one) and providing symbolism of the institution's academic life in pursuit of scholarly achievement

Constituting an integrated workshop for use of publications, manuscripts, archives, and other library materials with a physical presence that symbolizes the intellectual richness and excitement of the life of the mind

Other functions may be added in particular institutions. For example, a major media center may include a television studio, audiovisual equipment management, or language-laboratory facilities. Or a learning assistance center may be established to aid students in their reading comprehension or speed, writing skills, or study habits. Quarters for a historical society may be provided as an adjunct to an archive. Occasionally a student lounge or snack service, or the offices of an academic or administrative unit other than the library, is provided within the library building. And, occasionally, there is a library school within the library complex.

Not all the functions need to be provided within a centralized library building. In terms of functional operation, it is possible to house many of these functions in separate buildings, though to do so may be very awkward and more costly to operate. For example, the office of the head librarian could be in an adjacent building, as it is in a few institutions. The technical services of acquiring and cataloging materials can also be accommodated separately with some awkward communication, operational, and management linkages. The prospect of dispersion requires reviewing each of the individual functions with consideration given to the relative importance of placing each function within the particular site.

Beyond the above obvious purposes, a less tangible function is expressed by many academic institutions in these times with heavy emphasis on computers and other informational technologies. These institutions stress the importance of

"library as place"—where students seek out intellectual interaction, informational exchange, and socializing in an academic environment, and even find the library a refuge from a world dominated by slick entertainment, the media sound bite, and pervasive commercial values. Amidst these omnipresent conditions, the halls of academe offer a respite while the mental and social skills of young people mature into those of the leaders of tomorrow.

So it is that higher education is increasingly understood as a social activity, and the library provides the prime studious home with spaces specifically designed for such functions as: bibliographic instruction classes, learning assistance centers, computer labs, information-handling labs (some workstations with 4–5 student seats each), language labs, reading labs, writing labs, media centers, multimedia rooms, study centers for the visually limited, video and motion picture presentations, Web-site development, teleconferencing, academic text service, conference quarters, and a variety of group-study rooms. Its users want an inviting learning environment and thrive in a library building that successfully meets the needs of all its users.

What is successful architecture? What is beauty? What is good design? What is great architecture? The answers are in the eyes and mind of each individual. They differ depending on one's background, sophistication, understanding of historical roots, and sensitivity to form, space, texture, color, and scale. Architecture has been described by Sigfried Giedion as "the hope of escaping from transitory work and achieving a timeless rightness."

Only architecture that is effective internally and externally can be considered superior. It must meet local needs. It commonly will use local idioms and indigenous materials. It usually is an expression of the social and cultural conditions of the period and locale. It must function well. It should be handsome at least, or have authenticity and grace.

Successful architecture is a composition of selected materials, given a shape and mass appropriate for its function, and carefully set in its surroundings as a compatible neighbor. Its form provides interest and life while ornamentation often adds embellishment. The architecture of the building is the molding of shape, lines, styles, and shadows, encompassing the requisite engineering fabric so that the building is structurally safe and operationally sound. The building should work with existing landforms and characteristics. Architectural unity is achieved by honest form, not often by re-creating former styles. The resulting physical environment is known to be a major influence on people's lives.

First impressions often govern the public image of great buildings. The facade makes a statement and its image can be best remembered. To an extent, the interior function is taken for granted, though the interior must meet as rigorous a test for success in operational terms as the exterior does in terms of its physical presence. An academic or research library, as much as any building, should express human dignity and assert the centrality of access to information, including books that record human thoughts, successes, failures, theorems, and dreams.

> The New York Public Library is not . . . one great confusion of ornamental episodes. Any one who looks even hurriedly at the New York Public Library can hardly fail to be aware of an order in the disposition of its parts. A central pavilion pierced with three deep arches anchors the building to the fine terrace upon which it stands; from this pavilion two peristyles march equal distances right and left and end in identical little temples; and the blithe ornament dances across the marble walls in rhythmical ecstasies. The intention of the architect was clearly so to relate all of these that taken together they would present a unity; and if we are persuaded of that unity, finding it complete and without adventitious parts or discordances, it may happen that we will find in such unity a mode of beauty.[1]

Opinions can, of course, change (see fig. 1.1). Past centuries have produced a rich heritage of city and campus planning, architecture, and inte-

rior design. Every well-read individual can refer to dozens of outstanding architectural creations. The profession of architecture is long-standing and rich in tradition.

Local tastes and the circumstances in different parts of the world lead to unique solutions. Design idioms and interior decor preferences vary from decade to decade. Although there are multiple appropriate solutions for a particular locale and institution, the good ones combine functional excellence with a sense of propriety and beauty. Furthermore, although the needs of institutions shift over time, good buildings can serve for many decades. Even with newer and larger library buildings at Oxford, Cambridge, and Harvard, buildings of previous centuries are still in use and are of historical interest and significant emotional value. The different approaches to design in, for instance, Italy, Sweden, Australia, Japan, or Scotland all produce distinctive architecture—the best examples of each having considerable variety and, at the same time, basic architectural integrity.

Still, in any decade, striking similarities appear among the best academic library buildings from one part of the world to another. The form of the library building is dependent to a significant degree on current national or regional principles of functional requirements, standards of taste, and the economics of building materials and the construction industry.

1.2
Academic Objectives and the Library

The library is an integral part of the academic (or research) institution whose mission and goals

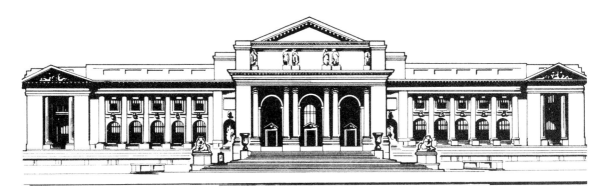

FIGURE 1.1   New York Public Library, Center for the Humanities.

constitute the framework within which the library plans and functions. Some institutions have carefully formulated goals and objectives; many lack a clear and current set. Whatever the local circumstance, the academic goals of the institution should be determined and used as the basis for setting the library mission, goals, and objectives that shape the operations.

The varying nature of academic programs as well as the changing views of academic imperatives, both influenced by new and emerging technologies, contribute to the complexity of sound library planning. In this century, major shifts have occurred in educational philosophy and goals. German universities were the first to emphasize research as a prime mission of the university, a development that led to the founding of Johns Hopkins University, with striking consequences for the future of American universities. Also, in the last third of the nineteenth century, the 1862 Morrill Act created a powerful partnership of American government and higher education in support of agricultural and technological development. The strong development of community or junior colleges as preparatory to upper-division collegiate programs, as well as providing terminal vocational studies, flourished only after the mid-twentieth century. There was the rude awakening in 1957 when Sputnik brought sharp increases in scientific and technological education. The enrollment boom of the 1950s and 1960s in the United States, followed by the temporary decline in the latter quarter of the century, provides its own influences. And, today, libraries and universities grapple with the striking consequences of computers and other technologies on educational and research endeavors.

With occasionally profound consequences, a continuing reexamination and change is taking place in many disciplines within the university. Knowledge in some fields is developing more rapidly than ever before. The means of creating, storing, transmitting, and accessing the record of that knowledge is dramatically changing. As technical, economic, and sociological conditions shape governmental policy, elicit foundation support, and induce faculty to conduct research programs in problem areas, so the need for library collections and services will grow correspondingly while becoming increasingly complex because of the explosion of information resources and computer interconnections. Although the emphasis of change will vary from time to time, many of the

factors of growth and of new teaching or research endeavors need to be reflected in the library program and in the physical accommodation.

Consider the influence of academic policies on the library. A practice at Bard College, Sarah Lawrence College, Washington and Lee University, and the University of Denver has been to require faculty office hours scheduled in the library. Pronounced examples of academic philosophy affecting the library are found at St. John's College, the University of Chicago, Stephens College in Missouri, Florida Atlantic University, Oral Roberts University, and the Open University in Great Britain, though similarly striking effects on the library building can be found in a large proportion of community colleges, many state universities, and some of the finest privately supported colleges, such as Swarthmore, Bryn Mawr, Earlham, Occidental, and Reed (figs. 1.2 and 1.3).

Changing attitudes toward smoking, ergonomics, access for the disabled, the intrusion of laptop computers, electronic networks, the effect of budget reductions, and the use of umbrellas, roller blades, and bicycles all have some effect on library design. In a few libraries pillows now replace some library chairs. Headphones for wireless reception are in use. The clicking of computers is heard. And the concept of a virtual library is discussed. Around the corner, in every generation, other changes will follow.

The significance of a shift in institutional or governmental policy can be seen in changes of just the past decade or two. During the 1980s and 1990s, American universities were under pressure to find ways to do business at less expense. The computer was seen as the means to that end. Libraries were asked to embark upon automation projects. A movement to combine the library administratively with the networking and computer operations of the institution was not uncommon. Support for the creation of systems to use the computer for bibliographic access, conservation (through scanning of collections), and networking contributed to the speed of change.

Shifts in federal support, the popularity of subjects, enrollment, educational philosophy, advancing technology, and the particular academic goals emphasized by the institution's president and academic deans create moving targets at which a library must aim. However the institution is defined, and to whatever extent its special purposes are emphasized, the library must reflect the nature of the institution it serves while striv-

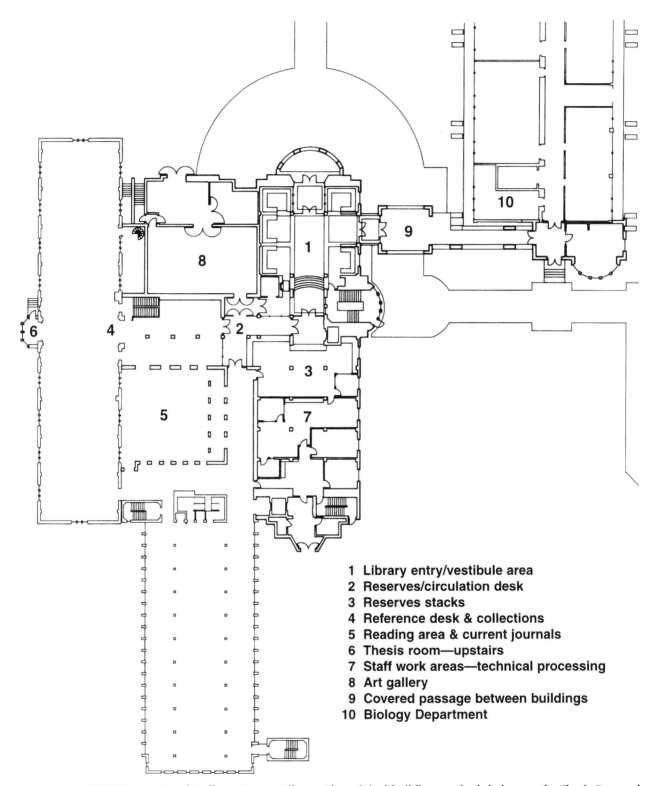

1 Library entry/vestibule area
2 Reserves/circulation desk
3 Reserves stacks
4 Reference desk & collections
5 Reading area & current journals
6 Thesis room—upstairs
7 Staff work areas—technical processing
8 Art gallery
9 Covered passage between buildings
10 Biology Department

FIGURE 1.2   Reed College, Hauser Library. The original building, to the left, houses the Thesis Room, the Reference Desk, and general collections. The reading room (5) is principally current journals; it is a very attractive room in which the brickwork of the original building is still visible. The newest addition (to the right) includes the entry (1, to the upper right) and the circulation desk (2, 3—combined with reserves) as well as the staff areas (7). (Courtesy of Zimmer Gunsul Frasca Partnership)

FIGURE 1.3 Occidental College, Mary Norton Clapp Library. Note special rooms: Cumberland is an open browsing room for selected current light reading; Jeffers is a general classroom; Braun houses fine books; and the Bill Henry Room contains books and memorabilia of an outstanding newspaper correspondent. Both the Braun and Henry rooms are opened by special arrangement. Four other rooms on the third floor are used for U.S. and California document collections.

ing to meet the current academic goals and those that will evolve for a good many years into the future. Those responsible for designing the library should try to look 20 or 30 years ahead, be balanced in their view, and make their product as adaptable as possible.

1.3
The Stages of the Building Project

The particular steps taken in a building project vary among institutions, and institutional requirements vary from one administration to another or even from project to project. Certain broad similarities exist, however, between the creation of a new or renovated library and the design of any other complex and expensive product. A logical progression flows from conception through design to execution and activation.

Following is a list of 20 stages that constitute the major steps in justification, design, and construction of a major library building. Many of these steps may be skipped or merged if the project is of modest size. In most cases, additional reviews and approvals will be needed beyond those indicated here. In a large university, one or several approvals may be required for every step beyond the seventh, including those of academic and business officers; representatives of plant operations; police and fire officers; city, county, and occasionally state and federal offices; and the trustees or regents, depending on the stage or issues. Trustee approval may be needed only for the program, basic building design, site selection, and budget, and it may include approval of the contract documents. On the other hand, there may be approval through construction so long as a specified dollar figure is not exceeded.

Before, during, and often after the project, there will be a parallel fund-raising effort. Fund-raising processes can begin before the sixth stage, but they seldom do. They typically move into high gear after the board of trustees has given program approval. The librarian, other university officers, and even the architect may be involved in the fund-raising effort. Periodic comparisons between the estimated project cost and the progress of fund-raising may be required and lead to a series of decisions to bring those together. With fund-raising success, this comparison can lead to an expanded project, such as adding a specially furnished room or providing for a major art purchase. Much more often it will lead to reduction in the building project as fund-raising falls short. In any event, the fund-raising or governmental appropriations must be clear before the fourteenth stage is concluded.

A typical list of stages in an academic or research library building project includes the following:

1. Define and analyze the facilities need, usually through a statement written by the librarian, occasionally with help from a consultant.
2. Consider options for avoiding, minimizing, or otherwise solving the facilities needs in broad program terms. (Treated in parts of Chapters 1 through 4 of this book.)
3. Review the academic plan of the institution to assure that the academic program matches and validates the library option that is being proposed.
4. Prepare a written library building proposal in terms of basic academic purpose, scope, and rationale for the specific size and project costs. (Treated in Chapter 3.)
5. Consider siting, the arrangement of the physical mass, traffic, and infrastructure issues relative to the campus master plan. (Treated in Chapter 11.)

6. Obtain review, negotiation, and approval by the administration, including the board of trustees or regents and, for a state-supported institution, offices of the state government. Such approval is a major hurdle in authorizing the project and may be required for multiple stages of the project and within specific construction or project cost limits.
7. Conduct staff education in preparation for the project, including a study of published literature on academic library buildings and visits to selected libraries.
8. Form the planning team within the institution. (Treated in Chapter 4.) The team usually includes representatives of the library and faculty, certain academic and business officers in the institution, possibly student representation, and such consultants to the institution as are deemed appropriate.
9. Prepare the formal building program. This document is a specification of the facility and site requirements in detail. (Covered in Chapters 5 through 8.) It must be approved by the library officers and principal academic and business officers. It sets the essential requirements that the architect is expected to meet in the design of the facility.
10. Choose an architect and approve the consultants to the architect. (Also covered in Chapter 4.) This choice may in large measure rest with the campus business office, the librarian, the president, the trustees or state government, and occasionally a donor. Selection of an interior designer should be considered at this time if this service is not provided by the architect.
11. Prepare schematic designs. This work by the architect includes site studies and a master plan dealing with an existing facility as well as development of the new building's mass, floor size, and vertical and horizontal traffic patterns. (Covered in Chapter 12.)
12. Prepare design development plans. The architect will advance the schematics, once approved, into more precise plans, including all walls, fenestration, and doors, and which provide the first mechanical and other nonarchitectural drawings. (Covered in Chapter 13.)
13. Prepare contract documents. This work by the architect constitutes the final architectural working drawings with plans, details, elevations, and complete drawings for demolition; for the construction site; for the

structural, mechanical, plumbing, and electrical systems; and for landscaping. Included is a volume of written business conditions and performance specifications on everything from hardware to the mechanical systems. (Treated in Chapter 14.) A similar level of documentation will be required for interior design elements, which may be part of this phase or treated as a separate phase.

14. Conduct the bidding process. Based on the contract documents, this process includes advertising for bids, analyzing the received bids, selecting the general contractor, qualifying the subcontractors, and signing the base contract with the general contractor or the construction manager if there is to be no general contractor. (Covered in Chapter 15.)

15. Construct the facility. During this lengthy process, the architect and the librarian or other institutional representatives review the progress on a weekly if not daily schedule. Performance validations, document clarification, and consideration of and action on requests for changes or additions come up frequently and need programmatic as well as budgetary input. (Covered in Chapter 15.) This stage often begins with a ground-breaking or cornerstone ceremony. (Covered in Chapter 16.)

16. Select and purchase furnishings. This stage should overlap construction and occasionally may even begin during the working drawing phase for items needing especially long lead times for acquisition. A detailed treatment of furnishings is not included in this book, though aspects of interior design are mentioned where appropriate in the chapters dealing with design. It is useful to have the interior designer, if there is one in addition to the architect, involved beginning with stage 11.

17. Legally accept the building and grounds on the part of the institution from the contractor. This short activation stage frequently requires numerous interactions among all the parties concerned. (Covered in Chapter 16.)

18. Occupy the facility. Furnishings, equipment, furniture, and books are moved in, data lines and phones are activated, the building graphics are installed, and the building is put to use. (Covered in Chapter 16.)

19. Dedicate the facility. This event is occasionally omitted, particularly for a building addition, though it can be a particularly important stage for fund-raising relations. (Covered in Chapter 16.)

20. Make warranty corrections. The last phase involves the completion of all deficiencies against the bid contract documents by the contractor and subcontractors during the period of warranty that follows stage 17. (Also treated in Chapter 16.)

These stages vary from project to project, some are short and some lengthy, a number may overlap one another. There are also many reviews, approvals, and financial checks during or between many of the later design stages. The flow chart, fig. 1.4, shows an elaboration of this progression.

Nearly all large and many modest academic institutions have an office for campus planning. It may be called the architects and engineers office, the facilities planning office, or the campus design and construction office. In statewide college and university systems, there usually is an office in the system headquarters that reviews and approves projects and sets some specifications and business conditions, and that is involved at certain times (fig. 1.5). At the other extreme, a small college or university may retain an architectural firm to provide consistency in planning and sound business management procedures for each individual building project. For this service, the architect is apt to charge an hourly fee. Whatever the arrangements, this role is very important and should not be left to the librarian to perform. Typically the fiduciary responsibility for contractual matters rests with a business or financial vice president within the academic institution.

Representatives of the library and the campus planning or business office attend most, if not all, project meetings between the architect and contractors. The planning office project manager is the official institutional representative or "owner" and, thus, is the architect's contractual client, though the library is the ultimate client. The librarian should be the prime academic officer providing the program and guidance on operational or functional requirements. During construction the architect has an official role as mediator and facilitator, a role that during the design phase is filled by the project manager. On large jobs the architect usually represents the owner in meetings with the general contractor. The architect prepares and administers the contract, but the "owner" must approve and sign all changes. The librarian is technically an advisor to, and a client of, the project manager and should voice any concerns.

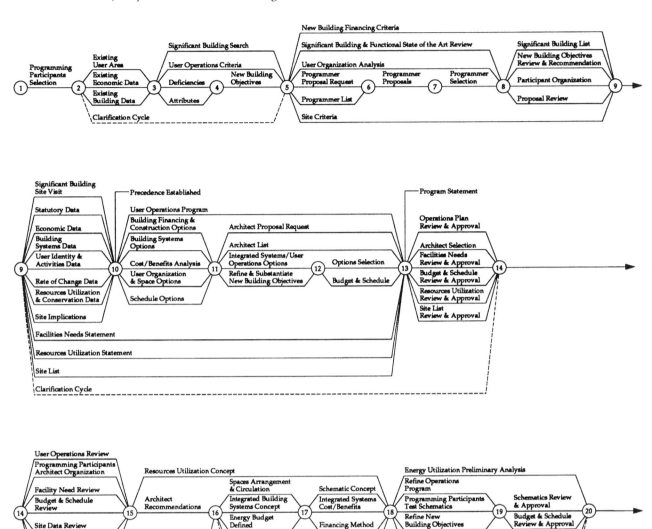

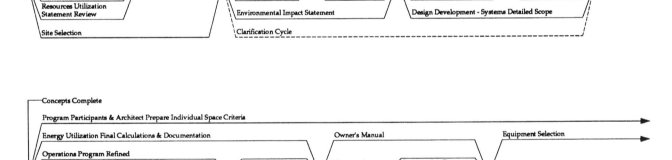

FIGURE 1.4   Project process shows one model of the planning process. Some aspects (for example, the operations program) may be firmly in place before this process is begun; other activities may be placed differently in some cases. Note the iterative nature of the process. (Courtesy of McClellan & Copenhagen)

	Client	Provost	Plant Services	Medical Center Support Services (Facilities)	Purchasing	Police	Safety & Health	Insurance Broker	Univ. Comm. on Land & Bldg. Dev.	Arch. Advisory Council	President & Vice Presidents	Trustees	County Planning Department	County Bldg. Dept. & Fire Marshal	City Government	University Facilities Office						Dir. Facilities & Properties	Controller	Anthropology Dept.
																Master Planning (Site, Landscaping)	Facilities Engineer (M/E Review)	Coordinator Med. Ctr. Projects	Principal Proj. Planner	Dir. Planning	Mgr. Constr. & Engineering			
Programming: Academic Program	○	○							○		○	○												
Program Feasibility Study	○	○									○					○		○	○	○	○	○		
Site	○	○		○					○		○	○				○	○	○	○	○	○	○		○
Target Budget	○	○									○							○	○	○	○	○	○	
Space Program	○	○	○	○	○		○		○									○	○	○	○	○		
Schematic Design: Early Schematic Review	○	○	○	○			○		○	○						○	○	○	○	○	○			
Schematic Plans (& Outline Specifications)	○	○	○	○	○	○	○	○	○	○	○	○	○	○	○	○	○	○	○	○	○	○		
Plans Review Meeting	○	○	○	○	○	○	○									○	○	○	○	○	○			
Environmental Impact Statement	○	○											○		○			○	○	○				○
Formal Budget	○	○									○	○						○	○	○	○	○	○	
Design Development: Preliminary Plans (& Outline Specifications)	○	○	○	○	○	○	○									○	○	○	○	○	○			
Plans Review Meeting	○	○	○	○	○	○	○									○	○	○	○	○	○			
Construction Documents: Final Plans - 50%			○	○			○									○	○	○	○	○	○			
Final Plans - 100% (and Specifications)	○	○	○	○	○	○	○	○						○		○	○	○	○	○	○			
Plans Review Meeting	○	○	○	○	○	○	○									○	○	○	○	○	○			

FIGURE 1.5 Project review checklist (taken from a Stanford University project). Clearly this checklist, generated for a project in the medical center, reflects the organization of a particular institution; a similar checklist reflecting local interests would be appropriate for a major library project.

Effective communication and sympathetic understanding among these individuals is exceedingly important. It is up to all team members to assure that contracts are followed exactly, that timetables are met for completing documents and giving approvals, and that financial constraints are followed conscientiously. Occasionally things can go awry in such a lengthy and complex process, particularly when individuals who were involved in the first stages of the project are replaced by others who are ill informed of earlier decisions. The business officer, library representative, or architect should inform the senior academic officers of any need to take corrective action should the project run into difficulties that they cannot resolve.

The business decision process can be complex. A large university may have at one time as many as 250 renovation and construction projects in planning or construction, totaling well over $100 million. The financial responsibilities are considerable. The business office, having responsibility for all building projects of the institution, should see that the architect and librarian are informed of the institution's business practices. Written decisions are important validation of oral agreements. It is customary for all directly involved offices to keep informed of the authorization stage, and about the decisions leading to the next stage, by having access to the decision record.

1.4
Defining the Building Problem

This section treats the need to define the building problem, an activity that precedes writing the program as discussed in Chapters 5 through 8. The following section summarizes the options available for solving building problems. Understanding the problems and their possible solutions is of crucial importance. It is clear from both successful and unsuccessful library buildings that basic success is relatively assured if project participants adequately define the needs of the institution, explore various options, select an appropriate direction, and follow a process leading to a well-executed construction.

Typical major facility problems include:

• lack of adequate space
• limitations of the present site

• poor environmental, physical, or mechanical quality of the building
• a lack of flexibility in the building when adjustments to new educational or study requirements are wanted

In an academic library, staff space usually runs out first, followed by difficulty with the book storage space, and finally a reduction of reader space.

For a combination of reasons, inadequate staff quarters is common. It may be difficult for the institution to recognize that major improvements in a library building can greatly increase library use. Although potential readers are psychologically driven from an inadequate library, they respond suddenly and positively to improved library conditions. This change means more work for circulation and reference staff. A new building often results in more gifts to the library and more gifts of book funds, resulting in increased acquisitions, cataloging, and preparation of materials for storage and use. Consequently the staff space, felt to be reasonable during the planning stages, turns out to be too small under the changing circumstance.

In all types of research libraries and most academic libraries, the most important space deficiency is typically inadequate accommodation for books and other library materials. This is almost always the most convincing condition influencing the decision of whether to embark on a library construction project. For one thing, the space problem becomes very obvious when the shelves are full and new materials are regrettably boxed, put on temporary shelves in corridors, or otherwise made difficult to find or impossible to access except by staff. Furthermore, every library user experiences the problem, not just the library staff. The case becomes extreme when substantial parts of the collection must be shelved in auxiliary quarters requiring a few hours or more for library staff to fetch a requested item. It is easier to determine the future shelf space needed than staff space, yet the calculations are not necessarily more accurate.

A shortage of reader space is less likely to be compelling, even though in educational terms it is as important for effective library use as adequate book or staff space. The consequence of students being forced to seek alternative libraries or to use classrooms or residence rooms for study is not easily determined. Many serious scholars will still use the library under the most adverse circumstances even without a place to sit and study in a quiet environment convenient to the books. Many take the path of least resistance and reduce library use; thus, the teaching process unquantifiably suffers, perhaps to a serious degree.

Other problem conditions can create unfunctional, unsatisfactory, or unpleasant conditions. In addition to space shortages, building inflexibility can limit an ideal deployment of functions. Relationships between functions may be distant or hard to explain to users. Use may be constricted or awkward for those whose physical movement is limited, for example, to wheelchairs. Utility capacities may be insufficient, and the environment may not meet reasonable preservation criteria for library materials, or it may be uncomfortable or unpleasant for the occupants of the library.

The assessment of facility inadequacy and space need may be completely or partially conducted by librarians. Such a study can benefit by comments from academic officers, faculty, students, and staff of the physical plant and business offices. The involvement of those outside the library, particularly members of the faculty library committee, has the advantage of eliciting their support and giving added weight to the conclusions reached. Their participation in the evaluation can also generate more widespread understanding of existing deficiencies.

Each institution will have its own administrative style governing the presentation of justification for a building project. In some cases a lengthy statistical document will serve the purpose; in others, a presentation based on the subjective pedagogical consequences, or a comparison with peer institutions, or a response to the academic plan and the goals set by the president for the decade ahead may be appropriate formats for the report. Some major building projects have received their blessing from chief administrative officers on the basis of a five- or ten-page statement; others have required massive reports. The result can be the same, depending on the management style, guidelines, and expectations in a particular institution.

One example may show how the nature of a building deficiency can be presented and at the same time show that the process of justification is no more or less important today than it has been in the past or will be in the future.

Harvard University built Gore Hall in 1841 as its first separate building entirely devoted to the library. A two-story wing with the first modern, tiered bookstack was added in 1877, followed by another addition in 1907.

Like his predecessor, the director of libraries at Harvard had been disturbed for many years about the limitations of Gore Hall. In 1910, only three years after the second addition was finished, the trustees of the university appointed an architectural committee to study the space needs of the library and to ascertain if there were stages of development that might temporarily alleviate the situation while promising some long-range relief. The committee conclusions of 1911 were as follows:

1. The Gore Hall site was appropriate.
2. As an alternative to a completely new building, one stack addition after another might be added to Gore until at some later time new "administrative offices" would replace Gore.
3. The initial stack addition would contain professorial study alcoves and seminar rooms as well as book space.
4. As units could be built, stacks would be added on three sides of a quadrangle with a court in the center.
5. Eventually Gore Hall would be removed and the main facade of the new building would form the final side of a quadrangle.

Furthermore, as their chief argument for razing Gore, the committee cited the librarian's statement concerning the inadequacy of the famous library building:

> The present building is unsafe, and has been declared so by insurance experts; the electrical wiring has all been added since the construction, and it must remain a serious danger.
>
> It is unsuitable for its object. The old stack was modelled after an English Chapel. . . . The whole construction is ill-suited to the working of a modern library, and no amount of tinkering can make it really good.
>
> The building is hopelessly overcrowded in almost all respects, and every week makes the situation worse. The quarters of the staff are inadequate . . . the general reading room for the students is too small, it leaks when there is a heavy rain, it is often intolerably hot in summer, the ventilation is bad

and must remain so with the present roof, and the room is frequently overcrowded. . . .

Finally, as to the books themselves. They have been shifted so often in order to gain space that at present practically every part of the library is equally overcrowded with shelves to their utmost capacity; books are put in double rows and are not infrequently left lying on top of one another, or actually on the floor . . . and the moving of books is always a matter of inconvenience and expense. We have now almost fifty thousand volumes stored outside of the building, mostly in cellars, and yet everyday we have need of some of these works and are obliged to send for them.[2]

After serving as the main library at Harvard for 72 years, Gore Hall was razed in 1913 to make way for the Widener Library building.

The written argument stating the nature of the building deficiency can be supplemented with photographs, statistical data summarizing the situation, statistical projections of needs over 10 to 20 years, and comparisons with peer institutions. Tours of the existing building might be offered to the faculty library committee, the president, and/or the provost, and visits might be made to one or two examples of good library buildings at comparable institutions.

Sometimes the need is so evident and the timing is so right both administratively and financially that an affirmative decision comes easily. If the president or a major donor takes the initiative, it may come quickly. In other cases there may be delays for years while the situation steadily worsens and, consequently, the argument for a major improvement becomes more convincing. The inadequacy of current library facilities relative to other needs is a matter for each institution to determine by weighing all the desired accommodations against what can realistically be afforded. The library, after all, must take its place among other institutional priorities, whether they be for capital expenditures, improvement in faculty salaries, scholarship aid, additional laboratory equipment, or other needs. It does no good to press for a new building or addition when the institution has other requirements that are universally seen as more immediate. Conversely, absolutely nothing is gained by waiting until the library situation is near catastrophic, for any administration will need time to be apprised of the situation, to weigh the priorities, to consider the available and feasible op-

tions, and to determine the means of financing the project.

1.5 General Consideration of Options

Consideration of various imaginative, unconventional, "blue sky," and even far-fetched possibilities for solving the library facility problem may be necessary. Some who are influential in the institution may believe that computers and information networks will replace books in a few decades. Others may feel that relying on other institutions for library support can stabilize local library size, or that there are so many unused books that one can easily weed a volume for every one that is added. Some may assert that the library should be housed in a number of different buildings on campus or that overflow might be placed in a former gymnasium or a former administration building. Or, the prospect of placing lesser-used materials in a building across the freeway some 20 minutes away may prove to be attractive. Depending on the receptivity of the administration to nontraditional solutions to library space problems, the library staff and the faculty library committee may need to give serious study to each one of these options along with others that may emerge. A reasonable short-term expedient or a means of moderating the required new space might evolve from this analysis. Chapter 2 treats alternatives to new construction.

The choice among options is made more complex if the campus is crowded with buildings, if the quality of some buildings is marginal, and if the institution is in a dense urban area. If the campus planners have saved land enabling a tripling or quadrupling of the library over the next century, they have done well. Some institutions have so many ad hoc building decisions, from one administration to the next, that a long-term rationale for library growth both centrally and in branches is difficult to achieve and maintain. In a dense urban setting, major limitations can be presented by the problems of buying land, converting land to different use, height and setback restrictions, parking or open space requirements, utility capacities, and, occasionally, historic site considerations. Again, each institution will need to study its own library and site problems to determine what options are available.

Campus planners and architects can be helpful for master planning in such difficult circumstances.

The age of the institution will also affect decision making. There is a difference between young and mature institutions. The latter will have built up research collections over a century or more, and the general deployment of laboratories, classrooms, and offices for academic disciplines will be fairly complete. The library pattern will have been formed, probably as part of a master plan, which should help in setting the future course for library space planning. Conversely, a young institution may have a more open and fluid campus plan. As the young institution looks forward to maturity, it cannot predict with certainty how the campus will grow—what enrollment patterns, percentage of majors by field, laboratory needs, or residential developments will occur. Therefore, the long-term prospects for library growth will be less clear than in an older institution. More attention will be required in assigning land for long-term needs to avoid limiting succeeding generations unduly. Consideration of probable branch libraries in 30 to 50 years will be especially important. The University of California campuses at Irvine and Santa Cruz are examples of good planning—one a centralized scheme and the other a cluster arrangement. And the tenth UC campus opening in 2005 at Merced will have 2,550 acres for creative planning.

Another kind of concern is found with a bifurcated campus. A few institutions, such as Rutgers and the University of Minnesota, have been unable to accommodate growth on a single campus and have therefore developed an adjacent or a nearby satellite campus that may become even larger than the original. One must determine if the new campus will house sciences only or professional schools, what student housing is intended, what the long-term plans are for the physical plant, and how intercampus transportation will be handled. Library space planning in this instance poses a compounded challenge. An option here is to start afresh on the new site. Some phasing advantages will accrue if the libraries on the old and new campuses can serve as safety valves when space pressures in one or the other become severe in future years. One of the two major library nodes may house centralized functions, such as the technical services departments.

Another basic consideration is the use of shared facilities. There are many examples of multifunc-

tional buildings, in which libraries share their facility with academic departments, audiovisual centers, computer centers, the president's office, classrooms, the student union, and so forth. Since prebiblical times, the usual pattern has been to have one or more rooms in a large building devoted to a library. This was true during the classical Egyptian civilization, in Greece, in medieval monasteries, and in all early colleges in the United States. Sometimes this library "apartment" was a wing in a college building or rooms on one floor or in one portion of a building. The first separate academic library buildings in North America were the University of South Carolina library (1840), the Gore Hall Library at Harvard (1841), and the Williams College library building (1845), followed by Yale University (1846), the University of North Carolina (1851), and Amherst College (1853).

Many examples of shared facilities still exist, although almost none among major colleges and universities where the main library is the minor or secondary building occupant. The campus may, on the other hand, include a megastructure with the library as one of the occupants, as at Simon Fraser University or the University of Wisconsin, Parkside. At Mission College, a community college in Santa Clara, California, the current plan is to remove the library from their megastructure (see fig. 7.27) and place it in a separate building with media services (a television studio and audiovisual facilities) to provide proper quarters for the library and growth space for the academic program.

Typically the library is the primary building occupant, with classrooms or other facilities, if any, occupying a small portion and having a separate entrance. This arrangement can be a mixed blessing. On the one hand, it provides expansion or "surge" space. If the library is to be a very prominent building, as at Colby College and New York University, the president's office may appropriately share such a monumental or symbolic structure. Collocating the president's office with the library may bring more attention to and support for the library program. Accommodation of the president's office within the library building can have certain advantages, as at Oklahoma State University where a handsomely appointed president's office (with fireplace!) was later available to the library as the director's office. There are academic and telecommunication advantages when a computer center or an audio-visual center shares or is adjacent to the library building.

On the other hand, joint occupancy can present traffic and security problems. And the ultimate eviction of those who share the building, even with functional compatibility, is often difficult. No universal recommendation can be offered except to give joint occupancy extra special consideration because its risks can be severe. Individual circumstances will dictate what is best.

A final basic consideration is the essential quality and grandeur of the desired structure. Although libraries should never be ugly, how important is high-quality construction and architectural grace? This is not easily answered. Time and costs, institutional goals, and the qualities of the design team are major factors. Considering that the answer is significant, especially in cost, the following questions should be asked. Should minimum funds be spent on the structure, finishes, and exterior appearance, or should an effort be made to build special quality into a building of such lasting importance? Should the goal be to harmonize in exterior design with other buildings in the vicinity? Or should the architect aim to create a visually distinct structure, one remembered by alumni and perhaps used in publications and other symbolic forms promoting the institution? Should the building be monumental in scale? Is there an imposing and suitable site? Should the construction of foundation and shell be of such high quality that the structure will still be sound after a hundred years? Or, should its life be thought of in more limited terms, on the assumption that this library will be outdated or radically changed and not worth preserving in its current configuration a century hence?

Institutional policies and trustee desires will shape some answers. Questions such as these can rarely be solved without conceptualizing the future in academic and business terms. Institutional objectives, related campus priorities, costs, and funding capacity will influence the course of action. However, except for a church, probably no other building on campus deserves as high a degree of architectural importance on an especially prominent site as does the main library. Nevertheless, for library management reasons, tower libraries, libraries with great central atriums, libraries that lack adaptability, security, or control of the environment, or monuments that are difficult to operate or expand must be guarded against.

1.6
The Span of Time for Which to Plan

The planning horizon will need to be established—how long will the new facility be adequate? Funding capacity provides a very real limit to the number of years. Other projects are awaiting their turn. There may be academic reasons for not planning too far in advance. The view of the future is always lacking clarity. Yet there are good library management reasons why a very short time span is undesirable. Some compromise must be found among these various forces. Because significant building projects consume anywhere from three years to over ten, it is undesirable to limit the program to accommodate library collections for as little as five or eight years hence. Some institutions, and some states, do not permit planning for space based on projections exceeding four or five years; this is undesirably short for the planning of a library building and is not to be encouraged. If a number of incremental additions are planned, then the period of time for any one increment can be shorter than is the case when an entirely new building is planned with no imminent expectation for incremental additions.

Even such large buildings as the Firestone Library at Princeton, the Sterling Library at Yale, or the Widener Library at Harvard were able to last little more than 20 or 25 years before some further space had to be found. Stanford University's main library was built in 1919, and despite constrained acquisitions during the Great Depression and the Second World War, barely 30 years passed before space problems were so severe that two more stack levels were added within the existing structure. Later an adjacent undergraduate library was built, an extended basement was added beneath the main library, a major subject collection was moved out as a branch, and a significant auxiliary collection was established elsewhere to accommodate overflow of collections. These additions met the need for 30 more years until a major addition more than doubled the library's size. Planning for this addition began in 1965, construction was completed in 1980, and it was projected to be full in the mid-1990s. With the closure of the old main library (a result of damage caused by the Loma Prieta earthquake), an auxiliary facility was constructed replicating the collections capacity of the old main library (now called the Green Library West Wing). Renovation of Green West together with the continued use of the auxiliary storage facility will allow a few more years before space will once again be a problem for the Stanford libraries.

Unless it is viewed as desirable that each leader of the institution be required to finance one or more library buildings, it is a good rule of thumb to build accommodation for the collections and people that will be adequate at least 20 years after occupancy. Twenty-five years would be 50 percent better. It is a more common practice to plan for 20 years from the start of the programming effort, resulting in a period of approximately 15 to 17 years from the date of occupancy until the space becomes limiting. If the institution can provide space approaching the longer time frame while providing a good-quality, flexible building with assured site space for later additions, then the institution will have been well served.

If a complete 20-year planning horizon is impossible, the alternative of choice is a phased building, such that building increments are added in logical steps over shorter periods of time. The main library at the University of California, Los Angeles is an example of such an approach, though the time increments have been longer than five years. The disadvantage is the obvious: Construction in and about a library is difficult for all involved, and multiple periods of construction and activation increase the project cost and the cost of library management. Financing is, of course, a major controlling factor. Every institution will have to find its own compromises between what is desirable and what can be achieved.

1.7
The Ultimate Size of a Library

A word about library growth. Academic and research library buildings do not necessarily have to grow if the student body and faculty size remain stable and if the academic program elements determining the size of the library staff can also remain static and if the collection size can expand off-site. However, even with the advance of networked databases, library collections do grow, especially in research institutions, and therein lies the major problem in housing libraries. This fact is so important that it bears emphasizing. Librarians and other academic officers responsible for libraries have yet to find a satisfactory way of preventing growth in library collections or even of appreciably slowing library space requirements.

This is growth due to the nature of learning. Information constantly expands. It is not always displacing prior knowledge, certainly not in the humanities and the arts and rather seldom even in the social sciences and much of the sciences. Although a college can plan on physical collections with limited growth for instructional purposes, the faculty will need access to additional materials in order to maintain their disciplinary skills. This need is true even in community and technical colleges. It is obvious with respect to a university, particularly because graduate students will be undertaking extensive reading in their field while preparing for orals and developing advanced papers or a thesis. Major graduate programs therefore require growing access to electronic data and text as well as physical book and journal collections that grow by many tens of thousands of volumes a year, carefully selected from current worldwide publications and the out-of-print book trade.

In general it has been the case that university library collections double about every 15 or 16 years. Although it may be that the growth of computer use and networks will diminish this growth rate, there is enough doubt that the computer will be a complete panacea for future library growth to suggest that the prudent planner should account for continued library physical growth. This doubt is based on ergonomics (people do not like reading extended texts on computers) and economics (the traditional book remains an elegant and relatively inexpensive way to record, organize, store, and access information).

It was once thought that the invention and promulgation of microfilm would be the answer to the constant growth of libraries. That view was held about 50 years ago, and the outcome is clear: Although microfilm can sharply reduce the storage space required for a fixed amount of information, it does little to contribute to smaller libraries because libraries continue to acquire newly published materials in hard copy format. Only in rare circumstances (such as newspapers) is the hard copy discarded when a microtext copy is acquired. The reason is largely ergonomic—the scholar prefers the far greater convenience of using physical text rather than the microform.

Computers have some of the same ergonomic limitations seen with microfilm. The text image is still poor compared to typical printed text. Viewing the text requires a machine, which remains a problem for many. Many students cannot afford their own computer, and many libraries in many parts of the world cannot afford to provide them. The machine requires power one way or another, it makes some noise, is sensitive to lighting conditions, cannot be used while one is slouched in a chair or lying in bed, is an object of interest to thieves, and so on. Although there is no doubt that machines will be used to access and process information, there is considerable doubt that they will ever totally replace paper and the printed text.

The computer enthusiast will point to the ease of use of the laptop computer, and indeed it is a wonderful instrument. In fact, this text is being written on a laptop with the author seated in a comfortable lounge chair. This particular laptop even has the word *book* in its name, and yet, rather than fitting comfortably in the crease of the lap as does a book, it opens to reveal a screen and a keyboard. Ergonomically, the book is more of a laptop device than this computer. And yet, here it is on the lap.

Reading and research will of course be done using computers. However, when lengthy text is encountered, the reader will usually print it out at some expense. Projections indicate that even where text is available electronically, there will be convenience and economic justification to obtain and maintain physical copies of this text in the library. Yet handbooks, indexes, and many other reference books will increasingly be preferred in online format. The power of the computer in this emerging model is in its capacity to search text and data files and to provide rapid and remote access to succinct information that can be specifically defined. When lengthy text is to be used extensively or read, the computer will continue to be inferior to traditional printed text. As recently pronounced by Peter Lyman, then University Librarian, University of California, Berkeley: "The computer is for research; the book is for reading."

The conviction that demand will continue for printed texts, together with the universal experience that books unavailable electronically will continue to be acquired, suggests that libraries will continue to grow well into the future. Although the geometric compounded rate of growth will decline as the size of the library grows, it seems clear that printed books will increase in number and continue in importance to academic and almost all research institutions well into the twenty-first century.

Keyes Metcalf in the first edition of this book made the following general prognostications, here slightly updated, with the full realization that they can be challenged, that details can be easily confuted, and that they should not be taken too specifically for any one institution. They do, in our judgment today, continue to offer sound advice.

1. The average strictly undergraduate library will continue to grow in the size and bulk of its collections and therefore its storage requirements; but its net increase, certainly by the time its collections approach the half million mark, will be reduced to something like 2 percent a year because of greater reliance on other libraries for little-used material, use of microreproductions of one kind or another, and greatly increased application of digitized and optical disk storage technology.

2. The demand for seating will for the next 25 years increase at a rate of about 1 percent per year, in addition to any increase in the number of students; this is to provide for increased intensity of use and for new equipment needed to access information. Evidence suggests that access to computer networks has reduced the need for library seating in largely residential colleges; similar reduction may be a fact for commuters as well. Where seating for 25 percent of the student body has been the traditional requirement, seating for 20 percent of the projected student body is currently acceptable in many institutions, and even less in some cases (especially for commuting campuses). However, it is predicted that this reduction has plateaued to a large extent, and the growth suggested here is from that new reduced plateau.

The recommended basic space per reader should be increased about one-fifth for prudent planning (or from the typical 25 ft²/2.32 m² to 30 ft²/2.79 m²) in order to accommodate new equipment and access for the disabled. The number of seats to be provided varies significantly from one institution to another, and is discussed in detail elsewhere. Staff-area needs will also increase at a rate of about 1 percent per year.

3. The average university library will increase in its space needs for collections more rapidly than will a library for undergraduate use, and, until any particular collection reaches at least 2.5 million volumes, that rate is likely to be not less than 4 percent per annum over that of the year before. The percentage of increase thereafter typically slows. Adverse economic conditions can, of course, temporarily depress this rate.

4. As was the case with the college library, an increase of 1 percent for seating accommodation, in addition to accounting for increased enrollment, is required for bibliographic and computer-aided instruction, audiovisual services, online computer searches, use of materials on optical disks or networks, and for traditional use of the library. Increased staff needs will be at least as high as the increase in the collections and reader accommodation.

5. The average large, mature research library (that is, one with over 2.5 million volumes), with few exceptions will increase no more rapidly than the undergraduate library group discussed under 1 above. The cost of space, the existence of national loan centers (such as British Library Document Supply Centre (DSC) and the Center for Research Libraries), and the use of technology, such as videodisk storage, will slow the growth rate for the very large research library. It will continue to grow, however, probably relying increasingly on some form of remote collection shelving for much of its growth.

These slightly updated predictions of 1965 are not offered as a guide for a specific library, but rather as a basis for discussion. Each institution should consider its own special situation; its relations with neighboring institutions; the present size, strength, and weakness of the collections; its recent rate of growth; the prospects for change in the composition and size of the student body; the quality and style of instructional requirements; and particularly the present stage of institutional development and prospects for the years ahead.

Is there an ultimate size? Librarians and academic officers may well wonder if there will ever be an end to the growth of academic and research libraries. Certainly it would be comforting to know that one might plan one last library building that will serve as long as any other building. Yet this is not feasible in the current nature of the academic or research library world. Faculty, researchers, and students need to have immediate shelf or computer access to nearly all the materials required for teaching, learning, and their immediate research. Although much of the heavily used materials for teaching and learning may gravitate to digitized electronic media, support in the form of a growing physical collection will continue to be required. At the same time, it will be increasingly necessary to purchase photocopies or facsimiles from a distance, rely on interlibrary borrowings, or visit other libraries that have specialized physical materials. As long as civilizations continue, publication will flourish, and materials available to researchers must increase.

Some libraries are embarked upon a program of compact shelving within the central library. There are several approaches to such a technique, the major issue being that of self-service, "public" access as opposed to closed and/or staffed access. In the latter model, very compact storage systems are possible involving specialized equipment and space. Even where public access is mandated, compact shelving utilizing a system of movable carriages can significantly increase the capacity of a given space, though access is reduced, floor load requirements can be limiting, and the cost of managing the collection increases slightly.

Another special solution is off-site storage in various forms. A growing number of libraries have auxiliary facilities into which they place less frequently used materials. Some (such as the Center for Research Libraries, the Harvard Depository Library, and the Northern and Southern Regional Library Facilities of the University of California) are accommodations for multiple libraries. Others (such as the University of London, Princeton, Yale, the University of Michigan, Stanford University, and the University of Texas at Austin) have auxiliary storage facilities on campus to handle the local overflow. It is quite probable that this pattern will spread widely among universities and some colleges. Together with compact shelving in the central facility and increased reliance on other institutions, this secondary-access collection is a common arrangement supporting access to larger and larger collections while extending the life of the main or central library building(s) on campus. However, as the size and use of these more staff-intensive access methodologies grow, the staff space required may grow at a proportionately greater rate than the collections and seating space need.

A trend toward stabilized collections size could be perceived if a national or regional center for serials and monographs is formed in the years ahead; however, this is not a prospect that can generally be planned as part of the collections growth problem, at least not in the United States. In other countries, the national library does fulfill this role to a certain extent, though it is not a very satisfactory solution to collection management for libraries at a distance from the centralized resource. Regardless of governmental programs, consortia, and reliance on off-campus or back-campus auxiliary facilities, faculty and students still need immediate access to a vast bulk of material relevant to their teaching and research. Time pressures in class require one- or two-day access to nearly all materials needed for class assignments. For research projects with a few weeks to complete, borrowing of some 5 percent of the needed materials can be tolerated if about 95 percent is readily at hand. If one looks at the Harvard University Library, which exceeds 12 million volumes, the addition of the Pusey Library in 1976 and the recent branch buildings for anthropology, art, education, music, and science indicate that the Harvard libraries do not yet have a static requirement for central space—even with the New England Deposit Library just across the Charles River and the Harvard Depository Library some 25 miles away at the Southborough Facility. There have also been major recent additions at the University of Washington; Washington State University; the University of California at San Diego, Berkeley, and Davis; Cornell University; Colby College; the University of Michigan; Occidental College; Princeton University; Vassar; and Yale. Branch libraries on university campuses grow slowly in number; seldom are there consolidations. It seems certain that university as well as college libraries will grow well into the future in their requirements for book collections and campus space.

At least for now, the largest academic library structure is the 1973 University of Toronto Robarts Library of 16 floors, over 5 million volumes capacity, and a gross area of 1,036,000 ft²/96,250 m². Although some at Toronto have felt the facility is too large, the collections and services will likely grow to exceed even this capacity. A cluster of facilities in the tradition of Oxford, Harvard, the University of Michigan, and Stanford is a common distribution of library services, and such a decentralized approach is a natural outcome of the growth of the institution itself together with library growth. Each institution should consider its local circumstances, relations with its neighbors, and current level of provincial, state, or federal support; a set of individual decisions will then have to be made as to the nature of the library building that is needed. Given the circumstances at very large institutions, such as Harvard, the University of Michigan, the University of Toronto, and Yale, one can quite safely say that the ultimate size collection will not be reached at least in the next 50 years. However, the ultimate size of a library building may already exist in several places.

1.8
Looking toward the Future

We live in a changing world. If the past can be taken as a guide, it is obvious that the requirements for a library building in 2000 or 2050 will be quite different from those in 1970 or 1950. Libraries planned more than 80 years ago are almost always so outmoded today as to be questionable assets. One very old university may serve as an example. Harvard University with over 90 libraries systemwide has only three research branches in buildings built before 1907. It is, however, reasonable to expect that well-built buildings with reasonable functional adaptability will serve academic institutions for many decades.

The cost of a new library building today is so great and represents such a large percentage of an institution's total capital investment that it is generally unwise to build deliberately for a few years only. Consequently, to last a great many decades, the building should within reason be as adaptable as possible.

The characteristics of adaptability may be summed up as follows. The utmost floor space should be usable interchangeably with modest alteration for any primary library function: reader accommodations, service to readers, space for staff activities, and housing for the collections. It follows that:

1. All floors must be capable of bearing bookstack live loads of 150 pounds per square foot (7.182 kN/m²). If movable shelving is anticipated, floor loading requirements must be double this amount. Certain other storage configurations may result in other loading requirements.
2. Floor heights must be adequate for any library purpose, preferably not less than 8 ft 4 in. (2.540 m). Where a building is protected by a sprinkler system, the floor to ceiling height should be not less than 9 ft (2.743 m), and where movable shelving is anticipated together with sprinklers, a minimum ceiling height of 9 ft 8 in. (2.946 m) is recommended.
3. Atmospheric and other comfort conditions, such as ventilation and lighting, must be

adaptable to any of these purposes with minimal change, but ceiling and floor treatments need not be identical throughout a building. It is to be expected that special environmental conditions designed for the preservation of collections may be zoned and therefore not terribly flexible in terms of the total building; ideally the building will be designed with an environmental base that is thought to be reasonable for preservation of collections, with special zones for unique situations accepted.

4. All library areas must be readily accessible; it is undesirable to have load-bearing interior walls in places where they might interfere with later traffic patterns. Floor level changes are to be kept to a minimum, and, where required, must be designed to accommodate book trucks and wheelchairs.

5. Power and signal service, closets, and distribution systems must be designed to permit future change, both in terms of capacity and in terms of distribution.

6. Security and access will need careful consideration to permit reasonable flexibility.

7. The building module should be economical in handling shelving dimensions, as well as carrel, study, office, and reading area dimensions. Interior arrangements must not seriously interfere with satisfactory capacity for books, for readers, and for shelving.

Relative to the last item, it should be obvious that any building has supports to hold up the roof, and in most buildings interior columns are a necessity. With more than one level, vertical transportation, heating and ventilation shafts, and plumbing facilities are required and will limit complete flexibility. The placement of the structural and fixed elements of the building is therefore an important part of the design process.

Although adaptability is a very desirable condition, it does not mean that the use of the space should not be carefully planned for the original installation. Some buildings in recent decades have gone too far toward uniform interchangeable modular bays. Carried to an extreme, complete flexibility results in averaging requirements so that few spaces are fully satisfactory because of flexibility-driven compromises; the building will look and function as if it were the result of an investment speculation rather than a building designed to be a library. A strong flexibility requirement will increase construction costs; the only reasonable justification for this extra expense is that it may save money in the long run. Even here, if change cannot be anticipated, the principal effort should be limited to the more inflexible elements of a structural nature.

Interior masonry or plastered walls, which are messy to remove, and permanent built-in installations of all kinds should be minimized. Heating and ventilation ducts, toilet facilities, and vertical transportation should be grouped in a core and provided in places where they are least likely to interfere with prospective changes in library functional-space assignments.

Even in a large building, the number of permanent core areas should be limited. A large building with up to 5,000 m² (say, 50,000 ft²) on each level can be planned with only one central core with satellite power, telephone, and data closets, fire service equipment, duct shafts, and exit stairs; the satellite elements not within the core can be placed at the building's periphery where they will be nonintrusive. Some architects have gone so far as to place secondary stairs and other permanent features outside the main building block as protrusions (see fig. 1.6) worked into the architectural appearance. Building protrusions such as these can simplify interior traffic patterns and arrangements but should not be considered essential, because with many buildings they would not be suitable architecturally. And, they add construction cost.

One important arrangement that may prolong the useful life of a library and prevent unnecessary expenditures later is to plan the building so that additions can be made with modest alterations, rearrangements, and minimal functional and aesthetic effect. This can be accomplished only by providing for future additions in the initial plan. It is recommended that the architects for every major library building make specific intentions known for the placement of at least one substantial building addition.

What changes in library needs can be anticipated? The way to attack this problem is to consider the past and what can be deduced from studying the present.

1.8.1 Lessons from the Past

Old library buildings are very different from those planned more recently. A brief summary should suffice. One hundred fifty years ago thick exterior and interior bearing walls, typically masonry, held

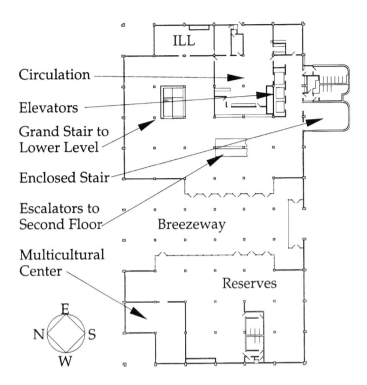

Circulation

Elevators

Grand Stair to
Lower Level

Enclosed Stair

Escalators to
Second Floor

Multicultural
Center

ILL

Breezeway

Reserves

FIGURE 1.6 California State University, Sacramento. Secondary stairs; designed in the late 1960s, the central library is based on a design that placed one major "core" element outside the main body of the building to the upper right. The concept is meant to simplify internal arrangements and traffic patterns, although the other aspects of the design can work against this plan. A later addition to the south was made more difficult because of the projected stairs and rest rooms. (Used with permission of California State University, Sacramento)

up the buildings, which were planned with little thought of flexibility. No library had elevators, steel shelving (shelving was typically wood in a cast iron frame), electric power or lighting, telephones, or air conditioning. Card catalogs were coming into use; the catalog in book form had been standard. There were no visible indexes. There were no typewriters or other copying machines, to say nothing of microfilm readers, computers, and audiovisual equipment.

Individual seating on a large scale was unknown. Compact storage, as we conceive it today, or even concentrated stack shelving had not been used. Except in libraries with a very limited clientele, there was, to all intents and purposes, no open access to the collections. Though it was not customary for most readers to have accommodations close to the books, some libraries had

a series of alcoves formed by tall bookshelving with a table in the center of each.

Of perhaps greater importance from the point of view of building, the largest collections in the United States in 1850 numbered about 100,000 volumes. By 1900 the number had grown to one million. Today there are many academic and research libraries of that size in the United States. The number of readers in academic libraries has increased at a similar rate due to the growth of student populations, the increasing emphasis on individual work and wider reading, and a deemphasis of textbook instruction.

Several basic changes in the physical structure of libraries are the direct or indirect result of changing requirements. We no longer need light courts or monumental reading rooms up to 50 ft (15.240 m) high for proper ventilation and natural light. This change alone has reduced cubage in areas open to the public by 50 percent or more. With good-quality artificial light available at reasonable cost, libraries are open and comfortable on dark days and after sunset. Although daylight is encouraged in parts of libraries for psychological purposes, if not for reading, ceiling heights can now be determined by factors other than the need for natural light and ventilation.

These changes make it practical to plan a squarish building without light wells instead of a relatively long, narrow, and irregular one. Such a squarish shape is desirable for the sake of reducing the area and cost of exterior walls and for shortening and simplifying internal traffic lanes. The choice, it must be admitted, may complicate aesthetic, site, and other problems.

What then have we learned from this brief picture of the past? Six things among others:

1. Major changes in construction methods and in mechanical and electrical systems have occurred, and more of them will undoubtedly be made in the future.

2. The size of library collections has grown rapidly and constantly and in most cases will continue to grow. However, space demands for shelving will abate somewhat in large libraries because of increasing use of compact shelving, greater access to electronic formats (though this remains to be seen), and greater use of auxiliary or warehouse facilities.

3. Library functions and public services have grown in number and in nature, especially in the latter half of this century. The proportion of staff devoted to different functions has constantly

shifted. As a result, a new building needs to be as adaptable as possible, although complete flexibility cannot be obtained or justified.

4. The demand made on academic libraries for seating accommodations has continued to increase in this century. Because of provision for access to new technologies, re-entry students, continuing education programs, students from abroad, changes in methods of instruction, broadening of the curriculum, and dormitory and home conditions that are not conducive for study, space demands for reading accommodations will continue to increase.

5. The quality of accommodations has continued to rise; more safe, accessible, comfortable, and convenient study conditions are being provided. The improved features include access to new technologies, better temperature and humidity control, improved quality of lighting, safer exiting in case of fire or other emergency, a larger percentage of individual seating, semiprivate accommodation, and improved access for those who are physically limited. None of these improvements has as yet reached its limits.

6. The atmospheric conditions and controls now available have been found to be very useful for the preservation of books, and continued improvements in this respect will undoubtedly be made, particularly in energy conservation techniques. Any building built today without satisfactory control of environmental conditions is already outmoded; within a few years non–air conditioned libraries should be a thing of the past in many parts of so-called developed countries. Innovative solutions, such as the 1982 solar-heated library at California State University, San Jose, shown in fig. 1.7, will be tried from time to time, but because of the value and importance of any significant library, systems based upon well-understood and widely accepted technologies

FIGURE 1.7 California State University, San Jose, Clark Library. Note that the entire length of the south wall just above window height on three floors was designed with solar collectors for building heat. Although the concept was notable at the time, it turned out to be of limited success; as would be the case in many climates, it required substantial supplemental heating. This heat source would not be adequate for full-time humidity control, where that is a requirement.

will continue to be the norm. The more common innovation will be to put together a complex system that works well and is easily maintained, within limited budgets.

If past experience means anything, the planners of academic and research library buildings should be guided by the following:

1. Because physical changes of many kinds can be expected to take place as the years go by, the utmost reasonable flexibility or adaptability is required.
2. Because long-term increase in space demands for collections and reader accommodations is almost inevitable, a building, to continue to be useful, must be so placed and planned that it can be readily enlarged at least once or twice.
3. Because accommodations will rise in quality, at least as far as the comfort of and service to the occupant and the preservation of the collections are concerned, overeconomizing is unwise; if the financial situation dictates a certain economy, the plans should be laid so that later improvements will not be unduly expensive.
4. Because technology is advancing so rapidly, the building should be able to accommodate increased use of wired and cable devices and an increase in devices using electricity.

1.8.2 Deductions from the Present

A few conclusions can be deduced that will help in planning academic libraries. These include the influence of governmental policy and of technological change. Only briefly referred to here, these particular program or design considerations will be dealt with in the appropriate places in following chapters.

Governmental policy controls an increasing number of the activities in any academic institution, whether it be publicly or privately supported. There are city, county, state, and national codes and standards for fire, earthquake, general safety, access, and general building construction. These by stages have become increasingly stringent; seismic bracing in active earthquake areas in the United States and access convenience for physically limited persons have been considerably increased in the past two decades. Professional standards may or may not be adopted or referenced in governmental codes, but they certainly can apply with nearly the force of law and administrative regulation. Promulgated by federal and state governments, the breadth of guidelines continues to grow, including, for example, the requirements of the Americans with Disabilities Act (ADA) or those of the Office of Safety and Health Administration (OSHA) in the United States. It is likely that more such measures will be developed to protect life and limb, assure full and equal access, maintain or improve the environment, economize on energy consumption, reduce pollution and waste, and otherwise assure safe buildings with minimal undesired consequences. All this, of course, puts an extra burden on academic institutions and their architects and engineers, and most mandates result in some increased cost. Each institution must work within those codes and standards that currently apply locally.

Technological change has been very great in this century and particularly so in recent decades. Indeed the situation is markedly more advanced than when the first edition of this book was published, for it was not until the 1960s that major library online computer systems were developed. It is now axiomatic that academic libraries in developed countries rely heavily on computer-based systems that automate large parts of the library operation: the purchasing, cataloging, reference work, circulation, interlending, faxing, and business operations. Today hardly an area of library operations remains, no matter how small the library, where a computer is not in use.

Although building accommodations for computer applications are woven into later chapters, a few statements are appropriate here. The Educational Facilities Laboratories asked a conference of experts in 1967 to assess the impact of technology on the library building. The conclusion was that "library planners can proceed at this time with confidence that technological developments in the foreseeable future will not alter radically the way libraries are used. In planning library buildings today, we should start with the library as the institution we now know it to be. Any departures in the future should be made from this firm base. To be sure, technology will modify library buildings. But the changes will involve trade-offs in space and demands for additional space, rather than less."[3] Although some of this sentiment remains essentially correct, it is also clear that the modern concept of the "library" is not represented by one building but rather by a set of smoothly coordinated functions and services, increasingly located in several places. Computer networking allows the library acquisition and cataloging functions to operate in a building separate from the book collections and public services. The staff of the collection preservation and conservation program, and even the library director's office (as is the case at Harvard University) may also be housed separately. And the integrated coherence of collection shelving in large research libraries is now broken up by the common use of auxiliary or storage shelving facilities.

The library building is recognized more than ever as a locus for educational effort in a social setting. The building must meet the need for the "library as place" within academe, as mentioned in the first section of this chapter. This intangible characteristic is often a major force in shaping the academic objective of the library building to meet the institutional goals for the years ahead.

The concept of a "library" is further broadened by viewing the library as a means for accessing information in digital form at places far beyond the library building itself. Some staff and some library users are able to make use of libraries from outside locations—with a personal computer linked to databases through telecommunication lines, enabling access to file servers and Internet services. Widely scattered people can use electronic mail, program software, and word-processing functions, and can access full text located elsewhere on the Internet. Thus some people speak of the "library without walls" or of the "virtual library," concepts that convey the idea that the "library" is not one building or even a local group of buildings but, rather, is all the information and library services that one can access and use from a personal microcomputer.

The definition of the "library" is therefore changing, and the implications for library buildings are great. If a major staff function does not have to be housed in the main facility for public use, a smaller building may result. Or a more remote location within the building may now be quite reasonable. The consequences of the computer create rather dramatic changes in the location and size of functional spaces within the building, in the particular local technical accommodations, and also in the size and perhaps even in the placement of the library building.

In various countries, some libraries will see a major influence brought by computer capacities. In others the impact will be modest or nonexistent for decades to come. However one plans, given the local situation, some pragmatic matters seem to be universally applicable, and some projections seem sound.

Everyone today would agree that technology will modify library buildings. Indeed, there are greatly increased electronic requirements, though some developments since 1967 have lessened the anticipated physical consequences of new communications technology. Microcomputers take less space, use less power, and produce less heat than did computers 20 years ago. Keyboards of terminals now make modest noise, and impact printers have been replaced with relatively quiet devices. Given major network services, local library file management does not require a large-scale computer using one or two thousand square feet and needing a double floor and separate power and air-conditioning sources. Distributed processing typically depends on minicomputers with modest physical demands. In nearly all academic libraries, terminals and/or microcomputers are ubiquitous, yet building consequences are very important indeed, though they are moderate in extent except for reallocation of space.

Other technological developments are also having considerable influence as the millennium draws to a close. Since the 1930s, microreproductions of one form or another have grown to constitute very large collections, such that in some libraries there are nearly as many bibliographic items in microtext as there are in book or codex form. It seems likely that the vigor of publication programs in miniature formats will continue, probably superseded by digital scanning and optical digital disk technology. Microtexts and digitized equivalents will not, we are convinced, replace the physical book to any large degree. At the same time the need for a photographic facility is limited to its utilization as a preservation technology, not as a means of saving space. Photographic arrangements were fairly common in large libraries in the middle years of the twentieth century; however, all but a few of the largest or very specialized libraries, historical societies, and archives now rely on commercial microfilming firms for filming to archival standards. Conversion to a scanning technology can be treated much like a photocopy or facsimile service within the library, though high-speed scanning involves equipment vaguely similar to that for high-speed microfilming. As with photography, scanning simply to save space does not make economic sense. Each institution will need to make a decision based on local circumstances in this regard.

Preservation of books requires much more stringent environmental control than was generally recognized as being necessary even 25 years ago. In 1967 it was thought that reduction in temperature from 80° Fahrenheit to 70° (about 27° C. to 21° C.) in a bookstack would double the life expectancy of the books; or, on another scale, life expectancy is multiplied by a factor of about 4.5 with every temperature drop of 15° C.[4] In 1994 it was calculated that reducing the temperature from about 77° F. to 68° F. (25° C. to 20° C.) while maintaining the humidity at 50 percent will increase the life expectancy of the book by a factor of approximately 2.8. If at the same time the humidity is reduced to 30 percent at the lower temperature, the life expectancy is increased by a factor approximating 6.4.[5] (See appendix D.) Temperature and humidity controls are very important for any library that has invested significant sums of money acquiring and cataloging physical materials that future generations will need to use. Exposure to light, damaging vapors produced by components of the building or furnishings, physically rough surfaces, and other preservation-related concerns are being viewed with greater interest in new building design.

Isolation chambers (for temporarily housing infested materials), paper casting machines, laminating machines, deacidification systems, and blast freezers are increasingly common in large research libraries. The rapid technological developments for treatment of particular book problems are welcome, though cool and humidity-controlled storage for the general collections will remain the most economical and effective approach to prolonging the useful life of the great mass of research collections.

The development of communication systems and devices, security systems, and information published in a wide variety of new formats create a great diversity in library management and put increasing demands on electronic and mechanical systems. Some machines produce heat and also require controlled temperature and humidity. Some machines are noisy, requiring the walls of their rooms to be acoustically treated. It is desirable to have such equipment as photocopy machines in convenient locations, provide ease of maintenance and replacement, and make arrangements so they are unobtrusive and acoustically isolated. One should expect to find in many

future libraries applications of mechanically accessed high-density book storage, closed-circuit television equipment, local area networks, fiber optics data communication, microwave long-distance or satellite transmission and reception, videoconferencing installations, and other developments not yet thought of or available on the market. The technological developments will continue to affect the planning of academic and research library buildings.

This chapter concludes with some forward-looking comments on a university library by President Claude T. Bissell of the University of Toronto:

> We must beware of a 1984 complex and, having starved our libraries in the past, of continuing to do so on the grounds that they will soon become obsolete. Technological change will mean that libraries will become even more central than they have been before, but they will also become more elaborate and more expensive; for they will need complex machinery, space in which to house the machinery, technicians to watch over them, and highly trained experts to use them.
>
> From these general reflections I turn now to comments on the specific changes that will take place in the library with the technological revolution; I shall have in mind chiefly large libraries associated with the universities. One used to think of the large research library in the university as mainly a storage depot, a cultural warehouse. That concept was modified some decades ago by the introduction of the compact storage concept whereby books rarely used were transferred to central concentration points. The use of various techniques of micro-reproduction further modified the idea of the library as a warehouse. One must not, however, indulge in science fiction fantasies of the abolition of the book; it is still the cheapest form in which to store knowledge, and will for most readers continue to be the *raison d'être* of the library. One must think too of the book as a physical object, in many cases as an *objet d'art,* which we will not readily abandon for an invisible world. Still the percentage of holdings in various forms of microtext will undoubtedly grow, and one can take some satisfaction in the prospect of space released from book storage for other purposes. . . .
>
> The profile of the new research library in the university is that of an active scholarly headquarters with a close working relationship between professional supervisors and users. . . . Again, I may illustrate the new concept by referring to our plans at the University of Toronto. We plan a research library which, in a fundamental sense, is a series of private laboratories for the graduate student and

faculty member, and where these are supplemented by small rooms for discussion and informal seminars. As the headquarters of the University, this library must not have an atmosphere of the puritan wake; it will be a place of activity, where the refinements of acoustics will release the human voice.

The best physical expression for this new type of research library has yet to be found. Thus far, changes in library structure have not been attuned to the new age. We have moved from the library conceived of as sarcophagus, a large elaborate tomb on which were inscribed the names of the illustrious dead, to the library as cathedral with an atmosphere of solemnity, grandeur, and mystery, to the library as combined head office and warehouse, with inevitable associations with that great archetype of modern architecture, the filing box. The new library must, to an extent, reflect the demands of the scientific age of which the marks are uniformity and repetition; but it must subordinate this to an expression of the unity of knowledge and the stubborn eccentricity of the human spirit. The library is a building that must be the chief symbol of the new university, the concentration centre of the systematic search for knowledge, which yet manages to cast a humorous and skeptical eye at man's pretensions to omniscience.

What will the next century produce of library transformations? Will off-campus contractual services significantly alter the need for staff space? Will full-text digital or fax transmission from afar meet a much larger proportion of the needs of library users than does interlibrary borrowing today? Will governmental law and policy make easier and less expensive, or more costly, the external access to copyrighted material? Will "distance learning" (e.g., courses taken at home via TV) become a major mode for undergraduate or continuing education? Will one or more regional or national central repositories become a major research resource, thus relieving universities of part of the library support for graduate research?

Deductions from the past lead us to be certain that books are here to stay, and will continue strongly to increase in number. The educational and research needs for large collections will continue. The techniques for housing books will not dramatically change. Easy access to library buildings will remain essential. Reliance will rapidly increase on electronic catalogs, bibliographies, other reference works, even full texts, and for distant transmission of or access to these data in digital form. Need for reader work spaces will remain strong. Need for staff spaces will in some functions diminish and in some increase, and this shift will vary among institutions. There will be change and more change, predictable in terms of one or a few decades but significantly unpredictable in the longer term.[6]

NOTES

1. Joseph Hudnut, *Architecture and the Spirit of Man* (Cambridge, Mass.: Harvard Univ. Press, 1949), p. 5.
2. William Bentinck-Smith, *Building a Great Library: The Coolidge Years at Harvard* (Cambridge, Mass.: Harvard Univ. Library, 1976), pp. 51–52.
3. *The Impact of Technology on the Library Building* (New York: Educational Facilities Laboratories, 1967), pp. 19–20.
4. *Strength and Other Characteristics of Papers, 1800–1899* (Richmond, Va.: W. J. Barrow Research Laboratory, 1967), p. 34.
5. *Isoperms: An Environmental Management Tool* (Commission on Preservation and Access, June 1994).
6. *The Strength of the University* (Toronto: Univ. of Toronto Press, 1968), pp. 134–38.

2

The Alternatives to a New Library Building

Before I built a wall, I'd ask to know what I was walling in or out.
                    —Robert Frost, "Mending Wall"

This chapter is intended to suggest possibilities for finding the best solution rather than to state arguments for or against various alternatives (though obvious arguments are noted). It discusses ways to maximize use of the library building. The chapter begins with academic master planning followed by a discussion of increasing the density of library building use, using shared facilities, moderating conditions through collection management, increasing the density of shelving through stack reconfiguration, using remote or auxiliary facilities, decentralizing library functions or collections, and capitalizing on interinstitutional or interlibrary dependencies—all of these serving potentially to postpone or moderate the demand for new space.

The expense of a new library building is often several times the library's annual budget; occasionally as much as 20 or more times larger. This being the case, alternatives to new construction providing satisfactory solutions to the needs of the library should be very seriously considered. The choice among alternatives must be based on three assessments:

1. Projection of the future of the institution and its teaching and research programs;
2. Projection of the future nature of the library, its collections, and its services; and
3. Assessment of the present and future quality and adequacy of the existing library space.

As an example, the condition of the University of Texas at Austin central library building in the 1970s constituted an especially clear case of need. The Tower, a campus landmark built in 1932, housed the main library on its lower floors. As a tower, it had inherent traffic problems for people, insufficient accessibility to some floors, and uncertain floor load capacity, and there was concern about safety, as the structure was not fireproofed and ductwork and wiring were exposed. Heat or smoke detectors, sprinklers, and alarm bells did not exist; there were no fire hoses until the 1966 fire on the twenty-second floor. Thus, despite faculty endorsement of centralized library collections for interdisciplinary scholarship, the third assessment above clearly called for a completely new structure.

This example concluded in a decision appropriate for the University of Texas. For each library space problem solved by a new building, several others are solved by additions, some by conver-

sions of adjacent nonlibrary space to library use, and many by renovations or extensive remodeling.

When a library building is first occupied, it should provide a suitable and relatively commodious setting. Within 10 years it may be relatively cramped, and some interior adjustments may be required. In 20 or 25 years it will have become quite crowded and a number of changes will usually be mandated—unless severe economic conditions restrain library growth. By the time the building is 50 years old, physical problems will appear, resulting from aging roofs, doors, windows, plumbing, mechanical systems, electrical systems, and interior surfaces. New technologies and codes may establish needs in terms of energy consumption, physical flexibility, access, environmental control, toxic substances, or structural design. Short of an extended period (50 years or more), major building components generally do not wear out. Yet they become inadequate for a variety of reasons: fashions, building standards, and operational needs change; remodeling and extensive maintenance work may be necessary.

Inadequate size is usually the most urgent consideration, and foremost is pressure from growth of library collections. Collections strictly devoted to undergraduate purposes, and particularly to lower-division students, can be maintained at a relatively static size through selective weeding. But faculty and occasionally staff work in peripheral areas of their fields to conduct research and publish: For these purposes, older books can be of supreme importance. Older works may also be valuable for documenting or prompting a different interpretation of a literary work or historical event, and thus the accumulation of carefully selected secondary materials contributes essentially to the growth and understanding of an advanced student who is trying to become fully steeped in a discipline. New acquisitions for the most part do not replace books already on the shelves.

Except for reductions resulting from changed operating methods, such as outsourcing (i.e., contracting outside the institution instead of having local staff do the task), the effects of automation, or a decrease in service levels, the staff of a library must grow as the collection becomes larger and more complex, and it will grow to the extent that additional formats need to be supported and use increases. Increased use suggests increased space is required for readers. Changes in teaching methods may result in larger demands on the library even with online access to international databases. Although demographic fluctuation for a decade or two may reduce enrollment, hamper the finances of an institution, and affect the vigor of the library program, cyclical patterns will shift and again the library will need more space.

Beyond the more obvious possibilities of dealing with library growth described in Sections 2.2 and 2.3, the several options can become complex and expensive. An academic master plan should be the guide to keep sights set on accepted long-term goals. Long-term costs need to be looked at in considerable detail.

In this connection, early use of a library building consultant, a local building inspector, and an insurance manager to advise on risk reduction and costs should result in excellent insight and wise advice for sorting out the alternatives and their consequences. For a detailed description of factors that should be considered in analyzing various shelving options, Chapter 6 should also be consulted.

2.1
Academic Master Planning

Perceiving shifts in teaching programs requires a very complete awareness of the curriculum. A grasp of the changing nature of research is also helpful, though difficult to obtain. Both have a direct effect upon the library program. Changes in technological, social, economic, and political conditions, and philosophical and moral attitudes also can engender major consequences for the library and its host institution. It has become increasingly common for libraries to have stated goals and objectives reflecting changing demands and influences. These program objectives constitute a library master plan ideally covering at least a five-year projection of what is expected in its collection development, its processing programs, and its public services. And the goals and objectives should outline broader direction for a decade or more ahead. A complementary set of phased objectives for the physical plant needed to house the library may be based on these goals.

Library planning for an academic institution can only be as sound as the planning for the entire institution, and the library should be recognized as a very important component of such institutional planning. Regardless of whether the institution as a whole has such a clearly documented academic master plan with a complementary physical master plan, the library needs to have such a plan.

From 30 to 50 years ago, it was rather common for surveys to be conducted by outside experts whose recommendations proposed changes to be realized in the years immediately ahead. It was found that the soundness of the recommendations, the understanding of them, and their effective implementation all depended on the extent to which the staff of the library and parent institution were involved and convinced.

In more recent years, often with some guidance by experienced outside consultants, key library staff have been deeply involved and frequently conduct the entire job of formulating long-term goals and setting down the phases for short-term objectives. This same rationale pertains when a library building program is written. A consultant may advise, question, and stimulate, but it is incumbent upon the local librarians to have a sense of authorship of the program. This is true because only the local librarians fully understand the institution's academic objectives, the historical conditions within the institution, the style and standards desired by the current administration, and the particular library response that is justified in serving such an institutional need. And they will need to follow through on issues long after the consultant has departed. Failing the obligation of authorship of the program, the librarian must ensure that the requirements suggested here are fully met, which will necessitate detailed involvement on the part of the librarian.

Colleges and universities are placing increased emphasis on planning as a defined function. Since 1945 planning departments have become common, sometimes divided into an academic planning office and a planning office for facilities. By whatever name, the academic planning office deals with the statistical conditions and trends of student matriculation, course enrollment, residence, and grading patterns. The facilities planning office is commonly part of the business office, dealing with the financial and legal aspects of space planning, the choice of architects and planners, the qualification of consultants and contractors, and facility project budget preparation and management. It assures that governmental as well as institutional standards are followed, that construction conforms to the bid documents, and that the process moves in a cost-effective and businesslike fashion. This office seldom gets into operational building maintenance affairs after the construction warranty period.

Both the academic planning and facilities planning offices are likely to have various master planning documents that can be useful for the library academic plan. In some institutions this planning procedure has become standardized and relies heavily on statistical formulation and annual completion of special forms. Some difference of opinion exists about whether this quantitative analysis assists or stultifies the academic planning process, though such analysis is fairly common in large, publicly supported statewide systems of higher education. If used wisely, quantitative data can support the planning process. Institutions considering future library requirements will need to develop planning processes within the existing institutional framework.

In New Jersey, North Carolina, Florida, Michigan, Indiana, Illinois, Wisconsin, Colorado, and Washington, it is clear that state planning for higher education represents a major activity. Because the number of students and the annual operating budgets for state-supported systems in places like New York and California are huge, there are public requirements for careful accountability. Such plans and their justification present constraints and certainly demand extra lead time in resolving a physical problem on a particular campus.

California may be cited as one example. The University of California in the early 1970s committed itself to a systemwide approach to library planning based on the concept of a university-wide book collection rather than nine separate campus collections. Planning data were gathered through meticulous studies of collections overlap, intercampus lending, and the amount of infrequently used materials. A master library planning document emerged to be reviewed by all campuses, the statewide academic senate, and the president's office. Balancing competing economic and academic forces led to a difficult conclusion, but one that was deemed to be feasible and desirable. A first tangible result was a statewide serial listing to supplement the published book catalogs; then came the system online library catalog, followed in 1980 by construction of the Northern California Regional Library Facility as an auxiliary bookstack building in Richmond. The facility was intended to substitute at least in part for more campus library construction and was a direct product of academic master planning. Since

its construction, a second storage facility was built in Los Angeles, and the Richmond facility has been expanded. The goal of limiting central campus library development was achieved until the later 1980s and early 1990s when major central library projects were approved for the University of California campuses at Davis, Berkeley, San Francisco, San Diego, and elsewhere.

Some independent institutions have done excellent planning studies, Swarthmore College being notable. The libraries at Columbia and Harvard have at times prepared extensive planning documents. This is not to say, however, that a major tome is always necessary or justified. A good understanding among academic officers and the principal library administrators may constitute such a sound understanding of the institutional future that a formal academic master plan document may not be necessary. Yet even then the individuals involved in judging the alternatives to a new library building must thoroughly understand and agree on this institutional framework and direction for planning, and a summary of academic objectives and standards should be written into the library building program document so that planners, architects, and, it is hoped, financing officers and donors will have a consistent understanding of these matters.

2.2
More Exhaustive Building Use

This section provides an overview of an alternative to a new library building. The next considers shared use of a building and is followed by four sections on alternative directions for management of book-collection space needs.

Careful study of the existing building may reveal areas where use of space can be increased, perhaps postponing the requirement for additional space. Increased space utilization must assure maintenance of legal exit aisles, maximum floor loading limits, adequate sprinkler clearance (where there are sprinklers), and access for the physically limited. Where maximum functional density is achieved, one may face problems of reduced air circulation, increased noise and consequent disruptions of staff operations, circuitous work flow, lessened aesthetics, and the loss of "sense of place," which can cause considerable morale problems. These and other issues need to be carefully evaluated in each case. Some increased use may be highly successful; some arrangements may entail alterations and rehabilitation costing more than can be justified.

Depending on whether the pressure is on reading quarters, staff work space, areas for information technology, or book shelving, space can be sought in appropriate locations. In some cases, a set of sequential moves may be needed. Questions such as the following may be asked: Is the main lobby large and could it therefore be partitioned to reduce its width or depth, maintaining a reasonably gracious entrance but providing new assignable floor area? Are corridors wide enough to accommodate a bank of carrels, a computer cluster, housing for certain reference works, workstations for hourly employees, or other use? (A consultation with the local fire marshal is urged where thoughts turn to use of a corridor.) Can exhibition areas be given up temporarily to meet certain other functional requirements? Can a coatroom be given up? Are student lockers used enough to justify continuance? Are there storage areas that can be dispensed with, or can bulk storage be moved to another campus building, freeing such library areas for priority needs? Can office partitions be replaced by open office landscape furniture techniques, increasing density while maintaining reasonable visual privacy and acoustical isolation? Can any administrative offices be relocated to another building? Could a student lounge and a staff snack facility be combined or reduced in size? Can some parts of the technical processes be decentralized to one or more branches? Can all technical processes be relocated to a nearby building, or provided by a contractor at a remote location? Can books be shelved tightly in a closed collection or a collection shelved in a classification scheme not currently used so as to free empty shelves? Can some cross aisles in the bookstack be filled in with shelves without eliminating major traffic patterns? Can shelving be made taller? Can shelves be added along the walls? Can oversized books be shelved on spines or moved to a folio or portfolio section in order to add shelves in a section to handle more octavo volumes? Is the use of major reading rooms intense enough to justify devoting the entire room to reading, or could some part be partitioned for work quarters or extra shelving for processing backlogs? Can shelves be moved closer together or can movable compact shelves be installed? (Refer to fig. 6.20.)

These and other questions can be raised during a critical look at increasing the use of present space. Although an excellent solution may be found in better use of existing space, it is important to consider the deleterious results of overcrowding as noted earlier. Overcrowding of staff quarters in academic libraries is one of the most frequent space pressures, perhaps because the librarian during programming was too modest in the assignment of staff space, failed to foresee the prospective needs, or did not convince the institutional administration that the staff size would need to grow as conditions change.

The building codes probably have changed since the building was constructed or last remodeled. Alterations costing more than 50 percent of the building's replacement value may result in a requirement to bring the entire building up to current building codes. (All new work will naturally be required to meet code.) This can mean that fire exits, access for the physically limited, rest rooms, emergency lighting, handrails, electrical circuitry, ventilation, and dead-end corridors, among other things, may require correction. A good way of determining the probable cost of substantial alterations is to have the structure carefully examined and a cost estimate prepared by a reliable construction contractor who should take into consideration potential code-driven costs. Such an effort is only effective where the scope of work is clearly identified.

A thorough review of current and potential building use, and answers to questions like those posed above, will strengthen the hand of the librarian requesting approval for remodeling, a building addition, or a new structure. The librarian should demonstrate that all reasonable alternatives have been considered and why these alternatives do not appropriately solve current and projected needs. The librarian must show that space now available is not being wasted and that continuing to operate in the present building bears demonstrable adverse consequences.

One other approach to a more exhaustive use of an existing building should be mentioned. This has been termed *outsourcing* in some contexts, and *contract services* in others. The concept is to arrange with an outside organization to provide specified services. The aims are often to reduce expenses, derive service from an organization with specialized talents not available in-house, and save some space and overhead costs. These management approaches are frequently used in business enterprises. In applying these ideas to an academic library, evaluate the pros and cons of contracting for a variety of technical processing tasks with an outside company, or of using a cooperative regional nonprofit service if one exists (e.g., the New England Document Conservation Center). In such cases, space would be gained within the current library building for all tasks subsequently done outside. A variety of problems or concerns stem from such an approach, and there are certain to be some offsetting costs. Nevertheless, there may be some sound applications of this concept, and the benefits are worth considering.

This concept represents the origin of the H. W. Wilson Company, Information Access Corporation, and CARL, with their indexing and abstracting services once conducted in-house by libraries. Library contracts for online services are common today. However, if this approach is pushed to the extreme, one might conceive of access to a collection of material in print format being purchased from off campus, or existing college and university book collections being "sold" to an outside organization in return for which the organization provides copies on demand, or loans from its off-campus warehouse to members of the academy who need specific items. This would in most cases be a desperate, even reckless, action with adverse long-term consequences. However, the Center for Research Libraries is a valued nonprofit organization built on exactly that concept. A service contract that turns over a valued educational capital resource to a management that has commercial business motives is dangerous. It does ease space pressures within the library building. Yet, in short order, it undermines the viability of the educational institution if carried to such an extreme. If the collections of a secondary nature, collections supportive of graduate or advanced study and research, are moved off campus, the very process of education is damaged, the instrument of research is crippled. Thus, while the institution must very carefully consider short-term problems and the long-term consequences, the concept may in selected instances provide a partial solution to building pressures.

2.3
Use of Shared Facilities

Nonlibrary functions within the library building have their advantages and disadvantages. One clear advantage of other occupants in a shared facility is the possibility of the library taking over more of the building as an alternative to building new library space.

Some institutions are housed in a megastructure, such as Simon Fraser University; the University of Wisconsin, Parkside; and Mission College in Santa Clara, California. Library expansion in such cases should be relatively easy if the building was designed for such expansion. Even in much smaller buildings where the library is the dominant occupant, a great many other functions can be housed in the same building. Various examples exist and almost any function is possible. These include the offices of the president, the alumni secretary's office, classrooms, a library school, audiovisual service not part of the library, the student union or other food facility, the university bookstore, the student counseling service, university press stock, a language laboratory, and a campus computing facility—even a college chapel! Classrooms have often been placed in a library with the idea that they would be removed later as the demands for space on the part of the library increased and a new separate classroom building could be made available. Other functions may be sympathetic with library service and provide educational value and building flexibility, one example being the "literacy center" in the 1998 Monroe Library of Loyola University, New Orleans. Perhaps the worst co-occupant would be wet labs because the investment in utilities would be wasted in later conversion to library usage.

Whatever the temporary occupant, the decanting of nonlibrary functions can provide a satisfactory alternative to new library construction. With any new building containing a library, it is desirable to anticipate greater eventual library occupancy and therefore design column spacing, floor load capacity, ceiling heights, lighting, and utilities that will work effectively and harmoniously with an expanded library. Many institutions have failed to be foresighted, and have opted for short-range values rather than recognized that higher education and many research institutions must plan for the very long term.

2.3.1 Future Displacement of Nonlibrary Functions

The decanting of neighbors will require providing the other function a home elsewhere some day, and there are difficulties in shared use of a building. These are summarized here as if a new building were being planned, because the availability and cost to take over more of the building may depend on the original plan.

The prime consideration is the main entrance, access, and control of exits. If book materials are to be inspected at the exit, it is desirable and almost obligatory to have a separate exit and entrance (perhaps off a shared lobby) for other functions in the building. One need only consider traffic generated by classrooms or the president's office to recognize the awkwardness of a shared entrance and exit. With book inspection, all occupants of the building sharing the same entrance and all their visitors of all types and ages and professions must pass an inspection desk to see if library materials are charged out. A book detection system in which the target can be neutralized when the book is checked out eliminates the need for inspection of library materials at the exit, making control of traffic less critical. However, it still should be noted how disturbing to library users a sizable amount of extraneous traffic passing by library study quarters can be. Additionally, the false alarms common to at least one of the widely used book detection systems are increased by the added traffic. When nonlibrary activities are assigned to a library, they should ideally be given a separate entrance and exit. Keep in mind that multiple building entrances can be very frustrating to the visitor if they lead to distinct functions that are not clearly defined.

The character of the entry is another point for serious consideration. The entrance to a building often helps define its function. This is certainly the case with respect to libraries. The size and quality of the entrance and lobby areas, presence of exhibits, artistic works, artifacts symbolic of the function therein, the nature of seating—all serve to define function, either intentionally or by chance. There is a certain character as one approaches classrooms, with their periodic hustle, bustle, noise, chatter. There is a different character as one approaches a college president's office, a bookstore, an alumni office, religious spaces, or a student union. The entry and immediate functions are intended to clarify and set the tone for the activities one is approaching, and imply suitable behavior. Because libraries should be distinctive on campus, a clear separation of entrances for disparate functions is therefore usually wise. Yet, architecturally, where is or which is to be the main entrance? Is there an approach to the building that would be regarded as the "front door," the major function therein? Should a single entrance to the building lead to a lobby serving as a traffic center into two or more functions, the library being but one? Can such a solution be implemented without seeming to subordinate one internal function to the other? Thoughtful and sensitive solutions need to be developed, with both the short- and long-term consequences contributing to the final arrangements.

Another potentially serious problem is the relocation of the nonlibrary function in a timely manner. If the institution's administration is in the building and if the building is one of the most attractive on campus, this staff may not be motivated to ask for other space in spite of the fact that their remaining causes library problems. Even classrooms may be hard to remove, especially if they have sloping floors or other special features. The primacy of library need, when justified, may be strengthened if all parties understand from the beginning the eventual assignment. The librarian must recognize institutional and building priorities and the difficulty of getting space with ideal timing. It would be unreasonable for the librarian to expect to displace nonlibrary functions if the library is only slightly pressed for space. Conversely, the library should not hold unneeded space just for the sake of having it later.

The Meyer Memorial Library at Stanford University is a case in point, originally having four extraneous occupants. The university chancellor had two rooms as an office on the top floor, and four language laboratories had quarters on the ground floor. All users had to go through the library exit control. In addition there are six small classrooms and the Disability Resource Center serving physically limited students on the ground floor, each with its own outside entrance. Only the laboratories and classrooms were initial occupants, and, after 30 years, the library's needs are not yet more compelling than those of the others (fig. 2.1). Indeed, to add complexity, a large open room (called the Forum Room) with a separate outside entrance, well off to one side of the entrance to the library itself, seats 125 persons for meetings, lectures, conferences, and computer and media presentations and has been shared by the library system and by others scheduled by the Registrar's Office—a bit awkward, yet workable, and a way to achieve maximum use of a versatile university facility.

Another approach to the general concept of shared entry can be seen with the Bibliothèque nationale de France and the National Taiwan Library as designed (the latter is not yet constructed).

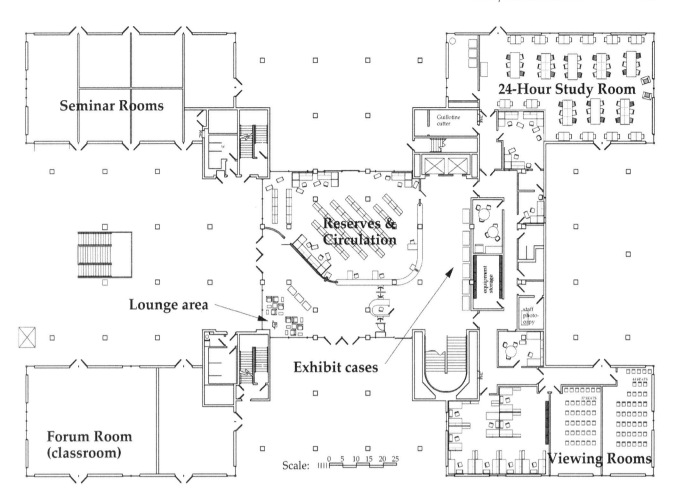

FIGURE 2.1 Stanford University, Meyer Memorial Library, ground floor. Originally designed to house undergraduate library services, the facility currently is heavily oriented toward technology with one entire floor devoted to computer clusters, media facilities, a computer-based language laboratory, interactive video, and the like. This diagram of a proposed alteration was subsequently realized with minor changes; the 24-hour study room was created from the former media library while the language laboratories on this floor have been converted to staff space and two viewing rooms for films and video. The major change proposed here is the introduction of the circulation and reserves function, which was originally on the second floor. The seminar rooms and the Forum Room remain much as they did originally. The entrance to the main research library (the Cecil H. Green Library) is to the left of this illustration, perhaps 200 feet away. (Used with permission of Stanford University Libraries)

Both national libraries have multiple "nonlibrary" functions within the building. Conceptually they are accessed from a shared circulation space. In effect, there is a library within the library building along with other activities. Megastructures containing major university functions along with the library share some of the same characteristics. This might be thought of as a shopping mall model; it works quite well for patrons and flexibility, provided the needs of flexibility are accounted for in the original design.

As for the physical aspects of shared space, the conversion of quarters taken over from another function may be relatively inexpensive because major structural difficulties seldom occur if the building was initially engineered to meet library requirements. For example, the floor loading and column spacing (where the requirements of access have been made part of the original design) should be suitable for shelving. Lighting and environmental control will need some reconsideration, and it may be a problem to create aesthetic continuity between original library space and newly occupied space.

Finally, although no one location in a library building is best for a temporary occupant, it is well to consider one wing, a small portion of the first floor, lower-level space, and the top floor so long as separate stairs, elevator, and entrance can be arranged. Special attention must also be given to horizontal and vertical traffic; good solutions must be found for each of the initial occupants. Individual circumstances will lead to the best interim solution.

2.4
Collection Management

Control of the active collection size may be a temporary palliative, but it needs serious consideration for two reasons. It can buy time for an institution to justify and raise funds for new space, and it also may show the administration that the use of present space has been optimized. Sound collection development policies are needed, as is wise professional judgment of which items to select and acquire. More rigorous selection, especially from proffered gifts of books and other materials, may improve the quality of what is added, and it can save space.

Culling the collection may be a reasonable step, saving shelf space with only slightly more reliance on interlibrary borrowing or electronic access to resources (see, for example, JSTOR at www.jstor.org or Project Gutenberg at www.promo.net/pg/). Although the authors are not yet persuaded that the advantages of electronic access outweigh those of traditional means, the fact remains that one possible alternative is the replacement of hard copy with digitized access, provided there is a degree of certainty that access will continue to be available at reasonable expense. In most cases, the space savings achieved through this approach will be modest, though this should change over time.

Often multiple copies of a title must be obtained for current use without a continuing long-term need. Retention of multiple editions of encyclopedias and other large works may not be necessary. Little-used classes of books in a branch library may be appropriate in the main library. Although there is expense to alter catalog records and book marks as such items are withdrawn or transferred from the collection, the space occu-pied by the average volume on the shelf is currently worth as much as US$10, and more in some cases. Suffice it to say that a librarian ought to achieve judicious weeding in part because of the space consequences.

The microtext collections may constitute as much as half of the bibliographic items held by the library. Microtext replacements of newspapers and other materials on exceedingly bad paper are common, and, as a byproduct, space is saved. Some microfilming (or digitizing) may be done for preservation purposes, particularly when the material is seldom used. Most microtexts are purchased, however, because they contain the text of scarce publications, expensive sets, or manuscripts that cannot be economically obtained in any other way. Still, faculty, trustees, and administrative officers may regard conversion of parts of the collection to microtexts or digital images as a solution to a request for a new building. The goal of carrying the Library of Congress around in miniaturized form in a shoe box has at times been cited as preferable to a new library building. However, experience over the past 60 years has shown that this is illusory.

Microtext and optical disks or videodisks can be space savers, and materials in these formats are certainly increasing in number. Microtexts have had a greater impact on library building design than has the provision of computer terminals; yet they seldom have replaced the book except in some college or science and technology libraries with severe space limitations. Journal runs, for example, can be replaced in microtext with great space savings. Digital technology is rapidly increasing in importance in libraries but it also has limitations. It is suggested that digitizing should not be considered as a panacea for growing libraries, but rather it is likely to be supplemental to traditional library collecting just as microtexts have largely been.

The handling of seldom-used materials is a different matter. Occasionally a relatively unused collection may be offered as a gift or deposit to another library with an active academic program in that field. Placing seldom-used materials in auxiliary shelving facilities (once called deposit libraries and often inelegantly and somewhat misleadingly referred to as storage libraries), or a shared service facility like the Center for Research Libraries can be helpful for local space pressures. Judgment of what materials are appropriate for removal from the active collection requires extensive knowledge of the ongoing educational and research endeavors that the library is designed to support. The published literature on weeding, relegation, and collection management can help one work toward a suitable conclusion for any particular institution.

Temporary removal of certain sets, serial runs, archival materials, or subject classes to another campus building may also provide breathing space for a few years while a building is being financed and constructed. One must remember the academic justification for parts of a collection and the related effect that weeding or relocating may have on the teaching and research program that cannot be quantified but may nonetheless be harmful. Careful consideration must be given to the consequences on the educational program and on research efficiency.

2.5
Stack Reformation

The preceding section dealt with management actions that give temporary relief, though in some instances they indicate desperation in housing collections. The physical alteration of the bookstack into a reformed pattern is another extreme action and one that is certain to be quite expensive. The means of reaching the highest stack density need careful analysis of operational and access issues and cost. Compact shelving is given more extensive treatment in Section 6.3.

As was mentioned in Section 2.2, you may find certain empty walls in a bookstack where shelves can be added. If there is more than one main aisle, it may be possible to fill in all but one, so long as the building code requirements for exiting are still met. You may fit vertical extensions onto the stack columns so that more shelves can be hung near the ceiling, though stools will need to be conveniently located. In these instances, changes can often be made without a structural engineer or a building permit. Of course, the added weight, sprinkler clearance, lighting, air circulation, the seismic resistance of the shelving itself, and other features may need review by experts.

In rare instances, usually where such an expansion was preplanned, a mezzanine or second tier can be installed in a bookstack. Still more ambitious would be narrowing range aisles to the minimum permitted by code or for wheelchair access, not less than 26 in. (660 mm), though the Amer-

icans with Disabilities Act (ADA) in the United States limits the aisle width to 36 in. (910 mm). A careful reading of the 1988 Uniform Building Code (still used in some locations) further limits aisle spacing to a minimum of 44 in. (1.12 m). A number of code authorities have accepted the less space consumptive requirements of ADA where an exception is requested for library stacks. Few libraries exist in the United States that will be able to increase capacity by moving shelving closer together. This is usually true even of shelving that is closed to public access, though local officials may grant a variance in such instances.

If there are no code limitations to aisle width, capacity can, in some cases, be increased as much as 10 percent by moving the shelving closer together. Changing range aisles usually entails emptying at least the range that is being moved (there have been libraries where fully loaded ranges were moved with special equipment), replacing the carpet or patching the floor, and relocating lights, unless they were running perpendicular to the range. In the case of the Yale Divinity Library, narrower aisles were achieved at the same time that the ranges were turned 90°, a technique that may save on lighting changes. In these instances a structural engineer should advise on the safety of floor loading, and a building permit may be required. For adding a second tier, coordination of vertical movement and structural relationships will be necessary. Where the second tier is technically a mezzanine (i.e., it does not have direct emergency egress to enclosed fire stairs), it is limited in some codes to an area equal to one-third of the basic floor area.

It should be stressed that reformations of the bookstack should be undertaken only after very careful analysis; they are seldom justified. They always cost a great deal for a modest amount of additional shelving. They increase the floor loading. They may detract from the good feel of architectural spaces. (At Wheaton College, Norton, Massachusetts, a 1923 central atrium of classic beauty was filled with bookstacks in 1961, an expedient that was reversed only 19 years later.) The traffic patterns may be made much more difficult, not only for those in wheelchairs. The movement of book trucks in very narrow aisles may be impossible, requiring stack shelvers to hand-carry books from a main aisle down the entire length of the range aisle for reshelving. Two people may not be able to pass in an aisle if it is as little as 22 in. (560 mm). An occasional oversized book will overhang the shelf and be hit by shoulders, hips, and book trucks. The lighting, which adequately reached the bottom shelves, may become inadequate for narrow aisles even when properly positioned. Even ventilation would be slightly impaired. Operational considerations, public relations, and architectural honesty as well as results of a cost study should be weighed.

Movable compact shelving is a still more expensive alternative in terms of cost per unit area, but it may be less expensive in terms of cost per item stored. Where the necessary floor load capacity is available, it may represent an excellent alternative. Compact shelving generally is free of the code limitations for minimum aisle spacing except for the infrequent access aisle. Installations of compact shelving have become common in university and research libraries. They are found in public as well as closed stack areas. They have been employed in multifloor installations. They have been used for books, artworks, and microtext collections. The Marston Science Library at the University of Florida has even used compact shelving technology for a large accumulation of map cases.

Movable shelving is widely accepted so long as the cost of such installations is justified. Examples of the sound application of compact movable shelving are where a building addition is not feasible or cannot be afforded for many years, where the site is ideal and conversion of adjacent space is not an option, where real estate values are high, and where existing physical conditions of column spacing and floor loading capacity permit it to be considered. In an older building being remodeled, the basement may be the only level that can structurally handle the weight. Since the 1960s, use of compact shelving in academic libraries has been increasing, though not for heavily used collections. Depending on preexisting conditions or the arrangements in a normal stack, the increase in capacity may be anywhere from 50 percent to as much as 130 percent. Where this has long-term importance, movable compact shelving may be an excellent and cost-justifiable solution.

As early as 1878, an English librarian designed a bookcase attached by several hinges to another stationary bookcase. The user then had to swing open the outer case as if opening a cabinet door. The movable case can have a single face accessible from the outside, or it can be double-faced so that when opened one can utilize the shelving on the back of the movable section as well as access

the fixed section behind. These cases have a floor wheel at the side away from the hinge, and they often have handles to facilitate moving. The weight in a double-faced hinged case filled with books is of course considerable, yet it moves with no more difficulty than a rather heavy door.

The installation of this type in the Center for Research Libraries (CRL), Chicago, worked quite well when installed with careful leveling and when the hinges and wheel bearings were kept clean and well lubricated. However, in 1981, CRL moved to its new Kenwood site and used conventional industrial shelving throughout. The 1992 second phase was with compact shelving, providing CRL a total of 130,000 ft^2 (12,077 m^2) so it could sell the original building and scrap the swing-shelving—though one full section of the unique shelving was retained as a museum piece.

Another type of compact shelving has movable sections that roll laterally on wheels or overhead tracks (that is, individual sections may be moved from side to side as one faces the shelves, thus exposing additional sections behind the moved sections). Perhaps the earliest example of this type of shelving was installed in the Bodleian Library at Oxford and dates from early in the twentieth century, although it was replaced when the 1946 building expansion was designed.

The most common movable compact shelving throughout the world is now the type where entire ranges of bookshelves move on tracks running perpendicular to the range. From Australia to Scandinavia, they are now widely used. The shelves are fixed on heavy carriages that move along tracks. The track in new buildings may be mounted flush into the floor, whereas in installations in existing buildings it sits above it. On top of the carriage are standard case, industrial or cantilever-type bookshelf units with rigid structure. Movement may be by hand lever or a crank, or electrically driven by motor. Safety features are incorporated in all that are motorized, generally including at least a kick plate that automatically cuts off electricity if a book on the floor or someone's foot is in the way, torque-limiting devices in the drive mechanism, and weight-sensitive flooring designed to prevent operation of the system when a person is in the aisle. Systems involving light beams, motion detectors, resetting procedures, and various interlocking devices are available. There even is a system available that can automatically move the carriages to a "rest" position where the space between the carriages is uniform within the bay of compact shelving in order to maximize airflow and sprinkler protection when the system is not in use (that is, the access aisle is used to create an equal space between each range).

Movable compact units have had some problems. Some shivering or other movement may result in an occasional volume dropping off the top shelf. A book that has inadvertently been shelved in front of another and may project out beyond the shelf can be crushed when the unit moves against the adjacent unit. Hand injuries can occur if, when not standing within the unit, a user attempts manually to stop a moving electrically driven unit by putting a hand between two ranges. This latter risk can be reduced by adding a pressure-sensitive strip along the vertical edge of the end panels that, if touched, will stop the motors, a safety feature offered by some manufacturers. Of course anyone standing on a bottom shelf to reach the top shelf would circumvent the protective effect of a kick plate or floor weight device. In this example, a torque-limiting device or some form of a motion detector or light beam may be required as an added protective measure.

Because from 10 to 20 seconds are required to open aisles in an average installation, and because only one person can use a bay of ranges at a time, it is clear that movable compact systems are for collections that are seldom used or that are used by staff only. This limitation can be partially offset by creating smaller blocks of movable shelving with shorter ranges or with fewer ranges per bay. Mechanical assist systems (that is, the type that are cranked open) can easily be up to 30 ft (9.114 m) long. Motorized systems have been installed up to double this length, though lengths of 30 to 36 ft (9.144 to 10.972 m) are more common. As most systems are accessed from one end, the systems with extremely lengthy ranges are less convenient for shifts, reshelving, and the like. And there is greater risk of mechanical problems due to torquing and twisting of the very long range.

The spacing of stack columns, the need for earthquake bracing, electrical requirements, and the arrangement of lighting are details to be studied. Floor loading requirements of 250 pounds per ft^2 (11.970 kN/m^2) are required, although some materials, such as phonograph records, may require as much as 300 pounds per ft^2 (14.364 kN/m^2).

Other compact arrangements have been tried from time to time. A drawer-type unit mounted on shelves was available during the third quarter of the twentieth century and before. The tiered stack in the 1919 Main Library (now the Cecil H. Green Library) at Stanford University had such drawers, which were removed in the 1970s because they were difficult to use.

Labyrinthian mechanized bookstacks have also been designed where an operator at a keyboard instructs a mechanical picker which bin to retrieve. Rotterdam University in Holland and the Medical Library at Ohio State University have installed this type. More recently, various forms of "order-picker" storage systems have been incorporated with success in facilities at California State University, Northridge; the Harvard Depository Library; the University of Alberta; and elsewhere. This technology makes a great deal of sense where collections are kept in accession order and by size, rather than by subject classification. It has been demonstrated to be one of the least expensive methods (at least in terms of the physical accommodation) of storing large collections.

Although those who are involved with "order-picker" systems tend to be avid supporters, the authors urge some measure of caution if such a system is contemplated. Our concerns revolve around system maintenance cost, life expectancy of the mechanical components, the cost of records changes necessary to place materials in this type of system, dealing with power failure, the cost to deliver materials to patrons, and the like. Regarding the cost of service, we are reminded of a story told by Professor Sidney Verba of Harvard who at the time had been doing research on the effect of religion upon politics. It seems he realized that he did not know much about Episcopalianism, whereupon he asked his assistant to fetch material on the subject. The next day some 11 books arrived at his office. He quickly determined that only a very small number were appropriate for his research; the rest had to be returned to the stacks (which in this case were all over campus and included materials from the Harvard Depository remote storage facility). If he had been able to browse the collection, he could have reduced the number of items checked out substantially, and the delivery cost would have been limited to his time only. Part of the argument of this story is that libraries need more complete cataloging information so that decisions about materials can be made more effectively before requesting them. With improved cataloging information, the cost of service from any of the storage systems requiring staff or machines to fetch materials should diminish. However, the trend appears to be toward streamlining cataloging information rather than making it more detailed.

A variation, which in terms of the physical plant may cost less than an "order-picker" system, is seen at the University of California Regional Library Facilities. Here it was decided to use extra-deep industrial shelving with open grate floors in what amounts to a tiered stack. With the open grate floors, the problems of air circulation are applied to one large space volume, much like the "order-picker" system. The materials are shelved by size, in accession order, two and sometimes three rows deep. Although the facility cost per volume capacity is low, the management cost for servicing the collections is substantial. The authors urge careful analysis of the operating cost and the effect of nonbrowsability on advanced students and scholars before choosing this type of storage system.

In considering compact shelving, it is essential to balance the consequences of operational conditions against the economic factors. Browsing is difficult in most of these systems and quite impossible in a few. This shelving may be very good for archive boxes but difficult for very large volumes. Some compact shelving requires fixed spacing of shelves, and, therefore, classified order of books may be difficult to maintain. Where the compact shelving will constitute housing for a separate auxiliary collection, the costs of changing catalog records and the extra staff to service such an installation need to be considered. The possibility of further expansion into another unit of compact shelving also needs consideration.

As with other aspects of library planning, the total operational costs may be difficult to determine. There is not only the determination of book storage costs on a per-volume basis when compared to land value and the cost per cubic foot of the building space, but also the difference in lighting costs, ventilation, staffing, and the effect on library clientele. It may be found that the short-term savings from compact shelving are nonexistent, particularly when factors other than initial construction costs are considered. A cost study should be undertaken to aid in the decision, and local political or budgetary factors will often have an influence as well. For example, there may be

an institutional budget for equipment while funding for a new facility may be impossible. Phasing of equipment additions or replacements to an existing space may be easier to achieve than phasing new space.

2.6
Decentralization of Resources

The deployment of libraries on a campus must in some measure reflect the singular conditions of the institution itself. However, the cost of operating a fragmented, scattered, decentralized library system is certain to be more than the cost of one physically in one place. That should be obvious. Why then even consider decentralization? There are at least five reasons.

1. Space in the one main library building has run out, and perhaps there is no land on which to build a library addition.
2. Campus academic quarters are spread widely over many acres or blocks, so getting to the single library building has become very troublesome.
3. The close and frequent student use of library materials in connection with use of laboratories, studios, or performance halls argues for juxtapositioning of the library with the supported academic functions.
4. The strength of a major academic department or a senior official forcefully urges a separate, an impressive, or a more independent home for that department, including its "own" library.
5. The fund-raising potential exists and adds to one of the other arguments for new, separate quarters.

This chapter does not argue the merits of decentralization; the policy on and planning for branch library quarters is dealt with elsewhere (see Sections 3.2.3 and 10.7). This section merely addresses decentralization as a way of postponing the necessity for a major central-library addition or even an entirely new building, the first of the five reasons listed.

Any decision to decentralize the book collections must take into account the operational master plan for the institution and the direction in which interdisciplinary areas are moving. Factors to be considered include institutional geography, transportation and parking, size and strength of departments, fund-raising opportunities, the need for large associated spaces, such as studios or labs, and the bibliographic separability of a subject field without the need for extensive duplication of materials among library units. Decisions are made more complex by the fact that traditional disciplinary boundaries keep shifting, slowly but surely. Fields change and today's discoveries become the historic base on which tomorrow's research efforts are built. This advancement occurs both in the traditional disciplines and in their interconnections, which themselves often emerge as new disciplines. The result can especially influence libraries in the sciences and technology disciplines.

The Harvard University Library has been moving toward increased decentralization for nearly 150 years. As late as 1887, 89 percent of the collections were in a central research library. Yet by 1927 as many volumes were housed in branches as in the Widener building. Today less than a third are in the central research collection, and even those are divided among the central cluster of library buildings known as the Widener, Houghton, Lamont, and Pusey buildings, together with those items stored across the river in the New England Deposit Library and in the Harvard Depository Library.

The controversy about the desirability of physical centralization versus decentralization continues on many campuses. A few have achieved substantial centralization, among them Queens College, Guelph, Johns Hopkins, Iowa State University, Michigan State University, Oklahoma State University, Rice University, Southern Illinois University, Tulane University, and the University of California campuses at San Diego and Santa Barbara. In some cases, the main or central library is physically restricted by the site but may be of good quality, and so branch libraries are unavoidable. Most large and long-established universities of high quality have many branch libraries. Several dozen and sometimes as many as a hundred may be distributed across the campus. The University of Tokyo has had as many as 312 different libraries!

Although there are very clear operational and economic advantages in a physically unified and logically classified collection, most university libraries have been decentralized to some extent. This is also true in some colleges. Subjects that frequently have been given their own quarters are art, music, engineering, and the sciences, and such

professional fields as business, divinity, education, law, and medicine. Completely desirable or not, decentralization does commonly occur. Furthermore, one can look to such old and respected universities as Cambridge, Oxford, Harvard, and Yale to see that dozens of physical branches would seem to be inevitable in the course of time. What has happened in those universities is only a degree more developed than in those like Cornell University, the University of Michigan, the University of Texas at Austin, Columbia University, the University of California at Berkeley and Los Angeles, Ohio State University, and the University of Illinois at Urbana-Champaign. Such physical decentralization can be a method for easing pressure on the central library building. Conversely, the creation of a new central divisional facility, such as a central science library or one for an arts cluster, may ease the pressure elsewhere.

Multidisciplinary and interdisciplinary interests argue for a minimum of decentralization, or at least for striving to keep decentralization limited to large units. It would in theory be desirable for an early fragmentation of a comprehensive library building to be the creation of a separate multidisciplinary science branch. If it is properly located and of a size that justifies at least three or four staff members with at least 10,000 or 15,000 volumes, the space may serve efficiently until there is justification to fragment again into a life sciences and a physical sciences library, and one of them is moved out to some other strategic location on campus. Those two might serve for another generation or more until further growth requires that the physical science library break into physics, chemistry, or the mathematical sciences, one of those staying in the original physical sciences branch and the others having a new location. Though such a planned and phased decentralization is logical because of its deliberate progression, in practice the availability of remaining land and existing buildings, the clout of certain disciplines and their fund-raising capacity, student course enrollment shifts, together with the general difficulty of adequate forecasting—all result in compromises from generation to generation from the ideal development plan. The logical planning of major branch units has at times been done well, as at Yale, the University of California at Davis, Florida State University, and the University of Georgia.

The separation of major research collections is in contrast to the development of small departmental libraries serving as "working" or convenience collections, sometimes as an adjunct of a seminar room or laboratory, and which duplicate in small numbers the book collection held in the main research collections. These departmental libraries are seldom spin-offs from the main library; they certainly are not satellites created because of central space problems. Rather, they are commonly the result of local faculty entrepreneurs, with the consequence being "underground," bootlegged, relatively ill-managed convenience collections. They are generally unauthorized and not part of the organized campus library system, though they are useful in limited fashion.

A decision to create a separate art or engineering library may be based on academic or space concerns, or both factors when combined with financial feasibility. In more than a few institutions, a professional library or the main library has moved to new quarters and, with advanced planning, the released space has served well as a branch library or for book storage.

If the library can monitor the shelf capacity and growth rate of each branch, and thus predict the date when the shelves of each unit will be full to working capacity, it will help determine whether other campus buildings or newly planned quarters may be utilized to meet this need. In anticipating physical fragmentation, it is desirable for the library to keep in close touch with the academic and campus space planning offices. A meeting each year with the appropriate academic staff may elicit indication of what is anticipated in five or ten years for physical relocations. It may reveal planning for new buildings in which a library might be added or relocated to solve problems elsewhere. Planning officers who are aware of difficulties in various disciplines may put such facts together with problems faced by the library to create new space or remodeled quarters that can solve both problems. In any event, library management needs to be aware of nonlibrary projects that are in the thinking stage so that its long-term plans fit campus programs.

2.6.1 Remote or Auxiliary Facilities

Secondary-access shelving, or storage, should be considered when a library has many books that are used infrequently yet are judged to be worth keeping. Such books can be housed inexpensively in a building on less valuable real estate, perhaps in a remote structure especially designed for them. (The cost differential in a remote shelving facility comes from lower land value, storage technologies with greater density, and the use of less-expensive finishes.) The University of California estimated the building cost at one-quarter the cost of normal shelving for the same number of volumes.

Such auxiliary shelving facilities exist at the University of London, Queensland, Sydney, Western Australia, the University of Michigan, and Iowa State University; specially designed facilities have been used by the University of Alberta, Cornell, Harvard, Princeton (fig. 2.2A, fig. 2.2B), Stanford (fig. 2.3), the University of Texas at Austin, the University of Virginia, Yale, and the University of California. Most of these facilities are within a couple of miles, usually on the edge of campus. However, the University of California Northern Regional Library Facility building is in Richmond, six miles north of the Berkeley campus, and the University of London Repository is some 20 miles (33 km) west, in Egham.

These auxiliary or storage facilities have a high density of book shelving, using narrow aisles, long ranges, and shelving by size divisions in order to approach maximum density. Furthermore, these facilities commonly use compact movable shelving, deep storage drawers, double-depth shelving, or some other arrangement to obtain a density of books much higher than that for normal access by the public. The facilities may or may not allow public access to the shelves. (In fact, public access is increasingly permitted.) The type of material located there may be almost any that is seldom used, including archival material, manuscripts, superseded editions, foreign-language materials, newspapers, dissertations, old textbooks, and so on. Rare, very valuable, unique, and especially fragile materials usually would be in a separately caged area of the facility, accessed only by designated library staff. With use of online public catalogs and automated circulation systems, infrequently used materials can be charged out to this auxiliary facility, obviating the costs of changing catalog records.

Cooperative storage with other libraries offers further administrative advantages through joint management and the possibility of shared transportation and elimination of some duplication among items placed there. Examples cooperatively used or jointly owned are the New England Deposit Library, Harvard Depository Library, the University of California regional facilities, and the Center for Research Libraries.

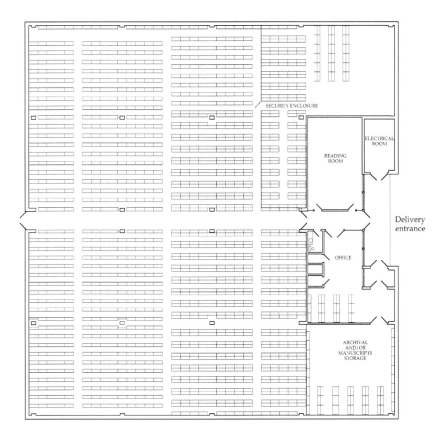

FIGURE 2.2B Princeton University, current storage library. In 1991 an extensive renovation project was undertaken with compact shelving replacing fixed shelving. The collection is still shelved by subject order, but the books are no longer shelved by size. This library is a closed site (no public access); the books are paged from the central libraries. With 10 ft. (3.048 m) high mobile shelving, the capacity was increased to approximately 675,000 volumes on 96,500 linear feet (29.413 km) of shelving. (Used with permission of Princeton University Libraries)

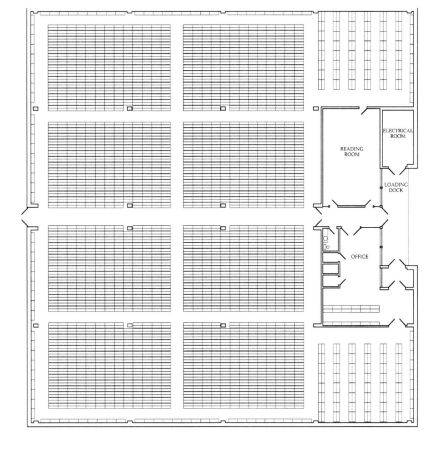

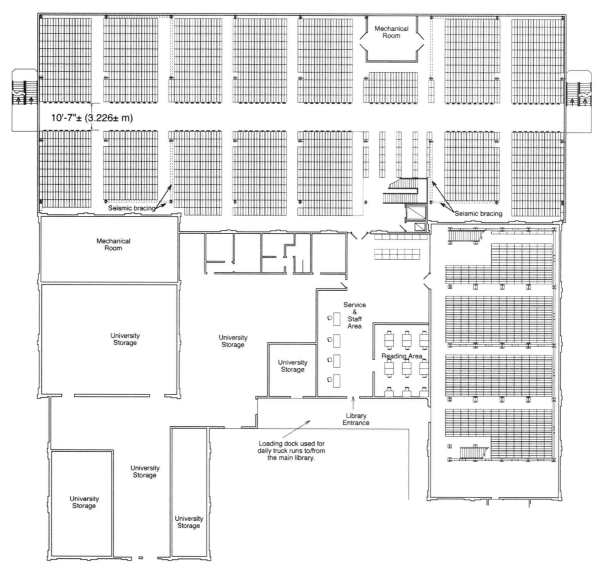

FIGURE 2.3   Stanford University. The Stanford Auxiliary Library is located within 20 minutes walking distance from the main research library in a building originally designed as a food commissary in the late 1960s and subsequently expanded toward the top of the figure in 1992 for library storage. With compact shelving on two levels, this facility has capacity for approximately 1.5 million volumes. Except for caged areas, the facility is open to the public with reading facilities provided near the entrance. Materials are also paged from the central libraries. All the compact shelving is motorized. Oversized shelving is provided in the upper right corner of the stack; folio shelving is in the Service and Staff area. (Used with permission of Stanford University Libraries)

The future of campus auxiliary facilities is assured. The size of college and university holdings and the cost of buildings create pressures toward this end. The future growth in the number of shared or cooperative storage libraries is less certain, because the administrative advantages may be offset by different desires in public accessibility, equity issues of uniform versus differential

space cost, needs of handling bulky or rare special collections, the speed with which space can be available when one campus needs it, and the graduated disadvantages of distance.

Whatever option is judged best for a particular institution, these facilities provide relief, perhaps enough to obviate the need for a new library building. It would not be surprising if, just as the

Harvard University Library found 50 years ago that half of its materials were not in the central library, all the larger university libraries may have half of their collections in a secondary-access facility within a decade or so into the twenty-first century.

2.7
Increased Interdependence

Since the early 1930s and particularly during the 1960s and 1970s, interinstitutional cooperatives and consortia have mushroomed in North America. A number of these focus on cooperative purchase arrangements that acquire an expensive or a hard-to-find item, which is then shelved in one location for sharing among all in that cooperating group. The Farmington Plan was a prime decentralized example, followed by the National Program for Acquisitions and Cataloging, which concentrated scarce resources obtained in the national interest for housing in the Library of Congress. Regional and national programs that ease the local rate of acquisition are likely to provide significant cost-beneficial ways of maintaining access to research resources without requiring as intensive an effort to add to local collections. In theory, this eases the pressure for frequent additions to library buildings.

Various models are still being developed and the exact shape of the future is uncertain. (Note the comments about outsourcing and contract services in Sections 2.2 and 8.3.) It can be asserted, however, that increased interdependence among research libraries within a country or continent seems essential over the decades ahead, given the economics of higher education. The Center for Research Libraries has provided important service since 1949, backstopping all its members with certain basic research materials as well as a wide variety of esoteric and scarce research resources. Since 1975, the Research Libraries Group has approached the same problem on a distributed basis, whereby each of its members is committed to maintaining selected current subject collecting responsibilities at a research level to assure all members future access to and preservation of those resources. The world has also looked to the British Library Document Supply Centre (DSC) as an extraordinary achievement and a service concept that is discussed and may be followed in other countries; the DSC already pro-vides considerable international service from its striking and specially designed 1972 building.

2.7.1 The Influences of Information Technology

The world of scholarship and its reliance on computer systems is changing so rapidly that additional attention must be applied to this modern phenomenon when considering the pressure on space within a library building.

College and university officers and boards of trustees may believe that increased sharing of library resources will obviate or at least moderate what to them may seem a continual need for more and more library space of one type or another. Indeed, the growth of interlibrary borrowing of materials has been striking since the advent of the major national and international online databases listing the combined catalogs of a host of local libraries. As a notable instance, the OCLC combined online listing of library holdings has provided an exceptional stimulus for requesting the loan or photocopies of materials needed for any and all educational and research purposes. Although interlibrary loans have been requested and granted for well over a hundred years, the interlibrary lending statistics within North America have taken a quantum jump in the last quarter of this century. A huge effort has been made to convert old card catalog records into machine-readable form, and to expand effective catalog records to include archival and manuscript collections, recordings of music and the spoken word, maps and cartographic records, and so on. Thus the interlibrary traffic has significantly increased and will continue to do so.

This interdependence among educational and research institutions is bound to increase further as the full text of fragile or heavily used materials or the corpus of a distinguished author is converted to digital form. Therefore, the prospect for further growth in interlibrary traffic, especially in online access through computer networks, is assured. Whether this growth will taper off and stabilize in another two or three decades is a matter for speculation. Yet stabilize it will.

Any use of online resources has its advantage in immediacy and cost-effectiveness in the sense of sometimes saving time traipsing to card catalogs and indexes and bibliographies. It also has its limitations due to the requirement for access to a network and/or fairly sophisticated equipment, or the necessity of suffering through delays of various origin in the process of acquiring the text online, of reading on a screen, of printing out the received material at an extra cost, of working through a copyright algorithm that may require an account or a credit card, or of using a format that lacks the cultural, artifactual, aesthetic, and bibliographic advantages of the book. Further, scholars and advanced students will for decades, perhaps for many, many decades, find that locally held research collections, strong if not comprehensive of research materials in their field of interest, including primary and secondary as well as the more fugitive materials, are the major academic asset to help their research, their publications, their careers. They must rely on printed collections in their local library stacks for far more than 90 percent of their needs, and thus interdependence, even digitally, has its severe limits.

Cost models have been prepared that are aimed at demonstrating the cost effectiveness of digital access to information. Some, including especially those who support Project Gutenberg, claim that access to texts in digital form is virtually free. When encountering arguments that claim cost benefit for digitally storing library collections, it is urged that the following questions be asked:

1. Is the available information of proven reliability, free of error, complete (with maps, tables, portraits, etc.), and of established authority? Can you be certain that you know what you are getting? Where archival quality is required, is that criterion met? The same can be asked of traditional technologies, though alteration and mutilation is generally more apparent in printed texts than may be the case with fully digitized texts.

2. What for students and scholars is gained, and what is lost? Is the fine hand of well-done penciled notes turned to ink-like black in the digitization process, or lost altogether? Is the ability to flip through the pages looking for an advertisement with particular features of importance? Is the time it takes to transmit the complete document an issue? (Time, of course, varies significantly depending upon the nature of the document and the nature of the connectivity.) Is the ability to search for a word or phrase the persuasive justification? If yes, then scanned documents are not enough and the cost of creation goes up markedly.

3. Is the full cost being considered for alternative technologies, including costs for copyright permissions, software, equipment, connection service or line, printing, storage, migration, frustration (if that can be quantified), and, where materials

are being digitized locally, the digitizing cost (scanning, OCR processes, editing for errors, keying, etc.)? Are the assumptions realistic? When compared with traditional technologies, it is fair to ask the same questions, including questions about processing cost and circulation transaction cost. It may be the case that, where materials are removed from the traditional collection for digitizing, there is a decision cost as well, especially if the material is destroyed in the process and a facsimile is not produced to replace the traditional form. If the digitization includes the production of a facsimile for the shelf, that cost would seem to be properly part of the cost of digitizing, as would the decision cost if there is one.

One professor in a research university, writing in 1992, commented on "Expectations for the Library of the 21st Century" as follows:

> The outlook of faculty who study books is going to be very different from that of their colleagues who receive most of their information in electronic form. Take, for example, the question of whether the importance of locally owned collections is likely to diminish in favor of access to remotely held collections. If the archive is on a file server, the distinction between "local" and "remote" becomes irrelevant. . . . But if I want to use the Mark Twain papers, I have to drive fifty miles to the Bancroft. For those of us who rely on printed texts, then, the answer to this question is a qualified "no." The widespread availability of books that are distributed electronically and printed locally may ultimately change the way librarians think about collection development. In the meantime, however, interlibrary loan is not an acceptable substitute for locally held collections. Everyone who does library research knows that you have to see what's available in order to understand what's available.[1]

Use of computer technologies to create the long-heralded paperless society remain to be proven, if indeed they ever will be. Even where access to digitized books is possible, it appears as though it will be cheaper to provide space at a one-time cost of about US$5 per volume in a storage facility, and make them available on a loan basis at a cost of about $2.50 (or less) per transaction than it will be to access and use the material through computers and printing on demand. Clearly there are exceptions as there are in nearly every library cost model; this aspect of interdependence will need special study in the years ahead.

To sum up, each of these approaches to interdependence has its costs. They are not free alternatives to a new library building; nevertheless, they can offer effective remote access to seldom-used resources, sometimes on a more economical basis than acquiring and storing them locally. They constitute but one of the options for mitigating the need for more library book collection space. And the reality of computer capacities, with their exciting plusses and sobering minuses, will be an important factor in designing the academic and research libraries for the coming decades.

There is much in the literature about OCLC, the work at Cornell University, Project Gutenberg, the Library of Congress effort to digitize vast resources, the Bibliothèque nationale de France and its digitization effort, and numerous other digitization projects. Digital access to information is current reality, and it must be supported within the library structure. However, other than the obvious need for connectivity and staffing expertise, and possibly an increased opportunity for outsourcing of functions made possible by computers, the full impact of this significant trend on library collections (and, therefore, on libraries in general) is one we can't fully predict, because it may be decades before digitization makes real inroads on the size of collections, especially monographs. Perhaps the result will be as with microtexts: It's an additional text source but only marginally replacing the printed volume. It would seem that prudent planning is best predicated on collections projections based largely upon historic collections growth; to do otherwise risks serious problems down the road.

Although many libraries find space advantages in microtexts and probably will increasingly in digitized data, keep in mind that there are some offsetting factors. The process of transferring printed materials to microfilm or digital format is costly, as mentioned earlier. The cataloging of the item is every bit as expensive as it was in the original format. Environmental conditions appropriate to microfilm may be more difficult to obtain. Any browsing or quick reference is difficult. Ambulatory use of a microtext is impossible, though many libraries make available fiche-to-fiche copiers and portable readers. Reader access is impeded where it has been necessary to rely on staff fetching of a particular item. Needing specialized reading quarters and arrangements for housing, microtexts are and will remain a very

important supplement to printed collections of books and journals, but they are rarely a substantial replacement for library space needs. Digitized technologies will have a significant impact on library operations where their costs can be afforded; however, most of the disadvantages of microtexts also apply to publications and other written and graphic material accessed through computers.

2.8
The Basis for a Judgment

Before embarking on a library building addition, a major renovation, or a new structure, any institution must give thorough consideration to building costs and the costs of administrative alternatives, including the prospect of implementing alternative technologies. Innovative solutions may obviate or at least postpone the need for new construction and may save an institution hundreds of thousands of dollars.

The best way to begin the process of determining the probable costs of library space alternatives is to consult an architect. Then have the existing structure carefully examined by a reliable builder in order to obtain an estimate of costs for modernization and remodeling. Questions of floor loading capacities, which often arise during such a review, must, of course, be resolved by a structural engineer. Let us take a hypothetical example. A library finds that the stack capacity of its building can be increased by one million volumes if compact shelving is installed in an unused basement. This shelving would postpone the need for a new building for an additional 10 years, but it would require the installation of a new stairway, sprinklers throughout the basement, and the removal of an unused coal bin. Old heating and water pipes would have to be torn out, including the removal of asbestos; a concrete floor should be given a new floor covering; new lights would have to be installed; and the ceiling would need refinishing and repainting. Add to this a need for flood protection, including a pumping station and redundant systems along with mandated code improvements, and the cost of these alterations plus the new shelves might amount to as much as it would cost to build an addition to the library large enough to house the same number of volumes. An addition might be preferable.

However, other factors may need to be considered. From the point of view of financing, it may be much easier to obtain funds for renovation than for new construction, although this is not always true. Possibly only a small addition to the building is practical at the present time and a larger one will be more feasible at some later date. A small addition now may use enough of the site to create very difficult design problems for a later larger addition. Yet, considering the rate of growth of the collections, the financial condition of the institution, the urgency of competing institutional space needs, and the national economic circumstances at that time, temporary expedients may make more sense. Renovation of existing space may be more easily phased to match a financing program.

On the other hand, providing for one million volumes in the old basement may take care of only a fraction of the total need for space that can be foreseen in the near future. A new building may be the only good solution, and, if so, renovation of the basement may be an expensive way of providing space that will become relatively useless as soon as the new building is constructed. If the new building will cost $15 million, each year that its construction is postponed might be regarded as saving the income on that sum. This income, at 5 percent, is $750,000, which means that renovation of the basement at a cost of $3 million, including compact shelving, may be an economical course of action if it enables the library to postpone construction for more than four years. Prospective increases in building costs and trends in business cycles should not be

forgotten. The practical nature of fund-raising at the time may be a crucial point, as are institutional priorities for financing new space. Finally, a good new building ought to enable a library to provide better services than are possible in an old one. It is difficult indeed to estimate how much this improvement is worth to the institution. All these financial aspects need to be taken into account in making the decision.

Many a librarian may be sure, both before and after reading these paragraphs, that only a new building or an addition can provide space of the kind and quantity needed. But the librarian's position will be much more convincing if, before asking for new construction, he or she has carefully investigated the alternatives, instead of waiting for others to do it. One ought to be prepared to demonstrate that the alternatives have been considered and that they will or will not be satisfactory. One ought to be able to show and document that the space now available is not being wasted and that the cost of continuing to live in the present building, including the cost of required rehabilitation work and the impaired efficiency in services, is greater than the cost of new construction. In the course of examining all the possibilities, the librarian may discover means of postponing such construction; if not, the examination ought to have provided compelling arguments for it.

NOTE

1. David Riggs, *Imprint* 14, no. 2 (spring 1995), pp. 19–20. Used by permission of the Board of Trustees of Leland Stanford Junior University.

3

Planning Preliminaries

Think of the end before the beginning.
—Leonardo da Vinci, *The Notebooks*

How much justification for new space is needed? Nearly every institution is pressed for space. If by chance there is enough total space, the right *kind* of space to serve the needs of the library, laboratory, museum, or classroom may be lacking. The librarian must prove that the need is critical and, further, that giving the library additional space will be better policy for the institution than any other arrangement. If the case is strong but not overwhelming, the library may have to wait until one or more other projects are achieved, or until other conditions—a considerable increase in student enrollment, a substantial growth in the book collections, or new program requirements for which no space is available in the library—make the need more persuasive.

Undoubtedly occasions will arise when the library has great difficulty because of minimal administrative support. Even when support is excellent, it is seldom advantageous for the librarian to press unreasonably for space too early, ask for too much, or hold on to unneeded space for even a few years while someone else's need is urgent.

Most institutions with reasonable and stable administrations provide more support to libraries accommodating of others who have immediate and pressing space needs. There is no point in being so bullish as to keep a secondary reading room that occasionally is occupied by one or two persons when nearby an administrative office of the institution houses people in intense and crowded conditions. After all, the library is not independent of the institution in which it operates and which it is designed to serve. The librarian needs to take a long-term view, as must institutional officers. The librarian must also be the library advocate in a timely and effective fashion in advance of the space problem becoming urgent. Yet the library must recognize that it is but one member of a family of functions that make up the academic or research institution.

One must keep in mind that the library takes its place in the long-range academic or operating plan. This institutional plan and its physical requirements form the touchstone. The library program and the decisions on major library policy issues must relate and be responsive to the operating plan of the institution.

Comparative statistics can sometimes help people understand the circumstance of library need. Comparisons of occupancy rates among various libraries of the institution can be informative. Comparison with peer institutions is almost always of value, more so if one looks poor and much less if one is among the leaders. In the former case, data from other libraries may show how much must be achieved to realize similar library collections and the required support space and presumably be competitive academically. With analysis of a dozen peer libraries, one may compare book space, reading space, staff quarters, and allocated floor area. And if one's own situation is in the lower half in terms of quantity, the story may be quite telling. For an institution apparently well situated, the concept of striving for excellence is important. In this case, it may be prudent to look at fewer peer institutions, selecting one for analysis where the comparison is striking, or, in certain cases, you may need to address the local situation without reliance on such comparative data. Without comparative data, the complaints of students, researchers, and faculty can be the most important evidence, as can the occasionally obvious need to implement new technologies with associated infrastructure, the results of a code survey, the effects of the Americans with Disabilities Act (or similar local law), evidence of traffic problems, lack of security, hazardous conditions that could lead to lawsuits, and the impact of library circumstances on the ability to attract and retain faculty and/or research staff, or the ability to attract graduate students. These and similar consequential matters may form the basis to justify a library building project.

But a word of caution. Valid statistical comparisons are difficult; the argument can backfire if the data are not demonstrably sound. For example, if stack capacity and current occupancy are not compared to a national standard, then the importance of capacity and occupancy data may easily be questioned. The determination of occupancy by readers can mean one condition if it is drawn over a 12-month period and a different picture if only peak use is tabulated or if it is taken by sampling only in the middle of the semester. Net area can be determined in several ways, so be careful in such definitions; the definitions of gross and net areas are dealt with elsewhere in this volume (Section 5.4). At this point it may suffice to say the obvious: Comparative statistics must be drawn up on a comparable basis, and, when well done, they can be more convincing than many pages of prose and passion.

3.1
Character and Nature of the Academic or Research Institution

It is essential to grasp clearly the character of the institution before determining the general library solution. One must study its history and talk with key faculty and administrative leaders. The crucial step in a building project is that of securing the understanding and support of principal academic

or research officers. This phase may require one or a few meetings with a dean, a provost, or the president of the institution. Or it may require preparation of a document to be reviewed, possibly revised, and approved by an advisory library committee, a library staff group, a committee on institutional program priorities, a committee on undergraduate or graduate studies, a committee on buildings and physical plant, a committee on traffic and parking, a committee on financial planning and priorities, a fund-raising council, and the trustees. Such detailed committee involvement is less common in independent research institutions than in academic institutions. Within the context of a particular institution, certain major policy decisions will be needed with respect to the library itself. These constitute the first through fourth and perhaps part of the fifth stage in a building project, as outlined in Section 1.3.

This treatment of the character and nature of the institution is divided into two aspects. The first is a set of seven characteristics of the institution that are likely to have the greatest influence on the library design. The following list assumes that the institution is academic in nature; a similar tabulation may be created for independent research institutions. The second aspect treats constantly changing institutional conditions as well as changing library program and administrative organization.

The seven most important institutional characteristics are:

1. The kind and nature of the institution and its specific academic program
2. The student mix in terms of educational preparation, economic background, and age
3. The nature of commuting and residential patterns
4. The size and diversity of graduate programs
5. The number and fields of research institutes and laboratories
6. The nature of developing or emerging educational programs, including changing pedagogy involving new technologies and other devices
7. The physical setting of the campus and the nature of its physical development

3.1.1 The Kind of Institution

Institutions have significant differences of purpose and character one from another if they are community colleges, colleges, universities, or universities with a particularly heavy emphasis on research. Likewise, there are distinct differences if the institution focuses on the liberal arts or aims to concentrate on science and technology, religious training, legal or medical education, or music theory and performance practice, or if it is a "service school," such as those supported by the federal government to prepare people for a particular service career. There must be a clear understanding of the institution's stated mission, its specialized character, its academic qualities and traditions, and its objectives for the next 10 or so years.

3.1.2 The Student Mix

It is important to know the percentage of students who are enrolled in lower-division programs, upper-division programs, extension programs, professional preparation, and graduate programs in the pure or theoretical disciplines. It is also significant to understand the percentage who have had strong academic preparation before coming to the institution and the percentage who may come from underprivileged parts of society and who may not have received good preparation for effectively utilizing libraries. Of less importance is the percentage from foreign countries, particularly those whose native language differs from that used in the institution. To a lesser extent the percentage who are over 25 or 30 years old may be indicative of somewhat different behavior and social needs that may affect library services, though such a factor may be temporary in the life of the institution. You also need to know the probable trend in the total number of students anticipated over a decade or two in each major program or subject. Each of these contributes to understanding the needs of students.

3.1.3 The Commuting and Residential Mix

It is similarly clear that there are differing library requirements if the institution is mostly serving a commuting population or a campus-residential population. The extent to which the on-campus residents are in sororities and fraternities in contrast to dormitories can be of significance, and institutions that have educational and cultural programs within the residence halls (such as theme houses devoted to Latin American studies or East European culture) also create different conditions for the library. To a lesser extent the commuting patterns, including the routes to and

from class, to parking, or to living quarters, can make a difference.

3.1.4 Graduate Programs

As suggested above, it will be very important to determine the extent of graduate and professional programs in the sciences, technology, humanities, social sciences, and other areas. Also it is important whether such fields as English, art, music, and drama focus on the literature and history of those disciplines or whether they are concerned with criticism and performance, such as would be the focus in studio programs, stage practice, and creative writing. Graduate programs are also affected more than are undergraduate programs by the proportion of students who are taking full-time studies and by whether the part-time students are employed on campus or in occupations in the surrounding community.

3.1.5 Research Institutes

There is another dimension of considerable importance if the institution has created research institutes or centers. These programs generally are devoted to theoretical or applied research and provide little or no instruction. They include faculty among their senior staff together with research associates, postdoctoral fellows, and research assistants often on foundation or federal grants. These institutes draw together faculty from a number of departments to concentrate on a particular social problem, technological challenge, industrial concern, or the like. Examples might be a center for environmental studies, a center for research on women, or an institute for research in international studies. Factors to be considered are the distance of such institutes from libraries with related research collections, the existence of library collections in the institutes, the degree of permanency the institutes seem likely to have in the institution, the source of funding, and the nature of their programs.

3.1.6 Changing Academic Programs

From time to time institutions add and drop courses of instruction or change the way existing courses are taught. These changes come about because of the dynamic nature of many academic disciplines, because of emerging technologies, and as a response to societal changes. Thus a traditional program in biology may give birth to a program in biophysics, another in the biopsychology of youth development, and a third in population biology. Or, a traditional classroom setting for the teaching of a foreign language may change to or be supported by an interactive computer cluster, perhaps in the library, with supporting documentation and staff. Such changes have great influence upon academic officers during their processes of planning for the future. Growth or reduction in continuing education programs also has its consequences. An understanding of these prospects is important in understanding the character and nature of the institution and its possible changes in the years ahead.

3.1.7 The Campus Physical Plant

The final factor is the density of campus buildings and the degree of high-rise construction and important lines of sight. The means and paths for moving people on campus above ground level or on grade or underground are related aspects. The environment is significant—whether the location has severe cold, a great deal of ice and frost, a heavy rainy season, an exceedingly hot sun, or earthquakes, as well as what the prevailing breezes are, and the general frequency and nature of storms. The institution's central or distributed maintenance and caretaking also affects the need for a library supply room, maintenance staff quarters, tool shop, and so on.

These and other issues contribute to a general understanding of the nature of the academic institution and thus of the character of library facilities that are appropriate for that institution. The seven cited areas would be quite obvious to those who have worked in the institution for several years and have been alert to its policies and operations. It is important for the architects and planners to understand them thoroughly. The more you understand about different institutions, even of the same kind, the more it will be evident how very different institutions are one from another. The difference in physical, educational, cultural, and social environment between Harvard and Yale is great, or even among schools within state systems, such as the campuses of the University of California. Community colleges and junior colleges also have distinct character, even within the same region.

3.1.8 Coping with Change

What are the optimal responses when an institution is rapidly evolving or changing in character? Generally, you should: (1) plan to accommodate

needs of each of the existing academic programs that seem to be reasonably well entrenched; (2) try to avoid expensive and special accommodation for programs whose future and financial support are doubtful; and (3) plan for reasonable flexibility in all accommodations. Remember that the building is being planned for a lengthy future, and it must be responsive to emerging educational conditions that will be important five and ten years from now or beyond. The librarian should ask senior academic officers for clarification when there is uncertainty about future expectations or when there are contrary or competing statements.

What if there are rapid changes in the current library program? Because libraries are not static enterprises, certain conditions will be quite different when the building is occupied than when the building was first being planned. Within a few years after occupancy, still other changes will come about, and changes will occur in the future. Libraries are changing more in the 1990s than anytime in the past century. The library may be starting a considerable program in bibliographic instruction; a new government documents department may be intended; the loan department may be renamed the circulation division; the library may now have one associate director and later utilize three assistant directors; the reserves function may be established online with plans to eventually remove this responsibility from the library totally with faculty homepages taking its place; the library may embark upon electronic publishing and the printing of texts on demand; or the concept of contracting for cataloging from a national vendor may be tried with the distinct possibility that much of this staff function will never return to the local library. Change in the library can range from the simple renaming of a function to the fundamental removal or installation of a function.

Those planning the building should recognize that such changes are to be expected in the future. One cannot plan extra space just on the chance that in five or ten years this or that new program will require extra staff. Yet, similarly, it would be unfortunate to plan without any foresight, leaving no options for library space adjustments. There are no simple answers to this quandary. The obvious response is to build in at least a small amount of flexible contingency in those parts of the building where conditions are most likely to change. Future flexibility in space allocations is an obvious need in carefully selected spaces in order to leave open options. Generally speaking, try to project the probable requirements of the library as they will exist in the next 10 to 15 years and design the building program that will best meet those needs.

Try to freeze the library building program in terms of areas, spaces, offices, and built-in furnishings—as it is envisioned at the time of building occupancy and immediately thereafter—and stay with that plan once it has been signed and given to the business officers and the architect. The librarian should not change program requirements in the course of building design unless there are very strong arguments to do so. Changes take extra time, they are certain to cost money, and they lead to uncertainty if not confusion in the entire planning process. Before the plans are finished, almost every architect will try to accept requested changes and may even recommend some when they are clearly advantageous. Remember, however, that the later in the design process change is proposed, the more difficult and costly it will be.

3.2
Major Policy Decisions Before Detailed Planning Begins

Once the college or university administration understands that it has a library space problem and once the general academic approval to correct that problem has been received, it is time for serious planning to begin. Until such a general understanding is held by major administrative officers and perhaps by the board of trustees, it may be a waste of time for the librarian to do detailed planning. An academic need has to be understood and a high priority assigned to it. At least 15 major policy decisions need to be resolved before going farther. Only when these have been decided by the institution should planning progress to the programming phase. Site considerations then become a crucial matter, as will be dealt with in Chapter 11.

Answers to the following policy questions may affect the whole enterprise. Advice on each numbered question is given here, or in other chapters in a few cases. Can a building be avoided or delayed? This is treated in Chapter 2. Length of time for which to plan? This is in Section 1.6.

How will future growth be handled? This is treated in Section 10.3. What site is desired and logical? This is treated in Section 11.4.

1. Is the financing strategy clear and is there a fixed cost ceiling?
2. Is functionalism to take precedence over the desire for visual significance or distinctiveness?
3. Should branches be centralized or decentralized?
4. Are faculty offices and classrooms to be included?
5. Will nonlibrary functions be included?
6. Will the library house a rapidly growing research collection or a more stable course-related collection?
7. Is access to the bookstacks to be open or closed, and is the book collection to be interspersed with the general accommodations for study and reading?
8. How will security and supervision be provided?
9. Is a divisional subject plan of service to be used?
10. What amount of seating is desired? Is smoking allowed?
11. Are computer, interactive video, and traditional audiovisual services projected? To what extent will these be supported in the library now and in the future?

3.2.1 Financing Strategy

The financing strategy provides such overriding constraints that it needs to be in the forefront of one's mind. No matter how persuasive the need, if the funds cannot be obtained, there will be no new construction. If the institution is embarking on a fund-raising campaign of several years, the trustees may have made strategy decisions about priorities and goals for scholarship aid, endowed faculty chairs, physical plant, or new programs. If there is state or federal financing, there may be automatic legislative limits to the amount of funding available. If one prominent donor has an interest in the library, it certainly can have an effect on the institution's goal. Guidance is required from the institution's president and financial officers about the maximum and the strategy for funding the library project. Can the library be the most expensive project in that decade, or the largest building the institution has undertaken? On the basis of experience, can individuals and foundations be counted on to provide certain percentages of the total cost and so many gifts in each range of donation for a project of this type? When and in what way is it best to launch the fund-raising?

In addition to fund-raising in the traditional sense, there is a growing body of experience in joint ventures of one kind or another driven by financial circumstances. For example, two branches of the Fort Lauderdale/Broward County Library in Florida share facilities with the north and south campuses, respectively, of the Broward County Community College. The County Library has also entered into a joint venture with Florida Atlantic University and Florida International University to provide library services within shared facilities. The main branch of the Broward County Library in downtown Fort Lauderdale supports the Urban Studies program including Architecture for Florida Atlantic University. Florida Atlantic, in turn, has entered joint ventures with additional community colleges. Those involved speak highly of this kind of relationship, particularly from the perspective of achieving more at less cost, even though some concerns have been expressed by faculty.

A joint university/city building was to be under construction in 1997 at the Helsinki Science Park in Niikki, Finland. In this instance, a university biological and biotechnology library with university lecture rooms and administrative quarters shares a building with a branch of the public library of the city of Helsinki, as well as a cafeteria, a bookshop, even a travel agent. In this example, the university wanted to have a public library branch in the building. Similar joint ventures are currently in early planning stages between the California State University, San Jose and the San Jose City Library. The University of Alaska, Anchorage (UAA) is also considering possible joint ventures; indeed, they currently provide library services for both UAA and Alaska Pacific University within the same building. It can be predicted that library joint ventures will be more common in the future, even though substantial differences remain between public and research libraries. In most cases, the institution joint venturing with a public or county library probably does not think of itself as a research institution, with limited exceptions. It seems likely that the most compatible libraries for sharing a facility will be those with rather comparable collections and overlapping clientele, or where one

has deliberately minor and separate quarters within the host's building. When the collections and clientele are quite disparate, a joint venture building is likely to be a move of financial desperation.

Another kind of joint venture was achieved at the Eastman School of Music. In this example, the university owned a strategic piece of land that was made available to a developer at low cost with the provision that the developed site would include a new Sibley Library at minimum cost to the university. This was achieved with apparent satisfaction for all; the upper floors of the new building are library with the programming controlled by the university, and the street level is commercial, essentially programmed by the developer. This is indeed a creative solution based on financial realities.

Clearly, if a joint venture is seriously considered, many questions must be addressed before proceeding with a facility design: Are the service needs of the different clientele so distinct that one will suffer within a shared facility? How will the different collections be arranged? Will this prompt moving more scarce, expensive resources into a rare books or other controlled-access stack? Are there different systems of classification and catalogs, or can and should the differences of historic ownership be made to disappear? Should upper-division students, graduate students, or teaching staff be provided more secure studies of some sort than would be desired if not in a shared facility? How is the financial arrangement to be made for new materials, staffing, maintenance, utilities, and so on? Who will be in charge of building operations and maintenance? Will security be managed to the standard of the more scholarly of the cooperating entities? What can be saved—can there be fewer seats than would be required for two (or more) separate libraries? Can there be fewer staff? Does the processing staff need to be in the same building? Is there to be one processing staff? Will a shared facility require an administrative agreement documenting the basis for much more than just the capital and operating financial arrangements? Is there sufficient political motivation to press this kind of an approach even though some will believe they are negatively affected?

3.2.2 Grandeur versus Functionalism

The degree to which the library building should be massive and imposing is a major policy decision. Some institutions have decided against making the library one of the most physically imposing buildings on campus. Examples are Arizona State University, the University of Minnesota Wilson Library, Stanford University Green Library, or the University of California at Berkeley Moffett Undergraduate Library as well as the recent addition to the Doe Library (their main library). Clearly, as all the following are mostly underground, monumentality was not intended with respect to the addition to the law library at the University of Michigan, the Pusey Library at Harvard, the planned expansion of the Lee Library at Brigham Young University, the Clark Library at UCLA, and the undergraduate libraries at the University of Illinois at Urbana-Champaign and the University of British Columbia (which has become the lower levels of the Walter C. Koerner Library, their main library), together with the recent addition at Berkeley.

Yet other institutions have wanted an imposing building, perhaps of striking architectural design to serve institutional purposes of publicity, recruiting, and symbolism. Examples of this sort would be tower libraries, such as those at the University of Massachusetts, Hofstra University, California Institute of Technology, Notre Dame University, and the University of Glasgow. Those with striking architecture include Butler University, the Geisel Library at the University of California at San Diego (exclusive of its recent, largely underground expansion, though the expansion itself is an excellent architectural example), Clark University, and Northwestern University. In each case there are those who claim that in certain respects the imposing design hurts the long-term functionalism. An institution may opt for impressiveness as in Yale's Sterling Library, quiet elegance as in Princeton's Firestone, the restrained symbolism of Dartmouth's Baker, or the charm of Scripps College.

Because this quality of symbolism, monumentality, or imposing character can greatly affect the architectural design and the cost, it becomes a very important policy decision that may involve the president and trustees more than any other of these major policy requirements. This particular issue is critical as it can easily increase the expense by 50 percent and it could as much as double the cost of the building. However, it should also be emphasized that an impressive site and beautiful building are entirely feasible at very near the cost of a utilitarian building. The central issues tend to relate to the design and the choice of materials together with the extent to which these features affect the way the building works as a library.

3.2.3 Branches

In universities and very large colleges where the present building is outgrown or where the campus is very extensive, collections may be decentralized, as is the case at the University of Texas, Austin (fig. 3.1). If this is done, there may be a central or main library for the institution and separate branch libraries for some subjects. Or there may be a research library and a separate undergraduate library. It may be desirable to bring some or all branches into a proposed new main library in order to economize on staff and operating costs, reduce duplication among collections, and serve interdisciplinary needs in better fashion. As is noted in Chapter 2, decentralization can take the form of providing separate quarters for the bulk of library collections in fields like music, art, or the sciences—fields where a relationship to laboratories, studios and performance quarters, or museums is an advantage. Decentralization can take the form of one central science library, or the subject can be broken down into the life sciences, physical sciences, and earth sciences, or broken down further by discipline. The variations here are many and the impact on annual operating budgets can be great. Local campus circumstances must dictate whether a centralized library is best or whether a carefully planned program of decentralization is warranted.

Because library space is added by significant increments, it may be the strategy to centralize to a considerable extent when a main library or major branch can be provided, then cope with the next 20 to 50 years by gradual decentralization, and, in the next phase of library development, plan for some increase again in centralization. The academic consequences of doing this may be problematic, however, and it is far better to have a sound academic plan to guide the physical development rather than for the reverse to take place.

For the next decade or two it seems reasonable that undergraduate libraries will continue to be provided in at least some of the larger universities, though there are examples where the original concept of an undergraduate library is substantially changing. At the University of British Columbia, the decision was made to close the undergraduate library in order to make better space available for the main collections. At Stanford

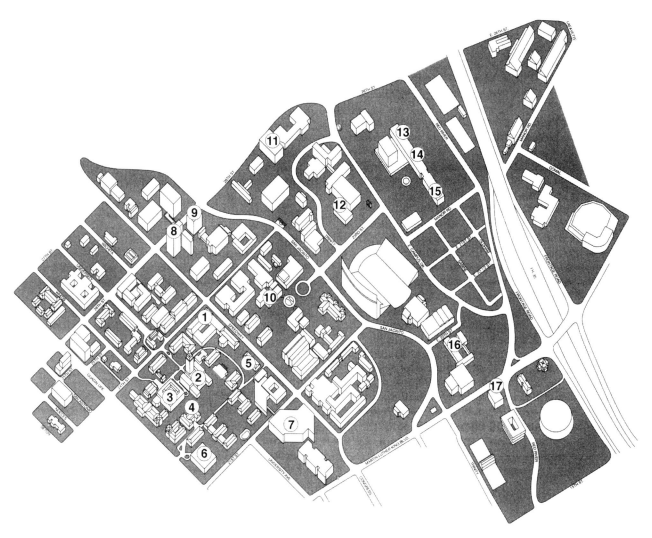

FIGURE 3.1 **University of Texas, Austin, as a decentralized library system. (1) Chemistry (Mallet) Library; (2) Life Science Library; (3) Undergraduate Library; (4) Architecture Library; (5) Classics Library; (6) Harry Ransom Center; (7) Main (Perry-Castañeda) Library; (8) Physics-Mathematics-Astronomy (Kuehne) Library; (9) Engineering (McKinney) Library; (10) Geology (Walter) Library; (11) Law Library; (12) Fine Arts Library; (13) Public Affairs Library; (14) Texas Collection Library; (15) Benson Latin American Collection; (16) Film Library; and (17) Collections Deposit (Storage and Preservation) Library. Note also the Lyndon Baines Johnson Library (the building to the left of 13 and 14), which is on campus, but is not one of the university libraries. (Used with permission of University of Texas Libraries)**

University, the undergraduate library is becoming increasingly a media and technology center rather than a separate collection in support of courses.

Only in very few universities will separate library buildings be provided for rare books and manuscripts and for archives. An increasing number of institutions have been using auxiliary or storage facilities over the past decade, and this trend will continue. Generally speaking, one can predict a very limited and gradual increase in the number of substantial branch libraries on cam-

puses of colleges and universities. If carefully defined and suitably coordinated, such branch libraries are seen to work effectively in old and large institutions, and there seems no reason to argue that they cannot sometimes be sound space-planning alternatives for smaller and newer institutions.

3.2.4 Offices and Classrooms

These may be useful inclusions in the library building. They are, in a sense, library space because faculty offices and faculty library studies may be one and the same thing. A faculty office may have a telephone and be used for appointments with students; the faculty study in the library may have a computer and be used for professional writing and research. Either of these spaces may be used for preparation of class lectures, seminar problems, tests, and so on. Many institutions combine these because it is difficult to justify an individual's having both a study and an office. The advantage of having faculty studies in the library is that they improve the faculty's use and understanding of the library. The disadvantage is that the enclosed spaces represent a library management concern (books will migrate to these spaces without being charged out unless an active stance is taken). A decision has to be made in each case.

Classrooms can be beneficial though they take away from space that otherwise could be used completely for library purposes. Libraries with mature programs of bibliographic instruction will find them very useful for those librarians offering credit courses, workshops, or short seminars on the bibliography of a subject. This type of teaching has become more important as accessing information has become more complex, which has certainly been the case with the digital library. Library tours may end by using a classroom for question periods or for slide or tape presentations and for hands-on network access. Faculty members find classrooms convenient in a library for seminars to which they may wish to bring books or manuscripts from Special Collections as examples and for discussion.

In some institutions, courses given by library professional staff are a fundamental educational offering. Indeed, some colleges and universities now regard classroom training facilities as central to the function of an academic library during a time when navigating the ocean of print collections, audio resources, electronic text, and visual materials has become so complex. Courses and workshops, sometimes short and sometimes long, are seen as very important because of the increasing complexity of informational resources needed for higher educational programs, the rapid development of and reliance on the Internet and World Wide Web, the universal nature of this changing intellectual environment, financial pressures within the institution, and the current needs of college graduates who will find themselves producers and consumers in the so-called informa-

tion age. Further, relying on the library as the chief informational repository, a new collaboration of professor, librarian, computing specialist, and student is producing new educational modules and software packages in a synergy of effort. And such groups require new collaborative spaces for creative effort as well as classrooms in which to teach with the results.

As one example, the 22-campus California State University system in the late 1990s recognized the convergence of campuswide instructional technologies and the need for professionals in library, media, and academic computing to play a strong role in teaching students and training faculty to access, manipulate, and use information in all formats. This team integrates information resources, including such services as instructional computing labs and classrooms, self-instructional labs, bibliographic instructional classrooms, multimedia development centers, electronic reserve book collections, OPAC, academic text service, and the traditional print and nonprint collections of various formats. Such an integrated program enables partnering and collaboration in instruction, and it requires classrooms as the library information hub shifts focus in significant measure from print-based activities to instructional training.

Thus, one or several classrooms in an academic library are now frequently required, each with interactive, networked, multimedia computers for the instructor and all students. When they are not assigned for class purposes, classrooms can also be scheduled by library staff for testing and evaluation of information systems, planning sessions, committee meetings, the library friends' club, or group interviews. The particular needs of the institution must be weighed before a decision is made.

3.2.5 Nonlibrary Functions

It is not unusual to use part of the library building for other than library purposes during the first years after its construction. For major spaces to be assigned to some other purpose, a separate entrance may be needed. The inclusion of such functions may help with the fund-raising prospects. As was explained in Chapter 2, it is important that any temporary function not be so specially designed (as are audiovisual departments or wet laboratories) that they cannot be relocated with ease and the space converted to library purposes at reasonable cost.

Including nonlibrary functions in the library is another major policy decision that each institution must decide given its local circumstances. However, the authors urge caution in combining the library with other functions because problems are bound to arise. In many small institutions this combination has been forced on the librarian with very unsatisfactory results for library services.

3.2.6 Collection Growth

Depending on the function of the particular library unit, a decision has to be made about whether the collection is to be a growing research collection or whether the size is to be relatively static. As noted elsewhere, as much as they may wish to be persuaded, the authors remain unconvinced that libraries can easily contain their collections growth as a result of digital access to information. There are examples, however, where library growth can be maintained, such as in small departmental teaching collections or in an undergraduate library providing the required and recommended reading with a limited core collection of items most relevant for the instructional program. Though an undergraduate or a departmental teaching collection can be viewed as having limited growth, there is some risk that a change of academic approach may require continued growth despite the limits of building designs.

Most library collections pose forecasting problems that are not as simple as the preceding examples. A decision will require balancing many factors, such as the extent of future reliance on microtext and digital sources, the potential for bringing some existing branch collections into the building, the intended growth of graduate programs, the long-term physical spread of academic programs and the concentration of buildings within a block or two of the library, and guesses about the nature of publishing in the years ahead. This decision is difficult for librarians and academic officers. Unless one or more forces will have a clear and dominant effect in the years ahead, the library will be wise to view the growth of the past 10 to 20 years as the best indication of the future growth rate.

3.2.7 Open- or Closed-Stack Access

A related policy issue is whether students, faculty, and others who are not on the staff of the library will be allowed stack access. Whereas a certain amount of access has always been permitted to the main book collections by certain classes of individuals, it was only after the middle of the twentieth century that in the United States and Canada most libraries permitted all students freely to use the books at the shelves. Security is still a concern because of the potential extra operational costs and the disruptive effects on the educational and research process when users abuse their library privileges. However, as the balance of expenses between books and staff has tipped toward the latter, direct access to the books has now become common. The advent of departmental or branch libraries and the undergraduate library facilitated direct access to the books. Once the undergraduates were well served, it became more reasonable to open the entire research collection to their use because students should no longer flood the research stacks, making them ineffective for the graduate students who have primary need for large and broad collections in their field.

Thus for about a half century it has been common in the United States and Canada to provide seating in the bookstacks for the convenience of students. Charging out a book and reserving it in a carrel or study have become common. But will this evolution over the past century continue or will disciplinary problems and book security difficulties again alter the course of history and increase the number of closed bookshelves for some readers? Given the value of research collections, their increasing brittleness, and the prevalent ethical atmosphere, some constraints on open access to the book collections are predicted. This may go hand-in-hand with increased digital access in some cases. Alternatively, the proctored reading collection (or "special collection") will grow at a rate greater than that of the general collections. There is already a trend toward the transfer of more rare and expensive volumes into special collections, including all eighteenth-century and even a good many rare early-nineteenth-century volumes.

Under any scenario, certain collections in any library supporting advanced education or research will have some collections with limited access, serviced by the library staff. Among such collections will be rarities, manuscripts, exceedingly small books, prints, very fragile materials, archival files, and some media. When planning library building spaces, each library must define which materials to include under such limited access, how large such collections are today, and how rapid will be their growth. Access to U.S. federal documents is a special case, due to the access requirements under which many libraries in the United States receive materials under the depository law.

3.2.8 Security

Another major decision is whether control of book circulation is to be handled at the public exits of the building or at the exit from the bookstack and reading areas. To the extent that access to the general bookstack is restricted, the entrances and exits to it must be controlled. If the stack is to be completely open and the readers admitted anywhere, inspection is conducted at the library exit rather than at or within the stack. Yet if stack access is to be controlled, as in the 10-story bookstack with 31 stack doors in Harvard's Widener Library, there obviously cannot be staff at each exit. Thus Widener uses two staffed entrance/exits; the other doors are locked and some, by code, have "panic hardware" permitting egress in emergencies. Although this panic hardware requires breaking a piece of glass to operate the door release hardware, thus sounding an alarm, it has not been found sufficient to deter impatient people who choose to ignore approved operational processes. Escapes from these unstaffed exits are a problem in a research library because some people will use them knowing that the library staff would rarely be able to move quickly enough to find out who the individual was and determine whether library property was involved. Surveillance television cameras at unstaffed, alarmed exits have been used with good results at the Perry-Castañeda Library at the University of Texas at Austin. Other institutions have had success with time-delay exit devices that do not permit the door to be opened less than 15 seconds following an exit attempt by hitting or pressing the door panic hardware that activates the door alarm. This time delay is not in effect if the fire alarm has been activated. According to one building code, time-delay exit devices are acceptable only where approved by the local building official, and only if the building is fully protected by an approved automatic sprinkler system and an approved smoke-detection system.[1]

A decision is also required on whether everyone is permitted into the building or whether security clearances will be used to sort those who are authorized from those requiring per-

mission. Decisions will also need to be made about whether electronic control systems will be used in some or all of these locations, both for automatic entrance checks as well as for screening books to assure they have been charged out for circulation. Each of these will affect the basic design in modest fashion but will have a considerable effect on staff facilities, traffic patterns, and the openness or compartmentation of spaces. One unusual method used for years at the Woodruff Library at Emory University was a revolving caged door in the elevator lobby, controlling outside access to the stacks. However, the proprietary software system necessary to operate this gate required management support the library decided it should not continue. So the revolving gate remained for many years, unused, the apparatus and mechanism to be replaced as Woodruff and Candler library buildings are given a major linking addition.

Many administrators of libraries, particularly smaller ones, branches, and those in rural areas, may feel that there is no need for exit controls of any kind either from the bookstacks or the building itself. If there is evidence that individuals at the institution will not take materials without authorization, one may forgo controlled exits, except for rare books and similar materials that can be controlled at the point of use. Even so, the design should allow future controls if changing circumstances require them.

The Lamont Library at Harvard University was planned so that during quiet times the attendant at the desk where books are regularly charged can also check any volume, whether owned by the library or not, that a student wants to take from the building. This procedure saves staff and, in many cases, saves a double check, one at the charging desk and one at the exit. Of course, electronic book detection systems have largely eliminated this need where they have been employed.

In large city libraries and in nearly all very large library buildings, exit controls are now commonplace. The very largest university library buildings, such as those at Edinburgh, Toronto, Chicago, and Texas, have relied on staffed exit controls separate from other service points. Any new library should be planned so that exits can be controlled easily, either by electronic checking of library materials or staff, without adding unreasonably to the cost of the operation of the library.

3.2.9 Divisional Subject Plan

During the 1940s and 1950s, large academic libraries often had separate reading rooms, reference services, and shelf areas for the humanities, the social sciences, and the sciences. This plan was implemented in greater or lesser degree in a large number of institutions; many have retained it and some have given it up. Stanford University tried this, gave it up, and is now using it again in the rebuilt West Wing of its central library building.

A different division is to separate reference books, current periodicals, public documents, microtexts, rare books, and manuscripts. It is evident that when the collections are divided along subject lines or by format, the plan of the whole building is affected, particularly if the reading areas are to be divided or the components are to be placed on different floors. It is sometimes possible to adapt an old building to divisional organization if there are a number of large reading rooms, though it is easier to apply a divisional plan in connection with a new building.

Some of the difficulties arising from the divisional plan are here mentioned, not in order to criticize but simply to state the problem. The number of service locations directly affects the operational costs, especially if service for the full opening hours of the building is to be provided in each division. The larger the number of units, the more difficult it is to determine the long-term space requirements for each division. Estimating total library space requirements is difficult enough. Estimating the long-term space requirements of individual subject-related units becomes much more difficult. Staffing costs and staffing flexibility may present other difficulties.

On the other hand, no one can deny that having specialists select and service books in a particular subject field is advantageous. This feature is one of the attractions of branch libraries, which are another version of a subject divisional plan. The point is that if a divisional plan is to be adopted, it should be in the program for the new building; final decisions on the number, size, and relationships of the units should be made in advance of schematic drawings if complications are to be avoided.

3.2.10 Seating and Smoking

Another basic decision concerns the amount and nature of seating to be provided. Regarding seating and other features of the library, the nature of the users will also require consideration. In addition to the faculty, staff, and students of a particular institution, will demand be placed upon the library from the general public, regional industry, special-interest groups, local schools, visiting scholars, and others? Will these factors contribute to the need for and character of the seating? What portion of this seating will include access to power and network connections for use with laptop computers? Seating suitable for reading with or without a computer may be for as little as 10 percent of the student body at a commuting institution and fully 50 percent at an institution with strong graduate and research programs. Furthermore, a decision is necessary on the proportion of the seats to be in the bookstacks, in the reference areas, and in other specified areas.

As individual readers enter a reading room, they will usually space themselves as far as possible from one another until the number in the room makes it necessary for them to choose a seat near somebody else. Some individuals will wish to sit in groups. Some like to be in very private spaces, almost as if they were closeting themselves, while others choose spaces as if they wanted to be in the center of traffic. In consequence a wide variety of seating options is desirable. Decisions are also needed on how many seats are to be provided in relation to various book collections and services, as well as the types of seating to be provided.

The nature of seating arrangements is dealt with more thoroughly in Chapter 7. Here it is stressed that these decisions will be a major determinant of the character of the building. Whereas individual carrels have been provided for the past 70 years, they have become so popular that in new facilities since 1950 a majority of seating has been at individual carrels or partially sheltered individual tables. Since the 1970s there has been a perceived reversal of student habits with somewhat more individuals seeking lounge furniture or open tables. Trends seem to shift, and each institution will have to determine what is likely to be most functional, keeping in mind that a considerable variety is needed.

Seating provided with computers is almost always filled to capacity even where the seating is arranged in fairly open and densely occupied areas. In the same facility, nearby carrels and tables without computers will often be largely empty. This phenomenon suggests that computer-based seating will need to be increased relative to other kinds of seating, and certainly most seating should be arranged so that computers can be supported in the future. It is also suggested that the use of computers as they currently are configured is not particularly compatible with traditional reading; consider the programming of reading alcoves or smaller spaces rather than single large reading areas, some of which can be dedicated to traditional reading, others to mixed or computer-supported reading.

Although individual seating accommodations at separate carrels or tables properly arranged will tend to keep the library quieter and help reduce some disciplinary problems, they can cost somewhat more than tables for several individuals and they also may require more space unless very carefully arranged. The disciplinary problems of carrels are of a different nature, although they can be even more troublesome to control. Defacing of property and other undesirable social behavior is easier if one is hidden from sight. On the other hand, some libraries have found that carrels designed with the side panels, or shrouds, extending beyond the front table edge create few acoustic or disciplinary problems.

A serious question relates to smoking policies. Discussions in the past debated the issues of air filtration, the effect of smoke on nonsmokers, maintenance costs, fire concerns, and other issues. However, with the growth of a nonsmoking attitude in libraries, largely for health reasons, this issue is disappearing. Where smoking is still allowed, it is urged that the benefits relative to the extensive negative aspects should be carefully considered. The authors of this book recommend no smoking in the library. This approach solves many problems!

3.2.11 Computer, Interactive Video, and Traditional Audiovisual Services

The notion of electronic connectivity is now almost universal in library planning, both within the library and between the library and outside sources. In the past it was thought that where the building was to be connected to a major computation center located elsewhere, on campus or off, and where it was to be linked to audiovisual source equipment located in some other building, then a minimum provision would be sufficient conduit capacity with distribution to all parts of the library building that in the future may need connection with these services.

Today it is common to have multiple connections plus the capacity to add more. And, it is common to require a distribution of office-sized phone closets complete with air conditioning to support file servers and other computer equipment used for everyday library services. Entire floors may be fitted with access flooring, as has been the case at much of the U.S. National Archives II located just outside Washington, D.C. (The 3-in. [76-mm] high, or slightly higher, raised floor is becoming common and is said, in some cases, to have the capacity to support library shelving even with seismic requirements.) Or, a strategy of how to provide signal and power to various points in the building needs to be established—even if conduit is not provided to every possible point. As much of the library as possible must be arranged to support electronic access and manipulation of information, stack areas being partially excepted.

There are of course a host of policy issues for accommodating these technologies in the building. Basic factors to be considered are: the educational purposes to be served, the variety of media desired, the expectations of computer literacy on the part of incoming students, and the extent of databases provided and the Internet links. Each decision will help shape the program. Yet the rate of expected technological change, the nature of these prospects, and the direction of shifting near-term academic goals should do much to give the program form and suggest the flexibility to be sought.

Another policy decision is where and how to distribute the connections for bibliographic, pictographic, numeric, chemical, cartographic, video, audio, multimedia, full-text databases, and combined informational sources. All of those databases can be given their unique outlets in the locations where they will be most used, or they can all be provided in unified fashion from the same locations—what some call the arcade model versus the commons model. Then again, there is the issue of proximity to library service points, especially to points where informational and reference assistance is provided. (Programming for this informational technology is discussed in Sections 5.3.9 and 7.3, and consequential design development issues are dealt with in Section 13.4.4 and elsewhere.) Financial conditions often limit the extent of providing these networked outlets; however, midterm goals can usefully drive the direction in which the policy should be implemented.

The provision of major media facilities in libraries is increasing; they are almost universal in community or junior colleges and are becoming more so in senior colleges and universities. Programmed learning centers and language laboratories may be included, whereas a campuswide TV studio and graphics facility is more likely to have its own building or be associated with the department or school of education or of communication.

However, if the institution plans to house within the library computer processors, data storage units, and other peripherals, and if it plans to include source equipment for a major audiovisual or media service, including language laboratory facilities or video capacity, these services will place demands on the entire building project. Thus, the probable educational goals of the institution and the probable methods of instruction must be reviewed carefully. The kinds and number of such special facilities must be determined reasonably precisely, the future changes judged, and the probable extent of centralized or decentralized facilities within the building or institution must be resolved. It must be determined whether such supporting space as a photographic laboratory and graphics design facilities are needed in support of the audiovisual services, such as may be seen at Eastern Washington University and elsewhere.

As a substantial example, the Library of Congress Madison Memorial Building utilized a 3-duct system laid on 5-ft (1.524 m) centers in the slab of most floors above the basement. To handle power, telephone, and coaxial cable, these ducts are 3 in. deep and 6 or 12 in. wide (0.075 × 0.150 or 0.300 m). Such an installation can be a very costly element in a contemporary building and yet, a library that cannot adapt to changing technology will not be able to support a key part of its presumed mission—that is, providing access to information.

In both information technology and AV installations, a very large number of technical as well as programmatic decisions need to be made. A consultant may be essential unless there is an in-house expert. In any such installation of substantial size, the cost implications and the influences on significant parts of the building will be large.

3.3
Library Staff Preparation for the Project

Planning a new library building is expensive and complicated. It is exhilarating and may be one of the most pleasant, demanding, frustrating, and satisfying activities that a librarian can undertake. It should not be undertaken without proper preparation. Some activities need to be done in conjunction with the design team, and these will be treated in Chapter 4. A number of things need to occur before the architect is chosen and the program is written. Because these may be underestimated or overlooked by library staff, they are given prominence here as they may critically affect the smooth and effective completion of a building project.

3.3.1 Developing Staff Competence

The chief librarian or library director must understand a good deal about building design and operation in order to play an effective role in the planning process. This role is important even if the library is large enough to have a full-time or part-time planning officer or architectural building projects manager on its staff. Therefore, whether the institution is small or large, the head librarian or the associate or deputy librarian must have the ability to guide and participate in the project from the program point of view.

Whoever this individual is, it will be important for responsibility to be so vested that there can be a voice of authority and clear direction to the project month after month and year after year. If the director is to serve this function, it may well require at least 10 percent of that person's time over the entire number of years required from planning through occupancy. If, in fact, this individual is going to handle all interior planning and furniture selection, review all construction change orders, and participate in most meetings with the architect, these activities can occupy from 50 percent to 100 percent of her or his time during substantial periods, depending on the speed of the project and the care and effectiveness with which it is executed. Indeed, large projects on the order of 300,000 to 600,000 ft² (28,000 to 56,000 m²) may require two or more individuals in the library, even if the institution has an effective architectural planning office that handles all business matters and resolves most of the problems with the architect and the contractor. This may appear to be an excessive use of the time of senior library officers when many other things almost certainly will be going on. Yet it is also true that the process is a demanding one if the results are to be satisfactory. When a building project may cost up to 10 times the library's annual operating budget, there clearly is reason for the chief librarian or the deputy librarian to give it the attention it requires. A different aspect of this point is dealt with in Chapter 4; however, this time requirement must not be overlooked.

3.3.2 Releasing Staff Time

What has been said about the chief library officer can also be said in somewhat lesser degree about every department head and unit chief in all staff sections that will be housed in the new or renovated facility. Institutional officers will understand the attention to the project that is required of the head librarian; similarly the head librarian must recognize that unit heads will need to be informed of basic planning practices, involved in the programming effort, and deeply concerned about the exact details in their spaces and the possible impact of small deficiencies on their operating effectiveness.

Although it is almost never possible to provide departments and units with extra staff during a building project, the library administration can relieve those units of some tasks in order to compensate for the priority of attention that must be given to a building project. This time spent on the part of departments will be spasmodic, which is, in a sense, a saving grace. It will not be as incessant as is the burden on the head librarian, who will have weekly if not daily issues needing to be resolved, week after week and month after month. It may be possible for the head librarian to reduce the frequency of certain administrative committee meetings during that time. Perhaps a departmental annual report can be written every two years instead of each year. Certain budget processes may be simplified during the course of building planning. Perhaps some salary savings can provide a bit of flexibility. However it is planned, the affected departments need to be involved and understand the basic criteria on which the design is based, and what the effects will be of space being planned for each particular department or unit.

A building project is a new experience for nearly all members of the staff. Furthermore, the pressures and nature of a building project vary so much from conventional library operations that alternative styles are required. In some instances the institution's architectural planning office may provide briefing sessions for some or all library staff who will be involved in the process. In other cases the head librarian, the deputy, or the planning associate may have the responsibility for the educational process that will help each unit to understand what is going on and to have confidence in the process. Occasional articles in a staff bulletin will be of help. Oral reports in selected staff meetings can be useful. Posting schedules and sketches in a staff room at various stages of plan development can help this educational process.

In order to have constructive and timely decisions, it is essential that the staff understand the processes and the rigorous and, sometimes, constraining nature of the planning procedures. A building is, after all, a way of expressing a philosophy of library service. A poor building can be exceedingly limiting and frustrating both to the staff and to its users. Conversely, a clear set of goals and objectives and a precisely drawn program expressing those components in terms of a physical structure can eventually result in a building that facilitates the operations in all library units and thus pleases staff, faculty, researchers, and students.

3.3.3 Study of the Published Literature

Because special problems are involved in planning a library building, some knowledge of these problems is a reasonable prerequisite to the writing of the program, to say nothing of their importance in the actual planning by the architect. Reading selected literature on the subject can be useful. Although this literature is extensive, it is not well organized for the purpose. This volume is not intended to make further reading unnecessary, and it includes a selected, annotated bibliography that should be helpful. As a result of their reading, those responsible should be aware of much of the terminology, the range of problems, and the kind of basic information on which decisions should be based. The literature should help, although the decisions must be determined by the local situation.

Who should become acquainted with the literature? Probably it ought to be kept in mind that "a little knowledge is a dangerous thing." If the study is too casual, and if the reader tends to consider everything as gospel truth, errors will occur. It is suggested that at least one senior librarian on the staff, including the head librarian if possible and certainly including the primary planning associate in the library, try to become acquainted with the more important materials in the bibliography, as well as more recent selected publications recommended by a planner or an architect. It is further suggested that this volume be placed at the disposal of others involved in the program writing and that their attention be called to the parts of it that fall within their special fields of activity, as well as to other pertinent published material.

If the institution's president or provost expects to take an active part in the building project, the attention of this officer should be called to the literature, especially to points of library philosophy and academic significance. Exposure to the literature is equally important for other officers of the institution who may be involved, such as the administrative vice president, deans, the business manager, maintenance officers, the chair of the library building committee, and later the architect and the architectural and engineering consultants. Time spent in reading the literature and learning of problems in buildings elsewhere will save a good deal of grief.

3.3.4 Visiting Other Library Buildings

There is no better way to obtain insight into library building problems than to visit other libraries. Few people have imagination enough to picture these problems without seeing examples of them, and a careful examination of the literature by itself is not sufficient. Ordinarily not more than six or eight libraries need be visited by any one person, and those selected should be examined carefully enough to make the enterprise worthwhile. On the other hand, interesting solutions to problems can be found in a great many libraries because each may offer unique arrangements. Thus it may be useful for all the librarians on the staff to pool their experience from places they have worked or visited in the past to indicate what good and bad conditions they can remember and describe.

More on this topic of visits to other libraries is provided in Section 4.6, because some of this visiting should be done with the architect in order that each may learn from the other.

As an example of what can be drawn from visiting other library buildings, the following list of design attributions was prepared in 1966 in connection with Stanford University's undergraduate library, the J. Henry Meyer Memorial Library.

Alcove arrangement—Quincy House at Harvard, et al.
Reference alcoves—Lamont Library at Harvard

Audio outlets on upper floors—Indiana University
Low-divided tables—University of Texas Undergraduate Library
Eye-height bookcases—Andover-Harvard Theological Library
Checkout desk—University of Michigan
Reserve card counter—Doe Library, University of California, Berkeley
"Character" of pavilions—Tower Library at Dartmouth, Alumni Room at Bowdoin College, and the Morrison Room at the University of California, Berkeley
Desks around light well—Air Force Academy
Bulletin board arrangement—Colorado College
House phone provision—Countway Library of Medicine, Harvard
Area signs—University of Santa Clara
Trash chute—John Carroll University, Cleveland
Bookshelf material and color—Washington University, St. Louis
Lighting panels—Richard Blackwell's speech at public meeting
Air conditioning—Washington University
Electronic pianos—Sinclair Library, University of Hawaii
Remote tape decks—University of California, Los Angeles

3.4
Cost Estimates and Fund-raising

Before drafting the building program, it is essential to have some projection of the approximate size and probable cost of the project. Funding officers will need to determine whether these totals are acceptable to the institution. Chapter 9 gives considerable treatment of estimating construction and equipment costs, qualities or features in the building that may have exceptional effects on the costs, the institutional policies for estimating costs, and special factors that might affect building costs. It is also essential to have preliminary estimates on probable increases or reductions in the proposed library's services, energy, and other projected costs and to ascertain whether these are acceptable to the institution.

With the general idea of the size of the building derived from estimates of needs for bookshelving, reading space, and staff space, and with a sense of the difficulty of the site and the quality of the intended building, the institution's architectural planning office can put together a preliminary building budget. Construction costs for the anticipated type of structure can be provided by reputable contractors and, of course, must be projected ahead until the time when the building is under construction. Recent experience at the institution and in the same part of the state or country will serve as a guide. There will also need to be a budget for equipping and furnishing the building, landscaping around the site, moving in, and, sometimes, staff consultants and related planning expenses. Because conditions change and vary from one part of a large country to another, this volume can merely suggest that recent data from the institution's locale are necessary.

Library building costs have been tabulated from time to time in various forms and places. Those for individual libraries are often recorded in library publications. Although these may be helpful, always remember that they may not include each of the six categories of expenditure discussed in Chapter 9 and are unlikely to be comparable with one another. One must remember the three basic cost factors: (1) time of construction and the economic climate when bids are accepted; (2) the size and location of the building and any soil or site problems; and (3) the type of architecture and the quality of materials to be used. In other words, it is difficult and seldom useful to compare costs of a proposed building with other libraries or other types of buildings unless it is done by architects or consultants who are able to delve deeply enough into the similarities and differences that affect cost in order to provide valid guidance for the current project.

The nature of the building concept has a powerful effect on the building cost and the ability to raise funds for its construction. Before Cornell University and the universities of North Carolina (Chapel Hill), Texas (Austin), and Chicago built their large, impressive main libraries, the library condition was so obviously unsatisfactory that it engendered a lot of on-campus support and support from those who had funds. A library space that has become desperate or truly shocking may be in the best position for effective fund-raising. Sometimes a grand architectural design can be an asset for raising funds, though a finely crafted and demonstrably economical solution also garners support. Concerning impressive buildings, a donor problem was expressed to Keyes Metcalf by a well-known librarian in these words: "It is far easier to get money for a monumental or memorial style building than for one providing for the day-to-day needs which will make it live as a library. I doubt if this would be the case if the librarian or someone else who could speak with authority was prepared and able to explain the situation clearly and dispassionately to the institution's administration."

Before turning to fund-raising for publicly and privately supported libraries, a few points should be made about "selling the case" regardless of the type of institution. The financial strategy for raising funds needs to be based on the magnitude and type of library program that has been adopted. This program is shaped by the answers to the consideration of alternatives to new construction that were treated in Chapter 2, together with decisions on the major policy issues outlined early in this chapter. Ordinarily an institution does not go far with planning until funds are in sight or it is believed that they will be readily available. There are cases, however, where schematic building plans should be drawn as part of the preparation for a campaign to obtain funds. The need for the new structure certainly must be made convincing in order that support from one or more sources can be solicited and can reasonably be expected to be forthcoming. A description of services that the building will provide is helpful. A brochure, well written and carefully designed, can be useful in explaining the needs and requirements of the institution. The use of such brochures is common in privately supported institutions. If the persuasive voice of someone who has real knowledge can be added at the critical and decisive moment, it may turn the tide. For instance, quoting a highly respected member of the faculty can provide real insight into the current situation and the correction that is needed. If the brochure is not printed, at least the required information should be readily available as institutional representatives work with governmental bodies, foundations, alumni supporters, and volunteer groups on the fund-raising campaign.

Following is a sample taken from a published appeal. Substitute the years of your choice, and this statement could be current.

A NEW LIBRARY LONG OVERDUE
The need for a new library building may be quickly sketched by enumerating a few disturbing facts:

- The present Library has occupied the same space since 1938; the second floor location is a remodeling of an earlier amphitheater lecture room, students' lounge, and classroom.

- Its reading space (12 tables, 100 chairs), adequate in 1938, remains the same; the number of readers has *quadrupled.*
- While its regular shelf space remains the same, the number of books, pamphlets and periodicals has *doubled.* (The excess has been accommodated by overcrowded shelves, improvised shelving in nooks and corners, and by piling books in almost inaccessible places. Now there is no more room for even these expedients.)
- Ten thousand volumes dispersed to departmental libraries are *not* available for student use on evenings or weekends.
- The Medical Library needs larger appropriations for purchases and for additional staff, but such sums literally could not be spent effectively at the present time. Where would they put more books? Where would they put more workers?
- The Library, designed in 1938 and fitted into existing space, contains no private study alcoves, no rooms for typing notes or dictating onto tape, no photo-duplicating laboratory, no seminar rooms for group discussions, no audio-visual room, no proper room for microfilm or microcard reading—in short, none of the special features of modern library planning that so enhance its effectiveness as a[n] environment for creative thinking.

The inadequacy of the present library facilities has gone far beyond inconvenience; it is already close to the point where it is putting a ceiling on the School's programs of advanced teaching and research.

Add to this the need evolving from new technologies, along with the notion that viable libraries will continue to grow and change well into the future, and the argument should be persuasive.

The architect will occasionally be brought into discussion with a major donor, and may make a presentation to the board of trustees, and prepare a written statement that can be used in fund-raising documentation. The librarian is frequently involved as the expert witness to the present conditions and to what is needed by the institution and intended in the building project. The librarian may be involved in meetings as a representative of the institution with those who can appropriate or give funds, sometimes meeting with a volunteer committee, joining the president to visit a major prospect, and always being ready to assist the principal officers of the insti-

tution with a tour of the existing facilities whenever requested. Guidance to fund-raising is widely available, including the following: *Developing an Effective Major Gift Program: From Managing Staff to Soliciting Gifts,* edited by Roy Muir and Jerry May (Washington, D.C.: Council for Advancement and Support of Education, 1993); *Wealthy and Wise: How You and America Can Get the Most Out of Your Giving,* by Claude Rosenberg, Jr. (Boston: Little, Brown, 1994); and *Educational Fund Raising: Principles and Practice,* edited by Michael J. Worth (Phoenix, Ariz.: American Council on Education and Oryx Press, 1993).

Fund-raising is a task carried by the president, the vice president for development, one or more members of the board of trustees, and perhaps a provost or chief academic officer. The librarian usually serves as staff to assist in the project, though in some private colleges and an occasional university, the librarian has been asked to play a more prominent role. In any event, nothing can be more important than assisting with the fund-raising, for without funds there will be no building no matter how dire the need and how admirable the design.

Financing strategy may well include a variety of sources and several types of monies. The strategy will vary depending on the nature of the institution. The publicly supported college and university will rely primarily on state appropriations, though other sources often are of great importance. Church-affiliated institutions may receive all or substantial construction funds from the church authority. Private professional schools may internally finance the construction. Bank loans or borrowing from endowment may be necessary. Most institutions use a mixture of funding sources. For instance, a medical center library in a university may have funding from the federal and state governments and perhaps the local city or county, as well as foundation grants, gifts from individuals, and maybe income from endowment, from the sale of real estate, and even from patient fees.

Funding sources may include public bonds, governmental appropriations, federal grants from programs specifically designed for academic library buildings, loans or gifts from private foundations, from private individuals, and from corporations, and very often a combination of these. The fund-raising strategy may include an incentive program to provide funds when matched by individuals, perhaps one dollar from the principal source for one, two, or three dollars raised from other sources. Although it is not normally recommended, both Harvard (for the Fogg Museum addition) and Yale (for the Seeley Mudd Library) have sold some of their collections to help cover building costs. In Yale's case it was the Brasher doubloon coin, sold for $650,000 in 1981 to help close a $1.5 million gap in funds for its $6.7 million social science and documents library.

In the financing of a publicly funded institution, most funds come from taxation. Federal legislation in the United States has from time to time made government support available, either by loan or outright gift, to public and private institutions for library building construction. State and municipal bodies have, on occasion, provided funds for this purpose. If the funds are to come from a government agency, institutional officers will develop the strategy.

The question almost certain to arise in the case of a large building is whether it will be constructed at one time or in stages. The answer may be complex, and the pros and cons need to be thoroughly analyzed. Phasing construction will add to the design cost and probably the construction cost, particularly where the construction activity is prolonged as a result. A building constructed in stages may be easier to finance, but planning is more difficult. One may not wish to build in stages; however, state policy for capital projects may require it.

If the funds come from a governmental body, a considerable hierarchy of offices must ordinarily be dealt with before an architect is chosen and the plans can be completed and approved. These actions are often quite political. The approvals may involve not only the chief administrative officers of the government concerned, the legislature, the finance and education departments, and the administrative officers of the institution but also one or more architects who are official representatives of the government involved. Threading one's way through the maze takes time and may be difficult. Capital funding approval can require five or more years of requests, justifications, and various preliminary approvals before being finalized by state or other responsible governmental authorities. The institution's administrative officers and librarians should seek all the help they can get to prevent the project from bogging down.

Government participation, whether it be federal, state, or municipal, also means acceptance by the institution of governmental rules, procedures, and standards, which may add a layer of difficulty as well as something to the cost. Forms will need to be made out extensively, extra inspections will be required, and frequent reports given. The accounting process will be rigorous. However, state or county building requirements and standards will usually apply even if governmental funds are not involved.

If governmental funds are not available, private funds must be sought. In spite of the unprecedented large gifts to institutions of higher learning in recent years, funds are not ordinarily easy to come by for new library construction. Whereas monies for "bricks and mortar" were quite popular gifts four or five decades ago, more recent experience is that they are currently among the most difficult funds to raise. The particular methods used by institutions vary greatly, and some are more sophisticated than others. A few institutions can rely on a relatively steady flow of gift monies for buildings and other purposes. Some have a particularly strong alumni network. Others must rely much more heavily on private foundations or local corporate resources.

One or more of the numerous private foundations that support facility projects may be a funding source. Foundations best known to academic and research libraries—Ford, Rockefeller, and Carnegie—are seldom prepared to make grants for new buildings. Yet there are hundreds of other large foundations, some of which will ordinarily be interested in a proposal of a new building, especially for a local institution. Some foundations do not, however, make grants to public institutions. Corporate donors also should not be forgotten, as a special interest may be developed for a specific area. For example, the newspaper reading room and stack might be of interest to a local newspaper publisher, or a science library could interest a major technically oriented firm. Local industries often will have an interest in supporting their neighboring educational institution, and a new library may well be an attractive opportunity.

If the present library is named for a donor who is still alive, that individual may not be in a financial position to repeat a major gift or may even be opposed to a new building. If the donor is deceased, but family members, even into the second or third generation, are living and their whereabouts can be ascertained, the family should be informed of or even consulted about the institution's need for a new building. The courtesy will be appreciated and the possibility of hurt feelings lessened. Sometimes the family is able and willing to contribute to the renovation of the original building. Many other factors will influence the fund-raising.

The rapid growth of libraries brings another problem in its train. A new library tends to be one of the largest buildings on the campus, and consequently very expensive. Only a comparatively few individuals will have the capacity to make a gift of the whole amount required. Large gifts tend to come as bequests, and a bequest seldom provides for library construction because the donor does not know, when the will is drawn, what the institution's needs will be when the bequest becomes available. Such a bequest is more likely to be specified for a professorship, scholarships, a book fund, or even a dormitory or athletic facility. Obviously, unrestricted bequests to the institution provide the desired flexibility.

It is rare that a building is named after a group of successive donors. There is one instance of a university library building with two names, honored scholars rather than donors. A donor may offer to pay for a percentage of the new library if the institution would wish to name it for that family or individual. In such cases the institution must decide whether a gift of one-quarter, one-third, or one-half makes the balance of the fund-raising feasible and thus can justify putting the name of one person on the building.

Certainly if an institution agrees to name a building for a donor who gives less than the full amount, the donation should be accepted with the understanding that the names of others who contributed toward the total sum will also be recognized in some appropriate fashion. This recognition may be in the form of a tablet in the entrance or plaques in individual rooms. The possibilities here are many. This approach was used successfully at Princeton University, where up to a thousand individual gifts are recognized in the library in this way, and at Brandeis University Library, where this method was adopted on a large scale. Donor recognition, important for the institution and for the individuals concerned, is treated in Chapter 15 as part of the dedication event.

For fund-raising purposes, an arbitrary value per unit of area may be put on a room, a carrel, an alcove, a courtyard, or other space to which a donor's name may be attached. The term "arbitrary" is used because the value will probably be higher than the actual cost. This value is properly based on a pro rata fraction of the project cost, including nonassignable space and space that cannot be "sold" to prospective donors, rather than the exact construction cost. These figures may be further inflated for very desirable spaces and deflated for those that are less desirable from a donor's point of view. Examples are given in Section 9.1.

A special college or university fund-raising campaign among alumni and friends may include the library along with several other needs. Such a campaign usually extends over a number of years and must be well planned and scaled in order to have a reasonable degree of success. Some institutions use professional fund-raisers who have experience with effective methods of presentation and appeal. It should be recognized that in such campaigns, the gifts will not come designated in exactly the proportion required for the needs requested by the institution. Some gift opportunities will turn out to be more popular than others. Unrestricted gifts can be assigned to the less-popular items. Some time ago a very large and successful fund-raising campaign at Stanford University was concluded without the proposed undergraduate library receiving the required major gift to lever the project. A year or two later two sisters made the gift that, together with about one-fifth of the needed funds by a grant from the U.S. Higher Education Facilities Act of 1963, covered the entire cost of the project. Though this building had been delayed four years, funding for most large projects is not as simple.

There are many amusing and sad stories about academic fund-raising, some of them resulting in eventual success and some in failure. Though it is by no means meant to be a typical case, the following statement from Saint Michael's College in Vermont is included to indicate some of the complexities, anxiety, and effort that are involved in fund-raising, nearly every instance of which has its unique set of episodes, and many are quite extraordinary tales.

The plan for financing of the construction was divided into three parts: A grant under Title I of the Higher Education Facilities Act, a loan from the same Act of 1963, Title III, and funds from the College Development Fund.

The grant in the amount of $300,000 had to be approved by the Vermont Commission on Higher Education Facilities which was established by the Governor of the State of Vermont. The State Commission will accept any application from any of the institutions, provided such applications are submitted on forms provided by the Commission. . . .

When the bids for the construction of the Library were opened June 9, 1966, it was revealed that the lowest bidder of six was $265,500 higher than had been anticipated.

The College set about trying to reduce the figure and arranging for the additional financing. We subtracted from the contract alternatives in the amount of $72,000. We adjusted the architect's fees according to the new contract and, on the advice of the New York Office of Housing and Home Finance Agency, we allowed only 2% instead of 5% construction contingency. We also found we could reduce the amount allocated for equipment cost in our original application by $20,000. Thus the original application for a loan of $595,500 was increased to $723,000 and the share of the College increased.

On October 16, 1968, Certificates of Project Costs were approved by the Office of Education. The eligible development costs were $1,349,895 (Title I) and $1,358,355 (Title III). This supported the Federal share of the grant of $300,000 under Title I and a loan of $718,000 under Title III of the Higher Education Facilities Act. Thus the financing was as follows:

Grant—Title I	$ 300,000
Loan—Title III	718,000
St. Michael's funds	345,307
Total:	$1,363,307

The financial problems in the construction of the Jeremiah Kinsella Durick Library were like putting your last one dollar bill on the dice table and knowing that the sevens and the elevens had to keep coming up with each roll.

Special arrangements with the Office of Education in Washington were reached [for] an escrow agreement establishing the account in a New York bank where funds that were to be approved by the Federal Government would be protected and the contract obligation of the College fulfilled. With this protection established, the contract was signed and ground broken. A short sixty days after the footings had been put in place, the Federal Government froze all construction funds and it was unknown, at this time, just when Washington might approve the additional funds for Education Construction.

As the first flowers of Spring, "the Snowdrops," showed their faces, the most welcome news came from Washington that our increase in the loan of $128,000 had been approved.[2]

It took over two and a half years after bids were opened to resolve the financing. It is sometimes very very difficult, as many can attest, though seldom are the stories publicized.

Notes

1. This qualification is per page 643/4 of the 1988 Uniform Building Code with 1989 California Amendments.
2. As quoted in Jerrold Orne, "Financing and the Cost of University Library Buildings," *Library Trends* 18 (October 1969): 150–65.

4

The Planning Team, with Architect and Consultants

Architecture, to state the obvious, is a social act—social both in method and purpose. It is the outcome of teamwork; and it is there to be made use of by groups of people, groups as small as the family or as large as an entire nation.

—Spiro Kostof, *A History of Architecture: Settings and Rituals*

The fate of the architect is the strangest of all. How often he expends his whole soul, his whole heart and passion, to produce buildings into which he himself may never enter.

—Johann Wolfgang von Goethe, *Elective Affinities*

4.1
The Building Planning Team

The building planning team will guide the creation of the distinctive nature of its particular project, just as the eventual building will control the operating practicalities for its occupants. It is truly a team effort, a group effort. Every member will play a crucial role, just as does each member of a symphony orchestra in achieving the total effect. Some teams will be quite small while others will have many members.

The team is composed not only of librarian and architect working together, though they are the most important of the group, but rather of a group of individuals whose skills are all required for and committed to creating an excellent library building. It is a team in the sense of teamwork, for, although each plays a particular role, the members will never all meet together at one time. It is made up of one or more committees, representatives of various offices in the institution, the architect and engineering associates, and consultants for specialized aspects of the work. These people must cooperatively work toward the defined building goal over a great many months. Very few of them, maybe only three or four, will work full-time on the project.

Because the team members have not worked together before and most of them have not worked on an academic or a research library, or a building for this particular institution, the team should be formed with special care. Team members early on should achieve a common understanding of the purpose and nature of the desired product. The creation of this group and their relationships are the subject of this chapter.

4.1.1 Planning Committees

The following planning committees are possible, though it would be unusual and probably unnecessary to use all of those suggested in any one institution. Indeed, better continuity usually occurs if fewer committees are used, though each committee can play a different role and be involved briefly at appropriate times. If several committees are formed, a coordinating or planning committee may be needed, with the roles of the subcommittees strictly defined and the responsibilities limited.

A trustees' building committee. A committee from the board of trustees may be desirable, particularly if the trustees expect to keep a tight rein on building design. Often trustees find that they can control the situation satisfactorily if the president represents them in planning a new building, but with the understanding that final policy decisions, especially those involving financial matters and public relations, will be referred to them before action is taken. Sometimes one or more trustees having special interest, knowledge, and competence in building planning can be asked to serve on a committee made up of representatives of other interested groups.

A committee of administrative officers from the institution. This committee is a second possibility. The president may want to be a member or even the chair, though often it is enough to be represented by an administrative assistant in whom there is confidence. Other members may include the treasurer, the business manager, the head of the building maintenance department, and the vice president in charge of educational policy. To these might be added other officers, such as the provost and one or more deans.

Faculty committee. Appointment of a committee of professors (sometimes also with one or more student representatives) is certainly not out of place, to ensure that educational interests receive proper primary consideration. This committee can include professors who are known to have special interest in the library, preferably those with some practical building knowledge and imagination. They should represent each of the major fields—science, the social sciences, and the humanities—if the building covers all such fields. Sometimes one professor is given the leadership of the project. This person may have served as chair of a faculty library committee, may represent special interests of the institution's president or chancellor or the trustees, and sometimes plays a crucial roll in private fund-raising.

A student committee. A separate group of students is sometimes useful in enlisting student interest and cooperation in the project. If a strong student council exists, it might be asked to appoint this committee. If not, the dean who deals most closely with students should select its members.

Library staff committee. In a large institution, this fifth possible committee can properly be appointed, often with the chief librarian as chair, but sometimes with a senior staff member in charge who has special knowledge of planning problems.

The librarian or a heavily involved representative should be a member of all these committees as a coordinating officer, if nothing else. Often several of these committees may not be of much direct help. The problems involved may not be fully understood by the committee members. Decisions may need to be made during school vacations and a rigorous schedule of sequential decisions must be met. However, remember that each group is deeply concerned with the results. Frequently, important help can come from one or all of the groups; including representatives of each in the planning process is a matter of first importance to the institution, if only to obtain the occasional helpful suggestion or point of view and to prevent unnecessary and destructive criticism of the building when it is finally erected.

If one or more of the committees are not appointed, the librarian or some other officer must have the responsibility of keeping in touch with all the groups concerned to make sure that their different points of view receive full consideration as planning proceeds.

4.1.2 The Question of Inside Library Help

Although a library staff committee may be used, many other patterns can be appropriate in a particular institution. A staff committee may be suitable if no individual on the staff has significant building experience. If one or two have broad experience in building planning, the responsibility for coordinating and involving staff departments and units may be a natural expression of the existing organizational structure, and a special committee may not be needed. In such a case the group of department chiefs may meet regularly, and the building project would be a natural topic to include on their agenda. The same may be the case for the director's council or cabinet. Yet it must be realized that the building will demand its own time; therefore, many extra group meetings must be devoted particularly to the building.

In the case of a departmental or branch library, the staff of that branch may in effect be a committee, or one or two representatives of that branch may work with one or two members of the central library administration as a committee. In this case, though, it must be made clear who has the final authority and who will be the speaker for the committee.

As an example, at Texas A&M University, one reference librarian with a degree in architecture worked almost full-time assisting the director of libraries with building construction matters. In many libraries there will be an individual who is good in planning and communicating, who is close to the chief librarian, and who undertakes this major representation. At Stanford University, when the project was begun to enlarge and renovate the main library, a professionally trained building projects manager was appointed to the library director's office. This new position, reporting to the director of libraries, continued for more than 10 years as the project effort moved along. Even after the main library was completed, other major library projects evolved that continued the need for a building projects manager. Where an institution is faced with a large project or has many branch libraries and other planning and renovation tasks, such a position can be the best use of funds. If in one year the project slows down while funds are raised or authorizations are obtained, the individual can usually be well used to plan furniture, review fire safety or earthquake hazards, check on compliance with standards for physically limited persons, or assess maintenance deficiencies in the library buildings.

Whatever pattern is chosen for the library, it is essential to establish clear lines of authority, to emphasize communication both up and down the organization, to meet decision schedules, and to announce results if they affect staff units. The process must flow in pace with the architects' and engineers' requirements. On the other hand, the library staff has a high professional stake in the results and has every reason to be involved on a regular and continuing basis.

4.1.3 The Question of Outside Help

The problem of outside help is complex. Often the first question is whether or not an architect should be employed to make a master plan for the entire campus, including the library site selection.

A master plan is desirable and too often not available. But if the governing board approves the site chosen by the master planner, the library architect, when selected, may feel that a better site exists and may properly recommend it. The librarian must also be given opportunity to participate in the site selection with the campus planning group and the architect.

The institution may have a supervising architect, as has been fairly common in smaller institutions. If so, this person will be involved before the selection of the design architect, and will be required to give approval for all new construction. The relationship between the design and the supervising architects should be carefully defined to avoid misunderstanding. Keyes Metcalf claimed that instances could be cited where disagreements between the supervising architect or campus planner and the library architect have caused serious difficulties.

Should one or more consultants from outside the institution be selected before or after the architect is chosen? In general, with the exception of the library building consultant, such appointments should follow the selection of the architect, who should have an opportunity to express a preference. Indeed, the architect usually selects, appoints, and pays the consultants. Sometimes the institution will want help from a consultant in selecting the architect. Circumstances alter cases.

Probably the most important consultant, from the perspective of this volume, is one who has special knowledge and experience in library building planning. Occasionally such a person exists within the library; much more frequently such a person is called in to advise and work with the architect. This outside consultant may be a librarian with experience in building planning or an architect with experience in the library field. Whether one is appointed in advance or only after consultation with the architect will depend on local circumstances.

Sometimes the architectural firm selected has had little or no experience in library planning but understands that it will work with a library or an architectural consultant. If the librarian has planning experience and the architect has limited library experience, an architectural consultant with library planning experience might be appointed. If, on the other hand, the architect has library planning experience and the librarian has little or none, it may be better to appoint a librarian experienced in library building planning. It sometimes happens, however, that both the architect and the librarian are inexperienced in library building planning. If the proposed library project is large, it may be worthwhile having both an architectural and a library consultant. Yet if only one is needed, other things being equal, a library consultant will be more useful to keep the architect informed on special library functions and problems and to provide the librarian a fresh perspective on local issues. Fortunately, there are, at least in North America, a number of experienced library consultants.

4.1.4 Briefing and Coordination of Efforts

Ideally all the individuals and committees mentioned above should be briefed by the librarian or, perhaps better, by the president or senior academic officer on the basic financial and education problems that the institution faces. The "ground rules" to be used in dealing with such problems must be clearly understood.

The entire planning group should be told what is going on, and full participation should be solicited. It is undoubtedly true that, when a large group is given an opportunity to comment, the floodgates may be opened to unnecessary remarks; but this procedure involves everyone in the proceedings, and the suggestions or criticisms of all will have been aired. The planning group members should be less likely to criticize the results than if they had not participated. The publicity obtained may also help in fund-raising, when needed.

Of course, if all these individuals and groups are involved, special care must be taken to see that their efforts are coordinated, that all understand what is and is not expected, and that their activities do not come into conflict with one another—something that can happen. This matter of underlying importance is too often neglected.

All the primary members of the planning team should be exposed to literature on library buildings, including at least portions of this book. By the time the planning participants are acquainted with the literature and have been briefed on the planning problems to be faced, the advisory committees should be appointed, and agreement should be reached as to the relationships and responsibilities of each group.

4.1.5 Visiting Other Library Buildings

When should other academic library buildings be visited? Depending on the degree of knowledge about academic library building planning, the principal members of the planning team may need one or several visits. As mentioned in Chapter 3, key library staff can benefit from a visit to two or three institutions when considering space problems, the philosophy of service, style of presenting these services, and alternatives to pursue.

Once the architect is chosen, visiting several academic libraries and perhaps a few special research libraries and a few of the larger public libraries will be important so that there can be a dialog during site visits among the representatives of the library and the architectural firm. It can be helpful if an academic officer or a member of the faculty library committee participates in these visits. In many instances in North America, the visits may need to include examples in the east as well as the west so the team can see good efforts of roughly the same scale.

There may also be a visit when the design development work is completed and before the interior finishes and furnishings are settled. At this stage of a project, it may be especially instructive to visit a few public libraries and even buildings other than libraries. Thus, depending upon the project and the individuals involved, there can be as many as three or four trips with each trip including one or more buildings.

What specific libraries should be selected? They should include very good examples, though one

can learn almost as much from an unsuccessful solution of a particular problem as from a good one. As to what is good or what is unsuccessful, even the experts often disagree and will emphasize different points. It is hoped that those who study this volume along with other literature on library buildings will know about the variety of solutions to particular problems, will have fairly definite ideas about their basic planning objectives, and will know what they want to look for. Here, we mention a large number of examples in widely differing locations. Yet new examples are constantly coming online.

Be sure to choose libraries of several institutions that are similar in character to your own—that is, in the number of students, the size of the collections, locale (rural or urban), and general outlook—because such institutions and larger ones are more likely to have dealt with problems that resemble yours. On the other hand, do not hesitate to go to smaller or larger libraries if they have something special to present.

Among the things worth noting when visiting libraries are first impressions, general appearance, traffic patterns and spatial relationships, portal control arrangements, OPACs, self-service circulation, online reserves for courses of instruction, support of technology in general, adjustability or lack thereof of chairs and other equipment, strategies for addressing potential staffing changes (such as outsourcing or functional grouping), table sizes, dimensions of individual seating arrangements, the use of reading spaces by students, crowded areas, aisle widths and shelf depths, informational and directional signs, coatrooms, arrangements for smoking (significantly less common in North American libraries than it once was) and snacks, heating and ventilating installations, window treatments, background sound, lighting, ceiling heights, and the use of color and glass. This list could be much longer—the interests and concerns of the visitor will obviously shape such a list.

What procedure should be followed when the libraries to be visited have been designated? One method is to have the librarian go first alone to one or two libraries and to suggest that the architect do likewise. Then a joint expedition is desirable, perhaps including a member of the faculty library committee and a representative of the institution's maintenance department. Probably not more than five should join in a visit. A larger number cannot easily keep together and see things that should be seen, and the librarian of the institution being visited is likely to be overwhelmed. The library consultant, if one is to be employed, may be included in the visit, for such an expert is in a better position than others to point out both satisfactory solutions of problems and failures.

It is a courtesy to make prior arrangements with all libraries to be visited. Ordinarily a half day is enough for one building. A large university building might require a full day, but not usually. Be sure to reserve time after the visit to talk and prepare notes. Photographs of selected features can also be helpful and can be used in discussions back home. The notes and photographs should be organized so that they can be referred to and made available to others during the course of the project. If the host librarian comments on good and bad points of the library, these remarks can be particularly helpful.

There is such a thing as getting too involved in details and seeing too many buildings. Yet visits are very useful and enhance communication because of the common experience. They should be undertaken selectively even when the librarian and/or architect have worked on other academic library buildings.

4.2
Selection of the Architect

The architectural firm is commissioned under contract to the institution (known as the "client" or "owner") to design a building that will accommodate all the functional components, will operate effectively for years to come, and will be an aesthetically pleasing contribution to the community. The architect brings to the design team a background that calls on centuries of architectural practice. The training and skills in site placement, building styles, form and materials, use of three-dimensional space, mechanical needs, and decoration are applied to provide a suitable environment for the library functions. From study or experience in design, the architect will be familiar with design theory and practice, technical problems and solutions, and detail issues, and must relate mass and form and space to good effect.

The architectural firm may include a wide variety of specialists, particularly if it is a large firm with 40 or more on the staff. The architect will supplement the firm's talents by hiring one or more consultants. These may be engineers or other specialists as required by the particular nature of the project. (In contrast to the planning team, the design team is composed of the architects, engineers of all kinds, cost estimators, code experts, landscape architects, graphics designers, interior designers, and often others.) The architect maintains overall responsibility for the performance of the building, its soundness of construction, its quality of materials, its cost, its basic safety for occupants, and its attractiveness. In simple terms the librarian defines the functions and quantities in the building and their interrelationships; the architect is responsible for creating its shape and its appearance—a building with "strength, function, beauty," to quote the Roman architect Marcus Vitruvius Pollio.

4.2.1 Criteria for Selection

The selection of a well-qualified and talented architect is essential if a good library building is to come into being. The characteristics of key personnel (as well as the firm in general) must be considered, though the architectural firm must be financially sound and devoid of suits that could affect its practice. The following 14 characteristics are essential:

1. Must be professionally competent and licensed.
2. Must be able and prepared to interpret and understand the needs of the client.
3. Must have the imagination and creative ability to produce a unique and satisfactory design that is responsive to the program, site, economic conditions, and other factors. A library is to be the result, not a structure that speaks as a testimonial to the architect.
4. Must be a good listener with a clear mind and must also have the ability to explain clearly the architect's point of view, both orally and in writing when needed.
5. Must understand the client institution, its standards, its problems, and its educational objectives. The firm need not have designed a library, though commissions for academic institutions would provide a useful background.
6. Must realize that the client's functional needs are to be directly served by the architectural answers. If the client's wishes and needs do not coincide, the architect is free

to try to persuade the client of that fact, but the primary task is to answer the client's needs functionally and aesthetically.

7. Must, of course, have good taste and a feeling for what is appropriate and must be prepared to plan a building so that the functional requirements of the inside are integrated and in harmony with the outside; must have a full understanding of the importance and weight of both function and appearance.

8. Must know the costs of constructing the building that is planned, and must not either underestimate costs so that extra time and money are required to solve the problem or overestimate so much that the client does not obtain as good a building as it should from the available funds.

9. Must have readily available engineering competence, which is highly important in producing good plans today.

10. Must be prepared to get help, when needed, from an architectural, an engineering, or a library consultant. Must be willing to work effectively with an interior design firm, if one is used, regardless of whether the architectural firm has such a capacity. Must be talented in seeking solutions and gaining agreement.

11. Must have a staff proportionate to the task the firm is undertaking, so as to be able to design the project and produce the working drawings and specifications in reasonable time, and not so busy that the commission is given poor attention or relegated to inexperienced staff.

12. Must have almost infinite patience; but if the client demands changes so late in the planning process that they cannot be carried through without extra cost, the architect must in due course say firmly that no more changes are possible.

13. Must always be ready to learn and must realize that genius alone is not enough.

14. Must be a person of integrity, prepared to admit that a distinguished building that is not functionally sound will not be satisfactory.

Beyond these characteristics other matters must be considered. The strictest of selection criteria for an architect is desirable for a building in the academic center of an institution or for a larger commission, whether it is for a new building or for the enlargement of an existing structure.

If a competent local architect can be found, certain advantages will result. The cost, other things being equal, may be less. Knowledge of building materials locally available, local building codes, construction firms, quality of specialized labor, and special community history and problems should be valuable. The client will not have to wait for days for a small but necessary consultation, something that can occur with a firm a great distance away. Architectural services will also be more readily available during construction when it is crucial for the architect to keep track of what is going on. For departmental or branch libraries and for remodeling projects, local firms are particularly good. Small firms may be entirely satisfactory and may offer distinct advantages deriving from extra personal attention. Of course, using a smaller local firm on a project of modest scope is a way to test a young and promising firm or one that the institution has not used before.

On the other hand, there have been excellent experiences with architects located more than a few hours away. The Stanford University campus plan by Frederick Law Olmsted and the Quadrangle architecture by Charles A. Coolidge in the Boston firm of Shepley, Rutan and Coolidge were designed by skilled professionals 3,000 miles away—in days before airplanes—and a hundred years later are considered superior and appropriate designs. An architect usually supplies contract administration during construction as part of normal services. If an architect from a distance is selected, a local representative must be available during construction.

It is reemphasized that the architect must be astute and candid about construction costs. It is suggested that an architect should not be selected until the institution has consulted former clients on this and other points. When cost is underestimated, unfortunate compromises result, possibly affecting the soundness of the whole campus building program. Too often failure to face up to the real cost leads to embarrassing situations. For example, Stanford University had poor cost planning for the Meyer Memorial Library in the early 1960s. Construction estimates based on finished design development plans were 5 percent above budget. Consequently, the architect was required to cut costs by 5 percent, and the problem was badly solved by reducing the planning module by 5 percent!

Money goes a long way toward determining space both in terms of quality and quantity. To avoid unpleasant controversy that, combined with other complaints, may have deplorable consequences, the architect should be told during the selection process that the institution wants as handsome a building as possible, but that there is a definite limit to available funds; within this limit the requirements stated in the program must be met and the results must be functionally satisfactory. A maximum construction cost figure can be stated. One important consideration in the selection of an architect is a conviction that the selected firm can design an excellent building that can be built within an agreed-upon budget. The more difficult the problem, the greater the challenge to the architect, and the firm can properly be told that it was selected because it was believed capable of doing the job required. The architect should, however, be prepared to speak up promptly if asked to perform a miracle and produce something that cannot be built within the proposed budget. Unfortunately, the dynamics of architect/client relationships often result in a lack of full candor in dealing with issues of this nature; the client does not want to hear that the project cannot be completed for the funds identified, and the architect does not want to tell the client this fact when a commission might evaporate as a result. Human nature to be optimistic in this setting is a problem. This topic will need direct attention if the finances are truly limited and the institution really wants full disclosure about cost reality.

Another question deserving special consideration is whether the architect should be experienced in library building planning. This factor is much less important than skill, competence, imagination, willingness to listen, ability to communicate, desire to find good solutions, and honesty in facing building costs. Ordinarily, of course, an experienced library architect is selected for major library projects. If the architect selected has not had library experience, and particularly if the librarian has never been through the process of planning a library or is not given a leading role on the planning team, it is of the utmost importance that a library consultant be called in. Given a strong and very able librarian, a skilled architect should produce a fine library on the first such commission.

A famous architect should be able to produce a superior library. Yet beware of one with such a strong sense of the exterior design that functionality is poor. A case is the award-winning Irvine Science Library at the University of California, Irvine, which is striking externally and fails internally despite the international acclaim of its architect. And this is not the only case produced by highly regarded firms. If the institutional goal is to create an architectural centerpiece, then perhaps reasonable compromise on functional aspects can be justified, and use of a world-famous architect should be sought. However, such compromise must be done with open eyes; the management of the institution will be required to make the building work for many years even if it is more expensive to do so.

4.2.2 The Selection Process

The institution may have a stipulated method for selecting an architectural firm. In some instances, an architectural competition may be chosen or even required. (This approach is discussed in the following section.) The institution should not be so wedded to a firm traditionally used that it must be given the library commission even if it fails to meet reasonable criteria. The librarian should play a major role in choosing the architect, perhaps as part of a small group representing the institution's business office or architects and engineers office. However, it is recognized that, especially in large, state-supported systems, the choice may be made at systems headquarters or even in another state office.

The selection process may begin with a list of 15 to 20 firms compiled from various suggestions, some from the librarian and most probably from the architects and engineers office. It may include some firms that have previously been used with satisfaction by the institution and some that have not been used. The specific criteria for selection should be determined by the group. All firms meeting the criteria should be asked to state their interest in the job and availability for interviewing, to describe their present workload, and to supply copies of their brochures and a list of professional experience.

This procedure may enable the institution to narrow the number down to six or fewer firms that will be asked to participate in an interview and for which references should be checked with previous clients. A visit to the architect's office is very useful before making the final selection. One may consider the key individuals who would be assigned to the library project, their experience and where they may be weak, what kind of support staff they have for computer work or specialized talents, the extent of the office workload, the nature of personnel relations, how businesslike is the office, and how much time and effort are required in getting to and from the office. One can discuss experience the firm has and try to evaluate whether that experience may be advantageous or disadvantageous.

The particular process of selection can have many variations. For example, one fine, old New England college states the following process:

> First, let me emphasize that we did not have a big formal AIA competition though I anticipate that many have construed it as such. We have followed a particular selection process of architects for the student union, science complex, the Theater, the recently completed dormitory and finally, the latest, the Library Addition and Renovation.
>
> Very simply, the philosophy has been something like the following: If architects are invited to make presentations to whatever selection committee may be involved, they invariably discuss their successes in short projects with which the committee members are unfamiliar. This places us in an even more embarrassing position as frequently committee members are untrained in architecture or construction and therefore are unable to intelligently evaluate what they're hearing. In an effort to avoid this situation, we follow a different routine.
>
> First, the Physical Plant Department recommends to the committee eight or so highly reputable architectural firms who are knowledgeable in the particular area. The committee after listening to the usual presentations will select three firms to continue. The three firms will each be paid [a nominal amount] and asked to spend at least one day on the campus meeting with various groups or individuals to become somewhat familiar with the design problem. They are then asked to return after a few weeks to study the problem and to make a one-hour presentation to the selection committee (usually plus the Buildings and Grounds Trustee Committee). The presentation is expected to focus on the design problem at our college. Since they are discussing their approach and alternatives to a problem which is better known and understood by the members of the committee, they are better able to evaluate the capability of the architectural firms.
>
> Following the presentations, the Trustee Buildings and Grounds Committee receives the recommendation of the Ad Hoc Committee and the Buildings and Grounds Committee takes the definitive action in making the final selection.

The acceptance by architects of this process has been uniformly positive. In all of the twelve to fifteen firms that were involved, there was only one who felt that they had been unfairly treated. In all honesty that firm did not make a sincere attempt to work with our requirements and the attempt at circumvention was poorly conceived. Obviously we do not award prizes nor do we widely publicize this procedure.

Sometimes a local firm will propose a joint venture if it is small or lacks particular talent. The employment of joint venture architectural teams has produced varying results, not all of which have been satisfactory. Such arrangements usually are a compromise in which a nationally prominent architect is brought in for the name and the hope of having a striking design. Pairing that firm with a local one is convenient for some practical tasks, is good public relations with respect to local employment, and may be necessary for political reasons because some states require selection of an architectural firm in the state on state-financed buildings. The working relationship between the two firms is critical and should be explored in depth. This is not to say that joint ventures are impossible arrangements for obtaining satisfactory buildings, but there are special problems that need exploration. An absolutely clear understanding of divided responsibilities and of who makes what decisions is critical in order that a joint venture work to satisfaction.

A donor's selection of the architect is almost always suspect. Harvard's Widener Library was the result of the donor's choice of a favorite architect located in Philadelphia. The firm had done the Philadelphia Free Library building as well as work for Duke University. After architect Trumbauer visited Harvard, two draftsmen went to Cambridge for about a week and returned with a first plan to show the donor. Apparently the donor's commitment of funds was pending while the initial design was undertaken. Mrs. Widener made an offer of the funds for the building plans, and the proposal was accepted. The agreement between the university and the donor indicated that it would be "a library building in substantial accordance with plans and specifications which had been prepared by Horace Trumbauer." Many of the building problems of the Widener Memorial Library (fig. 4.1) derive from such an unsuitable method of selecting and working with the architect; other, much more recent

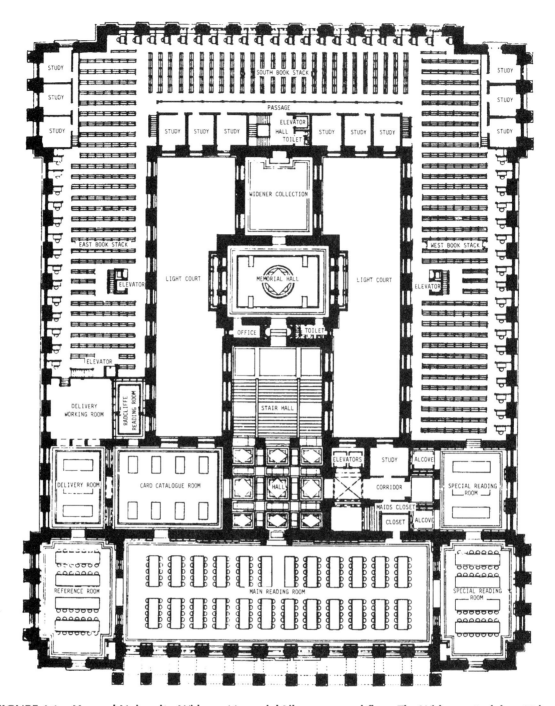

FIGURE 4.1 Harvard University, Widener Memorial Library, second floor. The Widener stack has 10 levels surrounding three sides of the building and two courts. The traffic pattern is simple, with only one range of stacks at right angles to the main aisle. Carrels (called stalls) are on the outside walls. Faculty studies are in the outside corners and on the south wall facing the courts. The ranges are 10 in. (1.270 m) on centers with wide bases, so that the available aisle width is only 26 in. (0.660 m). The main aisle, which is 48 in. (1.219 m) wide, seems adequate for heavy traffic. The aisles by the carrels are only 38 in. (0.965 m), but, with open carrels on one side and stack aisles on the other, seem wide enough. ADA is obviously not addressed, but then, ADA was not an issue at the time.

Problems with this fixed function arrangement include: (1) the main aisle is difficult to reach from the entrance; (2) the elevators are scattered and inadequate; (3) the stack aisles are quite narrow because of the wide (24 in., or 0.620 m) bases; (4) the distance from the entrance to the far end of the stack is over 400 ft (122 m); and (5) the main entrance is reached on the eighth of ten levels after going up five steps.

80

examples exist, including the Robert A. Millikan Library at the California Institute of Technology, where the architect was also selected by the donor.

In the last analysis, it is important that the institution and, particularly, that the librarian feel a suitable rapport with the principal architect and the project architect with whom work will go on in a close relationship. A mutual understanding can result in a satisfactory product; any sense that communication is not effective and that there is not a common understanding and confidence in one another is quite certain to result in an inferior product.

The importance of good architecture and the selection of a good architect cannot be overestimated. The architect's role is a major and demanding one. The American Institute of Architects (national headquarters at 1735 New York Avenue, N.W., Washington, DC 20006) and its chapters and state organizations (as well as similar organizations in other countries) distribute pamphlets that should be useful in selecting an architect or architectural firm. The following titles available in 1996 indicate their scope: *Architecture Books, Reference, and Gifts; You and Your Architect; A Beginner's Guide to Architectural Services;* and *Building Relationships: A Guide for Institutions on How to Work with an Architect* (this last item was out of print in 1996 and probably is no longer available). Do not hesitate to write to Washington or the local AIA chapter for information.

4.3
Architectural Competitions

Early in the twentieth century architectural competitions were not unusual for a library, particularly in the case of large buildings. This method is still used in the United States and in Argentina, Australia, Denmark, the Federal Republic of Germany, Finland, Great Britain, Japan, and, in 1980, China, for the Beijing National Science Library, as well as the Bibliothèque nationale de France (first expressed as a national goal on July 14, 1988, and completed about 10 years later). Indeed, competitions are today the usual process in western Europe for design selection of public buildings.

Competitions are and have been used from time to time in North America. Stanford University in 1993 began to use competitions. For major new buildings, the "University Architect" (the chief planning officer) assembles credentials from a dozen qualified architectural firms, with four being subsequently shortlisted and invited to prepare design solutions for the proposed project. One week before the final presentation by the firms, they are asked to submit written proposals for staff evaluation and reference reviews to assure that the project as conceived will be, in fact, buildable on time and within budget. Each participating firm receives a sizable stipend.

Stanford believes that the selection process has three advantages: (1) The simultaneous inclusion of trustee and administrative representatives makes this a community process instead of the usual serial sequence of design review as is known at most institutions. (2) The process leads to a higher level of design understanding because the university "has access to various alternatives in the formative stages of design development." And (3) competitions have led to the streamlining of the review process, thereby saving two to three months from the design review through the design development stage. The first advantage is intended to counter the "campus sprawl" that can result when an architectural firm is hired for a new project based solely on its portfolio and interview presentation, and by the time university trustees see a surprising and problematic design, it is deemed too late for a totally different approach.

When the project solution can be within very broad limits, competitions will produce a variety of solutions and thereby assist the institution in formulating more exact design parameters. On the other hand, this is a process that obviously can lead to designing a building from the outside in, rather than the preferable approach of designing from the inside out. Each process for selecting the architectural firm can have its advantages and perhaps its disadvantages.

Theoretically, competition has several other advantages. If a number of architects attack a specific building problem, the selected design should be better than if one firm is chosen in advance and told to do the best it can. A public competition attains more local publicity and thereby demands more attention and accountability of trustees and top officers of the institution. It calls attention to the building and provides publicity and extra excitement that may make fund-raising easier. It may allay criticism after the building is built; people will feel that every effort has been made to obtain the best possible plan. Further, it can circumvent a political situation when one architect is the presumptive firm for a project, especially so in the smaller countries or less populated regions where there may be few if any highly qualified firms. However, any particular competition may be criticized on various points as well, as has been the case from numerous sources in France and elsewhere.

Often arguments for an architectural competition are more political and theoretical than practical. It is generally possible to select a competent architect and work closely enough so that a fine building results without a competition. Except for the potential loss of an array of design insight, which can vary substantially from architect to architect, and except for circumventing a political situation, each of the advantages of competitions stated earlier can be met by a well-managed project with one firm chosen by the traditional process of interviewing, checking of references, viewing previous work, and having an evaluative presentation by the shortlisted firms. And, indeed, any one chosen firm can be asked to present several design solutions as part of the early schematic phase of designing—and, in fact, good architects will always do this at least as part of their own routine process in approaching any project.

Possible objections to competitions are these: The winner presented a plan that is dramatic or sensational but unfortunately not particularly functional. (It is striking in the exterior and potentially seriously deficient in the interior.) It is especially difficult to make changes after the winning design is announced. The architect claims the competition was won because of certain features in the plan and may be unwilling to alter them. The winner was selected by architects or political friends, not by librarians or occupants of the ultimate building. Public competitions are usually not judged by the client but by a group of judges, the majority of whom are architects and who may be more interested in architectural features than library function. The chief librarian can frequently be in a weakened position because of heavy involvement of higher authorities and the egos involved.

A successful competition is a complex process to manage effectively, assuring the result is truly the best for the owner of the building. Thus this approach can require a highly competent institutional planning office to guide and manage the process from start to finish, or the services of a firm to so manage it. The International Union of Architects (UIA) has issued instructions and recommendations to promoters of international architectural competitions. UNESCO published in 1981 "Revised recommendation concerning international competitions in architecture and town planning," a document used in organizing the 1989 competition and international fundraising effort for the Bibliotheca Alexandrina.

Two other points may be made. Competitions often take extra time—sometimes six months or more. And they are costly because of prize giving and other inevitable expenses. The winner's first prize is considered part of the regular fee if the building is constructed, but the other prizes and the expenses of the competition are all extras.

Certain better architects hesitate to compete because of the work involved and fear that their reputations will be damaged if they do not win. It has been said by many architectural critics that the best solution is almost never the winner of the competition. On the other hand, competitions can be very useful when local campus planning is minimal, where a "higher level of design understanding" is desired, and where a departure from recent stylistic traditions is desired.

There are two main kinds of architectural competition: (1) limited competitions, open only to a selected group of architects invited to participate, as in the Stanford case above; and (2) open competitions, to which one and all are invited. These may be local, national, or international in scope. The noted Polish-French architect Jan Meissner describes the following two types: project competition where the winner carries out the commission, and ideas competition where the winner is not supposed to carry out the project. And Meissner defines three different forms of eligibility: public competition, competitions limited to everyone within a country or region, and competition by invitation of a select few. (See his paper "International Architectural Competitions," delivered at the 1996 Beijing conference of the International Federation of Library Associations and Institutions.)

Attention is called to three library competitions, one in the United States and two abroad, which, although conducted many years ago, are still prime examples of successful events. Probably the most famous academic library in the

United States resulting from a competition is the Washington University Library (fig. 4.2). The original structures on the campus of that university were built largely to provide quarters for the St. Louis Exposition of 1904. Buildings added later followed the general architectural style of the exposition. Criticism was sure to arise if changes were made for new construction. In 1956 a limited competition was held in which three local and three nationally known architects were invited to participate, each being paid $2,500 with the understanding that the winner would receive the commission and the fee would be 6.5 percent of the total project cost. All the plans presented were for exciting buildings. The winner was a local architect, and the building is without doubt one of the better university libraries. More than one of the other plans submitted, although architecturally pleasing, would have been disastrous functionally and perhaps financially.

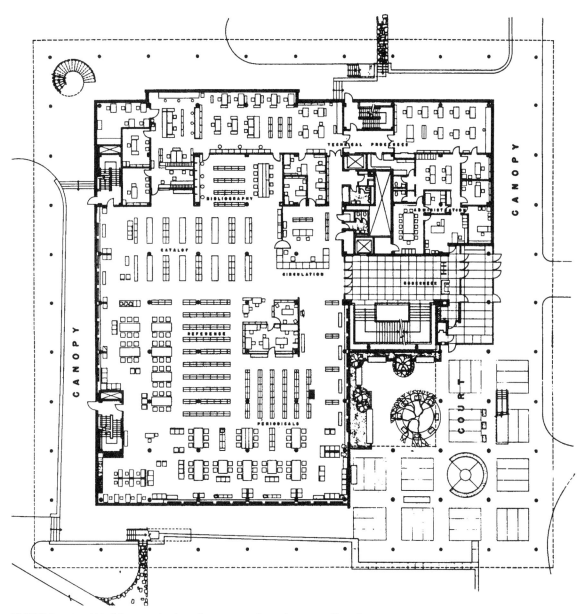

FIGURE 4.2 Washington University, St. Louis, John M. Olin Library, entrance level. This level encloses 55 bays. Levels 1 and 2 below it enclose 84, level 4 encloses 60, and level 5, the equivalent of 67. The entrance level is very effective aesthetically; but the essential services there are unduly restricted, a result that could have been avoided if the colonnade area were available for library use.

Trinity College, Dublin, in 1960 and 1961 had a competition for an addition to supplement its great early-eighteenth-century building, which is one of the finest libraries architecturally to be found anywhere in the world. Organizers believed that the publicity that would come from a competition would be useful in raising funds and that, although there was danger of serious criticism of any plan selected, this danger would be less if the plan could be selected from a large number. There were 218 submissions, and it is interesting to note that most of those that received prizes or honorable mention were, taken as a whole, functionally satisfactory. The winning design was built and is an exciting and distinguished piece of architectural sculpture. Yet it is extremely inflexible and is regarded by some as a functional disaster.

The third successful competition was for the Aalborg University Library, Denmark, serving four colleges that had been recently formed into the University Centre. In Denmark, competitions for choosing an architect for government building projects are normal. Many young architects participate, and a majority of the competitors are from Scandinavian countries. This 1974 open competition, sponsored by the Ministry of Education and Aalborg City Council, drew 37 proposals, which were judged by a board of architects and politicians. The competition was for a first-stage design, a layout proposal in principle for later stages, and design requirements for an integrated university center and housing development. Four prizes were awarded, five submittals were given honorable mention, and names of unplaced competitors were not revealed. A very satisfactory urban library resulted because of major involvement of library staff during the design effort.

As is usual, the Aalborg sponsors were not bound to use the first-prize winner but had the right to choose any receiving an award and to require modifications as they deemed best. It is not uncommon for the first prize to go to the outstanding design and the project to be awarded to the most economically viable proposal. The prize-winning Aalborg design group (architect, civil engineer, and landscape architect) was assigned the project, according to the principles of their competition submission but modified by specifications of the sponsors.

The Meissner paper cited earlier describes other competitions: for example, the Syrian National Library in 1974, and the 1993 Dubai Centre of Mr. Juma Al-Mijid. Occasional campus plans are the result of competitions (one in the 1990s was for the University of Cyprus, Nicosia), as are some major public artworks. All architectural competitions should be guided by the accepted rules distributed by national institutes of architects or the International Union of Architects (UIA), headquartered in Paris.

4.4 Architectural Fees

Fees vary by location and with the size and complexity of projects. A major part of the fees are for architectural and engineering services, though other consultants' fees should not be forgotten.

The architect's compensation is customarily based on a percentage of construction cost, although it may be a set fee plus office costs, a multiple of the technical payroll cost, a lump-sum agreement, or a per diem or hourly rate. Because design and consultation fees are related to the actual effort involved, there should be little basis for negotiating except possibly for a small differential based on the complexity or simplicity of the planned building.

Usual services performed by the architect for the average building assignment include, in addition to the architectural concept and planning of the library, engineering services for structural, plumbing, heating, ventilation or air conditioning, and electrical work. This work may be performed within the architect's organization or by outside engineers employed by the architect. What are known as "usual" architectural services are ordinarily divided into three groups:

1. Preliminary services, which include: (a) conferences to determine the scope of the project, the problems to be solved, and the general approach, and the preparation of schematic drawings; and (b) sketches, which include preliminary structural and mechanical design, preparation of preliminary or design development drawings of the approved solution together with outline specifications listing the materials to be used and preliminary estimates of cost. A "working" scale model may also be included.

2. Construction documents and specifications—also termed the "contract documents"—which include preparation of the contractor's

construction (working) drawings and specifications describing and illustrating in detail the work to be done, the workmanship, and the materials to be used; the preparation of structural, electrical, mechanical, and landscaping drawings and specifications; and assistance in preparing proposal and contract forms in securing bids and in awarding contracts.

3. Execution of work, which includes general administration of the construction work and necessary shop inspections; preparation as needed of additional large-scale and full-size detail drawings; checking of samples, subcontractors' shop drawings, and models or mock-ups submitted by contractors and subcontractors; issuance of orders for changes in the work required and approved by the owner; and checking of contractors' requisitions, issuance of certificates for payments, and final inspection of the work. The architect must also ensure that the preparation of "as-built" drawings is achieved in acceptable order, even if they must be prepared by the architect.

The architect's agreement with the client should make clear that the drawings and specifications, as instruments of service, are the property of the architect, whether the work for which they are made is executed or not, and are not to be used on other work except by agreement with the architect. However, in certain types of public work, the authority involved sometimes stipulates that the original plans and specifications are the property of the public authority in question. This is also the case for many academic and research institutions. It should be added that no service, oral, written, or graphic, should be furnished by the architect without assurance of adequate compensation.

When compensation for usual services is a percentage of the construction cost, it is commonly based on a percentage of the final construction cost, including fixed equipment and bookstacks, called the basic rate. Compensation for supplementary services is added to this. It used to be the case that basic minimum rates for institutional buildings, schools, banks, hotels, and theaters were recommended to be about 8.5 percent of construction cost for very small projects and as low as 5.5 percent for very large ones, plus 2.5 percent if they were renovation projects. These rates were designed to cover costs of the architectural services with about 50 percent additional for profit. The particular character of any project would affect the amount. (Warehouses might be

1.5 percent lower, while laboratories and hospitals could be 1.5 percent higher.) Although complete and adequate architectural services cannot reasonably be expected to be less under ordinary circumstances, long experience and outstanding reputation in a given field may entitle an architect to higher compensation.

The American Institute of Architects no longer recommends a schedule of rates because of antitrust legislation. Rather, since 1975, the AIA has published *Compensation Guidelines,* which is useful. A 1978 AIA leaflet entitled *Your Architect's Compensation: What It Covers and How It Is Derived* contains the following advice:

> You have a choice of services. First, you and your architect meet to identify, from a schedule of designated services, the specific items required to carry out your project. The decisions may be recorded on a special form. At the same time, you and the architect assign responsibility for carrying out each item of service—either to the architect, to yourself and your staff, or to special consultants. . . .
>
> The architect computes the cost of services. Once you and your architect have determined the general scope of services to your satisfaction and assigned responsibility for each item, the architect proceeds to compute the compensation. He or she does this by estimating the number of personnel hours and expenses needed to provide the services, and by adding amounts for overhead and reasonable profit and for expected reimbursable expenses. Normally the architect does this in-house, and only after summarizing the resulting figures by phase and for the entire project is there another meeting with you to review the amount of the proposed compensation and to complete and sign the owner-architect agreement. In addition to providing summaries, it may be appropriate under special circumstances for the architect to share details of the derived data. . . .
>
> The architect sums up this personnel data and adds amounts for share of indirect expense or overhead (all items not directly chargeable to specific projects, as derived from office accounting records), and for other nonreimbursable direct expenses, outside services such as engineering and other consultation, and profit.
>
> Profit is an important consideration. Profit is one main reason why the architect, like others who practice a profession or a trade, is in business. It is the tangible reward for professional and financial risk, and a return on investment. It is what is left of the total compensation after all expenses are deducted. The amount the architect includes for planned profit is derived in part from the nature of the project and the firm's financial goals, in part

from taking into account certain expenses which the architect cannot include in compensation. Such "risk" items could include a rise in overhead costs after an overhead factor has been agreed upon, direct expenses not to be covered in compensation, and administrative costs tied to consultants' payments. . . .

Now you are ready to discuss compensation. Having taken into account all the factors in computing compensation, the architect is now ready to discuss with you the amount and the method of compensation for your project. As an aid, the architect may use the AIA's special project compensation summary form on which to record this cost information. The form contains space for proposed amounts of compensation by phase, a column that shows the same data cumulatively, a column for anticipated reimbursable expenses, and added space for revisions.

You are now at a most critical stage of the cost-based system, for it is here that you and your architect fix the actual amount of compensation. What yardstick can you, as the owner, use to see that the compensation being proposed is fair to both you and the architect?

Some owners budget what seems to them to be a realistic figure based on past experience. First-time owners rely on careful computation by the architect combined with open discussion. If, after all, your figure is still lower than the architect's proposal, a way must be found to reconcile the difference.

If you are still unable to agree, what happens? The best route to agreement in such cases is to pull out once more the schedule of designated services form and review the various items. Some costs may be brought down—for instance, by transferring responsibility for the service item from architect to owner. (Coordination, however, should remain with your architect.) An increase in the initial retainer will lower the architect's level of receivables and may induce him or her to modify the compensation amount. Sometimes, a second look at an item-of-service description will indicate a higher than average commitment of the architect's time, thereby justifying higher costs for that item.

Also, as you begin to discuss the type of construction contract, keep in mind that some kinds of contracts (such as a negotiated contract or one with several prime contractors) call for more from the architect by way of personnel hours than does a single contract, stipulated-sum arrangement. If you are a client with many projects, consider aggregating them in such a way that one architect could provide the needed services for several projects on a more cost-efficient basis.

Finally, you may wish to reduce the scope of services to bring the architect's proposed compensation into line with your budget. But be sure that the reduction in services will not hurt your project.

On occasion you and your prospective architect may run into the problem of ill-defined scope. If the early phases of your project fit that case, consider asking your architect to help you develop a scope of services; meanwhile you are billed on an hourly basis or other "cost-plus" arrangement. Then, as your program gains in precision, you can call for an accurate, cost-based proposal.[1]

This statement is provided to give some comprehension of the financial and other concerns involved in an architect's contract. Information about additional architectural services and payment practices is provided in Section 9.2.5, Architectural and Other Fees.

4.5
Consultants

A major new building is a considerable undertaking. At the very least, the architect will typically employ structural, mechanical, and electrical engineers. Very often a library building consultant will be used. Usually a landscape architect will be involved. Often an interior designer is included, and there may be other consultants involved from time to time, as cited in Section 4.5.5. Because a college or university does not have a full range of expertise and even a very large architectural firm will not have all these specialists, the use of consultants is universal, although the number and choice of topics for consultancies will depend upon the individual project.

With the aid of the architect, identifying qualified consultants is easy for some specialties; other talents may be extremely specialized and scarce. Yet with inquiry of architects, contractors, or those who have planned similar buildings, the names of individuals or firms will be obtained. When necessary, it is far better to select the distant specialist than a local amateur because use of the consultant is justified only when significant new talent is brought to the project.

In each case needing a consultant, sound selection criteria are called for. They can be similar to the criteria for selecting an architect. In general terms one wants integrity and honesty, sound oral and written communication skills, highly professional and experienced talent, availability, and an interest in working on this particular project.

Consultants' commissions are commonly based upon a percentage of cost, a lump sum for a clearly specified amount of work, or an hourly or daily rate plus expenses, sometimes with a maximum. Fees will vary markedly, depending on the experience of the consultant and the scarcity of and demand for that expertise, but fees should almost never be the primary basis for selecting a consultant. If a planning team needs to bring in a special expert, the need must be an important one, and a consultant who seems to be expensive may ultimately save the institution a great deal of money.

As with selecting architects, a thorough interview and sometimes a visit by the consultant to the institution can be very helpful. Once the scope of the task is understood, the architect or the institutional representative should discuss the business aspects with the proposed consultant. A jointly signed document or contract is highly desirable even if it is merely a letter of understanding of the nature of involvement, what is expected of the consultant, and the basis for payment.

In deciding where it is important to have specialized expertise, one may look at significant errors or problems that have occurred during past building projects. Although there is no statistical frequency table that can guide, the following are frequent:

1. The whole project had to be postponed or given up because costs were underestimated. Cost overruns accumulated during construction.
2. The size of the building had to be reduced at the last minute. A costly change was required during construction to meet a local code.
3. The column spacing is so awkward that library reading or shelving capacity is lost and the columns fall awkwardly in passageways.
4. The lighting glares, reflects badly, or is very obtrusive in the peripheral field of vision.
5. Some types of seats are not used, or some writing surfaces or walls are covered with graffiti. The interior seems cold, unpleasant, or at least unattractive.

6. The ventilation or air-conditioning system is abominable for one reason or another. Vibrations cause disturbing sounds. The audio system components have not stood up for even three years of use.
7. Sunlight makes some areas very difficult to use because of heat gain; staff complain or readers will not use those areas.
8. The building was placed on the site in a way that makes it impossible or exceedingly awkward to build an addition.
9. Mezzanines are very awkward for housing part of the collection or using efficiently. A central well engenders antisocial behavior. Wasted space exists through monumental stairways or halls.
10. The library sounds noisy. People are easily distracted by sounds coming from various activities in the building or from adjacent offices.
11. Floors or walls have not worn well, and show excessive wear.
12. Security and traffic problems abound. Main entrance door hardware is constantly loose, and it is very difficult to find your way around the library without asking for help.
13. The introduction of new technologies is awkward or impossible. Adaptability is largely missing.
14. Acoustic treatment for the use of computers, meeting rooms, and separation of sound for group studies is lacking.

These and other problems can be found with unfortunate frequency in otherwise good, well-designed, and functional academic and research libraries. Though the preceding list is but a sampling, it may serve as a sober reminder that building a library is a complex undertaking and that use of consultants may be a requirement to eliminate or ameliorate what otherwise could be a very significant problem when the building is completed. At the very least, a good consultant should inform the institution of the potential problem so that a well-informed decision is made.

This section deals with the following consultants:

1. Library building consultants
2. Engineers

3. Landscape architect
4. Interior designer
5. Other consultants

4.5.1 Library Building Consultants

In the past half century, some individuals who had an extraordinary understanding of library building planning were called upon frequently as consultants. Angus Snead Macdonald, Alfred Morton Githens, Joseph Wheeler, James Thayer Gerould, John E. Burchard, Ralph Ellsworth, and Keyes Metcalf were pioneers. An experienced librarian-consultant, though rarely used in the United Kingdom, is more often used than not in some countries and certainly in North America. Even where the local librarian has considerable experience, a consultant has been found of distinct value as a means to confirm and refine beliefs.

Five questions should be answered in connection with library building consultants:

1. Why have a library consultant?
2. How should a library consultant be selected?
3. At what stage in the planning should a library consultant be selected?
4. What should the library consultant be paid?
5. What should the library consultant do?

Though the why and how of contracting for consultants has been discussed to some extent, because of the potential importance of a library consultant, each question will be addressed in greater detail.

Why have a library consultant? A consultant is ordinarily appointed because the institution realizes that without such a person it will have no one available, including the architect, who has had the desired experience in planning a library building. In spite of the large number of recent library projects, the typical librarian rarely has an opportunity to participate in the planning of more than one building during a career, and many architects lack enough experience with library buildings to qualify as a specialist. The administration of an institution may well appoint a consultant to place at the disposal of its planning team the knowledge and experience that would not otherwise be available or not available in sufficient degree.

Institutions sometimes have a local history or influential persons holding rather extreme views, which can make a consultant particularly useful. There may be a trustee who wants what his or her grandfather wanted, and only a monumental or a gothic building will satisfy. There may be a dean who thinks that audiovisual or computer support is more important than a library. There may be a professor who believes in excessive decentralization of library facilities or in seminar rooms for advanced classes in which basic collections of that special field are shelved. There may be a science professor who is convinced that no library is going to be needed in the future because of computer networks and other technological developments. There may be a librarian who is intimidated by videotext technology or the Internet, or who has had bad experiences with major book thefts. There may be special problems, and the institution's representatives who have the overall responsibility for the building may very often believe that an outsider could provide a needed balance.

In most cases a consultant is wanted because of the realization that special knowledge is not locally available, that the cost of a library building is great—it sometimes doubles the institution's investment in its library, amounting to as much as 20 times the annual library budget—and that mistakes would be extremely serious. Previously when libraries were planned, the librarian generally had comparatively little to say about the details; too often the architect went ahead without knowing library problems, and, being primarily interested in the aesthetic side of the matter, produced a result that was not functional. This is an age of specialists, and it is not strange that library building consultants should be more in demand.

The chief reason for a library building consultant, then, is to make available special knowledge of the functional needs and requirements in a library building, and to make sure that an effective advocate will speak for these needs as planning proceeds.

How should a library consultant be selected? Select a consultant with experience. Investigate and find out about the results of work done elsewhere. Keep in mind not only the consultant's knowledge of building planning but also his or her ability to influence people and make them understand the basic problems involved. An expert in library building planning who cannot get ideas across to the architect, to the other members of the planning team, and to the institution's administration may be pretty useless, however much is known.

The consultant should have the ability to explain the reasons for a point of view and to persuade others of the importance of carrying out the suggestions. The consultant must not be overly dogmatic, should be fearless in expressing views, must avoid undue aggressiveness, and must understand the local situation.

There must be enough understanding of the architect and engineer to avoid unsuitable and impractical suggestions. One must realize that planning a library building involves not only functional but also very difficult and critically important architectural and engineering problems.

The desirability of choosing the most appropriate consultant cannot be overemphasized. The person should be the right individual for the particular job, perhaps suitable for one institution and not for another. The consultant should not be chosen just because she or he works in the same city or state, although convenient accessibility can be helpful. The qualifications for a good librarian do not necessarily make a good library building consultant. Just because an individual is eminent in the library profession or is a successful administrator of a large library does not mean competence in planning buildings. Similarly, a good experienced architect may not necessarily make a good library building consultant. A planner with both architectural and library experience may be the most useful, to the institution as well as to the architect.

A successful public library building consultancy does not necessarily mean that the consultant can do the same on a college library or vice versa. Indeed that would rarely be the case. Problems of college library building planning and university and research library building planning differ greatly from those of public libraries, and in details will differ considerably from each other. Choose a consultant who seems to have the knowledge, the experience, and the broad-gauge mind that will assure an understanding of your particular problem and help in the places where you need help. If you need someone to influence your governing board, library committee, or administrative officers, rather than to help with the details of the building planning, choose someone who, in your opinion, can be persuasive. A poor selection may be worse than none at all.

At what stage in the planning should a library consultant be selected? If you are going to have a consultant, select one as soon as possible. The person can be of use in deciding whether you should build a new building or add to an old one, can help to select the site, and can properly give advice on the selection of an architect.

Normally the consultant should not recommend a specific firm, but can offer suggestions regarding the qualifications that should be met. If the consultant can be appointed early enough, before important decisions have been made that will be impossible or embarrassing or expensive to change, fundamental mistakes may be prevented. However, if one is not used at the beginning, problems may often develop that make the appointment imperative; better late than never.

Unfortunate developments sometimes arise, more often in a public, tax-supported institution than in a private one, where the governmental authority or the source of the building funds and the institution's administration, without consultation with the librarian or faculty library committee, decide on the amount of money to be made available for a new library, select the architect and the building site, fail to provide time for the preparation of a program or the employment of a library building consultant, and make basic irreversible decisions that almost inevitably bring about poor planning, an unsatisfactory library building, and a waste of funds. If the architect has had experience in library building planning, some of the hazards may be avoided; however, lacking such experience or a qualified consultant, the results can be and occasionally have been disastrous.

What should the library consultant be paid? There is no accepted schedule of payments for library consultants. As yet, library building consultants are not in an organized and accepted profession, and they may never be.

Three fairly definite methods are used in charging. One is on a percentage basis, the percentage varying according to what the consultant is expected to do. It may be scaled depending on the extent to which the consultant is involved in the procedure from beginning to end, as the architect is, being on call during the construction as well as during the preliminary planning and the contract documents stage.

The second method is an agreement by which the work will be done for a definite sum, or at least an amount not exceeding that figure, with consideration given, as the plans develop, to the amount of time spent. Ralph Ellsworth suggested one-tenth of 1 percent of the total project cost may be budgeted for the consultant. He noted that it may not all be used, since it depends on how many days may be required.

The third method is for the consultant simply to charge so much a day, plus expenses. The per diem may range widely according to the experience and the prestige of the consultant and the job at hand. The consultant may set a rate equal to what would be the person's full-time employment salary rate in a large organization. (This rate appropriately should be figured to include benefits—for vacation, sick leave, and personal time—which a salary in an organization covers.) A consultant may reasonably charge as much as twice the equivalent rate if very experienced. Further, the size and nature of the project may justify a smaller or larger fee. For instance, a branch library project costing $1 million might need a consultant, but 0.1 percent of the total, or $1,000, probably is not adequate budgeting for either the second or third method.

A consultant with a great deal of experience may feel that in a situation with complications of one kind or another, the rate for an experienced person is not adequate and that a somewhat greater per diem is reasonable. A team of consultants, working together and contributing among them expert knowledge in various fields, may require altogether a larger percentage of the total cost though perhaps less per day per person, and so on.

What should the library consultant do? The consultant should do everything within reason to help plan the best possible building, making knowledge and experience available to those concerned, using excellent judgment about when to push and when perhaps to hold back temporarily or permanently, if it is believed that someone else's voice on a particular point at a particular time can be more valuable. One should defer to the specialist in a field for which one is not particularly qualified, although if a definite opinion is held based on good authority, one should state the case quietly and persuasively. One should avoid butting one's head against a stone wall if there is a good way around it.

To be more specific, the consultant called on at the very beginning should first go over the whole situation in general terms, to obtain a firm grasp of it. Then she or he should try to learn enough about the institution, its history, its background, and its objectives, so that the framework of the library's requirements becomes

reasonably clear. These needs should then be translated into space requirements, with the understanding, of course, that the results will be an approximation.

A consultant may have basic formulas for use in this way. Different formulas are required for different types of institutions. For a small academic library, for instance, something like the following might help as a form of quick analysis: Ten to 12 volumes can be shelved in one square foot of net floor space, and in a larger library 12 to 14 may be a safe figure. (This is a range of 108 to 151 volumes per square meter.) Fifty square feet or a little more will accommodate a reader. This 50 ft^2 (about 4.7 m^2) will provide not only for reading-room space but for the staff to serve the readers, the processing work space, and the nonassignable space for the whole building as well. The two added together—that is, the space for books and for readers and services to readers—will give the total net square feet if no unusual special facilities are required, such as an auditorium, audiovisual areas, an exhibition room beyond normal lobby space, classrooms, more than a limited number of seminar rooms or faculty studies, and special lounges. These are extras and must be added to the previous figure.

With a very rough total of net space requirements available, the present building should be carefully investigated by the consultant.[2] With rearrangements within that building, can the space required for a few years more be provided or could a wing be added without leaving the building in an undesirable position aesthetically or functionally? The possibility and advisability of major alterations and an addition should always be seriously considered, so that no interested person can say that such alternatives were ignored.

At this stage, of course, it is desirable to reach a decision about the future number of years for which plans are to be made, for not only the present but also the future requirements are extremely important. Projected growth in book collections and the effect of digital technologies are the major determinants.

When a conclusion has been reached about the total space requirements, the problem of a site should be settled. Do not permit the decision on that point to be determined until you and the consultant know what is needed and can be sure that a satisfactory building of the size required can be placed on the plot selected. Be sure that thought is given to the next stage when the new building will be outgrown.

It will now be time to consider in detail the written program for the architect and make sure it is complete. It should provide, if not the exact size of each area, an indication of the required size in terms of readers, staff, and collections to be housed and the desired spatial relationships among the different areas. The role and content of the program are discussed in Chapters 5 through 8.

The program is a matter of greatest importance. If practical, the program should be written locally by the librarian on the building committee or by someone on the scene who is skilled in a task of this sort. It is almost impossible for an outsider to obtain the required information in a short time. But the consultant can and generally should take a vital part in the program preparation, primarily by asking the questions that should be answered and by making sure that important points are not omitted. In other words, the consultant should be the guide and critic rather than the author.

Sometimes a consultant may think that the task could be better done personally, and perhaps that could be the case; on the whole, however, if the program is written by those who have to live with the results, it should be much more satisfactory. The building committee and the librarian, for instance, will understand the program better if they have written it or taken direct responsibility for it. They will then be able to explain it more successfully to the faculty and students or the governing boards and the public in general, than if it is written by the consultant.

Help in selecting the architect, either after or before the program has been completed, can be provided by the consultant. But, as has been already noted, this must be done carefully, preferably confining suggestions to the type and characteristics of the architect to be selected and not recommending a particular firm.

The consultant, or the librarian for that matter, should ordinarily not prepare schematic drawings or preliminary sketches for the architect beyond those that indicate desired spatial relationships or minimal functional arrangements as program information, not design intent. It is not uncommon, for example, to record a typical office layout, or an acceptable arrangement for a service desk or processing area with its various components. Alternatively, it is important

for the consultant to see and discuss with the individuals concerned the drawings prepared by the architect, particularly those that have to do with spatial relationships and function, the adequacy of the space assignments proposed, and their capacity to fulfill the program requirements. There certainly should be involvement in detailed review of equipment layouts and traffic patterns, floor coverings, lighting, security, acoustic concerns, ventilation, and so forth. Furniture design could well be included, particularly sizes, and, to a limited extent, color and finish. (See fig. 4.3.)

If the architects and one or more members of the planning team go to other libraries to learn how to solve planning problems, it is useful for the visits to be made under the sponsorship and direction of the consultant, who can suggest libraries to be visited and points to be kept in mind during the visits. If the consultant goes along, which is sometimes desirable, attention can be called to important features, and causes, alternatives, and consequences can be discussed.

The consultant should be available by telephone and by letter as questions and problems arise, throughout the contract documents stage and preferably during construction as well, even if appearance on the construction site is not necessary.

It should be noted that it is always dangerous to attempt to give advice without knowing fairly intimately the local situation, including the climate, the terrain, the campus and its master plan, if any, as well as the general spirit and atmosphere, philosophy, and objectives of the institution. It is difficult to get acquainted with these without being on the spot. Consulting in absentia, either here or abroad, is not effective.

A final question in connection with "What should the library consultant do?" lies in how far this specialist/advisor should insist that the architect and the institution follow recommendations. For instance, should the consultant withdraw if major suggestions are not followed? Should the institution be asked to agree that it will not proceed without the written approval and the consent of its consultant? Because ultimatums almost never serve any constructive purpose—few people are infallible, and circumstances alter cases—the authors believe that a "yes" answer to these questions is too drastic. If a prospective consultant believes that the answer to these questions is yes, as some consultants have pro-

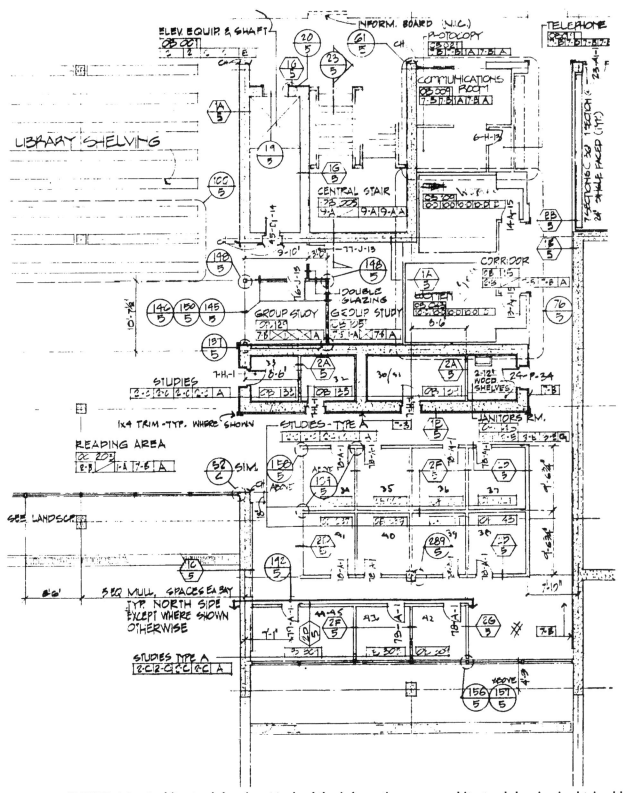

FIGURE 4.3 Architectural drawing. Much of the information on an architectural drawing is obtained by relationships to other drawings or the specifications as identified by a system of symbols and codes. To the inexperienced, understanding the drawing can be a frustration that can easily be circumvented with the help of a consultant.

posed, this should be specified and approved by both parties before the work is undertaken.

A consultant can, of course, always withdraw and refuse to be publicly associated with the project; however, Keyes Metcalf's experience with several hundred planning enterprises suggested to him that a procedure of this kind is seldom, if ever, necessary or justified. In the authors' experiences, architects as well as librarians and academic administrators tend to be very reasonable. They are all seeking the best possible results with the funds available. Although agreement is not always possible, compromises can be reached if people truly understand the case and communicate. The consultant is serving the institution. Only the institution will have to live with the result.

4.5.2 Engineers

An architect's contract ordinarily includes the foundation, structural, heating, air-conditioning, plumbing, and electrical parts of the work. If the architect does not have those who can supply these services within the firm, the architect will engage and pay for the appropriate consulting engineers. This arrangement is standard practice in the United States and elsewhere, though not universal. Where unusual circumstances suggest, special engineering consultants may be needed. Such services as soil and foundation investigation, acoustical engineering, data services, preservation-based engineering, and lighting design are specific and common examples. The institution may ask the architect to select the engineering consultant; the institution may properly challenge a choice of consultant if it has had poor experiences with the firm. At other times it may ask the architect to work with an engineer selected by the institution in order to ensure the desired results. If the institution takes the initiative, it must expect to pay for the additional cost, but, whatever arrangements are made, the financial implications should be examined and agreements should be reached.

A great many library buildings have had unusual problems. Unstable soil may require caissons being carried down to bedrock. The building may need to be designed to "float" in the soil because of lack of suitable subsurface conditions. Simmons College and Tulane University libraries had such problems. The heating, ventilating, and air-conditioning requirements in tropical climates, in very cold zones, or for portions of buildings housing unique materials may bring special prob-

lems. Library lighting and acoustical conditions are particularly critical in a building that must be conducive to serious and prolonged study. Each institution needs to decide whether these requirements are sufficient to justify hiring consultants who are particular specialists, beyond the architect's obligation to provide the solid and mechanically operating building meeting the basic needs of the institution.

Even though the institution ordinarily must leave it to the architectural firm to select its engineering consultants, the performance reputation of the chosen consultants can constitute one basis for judging among architectural firms. Critical aspects may be how long and well the architect and the engineers have worked together, how competent are the engineers, and how effective they will be as part of the team. A building can be overdesigned structurally as much as it can be underdesigned, and coping with such problems as earthquake forces or subsurface water conditions can lead to designs that may be unnecessarily expensive, depending on the solution chosen. Agreement on the qualities needed by engineers chosen by the firm thus becomes important in formation of the planning team.

4.5.3 Landscape Architect

Few architectural firms in the United States have on their staff a landscape designer; however, most large firms in Canada do include such services. If the firm does not provide the service, it will know firms in the area having good reputations, and commonly the architect will have a standing arrangement with one or more. The arrangement for this service is more flexible than it is for some other consultants.

The college or university may have used a landscape firm to work on a master campus plan to include roads, pedestrian and bicycle paths, outdoor signage, and lighting. The institution sometimes asks the architect to work with a landscape firm with which it has had good experience in order to ensure continuity of campus treatment. Coordination between the landscape firm and the architect is particularly important on matters of drainage and access routes, and it may be very important in terms of wind or sun screening. Good landscaping can enhance a good building design and can soften or mask mechanical necessities or an unattractive feature. Appropriate landscaping can be an important feature in almost every project (fig. 4.4).

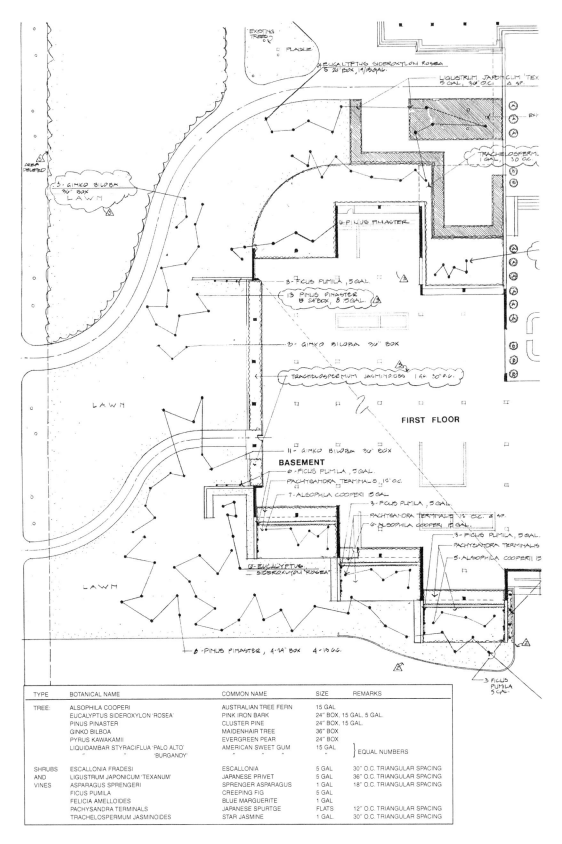

TYPE	BOTANICAL NAME	COMMON NAME	SIZE	REMARKS
TREE:	ALSOPHILA COOPERI	AUSTRALIAN TREE FERN	15 GAL	
	EUCALYPTUS SIDEROXYLON 'ROSEA'	PINK IRON BARK	24" BOX, 15 GAL. 5 GAL.	
	PINUS PINASTER	CLUSTER PINE	24" BOX, 15 GAL.	
	GINKO BILBOA	MAIDENHAIR TREE	36" BOX	
	PYRUS KAWAKAMII	EVERGREEN PEAR	24" BOX	
	LIQUIDAMBAR STYRACIFLUA 'PALO ALTO'	AMERICAN SWEET GUM	15 GAL	} EQUAL NUMBERS
	'BURGANDY'	"	"	
SHRUBS	ESCALLONIA FRADESI	ESCALLONIA	5 GAL	30" O.C. TRIANGULAR SPACING
AND	LIGUSTRUM JAPONICUM 'TEXANUM'	JAPANESE PRIVET	5 GAL	36" O.C. TRIANGULAR SPACING
VINES	ASPARAGUS SPRENGERI	SPRENGER ASPARAGUS	1 GAL	18" O.C. TRIANGULAR SPACING
	FICUS PUMILA	CREEPING FIG	5 GAL	
	FELICIA AMELLOIDES	BLUE MARGUERITE	1 GAL	
	PACHYSANDRA TERMINALS	JAPANESE SPURTGE	FLATS	12" O.C. TRIANGULAR SPACING
	TRACHELOSPERMUM JASMINOIDES	STAR JASMINE	1 GAL.	30" O.C. TRIANGULAR SPACING

FIGURE 4.4 Landscape plan. The landscape drawing showing plants must be viewed along with the grading plan. In this example, the lawn as shown to the left slopes down to the basement level. The resulting hand mowing eventually led to replacement of the sloped lawn.

4.5.4 Interior Designer

The interior design commission may be performed by the architect or by an independent design firm selected by the architect or by the institution. Such a firm may be retained and paid by one or the other. In any event, all concerned should know whether the consultants are working for the architect or the institution and who is financing their effort.

Interior designing is certainly within the accepted province of the architect, since it involves the design and purchase of furniture and equipment and may include wall colors, carpets, signs, and exhibit cases. Sometimes it is taken out of the architect's hands and turned over to the purchasing agent of the institution, on the grounds that the architect's commission may run, for this particular type of work, up to 10 percent of the total furnishings and interior finishing cost. However, if the furniture does not serve well, the effects on library operation can be quite unfortunate. The library building consultant, on the other hand, has the functional arrangements as a primary responsibility and can rarely be counted on to give satisfactory advice in connection with the aesthetic side of the problem.

Because library furniture and equipment is a special field in itself, an interior designer (not an interior decorator) who specializes in library work is sometimes called in as a consultant. Use of an interior designer is to be encouraged on any but the smallest of projects, or on projects where interior appearance is not critical (such as for a storage facility). A poor interior design can be a disaster; indeed, some work by designers independent of the architect has led to dreadful experiences.

In past years a furniture manufacturer may have done a layout as a marketing assistance. Occasionally the library building consultant may do it. Yet it will be far more satisfactory if a professional interior designer is given the commission. If an independent consultant is used, the firm should, of course, work very closely indeed with the architect and with the library consultant, if there is one, to assure compatibility of product and avoid any conflict in interest. Quality interior design is essential in producing an outstanding project.

Choice of the interior designer can be approached with criteria similar to those used in choosing the architect and with a selective process of references and interviews, as with the architect. The cost of interior design services is treated in Section 9.2.5, Architectural and Other Fees.

This volume does not try to deal extensively with the problem of furnishings and finishes. This is a matter with complexities of its own. However, the very early involvement of an interior designer with the architectural plan development can be a great benefit. The furnishings selected will need to be in harmony with the interior finishes. The interior designer may in fact have responsibility for the color of wall surfaces, the choice of applied wall surface material, and selection of carpet type and colors. This design professional may be involved with built-in furnishings (in place of the architect, which is more common), and always will have responsibility for movable furnishings, including their number, estimated cost or budget, distribution, orientation, design, texture, color, and construction details, whether anchored or not. Essentially, the domain of the interior designer is the complete specification necessary to place the order and have the material installed correctly and on schedule for all interior components of the project. Graphics or sign design as well as the selection of artwork can also be made part of the interior design contract. The scope of the individual contract needs to be carefully determined.

A number of American interior designers and architects who have had considerable library building planning experience have designed satisfactory carrels, with special features to fit the decor of the building as a whole. Some have designed chairs as well. But unless they are experts in work of this kind or have expert help, the results are not always sturdy and comfortable, even if they are aesthetically pleasing. The firm may use entirely stock items from one or various manufacturers, may use companies that are not specialists in library furniture and do exceedingly well by this choice, and will occasionally design specialty items when a satisfactory product is not already on the market. The interior designer may have access to types of furniture not otherwise readily available and should certainly be an expert at determining what—with reasonable cost and attractive design—is sturdy, comfortable, and functional, and has a satisfactory finish.

The choice of furnishings may come from ideas found in many sources. The institution may rely wholly or largely on the interior designer; it may also suggest features or small details that have been found suitable in other library buildings and that can be blended into the project design. As an example of such use of ideas from other institutions, the following lists the source of ideas for items or arrangements in the late-1970s design for Stanford University's Cecil H. Green Library:

> Reading areas—size and character of comfort based on the Tower Room at Dartmouth, Alumni Room at Bowdoin College, and the Morrison Room at the University of California, Berkeley
>
> Group study rooms—Northwestern University and the University of Chicago's Regenstein Library
>
> Directors' suite and personnel office—University of Chicago's Regenstein Library
>
> Reference staff offices—University of Minnesota's Wilson Library
>
> Reference desk—Harvard's Widener Library
>
> Compact shelving for microtexts—Rice University
>
> Sound system—Washington University
>
> Lighting—University of Denver
>
> Stack lockers—Washington University and University of Chicago's Regenstein Library
>
> Central service rooms on stack levels—Northwestern University
>
> Dissertation rooms for graduate students in the stack—Princeton University
>
> Administrative conference room—University of Utah
>
> Faculty studies—Cornell University and Harvard's Widener Library
>
> Card catalog arrangement—University of California, Los Angeles
>
> Card catalog split-level height—Harvard's
> . Arnold Arboretum Library
>
> New book display—Princeton University's Firestone Library
>
> Basement connection to an adjacent book-stack basement—Yale's connection between Sterling Library and the Cross Campus Library, and Harvard's connection between Widener and Lamont libraries

Good ideas are to be found in many places; there is every reason to copy, in concept if not in detail, so long as program need is met and harmony of design is achieved.

4.5.5 Other Consultants

The possible need for other consultants should be considered. There is, of course, an expense in retaining a specialist in any field. Doing so may result in extra effort and possibly some slight delay in the project; on the other hand, advice of a specialist can avoid some egregious errors.

There is no definitive list of what other consultants might be used. A few may be experts in specialty firms that are the chosen equipment suppliers, for example, a lock company or security system firm. Yet it is obvious that in seeking advice from a specialty firm, you may or may not receive entirely objective opinions, though there is usually no consultant fee because costs are covered by profit from the sale of equipment and installation.

The following are examples of consultants who have been used on major recent university library buildings in the United States:

> acoustics
> artwork
> audio systems
> code conformity (building, fire, access, etc.)
> computer facility design; network design
> construction management
> cost estimation, or quantity surveying
> design (sometimes shared by a master architect)
> energy conservation
> exhibition facilities
> food service
> fund-raising
> hardware
> materials testing
> move planning and coordination
> preservation environment engineering
> security systems
> signage or graphics
> technological applications (including but not limited to automation)
> value engineering

Although there is separate justification for each of these, and others can be considered, an explanation of one is provided as a sample. Acoustic problems can abound in libraries, though study and research clearly demand a nonintrusive environment. Computers, the activities of people, compressors, ballasts, air mixing and distribution boxes, door hardware, and chair glides on a hard floor are among the sources that can be extremely disturbing. An acoustic consultant is useful for large buildings, not necessarily for audio systems, but to check the architectural and engineering design by examining the plans in terms of area functions, materials, and electrical and mechanical system details (fig. 4.5). Advice

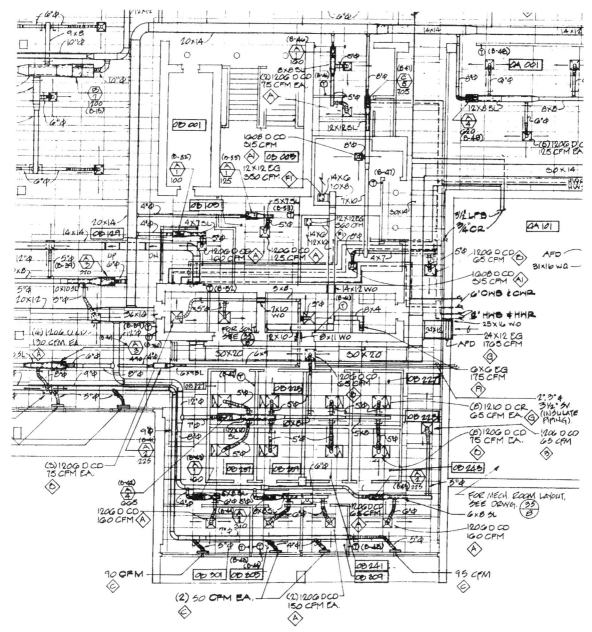

FIGURE 4.5 Mechanical system plan. An acoustic consultant would be interested in the potential sound transmission by ducts between offices and the speed of air delivery into a space and thus the sound it produces, both of which can be determined to a large extent from a plan like this. Other plans show the isolation of mechanical equipment from the building structure, which is also of great importance for acoustics.

This plan looks as though it treats potential temperature variation adequately with a thermostat in each enclosed study (the little "T" in a circle); it turned out that the studies along the lower edge are quite cold, perhaps because of the expanse of north-facing glass those studies enjoy. It is next to impossible to predict such a circumstance by looking only at this drawing and its associated references.

Preservation criteria for the environmental control, especially humidity control, are not addressed by this plan, which is based upon a periphery system of terminal reheat (that is, the air is heated for each space along the edge of the building based upon the demand for heat in that space). It may be that the problem of cold spaces noted above is partially due to a failure of some nature with the reheating system. Such a system does not maintain any form of constant humidity; at the time this system was designed, it was thought temperature control was the most important aspect of the design.

from an acoustic consultant may result in the introduction of increased amounts of acoustically absorptive material; changes in construction details to increase acoustic separation between functions; recommendations about the arrangement of noisy and quiet functions; and specification of alternative materials, systems, or devices for acoustic control and isolation. This example is not intended to urge the use of any or all consultants from the preceding list. It merely points out some options that are worth consideration.

The choice process in selecting any of these consultants can follow the general selection process used for architects or interior designers. The choice should be based on reputation for integrity, ability, and professional competence. References can be checked even if the individual has not worked on a library before. The individual may be retained as a consultant to the architect, or as a consultant to the institution. For instance, cost estimation can be done for the institution by the architect's separate cost consultant or the institution's cost consultant in order to confirm the architect's cost estimate. However, it is probably more common for the institution to hire directly a cost consultant to produce a confirming cost estimate.

The key question is whether the design team needs extra special talent to solve an important problem or to assist in a particularly sensitive area. The question should be openly raised and discussed, generally at an early stage in the design process. In general three approaches are possible if you have had bad experiences or seen problems others have had. Stay away from the problem altogether. Or ask the architect to specify, for example, highest-quality, heavy-duty fixtures— that is, overdesign the project to try to avoid the perceived problem. Or use a specialist consultant for guidance. The expense of the latter approach can make a good building an exceptional one.

4.6
Early Activities with Architect and Consultants

The matter of the relationship of the architect, the librarian, and the planning team is of primary importance from the time the architect is selected, during the planning process, and until the building is completed. If the architect was selected without the approval of the librarian, the whole planning process may have gotten off on the wrong foot. If, on the other hand, the architect knows that the librarian had an important part in the selection, the good rapport between the two may be a great help.

The first talk between them may be crucial, and every effort should be made by the institution's administration to see that a good start is made. If the president, in notifying the architectural firm of its selection, is able to, and does, say that the institution has great confidence in the librarian and hopes that the architect will work closely with the librarian and give due consideration to suggestions in regard to functional matters, the statement will help ensure a successful relationship. In one case in which the librarian recommended the architect who was selected, the president said to him, "Since you have recommended the architect, you should notify him of the selection." He did, and an important step toward the success of the building was taken.

A good atmosphere is created if the librarian has had a major part in the preparation of a good building program and the architect realizes this, and if the librarian appreciates and understands what his or her part in the planning process should be and understands that the architect is the designer to produce an aesthetically satisfactory and functional building. The librarian must, of course, be prepared to answer questions, and both parties should reach a mutual understanding of the part each is to play.

The architect must realize that the librarian's province is to provide access to information for the academic and/or research community conveniently, efficiently, and economically, and that the librarian or the library consultant is the expert for these matters on the planning team. The librarian should understand that the institution has placed the design responsibility in the hands of the architect, who is equipped and trained to analyze and interpret functional needs spatially and to translate this interpretation into what is inclusively called "bricks and mortar."

If the librarian presents to the architect functional problems and requirements and if the architect then studies them seriously and solves them, each of these important members of the planning team is fulfilling a proper role. Sometimes the librarian has contributions to offer in the architect's province and vice versa; but only if a clear understanding of the ultimate responsibilities of each one is reached will a completely harmonious relationship exist. In many large architectural firms, the principal architect or head of the firm is not the one who works directly with the librarian; this duty is turned over to one of the partners or associates who serves as the project architect. The architectural decisions mutually reached should, of course, be reviewed by the principal architect before their submission to the institution for approval. The closest possible rapport is important.

All this can be summarized by saying that misunderstanding between the architect and the librarian must not be permitted. The same holds true for the other representatives of the institution. The administrative officers and the planning committee members, individually and as a group, must also understand the place of each person concerned in the planning process. They should never be played off one against another. A first "kickoff" meeting with architect, librarian, business officer, institutional planner, director of planning, plant services representative, principal consultants, and others is commonly held to clarify precisely the project scope, the role of each individual, the time schedule required, and the financial constraints.

4.6.1 Matters of Timing

The planning period should not be extended indefinitely. Neither should it be hurried too much; under pressure the best of architects and librarians will miss important factors. It is very rare for a satisfactory library building to be planned and construction documents completed in less than a full year. Harvard's Lamont Library took more than a year and a half to plan, although both the librarian and the architect had been considering possibilities and thinking about the building for six or seven years. The same can be said for Stanford's Green Library. On the other hand, the planning process can be extended too far until all concerned become stale and unwittingly careless of important details. In the case of the University of North Carolina at Charlotte, in 1995, the chancellor was concerned about the state legislature's mood, which might have led to postponing the project, so an all-out push was made for groundbreaking—a calculated risk and not a unique situation. It is usually desirable, however, to have a definite timetable worked out in advance, and both the architect and the institution should be expected to keep to schedule.

The timetable should include dates for completion and approval of each phase, when bids are called for, and the date when construction should begin. Do not try to push the preliminary phases too fast, particularly if for any reason frequent conferences between the two groups cannot be scheduled. The time required for preparing construction documents will depend largely on the size of the architect's staff and the other work in process. Not less than six months is reasonable for a large building. Taking bids and assigning of the contract may require two months or more. And the construction for a building of 20,000 ft^2 (say, 1,860 m^2) may take at least a year, and for buildings over 100,000 ft^2 (say, 9,300 m^2), as much as 18 months or even two years or more, depending on geographical location and local labor conditions. Fast-tracking can cut the time of construction; any necessary phasing will increase the time.

Try to plan so that the building will be completed at the most advantageous time. A large college library should be finished in the spring or early enough in the summer so that occupancy can be carried out without too much pressure during the summer months and allow for a shakedown period before the college opens in the autumn. A smaller college library or a university branch library might attempt to move in during a term break of two to four weeks, but if the climate is severe, this may be difficult or impossible. An addition to a main library can probably be occupied whenever it is finished; a completely new university library building can be very time-consuming to occupy no matter when. Nevertheless, one must realize that delays are almost certain to occur so little reliance can be given to timing the occupancy precisely.

Be sure that before any work is expected from the architect, the contract with the architect is signed and agreement is reached regarding payments. The agreement should consider what will happen if, for one reason or another, such as a lack of funds or disagreement on the proposed plan, the building is never constructed.

After the program (in some countries called the *brief*) has been submitted to the architect and the firm has had an opportunity to study it carefully, the architect should be prepared to discuss with representatives of the institution all points that are not understood, aspects that need to be covered by more specific instruction, and program requirements that are judged to be too specific and on which the architect would like to propose changes. This is the time when most of the uncertainties should be resolved and definite decisions reached, if possible. The architect needs a clear understanding before preparing sketches for preliminary plans or setting to work on details that might have to be changed because of a failure to understand each other's wishes. Most difficulties come from failure on someone's part to make a point clear and to explain the reason for wanting what is requested. If neither party has had experience in library building planning, it is easy to see why neither one understands the technical language to which the other is accustomed. Preconceived notions of what is right and essential easily become so deeply entrenched that they are hard to change. It is very important for the success of the enterprise that all members of the library planning team keep in close touch with one another and with the progress of the architect after the problem is tackled and the firm begins to prepare sketches indicating the proposed spatial relationships and space assignments.

Nothing more than the most preliminary plans can be made before the site is selected. As early as possible, but not too early, the module sizes and the column sizes should be agreed upon. This cannot be done, however, until a decision has been reached on the size and number of floor levels and perhaps on whether a central utility and vertical communication core is to be used or whether these facilities are to be scattered. Make sure that in either case the core or cores do not interfere with present or prospective horizontal circulation patterns. Planning of the heating and ventilation system should not be delayed because it may take much more space than anticipated and reduce what is available for library purposes, thus complicating plans in other ways.

Before any planning is done and before the construction documents are begun, the team members should all clearly understand whether the consultation will be frequent, regularly scheduled at certain stages of completion, or on a floor-by-floor and trade-by-trade basis. The institution should not abrogate its rights for further consideration at this time. Neither should it expect to interfere continually with progress. It is customary and good practice for the institution's chief business officer formally to sign off on schematics, and later on design development drawings so

there is legal understanding when one milestone is met and approved and work toward the next is officially authorized.

Authorization for the construction contract documents means that the basic plans are agreed upon, but there are still what may seem like minor matters where the librarian's opinion should be given consideration. These will include, for instance, the location of doors and the direction in which the doors swing. The placing of light switches is another example, as may be the selection of hardware and plumbing fixtures. As the construction contract documents are prepared, it may be found from time to time that an unexpected six-inch (0.150-m) difference in space available will require decisions regarding how the space is to be used or how to deal with the lack of it (fig. 4.6).

Meanwhile the furniture and equipment should not be neglected. Too often decisions on these matters are delayed, with the result that the design and selection process is hurried, and in too many cases the equipment is not available when the structure is ready for it. What part of the equipment will be in the general building contract? What are the architect's responsibilities for the furniture design and selection? Be sure that the delivery timetable is understood so that as construction is completed, the furnishings arrive. Shipments must be made at the optimum time to avoid interference with the building construction or furniture storage problems, and yet not delay the opening of the structure.

4.6.2 Study of Publications

Just as the library staff should be prepared by reviewing selected publications on the planning of academic library buildings, so the architect and consultants should conduct such a review. This will promote good understanding of the terminology, processes, practices, and attitudes of the other professions making up the team. Librarians might look at architectural and interiors magazines while the architects might look at some library periodicals, such as *Library Journal*. It is hoped both will find this volume of fundamental help.

However, the published literature is extensive and uneven in quality. Thus it may be that each individual can recommend key articles and a few most important chapters in books that the others should consider reviewing. This process can be

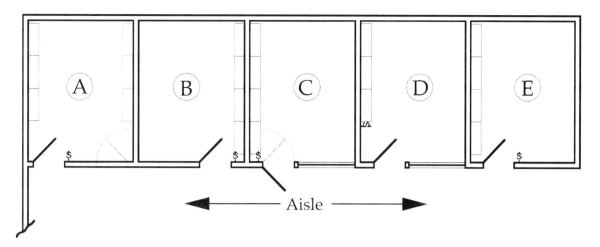

FIGURE 4.6   Door swings. Architectural drawings seldom show furnishings (shelving here), light switches (the "S" at the wall), and door swings on the same drawing, but each can affect the other. The doors suggested in A are so close to the wall that a fourth section of shelving cannot be added behind the door. The suggested door to the right could provide a useful corner at the end of the aisle. Door B occupies important space in a small room; it would be better if it swung out. In either case, door B would not meet ADA requirements. Door C swung out works well where there is a window in the aisle wall (which forces the switch to the shelving wall). The alternative door C makes the switch very awkward; if the switch is moved as in D, a section of shelving is lost (or the switch is hidden in the shelving). Door E, without an aisle window, probably works best for doors swinging in or out, particularly relative to the light switch. Having the door swing out, as in C, is probably best for handicapped access when a desk or other furniture is taken into consideration, but such a door can affect traffic in the aisle. See also figures 13.1 through 13.6 for other door swing and related space issues.

useful throughout the course of the project. Some useful works are cited in the appended bibliography, yet more recent publications may do a better job or deal with a more modern technology.

4.6.3 Visits on Site

It is well for several if not most of the planning team, when it is finally formed, to spend some time early on visiting and getting to know the architect's and consultant's key staff, just as the architect and consultant should visit the client's facilities and get to know key staff. Principal representatives of the library should be involved to some extent in conjunction with early meetings. No matter how brief the introductions, it can help early understanding and thus get the project started on a good footing.

Because buildings are three-dimensional spaces for human actions, it should be obvious that, as noted earlier, no publication, no matter how carefully written, can convey as much as seeing li-

brary buildings in use. Thus visits to key libraries are exceedingly important. If some college or university business officers question the value of that expense or time, they should be reminded that floor plans of their laboratories or libraries convey very little indeed of the actual physical appearance—the color and texture of materials, the shadows and glares, the human activity, the clutter, and other visual and auditory conditions. Reading may come first but visits to a selected number of libraries should not be neglected. Because a library building involves huge amounts of money and a great deal of time for fund-raising and for design and construction, the expenses of site visits by three, four, or five principals in the team are a modest investment for the potential of a very great payoff. Indeed the expenses of a cross-country trip are really nothing compared with the magnitude of the project and of the time and salaries of involved individuals who will use that time even if they were to visit four or five sites all in the same state.

4.7
Amount of Time and Degree of Involvement

It is important for the college or university to realize the amount of time that will be required for a successful project. As has been mentioned, the librarian or a principal associate to whom responsibility has been given should expect to spend anywhere from half-time to full-time on this project during the programming and early design phases. The time commitment can taper off during the contract documents phase and during construction, but activation will require another surge of staff time on the part of the library. Even when library staffing is tight and operational budgets seem inadequate, the library must give priority to this commitment of staff time throughout the entire project. Major long-term consequences derive from the extent and quality of this involvement. Communication flow within the institution and within the library is every bit as important as are the meetings with the architects and consultants. The involvement must be substantial and measure up to the magnitude of the task.

The design of meetings can be very important. Regular meetings with the architect will need to be called by one individual in the institution, the agenda will need to be set and issued to all concerned, the objectives of the meetings will need to be clearly defined, and the results and decisions will ordinarily need to be documented and distributed to all present and other concerned officials. Attention needs to be given to the size of the group. More than 10 or a dozen can easily result in poor interaction, some being too timid to speak up or some wasting their time if they are needed on only one small aspect. Consider briefer meetings, scheduled well in advance, with fewer people in attendance. Or, schedule certain topics to be treated with specified people present (e.g., a lighting specialist) at a designated time within the meeting.

The psychology of public meetings can lead to bickering and attention to irrelevant matters if the purpose of the meetings is not clear. Too many building planning groups get off track and poor feelings result. This can be the case for small projects just as much as for large projects, and it can be even more difficult with respect to branch libraries, where there are both library representatives and faculty departmental representatives

and perhaps representatives from a dean's office. Though these may be small projects, there is frequently need for even more effort on communication and the conduct of meetings.

In general, the institution's planning officer assigned to the project should arrange meetings and preside. Meetings need to be conducted with some deftness so that firm direction is taken while at the same time there are ample opportunities for the participants to express their points of view and contribute to the conclusions of the meeting. Sometimes a meeting may be deliberately staged as a brainstorming session. The interactive method of conducting such meetings, with a carefully prepared agenda, the use of a facilitator, a public record on flip charts, and a recorder, may be the best method. (A useful book is *The Fifth Discipline: The Art and Practice of the Learning Organization,* by Peter M. Senge, New York: Doubleday/Currency, 1990. Note especially Chapter 12 on "Team Learning.")

As indicated in this chapter, there may be a great many consultants. Each of these will be involved for varying amounts of time. A library building consultant may be involved for the entire process. Engineers and interior designers may be involved for considerable periods. Others may be briefly involved, perhaps for only one or a few meetings. In each case, the role to be played needs to be explicit for all concerned. Each consultant will need to be adequately briefed before being involved, especially before any sizable group meeting; the definition of services rendered must be precise, and the basis for concluding the consultancy must also be agreed upon.

A final word about involvement. The documentation of many decisions on building projects is exceedingly important. Dozens of people are involved in a small project, and there will be more than a hundred involved throughout a large project. The number of people involved means that the written record of meetings is essential. Minutes of important meetings must be prepared at once and distributed promptly. Major questions from one individual to another may deserve to be in writing with responses also in writing. Any action that involves a policy matter, a financial commitment, a design criterion, or an authorization must be in writing. Some interpretations or elaborations should be in writing.

Some planning offices and some architectural offices have very formal documentation patterns. A specific numbering and lettering pattern may be followed. Forms may actually be used for certain kinds of documentation. This is not needed for many projects, or by smaller institutions or architectural firms. But it is needed in cases where formality has been found to be necessary, and it is well for the architectural firm and the institution to agree on a pattern of documentation at the very beginning of the architectural work.

4.8
Who Has the Last Word?

It is obvious that sooner or later, and probably the earlier the better, some kind of an agreement should be reached about who makes the final decisions relating to architectural style, aesthetics, and function. Often five different individuals or groups may be directly involved:

1. The architect
2. The librarian
3. The donor, if there is one
4. The institution's administration represented by the president, or, through the president, the board of trustees
5. A special committee appointed by the administrative authorities to take the responsibility

Which one of these individuals or groups should have the last word? Certainly, architecture is primarily the responsibility of the architect, but it is obvious that the administrative heads of the institution cannot avoid their share of interest and responsibility and, in the final analysis, must approve decisions by the architect or others. The institution may, if it desires, delegate the authority and responsibility to a special committee made up of administrative officers, perhaps members of its own board, other officers of the institution, one or more consultants, or a faculty group. It may defer to the donor or leave the matter to the librarian.

Whatever is arranged, the architect should keep in touch with the librarian, or some other person assigned to the task of thoroughly acquainting the architect with the functional needs of the library, with the understanding that any disagreement they cannot resolve should be referred to the administrative authorities.

The librarian is the library operations expert, and the functional aspect of the building should be regarded by the architect with as much seri-ousness as it is by the institution. Generally, the librarian or consultant is more familiar than the architect with the details of satisfying the functional aspects. The library representative and the architect can, if they cooperate, be of immeasurable assistance to each other.

The architect should be the one finally to recommend the methods of satisfying these functional necessities as well as the appropriate style and aesthetics. Having been selected on the basis of its competence and acquaintance with the problems involved, the firm is, or at any rate should be, the expert on the team for these matters. Its recommendation should be submitted to and approved by the responsible person or persons designated by the institution.

In too many cases deference to the principal donor has brought results that are not happy. This does not mean that the donor's wishes should not be given full consideration or that the donor should not be kept informed about the situation. Donors certainly are entitled to explanations if it proves impossible or undesirable to conform completely to their wishes. Unfortunately, not enough donors take the attitude that Thomas W. Lamont took in connection with Harvard's Lamont Library. The plans and model of the proposed building were placed before him, and he was asked to express his opinion. His reply was simply, "I like it, but if I didn't, I wouldn't say so. I want what the College decides that it needs."

The administrative authorities have a responsibility to the institution. It is to them ordinarily that complaints will come—often for decades—if the results are not satisfactory. With the shift in recent years from what is often called traditional architecture to a variety of contemporary and modern styles, some alumni of academic institutions have been upset by new buildings. They may be tempted to withdraw financial support; their voiced criticisms may discourage others with capacity to give. A few write letters to the alumni magazines and to newspapers, doing what they can to arouse antagonism in the hope that it will bring about changes. Although it is true that some architectural atrocities have been perpetrated in library planning in recent decades, it seems equally true that as one becomes more accustomed to new styles, one is less likely to be offended by them. On the other hand, poor planning of interior functions may forever be a curse.

Sooner or later the institution must face the problem of the effect of architectural style on costs. To build a Gothic library today is so expensive as to make its desirability questionable. Anyone who has seen the previous main library in the University of Pittsburgh's Cathedral of Learning or the Sterling Library at Yale will understand this point and will also realize the functional problems that may arise from such a design today.

It should be added that a great argument for modern or contemporary architecture, as some prefer to call it, is that it can be simple, with good lines, functional, and relatively inexpensive to build and to keep in repair. But if the architect goes to extremes in an attempt to produce something different and the results are not functional, are more expensive, and do not stand up physically, there is no excuse for the product.

If the architect recommends a practically all-glass building that will require double windows and also sun protection of some kind on the inside or out or both, the net results in comfort and operating costs should be carefully considered. If irregular exteriors are planned with unduly large amounts of expensive outside wall areas that add to the construction costs, their desirability should be weighed (see fig. 4.7). If the architect proposes a slanting roof with unusable attic space

not required for the mechanical services and it adds a small percentage to the cost, its desirability should at least be questioned. These points are brought up to call attention to decisions to be made, not to object to any particular style of architecture. It may well be that the additional expenditures are worthwhile for symbolism or pride, but they should be incurred with open eyes.

From wide personal experience and from conversations with other librarians and library consultants, Keyes Metcalf had the distinct impression that (reversing the trend of the first decade after the Second World War) there has been an unfortunate tendency on the part of some of the more capable and better-known architects to attempt to attract attention by glamorous and exciting buildings that subordinate function to other features (fig. 4.8). Late in this century, atrocious library buildings continue upon occasion to be constructed. They ignore the fact that most academic institutions must choose between a building that is primarily functional and one that will be more expensive, flashy, inflexible, quickly outgrown, and difficult to explain a generation hence when it will require an addition or even a replacement. Without question we need to welcome new architectural concepts

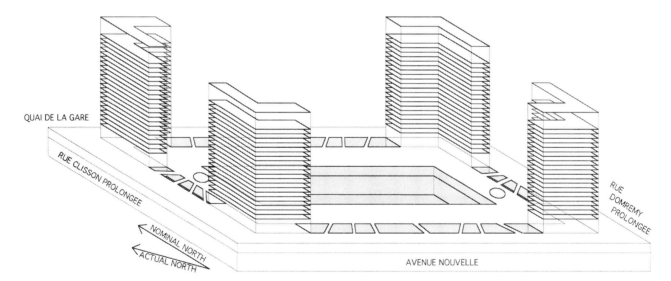

FIGURE 4.7   Bibliothèque nationale de France. Although this isometric presentation is visually distorted (which is a product of the drawing technique), the concept of four towers and a central sunken garden is clear. The original design concept was intended to provide a view of the national treasures in the towers for visitors to see from the street, the main plaza level, and from the reading rooms below; preservation and operational efficiency were not the guiding concerns in the concept. In addition to the grand central garden, there are secondary depressed light courts between the towers. This building is an example of extremes when it comes to exterior surface (and elevators) relative to the programmed contents.

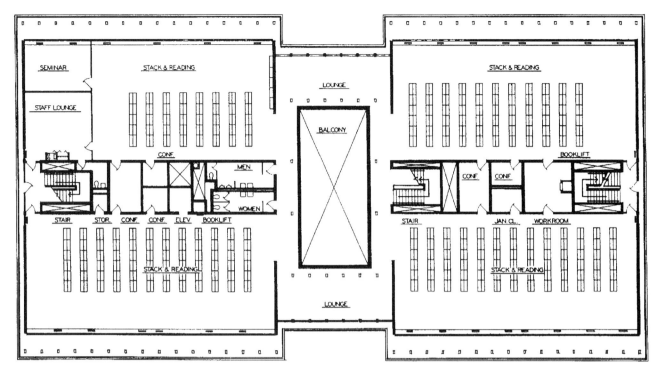

FIGURE 4.8   Butler University, Irwin Library. Although this 1963 work of Minoru Yamasaki and Associates is an attractive example of his light, windowed style, with three levels of exterior repetitive vaulted-roof colonnade, its weaknesses include excessive windows (the entire east and west walls), constant maintenance problems from extreme narrowness and height of entrance doors, security problems due to safety doors on north and south sides, extremely limited and inflexible office and technical services areas, and a large light well limiting flexibility on the upper two floors.

and more economical construction methods. We should not object to radical solutions just because they are new and different. Yet, there is no excuse for unattractive, unfunctional libraries; the famous aphorism is still true that form follows function in truly great architecture.

Given the above, it is still obvious that the final responsibility for architectural style and aesthetic problems lies with the institution's administration. The institution can accept or reject final plans. It does not have to build the building as designed. It can even begin again with a different architectural firm if it wishes and can justify to itself the extra time and costs.

From the librarian's point of view, if the building planning can begin from the inside, the result should be a better building functionally. For the architect to plan the building with the site and facade uppermost in mind, before knowing a good deal about the functional requirements, can be a serious mistake. Although a few architects may be inclined to think that function is sec-

ondary, that a modular building gives infinite internal flexibility, and that planning from the inside out is impossible and illogical, the result is unlikely to be as useful a library as one that is planned with function uppermost in mind. Functional planning should be considered a challenge. Compromises may have to be made in connection with it, yet they should be reached only after the people directly involved have given full consideration to the consequences.

The Lamont Library building was planned almost completely from the inside out. The architect, when asked to comment on this statement, wrote as follows:

> The architect's point of view on "planning from the inside out" should and I am sure does consider that a building is ideally a complete and homogeneous entity and has no inside that can be separated from the outside, any more than natural objects have bones or veins that can be separate from the skin. That the exterior of Lamont fits the inside is not a result of accident but of the disposi-

tion of the functional elements inside so that their expression on the outside results in some architectural unity.[3]

This principle would have held true for Lamont regardless of the style chosen. The basic disposition of the planned elements was decided long before any final decision was reached in regard to the style of the facades. The architect then made several studies and models, some more contemporary than others, which were presented for review at a meeting of the governing board. From these studies a final exterior design was selected and approved, but this step was not taken until some time after the major part of the inside planning was finished. The surest sign of a first-class architect is his or her ability to design a building that is functional and also distinguished architecturally.

The "last word" should never become an issue if the right architectural firm is selected and good creative work is conducted by the planning team. The architect and the rest of the team will sincerely want to provide the institution with what is suitable. Cooperation and understanding of each other's problems are prerequisites for the best results. Misunderstandings are the sources of most difficulties that arise. An architect should not be selected unless the institution is convinced that a good understanding will be achieved. A good library consultant can sometimes help to bring about a meeting of minds.

In spite of Charles A. Cutter's well-known statement to the contrary, architects and librarians should *not* be considered natural enemies. Very satisfactory and highly rewarding working relationships can be and usually are achieved. If the architects and the librarians really understand each other, there should be no conflict of opinion. The architects, realizing that they must take the first responsibility for form and beauty, and rarely being authorities on the proper function of libraries, should leave that responsibility to the library experts.

NOTES

1. AIA Document 6N902, copyright 1978 by the American Institute of Architects.
2. The term *net* as applied to area of a building is net of elevators, structure, stairs, traffic areas, janitor's closets, mechanical rooms, electrical closets, duct shafts, etc. For a good-sized library, net area will be about 75 percent of the gross area, though this percentage will vary depending principally upon the space allocated to traffic circulation.
3. H. R. Shepley, statement prepared for use in the first edition.

5

General Programming

*No house should ever be on any hill or on anything. It should
be of the hill, belonging to it, so hill and house could live
together each the happier for the other.*

—Frank Lloyd Wright, *An Autobiography*

In nearly every significant building effort, the program document is considered a major benchmark establishing the functional specifications for a new or renovated facility. Programs may take many forms, ranging from a brief memorandum of scope and objective to a complete set of documents setting down the expectation and design requirements of the institution. As is the case in many fields, each project justifies its own level of programming effort. For the purpose of this chapter, the program elements assume that the project is of considerable significance and that the program is a written document prepared to establish the scope of work for the architect and other consultants.

Earlier chapters, particularly Chapter 3, speak of elements that will ultimately shape the program. Certain of the more important elements are reviewed in this chapter. The following chapters address more specialized programmatic aspects of libraries, while two appendixes deal with formulas and equipment and a third deals with preservation-based considerations.

5.1
The Question of a Program

Before the task of preparing a program is undertaken, four points should be considered: What is the purpose of this program? Should it be a written program? Who should write it? Who should approve it?

5.1.1 What Is the Purpose of a Program?

The program's purpose is to clearly communicate requirements of the project to the architect, business officers, library staff, and others. It also serves as an educational instrument, a basis for negotiation, and a formal administrative statement of understanding. This definition of a program deserves some elaboration:

1. The preparation of a program is the best way the librarian, the library staff, and the institution's administration can state the essential needs of the library and make all concerned confront them.
2. The program provides opportunity to point out to administrators and faculty the requirements of the library and to obtain their formal approval. This approval is a matter of first importance.
3. The program states the basic criteria on which the architect can plan a satisfactory building. On occasion the architect's fee may be adjusted if program changes occur; thus the document serves as a fee control mechanism.

5.1.2 Should There Be a Written Program?

A written program is strongly recommended and is almost universally prepared for any significant project. Without one the advantages that can and should come from the points above will be lost; the architect will be too free to explore all manner of topics without guidelines. With a lack of clearly defined direction, it can be difficult for the librarian and the institution to bring their influence and ideas to bear on those who design the library.

5.1.3 Who Should Write the Program?

Ideally, it should be written by the senior responsible librarian who has the advantage of clear understanding of the problems and requirements for the services to be provided in the particular facility. In the case of a major branch library, such as engineering, art, or music, the branch librarian should be responsible for or fully involved in the program content.

In some cases, competent librarians are not equipped with sufficient background for the preparation of a program, although some could with time and effort acquire it. In other cases, the librarian's time can be spent to better advantage in other ways. In a large library, a senior assistant may be assigned the task of writing the program. In still other cases, a building expert or nonlibrary administrative officer may be given the task. If this is done, the person selected should work closely with the librarian and library staff to incorporate their special knowledge. In any case, the librarian should be closely in touch with the preparation of the program, and the librarian should approve and support the program before it is passed to those giving final approval.

Program writing in most cases should not be a one-person task. It should be a compilation of the best information the institution can gather, and those responsible should not hesitate to call for help from others. An experienced library consultant may be useful. Sometimes the consultant is asked to write the program; an outside expert can help, but it is nearly impossible for a consultant to know and understand the institution as well as the program writer ideally should. On the other hand, the consultant should be more familiar with the nature of programs—their content and format. When a consultant is involved, interpretation and support of the program with other members of the design team may be stronger as well.

Engineering and technical help from the staff of the institution or from outside should be made available to whomever writes the program, because any statements dealing with engineering problems—such as site limitations, construction, electrical services, data networking, plumbing, heating, ventilating, and air conditioning—

should be examined and approved by someone who has more than a layperson's knowledge of what is involved. This is necessary in part because specific program requirements can result in very real cost and ongoing maintenance obligations. This fact should be anticipated as much as possible. On the other hand, added facility cost may be offset by substantial operational cost savings or other important advantages; cost decisions at the program stage must not be based upon anticipated facility cost alone.

5.1.4 Who Should Approve the Program?

If the architect is to pay proper attention to the completed program, it must be evident that it records more than the hastily prepared ideas of the librarian or an outside consultant. It must be considered an official document of the institution and its administration. Thus, for a major project, the program should be approved at least by the chief librarian, the library committee of the faculty, the administrative officers, including the president, and, perhaps, the governing board. Of course, smaller projects do not need the full weight of this formal process, but a broad base of approval and support is always important.

After understanding the necessity of these formalities, the design team should also understand that the program is not a bible that cannot be changed as planning proceeds and that mutually agreed-upon alterations are to be permitted and encouraged if they represent improvements that are cost beneficial or justified by their own merit. With care the entire design process should evolve toward the best possible solution within the constraints of time and money.

The architect will often wish to consider the program unchangeable in order to prevent the librarian from altering the ground rules too late in the planning process. There should be a definite understanding that, up to an agreed-upon point in the planning process, both sides are free to question the program and propose changes if they believe a better building will result. Usually the conclusion of the schematic phase represents the last opportunity for change without potentially costly results. There should also be an understanding that the time must come when further changes cannot be made without an addition to the architect's fees, just as there should be an understanding that the plans submitted by the architect must be satisfactory to the institution and represent a building that can be built with the funds available.

5.2
Establishing Policy

A number of major policy decisions should be addressed before writing the facility program, some of which overlap with those dealt with in Section 3.2 and elsewhere. Not all these issues need be agreed upon at this stage, but those that are not must be resolved at an early date in the design process. These policy decisions, many of which will affect the whole enterprise, should answer at least the following questions:

1. How far into the future should library needs be projected? Will new technologies augment or replace the need for a physical library in the future? See Section 5.2.1, Future Needs of the Library.
2. What provisions or options are anticipated for growth beyond the life expectation of the facility to be programmed? To what degree should short-term flexibility be considered? See Section 5.2.2, Flexibility for Long-Term Growth and Short-Term Change.
3. Can or should a new building be avoided by undertaking alterations, additions, decentralization, reorganization, or other means? Should any of these possibilities augment a new facility, either now or in the future? See Section 5.2.3, Alternatives to New Space.
4. Where will the structure be placed? See Section 5.2.4, Site Selection.
5. Will nonlibrary facilities be housed in the building? If so, will this be temporary or permanent? See Section 5.2.5, Nonlibrary Facilities.
6. What percentage of the user population will be provided reading space? What will be the nature of reading provision? See Section 5.2.6, Accommodation for Readers.
7. How much emphasis is to be placed on environmental control and energy conservation measures? What is the nature of the materials to be housed? What is the understanding about smoking in the library? These issues and others are covered in Section 5.3 dealing with the front matter.
8. What constraints on the external appearance will be caused by the library's setting?

See Section 11.4, concerned with Library Site Determination.

5.2.1 Future Needs of the Library

Assessing future needs, considered in Chapter 1, involves the dynamic character of libraries. The effect of technology on library growth is not yet fully understood; the authors of this volume believe (as discussed in Chapter 3) that with few exceptions, library collections will continue to grow indefinitely, though the growth rate for reference books, technical journals, technical reports, and, perhaps, certain classes of books may diminish over time. Still, it is our conviction for many reasons (see comments at Section 1.7) that prudent planners will project most collections growth based upon historic records. As new technologies evolve, service and access to these collections are changing. It is certain that multiple forms of information storage and access will need support, including both traditional and computer-supported information systems.

Each increment of new space includes a considerable expense for related operational adjustments, which should contribute to the formulation of a realistic planning horizon. Leading up to construction, the old building is affected by excessive crowding. Just as space is at its greatest premium, areas may need to be cleared for construction. During construction, there may be various inconveniences, especially where the construction site is juxtaposed to the existing library. After construction, shifts and other disruptive activities will be needed to put the new space into service, and there may be a period of remodeling within old parts of the library. All these elements, each of which will result in tangible costs, tend to suggest that ideally there should be a constant and quiet incremental growth of a facility designed to minimize disruption and massive shifts of collections, staff, and reader services (an ideal that is probably not possible), and, lacking the ideal solution, a facility should be planned for a considerable period with sufficient internal flexibility to adapt to the evolution of new technologies.

If one calculates that the collections are growing at a rate of, say, 3 percent per year, each increment of five years will add about 16 percent to the project budget for stacks. Because stack space relates roughly to needs for reader and staff space, these spaces will grow as well, but probably at a lower rate than the collections. In any case, stacks generally represent the largest single element of a library facility. With building construction cost in the multimillion dollar range, it is easy to see that planning for five or twenty-five years will significantly alter the initial facility cost. It may also be argued that the cost of money is nearly balanced by the cost of inflation; thus, the cost of a larger building now or later is nearly the same, and the management cost from construction, activation, and library operations should be less if done earlier. However, most institutions have limited resources and many projects worthy of funding. The decision of how far into the future one should plan must therefore reflect institutional priorities and funding capability. Although the authors suggest that 20 years is an appropriate period for most planning projections, factors beyond the responsibility of the librarian must be considered. See Sections 1.6 and 1.7 for discussion of rationale for an appropriate projection period.

Information technologies are rapidly changing the ways in which information is accessed, managed, preserved, stored, and acquired. Although one can look only so far ahead and be sure of precise needs, sometimes only two to three years, a building should and can accommodate changing uses. Planners will need to consider projected needs under shifting circumstances. Will electronic reserves replace paper-based reserves in the near term, and, if so, how will the shelving capacity be used? Will faculty homepages replace the reserve process altogether? Will the library be expected to staff faculty homepages for copyright compliance? Will electronic publishing encourage acquisition of library materials in hard copy as needed rather than in anticipation of need, thereby reducing the rigor and staffing of the selection process? Will the library be funded to print a single copy of an online text that, in anticipation of subsequent use, will be placed on the shelf after its initial use? Will students pay for a printing service with debit cards or other technical devices, or will the library need to have a cashier? How will laptop computers be accommodated in a traditional library setting? Should all carrels be tied into power and signal wiring systems, or should some reading areas be intentionally lacking in computer support to ensure quiet? How extensive should be ports or taps into the local area network? How will libraries provide access to electronic journals and reference works? These are but a few of the questions emerging from the era of digital technology, most of which will be answered differently depending upon local circumstance. The ability to change and add electronic capabilities in nearly all parts of a library building is a prime planning requirement along with provision for relatively traditional library functions.

5.2.2 Flexibility for Long-Term Growth and Short-Term Change

What is flexibility? It is the provision of adaptability to address changing needs. What characterizes a flexible library? Principally, it is the ability to assign to any part of the facility the collections, readers, service to readers, staff activities, or unrelated activities, such as classrooms and offices. Section 1.8 outlines the major factors to be considered, and Section 5.3.5, Module and Structural Flexibility, will deal more fully with some of the details that may affect flexibility.

One thing a librarian can be sure of is that in nearly every case, library space needs will increase as years go by. Possible exceptions include a few undergraduate libraries or certain branch libraries where an institutional policy establishes a firm maximum collection and accommodation for staff and readers. Special libraries (i.e., corporate libraries of business and research and development firms) also feel pressure to maintain their collections with minimal growth, relying heavily on information brokers and Internet services for current research. However, the general rule is growth. Even if the number of clients does not increase, the book, microtext, compact disc, and other collections will grow. So far, no healthy research institution has for long maintained an absolute limit on library collections, although with the growth of remote storage facilities and with the limitations of the central campus, this may change for particular facilities, even though the total collection will continue to grow. At the time a new building is planned, even if an agreement seeking to restrict the ultimate size of the collections has been reached, a way out must be provided for the successors of the planning process. It is very important to plan almost all new libraries so that they can be added to.

5.2.3 Alternatives to New Space

As the potential for alternatives to costly construction is such an important issue, Chapter 2 is devoted to this topic. Here it is only necessary to suggest that, in programming and the early design phases of a new facility, as many options for future alternatives as possible should be maintained and developed.

5.2.4 Site Selection

Although thought will undoubtedly be given to site selection long before this stage is reached, in many cases there are options, or configurations of the site, that may require review and consideration even into the early design phases. Chapter 11 is devoted to site considerations. However, aspects of site selection should be thought about during the early programming phase. Is the facility totally new or is it thought best to add to the existing library on available land? Should the institution adhere to a philosophy that the library should be at the heart of the campus? Or should the philosophy be that the library is better sited between the academic campus and major residential or parking facilities? Is the structure to stand alone, be attached to an existing facility, or join two or more facilities? Is the program to address the total library, or just the new addition? Is there a desire to create a special configuration of buildings forming a court or quadrangle or giving direction to exterior space? Are there historical, archeological, environmental, local ordinance, or other factors to be considered? What is the influence of access and external traffic? These and other questions are addressed in Chapter 11. The programmer should be familiar with these issues as the initial programming decisions are made.

5.2.5 Nonlibrary Facilities

As a result of library growth, it is usually desirable to construct a building considerably larger than necessary for the first five years or more; the additional space will inevitably be needed later. But any new, rapidly growing institution will almost always have greater space demands than can be readily met. It has thus become fairly common to use part of the library building for other purposes during the first years following construction. These purposes may be of almost any kind, including administrative quarters, classrooms, separately administered audiovisual or multimedia departments, and computer centers. Some institutions have considered using surplus space planned for future need as rental space for commercial activity. Even entire campuses have been constructed in a single building with integrated plans for expansion involving multiple shifts of space assignment as the library grows (e.g., the University of Wisconsin, Parkside).

Three points should be made in connection with the proposal for use of library space for other purposes.

1. A multiuse facility that is intended to be fully occupied in future years by the library should be built to library standards for floor loading, module size, ceiling heights, and so forth to ensure the flexibility to accommodate the eventual library expansion. In such planning, there is always a risk of code or technology change that will render such plans obsolete or reduce their efficiency.

Note in particular the recent code-driven requirements for increased stack aisle widths in the United States from as little as 24 in. (60 cm) to 36 in. (90 cm) or as much as 44 in. (110 cm), depending upon circumstance and the code authority. It is also notable that this code-driven change reduces the efficiency of a stack throughout. To accommodate the same amount of material, the space required in the worst condition with 10 in. (25.4 cm) shelves must be 1.45 times as large. For a large library, this is very significant. This fact makes compact shelving more attractive as a space-efficient alternative; it is often prudent to include floor load capacity throughout the anticipated library space with capacity to accommodate compact shelving.

2. If the library exits are to be controlled and if books and papers carried by library users are to be checked at the exits, it is desirable and almost obligatory to have separate access to the library and nonlibrary areas, irrespective of hours of operation.

It should be noted that separate, internal controlled-access points can generally be developed within a building with a single main entrance from the outside. It is sometimes irritating to the user to approach a building with two distinct entrances and no clear indication of which is the library. It is also irritating for the user of the other part of the building to have to walk around the building only to reenter the same structure. However, if no other way can be devised than to have a positive separation of the functions outside the library control point, then it is strongly advised that nonlibrary activities assigned to library space be given a separate entrance and exit (fig. 5.1).

ADMINISTRATION

OFFICES

DOCU-
MENTS
OFFICE

OPEN STACKS

NORTH

BIBLIOGRAPHY

SOUTH READING BAY

REFERENCE

NORTH READING BAY

CARD CATALOG

REFERENCE
LIBRARIAN

PERIODICAL INDEXES

CONTROL DESK

CATALOGING
ROOM

ELEV OFFICE

LOBBY

CURRENT
PERIODICALS

OFFICE | LIBRARIAN | SECRE-TARY

NEWSPAPER
ROOM

FIRST FLOOR PLAN

ENTRANCE

FIGURE 5.1   Bowdoin College Library. For a first-time visitor, the two entrances (the second one is near the administration offices) could lead to confusion. When the library became overly crowded, an underground addition to the east (connecting with nearby stack floors of the former library) was chosen over conversion of the college administration office space.

Too often this is not the case, as is illustrated by 10 classrooms in the Lamont Library at Harvard, the Family History center at Brigham Young University, the writing center at Western Washington University, and the three lower-level classrooms at California State University, Sacramento, where access to the building is through the entrance lobby and past a library control point. Such a configuration will necessitate checking the students who have participated in nonlibrary activities and are leaving the build-

ing, just as though they had been using the library and library books. Although book detection systems reduce this concern, they are not a panacea. Closing the library must also include clearing the classroom space. Assignment of classroom activities must be restricted to library hours. In an era of concern about book theft and vandalism, adding unrelated functions within the library confines is a poor security decision.

3. Many librarians have emphasized that, once extraneous services have been permitted into the

library facility, it is almost impossible to decant them later, even when the library is in desperate need of space. The institution's administrative staff often find the library one of the most attractive buildings on campus. Administrators hate to ask for other space, knowing the needs of other parts of the institution, and they tend to maintain possession of their quarters although they are no longer welcome. Classrooms are almost always in great demand; the library will find it hard to reclaim the space once they are installed.

When an institution is pressed for space, and there is hope of obtaining additional space within the library facility or by new construction, the librarian must be able to prove that the library need is greater than that of others, and that giving the library additional space will be a better solution for the institution educationally than making any other arrangement. There will undoubtedly be occasions when the library will suffer, but it will not add to its prestige or popularity with administrative officers or with the institution as a whole if it holds space urgently needed for other purposes for the sake of having it available later.

5.2.6 Accommodation for Readers

Planning for seating accommodation for readers involves four basic questions:

1. Who are the readers? Can and should they be divided into different groups with different types of accommodation for each? If so, can a formula be found and used for the number of places and the space per place for each group, and, from these, can the required net space be calculated?
2. Should there be different rooms or areas for different subject fields, different forms of materials, or different types of use, and, if so, what fields, forms, and types should be considered?
3. Should different types of seating be used for different groups of readers or for different reading areas?
4. After the decisions have been reached on these three points, how many seats should be provided for each group in each area and with each type of accommodation?

These questions are addressed in the various sections of programming. Sections 7.1 to 7.3 deal with general aspects of questions 2, 3, and 4,

while Sections 7.4 to 7.14 deal with those specialized aspects associated with unique collections or fields. Layouts and arrangements are covered in Sections 12.5 and 13.4.

College and university libraries can expect to have demands for accommodation from five distinct groups of users—undergraduates, graduates, faculty members, visiting scholars, and others, including staff and the general public—although not every group will necessarily be represented in each library. These groups differ widely in library use; in order to estimate the number of seats that ought to be provided in a new library facility, one should estimate the needs of each group separately and then total them.

Undergraduates. In most academic institutions, undergraduates are more numerous than the other four groups combined. This statement does not mean that their use of the library will be proportionate to their numbers or that the percentage will not change; use will depend upon the nature of the library being planned and the character of the institution and its objectives.

No definite formula can be proposed to determine the percentage of undergraduates the library should be prepared to seat at one time. Institutions and libraries differ widely in the amount of use expected at periods of peak demand, and future estimates are still more difficult to make because of uncertainty about the effect of new technologies, use patterns in the new facility, changing academic programs, and the changing size of the user group. Change of admissions regulations, library lending policies, pedagogical trends, demographics, the job market, and other social and economic factors will all affect library use; the student body is constant neither in size nor in other characteristics. It is not easy to forecast how much a fine, new, comfortable, and attractive building will increase the demands for seating. Furthermore, the effect of other possible additions to the institution's building plant should not be forgotten. A new student union, study or library rooms in residential halls, small private study accommodation connected with dormitory suites, related branch libraries or studies in academic departments—all will influence peak library loads. In spite of all these uncertainties, some estimate must be made before the program is finalized and plans for a new library are prepared if the institution expects to provide a building large enough, but not unnecessarily large, for a reasonably long period.

It is suggested that the administrative officers of the institution should be responsible for projecting student enrollment during the period for which the proposed building is designed, and that they should also indicate any plans for changes in admissions and educational policies that will affect library use. In the past it was fairly certain, at least in the United States, that the numbers of students, and thus library use, would increase even without policy changes. However, the student population has recently decreased or remained steady at many institutions. This should be followed by an increase in the college age population that should peak during the years 2010–2015. Demographic studies have not, however, proved to be particularly accurate as predictors of enrollment, even in the short term, and should be used with caution. Even so, when a well-planned, comfortable, and attractive building is provided, it can be predicted that there will be a dramatic increase in use, perhaps as much as doubling or tripling if the space provided makes the increase possible.

Other important factors may sooner or later bear on the number of required seats. Is library service to undergraduates to be centralized in the proposed enlarged or new structure? If the university is a large one with departmental libraries, how much of service to undergraduates will be provided outside the main building? Is it a residential institution with students living in the immediate neighborhood who can be expected to use the library heavily in the evening, or does the student body largely commute, leaving the campus as soon as possible after classes are over? Are there a large number of evening students? (They are often very numerous in a city institution; however, if both day and evening students commute, it is unlikely that they will use the facilities at the same time.) Is the university in a city where there are many attractions outside the campus, or is it in comparatively rural surroundings where few outside activities attract the students, particularly during weekday evenings? Do most of the students live in dormitories on the campus? Do the dormitories provide an atmosphere conducive to study? Does the institution provide special reading rooms and library collections in the residential halls, as is done in the Yale colleges, the Harvard "houses," and the larger dormitories in many public and private institutions? What are the library hours: open until midnight on weekday evenings or only until 9 or 10 o'clock? If the library is in a residential institution with heavy evening use, do some students spend the early evening at the library, while others go to the movies first and then to the library from 10 to 12 o'clock, reducing the percentage who can be expected at any one time?

The following additional questions should be considered by the program writer, although, like those that have been suggested above, there are no answers that can be translated into exact figures. Does the library expect to be able to take care of peak demands that tend to come just before and during the examination period or during the reading period, if there is one? These are the periods of heaviest library use. They may also be those when the students are most anxious to study and when dormitory rooms may be more suitable for that purpose than at other times. At these times students may be willing to study at large tables in a reading room with chairs closer together than at other times in the academic year. However, it is common for students to perceive the reading area to be full even if only half the chairs are taken at tables. Is the institution prepared during peak loads to have students use facilities outside the library, such as study halls, seminar rooms, and classrooms, on the basis that it cannot afford to increase the size of its library by as much as 20 percent for the convenience of its students during perhaps three or four weeks in the academic year?

Does the library encourage students to study using their own books in the library, believing that a more studious atmosphere will prevail there than elsewhere and that study with reference material immediately at hand tends to be especially advantageous? Is it the expectation that computer clusters in the library will be used for study as well as the completion of assignments? Are there alternative sites for this activity? It may be that the requirements of copyright control will influence the degree to which access to information is freely distributed on and off campus; systems dealing with this issue are emerging. It is possible that use of certain materials will require dedicated networks—where this is the case, such use would seem to make the most sense in the library, except possibly where library hours are very limiting.

Does the institution expect to assign seats in the library for honors students or graduate students? Whenever a seat is assigned to one student exclusively and use by others is prevented or discouraged, the total number of seats required is increased. Assignment of seats to undergraduates is generally not recommended; an exception might be for a liberal arts program that requires a senior thesis (as at Reed College in Portland, Oregon). Very few institutions can afford a seating capacity large enough for this purpose.

All the foregoing questions suggest problems that ought to be considered, though they may do little to help the program author decide on the number of seats for undergraduate students. In 1968, Keyes Metcalf suggested that in institutions with students of the highest quality, located in a small town or rural area, the library should be prepared to seat at least one-half of the undergraduate student body at one time. This recommendation echoed that of W. W. Bishop, who recommended as early as 1920 that libraries be prepared to seat one-half of the entire student body at one time. At the other extreme, California's standard for the CSU system is currently set at 20 percent; Association of College and Research Libraries (ACRL) "Standards for College Libraries, 1995 edition" (*C&RL News,* April 1995, pages 245–57), with up to 50 percent of the full-time equivalent student body living on campus, also suggest seating for 20 percent of the total student population. However, for a substantially residential campus (more than 50 percent FTE students), the traditional figure of seating for 25 percent is stipulated. A figure of 20 percent is more realistic than 25 percent for most institutions, and some argue that a figure closer to 15 percent for nonresidential college campuses is adequate. Some notable library consultants suggest that for a commuting campus, the library can be planned for as little as 10 percent of the full-time equivalent student body. The ACRL standard for community, junior, and technical college learning resource programs (*C&RL News,* May 1994: 274–87) is for seating 10 percent of the student body. Clearly, interpretations of the type of questions outlined in this section will lead to a fairly broad spectrum of seating proportions for different institutions.

As a confirmation of the multiple influences described, librarians at Sweet Briar College feel that providing for 23 percent of the student body is very inadequate. At Washington and Lee University, 40 percent of undergraduates have library seating and that is "about right." The University of Florida seats only 1 percent because of space limitations; they feel it "should" seat 25 percent.

The University of Miami believes 12 percent would do. The University of Central Florida believes 10 percent is the reasonable goal because its 26,000 students commute. The University of North Florida seats 8 percent and says it is enough. Duke University says 10 percent would be adequate if they could be at "nice" seating areas. The U.S. Naval Academy Library seats 50 percent, which is adequate. Mount Holyoke College Library seats about 48 percent (plus 24 faculty studies) and that is adequate in its case.

Some time ago at Harvard University, with an outstanding student group in a metropolitan area, the librarian estimated that three out of eight undergraduates should be provided study space in either the house libraries, departmental libraries, the research library, or the undergraduate library. At Stanford University, assuming that about 75 percent of the undergraduate library and 25 percent of the research library seats are used by undergraduates, seating is provided for about 25 percent of the undergraduate user population plus what is used by undergraduates in various branch libraries. Although there are times during the peak periods when students feel they cannot find a place, there have always been at least a few empty seats. Even so, a student may end up using a study space in a building other than the one preferred. As it turns out, considerably more than 25 percent of the seats in the research library are being used by undergraduates at peak times.

At the University of Florida, Metcalf suggested that at the time of the peak load, up to 75 percent of the students could be expected to be studying at one time and that one-half of this 75 percent would, or at least could, properly use their own rooms for this purpose. This would leave 37.5 percent to be cared for elsewhere. It was then suggested that one-fifth of this number, or 7.5 percent, might well be cared for in reading or study rooms in the residential halls, and that, of the 30 percent remaining, one-third would find their study facilities in departmental libraries, leaving 20 percent to be cared for in the central building. It is interesting how this percentage as a national standard has remained relatively constant over the years, while the actual seating at the University of Florida has suffered because of space limitations.

Manual four of the *Higher Education Facilities Planning and Management Manuals,* prepared by Dahnke, Jones, Mason, and Romney, provides a general guide for each discipline and user group. Of course, adjustments should be made for other factors, but the outlined approach is a useful way of considering seating requirements. See appendix B.

Accommodation for students in professional schools may include law, medicine, divinity, education, public health, pharmacy, nursing, veterinary medicine, architecture, engineering, home economics, agriculture, and physical education, among others. Library needs of these diverse fields are by no means identical and demands for seats will vary. Students of law and divinity are typically very heavy users; education and medicine less so; and the others much less, although local academic emphasis could change the order suggested.

Little has been said of departmental libraries for disciplines in the arts and sciences—that is, the humanities, social sciences, physical sciences, and their subdivisions. Departmental libraries tend to multiply, and their cost to the institution can become very high. At Harvard University there are over one hundred libraries in all; similar situations on a smaller scale are found at many large universities. In too many institutions some departmental libraries have simply grown up without involvement of the university library system while others are recognized and supported as part of the university library. See discussion of these in Sections 7.15 and 7.16.

A study of the circumstances should be made for any particular institution; the foregoing statements can at best provide guidelines that may help in solving the problem. No clear rules can be suggested for determination of needs, but most of the factors involved in the consideration of how many seats to provide have been outlined, and it should be emphasized that each institution must consider its seating requirements carefully, with the future in mind.

Graduate students. Compared to undergraduates, graduate students in arts and sciences, and those working for advanced degrees in professional schools, represent somewhat different problems. In larger institutions, each graduate professional school is likely to have its own special library. The percentage of students requiring seating at any one time may be determined after consideration of the points presented earlier, but with a separate calculation for each program. As suggested by the tables in appendix B, the percentage of seats required will generally tend to

be larger for graduates than for undergraduates, particularly in law schools where 50 percent or more may need to use the library at one time. The Association of American Law Schools continued in 1995 to recommend seating "with generous table or desk space" for 65 percent of the student body. City institutions with many part-time students will usually be an exception to this statement, though, in such settings, the local legal community will represent a significant user group unless public access is limited. In a medical school the percentage will typically be considerably smaller, as so much time is required in laboratory and clinical work, yet research and hospital staff must be considered. Similar factors are to be considered in engineering and technological institutions. Those working in the physical sciences resemble medical and engineering students; they spend much of their time in laboratories, so library demands are decreased. The ability of the scientist to be current by use of the computer is becoming a greater reality as well, though there is still need for library support. Of course, the theoretical scientist may be an exception, but it is seldom that this type of research accounts for more than a small fraction of the user group.

Graduate students in arts and sciences, particularly in the humanities and social sciences, ordinarily require seats for a percentage of their number little, if any, less than those usually required in a law school. Graduate students in the humanities and social sciences working for doctorates will make the largest demands on the library in the percentage of seats required. In these fields there is ordinarily a great difference between those doing the first and second year of their work toward the doctorate and those who are engaged in writing their dissertations. Many academics believe that any scholar writing a doctoral dissertation in the humanities or social sciences should have an assigned library seat, preferably at an individual table or in a carrel, with a bookshelf and security for personal papers, for the full period of this task. For instance, the University of North Carolina, Chapel Hill, provides 500 of these graduate student studies in its 1983 Davis Library. Security, in this case, must be more than low partitions; a locking door and full height walls or a locker will be required.

Let us say, then, that in the average institution there should be a seat in the library for every doctoral candidate actually working full-time on a dissertation in the humanities and social sciences; for others working for the Ph.D. but not yet engaged in writing the dissertation, one seat for every two full-time students is sufficient; and for those working for the master's degree, seating for about 40 percent is sufficient in many universities. As with previous seating figures, circumstances vary; these estimates should be used as guides only. This subject is one on which an experienced library consultant may be helpful.

Faculty. The needs of faculty members differ from those of undergraduate and graduate students. Customs and study habits vary among institutions and disciplines, and they are changing with the revolution of networked access. If adequate library facilities for faculty have been provided in the past, it is probable that many faculty members will prefer to do much of their research and lecture preparation in the library. In other institutions where library facilities have not been satisfactory, particularly if faculty have suitable offices elsewhere, many will have developed patterns of doing their research outside the library. The private study at home is, of course, favored as the likelihood of being disturbed is much less. However, as houses and apartments become smaller, they become less suitable for study. With children at home, the residence may not be a satisfactory place to carry on research. Faculty who are still working on their dissertations find satisfactory quarters on campus for research are of great importance.

Where faculty typically have a departmental office, there may be some institutional concern about providing a second place where faculty can disappear. Some feel that to generate a cohesive academic atmosphere, faculty should be encouraged to be in their offices, available for student consultation as much as possible. In such circumstances the introduction of special library faculty accommodation may be undesirable. Yet many college and university libraries do provide some faculty studies, including 24 at Mount Holyoke College Library, many at such universities as Harvard and Stanford, and even 24 specifically for emeriti in a suite at Wake Forest University's Reynolds Library. Clearly, the institution's policy regarding the use of faculty offices is an important factor. Whether or not such use is a consideration, many faculty will request a quiet study in the library as well as an office elsewhere. Many universities have felt that they could provide library studies for senior members of the faculty only, although this group generally needs such accommodation less than their juniors.

Although the number of faculty may exceed 10 percent of the students in a few institutions, they can probably be left out of calculations of seating capacity in the regular open reading areas of the library. This omission is not because they do not read, but because their heaviest library use tends to be in quarters specially assigned to them. Where this is not the case, as in the reference room, a computer cluster supporting the public catalog, or the current periodical room, faculty are not likely to stay long or to add to congestion. Times of peak library usage by students are generally avoided by faculty.

Although special faculty reading rooms are not unusual, their value is questionable and they are not here recommended. Faculty members doing research or preparing lectures prefer to be alone rather than in a reading room, even if its use is restricted to their colleagues. The desirability of a small social area for use by faculty and graduate students may be worth consideration, though this is far more prevalent in the departmental quarters. However, careful thought must be given to this concept because of the likelihood of demand for refreshments.

Another approach is to provide faculty studies as mentioned above, or the type of cubicle or carrel provided for graduate students. The dividing line between graduate students and faculty is not always clear; in the case of teaching fellows, the facilities ordinarily assigned to graduate students are usually considered adequate, but for the more senior professor these are seldom satisfactory. If quarters for the faculty in the library are intended as studies only, which the authors recommend, the number and size can be greatly reduced from what would be required if they also function as faculty offices. Most professors doing administrative work or frequently consulted by students do not like to do this work in their library studies, and would prefer an office in a departmental or other building. Office functions provided in a library will lead to demands for special consideration for access when the library is closed, and, of course, consideration of office support functions must be given. Included here would be secretarial space, phones, photocopy areas, supply storage, and the like.

Faculty members in the physical sciences are better satisfied if their studies or offices are in the buildings that are considered their headquarters. The same will be true for a certain percentage, varying in each institution, of those in the humanities and the social sciences. In general, there is less demand proportionately for library faculty studies in colleges than in universities.

A number of libraries with studies have had concerns in assigning them because of high demand, while frequently their level of use is less than anticipated, especially where suitable offices are provided. Yet, they do have a place in the library program. They may be assigned for limited periods only, and assignments renewed only when the need is clearly demonstrated. On the other hand, it should not be forgotten that much valuable research is greatly facilitated by library faculty studies. In a few institutions, as many as 10 percent of the faculty may have library studies. Because local attitudes and concerns will affect the final decision, this problem could be placed before the library committee.

Visiting scholars. Although visiting scholars are a comparatively negligible factor in most institutions, they are significant in larger research libraries, particularly those with exceptional original manuscript or archival collections, and perhaps those in large cities or on the way to and from "vacationland." Because faculty in all colleges and universities visit other libraries, as do graduate students, academic libraries should be hospitable to such visitors as a *quid pro quo*. In providing access to both general research collections and to rare book and manuscript reading rooms, reasonable needs of visiting scholars should be accommodated, and they must be considered seriously in building planning. Only local experience can serve as a basis for estimating the requirements. The basic requirement is for a reading position at a table where library materials may be used for long hours or many days without interruption or disturbance. The Folger and Huntington libraries are exemplary instances of libraries that provide for visiting scholars.

At Harvard University for a large part of the year, both summer and winter, the central Widener Library could make good use of 25 studies for visiting scholars, in addition to 50 carrels. An equal number of both studies and carrels would be useful in its departmental libraries in addition to the Houghton rare book and manuscript accommodation. At Stanford University half that number would suffice, though at Stanford it has been suggested that, because most visiting scholars are faculty at other institutions, the combination of carrels and studies would result in an allocation headache; all studies or even all carrels with lockers would be better than a mixture. It is suggested that accommodation suitable for graduate students will be satisfactory for visiting scholars using general research collections in most institutions, and that very few academic institutions will be able to justify space for a reading room dedicated to visiting scholars.

Others, including the general public. When an institution must provide open access to any visitor, as is the case at the University of California, Los Angeles, and Concordia University in Montreal, the effect of the public can be significant, perhaps limited only by parking and access from off campus. It is more often the case that casual visitors can be ignored in estimating seating, yet they should not be forgotten because of the problems they may present. Their number is not necessarily negligible. In nearly all college and university libraries, alumni of the institution are welcome. High school and college students from local institutions can be expected to pour in unless they are actively discouraged from doing so. Here the decision of what to do with or about them is a matter of policy for the institution's administration after the librarian has set forth in detail the effect on the library. Certain aspects of public access may be established by law, such as is the case for government documents depository libraries in the United States. In Ontario, Canada, and many other areas, all libraries supported by public funding are legally required to be open to all residents. In most cases, however, the seating capacity provided for peak student loads will be sufficient accommodation for other visitors.

5.3
Front Matter

The principal reason for expending considerable effort to prepare a program statement is to record in one document the basic information necessary to establish the scope and character of the building project. The program will not answer all questions, and continued involvement will be required of the librarian and other members of the project team. As stated before, the program forms the basis for the development of a project budget as well as design fees for the various consultants.

It also provides basic information of which the architect should be cognizant during the design period. Although the detail of the program will vary with institutional circumstance and the size of the project, it is suggested that the following general topics be considered for inclusion in what is often called front matter: Goals of the library; Site concerns and access; General relationships of major functions; Aesthetic versus functional concerns; Module and structural flexibility; Security; Interior design concerns; Environmental control; Adaptability and the support of technology; and Codes and standards. Each of these is discussed in the subsections that follow.

Much of this volume consists of discussion related to the concerns outlined above. Marcus Vitruvius Pollio, the Roman architect and engineer, wrote in his *De Architectura Libri Decem,* at the time of the Emperor Augustus, of the three essentials in building, which he called *firmitas, utilitas, venustas,* in that order. They can be translated as strength, function, beauty. The intent of the program front matter is to establish the basis for the interrelationship of these essentials in building as they are shaped by the design process. Clearly, all aspects cannot be resolved by a program document, for if they were, the design would no doubt be complete, the building constructed, and the library functioning smoothly in its new quarters. The purpose of the program is to identify the problems, not the solutions. Nevertheless, direction should be established with the expectation that there will be change and compromise over the months, indeed, years to follow.

5.3.1 Goals of the Library

In most cases it should be assumed that the project architect has had little experience with libraries, particularly the libraries of the institution for which the program is being written. In a statement of library goals, it is useful to outline briefly the recent history of the library in its institutional setting. Important is the nature of the library as a teaching instrument, a central research facility, a research branch, an undergraduate library, a learning resources center, a storage library, a rare books library, or other special library. Trends in growth of the collections, the student population, the characteristics of use, the application of information technology, and the influence of future facilities on these factors all warrant discussion. Then, with suitable caution, it may be

useful to describe the librarian's view of this particular facility 10 or 20 years in the future.

There will be facilities goals as well, which should be discussed in succeeding paragraphs. For example, you will want to provide quarters that will, as far as possible, ensure the preservation of the collections. Suitable comfort for readers and staff is a likely goal. Convenience of access and operations, and effective, efficient utilization of space certainly are reasonable requirements.

In some cases there will be need for phasing a project to permit partial activation before completion. This is particularly true in the event of a major addition to a building that is to be significantly remodeled as part of the same project. To facilitate the arrangement of a library that is to be expanded into new contiguous space, part of the project may be a master plan that develops the direction of future renovations while limiting the main project effort to only the new addition. In this case the second phase, or the renovation of the existing building, may be treated as a separate project. Because of the timing and the different requirements between new and renovated construction, it may make considerable sense to keep the two phases distinct, including perhaps even separate contracts with the architect. Indeed, the two projects could involve different architects.

A renovation project will likely require phasing. Although the program does not need to spell out the exact phasing requirements, the fact that phasing will be necessary to provide for ongoing library operations should be established.

5.3.2 Site Concerns and Access

Chapter 11 covers the major aspects of siting and preparing a master plan from the planning and design point of view. The program is an excellent instrument to establish guidelines for site selection or, if the site is known, to describe significant factors that must be considered during the design of the building. The program should state the source of existing site data, such as weather, soil tests, traffic patterns, surveys, utility locations, and the like. Should these vital pieces of information be missing, it should be established either that the architect is expected to obtain all the necessary data or that the institution will gather this material.

Where proposed construction is connected with existing structures, the needs should be detailed. The program may speak to floor connections, sun or wind conditions to be preserved or avoided, and perhaps the character and function of the connecting element. If there are vistas of historical importance, they must be mentioned here as a feature to be preserved.

Policy or local sentiment, where it affects building design, should also be detailed. Does the institution maintain a certain architectural character as at Stanford University where sandstone and tile have been part of the design almost without exception? Are there historical elements that must be preserved as at Concordia University, which had to preserve an older facade? Does removal of a parking lot or a tree require the replacement of such items in other locations as part of the project? The University of British Columbia was required to preserve trees within what was then known as the Sedgwick Library (now part of the Walter C. Koerner Library). Are there limitations of height? Is flooding or other natural disaster of special concern? How many deliveries a day or week are made to the library? How large are the vehicles? Does special parking for handicapped, staff, visitors, service personnel, or library vehicles need to be provided? What is the anticipated system of trash removal? Will there need to be a curbside book return? How many library visitors a day or week are anticipated? Will site lighting or remote signs be part of the project? Is bicycle parking for staff and users to be part of the project? If so, how much? Should there be benches, lighting, or other site features? Are there to be underground connections to other facilities? Is a part of the project to be artwork, some of which might take the form of a sculpture or fountain? If there is need for irrigation systems, should automatic timers be included?

Many site features may be established by the local environment or institutional facility standards. Where this is the case, the proposed questions may not require elaborate discussion. Clearly, the overall goal must be to develop a facility that works well with the site in response to the architectural fabric, traffic patterns, environmental conditions, and the site's natural features. Reference should be made to known documentation of site features, including archeological remains, and any specific requirements that may be suggested by the questions above should be stated.

5.3.3 General Relationships of Major Functions

A complete program should always include a concise but careful statement of desired spatial relationships between the different services as well as a description of how the library is to operate and will be administered. Supplementary information, including perhaps a library organization chart and library phone book, can be useful. A description with an illustration to outline the flow of materials coming into the library through the technical processing offices as well as being used by patrons of the library is important in helping the architect to understand.

In preparing the statement on spatial relationships, the librarian has the opportunity to reconsider the library's organization and operation. Just because work has been handled in a certain way in the past does not necessarily mean that old practices should be continued. This is the time to study the problems involved; it may be the ideal time to institute improvements that an old building may have prevented. The convenience of faculty, students, and staff should be kept in mind as well as the cost of services rendered. Relationships with any nonlibrary functions that are being programmed for the building should also be considered. The arrangements decided upon may have a great effect on operating costs for security, maintenance, services, and processing additions to the collections. Other things being equal, the fewer service desks and control points to be staffed, the better. The shorter the distances staff travel vertically or horizontally, the better. But the building should not inconvenience readers or reduce service quality for the sake of staff convenience.

In arranging spatial and functional relationships, the various uses made of the library by students and faculty must be kept in mind. They may include the following: use of computer resources for word processing, communications, homework assignments, and entertainment; reserve books for use in or outside the library; general recreational and collateral reading, the latter in connection with course work; preparation of reports of various kinds and research work; and use of the World Wide Web, current periodicals and newspapers, manuscripts, maps, microtexts, audiovisual materials, computer data files, the reference collection, catalog, and so on.

Of course, other uses of the library or outside factors (such as site configuration, logical entrance points, delivery locations, preservation of a heritage tree, and the like) may influence spatial relationships. For all of them, the shorter the distances to be traveled by everyone concerned, the better. Even walking on the level through reading areas is likely to be disturbing, and traffic up and down stairs can be noisy. Visual and auditory distraction of readers should be avoided as far as possible. The use of computers, photocopy machines, and toilet rooms should be considered in planning their arrangement relative to areas where quiet is desirable.

The staff side of the picture is also important. Spatial relationships have a great deal to do with staff effectiveness. Salaries are often the largest single expenditure in libraries. If in a large library staff members have to walk considerable distances frequently or go up and down stairs often, the time consumed is a distinct intrusion upon effective working time. Once or twice a day might not be serious; it is the total amount of travel that counts. Pushing one truck loaded with books each day from the mail room to the acquisition department is not serious, even if the distance involved is one hundred feet. But if the circulation desk is adjacent to the entrance and the service elevator or lifts are one hundred feet away and 10 truckloads of books must go back and forth each day, the configuration may not be cost effective.

The relationship of staff functions to the user is yet another topic to be considered. In the first edition of this book, Metcalf pointed out that few, even advanced scholars, enjoyed facing the 12 card catalog trays under "William Shakespeare" in the Widener Library at that time, or the 87 trays under the heading "United States," or the 14 trays listing the material on "Bible." Access to bibliographic information via the computer can magnify this type of problem such that the amount of information available is overwhelming. Unless a reference librarian, equipped to handle the situation and available to assist, is close at hand, many will give up in despair. Unless scholars can find a good reference and bibliographical collection, including online substitutes, with an experienced and helpful librarian readily available when help is needed, they will be handicapped, if not baffled, in using the library and library-related computer resources. As the library grows larger in area and collections, and the digital information world expands, these problems tend to increase in magnitude. The climax of it all for those seeking printed texts is in the bookstack if it lacks logical arrangement.

Description of these relationships can take many forms. One that is quite useful involves a graphic vocabulary of circles and lines to express the various relationships. Rectangles are also used (fig. 5.2), but circles avoid the temptation to start actually designing a building, an exercise best left to the architect. Circles may be sized to simulate the proportionate space represented by each function, but absolute accuracy is not necessary nor desirable at this stage. Critical relationships, where two functions essentially are to be juxtaposed, may be circles connected by a thick solid line; important, but less critical, connections can be represented by a thinner line. Frequent though even less important relationships could be shown by a dashed line. Other factors, such as security boundaries, noise, or outside influences, can be shown with either simple graphic techniques or brief statements. Using tracing paper or drafting software on the computer, you can quickly explore a number of possible relationships and discuss or ponder their merits until you arrive at something close to expressing the needs of the specific institution. When the architect begins work on the project, there will no doubt be a period of testing the stated relationships, which should be viewed as a positive contribution, for the architect may discover factors that the librarian or others missed.

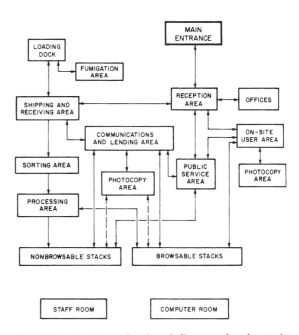

FIGURE 5.2   Organizational diagram for the University of California Northern Regional Library Facility. This is essentially a bubble diagram (without the application of relative size for the functions) showing functional relationships of the various building components.

The intent in exploring spatial relationships is to develop a picture, either textually or graphically, of those functions that have close connections with the organization and service patterns of related functions. Discussion of the problem can begin with the central or key services, that is, the circulation desk, the reference desk, the reference and bibliography collections, the periodical indexes, the networked computer cluster, and the card and/or computer catalog—services to which the reader will naturally turn to unlock access to the world of information. These key services should be easy to find. Users should be able to reach each one or go from one to another without traversing great distances horizontally or vertically. If there is a general reading area for the use of reserved books, privately owned books, or after-hours computer use or study, it should be easy to find.

A common use pattern is represented by finding a book on a specific subject. The typical first step is to ascertain its location. The reader may obtain a citation in the reference or bibliography collection, go to the online catalog to learn if the library owns it, and, if so, discover its shelf mark or call number and hence its location on the shelves. In some cases, help may be required in this process. Once the book is found and the reader decides to check the book out, the next step involves a visit to a circulation desk or perhaps a terminal supporting a self-charge circulation system. The final exiting of the library involves some form of confirmation that the book is properly charged out, either by staffed inspection or through use of a book security system. This can all be summed up by saying that if each of these staffed central services—excluding, of course, the main bookstack and remote computer stations for charge out, reference, and the online catalog—can be near the entrance and readily found, a large part of the design battle is won. Ideally, access to the stacks and computer-supported services will be provided in proximity to the entrance as well.

Of equal importance are the requirements for the processing staff that selects, orders, receives, and catalogs books, serials, and the multitude of other library materials. Their work is closely involved with the reference and bibliography collections and the catalog. While need for access to the public catalog is reduced by the advent of computer-based cataloging, where there is a large card catalog that is unlikely to be retrospectively converted to machine-readable format, or where the card catalog is being actively maintained, it is important to have the technical processing quarters as close as possible. Juxtaposing the processing area with the reference collection space is also desirable. Such an arrangement will reduce the need for duplication of expensive bibliographical collections and work will be simplified and speeded up. However, when the necessary bibliographic tools can be purchased in duplicate sets or accessed online, and when the entire cataloging activity is done through computer terminals, the need for adjacent location is less essential.

For very large library systems, particularly where centralized processing is the accepted practice, consideration may be given to placing this activity in a separate building, perhaps related more to a delivery dock than to the operating library. The University of British Columbia, New York Public Library Research Libraries, Rutgers University, and Stanford University are examples, with parts of technical processing located in separate buildings. Some, including the authors, may question the philosophy of such a division because the collegial atmosphere of staff would be difficult to maintain, though there are cases where separation is the best choice. The notion of "them" and "us," which is often prevalent even when departments exist in the same building, is considerably greater where totally separate quarters are developed. (An extreme form of separated technical processing is the result of outsourcing, comments on which can be found in Section 8.3.)

Answers to the following questions will bring out many of the relationship issues. Others will be based on local situations and details of organization; the librarian will have to be alert for them as the program is prepared. In the following paragraphs, as elsewhere in this volume, questions are deliberately posed without answers because for each institution the answers will be unique. Also, the planners and program writer must subject their work to this type of questioning if they are to be confident in their responses to the questions of critics (and critiques) of the project.

1. What functions should be close to the entrance lobby? Functions that warrant consideration include a library access privileges desk; the circulation desk and related staff quarters; an entrance/exit control portal; the entrance to the government documents, reference, bibliography, rare books, and current journals and newspapers

areas; the reference and reserve book desks with their related space needs; the card catalog and other catalog devices; display area; a networked computer cluster; a light reading or browsing area; access to the rest of the building via stairwells and elevators; and perhaps the library administration and personnel office, and also the development office where this is a library function. Although it may be desirable to state the ideal arrangement of functions to be placed near the entrance lobby, some compromise is almost certain. Priorities will need to be developed, and the list of functions near the entrance will need to be limited. In most cases, such functions as reserve books, the administrative offices, or rare books can be somewhat more remotely located, provided the route to them can be clearly identified by the library visitor.

2. If space can be provided, should the quarters for the technical processing departments be on the same level with some of the services listed in question 1? Or can the space be better used for other reader services functions? If space cannot be found for all the processing departments there, should they all be housed one floor above or below or elsewhere, or can they be divided, with accommodation for those functions most closely related to the reader service functions located on the main floor and the others elsewhere?

3. What should the spatial relationship be between the shipping and receiving room and those areas that handle quantities of incoming or outgoing materials, such as that generated by the acquisitions department, a gift and exchange department, bindery preparation, or serials processing? If they are on different levels, should they be sited one above the other close to the service elevator? It is suggested that in an academic library much less material is transported between these departments than between the central book return and discharge area and the stack areas. If the same elevator is used in both forms of traffic, the convenience of returning books to the stacks should be given priority. Usually the movement of materials to and from the shipping and receiving area can be batched to avoid conflict with other operations.

4. Should the administrative offices be on the same level as the major public services? There is a great difference of opinion here. Some librarians, especially in colleges and smaller branch libraries, want to be close to the operational reader service areas so as to be more readily available to the public. Some feel it is of first importance to be adjacent to the acquisition and catalog departments, and some prefer to be at a distance from all operations to make it easier to carry on administrative and sometimes scholarly work undisturbed by routine problems. In any case, it is desirable to provide accessibility without necessarily going through a control portal in most cases, although this is certainly not essential. Such an arrangement removes the need to provide access to the collections for visitors unaffiliated with the institution when they arrive to see the business manager, personnel officer, or the director. This question is probably of greatest concern in very large libraries, and separate access is typically more of a concern for private than public institutions where anybody can enter the general stack areas. The more important issue is that these offices should be easily found by a visitor.

A related question is whether the associate and assistant librarians should have offices adjacent to the chief librarian's office, in order to facilitate consultation, or close to the departments or the staff they supervise? For instance, if an assistant librarian is in charge of public services and the library's administrative suite is on the second floor, should the assistant librarian have an office next to the reference and circulation departments or on the second floor next to the chief librarian? Often this decision depends upon the current administrative style; what is done today may change a year from now. Because of this, it is suggested that the arrangements be made with flexibility in mind. This issue is more important in the administrative area where space is more limited in size and configuration than in larger operating departments.

5. If the library is to include an exhibition room or a rare book room to which it wishes to attract visitors, especially friends of the library, should it be placed near the entrance so as to be readily accessible, or will space elsewhere in a quieter location be satisfactory? Should a basement level without windows be considered where special protection of books and manuscripts from sunlight would not be required, and where temperature, humidity control, and security might be easier to provide (but where flooding may prove a hazard), or would a top floor be preferable where, except for roof and overhead plumbing

leaks, one might expect the hazard of water to be minimized?

All too often, rare book collections are soaked. Unfortunately, due to the consequence of deferred maintenance, rooftop mechanical rooms, sprinkler systems, and the like, placing these materials higher in a building does not remove the potential of water damage. In establishing the location for such a facility, keep in mind that elevator access is probably required for handicapped and elderly visitors. Also, this is often an area that attracts visiting scholars and people with little or no need for general access to the main collections. Because of this, the rare book room is often another candidate for placement outside the main portal control point. Size and local circumstances will greatly influence its location.

6. How important is it to place a large percentage of seating on the entrance level, or, if that cannot be arranged, one level up or down to avoid unnecessarily heavy traffic on stairs or elevators? This arrangement should make for a quieter and less restless building where reader populations are large, though at the same time it increases the difficulty of combining accommodations for books and readers in proximity. Of course, closed stacks dictate large, centrally placed reading areas, while the concept of an open stack is, in part, to place the reader as near the collections as possible. Many factors, such as the distribution of the collections, the nature of the user group, the size of the library, and so on, need to be considered in reaching a conclusion on seating distribution.

These questions might be added to almost indefinitely; it is hoped that the basic general questions have been suggested. Posing the questions and, in a few instances, suggesting possible answers is not meant to dictate decisions but to clarify the issues.

5.3.4 Aesthetic versus Functional Concerns

Although there may be some risk in establishing guidelines for aesthetic versus functional questions, it is nevertheless useful to formulate a statement on the issues, with recognition that the design team will test various options and possibilities. Obviously, the building should house the library staff and collections adequately and provide sufficient accommodation for the readers. But these alone are not enough. Other issues must be dealt with in planning a new structure, and

they can rarely be solved without deciding priorities, which in turn should be based on the objectives of the institution. It can readily be agreed that the library should not be ugly. But how important is its architectural style? Should a minimum of attention be given to the appearance, or should an effort be made to have it harmonize with other buildings in the vicinity; or should the architect aim to create an outstanding structure on the campus? Should special attention be paid to its interior design? Should the construction be of such high quality that the structure will be sound after a hundred years, or should its life be thought of in terms of a limited period, on the assumption that it will be outdated and not worth preserving thereafter? Costs too often have more influence than one might wish in determining the answers. Codes and local ordinances often dictate a certain level of quality or style. Other factors, some of which are discussed elsewhere in this section on program front matter, will influence the aesthetic and functional quality.

No attempt will be made to write dogmatically on architectural style and aesthetics, important as these are in determining the success or failure of a library building. Local conditions, traditions, and aspirations create circumstances where choice is appropriate from among a very wide variety of design styles. Architectural propriety and aesthetics are not exact sciences. However, they are basic, and they should not be completely subordinated to the functional aspects of the program; yet the beauty of a building should not conflict with its satisfactory operation. The ideal is to strike that delicate balance between the architectural requirements for aesthetics, the functional requirements as established in the program, and the resources to achieve both.

Traditionally library buildings have tended to be monumental in character. This distinction follows from their physical size and the importance attributed to them, which has often resulted in libraries that are the central, most conspicuous, and largest buildings on the campus. The donor, wanting perhaps to perpetuate a family name, asks for an architectural gem, and incidentally a monument. The governing board may take advantage of an opportunity to build something quite special on a campus otherwise largely comprised of utilitarian classroom and dormitory buildings, and encourages or gives tacit approval for a structure of some monumentality. The library is probably used regularly by a larger percentage of the students and faculty than any other building, with the possible exception of a student union or the chapel in a church-affiliated institution. The architect naturally takes advantage of an unusual opportunity for a fine building. Because of the long-term inertia derived from the desire for monumentality, the impact of such a design should be clearly understood so that the decision appropriate to the institution can be reached. High ceilings, which historically have been associated with monumental structures, add cost that may limit the ability to provide a facility that meets the programmed operational needs. Tower libraries may add to the difficulty of managing the collections and thus may add to the ongoing operational cost, as well as make the collections more difficult to get to from the central service points. Future expansion of a monumental structure is often much more difficult to accomplish in an architecturally satisfactory way. Flexibility for alternative uses may be severely restricted. The cost for monumentality is generally high, and the advantage of such a structure should be carefully weighed against the disadvantages.

The librarian may go along with the architect in striving toward monumentality until it is found that the funds required are needed to provide useful floor area for library purposes; then a loud protest is generally heard. To avoid an acrimonious debate, the various points of view should be assembled and some agreement reached on what is most important for the institution as a whole. The direction of such an agreement should then be incorporated as part of the program statement.

This commentary is not meant to assert that monumentality is bad. As long as the design serves well the internal function, a striking, imposing, and even flamboyant exterior may in some places be entirely appropriate. This has been achieved with success in many instances. However, the University of California at San Diego, Clemson University, Furman University, Harvard's Widener Library, Northwestern University, Princeton's Firestone Library, the U.S. Naval Academy's Nimitz Library, and such tower libraries as those at the California Institute of Technology, the University of Massachusetts at Amherst, and the University of Pittsburgh—each in its way is monumental, but not all are functionally successful today, certainly not Harvard's Widener nor Cal Tech, and a successful tower library has yet to

appear. It is a fine architect who can pull off the great interior within monumental clothing.

5.3.5 Module and Structural Flexibility

Basic to the design of any modern building is some form of a dimensional module. In libraries the standard dimensions of shelving, together with the needs for aisle space as well as furniture dimensions, structural and mechanical requirements, and possibly parking space (as was the case for the new addition of the Holland Library at Washington State University and the plans for the National Taiwan Library) should be considered in establishing an appropriate building module. A carefully selected module will ensure a certain degree of flexibility or adaptability, particularly if anticipated future changes in the assignment of space can be accommodated. Other forms of adaptability include provisions for future expansion or deployment of functions or collections, the provision of utilities and environmental control that will permit a broad range of specific uses, and the planning of fixed elements to minimize the difficulty of future alterations. A building designed with modules can also be built more efficiently and accurately because of the simplification of dimensions.

Modules vary in scale from the small size of a specific building unit, such as a brick, to the dimension of a ceiling grid with lighting and mechanical systems included, to the shelving unit required to house a book, or to the structural column spacing. Other elements can be considered as the basis for a module, but at this stage of the project design only the concept of desirability for a module should be established.

The most important factor for layouts and future flexibility will be the column spacing. Thus the modular system, as the term is used here, is a building supported by columns placed at regular intervals. All weight-bearing elements, including shear walls as required in earthquake areas, are assumed to be in a regular pattern as established by the module. To simplify the discussion, we will assume that fixed elements, such as shear walls, will be carefully located so as to have minimal effect on future space reallocations; columns act as the immovable framework within which all functions must be arranged.

A rectangle—usually, but not always, a square—defined by four adjacent columns is known as a bay. The modular building then is made up of identical bays, any one of which may be furnished as part of a reading area, filled with ranges of shelving, divided by partitions into offices, or combinations of two or even three of these. No difficult structural alterations should be required when a bay that has been serving one of these purposes is assigned to another; there can be a shifting of furniture, shelving, and partitions, which may be without power and data cables (dry) and demountable or supplied with power and signal (wet) and more difficult to remove.

This flexibility is a major virtue of the modular system, and it appeals greatly to those who have attempted to adapt to changing needs within one of the traditional structures characterized by massive interior walls and multitier stacks, even when those fine older buildings do have some form of a module, which they usually do. A revolution has occurred during the last half century, thanks in large part, as far as libraries are concerned, to the efforts of the late Angus Snead Macdonald, Ralph Ellsworth, and other forward-looking librarians, architects, and builders; the modular system is now prevalent, although not universally used. To sum up, a building consisting largely of space that can be used for almost any purpose without extensive or expensive alterations should in the long run save money and prevent complications that so often arise as space requirements change. The modular system or some adaptation of it is now generally standard in libraries.

Like most innovations, however, the modular system is not a panacea; it has its faults and its pitfalls. The fundamental objection is that no one column spacing or bay size is ideal for all purposes; the module that is almost perfectly adapted to one function, such as book storage, will not be equally well suited to another. Metcalf once suggested that it might be desirable to construct one-third of a library in bays designed for book storage, one-third in a module well adapted to reading areas, and one-third in a reasonably satisfactory all-purpose size. This seemed a more promising procedure at the time it was proposed than it does today, when there is an increasing tendency to bring books and readers together in a single area. However, circumstances no doubt exist that make such a suggestion appropriate. A combination of different bay sizes was used in Harvard's Lamont Library (fig. 5.3) to take advantage of the useful features of the modular system and at the same time avoid the handicap

that it often brings in its train. The attempt to attain flexibility entails certain sacrifices and some inflexible features, such as columns at regular intervals.

If the optimum module size for a new library is based on the present nature of the library collection and its clientele, it must be recognized that many institutions change so rapidly that the size desirable today may be wasteful 10 years hence. There may then be an 8 percent to 10 percent loss in space utilization, particularly if an addition is built without change in bay sizes. For instance, if a bay size suitable for an open-shelf undergraduate collection with stack ranges 4 ft 6 in. on centers is used for what becomes a large research collection where 4 ft 2 in. on centers may be adequate, some 8 percent of the stack area will be devoted to unnecessary aisle space. This example is based upon stack dimensions that are not possible where handicapped access standards are met, but the point remains valid.

"On centers" is the distance between the center of the uprights in one range to the center of the uprights in the next parallel range. The term is also used in connection with table and carrel spacing. Where there is a row of tables or carrels equally spaced, it is the distance between the edge of one and the corresponding edge of the

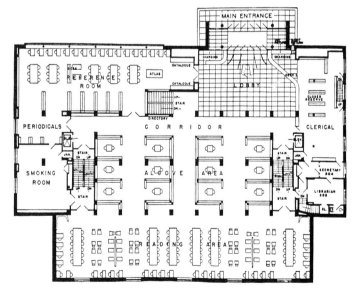

FIGURE 5.3 Harvard University, Lamont Library, third level, showing column spacing. The columns are irregularly spaced to make possible large reading areas and a lobby without obstructions, but the building is basically modular with columns 13 ft (3.962 m) on centers from east to west.

next one parallel to it (fig. 5.4). Column spacing is generally spoken of in a similar way.

Cases can also be cited in which the modular system has caused a librarian to suppose that because the building was assumed to be completely flexible, layouts did not need to be planned carefully in advance, so long as the total floor space was sufficient. The result has been a great deal of shifting that ought not to have been necessary; it is expensive, even with a modular system, to replace floor coverings, change lighting fixtures, rearrange air handling ducts, relocate outlets, and move temporary partitions.

Totally modular buildings have sometimes resulted in serious acoustical problems because the movable partitions and bookcases on which they depend to divide up each floor have not proved adequate barriers to sound. Of course, a modular building need not have movable partitions, and even where movable partitions are used, there are often ways of reducing the acoustic problems.

In spite of the difficulties, the modular system is undoubtedly here to stay, and should be used with care in most new library construction. Its advantages can be summarized as follows:

1. It simplifies the task of estimating costs, with more accurate results.
2. It saves time on the site because materials are acquired in suitable standard sizes, and it reduces cutting, patching, and wasting materials.

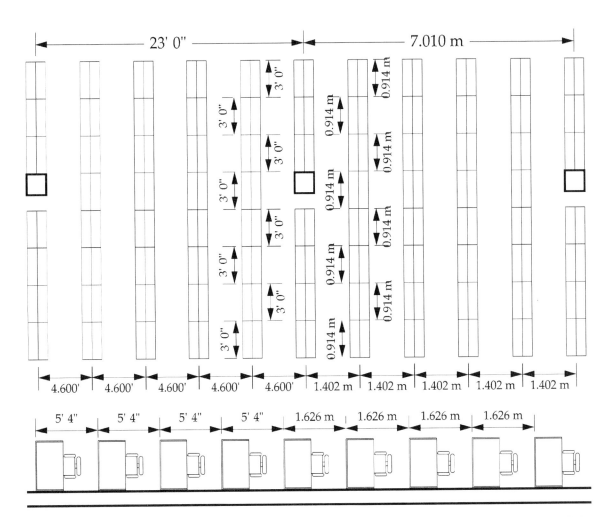

FIGURE 5.4 **"On centers" refers to equal spacing between objects, either relative to the center of the object (as illustrated with the building columns and range centers), or from the edge of one object to the edge of the next (as with the sections of shelving and carrels). In all cases, the objects can be said to be dimensioned "on centers."**

3. It simplifies supervision and reduces construction error, as much of the work is routine.
4. It should improve the finished product because more of the work can be done under factory controls rather than field conditions.
5. It provides more flexible space adaptable for any purpose.
6. Where prefabrication is anticipated, standardization with a modular design is essential, and in most other cases it facilitates some of the planning processes.

By the time the program is being written, the administration should have decided whether it wishes to require the use of a module system. The program writer should hesitate to give definite instructions to the architect, unless there is some special reason for it. Usually, if the module system is to be used, the architect should propose the dimensions and say whether or not the bays should be square. The program, however, can properly outline the need to analyze the alternatives, with the involvement of the architect and other consultants. Factors to be considered can also be detailed, including information on the anticipated dimensions of shelving units, a range of acceptable aisle spacing, the desire to include modular division for other functions (such as offices or faculty studies), and the extent of flexibility desired. There may be zones of the building that are treated differently, especially if large areas are to be assigned to special functions or unique stacks, such as archival storage, map rooms, or movable shelving.

The program writer is urged to find other specific requirements that should be established early in the project by reading Chapters 6 and 7 and appendix B, where various modular considerations are discussed. In many cases it will be sufficient simply to state the requirement to establish a module suitable to the most frequent library spacing conditions and the structural and mechanical needs of the building.

5.3.6 Security

Security in libraries takes many forms, ranging from sophisticated intrusion alarms to concern about the use of windows. Planning for a secure facility will include aspects of layout and internal arrangements, where there may be several interior zones with varying degrees of security.

Other aspects include the book control and charge-out system, exit alarms, book-detection systems, panic buttons, emergency phones, fire pull boxes, sprinkler systems, and radio systems. Use of "smart" building controls are particularly helpful for security conditions. Such factors as the speed with which police or fire personnel respond to an alarm, the hours of operation, the exposure to vandalism, the value of the collections, and the philosophy of how the library should serve the user can all play a role in shaping security aspects of the facility. Because many of these factors change with time, provision for flexible response to security needs is of considerable importance.

In developing the program requirements for security, the following general aspects should be considered:

Site aspects. Outside the building, is planting to be maintained so as to minimize places to hide? Are lights to be provided? How do fire trucks or police vehicles approach the building? In most cases these site aspects can be developed as the design progresses, and usually a simple program statement of the need to incorporate security aspects into the design will be sufficient. Such details as a bike rack that permits locking bikes to a solid object might be a specific requirement. Another requirement might be the avoidance of such objects as open fences, columns, or fixed furniture near the main entrance so as to discourage securing bikes where they will influence traffic. External devices for fire annunciation may be required by the fire department; some mention of these, unless they are covered in a published institutional standard, should be made along with any requirements for interior annunciation. Safety kiosks can be useful at well-lit places near major building entrances or crosswalks, for people to call police in any emergency situation.

Structural aspects. The building envelope, or shell, warrants consideration. In some cases, the use of glass is an invitation to vandalism. However, the psychological cost of a windowless building is great, and the institution that feels it must have solid, window-free walls is unfortunate. Windows that can be opened offer easy removal of library materials without control. Reading porches near ground level amount to another building entrance, and remember that students rise to challenges so that even a second-floor porch is an invitation.

Where glass is desired but vandalism is great, glazing materials, such as laminated glass or Lexan, can add significantly to the security, but will also add significantly to the cost. Tempered glass may seem like it is stronger than normal glass, but it is not; tempering simply makes the glass break into small pieces rather than large shards. Smaller windows are of course less expensive to replace if broken; one may have to wait a month or two for delivery of a large-sized replacement. To a large measure, energy concerns may dictate the amount of glass permitted. Local building codes may also help determine the maximum and minimum glazing.

Where the library is to be an addition to another building, roof hatches and rooftop mechanical systems will need to be carefully considered for required service access, which may also present security problems. Air intakes that are accessible to a pedestrian may represent an invitation for a smoke or stink bomb. Remember that student pranks are traditional and that mass student protests and riots have occurred periodically in all countries throughout history.

Entrance doors often are double doors with panic hardware on the inside. Such doors always represent a security problem as, unless there is an astragal or a separate lock of some kind at the floor or overhead frame, they can easily be opened with the simplest of tools. With an astragal on double doors, there is nearly always a problem of banging or having the doors close out of sequence such that one leaf is not fully closed. One good solution where double doors are considered desirable is to make the exit arrangements such that they are not a required exit. In this case most code authorities will permit a form of positive locking so that the doors cannot be opened without a key. A second solution is to have several single doors rather than double doors. Even with panic hardware, single doors are far more secure than a double door.

Emergency exit doors that normally would be locked, which in many cases must always be free opening from the inside, should have a local buzzer or bell type of alarm. There are a number of examples where the local authorities have permitted a lock release delay system (such as the Von Duprin) that may improve security at exit doors. With this type of system, the lock will not release for a brief period unless the fire alarm has been activated, in which case the door immediately releases. Some argue that this system negates some of the principles of an emergency exit, particularly for a person being physically accosted.

In a large library where a high probability exists that staff will not hear the local alarm at the exit door, a remote alarm and an annunciator panel will indicate the particular door that has been compromised. The remote alarm should be set up so that if a key is used to open the secured door, the alarm does not go off, or the indication of alarm is simply a blinking light. The remote annunciator panel will need to be located in an area certain to be staffed during all hours of operation. After hours, this alarm can be transmitted to a central communication or campus security office.

Internal aspects. Internal arrangements, previously discussed in terms of functions, can also have considerable influence on security. Some libraries have a goal for all areas of the stack to be within sight of staffed positions. Although this may be extreme, and even impossible in a large library, some aspects of this notion are beneficial. Major service points should be within sight of each other, and some reading accommodation should be provided in a supervised area. Usually greater supervision is found in reference, current periodicals, and general reading areas on the main floor. Stack reading areas should probably be large enough to ensure their use by several readers at any given time, but not so large that they become overwhelming seas of carrels or tables. Where the security of readers in the stacks is a great concern, television monitors may be warranted in selected locations. The librarians may prefer to schedule reshelving during the evening to increase security or to finance a group of roving proctors, perhaps students, to frequent the more remote reading areas. Even though proctors are an expensive solution, many will argue that they are more socially acceptable and even more effective than television monitors. However, some libraries, including the Perry-Castañeda Library at the University of Texas at Austin, have found television to be effective when the monitors are located at the staffed exit-control portals in full public view. To plan on the basis of human security may prove expensive to change; building flexibility may be reduced.

Determination of whether the point of control will be at the building entrance, department entrance, or stack entrance is in part a security decision. At the University of Chicago Regenstein Library, provision for portal booths was made both at the stack entrance and off the lobby. The building opened with the control point at the stack entrance, but after a rash of arson attempts and vandalism, the control point was moved to the lobby. Flexibility to make such a change may be a prudent program requirement. If nothing else, conduit might be stubbed out to permit such a change with minimal utility and signal alterations.

Many libraries have a book detection system. Several different systems are on the market, and each has slightly different facility requirements. The major distinction is a matter of permanent book targets or targets that can be shielded or disarmed as part of the charge-out process. In either case, a library book that is not properly processed, either by being passed around the detection device or by being deactivated, will set off an alarm, lock a gate, or both when it is removed from the library. If there is any reasonable expectation that such a system will be required, conduit access to power should be provided. Representatives of the manufacturer can be helpful in regard to layouts and utility requirements. Some systems work best where there is clear separation from photocopy machines and computer terminals. Most of this work can be done in later design stages, but the basic requirement for such a system should be established in the program.

Where a large library is being planned, there will probably be staffed areas that are not centrally located. In this case remote service points can become very lonely and seem rather dangerous, especially if staffed by a timid soul. A panic button system may be one way of providing psychological or actual security for isolated staff. When pushed, the panic alarm should sound at a central location staffed during all hours of operation. It should not be so loud that the entire library will be disturbed. Then, according to policy, the police can be called, a staff member can call the panicked person to get a description of the nature of the concern, or a staff member can visit the site of the incident. In the event there is more than one panic button, an annunciator to determine the location of each activated panic button is required. Also for personal security, duress alarms are sometimes placed in women's rest rooms so, in case a woman feels threatened, she can send an alarm. With regard to monitoring remote parts of a library, one possibility is an audio system activated by noise above a certain

threshold, so a scream or other loud noise opens two-way communication for service desk staff to hear what is happening and respond to it. (See also comments regarding vandalism and injury in Section 13.2.5.)

The local fire code probably requires fire alarm pull boxes at specific intervals within the building. These too, according to policy, can be used in a panic situation. Public phones at obvious or central locations throughout the building aid this form of security as well. However, experience with intercom systems or a house phone system indicates that they are seldom used, that maintenance of privately owned phone systems is usually difficult, and that eventually they fall to total disuse. Phones in the library generally ought to be those provided and maintained by the local telephone company, or by a reputable company with a demonstrated record of excellent service.

A public address system, if strictly limited to defined uses, such as closing and genuine emergencies, is a useful security device in a library. In a large facility care should be taken to keep phone lines and speaker lines electromagnetically isolated. Long runs of phone lines with a public address system can in certain circumstances result in the broadcasting of phone conversations or the clicking of phone equipment. At closing time a public address system is particularly useful for clearing the building of readers. The largest libraries must often rely on such a system combined with intrusion alarms, as the stack area may be so vast that clearing the building by a staff walk-through is virtually impossible. If a public address system is to be part of the building project, its operational location and the distribution of speakers should be generally addressed in the program. Staff areas and small public service units probably do not need to be covered separately, if other emergency signals can be heard in them. Where there are a number of enclosed studies, it may not be economical to include each of them within the system, and the speaker system will usually penetrate offices and other small rooms if the speakers are properly located. Major stack and associated reading areas are certainly candidates for such treatment.

The program or institutional standards should be quite specific about the documentation required for any systems, particularly electrical and mechanical systems. Without proper documentation of the various features, future maintenance and repairs will be difficult at best. An operations manual, including maintenance instructions, detailed wire labeling, and wiring diagrams, should be required of the contractor and engineers by the contract documents.

Some institutions prefer not to define in writing the details of intrusion alarms too specifically. These systems generally are a combination of motion detectors and door contacts, although many other devices may be employed. Several varieties of motion detectors are in common use in libraries, including ultrasonic, radar, infrared, and light beam detectors. Each device has its weaknesses and strong points, and each situation will require special consideration. Requirements for a display area for rare books may include special laminated glass, vibration detectors in the cases, weight sensors at each display, and motion detectors within the space. In some cases television surveillance or a guard may be appropriate, as is the case at the University of Texas at Austin, Ransom Humanities Research Center where a Gutenberg Bible is on display. The field of intrusion alarms is changing rapidly with changing technology. Because of this, it is recommended that where such devices are deemed essential, a security consultant should be added to the design team. The program then should state the security requirement for alarm systems in general terms only, and the contract documents in regard to intrusion alarms should only detail conduit runs, outlets, and phone line sites. The actual security devices should be contracted for separately, probably from the firm that will maintain them. This procedure is recommended because of the fairly large and often public distribution of the general contract documents. Where security is a serious concern, the documentation should be more limited. However, there should indeed be documentation just as there is for all the other building systems.

Fire protection. Fire protection is another aspect of security. As with pull boxes, other aspects of fire protection will be established by local codes. Usually included in the code is a table of maximum floor areas for specific methods of construction. Generally the floor area allowed is larger where there is a positive means of fire protection, such as a fire suppression system.

Several types of fire suppression systems exist involving both water and gas. Water-based systems are generally the recommended approach to fire suppression; gas systems are expensive, less reliable, and difficult in other ways. Some gas-based systems are essentially lethal (CO_2). Those that are not lethal involve gas that is very costly, or that is difficult to obtain (Halon, the use of which is no longer legal in new systems; FM200 and FE-13, which are near replacements for Halon; and, to a lessor degree, Imeron, which is composed of elements that occur naturally in air—the latter three costing up to $5.50 or more per cubic foot or $0.19 per liter of space to install). The installation cost for a gas-based fire protection system with an 8-ft (2,438-m) ceiling can thus be in the order of $44 per ft^2 or $473 per m^2—expensive enough to suggest that use in libraries will be very limited.

The major features of gas-based systems include the following:

- Gas-based systems are effective at fighting hidden fires or fires involving electrical equipment. Halon, for this reason, has often been found in major computer installations.
- Halon was originally developed for use in submarines. As a system that can be relatively nonlethal, such an application makes a lot of sense. FM200 is a close substitute that can achieve similar results. For certain applications, FE-13 and FE-36 are also reasonable substitutes for Halon, the latter being available in handheld extinguishers.
- A completely sealed space is required for Halon, FM200, and FE-13 suppression; Imeron requires initial venting of the space (to allow enough space for the gas being introduced), followed with complete sealing of the space after about one minute. To be effective, this involves careful design of the mechanical system, doors, and other features. As the gas itself is expensive, facilities that are designed based on gas fire protection are usually broken up into a number of small spaces separated by fire walls.
- Interconnections with duct louvers and magnetic door hold-open devices are also required so that when smoke is detected, the space is sealed, the gas is released, and a fire signal is sounded.
- If a fire starts in an adjacent space and burns through the wall, a suppression system based upon a specific volume of space will no longer work in the resulting larger space.
- The fire might reignite once the gas dissipates. Generally, gas-based systems have a single charge adequate to deal with one fire circumstance; subsequent reignition can only be dealt

with using fire hoses. The gas does not remove combustible materials, and it may do little to cool down the fire site. Many fire regulations require that a fire site be wetted down following suppression by a gas-based fire system. Once combustible material is soaked, it is far less likely to reignite. Thus even a gas-based system does not guarantee absence of water during a fire, and application of water by fire hose is far more damaging than application by overhead sprinkler.

- Accidental discharge is not uncommon. Once discharged, the system is no longer able to suppress a subsequent fire until it is re-charged at a current cost of US$3 to $6 per square foot (or US$32 to $65 per square meter). Halon substitutes are substantially more expensive.
- Halon is a form of Freon, which is banned in most parts of the world because of environmental impact. Although some of the substitutes will address this problem, they are not fully compatible with existing Halon systems; most require higher concentration of gas, and some are toxic. FM200 (made by Great Lakes Chemical Corporation) currently appears to be the closest current replacement for Halon; it is nontoxic and it does not harm the atmosphere. It is also said to have the capacity to extinguish a fire in a matter of seconds. FE-13 is a Halon replacement made by Du Pont that may be specified for spaces with high ceilings or in areas that can get very cold; although there may be uses in libraries, it is generally not the current choice of fire protection engineers. FE-36, also from Du Pont, is only used in handheld portable extinguishers. FE-36 is the only agent currently available in handheld extinguishers that simulates the function of Halon. Imeron is said to be nontoxic in the concentrations specified for fire suppression, but, at higher concentrations, it can be toxic. Imeron takes substantially more space for storage of the gas, and, as much more gas is required for fire suppression, it takes longer to put the fire out.

A Halon system once was regarded as the best fire suppression system available. Few libraries have been able to afford Halon or its substitutes for more than very limited space containing their most valuable materials. Concern about reliability, concern about having enough gas on hand for repeated ignition of a fire, concern about human access to the fire scene, concern about effective and meaningful testing, concern about excellent design to fully support a gas-based suppression system, and concern for the methods of fire suppression once the gas is spent—these all suggest that a fairly standard, easily designed, reliable water-based system is the best approach to fire protection, even in most rare book libraries. The application of a gas-based system is additionally questionable in most circumstances because of the high probability of fire control with fire hoses.

Although many librarians remain strongly against the use of a water-based fire sprinkler system, the authors are convinced that the potential fire damage in a library without a sprinkler system substantially exceeds the potential water damage from sprinklers. However, we would be the first to admit that where there is water, someday there will probably be a flood. With modern techniques of freeze drying, flood damage can be limited. Fire damage, on the other hand, results in absolute loss. The likelihood of a fire is almost as certain over the years as an accidental flood caused by sprinklers, and the absence of sprinklers by no means guarantees an absence of flooding.

Several things can be done to limit the flood effects of sprinkler systems. First, it should be understood that, unlike gas systems, when sprinkler heads go off, they do so individually as the heat of the fire melts a fusable link or otherwise activates individual sprinkler heads. Short of a roaring inferno, which is unlikely with an operational sprinkler system, few heads are ever likely to be set off simultaneously. When one sprinkler head goes off, a water flow switch activates the fire alarm, which in most cases results in rapid response by the campus security service and the local fire department. Officials then can turn off the water as soon as it is determined there is no fire danger or, in the case of flow-control heads or a Firecycle system (a proprietary system from Viking), the system or heads are shut down automatically as the area cools down.

Water detection devices placed at various locations about the floor, such as under bottom shelves, further reduce the risk of loss due to flooding. These devices may be as simple as a fixture containing a sponge that swells when wet to activate a microswitch. Floor drains, particularly in basement areas, often lead to sumps where a high-water alarm can be provided. None of these alarms will be effective unless they link to a remote annunciator at a communications center staffed to respond to alarms 24 hours a day.

Perhaps the most useful alarm system is the product-of-combustion, or smoke detection, system. In the event of a fire, the system devices, if properly distributed, will usually detect smoke and activate an alarm several minutes before the heat buildup is sufficient to set off a sprinkler. In many cases this means the security service or fire department will be on the scene before the fire activates a sprinkler head. An air sampling detection system, though it costs more, is said to be even more sensitive to products of combustion, resulting in the most rapid response possible to the start of a fire. Air sampling detection systems are designed to check the number of particles per unit of air of a size found in smoke (which are much smaller than dust particles).

Several different kinds of sprinkler systems exist. The most common is the one that has been implied in the preceding discussion. It is always filled, or "charged," with water under pressure, and, once a head is activated, the entire sprinkler zone must be turned off to replace the head and stop the water flow. Special wedges can be used to stop the flow of an individual head manually, but they are not very practical in most cases.

Another system, which has been in use in the Bancroft Library at the University of California, Berkeley, the Music Library at Stanford University, and Western Illinois University at Macomb, is a pre-action system that requires both the activation of a product-of-combustion detection system and a sprinkler head before water is present in the space. In this case the sprinkler feeder line is charged with compressed air. Water enters the system only when smoke is detected, and it is released only after the heat buildup activates a sprinkler head. Such a system can be further refined by adding sprinkler heads that turn themselves off when the temperature drops (this is the "flow-control" head mentioned earlier). In the past these heads had a tendency to leak and were usually not recommended for libraries, but it is the authors' understanding that more recently these heads have become fully reliable. In any case, even if they leak slightly as they might after activation, they result in a minimum of water flow in the event of a fire, and it does not take long to replace a head following an event. It should be noted, however, that not every fire authority will permit the use of such heads; they may not carry the full endorsement of the Fire

Underwriters. The concern of fire authorities is that they may cool the fire down, but not put it out and not have enough flow to trigger a fire alarm. The concern is that in this mode, a fire could continue for considerable time without complete elimination. Where allowed, such heads may make a lot of sense, especially in combination with a pre-action system (which should set off an alarm when the system is charged with water, thereby eliminating the concern about a lingering fire without an alarm).

Other fire protection conditions are important, too. Mechanical systems need to be designed to separate major areas in the event of a fire and to exhaust smoke while limiting the provision of fresh air in a fire zone. Compartmentalization can be an important concept in fire resistant construction; however, without additional fire protection devices, the risk of loss due to fire is only reduced to the size of the compartment. Finally, the reduction of combustible materials in libraries will reduce fire risk. If it is decided not to install sprinklers, then the designer should question the use of such items as wood furniture or book trucks, carpets, combustible drapes, and combustible wall or ceiling surfaces. In a library oriented toward people, this decision may be difficult to face.

Managing the Library Fire Risk by John Morris describes in considerable detail the risks and options for fire security. If you are undecided about what the fire protection requirements should be, this book can be a great asset. The program document should state all expectations at least in terms of general security requirements. Local fire codes also specify the use of fire retardant materials, and may limit the use of materials, such as polyurethane, that give off toxic fumes when smoldering.

5.3.7 Interior Design Concerns

Much of this book addresses interior design concerns from various points of view. A basic design criterion is that reasonable personal comfort should be achieved by conditions that enable the occupant to be unaware of such matters as air quality, drafts, lighting, glare, visual and auditory distraction, and chair and table configuration, and to use the library while being oblivious to the physical surroundings. Indeed, the physical surroundings ideally would promote and improve the quality of research or other work in the library.

Specific aspects that might be established in the program, aside from detailed space requirements, include acoustic quality, ergonomic issues (including the provision of adjustability), durability of surfaces and furniture, the desire for mock-ups of especially important features (such as lighting, service desks, or carrel arrangements), who is to do furniture layouts, the general "feel" of the space desired by the institution, and whether an interior consultant will have defined contractual responsibilities.

The architectural and functional qualities of the library will be greatly influenced by the interior design, and, obviously, the interior design will need to reflect these desired qualities. A building, even if handsome to look upon, will always be regarded unfavorably by users if it is not successful functionally, just as will one that is successful functionally but unattractive or so extreme in its architecture that it becomes outdated while still new. This does not mean that a good library building must be traditional in style; quite the contrary—the use of imagination and a contemporary outlook in the planning and design may make a significant contribution toward the success of the building. Indeed, the building should reflect the period of its construction, even if outwardly it is Georgian, colonial, or gothic in style.

Architectural propriety, aesthetics, and the interior design for a new building are governed to some extent by the financial situation. Funding capacity will significantly influence space in terms of quality and quantity. To avoid controversy, it is suggested that the architect be told when selected that *the institution wants as handsome a building as possible, inside and out, but that there is a definite limit to available funds; within these limits the requirements stated in the program must be met and the results must be functionally satisfactory.*

Several basic conditions are desirable in the interior arrangements of any library. The interior should be a comfortable place in which to study. In staff areas, consideration should be given to alternative arrangements and business practices that reduce repetitive motion. Workstations should be broadly adjustable not only to provide ideal conditions to any individual, but so an individual can change posture from time to time. The interior should be well ventilated, well lighted, and quiet, but not silent. A feeling of restlessness in the public areas should be avoided as should one of deadness. The space should be so arranged that good library service can be provided easily, quickly, and inexpensively. It should have sufficient flexibility or adaptability to allow changing operations or other features as the library evolves. The space should be designed with materials and features that support preservation of the collections (see appendix D for details on this topic). Finally, it should have a layout in which users can find their way around with ease. These various factors may differ in importance in different parts of the building, according to the specific activity in each part.

Even when the architect is not to do the interior design, the goals of the institution should be established, and the program represents an excellent starting point. However, interior arrangements and selection will be influenced by the architectural design; thus, any statement is likely to be altered as the design progresses.

The desired "feel" of a space is at best difficult to establish in words. Words such as *inviting, stimulating, low-key, quiet, durable, pleasant, easy to maintain, vandal resistant, student proof, conducive to research or reading,* and *comfortable* are common descriptions of the desired effect. Some librarians might prefer bold, bright colors, and others more subtle hues. An art librarian might wish an absence of color so as to provide a minimum of contrasting stimuli for the color found in the art books, prints, and other materials. Color is certainly one of the most important aesthetic features of any space. Libraries in the past were too often drab in their general effect. The walls, the bookstacks, floors, and furniture all tended to have an institutional aspect. This conventionality was completely unnecessary. Different colors on different walls of a room can give an effect of larger size. Bookstacks of different colors on different levels can add to attractiveness, to say nothing of making it easier for students who go to sleep to recognize where they are when they wake up. Bright colors, some argue, stimulate students and more study results. Others claim that such conditions are distracting and that quieter colors are more suitable in a library. A mixture of strong colors in some areas and quiet ones in others may provide an acceptable compromise. It is likely that the direction will not be clearly established in the program, but where there is a local or an institutional philosophy, some statement should be made. The matter is for local decision, and that decision is not necessarily totally irrevocable. Repainting, after all, is possible.

Texture is another factor that influences aesthetics. Carpet adds this texture as well as softness and acoustic qualities. Other materials, largely because of their texture, can also make a space feel richer. The use of brick, wood, fabric panels, exposed concrete in its many forms, acoustic ceiling materials, and smooth hard surfaces, such as glass, chrome, painted gypsum board, or plaster, all will shape the aesthetic quality of the building.

Scale is still another aspect of aesthetics. Together with proportion, scale can make a space feel too large or too small. An excellent example of the effect of scale may be seen in the Philadelphia City Hall where all aspects of the building are of a giant scale; the net result is that the building at first glance looks much smaller than it really is. This quality is particularly deceptive from a distance where it looks like it should be a short walk to the building, but it may be a mile or more. The same quality can be experienced with interior space where a standard brick wall will look like a larger surface than a wall made of cinder blocks or elements of a larger discernible dimension. This fact has been used historically in church architecture to interesting effect.

Lighting can affect scale and highlight texture to alter the mood of a space. All these factors can serve as relief during tedious hours of reading. A view to the outside can often do much the same.

It would not be proper to establish strict guidelines for these factors in the program. Such elements as color, texture, light, scale, and proportion will evolve as the design progresses. The program might state, however, that carpet, for example, is a desirable feature, that an exterior outlook from reading areas is desired, or that reading areas should not be so large as to be overwhelming. Where typing or conversation is anticipated, acoustic separation of spaces may be a program requirement. The heating, ventilation, and air-conditioning needs discussed later certainly represent a requirement. Durability and flexibility obviously are important.

The question of having built-in or freestanding furniture is important. Freestanding furniture usually results in greater flexibility to respond to change while built-in furniture usually has a quality of being more strongly related to the design and thus "belonging." Typing surfaces generally transmit less noise if they are freestanding. However, a small enclosed carrel or workstation uses space more efficiently if the work surface is built

in. In most cases the decision can wait for later stages in the design, but where the use of existing furniture is anticipated, it is important to establish this in the program. In this case thought should also be given to whether any or all of the existing furniture is to be refinished to more nearly match the new decor. There may be furniture especially associated with some aspect of the library that will need special consideration as part of the design. This is quite common for rare book rooms, though other areas may be involved as well. Some institutions may require that certain furnishings or even all furnishings must come from a specific source. The California State University system, for example, once required that its furniture be produced by the penal industries in the state. Other institutions may have selected a specific carrel, book truck, or other element that should be matched exactly.

Another important aspect, related to both space in general and interior design, is the design of the directional, informational, and emergency signs and graphics, often called "signage." Most building graphics should be sympathetic with the building and its furniture, but not blend in to the degree that they are not noticed. Perhaps the most important programmatic aspect of graphics is to establish the scope of the work and who is to prepare the text and undertake the design and installation.

Library signs, or graphics, represent a challenge. There is always more information to be conveyed to the user than there are appropriate graphic devices to use. Care must be taken to avoid graphic clutter. A graphics system that can easily be adapted to change at reasonable cost is usually a requirement. A directory that can only be changed at considerable expense will no doubt always be out of date. Names on rooms, diagrams of stack arrangements, campus maps showing branch libraries, and bins holding library handouts will all change. The ideal arrangement is to have a system that can be maintained by the library or, in the case of a small college, within the institution. Without this capability, graphics problems will almost certainly be constant.

Room numbering generally is not thought about until the end of the project. However, if nothing is said, the architect will establish room numbers in the contract documents that usually will not relate to the final room numbering scheme. This way of work almost always leads to confusion during the final stages of the project, when the phone company is looking for a room designated on the drawings as B16, but labeled on the door as 103. Movers and workers in other trades will have the same problem, which can be easily avoided if the architect is required by the program to establish a room numbering schedule compatible with the library and institution.

Artwork in or on the exterior of the building helps create the design "feel," the aesthetic character. There is no doubt that the eight-story Jerome Library mural that has dominated the Bowling Green University campus since 1966 creates a style signature. The works of art add markedly to the feel of libraries at Mount Holyoke College, Rollins College, and the universities of Central Florida, North Carolina (at Chapel Hill), and Oregon, and UCLA's Powell Library. The sculptural space of the huge oval canted window at Southern Utah University's library is architectural art. Such features of the building are not spaces, yet they should be defined in the program as to importance, magnitude, frequency, or other factors to convey to the architect the expectations of the institution. Otherwise the architect or interior designer may be given a budget and a mandate to add art as deemed appropriate. (See related budget comments in Section 9.2.3.)

Other aspects of interior concern are found either in this section, the following section, or Chapter 6. While much of the interior design will and should evolve with the project, those aspects deemed important enough to be general requirements of the project should be established clearly in the program.

5.3.8 Environmental Control

Any building will create a controlled environment to some degree. However, without thoughtful specification, the nature of the environment may discourage use of the facility or promote deterioration of the materials housed. Appendix D provides specific guidelines and an extended discussion of the various issues of environmental control.

In planning an environmentally functional building, two essential points must be considered. The balance of this section discusses in greater detail the two issues with emphasis on the first, as this is a topic with which the designer may not be familiar.

First, the building should provide quarters that will as far as possible ensure the preservation of the collections. Proper atmospheric conditions—temperature, humidity control, filtered air, and the control of light—are important here. Other issues of interest to those concerned about extending the life of the collections are fire protection systems, the selection of building interior materials to minimize the off-gassing of damaging chemicals, flood protection, the design of the book return system, the control of food in the library, and other similar design and operational issues. Optimum conditions of environmental control can be expensive, both in terms of initial cost and in terms of operating cost. It must be decided how much emphasis on such matters is warranted by the quality of the collections, the nature of local weather patterns, air pollution levels, and preservation goals of the library. The presence of rare and irreplaceable materials, particularly in a humid industrial region or in a region with wide changes or extremes in temperature and humidity, should make the answer obvious.

Second, comfort of the readers and staff will need attention in any new facility. Although we have all experienced difficult environmental conditions, and can usually continue to function, it is clear that the efficiency of staff and scholars will be improved as the environment approaches ideal conditions. Preservation and comfort, taken at their ideal levels, are not always compatible. Some level of compromise will probably be necessary.

Paper produced over the last two hundred years of rising industrial technology has been subject to the impact of temperature and humidity. Most readers no doubt have observed the effect of leaving the daily newspaper out in the sun for a day or two. Although much of the discoloration is caused by light, heat is also involved. If left in such conditions for a longer period, the paper will become so brittle that it will fragment when touched. The same is happening, although much more slowly, to the vast majority of the collections held in libraries. Microfilm, magnetic tapes, and other library materials are also subject to deterioration due to poor environmental conditions.

It has become increasingly apparent over the past two decades that the majority of library materials are also slowly being destroyed by abrasion and chemical reactions encouraged by light, air pollution, biological infestations, temperature, humidity, and acids in the papers commonly used by the publishing industry. In testimony on behalf of the National Conservation Advisory Council to the Department of Energy as reported in *His-*

tory News, May 1980, Peter Waters said: "Fluctuating temperatures and relative humidities . . . inevitably trigger chemical reactions in paper and binding materials, expressed in rapid acceleration of hydrolytic and oxidative energy. For example, at 68° F. (20° C.) and 50% RH [relative humidity] we can calculate that a particular paper may have a life expectancy of two hundred years. At 95° F. (35° C.) and 50% humidity, the life expectancy is reduced to about sixteen years. At 50° F. (10° C.) and 50% RH, its life expectancy is increased to 1,260 years."

More recently, Donald K. Sebera at the Library of Congress developed the concept of the "isoperm," a unit measuring the effect upon the life expectancy of paper based on chemical reactions within the paper itself (found in *Isoperms: An Environmental Management Tool,* Commission on Preservation and Access, June 1994). See appendix D for a discussion of the isoperm as well as a table of isoperm values as prepared by Sebera. In that discussion it can be seen that the isoperm is a very powerful tool for justifying appropriate temperature and humidity values because of their long-term effect on the life of the collections. If you are considering preservation-based environmental criteria, review appendix D with care.

Even where preservation issues form a solid foundation for setting environmental criteria, the limiting factor for temperature and sometimes humidity control is usually related to the comfort of people or to the cost of energy. In a library where books and people are closely associated, the temperature minimum should be that of a reasonable minimal comfort level for readers who must remain relatively inactive for hours at a time. Typically, the ideal temperature range for this condition is specified as 68° to 72° F. (20° to 22° C.). However, local customs of clothing and other factors can influence this range. At the lower end of the comfort range, drafts can result in a sense of coldness lower than the actual temperature, a circumstance that is greater with lower humidity. A person sitting under an air register creating a draft will feel cold even though the temperature is accurately maintained at 70° F. or 21° C. Conversely, a space with no perceptible air movement or with higher humidity will feel stuffy when temperatures rise in the summer even though engineering calculations demonstrate sufficient air changes.

In a closed collection, such as a typical archive or collection of rare materials or perhaps a book

storage facility, the minimum temperature is more related to concern for condensation when materials are removed for use in a warmer room. Here, if one can be reasonably certain that the temperature in the reading room will not exceed 76° F., or 24.5° C., with an RH of 50 percent, then the storage temperature could be as low as 57° F., or 14° C. Lower storage temperatures are, of course, possible, but special consideration for the removal of materials for use will be required.

The energy cost for creating an environment suitable for reasonable preservation of library materials is often significant, particularly where an older building is being used to house major collections. Much can be done to reduce this cost, including installing superior insulation as well as the glazing; using structural mass to absorb heat (as in a cave); providing a good seal at windows, doors, and construction joints; and reducing the quantity of heat sources within the controlled space. For example, the 1973 University of Toronto Robarts Research Library was given 12-in. (305-mm) concrete walls to meet common winter conditions of −10° F. (−23° C.) and 28 percent RH without developing interior surface condensation; its Fisher Rare Book Library was designed to accept 40 percent RH minimum for preservation of collections; and some walls were precast with a separate insulation liner wall.

The calculation of energy use for a given facility is complex; it is best left to a mechanical engineer. However, the program statement outlining environmental conditions relating to preservation should not be made without the realization that there will be associated cost. It is because of this that a compromise will often be reached during the design process. Clearly, the priorities and goals of the institution must be well established before such a compromise is considered.

Another preservation concern is air pollution. Nearly all impurities, both gaseous and particulate, are harmful to books. For libraries located in regions with urban air pollution, the gaseous pollutants are likely to be the more serious problem. Of particular concern are sulfur dioxide, nitrogen oxides, and ozone, although other pollutants can cause deterioration of library materials. Do not assume that a library in a rural area is free of pollutants as there are indeed natural sources of air pollution. Particulate matter is perhaps a more superficial problem than the oxidizing and reducing gases (depending upon its chemical composition). Still, all dust has sharp edges and, together with perspiration and skin oils, will cause disfiguring damage over time. Maintenance costs for dusting shelves and books are, of course, reduced with proper filtration of the air.

Clearly, some form of air filtration should be considered in most libraries for both preservation and maintenance. A considerable array of filtration forms is available, including fabric, cyclone, electrostatic, alkaline water sprays, and activated carbon. Because of the production of ozone, electrostatic precipitation should be avoided in libraries. It should be noted that the Library of Congress does not permit the use of oil or viscous impingement filters because of concern for the production of polluting aerosols. Pollution levels and filtration are also treated with greater detail in appendix D.

As already suggested, light can also cause accelerated deterioration of library materials. The degree of deterioration is related to the intensity, duration, and spectral characteristics of the light. Years ago the original manuscript of the United States Declaration of Independence was displayed where it was exposed to indirect sunlight. As a result it is nearly illegible today, thus serving as an excellent example of deterioration caused by light.

The preservation aspects of light are perhaps as important as the comfort aspects. Although most light is converted to heat, library preservation experts suggest special concern for the effect of that critical fraction of light that is responsible for photocatalyzed degradation. The activation energy level of light from the ultraviolet end of the spectrum is considerably more damaging than the infrared end of the range. It is interesting to note that most fluorescent light tends to have a far greater component of ultraviolet than do incandescent sources, though variation between specific bulb brand and type can be significant.

In areas where this is a justified concern, fluorescent tubes with filtering lenses or tube-type filter shields can be specified to minimize the ultraviolet component. The architect should also select the particular fluorescent bulb based upon ultraviolet output data, which can be obtained from the manufacturer; it is a mistake to assume that the name alone indicates superior quality in terms of ultraviolet output without supporting data. The same "warm white" from different manufacturers will have quite different ultraviolet output.

In determining the specification for the various forms of ultraviolet control, maintenance routines should be reviewed. Special fluorescent tubes, for example, look like normal tubes even though they can cost five times as much. The institution's maintenance department may simply not replace them with the original specification, or a natural mistake could be made and never detected. Some experts claim the tube type of filter shield has a limited life expectancy; however, if the lights are off most of the time, this should not be a serious factor. Their advantage is that they can be seen. Thus the responsible librarian should be able to easily determine the status of ultraviolet protection. Probably the best protection is through the use of special lenses that provide the appropriate ultraviolet filtration, but such a requirement may preclude a superior light fixture that does not have a lens to provide filtration. When preservation is a concern, the lighting consultant or electrical engineer should also determine the spectrum of other light sources, such as metal and quartz halide fixtures. In all cases, the arrangement of the collections should never allow direct sunlight to fall on shelved materials unless preservation is not a concern.

Deterioration resulting from exposure to light can easily be reduced to a minimum through various other means. Although there is a distinct cost, individual range aisle switching in the stacks dramatically reduces the time of exposure for shelved materials. Such a system often can be justified on the basis of energy conservation. A low-voltage switching system or other device may be desirable to permit turning off or on all the lights from one or more central points. One advantage of low-voltage switching is that where electrical consumption is monitored in the interest of minimizing peak loads, it is a relatively simple matter to turn off all the range aisle lights as the power use approaches a predetermined level. Then, the library patron can simply return to the range end to turn on currently needed lights. With increasing public awareness of energy cost, such a system may be considered an extravagance if one assumes strict patterns of turning lights off when they are no longer needed.

Another switching system that has been suggested by energy consultants utilizes timers for the range aisle lighting. Such a system is probably fine in a closed-stack or warehouse facility, but it could lead to considerable frustration in an open-stack area. With proper staff training, use of timers in the closed-stack area may be considered an extravagance. Another arrangement is motion-activated range aisle lighting, which has to work from both open ends of the aisle. This motion-sensing system must be designed to work as a person steps in to use the first section in the aisle and yet not be so sensitive that every aisle lights up as people merely walk down the main aisle.

An instance is the Richter Library, University of Miami, which in the early 1990s converted to sensors in the middle of stack range aisles, supplemented with some permanent lights on the cross aisles. Originally Richter had stack lights controlled by a central switch located alongside the elevators. Because all stack lights were therefore on whenever the building was open, the electrical cost was high, and aisle "string-pull" switches were added in the early 1980s. Yet users tended to leave lights on, and janitors who cleaned at night typically left all the lights on when they departed—thus the motion sensors. The early 1990s addition to the University of California Southern Regional Library Facility, on the UCLA campus, has well-tuned motion-detection aisle lighting located slightly in from both ends of stack aisles.

Reduction of light levels in reading areas and stacks from levels specified 20 or more years ago is common as institutions have sought energy economies. This change is beneficial from the preservation point of view. Seating can be developed with individually switched task lights permitting lower ambient light levels, which can be an advantage where computers are anticipated, even though some degree of flexibility may be lost. With glare-free lighting, a level of 50 footcandles (say, 500 lux) is quite adequate for most library tasks. Even 35 footcandles (or about 350 lux), if maintained, works well in most cases.

The exact lighting level historically has been a very controversial subject. Lighting intensity, referred to as footcandles, lux, lumens, or lamberts (a lambert equals one lumen per square centimeter and 10.76 lux equals one footcandle, or one lumen, per square foot), should always be measured in terms of "maintained" intensity—that is, the amount available after several months of use, which usually can be estimated at approximately one-third less than in a new installation. The exact amount may vary from 25 percent to 40 percent, depending on the ballasts and fixtures used and how much the ceilings and surrounding surfaces darken as time goes on.

Over the years following the introduction of electric light, recommended light levels contin-

ued to increase in the United States from initial exceedingly dim levels akin to the use of candles and kerosene lamps to equally excessive brightness. As recently as 1970 the authors witnessed lighting in a library rest room that exceeded 180 footcandles (1,936 lux)! With today's energy concerns, the recommended lighting levels are generally returning to a reasonable level. Although there are many variables and caveats that will need thoughtful design input from the architects and engineers, the 1993 edition of the *Illuminating Handbook* (issued by the Illuminating Engineering Society of North America) suggests 5 to 10 footcandles (50–100 lux) for inactive stacks, stairways, corridors, and microtext reading areas; 20 to 50 footcandles (200–500 lux) for active stacks, book repair and binding areas, cataloging, circulation desk, audiovisual areas, and map, picture, or print rooms; and from 20 to 100 footcandles (200–1,000 lux) for reading areas and private offices, depending on the nature of detail, point size of type, age of the readers, and other factors. The program should provide guidance on these conditions.

Design considerations for lighting are discussed in later chapters as the design process is developed. Appendix D should also be consulted for its discussion on light. It should be noted here, though, that in addition to light levels, the quality of light in terms of glare, color, shadows, contrast, and aesthetics is extremely important. Glare especially can render a workstation nearly useless, even though the measured light level is sufficient. Computer monitors with cathode-ray-tube screens are especially affected by glare. Their placement and lighting must be carefully considered in the design process.

The librarian may wish to specify a requirement for a mock-up of the proposed lighting. This can often be done at nominal expense, and it can be very instructive of the nature of the proposed lighting system. The design contract for any major building project should provide for such services as well as additional studies or alterations to the lighting design that result from viewing a mock-up configuration. If such services are not clearly established in the architect's or electrical engineer's contract, there may be subsequent fees for extra services. Although this is not necessarily bad, all concerned should realize the budgetary implications.

Acoustics is one additional aspect that relates to the mechanical/electrical system and thus environmental control, though it has little to do with preservation. It is commonly thought that a library should be quiet, and, in a general sense, this is certainly true. However, a library can be too quiet. When this happens, every turning page or footstep can be heard by others. Sharp noises of any kind will become a distraction that, in the worst case, will render a library useless for more than a very few well-spread-out users. To avoid this circumstance, some level of ambient sound is necessary and desirable. Probably the best form of background sound is the gentle whoosh of air entering the space through the duct system. A system that is exceptionally quiet should be avoided. Where it is anticipated that the mechanical system will be cycled or turned off for limited periods to conserve energy, an electronic white sound system should be considered.

White sound is not always received with enthusiasm; however, it does have a place in library design with the possible exception of music libraries. A common problem with white sound results from a system design that covers all extraneous noise. Such a system generally does not sound good, and it is usually perceived to be too loud. It is suggested that the engineer be required to design a system that can be adjusted in various areas of the building. Such adjustment will permit a variety of acoustic perfume; for those who cannot stand it (which may be 50 percent of the user group) the volume can be placed at a minimal level. For others, reading areas can be provided with somewhat higher levels. It is likely that no one will like a background level that covers all noise; thus, the highest level probably will never be used.

A number of years ago, the sound level was measured in reading spaces at Stanford University. The quietest was found to be about 30 decibels, which was so quiet it was distracting. The level that students regarded as best was about 45 decibels. At that level, quiet conversations, foot traffic, and other unwanted noise were nearly completely masked. The range of 40 to 45 decibels would seem to be a prudent goal for open reading areas. Of course, closed carrels, remote reading spots, and the general stacks can be less. And one would expect the lobby and the staff room might, on occasion, be higher.

In any major library project involving significant reader space, an acoustics engineer should be consulted for both background sound and the control of sound, which, except perhaps for duct insulation, vibration isolation for mechanical equipment, acoustic separation from an adjacent subway system, separation between group studies or classrooms or conference rooms and quiet reading areas, or carefully selected lighting ballasts, is generally related to interior design concerns. When a row of offices shares common walls, special considerations for acoustic isolation should be required.

Concern for such detail at this programming stage of the project may seem excessive. However, if no mention is made of institutional requirements for such things as individual range aisle switching, strict temperature and humidity controls, filtration of ultraviolet light, or appropriate filtration of the air, adding such requirements later in the design process may be regarded as a program improvement with associated increases in design fees and estimated or actual construction cost. Where tight budget control is not a concern, the design team obviously would have the luxury of exploring each of these issues later in the design process. It is more common, though, that a statement of design requirements, or a program, must be established in concert with a fairly fixed project budget. Then any change in the scope of the project must go through an often difficult approval procedure, and trade-offs may be required. Clearly, time spent in formalizing specific requirements at the program stage can and will minimize financial and functional surprises later!

5.3.9 Adaptability and the Support of Technology

One key to adaptability is the ease with which our successors can alter the library to serve new and changed functions, and one of the most pervasive changes currently is and will continue to be the addition of electronic technology, particularly the computer and its telecommunications connectivity. This change is hardly complete, even with the provision of online catalogs and CD-ROM products and computer-supported teaching facilities and a computer cluster for doing Internet searches and homework; technology will continue to change and require new infrastructure well into the future, and the nature of its requirements will change as well. Reasonable steps to assure that such change can be dealt with economically are appropriate and should be required of the program, even though absolute flexibility is seldom possible or practical.

Section 13.4.4 deals with some of the technologies that may be considered. It is quite clear that telephone/data closets must be of substantial size, often approaching office size. They should be stacked one above another to provide easy vertical access. A main phone/data room in a large library may be several times the size of a typical phone/data closet. The capacity to pull wire of many varieties, including fiber-optic cable, to nearly any point on the floor should be understood, and a means to do this to each reading station at tables or carrels should typically be part of the requirement, even though the wire itself may not be installed for each seat. This may mean that all public areas exclusive of the stacks themselves should have a raised floor (as at the U.S. National Archives II), or a system of cable trays of one kind or another should be specified. Alternatively, interior arrangements should be made so that services can be provided off of columns, walls, or other vertical elements.

Power, its distribution, service capacity, stability (that is, without voltage fluctuation and without interruption) warrant consideration as well. Where data signals are provided, there should also be access to power for both laptop and desktop computers. Access, either now or in the future, to printers, scanners, various forms of disk readers, and the like will also be required. The typical power requirements for a workstation have increased over the past two decades from two outlets to six or more. The expectations of the program writer in this context should be expressed.

Along with the advance of technology is the creation of heat. Although new computers are becoming more efficient, over time, there will be more of them. And, they all produce some heat. Sound attenuation is another problem. Keyboards still click, and computers on occasion emit louder signals, such as for receipt of e-mail. It may be that some areas of the library should be designated as traditional "quiet" zones without computer support.

Technology also adds a layer of complexity to the process of accessing information, indeed, several layers. It is becoming increasingly important to provide the capacity to teach, both one-on-one and to groups up to a normal class size. Lighting also contributes to good technology support of information access.

The institution may have facility design standards that address some of the need for adaptability of technology, and they should be cited or included in this front matter. For example, all telephone conduit going from above the ceiling to a telephone service outlet in the wall may be specified to be no less than ¾ in. (19 mm), which was not uncommon recently. Many institutions now mandate a minimum size of 1 in. (25.4 mm), and a few, including the University of California at San Diego, require a minimum of 1½ in. (38.1 mm). The institutional requirement may also mandate a 4 in. by 4 in. (101.6 by 101.6 mm) box at each telephone service outlet where 2 in. by 4 in. (50.8 by 101.6 mm) was common in the past. Institutional standards may also address the size of telephone/data closets, the size of connecting conduits, and other features. Certain structural systems, including, for example, a precast post-tensioned structural concrete floor system, may preclude the future creation of openings for ducts to service an addition or a zone of the building with increased heat load; some specifications or institutional standards may therefore disallow such structural solutions. If they don't, the program author may want to preclude structural systems that do not permit relatively easy alteration and adaptability. Where institutional standards do not exist, it is suggested that standards from another institution might be sought and considered.

Where the building is a renovation, there may be limitations on the criteria that can reasonably be required. In some cases, installing a raised floor over an existing floor, as was done in several locations within the Meyer Library at Stanford, may be the answer. In other cases, flat wire may be a consideration. Or, overhead distribution of cables may be accepted, with power poles to get to the floor below or holes drilled where needed to get to the floor above. Cable raceways are available that can be treated as a chair rail along walls for both power and signal.

With some clever care, the designer can find ways to retrofit an existing building to support modern technology, though the flexibility one would wish to have may never be available. As an example of ingenuity in dealing with an existing building, the old main library at Stanford (currently the Green Library, West Wing) was designed in 1919 with a central vacuum system. Although the vacuum itself did not remain effective for long, its system of tubes all leading to a nicely centralized vacuum room served for many years as the major means of installing phones throughout the building. And, of course, the original vacuum room became the main phone room for the building.

5.3.10 Codes and Standards

Problems are common where there is no control over construction requirements. Buildings often restrict access for handicapped persons in numerous ways. Buildings not infrequently collapse or are severely damaged because of faulty construction, faulty engineering techniques or materials (sometimes triggered by earthquakes), unprecedented floods, and hurricanes. Electrical fires are frequently started as a result of poor construction quality, and the fire may spread rapidly through the structure for similar reasons. Energy consumption, especially in older buildings, is often excessive, resulting in the need for costly retrofitting of more efficient equipment or insulation. Qualified architects and engineers should be able to avoid such problems; however, a building of any size is a very complex construction, and it is easy to miss details that can result in serious problems.

Codes and standards represent essential minimal criteria for developing a sound project. However, even codes and standards will require thoughtful application. Combined with the code authority (often a city or county building inspector, fire marshal, or health and safety official), they represent some assurance but no guarantee that the result will have lasting quality. Codes generally have the force of the law. Standards may be legally enforced only in certain cases; for example, where there is federal funding, some standards take on the quality of a code. In other cases, standards represent minimal guidelines.

Local governing agencies will generally require that the project satisfy certain specific codes and standards. Typically these include the building, fire, electrical, elevator, and handicapped access codes or standards, lighting standard, and zoning ordinance. Governmental regulations or laws may also pertain to and limit construction on sites with archeological relics and on buildings that have been given a historic classification. An institution may also have its own facilities standards that detail procedural requirements, mechanical specifications, energy consumption goals, lighting standards, architectural limitations, or access requirements. To establish a clear understanding of the institutional requirements as well as those of the local government authorities, it is suggested that a tabulation of all the applicable codes and standards be included in the program. A statement that all appropriate codes and standards are to be met may not be sufficient, particularly if the institution requires application of standards that otherwise could be considered optional.

Besides codes and standards aimed at safety and legal requirements, many U.S. states and institutions have planning guidelines or standards used to determine (or sometimes suggest) space allowances and test specific proposals of projects they finance. The second edition of this book listed a dozen of these state planning guides on page 601. This edition includes in appendix B, Formulas and Tables, the 1983 University of California Library Facility Planning Standards.

The front matter of the program, then, should contain as much information about the history, goals, operations, design criteria, and module, site, security, and legal requirements of the project as practical. The amount of detail required depends on local circumstance, but usually a huge volume is not needed. It should clearly establish the scope of the project. The next section discusses the detailed space breakdown, which completes the programmatic description of the project.

5.4
Detailed Space Breakdown

There are many ways to write a program, and the format selected by a given institution may vary substantially from the one suggested in this chapter. (See appendix A for some of the variations.) The intention of the information presented is that it be used as a guide. It is essential that those responsible for preparing the program should weave into the final product those elements that are unique to the given situation. Because of this, nearly any guide will have exceptions at some point.

As has been suggested before, the program establishes in writing the goals and scope of the facilities project and the basis for the design fees, project budget, and, ultimately, the entire project. However, it must be understood that it represents a snapshot that does not easily change. At the same time, the operations of the library and the academic program of the institution will indeed change. The front matter should establish sufficient flexibility in the proposed facility to permit minor changes as the project progresses. At some point, though, changes will add to the cost; thus, the degree of accuracy that can be put into the program can easily affect the final cost.

The funding, design, and construction of a major project can take four or five years. Initial staffing, collections, and reader accommodation will need to be projected, together with anticipated growth, for another 10 to 15 years. The detailed space breakdown, then, should represent anticipated space needs up to, and in some cases beyond, 20 years into the future.

In a major project it is useful to begin the detailed space breakdown with a tabulation of space requirements by major departments, further broken down into each particular function, room, or other area. These space data are developed in terms of net space, which excludes the space required for walls and columns, mechanical rooms, duct shafts, stairs and other forms of circulation, janitor's closets, and other space that is not assignable to library functions. The gross area calculation will include a figure for all these unassignable elements added to the itemized net area requirements.

The ratio of net to gross area is one measure of the efficiency of a building, but it should be cautioned that this ratio can be misleading. Smaller buildings typically will result in a net-to-gross ratio of about 60 percent to 70 percent, while larger buildings will range from 70 percent to 75 percent or even 80 percent. A warehouse facility with limited corridors and minimal support space might have a ratio as high as 90 percent, provided stack cross aisles are included in the net space. Because of the variations in determining exactly what is included in the net or gross area, different planners will develop different figures for similar buildings. Thus the usefulness of this form of efficiency data is limited. Yet, once the net space is tabulated, the anticipated gross space requirement can be established by dividing the net space by the projected efficiency ratio expressed as a decimal. (For example, 50,000 net divided by 65 percent efficiency gives 76,923

gross.) This figure and current local construction costs for a given quality of structure then become the basis for the construction budget.

In a major library project, the groups tabulated in the proposed synopsis of space requirements might include (in no particular order) the library administration, book selection, ordering or acquisitions, cataloging, business office, building service quarters, government documents, circulation and interlibrary services, reference, computer lab, information technology classroom, special collections or the rare book area, the archives, the catalog and national bibliographies, exhibit or museum-type quarters, general reading areas, studies, and the book collection stacks. Such elements as a preservation studio, language lab, audiovisual or media center, computer facility, hand printing-press shop, and the like should also be tabulated where they are part of the project.

Following the summary tabulation, the program might contain in outline form a tabulation of each discrete space, together with reference to the page on which the detailed space information can be found.

Finally, each room, area, or other space should be described clearly. The description should include a succinct statement about the function, location, furnishings, built-ins, and any special concerns about the space. Requirements should be described for technology power and signal hookups, clocks, drapes, shelving, carpet, special environmental or mechanical features, unusual equipment, security systems, acoustic control, and the like, where they are particular to the function being detailed.

The following three chapters discuss the requirements of many of the spaces found in a library. They should help in glossing the detailed space requirements for the program. The program writer may also find it useful to read other programs, which often are available at neighboring institutions or where similar projects are in process.

6

Programming: Housing the Collections

The true university of these days is a collection of books.
—Thomas Carlyle, *Heroes and Hero-Worship*

Accommodation for readers, service areas, and service staff usually requires the greatest library space. The area required for housing the collections runs a close second, and may even exceed it in libraries having very large research collections and limited clientele.

The shelving of collections is especially important, given the cost and effort to assemble good teaching and research materials. Collections must be housed for convenient access while being protected for future generations. Collections may be placed in underground quarters, as many libraries have done. They may be grouped in a rather dense cube of stacking, as at Columbia University or California State University at Northridge. They may be housed in towers, as in the four at the Bibliothèque nationale de France measuring 80 m (262.4 ft) tall. They may in part be on public display, such as at the Beinecke Library at Yale. The configurations are of endless variety and will be discussed in Chapter 11. This chapter deals with shelving types and their design details, with economy of spatial use of bookstack ranges and aisles, and with particular space requirements of books and other formats of library materials.

Although shelving is expensive, it is a small cost compared to the project cost of the shelving floor area, which can be as much as 20 times the shelving cost per volume. The building shell, with its walls, floors, ceilings, lighting, and ventilation, is the greatest single project expense. To save even a small percentage in floor area used for shelving books is worth considerable time and effort. Still, over time, the relative costs of various building components and bookstacks will vary. Construction techniques and their costs as well as shelving designs and fabrications and their costs evolve. So, in the following sections, though comments about cost are reasonable today, be assured that the architect and the owner must figure the costs at the time that any project goes into construction.

6.1
Bookstack Shelving

Bookstack shelving involves a language of its own, which may initially be almost unintelligible to architects who have not had experience in planning library buildings. The same is true for administrative officials, faculty library committee members, and even some librarians. Definitions of many terms used in this section can be found in the glossary.

Each of 14 elements is discussed from a programming point of view in this chapter: the materials used; the option of multitier as opposed to single-tier stacks; stack types; stability; types of shelves; section lengths; shelf depths; aisle widths and range lengths; the height of shelving; stack lighting; color and finish; finished bases, end panels, and tops; stack accessories; and vertical communications. Additional information on many of these factors is given in Chapters 12 and 13 on the design phases of the building project.

6.1.1 Materials Used

Standard library shelving today is generally built of 18-gauge steel, unless the shelving columns and width of the shelves are more than normal. As the American Library Association *Library Technology Reports* point out, gauge is a range of thicknesses that can vary 10 percent to 12 percent, so specifications should give thicknesses in mils or inches rather than gauges. Wood is occasionally used, most commonly where a special effect, such as richness of appearance, is desired. Wood is sometimes used just for the end panels of ranges to provide harmony with nearby furniture. Where preservation of the library materials is a concern, wood shelves should be avoided. Where wood is required for important aesthetic reasons, the use of a sealant is an absolute requirement to prevent the emission of acidic vapors common to wood. In some cases wood shelving can be constructed at lower cost than standard library shelving, but it is generally less

durable, may increase fire risk, may be subject to color fading, and may be more difficult to brace properly in earthquake country. Other materials, such as plastic and glass, have been used in special cases, but they currently represent the exception rather than the standard.

The recommendation of materials to be used should be left to the designers in most cases, with steel being the choice lacking a very strong case for an alternative. Currently available finishes for steel shelving include a dry powder system that exudes fewer volatile solvents over the life of the product, a factor believed to aid the preservation of library materials. However, the end product must meet the criteria of budget limitations, flexibility, structural integrity, and durability as established by the librarian.

Where choices of materials or manufacturers exist, and the project is of significant size, it is suggested that full-sized samples should be required for review and approval. For wood shelving this would make sense only for a major installation, but jointing samples should be examined, and the construction closely specified.

6.1.2 Single Tier or Multitier

The structural configuration of shelving can be freestanding or nonfreestanding in single tier or multitier.

The basic type of stack installation is the single tier, meaning the shelving column or other stack structure on one floor does not hold up the shelving on the floor above. Each rank or section of shelving rests on a structural floor of the building. This is known among many librarians as "freestanding," but many stacks that librarians refer to as freestanding are not so regarded by the manufacturers. The latter say that double-faced shelving units with 8- or 9-in. (203- or 229-mm) adjustable shelves over a 20-in. (508-mm) double-faced base as well as 10- or 12-in. (254- or 305-mm) adjustable shelves over a 24-in. (610-mm) double-faced base are, in fact, freestanding. They otherwise insist the design is not "freestanding" and must be floor-anchored or top tie strutted. Depending on the nature of a particular installation, they may insist on special reinforcement to provide extra stability. In earthquake country, there should be no freestanding standard shelving in this context. To meet California earthquake codes, for example, all full-height shelving requires the equivalent of a gusset at each upright with floor anchor bolts on each side. Top bracing designed to take all deflection out of the uprights may be substituted for the gussets.

Many architects and some librarians consider what they call a freestanding stack with a wider base as more flexible, more easily moved, and more satisfactory than a stack that is fastened to the floor or otherwise attached to the building structure. The authors disagree with them on this point and recommend the nonfreestanding single-tier type in all concentrated bookstacks. Almost any bookstack, whether it is fastened to the floor or not, will damage the floor covering beneath it. If the stack is moved, the flooring will have to be replaced or at least patched because of damage caused by the "punch" load from the uprights, which may amount to 900 pounds per ft² (43.091 kN/m²), the indentation made by the finished base, or the retention of color in the floor because it has not been exposed to light.

Shelving units have been designed with a base that distributes the load, which, installed with a neoprene (an oil-resistant synthetic rubber) gasket, is said to refute this statement. Even if this installation is found to be possible, the added cost of a special unit with a wider base should be determined. If the flooring is installed around the stack and not under it, you are even worse off when stacks are moved. Some engineers will recommend that carpet not be placed under stacks because of the extra "cush," which, particularly in an earthquake, can result in less stability. In a building project, the cost of fastening the stacks to the floor is almost negligible, and considerable although not complete flexibility is still provided.

The authors are as yet unwilling to recommend any full-height bookstacks that are not fastened to the building structure in some manner, even when a broad base is used; at least several manufacturers concur on this point. Without fastening, the stack can tip over, one range falling against another until the whole group goes down like dominos. This has happened more than once. With a narrower base, additional provision for stability is desirable, which will be discussed later.

Multitier bookstacks are very different in structure. They comprise a system of shelf uprights or columns and floor decks that is self-supporting. Each level of stack supports the levels above, the Hoover Tower at Stanford University being an exception where intermediate levels are on structural floors. The top level sometimes also supports a reading room on the top floor of the building, as in the New York Public Library, even the roof over the whole stack structure or the glass walls enclosing the stack tower, as in the Beinecke Library at Yale University. With the exception of various compact shelving systems, a multitier stack represents as concentrated shelving space as can be found, housing the most book volumes in a certain volume of space.

A tiered stack installation, because of its structure, should be considered a very permanent component of the building, one that cannot easily be moved or altered. The support structure can be based on a variety of modules related to the length of a section (see Section 12.3 for extended discussion of modules) and on the dimension between range centers. Generally, in countries using English measures, the sections are 3 ft (0.914 m) long, resulting in an upright every 3 ft in the direction parallel to the shelves and usually half as far again, or every 4½ ft (1.372 m), in the other direction. Allowing for access requirements for disabled persons, the longer dimension is increased to a minimum of 4 ft 8 in. (1.422 m) for 10-in. (0.254-m) shelving and 3-ft (0.914-m) range aisles, exclusive of "growth." A section in metric countries is typically .9 or 1.0 meter, or about 3 ft or slightly over 39 in. Tiered stacks have been constructed with support uprights as much as 9 ft (2.743 m) apart in each direction, giving greater flexibility of use for the space between uprights. Spans of up to 6 ft (1.829 m) for main cross aisles are easily accommodated. Because the uprights are actually part of the shelving, they do not get in the way until an area must be opened up for another use; then one must deal with a forest of columns.

The floors above can be thin: Cellular steel pan decks are 1⅝ or 3 in. (41 or 76 mm), and reinforced concrete decks are normally 3½ in. (89 mm) thick. The typical height of a single level of multitier stack in academic and research libraries is now 7 ft 6 in. (2.286 m). Where a fully sprinklered building is required, this may represent a problem as some fire codes require 18 in. (0.457 m) vertical clear space between the top of any combustible material (books) and the bottom of the sprinkler head. If this requirement is enforced, the useful shelving height would then be about 5 ft 6 in. (1.676 m), which represents fully a 25 percent reduction in shelving capacity. As an alternative, many fire authorities accept sprinklers in each range aisle.

Although the tiered stack installation is part of the building structure and generally regarded as lacking flexibility, it is amazing what can be achieved by removing the shelving. During World War II the subbasement of the Littauer Center at Harvard, which was part of a multitier bookstack, was used as a radar teaching laboratory, and in it thousands of students received their training. In the Bancroft Library at the University of California, Berkeley, tiered stack space has been opened up for faculty studies and reading areas. The Government Documents Library at Stanford has used tiered stack space for a microtext and reference reading area. In all these cases, the solutions work well even though they are clearly affected by the column system. The resulting space assignment is less efficient than in modular buildings designed for freestanding stacks, but where there is no good alternative, multitier stack space can be used for other purposes.

Multitier stacks entail other problems. If wider shelves are needed, they can be used only by narrowing the range aisles. This change often is not satisfactory, because the deeper the shelf, the wider the aisle should be. Code requirements for handicapped access also can be compromised.

Because the floor-to-floor height of multitier stacks is less than the typical building floor height, architects can place three multitier stack levels next to two regular-height floors, or two levels of stacks for every building floor level. The result is that all intermediate stack levels will require ramps or elevators dedicated to the stacks for people in wheelchairs and for book trucks.

Multitier bookstacks have been made with ventilation slots between each level, because forced ventilation and air conditioning were not available, and planners realized that books deteriorate more quickly in stagnant air. Pencils, call slips, and, all too often, books fell through these slots. Where they exist, they represent a serious fire hazard by simulating a natural chimney flue. Several libraries have undertaken to correct this situation by sealing the floor-to-floor openings with special metal plugs, but, to be effective, open stairways and other penetrations must be isolated by a fire division. Such a reduction of airflow may also require the installation of a forced air ventilation system. Clearly, corrective action in this case is expensive, but it represents only a small fraction of the value of the collections that are being protected.

Multitier stacks built today do not have ventilation slots. If the stairwells and elevator shafts are enclosed, a tiered stack is hardly more of a fire hazard than other parts of the library building, although some would argue to the contrary, particularly where there is no fire suppression system. Indeed, if a significant fire were to occur on a lower level of a tiered stack, there could be a risk of collapse due to the loss of strength in the unprotected steel columns. Tiered stacks that have expanded metal grate-type catwalks, rather than a solid floor/ceiling, present a fire risk at least equal to the older tiered stack system with ventilation slots.

A combination of multitier and single-tier stacks is sometimes arranged. This plan was adopted in the Lamont Library, where every other level has a floor strong enough so that the uprights can support a metal pan floor above together with its single-tier bookstacks. The result is that a fixed stack on one level holds up a single-tier stack above it, thus giving flexibility in half the installation. A similar construction was used in the Engineering and Biology Libraries at Stanford University. This type of construction can be used to advantage as a means of providing future expansion of the shelving capacity, when the initial construction budget could not afford the complete stack installation. In this case fixed elements, such as elevators, stairs, and mechanical systems, must be arranged to provide for the easy future installation of additional levels. Yet planners must remember the limitation of flexibility, as mentioned above.

It is generally considered that the cost of a multitier stack is less per volume housed than that for a single-tier stack. Multitier construction in a tower stack is undoubtedly cheaper than a large single-tier installation of the same capacity, but this would not necessarily be true with only two or three levels of tiered stack with a reading room above. The nature of tiered stacks also suggests limited reading accommodations in the stack itself, which is often quite contrary to the philosophy of what the library should be. Of course, in closed stacks or storage facilities, this limitation is not a problem. In most cases there are ways of minimizing the effect of separate stack and reading facilities. If the decision to use multitier stacks is strictly based on economics, an engineer should calculate the savings in cost that might result from the reduction in the size of the building columns that would be made possible. Construction cost for floors and columns and ventilation arrangements must be considered. Where earthquakes are a possibility, the requirements for lateral bracing must be studied.

6.1.3 Stack Types

What type of shelf is to be used after multitier or single tier has been selected? There are four main types: four-post (also called industrial or commercial), case, bracket, and movable. The first three are discussed here; the movable is treated in Section 6.3.3. Until the 1960s case shelving was known as standard library shelving; bracket-type shelving has become the standard configuration today. With few exceptions, all shelving must be adjustable so staff can quickly alter the shelf spacing as collections grow or need to be shifted.

1. *Four-post, industrial, or commercial shelving.* Four-post shelving is used on a large scale in storage warehouses, music libraries for phonograph records, archives, manuscript collections, and elsewhere. (See fig. 6.1.) It is generally baked-enameled steel, often phosphatized to resist rust, and, although plain and unadorned, it can be very attractive. The standard color is gray or tan. Other colors can be obtained, sometimes at added cost. The shelves are adjustable by the use of hangers or special clips, but time and effort are required to empty and remove the shelf, reset the hangers or clips, and reinstall and reload the shelf.

Four-post shelving is most suited to installations where adjustment is not necessary. Because the bolts often used in the past can be a hazard to bindings, they should be carefully detailed in the specifications. Usually a "starter" section is constructed as a discrete unit, which is then fastened to adjoining add-on or "adder" sections to form a range. With a narrow beaded or T-shaped post specified for the front support, a single post serves to hold the shelving on both sides. Beaded posts (0.3 in., or 7.6 mm, wide when holding adjacent shelves) are superior to the more common T-shaped or L-shaped post (usually 3 in., or 76 mm, wide when holding two adjacent shelves) for library use; they interfere less with access to the shelf by eliminating front posts behind which a small book can be lost.

Because of the time and labor required to adjust shelves, four-post shelving is in nearly all cases considered unsuitable in a growing collection classified by subject. Where collections are housed in one quite permanent location by size

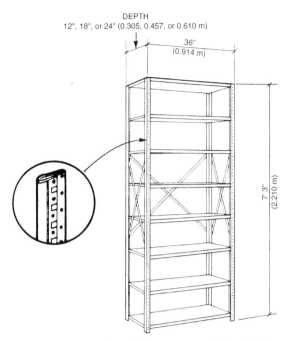

FIGURE 6.1   Industrial or commercial shelving. Adjustable with nuts and bolts or special lugs (see fig. 6.2); dimensions vary depending upon manufacturer. Inexpensive, it is often used for storage of little-used materials for which shifting is unlikely. Because the angle post and bolted fastenings can be hard on books and people, solid side panels and beaded front posts (inset) are superior for library storage.

groupings, four-post shelving may be an economic choice, though flexible use of the shelving will be lost.

However, the initial cost of four-post shelving may be no more than half that of other types of shelving, and it may provide excellent shelving for three types of materials: (1) material laid flat on shelves, such as newspapers, portfolios, and other oversized volumes; (2) boxed archival materials, such as manuscripts, photographs, and boxed microtexts; and (3) materials, such as phonograph discs, which are held upright by a number of vertical dividers fixed quite rigidly on each shelf. Such shelf dividers can be specified to create bins (see fig. 6.15), but with this configuration fasteners must be looked at carefully. With bins, the shelves really are not adjustable unless the dividers can be removed from the slotted shelves.

Four-post shelving is available with solid sides (see fig. 6.2) and backs or the X-bracing as shown. In a range of units, perhaps 50 percent of the sec-

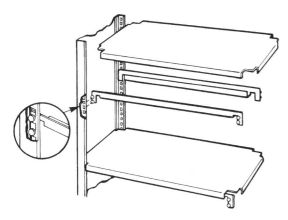

FIGURE 6.2 Industrial or commercial shelving. Even though the clip system (and this is but one example) permits somewhat easier adjustment than bolts, materials can still be hidden behind the front upright at the shelf ends. A filler can be used, but shelf capacity will be affected. With a 36-in. (0.914-m) shelf, the loss of an inch (25 mm) at each end represents about 6% of the capacity. This type of shelving is best for materials that do not require support at the ends, such as boxed materials or elephant folios shelved on their sides.

tions will require a brace at the back. All the side supports will require bracing of some kind, which generally means more bolts to be concerned about. Because some four-post shelving normally comes with 1.5 in. (38 mm) minimum vertical spacing for shelves and stack column heights several inches higher or lower than the standard 7.5 ft (2.285 m) typical of library shelving, be careful to require exact dimensions, including overall height and adjustability, as part of the specification. It is also important to be aware that the dimensions of the shelf are typically exact; the length of a range will be longer than the sum of the shelves because the thickness of the supports and bracing must be added. This added dimension is called "growth."

2. *Case shelving.* There are two versions of case shelving, one with slotted and one with solid end panels.

Slotted-style case shelving has solid end panels separating sections that are the full depth of the range (see fig. 6.3), and the shelves are attached by sliding their ends into slots in these panels. They may be locked in, or have notches in the bottom edge to fit over shelf pins. They always have canopy tops. There usually are no

backs, but backs can be installed and, when used, add to the stability, which is already good. Slotted shelves are a little more difficult to adjust than bracket-type.

This style of shelving is often used for legal folder and X-ray file storage. It has library application similar to the standard four-post industrial shelving for archival storage and the storage of other materials. It is a more stylish, attractive product, and it is more easily assembled than other shelving types. Where sway bracing is not required, as is the case with the product of some manufacturers, one shelf may serve two faces of the shelving range.

Slotted-style case shelving has been used in many rare book rooms and in some reading rooms, instead of wood shelves. The percentage installed in concentrated bookstacks has been negligible in recent decades because this style uses more material and is thus generally more expensive than the other shelving types. It is somewhat more stable in both directions and in most cases does not require the extra bracing typically found with bracket shelving. Because of its characteristic rigidity, it has been used for systems on movable carriages. In earthquake zones, though, the advice of a structural engineer should be sought regarding bracing. Finally, it is somewhat less adaptable to configurations with different-sized shelves or stack carrels than bracket-type

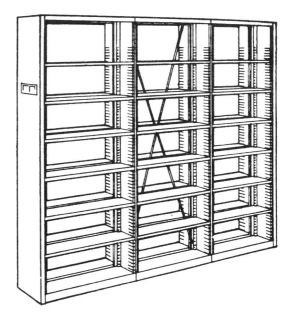

FIGURE 6.3 Slotted shelving. The sway brace shown in the center section is not necessary with a solid back panel or welded corners in each section.

shelving. Its strongest feature is the furniture-like quality of appearance.

The more common version of case shelving used today is an enclosure of steel open only in front. This shelving has solid backs and ends, a canopy top, and base shelves, which contribute to its cabinetwork appearance. Its appearance is similar to the slotted-type case shelving. Its shelves, fastened at either end to the closed upright panels, are more difficult to adjust than the slotted type, but many people feel it is the most attractive type of steel shelving and employ it for special purposes (see fig. 6.4).

Case shelving has the advantage of being so constructed that glazed doors can be attached more readily than with other types of steel shelving (see fig. 6.5). Although this adds to the cost, the addition of doors has merit where there are special concerns about security, dust control, or perhaps even added protection from dripping water. Doors, when securely latched, would keep the books on the shelves in an earthquake. However, if air circulation around the books is a concern, the doors may represent a negative feature, although this should only be a problem where materials in the case are exuding acidic vapors that might affect otherwise stable papers. Vents at the top and bottom of doors will not help air circulation unless input ducts feed the back of all cases, forcing air through the shelves to reach vents. Wire-paneled doors help some with air circulation and are good for security, though not with dust control.

If fine wood shelving is not used in rare book areas, the case or slotted type should be considered, with special attention to finishes to avoid those that accelerate deterioration of the collections. As with any library shelving, an effort should be made to avoid sharp corners or places where the text block of a book can be "knifed" when shelved. Solid backs are of prime importance in these areas to prevent loss and damage.

3. *Bracket shelving.* Central-column, cantilevered, bracket shelving has been for many years

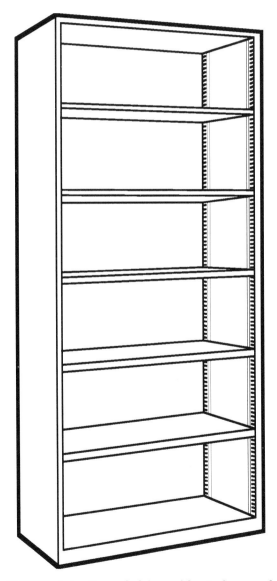

FIGURE 6.4   Case shelving without doors, adjustable by setting four clips per shelf in the vertical strips.

FIGURE 6.5   Case shelving with doors. Note that spines of many volumes will be hidden from view. In cases of this style, locks are usually used.

by far the most frequently used type of library shelving; it offers the best available combination of satisfactory performance in storing a variety of library materials at reasonable cost. A great majority of librarians prefer it.

The bracketed shelf assembly is hung cantilevered from the column uprights (see fig. 6.6). These uprights are formed in several shapes, the most common being a squared tube, a tube formed with two **C** shapes, and an **H** shape that also may be constructed from **C** forms. There are two general frame types consisting of the rigid frame and the starter and adder frame. Rigid frames provide the complete support for a single section; there are exactly as many frames as there are sections in a range. With starters and adders, the column uprights share the load between two sections so an entire range requires one more column than the number of sections in the range. There are also columnlike strips, sometimes called pilasters, that can be attached to walls to support shelves. Where this is done, care must be taken to ensure that the wall is strong enough to support the weight of fully loaded shelving.

The columns have elongated holes arranged vertically on 1-in. (25-mm) centers to permit easy adjustment of the shelves, which engage these holes. These holes typically are varied in shape every two or three to facilitate relating one side with the other. The shelf itself typically has one or two hooks and one lower lug at each end of the shelf. It is possible, if you are strong, to adjust the height of a shelf loaded with books, or even to move it to another section.

There are two general varieties of bracket shelves. One has plate brackets that grip the shelf at each end and rise above its surface, forming bookends. The other has a bracket that is flush with the top surface of the shelf, enabling books to be placed flat across two shelves without an intervening bracket. One is supported from above, the other typically from below, although there have been flush brackets that support the shelf from above. Both types of brackets can be removed from the shelves for storage unless rivets are used as fasteners.

As with other shelf types, bracket shelves are available with dividers, which may be useful for technical reports, phonograph discs, and other materials that need frequent vertical support. Divider shelves have the back flange turned up to engage and hold vertical the divider sheet, which can be a serious disadvantage in the general stack

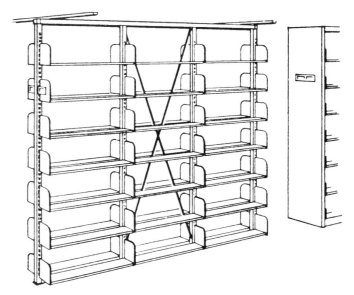

FIGURE 6.6 **Bracket shelving. Open base, no end panel or canopy top, but with sway bracing and strut channels for top bracing. The X-bracing can be replaced by other types of bracing, including rigid frames and specially designed structural spreaders (large horizontal bars between the section uprights). The range to the right shows a finished end panel, base, and canopy top. Note the flat range-finder cardholders. A wider bottom shelf and other structural features may be added to make this shelving freestanding, but floor attachment is always recommended for full-height shelving. This example is essentially the same as tiered-stack shelving (see fig. 6.10).**

as it prevents "shelving through" for the occasional wider/deeper volume.

Steel book trucks have been made with end supports so designed that bracket shelves can be hung on them and six shelves moved at a time from one section of a stack to another without handling a single book individually. It must be added that this is not easy to do and requires the services of a powerful individual.

The decision to use bracket, case, or industrial shelving depends on judgments regarding appearance, utility, and cost. Case or slotted shelving, as already noted, is almost always more expensive. Bracket shelving is more flexible, but, as will be explained in the following discussion, it may require more bracing to assure stability. All types are available in both multitier and freestanding installations, although it should be noted that the previous discussion of multitier stack was based on bracket-type shelving. With the other types of shelving, the support for the multiple tiers will vary, and the ability to use portions of a tiered stack with the shelves removed may not be practical.

It might be said that practically every stack manufacturer offers shelving with special features, for which advantages are claimed in strength, ease of installation, adjustment, finish quality, durability, and safety. Competent engineers are at work trying to improve each line. Unquestionably, progress has been made. As with new lines in automobiles and computers, cost should be kept in mind and weighed, and you should make sure that a change is a real improvement before reaching a decision to purchase.

6.1.4 Stability

Stability is of great importance. Many methods can be used to make the stack more stable where the stack is not part of the building. (Multitiered is, in effect, part of the building.) Where stability is a critical issue, as in earthquake zones, the advice of a structural engineer should be sought on any significant installation. Many manufacturers have developed engineering calculations to demonstrate the earthquake resistance of their product with special bracing techniques. Where this engineering work does not exist, it can be established as a requirement in the program. However, it should be realized that for small installations or the reuse of existing shelving, a complete engineering analysis is relatively expensive. Yet the

authors cannot recommend an alternative to engineered design. Though not nearly as authoritative as a structural engineer, a library building consultant can often be found with useful experience that may help. Further, the literature has good information on structural bracing; an intuitive approach in some countries or regions is the only practical and timely approach. If it is decided that stability bracing should be provided without an engineering analysis, the bracing should be as stout as practical.

Longitudinal bracing to prevent a range from collapsing end to end is generally approached in three ways within the shelving construction. First, there is the unit-constructed, welded frame where each section is a discrete structural unit. Manufacturers of this type of system claim to achieve adequate longitudinal range stability with their welded top and bottom horizontal spreaders between the column uprights. Special supplementary welding and/or additional cross members may be provided in extreme cases. The welded frame technique is not suitable as a retrofit for existing shelving.

The second and third techniques for adding longitudinal stability are common where starter and adder shelving is employed. The first of these uses one of the most common methods of providing stability through the use of sway bracing. Heavy cross rods forming an **X** (see fig. 6.7)

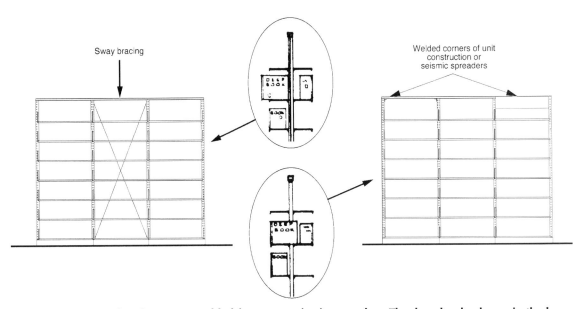

FIGURE 6.7   Sway bracing versus welded frames or seismic spreaders. The deep books shown in the lower inset are only possible where there is no intrusion of X-bracing or seismic spreaders. Full use of the space between the backs of opposing shelves may save up to 4% of the total stack area. The 7 ft 6 in. (2.286 m) height and 3 ft (0.914 m) width per section unit (as drawn) are standard in the United States.

connect the two uprights at a section of shelving. On relatively shallow shelving nominally 8 or 9 in. deep (203 or 229 mm, found in many libraries), a book 9 in. (229 mm) deep will run into the bracing. When sway bracing is used, the space at the backs of shelves is frequently unavailable for deep books.

To clarify, bracket shelving in double-faced sections generally has 2 in. (50 mm) between the back of the shelf on one side and that on the other side; consequently, with a shelf 7 in. (178 mm) deep on each side, if there is no sway bracing in the way, it is possible to house a book 9 in. (229 mm) deep anywhere except where there is a similarly deep book on the other side. A shelf that measures 7 in. (178 mm) from front to back is said to be nominally an 8-in. (203-mm) shelf; 1 in. (25 mm) of the space between shelves is included in the nominal shelf dimension. Using this space for books is what was earlier referred to as "through shelving." Studies indicate that only 6 percent of the volumes in a college or university library, or about nine volumes per single-faced section on average, are 9 in. (229 mm) or more deep. Of course, sway braces are not used for every section. Some manufacturers recommend at least one sway brace in every five sections and preferably a larger percentage than that; still you cannot be sure that the unusually deep books will not come in the sections where there is sway bracing.

Sway bracing is probably the cheapest method of adding extra stability. It has not been unknown for sway bracing to get out of order and come loose; it needs regular inspection and occasional tightening. Under severe longitudinal force, the hooked ends of the rods have been known frequently to rip out of the column uprights; it is essential in any area of earthquakes to bolt the sway bracing ends.

The last method of providing longitudinal stability is to install oversized spreader bars (also called tie bars or tie channels) between the vertical columns in a range. These may be installed at the top of each section and near the base. This was the choice for the Green Library East Wing at Stanford University. As with sway bracing, these heavy horizontal spreader bars limit the possibility of through shelving; however, some librarians prefer this limitation to that provided by the X-type brace, which is less predictable in terms of its location relative to the collections. The bottom spreader bar can be at a height that would permit the shelving of large volumes flat

on the full, double-faced depth of the base shelf. It is likely, though, that the spreader bar will be too big to be concealed beneath the base shelf. At least one manufacturer has called this type of bracing "brace-built" construction. Bracing of this type is generally required only in earthquake areas.

More than 90 percent of bookstack shelving installed in library public areas is of a closed-base style. A finished base—that is, a bottom shelf with the front flange extending down to the floor, with its top surface 3 or 4 in. (say, 100 mm) above the floor and with similar treatment at range ends—gives extra strength in both directions. This shelving, of course, provides bracing for the full length and width of the range and also gives a more finished appearance. Because it closes the base, dust and stray books cannot get under it (see fig. 6.8). Where carpet is not desired under the shelving, the closed base provides a vertical surface to work to. A closed base is, of course, an

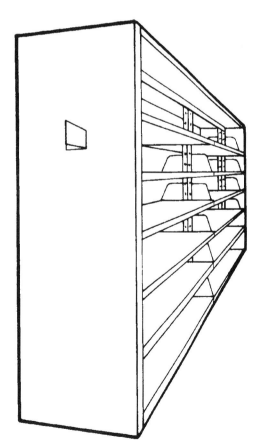

FIGURE 6.8 End panels, closed bases, and canopy top. Note projecting range finder.

added expense. Like other features that have been described, it is not required for stability in a multi-tier stack, although it may be desirable for other reasons.

Lateral bracing to prevent a range from collapsing frontwards or backwards is increased by using a wider base bracket and shelf. Some manufacturers recommend a double-faced base shelf 20, 22, or, in some cases, 24 in. (508 to 610 mm) wide, even if the shelving above is 4 in. (102 mm) narrower from one face of the range to the other. This feature also adds cost, both in terms of the shelving, and, where a wider base shelf is not required for the collections, in terms of floor area.

A second method for dealing with lateral forces is to bolt the base to the floor. Shot-in anchors are occasionally used, although some engineers will not accept these fasteners because of uncertainty about their pullout strength. Where flooring such as carpet is planned, the extra thickness results in a connection with lateral loading cantilevered off the floor. The added dimension of the carpet, together with its springlike quality, may require avoidance of carpet under the shelving for structural reasons.

A third method involves the installation of gusset plates or strap bracing from the base to the support columns. Gusset plates are common with rigid frame-type shelving, while strap bracing was an early solution for starter and adder shelving that is not commonly used today. It, too, adds to the cost, and, in some cases with strap bracing, it blocks the installation of a shelf where the bracket is attached to the column. The gusset plate installed between two half columns is a better installation in this regard. It will add about ⅛ in. (3 mm) to the length of the range for each gusset plate, a point that should be considered in determining the building column or bay dimensions. Where strap braces are used, the fasteners can also be a concern as they may have sharp edges that could damage books. If strap bracing is specified, it is recommended that the librarian should see a sample before a final approval is given.

A variation of the gusset plate is a T plate, which can be placed on either side of a shelving column. This solution does not add to the overall length of the range. The T is placed upside down such that its "leg" runs along the side of the column to which it is bolted. At the floor are flanges that allow bolting the cross member of the T to the floor. All this structure essentially

disappears into the center of the shelving or beneath the base shelf. This approach has been used to good effect on older starter and adder shelving installations in combination with X-type sway bracing.

Manufacturers' bookstack trim items, usually considered for their aesthetic value, can contribute to strengthening a shelving installation. A finished or canopy top (see fig. 6.8) provides extra stability in at least the longitudinal direction. Further lateral strengthening is provided by finished end panels. The end panels and canopy top, together with closed bases, produce what appears to be a more finished job, resembling a case in appearance. They are often considered very desirable if not essential in reading rooms, although more than one librarian prefers bookstacks without finished end panels because more of the books can be seen and the installation gives a lighter, warmer appearance. Further, canopy tops limit the useful height of the top shelf. The cost of end panels and canopy tops is significant. The cost will depend on the length and width of the range as well as the design of the end panel. Ten to 20 percent of the total shelving cost is not unusual.

Finally, one of the most effective methods of laterally strengthening basic shelving installations is to use steel channels running from the channels at the top of one range to the adjacent ranges. These are called strut channels (see fig. 6.6 at upper left). Some think that they do not look good, and architects often object to them, but, if the bracing from one range to another is placed anywhere except immediately adjacent to the cross aisles, it will rarely be noticed. Standard channels provided by shelving manufacturers are comparatively inexpensive and, if extended to some part of the building structure and very securely fastened, are an excellent method for bracing stacks against overturning. However, where earthquake codes are to be met, the strut channel and its connections will require structural analysis.

Use of strut channels is not recommended in reading rooms, particularly if they can be looked down on from above. At the Millikan Library at the California Institute of Technology, struts were installed consisting of heavy square-tube structural steel with heavy steel mounting plates provided to bolt the system to the building structure. This installation was conceived and installed after an earthquake induced shelving collapse. A similar installation in a reading room could become a major design feature to overcome the concern about appearance, but of course it would be more expensive than the standard strut system.

The decision on bracing involves three major points: safety, cost, and appearance. In some cases the utility of the shelving installation will be affected. As noted earlier, the authors are unwilling to recommend any freestanding stacks that are not firmly fastened to the floor for absolute safety. Stacks should not sway in any direction. All the special devices just described will help. They will all cost money, sometimes adding up to more than 25 percent of the basic installation. The cost must not be a deterrent if bracing is necessary. It should be emphasized that the decisions here may change the practical or actual dimensions of the range spacing, thus influencing the ideal column spacing in the building.

The program should detail the type of shelving required to house the collections as well as the nature of the bracing desired. For various reasons, the librarian may wish to specifically avoid certain kinds of bracing while favoring others. The final decision on exactly what the bracing is to consist of cannot be made at the program stage in most cases, but the degree of its need should be clearly established. The implication of various alternatives should be explored during the design phases.

6.1.5 Types of Shelves

Standard library shelving is constructed as a flat shelf with plate-type brackets that usually are clipped to flanges at the shelf ends. Assembly of this type of shelving often requires persuasion with a rubber hammer; the process is noisy. In the past, shelf ends have been formed by folding up the same sheet of steel as the shelf, and there have been examples where the shelf ends were bolted to flanges on the ends of the flat shelf; both types worked quite well and are quiet during assembly, but are uncommon today. The folded type of shelving also stacked neatly for storage with one shelf nesting easily into the next. The other types require at least partial disassembly for the most compact storage.

In the past a bar shelf was also commonly used. Other shelves that are used for special installations include journal display, newspaper, and divider shelves. Commercial shelving also is available in several shelf configurations, as is case or slotted shelving. Bar shelving was popular

because it was supposed to be stronger, and the slots between the several bars of one shelf were supposed to provide for ventilation that was desirable in humid climates (see fig. 6.9). Today they are not so well thought of by most librarians. They tend to damage books. A heavy volume that has rested on a bar shelf for years will often show indentations on the binding from the bars. Small and thin volumes sometimes fall between the bars. With good mechanical ventilation the bars are not needed for air circulation.

Flat shelves are strong enough for normal library loads. Where heavier loads are anticipated, as in a shelf designed to support the weight of tall piles of journals awaiting gift processing or large cartons with shipments to or from a bindery, additional strength can be provided by requiring heavier-gauge steel or by adding a separate steel channel under the shelf at the front edge. (See Section 6.6 for the weight of phonograph discs.) Where the width of the section is 4 ft (1.219 m)

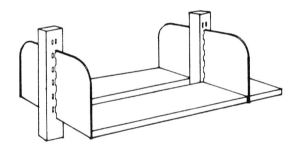

SOLID SHELVES

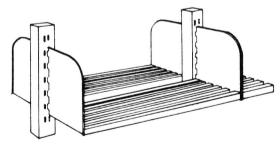

BAR SHELVES

FIGURE 6.9 Bar and solid, or flat, shelves. Bar shelves are no longer manufactured in the United States. They are not generally recommended as they tend to damage bindings, and the ventilation they provide is seldom necessary. However, fire authorities may favor such a shelf in compact shelving installations with overhead sprinkler systems.

or more, special consideration of the shelf strength is required.

A variation of the flat shelf, once produced by at least three manufacturers, has a single slot running nearly the length of the shelf that is designed to accept a specially made book support. One would expect this shelf to be stronger than the standard flat shelf because of the extra bends in the metal, but this is not necessarily the case. In fact, some would argue that these shelves definitely are not stronger. Another variation on the normal, flat-base shelf is one used for bottom shelves that slopes down toward the back. Although it permits easier viewing of the book spine in the stacks, smaller volumes will have a tendency to slip out of view, and it is impossible to store the occasional oversized volume on the base shelf.

For journals, there are sloping display shelves, which are either fixed or hinged. The hinged display shelf permits access to earlier issues of the journal or other periodical housed on a flat shelf with inverted or flush brackets that is hung under the display shelf. This movable display shelf can be Plexiglas or other clear material so the user can see the earlier issues. Although rubber bumpers will help, this type of shelving tends to be noisy when used. Capacity is seriously limited, as only about 15 titles per single-faced section can be displayed, whereas as many as 45 titles per section can be placed flat on flush bracket shelves. Another technique is to stand the current issues in boxes, eight per shelf. This method will house either 48 or 56 periodical titles per section, depending on whether the seventh shelf is considered too high for convenient access. Visibility of the current issue is popular in some libraries as a method of serving clientele, yet capacity is obviously sacrificed.

Special shelves for newspapers, microtexts, compact discs, films in canisters, and other media are also available. The newspaper shelves are heavy and cantilevered, as discussed elsewhere. Most manufacturers also produce a shelf that can create a desk, carrel, or consultation surface in a standard stack section. This extra-deep surface is built with extra strength and is often used to advantage in multitier stack installations. Because these units are deeper than normal shelving, the aisle space may limit their utility in normal stack configurations. With such units it is essential that the shelving structure be well braced, or troublesome movement of the range will occur as weight is placed on the edge of the carrel unit. One manufacturer produces a unit with support legs at the front edge, which would eliminate this concern. Where space is minimal, legs get in the way.

6.1.6 Section Lengths

Sections 36 in. (0.914 m) long are standard in the United States. This length is from the center of one upright to the center of the next and thus is considered a nominal or gross length. The net length is usually about 35½ in. (0.902 m), but this varies depending on the type of shelving and the way the uprights are fabricated. *Note that commercial or industrial shelving is often fabricated with the actual dimensions of the shelving being of full measure.* The space required for the uprights in most commercial shelving, called "growth," is about 1¼ in. (32 mm) for the first section and ½ in. (13 mm) for each additional section, plus a nominal safety factor of ¾ in. (19 mm) per range. As noted earlier, growth of approximately ⅛ in. (3 mm) per gusset is required where they are used in standard library shelving. Uprights designed for tiered commercial shelving will often consume more space.

In countries using the metric system, sections are usually 1 m long, or slightly more than 39 in. Shelving that is no more than 30 in. (0.762 m) long, or even shorter, is also used because it may fit into the space available. One should strive for no more than two or at most three different shelf lengths in any installation. The Boston Athenaeum has some 30 different shelf lengths in the same building, resulting in considerable inconvenience when shifting the collections.

In stacks designed for archival storage, sections 42 in. (1.068 m) long have been used to reduce the unused shelf space where boxed materials are housed. The "record storage box" is 13 in. (330 mm) wide by 16½ in. (419 mm) deep, and 10½ in. (267 mm) tall. The common Hollinger manuscript box is 5 in. (127 mm) wide, 12½ in. (317 mm) deep for letter size or 15½ in. (394 mm) deep for legal size, and 10½ in. (267 mm) tall. These manuscript boxes come also in half widths. Therefore, three record storage boxes fit comfortably on the 42-in. (1.067-m) shelf, as do eight of the full manuscript boxes. Of course, different box dimensions would suggest consideration of other shelf lengths.

The length of the sections in a modular building can affect bay sizes. Where bays are calculated on multiples of the section length, anything that influences their size can be a matter of great importance in a library with large collections. Adherence to the U.S. Americans with Disabilities Act can result in bay sizes related to the depth of the double-faced section plus the required access aisle as much as the length of the section. Section 12.3 deals with this in detail.

Shelves longer than standard should not be dismissed without further consideration, while shorter shelves do not make much sense unless dictated by the building. The Widener Library at Harvard has 40-in. (1.016-m) sections throughout its stacks. For a small library, any shelf length that is not standard may be undesirable because special tooling may be required if shelves are not in stock or if the manufacturing process must be altered. Special shelves may be even more of a problem later if a few extra shelves are needed. However, most manufacturers can make custom lengths that, in quantities of one hundred or more, are generally not much more expensive. For limited quantities, one manufacturer has made a two-piece adjustable shelf that, even though it is expensive, may permit limited shelf replacement or additions where unusual dimensions are encountered.

There have been installations of shelving 48 in. long (1.219 m) for which considerable reduction in cost is claimed. Because six sections 48 in. long have the same capacity as eight sections 36 in. long, the number of shelves is reduced by one-fourth and the number of uprights by two-ninths in a range 24 ft. (7.315 m) long. The reduction may lead to a shelving cost savings of as much as 15 percent, even after allowing for the heavier-gauge steel required because of the longer span. The actual savings can be much less, depending on the manufacturer. Experience demonstrates that 48-in. shelves of standard gauge and without reinforcement will on occasion bend. Before concluding that using the wider range is a true cost-saving technique, a careful study should be undertaken, but it may well be worth consideration.

Long shelves suggest another problem on which more information is required before longer sections can be recommended, even if it can be proved that they cost less. This is the matter of inconvenience, if any, to the user. It seems that one can with ease scan back and forth over a 36-in. or even 40-in. (0.914- or 1.016-m) section, whereas eye motion and even rocking between the feet is more awkward over a wider section. It seems doubtful that the human body can use to advantage a 4-ft (1.219-m) or longer shelf.

The basic problem with long shelves is this: When a shelf is at eye level or immediately above or below, one can readily move along, at least for the length of a 4-ft (1.219-m) shelf, but as one gets lower in the section (or higher using a stool), it is quite a different proposition. When searching the bottom shelf and probably two shelves above it, even a young and agile person may find that hitching along will be difficult. For an elderly user with bifocal glasses and a lame knee, the situation may not be too happy. However, a 15 percent reduction in cost, if real, might make inconvenience to a few seem somewhat minor.

There probably is no completely satisfactory answer to the advantages and disadvantages of longer shelving. Anyone working on this aspect of the problem should keep in mind that the cost of the bookstack shelving probably represents no more than 5 percent of the total building cost. A savings anticipated through the use of longer shelves can normally be equaled by lengthening the range by as little as one section or reducing the distance between range centers by between 1 and 2 in. (25 and 50 mm). Associated problems may result from adjusting accessories, such as stack carrels, lockers, and sloping periodical shelves.

6.1.7 Shelf Depths

Shelf depth is fully as important as the length of shelves, if not more so. In this volume the dimension used will be the actual shelf depth unless noted otherwise. This is 1 in. (25 mm) less than what the stack manufacturers call "nominal" depth except in the case of commercial or industrial shelving and for shelves with backs where the actual and nominal depth of the shelf are the same. For base shelves, which are continuous through the section, the nominal and actual dimensions are nearly equal; in some cases, the actual shelf dimension is between ½ and ¾ in. (12.7 and 19.1 mm) deeper than the nominal dimension, which can be a sticking point with strict code interpretation if not accounted for.

Standard shelves are typically 7, 9, or 11 in. (178, 229, or 279 mm) actual or 8, 10, and 12 in. (203, 254, and 305 mm) nominal. Note that the metric equivalents, here converted from standards in the United States, are likely to be 200, 250, and 300 mm. In Canada, shelving of from 7 to 12 in. in 1-in. increments is considered standard. Shelving for atlases, music conductors' scores, many books in the fine arts, many reference materials, and other large-size volumes may require additional depth, and shelves varying from 11 to 17 in. (279 to 432 mm) actual depth are occasionally required or desirable. Rare book and archival collections should use deeper shelves to protect these most valuable materials, not one of which should be allowed to overhang the shelf. Shelves as narrow as 4 in. (102 mm) are available for reels of microfilm, though it is not at all economical of space and other provisions are commonly made. And divider-type shelving is typically 9, 11, and 13 in. (229, 279, and 330 mm) actual depth, although other sizes may be available.

To clarify, as bracket shelves have a 2-in. (50-mm) space vacant in the center of a range, a 7-in. (178-mm) shelf without a back stop, sway bracing, or other structural restriction can house a book 9 in. (229 mm) deep anywhere, unless the volume behind it is more than 7 in. (178 mm) deep. This arrangement will take care of about 94 percent of all books. An 8-in. (203-mm) "actual" shelf will take care of a 10-in. (254-mm) book in nearly all cases and will be adequate for 97 percent of all volumes in a general collection.

At least four stack manufacturers have provided an 8-in. (203-mm) actual, 9-in. (229-mm) nominal, shelf as a standard unit. Where there are no structural limitations, 8-in. (203-mm) actual shelves are perhaps best for most stacks, and no difficulty or undue cost is involved in fabricating them for any but very small orders. Collections having large books may require 9- or even 11-in. (229- or 279-mm) actual depth shelving.

The advantages of bracket shelves include the ability to use them with standard accessories and to use shelves of different depths on the same upright, something that is impossible to do with slotted, case, or commercial shelves without special arrangements or significant effort. With standard library-type shelving, the construction cost of the floor area occupied by bookstacks and their aisles is some 10 times the cost of the stacks themselves. Thus, where deeper shelves are used, the associated space cost can be significant. This should be kept in mind when structural bracing devices force the use of the next larger shelf. However, there may be no reasonable alternative.

It has been noted that deeper bottom shelves are suggested by stack manufacturers for reasons of stability. They may claim that this shelf does not interfere as one goes up and down the stack aisles because it is at shoulder height that the full

aisle width is necessary. Ignoring for the moment the need for handicapped access, any stack aisle that is 30 in. (0.782 m) across is wide enough for a person to get through safely without bumping into the shelves at either side. Others would argue that, with a wider base and less aisle space at the floor, for example 27 in. (0.686 m), the same is true. Metcalf commented that it is possible for most people to squat down in a 30-in. (0.782-m) wide aisle. The same is generally true for a 27-in. (0.686-m) aisle with a wider base shelf where the aisle dimension is measured at the base.

The primary reason for widening an aisle is to reduce the inconvenience when two persons pass in it and to satisfy the minimum code requirements for handicapped access. In either case, a wider base shelf serves as a bumper or protector for the occasional volume that is unusually deep and therefore sticks out slightly from the shelf. Where minimum 36-in. (0.914-m) range aisles are required, the difference of 10-in. versus 12-in. (254-mm versus 305-mm) nominal depth shelving represents a potential savings of 6.67 percent. Where deeper shelves are required because of the collections or for structural reasons, the savings are nominal.

On the other hand, if you are prepared to use ranges that are only 16 in. (406 mm) actual from front to back rather than 24-in. (610-mm) double-faced base shelves, which is not uncommon, the savings are more than 13 percent for the affected stack area. Such a shelving configuration requires separate shelving for oversized volumes, but, in absolute terms of space efficiency, a case can be made for its use in many stack areas. Of course, there is no reduction in the amount of shelving that must be bought, but the narrower shelves should cost less per linear unit. As the shelves become narrower, more materials will need to be housed in special areas with deeper shelves. In an open stack with classified collections, this may result in one of three arrangements: (1) shelving the book on its back, allowing it to overhang the shelf, a very undesirable condition; (2) placing the book on the bottom shelf of that section or at the end of that range; or (3) gathering all such folio or large books in a separate stack area with special shelving. For the second and third arrangements, libraries may use book dummies that take up shelf space. Or they may rely on catalog records noting folio or portfolio volumes, and stack guides showing where these are separately shelved. In fact, if only 94 percent of all books can be housed in a 16-in. (406-mm) actual depth range, then each standard single-faced shelf will average about one and a half dummies. At best this is an inconvenience, and it will add to the linear shelving required, perhaps offsetting the savings.

As has been stated, an argument for the wide bottom shelf is that the larger books can conveniently be shelved there. With a 24-in. (610-mm) double-faced base shelf and 9-in. (229-mm) actual shelves above, it is rare when more than two or three volumes are on the base shelf; some argue that this is poor use of space and the extra-deep shelf. Those subjects that are heavily skewed toward larger volumes, such as art and music and reference collections, should have deeper shelving. Even with 9-in. actual depth shelving over 24-in. double-faced base shelves, book dummies will still occasionally be needed, but they will be relatively infrequent. It could then be argued that the reader is best served with slightly deeper shelving, although Metcalf was absolutely right when he pointed out the facility cost associated with such service.

Many librarians agree that oversized books can properly be segregated and that to do so is less expensive and as convenient as keeping them more nearly within their specific subject sequence. As suggested earlier, there is by no means total agreement on this issue. To determine the course to be taken, each institution must weigh the advantages and disadvantages in view of the goals for the library and the physical nature of the particular collections.

To summarize, it is suggested that bookstacks should be finished with book preservation as a criterion; that they should always be fastened to the floor and/or top tie-strutted (except for low shelving often found in reading rooms); that they be strengthened in ways other than by sway bracing where practical; that where sway bracing is used, accommodation of deeper books be accounted for; and that consideration be given to the alternatives of equipping the sections with shelves of the same width throughout, with only minor exception. As to depth of shelves, Metcalf suggested that most of them need be only 7 or 8 in. (178 or 203 mm) deep actual measurement, unless the bay size is such that columns will obstruct the aisles. Although 7-in. (178-mm) shelves may be suitable for literature and a few other subject groups, 8 in. (203 mm) provides greater flexibility. Reference and engineering collections should be on 9-in. (229-mm) shelves, and music

or art collections or rare books on 11-in. shelves. The greatest flexibility for a general stack area is provided by 8- or 9-in. (203- or 229-mm) shelves with, some would argue, a 24-in. (610-mm) total, front to front, base shelf. If the building module is to be uniform, it is recommended that it accommodate the deepest shelving anticipated for a large percentage of the collection, with any difference between nominal and actual dimensions accounted for. It should be said that where shelves are not deep enough, volumes will protrude into the aisles and be damaged by passing bodies or book trucks, a phenomenon that can be essentially avoided with a deeper base.

6.1.8 Aisle Widths and Range Lengths

Two principal aisle widths must be considered: range aisles (running parallel to the ranges, and between the range faces) and cross aisles (the main access aisle to the stack area, or the aisle that runs perpendicular to the range aisles). The U.S. Americans with Disabilities Act (ADA, 1991) states that library range aisles must be a minimum of 36 in. (0.914 m) clear with 42 in. (1.065 m) preferred. Main or cross aisles typically are larger. ADA states that the minimum width for two wheelchairs to pass is 60 in. (1.524 m). In much of the United States, a restrictive reading of the Uniform Building Code in the section dealing with aisles (Section 3315) requires a minimum clear width of 24 in. (0.610 m) in areas serving employees only, 36 in. (0.914 m) in public areas where furnishings are on one side of the aisle, and 44 in. (1.117 m) in public areas where furnishings are on both sides of the aisle. In California and elsewhere, most code authorities accept the minimum stack aisle required by ADA, including in staff-only areas, though this is not universal. This is a very important point needing clarification early in the planning process; the difference between 36-in. and 44-in. aisles is significant in terms of formulating project budgets and space requirements and can be a factor pressing libraries to move much more fully into compact shelving. And, where politics play an important role, the issue needs resolution with care if excess cost is to be avoided. This is not a trivial issue.

In many areas, the controlling factor establishing minimum aisle width is the building code, such as cited above. For a research collection, aisles of even 36 in. (0.914 m) are excessive, but codes must be met unless a variance can be obtained.

Wheelchairs and firefighters can negotiate substantially narrower aisles. Where 44-in. aisles are required by code, it can usually be argued that a minimum clear aisle width of 36 in. (0.914 m) is acceptable. It is recommended that the architect or project manager should talk persuasively with the code authorities in the event more than 36-in. aisles are mandated. In the stack space, the savings can be substantial: reducing the aisle space from 44 to 36 in. (1.118 to 0.914 m) saves about 12 percent with 24-in. (0.610-m) double-faced base shelves, and 12½ percent with 20-in. (0.508-m) base shelves.

Where the local authorities do not establish the minimum width of the stack aisles, or where wider aisles may be appropriate, their width warrants further discussion. Before a final decision is made on shelf depths, range aisle widths should be considered, as the two are closely connected in a modular building. Various factors are important, particularly the bay size available, the amount of use, and the extent of provision for wheelchair access. Whether access to the shelves is open or not makes a difference. Aisles 36 in. (0.914 m) wide are sometimes called standard for open-access stacks, but every inch that this can be reduced (with 24-in. (0.610-m) double-faced base shelves) saves 1.67 percent of construction costs for the space occupied by the stacks.

To use a commonly accepted formula of 15 volumes per square foot, a stack with a 1,500,000-volume capacity requires 100,000 ft² (9,300 m²). If the range depth can be reduced by 2 in. (50 mm), it should save 3.33 percent, or 3,300 ft² (310 m²) of floor space, and if aisle width is also reduced by 2 in. (50 mm), the total savings will be 6.67 percent, or 6,700 ft² (620 m²), which at $150 each would be $1 million. This is not to say that the savings are necessarily desirable. In many circumstances it would not be worthwhile or very wise. Weigh your local situation and then decide.

Aisles should be wide enough so that the bottom shelves can be adequately lit (more of that later); so that the user can squat down and read labels on the bottom shelf and select and remove the desired volumes; and so that in a busy stack two persons can pass each other without too much difficulty. Shelving the collections will be easier if the aisles are wide enough to accommodate a book truck. This problem can be eased by making the trucks narrower, but their capacity and stability are reduced. Another alternative is to reshelve books from a book truck parked in a wider cross aisle. This works best in a large collection where the number of items being returned to a particular range seldom exceeds a small armload. Major stack shifts, however, would remain a problem. The University of British Columbia library once shifted books from a large truck to a small square truck and then to the shelves, because of aisle width and distance from the main sorting area. Probably for ergonomic reasons dealing with repetitive motion and handling, this practice has been stopped. For heavily used shelving areas, much can be gained by being able to reshelve books directly from a truck.

The human limitation for being able to squat down depends a great deal on size and agility. To what extent should the aisles be suitable for elderly, stiff, rotund faculty with bifocal glasses and poor eyesight? An occasional low stool can be a help, and adequate lighting is important. Again, the decision must be made locally.

Range lengths play a key role in convenience of use and in both construction and operating cost. Other things being equal, the larger the book collection, the less any one aisle is used. The length of range aisles affects both the amount of use and the total stack capacity very considerably, as can be seen later. It is suggested that aisles in a reference room or in an undergraduate open-access stack, with no more than 100,000 volumes, should not be less than 3 ft (0.914 m), and ranges not more than 24 ft (7.315 m) and preferably only 18 ft (5.486 m) long. In a heavily used reference collection, a 40- to 42-in. aisle (1.016- to 1.067-m) is better still. A strict reading of the needs for handicapped access suggests an aisle of 42 in. (1.067 m), which will easily allow a wheelchair and another person to pass and the person in a wheelchair to easily withdraw a book on lower shelves at the side of the chair. The minimum width a standard wheelchair can negotiate is 27 in. (0.686 m), although 28 in. (0.711 m) is preferred. Where the base shelf is the same size as upper shelves, a wheelchair will require more room for finger space. With minimal aisle space, the occasional volume that sticks out will be a problem.

In a large collection with limited use and where the code permits, 33- or 34-in. (0.838- to 0.864-m) aisles are adequate; 32 in. (0.813 m) is not impossible. In a very large library with open access to relatively few readers, 30 in. (0.762 m) is not too unsatisfactory. And as little as 27 in. (0.686

m) has been used with reasonable success where the shelving is provided with a 24-in. (610-mm) double-faced base. Storage collections and other stacks closed to the public have been successfully arranged with 24-in. (610-mm) aisles, but this only works where the volume of transactions is small. With a 27-in. (0.686-m) aisle and a 24-in. (610-mm) double-faced base shelf or a 30-in. (0.762-m) aisle and 18-in. (457-mm) overall double-faced base, 48 to 51 in. (1.219 to 1.295 m) can be achieved for the center-to-center range spacing for large, little-used collections. And 51 to 54 in. (1.295 to 1.372 m) on centers can be considered standard, depending on the base size. The effect of this on column spacing is a matter of considerable importance and is discussed in detail in Chapters 5 and 12.

The desirability of short ranges in parts of the library with very heavy use is important, as has been mentioned, but a very large, comparatively little-used collection is a different proposition. In the past, a 30-ft (9.144-m) length has generally been considered the outside limit for any library. However, the National Library of Medicine has ranges up to 36 ft (10.972 m) long, and the Cecil H. Green Library at Stanford University has ranges up to 42 ft (12.802 m) long without a problem. The storage levels of the Lamont Library at Harvard have ranges as much as 51 ft (15.545 m) long, and the ranges have been quite satisfactory for the use to which they have been put.

Let us explain consequences. If the 51-ft (15.545-m) ranges had been divided by two cross aisles 3 ft (0.914 m) wide, or one cross aisle 6 ft (1.829 m) wide, the number of sections would have been reduced from 17 to 15 in each range. Accommodation of 17 sections is over 13 percent greater than 15. If 13 percent is gained in capacity by narrowing ranges and stack aisles, and this 13 percent is added to the 13 percent obtained by lengthening ranges, the result is a total increase of over 27 percent. However, it would be a mistake to narrow the aisles and lengthen the ranges in this way in an open-access, heavily used stack; this increased capacity would not be worth its costs in inconvenience. Give full consideration to the anticipated use.

The width of cross aisles is also an important factor. The difference in capacity with cross aisles 6 ft (1.829 m) wide instead of 4½ ft (1.372 m) is nearly 6 percent, with 21-ft (6.401-m) ranges. A 3-ft (0.914-m) instead of a 6-ft (1.829-m) aisle would add over 11 percent to the capacity. Again,

use and codes should be kept in mind; do not overeconomize. You will regret it.

Cross aisles can always be inserted in a long range, if finished bases and sway braces do not intervene, by simply removing the shelves and perhaps adding a piece of floor covering. Relocation of the sway braces and removal of the finished base are usually possible. The reverse is also possible if the uprights do not contain light switches, if they are notched so that shelves can be attached, and if the aisle is an exact multiple of a standard shelving unit or the space provided is sufficient for the frame of a unitized shelving section.

6.1.9 Height of Shelving

The U.S. Americans with Disabilities Act states that library stack height is unrestricted, though library magazine displays are specifically limited to a maximum reach height of 54 in. (1.372 m), with 48 in. (1.219 m) preferred. This could seriously limit the height of traditional journal display shelving. Local interpretation will control whether the term "library stack" includes journal display shelving in a common stack arrangement. The standard full height for library shelving in the United States and Canada is 7 ft 6 in. (2.286 m). Four-post shelving really has no standard full height, though 8 ft (2.438 m) is not unusual, and this height works well with archival materials. Many dimensions of shorter shelving units are available.

Multitier stacks are designed with floor-to-floor levels of different heights. They have often been 7 ft 6 in. (2.286 m) on centers vertically—that is, 7 ft 6 in. from one floor level to the level of the next floor. If 3 in. (76 mm) is lost in the floor thickness, each floor is 7 ft 3 in. (2.210 m) in the clear. Sometimes they have been only 7 ft (2.134 m). At least one multitier stack, that at Pennsylvania State University, is less than 6 ft 8 in. (2.032 m) in the clear. Too often lights in the aisle are so arranged that the top few inches of shelving are difficult to use because of the physical intrusion of the light fixture. (See fig. 6.10.) This condition may be aggravated by a sprinkler system. In recent years the full 7 ft 6 in. (2.286 m) clear height has become more or less a standard, but if sprinklers are anticipated, it may not be sufficient. Some fire code authorities will insist that the sprinkler heads be 18 in. (457 mm) above the highest book. This would suggest that if 7 ft 6 in. (2.286 m) of shelving is desired, the clear height must be more than 9 ft (2.743 m). Or

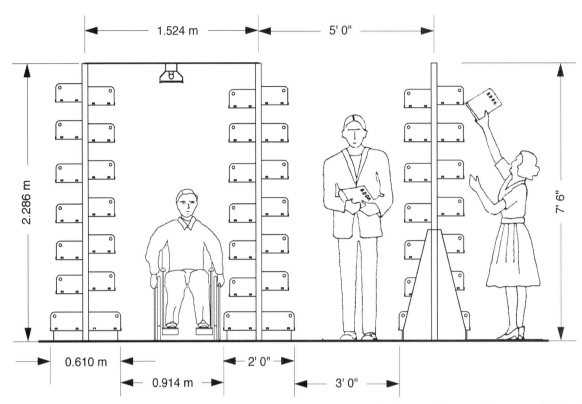

FIGURE 6.10   Shelving of standard height (tiered suggested to left; freestanding to right). Top shelf of seven is 6 ft 4 in. (1.930 m) high. This is the lowest possible height with a 4-in. (102-mm) base and shelves 12 in. (305 mm) on centers. Anything higher would require a stool. Anything lower would decrease capacity by one-seventh or require reduced shelf-to-shelf spacing. The 12-in. (305-mm) spacing should work for 90% of general collections, while 11-in. (279-mm) spacing will provide for only 79%. This arrangement will not apply to all collections; art, music, reference, and science collections often require six rather than seven shelves in a standard section.

Note the spacing as illustrated meets ADA requirements. Note also the seismic gusset shown on the freestanding shelving to the right.

more frequent heads may ease the problem. Local code authorities should be consulted in this event as it may be possible to seek a variance. The possible adverse effects of a variance in the event of a fire should be considered if this direction is to be taken.

The 7 ft 6 in. (2.286 m) total height for shelving is not so high that those using the stack cannot reach the top shelf. Most people can reach up to get a book off a shelf 6 ft 4 in. (1.930 m) from the floor, although it will be very difficult for those who are only 5 ft (1.524 m) tall. (See fig. 6.10, person in right aisle.) If the top shelf is higher than that, it is unreachable by so many people without the assistance of a stool or ladder as to make its position inadvisable in most cases.

Studies have shown that some 90 percent of all books are no more than 11 in. (279 mm) tall. A standard steel shelf (excluding commercial shelving) is not more than ¾ in. (19 mm) thick, including the formed edges, and if shelves are placed 12 in. (305 mm) on centers, a book measuring 11 in. (279 mm) can slide in between. With seven shelves, counting the base, placed on 12-in. (305-mm) centers, and with the top one at 6 ft 4 in. (1.930 m) above the floor, giving a 14-in. (356-mm) margin there below a clear 7 ft 6 in. (2.286-m) ceiling, the top of the bottom shelf will be 4 in. (102 mm) above the floor. This makes possible a 3- or 4-in. (76- or 102-mm) base, allowing space for a raised base shelf or kick plate, both of which provide important protection for the books from feet, water, brooms, floor polishing machines, or vacuum cleaners. A canopy top will usually reduce the maximum clearance for the top shelf by at least 1 in. (25 mm), though it is not needed close under the ceiling unless there is concern for potential water leaks.

If the distance between shelves is reduced by 1 in. (25 mm), that is, to 10¼ in. (260 mm) in the clear, eight shelves including the base will still not be possible without raising the ceiling several inches. Equal spacing on the shelves would require a clear height of a little over 91 in. (2.328 m). Unless the ceiling must be higher anyway, there is little to gain from it. The eighth shelf, if made possible by the higher ceiling, would be 6 ft 9 in. (2.057 m) above the floor and beyond reach of most people shorter than 5 ft 4 in. (1.626 m). Some 21 percent of the volumes will be too tall for this configuration. This is enough to make 11-in. (279-mm) shelf spacing for the general collections undesirable, although there will be some areas in most collections where, with careful adjustment of the shelves, an extra shelf can be added.

With few exceptions, notably for phonograph discs, archives and manuscript collections, facilities with compact shelving, and installations with sprinklers, 7 ft 6 in. (2.286 m) in the clear seems satisfactory for academic and research libraries. A tiered stack that is much less than 7 ft 6 in. (2.286 m) clear height will be inconvenient, if not dangerous, for very tall people. Harvard's Widener Library, with 7 ft 2 in. (2.184 m) clear stack height, can use only six shelves, except in the literature sections. If it could use seven, capacity would be nearly one-sixth greater, and more than 300,000 additional volumes could be stored.

In a stack that is not tiered, the floor-to-ceiling height must be somewhat greater if one is to install a shelving unit 7 ft 6 in. (2.286 m) high. As suggested earlier, the minimum ceiling height may be established at 9 ft (2.743 m) by the requirements of a sprinkler system and standard-height library shelving. Should an upper limit beyond that be considered for ceiling height in nontiered shelving arrangements? It depends on why the extra space is provided. The higher the ceiling, the greater the cost for a given floor area.

Where sprinklers are not a factor, a ceiling height of 8 ft 6 in. (2.591 m) would allow an eighth shelf, which could be devoted to storage for less-used books. This addition would be comparatively inexpensive cubage, though it might also be confusing, even if this top shelf were a different color, as it would require a single horizontal arrangement for books. Location notation may be required in the catalog, which, if it must be added, is at some cost. This type of storage is not recommended in most circumstances. However, if the entire collection is less-used books, the extra shelf serves to advantage. Even in an open stack, where space is at a premium and there is little alternative, the added eighth shelf on over-height frames can work, provided sufficient stools or low stepladders are available, but the result is obviously an inconvenience. Providing the possibility of adding an eighth shelf at a future date may be viewed as a form of insurance against the day when the library runs out of shelf space. It should be noted that doing so will increase the floor loading and make lighting the lower shelves more difficult, factors that must be anticipated in the initial design if eventual use of an eighth shelf on extended uprights is a possibility.

A bookstack area with 7 ft 6 in. (2.286 m) clear height is high enough for readers in carrels or desks anywhere in the stack, and, in fact, is adequate and satisfactory for small groups if care is taken to place them where each person can look out in some direction for a considerable distance. Larger groups require a somewhat higher ceiling to avoid a feeling of discomfort. In the Lamont Library there are two mezzanines 91 × 45 ft (27.736 × 13.716 m). Each provides seats for 75 readers who work in comfort with a 7 ft 9 in. (2.362-m) ceiling, and each seat provides a view in at least one direction, although some of the seats are over 75 ft (22.860 m) from any window. At Princeton University, 8 ft 4 in. (2.540-m) ceilings on the stack levels permit adequate height for rooms for human occupancy that are as much as 25 × 36 ft (7.620 × 10.973 m) or even 25 × 54 ft (7.620 × 16.459 m) in size.

Manufacturers of library shelving provide standard heights of 3½, 5½, 6½, and 7½ ft (1.067, 1.676, 1.981, and 2.286 m). Commercial or industrial shelving is manufactured with slightly different standard heights of 6, 7, and 8 ft (1.829, 2.134, and 2.438 m). Some library stack manufacturers offer other heights, and in any significant shelving order a custom height is entirely feasible at reasonable cost. At least one manufacturer of commercial shelving has provided heights of 39, 51, 63, 75, 87, 99, 111, and 123 in. (0.991, 1.295, 1.600, 1.905, 2.210, 2.515, 2.819, and 3.124 m), none of which is exactly equivalent to standard library shelving.

Collections of newspapers, microtexts, phonograph discs, oversized books, and film reels will require different shelving configurations. These are discussed in Section 6.6. A few of these collections can be efficiently accommodated on industrial shelving, and, as 8 ft (2.438 m) is a standard height for this type of shelving, it may be prudent to provide some space that will permit the use of 8-ft (2.438-m) shelving. Of course, all these collections can also be housed on various forms of bracket shelving, and the only reason to consider industrial shelving is the cost saving of the equipment.

Where a future installation of movable compact shelving is a possibility, provision for a track system and false floor may be desirable. With one system, the clear height required, including lights but excluding sprinkler clearance, is 8 ft 6 in. (2.591 m). More on compact shelving later.

There is no precise upper limit for ceiling height in a stack area, except that extra height may look awkward and be wasteful, costs more, and, where the lighting is ceiling mounted, becomes less efficient as it becomes higher. Stanford University's Branner Earth Sciences Library is a case in point, where the ceiling over the general collections is about 20 ft (6.096 m) above the floor. However, if the floor is designed for additional weight, extra ceiling height can be considered as a form of future expansion. Basement spaces in particular, where the floor loading is not such a problem, can be constructed to permit the future addition of a second tier of shelving. Where this is the plan, there will be advantages to installing the initial lights on bracing struts supported by the shelving itself. Planning stairs, elevators, and other services and utilities for this form of future expansion is important, too.

6.1.10 Stack Lighting

The question of library lighting in its broader aspects is discussed in Chapter 13, which deals with the design development phase of a building project. In Chapter 5 lighting is discussed in the general terms that the front matter of the program might detail. Here the special lighting problems in relation to bookstacks are considered.

With relatively narrow aisles, lighting has always presented a problem, particularly for finding books on bottom shelves. The narrower the range aisles and taller the ranges, the more difficult it is to light the bottom shelves properly. There may be good light on the floor, but the backs of the books are at right angles and receive little light, perhaps as little as 1½ or 2 footcandles (21.5 lux), though more is usually possible.

Because buildings cost so much and lighting in a library is crucial, we mention attempts over several decades to find excellent stack lighting. Early solutions were a combination of skylights and glass floors. If energy resources become scarcer, it is entirely possible that there will be a return to the use of some natural light for shelving areas to augment artificial light sources, though heat and preservation of the books will be a concern. Natural light, in its full spectrum, is damaging to books. Careful filtration may help, but, of course, this will reduce the amount of light. Glass floors, although an interesting concept, have caused problems as well. There have been cases of the glass breaking, which would be a terrifying experience for anyone. And after years of use, their surface becomes so abraded with dirt that it is rendered nearly opaque. Glass also is notorious for producing static electricity, which is an irritation. New techniques to light stack areas with sunlight may be developed, but librarians should be cautious and consider the preservation and practical aspects with great care.

Fluorescent tubes housed flush with the ceiling or suspended close to it and protected by baffles or a form of plastic came into use in the early 1940s and provided by far the best stack lighting then available. They used approximately 40 percent as much current as incandescent bulbs to give the same intensity of illumination, and this illumination was spread over the entire length of the aisle. Fluorescent tubes seemed to be almost perfect for heavily used stacks, where they were required during all the time the library was open. Because of the lower cost for current, there was no need to consider installing individual range aisle switching or time locks that would automatically turn them off after 10 or 15 minutes, as was sometimes done with incandescent bulbs. In the past, people notoriously failed to turn off lights when they were through with them, perhaps because of a general uneasiness about dark areas. This attitude may be changing in some libraries where general brightness of main aisles and a lack of nooks and dead ends give people more comfort. With the possibility of continuous lighting, wiring and switches were simplified and became less expensive, proportionately.

Fluorescent lights still had four problems:

1. If they were used for short periods only and were turned on and off frequently, they burned out quickly.
2. Because the light from them did not carry out from the ends very well, a nearly continuous row was required for good stack lighting.
3. A continuous row of regular, 40-watt, 4-ft (1.219-m) tubes gave out more light than some librarians believed was necessary.
4. Regular wiring is fixed, and if the ranges were shifted to perhaps four instead of five ranges per bay, rewiring became necessary.

Because of these problems, it was reasoned that, if the ceiling height was increased to make other space on the same floor more usable for the concentration of readers or for other reasons, then the light fixtures could be placed at right angles to the aisles. By doing so, flexibility was increased in terms of shelving placement (the fourth problem above), and adequate lighting could be provided by placing rows of lights as much as 6 ft (1.829 m) apart instead of the approximately 4 ft 6 in. (1.372 m) associated with range aisle spacing (which would be more like 5 ft in many libraries today due to current code requirements). Installation, maintenance, and energy costs were thus saved. Various ceiling patterns have been used that accomplish a similar effect, including diagonal and square patterns.

The energy crisis of the 1970s, however, may have changed this approach, at least temporarily. Normal 4-ft (1.219-m) fluorescent fixtures are now three to four times more efficient than incandescent fixtures in terms of lumens per watt. With regular ballasts, two 40-watt tubes draw about 92 watts, which can be improved by using energy-efficient ballasts and tubes such that the same light can be obtained from about 75 watts. The 4-ft (1.219-m) tube now lasts about 20,000 hours, compared to perhaps 1,000 hours for a standard incandescent bulb, and up to 2,500 hours for the long-life incandescent. Although frequent cycles of on-off use will shorten its life, the modern fluorescent tube still has a significantly longer useful life than the incandescent bulb. The energy savings by turning the fixture off, even if only for a few minutes, are considered greater than the cost of more frequent tube replacement.

The payback period for the additional cost of individual range aisle switching, which results in energy savings, is generally found to be favorable. Recent developments in light fixtures, particularly the use of specially designed library stack light fixtures, have increased further the efficiency of fluorescent light. The comparative cost of the fluorescent tube has dropped to a point where it is considerably lower in terms of lumen hours than the incandescent bulb.

A row of single-tube fixtures running down the center of a range aisle is hard to improve upon, even though the light levels may be greater than some regard as absolutely necessary. Because of this, it is now recommended that for general stack lighting, serious consideration should be given to individual range aisle lighting with local switching.

Light fixtures can be mounted at the ceiling, suspended from the ceiling, or mounted on or hung between the ranges themselves. Two configurations are shown in fig. 6.11. In a stack with a high ceiling, such as a warehouse, it is suggested that lights mounted on struts between the ranges would be most efficient. Mercury vapor or other high-intensity lighting sources are not much more efficient, and, because of the placement that they require, the lower shelves will be difficult to light adequately. Of course, any form of general illumination must be all on when the stack is in use. General illumination only makes sense where energy costs are of concern in heavily used shelving areas, for example, in a reference room. Even then, be aware of the problems of ultraviolet light that can occur with both unfiltered fluorescent and mercury vapor light sources.

Regarding illuminating the bottom shelves, a comparison test of seven lighting systems was undertaken in 1977 by a California lighting manufacturer. The light fixtures included the Parabolume, or reflective lens, a fixture with a refractive grid, and an extruded aluminum fixture manufactured by the particular company. While the cost comparisons and other features were carefully outlined, one point of special interest is that in no case was the light level on the bottom shelf less than 7.7 footcandles (82.851 lux), and in most cases it exceeded 10 footcandles (107 lux). This was in a 36-in. (0.914-m) stack aisle with the light fixtures mounted 8 ft (2.438 m) above the floor. A light-colored floor will help to reflect light to the backs of the lowest books. However, with improved lighting fixtures, this may not be

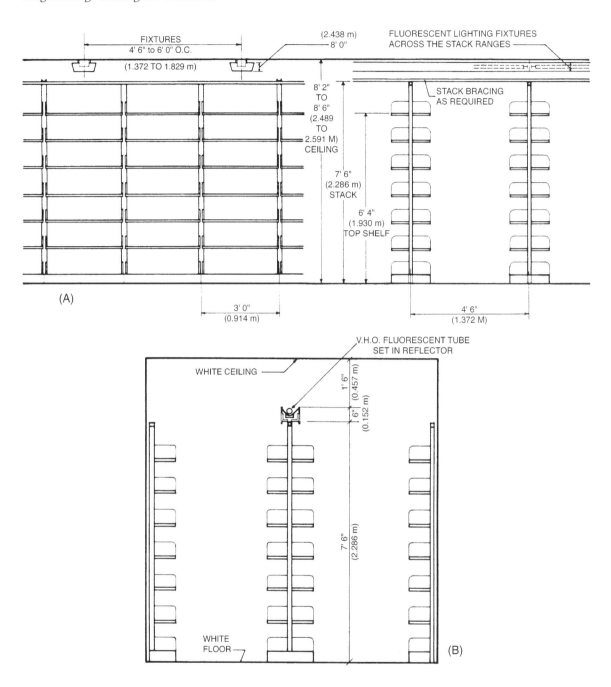

FIGURE 6.11 **(A) Lighting at right angles to ranges. Provides good lighting for the lower shelves and permits a future shift in range spacing. All the lights must be on when the stacks are in use. With ADA rules as well as structural requirements for seismic loads, shifting ranges to increase stack efficiency may never be feasible. The clear ceiling height must be at least 8 ft 2 in. (2.489 m) and preferably 8 ft 6 in. (2.591 m) to prevent heat damage to books on the top shelves.**

(B) Fluorescent light on the top of a stack range. This is not as efficient as a direct down-light fixture in the aisle between the ranges, but it is an alternative. Ultraviolet radiation is minimized by this approach. A white ceiling and a very light floor are required, with the tube set in a specially designed reflector. Individual range aisle switching could be accommodated, although two rows of light fixtures would need to be on for the use of any range aisle. The switching would thus be somewhat more complex than for an overhead aisle fixture.

a critical point, depending on the arrangement of the fixtures.

If the stack area has a clear height of 9 ft 6 in. (2.896 m), an indirect light fixture placed on the channel or canopy top over a range can be used and can provide completely indirect light. One of the advantages of indirect light is that the reflecting surface absorbs much of the worst part of the light spectrum as far as preservation issues are concerned; filtration of the light source becomes much less important. However, where individual range aisle switching is desired, this system will not be effective. Some of the light is absorbed by the ceiling, resulting in lower light levels per watt. Except where a special effect is desired, this is not a very practical system. Dust accumulation on the reflecting surfaces of the indirect fixture is another problem.

6.1.11 Color and Finish

Shelves used to be almost exclusively black or khaki-colored. A dozen or so colors are now typically available, although these will vary with each manufacturer. A different one can be used for each stack level if desired, and contrasting colors for book-return shelves or other special shelving can be selected.

Color can be used to introduce variety to satisfy the notion that some people like intense colors while others prefer quieter tones. Designing different colors for each floor or zone of a large building, however, means the parts are less interchangeable. Lighter colors are said to be helpful for improving the light level, although the effectiveness is limited with filled shelves. Even so, where preservation is a major concern, consider light-color shelving and flooring so that the lighting levels can be minimized and still be effective. Dark shelves show dust more than do light ones, but they also tend to show off the spines of books better, as they compete less for the attention of the eye. In a stack with shelving of a light or bright color, the shelving itself becomes a prominent visual element. While the lighting levels with dark shelving may be slightly lower, the reduced distraction of color contrast may make the spines easier to read. Except for paperbacks, books tend to be fairly dark.

Of greater importance from the functional point of view is the finish. Preservation experts advise that products that minimize the vaporizing of volatile organic compounds (VOCs) and the off-gassing of acidic and other gaseous materials should be selected. Where preservation is a prime concern, this applies to basic construction and trim materials as well as the finishes applied throughout the facility. For ideal preservation conditions, wood shelving and carpet (because of off-gassing and dust problems) should be avoided. Where wood is mandated, solid wood is preferred to plywood and laminates because of their glues, and, for the same reasons, plywood is favored over particle board with laminate. Where plywood must be used within the stacks, exterior- or marine-grade products are thought to be better than interior-grade products for off-gassing.

For metal shelving, the current thinking is that dry powder paint processes are best in respect to preservation. This process electrostatically applies a fine powder that is fused to the metal with heat. One side effect of this process has been that custom colors are very difficult to achieve. Other finishes that are favored by preservation experts (though not typically used on shelving) include epoxy and acrylic paints. Providing a "burn-in" or curing period before moving into a new space also helps for materials that dry out or complete their chemical changes in a relatively short time. Where there is no choice but baked enamel, consider colors other than white to ensure that maximum baking can be applied (the risk is that white may be underbaked to avoid discoloration).

The finish must be hard enough to resist chipping and abrasion; if it does wear away, the underlying steel may rust, with distressing results. The *Library Technology Reports* in its November–December 1990 treatment of library shelving includes testing of paint finishes, which may be useful in making a selection of a shelving product. (This evaluation showed considerable variation in the finishes of 11 U.S. manufacturers.) The architect's specifications should ordinarily require some form of finish test before acceptance of the product. Furthermore, because some stack installations have not been satisfactory because of poor paint quality, recent installations elsewhere should be checked.

6.1.12 Finished Bases, End Panels, and Tops

These components were discussed earlier as contributors to stability. Should they be used and should end panels and tops be 16, 18, or up to 24 in. (406, 457, or 610 mm) deep to match the double-faced base, as sometimes recommended to provide greater stability? Each library must decide for itself what depth of shelving it prefers to have, but the following factors should be kept in mind.

Bases, end panels, and tops present a more finished-looking result and all are stabilizing factors. There is no place under the bases for dust and dirt or stray books to collect. Just as the cost of shelving goes up nearly 10 percent with every 2 in. (51 mm) added to its depth, the addition of canopy tops has a similar effect. Yet the cost of space is much more important than the cost of shelving. Where cost is a concern, you might equip only those areas where the finished appearance is of greatest importance.

Uniform color is urged for all bookstack components except book return shelves, certain accessories, and end panels, where color may be varied, perhaps by floor, alternating ranges, or type of collection or to indicate where main cross aisles are located or where carrels or folio shelving can be found. Like tops, finished end panels can add 10 percent to the shelving cost, the exact figure varying with the panel and the length of the ranges.

6.1.13 Stack Accessories

Almost all bookstacks require accessories, such as range label holders and book supports. Other features that may be regarded as accessories include pullout reference shelves, shelf label holders, stack-mounted carrels, work shelves or counters, shelf dividers (used only on shelves designed for dividers), newspaper racks, divider film reel shelves, filmstrip trays, solid back panels, coat racks, and lockers. A Seismoguard™ shelf restraint device is designed with a steel bar that drops in front of the books at the onset of a strong earthquake. This novel seismic product is in use at the Getty Trust, Loma Linda University, and UCLA's Biomedical Library. Each of these classes of accessories should be considered. They cost money but will cost more later if they are ordered separately or in small quantities.

Color variation in some accessories can be helpful to add a color accent, if that is wanted, and to create findability. Unless the frame is made of brass or another natural metal, it is useful for the color of the label holder to draw the eye to this device, which holds important information. Similarly, color can be useful for ease in locating reference shelves and work shelves, and possibly for book supports. It is an interior design decision whether you wish the bookends to stand

out by virtue of having a different color. It should also be clear that the finish of the metal (for preservation and durability concerns) should be the same as that for the stacks.

Range label holders can be flat against range ends, stand out at right angles, or be wedge shaped, so as to be in view as users walk down the cross aisles. (See fig. 6.12.) If they project into the aisle space, they should be very high; 6 ft 6 in. (about 2 m) is enough so that tall people should not bump their heads or shoulders on them. The flat variety should be large enough to contain all required information. The projecting type should be of a size to hold classification information that can be read from about 12 ft (3.658 m). This is particularly important with all open-access stacks, letting the person look ahead at two or three range indicators without having to slow down while walking to the desired subject or classification number.

Standard-size range label holders designed for a 3 × 5-in. (76 × 127-mm) card do not give enough space for all the information that some libraries wish to place on them. Although larger label

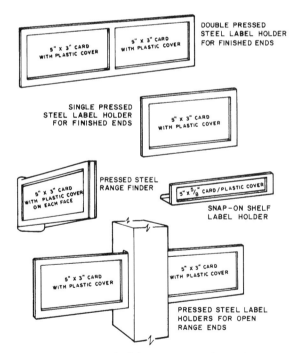

FIGURE 6.12 Shelving accessories. Common range aisle and shelf label holders for 3 × 5-in. (76 × 127-mm) cards or ⅝ × 5-in. (15.9 × 127-mm) labels. The plastic covers are optional. Note that the "pressed steel range finder" projects into the main aisle, conveniently visible from some distance.

holders are usually not carried by the library shelving companies, it is possible to achieve the size desired with a custom design. In this case the label holders may or may not be part of the shelving contract; they may perhaps be part of a graphics contract.

Label holders are desirable at both ends of a range, with one for each side of a double-faced range. Some libraries require both the projecting and flat label holder. In this configuration, the projecting label holder contains the book classification numbers for the range. The flat label holder is used for a verbal description enumerating the subject contents of the range and perhaps for more general information, such as "Return books to the red shelf" or "Turn off the lights when not in use," and the location of folio or portfolio volumes. Range numbers are also useful, particularly for emergency and stack maintenance purposes. Occasionally, directional information may be placed in these label holders.

Shelf label holders are particularly useful where unbound journals or newspapers are stored flat on a shelf. They typically display the title of the serial housed in a specific location. In the general stacks, shelf label holders are not useful except in rare circumstances. They are used occasionally in reference collections, particularly where a great proportion of the shelving may be along walls, making it somewhat difficult to introduce range-end label holders. Shelf label holders should be easily installed but not easily moved once installed. The quantities required will obviously depend on their intended use. In an area of unbound journals housed flat, three and one-half label holders per standard shelf are generally adequate. In a newspaper area, two per shelf are sufficient.

Book supports must stay put where they are wanted, yet at the same time be easily shifted. They need to be so made that they will support books of various heights and not present front edges that may knife books when shelved. (See fig. 6.13.)

Wire book supports are suspended from the shelf above by sliding in the channels at the front and back of the shelf; they are grasped, squeezed, and moved by one hand. It is important that the wire is strong and springlike enough to prevent bending. If the supports bend too easily, they are useless. Properly constructed, they represent an economical book support that many librarians prefer. Unless there is a canopy top that will carry a wire book support, the top shelf will

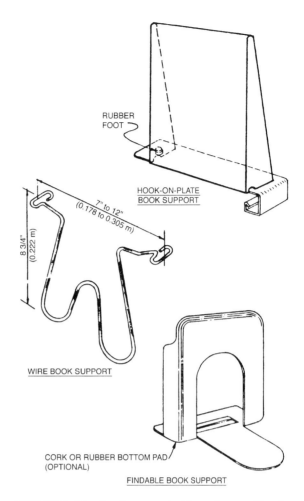

FIGURE 6.13 **Book supports. Three types of book supports are shown. The wire support attaches to the shelf above, the hook-on-plate support attaches to the immediate shelf, and the findable book support is suitable for any shelf. For large volumes, the hook-on-plate support is improved with an extended and turned-down back tab. Note that the rubber plug, cork, or other friction base is designed to inhibit the support slipping along a metal shelf because of the weight of leaning books. Bricks covered with acid-free paper or buckram or fixed supports constructed of wood have sometimes been used in place of these standard book supports. Note that wood is not recommended where preservation environments are prescribed.**

require another type of support. Wire supports fail the design requirement of not knifing a book. They can be lost between books. And standard 6-in. (152-mm) wire supports are almost useless where tall and short books are intershelved because the latter will frequently slip out to the right. Some manufacturers have available an optional 9-in. (229-mm) wire support especially useful in such cases.

The hook-on-plate support is designed to fit into the front edge of the shelving. Because these supports are slightly more difficult to adjust, cost more, and occasionally have a tendency to scrape the paint, they are not always popular. They are formed with a front flap that adds to the stability and prevents them from being lost between books. They can easily be made in several heights. An improved design, recommended for large, heavy books, is at least 9 in. (229 mm) tall, with a front flap and a tab that projects down at the shelf back, but this may be a custom design adding to the cost. This type of book support, with the added back tab, works well for art libraries where the volumes tend to be large and the tab gives greater stability for their support. An advantage of both the plate and wire supports is that they do not work on normal home shelving. Because of this, they tend to stay in the library.

Perhaps the most common book support is the "findable" plate type, which will work on any shelf. This support must always have the "findable" front flap or folded edges, for otherwise it can easily be lost between two books or inside a volume. A cork or rubber pad can be added to the bottom of the support to improve its grip on the shelf surface, though this is not as certain a support as is the hook-on-plate type. A magnetic strip affixed to the book support base has been used to good effect in compact shelving installations at Stanford University.

All the book supports are available in different sizes. The findable type is usually 6 or 9 in. (152 or 229 mm) high; the larger one is probably more satisfactory in most cases. It is recommended that a sample be required before final approval. Because full shelves of bound journals do not need book supports, five book supports to a single-faced section are usually an adequate quantity, but one per shelf is no doubt the typical specification, perhaps to make up for previous deficiencies or to replace those bent or stolen.

A few libraries have preferred to use bricks or concrete blocks covered with heavy brown paper or, better still, with buckram for book supports. The Houghton Library at Harvard has done this but has used decorative glass bricks in its exhibition cases. A disadvantage of a brick or block is that it will reduce the total available shelf length, and 5 percent to 10 percent of the stack capacity can be lost until the shelf is about

full and no bookend is needed. The use of such blocks is recommended only in small installations of very special materials.

Pullout reference shelves are mounted under a standard shelf, usually at counter height. (See fig. 6.14.) They have been used where space is at a premium, and they are a convenience midway in very long range aisles. However, in metal shelving they tend to produce noise, and the useful surface, which is no deeper than the standard shelf, is quite narrow. They also reduce the aisle space when in use, and wire book supports cannot be used on the shelf below. Custom pullout shelves at the U.S. National Archives II overcome the problem of depth; this particular example is both substantial and useful. Pullout reference shelves have been effective at Rice University's Fondren Library in a bibliography room with wooden shelving and aisles 51 in. (1.295 m) wide.

Regarding counter-high shelves in bookstacks, most librarians prefer to find other methods of providing a reference counter or minimize the importance of the need. Chance will usually provide a partially empty shelf nearby. At the Berlin Staatsbibliothek, there are many reference shelves in the stack where a reader can switch on a little

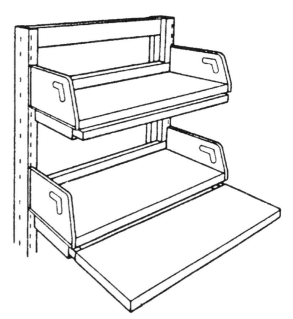

FIGURE 6.14 Sliding reference shelf. The slide mechanism is suspended under a standard shelf, allowing the reference shelf to be pushed out of the way when not in use. These shelves tend to be shallow and noisy, and often are left in the pulled-out position in the stacks.

light to illuminate the empty shelf, and peruse a volume.

Stack-mounted carrels are available in several forms. In ranges with sufficient spacing, they can represent an economical seating arrangement. They have been used effectively at the end of dead-end ranges (along a wall) where the shelves on the facing section are removed to provide space for a chair. They are usually 24 in. (610 mm) deep and limited typically to the standard shelf width, although other widths are possible.

By placing such carrels in a row, side by side, an index table configuration can be created out of standard shelving units. Combined with solid back panels for stability and visual separation, such a configuration can provide relatively comfortable accommodation with greater efficiency (three shelves can easily be above the carrel surface) than the standard index table. However, unless the shelving is well braced, it will seem to be unreasonably flexible, much more so than a regular index table. This type of unit can be useful in a technical processing area for some of the large sets of bibliographies and book catalogs and is occasionally seen in public areas of libraries. As reference resources gravitate toward computer-based technologies, increasing the efficiency of traditional index tables makes sense in most cases.

The work shelf or counter is essentially a variation of the carrel, cantilevered and at counter height. When certain sets of volumes are heavily used, these counters can be operationally essential, perhaps arranged in a row below or in front of the volumes. Reference collections in public areas or in technical processing quarters are instances. A variation on this counter is to have two regular shelves on each side of a double-faced range placed at counter height and remove the next shelf above for head room. This is a flexible and convenient arrangement when the double-faced shelving is in the needed location, and in this condition the shelves below the counter can also house the heavily used volumes.

Divider-type shelving, discussed earlier, is particularly useful for collections of fairly thin materials that tend to flop over. (See fig. 6.15.) The dividers do add risk of knifing materials. Because the back of the shelf must turn up to support the divider, the two inches of space between the back edges of the shelving in a double-faced range are lost. Divider-type shelves are not recommended for books, but variations are suitable for phonograph discs, issues of journals, technical reports, and the like. Shelving designed for the storage of film reels is another type of divider shelving.

Newspaper racks hold a current issue on a stick placed in a rack. (See fig. 6.16.) This type of newspaper storage is also available in furniture-like holders. The rack provides easy access to the

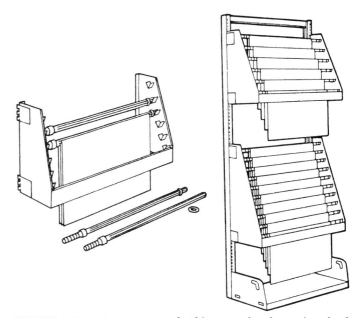

FIGURE 6.16   Newspaper rack. This type of rack requires feeding the newspapers down through a narrow slot. A rack that holds sticks (shown at left) by one end (see figs. 6.17 and 6.18) is easier to use, but unless the sticks are sturdily built, breakage may be more of a problem. Note that this type of rack cannot realistically be used above about 4½ ft (1.372 m), for the average person will have a great deal of trouble feeding the long sheets into the rack upon reshelving. Thus, this illustration is unlikely as shown except for rather seldom used storage, and that would be an odd use of such a rack system.

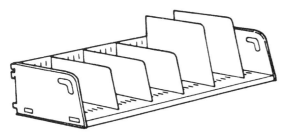

FIGURE 6.15   Divider-type shelf. This type of shelf is often used for phonograph records, music scores, technical reports, and other thin materials requiring additional support. The dividers can knife materials carelessly shelved.

newspapers housed, but replacing the stick and newspaper in any but the front position on the rack is often a little difficult as the pages tend to curl out. Architects frequently use what they call a "plan rack," which is similar. The type that holds one end of the stick is easier to manage. (See figs. 6.17 and 6.18.) Many librarians prefer to simply place the current issue of a newspaper flat on a shelf, which seems to work well in most cases. Probably the greatest advantage of placing the newspaper on a stick is that it is less likely to get out of order, and, of course, it is more difficult to fold up and walk off with.

Filmstrip trays also duplicate storage that is available as a furniture item. Essentially, a filmstrip tray is a sloping shelf with dividers going from end to end that permit storage of filmstrips in canisters.

Solid back-panels represent an expensive way to add bracing to shelving, and, like sway bracing, they prevent flexibility for shelving through. They can only be recommended where there is a desire to create separation from one side of a range to the other, perhaps behind stack carrels or in a range that serves as a wall for security or complete visual separation.

Shelf-hung lockers work well in stack areas near reading areas. They are generally preferable to assigned carrels with lockers. Any lockers in a library represent a management issue in that they provide places for library materials to disappear without a charge-out record. They also tend to encourage the storage of nonlibrary items, such as food, which can become a serious problem. Lockers that can be seen into, either through a grate or a glazed panel in the door, may reduce

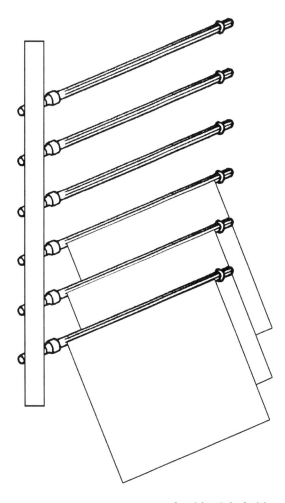

FIGURE 6.17   Newspaper rack with sticks held at one end. Some racks of this design have had problems with breakage. If the fixed bar is slanted away from the viewer toward the top, the papers will not interfere with each other; otherwise, they will bend themselves over the bars and papers below much like ties in a tie rack.

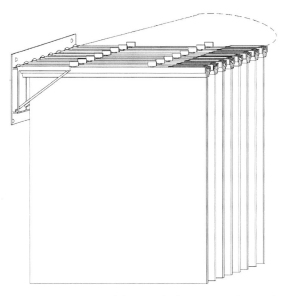

FIGURE 6.18   Architectural plans rack. This rack, which can be either wall mounted or movable, is very sturdy, easy to operate, and effective at holding large-format sheets of paper. The sticks are clamped to one edge of the paper with turn-screw knobs. The sticks are held at one end by supports that can swivel, thereby permitting easy replacement of an individual stick. Each stick can have a label holder (as shown on the top edge) so that individual titles can be easily found. Such a system may be suitable for newspapers in some libraries.

the need for routine inspection. In any case, the keying should be set up with a master key to facilitate routine checks for library books that are not charged out, and the published policy should state that the library maintains the right of inspection. Grouping lockers in clusters makes it more efficient for library staff to make periodic checks. The lockers work well with combination locks with a master key, so designed to permit changing the combination when the locker assignment is changed. Experience with coin-operated lockers has been mixed. In at least one case, an enterprising student bought all the keys at the beginning of a school term and then sold them to fellow students at a tidy profit! Normal key locks result in a constant process of replacing keys and rekeying the locks, which can be an irritation; they are common, though not recommended.

Consideration should also be given to the noise produced by lockers. Placing them a range or two away from an open reading area tends to help. The typical size of a shelf locker is 36 in. wide, 12 in. deep, and 18 in. high ($914 \times 305 \times 457$ mm) with two compartments in each unit. Where ranges are designed for minimal aisles and shelf size, their depth may be a problem. Also, a separate locker facility may be desired with dimensions sufficient to house a laptop computer or perhaps a briefcase, as the shelf locker is too small for some books, a box of research notes, and these items.

Alternatives to shelf lockers include lockers at the carrels, separate banks of lockers, or small book trucks that are designed to serve as rolling lockers. There is no magic formula for the quantity of lockers needed, although it is clear that a library planned for extended research probably would have greater demand for lockers than one planned mostly for course-related support. An undergraduate library might have sufficient locker capacity if lockers number about 10 percent to 20 percent of the seating count, while a main research library might find that 50 percent to 60 percent or more would be an appropriate number, depending on several local circumstances, such as the percentage of commuters. Where lockers are primarily for library-related purposes, they should be located inside the library exit control. With some security systems, books kept within the library do not need to be checked by the exit attendant, and readers find repeated access to a locker more convenient if it is proximate to their study area. However, where lockers serve the nonlibrary storage needs of commuters, the per-

centage may be greater, and the lockers are best treated as unrelated to book collection use and should generally be located outside the library exit control.

6.1.14 Vertical Communications

Vertical communications in a bookstack may include stairs, booklifts, elevators, ramps, pneumatic tubes, and endless-belt conveyors. Slides and chutes may be used to return books to lower levels, and various forms of electronic devices have been used for paging books.

Stairs take space, and sometimes confuse the user if they go around several corners and terminate on different levels in different orientations. They should not be too wide or too narrow, and if possible neither too steep nor too gentle. (See fig. 6.19 for stack stair types.) They ought not add to fire risk by making a chimney, and they should not be so hidden amidst shelving as to be difficult to find. Too many libraries have stairs that are very noisy, a problem compounded by door hardware that produces harsh, sharp sounds whenever opened. An exceptionally good example is the University of Central Florida Library in Orlando, a 1965 structure with a 1983 addition in which the stairs are very wide and carpeted, sound is deadened by acoustic panels, and the doors are kept open on fire-activated magnets.

Usually the stairs required for emergency egress plus a main public stair are sufficient for vertical communications in terms of stairs. However, where emergency stairs are used, special attention to stack security will be required both for separation between discrete stack areas and for the exiting process. Signs that indicate "Exit" will need to have "Emergency Only" added, and graphics indicating the route to the circulation desk or lobby may be required. The actual emergency exit door, while it must always open freely from the inside in most code jurisdictions, should have at least a local alarm. Provisions for the possible future addition of remote alarms and even television surveillance may be prudent, even if they are not intended as part of the initial operation. Where allowed, a delayed-action emergency exit lock system interconnected with the fire alarm system should be considered. This type of lock activates only after a 15-second delay (except when the fire alarm is activated), which generally is enough time to allow a staff member to meet the exiting person. Such a system must also be connected to a remote alarm system so that the staff

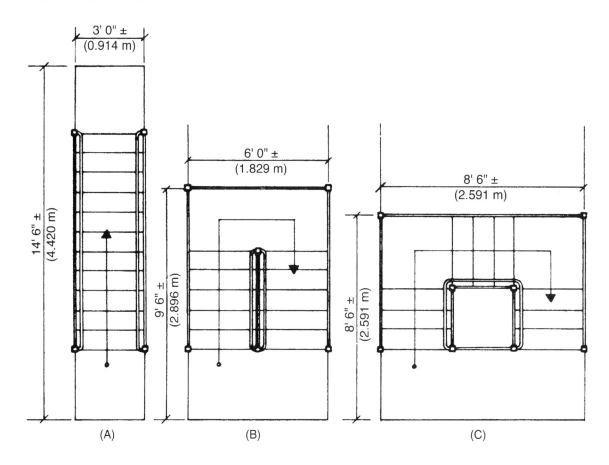

FIGURE 6.19   Stack stairs. (A) Straight-run minimum stair; (B) stair with one turn and intermediate land-ing, which has the advantage of the same relative position and orientation on each floor; (C) stair with two turns and intermediate landings. All three examples are for tiered stacks; normal floor-to-floor height will require more space, as would an enclosure for fire separation. In these examples stair B requires 31% more space than A, and stair C is over 65% larger than A.

member knows when to start running even if the local alarm cannot be heard. In many libraries, this arrangement is well worth the extra expense.

Booklifts are sometimes installed because of the lack of funds for elevators, but unless there is an attendant at both ends, the booklift will at times be irritating. Staff will not be saved from climbing the stairs, and, unless the lift is designed to receive a loaded book truck, the books will be subjected to unnecessary handling at each end of the line. Some code authorities will not permit a lift of sufficient capacity for a book truck as they reason that such a capacity would permit the use of the lift for people. They will then require all the safety features found in an elevator, and the supposed economy of the lift would be lost. If a book truck lift is desired, it is suggested that the local code authorities be consulted before a final commitment is made.

An elevator, even if it is just large enough for a fairly thin attendant and a book truck, will save weary hours of labor and wear and tear on books. It will also provide stack access for a person lim-ited to a wheelchair or crutches or a senior fac-ulty member with heart problems. Its use can be restricted by having it operated only by key. In order to facilitate a wheelchair, the standards for handicapped access suggest a minimum cab size of 4 ft 3 in. × 5 ft 8 in. clear (1.295 × 1.727 m) where the cab door is in one corner, or 4 ft 3 in. × 6 ft 8 in. (1.295 × 2.032 m) with a center door, which is somewhat larger than the thin atten-dant and book truck would require.

Ramps have a few advantages over elevators. They are generally open and seem friendly and safe. They are reasonably quiet places. They are available every minute. They do not have me-chanical failures. And they can serve as emergency exit routes. Some libraries, such as the Engineering Library in the Bechtel Center at the University of California, Berkeley, have introduced a system of ramps to provide for vertical movement of both books and handicapped persons. Considering that a ramp for wheelchairs should not be steeper than one in twelve and that ramps with less slope are often recommended, the space required is considerable. Excluding landings, a ramp required to negotiate 8 ft (2.438 m) vertically will need to be 96 ft (29.260 m) long. At least one standard requires a landing for every 2 ft 6 in. (0.762-m) rise, which, in our example, would result in three landings plus top and bottom landings. Based on the same standard, this requirement adds 5 ft (1.524 m) per landing, for a total length of 121 ft (36.880 m). With a minimum width of 3 ft (0.914 m) clear plus a minimum of 6 in. (152 mm) for rails on each side, the required ramp thus would consume at least 424 ft^2 (39.39 m^2). Steeper ramps can be found in libraries; yet with a fully loaded book truck, they can be extremely dangerous, and they do not comply with the requirements of new construction and access. At $150 per ft^2, this ramp costs nearly $8,000 per vertical foot (or over $26,000 per vertical meter); a typical library with 14 ft (4.267 m) from floor to floor would thus cost about $112,000 per floor for a ramp. The cost for a system of ramps of any extent could easily equal or exceed the cost of an elevator.

Pneumatic tubes to carry call slips from the circulation desk to stack stations have been used for many years. They can be noisy. At the University of California, Los Angeles, a pneumatic tube was installed to move books between the two main library collections a block apart. In this case there were problems initially with the abrupt changes in speed, which seemed to be causing damage to some materials. For paging books, it is now possible to use pocket radio pagers and computer terminals in place of Telautograph, Teletype, or pneumatic tubes. However, hard-copy transfer of the required information results in less error than a spoken or copied message. Before installing mechanical transport systems, the authors strongly recommend that the design team investigate several installations of the exact design or model that have been operating for over a decade, if at all possible. Specially designed systems typically become white elephants, a consequence made even more compelling by computer technology.

Endless-belt conveyors have been in use in libraries at least since early in the twentieth century for both vertical and horizontal transmission of books. Almost all are quite noisy. Too often they go out of order, generally because they are too complicated, having been made to turn too many corners, run on different planes, and receive and drop books at many stations. The more satisfactory installations have usually been the simplest. At least one elaborate example (the Library at California State University, Long Beach) was, in the 1980s, successful. However, as with many such custom-designed devices, its operations became faulty, parts became no longer available, and the entire conveyer system was taken out within a decade. Of course, endless conveyors are now used on a large scale in industry, and manufacturers now know much more about their problems. Such a system probably should be at least considered in a library with a proportionately large user population where circulation rates are exceedingly high. Other aspects of vertical communications are discussed in the chapters on the facility design, particularly Section 12.4.

6.2
Space Requirements for Books

This section deals with space requirements for book collections in terms of stack sections and floor area. It will not attempt to discuss book storage in reading areas, storage of nonbook materials, or compact storage. All these aspects are discussed in subsequent sections. This section is concerned only with books, pamphlets bound as books, and bound periodicals stored in standard bookstacks.

Space for staff and readers frequently becomes inadequate first, but, although books cannot talk and complain, lack of space for them is more evident visually and often receives greater attention. Additional seating accommodation is needed for a limited number of hours only during the school year, and, if students cannot find seats in the library, they may go to their rooms or decide to do something else rather than read or study. The librarian works on the principle that space can always be found for one more staff member and hesitates to complain. But the books, although not vocal, suffer physically; their suffering is easy to demonstrate, as is the resulting poor service.

The shortage of stack space too often may be the result of an overestimation of its capacity at the time of construction. The fault may lie with a too optimistic librarian or with an architect who has tried to crowd more capacity than is practical into the limited space that can be provided from the available funds. Or the fault may rest with those responsible who have failed to realize that, with subject arrangement, shelves become uncomfortably crowded by the time 80 percent of the total space is occupied and become almost unusable when 90 percent is used. But other factors may be to blame.

Cornell University in 1990 projected the size of its library 30 years hence, taking into consideration the effects of information technologies. We quote its report:

> For the conventional analysis we employed traditional library standards: State University of New York standards for the land-grant colleges and the generic national standards of Leighton and Weber (1986) for the endowed libraries. We frequently customized the Leighton and Weber standards to fit our local situation, especially when they seemed much too liberal for one of Cornell's libraries. For example, the industry standard for shelving density is 10 volumes per square foot but most Cornell libraries had densities of 12 to 20 volumes per square foot. We based the growth of collections estimate on the rate of increase for the most recent five-year period, using an annual incremental volume increase, not a compounded growth rate. We believe acquisition budgets will grow in a more modest linear fashion in the future even though library material costs are expected to rise in a non-linear fashion. . . . We thus believe the Library's average annual growth will drop from the present 2.2 percent to 1.6 percent by 2010.[1]

As the year 2020 approaches, Cornell will be able to prove the soundness of its planning model.

Collections historically have grown more rapidly than anticipated, geometrically, or exponentially, rather than arithmetically. Although this is not true in all cases, the exceptions tend to be those collections, such as in the physical sciences and engineering, where policy requires essentially the removal of a volume for every book added, a practice that may become more common as more remote storage facilities are developed and institutional budgets are restricted. Even so, it seems to be difficult to understand in advance that faculty and students will not be content in most cases with a fixed collection of, for example, one million volumes any more than

they were earlier with half that many, and that they will demand more.

Disagreement often arises in regard to how many volumes can be stored in a given amount of space, and the optimists who tend to overestimate the number usually prevail. Any formula or standard should be used with discretion and concern for local circumstances, including the most generous. In order to decide how much space will be needed for books in the bookstack of a new building, eight basic questions should be considered.

1. *What is a volume?* Methods of counting library holdings are far from uniform, though a physical rather than a bibliographical count is most common. Some libraries call anything with over 50, or perhaps 100, pages a volume and, if it has fewer pages, a pamphlet. Some would count six pamphlets as a volume, while others call anything that is cataloged as a separate item a volume. Some in the past insisted that a volume must have hard covers. Most library collections contain numerous unbound and unprocessed items that have not been counted and may be forgotten, but they must be housed, preferably on regular library shelving. Space requirements may be affected by an unusually large proportion of oversized volumes in such fields as music and fine arts, or by collections of unbound newspapers, or by a policy of binding periodicals into unusually thick volumes. If space requirements are to be estimated with any degree of accuracy on the basis of the number of volumes to be shelved, then a volume must be defined.

In one definition, outlined by the U.S. Higher Education General Information Survey (HEGIS) in 1971, a volume is "a physical unit of any printed, typewritten, handwritten, mimeographed, or processed work contained in one binding or portfolio, hardbound or paperbound, which has been classified, cataloged, and/or made ready for use." This definition is still useful. A more detailed breakdown of types of material is always desirable for accurate space planning. Do not forget materials that have not been fully processed for use but that may be housed in the stacks.

2. *How tall and, even more important, how thick is an average physical volume?* This is as complicated as the preceding question and depends in part on the answer to that question. A figure must be determined in order to use the number of volumes as a basis for capacity estimates. Height and depth, as well as thickness, are involved, at least indirectly. The height and depth parts of the

problem were carefully studied in the 1930s and 1940s by Henry B. Van Hoesen and Norman L. Kilpatrick (table 6.1) and by Fremont Rider (table 6.2). Publication patterns in recent decades have probably not significantly altered these percentages.

Thickness depends partly on the subject (see table 6.3); partly on binding policy, particularly for periodicals and pamphlets (some libraries never bind a periodical in volumes more than 2 in. or 51 mm thick); and partly, as already noted, on the policy adopted for defining a volume. The proposed thickness of a typical volume may vary from country to country, century to century, or sometimes even decade to decade. Anyone planning the housing of Oriental collections will find that the traditionally slim Chinese fascicle or ts's (satsu in Japanese) will amount to almost twice the number of Western-style volumes for a given space. For the National Taiwan Library, the program is based on discussions with staff who defined their collection as 6 percent Western at 24 volumes per shelf, 9 percent Japanese at 30 volumes per shelf, 60 percent Chinese at 35 volumes per shelf, and 25 percent bound journals at 24 volumes per shelf. The resulting projection for their general collection is at a rate of 31.14 volumes per shelf, each shelf being 3 ft (0.914 m) wide and, for the purposes of this projection, full.

The thickness of paper at different periods has its effect. Various styles of binding will result in various additions to the width of the text block, and this makes for great differences when totaled for thousands of volumes. Collections that have survived a flood will tend to require more shelf space due to their warping and deformation. Other variables can modify the space required for a volume in any specific instance.

There was probably a larger percentage of quarto and folio volumes in the eighteenth century than there is today. Fine arts volumes tend to be taller than others, while music volumes are likely to be taller and thinner than the norm. If volumes are over 11 in. and under 13 in. (279 and 330 mm) high, six shelves at the most will be possible in a standard-height 7 ft 6 in. (2.286 m) section. If they are over 13 and under 16 in. (330 and 406 mm), only five shelves can be used. If over

TABLE 6.2   Measurement of Book Heights*

Metric depth × height	Imperial depth × height	percentage	Cumulative percentage
130 × 200 mm	5 × 8 in. (or less)	25%	25%
150 × 230 mm	6 × 9 in.	29%	54%
180 × 255 mm	7 × 10 in.	25%	79%
200 × 280 mm	8 × 11 in.	11%	90%
230 × 305 mm	9 × 12 in.	4%	94%
255 × 330 mm	10 × 13 in.	3%	97%
over 255 × 330 mm	over 10 × 13 in.	3%	100%

* This is Rider's 1949 study to include depth as well as height of books. From Fremont Rider, *Compact Book Storage: Some Suggestions toward a New Methodology for the Shelving of Less Used Research Materials* (New York: Hadham Press, 1949).

TABLE 6.3   Space Requirements for Various Classifications of Books When Shelves Are Filled Solidly*

Kind of book	Vol. per foot of shelf	Vol. per single-faced section
Circulation (nonfiction)	8	168
Fiction	8	168
Economics	8	168
General literature	7	147
History	7	147
Technical and scientific	6	126
Medical	5	105
Law	4	84
Public documents	5	105
Bound periodicals	5	105
Art (not including large folios)	7	126

* Table 6.3 is adapted from one in common use by stack manufacturers. It was used by Wheeler and Githens, who suggested that 125 volumes per single-faced section should be considered practical working capacity. From Joseph Lewis Wheeler and Alfred Morton Githens, *The American Public Library Building: Its Planning and Design with Special Reference to Its Administration and Service* (New York: Scribner's, 1941), pp. 414–15.

TABLE 6.1   Measurement of Book Heights*

Group	Size mm	Size in.	No. of vols.	Percentage of the whole	Cumulative percent
I	up to 190	7⅞ or less	88,582	25.00+	25.0
II	230	9	101,924	29.00+	54.0
III	250	9⅞	86,262	25.00−	79.0
IV	280	11	38,315	11.00−	90.0
V	298	11¾	14,777	4.00+	94.0
VI	330	13	10,348	3.00−	97.0
VII	400	14¼	7,268	2.00	99.0
VIII	450	17¾	2,377	0.60	99.6
IX	over 450	over 17¾	119	0.04	100.0

* Computations based on measurement of 350,000 volumes at Brown University Library, reported in 1934 and 1935.

16 inches and under 20 (406 and 508 mm), four can be used, but extra-deep shelves will be required, and it is desirable to shelve books of this size on their sides to prevent unnecessary wear and tear. The effect of tall volumes on capacity is great.

It is obvious that total capacity per section is a matter of great importance in determining space requirements. Although conservative, a formula of 6 volumes per linear foot (or about 20 volumes per meter), including modest space for growth, has been suggested as a basis for comparing shelving arrangements. Ignoring the space required for collection growth, 10 volumes per foot is closer to what most academic libraries experience, or even more in some cases.

If it were possible to insert one additional volume per linear foot (about 3 volumes per meter) beyond the 6 (20 per meter) provided by this formula, the capacity would be increased by 16⅔ percent, which would provide space for an additional 167,000 volumes in a 1,000,000-volume stack. The construction cost for the floor area required for that many volumes would probably exceed $1.5 million today. However, arbitrary adjustment of the figures used to calculate the shelving capacity in order to reduce construction costs must not be permitted without a clear understanding of the implications.

3. *Is there a satisfactory formula for capacity that can be used?* No. Many different formulas have been used to determine space requirements. They vary widely. The "cubook," proposed over 60 years ago by Robert W. Henderson of the New York Public Library, has been used;[2] it was used in planning the National Library of Medicine. This formula provides for 100 "cu" or "average"-sized books per standard single-faced stack section; it goes one step farther and assumes that a section of this kind occupies 10 ft² (0.929 m²) of floor space. This gives 10 volumes per ft² (108 volumes per m²) of floor space in a bookstack, which is quite conservative for most libraries.

At the other extreme, some architects, under pressure to provide more stack capacity than their clients can afford or from lack of experience, have used estimates of as much as 175 volumes per single-faced section and 20 volumes per ft² (215 per m²), even when subject classification was to be used. Collections arranged by size and stored by an accession number or its equivalent might fit into these estimates, as will be shown in Section 6.3. The authors have seen a full section of

traditional Far Eastern materials with 295 volumes by count! But this is exceptional unless, as mentioned above, one is developing a building program to house such collections.

In between these extremes, a typical formula suggested by the University of California and the *Higher Education Facilities Planning and Management Manuals* (May 1971) proposes that a standard single-faced section will require 8.7 ft² (0.808 m²) and house 125 volumes. This works out to a little over 14 volumes per ft², which is certainly possible in many cases but not all. With the width of range aisles mandated by recent codes, the area required per single-faced section will almost certainly be larger than 8.7 ft² (0.808 m²). Indeed, with 12-in. (0.305-m) base shelves, ranges eight sections long, 36-in. (0.914-m) range aisles, allowance for 1-in. (25-mm) "growth" in the depth of the base shelf in a double-faced section, and 44-in. (1.118-m) cross aisles at each end, a single-faced section will require almost exactly 10 ft² (0.929 m²). This works out to 12.5 volumes per ft² (129 volumes per m²).

In a music library with shelving deep enough to house phonograph discs and provision for full access by handicapped persons, the floor space required will be nearly 11 ft² (1.022 m²) per single-faced section. But, depending on how volumes are counted, a music library may have as many as 120 "volumes" per standard shelf. Assuming six shelves per section, this works out to about 65 "volumes" per ft² (or 700 per m²). A similar calculation for a reference collection, assuming 18 volumes per standard shelf, six shelves per section, and 11 ft² (1.022 m²) per section, which is not especially generous for a well-used reference area, would suggest a capacity of less than 10 volumes per ft² (or 108 volumes per m²). Formulas for capacity are dangerous. Each is merely an attempt to generalize for a particular type of collection in a type of institution with an average current mix of volumes in such a collection. And none of them is completely satisfactory.

4. *Are the books to be shelved primarily by subject, with perhaps limited segregation by size for oversized volumes, or primarily by size?* Shelving by size is discussed in some detail and its effect on capacity is indicated in Section 6.3, dealing with compact storage. This section deals with the first alternative, shelving primarily by subject, which might be said to be essential in an open-access academic library and is common in many independent research libraries.

5. *How much space is occupied by the present book collections?* This is the essential question that must always be answered to give a firm basis on which to make further computations. It is always safer to measure the collections in terms of the number of standard sections that they would fill if each shelf were filled to capacity.

This is not as difficult as it might seem, particularly if the shelves are well filled at present and a minimum of library materials are in circulation. It need not be done with a tape measure; careful eye estimates of empty space that amount to a full shelf are almost always sufficient. The chief task is to count up the vacant spaces, in terms of sections, and subtract the number from the total sections now available. The remainder will be the desired figure. Do not forget to include all the library's collections, not just the regularly classified ones; small and uncommon caches may deserve to be measured more exactly. It will be suggested later in more detail that if 50 percent is added to this figure, the result will be the number of sections that the present collections would fill comfortably and leave room for modest growth. Doubling the shelving filled to absolute capacity will normally provide a good growth figure, accommodating the collections for about 20 years in many cases. But, as with other formulas, this factor needs consideration and adjustment to reflect the nature of the specific library and recent growth experience.

6. *At what rate are the collections expected to grow in the years immediately ahead?* Any formula used for this purpose must be based on (1) the nature of the collections, (2) the present rate of growth, and (3) changes in that rate which can properly be expected. The third is particularly judgmental.

In this era of rapidly advancing technology, will developments in videodisk storage or digital transmission of information enable libraries to slow their rates of growth? This basic question has been asked for several decades. With few exceptions (most notably certain college and undergraduate libraries), the answer appears to remain negative in spite of the fact that libraries will continue to benefit greatly from the new technologies. Microtexts, for example, have preserved for posterity large collections of newspapers that were published on disintegrating paper stock and took a great amount of space. They have also enabled libraries to acquire large collections of other materials. The compact disc and other high-

density digital storage media along with the World Wide Web and other networks may hold promise of even greater space savings, assuming that access to this digital information represents materials that would otherwise have been acquired. Counter to this proposition is the notion that the typical scholar will print out much of the information for use, especially lengthy texts. If this latter practice holds, the printed collections will continue to grow over time, though the source of the printed material may well be digital. To speculate, a library might even contain a print shop and a modest bindery.

To date, the growth of regular stack collections in libraries has continued in almost all cases, and there is no certainty that the rate will dramatically diminish as the result of miniaturization or increased networked information or interlibrary cooperation coupled with improved communication systems and devices in research libraries. The authors would be pleased to be proved wrong on this point, but history and our current experience tell us that the book as we know it will continue to proliferate in numbers well into the twenty-first century, if not indefinitely, and that libraries will continue to buy and house books.

All libraries do not grow at the same rate, and they will not continue to grow at the present rate. Special libraries in corporate settings tend to grow fairly slowly, frequently relying upon information brokers and online resources to support the research needs of the organization. In the academic world, relatively young institutions or new programs in older institutions may grow for a time at a rate of 10 percent or more per year. Today, in the United States, the more typical rapid growth rate is about 4.5 percent per year. From the data gathered by the Association of Research Libraries through 1995, the figures in table 6.4 may be calculated for large academic libraries (with a few minor adjustments to account for obvious glitches).

Intuition tells us that the largest libraries should be growing at the slowest rate, which is demonstrated, and that smaller libraries should be growing at the most rapid rate, which interestingly is not currently the case. It is especially interesting to note that the average growth rate for the most recent five years is generally greater than that over a ten-year period; growth rates appear to have increased. For the total set of libraries, the 1995 holdings are over 356,000,000 volumes; at a growth rate of 2.94 percent per year, over 10,000,000

TABLE 6.4   Growth Rates for ARL Libraries through 1995

Range of collection size (volumes)	Number of institutions	Most recent ten-year average growth	Most recent five-year average growth
1–2 million	17	2.74%	3.58%
2–3 million	52	2.88%	3.11%
3–4 million	15	3.15%	3.18%
4–5 million	7	3.50%	4.23%
5–6 million	7	2.41%	3.14%
over 6 million	10	2.10%	1.97%
all together	108	2.65%	2.94%

volumes are added per year. It is clear that libraries are continuing to grow rather substantially. (Note Cornell University's growth rate, quoted earlier.)

It is suggested that, in most cases, the best data for projection are found in the individual library's statistical history. The current growth rate should at least be projected as a compounded percent annually over the anticipated life of the programmed space, unless known factors would suggest otherwise. For a very young library this type of projection would be too high; it may be more accurate to project a growth rate in terms of absolute volumes per year in this case, with some adjustment for anticipated budget changes.

Other factors may also affect the rate of a library's growth. Increase in the size of the student body has a relatively slight effect on a large university library, but it may be a factor of considerable importance for a small college. By the same token, declining enrollment may imply a reduced growth rate. One standard suggests that 50,000 carefully chosen volumes are required to support the instructional program of even a very small college and may be adequate for as many as 600 students; for each 200 beyond that number, at least 10,000 volumes should be added. It is emphasized that these are minimum figures and that strong institutions will demand considerably larger and richer collections.

Broadening the curriculum ordinarily calls for extensive additions to the library. So does the development of honors courses for undergraduates. These facts are closely related to the adoption of more selective admission requirements and improvement in the quality of the student body. Moreover, a new, attractive building, with the improved services it makes possible, is sure to stimulate a significant increase in library use, which

in turn will result in pressure for an increase in the size of the collections. This has been experienced repeatedly. It is also not uncommon for a new facility to generate more gifts to the library, which will swell the collections at a pace somewhat more rapid than the historical statistics may suggest.

When a university undertakes advanced instruction and research in a new field, its library almost certainly will be called upon to add thousands of volumes that would not otherwise be required. Meanwhile, the breadth of collecting demanded by the older fields of research continues to increase; it is no longer sufficient to buy books and periodicals from the United States and Western Europe. Nations in all parts of the world are becoming increasingly important sources of library materials as their scholarly programs multiply.

In this connection attention should be called to the fact that good research material in a library helps an institution attract better faculty, and, in turn, a good research faculty tends to insist that a library improve and enlarge its collections. Clearly, there must be a sound understanding of the academic and program goals of the institution as a whole in order to shape a reasonable projection of the growth of the library. Equally clear is the fact that any projection is an informed guess and that it will in almost all cases be somewhat off, which suggests that options and contingencies must be part of the planning process.

Estimating growth, then, is something that must be done for each library individually in the light of its present situation and its institution's plans for development. No one formula can be proposed, and, if any general advice is in order, it is that estimates nearly always prove to be too low rather than too high.

7. How full does the library propose to fill its shelves before the situation is considered intolerable? Librarians will not agree on the answer; some will say, "When the shelves average over 80 percent full," because when that stage is reached, a great deal of shifting is required whenever large sets or a considerable number of single volumes in a limited subject field are acquired. It is suggested as a basis for discussion here that 86 percent be considered complete working capacity, leaving an average of 5 in. (127 mm) vacant on each 36-in. (914-mm) shelf (actually about 35.5 in. or 902 mm in clear measure). New space should be available, not just planned for, by the time that figure is reached, or the growth rate should decline to zero, which in most cases is simply not practical. Staying within a reasonable working capacity is particularly a problem for branch libraries. For an active, growing library, the cost of labor required for shifting, plus the resulting inevitable wear on the books, is so great once the working capacity is reached that it will be uneconomical to permit further congestion. If any figure other than 86 percent is adopted, similar computations to those presented below should be made.

As an illustration, using 1995 U.S. dollars, the typical cost for new, central library stack space is roughly $10.00 per volume. The cost to shift a book will vary substantially depending upon staffing and supervision cost, but a figure of $0.10 per volume is reasonable. If three sections of 125 books each must be shifted in order to add a set of 10 volumes to a particular shelf and to reasonably spread out the remaining open working space, then the cost of shifting alone for adding these 10 volumes to the stacks is $37.50, or nearly $4 per volume added. It takes little imagination to see that this is expensive, and such cost can be anticipated as the collections exceed working capacity.

If the library shelves are 75 percent full and the collections are growing at the rate of 3.5 percent a year compounded annually, the available capacity (86 percent) will be reached in almost four years. Four years is none too long a time in which to obtain funds and to plan and build a new library or an addition. In too many cases a considerably longer period will be required. A period of 10 years from the first proposal to the activation date is not unusual in all developed countries. In fact, the great majority of library buildings taking over 10 years are in the largest countries of the world, and exceptional cases run to 20 years.

Further, the time taken for major additions to the main library took just about the same time as did a new main library building. This gives some idea of a desirable timetable, but if it cannot be carried out on schedule, shelves are bound to become overcrowded, books will be damaged, and costs for shifting will mount rapidly. It may be necessary to place in some outside temporary storage, or even permanent storage, volumes selected by subject or by the amount of use they are expected to receive. (See Chapter 2, Alternatives to a New Library Building.)

Tables B.13 and B.14 (in appendix B) show the length of time required to fill shelves to their working capacity at different rates of growth. It should be noted that in a storage library, if the books are added to the shelves by an accession number or its equivalent (fixed location), the working capacity can be essentially 100 percent. However, it must be cautioned that this leaves no room for error; additional space should be available well before 100 percent is reached lest the materials be piled on the floor. Even here, 86 percent may be a prudent planning target, although 90 percent to 95 percent is probably more easily justified.

8. *How long should the new building be expected to be adequate before it is replaced or enlarged, or an alternative space arrangement is activated?* This topic is discussed in Chapter 5. Because it is an important issue, additional comments are made here. The question of the time span for planning a new facility must be answered in accordance with the institution's general building and planning policies; one may suggest only that it is unwise and generally impossible to attempt to plan for long years ahead, just as it is usually unwise to plan for very short periods. If a new building includes satisfactory provision for the construction of an annex or annexes when they are needed, it should not be necessary to construct extensive and expensive stack areas a great many years before they will be used.

Some tax-supported institutions have been unfortunate enough to be subject to governmental regulations, made because of pressure for funds from many directions, that forbid new construction that will be sufficient for more than five years. For a research library, this is undoubtedly a penny-wise and pound-foolish policy if a long-term view is taken. It should also be remembered that in such cases, if space requirements are based on the date when planning begins, and some years must elapse before the new quarters are ready for occupancy, the library will be beyond suitable capacity when the move finally takes place. The state of California permits planning of library collection needs 10 years past the anticipated project completion date. In planning its new building, the Royal Library of The Netherlands was exceptional in its wisdom of programming requirements for housing the collection 50 years ahead, projecting from 1970 to 2020.

To summarize: What can be done in estimating bookstack space requirements? Here is one possible approach in terms of a specific library, assuming that the eight questions have been answered as follows:

1. A volume is any physical unit of material that is to be shelved in the bookstacks being planned.
2. The height and thickness of volumes are such that the number now at hand fills completely the 2,000 single sections noted under answer 5 below.
3. No formula for a definite number of volumes in a section is selected, as the figures used in answer 5 below are considered more accurate. (It is desirable, however, to compare the 2,000 single-faced sections with the count of volumes that are believed to be in the library.)
4. The books are to be shelved primarily by subject.
5. The present book collections would occupy 2,000 standard-sized single-faced sections, 3 ft (0.914 m) wide and 7½ ft (2.286 m) high, if the shelves were completely filled to absolute capacity.
6. The collection is expected to increase in size by 3.5 percent each year compounded annually.
7. The stack is to be considered full to working capacity when the shelves on average are 86 percent full, leaving approximately 5 in. (127 mm) unused space on each shelf, and additional space should be available not later than at that time.
8. It is hoped that the new building or additional stack area will be adequate for 15 years from the date on which the estimate in answer 5 above was made.

Given these answers, the required stack capacity in the new building could be calculated as follows:

Two thousand single-faced sections, increasing at the rate of 3.5 percent a year compounded annually, will fill completely 3,350 sections at the end of that time. Because the new stack is to be considered full to working capacity when the shelves on the average are 86 percent full, the number of sections required for the new construction will be 3,900.

Another extremely important factor suggested under answer 7 above should be repeated here. When the shelves are 75 percent full (using the proposed rate of growth), which will be about

four years before working capacity is reached, the next campaign for more space should begin. With a faster growth rate, the time to start planning will be reflected by a smaller percentage of absolute capacity; that is, if the growth rate were 5 percent compounded annually, the time to start planning new capacity would be when the shelves are about 70 percent full, which again would provide about four years. For a 10-percent growth rate, the time for planning is when the shelves are about 60 percent full. That will be only 11 years from the present, 7 years from activation of the currently planned facility, if the space requirements are based on the space occupied by the collections at this time and the facility can be actually programmed, designed, funded, constructed, and activated in a four-year time frame.

Planning for only 15 years beyond the present need is probably an altogether too conservative approach. The dilemma of those institutions restricted to 5-year planning projections can easily be seen from this sketch. Space for 20 to 25 years from the present is undoubtedly more desirable.

Tables in appendix B will give an indication of the desirable schedules for planning new space when different rates of growth are used.

6.2.1 Square-Footage Calculations (Space Requirements)

So far the discussion has dealt only with the number of standard sections required. The number of these sections does not determine the floor area required because, as was seen in Section 1, variations are possible in distances between range centers, which are affected in turn by shelf depths and aisle widths. Variations are also possible in the length of ranges between cross aisles and in the width of cross aisles. The space required for vertical communications, such as elevators, lifts, stairs, ramps, supporting columns, air ducts, and other services, should not be forgotten, although these elements are normally not counted as part of the net space. The "density of reader population" or the use factor is important as has been noted; aisles in a relatively small stack used by many scholars need to be wider and shorter than those in a very large stack to which proportionately few persons are admitted. The requirements for handicapped access may also have a significant effect on the overall space need.

The generous "cubook" formula suggests 100 volumes and 10 ft^2 (.93 m^2) per single-faced section. A much more compact arrangement is feasible if public access to the stack is severely restricted. If ranges are only 4 ft (1.219 m) on centers (which cannot be done where handicapped access must be provided) and 30 ft (9.144 m) long, and 125 volumes to a section are estimated, 15 volumes per ft², or even 17, are easily possible (160 or 180 volumes per m²). This is generally regarded as quite dense storage for normal stack arrangements. The trend, at least in the United States and Canada, is for increasing use of stacks by undergraduate students, and the average college or university can expect its stack population to increase rather than to decrease. The educational value of stack access is a major pedagogic and scholarly consideration.

It is tentatively suggested, therefore, in order to provide a basis for estimates, that 10 volumes per ft² (108 volumes per m²) of floor space be used for small undergraduate collections with completely open access. Not more than 12 volumes per ft² (129 per m²) should be used for larger undergraduate collections of up to 100,000 volumes. Thirteen (140 per m²) is safe for considerably larger collections, and 15 (160 per m²) might be used for universities with great research collections and open access for graduate students and faculty only. Handicapped access will generally imply a reduction of these figures depending on the specific circumstances, particularly for the denser capacities. Where handicapped access requirements do not mandate extra aisle space, using shelf spacing to maximize capacity can result in up to 20 volumes per ft² (215 per m²) in a great research library with limited stack access, narrow stack aisles, long ranges, and a minimal base shelf. The chapters on design, particularly Chapter 12, as well as appendix B should be consulted for layouts.

Estimating the space requirements for a library's book collections is but one of the problems that must be faced when a new building is programmed. If a completely satisfactory formula could be provided for such estimates, the task would be greatly simplified, but experience suggests rather that the first rule should be *Beware of formulas*. Libraries differ, and there is no satisfactory substitute for consideration of the individual case by an expert librarian, library consultant, and architect. The figures that have been given here, if not accepted blindly, should be useful in making preliminary estimates of space for book collections, and they give at least some indication of the problems involved.

Finally, remember when in doubt another basic rule in library planning: *A healthy library tends to outgrow its bookstack space and its building sooner than expected.*

6.3
Methods of Increasing Capacity

Chapter 2 discusses the possibility of increasing stack capacity by a number of methods as an alternative to new space planning. As many of these techniques may be desirable as part of a proposed facility, either upon activation or as a future option, the physical aspects will be further discussed here, particularly in terms of a program statement.

As detailed in the preceding section, it is not easy to define a volume precisely or to determine the average thickness of volumes in a library. Here, in order to simplify matters, two formulas will be taken as a base; these are arbitrary and debatable and by no means satisfactory for all institutions, but they will make it possible to compare book capacities resulting from different shelving arrangements. For a discussion on book sizes, Section 6.2 should be consulted.

The first of these formulas is that *6 volumes equal the average comfortable capacity per linear foot of shelving (or 20 volumes per meter) if the collections are classified and space is provided throughout for growth.* This formula is commonly accepted and is often very conservative for a college, university, or research library. It means that a standard single-faced section 3 ft (0.914 m) wide, 7½ ft (2.286 m) high, with seven shelves, including the base where possible, can hold 126 volumes. The figures will vary, of course, from subject to subject within the same library. Bound volumes of periodicals ordinarily take more space than monographs, which will be of special interest where they are shelved separately. Seven shelves of quarto or folio volumes cannot be provided in a section, but six volumes per linear foot (20 per meter) is a figure conservative enough to make up for the extra space occupied by the 5 percent to 10 percent of the ordinary collection that is oversized and still provide a reasonable amount of space for growth. Newspapers in their original form should be dealt with as a separate or distinct group as should other nonbook materials.

The second arbitrary formula that will be used here provides that *15 volumes can be housed per ft²*

(160 per m²) of stack floor space. This matter was also discussed in the preceding section, and more is said in the chapters on design, particularly Chapter 12. It should be noted that this is a fairly dense capacity for an open-access stack; 12 or 13 volumes per ft² (130 or 140 per m²) may be a more satisfactory figure to use in an open-shelf college library, and some planners are currently using 10 volumes per ft² to provide for handicapped access.

Three basic methods can be used to increase the storage capacity within a fixed floor area. Each has its advantages and disadvantages. The total cost of housing any given number of volumes may be reduced under some circumstances, if not all, by any of the three, and savings in space and cost may be even greater if a combination of two methods is used or even all three. The most significant problem is whether or not their disadvantages overshadow the anticipated savings resulting from their use.

The three basic methods can be characterized as: (1) methods of shelving more books in the existing or standard library sections; (2) methods of devoting a larger percentage of the available floor space to standard shelving; and (3) methods of increasing the capacity of a given floor space by using special kinds of shelving.

6.3.1 Shelving More Books in Standard Sections

There are five options, all of which will increase the weight of the collections; thus it would be prudent to consult a structural engineer, particularly about an existing stack where more condensed storage procedures are being planned.

a. *Higher sections.* One method of increasing capacity without abandoning standard shelving is to increase the height of the shelving. This can be done, of course, only if the ceiling height is sufficient, there are no code limitations related to sprinklers, and the shelving can be properly braced. If, as in many bookstacks, there are no sprinklers, no particular concerns about bracing, and an 8 ft 6 in. (2.590-m) ceiling (which is lower than the ceilings in most areas of modern libraries that are used for both book storage and readers), the capacity theoretically can be increased by more than 14 percent. This move does not call for giving up a classified arrangement with open access, but it places the top shelf out of reach of all but the tallest readers unless footstools are used.

It also may require heavier-gauge shelving uprights at a somewhat higher cost.

In warehouse buildings, where shelves are closed to the public, the disadvantage is much slighter. The rare book stack in the University Research Library of the University of California, Los Angeles, and the collections housed in the California State Archives in Sacramento are but two examples of extra-height shelving that work fairly well. Auxiliary or storage libraries are discussed elsewhere.

b. *Books may be shelved by size.* If books are shelved by size and the system divides them into five or more groups—for example, books less than 7 in. (178 mm) high, those between 7 and 8 in. (180 to 203 mm), 8 and 9 in. (200 to 229 mm), 9 and 11 in. (229 to 279 mm), and those over 11 in. (279 mm)—it should be possible to place on the average eight or nine shelves per standard section. If the average is eight and a half compared with seven shelves on the average for regular shelving, the shelving available has been increased by approximately 20 percent (Fremont Rider has calculated the figure at approximately 25 percent), which would bring the average capacity per section up to 150 volumes. If combined with the chronological arrangement described below, the figure will rise to 200, a total increase of 60 percent.

This technique has been used at the storage facility at Princeton University for a number of years with support of the faculty (materials are stored in subject order). Other facilities combining shelving by size and by chronological order include the Northern and Southern Regional Library Facilities of the University of California, the Center for Research Libraries, and many reference and research libraries of the United Kingdom, countries on the Continent, and elsewhere. It often comes as a shock to an American librarian to discover the prevalence of shelving by size abroad; foreigners are often equally surprised to find that great American libraries shelve nearly all their books by subject. A decision one way or the other, particularly if chronological shelving is involved, usually will have significant influence on the thinking for seating arrangements and open versus closed stack access.

c. *Fore-edge or spine shelving.* A third means of increasing the capacity of a given area is to shelve books on their fore-edge. The classification or sequence number is conveniently marked on the spine. Where conservation of library materials is a concern, this technique is a mistake as the weight of the text block will eventually cause severe damage to the binding. Alternatively, the volumes can be shelved on their spine, with the sequence number marked on the top edge or with cards indicating the sequence numbers inserted in or between the books. However, either of these variations is a stopgap measure when other alternatives are not appropriate. It has been adopted for infrequently used materials at Yale University and elsewhere. A variation is to pile books flat one on top of another, top edge showing; however, this makes misshelving easy.

A method of saving still more space has been suggested in which books are not only placed on their fore-edges, but their margins are sometimes cut down with a power-driven paper knife, and the remaining text is boxed in inexpensive cardboard containers. Any good conservation officer and most librarians should strongly object to this technique! It is a desperate and irreversible action to take.

It is estimated that fore-edge or spine shelving, if used in conjunction with arrangement by size, will increase by at least 50 percent the capacity per section made possible by the chronological plan. It may bring capacity up to at least 250 volumes per section, an increase of 100 percent over the subject-arrangement plan, and provide for 30 volumes per square foot of floor space instead of 15 (or 320 as opposed to 160 volumes per m²). Where this technique is employed to its fullest, the spine labels will be readable only on the lower shelves; card insertion with call numbers will be required on the upper shelves. With more than an occasional volume shelved on its spine, shelf reading is difficult, as is finding an item.

d. *Shelving two or three deep.* Books can be shelved two deep, that is, one row behind the other, on shelves 12 in. (305 mm) deep, or three deep on 18-in. (457-mm) shelves. As some individuals have done with their personal collections, libraries, because of lack of space, have occasionally resorted to the two-deep plan as a temporary last resort. The inconvenience to users is extremely serious, and it compounds the task of maintaining shelf order and keeping control of inventory.

For lesser-used collections, the problems may be tolerable. The Northern Regional Library Facility of the University of California, opened in 1982, was designed for double-depth shelving—the hidden row for seldom-used archival boxes and the front row for monographs, shelved by size in continuous ribbons, as a set of five or six exceedingly long horizontal layers of books. The facility currently double-shelves books as described here. The Southern Regional Library Facility of the University of California achieves high density through 18-in. (457-mm) deep shelves and 30-ft. (9.144-m) high warehouse-style shelving, the books being double-shelved in accession number order. The exceedingly high shelving is reached using tall stepladders.

When President Eliot of Harvard University proposed cooperative storage for the Boston area, which came into being 40 years later as the New England Deposit Library, he suggested that the "dead books" be shelved three deep, which is even worse—several times as unsatisfactory as two deep. The procedure will, however, increase capacity materially. Two-deep shelving, where books are on 12-in. (305-mm) shelves, with no change in aisle width, could bring the total up to as much as 400 volumes per section or 50 per ft² (540 per m²), assuming the arrangement is also chronological and by size. If the three-deep plan were adopted and the distance between range centers were increased from 4 ft 6 in. to 5 ft 6 in. (1.372 to 1.676 m), as would be desirable if not necessary, capacity would rise to 600 volumes per section and, in spite of the reduced number of ranges, more than 60 volumes could be housed per ft² (or 650 volumes per m²). If long-term use of this configuration is anticipated, a wider aisle permitting direct removal of the contents of a shelf to a book truck is desirable; if employed, this would reduce the capacity calculated here.

A variation of this scheme is to shelve boxed materials with the box sized to permit double or triple rows of books. The Harvard Depository Library and the automated stack at California State University, Northridge, use this method. Increased aisle width to permit handling the boxes is still desirable, if not mandated.

e. *Books are arranged in fixed location, chronologically by date of receipt.* By this method, shelves are filled to capacity one after another as the collection grows. This has been the traditional plan in many large libraries and small ones where closed stacks are common. It facilitates the use of each linear unit of shelving to full capacity. Once shelved, a volume need never be shifted. Many library remote storage facilities use essentially this technique, though it has serious service consequences even in lesser-used collections.

The arbitrary and conservative figure of 6 volumes per linear foot (20 per meter) proposed for this discussion will fill a stack to something like three-quarters of the absolute capacity. With chronological arrangement the same stack should accommodate 168 volumes per section. Still, some factor for growth for the entire collection should be added; it is suggested that reasonable capacity might occur when 95 percent of the shelves are full. This leaves little room for timing error; a smaller percentage working capacity may be prudent. All things being equal, assuming a very accurate analysis of the average book size, 95 percent of the absolute capacity will represent a contingency of about one year in most cases, depending, of course, on the growth rate.

The chronological plan should not be used with a subject arrangement, except in one special circumstance. If the library decides to change classification schemes, the existing collection can be compacted to fill all available shelf space (except for serials, which may continue to grow in the old classification scheme). Volumes in the new classification can then begin in the emptied shelf areas. It is hoped this would happen only once in a century. Yet when it does happen, a saving of shelf space may occur unless the available shelves are already practically filled to capacity.

If a fixed-location, date-of-receipt arrangement is adopted, the only way to use the stacks is through consulting the catalog; all the advantages of classified collections relative to the shelving arrangement must be forgone. Unless the location number appears on the spine of the book, misshelved volumes may never be found. Although readers may still be permitted open access, the disadvantages of open access would result without any of the manifold advantages it normally offers. Having a carrel or study near the specific collections of interest would no longer make sense. The possibility of a serendipitous discovery of an important or useful volume is all but lost; the only means of browsing a subject collection is the shelflist or catalog, which usually is less than satisfactory. Many readers will be interested in several books at once on the same or related subjects. Because these books will seldom be acquired at the same time, the attendant or reader in a fixed-location stack may have to go to widely separated areas for them, taking more time than would be required under a subject-classification system. This is one reason for slow service in many libraries that do not shelve their books by subject.

To be weighed against these considerations, the great advantage of the fixed-location arrangement is its saving in space. Use of this shelving alternative may be most easily justified in a large, seldom-used storage collection, particularly one housed at a remote location and accessed by staff rather than readers. The space required for books in chronological order of accession with a planned contingency of 5 percent is about 78 percent of the space needed for a classified plan with moderate provision for growth. This change alone might save more than $2 million in construction for a one-million-volume capacity.

The ultimate capacity of classified collections in storage on normal shelving can be achieved if, say, every 10 or 12 years all classified volumes are compressed fully to fill every shelf. That subcollection could be called set A, or some such designation (using a manual process to mark catalog records, or a digital wand to read classification bar coding on spines and thus to modify computer records). Collection sets B, C, and so on follow a decade or more later, causing relatively modest inconvenience, especially in subjects with the shorter "half life" of major educational usefulness.

In the United States and Canada at least, scholars and librarians are, for the most part, convinced that open access and subject arrangements are of vital importance and that the cost is not unreasonable. Where graduate programs exist, the classified shelving is also of significant research advantage in auxiliary or remote storage facilities of less-used volumes.

Five methods have been described by which, without making a basic change in standard stack installations, the capacity of a given area can be increased. To double the capacity by shelving books chronologically, by size, and on their foreedge or spine may save as much as $5 million in the construction of a one-million-volume bookstack if construction costs are approximately $150 per ft^2 (or $1,614 per m^2). As has been noted, various combinations of these methods are possible; the total number of plans that might be adopted is therefore considerably greater than five. And the exceptionally high stack or automated stack results in exceptional density of stored volumes. This is treated further in Section 6.3.3.

All these methods will increase the possible floor loading, which must be considered both in existing facilities and when programming a new facility where some form of compact storage is anticipated. Each institution must carefully consider its service methods and requirements before deciding to adopt one or more of these procedures. No one of the five is recommended for an open-access library, although some would clearly be more difficult than others. Their use in a closed-access stack for any but little-used collections is decidedly questionable. These methods should be compared with procedures that will be described below.

There is another, though deceiving and misguided, method of thinking that more books can be shelved in existing sections. It constitutes cheating on the future. The method is simply to decide that, though fixed locations are not to be adopted, a larger percentage of each shelf may be filled without too great difficulty. If seven volumes instead of six are shelved per linear foot (23 rather than 20 per m), the working capacity will be only seven-eighths of complete capacity, yet the estimated capacity will have been increased to 147 volumes per section. There will still be room for a 14-percent increase in the bulk of the total collection before the absolute capacity is reached. However, as pointed out earlier, experience has shown that whenever shelves of classified books are filled on average to 80 percent or more, library service begins to suffer. Constant shifting of books is required because of unequal growth that is impossible to predict; individual shelves and sections overflow; and space has to be found for expansion of entire subject classifications that are growing more rapidly than the collections as a whole.

It should be added that institutions all too rarely provide additional shelf space as soon as it is needed; often they delay until books have to be piled horizontally on top of other books or on window ledges, or shelved on their fore-edges in order to add an additional shelf, a procedure that inevitably damages the books and impairs service. For this reason *the authors strongly recommend that, in estimating stack capacity, a more conservative figure (125 volumes in our example) per section be used. Also, as a rule, the library should begin planning for additional space or alternative measures as soon as the library stack is filled to two-thirds or, at the most, three-fourths of complete capacity, depending on the* *growth rate and anticipated planning time as shown earlier.*

6.3.2 Devoting More Floor Space to Regular Shelving

There are three options:

a. *Shallower shelves.* If the depth of shelves is decreased without changing aisle widths, the center-to-center spacing could be reduced, making it possible to install more ranges in a given floor area, thereby increasing the capacity. This issue is discussed in Section 6.1, but it is of sufficient importance to warrant further discussion here. A large percentage of the double-faced shelving installed in college, university, and research libraries is 20 in. (508 mm) from front to back, often with bases or bottom shelves and end panels 24 in. (610 mm) wide. The justification for this width is to increase the flexibility to house the occasional deeper volume within its subject sequence and to provide greater stability.

The argument for narrower shelves suggests that about 94 percent of all general collections in college and research libraries measure not more than 9 in. (229 mm) from fore-edge to spine. If one accepts the fact that the remaining 6 percent of the collections might be housed in separate, deeper shelves, then shelving that is actually 7 in. (178 mm) deep, together with the 2-in. (51-mm) space between shelves, should be sufficient for most volumes. This proposal results in a range 16 in. (406 mm) deep rather than 20 in. (508 mm) or more as is common. Provided there is no sway bracing, and provided two 9-in. (229-mm) books do not occur exactly opposite each other, this scheme no doubt works. It would require the user to check at least two locations to find an item if it is not at the first place checked. Occasionally two 9-in. (229-mm) books will occur back to back and each must project into the aisle by one inch. If dummies are used (a wood block indicating that the volume with the specified call number is located elsewhere), the anticipated space savings would be slightly reduced. Assuming no dummies, bracing, or back-to-back volumes, the space savings for the proposed 94 percent of the collections would be 7 percent (based upon 36-in. (0.914-m) range aisles, 1-in. "growth" space in the range depth, and going from 20-in. to 16-in. (508- to 406-mm) shelving).

It is possible and perhaps even more acceptable from the service point of view to use narrower shelves in conjunction with size arrangements. Further, it should be noted that newly purchased shallow shelves cost less than deep ones. Finally, some small percent (usually less than 3 percent and often less than 1 percent) of volumes will require special shelving in any event. It is thus suggested that in planning a new stack facility, or considering new arrangements for an existing facility, narrower shelves of 7 in. actual or 8 in. nominal (178 or 203 mm) dimension should be considered. Of course, in an existing facility, a change to narrower shelves would be a costly alteration perhaps limited by the structural module, lighting, and other features, factors that will restrict this approach to new facilities in most cases.

b. *Narrower aisles.* The standard width of aisles in academic libraries in the past has ranged from 30 to 36 in. (0.762 to 0.914 m). With application of the Americans with Disabilities Act, the standard has become 36 in. (0.914 m), 42 in. (1.067 m) where handicapped access preferences are applied, or 44 in. (1.118 m) in public areas where a strict reading of the Uniform Building Code has been applied in the United States; in housing infrequently used books, particularly in closed-access stacks, the width may well be reduced considerably provided wheelchair access is not required. This topic was discussed in Section 6.1, but bears additional brief comment. Combined with shallower shelving, ranges have been installed on as little as 40-in. (1.016-m) centers instead of 54-in. (1.372-m), which, excluding the effect of bracing, dummies, and back-to-back larger volumes, increases the capacity for about 94 percent of the general collections by 35 percent. On this basis, without resorting to any of the other procedures that have been considered, the capacity per square foot will become approximately 20 volumes instead of 15 (or 215 as opposed to 160 volumes per m²). It should be noted that narrow aisles increase the difficulty of lighting the bottom shelves adequately, and that stack management as well as user service may be affected. The resulting scant 24-in. (0.610-m) aisles are suitable only for very low use materials.

In Dublin, the Trinity College Library uses a colonnade under its famous Long Room as a stack area, with ranges 40 in. (1.016 m) on centers; the arrangement is by size, with the result that some 30 volumes are housed per ft² (320 volumes per

m²). In the New England Deposit Library, with shelving 44 in. (1.118 m) on centers and aisles 26 in. (0.660 m) wide, capacity increased by 23 percent over standard shelving, in addition to the gains resulting from arrangement by size. Much of the Newberry Library and the south wing of the Cecil H. Green Library at Stanford University have ranges 48 in. (1.219 m) on centers. Harvard's Widener Library has a heavily used stack with ranges 50 in. (1.270 m) on centers.

The authors suggest that, where code and circumstance permit, aisle widths be carefully considered with present and prospective use in mind. They are not easily changed once installed. For a heavily used stack open to a large undergraduate group, 36 in. (0.914 m) is recommended; where handicapped access is not mandated, 32 to 34 in. (0.813 to 0.864 m) is adequate for a collection of 500,000 volumes and over if the use is not heavily concentrated; and 30 in. (0.762 m) is enough for a limited-access collection of over 1,000,000 volumes. These dimensions can be reduced by 2 to 3 in. (51 to 76 mm) if the measure is at the base and the bottom shelf is 2 in. (51 mm) wider nominally than those above it. Handicapped access, however, may suggest a minimum of 32 in. (0.813 m) clear aisle space or more depending upon the local code, although many wheelchairs can negotiate aisles as narrow as 27 in. (0.686 m) where the base shelf is larger than the standard shelf. In a storage stack for less-used books, 26 in. (0.660 m) will do, but less than 24 in. (0.610 m) should not be tolerated.

Before deciding on aisle widths, the planner should consider range lengths; other things being equal, the narrower the aisle, the shorter the range should be. Both factors are part of the same problem.

With shallow shelving and narrow stack aisles, special provision should be made for deeper shelving for the limited number of oversized volumes. This can sometimes be done by placing them along end, elevator, and stair walls that are adjacent to wide aisles. In this case, be careful not to so disguise stairs and elevators that they are difficult to find. Another option is to set aside bays where one less range than elsewhere is installed.

c. *Lengthening ranges and reducing the width of cross aisles.* Some people have asserted that no range in an open-access stack should be more than five sections or 15 ft (4.572 m) long. This may be valid for a small undergraduate collection, though it could well be disputed even there.

Indeed, short ranges interrupted by cross aisles only complicate shelving arrangements, particularly in a large stack area. If the ranges are clearly labeled and if floor plans are readily accessible, with broad subjects or classification segments clearly indicated, long ranges may be more satisfactory than short ones, because they may simplify traffic patterns and enhance comprehension of collection deployment.

Ranges 33 ft (10.058 m) long will provide 10 percent more shelving in the same floor area than two 15-ft (4.572-m) ranges separated by a 3-ft (0.914-m) cross aisle. A range 36 ft (10.973 m) long will provide 20 percent more shelving than two shorter ranges with a 6-ft (1.829-m) cross aisle between. On the other hand, long ranges add some degree of difficulty for reshelving returned books or shifting a collection, especially where the aisle is too narrow for removing books from a book truck.

Additional discussion of this topic may be found in Section 6.1.

6.3.3 Increasing the Capacity with Compact Shelving

As outlined in Chapter 2, several special kinds of shelving can be used with the normal subject arrangement of books or with one or more of the other procedures suggested above. Not all combinations are practical. Books cannot be shelved two or three deep on some of the special shelving that is described below; in effect, these special shelving devices are a means of achieving the savings of space that two- and three-deep shelving provides without most of the disadvantages. Except for warehouse or order-picker shelving, the height of ranges of special shelving should not be increased beyond the standard height because the shelving generally does not lend itself to use with the aid of footstools. In spite of this statement, higher than standard ranges have been used with special shelving at the University of Wisconsin Library and elsewhere. Four general methods are discussed.

a. *Hinged shelving.* Hinged shelving was first used in England in 1878. The first major installation in the United States came in 1951 at the Center for Research Libraries where it made possible an increase in capacity for a given floor area of up to 75 percent over the standard 125 volumes per section. To this possibility can be added the savings that result from shelving by size if

that procedure is also adopted. This hinged shelving is a custom installation designed by Angus Snead Macdonald. His proposal was accepted before the design had been completely perfected, and the shelving is not as satisfactory as it might have been if a rush order could have been avoided. This shelving consists of double-faced sections hung on each side of standard sections; each range, therefore, has what amounts to three-deep shelving on both sides. Because the hinged sections are nearly 3 ft (0.914 m) long and are deep enough to accommodate books on both sides, the aisles had to be nearly 40 in. (1.016 m) wide; the hinged sections thereby lost part of the gain, but provided considerably larger capacity than would be available with ranges no more than 40 in. (1.016 m) on centers. No library is known by the authors to have copied this design.

A variation of this concept consists of swing units occupying a little less than half the length of a regular section. These units are hung at both ends of each section. The swing units have been offered in either single- or double-faced shelving. The latter, like the installation at the Center for Research Libraries, makes it possible to shelve books three deep on both sides of each range and provides access to books on the inside rows without individual handling of the books on the outer row. Because these units are only half as long as those designed by Macdonald, the aisles need not be widened, and there is less weight to contend with in the movable portion. As pointed out in Chapter 2, hinged shelving typically must have wheels that roll over the floor to assist in carrying the weight. Because of this, carpet may not be appropriate in installations of this type. No academic library in the United States is known by the authors to have this type of hinged shelving.

b. *Drawer-type shelving.* Drawer-type shelving when first introduced by the Hamilton Company of Two Rivers, Wisconsin, was called "compo." The University of Wisconsin at Madison in 1951 stored some 500,000 volumes on new open-stack shelving of this kind. *Library Technology Reports* record that by 1988 only two-thirds of this installation was used because the top drawers were wobbly and full drawers tended to bind. The University of Arizona Library satisfactorily installed a multitier drawer system in the late 1950s, as did Illinois State University at Normal, though a few drawer tracks warped after some years. Similar units called Store-Mor Drawers were also made by W. R. Ames Company of Milpitas, California, and C. S. Brown and Co. of Wauwatosa, Wisconsin. No company known to the authors now makes this type of shelving.

c. *Movable shelving.* Ranges of sections are compacted so that only a single range aisle exists at one time in a bay of perhaps 10 movable ranges, though the number of ranges generally relates to the building structure. When a person wishes to use a range different from the two in the open aisle, the bank of ranges rides on tracks or rails moving perpendicular to the range length so the desired aisle becomes the open one. This type of compact shelving is increasingly common for lesser-used, or at least not heavily used, collections accessed by students, faculty, and others. Even for parts of the general collection of a university, movable shelving has sometimes been found suitable. In one study (University of Mississippi) of use in a relatively large public stack, 76 percent of the users did not have to wait for an aisle to become available, the infrequent delays averaged less than a minute for users, and delays were encountered by staff shelvers no more than one or two per hour. Movable-compact shelving should not be used for relatively small, heavily used collections, especially those with public access, because one user of the bay will tie up use of all books in that bay and might feel discouraged from browsing among the volumes of the particular subject being explored. The latter point is a serious handicap for any student at any level.

Movable shelving is used now throughout the world by over 2,000 libraries for selected collections or parts thereof. In 1984 the Sixth Stack Addition of the University of Illinois at Urbana-Champaign was equipped with 55 miles (88.5 km) of movable-compact shelving on seven floors, said to be the first major library building designed specifically for such shelving. The James Madison Memorial Annex of the Library of Congress, the National Library of Medicine, the Bibliothèque nationale de France, and the new U.S. National Archives II have very large installations. In the 1997 St. Pancras building for the British Library, a major proportion of the book shelving and shelving for very large flat materials is in compact shelving, moved by hand turning of mechanical-assist cranks. In the major 1995 addition to the University of California, Berkeley, main library (Doe Library), two-thirds of the book-stack collection of 1.9 million volumes are housed in movable shelving, with the remainder in conventional fixed shelving. And Cornell University

has projected that 12 percent to 18 percent of all library collections will be stored in remote facilities or compact shelving by the year 2010.

The 1980 Library of Congress Madison Building movable-shelving installation incorporates louvered end panels and canopied tops to facilitate air circulation, three-phase 208-volt motors for greater reliability, full solid-state controls, dual reset buttons, tracks set flush with the finished floor, and an additional safety arrangement using solenoid-activated brakes on the motor shaft that must be released before a shelf unit can be moved.

Though design variations will be mentioned later in this section, the dominant perpendicular-moving type is here given major treatment because it is now so widely used around the world. Compactus shelving was designed by Hans Ingold in Zurich, Switzerland, in the early 1900s. It consists of carriages upon which standard or special shelving is placed. The carriages ride on very low tracks set into or on top of the floor; in the latter case, the surface of the floor is slightly raised to accommodate the tracks. The system in effect provides shelving ranges that can be pushed tightly together so that a given group of ranges (a module or bay) will have a single aisle. The space utilization—depending on the aisle width, the range length, and the number of movable ranges—will usually increase capacity 100 percent, and sometimes much more over standard static shelving in the same amount of space (see fig. 6.20).

Movable carriages can be braced either by special guides that grip the rails or overhead fixed beams with rollers on the shelving units, or by use of an overhead pantograph or collapsing beam system that can carry wires and lights as well. Some manufacturers may recommend a combination of bracing techniques in areas vulnerable to earthquakes. Where energy conservation is a concern, the pantograph or range-mounted lighting system offers the same advantage as range aisle lighting; without it, an entire bay must be illuminated for the use of a single aisle.

This type of compact shelving can be manual (that is, where the operator grabs a handle and physically pulls or pushes the range), "mechanical assist" (where added leverage is provided, generally with a crank and drive-gear system), or electrical (where the operator simply pushes one or more buttons to move the ranges). Without mechanical assistance, the totally manual system is limited to fairly short ranges, often no more

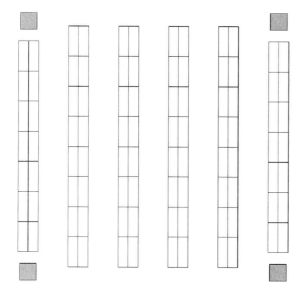

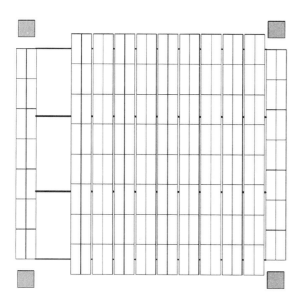

FIGURE 6.20   Standard versus compact movable shelving, of which the entire range is moved to relocate the aisle. In this example—a 25-ft (7.620-m) square bay, no more than 12-in. (305-mm) base shelves, and range aisles meeting ADA requirements—the shelving contained within the column centerlines is 78 section faces with fixed shelving and 158 section faces with compact shelving, or slightly more than double the capacity of fixed shelving in this case. Note that in the compact shelving arrangement, only the shelving along the column lines is fixed.

than three sections. A problem with manually operated ranges is that a strong person can cause the ranges to move too rapidly, resulting in shifting and eventual dumping of materials. Manual systems are generally not recommended for this reason, though they have been used (for example, at the University of Illinois).

"Mechanical-assist" shelving is quite a different matter. With "mechanical assist," ranges up to 10 sections long can be easily accommodated. With proper gearing, as little as 2.4 lbs (1.1 kg) permits moving 10,000 lbs (4,545 kg). Adding up the total number of sections to be moved with fairly full shelves, it is easy with "mechanical-assist" design to move 30 sections, quite easy to move 50, requires real effort to move 70, and 80 is nearly beyond human capacity. The problem is that even with a mechanical leverage system and steel wheels with excellent bearings riding on steel tracks, the force required to overcome the inertia of loaded ranges of books is significant. In a system with as many as 10 sections, it is easy to move a single range, and two or even three at a time are possible, but if the aisle needs to be relocated 10 or so ranges away, a considerable amount of cranking is required. Of course, with longer ranges a motorized system will be required. With motors the ranges can be 60 ft (18.288 m) or even longer.

Also, safety is a factor and should be considered when utilizing mechanical leverage systems, especially in public areas where misuse can occur. The safety risk results from the lack of automatic safety features, though such features can be specified and provided. Unlike the totally manual system, with the "mechanical-assist" system, the speed of the carriages is controlled by the speed at which the operator cranks. It is not easy to crank the system fast enough to cause any alarm in terms of speed; thus, speed is really not a problem.

Movable compact shelving is not always operational, even in quite recent installations. The University of Illinois is said to have one and a half technicians employed to resolve mechanical problems that crop up. Many libraries use a maintenance contract to provide for regular inspections and emergency calls. Although the authors have not heard of a fire in any compact shelving installation, the sixteenth edition of the *Fire Protection Handbook* (section 11085) considers the motor of an electrically operated unit to be a potential ignition source. A 1978 test for the Library of Congress indicated a low probability that automatic sprinkler protection would limit flame spreading. Therefore it was concluded that use of sheet metal panels to subdivide bays and some openness at the tops of sections should help limit fire. This conclusion was partially confirmed by research done in 1990 for the National Archive II with quick-response fire sprinklers, shelving designed for transfer cases with solid, deep shelves, and where a fire stop was provided at every sixth range. In the more recent study, confirmed with tests at Underwriters Laboratories, it was determined that a fire started on lower shelves could be contained.

The U.S. National Archives II research discovered an even better approach to fire protection. It was determined that the best fire protection devised to date can be obtained through a combination of quick-response fire sprinklers and an electrically driven system that automatically moves the carriages to a rest position when smoke is detected (or at a specified time after closing). The rest position distributes the open aisle space equally between all the ranges, leaving 4 to 5 in. (102 to 127 mm) open between each range. With this system, fire damage can be contained and minimized. Conservation experts appreciate the improved air circulation that also results from this system.

There have continued to be occasional injuries resulting from movable-shelving systems, just as there have been injuries from nearly any mechanical system. However, safety features that have been developed for electrically operated movable-shelving systems, if employed and maintained, will make it nearly impossible to incur a serious injury in normal operation. A completely passive safety system should be employed in any electrically operated movable-shelving system so that no conscious effort by the operator is required to ensure proper safety. A key feature of one passive system is incorporated in the flooring (safety floor) that fills in the space between the tracks and consists of panels that, when depressed, activate a micro switch that turns off the system. Other systems use light beams, motion detectors, and other devices to achieve similar results. A "safety sweep," similar to a hinged base plate or kick plate, or a light beam at the bottom edge of the shelving can be added that will stop the system if a stool or book is left on the floor. A second pressure-sensitive strip is sometimes installed at a higher (waist high) level

to stop the system, but it may affect the adjustability of the shelf involved, and, at waist height, the strip is less passive than the floor system. The shelving would in effect already be pressing against you unless you knew that the safety strip was there and consciously pressed it. Vertical safety strips can be installed at the end panels to reduce the chance of the system closing on an arm or fingers of an operator standing outside the range aisle.

The activation of range motion is safer using a constant-touch button, rather than a press-and-release button. A plug-in cable across the aisle entrance is another technique, the electrical circuit becoming inoperable when the cable is unplugged so one can enter that particular aisle. Systems of lights can be employed to indicate when the system is in use. At least one manufacturer offers a torque-limiting feature on the drive mechanism that, when properly adjusted, prevents serious injury even if all the other systems fail. Even with multiple safety features, injury has recently occurred when components of the safety system failed and the defects had not yet been detected. Design improvements are still needed.

It should be noted that some safety systems have an automatic reset feature, while others require staff intervention. A typical safety system activation requiring staff intervention occurs when the range closes on a book left on the floor; the attendant will need to operate the system mechanically or use a special safety override circuit to open the aisle enough to enter it and remove the book. Without the special override circuit, the attendant must go to the master control panel, which is often in another area, to reactivate the system. This inconvenience can be reduced by providing reset buttons at the shelving units. To ensure proper use of the reset buttons and the override circuit, keyed operation is desirable. As can be assumed from the comment above, in the event of power failure, most motorized systems can be operated manually, although it is not particularly convenient or easy to do so with long ranges. As with any significant engineering advance, the state of the art of compact-movable shelving designs has not yet reached a high degree of perfection. Yet, for library book space utilization, they are justifiably now widely used.

When this type of system is installed in an existing space, the tracks and infill floor will add 2 to 3 in. (51 to 76 mm) to the overall height of the shelving. A ramp at the edge of this flooring is installed to permit wheelchair or book truck access. In a new building, the floor slab can be depressed to provide for a completed floor installation that is level or the track can be set into the floor slab. The carriage itself will add about 5 in. (127 mm) to the height. With at least one manufacturer, the minimum depth of the carriage, front to back, is 18½ in. (470 mm) including bumpers, which suggests a minimum shelf size of 9 in. nominal dimension. The carriage can be up to 48 in. (1.219 m) deep or more, which is useful for microtext cabinets, map cases, newspapers, or oversized book storage. Standard shelving, four-post shelving, case shelving, or even file cabinets may then be mounted on top of the carriage. With standard 7 ft 6 in. (2.286-m) shelving, the overall height installed in an existing space will be a little over 8 ft (2.438 m); an estimated 8 ft 2 in. (2.489 m) is safer where dimensions are critical. To this must be added another 6 in. (152 mm) where a pantograph, or beam bracing, or lighting system is installed. A pantograph system for wire management only may add about 4 in. (102 mm) to the height.

A typical installation places the ranges perpendicular to a wall and within a column bay. The power requirements and wiring for the controls are then done through a duct on the wall. Generally, fire code authorities will view the system as furniture and allow ranges of any length. Other local authorities may view the units as built in; thus, the range aisle length may be limited to that allowed for a dead-end corridor or, in the United States, 20 ft (6.096 m). In this case the planner may wish to arrange modules of movable shelving with one cross aisle in the middle of 40 ft (12.192 m) or with cross aisles at each end with an overhead wire management system.

One additional advantage of the movable-carriage system, beyond the potential space savings, is that it offers the possibility of superior protection for the collections when an aisle is closed, as it amounts to a closed cabinet. The safety systems can be integrated with the building security systems, and the electrical aspects can be locked off if provision is made for a key-operated master switch. In the recent underground addition to the New York Public Library Research Library, the electrical movable ranges were combined with a security system for the storage of rare books in an otherwise general stack. The system requires a staff member to swipe a special card through a slot and enter a PIN (personal identification number) before the system can be used. After use, the system automatically returns to the closed position and cannot be used again until the security system is activated.

The systems that detect the presence of a person can also automatically operate the building overhead lighting for the module or, better yet, the range lighting for the open aisle when a person enters an aisle, thus saving energy and maintenance expense.

d. *Design alternatives of movable compact shelving.* A variation of the movable-carriage system provides rows of mobile units in what would otherwise be aisle space. In this installation individual sections are moved manually, longitudinally along the length of the range, to provide access to sections that otherwise would be hidden. The movement somewhat resembles methods used in solving Chinese puzzles. The shelving capacity gained is somewhat less than that gained by the hinged shelving described earlier or by the movable-shelving system described above, as, except for the innermost unit, one section in a range must be left vacant. (See fig. 6.21.) As with the manual movable-carriage system, where a number of sections must be moved to create access to a hidden unit, a fair amount of pushing will be required. Where access to inner shelving is needed, only one person at a time can use the system. Because collections of very large books shelved flat are less used than are common sizes in most libraries, this type of shelving may be useful for housing flat elephant folios and other oversized volumes.

FIGURE 6.21 Longitudinal compact shelving. Here the section is moved from side to side to provide access to hidden sections. In this illustration there could be two movable sections. Although less efficient of space than the movable range, sections of this type may be useful in some cases.

The technology exists to manufacture two additional types of movable shelving, which might be called the "carousel" and the "monorail." The carousel provides perhaps 100 ft (30.480 m) or more of shelving that traverses an oval-shaped track. The shelving can be programmed to stop at specific locations at an attendant station. Also, the format can be designed to operate in a vertical or horizontal configuration. Monorail shelving consists of an overhead track that carries shelving modules. The configuration can provide very dense storage in a large area. Individual shelving modules can be switched to a spur track for access. Like the carousel, the monorail has specific units that can be programmed to arrive at an attendant's station. Both of these systems at this time would be custom installations, and they probably would prove to be expensive to install and maintain. Other systems are likely to be found more suitable for library storage.

Finally, there is a warehouse type of system called the "flow rack," in which containers are housed in racks 15 to 50 ft (4.572 to 15.240 m) long that are stacked from 20 to 40 ft (6.096 to 12.192 m) high. The containers are circulated on these racks and are retrieved, using photo sensors and bar codes, to an attendant's station. Although such a system is quite costly, there may be cases when land values, construction costs, and utility costs warrant its consideration for its exceptionally dense capacity. Careful analysis, including cost projections over a 10-year period for these compared with proven systems, would seem to be necessary.

e. *Movable access of stationary stacks.* Warehouse storage techniques, used for many years, suggest that an alternative to other methods of compact storage is to provide shelving that is 15 or 18 ft (4.572 or 5.486 m) high or higher, together with a mechanical means of accessing the collections. Such a system is sometimes called an order-picker system. Two distinctive systems have evolved—one has a mechanical device that picks totes and delivers them to a staff station where items are manually removed from the tote (as at California State University, Northridge); the other uses a lift on which a staff member stands and, moved horizontally and vertically by the lift, manually removes totes from the shelving rack or material from the tote (as at the Harvard Depository Library, the Ivy Stacks of the University of Virginia, and the Northwest Ohio Regional Book Depository). Each would be suitable in a closed-storage collection where shelving in the most compact manner—that is, by size and in chronological or random order—is appropriate.

The California State University, Northridge, conducted a cost analysis and concluded that a semirobotic stack would save building construction costs and save students some access time. Therefore, the 1991 addition to its Oviatt Library uses a robotic crane that retrieves bins in an 8,000-ft^2 (743.2-m^2) stack 37 ft (11.278 m) high (within a 40-ft-high room, or 12.192 m), designed to hold one million of the least frequently used volumes. The annual maintenance cost of the Kenway Mini-Load system was calculated to be one-quarter the cost of caring for volumes in traditional library stacks. Although browsing is totally lost, many students enjoy the ease and apparent wizardry of typing a code into a computer that directs the crane to the appropriate storage bin. The large bin is mechanically fetched and brought to a central work area, then placed on a conveyor belt that moves past a stack attendant, who removes the desired book and forwards it by mechanical delivery system to the appropriate circulation desk. The pros and cons of this university library structure are still being evaluated.

The Bordeaux, France, city library uses a variant robotic system for lesser-used books. These systems will continue to be considered, and occasional future applications of automated stacks can be expected.

At the Harvard Depository Library, materials are also stored by size in totes. The totes are held in double-faced racks approximately 32 ft (9.753 m) high. Access to the totes is provided by a machine that looks like a forklift, but with a platform for the operator that can be lifted to the desired height in the range. The platform is large enough to include a photocopy machine; requests for journal articles can be filled without removing the item from the stack area. Books, of course, are removed from the tote and brought to the processing area for shipment to the requesting library. The building, including the loading dock and staff work area, is designed with the capacity to easily add additional stack modules.

The facility cost for order-picker storage systems is substantially lower than that for compact storage systems—approximately $3.00 per volume capacity as opposed to about $5.00 per volume capacity with compact shelving and $10.00 or more per volume capacity in traditional fixed shelving (in mid-1990s dollars). In 1997, the Harvard Depository Library charged $3.06 per year for what it calls a BSF (1,296 in.^{3} or 21,000 cm^3).

At that time a BSF accommodated about five items; rounding off to five, this clearly approximates a rental of $0.60 per year per item, which, based on an initial cost of approximately $3.00 per item, suggests that maintenance and energy costs are included in the rent (which certainly is reasonable). However, service and management expenses are not trivial; Harvard charges $2.89 to retrieve an individual item plus delivery costs (which are charged by trip rather than by item). Although most delivery costs are reasonable, an emergency delivery during business hours is $116. After-hours emergency delivery is over three times this amount. If only a few items are delivered, this can be a pretty costly service.

Since 1990, use of the collections at the Harvard Depository Library has varied from less than 5 percent of the total collection held to over 6.8 percent per year; the average annual use has been about 5.5 percent. This is equivalent to about one use of a given item every 18 years, which makes the cost per circulation more rational, particularly when spread over time. Local circumstance needs consideration to accurately demonstrate the cost relative to traditional technologies. Clearly service of heavily used collections using this methodology would be expensive.

The 1994 Ivy Stacks of the University of Virginia is a similar design but with heavier-gauge shelving and the tops of the corner posts anchored in an improved fashion. (See fig. 6.22.)

This facility has a stack with 9,825 ft² net (912.7 m²) and a "head house" of 1,181 ft² net (109.7 m²) to provide the necessary staff and utility spaces. Overall the building achieves a 78 percent efficiency. Shelving is in eight ranges of 39 sections each; four 4-ft (1.220-m) aisles handle movement of the order picker. The shelves are 32 and 36 in. deep × 54 in. wide and generally spaced apart 16 in. vertically (0.813 and 0.914 m × 1.372 m spaced 0.406 m apart). A notable feature is the 5¼-in. (13.34-cm) void in back of each range, provided for conduit of the sprinkler fire-suppression system, and for smoke detection and air circulation. Volume capacity is estimated at 1.2 million. Most of the tote boxes, with tops, are special sizes to handle specific materials.

Essential to this type of storage system is establishing a record of the location of any item. The system generally requires machine-readable bibliographic control and bar codes, both of which are frequently missing from less-used materials. Thus, part of the expense of this kind of system is the creation of necessary records. If the record process breaks down for any reason, the items involved will be essentially lost.

Arguments supporting the use of this type of system include:

- Books can be housed in as little as one-third the cubic space required for standard shelving, so building construction costs are saved, off-

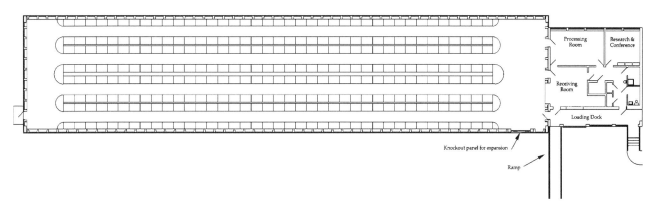

FIGURE 6.22   University of Virginia, Ivy Stacks. Each shelving unit is 4½ ft (1.372 m) wide. Those along the walls are 32 in. (0.813 m) deep, and the rest are 36 in. (0.914 m) deep. The total stack room has outside measurements of 45 ft 8 in. × 215 ft (13.919 × 65.532 m). The stacks go vertically to the underside of the structural ceiling, which is approximately 35½ ft (10.820 m) above the floor; each has 22 shelves. The mechanical room serving this facility is above the loading dock and service spaces at the end of the stack room. Note the provision for future expansion with a knockout panel near the service module. (Courtesy of Osteen Phillips Architects, Project Architects; Ekstrom + Associates, Design Architects; 2rw Consulting Engineers, PC, Mechanical and Electrical Engineers; St. Claire, Callaway and Frye, Structural Engineers)

setting or more than offsetting the cost of the mechanical system.

- Stairs, elevators, and booklifts are not required for human stack access.
- The space need not be finished for human occupancy; savings may be realized in finishes, lighting, air conditioning, and ongoing energy costs.
- Much lower temperature tolerance can improve the longevity of paper, and thus of books and many other library materials.
- Where collections are to be paged anyway, there may be staff savings.
- Bins may provide better physical safety of library materials during such emergencies as flood and earthquake.

Other advantages no doubt can be discovered, but these must be weighed against the significant cost of the system, the access implications, and what happens when this complex device fails to function.

With any of the compact storage techniques, the weight of the system must be considered. With movable-carriage systems a floor load in the range of 300 lbs. per ft^2 (14.364 kN/m^2) should be provided for. With the order-picker systems, the potential floor loading can be substantially greater, while with other systems of increasing capacity, somewhat lower floor loadings are possible. Also, all the movable-shelving systems are costly, but local analysis may demonstrate that their cost is less than that of additional building space with standard shelving. It is clear that they can add significantly to the capacity of a given space.

Against the advantages of special types of shelving, the following drawbacks must be assessed:

1. Books are not as readily available to the reader as they would be on standard shelving, although in most cases they can be publicly accessed. Most of the systems are not appropriate for heavily used collections. Browsability is always impaired, and, in several of these systems, it is impossible. As one highly regarded building consultant in the United States has stated, "Creating browsability in storage buildings defeats their purpose." One can also argue that denying browsability in seldom-used book collections defeats the goals of higher education, at least at the graduate level and for all advanced scholars.

2. As ranges roll, sections swing out, or drawers pull out, there is danger of books falling and becoming damaged. The extent of this danger depends on the design, and is probably greater with hinged shelving and fully manual compact shelving than with the other systems. Even with the safety devices on a motorized-carriage system, the carriage will not stop instantly; there is risk of injury to people and damage to an item left on the floor.

3. All types of special shelving have moving parts, and anything with moving parts may sooner or later fail. Design and quality of construction are vital considerations. The motors, hinges, rollers, and other parts, if well made, should be capable of standing heavy use for many years. When they do fail, means of repair or replacement must be convenient and expeditious.

4. As already mentioned, the cost per linear unit of shelf, all things considered, is much greater for any of these types of shelving than for standard ranges. This is inevitable in view of the moving parts and the heavier construction required, or, in the case of order-picker systems, the specialized equipment needed to support access. The cost may cancel out a large number, but not necessarily all, of the advantages resulting from increasing the capacity, particularly when added to the other disadvantages. Typically, space for a single book can be created for about $10 in traditional stack space or $5 in a compact storage facility using movable shelving, and it has been suggested $3 per volume is possible with an order-picker system. These current guideline figures exclude operating cost (utilities, insurance, stacks and facilities maintenance, collections maintenance, and access cost) and land cost; they are only the initial facility cost.

Two major questions need to be answered before you reach a decision on whether to use any method of compact shelving.

1. Is the resulting inconvenience great enough to outweigh the saving in space that will be achieved? Capacity can be increased, and the options all have their disadvantages. Anyone considering one of the alternatives definitely should consult libraries that have had experience with it, although a few of the techniques are so unusual that examples may not be easily found. Included here are the more elaborate mechanical systems, where the best advice may come from warehouse facilities rather than libraries.

2. What is the actual monetary saving that can be anticipated from adoption of any specific plan? Local conditions, including land value, construction cost, salaries, anticipated service, and utility costs, as well as political or budgetary con-

straints, must be considered. Local codes, potential for earthquakes or floods, conservation concerns, access for handicapped persons, and the nature of the materials being stored all play a role. Are there other alternatives, such as microfilming, recording on a videodisk, or weeding for discard?

Many mistakes have been made in the name of economy. There are libraries that could have used one or more of the methods of compact storage to advantage, but have failed to do so. Others have used one or more of these methods with unfortunate results. There may be two rules: (1) Any shelving other than the typical standard design limits a degree of future flexibility. (2) Any shelving with electronic or moving mechanical parts is certain to malfunction at some point.

It is not easy to estimate costs accurately, and it is difficult indeed to weigh costs against convenience and academic benefits. What, for instance, is the dollar value of open access and collections classified by subject? Still, it is likely that over the next few decades, there will be a far greater interest in library storage facilities with some form of compact shelving. Studies, such as one commissioned by the University of California in 1979, will be more common. In this study, factors of land value, construction, equipment installation, maintenance, and staff costs were analyzed for some 18 different compact storage systems. Although local conditions play an important role, it is interesting to note that this study recommended the use of an order-picker system. The final decision, however, was to install double-depth regular shelving in a tiered stack arrangement with open grate floors. Indeed, each institution must reach its own conclusion on the basis of the economics and technology of the time. This volume can provide no firm answer; it can only indicate the questions that ought to be asked.

6.3.4 Microreproductions and Digital Technology

As implied above, compact shelving should not be dismissed without pointing out that microreproduction and digitization of one kind or another are now used much more extensively than all forms of special types of shelving put together. This is not the place for a definitive discussion of this important topic, except to note:

1. These two technologies represent greater space savings by far than any of the methods described in this section (provided

paper-based copies are not also placed in the collections).

2. The inconveniences connected with a machine-projected text and the dislike that some scholars have for reading at length from a computer screen must be kept in mind. Many texts will be printed for reading; who will pay for this service? It may be less expensive to have a text shelved in paper form in the library than to have it specially printed for each use.

3. To replace material already in a library with microfilm, access from network sites, or compact disc or videodisk storage may cost more than the savings in space are worth, unless the material is reproduced in a fairly large edition. The effect of copyright law and the fees to be charged by owners of information remain largely unresolved.

4. Reading machines, computers, and video terminals are expensive, are not very portable, and involve extra reading area. Do institutions accept the extra expense of this infrastructure? On the other hand, personal computers and smaller portable laptop computers are now heavily used and increasingly popular and common. The California State University systemwide standards have reverted to a simple 25 ft^2 per seat based on their current belief that computers do not add to the space needed per reader.

5. The use of microreproduction, in one form or another, will undoubtedly continue to increase rapidly in the years ahead, but not rapidly enough to reduce present requirements for storage areas for collections. In most cases, this type of technology will supplement rather than replace the book as we know it. Although growth rates will be moderated, collections will continue to grow for the indefinite future.

6.4 Shelving in Reading Areas

Chapter 7, in dealing with housing readers, outlines some two dozen different types of reading areas, many of which require book shelving on a larger or smaller scale in nonstandard sizes and with different spacing. Some of them require storage for nonbook materials, which will be considered in Section 6.6. Shelving in reading areas, speaking in general terms, tends to differ from regular bookstack shelving in four ways.

1. *Attractiveness.* An effort may often be made to make this shelving aesthetically more pleasing than stack shelving, as it is in constant view of library users. Such conspicuousness may make it desirable to use shelving of a more attractive or stimulating color than that in the main stack area, or to install case shelving instead of the bracket type to give it a finished appearance, or to use special end panels or even shelves constructed of wood and finished as fine furniture. If the latter costs more than can be afforded (it may double the cost, particularly if oak, walnut, or a special design is used), the addition of finished-wood end panels can dress up an otherwise utilitarian shelving system. Finished bases or base supports of special design are desirable in many cases as are canopy tops. Each of these distinctly adds to the general appearance of the space.

2. *Aisle width.* If floor cases or shelving are used, the spacing between them is usually wider than that required in a bookstack. Books ordinarily placed in a reading room are there because they are heavily used; with heavy use, wider aisles are advisable, the width depending on the amount of use. A width of 3½ ft (1.067 m) might be considered a minimum, and up to 6 ft (1.829 m) is not unusual, depending on local circumstances and the length of the ranges.

If wall cases are arranged with adjacent tables for users, it is obvious that chairs should not be placed so as to back into the aisle in front of the shelving unless additional space is provided. Furthermore, the aisle should be wide enough so that the reader can consult books on the bottom shelf without obstructing the aisle. This probably means a width of at least 4 ft (1.219 m). At least 5 ft (1.524 m) is indicated if a chair on the shelving side of the table is used. Although these dimensions can be squeezed a bit, reduction will result in increased inconvenience and disruptions under heavy use.

3. *Shorter shelving.* The height of the shelving presents another question. Wall shelving or shelving dividing a large space can go up to the standard height of 7 ft 6 in. (2.286 m), although it may well be held down a few inches if reference books, which tend to be large and heavy, are to be stored. Six shelves 13 in. (330 mm) on centers, instead of the more common 12 in. (305 mm) recommended for most stack shelving, may be

desirable, and with a 4-in. (102-mm) finished base, the top shelf will be 69 in. (1.753 m) above the floor. That distance will be considerably easier for a short person to reach than the 76 in. (1.930 m) proposed in the bookstack for a seventh and top shelf. This is not intended to suggest that the shelves may be fixed; it is still of great importance to have adjustable shelving. The six shelves and a 2-in. (51-mm) molding or canopy at the top will result in a total height of 84 in. (2.134 m).

Some believe that keeping reference collection shelving the same height as the stack shelving will link them beneficially in the minds of the users, especially if one is visible from the other. Further, the full standard-height shelving unit will offer a little greater flexibility to accommodate the occasional collection that is slightly higher than the average volume. Many architects and librarians will prefer to have wall shelving in a reading area built into the wall because of the pleasing recessed appearance. (See fig. 6.23.) Some librarians feel that wall shelving in a reading area is often undesirable because readers going back and forth to consult the heavily used volumes make the whole room more restless and noisy, even with good acoustic protection. On the other hand, a library reading room without books in sight suggests an unwelcome study hall atmosphere.

When freestanding shelving or cases are used, height is a problem. If the room is high and spacious in appearance, freestanding shelving of the same height as the wall cases may be indicated. If the shelving is reduced to approximately 6 ft (1.829 m) in height, only five shelves instead of six will be available, but a more open feeling can be obtained. This is treading on the territory of the architect and the interior designer and is mentioned simply because it is a question that must be decided sooner or later, and there is a distinct space implication that should be reflected in the program. To go down to four shelves will place the finished top at about 4 ft 10 in. (1.473 m), which would make it possible for a person of average height to look over the top and, in turn, would mean that heads will be bobbing up and down as people walk through aisles, which may not be unpleasant at a distance but may be disconcerting nearby. The fifth shelf avoids this and increases capacity by 25 percent, other things being equal.

A height of three shelves will, if carefully controlled, bring the finished top to a level where

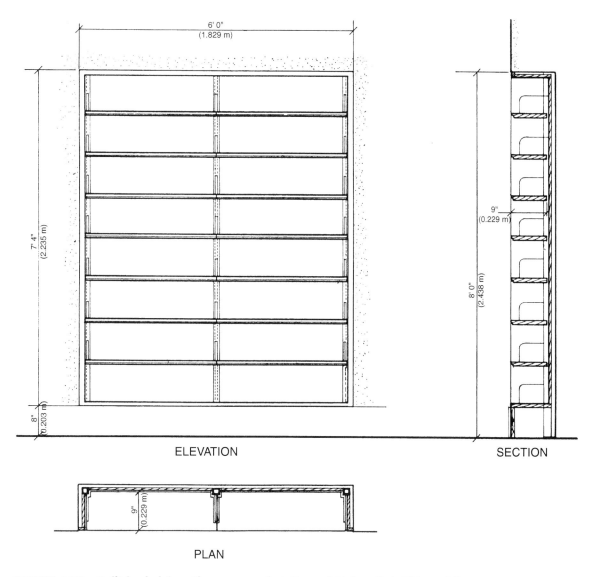

ELEVATION   SECTION

PLAN

FIGURE 6.23   Built-in shelving. Shown as used at Harvard University's Littauer Library.

it can be used as a 43-in. (1.092-m) consultation counter, with definite advantages. In a large reference collection, alternating high and low shelves in either adjacent sections or ranges can assist the use of those typically larger and heavier volumes, particularly where only a short consultation is required. Use of this configuration of shelving will, however, result in readers standing at those counter-high sections obstructing access to some volumes by other users; it may not be an appropriate approach in a busy area.

4. *Deeper shelving.* A final question deals with the depth of the shelves. As already noted, reference books tend to be thick, heavy, and tall. They also tend to be deep, and, as a result, many reference shelves have been specified a full 12 in.

(305 mm) deep with, some would argue, unfortunate results. The number of books over 10 in. (254 mm) deep is extremely small, except for atlases and a limited number of books in fine arts and a few other disciplines; the disadvantages resulting from shelves too deep, particularly lower shelves, may be so great that shelves of a 10-in. (254-mm) nominal dimension in metal bracket shelves or 11 in. (279 mm) in solid-backed wood should be considered. When a 12-in. (305-mm) bottom shelf is used and a 7- or even 8-in. (178- or 203-mm) deep volume is shelved on it, the volume will sooner or later be pushed back and be difficult to find and remove. The same will happen, of course, to a lesser degree on 10-in. (254-mm) shelves.

One means of obviating this problem where a whole shelf of smaller volumes occurs is to place a length of wood, well sealed for preservation reasons, as a block at the back of the shelf. If this is very common, one must ask about the value of providing deep shelves and then blocking the back; however, the deeper shelves do provide flexibility to accommodate deeper volumes when collection shifts occur. If a substantial portion of the collection is larger than normal, the advantage of having a single standard shelf dimension in the reading area has merit. A program of shelf reading and collection maintenance should reduce the likelihood of "losing" volumes. The block at the back of a shelf works well where the top shelf for reference or bibliographic volumes has to be set at 76 in. (1.930 m) or higher. In such a case the block can be of a dimension to require such books as the U.S. *National Union Catalog* and large-library-published catalogs to overhang the top shelf by an inch, thereby letting the user push up the volume and grasp it between thumb and fingers, since short people could not reach to the top of the spine. This is much easier on the spine of the book, lessening wear or damage. Of course, a narrower top shelf can also create such a useful overhang.

A word of caution should be given in connection with the last three points about aisle widths, height, and depth of shelves. Any change from the standards used for stack shelving—that is, wider aisles, deeper shelving, and reduced height—reduces the volume capacity per unit of floor space. Although reference collections are ordinarily classified and shelved by subject, it is customary and desirable to fill shelves fuller than those in the stacks, removing old and outdated material when new books are received. (Reference librarians are hesitant to relegate older volumes to the stack and readily find grounds to avoid discarding from the reference collection, just as librarians tend to find reasons for not weeding for discard or transferring books from the main stack collection to storage until there is no alternative. Both these actions, of course, take time and some expense.)

It is suggested that 100 volumes per standard-height reference section with six shelves 3 ft (0.914 m) long be considered full capacity, instead of the 125 figure used in regular bookstacks; that this figure be reduced to no more than 85 volumes for five shelves, to 65 to 70 for four shelves, and to 50 for three shelves. When it comes to square footage capacity, it is suggested that, with double-faced, freestanding, standard-height shelving units, if the ranges are 15 ft (4.572 m) long with 3 ft (0.914 m) of cross aisles charged against the shelving, and if the ranges are 6 ft (1.829 m) on centers, no more than 8 volumes per ft^2 (86 volumes per m^2), instead of 15 (160 per m^2) in a regular bookstack, or 12 (130 per m^2) in an open-stack undergraduate library, be considered capacity. Where the use of lower shelving is anticipated, this figure must be adjusted downward or a contingency factor should be added.

6.5
Shelving for Oversized and Miniature Volumes

6.5.1 Oversized Volumes

Section 6.2 states that 90 percent of the general collection volumes in research and academic libraries are no more than 11 in. (279 mm) high and that with standard shelving of 7 ft 6 in. (2.286 m) in height, seven shelves can be used for volumes up to that size. With the same stack height, six shelves 14 in. (356 mm) on centers, leaving room for books up to 13 in. (330 mm), can be provided for; this will care for 7 percent of the remaining 10 percent, leaving only 3 percent more than 13 in. (330 mm). It should be noted that if minimal shelf depth for the main stacks is provided, the shelving for oversized volumes may need to accommodate more than 3 percent of the collection because of the depth limitation. The 11- to 13-in. (279- to 330-mm) volumes may well be segregated and placed on deeper shelves vertically spaced 14 in. (356 mm) on centers.

Do not overestimate the proportion of volumes over 13 in. (330 mm) high, though it will always be larger than 3 percent in collections of art history. The 3 percent proportion was determined over 40 years ago in a rather mature university library collection. Folios and elephant folios may have been published more often 50 or 100 years ago. They were expensive scholarly works issued in relatively few copies, so libraries today can seldom find them on the market. Further, undergraduate collections will have very few, if any. Collections in the fields of art, anthropology, archeology, geography, classics, and philology may have more than others. Unless a research library has a good base of oversized volumes, only 1 percent or 2 percent may be sufficient, depending on the fields of graduate study. By far the best basis for determination is to count the current exact holdings and project growth. Conservatism is recommended.

It is desirable to segregate folios, portfolios, and elephant folios on shelves where they can be laid on their sides, which will reduce damage from warping and save the heavy text block from pulling out of the binding. Even where the base shelf in the general stacks is intended for this purpose, there will be need for some concentrated storage of larger volumes. Shelving these volumes will require extra shelf depth, at least 12 and preferably 14 in. (305 and 356 mm) or more to prevent books from protruding into the aisles and being damaged.

With a little ingenuity, a place for this special shelving can be found. At the end of a bookstack, there may be a wider aisle where the extra depth will not be troublesome. Close to a large table and to the elevator would be advantageous. Generally, other locations will suggest themselves as the design effort progresses. It is further suggested that, when bracket-type shelving uprights are used, the deep shelves be of the cantilever or flush-bracket type, so shelf ends will not interfere with spacing shelves closer than the bracket would permit, and much space will be gained thereby. Ideally, only one or two volumes would be placed on each shelf; a greater number will lead to much greater damage to the volumes through use no matter how careful. A very few ranges of this kind will provide for the extra-large volumes in most libraries, except for the newspapers, which will be dealt with later. Elephant folios, such as the Audubon *Birds of America,* or tremendous volumes, such as the set that Napoleon sponsored about Egypt, may require special treatment or custom-built housing. Industrial or commercial shelving is often used for these giant volumes. It should be noted that shelving for those very heavy volumes must not exceed shoulder height; 5 ft 4 in. (1.626 m) should be considered a maximum height for the safety of the user. Ideally, only one or two volumes would be placed on each shelf. This is one of the penalties resulting from riches of that kind—a sort of supergraduated tax.

6.5.2 Newspapers

Most American libraries and those in other countries do not preserve and bind large quantities of recent newspapers because of (1) their bulk and awkwardness in handling or photocopying, (2) the cost of binding, (3) the space they would occupy and its cost, (4) the poor quality of the paper on which nearly all are printed (they often fragment in a generation or so and leave the library empty-handed), and (5) the availability on microfilm of most large city newspapers of importance worldwide and, in the future, in digital format at a cost little, if any, exceeding that of binding.

But there is still a large collection of newspapers in bound and unbound form in libraries throughout the world, and the storage problem is great enough in many cases to make special newspaper shelving desirable to increase the storage capacity for a given floor area for this material. Libraries also tend to keep runs of local papers, including the student newspaper, where conversion to microformat may be costly or generally not justified except when use is very heavy or for archival historical purposes.

Bound or unbound newspaper volumes will last longer if they are shelved flat. Most papers today are no more than 25 × 16 in. (635 × 406 mm) when bound, and many are in tabloid form, measuring about 15 × 12 in. (381 × 305 mm), though some popular papers in some cities fall in between. Shelves 16 in. (406 mm) deep in actual measurement are sufficient for most. If these shelves are cantilevered from the uprights using flush brackets, four (or more, in the case of tabloids) vertical rows lying on their sides will go in three sections each 3 ft (0.914 m) wide, and if ranges are placed half again as far apart as standard shelving and are made from 32 up to 36 in. (0.812 to 0.914 m) from front to back, they will increase the capacity by nearly 80 percent over that obtained when papers are shelved on standard stacks going through from the front to the back of a range. (See figs. 6.24 and 6.25.) The same can be said about housing significant collections of other oversized volumes. Note that the brackets supporting the shelves, even though flush with the top surface of the shelf, do project down in such a way that there may be some risk of damage to the top volume in a stack of several if it is carelessly pushed back and if it straddles two shelves. This type of shelving configuration may suggest the use of shelf label holders described in Section 6.1, particularly where unbound volumes are housed.

A library may provide special shelving of the kind just noted if it expects to keep permanently

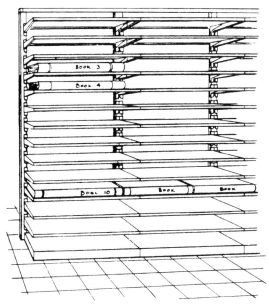

FIGURE 6.24 Newspaper shelving. When the length of a set of books is less than that of the shelf, books may overlap the shelf and thereby increase its total capacity. This is possible with specially designed shelving where the shelf support does not project above the end of the shelving. Shelf labels may be useful with this shelving technique.

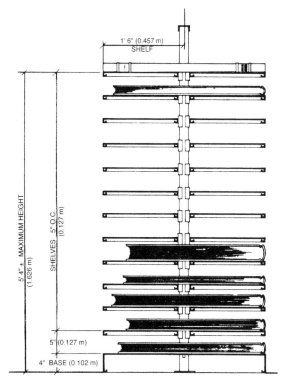

FIGURE 6.25 Elephant folios on newspaper shelving. Note that a label holder is useful for the extra-tall volume on the top shelf in the illustration because the spine cannot be read.

any large number of bound newspapers. For heavy bound volumes or portfolios, special shelves with a set of built-in rollers can be used but are very expensive.

A few older newspapers, and a limited number still being published, are 36 in. (0.914 m) long and more than 18 in. (457 mm) deep. They can be "shelved through" on back-to-back shelves as described above, with their length at right angles to the range. As with giant books, because of the weight of these volumes, they should not be stored above 5 ft 4 in. (1.626 m). Hanging file folders are available that can be adapted to conventional shelving for this storage purpose, as can be seen at the University of Pennsylvania Van Pelt Library. Yet the papers tend to slump in their open envelopes. At Rice University Library, one complete month of most U.S. daily newspapers has for many years been shelved in hanging files (with a freestanding vertical rack with holding sticks for the latest issues of local newspapers). Each newspaper has a separate file for each day of the present month, and below that another file labeled for each day of the preceding month. This permits the reader easily to locate any issue and simplifies the reshelving.

On the other hand, if a library expects to hold its newspapers unbound and discard them in a few months, special shelving is not worthwhile, and those that are kept can be placed on regular shelving, going through from front to back of a double-faced range. Alternatively, unbound newspapers can be shelved folded in half, as they are usually delivered or sold. In this case, they commonly measure 12 in. (305 mm) × 14 in. (356 mm) and it is best to shelve the larger dimension along the face of the shelf so the reader can easily select one or more days. Thus, regular bracketed 12-in. (305-mm) shelving comfortably houses two piles of issues per shelf. Note that both aisles by a double-faced section are useful, whereas half of the range aisles are waste space if the shelf contents are "shelved through" on back-to-back shelves. It is recommended that, with the common use of microfilm for most newspapers, special shelving of the cantilevered type should be minimized in most libraries.

6.5.3 Atlases

Atlases represent another common type of oversized volume. Publication of them will not soon decrease, and many of them are used frequently. Those kept in a reference collection are generally stored in specially designed atlas cases, sold by library-equipment supply houses or built locally to special order. (See figs. 6.26 and 6.27.) These units typically have rollers or trays that reduce the need to slide the volume over a shelf surface. The shelf width and depth and center-to-center spacing of the shelves must be selected to handle the largest single atlas so that subject arrangements are not interrupted by the need to place the larger volumes out of sequence. Individual shelf labeling will greatly assist keeping the collection in order and will help users find the desired volume. The units also typically have a sloped top for brief consultation of an individual volume, but, as is the case with the storage of all large books, it is very important always to have a good-sized table nearby for more extended reading. Because superseded atlases still have scholarly usefulness, the collection will grow, and all but the most heavily used may be housed in a section of the general bookstack or in a map room. A map room, if there is one, may store atlases on shelves similar to those discussed above for newspapers or oversized books. Heavy atlases, wherever possible, should be stored horizontally.

6.5.4 Unabridged Dictionaries and Bulky Reference Manuals

Unabridged dictionaries can be used to advantage on a slanting-top, standing-height consultation table. (See fig. 6.28.) The programmer will need to identify the frequency and general location for these units to ensure that they are included in planning for the furniture. Where a number of small reading areas are planned in an open stack, it may also be convenient to provide for briefly consulted and heavily used subject dictionaries on a shelf near the subject reading area. Larger reading areas and the general reference area, or a central location on each stack level, may be the most appropriate location for a special dictionary stand. These stands are appropriate for any briefly consulted and heavily used tome; a counter may be best if several stands are needed, as for large manufacturing or computer science reference manuals.

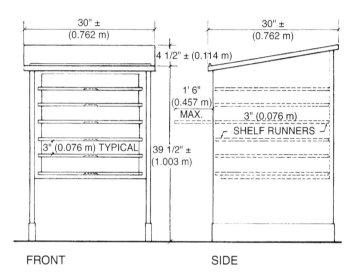

FRONT   SIDE

FIGURE 6.26 Atlas case, front and side elevations. Shelves (nonadjustable) are constructed to pull out for ease of use. Some atlas cases have rollers on the shelves to ease the removal of these heavy volumes.

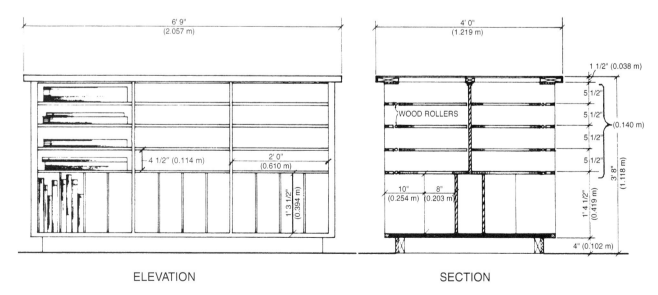

ELEVATION   SECTION

FIGURE 6.27 Custom-built atlas case, designed for the Lamont Library at Harvard University.

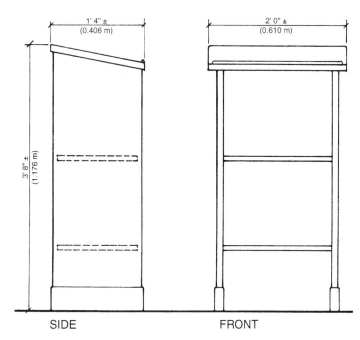

1' 4" ±
(0.406 m)

2' 0" ±
(0.610 m)

3' 8" ±
(1.176 m)

SIDE   FRONT

FIGURE 6.28   Dictionary stand, front and side elevations. Note slanted top to aid use.

6.5.5 Miniature Volumes

Fortunately, miniature volumes are so few in number as to prevent their being a serious problem, but this warning seems desirable. When a volume is much, if any, under 6 in. (say, 150 mm) high, it should not be shelved on regular stack shelving because of (a) the potential for being inadvertently pushed behind larger books and lost for long stretches of time, (b) its slipping out from wire bookends, and (c), due to the very uneven support of much larger adjacent volumes, its causing warped bindings. Miniature books are also prone to be removed from the collection without authorization because of the ease with which they can be slipped into a pocket and the temptation they seem to present to the light-fingered.

Special housing should be provided for miniature volumes in a secure area. Some librarians prefer to use boxes that will hold a group of volumes of approximately the same size. One method is to use three different-sized boxes, each 10 in. (254 mm) long—one for those under 6 but over 5 in. (152 to 127 mm) in the largest dimension, one for those between 5 and 4 in. (127 to 102 mm), and a third for those with neither dimension over 4 in. (102 mm). Alternatively they can be kept in accession number order, perhaps loosely laid in piles in boxes, each holding 20 or 25 volumes, or

in numbered envelopes rather closely filed. These boxes can be placed on standard shelving but should, in general, never be in areas of open access.

6.6
Nonbook Materials Requiring Special Housing

Practically all libraries have collections of material for which special storage facilities, differing from those for books, are desirable. They are discussed below under various headings.

6.6.1 Current Periodicals and Other Serials

Unbound issues of current periodicals present a special shelving question. The basic decision to be made is whether to provide what is known as display shelving so that the cover of the magazine can be seen and readily identified, or, in order to save space, regular library shelving on which the periodical is placed flat or in pamphlet boxes. The decision may be to display selected, more popular titles, and house the bulk of the collection in the more compact shelving. Some libraries display only the current issues or week's receipts and house all the back files on standard or flush bracket shelves.

Journal cover display shelving, described in Section 6.1 and illustrated in fig. 6.29, is somewhat more expensive and requires considerably more space than other forms of journal storage. Where the height of journal display shelving is limited to meet access codes, the space penalty is even more severe. Furthermore, those with movable shelves (type 1 in the illustration) tend to be noisy unless sound deadening buffers are provided. Six journal display shelves per standard-height section are generally considered the maximum; with three and one-half titles per shelf, the capacity is 21 titles per single-faced section. (A more common maximum is five shelves high as illustrated and 3 titles per shelf.) At 10 ft^2 (0.929 m^2) per section, which is probably too little for most journal display shelving in heavily used areas, the more ambitious maximum results in 2 titles per ft^2 (or 23 per m^2). A more realistic evaluation suggests 15 titles per section face and 12 ft^2 (1.115 m^2) for a total of 1.25 titles per ft^2 (or 13.5 per m^2). Even so, many librarians feel that the advantage of service to the reader justifies this type of storage.

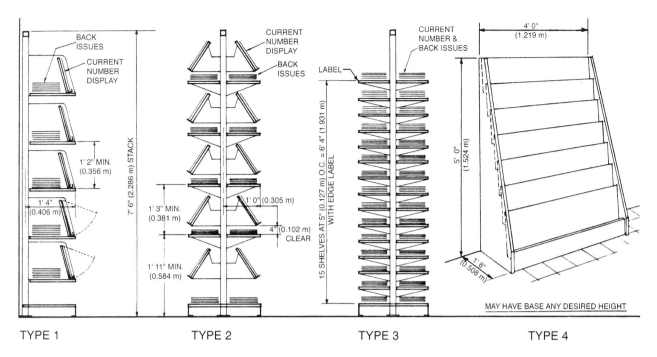

FIGURE 6.29   Shelving for current issues of serials. A variant of type 4 is possible with flat shelves for back-issue storage under fewer slots (as used at the University of California, Santa Cruz Science Library). Access standards for display shelving often dictate both maximum and minimum heights for the shelved materials that differ from the heights in this illustration.

Other things being equal, journal display shelving is to be preferred, but in a library with many hundreds or thousands of current periodicals and other serials, it may be undesirable to use it, except in limited quantity, because of the space it requires if not because of its cost.

The generally preferred configuration for housing large numbers of unbound issues of journals on standard shelving is to place the issues flat on shelves, often with the spine of the issue parallel to the aisles, and to have the shelves fairly close together, perhaps no more than 5 in. (127 mm) apart vertically on centers. Flush bracket or cantilever shelving works best for this arrangement. Labels should be attached to the shelves to make it easier to find the desired title (a practice that is often true of journal display shelving as well). Typically, a section of shelving of this type will hold 14 shelves, if not limited by the height of the end bracket; assuming an average of 3 titles per shelf, a single-faced section has capacity for 42 titles. The slight reduction of capacity per shelf is due to the suggested orientation; 3½ titles per shelf should be possible where the spine is oriented perpendicular to the aisle. For the sake of com-

parison, if we assume 10 ft² (0.929 m²) per section, the capacity is increased by 200 percent over the display shelving (or 233 percent at 3½ titles per shelf).

A third storage technique is to house the journals in pamphlet boxes placed upright on standard bracket shelves. Only seven shelves per standard section can be used. Assuming that 4-in. (102-mm) wide pamphlet boxes are typically used, 8 titles per shelf are possible, with a total capacity of 56 per section—yet another 33 percent gain in capacity (or 14 percent over the 3½ titles per shelf model). It should be noted that narrower pamphlet boxes will suffice for many titles. Given a fixed floor area, this represents an increase of 267 percent over a full-height journal cover display system—even more where the display shelves must be lower. However, journals housed upright in boxes do tend to curl; many librarians feel that the damage that results is not worth the more economic use of space. Furthermore, where display shelving is not used for a particular title, it is sometimes more difficult for the reader to see if the most recent issue has been placed on the shelf.

A variation of the pamphlet box system involves the use of specially designed hanging files that fit into shelving units. The advantage of the hanging file is that its width is essentially adjustable to the thickness of a given title, but the materials still tend to curl. As noted earlier, newspapers are sometimes housed in this type of unit.

Slotted, divider-type shelving is another alternative similar to the pamphlet box. The advantage of slotted shelving is that the dividers can be placed much closer together (1 in. or 25 mm), thereby adding support and increasing capacity.

The key factor, which should not be forgotten, is the amount of use that can be expected relative to the number of titles in the collection. Current periodical areas are among the most heavily used spaces of the library, though this will change in some libraries as more journals are available online. Aisle width should be larger, particularly for a small collection with large proportionate use. It is suggested that for display shelving or even more compact standard shelving in a heavily used periodical area, 10 ft^2 (0.929 m^2) per single-faced section be considered an absolute minimum; in many cases as much as 15 ft^2 (1.394 m^2) is appropriate. Larger collections, where the proportionate use is less, can be housed in shelving arranged with the same spacing as the general stacks, except where absolute minimal stack spacing has been employed.

In any case, in a large library, current unbound periodicals should be housed separately from the main collections and provided with their own reading area. Current issues of quarterlies are commonly so handled, while less-frequent serials may be shelved with the bound volumes of that title in the general stacks. Many large libraries accept the compromise suggested at the beginning of this section and use display shelves for a few hundred of the more popular titles or, in some cases, the current week's receipts, and standard or flush bracket shelving for the back files and less-used issues. This has the disadvantage of resulting in two alphabets or, in the case of temporary display of recent receipts, double handling. Nevertheless, faculty and students soon get used to it, some prefer it, and, if there is an attendant to step in when help is needed, problems will be minimal.

A variation of this compromise is to display the popular, most-used titles on display racks, and the remainder of the collection on standard shelving behind a staffed service counter. Loss and mutilation are prompting this in a few academic libraries. Unless the service counter serves other functions, this solution is expensive. However, if students have to sign up for the material taken to a nearby area, loss and confused shelving can be largely avoided and at least part of the extra cost canceled. The method will result in less use of closed-shelf titles because it severely discourages browsing, which is of great educational value with current periodicals.

Because loss and vandalism with current periodicals are continuing problems, duplicates of certain titles on the display racks are often kept behind the scenes for binding and permanent preservation. (Shelving duplicates should not be forgotten when writing the program.) Another decision that could significantly alter the program is whether or not the runs of bound journals are to be placed in their subject classification in the general stacks, placed in the same area as the unbound collection, or replaced with microtexts or digital access in lieu of binding. In planning the current periodical area, keep in mind that many journals of the future may be viewed on a screen rather than in hard copy. This is one area where flexibility is important.

6.6.2 Manuscripts and Archives

For manuscripts and archives, acid-free boxes of several standard sizes are desirable, as it is rarely wise to bind the loose sheets into volumes, and more protection is ordinarily needed than tying them up with brown paper and string and placing them on standard shelves. At least two types of boxes are frequently used: The larger "records storage box" often serves for the shipment or transfer of materials, which are then kept in this container until sorted and processed and placed in smaller "manuscript boxes." Some comments about such arrangements were given in Section 6.1.6, yet further considerations are needed.

Although acid-free boxes are available in a variety of dimensions, one major source produces records storage boxes that are 10½ in. (267 mm) high with a lid that slips over the top that is about 16½ × 13 in. (419 × 330 mm). There are handholds on each end, and the box should be placed on the shelf with one handhold facing out for easy removal. With standard shelving these boxes can be "shelved through," but in this arrangement only two boxes per double-faced shelf are possible, or six boxes per single-faced section (manuscript shelving can be seven high, but six is preferred for handling potentially heavy boxes, and six shelves per section are used in this illustration). If we assume that each section requires 10 ft² (0.929 m²), it works out to about 0.6 boxes per ft² (or about 6½ boxes per m²). If the shelving is deep enough to accommodate 13-in. (330-mm) material, two boxes can be placed on a single shelf with the handholds facing the side. Given the same area per section, this approach doubles the capacity.

If 15-in. (381-mm) nominal shelving is provided, the two boxes can be placed on a single shelf oriented correctly for easy use (with the handhold facing the aisle), although they will protrude somewhat into the aisle. Considering that the materials are protected by the boxes, this should not present a serious problem, provided the aisle width will accommodate the loss of space and still meet the applicable codes. If we assume that ranges are set up for 15-in. (381-mm) shelves and require 11 ft² per single-faced section (1.022 m²), the capacity is increased by nearly 80 percent over the shelved-through model, but it is decreased by 9 percent from the two-per-shelf model with less desirable orientation. By increasing the length of the shelves to 42 in. (1.067 m), a standard size with many manufacturers, three boxes can easily be housed endwise on a 15-in. (381-mm) shelf. Adding a proportionate floor area for the added length, we find that the capacity is again increased to over 1.4 boxes per ft² (over 15 per m²) for a gain of about 133 percent over through-shelving in standard sections. (See fig. 6.30.)

As the size of the boxes seldom changes, this can be an ideal area in which to use commercial or industrial shelving. Remember, however, that the space economies suggested will be somewhat reduced if the building module does not readily adapt to the spacing requirements of larger, wider shelving. Also remember that even though archival storage is usually in a closed stack, because of the size of and security for the records storage boxes, the aisles will need to be somewhat wider than those required for closed access book storage. It is suggested that the minimum aisle width for this type of storage where codes do not mandate wider aisles should be 30 in. (0.762 m) clear of obstructions; a wider aisle would make handling of the boxes safer. Often a rolling stepladder, which must be able to enter the aisles, is desirable for boxes stored on shelves above head height.

Smaller manuscript boxes may also be obtained in a variety of standard sizes; one common variety is 10½ in. (267 mm) high, 12½ in. (318 mm) long, and 5 in. (127 mm) wide for letter-sized papers, and 15½ in. (394 mm) long for legal-sized papers. As with records storage boxes, manuscript boxes can be "shelved through" on standard shelving where it is not desirable to have the boxes project into the aisles. In this case, because of the space required by the shelf columns, a double-faced shelf can accommodate only six boxes. Using 10 ft² (0.929 m²) and seven shelves per section, this results in about 2.1 boxes per ft² (22.6 per m²). Using 15-in. (381-mm) deep shelves, 36 in. (0.914 m) wide, assuming 7 boxes per shelf (the additional box is possible because of the lack of shelf uprights in the shelving space), and increas-

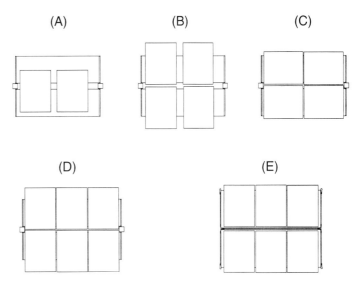

FIGURE 6.30 Archives and manuscripts shelving. In all cases the boxes shown are standard, 13 × 16½ in. (330 × 419 mm, though European standards may differ). Diagrams A, B, and C represent standard 12-in. (305-mm) deep shelving. Note that if the aisle space is minimum, configuration A may be required (and shallower shelving is possible). With B, the boxes are oriented correctly, but there is a considerable amount of wasted space and the boxes project into the aisle quite substantially. Arrangement C is a good use of space, but the boxes are not oriented correctly for easy management.

With a 42-in. (1.067-m) wide shelf as in D, the boxes can be correctly oriented and space efficiency maximized. Shelving type E is four-post shelving, 15 × 42 in. (381 mm × 1.067 m), usually less expensive than cantilever library shelving, and it works quite well for this purpose. Note that if projecting boxes are avoided, the next deeper shelf size (typically 18 in. or 457 mm) will not be as space efficient.

ing the required floor area proportionately, results in a capacity of nearly 4.5 boxes per ft² (48 per m²) for an increase of over 110 percent. The capacity on shelves 42 in. (1.067 m) wide and 15 in. (381 mm) deep can be 8 boxes per shelf but no greater capacity per ft² (per m²). Again, industrial or commercial shelving is well suited for this type of storage. Additional capacity can, of course, be achieved through the use of a compact-shelving system.

In a number of archives, double shelving of records storage boxes on 30-in. (0.762-m) deep shelving has been found to be acceptable, especially for records and seldom-used archival collections (Delaware Public Archives and Records Center is an example). Taller shelving with eight (or more) shelves per section has been used as well, but because of the required use of a ladder, it is not popular (California State Archives). Both of these techniques can easily be used to increase capacity substantially. The double shelving in more nearly standard-height shelving with tiered stack construction would be an especially efficient use of space, and, with records storage boxes in a closed stack, would be more easily staffed than double-shelved books (discussed earlier).

With the possible exception of state archives and records centers where collection activity is mandated by law, estimates of the amount of shelving that should be provided for manuscripts and archival records storage will be difficult to determine because the growth of these collections is generally more uncertain than that of books. Because of this, for most academic libraries the partition or caging separating this shelving area from general shelving areas should allow for future adjustment of the manuscripts and archival stack space while maintaining security for the collections. A common technique to accomplish this is to use very heavy wire-mesh caging fastened directly to the shelving columns in panels that project to the ceiling. If done correctly, these panels can be relocated at modest expense if the archive and manuscript collections grow at a faster rate than projected. Use of this technique will, of course, mean that the environmental conditions of the adjacent stack areas will be similar. For security of collections, caging must be very snug to the floor and quite close at walls and ceiling. The means of fastening the cage panels should also be carefully reviewed, and emergency egress requirements must be met in each stack area.

6.6.3 Pamphlets

Pamphlets are acquired on a large scale by some research libraries but to a small extent in most libraries. They may be kept in one of four ways:

1. In vertical filing cases, preferably near the reference or service desk, with their access restricted. Material in these files is generally kept for limited periods only and then discarded. Pamphlets kept in this way often get hard use and tend to deteriorate.

2. In inexpensive pamphlet binders, preferably acid-free, classified and shelved by subject in the bookstack. This is common practice. In engineering and other scientific libraries where there may be a large collection of technical reports, divider-type shelving is sometimes used to provide physical support.

3. Bound in groups in pamphlet volumes by broad subject or author or issuing agency and shelved in the bookstacks. This is quite often done when large collections of pamphlets on a single topic are acquired en bloc.

4. In pamphlet boxes, similar to those used for manuscripts except they are typically open-topped and small enough to fit on a standard shelf. They may then be classified by subject and kept in a separate pamphlet-box file or scattered in subject locations in the stacks. This approach postpones the day when binding or covering is done to physically protect the item, may still require individual circulation and ownership marks, and may cause future management problems. The pamphlet-box file is a useful alternative for large collections of technical reports that offers more shelving flexibility than the divider-type shelf, principally because divider shelving has serious drawbacks for book storage resulting from the upturned flange at the back of the shelf. Also, the dividers on divider-type shelves tend to be hidden by the shelved materials; eventually knifing may cause damage to the materials.

6.6.4 Microfilms, Microfiche, and Other Microreproductions

Microtexts are commonly found in two and sometimes five types: reel microfilm, microfiche, microcards, microprints, and strip microfilm. There are advantages in making special provision for each, although some of the forms will be held in small quantities and two forms are no longer produced.

Microfilm in 16- or 35-mm format represents the bulk of microproduction in the United States if not abroad. Storage conditions should be rigorous for archival collections and should also be carefully designed for public-use collections. American National Standards have been adopted for both conditions and are summarized in the January–February 1991 *Library Technology Reports*. No film should ever be close to radiators, direct sunlight, or other sources of heat.

Storage techniques for housing public-use collections are basically the same for both film sizes; for the sake of comparison of several storage techniques, the housing of 35-mm microfilm will be discussed here. Reels of film are generally individually stored in cardboard boxes, preferably acid-free, which are 4 in. (102 mm) square and a little under 2 in. (51 mm) thick. The reels should always be housed vertically, on edge, rather than flat. (Formerly, metal canisters were used to house individual spools of roll film, and such canister housing continues in some parts of the world.) Shelving manufacturers offer a special shallow shelf with a turned-up back that can be placed in standard shelving uprights. If one assumes a capacity of 20 reels per shelf, and 14 shelves per section placed 5 in. (127 mm) apart, the capacity of 280 reels results in about 28 reels per ft^2 (301 per m^2) of floor space if stack spacing is arranged for 10 ft^2 (0.929 m^2) per section.

To use normal bracket-type shelving, some libraries utilize rather small, open-fronted plastic bins that may house these individual boxes horizontally five tall, though film conservation argues for reels to be housed vertically so long as the reel itself extends beyond the film. In this arrangement, seven rows with reels five tall result in 35 reels per shelf and usually six shelves per section, a total of 245 reels—not quite as efficient as with special shelves, and yet the extra cost of those special shelves is saved.

A second common method of increasing capacity involves storage of several boxed reels in a larger box, which is then placed on standard shelving. One such box widely used is 4⅛ × 4⅛ × 10¼ (105 × 105 × 260 mm) and holds six reels of microfilm. These boxes can easily be stacked two high on a standard 10-in. (254-mm) nominal shelf. Some libraries prefer not to stack them, but they are light enough to allow easy shelving or removal even when stacked. A three-high stack is awkward, though. Stacked two high, a standard 3-ft (0.914-m) shelf will hold 16 boxes. With seven shelves per section, the capacity is 672 reels, which, given equal stack spacing, represents an increase of 140 percent over the shallow shelf solution. Deeper boxes are available that, given the flexibility to adjust aisle widths, will increase the capacity further. However, the larger boxes will be more difficult to handle if stacked; individual shelves for each row of boxes are recommended.

A third common storage technique involves the use of metal cabinets. Again, a variety of sizes are available; one example is 23¾ in. wide × 28½ in. deep (603 × 724 mm) with each drawer having flush handles and containing five rows of 16 boxes each. In its maximum capacity configuration, it contains 11 drawers in the basic unit, which is 55¼ in. (1.403 m) high with a possible additional 5 drawers of over-file storage. The total height then is 90½ in. (2.299 m), which is virtually the same as that for standard shelving. Clearly, cases of this height must be braced in a way similar to shelving in order to minimize the risk of their tipping over.

Another common cabinet configuration is 20¼ in. (514 m) wide and 29¾ in. (756 m) deep with each drawer containing four rows of 15 boxes each. This particular product with 11 drawers is 62.25 in. (1.581 m) high and has handles slightly projecting, enabling use of a locking bar if the library wishes to secure the contents. Because of the space required by the drawers, the aisle space must be quite generous. Assuming that the floor space required for a single cabinet is 2½ times the area of the cabinet, a factor that may vary depending on the layout, then the area required for each cabinet is approximately 12 ft^2 (1.115 m^2). One unit of this type will hold, according to the manufacturer, 1,330 reels of film, which works out to 111 reels per ft^2 (1,195 per m^2), for a 258 percent increase over shallow shelving.

There is also a storage unit designed with shelves slightly deeper than a roll of microfilm. The shelves are mounted on overhead tracks such that one of the slender shelving units can easily be pulled into the access aisle for shelving or removing an item (fig. 6.31). This unit occupies 25 ft^2 (2.323 m^2) and, in its maximum configuration, holds 4,284 reels of 35-mm film (according to the manufacturer and probably without boxes). At 171 reels per ft^2 (1,844 per m^2), this is an exceedingly efficient storage methodology. The equip-

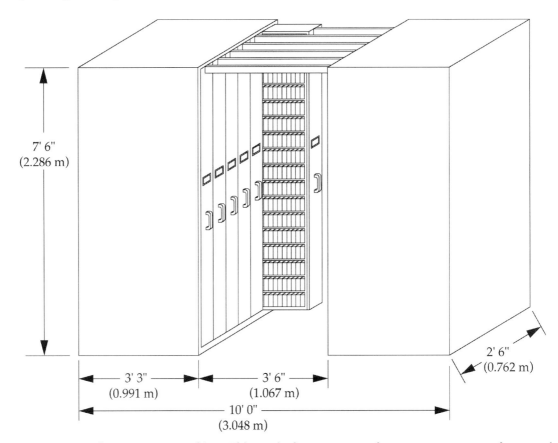

FIGURE 6.31   Microtext storage cabinet. This particular system may be set up to accommodate a variety of media; it need not be used solely for microfilm. However, as a microfilm storage technology, given the space appropriate for such a system, this is a very efficient arrangement. Being no more than standard shelving height, lighting and fire protection systems should not be a problem in most cases. The Gemtrac high-density media storage system is manufactured by Russ Bassett Corp., Whittier, California.

ment, however, is expensive—its list price exceeds $2.00 per reel capacity. Applying $150 per ft^2 ($1,615 per m^2) for the space, this works out to about $0.87 per reel for a total of nearly $3.00 per reel stored. Compared to standard shelving with shallow shelves (for this exercise assumed to cost $200 per section), with a capacity of 280 reels, the cost per reel is $6.07, including the cost of the floor area. For reels stored in six-reel boxes on standard shelving (also assumed to be $200 per section), the cost drops to about $3.00 per reel, including the archival microfilm cases for six boxed reels and floor space at 10 ft^2 (0.929 m^2) per section.

The major difference reflecting comparative cost is in operating budgets, which pay for the equipment, and the space is provided from other budgets. In this case, the operating budget is fa-

vored with less-expensive equipment, even though it takes more space; for operating budget expense, standard shelving and boxed reels are clearly the way to go until there is no choice but to buy the more expensive equipment to save space.

Many feel that cases offer greater accessibility than boxed materials on shelves; therefore, in some libraries a handful of frequently used titles may be in cases while the rest are on shelves. There certainly will be circumstances when the dimensions of the case will be more appropriate for a given space than shelving. Finally, the case has a more finished appearance than shelving, and it can be locked. A special purchasing agreement may significantly alter the results of the cost analysis.

Yet another general type of storage is the carousel unit consisting of a framework of slots for roll film that forms a circular or square column mounted on a lazy Susan base. Most carousels are designed for 16-mm film, but for comparison a unit that will house 35-mm film is discussed. The example is 17⅜ in. (0.441 m) square and 62¾ in. (1.594 m) high. The clear circular space required for rotation is a little over 24½ in. (0.622 m) in diameter. This particular unit holds up to 360 rolls of film. The great advantage of this type of unit is that it places within easy reach and simple access a good number of microfilm units, which is of particular benefit where a single reader station or perhaps a pair of reader stations are juxtaposed to the storage unit. Clearly, this easy access would be of special importance to a business function that relies heavily on microfilm records, though it probably makes sense for very few uses in a library. If a library set of less than 1,000 reels is heavily used at one or two reading machines, such as for a localized staff function, this is a very convenient solution. Plausible applications might be for a heavily used collection of, for example, the *New York Times* or *Chemical Abstracts*. For general storage there are more efficient systems.

Warning should be given here that no library should store in its building nitrate microfilm in any form because of its explosive qualities. All films acquired should be examined to make sure they are made of acetate or another nonflammable base. Also remember that acetate film will dry out and become brittle and that it can be easily torn or damaged if subjected to low humidity. High humidity also results in damage that can be irreversible. Environmental control for a microtext collection is particularly important.

Microfiche (typically 105 × 148 mm) may represent, next to books and perhaps microfilm, the largest library bibliographic collection in sheer numbers. For example, the Human Relations Area Files constitutes one large set issued on fiche. Although small collections of fiche are frequently available for public access, large collections are generally housed so as to encourage or require access through a library staff member because of their small size and ease of misplacement. Publicly accessible collections may be housed in binders, tabletop stands, flip files, drawers in cabinets, or small boxes. Their use seldom affects the facility space requirements except that counter space or a special consultation carrel may be appropriate. Few libraries now house fiche (or, for that matter, roll films) along with books in their subject classification on standard shelves, though

the University of Guelph and Earlham College have found this advantageous. In large collections it is almost universally the practice to centralize the collections within the main library and in major branch libraries for control and because of the equipment needed to use the materials.

One typical system for the bulk storage of microfiche involves boxes that may be placed on standard shelves or housed in a special cabinet or rack. An example for 4-x-6-in. fiche is a file box with a follower block that is 5 in. high, 6½ in. wide, and 12 in. deep (127, 165, and 305 mm). This particular box holds some 500 fiche in protective envelopes. A standard shelf 12 in. (305 mm) deep nominally would hold five boxes, and with the shelves placed 7 in. (178 mm) on center, 12 shelves could comfortably be placed in a section, resulting in a capacity of 35,000 fiche. Assuming 10 ft² (0.929 m²) per section, this obviously results in 3,500 fiche per ft² (37,700 per m²). It should be noted, however, that a box this size filled with fiche will be fairly heavy and, if dropped, will require refilling. Also, in order to withdraw a single item, the box must be moved to a table or consultation counter, which, in a heavily used collection, may suggest either additional staff time or additional space devoted to consultation areas. This situation may suggest the use of pullout reference shelves (see Section 6.1).

Another common system for housing microfiche involves a cabinet similar to that used for roll film but with a different drawer configuration. Over-file storage is not available for fiche, although other forms of storage can be devised in this otherwise wasted space. As with other equipment, there is a considerable variety from which to choose. One example is a 10-drawer cabinet with three rows of fiche per drawer that is 57½ in. high, 21¼ in. wide, and 28½ in. deep (1,460 × 540 × 724 mm), which holds up to 36,500 4-x-6-in. fiche in protective envelopes. Use of the same assumption proposed for roll film cabinets suggests that about 10½ ft² (0.976 m²) per cabinet should be allowed, which results in a capacity nearly equal to the shelved boxes. Of course, other examples will result in different conclusions; the illustration is meant only to demonstrate a way of viewing the alternatives. And cost will be a factor; cabinets tend to be quite expensive, but systems of boxes are not necessarily cheap. Local analysis is suggested.

Other storage devices include safes (which might be considered for master negatives), fiche carousels, tabletop flip stands, binders, and various specialized items.

Filmstrips, which are not particularly common, at least in microtext collections in the United States, are sometimes stored in filing cases wide enough to hold a strip 35 mm, or about 1½ in. high and up to 8 in. (203 mm) long. Filmstrips may be stored on sloping tray shelves, which hold 98 canisters of film, or in special cabinets. When a library has a collection of this type, the facility requirements may reflect the existing means of storage unless improvements are specified.

Microcards were designed to be stored in standard catalog trays for 3-x-5-in. (76-x-127-mm) cards. Cabinets similar to the fiche cabinets discussed above are available. Microprint cards or sheets, which are 6 × 9 in. (152 × 229 mm) in size, can be placed in filing drawers designed for that size card. They often have come from the publishers in boxes designed for the purpose, and these boxes can be, and ordinarily are, stored like books on regular library shelving. These opaque microcards and microprint cards are no longer produced, though many academic and research libraries will have collections.

All the storage techniques discussed here, including cabinets, can be adapted to compact storage, such as the carriage type of movable shelving. The increase in capacity would be similar to that found for books, as discussed in the previous section.

A key question for all this material is projecting how much space to provide for future growth. Though microfilm and fiche continue to be published throughout the world, the growth of microtext collections is likely to taper off as digital formats take over. However, at present, the heavy use of these formats during the second half of the twentieth century leaves considerable collections in libraries. And the use of several of these formats seems likely to continue until some other technology begins to dominate the market. Microfilm remains less expensive to create than digital scanning of materials, and archival quality can be obtained; as this is written, digital conversions have not yet been considered of archival quality (though this will almost certainly change). Local statistics of growth rates are probably the best guide. It is suggested (1) that space should be provided for at least double the amount of that currently occupied; (2) that if this projection ends up being high, other formats can be stored in the same space; and (3) that the shelving area

be so arranged that allocation of space to microtexts can be substantially increased or decreased in the future, or that these collections can be moved to more compact storage techniques at a future date.

6.6.5 Phonograph Records and Tape Recordings

Phonograph records are widely collected in the fields of music, drama, poetry, ethnology, political and governmental speeches, media interviews, and language instruction, and for historical purposes as archives of recorded sound. Such collections require specialized storage devices, often made up of standard shelving units with divider-type shelves, although the programmer should be aware of distinct problems with large collections. First, phonograph records are heavy! A 3-ft (0.914-m) shelf of bound journals may weigh about 105 lbs (48 kg), while a shelf full of 12-in. (305-mm) LPs will weigh about 145 lbs (66 kg) and 12-in. (305-mm) 78s will weigh 200 lbs (91 kg). Normal shelves are often designed for a maximum load of about 120 lbs (about 55 kg); thus, stronger than usual shelves must be provided.

The second problem is that phonograph discs need support to prevent warpage. Partly because large standard bookends only come at the end of a shelf, these supports are never satisfactory in holding the discs vertical to enable easy removal of any one record. This is why divider-type shelving is common; however, normal shelf dividers become hidden as the shelf is filled, thereby presenting a risk of damaging the materials as they are reshelved. Custom shelving designed with dividers that extend to the front edge of the shelving and have some width so that they can be seen will provide a superior means of supporting the discs. If commercial/industrial shelving is used, the method of attaching the dividers must avoid exposed bolt, rivet, or screw heads on the shelf surface in order to minimize damage to the housed materials.

The third problem is that a 12-in. (305-mm) disc in its protective jacket is actually more than 12 in. (305 mm) in dimension. Therefore, to avoid having the materials project into an aisle, the next larger shelf size is required. This is usually 15 in. (381 mm) nominal depth in standard shelf units; 13 in. (330 mm) would be preferable but it is not a standard shelf size for most manufacturers. As with oversized book storage, the size of shelf chosen will affect the space required for ranges.

Finally, phonograph discs, and tapes for that matter, are dramatically damaged, if not destroyed, by extreme heat. Temperature control is essential. Many older discs are extremely fragile as well. In earthquake country, in addition to the normal shelf bracing, there must be some means of keeping the materials on the shelf during a tremor, particularly if the collection has significant historical value. This consideration may suggest case shelving with latching doors, although other devices may be used. Compact shelving is excellent in this regard.

Phonograph disc space requirements cannot be projected in ways similar to those of books, since the market has shifted from records to tape cassettes and compact discs. The area requirements for individual units of shelving would be similar to those for book shelving, although the greater depth requirement needs to be added. Custom shelving may be the best solution where maximum capacity for a given area is desired, but for the purposes of the program, standard shelving requirements should suffice for all but the largest of collections.

An exceptional problem in a library concerns historical recordings on flat discs, wire, cylinders, and other media that require antiquated playback and recording machines for their current use. As one example, the Bibliothèque nationale de France, with its collections of over 900,000 sound recordings and 40,000 videotapes, requires a collection of 400 original machines to play the old originals today. Enclosed cabinets or case-type shelving with locking doors offer the physical security needed. Each collection of such equipment will need special attention.

Open reel tapes are typically stored in their boxes on standard library shelving. Tape cassettes can be housed in card catalog cabinets or in cabinetry similar to the microtext cabinets discussed earlier. There has been some controversy about the effect of storing magnetic tapes on steel shelving or in steel cabinets because of a possible magnetic field that could alter the stored information. Where this is viewed as a valid concern, nonmetallic shelving or cabinetry should be specified. The authors decline to make a recommendation here except to note that a lot of magnetic tape is stored in or on steel shelving. However, it is generally accepted that magnetic media (i.e., tapes) should not be housed near motors or transformers, and yet the authors are not aware of any problems resulting from storing magnetic-based materials on steel shelves in electrically moved compact shelving.

6.6.6 CD-ROMs, Compact Discs, Videotapes, Videocassettes, Optical Disks, and Other Digital Media

In recent decades, these formats have become very popular indeed, with the compact disc and videocassette dominating the home music and motion picture market. The compact disc measures 5 in. tall × 5½ in. deep (127 × 140 mm) and is less than ½ in. (13 mm) thick, so a lot can be housed in little space. The videocassette in protective plastic case measures 8 in. tall × 5 in. deep (203 × 127 mm) and takes about 1¼ in. (32 mm) of shelf space. Other storage media are evolving annually: The DVD system is to be similar to the compact disc in size and format; recent high-density computer storage disks will fit into a pocket and yet they can hold a gigabyte or more; magneto-optical disks are available in both the pocket size and the larger compact disc size. It can be expected that most libraries will eventually have some of each in their collections.

These media do not need to be stored under rigorous atmospheric conditions; the January–February 1991 *Library Technology Reports* gives a good review of desirable storage conditions for magnetic media. However, like audiotape, they can be destroyed by extremes.

Equipment problems now and in the future with respect to utilizing obsolete computer programs, equipment, and databases should be modest in comparison to the problems of older audio storage technologies, at least initially, though they will exist. For example, an education library may well need to have an array of the oldest equipment one could expect young teachers to be faced with in their teaching assignments. This will almost certainly be antique compared to that in common use in the library.

Data that are migrated from one technology to another often lose format information and, because of this, older technologies may be required in research libraries to allow viewing of the original format. Program information, such as the hidden notes and formulas in a spreadsheet, is generally lost in a migration process, and could be of great importance to a scholar of the future. It should not be concluded that digital storage will remove the need to maintain and provide access to antique equipment in the library!

The technological world is rapidly changing. Thus, academic libraries in the future may need to house increasing archival collections of magnetic computer tapes or high-capacity disks, if such materials are not kept in a separate data archive. In a few short years pocket-sized computer disks have gone from a capacity for much less than one megabyte to over one gigabyte; the capacity for a similar-sized object has thus been increased over 1,000-fold. It is increasingly likely that materials will be stored on such disks for future use, and this kind of storage is likely to be found in libraries. For example, these collections could include archived library administrative records, or programming needed for the study of the history of computer science, or the product of scanning materials for electronic course reserves, or a fully digitized set of architectural drawings for a campus building. Publications that contain a supplementary floppy disk or consist mainly of magnetically stored information may be of sufficient quantity in the future to require special housing with attention paid to keeping them separate from magnetic-based security discharge stations.

Currently floppy disks are limited in number; tabletop equipment can easily accommodate the need. It may be predicted that this circumstance will change. When more information is needed for the building program, local vendors or the institution's computation center can help in visualizing the future more clearly. This is a technical matter and constant developments in miniaturization and packaging are altering and often easing the specifications for housing and performance. And, in most cases, the quantities of newly devised storage techniques are small in the total scheme of things; assuming some room exists in the program for changing the way things are shelved, no serious problems should result from new developments. We suggest that because of the vulnerability to change of both digital magnetic and magneto-optical information, there will be a need to accommodate such materials in a special collection with supervised access; it is quite possible to expect that only copies of this material would ever be circulated, especially if it is unique or nearly so, and that the copy can be quickly made on demand when needed.

In libraries, one method of housing these materials is to use narrow regular shelving (such as 7 in., or 178 mm, nominal) for the videocassettes, and with dividers to hold the compact discs upright and facilitate selection of a particular one.

Another method is to use display racks if the library wishes to provide direct access to these materials. The CD-ROM discs are sometimes kept at the staff service desk; in other cases they are kept in a CD-ROM drive or array dedicated for reading that particular disc or set. At present there are a relatively modest number of CD-ROM discs to present library housing problems. Yet the future is certain to include substantial growth in this and similar formats.

Display furniture racks are popular in public libraries and are often used in collegiate undergraduate collections or for promoting use of small popular collections, such as paperback books, videocassettes, and sometimes compact discs. In some instances, the empty jacket is on display, and, for security reasons, the contents are available upon request at a staff counter. One major equipment company provides a variety of wall-anchored and freestanding racks of a tall columnar design. In this case the display column is 68¼ in. (1.734 m) tall. The three-column design is 32 in. (813 mm) square, the four-column one 38 in. (965 mm) square, and the six-column configuration 49 in. (1.245 m) wide. Varying from most shelving, this display rack is of 20-gauge sheet metal. It is powder-painted black, and has clear acrylic panels to hold but not cover the displayed material.

The cabinetry described earlier for microfilm can be configured for CD-ROM, videocassette, and other formats. As a comparative example, the system that was last described for microfilm with pullout units of shelving suspended on overhead tracks, can, in its maximum configuration, be set up to house up to 11,232 4-mm DAT tapes, 7,200 audiocassettes or 8-mm tapes, 3,240 BETA tapes, 3,240 VHS tapes in sleeves, 2,520 VHS tapes in cases, 8,960 compact discs, or 1,232 ¾ U-Matic cassettes. Many other cabinet types are available, each with its own capacity, set of dimensions, and cost.

Developments in information technology will require continuing attention for their influence on library collections, services, and building accommodations. These are rapidly changing technologies, and one can expect radical format and equipment changes that may add complexity for housing library collections of this type of material.

6.6.7 Slides, Photographs, and Prints

Slides are sometimes housed in cabinets similar to card catalog tray units. Other techniques include placing them in pocketed albums or in a group of covered boxes housed on shelving. Safety can be a concern, especially if there are glass slides or glass photographic plates. Photographs and prints are generally stored in filing cases selected for the purpose, and the important decision relates to the suitable size of the filing drawer and the total capacity to be provided. The objects cannot be housed above shoulder height without requiring use of a stool or ladder. As with other filing cases, a factor of two and a half times the floor area covered by the case itself should generally be sufficient for programming, provided space needs for sorting and viewing tables are separately provided. Floor weight should be no problem in a normal installation. If the librarian has no special knowledge of the problem, it may be advantageous to consult with dealers and libraries with special collections in the field that have recently installed equipment.

6.6.8 Maps and Broadsides

Sheet maps, architectural drawings, plans, large aerial photographs, and broadsides are generally placed for protection in large acid-free folders and stored flat in drawers in cases designed for the purpose. These drawers may be as little as 1 in. (25 mm) deep, on the basis of a limited number of folders per drawer, which will be easier to handle, particularly the upper drawers. A commonly available case made of steel is fabricated in units of five drawers; the cases are typically set up with two or three units plus a base, which permits use of the top surface for sorting or viewing the maps. Cases have been put together that are 6 ft (1.829 m) high or higher, but at this height sheets and folders stored may be damaged when they are removed from or replaced in the cases. When a drawer is so high, one's vision is cut off unless a stool is used when filing. The authors do not recommend stacking drawers over about 4½ ft (1.372 m) so most people can look into the drawer and remove the maps.

Weight can become a significant factor when map cases are assembled to greater heights. Deeper drawers, each containing more folders, have a much larger capacity; however, a 1-in. (25-mm) stack of large sheets is very heavy, and getting materials in and out becomes more difficult as the individual stack of sheets grows. It is suggested that 1 in. (25 mm) of materials per drawer, which would be about 100 sheets including folders, should be considered capacity and that 15

drawers in height should be a reasonable limit.[3] In any region subject to earthquakes, the drawer units should be bolted to each other and to the base. The individual drawers can be made secure by attaching a vertical hinged device to the left-hand edge of the cabinet to cover the 5- or 10- or 15-drawer banks. The device (one of which is called the Multi-lock) moves out of the way for use of the drawers and can be used with small padlocks if user access is to be restricted.

Some companies design drawers in which folders are shelved vertically, as in a correspondence filing case. One such product for maps is a cabinet (used for a large map collection at the University of California, Berkeley) that uses folders to keep the sheets from dropping down into the cabinet. They are said to have a capacity similar to that of the more traditional map cases, but that the process of pulling and returning individual sheets is easier. Architectural plans racks are similar, but in general these are not as satisfactory as flat drawers, certainly not for any sizable collection.

Roll maps present a different problem. Libraries often must store quantities of them for private study or use in classrooms. They can sometimes be fitted into frames that hold them in place vertically and might be said to resemble racks for garden tools or umbrellas. They can also be stored horizontally on brackets, but to prevent sagging, they may have to be frequently rotated. Tubes or honeycomb-type bins are excellent possibilities for convenient horizontal housing, though the vast variety of sizes constitutes a minor problem; if the storage unit is designed for the largest map, space will be wasted. The authors have frequently seen rolled maps simply stashed vertically in a closet. Although they are out of sight, access to items hidden in the back is difficult. An umbrella rack or a similar larger and heavier frame can work for smaller rolled maps, and in some cases a means of hanging larger rolled maps from a ceiling-mounted frame may be possible.

There are examples of roll map storage built into standard shelving units that have notched racks designed to accommodate a pole that in turn holds a rolled map (see fig. 6.32). Another approach might consist of a single shelf at baseboard height with a back panel where both the shelf and back panel slope away from the access aisle. Lumberyards sometimes use this kind of storage for trim lumber, which can be quite long, but stored on end with the long dimension being

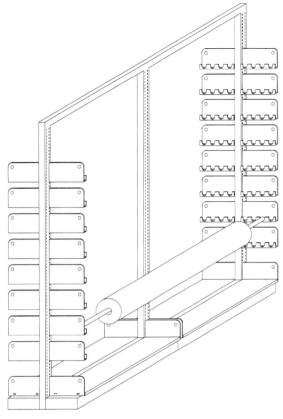

FIGURE 6.32   Map storage. Using custom brackets designed to hold relatively stout rods or pipe, an effective roll-map storage system can be developed in standard shelving.

vertical. The recommended solution is left to the devices of the map librarian; it is a detail that should be brought out in the program and can greatly influence ease of use, as well as required floor area, for the map collection.

The shelving equipment for reading areas and nonbook materials is ordinarily not large enough in quantity to affect module sizes seriously, and therefore it is not discussed in detail in Section 5.3.5. However, bound newspaper collections, institutional archives, reference collections, and even the microtext collection can be so large that the module size will be of importance where shelving methods vary from standard shelving dimensions. It is suggested that if two ranges of deeper shelving can take the place of three ranges for regular books, the stack module selected will work out to advantage. This may provide an aisle a little wider than absolutely necessary, but it avoids involvement with supporting columns. The lighting configuration must, of course, be suitable for variant shelving arrangements.

NOTES

1. Michael Matier and C. Clinton Sidle, "What Size Libraries for 2010?" *Planning for Higher Education* 21 (summer 1993): 11. Reprinted with permission of the Society for College and University Planning, 4251 Plymouth Road, Ann Arbor, MI 48105-2785, e-mail <scup@umich.edu>, Web <www.scup.org>.
2. *Library Journal* 59 (November 15, 1934): 865–68, and 61 (January 15, 1936): 52–54.
3. See C. E. LeGear, *Maps: Their Care, Repair and Preservation in Libraries,* rev. ed. (Washington, D.C.: Library of Congress, 1956).

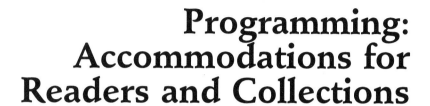

7

Programming: Accommodations for Readers and Collections

For solitude sometimes is best society, and short retirement urges sweet return.

—John Milton, *Paradise Lost*

While Section 5.2 dealt with accommodations for readers in terms of who and how many, this chapter addresses the specific needs of readers in the bookstacks, in general reading areas, and in reading areas for materials in various subject fields and formats.

Many different types of accommodations are available to the present-day reader. In many older academic libraries, all seating was in one or more large rooms, where books, except for those shelved around the walls, were brought to those who requested them. This concept still has merit where maximum collection security must be achieved and closed collections are planned. As libraries grew larger and readers increased in numbers, additional reading rooms came into use for current periodicals, public documents, reserve books, rare books, manuscripts, and other limited purposes. As time went on, divisional reading rooms for groups of disciplines—the humanities, social sciences, and physical sciences—and for more limited subjects—such as fine arts and music—came into use, particularly in larger libraries. In the meantime, an increasing number of libraries in the United States and elsewhere began to open their bookstacks to many if not all readers. In due course, accommodations were provided in carrels adjacent to the books, and finally individual table seating has, with certain exceptions, been made available throughout the library. Each arrangement and each room or area has its purposes and its advantages and disadvantages.

Another model driven by the need to maintain maximum control over the collections leads the modern independent research library to be more nearly that of the historic library described above. In this case, the main body of the collections remains in a closed stack, and the materials are paged for the user. Such an arrangement can save considerable space where the collections are arranged by accession number and by size rather than by subject classification. Though we know of no United States academic library as a whole now using this model, most private and special research libraries (including archives, rare books, and many storage facilities) find it advantageous.

As one example, the British Library, in its 1997 quarters next to St. Pancras Station, has arranged its services so that "readers will gain access to the catalogue through some 150 computer terminals where they will order books automatically with a swipe of the new bar-coded reader's pass, and machinery in stacks will print the search requests that the library assistants will use to locate materials on the shelves. A light on the reader's desk turns on to announce that his or her books (or other materials), routed to the correct reading room by optical scanning, have arrived. Every reader's place will have facilities for a portable computer, and there will be storage facilities for personal property. . . ."[1] (At the Library of Congress where the collections are closed but arranged in subject order, consideration was being given, in late 1996, to alternative shelving arrangements that might allow accommodation of more materials in their central facilities. Certainly one of the shelving techniques to be considered will be shelving by accession number and size rather than by classification.)

The sociology of seating arrangements is enlightened by several researchers who have shown what are regarded as good and poor arrangements. Some results will be summarized. People prefer sitting across from one another but not directly. Chairs side by side are acceptable to most people; 15 in. (381 mm) between chairs is the most satisfactory distance, 9 in. (229 mm) is close, and 3 in. (76 mm) is quite unpleasant. Most people but not all prefer a semi-isolated space, giving at least a sense of privacy. A person whose personal space is encroached upon by another will move the chair away a bit, may set up psychological protection with notebook and papers, and ultimately will seek a more protected seat the next time. Unless they are good friends, most people do not relish the feeling that someone is staring at them; they may feel awkward and perhaps self-conscious when reading and taking notes. This is so even in a college library where the reader will know a much higher percentage of library users than in large institutions.

Yet many prefer to feel they are part of their group; they study in comfort because their chums are there also; they are not losing out on a rap session or game. Complete isolation is for some quite unwelcome. Extroverts will wish more group inclusion and will sit closer together than introverts. More or less taking over a room or area is a way for a group of friends to gain psychological encouragement and guard against undue invasion of personal space, not merely to be with friends who can explain a study problem or with whom one may gossip about classmates. Further, at least two kinds of study require or benefit from work in pairs, one being joint research and writing projects and the other being introductory practice on computers where peer consulting is common and beneficial. And, of course, the visually handicapped frequently arrange for a person to work along with them.

These factors affect seating arrangements. Yet they are of varying importance in different types of institutions and different countries. An experienced consultant has written: "I worked on a 4,000-seat library for Ewha Woman's College in Seoul, where I introduced the question of whether an area 5 ft × 5 ft (1.524 × 1.524 m) per seat would be needed. The faculty there did a quick-and-dirty analysis, and on the assumptions (1) that Koreans are used to much denser population concentrations with considerably less 'private space' available to individuals, and (2) that women feel less invaded by proximity with other women, they could pare that dimension down to 4 ft 10 in. × 4 ft 10 in. (1.473 × 1.473 m) each. Now you multiply that out. I was really surprised that such a thin slice on the two dimensions, times 4,000 seats, saved us constructing 6,555 net square feet (609.0 m²) of floor space, plus of course the gross allowance that implies."[2]

Furthermore, seating preferences are conditioned by other factors in study places—sound and light quality, density of overall seating and occupancy, the degree of familiarity readers have with each other, cultural mores and traditions, the variance in personalities (from the campus clown to the Phi Beta Kappa prospect), and even the difficulty and nature of the reading matter. Variation in seating options is thus needed. Varying degrees of privacy are useful. Planners should realize that studying can be hard.

Reading areas can be separated by shelving instead of full-height partitions. In using shelving to divide space, it should be realized that such a technique may not be suitable in busy, crowded libraries unless sufficient space is provided to access the collections without undue disruption for the reader. Used to divide space, shelving needs to be carefully plotted to maintain a logical sequence of the collections. This shelving should sometimes have solid-back panels or a divider partition down the center of a double-faced range to shut out vision. Back panels can be provided by most shelving manufacturers or constructed of Masonite™ to form a simple, inexpensive divider. Sometimes, for acoustical purposes, glass or clear plastic can be placed above the top of a case running up to the ceiling; however, a single sheet of glass will transmit a fair amount of sound. Laminated glass is better and double glazing is best for good acoustical separation, but these add to the cost and probably make little sense over shelving. Where there is a suspended ceiling, sound often passes freely over partitions. Often a number of stack ranges running parallel to the reading area will provide an adequate visual and acoustic barrier.

Because library staff are an expense, the architect should be informed in the program that the special reading areas requested must be arranged, if practical, so that they will not require additional staff for supervision or service. A service desk is hard to defend unless the attendant can be expected to be kept reasonably busy.

The desirability of providing multiple reading areas depends to some extent on supervision policies, which are discussed in the next chapter. The different types of rooms and reading areas in common use in academic and research libraries will be discussed in this section.

7.1
General Seating Accommodations

As the years go by, a larger and larger percentage of academic library seating accommodation is being placed in stack areas or very close to major book collections. In the United States and Canada, it is common that more than half of the total seating is in the stacks, including open and closed carrels, alcoves, "oases" (as seating clusters located amidst bookstacks may be called), studies for advanced students and faculty members, and so on. Ten types of general seating arrangements are possible. They are discussed also in the chapters on the design phases, as well as summarized in Section III of appendix B.

7.1.1 Standard Library
Reading-Room Tables

At least some large tables for multiple seating should be provided in any library. It is recommended that these tables be at least 4 ft (1.219

m) across. If task lighting is provided in a fixed position at the center of the table, a width of 5 ft (1.524 m) or even more in some cases may be appropriate. The depth as well as width of reading position is important particularly where the table will be used to read large volumes and wherever laptop computers will be used in addition to the books and papers needed during a research project. At least 3 ft (0.914 m) should be assigned along the side for each reader, and readers should never be placed at the ends of the tables. There should be at least a 5-ft (1.524-m) aisle between two parallel tables, although a 4½-ft (1.372-m) aisle is possible if the tables are only 6 ft (1.829 m) long. A 6-ft aisle is preferable if the tables are continuous for as much as 15 to 18 ft (4.572 to 5.486 m).

The authors usually prefer four-person tables of 4 × 6 or 4 × 7 ft (1.219 × 1.829 m or 1.219 × 2.134 m) because of the flexibility they provide. These tables can be arranged in a line when the space required by cross aisles is considered a luxury, or they can be placed as individual units. Such a table will provide sufficient space for the occasional student to spread out a large project. Furthermore, with tables of this size, the impression that all seating is full will be kept to a minimum. The structure of any multiple seat furniture must be stout enough to avoid what might be called "writers wiggle." If armchairs are provided, the arms should easily clear the apron and underedge of the table. Keep in mind also the need to provide a few tables that may be slightly higher for use by a person in a wheelchair or motorized cart; the quantity of such accommodation is spelled out in the U.S. Americans with Disabilities Act as 5 percent of fixed seating, tables, or study carrels, or a minimum of one of each element of seating.

Architects often recommend round tables, but they result in wasted space and reduced flexibility, and so should be discouraged, except possibly in rooms for the use of current periodicals or for what might be called "aesthetic relief." On the average, they will be used less than other tables with the same number of chairs. Tables provided for outdoor reading areas are often round. Care must be taken with exterior tables to provide a surface on which users can take notes; an open wire fabric or grille is not suitable for an outdoor area where much writing is expected. Many of the disadvantages of round tables also apply to square tables for four persons.

One must learn from history. Until about 1950 practically all seating accommodations in libraries were at reading-room tables, generally in fairly large reading rooms. One of these tables accommodated from four up to perhaps twelve or even more readers. In a few libraries these tables were 4 ft (1.219 m) across with one chair on each side every 3 ft (0.914 m). This arrangement was considered quite satisfactory. But in many college and university reading rooms, in order to increase the seating capacity, tables were 3½ or even no more than 3 ft (1.067 or 0.914 m) wide, and in a few cases even less. Too often, in order to increase capacity still further, only 2½ or even no more than 2 ft (0.762 or 0.610 m) on the side were assigned for each reader. This resulted in such crowded conditions that it was almost impossible to fill all the seats, and the total use might have been greater if more space had been allowed for each reader. To make matters worse, the tables were crowded together, sometimes with several long tables in the same line without a cross aisle in between, and with an aisle no more than 3½ or 4 ft (1.067 or 1.219 m) between two parallel rows. The arrangement was very unsatisfactory. Even with ideal arrangements, students will tend to view a table with every other seat occupied as being in full use, except during the week preceding final examinations. With minimal space arrangements, serious study with full occupancy is virtually impossible. Students usually would rather sit on the floor than be forced into such minimal accommodations. Still, a mystique exists in a grand, large old room of stunning architectural design, a student body gathering place of the young scholar with books, a study hall today of which the Duke University "Gothic Reading Room" is a classic example.

7.1.2 Reading-Room Tables with Dividing Partitions

As a cross between a carrel and an open table, the divided table is provided, with low partitions in front and often at the sides of each reading position. (See fig. 7.1.) Some librarians refer to this type of accommodation as a mock-carrel. At least a degree of privacy is obtained in that the reader's "turf" is clearly defined. If the divider is 8 in. (203 mm) high, a reader with head down to read a paper flat on the table will see little or no nearby distracting motion. And the partition can provide a good location for power and signal service for portable computers.

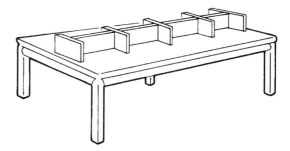

FIGURE 7.1 Divided reading table, or index table. Extending the tabletop dividers to the table edge would make what is sometimes called a mock-carrel. See fig. 7.24 for a more common index table configuration.

With somewhat higher dividers it is possible to provide task lighting hung from the partition in front, but this form of lighting tends to result in unpleasant reflective glare. With the higher partitions the student in effect faces a blank wall; where the side partitions are also high, the user cannot see out without leaning back in the chair, and then the next-door neighbor is uncomfortably close. In the case of tables for only four, or with low partitions, this problem is largely avoided.

As used at the J. Henry Meyer Memorial Library, Stanford University (fig. 7.2), and at the University of Texas, Austin, Undergraduate Library, the mock-carrel serves those students who prefer to be able to look around while at the same time feeling a need for a well-defined spot. The table with high dividers, on the other hand, serves the same function as a line of carrels placed side by side, but with a great deal less flexibility for future arrangements. As with open tables, it is essential that the structure be stout to avoid movement as a vigorous writer works. The minimum dimensions of the divided work surface should be similar to those provided in carrels.

7.1.3 Slanting-Top Tables

The only difference between these tables and those described above is that their tops slant downward toward the reader; the slant makes it easier to read a volume that lies on the table and also helps to prevent the glare that too often reflects from the table into the eyes of the reader. (See fig. 7.3.) Index tables are often a variation of this type of table, with a double-faced set of one or two shelves running down the center. Another variation is a table designed for reading exceptionally large volumes, such as might be

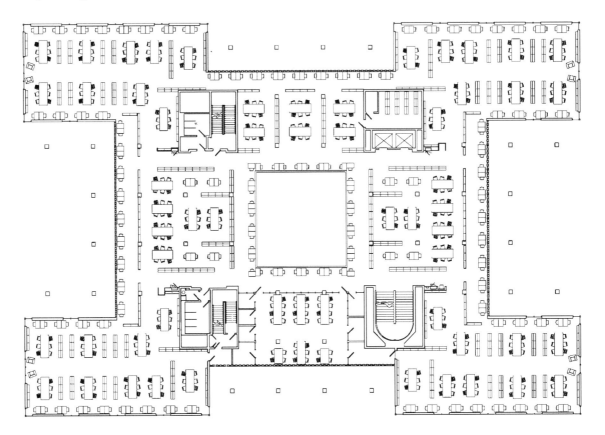

FIGURE 7.2 Stanford University, the J. Henry Meyer Memorial Library (third floor). Originally accommodated a mixture of seating, including 230 at carrels (33%), 76 at lounge chairs (11%), 150 at mock-carrels (22%), 214 at tables (31%), and 22 in small studies (3%) in approximately 23,000 ft² (2,140 m²). Subtracting the area provided for shelving, the seating worked out to be about 27 ft² (2.5 m²) per seat, including circulation space. Since the original layout, shelving has been added to accommodate changing needs. (Courtesy of Stanford University Libraries)

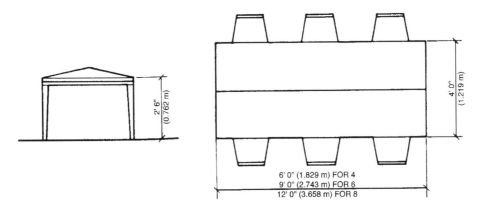

6' 0" (1.829 m) FOR 4
9' 0" (2.743 m) FOR 6
12' 0" (3.658 m) FOR 8

FIGURE 7.3 Slanting-top table. Avoid a steep slant, which will necessitate a front-edge molding that may be picked at and mutilated and in any event creates an uncomfortable ridge when a reader is taking notes.

found in the art library or a newspaper reading room, whose reading surface is of increased size.

If the slant is too great, the book tends to slide down into the reader's lap, unless there is a molding or stop of some kind to prevent it. Where such a very low molding is specified, it must be of a durable design as some readers will tend to pick at it and, in many cases, ultimately mutilate it. A limited number of tables of this kind can be useful, as at least some readers prefer to work with their books slanting slightly toward them. In the original furnishings for the Lamont Library at Harvard University, about 3 percent of the seating accommodations were of this type. The authors seldom find this table to be necessary.

7.1.4 Tables in Reading Alcoves

Tables resembling those described above may be placed in alcoves with books and shelving on at least two sides, a third side often being an outside wall with a window and the fourth opening into a larger reading or stack area (see fig. 12.11). A nest of four individual tables or carrels in a pinwheel arrangement can sometimes be used to advantage with an alcove if it has inside measurements of at least 11 ft (3.353 m) and preferably 12 ft (3.658 m). Additional space is required where the individual tables or carrels are larger than the 2-×-3-ft (0.610-×-0.914-m) tables illustrated, as may well be the case in graduate research libraries and even certain undergraduate libraries or where computers will be used.

The above arrangement has the advantage of placing the readers close to books. Alcoves adjacent to large monumental reading rooms were common in nineteenth-century and a few very early twentieth-century buildings, with a central hall going up to the roof and one or more levels of balcony or gallery alcoves on mezzanines along the sides. Although the passageways between the reader and the bookshelves were generally narrow, the number of readers wanting to consult the books in any one alcove was small enough so that their movement was not too disturbing. If the alcove has the proper dimensions, this is an economical arrangement for book storage and reader accommodations as far as floor area is concerned.

One problem in connection with alcoves, at least in the eyes of some librarians, is that they have occasionally been arranged in what amounts to a maze. Supervision is usually impossible. In some circumstances encouraging reasonable reader discipline is difficult. Such an arrangement makes management of the collections somewhat more difficult, and the reader seeking a seat may feel some degree of frustration in wandering from alcove to alcove looking for a suitable spot. (Consider these problems in fig. 7.2.) As an illustration demonstrating practical concerns and a potential shift in policy, Harvard's Lamont Library in the late 1990s considered plans to remove their alcoves in favor of a more straightforward arrangement in order to maximize book capacity, to improve access to books without disturbing readers, and, perhaps most important, to provide space for special carrels with network access.

On the other hand, many students like to discover a place that may not be so obvious; they like the maze character and nooks and crannies. Although disagreement no doubt exists on this issue, many, including Keyes Metcalf, have argued that it is exceedingly important to develop the simplest possible traffic circulation patterns throughout a library, particularly in main corridors, bookstacks, and reading areas. This point of view has much merit, even though there may indeed be valid circumstances that lead the design toward a mazelike solution. Also remember that emergency egress and certain aspects of security are facilitated by clear and direct circulation patterns. Graphics in the form of directories, floor plans, and directional signs are always a poor substitute for an obviously simple and direct arrangement. Finally, some librarians feel that alcoves introduce an undesirable level of inflexibility, particularly in a general reading room. The means of creating the alcoves can play an important role relative to long-term flexibility. Also, depending on how the carrels or tables are constructed, the pinwheel arrangement may be inflexible, may be susceptible to rearrangement by users unless the furniture is fastened down, or may incur added cost to ensure flexibility and discourage creative arrangements.

7.1.5 Individual Tables or Carrels

In the past, individual tables or carrels in a reading room or stack area were placed with an aisle on each side so that each table was at least 2 ft (0.610 m) from an adjacent one. (See fig. 7.4.) Tables so placed take somewhat more space than other arrangements, particularly if adequate aisles are provided. However, if individual tables are against a wall and at right angles to it, with an

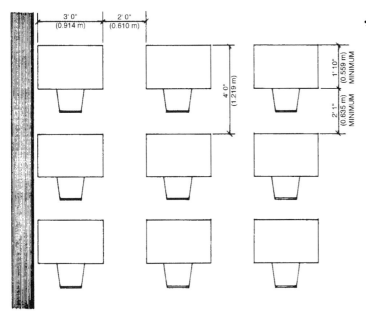

FIGURE 7.4   Individual tables once common in reading rooms. These are exceedingly small tables for anything but reading. The arrangement is not recommended because it does not meet ADA standards (the space between tables at the chairs for at least 5% of the seating and for the aisles must be 36 in. [0.914 m] or more), and the arrangement is not very efficient (putting two tables side by side and back to back could create an arrangement that meets ADA requirements within the same space).

aisle on one side only—one that is required under any circumstances—floor area can be saved.

Over the past few decades, the use of individual tables of the open-carrel type in reading rooms or stack areas increased to 50 to 75 percent or more of the seating capacity in an academic library. However, there are those students who prefer tables for four or more readers or other accommodations; it would likely be an error on the part of the planner if individual tables or carrels represent over 65 to 75 percent of the accommodations. People vary greatly in their preferences.

Individual tables or carrels present six decisions. How large should they be? How can they best be separated from their neighbors? How can lighting be provided to minimize shadows and reflective as well as peripheral glare? How can power and signal wire service be provided? How much space do they take including circulation space? What happens to the overall cost figures when they are used? The discussion here will be extended in the chapters on lighting and information technology.

The customary minimum dimensions are 36 in. (0.914 m) by at least 22 in. (0.559 m). Individual carrels as large as 42×24 in. (1.067×0.610 m) have been used in undergraduate libraries. Even though students no doubt like them, many librarians would consider their size luxurious. For a student working on a major paper or a thesis, though, it is none too large. In fact, at Stanford University's Cecil H. Green Library, carrels with a working surface of at least 8 ft² (0.743 m²) were specified for the open reading areas. These are well used and liked by the students, although they probably represent the upper end of the scale of carrel size, with the exception of carrels for computer use and carrels provided in rare book, newspaper, microtext, and art reading areas, which may be in the order of 10 ft² (0.929 m²) depending upon their design and use. When it is affordable, many faculty and advanced students would be benefited by $4 \times 2\frac{1}{2}$ ft (1.219×0.762 m) or 10 ft² (0.929 m²) of reading surface. For writing a major paper, the dining room table at home is often commandeered.

Some librarians feel that an undergraduate student, working with one or two books only or with one book and a notebook, can manage in a pinch with a table 30 in. (0.762 m) wide by 22 in. (0.559 m) deep if the tables are not placed side by side. This size is exceedingly small; the authors recommend against the use of tables this size except in very unusual circumstances. Consider that if the carrel table surface is cramped for the typical task being undertaken in college, students will take over tables to gain extra space and carrels may thereby be underused. Yet this is not because most students prefer an open table to the carrel, but rather that the carrel was not sufficiently sized.

In the Lamont and many other libraries, individual tables or carrels are placed frequently at right angles to the walls of the reading areas. In Lamont they are 4 ft 4 in. (1.321 m) on centers and attached to the walls to prevent their being moved. (One problem that often results from small tables is that they are easily moved, creating an untidy appearance. This problem is reduced where there are electrical connections that limit the possibility of creative arrangement or where the units are sufficiently heavy to discourage movement.) Similar individual tables can be placed on both sides of screens and at right angles to them in a reading area. Then, with a partition the same height in front and back but with an open aisle on the fourth side, practically individual accommodations are obtained and, again, no undue amount of space is used. Fig. 7.5

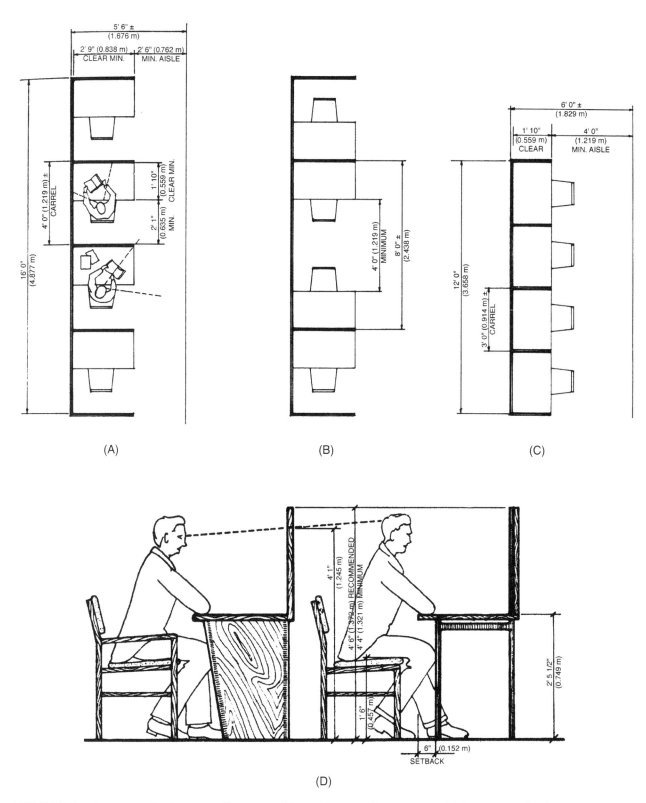

(A)

(B)

(C)

(D)

FIGURE 7.5   Open carrels along a wall or a partition at least 52 in. (1.321 m) high. (A) Carrels along a wall facing the same way (recommended, though ADA must be met). (B) Carrels along a wall in pairs. In both examples the space for the chair is very constricted, requiring the setback of 6 in. (152 mm) shown in D. (C) Carrels facing a wall (not recommended). (D) Carrel elevation to show desirable height of partitions to prevent visual distraction.

illustrates that partitions at least 4 ft 4 in. (1.321 m) high are required to prevent all visual distraction. Arrangements of this kind have been used on a large scale in a number of libraries. Central libraries of the University of Wisconsin and Brigham Young University in Provo, Utah, provide good examples.

Double carrels with adjacent readers facing in opposite directions are another means of providing almost individual accommodations. Carrels of this kind can be found at the Douglass College Library at Rutgers University, and at the Uris Undergraduate Library at Cornell University. If they are staggered, they give more seclusion and take very little more space. Various arrangements for double- and triple-staggered carrels are possible and are described in Chapter 12.

Individual seating can also be provided in almost any bookstack by omitting two ranges of shelving and replacing them with one double row of carrels, with a screen running between the double rows. (See figs. 13.18–13.20.) If ranges are 4 ft 6 in. (1.372 m) on centers, the tables or carrels can be 3 ft (0.914 m) wide, and there is still space for a 3-ft (0.914-m) aisle on each side before coming to a bookcase. If the ranges are only 4 ft 3 in. (1.295 m) on centers, the tables and aisles must be reduced to 34 in. (0.864 m). Both configurations provide minimal reader space, but they are probably adequate as supplementary seating or seating in an essentially undergraduate library if heavy computer use is not expected. Although it is true that readers will occasionally come down these stack aisles to obtain books, the number of persons using any one aisle should not be great enough to cause much difficulty. There are many seats of this kind in the Louisiana State University Library in Baton Rouge and a still greater number in the Louisiana State University Library in New Orleans (see fig. 7.6). These double rows of carrels can also be placed in reading areas between parallel rows of standard reading tables.

Another arrangement is to place individual seating on the periphery of a bookstack, preferably adjacent to the outside aisle or even at the end of a blind aisle along an inside or outside wall. If tables are next to a window, so much the better, although glare may sometimes be a problem. Either the window should not go to the floor or some form of a modesty panel should be provided. Long rows of tables or carrels, with a window for each, can be found in Cornell's Olin Library as well as the libraries at UCLA and the University of Utah. (See fig. 7.7.)

Individual carrels placed at the end of blind aisles can be arranged within the range spacing. If ranges are as close as 48 in. (1.219 m) on centers, the chair must be fairly small and without arms in order for a reader to get into it easily, and the table leg next to the aisle and the reader should be set in at least 6 in. (152 mm) toward the back of the table. (See fig. 7.8.) With range space meeting the handicapped access standards as required in the United States, this accommodation is even more attractive. This usually means that the tables must be fastened to the wall or floor to keep them steady. With carrels on 51- to 54-in. (1.295- to 1.372-m) centers, there is adequate room for an armchair, particularly if the carrel is not more than 23 in. (584 mm) in depth; 21 or 22 in. (533 or 559 mm) is possible but hardly desirable. This minimal depth is tight for use of a portable computer, though the degree of privacy can make these popular carrels; greater depth is of course possible with more generous range spacing.

Nonrectangular carrels and tables in the form of an L or a modified L represent another approach. Generally, they result in somewhat greater space requirements, but, with careful design, they can create a very pleasing atmosphere with less formality than the previous examples. Where task lighting is provided under a shelf, this type of carrel can be arranged so that light comes across the book at an angle, which reduces the reflective glare that is always a problem with this kind of fixture. One example, patented by Marquis Associates of San Francisco, may be found in the Cecil H. Green Library at Stanford University and the California Polytechnic State University Library at San Luis Obispo.[3] This particular form can also be used to incorporate a high-intensity kiosk-type ambient light fixture in the center of a pinwheel arrangement, although other arrangements can be developed similar to the standard rectangular carrel. (See figs. 7.9 and 7.10.) It should be noted that L-shaped carrels tend to be right- or left-handed; thus, a mixture of the two orientations is recommended. Another variation of this general pattern may be found along a wall at the Lilly Library, Earlham College, in Richmond, Indiana.

With careful planning, individual freestanding tables or carrels can be provided in approximately the same area as regular seating accommodations,

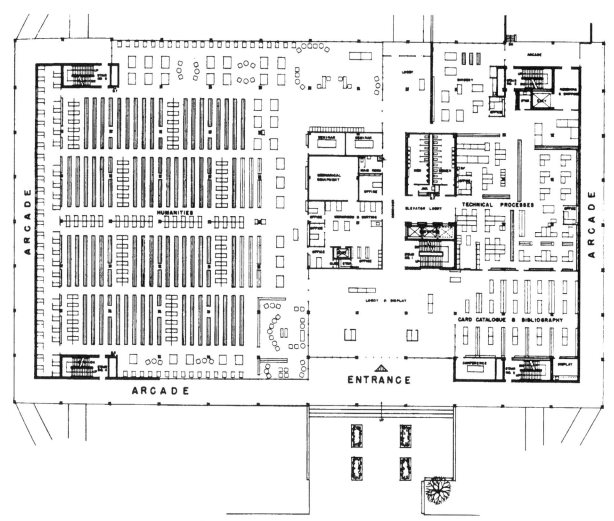

FIGURE 7.6 Louisiana State University Library, Baton Rouge. An example of the use of double rows of carrels. A lot of space is devoted to circulation in the arcade and entrance lobby, perhaps at the expense of constricted space in other areas.

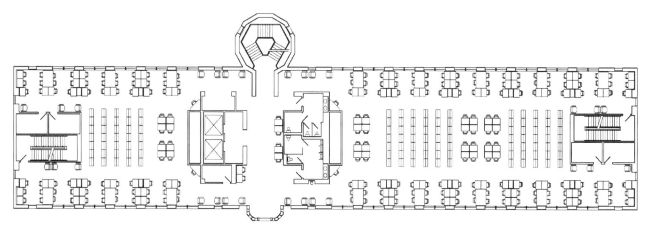

FIGURE 7.7 University of Southern California, Leavey Library. The arrangement on upper floors that arrays much of the seating at tables, carrels, and lounge chairs along the exterior walls with the stacks arranged in the interior of the building. (See vertical relationships to other floors: figs. 7.22 and 7.23.)

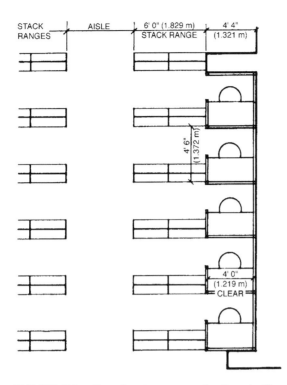

FIGURE 7.8   Carrels at range ends. Carrels like these, without doors but in an area with acoustically treated walls and ceilings, have been used successfully for typing and computers. They also provide an excellent sense of privacy in a minimum of space, although the spacing as shown is not enough by some standards (it does not meet ADA requirements). (Courtesy of Stanford University)

with similar table area assigned to each seat in a large reading area. Nonrectangular carrels require some additional space, though it should not be substantial. The furniture cost will be higher as it costs more to construct four individual tables or carrels, each with its own structural support, than it does to construct a single four-person table. Although all seating should not be at individual carrels, the advantages of carrels are significant, and in most cases the added costs are justified. Carrel and individual table arrangements are discussed again in Section 12.5 on the schematic design and in Section 13.4.2 on design development.

7.1.6 Tablet Armchairs

Chairs of this kind (see fig. 7.11) have been used for many years in classrooms. Thomas Jefferson designed one for his own study, apparently finding it more convenient for certain types of work than a table and regular chair. There is no reason why tablet armchairs should not be used, although they typically are not very decorative and they tend to result in a confused and irregular traffic pattern. Until 1983 in the Music Library at Stanford, where space was severely restricted, a few tablet armchairs were placed in range aisles. Although this use is extreme, it does illustrate possible supplemental seating where there are few alternatives. The College of Agriculture Library of the University of the Philippines in Los Banos

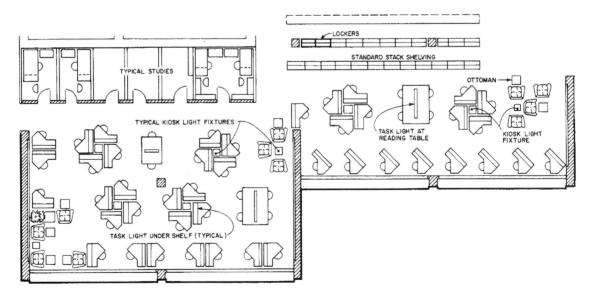

FIGURE 7.9   Stanford University, Cecil H. Green Library reading area. An example of a variety of seating accommodations. Note that the arrangement of lounge chairs is designed to discourage conversation. The lockers are slightly removed from the reading area to help control the noise they often produce, and the collections are located well away from the windows. (Courtesy of Stanford University)

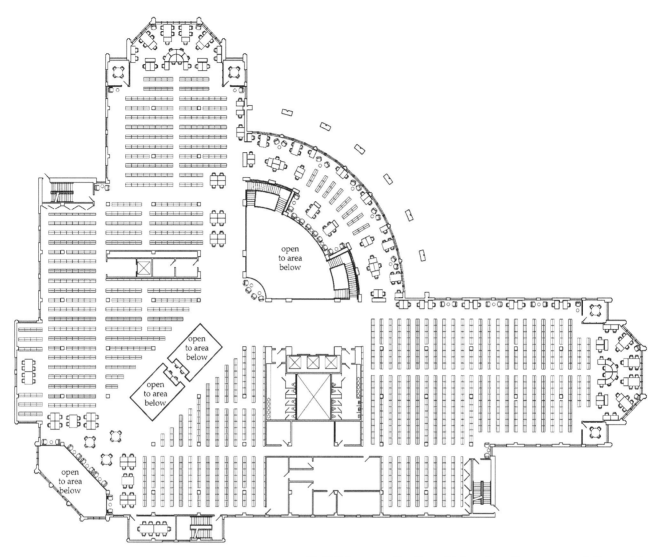

FIGURE 7.10   Fordham University Library, second floor. This example is of a library with a particularly high proportion of shelving relative to seating, and yet the seating is grouped in arrangements with variety and interest. Note the open area to the floor below at the lower left corner as well as diagonally up and to the right from that opening (with two smaller openings between); in two cases the edge of the opening is used for lounge seating, and, at a bridge, carrel seating is provided. (Courtesy of Shepley Bulfinch Richardson and Abbott Architects)

FIGURE 7.11   Tablet armchair used in place of chair and table. A tablet that slides on and off the arm is used with an attractive chair for a multipurpose meeting room in Stanford University's Meyer Memorial Library. A much larger arm, such as Thomas Jefferson designed, would be more suitable but would take more space, be less stable, and, perhaps, not be aesthetically pleasing.

placed tablet armchairs on three walls of a large reading area as close together as they could stand, just over 2 ft (0.610 m) on centers, and the librarian has reported that they have been heavily used. And the Mount Holyoke College Williston Library Miles-Smith Science Wing of 1992 has provided upholstered lounge chairs with removable large writing boards, to be spread from one flat wooden chair arm to the other, which perform the same function, and these are popular with students. There may be a place for tablet armchairs in a library, and some lounge chairs have an arm wide enough to serve somewhat the same function, though to one side.

7.1.7 Lounge or Semi-Lounge Chairs

Without a table or a tablet arm, lounge chairs in a library almost always stir up a controversy. (See fig. 7.12.) Some librarians feel that they are often

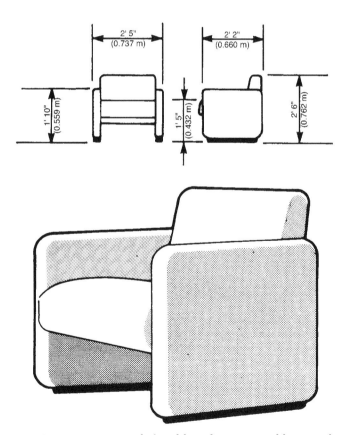

FIGURE 7.12 Lounge chair. Although some would argue that such a chair is unduly expensive, uses an unnecessarily large amount of floor space, and encourages slumber, they are popular in libraries and they do add comfort and variety in seating. Use of footrests is recommended with this type of chair. Note that the dimensions are typical but will vary greatly.

too large, particularly in browsing areas, and therefore take too much space, are unnecessarily expensive, and encourage the occupant to slumber and to stretch out and obstruct the aisles. Students like to arrange lounge chairs to create nests or, in effect, a bed. One chair is often used as a footrest for a second chair, a situation that can largely be avoided by providing proper footstools or, in problem areas, securing the chairs to the floor. On the other hand, many feel that a chair with a padded back, padded seat, and perhaps padded arms, if properly designed, may be more comfortable than a regular library chair, and they should require no more space than a chair with its associated table or carrel. (Padded arms will ordinarily wear out before the rest of the chair. Beanbag chairs are similar in use of space, and several academic libraries have also found these popular in small areas.)

A number of lounge chairs can be used to advantage in current periodical rooms and in other areas. Almost always a certain percentage of readers, if not taking notes, prefer to sit in a somewhat larger and more comfortable chair. A great many of these chairs have been used in libraries, not only in the current periodical area, but in browsing areas and even in the stacks. Public multiseat furniture (couches, sofas, or love seats) should not be used at all in reading areas or bookstacks, although they are useful in special-purpose rooms, such as the Stimson Room of Mount Holyoke Williston Library (used for readings and teas).

If 8 to 10 percent of the total seating accommodation is of this kind, the number should be quite adequate in most academic libraries. Lounge chairs usually can be purchased for little more and sometimes less than a chair and an individual table or even a chair and a section of a larger table. They are sometimes used to break up the monotony of a long row of tables or carrels. They can be used successfully in pairs or even in clusters of three or four if they face at least slightly away from parallel or are provided with small side tables, preferably 12 to 24 in. (305 to 610 mm) wide to give a place to rest books and at the same time to separate two readers, thus reducing the likelihood of conversation. Single units of two or three chairs with associated tables are possible, but they reduce flexibility for future arrangements. If footstools aren't provided, small, unattached tables will tend to be used for this purpose.

7.1.8 Enclosed Carrels or Dissertation Rooms

In some cases carrels are completely closed in by walls of some kind; if so, they must be larger in size than would otherwise be necessary in order to prevent claustrophobia. One major university has many of these with one wall being a grille, providing the occupant a very unpleasant zoo-cage feeling. Where they are not properly designed with adequate light, ventilation, and size, they have seldom proved satisfactory. However, where there is a desire to provide full enclosure so that the user can lock the cubicle, leaving papers and books spread out and secure, then closed carrels make sense even if some must be located within the interior of the library without a window. Location of enclosed carrels would be ideal along an exterior wall, each carrel with a window; but as a number of functions would ideally have a similar outlook, some compromise is usually necessary. The University of North Carolina (Chapel Hill) Davis Library solved that with six vertical "study towers" that extend the perimeter of the building, providing six floors with 12 to 14 enclosed graduate carrels, each with an outside window; an open well in the center of each tower on alternate floors was intended to diffuse light and provide a feeling of spaciousness. For ventilation the carrel walls may be designed to come short of the ceiling, but this can cause a problem if there is sufficient space for an intruder to climb over the wall, as there initially was in Stanford's Green Library East Wing. The door can be fitted with a louver or undercut an inch or two (25 to 50 mm) to further aid ventilation.

The dissertation rooms at Stanford are 5 × 6 ft (1.524 × 1.829 m), with the work surface being the full width of the cubicle and 30 in. (762 mm) deep. Each cubicle is provided with a two-drawer file, and the equivalent of one single-faced section of shelving mounted on the inner wall, and a door fitted with a glass panel. Typing in such a cubicle is a problem acoustically; in this case certain blocks of dissertation rooms might be assigned for those who insist upon typing. Laptop computers generally do not present that problem. Clearly, these rooms should not be near open reading areas, but where they can be well isolated acoustically, such as where a double row of cubicles displaces three ranges of shelving in a large stack area.

Similar units may be found in the Firestone Library at Princeton University. They are well used

at both institutions. As with all seating arrangements, care should be taken to provide for handicapped access. Providing full access will affect the door as well as the height of the work surface. The doors on the Princeton cubicles are sliding, which, if they are wide enough, would work well for this purpose. Four-person cubicles have also been used with good results at Princeton (see fig. 7.13).

7.1.9 Studies of Various Sizes

Ordinarily for one or two persons, these are often referred to as faculty studies. (See figs. 7.14 and 7.15.) Most academic institutions feel that they should provide individual studies for faculty

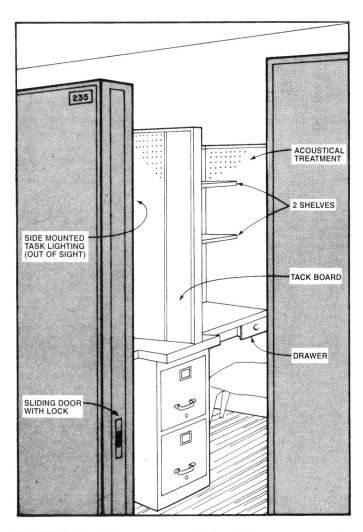

FIGURE 7.13 A four-person cubicle, with two seats to the right of the door. This configuration can be arranged at range ends, somewhat similar in plan to that shown in fig. 7.8, or more like the typing room in fig. 7.33.

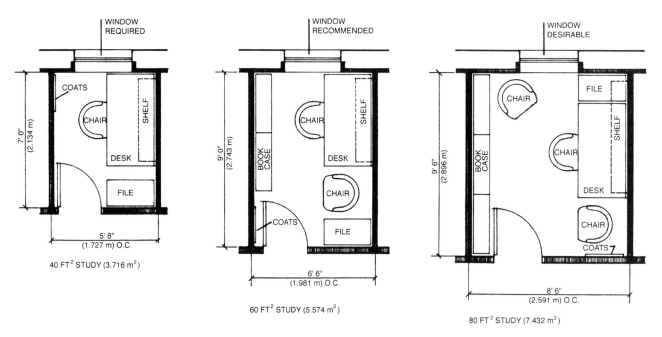

FIGURE 7.14   Faculty studies of different sizes. The study at the left is the minimum size for a completely enclosed room, and a window is required. The one in the center is adequate if there is a window, but it might be unpopular without one. The size of the right-hand study is generous; though a window is desirable, it can be omitted if there is a clerestory window opening into a lighted bookstack or other area.

members only. Independent research libraries often provide some for selected long-term fellows or visiting scholars with special needs. The studies may be essentially like the dissertation rooms described above, or they may be a good deal larger, with added shelving, a coatrack, a side chair or a lounge chair, increased file space, and a typing or computer stand. A reasonable minimum size can be 65 ft² (6.039 m²) to 70 ft² (6.503 m²); studies with a window can be smaller. They should be provided with full-height walls for acoustic privacy and, like the dissertation room, have glass either in the door or next to it. The glass aids the closing procedure (a light left on in a study can readily be seen), while giving the occupant of the study a slight sense of greater space with the door closed.

The preceding paragraph speaks of file space and does not mention the desk or writing surface. Yet, the latter is by far the most important furniture and must be large, 3 × 5 ft (0.914 × 1.524 m) being minimal and a larger table as long as 6 to 8 ft (1.829 to 2.438 m) being that much more useful. File drawers are useful for work that is finished, to be pending for months, or of potential historic interest. However, the flat open working surface is for the current projects—a

pile of student papers, drafts of an article, lecture notes of this week, current bibliographical drafts, a book open to a passage being studied, active committee files, and so on, each representing one facet in the life of an active teacher and scholar. A few of the book shelves may be used for such segments of work in progress. In contrast to the graduate student who concentrates on the chapters of a thesis or dissertation, most professors in colleges have multiple involvements that require juggling to keep all moving forward each day; a visual reminder of the several immediate tasks made possible by a large work surface is a great advantage.

Even though very satisfying philosophical arguments can be made in support of faculty studies, their real need is sometimes more political than actual. This is not to suggest that a library should have no faculty studies; Harvard's Widener Library and Stanford's Green Library each have over one hundred. Many of these spaces will not be heavily used, particularly where faculty have individual offices elsewhere; yet studies are always in demand, at least in terms of assignment. And, in point of fact, some will be constantly used and heavily packed with the materials needed by a teacher or scholar.

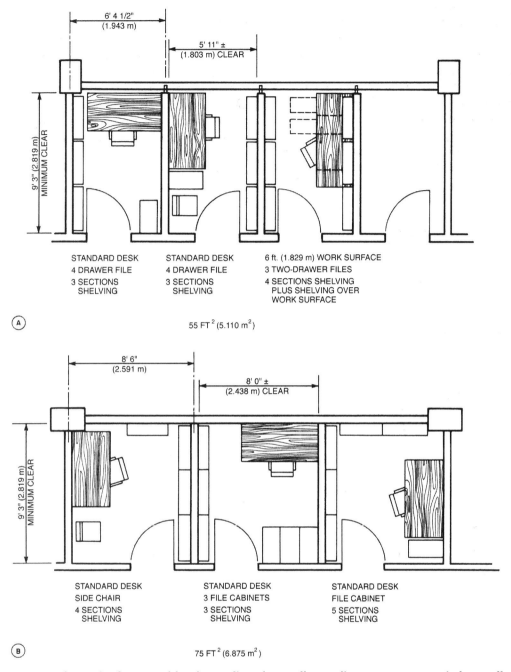

STANDARD DESK
4 DRAWER FILE
3 SECTIONS
   SHELVING

STANDARD DESK
4 DRAWER FILE
3 SECTIONS
   SHELVING

6 ft. (1.829 m) WORK SURFACE
3 TWO-DRAWER FILES
4 SECTIONS SHELVING
   PLUS SHELVING OVER
   WORK SURFACE

(A)   55 FT^2 (5.110 m^2)

STANDARD DESK
SIDE CHAIR
4 SECTIONS
   SHELVING

STANDARD DESK
3 FILE CABINETS
3 SECTIONS
   SHELVING

STANDARD DESK
FILE CABINET
5 SECTIONS
   SHELVING

(B)   75 FT^2 (6.875 m^2)

FIGURE 7.15   Alternative layouts of faculty studies. The smaller studies (top) are on a window wall while the larger studies (bottom) are in an interior space. Both examples are based on a building bay module of 25 ft 6 in. (7.772 m).

Faculty studies are on occasion set aside for faculty emeriti, as is the practice at Western Washington University. The Wake Forest University Reynolds Library has a suite of eight studies reserved for its faculty emeriti. Visiting scholars also need consideration. Faculty visit and use research libraries other than their home library, and the reciprocity of accommodation should be recognized in reasonable number and quality. Along with the planning for the facility, a very careful assignment policy should be established, ideally with faculty support. This policy should include a means of reassignment to other persons or uses in the event a study is not used. It should also be realized that the addition of significant numbers of closed spaces like studies or dissertation rooms will measurably increase the collection management function, as each space represents a niche that can house library materials not properly charged out, which, in turn, means that another reader will not be able to find them. Clearly, faculty studies and dissertation rooms need careful planning.

7.1.10 Other Seating Options

There is one or more miscellaneous seating type for every standard library seating accommodation described. Swarthmore's library has a reading pit, which is a depressed floor area with steps serving as casual seating accommodation. The Penrose Library at the University of Denver once had a furniture form that was just the reverse; it formed a stepped mound, which, being covered with carpet, provided a popular seating area. Carpet-formed tiers with a few pillows create the Tower Lounge at Rollins College Olin Library, a feature just below the Tower Room with its more

formal tables and chairs that have a grand view of the college lake. Carpet itself can be thought of as providing potential seating; in fact, some students rather like sitting on the floor in the stack right where they find the item they wish to read. The Hillis Library at Radcliffe provides cushions for students to spread about on the floor at peak hours. Double-deck carrels (see fig. 7.16) have been used to good effect at Clemson University, the University of Florida, Furman University, and elsewhere, and the authors have seen one carrel designed to hang off the edge of a balcony (although it was not built). With eight benches and a fine stained-glass window, the Regent University Library has a lovely small chapel, located next to its Special Collections and Archives.

The point is that the librarian should be open to suggestions from the designer even though a great deal of thought will have been put into the program detailing the exact needs of the library. As long as there are active imaginations, there will be new and unique solutions to the problem of seat-

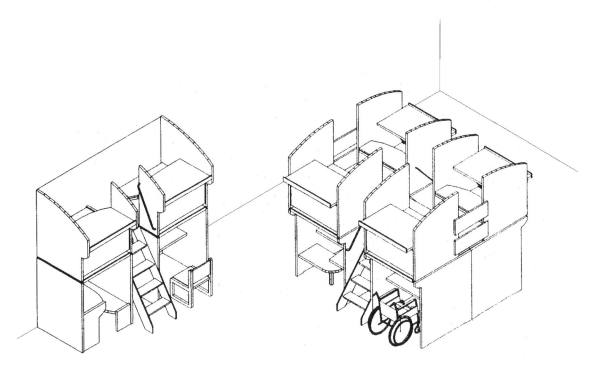

FIGURE 7.16   Double-deck carrel. Both freestanding and wall versions are available. Although students like this seating accommodation, those responsible for retrieving materials to be returned to the shelves are less enthusiastic.

Note that the normally recommended ceiling height for such a carrel is 11 ft (3.353 m). Lighting of work surfaces needs special care. The full height of this particular carrel is 9 ft 1 in. (2.769 m); the floor of the upper carrel is 4 ft 10 in. (1.473 m) above the building floor. These carrels are a full 4 ft (1.219 m) wide with upper and lower carrels having 10-ft² and 8-ft² (0.929-m² and 0.743-m²) surfaces, respectively, making them oversized and contributing to their popularity. (Courtesy of Mohawk Midland Mfg.)

ing. The librarian should review unusual solutions in the context of cost, functionalism, potential popularity, and flexibility. There is still merit in providing what has worked well historically.

7.2
Reference Rooms or Areas and Bibliographical Collections

Reference service, and related book collections and computer terminals, are preferably placed on the entrance level where space is at a premium, close to the main entrance lobby and the catalog of the local collection. Except for libraries with a totally online public access catalog (called an OPAC), this reference center should not be far from the professional staff of the processing department, though this requirement is being rapidly reduced with the advance of digitally based processing. Indeed, in a growing number of academic libraries, the main technical processing quarters are in totally separate buildings, or even to a large extent managed and staffed by separate outside vendors.

In many older university libraries, large reference reading rooms seating hundreds can be found, although many of them have been converted to other functions as the main library is altered to suit the philosophy of open-stack access. In a number of cases, the old monumental reference room now serves as a rare book reading room, an undergraduate library reading area, or, in at least one case, a map room. These reading rooms were originally designed to be filled with large reading tables and to have walls lined with bookcases. Impressive large reading rooms still exist and are valued at Columbia University, Duke University, the University of Florida, Harvard University, UCLA's Powell Library, the University of Washington, and others.

One reason for making these rooms so large was to provide sufficient wall shelving for the reference collection. It was not uncommon for freestanding shelving to be added between the tables to make up for the limitations of the wall surfaces; and, as shelving is added, it is never difficult for reference staff to fill all the available shelving with reference books and then look for more. The rooms almost always give an impression of restlessness and tend to be noisy. Lighting them usually is a problem, at least after dark; in many cases general lighting from the ceiling and from skylights or windows has been supplemented by lighting over the bookcases and by table lamps or, in current jargon, task lighting.

As to the optimum size of a reference area, even in a great university library, it is unlikely that more than 50 readers will use the reference collection at one time for reference purposes, and it is suggested that, unless a good reason can be found for a larger number, fewer than 100 seats are adequate for reference space in an academic library, except in cases where the space is expected to be used for other purposes as well. Obviously a room seating no more than 50 persons, with 30 or even 35 ft^2 (2.787 or 3.252 m^2) per person allowed, will not have enough wall space for the shelving required by a large reference collection. The valuable periphery of the room might therefore be used for individual seating, with seats along at least two or three of the walls, and the books might be concentrated in double-faced floor cases, either in the center of the room or at one end or side. (See fig. 7.17.)

If books are at one end or side, and if the space is high enough, a mezzanine over the reference collection may make comparatively inexpensive additional floor area available and also absorb under it some of the inevitable noise. However, the problems of access and collection management need to be considered; for example, will elevator access be required and will a copy machine be needed on the mezzanine? There are other techniques to deal with noise, and, with the addition of a mezzanine, particularly one supported by the shelving below, a certain amount of flexibility will be lost.

Careful study should be given to the spacing of the reference bookcases. If they are kept down in length to 15 ft (4.572 m) for instance, and if there is a good cross aisle at each end, there seems to be no reason why reference collection shelving should be more than 6 ft (1.829 m) on centers even if the shelving is made extra deep, except perhaps as the building module may dictate. Because reference books on the average are larger than others, it is quite customary to provide shelves for them up to 12 in. (305 mm) in depth, and usually only six shelves per standard section, but this would still leave an aisle 4 ft (1.219 m) wide, which is enough to enable two persons to pass readily on the occasions when two readers are working in the same aisle at the same time. If the aisles are dead-end, the length of the ranges should not exceed 9 to 12 ft (2.743 to 3.658 m).

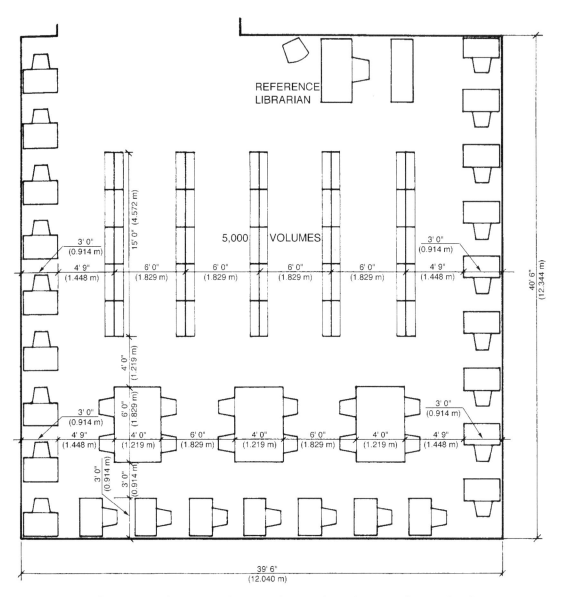

FIGURE 7.17   Reference area for 5,000 volumes and 37 readers. This area of 1,600 ft² (about 150 m²) provides approximately 20 ft² (2.79 m²) for each reader and 10 volumes per ft² (108 volumes per m²), if figured at 100 volumes per section for the collection. This can be considered as minimal spacing; it does not include elements often found in a reference room, such as index tables, an atlas case, or computers, all of which will add to the space requirement.

Many of the library book catalogs and other bibliographical and reference books are quite heavy. Because of this, it is desirable to have the reference shelving and the associated reading positions and photocopy machines closely juxtaposed. One technique that has been used with success is to alternate full-height and counter-height ranges to provide a convenient consultation surface for those volumes the reader may not wish to carry very far. Such a configuration

justifies reduction of seating at tables and carrels because much use will be standing. It also serves to visually open up the space, although there is a reduction in the absolute book capacity. The low ranges may, however, be considered as a form of flexibility, as they could be replaced with full-height ranges as a need for additional capacity becomes convincing. Counter-high reference shelving appropriately arranged allows the reference librarian at the service desk to easily see if a student is having trouble finding something, which can be a benefit for active reference service.

Other devices have been used to provide what amounts to a consultation surface, including ranges where each shelf up to counter height is essentially 24 in. (610 mm) deep, with 10- or 12-in. (254- or 305-mm) shelving above. Another method is to provide pullout reference shelves at counter height. In both of these approaches, the depth of the usable surface is hardly adequate, and the pullout shelves tend to be noisy unless the shelving is wood. An exception may be seen in the stacks at the U.S. National Archives II where excellent pullout shelves of special design were made part of the project. There are probably better solutions than the typical pullout shelf or the shallow fixed shelf; the authors prefer the close placement of tables or the use of mixed high and low shelving in most cases, except where index tables are appropriate as discussed later. As a rule, with a fixed number of library visitors, the larger the reference collection the narrower can be the spacing of ranges, because persons using these volumes will generally be distributed so as not to crowd in one area. A small collection needs the generous spacing because crowding will more likely occur.

There is less reason to provide for any large amount of growth in a reference collection than elsewhere, as older volumes can frequently be shifted to the stack when new ones are acquired. It is generally feasible to estimate 100 volumes to a single-faced section, with six shelves each 3 ft (0.914 m) wide. Counter-height units would, of course, hold no more than half this amount. Metcalf suggested that a well-selected collection of 10,000 volumes, particularly if the bookstacks are open access, should be sufficient for most central reference book collections in large libraries if the bibliographical material discussed below is provided for elsewhere. This size is probably too restrictive for many general university libraries. On the other end of the scale, several major research libraries have reference collections of 30,000 to 50,000 volumes or more, although this number includes the bibliographies, indexes, and published library catalogs. Many would argue that today a reference collection of 25,000 volumes, including bibliographies and indexes, would be about the right size for most large libraries, 10,000 for colleges, and under 1,000 for branches. The decision about the size of a collection to provide clearly must be a local one. Although reference

works continue to be published, developments in online databases, CD-ROM, and other digital resources suggest that information access by computers may lead to a gradual reduction in the size of large reference book collections over coming decades.

Seating in a reference area where open-access stacks are provided should not encourage long-term research, particularly if only 50 to 100 seats or less are provided, as suggested earlier. The authors prefer a mix of seating in the reference area with perhaps 70 percent at tables, 30 percent at carrels, and no lounge chairs. The carrels probably should not be provided with a shelf, as this would suggest long-term use. Photocopy stations should be convenient for both staff and patrons. And provision for considerable access to computers should be made, as will be discussed in the next section. An area of 30 ft^2 (2.787 m^2) per reader is generally sufficient, though for special software requiring very large screens, a larger carrel designed for computers used by two people working together on large-screen multimedia tasks will require more space, perhaps as much as 45 ft^2 (4.181 m^2), though some library administrations question this allocation of space. Keeping in mind that this is not a research location, there are ways to minimize the footprint necessary to support various technologies. For handicapped persons perhaps 5 percent of the tables and carrels should be high enough for the arms of a wheelchair to fit under (as mandated by the Americans with Disabilities Act in the United States). A few rooms off the reference room may be desired to provide for such activities as group instruction on bibliographic access, reading to the blind, special equipment for the partially sighted, or simply typing or composing at a PC, although the last can be provided for elsewhere in the building.

The requirements for the reference desk should not be overlooked. Generally, the reference desk should be visible from the entry area, close to the card or computer-access catalog, and convenient to the staff area. Ideally, it should be placed to facilitate directing a patron to the desired materials and to provide some degree of control over the reference collections and seating areas. Depending on the distance between the reference desk, catalog area, and front lobby, an information desk may also be needed. Details should be thought out and described—such as a ready-reference collection, computer terminals with or without slave monitor screens for patron viewing, phones, a counter or sit-down desk (part of any service desk must be sit-down height to accommodate ADA in the United States), the number of staff to be accommodated at peak use, provision for handouts, a place for a location diagram of the collections, other graphic needs, provision of a seat or several seats for patrons, and drawers for special catalogs and normal desk supplies. Although some of this detail can be established in the design phase, as much information as possible should be provided in the program. More comment is provided in Section 8.2.

Remember that the necessary conversation by telephone and between library users and reference librarians can be disturbing. This should be kept in mind in selecting the room arrangement and particularly the location of the reference desk. The reference room should probably be considered for carpeted floors, acoustical ceilings, and perhaps the introduction of background sound, either air conditioning or electronic white sound.

Fig. 7.17 demonstrates a configuration for a minimum reference area allocating 30 ft^2 (2.787 m^2) per reader and 10 volumes per ft^2 (108 per m^2). This illustration is not intended as an objection to larger or more monumental reference space but to demonstrate an approach to a minimal reference room. Note that the carrels are a smaller size; many research libraries would prefer larger carrels. Also, there is no provision for computers, video terminals, or microtext readers, which would likely require larger units together with space for operating documentation. Furthermore, the space happens to be column-free, and without a catalog, dictionary stand, or atlas case (assuming the unit behind the reference desk is the ready-reference collection). It assumes that the bibliographies and indexes are separately housed and that the copy machines and the associated staff office or offices are located nearby. Clearly the illustration does suggest the basis for a formula that provides a point of departure for discussion by the librarian and the facilities programming committee.

For a much larger and heavily used collection, fig. 7.18 illustrates what might be an actual reference space where approximately 34 ft^2 (3 m^2) are provided for each reader, and 5.37 volumes per ft^2 are allowed. Although neither fig. 7.17 nor 7.18 is ideal, each demonstrates different points of view. Note how use of this area in fig. 7.18 has evolved over its first 15 years. Copy machines, microfiche readers, and CD-ROM stations have

been added. Informal and formal instructional areas have been formed, and one bay of the reference area has been converted into staff quarters for interlibrary borrowing and lending.

The situation for bibliographies is very similar to that for the reference collections, but the number of bibliography volumes to be shelved can probably be cut to one-half that allowed for reference in most libraries. This general advice will become even more sound as bibliographical information is made more readily available in computer-supported formats. For both reference and bibliography, half the seats may be individual, with the others at tables that provide more rather than less than 6 ft^2 (0.557 m^2) of table surface per reader. The key is to distribute seating so that, unless a reader is using a volume on a counter, that reader can find an empty seat close at hand, facilitating the efficient use of books that may be heavy, large, and needed for just a few minutes. In all cases where there are multiple seating positions at a table, joined carrels, or other specialized seating, the specification must ensure that the furniture is sufficiently sturdy to avoid "writer's wiggle."

Special equipment can be very useful for the most heavily used volumes—index tables and counters, particularly—for such reference types as selected dictionaries, directories, biographical sources, abstracts and citation indexes, book review indexes and digests, and a few such large sets as the catalogs of great libraries. (See fig. 7.18.) The special tables or shelving adjacent to counters may require several hundred additional square feet (20, 30, or more square meters) of space in a large library. Therefore, you should determine whether a title or set will typically be used daily and whether it will be used for a few minutes (suggesting the counter arrangement) or for 15 or 20 minutes or more (suggesting the index table arrangement). For instance, readers and library staff frequently consult bibliographical books at stand-up consultation counters, which can be provided as described earlier. A counter that has no shelving beneath may in some cases be equipped with high stools that can be pushed underneath.

If the reference and bibliography collections are located as they generally should be, adjacent to each other, near the public catalog and entrance lobby, they are likely because of the type of use as well as their location to have a restless atmosphere. It is not bad that this may discourage the general reader seeking a place to study. Remem-

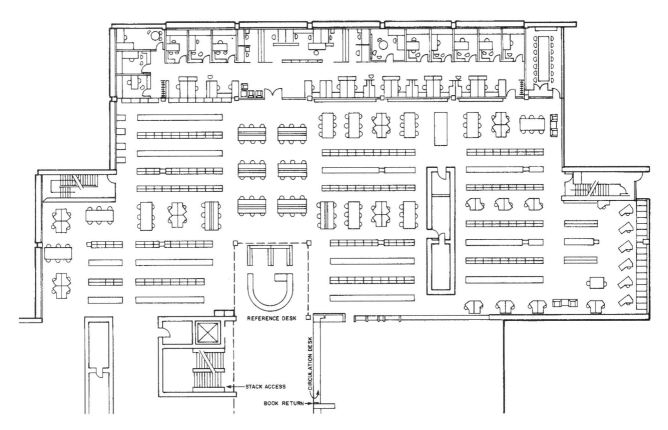

FIGURE 7.18   The reference room of the Cecil H. Green Library at Stanford University provides approximately 7,450 ft² (692 m²) for a capacity of 40,000 volumes on a combination of full-height and counter-height shelving (the counter types are shown here without section divisions). This works out to 5.37 volumes per ft² (57.8 volumes per m²). The 163 seats (including the eight index tables as seating) occupy about 5,550 ft² (516 m²), or 34 ft² (3.159 m²) per seat. The service counter and the ready-reference collection behind the counter are not included in this calculation. In this example, space utilization efficiency was not the primary goal.

The room includes bibliographies, catalogs, indexes, a small atlas collection, and online catalog terminals as well as CD-ROM stations.

Note the structural elements (heavy walls) required in this design to meet the applicable earthquake code. One such element severely hampers the reference collection traffic flow and visibility. Subsequent to the original design as illustrated, the protrusion to the right was converted to the Inter-Library Loan office, and the shelving to the right of the structural element is now all full height. Plans are currently in the works to dramatically change the whole reference milieu; flexibility to deal with change in any library design is critical! (Courtesy of Stanford University)

ber that undergraduates, when looking for a place to study, will sit almost anywhere they perceive an attractive empty space. Seating accommodations in a bibliography area sometimes have to be restricted to discourage their use for general reading; for example, low stools without backs are suggested at index tables or other specialized equipment, as are chairs with no arms. And you should try to assure that seating is not more comfortable or attractive than that provided among or adjacent to the general collections.

If the bibliography area can be adjacent or close to the acquisitions and catalog departments as well as to the subject specialists, collection curators, or book selectors, it should be possible to avoid a good deal of duplication of expensive bibliographical and reference material. Of course, where this material is replaced with electronic information storage and distribution, the need for proximity of the technical processing functions is reduced or even eliminated. Even though this technology will surely provide future alternatives for the functional organization of the library, it is prudent to provide for systems as they are known and understood today. Flexibility for adjustments in space assignment and space use, however, must be a basic part of any new facility. This is discussed in Section 5.2 in some detail.

7.3
Computer Facilities

Over the past half-century the use of information technology in academic and research libraries has grown steadily. Although many libraries around the world as yet have little or no use of computers, this section describes the provisions in public areas that thousands of libraries have already made or are in the process of making for staff and library users.

There are three basic concerns in planning for use of computers. One is the provision of power and signal lines, which is treated in the chapter on design development (see Section 13.4.4). The second is the allocation of space for use of computers, and the third is the effect of continuously evolving change on the philosophy of library service and operations. Both topics are addressed in this section.

7.3.1 Space Requirements

The space requirements for computers are not large in terms of each reading position; they are, however, significantly incremental over traditional reading positions, as will be explained.

In the public areas of the library, computers currently serve four major functions: library catalogs, instruction for library users, distributed data access, and special group or classlike clusters.

Library catalogs. Libraries that have converted card catalogs to an online form (commonly called an online public access catalog, or OPAC) need to provide sufficient catalog terminals to meet reasonable peak demand of all library users. If few students have personal computers (PCs) with network access, the library needs to provide more terminals than it would if many students have their own PCs and can access bibliographic information before leaving their dorm room. On the other hand, if use of the catalog by the general public is substantial, more terminals may need to be provided even if most students have their own PCs. In addition, use by faculty members, administrative staff, visiting scholars, research associates, and library staff must be considered. Thus it is easy to see that the total number of dedicated OPAC computers or terminals will vary greatly from institution to institution, and no general standard can be suggested.

The second edition of this text suggested one catalog terminal per 1,000 daily patrons. Experience suggests that such a quantity is quite low for most libraries, particularly where terminals are distributed throughout the building and where they are used for e-mail, citation and full-text searching, and network surfing. The main research library at Stanford University (the Cecil H. Green Library) has about 1,500 daily visitors (with peaks of 3,000 visitors) and over 50 public computer "kiosk stations" distributed throughout the building. About 35 of these terminals are clustered where the card catalog once was. This allocation suggests a formula of one full-service terminal (including those distributed throughout the building) per 30 average daily patrons. Reports indicate that this quantity is adequate for the average flow of visitors, but less so for peak demand levels. Some libraries have experienced serious problems when the terminals approached the end of their useful life and began dying before they could be replaced, suggesting that equipment should be renewed routinely, perhaps every two years.

The J. Henry Meyer Memorial Library at Stanford, largely media- and course-related, has 900 average daily visitors, 1,800 visitors at peaks, and about 15 full-service computer kiosks, suggesting one terminal per 60 average daily visitors. In the Meyer Library, 10 of these terminals are near the entrance and the balance are distributed. Substantial clusters of computers are available for homework and can also access the OPAC and networks.

The number of terminals is also greatly influenced by the total resources provided online. For instance, if the library catalog is limited to local library collections, fewer terminals may be needed than if access is provided to libraries of other institutions in the region, to a local network, or to a national combined library catalog. Further, providing commercial bibliographical services online increases the potential use and will justify an increase in the number of available terminals. Recent experience may be the best means of projecting use for the near future. You can also consider the peak number of persons using the card catalog at one time, and judge whether that might suggest a minimum number of computer terminals in a central catalog area.

From the example cited, it can be seen that the need for full-service kiosks will differ between a research library and a course-related or college library. And, the number will vary depending upon access to a computer cluster that may be regarded as separate from the full-service kiosks available for OPAC access. As a bare minimum, it would be prudent to plan for at least one terminal per 100 daily visitors, and the need may be evident for many more. The planner using this figure as a basis should insist upon the capacity to at least double this number even if this quantity is not initially realized.

Libraries find it a great service to their clientele to provide a small number of printers at some well-marked location beside the central bank of terminals. These printers will be used to print short lists of chosen citations with the shelf locations, or lists selected from available bibliographies and indexes. The printers should be located close to a regularly monitored service desk because staff will often need to replace paper, either because self-service has not worked well or because of the delicacy of some equipment. It may also be well to include one or two plug-in stations for users who may bring their laptop and wish to begin their current task in this bibliographic center of the library. A common model is to have two computers per printer with the computers placed on either side of a shared printer.

Printing is a particularly difficult issue, and it is going to become increasingly difficult. Faculty, and, for that matter, librarians, feel that students should not be required to pay for bibliographic information (where this may include not only catalog data but also full text). However, with limited budgets, how does an institution deal with this issue? The solution currently in place at Stanford University is to provide a minimum capacity to print on-site with two printers in the Cecil H. Green Library and only one printer in the Meyer Library, associated with the full-service kiosks. All printing is currently provided without charge, but the patron must walk to the printer and perhaps deal with a queue. The publicized alternative is to e-mail the citation, text, or other material to the user's personal account, and perhaps to print it on her or his own printer or the dorm printer. This model leaves much to be desired; it is mentioned only as a suggestion of how one institution is dealing with this difficult issue. It can be predicted that this situation will eventually change.

Note that the terms *computer* and *terminal* are used somewhat loosely in this discussion. In the past, all catalog access was through terminals with networked connection to a central computer. Today, microcomputers, commonly called PCs, not only serve the function of a terminal, but also provide access to other kinds of information and provide the capacity to do more things with that information. What was once called a "dumb" terminal is gradually being replaced with desktop computers and networked access, though laptop computers (also known as notebook computers) and the new, inexpensive "network computers" create another species of networked capabilities. This model suggests that anybody with a networked computer should be able to access the OPAC. By the same token, as the dumb terminals are replaced, the power and capacity of the dedicated catalog computer are increased, making it more attractive for patrons who do not have their own computers.

The next question is the location and specific placement of the OPAC terminals. The central visible location for the card catalog is also the best location for a centralized component of the online catalog with proximity to staff at the reference desk, the information desk, and the circulation or loan desk for both assistance and support. Visibility and closeness to the building entrance are usually assured with the historic card catalog site as well. Of course, other networked computers throughout the library will augment this centralized catalog area; however, the more remote OPAC terminals will lack the same level of staffed support or proximity to volumes of bibliographies and reference works.

As to the deployment of the main cluster of these terminals, some people like to stand at a counter and this may be best for a majority. Counter-high terminals discourage use for extended periods, which is appropriate for most users of the catalog. The terminals can thus be quite close together. However, some people will need to sit down while they work in computer listings for many minutes, just as they would flip through catalog cards to prepare a bibliography or select titles to help in a class project. People in wheelchairs will require terminals at table height as well. If bibliographic or textual data are included in terminal access, you can project more lengthy individual use of the terminals, and thus a somewhat larger proportion might be at sit-down carrels or tables, preferably spaced to give more linear distance and more isolation and quiet for those needing lengthy use of the available databases.

As a guide, it is suggested that allocation of space as follows is reasonable: 20 ft² (1.858 m²) for computers or terminals at counter height, an additional 10 ft² (0.929 m²) for each printer, 20 ft² (1.858 m²) per counter-height site to plug in laptops, 35 ft² (3.252 m²) for computers at sit-down height with space for note taking, 25 ft² (2.323 m²) for sit-down computers without note-taking space, and 25 ft² (2.323 m²) per site to plug in laptops at sit-down height. All these spaces include some space to access the seat (so to speak), but exclude rest rooms, structure, and so on that make up gross space in the architectural sense. (See fig. 7.19.)

A major failing in many libraries is the provision of terminals at normal counter or desk height, often with stools or chairs of normal height. Remember that the keyboard is a distance above the working surface, so the stool or chair must be comparably higher unless the working surface on which the terminal or keyboard is placed is lower to compensate. Light sources are another condition that is often detrimental to use of terminals. Natural and artificial light should be controlled so as not to reflect off the terminal screen or so that the terminal user finds a bright source within the field of vision. These last few points are dealt with further in Section 13.4.4, on design development.

Instruction for library users. Bibliographic instruction for all library users has become increasingly necessary as OPACs have replaced the familiar card catalog and as the variety of library collection formats and the multiplicity of bibliographic and information sources become more and more overwhelming. Some libraries conduct elementary instruction to groups of students in a formal classroom setting outside the library, and others by standing in the catalog and reference collection areas with the students. In other instances, an alcove or other area in the reference room is devoted to this informal purpose, perhaps equipped with a large-screen terminal and a flip chart for the instructor's use and seating not more than eight or ten so the students can see the screen.

However, in this age of information technology, most such instruction is best where the beginner can have hands-on use of a terminal and follow the instructor's guidance and can practice search, select, display, download, forwarding, and print command operations. In cases where a formal computer classroom setup is desired, this area or room should be near the public catalog and the central reference and bibliographic col-

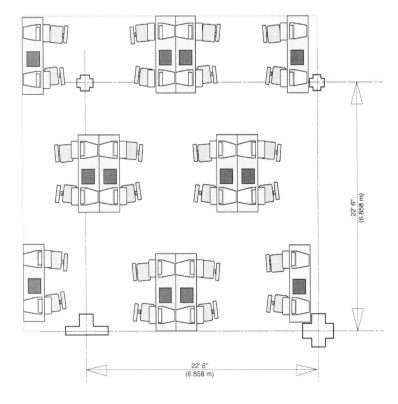

FIGURE 7.19 OPAC catalog arrangement proposed for the University of California, San Diego, Biomedical Library. In this diagram, there are 24 stations in approximately 800 ft² (74.322 m²), or approximately 33 ft² (3.066 m²) per OPAC with shared printer (shown as the dark squares between the monitors). Some stations are required at a height suitable for wheelchairs, which should be possible within this space allocation.

22' 6" (6.858 m)

22' 6" (6.858 m)

lections. Libraries have usually found it best to conduct such instruction in small groups, like sections of a class. The instructor will need a terminal connected with one or more overhead projector(s). Overhead transparencies or a laptop connected to an LCD plate or an LCD projector may also be used for certain instructional information. (An LCD [Light Conducting Diode] plate is a device that can be used in conjunction with an overhead projector to project the screen of a computer for a larger audience; other, more expensive technologies—the LCD projector, for example—exist and may become common in the future.) The pupil's terminal is often on a long bench or lengthy table, arranged to facilitate the "spaghetti" of wire management. The ideal arrangement has the student facing the front of the room, though greater space efficiency is possible with students facing the wall around the room or perhaps face-to-face down the center of the room; the authors recommend the former approach for planning purposes. This array of students will require about 35 ft^2 (3.252 m^2) per student plus space for shared printers, handouts, teaching space, the teaching station, and other features. In any arrangement, the teacher must be able to walk behind students for viewing and comment on each screen display. (Although the authors find this risky if not shortsighted, some institutions argue that flat screens and small CPUs as found in laptops enable keeping the old, smaller square footage planning per student.) Occasionally facilities are arranged with rear projection rather than overhead projection (as in the Meyer Library flexible classroom at Stanford). (See figs. 7.20 and 7.21.)

When a library finds frequent need for instructing groups of more than 15 or 20, there may be justification for a large classroom in the building, though in many instances the library staff merely schedule use of a technically adequate classroom in another building. The disadvantage of the latter arrangement is the occasional need for the library instructor to carry or truck to the classroom an armful of illustrative reference volumes of one type or another to use in conjunction with the online information.

Distributed data access. It is desirable for library users and staff to have accessible terminals at the point of need. That is, if a student or researcher is working in the bookstack and wants to find a book (perhaps a reference found in the book in hand), it is convenient to be able to use a computer nearby, rather than go to the central catalog area to conduct such a search. One or two such terminals will be appreciated on each stack floor, in the current periodicals area, in the government publications service area, in special collections, and so on. Obviously, equipment cost may be limiting, though space and utility ports or outlets can provide for such connections even if the equipment must wait.

It should be obvious that libraries are today in various stages of moving from the precomputer to the fully developed computer era. Even libraries with the most advanced use of computers are certain to experience further development over the years ahead. The target is moving in terms of technology to be planned for and accommodated. Yet there can hardly be debate as to the trend. It is desirable to plan for very extensive use of computers, and therefore to plan for very wide distribution of data access throughout the building. More will be said in Chapter 13 on this point.

Group or classlike clusters. Libraries house some (but not all) of the groups of computers on a campus. (The word *cluster* refers to a grouping of terminals, often in a room or semiopen area and often of the same equipment, with or without an instructor's position and usually with some type of human technical assistance close at hand to help solve systems or software problems.) Independent research libraries may have no need for such classrooms. However, all colleges and universities provide for groups of from 20 to 100 or more users in a single cluster, some in various academic buildings, some in dormitory or residence halls, and usually one or more in the library. Though a large university may have less than half in library buildings, even so there may be five or six library clusters.

The functions fulfilled in these clusters will sometimes be required by members of the faculty for their scheduled classes, for classes to work independently on projects or assignments without an instructor present, for use of advanced equipment with multimedia capacity, for librarians to provide occasional scheduled workshops on use of online catalogs and other databases, or for group instruction of staff or library users about evolving software and new hardware. Every generation of students will need elementary and intermediate instruction, and then opportunities for advanced instruction; every year faculty will develop new instructional modules and will take

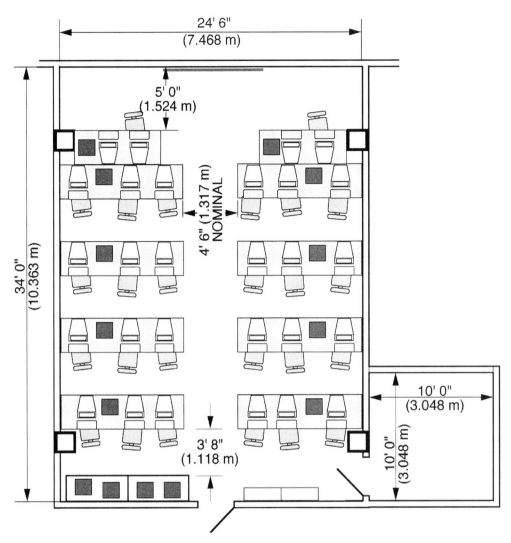

FIGURE 7.20   **Plan for a computer-based teaching space for an existing building. Conceptually, this is similar to the "Teaching Theater" at the University of Maryland. Note that this plan is based on 35 ft² (3.252 m²) per student. The space could accommodate scanners or other equipment at the computer desks plus shared equipment at the back (entry side) of the room. The storage room would accommodate specialized equipment as well as a file server. All wire management can work off the walls. The typical table is 32 in. × 10 ft (0.813 × 3.048 m); the space between tables is 40 in. (1.016 m). At the front of the room is a projection screen that could support projection of various forms from a cart as well as ceiling-mounted projection. The shelving at the back of the room is for reference documentation and handouts.**

advantage of new equipment or software or develop their own new multimedia instructional programs. Different campus clusters may offer one or several of dozens of possible hardware configurations and a selection of supported software from literally thousands of software resources, each with particular advantages.

The number, size, and location of these clusters will be locally conditioned by the stability of or change in information technology systems, by the evolution of class instruction, and by the status and use of specialized digital audio and video configurations. No planning guidance can be given except to state the obvious—that planners must understand thoroughly the current and projected needs of the faculty, as well as the thinking and expectations of campus and library planners of these systems. National and even international developments can be helpful in these projections. Do not forget the needs of those using wheelchairs

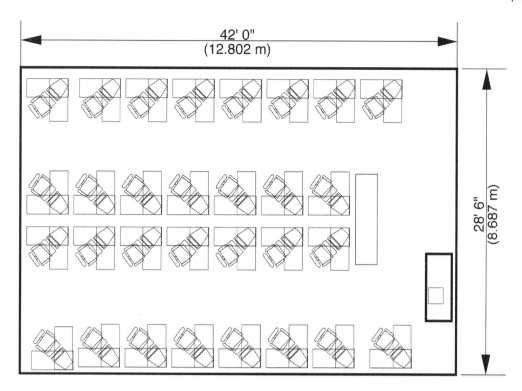

FIGURE 7.21   Although more schematic than fig. 7.20 (no entry is shown), this layout of a computer classroom within the dimensional characteristics of an existing building provides seating at about 40 ft² (3.716 m²) each, including the teaching space. This arrangement, based on a philosophy different from that of fig. 7.20, could support fairly complex workstations for each student. The apparently large space between the backs of the computer stations accommodates flexible (and probably not pretty, though clever design could address this) wire management. The large open aisles can be used for portable equipment on carts. Such an arrangement is planned at Western Washington University's Wilson Library in response to successful use of such an arrangement elsewhere on campus. (Courtesy of Western Washington University)

and motorized carts. And, again, look for constant further development, and be sure to plan for spatial flexibility and adequate communication connectivity.

At large universities, recent experience is that remodeling and upgrading of wiring may be needed at least every decade. Conventional wire networks are upgraded to Local Area Networks (LANs), to Ethernet cable, then to fiber optics, and to accommodate Integrated Services Digital Network (ISDN) requirements for voice, data, and video over one line. Cellular voice and data transmission may be common if not dominant. Distributed client servers are common (that is, minicomputers in closets or secured rooms with excellent connectivity to the network, large storage capacity, and the operational capacity to support a number of remote microcomputers via the network). The necessary use of reception dishes

on the top of library buildings may be replaced by smaller, hidden, even internal reception devices. Predictions are that communication systems will become smaller, more diverse in nature, gradually less expensive, and more universally accessible, and that their technology will keep evolving for decades to come. Clusters in library buildings need to be planned with these expectations in mind.

For each of the above types of computer provisions, there are many current installations that are badly laid out, that use the wrong furniture, and that are confusing as to function for persons first approaching the location. The authors have seldom seen really well designed arrangements, at least not at any of the large universities they have visited. Yet the field is changing rapidly. In the future, you should be able to visit a variety of facilities and, having seen and evaluated several recent installations, develop improved arrangements to meet the local need.

One facility, which opened in 1994 with heavy emphasis on computer use, is the University of Southern California's Leavey Library with 104,000 gross ft² (9,662 m²). (See figs. 7.22 and 7.23.) This undergraduate "teaching library" can shelve over 120,000 volumes and 270 current periodicals on the entrance level and upper three floors. The course reserve collections are accommodated in compact shelving behind the circulation desk on the entry level, and information technology occupies the lower (basement) level (40 percent of the total building), open 24 hours per day, called the "Information Commons," where online reserves of class notes, journal articles, book chapters, exam files, syllabi, and so forth are available on the World Wide Web. This lower level provides a 50-seat multimedia networked auditorium, 100 multifunctional workstations where students can work individually or in pairs, 17 small rooms with whiteboard and laptop Ethernet connections for collaborative projects and group study, a centralized printing area supporting remote printing from workstations throughout the building, two interactive computer training rooms (one for 15 and the other for 25 persons) for online bibliographic instruction and information access and analysis using computer technologies and networks—all supported by nearby library staff to provide "navigation" assistance and computer consulting plus reference service using a 5,000-volume collection (fig. 7.23). And on the first (entrance) level is housed the USC Center for Scholarly Technology to support faculty and librarians in designing and testing instructional and information-access software. This Leavey Center for Scholarly Technology provides a computing "discovery center" where students and faculty can explore the latest

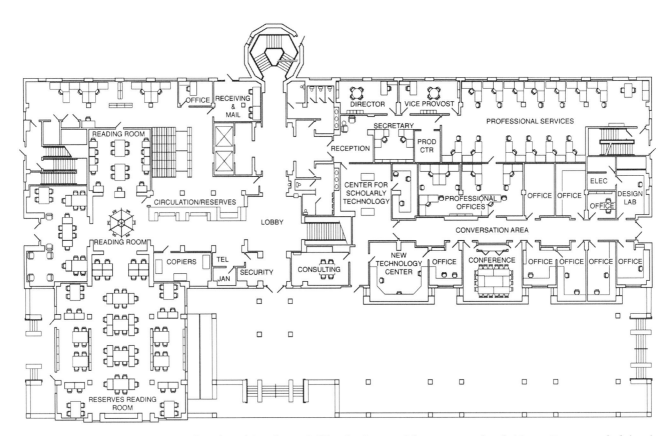

FIGURE 7.22 **University of Southern California, Leavey Library, entry level. Note: Compact shelving is used for reserves behind the circulation desk. Also, 24-hour access to the Lower Level "Information Commons" (see fig. 7.23) is through the first-floor lobby, with other entry-level areas then locked. The large area to the lower right is an outdoor terrace. To the left of that terrace are stairs and a ramp for access to the main entry. (Courtesy of the University of Southern California and Shepley Bulfinch Richardson and Abbott Architects)**

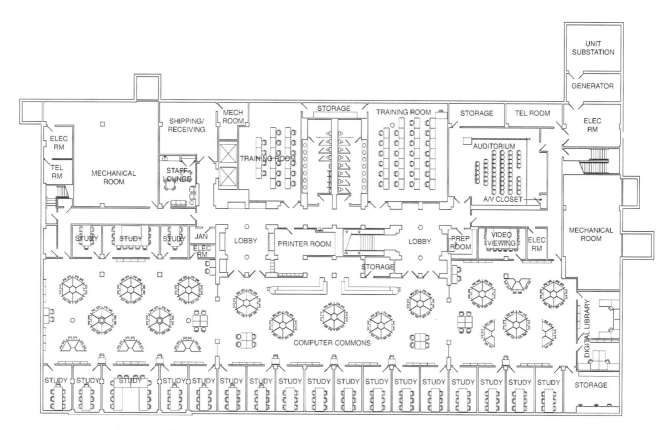

FIGURE 7.23 University of Southern California, Leavey Library, lower level. The large open area was at first known as the "Computer Commons." Note the large number of group study rooms. Note also the configuration of the three teaching rooms (upper part of plan) as variations relative to figs. 7.20 and 7.21. (Courtesy of the University of Southern California and Shepley Bulfinch Richardson and Abbott Architects)

hardware and software, a multimedia "exploritorium," and an instructional technology and imaging facility. This is indicative of what all academic institutions are doing during the 1990s in greater or lesser degree. (See other examples in Section 11.5.) In planning a new library or renovation, visits to several such installations will be helpful and are recommended.

To underscore the dynamic nature of information technologies in libraries, one may note changes in the USC Leavey Library after its first three years, largely driven by student use patterns and not by the technology. Students asked so many computer questions at the reference desk and reference questions at the computer help desk that these two service points were combined on the lower level and renamed the "Reference Commons." This Commons now has a modest reference book collection, with course reserves and current periodicals now up on the entrance level. Also, librarians felt a need to double the size of this new Commons, so the second level may be turned into another such area. Further, students

wanted a "quiet floor" with no computers, so the fourth level is slated to meet that expressed need.

7.3.2 Effects of Computer-Driven Change on Library Philosophy

Just as predictions of collections growth are certain to be slightly off, the comments that follow, coming from a somewhat clouded crystal ball, will not be totally correct. Still, at the risk of error and to encourage consideration of this important subject, a few thoughts are offered. Although technical problems currently exist with some of the activities suggested below, one can predict that these will be managed over time.

The computer is fundamentally changing the way libraries operate. With today's technology, it is possible to look up citations to library holdings from any place in the world (provided appropriate access protocol is met). Information that is stored digitally, either as a digital copy of a paper product (similar to a digitized facsimile) or as a fully digitized text, can also be accessed from any place. Library privilege can be controlled with cards containing bar codes or magnetic strips with unique information for each patron. These cards can control entrance gates, complete checkout transactions, be tied into financial resources to operate photocopy machines or laser printers, and the like. Self-service circulation is a reality in a growing number of institutions, and self-discharge of library materials is being tried.

Online building directories, sometimes called computer kiosks, are seen now in many libraries. Computer-driven signs used for announcements are seen in a few libraries (the Meyer Library at Stanford University is an example). Libraries are providing access not only to catalogs, but to local networks and the World Wide Web to anybody who enters the library. The local networks support electronic mail and provide access to specialized servers for various purposes, including controlled access to certain information (as in providing access to proprietary or copyrighted materials).

Books are being scanned into computer databases even though this is an expensive process. It can be expected that digital facsimiles of older materials will eventually meet archival preservation standards, and that digital scanning will be accepted for preservation where microfilming has for many decades been the medium of choice. The facsimile transmission of material, even paper-based text, is initially digitized, and then sent by wire to remote locations. The quality of these transmissions using the Ariel document delivery system is significantly better than the more traditional facsimile. Increasing amounts of material, especially journals, are available online from anyplace, usually with associated fees or access protocol.

For a long time, library materials have been purchased, cataloged, and controlled using computer technologies. The advantage of distributed access and greater control over the catalog using digital resources is clear; computer-based catalogs (OPACs) are here to stay, even though there are critics of this technology. The need to have technical processing staff quarters next to the reference room and the catalog is diminishing rapidly; indeed, it is at a point where many institutions could consider separating these functions, even though such a choice would not be made unless space is at a premium in the central facility. Systems supportive of online reserves have arrived, and faculty generate their own homepages or Web sites (which may in time largely replace the traditional reserves function).

Use of the library is actually increased with the introduction of computers. Certain materials will be available only through computers; other information will be available both through computers and in paper or microfilm or other formats in the library. Access to an ever greater world of citations drives use of the library to some extent. Scholars are using computers to write, to calculate, to communicate, to store, and to process information.

With the rush of technology comes a concomitant awareness of ergonomic, economic, and operational issues. Repetitive motion injury is a real concern in libraries as in any workplace. Concerns about low-level electromagnetic radiation have been largely dispelled, but they linger with staff who must be around computers much of their working day. Eye strain remains an issue.

Cost is certainly a problem from a multitude of angles, including the cost and distribution of equipment; the cost of dealing with copyright; the cost of storing, transmitting, manipulating, and, often, printing information; the cost of frequent upgrading to new generations of software and hardware, and so on. A very large portion of the world's population does not own a computer, and even fewer are networked; providing access to the disadvantaged remains a concern. Maintenance of artifactual information is a problem; books and other information resources can themselves be works of art or contain information that does not appear in a scanned or digitized text. Maintenance of a historic record can be an issue for some fully digital materials—how can the scholar be certain that a particular item has not been revised or altered by others? Ongoing expenses would be incurred if certain e-mail messages need to be archived for legal or historical purposes. Some are concerned about the social implications of computers—might the future support a society of scholars in some fields who never need to leave their home?

From this stew of change we will make the following 27 predictions, some or all of which will influence the shape of academic and research libraries in coming decades and will in varying degrees affect programming and design of library functions in public, technical, and administrative domains:

> Libraries will continue to change operationally and physically well into the future, if not forever. A facility that is designed to adapt to change is more important than a facility perfectly designed for the best tech-

nological device currently available. Whatever the technology, it will eventually be outdated, and its configuration or size or location will change.

The "library as place" will remain universally admired in nearly all institutions in societies in all countries. The significance of the library as a place in which people meet, consult, socialize, discuss, and study together will be constantly reaffirmed. Many thoughtful observers see the library as an antidote to the fragmentation of societies today, to the loneliness and isolation many students feel—a place providing a balance to the cold realities of technological life. This social significance of libraries in the Information Age will in coming decades be as important as its traditional functionality.

Most, if not all, of what goes on today in the library will continue to happen in the future, though the proportion of seats with computers or signal ports with computer support will increase dramatically. The day may well come when nearly every seat in the library will have the capacity to support a computer.

Collections in research libraries will continue to grow indefinitely. This prediction is based upon cost, ergonomics, and other issues related to the educational and research usages of information. Certain types of collections, however, will be largely replaced with digital formats over time, especially materials that are relatively short (most technical reports, for example), distributed to audiences by mail (journals and possibly newspapers), digitized to preserve intellectual content (replacing microfilm), or used more for brief lookup than for general reading (reference works, bibliographical databases, and some government documents).

Increasing collection quantities (perhaps even an increasing percentage) will be found in closed-access stacks, shelved in accession order. This will include remote storage facilities, special collections, and other materials. However, for the main centralized and branch libraries of the academic or research institution, the authors advocate continued support of open, subject-arrayed collections.

There will continue to be those who will resist change, and who will not use a computer unless they have no choice. Some of these folks will be important contributors to society or the local community; their needs will have to be met in one way or another. Resistance to computers comes from personal philosophy, mechanical aptitude, or attitude, as well as from technical, ergonomic, and economic problems with databases, software, or hardware. Some users place a very high value on being able to hold and read paper-based materials for a number of fairly obvious reasons. Most historical publications in most fields will not be available online for decades, perhaps for many decades. Some will feel that communicating in person or by phone simply cannot be replaced by communication by computer. Some will express and experience extreme discomfort from computer display terminals or keyboards or mice/trackballs, and will seek alternative information sources or devices to complete the required work. Some will not be able to gain access to library terminals when they have time to do their work. Many may not be able to afford a computer, or other costs passed on to the user, including printout products and access to resources requiring an account number or a credit card.

For these and other reasons, it is predicted that a considerable fraction of library use will continue to be traditional as long as such an approach is possible. Catalog cards will continue to be used as long as they are available. Likewise, journals, books, and other materials will continue to be heavily used and much preferred as long as they are available.

On-site academic library use will gravitate toward research and away from course-related work. This will become a real trend as electronic reserves become common and undergraduates find that they really do not have to go to the library to do the required reading or prepare basic research theme papers. This may result in an increase in maturity of the typical library patron, a fact that would be welcome in many places. On the other hand, as the greater community gains off-campus access to library information, there will be increasing pressure to allow physical library access to that community, which may well offset the prediction of reclusive (at least in terms of library use) students. We do not predict a reduction in library visits in the future, but the source and nature of those visits may change.

Staff presence will often be required at the library entry for security reasons. There are many ways of providing an appropriate level of security; a portal monitor will not always be required. However, if there is no staff presence in the area of the exit/entry, the psychology suggesting that the institution does not care about its collections will be problematic.

Self-service circulation, holds, renewal, and checkout activities will be increasingly used. Current examples suggest that staffed service points will also be required well into the future for a number of reasons, including both technical and social. It is suggested that although the size of service desks for these activities may shrink, they will not go away, and their location near the entry still makes sense.

A computer cluster will take the place of the card catalog in virtually every library. In libraries with very large card catalogs, the OPAC computer cluster will probably not occupy the entire space vacated by the card cabinets. Thus, it can be predicted that other functions, including reference or information desks or both, e-reserve terminals, photocopy and laser printing facilities, and exhibits, will fill in the space.

As the computers used for access to bibliographic information are increasingly used to provide access to other online resources, there will be a movement to maintain simple, dumb OPAC terminals that only support the catalog. This prediction is made simply to assure bibliographic access quickly to anybody entering the library. Terminals of this description can also be placed with security confidence outside the area controlled by the library.

Until the technology changes considerably, computer-driven information kiosks will not be heavily used while there is also a paper-based information and directory system; the computer is slow, the spelling has to be precise, and the user has to accept the prospect of others knowing who is being sought. Because of this, with current technology, it is predicted that computer directory kiosks will not replace more traditional technologies. However, the information available on the kiosk will be available on the network; visitors can find directory-type information before entering the library. Thus, the traditional directory will increasingly become a tool for the new visitor.

Computer-supported technologies will increasingly be used as tools for teaching in virtually all fields. Because libraries will continue to serve the process of accessing information (using increasing computer resources), it makes sense to combine a large fraction of the computer and other information resources of the institution for both teaching and information access. Thus, language labs, computer labs, interactive media centers, and the like may well be located in the library building. This suggests teaching space within the library not only for teaching information access, but for teaching all manner of other subjects. Additional computer resources (and teaching space) will continue to be outside the library, allowing the library to operate fewer hours than the main computer center supporting institutional administrative functions, interinstitutional telecommunications, and certain large-scale research needs on a mainframe.

The concept of a reference desk will continue. The reference librarian will become a computer and network expert as well as a general subject specialist and will be even more a teacher of information skills. Supporting equipment will be close at hand for both the librarian and library visitors. Traditional reading space in the reference area will be in part displaced by computer stations connected to various networks and information resources.

Reserve operations will work with faculty to deal with copyright permissions and royalty issues, and they will have equipment for high-speed scanning of lecture notes, tests, and other material where copyright is not a problem. The most heavily used reserved materials will to a large extent be available online through e-reserves. The reserves staff will include an e-reserves coordinator, and the work area will include scanning equipment. As with the circulation desk, the reserve desk should shrink in size. Combining reserve and circulation functions often will be attractive as procedures and operations are streamlined by computer-driven changes.

Interlibrary lending and borrowing processes will increasingly become digitally based, particularly as materials are scanned that are frequently requested by others. We do not foresee a reduction of this operation. There is the equipment needed for scanning and transmission of information which often requires the space of a workstation; more similar equipment may be required in the future. Indeed, with increasing access to bibliographic citations, it is easily predicted that this activity will substantially increase over time; additional staff space in this area will be put to good use. Its location, with digital communication and facsimile technologies, could be almost anyplace as long as staff can easily fetch materials from the collections.

In addition to teaching spaces, student scholars will seek increasing numbers of small-group study rooms. These should be set up to support networked connections as well as chalkboard and seating for four to six. Acoustic isolation is important.

Buildings will become "smart." Environments will be controlled with digital systems, locks will be increasingly managed with computers, security systems will be controlled digitally, and so on.

There will be fewer administrative support staff in the future. With computers, answering machines, and other technologies, the requirement for secretarial support is diminishing and will lead to fewer positions or to full-time positions becoming part-time. However, the space required per person has increased; the space savings is minimal.

The capacity to support distributed online serials check-in and payment will in some cases cause this traditionally centralized function to be dispersed, particularly in large academic libraries with multiple branches.

Interest in document delivery will not go away, and probably will increase as faculty and others spend more time at their computers in their offices. The ability to scan and transmit text to the office should diminish the need to physically deliver relatively short items. This activity will probably add to the space requirements for interlibrary and intralibrary loan.

As texts become digitized, acquisitions based on the fear of having materials go out-of-print will diminish. Some fraction of acquisitions in the future will move toward purchasing materials when needed rather than in anticipation of need. This should fine-tune the rate of acquisitions growth; collections will still grow, but perhaps at well-defended reduced rates.

If materials are never out-of-print, some college libraries should reduce somewhat their anxiety over a preservation-quality environment for newly acquired materials. Over time, it may be that substantial portions of new library buildings can be designed with less stringent environmental control, thereby saving both initial cost and ongoing energy cost, though controls needed for human comfort will, of course, continue. This could apply especially to storage or auxiliary collection shelving facilities.

Materials will increasingly become available through the network rather than through the mail. Alternatively, a CD-ROM, DVD-ROM, or other storage device will be delivered containing the desired text. Libraries may decide to print the text and shelve the printed copy as a book. Thus, the library may become a print shop. At the same time, it is probable that many libraries will set up a regular program for digitization of selected materials (e.g., fragile, heavily used, extremely valuable, or very scarce research items), placing them on the local network, making them available on the World Wide Web once copyright issues are resolved, and enabling a student or scholar to download an entire major publication onto a personal disc (or discs) for storage and ready use.

Libraries will have a continuing need for technical system support, so a systems department staff will require space for managing library servers, telecommunications, software and hardware changes, and so on. Once there is a rather full, library-wide application of integrated information technologies, the needed staff size may remain relatively constant, but we do not see any chance for much reduction in staff over the next several decades. Continuing a philosophy of distributed data and processing, libraries will not need major machine rooms, as in a central institutional data center.

Library building remodeling will need to include space for vertical wire and cable chases as well as the means for horizontal runs, and, in general, to achieve a substantial upgrading of power and signal capacity and rather universal location of ports or outlets in order to meet expanding needs. Even fairly new library buildings will require physical modifications to meet changing specifications of new technology—a change from Ethernet to fiber cable to ISDN is a case in point. This will be prompted by the desire to gain new operating features or price economies, or to meet changes in mandated national or institutional standards.

Microwave dishes on library buildings are likely to become universal as long-distance data transmissions become increasingly common and as this technology becomes more cost-efficient relative to land wires and cables. Cable TV, videoconferencing, and other such usages may favor this means of telecommunications. Conferencing may be widely used for certain technical training sessions, replacing some of the cross-country airline travel to attend technical briefing sessions or expert classes.

7.4
Current Periodicals and Newspapers

To accommodate easy use of current periodicals, there must be nearby seating for some 3 to 5 percent of the total readers, or, in some cases (e.g., physical and life science branch libraries), even more. Much of this capacity may be in lounge chairs (perhaps 60 to 70 percent), ideally with footrests, such as hassocks or ottomans. Without footrests, students will turn the chairs to create the desired comfort, which results in undue wear on a fairly expensive piece of furniture. The periodicals area should be near the entrance if possible. If use of current periodicals is not sufficient to fill all the seats, they are likely to be occupied by readers using their own material.

A self-service photocopy service will be very popular in any library and must be easy to find and often convenient to the current periodicals, with paper cutter, stapler, space for one or two book trucks by each machine for volumes ready for reshelving, and perhaps even a vending machine for prepaid debit cards. Because paper will frequently be wasted and discarded, one or more large paper recycling barrels must be near the machines. Heat from the machines and from people waiting to make copies means that the ventilation should be exceptional. And, given the noise produced by people using this service, its

location is often partially cut off from adjacent functions so the latter will not be disturbed.

Despite convenient self-service copy machines, and because of theft and vandalism, the periodical area probably will require supervision, and in many cases special provision for controlled access to some, if not all, of the collections will be desired. This may involve controlling access to the reading area, storing periodicals in shelving behind a service desk as reserved materials, or housing the collections in a separate closed stack and either paging the materials or providing for controlled access and special charge-out procedures for the reader. Northwestern University is an example with a self-service, controlled-access stack. In any case, the degree of collection control for current journals is an issue to be decided and fully explained in the program.

Special provision should be made for periodical indexes, if they are to be kept in this area instead of in the reference or bibliography area. If they are in book format in the latter area, they should be as close as possible to the periodical shelving. Libraries use large index tables, or bibliography ("bib") tables, for these indexes as well as for selected abstracts, bibliographies, catalogs, and directories. These tables may be up to 12 ft (3.658 m) long and about 5 ft (1.524 m) wide—this is a critical dimension—with two double-faced shelves down the middle; the reading area is sometimes flat, sometimes gently sloping on each side. The tables must be very sturdy, of course, because of the weight of the materials and their heavy use, and should have a stool for each 3 ft (0.914 m) of table. They are excellent for short use of the most heavily used indexes or reference sources. (See fig. 7.24.)

Even though little space may be required, provision should be made for the public display of a file or catalog of holdings of periodicals and newspapers and perhaps some other high-frequency serials. This display often is in the form of a microfiche serials record, a visible index (a set of large, rigid panels with each serial listed on one movable strip), or a card file. Increasingly, periodical holdings are available online. In that case, the terminal might be placed on the periodical service counter or beside the staff desk for self-service use, but placed on a revolving tray, or lazy Susan, so the staff assistant can view the screen to solve problems. Near this service desk area, depending upon the distance from the general reference collection, there may also be shelv-

FIGURE 7.24 **Index table for selected bibliographies, indexes, abstracting services, and directories. Other examples have sloped reading surfaces. Many libraries provide stools rather than chairs at these tables to discourage long-term seating.**

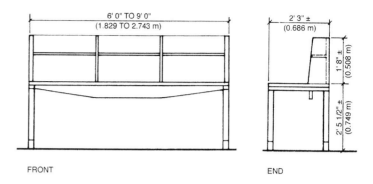

FRONT   END

ing for books, such as periodical directories and perhaps a few basic dictionaries.

Smaller libraries and many university departmental or branch libraries find it possible and advisable to combine in one area the reference, bibliography, and current periodical collections. Section 7.14 of this chapter gives further comments on the topic of divisional or departmental libraries.

Some libraries prefer to have the bound back files of their periodicals close to the unbound current issues. After all, the reader who is working on topics of the past few years may move constantly from bound to unbound and back, so proximity has advantages. And bound files may be served by the same staff that cares for the current numbers; in these cases, they are shelved close at hand, on the same level (often a difficult location to achieve) or perhaps on the level directly above or below, with a stairway making convenient connection between the two. This arrangement can be particularly desirable for the heavily used titles recorded in the standard periodical indexes. Because of the additional weight of the bound volume, more table or carrel seating should be provided in proportion to lounge seating. But remember, in arranging for the seating accommodations for periodical reading, peace and quiet and comfort are desirable, and the readers' purpose is quite different from that of students who are consulting standard reference works. One advantage of maintaining a separate bound journal collection is that this collection may be more adapted to compact storage technologies than are other collections, either now or in the future.

Other libraries array their bound journals by subject classification together with the related monographic collections. Scholars argue that they welcome having "their" materials close to "their" carrel, which is more practical with full subject classification and distribution of bound journals.

Once this system is implemented, faculty pressure will likely be to maintain this distribution of the collections. The decision on this matter largely relates to the concept of service held by the library.

Many libraries subscribe to only a few newspapers and keep only the current issues of most of them, sometimes discarding the others after a week or a month, or after a replacement microfilm has been received. Because of their size, newspapers placed on a regular library table tend to interfere with readers on each side and perhaps even across the table as well. A small individual table is hardly wide enough for comfortable perusal of a newspaper. If taking notes is required, further complications ensue. Some individuals find it convenient to read a newspaper seated in a not-too-large easy chair, although newspapers mounted on a stick may make this difficult. Others may prefer to read at a stand-up counter, an oversized carrel, or a large table. Some libraries anchor the current issue of the 10 or 12 most popular newspapers at 10 to 12 sloping table positions. (The Kanazawa Institute of Technology has an elegant arrangement of this design.)

The various possibilities should be considered and a decision reached so that the architect can plan the space satisfactorily. A few of each reading option may be best, though room aesthetics should be given consideration. It is obvious that the area required for each reader is larger in a newspaper room than elsewhere; an area of 40 ft² (3.716 m²) per reader should be adequate in most cases. The total number of readers will rarely be large at one time.

In a state university library, if local papers from throughout the state are made available, a considerable amount of space may be required for newspaper reading, and sometimes a special room is provided. A journalism departmental library may also have special requirements. Always remember that additional rooms present complications, particularly if they have walls and doors, and that small rooms may tend to be more difficult to keep quiet and orderly than large ones. At any rate, if a library is to have current newspapers in their original form, some provision for them and for those who use them and wish to copy excerpts from them is required.

Back files of newspapers are generally provided today on microfilm. The future may find back files housed on optical disks or other digital media. For either of these, some form of reading machine is required, with special seating accommodations that are discussed in Section 7.11. If the seats can be close to the storage place for microfilm and other reproductions, and also close to a service desk, so much the better. Of course, future use of terminals will not require the collections nearby, but occasional reader need for assistance may suggest a close service desk, at least until a technological literacy has developed among library users.

Many university research libraries are still plagued by back files of newspapers, generally but not always bound. Those issued before the wood-pulp age (which began gradually about 1870 and was almost universal by 1880) are still treasured and should ordinarily be kept in or transferred to the special collections department or to a library that is ready to preserve them. Heavy use will wear them out more rapidly than it will books, because the strain on the paper increases geometrically as the sheet size increases. These newspapers should be given special care and should be microfilmed if heavily used. Microfilm copies are even more strongly recommended for wood-pulp newspapers, because the life of the original is limited at best and because the cost of binding and storage space is often greater than the cost of the film. Methods of microfilm storage and shelving for bound newspapers are discussed in Section 6.5.

7.5
New Books, Light Reading, Viewing, and Browsing Rooms

New books are often withheld from circulation for a week while they are placed on view, and arrangements can be made to reserve them for future borrowing. The light reading collection of current popular books is generally a circulating collection with a fairly limited circulation period of perhaps one week; in some libraries the books are referred to as the "7-day books." Although the light reading collection is considered a useful invitation to a general education, the new book collection is less compelling today than it was in former decades when major libraries added far fewer new titles each week. Usually few people check weekly the new acquisitions, and, in some institutions, the subject curator may post or issue a "new acquisitions" list to interested departments. Each library must determine the educational value of this extra staff process and the need for this shelving space.

It is not recommended or proposed that a special room be provided, even in a very large library, for new books or a light reading collection. Rather it is customary to place the collection in a prominent position, often adjacent to or even in the main lobby, in order to make them visible and easily available, and to give the library user a collection to browse while waiting for a search, a paged item, or a friend. The books should be placed within the exit-controlled area, or the loss rate will be high. Libraries should provide a small amount of seating nearby, perhaps of the lounge type. Side tables on which temporarily to place personal belongings or the campus newspaper may be useful. If there is an annunciation panel to tell a patron of a completed service transaction, it is well to have it within view of this seating area. A location near the circulation desk is often suitable, particularly in a closed-stack library, and the inviting view of a small collection together with a few comfortable chairs can be developed as an attractive area in a building that otherwise is all business.

Television has become popular in some libraries as it has become universal at home. An area just off the lobby or fairly near the circulation desk, browsing area, or other lounge is sometimes devoted to large-screen presentation of local TV or cable channels, often with news reports, travel films, or local educational programming being offered for many hours. One example is the "current events alcove," step-seating in a sunken viewing area in the lobby of the 1992 Kapiolani Community College Library in Honolulu. Naturally, this function with adequate sound must be isolated from areas where business conversations or serious study take place. Artificial light will need to be muted, and a low ambient level of illumination can be recommended, though the design may be sufficient to provide for general reading if this area is converted from viewing.

Community colleges and other institutions that serve a predominately commuting student body may find this a means of attracting, or enticing, students to enter the library and helping them feel "at home" in an educational setting that may in other respects seem rather pedantic or formal or forbidding to some students. A viewing area may, on the other hand, be considered an effort to compete with a student union. In cases where there has been an effort to meld academic, social, and recreational activities, such as the Johnson Center of George Mason University, the viewing area may be considered just another educational medium, along with the motion picture theater, computer lab, and game room. Each institution must decide whether this feature of contemporary living is a programmatic benefit to an academic library.

Popular in college and university libraries for many years, a browsing room is essentially another means of providing seating close to larger collections of popular books and classics, intended to encourage general reading. Perhaps the earliest browsing room was the Farnsworth Room at Harvard, located from 1915 through 1948 in the Widener Library and later moved to the Lamont Library. The movement for browsing rooms spread rapidly, and they were established throughout the country, often in a room with handsome fittings and more spacious accommodations than most others in the library. They might be thought of as an example of an idealistic personal library, and their physical scale and homelike furnishings contribute to their continuing popularity. It was soon found that browsing rooms that had funds available for the acquisition of new and popular books were most used. Sweet Briar College Library has a charming "browsing room," equipped with two couches and a dozen soft chairs, which now features CDs for student listening. Smoking, often prohibited elsewhere, was once generally permitted, which naturally made the rooms popular, although views on this point have changed in many libraries. The Linonian and Brothers Room at Yale and the Morrison Room at the University of California, Berkeley, continue to be glamorous examples.

With the opening of the main collections to student access in many libraries, the whole book-stack has been made available for browsing, and many buildings have been planned without a separate browsing room. Other libraries, such as at Stanford and Princeton, have followed the example suggested above and placed in or near the entrance lobby a small collection of perhaps 200 to 400 volumes of attractive and popular books, inviting browsing and use, an invitation to a liberal education. The several Yale College Libraries and Harvard House Libraries perform similar functions, each with 3,000 to 10,000 volumes. Undergraduate libraries also in part meet this need.

Although a browsing room or area costs money for books, the space it requires may be used to good advantage if it serves general education purposes, advertises the growing library collections, relieves pressure on other rooms, adds to the total use of the library, or provides for future flexibility in a critical area. If a degree of oversight is supplied by staff at the building exits, the extra operational expense is nominal or nonexistent. The philosophical need for a specific area for this function must be determined locally. The authors have no formula to suggest for the ideal size or seating capacity, though it should be small and comfortable enough to be inviting and homey, and offer a relief from academic pressures.

7.6
Reserved-Book Rooms

Practically all libraries in institutions of higher learning have found it necessary to segregate most if not all printed materials that are required reading for courses. These materials are "reserved" for short loan periods to maximize access, and staff generally service the material. Since this type of service originated in the 1870s, the reserved-book system has spread and increased in scope, in spite of widespread discontent with its results. Today a trend toward online class material, or "e-reserves," will certainly lead toward a gradual shrinkage and perhaps virtual elimination of the space devoted to this function.

Some institutions have found it possible to place all reserved books on open shelves and to rely on the students not to misuse them and to sign for them if they are taken out of the library overnight or over the weekend. Others have decided that it is better and less troublesome to put them on restricted shelves, where students have to sign for them either after helping themselves in a suitably restricted area behind the desk or by asking for the book by call slip. (See fig. 7.25.)

Many libraries divide their collections into "open reserve," for what they sometimes speak of as collateral or recommended reading, and "closed reserve," for assigned or required reading or for books used by large classes where there are multiple copies but still not enough to go around during peak demand.

Online reserves will rapidly change the mix, especially for the required material or "closed reserves." With software designed to deal with copyright issues, electronic reserve services will include course packs, produced typically by the campus bookstore. Even without copyright software, many heavily used reserve items are being made available online. Faculty are increasingly creating homepages on which course notes, bibliographies, and other materials that in the past have been held in a reserve collection, are now available with or without library involvement. In these cases, students will be more concerned about access to terminals in computer clusters, or ownership of PCs or laptops with accessible network ports in dorms or the library, rather than about competing for materials on reserve, as has typically been the case. And, the materials will be available 24 hours a day with all students being able to use the assigned materials simultaneously if sufficient connections exist. One potential problem revolves around the need for fairly sophisticated computers to access and read electronic reserves when tone illustrations and perhaps colored graphics are involved. A different set of expenses is faced in this service model, but building area needs are certainly reduced. It can be predicted that the advantages of electronic reserves will be largely developed over the next decade, and that there will remain a core of texts that will need to be accommodated in a physical reserve collection of one kind or another.

Libraries vary greatly in their use of reserved-book areas and may over time shift at least in

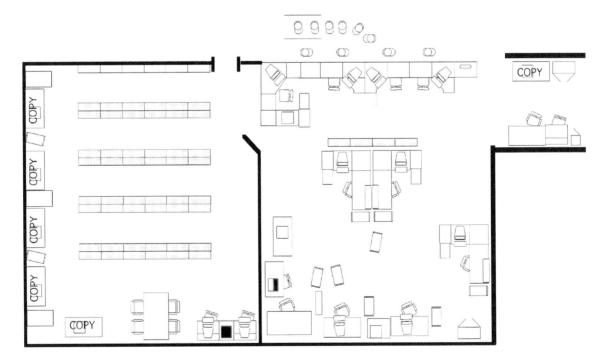

FIGURE 7.25   Conceived as a self-service reserves area juxtaposed to the circulation desk and circulation staff area, this plan was developed by library staff at Western Washington University. A very similar arrangement can be found at the University of Victoria McPherson Library. The reserve shelving is to be counter high (high enough for three shelves with 12 dividers per shelf). A magnetic-based theft detection system is proposed at the entry to the area, and the circulation station next to the entry would be the one station always staffed. Note that for ADA, accommodation of wheelchair access at the checkout station is required. (Courtesy of Western Washington University)

degree from open to closed and closed to open arrangements as well as from physical holdings to digitized holdings supported with computer-based reading stations or through custom printing at the bookstore. The percentage of material in each group varies, but it is predicted that the physical holdings will diminish over the next decade as more of the most heavily used material is made available online. It is suggested that plans be made so that electronic, open, or closed reserves can be put into effect.

Few if any large institutions have been able to avoid closed reserves for long periods. If there are to be closed reserves, a special secured shelving area must be provided convenient to support staff. If students can select their books at the shelves, wide aisles are desirable, but if the library attendant pages the books after a call slip is submitted, standard-width aisles are in most cases possible.

The size of reserves varies greatly but can usually be kept comparatively small. A college may have a maximum of 4,000 to 5,000 books and photocopies, but in a few universities, more than 6,000 are required at one time on closed reserve. The quantity may be sharply reduced, particularly for journal articles, example examinations, course notes, syllabi, and the like depending on the prevalence of the use by instructors of course "readers" or course "packs"—that is, article and chapter extracts gathered in a binder and sold by the campus bookstore to students of a particular course. The quantity also depends on pedagogical methods, the proportion of assigned readings that are available online to the students, the number of undergraduate students, the number of courses in the current semester, and library practices—such as the proportion on open shelves or a decision to keep all except one copy of each title on closed reserve year-round to save labor.

Because these volumes can be shelved tightly together or, in the case of multiple copies, perhaps turned on their sides and stacked, it should be possible to shelve up to 175 volumes in a standard single-faced section of closed-access shelves, so that 15 double-faced sections may be adequate for 5,000 volumes and videocassettes or other materials. A smaller quantity of shelving will be required in most institutions except where other types of reserved materials—such as headphones, current issues of current journals, and the like—are maintained in this controlled area. In branch libraries, one shelf for each two courses may suf-

fice. If insufficient space is provided, the results may be serious; this is one area where it may be prudent to include flexibility either by adding a contingency factor to the amount of capacity needed or by placing the shelving in such an area that by shifting a cagelike partition, adjustments can be made in the quantity of shelving available. This will become less of an issue with development of electronic reserves, but the space occupied by shelving may become a processing area for scanning texts and other activities.

A problem that often arises is whether these books are to be used only in a special reserved-book room and taken out of it only overnight or over the weekend or whether, after being signed for, they may be used anywhere within the library building or even elsewhere for a limited period. The latter system has many advantages and is generally preferable, as it makes it unnecessary to provide a special reserved-book reading room, and readers are free to select the type of space and seating accommodations they prefer. Furthermore, the potential savings of staff time resulting from the possibility of combining the main circulation desk with the reserved-book function could be significant. Such a savings would be difficult to achieve with a separate room. However, it has the disadvantage of making it easier for students to hide books for their own use or for that of a friend at a later time. This is another decision that must be made locally.

If the books are to be used within a special reserved-book room and withdrawn from it only during limited hours, the room should, in most institutions, be the largest reading area in the building. It is sometimes said that well over 50 percent of all the use of library books in most undergraduate college libraries is of reserved books. Sometimes the reserved-book room is provided with its own entrance and can be kept open after the rest of the library is closed for the night. Careful consideration should be given to planning a library to make this possible now or later. (See point 5 in the following section about study halls.) Though students should generally be able to plan well enough to get through required study in regular library hours, this, of course, may be less true where the economy forces budget restrictions leading to dramatically reduced library hours. Do not forget to provide for photocopy service and a quick-access catalog to the books on reserve. Rest rooms should be available, particularly during the late evening or night hours.

7.7
Study Halls

Students' rooms in dormitories or other living areas have usually been unsuitable for serious study. Yet in the past decade, with most undergraduates having personal computers or access to them in the campus residence halls together with network connections, students now do quite a bit of studying in these residences. The students are thought to be significantly more serious and intense than ever before, partly because of the cost of attending college. The more prestigious institutions find that huge, wild parties are fewer; students need to study—to graduate and begin their careers. Nevertheless, remember that the styles of student life as well as students' habits and diversions, go in waves. Student life in each decade of the past century has had a distinctive character, quite different from the previous ones.

As a result, the library as a place, in part a study hall, can provide a dependable home for learning. And if the library is adequate in size, attractive, comfortable, convenient, and quiet, it will be heavily used by students reading their own books and papers or materials such as course reserves previously charged out of the library. And, with access to computers, reading as well as writing, communicating, and game playing will occur even well after the library closes. In many libraries this may represent half the total use of the library. To the authors this use seems entirely proper and suitable. It has two major advantages. A studious atmosphere is provided, and staff support, software support, dictionaries, encyclopedias, and other useful reference and general books are close at hand, at least while the library is open.

One of the most serious problems in an academic institution stems from the limited number of hours when its physical facilities are used to their full capacity. This is especially the case when as much as 80 percent of U.S. students in all types of collegiate institutions live off campus and commute to campus. Part-time and evening students, and those age 18 to 22 who live in rented rooms or apartments away from campus or live with their parents, are going to use the library before, between, and after classes, and then depart. Yet the library must care for peak loads, both for the predominately residential and the predominately commuting institution. In both cases, library reading areas available to any student for long hours should tend to reduce space requirements elsewhere in the institution. One

reading area seat for every five or even four students, occupying from 25 to 35 ft^2 (2.323 to 3.252 m^2), goes farther toward providing suitable study facilities than an equal area added to dormitory accommodations, because at a largely residential institution, the space there has to be provided for each individual rather than every fourth or fifth one. (See Section 5.2.6 for extended comments on the proportion of student seating.)

Most students and faculty members find that with a little planning they can complete the work that needs to be done in the library during the fairly long hours of operation. A significant exception is in a library that supports laboratory research, where the research project may be scheduled on a 24-hour basis; this is a special problem of security in scientific and sometimes engineering branch libraries. Another exception are those students in residential institutions who are convinced that they study better in the middle of the night than before a 10 or 11 o'clock library closing hour and are constantly advocating longer library hours. As mentioned earlier, it may be claimed that the dormitory rooms are not suitable for study because of noise and visiting until perhaps 1 o'clock in the morning, and by that time, if there is one roommate who wants to sleep, the situation is no better unless a private study for each student is provided. Five possible solutions of this problem are suggested.

1. Library hours may be extended, at least from Monday through Thursday evenings, until 11 o'clock and perhaps to midnight or even later, particularly before and during examination periods. Where there is a separate undergraduate library, its hours are often longer than those for the main research facility. Many academic libraries are open until midnight, but some students seem to be almost as unhappy as ever. The library is faced with the cost of staff service for longer hours and of the utilities required to light and air condition the building, as well as with security and safety issues.

2. Study halls or residential library space may be provided in the dormitories, perhaps in the dining hall, and can be kept reasonably quiet with the aid of proctors if need be. A special study hall or dorm library represents just that much more space that is used for very short hours—one more factor in the inefficient use of academic space that has been prevalent but is becoming more difficult to defend.

3. Entire floors of living units, or even entire buildings, might be designated as quiet zones,

and students who choose to live in these quarters are expected to maintain a reasonable study environment. A number of institutions have tried this with mixed results, although, with appropriate peer pressure, it may help the situation.

4. Dormitory rooms may be enlarged by providing individual study accommodations for each occupant or by providing a larger percentage of single rooms. However, to do either of these for every student will cost far more than adding space for more library seating for use during regular library hours and will fail to provide the studious library atmosphere or reference books and other printed material that may be wanted. With the popularity of loud music, the intrusion of neighbors is nearly impossible to avoid. On the other hand, some institutions have borrowed funds for dormitory construction and are paying the interest and amortization on the resulting mortgage from the rental rate. The library normally does not have this funding advantage; thus, there is a temptation to build more elaborate residential halls and restrict the number of library seating accommodations, though this is a questionable procedure.

5. A section of the library can be separated from the rest of the building and have its own entrance open after regular closing hours. A number of academic libraries have tried this solution and keep one room open for long hours or even for all 24. At Bennington College, no library books, except perhaps a dictionary, are available, and there is no attendant of any kind. At Stanford the Meyer Library closes at midnight (or 1:00 A.M. before and during exam week), yet one large outside-accessed room is available all night for study use without staff, but with an emergency phone in the room. It is said that this space is fairly well used. It would, of course, be possible and comparatively inexpensive in a large institution to keep a single attendant on duty to give a bare minimum of supervision and make it practical to supply those who use the room with the library books and computers they are most likely to want—that is, reserved books and reference material and the technologies necessary to support access to this material. The attendant may be a student-employee who can read and study most of the time. This modest level of staffing would obviously improve the utility of the room while reducing the likelihood of vandalism.

It is important to remember that if an all-night or late-night room is to be provided, it should have its own entrance, arranged so that it can be cut off from the rest of the building at night when the remainder of the library is closed, but with the outside entrance closed in the daytime so that the room can be used without an extra control point during regular hours of operation. This problem has been well solved in the University of Chicago's Regenstein Library, and at Indiana University, Hofstra University, Earlham College, and Georgetown University. The aesthetics of such rooms usually leave a great deal to be desired, and vandalism can be a problem.

7.8
Special Collections: Rare Books, Manuscripts, and Archives

A reading room for rare books should be arranged to assure extra protection of these unique or particularly valuable materials. The number of readers at any one time tends to be small: one to two dozen in large universities, somewhat more in the larger independent research libraries, and much more in the larger national libraries. The arrangements must be designed to recognize that these segregated materials are of special long-term educational and research importance, probably for centuries to come. The care with which the collections are housed and serviced will encourage future donors of collections, will make an educational impression on professors and students as well as library staff, and will have demonstrably beneficial consequences on the materials themselves over a period of decades. A distinction can be made, if the library wishes, between the rigorous conditions for storing and handling rare, valuable, and often fragile published materials and the especially exacting conditions for unique materials. Most attention here is given to the former; for the latter, reference is made to Mary Lynn Ritzenthaler, *Preserving Archives and Manuscripts* (Chicago: Society of American Archivists, 1993), Chapter 7 of which gives good advice on storing and housing such materials as manuscript documents, maps, and glass plate negatives.

The books should not be on open-access shelves, with the exception of certain reference books; if housed in the reading room, the rarities should be in locked cases or shelved in a closed area behind the service desk. The size of rare book collections varies tremendously from one institution to another. Some institutions have comparatively few rare books and seem to be not particularly interested in them. On the other hand, some comparatively small private institutions have received, as gifts from generous friends and alumni, large, distinguished collections of rare books. Such colleges as Colby, Dartmouth, Mills, Occidental, and Vassar are examples. The size of the institution may therefore have little to do with the size of the collection, though the older institutions tend to have larger collections.

Five problems of importance come up in connection with planning a rare book room.

1. *How many readers and how much space per reader should be provided for?* Perhaps the most important aspect is that the reading area should not be so large that it is difficult to supervise. In the Houghton Library at Harvard, where a considerable proportion of the rare books belonging to the university are housed, there is a reading room approximately 30 × 55 ft (9.144 × 16.764 m), which can seat up to 35 readers. Including the service desk, this works out to about 47 ft^2 (4.366 m^2) per reader. Within the room, microfilm reading machines and relatively "noiseless" typewriters (which today would likely be a personal computer or laptop, or in some instances an electric typewriter with an acoustic hood) are provided for use by readers. Photocopying is arranged with the staff, never self-service. When the room was designed, the planners felt that it was as large as could be supervised from a desk at the center of one of the long sides of the room. The desk is on a raised platform to provide the attendant with a better view of the readers. This room, particularly in the summer, is frequently filled to capacity, but it must be remembered that the Houghton Library has one of the great rare book collections in the world and one that has always emphasized usefulness to scholarly research rather than the acquisition of rarities for their own sake.

The Chicago Regenstein quarters for special collections seat 24 in one reading room plus a small typing and microtext reading room, three private studies, and three small seminar rooms. Indiana University's Lilly Library seats 28, with a small adjoining room for typing and microtext use. Yale's Beinecke seats 60 plus a similar number in special purpose rooms. The University of Illinois can seat 83 and has a microtext reading room as well. The Spencer Library of the University of Kansas has 67 individual studies plus separate reading rooms for rare books, manuscripts, maps, university archives, and regional collections, for a total of 109 seats. Still, only a few libraries will have to provide seating for 30

for use of special collections and rare books unless a practice of class projects for advanced students is instituted.

Reading positions in a rare book reading room must be at open tables arranged for maximum supervision from staff areas. It is common to provide fairly generous individual tables, often with task lighting, computer ports for laptops, and several foam wedges equipped with snakes for holding large and small books. A few larger tables are desirable as some rare books are exceedingly huge, or to accommodate very large prints and architectural drawings. Chicago's Regenstein special collections reading room and Harvard's Houghton Library reading room have laptop outlets that are in great demand, plus network connections that are to be activated. The same laptop popularity exists at the University of California Bancroft Library and the University of Kansas Spencer Library, for note taking and transcription rather than for Internet access. Incidentally, scanning is on the increase, handled by staff as are photocopy requests, so long as there is legal clearance and the physical item will not be damaged.

Although some prefer tables arranged so that staff can see down the center of a table with readers facing each other, the more common arrangement is for all readers to face the staffed service station. Although there may be aesthetic justification, most rare book librarians prefer not to have lounge seating because of the implied casual use of valuable and often fragile materials; however, two or three comfortable chairs may add atmosphere and provide a spot for brief talk with a donor or professor within the room itself, as at the University of Virginia Alderman Library McGregor Room. Space should not be forgotten for specialized equipment as is locally useful, a microfilm reading machine, or a Hinman collator in a few instances. It is suggested that at least 35 and preferably 40 or even 45 ft^2 (3.252, 3.716, or 4.181 m^2) per reader be provided, with good separation between any two readers.

2. *How much shelving is required?* One should admit from the start that few rare book collections can hope to be shelved indefinitely within the reading area assigned to rare books; they will have to be provided for in secure but otherwise regular bookstacks, with appropriate environmental control, preferably as close as possible to the rare book reading area. Of course, provision for housing elephant folios may be required. The shelving area can sometimes be on the same

floor, sometimes directly above or below, preferably with ready secured access for the staff to go between the two by stairs or elevator, or both.

Numerous factors will influence the growth of rare book collections in the future. Increasing efforts at preservation of brittle papers may argue for special housing and handling of many books, even though they may not be literally as precious. However, as the years pass, these and other older out-of-print books will increase in value and eventually be considered rare. It should also be remembered that the practice of giving rare books to academic libraries is something that often is cultivated, and that first-class accommodations for rare books help to attract gifts. Because of these factors, rare book collections will generally tend to grow more rapidly than other parts of an academic library.

The Department of Special Collections in Chicago's Regenstein Library opened with 1,758 standard double-faced sections with some special shelving; it moved into its new quarters with 100,000 volumes and 3 million manuscript pieces, and had initial room for 250,000 volumes. The Houghton has a 225,000-volume capacity; there is that much again both under Lamont and in Pusey next door. The Spencer Library at the University of Kansas began with a 670,000-volume capacity, the Lilly at Indiana with 300,000, and Yale's Beinecke with 800,000. Many other universities have 50,000- to 100,000-volume collections, and quite a number of colleges have several thousand and are growing rapidly.

3. *How should the collection space be arranged?* Some libraries have found that having the rare book area divided into a considerable number of separate rooms has made it easier for them to attract gifts of rare books from donors who want to have their names and their collections perpetuated. However, separate rooms will lead to reduced long-term flexibility and potentially to a more difficult problem of supervision. Another technique is to provide alcoves that can be named. A third possibility is the provision of specially designed and secured cases to house named collections, with a donor designation to perpetuate the donor's name in a dignified way.

Exhibit space is essential to the functioning of these special collections, for reasons of education, publicity, promotion, fund-raising, and donor relations. It should be in a prominent and secure public area, with cases deployed to minimize crowding, at least some portion of the cases with superior environmental control, case interiors easily accessible when mounting an exhibit, and free of any reflection on glass. Some if not all cases should be of sufficient height for quarto volumes and sufficient depth for a good-sized folio. See extended comments in the next chapter, Section 8.7. Visits to special collections quarters and discussion with experts are advised in designing for special collections. In order that the exhibition quarters can be accessible to the public without needing to gain entrance permission, so these quarters can be used for special occasions when the rest of the library may be closed, and so that the exhibits can serve as publicity and entry to the special collections reading room, these special collections quarters are often placed at or off the entrance without going through building entrance or an internal control, although this is not everywhere necessary. The University of California at Berkeley, the University of Chicago, Duke University, and Princeton University have resolved this through entry solutions, as have Harvard, Indiana University, and the Universities of Kansas, North Carolina (Chapel Hill), and Texas (Austin) by use of separate buildings.

Except in fairly small institutions, the planner must be careful to avoid combining exhibit and reading functions. In smaller libraries, the room will have several functions that can usually be combined without too much difficulty. At one time it may be used for class seminars, or for single class sessions when various rare materials are to be used by the instructor. In many cases the room is open to the public as publicity for the college, perhaps staffed by a student attendant. It may be a room to which campus visitors are brought to see examples of manuscripts or printed treasures that students can use, or for donors to see the room and materials with which their donations will be associated. Or the room may be used for small receptions, for the library "friends," for a student book-collecting club, and similar educational and appropriate social occasions. And some students and others will at times come to the room for serious study of rare materials housed there, using the area as a supervised reading room. When planning these quarters, determine whether such multiple use of the room is feasible, or whether some separation of functions is desirable. Where collection display cases are provided in a reading area, they should be supplemented with a separate exhibit area that can be open to the general public.

All these possibilities require special design, and if the material is to be shown as the donor undoubtedly wants it to be, supervision and control may be greatly complicated. Ideal environment for the long-term preservation of the materials is different than one would expect to find in a multi-use room. Experience in some institutions that have faced the problem on a large scale has been that donors, when the problems are properly presented to them, come to realize that if they want to have their collections used and their names remembered favorably, the collections should be shelved as far as possible with similar material on the same subject. Perhaps each item could be identified by a bookplate and also listed in a printed catalog of the collection.

Nothing is so sure as the ultimate stagnation and death of a collection that must be kept in a room by itself, without an attendant to make it readily available and without funds for enlarging it and keeping it up to date. Even when a collection is donated with a supporting endowment, in an inflationary age an endowment fund tends to decrease in purchasing power over time. Such support should not in most cases be sufficient to justify a separate collection.

Even so, quite a number of universities have special rooms that they do not consider white elephants. They may be tourist attractions, encouragement to friends or donors, or locations for seminars or receptions, and their educational, historic, or at least inspirational value should not be ignored. Examples can be found at Harvard, Indiana, Stanford's Hoover Institution, Texas (Austin), and elsewhere.

Metcalf has written of the summer of 1908 when he had charge of moving the Oberlin College Library into a new building and was finally bold enough to ask the librarian why he placed in his new office an unimpressive old mahogany bookcase filled with a miscellaneous collection of books. He replied, "In my early years here I accepted this collection as a gift with the condition that it would always be kept together in this bookcase. The library was poor in those days and welcomed almost anything that came to it as a gift. I have been glad to have it ever since, not because of the case or its contents, but because it reminds me day by day that gifts of this kind with strings attached are undesirable and should never be accepted. With it here before me there is no danger of my making a similar mistake again."

4. *What about the importance of providing the optimum atmospheric conditions for the preservation of the material?* Books deteriorate, even if they are not heavily used, particularly if they are printed on poor paper, as many of them are. One way to prolong the life and usefulness of any volume—and this is of special importance for rare books and other materials difficult or impossible to replace—is to provide an even temperature of 70° F. (21° C.) or less, and a relative humidity of roughly 35 percent, together with excellent air filtration and circulation, control of light, fire and flood control, and control of pests. These points are discussed in greater detail in Sections 5.3.8 and, to some degree, 13.2.1. See also appendix D.

In such quarters, it is ridiculous to include a fireplace, even though having such a feature may provide atmosphere. The inclusion is in such conflict with sound environmental conditions for rarities that it gives a most conflicting message. Even so, a number have recently been included in such quarters, an example being the Boston College Law School Library's Coquillette Rare Books Room, where a rose marble mantelpiece, once in the White House, had been given to the college during the Truman administration.

5. *What degree of security is appropriate for the collections and their quarters?* Local circumstances will play a large role in determining the nature of the security necessary. The program should spell out the requirements. Questions that should be answered include: Is there need for a vault or strong room? Should there be intrusion alarms, and, if so, where and of what type? Should there be door contacts and other forms of perimeter protection of various areas? Should there be other kinds of alarms, such as high- or low-humidity alarms, smoke detectors, water alarms, panic buttons for the staff, or special alarms in display cases? How should the various alarms be controlled—by electronic systems, video, clocks, keys, touch pads—or should they always be active? Should there be special keying? special doors to lock off areas? special glass? Many of these issues are discussed in Section 5.3.6. Do not forget to think through how the alarms will be responded to and where their signal should be seen or heard.

Manuscripts, archives, and original typescripts present very much the same problem as rare books. Not much provision needs to be made for seating accommodations, although in large departments of special collections it may be desirable to service manuscripts, archives, and photographs in a different room from the rare books. This may be justified when the special collections are frequently used by more than about 20 persons, because these unique materials may then be more rigorously supervised in a separate room. Staff procedures and rules of use can differ among manuscripts, archives, and photographs. However, adequate supervision and control of these collections can usually be provided in the rare book room. Each library must judge this for itself, yet, given the recurrent news stories of theft of rare materials, it may be prudent to plan new quarters supportive of rigorous security conditions. Suitable atmospheric conditions are also important, and ideally would be more stringent than for the other rarities.

If archival records represent primarily the academic and administrative history of the institution to which the library belongs, one of the great problems is collecting them and preventing their loss through neglect in the departments where they originated. At the time of change in an institution's administration or when professors transfer to another institution, go off to Washington, to war, or elsewhere, departmental and other records tend to disappear. The administrative officers of an institution hesitate to allow what they consider confidential records to be removed from their supervision and want to hold them in their own quarters. One hazard after another may come up. A program for discarding as well as collecting is essential. Every institution should make provision somewhere for its archival material and for the proper supervision of its use. Perhaps the most intensive use of archival and manuscript material for colleges and universities is for doctoral dissertations and sometimes for master's theses. As with manuscripts, special problems of literary property rights are involved, and control and supervision must be provided and copying authorized.

Accommodations for readers of rare books, manuscripts, and archives are often and quite reasonably combined in one room, as indicated above, in order to reduce overhead expenses; the same area per reader is appropriate for each group. Many if not all of the reading positions should be equipped with power and signal ports for use with laptops or other computers. Although task lighting is often necessary and desirable when handwriting in manuscripts is faint and textual defects of print difficult to decipher, the planner must be careful that local light fixtures do not get

in the way when the reader turns pages, risking damage to leaves. This suggests that any necessary task lighting be on a flexible arm that can be moved out of the way, or that only a quarter of the reading positions have task lighting so scholars with need for extra light must seek them out. The program statement may need to address some such practical arrangements for the special collections.

Finally, note that archival records come in various formats. One extreme case may be instructive. The U.S. National Archives in College Park (known informally as Archives II) divides its research center into eight separate rooms: textual, motion picture and sound and video, library, cartographic and architectural, still picture, electronic records, microfilm, and classified records. Each has its special needs for housing and providing service for materials in a distinctive format. In total, these eight rooms use 60,247 ft² (5,597 m²) for an average gross space per researcher of 154 ft² (14.3 m²), a figure that includes the necessary area for all public service staff, all equipment needed for public use of the materials, registration, display, and circulation space. Although each archive in a college, a university, or an independent research library will have varying amounts of such formats, it is instructive that the above list of eight is in descending order of the amount of space allocated in Archives II.

7.9
Public Documents

Many universities provide special accommodations for the storage and use of public documents because they are unable to catalog them or do not want the expense of cataloging them. At the same time, because specific documents can be difficult to find or find out about, especially U.S. governmental papers and reports and statistics, a trained staff to service them is often required and a special reading area for documents may be desirable. For a U.S. depository library, the documents collection must be accessible to the general public. In this case access to the collections should ideally be kept separate from the general building controls to maintain control over the more restrictively accessed collections.

If a library attempts to collect public documents on a large scale, their bulk increases rapidly, and a good deal of shelving may need to be assigned for them. The growth rate for documents can vary dramatically with a change in the political world. The reading space required, on the other hand, is ordinarily not extensive, particularly if documents used for assigned or collateral reading are placed on reserve during the period when they are in demand.

Special provision of some kind must be made for documents in most cases, however, unless they are cataloged in full. This is true even with U.S. documents that can be arranged by the Superintendent of Documents number. The more limited number of documents from other countries or from state and municipal governments is often more difficult to know about and locate without help from trained library staff. United Nations documents present problems of their own, whether in their original form or in microreproduction. It should be noted that public documents are being distributed in microformat in even greater proportions, which indicates the need for microtext readers.

U.S. government document publication online is growing rapidly, although bills and other legal instruments may not be so issued because of continuing concern with authentication. Many newly issued federal government documents are currently becoming available online, with a trend clearly established. Although perhaps slowly and erratically, states and foreign countries will probably follow this lead because of advantages in cost and accessibility. The time may come when there is no need for a separate government documents collection with dedicated staff, and the expert document librarian will be found at a general reference desk. However, it would be foolish to surmise that this trend will soon achieve a complete conversion to digital media. Many governmental agencies and countries will be very slow to change. Further, for most universities the continuing space and management problems are created by historic collections that are not online and many of which have not been cataloged. For many research institutions, these older documents are significant in number and very important. Still, we can imagine continuing and growing pressures to consolidate government document departments into a general reference and information unit, even if the outcome is not ideal. Even now, in smaller institutions, documents are serviced by the reference staff. Each institution must determine the best service and staffing arrangements.

If the use of public documents is largely limited to a special reading area, its relationship to the storage area for the material may be very important. If the collection is large, it will probably be in the main bookstack; if the use is restricted or more accessible than the general collections, it should be in a portion of the stack that can be cut off from the rest of the shelving area. This is particularly important where the documents department has a separate entrance and control point, as the documents staff will not want to be responsible for checking out general collections. Document collections often include unbound material, and housekeeping will be difficult. Because trained librarians are often required to assist patrons in finding an item, the reading, reference, and staff areas must be close to the stacks. Ideally, a significant portion of the collection should be housed on the same floor.

Seating for a documents area is much like seating in the general reference area, because use of these collections is fairly short term. A mixture of seating similar to that of the reference area—at carrels, probably without shelves, and open tables with sufficient surface to unfold a large map—is probably appropriate. The floor area required for each document reader is similar to that required for general reading, or about 30 ft^2 (2.787 m^2), except that provisions for microtext reading should be somewhat larger, with a minimum of 40 ft^2 (3.716 m^2) per reader provided. The number to be provided for depends almost altogether on the service patterns adopted. With the recent shift of the U.S. Government Printing Office to microformat and now to digitized online distribution, the need for a microtext storage and reading area and for an adequate number of terminals and laptop ports associated with the document collections is common. The user requirements for microtexts are discussed below, computer facilities above.

7.10
Maps

The use of a map collection in an academic or a research library is ordinarily not large, although it may be important. Because map storage requires special equipment and maps are often very cumbersome and awkward to use, a separate map area is frequently provided, though sometimes it is in one part of the reference area. In an undergraduate or a small college library, a map and atlas case, together with a few nearby tables, may suffice; separate rooms and large collections of sheet maps may well be an unnecessary luxury. Atlas cases may be locally designed and constructed or purchased from a library-equipment firm. In addition to material that can be so housed, many institutions possess collections of the United States Geological Survey topographical maps and those from other countries. Others have large collections of historical maps in either flat sheets or rolls, the latter being used from time to time in classrooms. A considerable number of American institutions acquired the Army War Maps after the Second World War, and these alone take a great deal of expensive equipment and space for housing.

A careful estimate should be made of the prospective growth of the map collection (see Section 6.6.8) and the amount of use expected. Because the transportation of sheet maps is difficult, facilities for use should be as near as possible to their storage location. In selecting a suitable location for a map room or area, remember that service by staff members will be needed. Map filing cases can be very heavy and present a serious floor load problem. It is a mistake to overcrowd in space assignments, as shifts to provide more space at a later time will be difficult and expensive to arrange. Space per reader is suggested of 35 ft^2 and, preferably, up to 50 ft^2 (3.252 m^2 to 4.645 m^2), including perhaps a light table, which will probably require at least the 50 ft^2. Unless there will be class projects, the number of readers provided for need not be large, and the total space for them should be generally less than that for map storage.

Large tables may have a slot just inside the front edge or a special sheet rolling device, as may be found on an old-fashioned architect's drafting table, so a person can bring the far portion of a sheet closer without leaning on and creasing it. The conditions for housing maps and similar large sheet materials were discussed in the preceding chapter, though it is here emphasized that very scarce or unique sheet materials that have archival importance will need somewhat different housing both physically and environmentally, as discussed in the Ritzenthaler book referred to in Section 7.8 in this chapter (see also appendix F.3.c).

Because of the size of these materials, the local intensity of use, and the challenge of fitting map cases into module dimensions often selected for economical housing of regular book collections, designing good map facilities can be a challenge. Visits to libraries with very good arrangements for maps can be informative and helpful. Good examples are the University of Michigan where the top-floor map collection room has fine arrangements, the University of California campuses at Davis and Santa Barbara, and the major facility in the Library of Congress Madison Building.

7.11
Microtexts

Practically all college and university libraries have accumulated microreproductions on a fairly large scale, and these collections of microfilm and microfiche are continuing to grow. Each of these requires special equipment for housing as well as for use. Although digital technologies will no doubt eventually supplement the microtext collections, it is still reasonable to assume that these collections will continue to grow in use and bulk for years to come, given their economy and archival standards.

The amount of use and the size of the collection of microreproductions do not depend primarily on the size of the library's other collections. Indeed, even though a large library may have a considerable number of microtexts, their use in such a library is often far less proportionately than in smaller libraries. Microtexts will be much more heavily used if individual titles are cataloged, if the library is weak in older or primary research materials, and if there is an easily found, well-designed area equipped with very good machines. Because these microtext collections do not attract crowds like other discrete collections, the reading quarters are typically placed below or above the main floor. However, it may be prudent to plan sufficient flexibility into the housing and reader facilities so that future adjustments in use and space assignments can readily be made as other technologies are implemented.

Too many microtext reading quarters in colleges and universities are quite unsatisfactory. One must recognize that this is not just another reading room; the materials being used and the characteristics of the reading equipment create a unique study condition. It is desirable but not essential to provide a darkened room, except perhaps occasionally when readers must use poor copies of difficult manuscripts. A darkened room will enhance the ability to see the projected image, but almost any convenient space without an excess of light is satisfactory. It should be obvious that, as with video display terminals, a reading machine should not be placed so that the sun or a bright light of any kind will shine on the reading surface. Positions of reading machines with vertical or nearly vertical screens must be arranged to avoid reflecting more distant bright light sources; for example, the screen should not face an exterior window. Adjustable task lighting for note taking is required.

Although some libraries have distributed their microtext collections and reading machines throughout the book collections in their appropriate subject classification, most librarians would argue that it is essential to centralize the machines in one location in the main library building and in research branches where an attendant is available to assist the patron, replace light bulbs, and ensure that proper maintenance procedures are undertaken. Most large libraries will have a mixture of reading machines, each with its advantages and idiosyncrasies, often requiring staff assistance. Generally the staff find it advantageous to group machines that serve the same type of microtext, especially because one or more machines will frequently be out of order. But all can very satisfactorily be in the same room. Some machines will be reader-printers, usually with a debit card attachment for payment for the copies made. Also, grouping the machines enables users to find the unused machine without touring the facility. And it may be argued that the small size of the reproductions makes them easy to misplace or lose, and that some supervision is desirable. All this suggests that the microtext reading area should be near a desk where a staff member is regularly on duty.

Lighting has been mentioned. Consider that nearly all the machines are large, heavy, and not easily moved. An additional consideration is the need to provide for both right- and left-handed readers, who will use surfaces on opposite sides of the machine for taking notes or comparing a microtext with that of a book. Because the bulk and weight of a reading machine generally limit its position, reading comfort must be supplied by the chair, which should permit the reader to shift position. For microfilm machines, the relationship of the chair and table must let the user sit high enough to use the transport knobs or levers

with comfort. This last point is important because users will frequently search for a lengthy time through a newspaper or other file seeking an elusive story or article, and regular chairs are quite wrong for reading film in a machine on a typical desk or carrel or counter. Although Stanford's Green Library microtext reading room is close to ideal, the seats are most unsatisfactory.

Booth or carrel arrangements with surfaces at least 30 in. (0.762 m) deep and up to 5 ft (1.524 m) wide will provide good flexibility. Note especially that reading equipment can be quite deep; even 30 in. (0.762 m) may not be enough for some equipment. Narrower carrels can effectively be used with pullout boards or L-shaped extensions. As mentioned, be sure to provide for the left-handed reader, with both note-taking space and a low-intensity, rheostat-adjustable lamp on the left as well as the right. If accommodation cannot be provided for both types of readers, then one in ten should be set up for the left-handed. A minimum of 40 ft^2 (3.716 m^2) per reader is suggested. Enough noise will be created by rewinding film and machine cranking that sound control is not a high issue, yet it is well to separate this function from spaces where quiet conditions are needed for effective study. Storage for microtexts is discussed in Section 6.6.4, and future growth must be estimated.

7.12
Audiovisual, Learning Resources, and Music

Many libraries provide special accommodations for varying media, at least in their music collections. There are a variety of reasons for this. Music material, particularly music scores and sheet music, tends to be outsized and requires special equipment. Compact discs (CDs) and other digital resources, phonograph discs, and tapes used in connection with music courses can be an important part of the program of the music department, and their special storage and use should be provided for somewhere in the institution. For other departments, motion picture film, videocassettes, laser discs, and other digital sources may be exceedingly important, or a program in oral history or recorded lectures will result in accumulations of tape cassettes and playback equipment. Some libraries will collect substantial numbers of slides, filmstrips, educational kits and games, and realia.

A major media service will also need to house and service VCR cameras, motion picture and slide and film projectors, camcorders, overhead projectors, opaque projectors, tape recorders, disc and tape players, and so on in seemingly never-ending variety.

We treat here the common needs of audiovisual sections, but not the greater variety of a broad media center, which often, but not always, is separate from the academic library. This field is changing almost as fast as other information

technologies, so it is wise to visit several recent installations to find good solutions. Currently California State University, Bakersfield (fig. 7.26) and the University of North Carolina at Charlotte have exceptional extensive media facilities, and the libraries of state universities, such as Washington State, often are ahead of the crowd. The details of layouts and technical data are beyond the scope of this book; only general principles and cautions will be covered.

One example of automated audiovisual service is that of the Kanazawa Institute of Technology in Japan. This exceptional library building has a

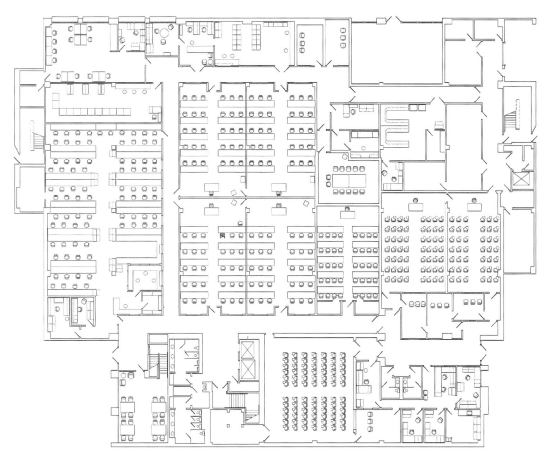

FIGURE 7.26 California State University, Bakersfield, Stiern Library, lowest of five levels. Note the variety of classroom seating arrangements. The right-hand third of this floor serves Instructional Television, with two classrooms, each with small adjoining observation rooms. The large classroom in the lower center serves, with movable seating, for group viewing of computer use and for presenting live television performances.

The rest of this floor houses a variety of information technology services. In the center are five classrooms, the smaller one (seating 40) for bibliographic instruction. Moving clockwise from the main stairs at the bottom of the plan, there also are an after-hours study room (lower left corner), a large 82-position microcomputer cluster lab with support offices, a long, narrow room for campuswide video distribution, a room with 12 multimedia workstations (upper left corner), a multimedia service center (four rooms along top of plan), and an interior meeting room seating 12 in conference style. (Courtesy of California State University, Bakersfield)

media collection of over 10,000 videocassette and audiocassette tapes, open-reel films, phonograph records, and slides. A user can select the desired materials with only a few keystrokes on a terminal keyboard. Then, "intelligent" robots process the input and automatically retrieve, load, and play the selection as a feed to one of the small-group listening/viewing rooms or an individual, semienclosed chair booth equipped with stereophonic audio output. A single technician services all the equipment, an arrangement that can be very economical of staff in a heavily used audiovisual department.

At UCLA's Powell Library, the media area has been arranged with a raised floor that has been added to the existing building. Behind a staff counter, the collection and playback equipment are conveniently arranged. The patron asks for a particular item and is assigned a carrel within a room of about 50 carrels, each equipped with a video monitor, earphones, and controls that permit stopping, backing up, and replaying segments of the video. Along the side of the room are small open-air viewing rooms suitable for two to four students. The viewing rooms are well isolated acoustically, even though there are large glass panels between the listening rooms and the main room.

A similar arrangement can accommodate a language lab, though video is less widely used for language training. A raised floor is a significant advantage for this function as well, and the lab may be arranged to accommodate class instruction with a teaching station. Some major electronics manufacturers (for example, Sony) have complete systems available for language labs and media centers; where such a system is contemplated, the specific requirements of that system must be met.

Most institutions have collections of videotapes, slides, and other related sources that may not be produced in-house, but that require organization and storage. Recorded poetry, dramatic readings, and recordings for modern-language instruction are common uses of this type of medium. These collections may run to over 100,000 items in exceptional cases. There may be very close ties with one academic department, perhaps with a member of the faculty serving as the collection curator or advisor to use, develop, promote, monitor, secure, and advertise this special collection. Each institution will have its own reliance on such audiovisual materials; thus, this section of the building programming is locally distinctive.

It is often thought that a collection of audiovisual materials can be housed and serviced better in a library than elsewhere. Material of this kind is costly, fragile, easily mishandled or lost, generally not well cataloged, and not easily browsable. Furthermore, a certain amount of service staff and supervision is desirable, and this may require another service point unless service points can be combined. Advantages of combining audiovisual media within the traditional library are the reliance on specialized technical staff, the common security procedures for these materials, the similarity of budgeting for most of these materials, the occasional copyright issues for unique and locally recorded materials, and the degree to which users of media will need simultaneously or sequentially to use correlative material elsewhere in the library. For example, there is use of French texts with French films, art volumes when working with art slides, musical scores when listening to music on CDs or discs, and so on. Language instruction may rely on several media, though accommodations for a language laboratory often are separate from those provided for general audiovisual material.

If the library is to have audiovisual production facilities, which a few library buildings have (for example, the Bakersfield and Charlotte libraries mentioned earlier), then a significant added programmatic need is established. Questions (many outlined in the *Higher Education Facilities Planning and Management Manuals*) that should be answered include the following:

1. Is a central audiovisual production and service facility desired as part of the library? or at least the library building? Is the service of a size and nature that it can be combined with another function?
2. Are instructional facilities (lecture halls, classrooms, language laboratories, filmmaking, television and radio studios, teleconferencing, and the like) to be included in the central facility?
3. What is the market area for audiovisual services? Campus? Multicampus? Local or regional industry? Statewide? National?
4. To what extent will the audiovisual service engage in the production of instructional materials and of radio and television programs?
5. Based on the answers to the preceding questions, how many and what kinds of professional and technical staff are required to operate the services and production operations? What are the clerical staff support

requirements? What amounts of film, tape, slides, and other materials need to be stored, maintained, and retrieved? What type and amounts of storage are required for equipment, such as television monitors, recorders, and projectors? Will equipment be repaired and maintained in-house? Will graphic arts services be supplied? Will the facilities be used for training in communication arts and education? Will faculty offices be required?[4]

Clearly, the concept of a centralized audiovisual facility in the library can mushroom into a substantial program element, some of which goes beyond functions normally associated with a library. Growth and development of programmed learning techniques, including computer-aided instruction, will continue to have a significant influence on the nature of college and university facilities.

Major media or learning resources centers exist in many libraries of community or junior colleges and sometimes in colleges or state universities. These quarters may occupy as much as a third of a community college facility. One good plan is shown in fig. 7.27. The variation among institutions in terms of the types and amounts of audiovisual facilities and the organization of these

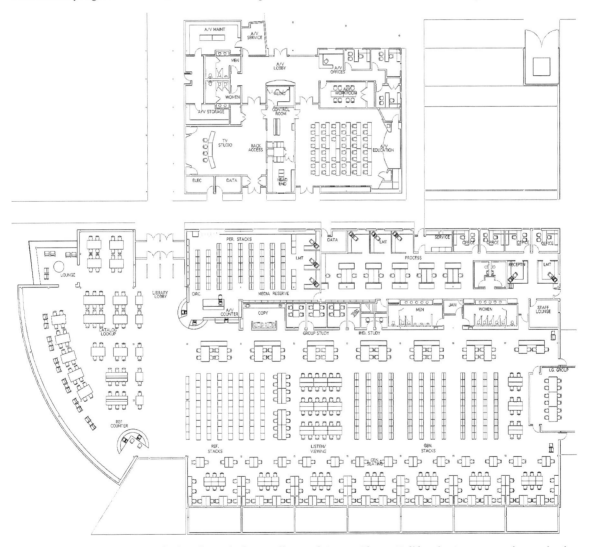

FIGURE 7.27   Schematic design for Mission College of Santa Clara, California (a community or junior college). This layout is based on the production arm of the media center with a studio across an exterior arcade on the upper side of the sketch. The library, with a module of 25 ft 6 in. (7.772 m) from left to right through the stack area, and varying modules going from top to bottom, shows seating for 140 at carrels, 194 at tables (one of which is round), 12 at index tables, 20 at lounge chairs, 12 in group study rooms, 12 in a seminar room, and 3 in studies for a total of 393 seats. (Courtesy of MBT Architecture)

facilities covers an enormous range, the upper limits of which go far beyond the scope of this book.

The number of readers to provide for will be a difficult decision where there is no history of audiovisual service. It is suggested that the number of seats provided for the general reference collection may be an appropriate minimum quantity for the audiovisual area, although this suggestion should be taken with care as individual institutions will have significantly different emphasis on the use of this type of material. Where class sessions are scheduled into the media service facility, one or more of maximum class size will naturally be required. In most cases there should be provision for some modest degree of maintenance for the equipment, including a separate room to store minor components, test and repair equipment, and house machines needing work. Provisions for the secure storage of portable projectors, screens, television monitors, and the like is also usually necessary and can occupy a large room with tall, deep shelving and other furnishings.

Reader stations for audiovisual quarters may take the form of tables or carrels especially designed to accept terminals, rear-screen projectors, tape decks, record players, and the like. A centralized facility for playback of audiovisual materials has been used in a number of institutions, and such a facility continues to have merit for certain types of material, including recorded lectures, or a traditional language laboratory–type function. In this case, reader accommodations need not exceed those provided for a normal carrel, or 25 ft^2 (2.323 m^2) per position. The teaching power of interactive video and computer-based language equipment is replacing traditional distributed audio in many language programs. The most common current technology for interactive video involves stand-alone computers tied to a video source; these require about 35 to 40 ft^2 (3.252 to 3.716 m^2) per position, or more depending upon the arrangement. A proprietary computer-based system is available that is set up much like a classroom, ideally with a raised floor for wire management, and with the seats all facing the front of the room; in this case, the space per seat will be more like 25 ft^2 (2.323 m^2) per position plus the space required for an instructor and support equipment. As video image and audio sound streams become feasible through data signal lines, computer clusters may reduce this space need, provided acoustic separation from more traditional library use is possible.

With noncomputer technology, music, poetry, and perhaps even language exercises are used by students who need to play the material at their own pace, often backing up and repeating a passage. Although this can be done in a centralized playback facility, it may be less staff intensive, less expensive, and more dependable to provide individual playback devices over which the student has direct control. (Self-service equipment should not be used for archival materials that need special care in handling.) In addition to playback equipment where independent playback is provided, there should be sufficient space to refer to a related text or music score and to take notes. From 35 to 40 ft^2 (3.252 to 3.716 m^2) should be provided per position, ideally in an area that has some supervision and where sound isolation is not a problem. Small groups can be accommodated in separate rooms or by the use of a centralized playback facility that can transmit the signal to multiple listening or viewing positions. Many academic library group-study rooms are equipped with video, audio, and television equipment (for example, the library of the University of Hong Kong, Kanazawa Institute of Technology, and many in the United States).

As one example, Stanford's Meyer Library (1966) was designed to have an audio room with 50 positions, each of which could access central programs or sources independently controlled. In addition, 262 seats, or 17 percent of the library proper, could receive programs from several of 34 audio room central sources. There also were two soundproof listening rooms for nine persons, not requiring earphone use, and four language laboratories; and the music library was two buildings away. Twenty years later, the media and computer collections and services had greatly expanded and taken over the entire second floor, with a single service desk behind which were reserved materials. In the most recent change, the media collections have moved back to the entry level, accommodated in expanded space along with the closed reserves behind a new circulation desk. The desk on the second floor has become largely supportive of computer- and equipment-related service. A cluster of interactive video stations has been installed along with more traditional video, audio, and computer stations, and three different computer-based classrooms have been developed, each with raised floor, but each quite unique. (See fig. 7.28.) Each institution will decide the best pattern for its academic programs and trends.

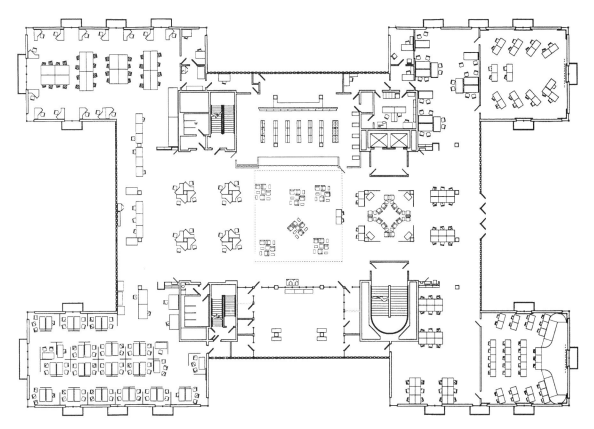

FIGURE 7.28 Stanford University, J. Henry Meyer Memorial Library concept sketch for changes on the second floor. The two proposed classrooms to the right were built largely as illustrated except that the floors in these classrooms as well as a third classroom in the lower left corner (not shown) are raised about 3½ in. (88.9 mm) to accommodate wire management. This approach results in a short ramp just outside the room. Note that in the classroom to the upper right, faculty felt strongly about having the capacity to wander freely about the room. In the classroom that is not illustrated, beanbag seating and laptops are now used together with a high-quality rear-projection system and a secured equipment storage area to further extend the flexibility of the room. (Courtesy of Stanford University Libraries)

As all audiovisual and computer equipment is attractive to those with light fingers, security of the area and equipment must be carefully established. It should not be forgotten that this equipment all produces heat, and that the materials being used are all dramatically damaged if exposed to extreme temperatures. This will be one area where special attention to the current and future mechanical and electrical systems will be required. For example, underfloor electrical ducts or grids may be needed. Headphones, portable playback devices, cassettes, CDs, tapes, or records can be charged out in a fashion similar to that established for closed-reserve books, with shelving for these items provided behind a service desk. Shelving for these materials is discussed in Section 6.6.

The program statement for a music library may contain several unique elements not found in other libraries beyond those already discussed. For example, some music faculty will be absolutely opposed to any form of what Metcalf called acoustic perfume, or white sound. If open-air listening is required, acoustic isolation is a must. Earphone listening, though it is not ideal for the scholar, does save space and expense, and listening stations can be easily distributed through the library. Some acoustic leakage occurs with headphones; thus, reading areas should be somewhat separated from listening areas. Open-air listening might be limited to a seminar room where a piano or an electronic keyboard may be desirable. With earphones, electronic keyboards have been found satisfactory within general reading quarters, such as at University of Glasgow Library. Chalk or marker boards in the music library may be scribed or permanently marked with staff lines to facilitate the writing of music.

The music library will sometimes have its own technical processing staff, at least for cataloging of materials including sound records, even where the library system has centralized processing. Compared to those in other libraries, the secured stacks, reserves, or noncirculating collections are often larger than is normally the case in proportion to the open collections (the exception being a rare book library where none of the collections circulate). Because of this, use of the collection is more staff intensive than that of many other collections. Digitized materials, including the great growth in computer music, are further diversifying the media and equipment needed for an academic music library, especially one with doctoral programs. Information technology has touched here as much as it has medical research libraries with the growth of medical informatics.

7.13
Distance Education

Instruction conducted from campus to distant locations has a long history, yet it has been strongly aided by television and, more recently, by computer technologies and by pressures upon state-financed institutions of higher education. The large areas and relatively sparse population in a state like Alaska make this a compelling educational style. The state of Wyoming finds that 23.4 percent of the total university enrollment is at off-campus locations.

Although the library is a crucial element in these programs, the physical infrastructure is a combination of three essential players, each having a high degree of modern technology. One player is the teacher in the campus classroom, another is the campus library, and the third is one or more remote locations, for example, community colleges, adult learning and continuing education centers, businesses, public libraries, local schools, distributed extension offices, and even the homes of students. Brief comments will be given on each of these three.[5]

The campus classroom may be in the library, though it usually is in a media or learning resources center and is used by various departments of the university offering distance education programs. The classroom may or may not include workstations for campus students, though it will

usually be more satisfactory to conduct the class solely for distant students. Videoconferencing technology enables students and teacher to see each other under the instructor's control. (Television cameras can focus on the instructor, on the teacher's computer screen, or on other illustrative or demonstration material, and, when a student presses a button to comment or ask a question, the student's image will be displayed on all monitors.) Audiographics enables the teacher to transmit visual images of printed or graphic materials with audio to accompany. A computer workstation enables the teacher to monitor computer-managed learning, conduct tests online, transmit electronic messages and databases, modify the curriculum, and so on.

The library will support e-reserves, utilize computer and scanner and printer to receive and send sources requested by the student, and maintain telecommunications and databases so that students can search OPACs, full-text publications on the Internet, and so forth. Interactive desktop televideo can personalize some of these requests and responses. Support of satellite campus centers via overnight delivery of library materials is sometimes accommodated by the library, as is the case for the Vancouver campus of Washington State University (which is housed in a Vancouver community college campus). Thus the university library retains the role of providing access to information; the library facility implication is the accommodation of a variety of information technologies within the library building. Rather than being distributed at several service areas, the interactive technology is usually at the quarters of library staff devoted to "extended library services" for off-campus students supported by the general collections, interlibrary loan operations, rooftop antennae, broadcasting ability, scanning capacity, and possibly videoconferencing facilities.

The remote locations should ideally be provided with the same or compatible equipment for sending and receiving audio, video, and digital signals. Obviously, education can be received with partial systems, as was the case with the old correspondence course. Yet inferior technologies put the distant student at a handicap. If the remote location is designed for many students to attend at once and if there is a local tutor (a teaching assistant, such as a local public librarian, or a corporate representative in a business setting), the sight lines from each student position to the front of the room will be important, as in any electronic classroom. In these cases, it may be useful to slightly sink the monitor into the desk or work counter, one example of this being in the "teaching theater" used by Library and Information Services and many other departments at the University of Maryland, College Park.

Video teleconferencing facilities vary greatly depending on the scale and nature of the instructional/management requirements to be supported. Though it is hazardous to suggest particulars of such facilities, which vary greatly in size and complexity, a few points can indicate some of the points needing attention. (And planning of such facilities should be by a qualified consultant unless the institution has an expert in-house.) At the low-cost end, a multimedia computer with PC video, microphone, and camera feed at each end enables the teacher and the distant student to see and work together via a desktop Internet connection using a standard analog line. Moving to ISDN lines at 128 kilobits per second improves quality and speed for a price.

For small and medium-sized groups, a quality setup would have suitable table(s) and seats and at least one teacher's lectern, one or more roll-about monitors, people camera(s), document camera, sufficient microphones, phone line, multiple ISDN lines and/or microwave link, data and graphics port, Codec equipment (to support signal compression/decompression at 128K or 384K transmission speeds, or 15 or 30 frames per second), and superior lighting and HVAC and acoustic design. In general that would equip a room such as that illustrated in fig. 7.29. Where students are to use PCs or laptops, network connectivity and power at each work position are required. Viewing of motion pictures adds another equipment dimension. Because these are expensive facilities, scheduling can be demanding. Therefore, spare equipment is necessary as backup to minimize downtime. For use with scientific and technical classes requiring demonstrations using various equipment, a revolving instructional stage enables

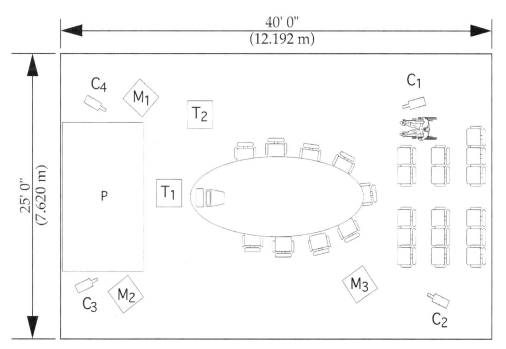

FIGURE 7.29   Sample of small video teleconferencing studio and teaching room at the teacher's location. The teacher is at T1 in front of a computer workstation on the table around which students sit (with any student overflow beyond the table). Ceiling-mounted cameras C1 and C2 view the teacher, and the two overhead monitors (M1 and M2) give these students views of material on the teacher's PC screen. Cameras C3 and C4 pick up input by the students around the table.

Alternatively, the teacher is at lectern T2 when the stage or platform (P) is used for other types of class presentations, such as small musical or dramatic groups, certain lab demonstrations, or the instructor's use of wall maps or other large-format sheets or realia.

Remote location(s) can have similar audio-video receiving and transmitting capacities, or merely be passive receiving sites (with or without a local tutor), in which case the M3 monitor enabling the teacher to see the distant persons is superfluous.

one class presentation to proceed while equipment for the next experiment is being set up behind the scene, as Stanford University arranged in its 1998 Regional Teaching Facility in the Science and Engineering Quad.

Distance education can save some university costs for faculty and facilities. Its use has grown in recent decades. And a growing number of libraries of state universities have been deeply involved, yet the service models are not fully developed and certainly the utility of information technologies will continue to develop. The simple matter of communications connectivity in Alaska between the university and the remote village remains a limiting factor that may be vastly improved in the future with satellite technology. The growth of digitized resources will certainly be an advantage to this method of teaching as will the development of fully digitized course packs and other supportive information. The prospect that video technology will merge with digital technologies is also potentially important. Any library planning effective support for distance learning must seek current publications on standards, programmatic design, service evaluations, and technological support, and also should visit and consult with those whose broad experience can help others.

7.14
Fine Arts, Pictures, and Prints

A considerable portion of collections for fine arts and related fields consists of large volumes with pictures and prints, outsized in shape and difficult to deal with. Along with mounted photographs and slides, each of these requires special equipment for service and for storage. In this fairly distinct and well-defined discipline, faculty tend to want a departmental library, as they do in music. Many of the advantages of such an arrangement can be made available in a special room in the main library, and this practice is sometimes adopted, more frequently in a college than in a large university library. The decision, as with audiovisual materials, may depend on the size of the institution, the number of majors and graduate students in the department and the vigor of the department, the size of the collection, and the geography of the campus.

Reader positions will usually consist of little more than oversized carrels and open tables, although computers and laptop ports are essential

and occasionally a slide projector may be required. Photocopy service will be expected. Seating accommodations for each reader should amount to at least 35 ft^2 (3.252 m^2); special tables have been designed to facilitate the use of large folios. Some designers may insist that the colors and quality of light in this area are more important than in most in order to be able to properly view the art collection, even as table surfaces are background to the viewing of color-illustrated books. In the art library at Stanford University, for example, the only colors allowed are white, black, or gray to avoid influencing the color perception of the human eye. Of all branch libraries, the art library is the most likely to have very rare and expensive volumes, and, therefore, it will need caged or otherwise locked or secure shelving for part of the collection. The proportion of quarto and folio shelving will need to be great.

7.15
Subject-Divisional Libraries within the Main Library

In many institutions, particularly in large universities, a constant and perhaps inevitable struggle takes place between advocates of a centralized library and those who demand a number of departmental collections. Some universities have sought to compromise by establishing service centers for broad divisional collections in the central library instead of a larger number of departmental libraries. The most common plan is to have service centers for Humanities and Social Sciences, and often also for the Sciences. An entire floor of the building may be devoted to one subject division, with a staff reference and lending service for that division. This has worked out fairly well in some of the large and middle-sized institutions. It provides staff assistance and supervision readily at hand, a convenience to the students. This plan and the need for a decision in connection with it are discussed in Section 3.2.9; the question should be resolved before getting into the building planning process. If the subject-division library plan is adopted, it may completely change seating arrangements throughout the library and affect provisions for catalogs, reference books, periodicals, photocopying services, shelving, graphics, and perhaps faculty studies and staff areas.

A strong selling point for this plan is the availability of subject experts on the library staff who form the collections, answer reference and informational questions, and have offices there in which meetings and conferences with students and faculty are convenient. It reinforces the culture of the disciplines therein served and facilitates interactions among people with similar research or educational goals. In physical terms, this entails provision of nearly all the public service functions in each of the subject-division areas, or floors. When a complete OPAC exists, there are not more terminals but rather a distribution of most of the central computer cluster that would otherwise exist without the subject divisions. All the special equipment and services that would be found in subject departmental libraries for these disciplines are here gathered in convenient relationship. Including group-study rooms, faculty studies, and specialized subject staff strengthens this plan.

A subject-division plan should not dramatically affect floor area requirements for each seating accommodation, except as any subdivision results in the provision for unit peak loads, resulting in an increase in total requirements. In effect, some pressure on seating and staff space will result from duplication of services, which will vary significantly depending upon the scope and scale of the unique division. In terms of the duplication that results in some reference books and staff services, some extra space will likely be required to provide for the subject divisions in a central library building, though there is a clear net reduction in space over what would exist if there were several separate departmental branch libraries serving the same range of disciplines.

7.16
Departmental Branch Libraries

Section 2.6 discussed the decentralization of library resources as a strategy for saving the necessity for a new central library building. This section provides issues to be resolved if the decision has already been made to create or rehouse a departmental library.

In addressing this issue, we draw a distinction between reading room library collections of academic departments and branch libraries located in or beside the quarters of academic departments. The former are small specialized collections often unauthorized and almost never under the financial and management oversight of the university library administration. They might be called clandestine, yet to the faculty and their advanced stu-

dents and research associates they can be very handy, and may sometimes be used for seminars or small social functions. We are not discussing these collections. The authorized organized branch is part of the university-wide library system. We call this latter type a departmental branch because their subject collections and any specialized services are designed specifically to meet the needs of an academic department, or sometimes two or more closely related and closely located departments.

Professional schools, such as business, law, and medicine, commonly have separate libraries similar in function and space character to very large departmental libraries yet they usually also include space required for the related technical services, administrative, and, sometimes, business staff. These professional school libraries may be housed in separate physical structures—buildings of their own—as are some departmental libraries, though inclusion within a large building of the school is more common. (See fig. 7.30.)

Most very large universities experience pressure for departmental library collections, and this comes from one of two sources. The central library building may have become so full that the least costly solution may be to remove part of the collection that is thought to be most easily separated. Or, most often, the campus has grown so that the distance from the main library building to other academic buildings, such as laboratories, argues for a branch. In both cases, the argument for a branch may be reinforced by the faculty view that their subject has special conditions not adequately met by the centralized library with what may seem a homogenized service.

The most common subjects for such branches are art, music, education, biology, chemistry, geology, mathematics, and physics. When there is a school of architecture, engineering, forestry, information science and librarianship, or nursing, a departmental or school library is common; the preceding list does not by any means suggest any limit on the subjects covered by such separate library units.

Table 7.1 illustrates a review two decades ago of science and technology libraries in 75 North American university libraries.[6] A more recent tabulation would find somewhat different data but not a radically altered picture.

What special provisions can be found in a branch? Examples will be given; however, these are merely indicative of the wide range of questions that should be raised and answered in program-

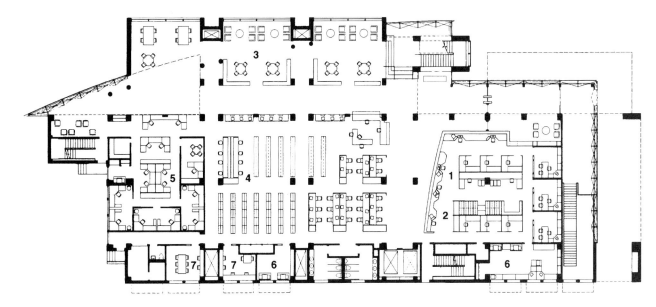

FIGURE 7.30 Vanderbilt University, Eskind Biomedical Library, first floor. This 80,000 ft² (7,432 m²) library has cable and wire trays below the ceilings throughout the library, accessible via flip-up boxes in the floor above. Thus, as use of information technology evolves, there can be gradual replacement of the bookstacks by computer workstations. Functional layout: (1) circulation, (2) documentation, (3) reading, (4) reference books, (5) reference department, (6) other staff quarters, (7) group studies. Note atria in upper left and right, which link this level with the upper floors. (Courtesy of Davis Brody Bond, LLP Design Architect, Thomas Miller & Partners, Architect of Record)

TABLE 7.1 Composite Data for 75 North American Science and Technology Libraries

Discipline	Size		Seats	Volumes	Current Serials	Total Staff
	sq ft	sq m				
Engineering	10,739	998	130	103,108	1,115	6.81
Biology	8,286	770	64	65	744	4.18
Geology	6,033	560	67	71,605	1,046	5.31
Physics	5,342	496	75	58,181	502	4.43
Chemistry	5,268	489	72	43,970	296	3.66
Mathematics	4,543	422	62	49,353	624	4.33

ming any departmental library. Note that all these subjects will make heavy use of information technologies and will need networked PCs. Some will need workstations, all must have laptop ports, and some may have multimedia requirements.

As was indicated just above, the needs in art and music are conditioned by the extra size of large portions of the book collections and by the nonbook materials, which are heavily used. These conditions affect the shelving, the reading quarters for students, perhaps the circulation or lending of the materials, the size of the staff, and the reliance on rare book materials. In other subjects, are these same conditions significantly important?

Will a journalism department have a broad array of currently published newspapers, with spatial consequences? How will this influence the design of spaces? Will the law library need to seat a very large percentage of the students, and medicine to house and display the current issues of serials in a fashion seldom used in the central library? (The display of current issues of the major journals in some fields may be handled by placing the receipts of one week on an open table or special display racks, replacing the displayed issues each week.) Chemistry will find that journals are 90 percent of the collection, and there may be a special work area for paper and computer use of such huge sets as *Chemical Abstracts, Beilstein Handbook of Organic Chemistry, Gmelin Handbook of Inorganic and Organometallic Chemistry,* and *Sadtler Spectra.* Questions on each aspect of the departmental library will bring forth a unique mix of conditions, sometimes subtle and sometimes not, yet all of great importance in programming.

Sometimes departmental libraries may economically be combined into related groupings of subjects. Thus, a very large university might have departmental libraries for electrical, mechanical, and chemical engineering, and it may be decided to provide an inclusive engineering library to serve all the departments in a school of engineering. Or a physical or life science library may be planned. The variety of options is wide, and local campus planning and academic circumstances plus financial considerations will guide the decision.

The Grainger Engineering Library at the University of Illinois at Urbana-Champaign is a case worth studying. (See fig. 7.31.) Opened in 1994, Grainger occupies an entire building with 92,000 net ft² (8,547 m²) and has space for 330,000 vol-

umes, receives 1,300 journals, and seats 1,200 or 15 percent of all the 7,400 students and 515 faculty members in the College of Engineering. It provides spaces for conferences, group study, and seminars, and includes a multimedia laboratory, a digital imaging laboratory, usability laboratory, writers' workshop, and instruction room, as well as microcomputer and workstation laboratories. Besides the regular reference collection, there is an ANSI and non-ANSI standards collection and microtexts of U.S. Department of

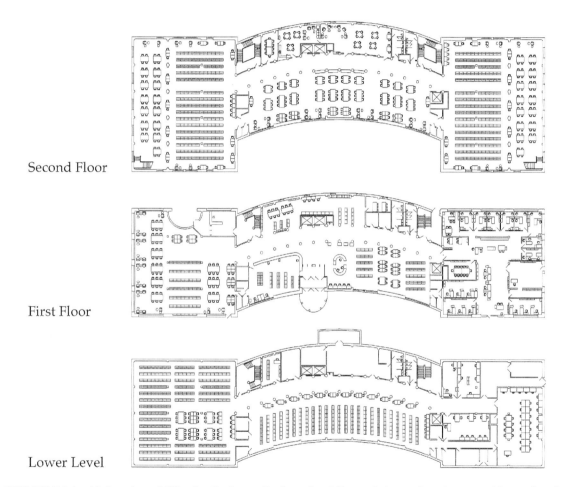

Second Floor

First Floor

Lower Level

FIGURE 7.31   **University of Illinois, Grainger Engineering Library Information Center, with seating for 1,200 and shelving for 330,000 volumes in 92,000 ASF (8,546 m²).**

LOWER LEVEL: Computer and Multimedia Lab occupies the room on the extreme right. Left of it is the Digital Imaging Lab. The Server Room is in the upper right corner, and just left of that is the Information Retrieval Research Lab.

FIRST FLOOR: Left-hand block holds current periodicals. Right-hand block is staff offices. Central section includes areas for circulation, reference, online searching, microcomputer lab, disability lab, and microtexts. Note the provision of two entrances, each with a staffed desk.

SECOND FLOOR: Note the large "Commons" room at top of central section.

(Continued)

FIGURE 7.31   (Continued)

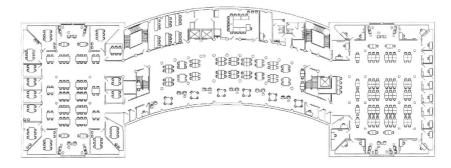

Fourth Floor

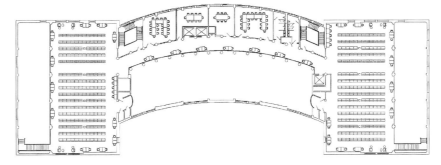

Third Floor

THIRD FLOOR: Central section of this mezzanine includes four rooms for seminars and conferences.

FOURTH FLOOR: Left-hand block has table seating and group studies available to students. Right-hand block has student carrel seating, as well as offices and studies assigned only to faculty. Central section includes a small communication skills lab as well as two instructional labs on either side of a room used for instructional preparation.

Energy and NASA publications, while nearly every table, carrel, and desk is wired for network access so library users can bring laptop computers and access all the systems, networks, and databases.

Other good examples will be found in large university systems. Yet a great many occupy hand-me-down space, or were planned by those with little or no library knowledge, so care must be exercised when seeking instructive models.

Because the central library built on most U.S. campuses in the past 50 years has a high degree of flexibility and meets reasonably high building code standards, and as central campus areas are built up, it seems probable that a substantial part of future library growth on these campuses will either be departmental or subject-cluster branch libraries or will be auxiliary or storage libraries. Though each branch unit is smaller than the main library, in aggregate they amount to a good deal of space and need just as careful planning as does the main library if they are to be academically sound and economically a wise investment.

7.17
Group-Study Rooms, Seminar Rooms, Typing, and Smoking

7.17.1 Group-Study Rooms

Working in groups is favored by many students who, at least on occasion, like to study with others. This seating type has increased in popularity in recent years, and, in most new libraries, it represents a somewhat greater fraction of the total seating than in the past. Students sit in twos or in larger groups of up to eight to discuss their assignments or work on a joint project. This is especially the case in scientific and engineering fields; and technical schools in particular have found it desirable to have in the libraries small rooms where students can talk over their work without disturbing others. With group study rooms, there is far less excuse for whispering in the open reading areas. It is suggested that every library should have one or in some cases a considerable number of these rooms (departmental libraries and subject-divisional plans included)—if possible, at least one or more on each floor. They should seat not less than four and generally not more than six. Seating for four is probably ideal, as larger groups tend to be rare outside an organized seminar and one-third of the space is wasted if a room for six is always used by four or fewer working together.

The rooms can be as small as 11 × 8½ ft (3.353 × 2.591 m) for four students, and would work for six students in a pinch, although this is minimum spacing; a few extra inches would help. Slightly more space will be required for handicapped access. (See fig. 7.32.) Rooms should be equipped with one table, four to six chairs according to size, and a chalkboard or marker board. The table need be no more than 3 ft (0.914 m) deep instead of the 4 ft (1.219 m) recommended for regular reading room tables. The minimum spacing of 2½ ft (0.762 m) on each side can be tolerated, although 3 ft (0.914 m) is more comfortable and should make it easier for a person in a wheelchair or motorized cart. The door or a panel next to the door should contain a large section of glass to permit easy supervision (so they will not become lover's nests) and ease in determining if the room is available.

The walls that adjoin other similar rooms or reading areas of any kind should be acoustically treated, including double glazing where there is glass and continuing the walls through the ceiling to the underside of the floor above. If the door opens into a part of the bookstacks where no seats for readers are close at hand, the need for special acoustical protection will be reduced.

7.17.2 Seminar Rooms

These book-lined spaces were copied from German university libraries. Most college and university libraries built before the Second World War contained a considerable number. Specialized collections were kept in these rooms and were made available to faculty and students. Small advanced classes and discussion groups met in them. Oberlin, a liberal arts college, made provision for some 15 seminar rooms as early as 1908, not unusual at that time. One difficulty typical with this arrangement comes from the fact that, if the rooms house books, the books are not available while the seminars are in progress, and the rooms are likely to contain more and more books because of increasing pressure for additional shelf space. To avoid this dilemma, a limited number of small rooms without shelving may be placed adjacent to other rooms or areas filled with collections on limited subjects gathered together for use by advanced students. Princeton's Firestone

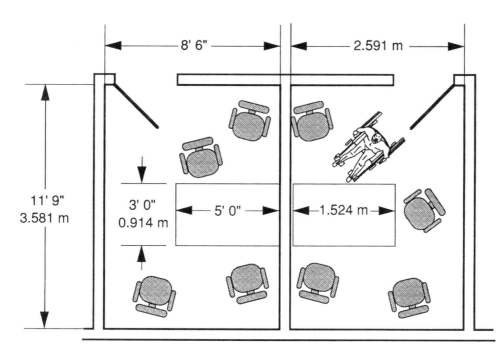

FIGURE 7.32 Group study. Although the example is slightly larger than absolutely required in many cases, the larger size should accommodate wheelchairs.

Library has 10 such graduate seminar rooms. In this way collections can be made available to others when the seminars are in progress.

A slight variation of the seminar room might be called a subject reading room, and Princeton's Firestone Library has another 10 of these graduate study rooms. In this case a room is set up with reading accommodations and a collection relating to a specific topic. It is intended as a research or reading area rather than a seminar or teaching room, although a seminar could take place there, and provision may be made for a staff attendant to add oversight to the room and to assist readers when they have bibliographic or research questions. The staff member may be a graduate student assistant, and the staffed hours may be quite limited. In some cases use of the room is open to any student, while in others it may be limited to those majoring in the specific field. Philosophically, one can argue that such a facility promotes collegial interaction and a sense of academic support, during a period that may seem very lonely to the graduate student.

In the Princeton example, the rooms are mainly in the humanities and in area studies, Arabic being the last one created. Some of the graduate study rooms have no books while others have several shelves of books and periodicals that are general-stack duplicates and do not circulate. A few unique serials go to these rooms until they are bound and shelved in the open stack. Most rooms are locked; students can leave their possessions there, with keys being issued only to faculty and graduate students in the department. Only one has assigned carrels as well as lockers where students can provide their own lock and secure their laptops. Some have assigned shelf space to which students can check out items from the stacks.

There is educational merit in the concept of encouraging students of similar interests to work together (known as peer counseling) in a specially provided area or room. Graduate students benefit by working collaboratively or alone in the same space day after day and away from the undergraduates. These rooms will not usually be heavily used, yet they are judged to be important in graduate life, providing a home for those in individual disciplines—a tangible "sense of place" was one academic value mentioned at the beginning of the first chapter. Fund-raising efforts may be quite effective with both seminar rooms and subject reading areas.

When either the seminar room or subject reading room/area plan is carried out, it may involve some duplication of materials. If the rooms are not exclusively assigned to any one discipline, it should be possible to schedule classes in them for so many hours a week that they will not be an extravagance. So much the better if they are placed immediately adjacent to the bookstacks or, in limited quantity, near special materials, such as the reference room, public documents, or technical reports, so that books from the main collections are readily available. Simply as small classrooms, they take space the construction cost of which must be figured at or higher than $100 per ft^2 (or about $1,100 per m^2). Unless used a considerable number of hours each week, they tend to be a luxury.

Although there are more instructional rooms in academic libraries, many fewer seminar rooms (used by faculty in a seminar mode) are being provided in American libraries built since the Second World War. They can, however, represent flexibility or surge space that can be used for other library purposes later, particularly if their walls can be easily removed. Acoustically they should be treated in the same manner as group study rooms, which may make the walls slightly more costly to alter. However, rooms such as these can be used for special projects, small conferences, or committee work, or they can often be made into several smaller rooms for group study or faculty assignment, which may sometimes seem desirable. They can be planned with these possibilities in mind.

7.17.3 Typing

Microcomputers have replaced the typewriter to a large extent in the academic and research libraries of many countries. In these cases, publicly accessible computers or terminals may be distributed throughout the library. Computers very often generate conversation between users trying to understand system or software characteristics or class problems being done on this equipment, so, in general, microcomputers should not be placed in an open reading room where computers are not in general use. See Section 7.3 for extended treatment of this use of computers.

In cases where typewriters are still used, there are four quite different but possible arrangements:

1. *In a regular reading room.* In general this is not recommended, but in a rare book reading room, where supervision of the library

materials in use is deemed essential, it may be required. The Bancroft Library at the University of California, Berkeley, still provides noise shields for typewriters but they are rarely used because laptops are now common. Without some form of noise control, typing in an open reading area is likely to be intolerable, whereas the softer clicking of laptops is usually acceptable. In most cases laptop computers have replaced the need for typewriters in rare book reading rooms.

2. *Typing rooms where from two to a dozen or more students using typewriters or computers are seated.* Possible arrangement of one of these rooms is shown in fig. 7.33. Such a room concentrates and segregates the noise, but necessitates acoustically treated walls and seclusion. If the room provides for too many users at once, it will be a bit of a zoo at certain times of the year. Tables or carrels separate from the walls and each other will help to reduce the transmission

of sound. Some positions for personal typewriters or computers should be provided even where the library provides equipment.

3. *Regular carrels in the bookstacks.* This solution is often possible if the use of typewriters is confined to one side of one stack level or to a specific stack area, and if only those who expect to use typewriters are assigned to this particular area. In a typical tiered stack, the pounding of a typewriter is likely to be transmitted through the structure and this approach may not work well. At the University of California, Los Angeles, main research library, individual typing stations were provided in the center of a large stack area so that the books themselves absorb most of the typing noise (though computer ports are now gradually being installed). This arrangement worked well there.

4. *Special acoustically protected individual typing cubicles or carrels.* Various arrangements are possible. In addition to quiet floors and acoustically treated ceilings in these cubicles, acoustic material of one kind or another is often placed on the walls. The carrels do not require doors if they are placed at the end of a stack aisle, as they were in the Wellesley College Library with

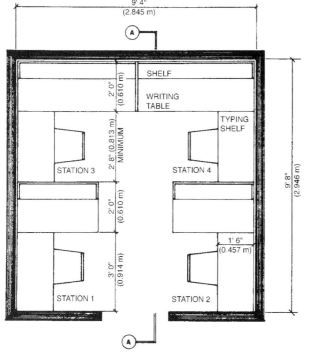

PLAN

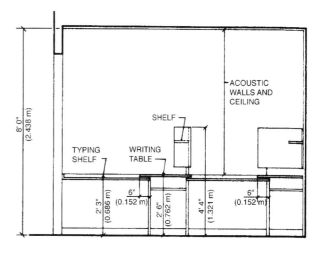

ELEVATION A - A

FIGURE 7.33 Typing room for four. Although such accommodation was once thought to be minimum, because of the significant reduction in typing (virtually zero in most U.S. libraries), such an accommodation for typing alone may be generous. Replacement of the typing shelf by an articulated computer stand with an adjustable keyboard surface would adapt this plan for a small computer cluster with reasonable accommodation, although the typing table should be 30 in. (0.762 m) deep rather than the 18 in. (0.457 m) shown here.

complete success. (See fig. 7.8.) They can be held down in size and still be acceptable, although at least a few should provide for use by a person in a wheelchair.

The use of typewriters and portable personal computers suggests that storage lockers would be convenient and desirable. Lockers of this kind are available with either combination or key locks, each with a master key. In some institutions they are rented for a nominal fee.

7.17.4 Smoking

This in any library is a problem, as was discussed in Section 3.2.10. This is particularly true with increased use of carpet throughout the library. There has always been a demand for smoking accommodations. Smoke detectors and alarms will serve as an effective deterrent. Some institutions permit smoking only in private offices or areas specifically set aside for smokers; others have no specific rules. Some regions and some countries are populated with greater numbers of smokers. Other regions have accepted the norm that smoking is not acceptable in public areas. Many states in the United States have passed laws to protect the rights of nonsmokers to breathe clean air, and many academic institutions have now banned smoking in all academic buildings.

There are three obvious objections to smoking: the fire hazard for paper products and furniture as well as buildings, the dirt and soil that inevitably result, and the now-universal recognition that smoking is a health hazard and that such smoke is clearly harmful even for the nonsmoker. Even where there is no actual fire, damage to tabletops, upholstery, and floor coverings is almost inevitable.

Where there are no legal restrictions or institutional rules governing smoking, the library planner should keep in mind the problems associated with the habit. A growing number of people dislike studying in a room filled with smoke, and yet there are still those who find it difficult to study for any considerable period of time without smoking. Because of them, it was once common in the United States for a library to permit smoking in specified areas, which experience tells us will reduce illicit smoking. The University of Minnesota Wilson Library had excellent smoking rooms by the stacks on most floors, now still popular study places. The University of Michigan Shapiro Undergraduate Library for years permitted smoking throughout the building and the

ceilings showed the result. However, by the early 1990s most U.S. academic libraries changed to a policy of no smoking, sometimes as part of a campuswide policy. Typical experience has been that this policy works well, though some butts are found in stairwells when it is bitter cold outside.

When provided, smoking areas or rooms should, of course, not have a fire detection system activated by smoke; where fire detection is necessary, a rate-of-heat-rise system is the only practical approach in areas where there may be heavy smoking, even though this form of fire detection is less effective. If the building is air conditioned or if there is forced ventilation, special care must be given to the ventilation in smoking areas. No extra floor area per reader is required in smoking areas.

7.18 Summary of Seating Accommodations

There are three major questions to be dealt with in deciding upon the type of seating accommodations.

What do the readers want? One can be sure that not all readers want the same thing and that a variety of reading accommodations are desirable. The problem comes in determining the number or percentage of each and their distribution, and all 10 types of seating should be considered.

Studies done in the past indicated that over three-quarters of all students prefer individual accommodations, although this finding is likely to vary, depending on local customs as well as the exact nature of the accommodations. (This excludes seating for use of reference books and current periodicals.) Indeed, this percentage has probably gone down somewhat in the past decade. During a late 1990s tour of libraries along the east coast of the United States, it was observed that there is much use of group studying, more than would have been seen 20 or 30 years ago, yet the impression was that the percentage of students studying alone or studying quietly near a buddy at a table for two or four was still something like 75 percent. They spread out, so getting exact proportions is not at all easy; and, in contrast, it is easy to see groups sitting and actually working and talking together, sometimes in "group study rooms" and occasionally in a large room aimed at that purpose, like the University of Miami Richter Library "zoo."

At the University of Minnesota, informal observations over the years suggest carrel and individual tables 2 × 3 ft (0.610 × 0.914 m) and 3 × 4 ft (0.914 × 1.219 m) tend to fill to between 90 and 100 percent of capacity. Open table seating rarely fills to more than 60 percent, and the table suffering the most is of six seats where three students "fill" them with one person at each corner on one side and the opposing center seat—particularly during winter months when students pile coats on the adjacent seat. Individual seating can, of course, be provided in dormitory rooms in a residential institution, but, as noted before, it is usually more expensive to provide satisfactorily for every student in a dormitory than for, let us say, every fourth student in the library. One thing that is certain is the strong tendency toward a large percentage of individual seating in libraries, often with as much as 75 percent of all the seats individual in character. There should be a quantity of seating at tables, too. And, though we have not repeated it in most cases above, one must always remember the needs of the person using a wheelchair or motorized cart, the left-handed person, individuals with bad backs or stiff legs, weak of sight or hard of hearing, and so on, for some accommodation must be given to such needs, no matter how infrequent, in all parts of the library.

Two examples from Stanford University can provide a comparison. The student seating percentages were determined by judgment—the undergraduate Meyer Library before it opened in November 1966 and the Green Library East Wing before it opened in January 1981. Note in table 7.2 that the Meyer clientele is about 75 percent undergraduates and 15 percent graduate students, while Green's clientele is about 50 percent graduate students and 15 percent undergraduates. (The Meyer Library seating after the mid-1990s is not given here because a major change transformed the library into predominantly a media center, and other temporary uses reduced the traditional library space to one floor.)

Experience in Meyer during the 1970s was that rarely were more than half the seats used at one time and that the proportion of flat tables was too high. Experience in Green suggests that the proportions are reasonable; the level of use often approaches 100 percent. Note that even in Green, the number of individual carrels is substantially less than the 75 percent suggested earlier; in categories 1–7, the individual accommodations are exactly 75 percent.

Tilburg University Library (Katholieke Universiteit Brabant) provides a different example, from 1992. With 9,500 students at that time, the new library was equipped with seats for 10.5 percent. And of these 900 seats, 3 percent were at language booths, another 3 percent at consulting stations, 6 percent at various sitting areas, 7 percent at cubicles (half open and half enclosed), 8 percent in study rooms, and 73 percent at two-person open study tables. A more recent example is Emory University, which opened a major addition to the Woodruff Library in 1997, the total building having 731 public work positions. Of these, 40 percent were at open tables for four persons each, 10 percent were divided among 10 group study rooms, 27 percent were at carrels, and 23 percent were at four different wired locations—that is, 19 at stand-up OPACs, 21 at surfaces

TABLE 7.2 Seating Allocation in Two Libraries

Type of Seating	Meyer Library		Green East Wing	
	No. of seats	Percentage	No. of seats	Percentage
1. Flat tables for two or more	468	30	126	12
2. Tables with low dividers	208	13	0	—
3. Slanting-top tables	0	—	0	—
4. Individual tables or carrels	565	36	424	41
5. Lounge chairs	163	11	68	7
6. Enclosed carrels	0	—	107	10
7. Group study rooms	0	—	64	6
8. Reference collection	60	4	164	16
9. Current periodicals	40	3	44	4
10. New books and light reading	12	1	6	1
11. Study hall	32	2	0	—
12. Microtexts	4	—	29	3
Total	1,552		1,032	

wired for laptop/notebook use, 38 at multimedia workstations, and 95 at multifunctional terminals on open carrels arranged in four-carrel and six-carrel semicircular clusters that facilitate wire and cable access through the open side of the cluster.

It seems that the *quality* of the individual position may be just as important as the basic type. That is, the degree of comfort, the size, the degree of privacy, the bookish surroundings, the natural and artificial light, amenities (such as a locally controlled light or a footstool)—these give a sense of private prestige space and will draw students. Except during the "forced feeding" of pre-exam days, a library is, after all, competing as a drawing card against the student union, dorm room, local pub, and other options. The "bloom" wore off Meyer after a very few generations of students, as is the experience in many other libraries; its recent efforts at refurbishing have been welcomed by students. Green, as the new kid on the block, became immediately popular. Maintaining attractiveness in any new library is not easy and yet is a factor in its continued effectiveness as an educational institution.

How much space do the different types of seating accommodations take? This is a matter of considerable importance, both financially and in terms of how the reading positions are to be used. On one hand, with a total project cost in the range of $150 per ft² (or about $1,600 per m²), the difference between 25 ft² (2.323 m²) and 35 ft² (3.252 m²) for each reader station represents a potential savings or cost of $1,500 per reader. On the other hand, insufficient space for the reader simply will accommodate seating that will not be properly used. As already suggested, the space requirement for readers will vary depending upon the nature of use, with the recommended range running from 25 ft² (2.323 m²) per reader in typical undergraduate libraries, to 30 to 35 ft² (2.787 to 3.252 m²) for use by a master's candidate, to perhaps 50 ft² (4.645 m²) per reader in a law library or where a student is expected to write a thesis. Faculty studies are typically larger, being often as much as 75 ft² (6.968 m²) or more. More space should also be allowed per reader in special areas, such as for using portable personal computers, microtexts, newspapers, reference collections, maps and atlases, archives, and rare books.

One architect with a great deal of library design experience in the 1990s has summarized that, whereas 20 ft² to 25 ft² net (1.858 m² to 2.323 m²) was the old standard, with information technology it is now 40 ft² to 45 ft² (3.716 m² to 4.181 m²), and even 60 ft² of net (5.574 m²) for collaborative use. The library net-to-gross efficiency is everywhere driven down by the technology of the digital age and perhaps in some cases by improved environmental control and improved access.

The determination of the space requirement, as already outlined in this chapter, includes consideration of three points: (1) the desirable amount of working surface at a carrel or table; (2) the aisle space required for access to the seat; and (3) the extra space for psychological "air space," for comfort, and for special equipment, particularly in a closed carrel or study. The range of space recommended above should normally be sufficient to provide for these three points. Excluded from these space recommendations is the space required for readers in other parts of the library, such as lobbies, public service areas, public catalog rooms, rest rooms, corridors, stairwells, elevators, and nonassignable and architectural space in general, to say nothing of exhibition space and areas used for what might be called nonlibrary purposes.

What level of detail should be programmed? Aside from the number of readers to be accommodated, the area to be provided for each reader, and the mix of seating accommodations, there are other features of reading positions that are very important. Most important is clarity as to the function and the environmental character of each type of seating space. For instance, lounge chairs should be arranged to either promote or discourage conversation, depending upon the circumstance. There may be need to provide for media access for work in pairs with an especially quiet environment. A mock-up of reading positions with their lighting configuration is probably desirable in all but the smallest library project. Special consideration for the needs of the handicapped should be detailed; even though physically limited persons will almost never constitute as much as 5 percent of clientele, between 5 and 10 percent of the reading positions spread among the library areas and functions should provide for full access by handicapped persons. Although it may seem like a small point to include in the program, outlets for such equipment as microtext reading machines and fixed and portable computers must be specified as to where the connections are to be made and how they will be done; to leave these critical matters to the design development or working drawings phases is to court user dissatisfaction and managerial inefficiency and headaches.

The materials used to fabricate the reading positions should be durable and refinishable where damage is likely to result. Anything that can be picked at should be avoided, which includes exposed screws or raised caps over fasteners. The chairs should be exceptionally strong but comfortable enough to allow a person to sit for several hours at a time. While armchairs are generally preferred, a quantity of armless chairs should also be provided for those who like to curl one leg under them, a position that many find comfortable and that is often impossible in an armchair. Where carpet is used, sled-base chairs are preferred as they tend to be easier on the carpet. (In this case, glides attached to the base of the sled defeat the intent of the design.) Because of power or signal outlets, some furniture must be bolted to the floor or otherwise restricted in placement, such as by a short-chain tether. Colors of the reading surface should not represent dramatic differences from the colors encountered in printed texts; too dark and too light both tend to be distracting to the eye.

Discussion of what might be regarded as trivia, such as clocks, dictionary stands, globes, wastepaper baskets, pencil sharpeners, sun control, locks on equipment or doors, notice boards, coatracks or hooks, emergency phones, and any other devices or equipment important to the support of the reading area, is appropriately part of the program. Although these aspects have not been discussed to any degree of detail in this chapter, they should not be left totally out, especially if the resulting budget is to cover their expense.

The program should include designation of any exceptional existing items of equipment or furniture. Examples might be a large hand printing press, an extra-large historic rolltop desk, a grandfather clock, or a noteworthy and exceptionally heavy piece of sculpture. However, reuse of existing furniture should generally not be part of the initial programming, though reference might be made to the fact that this will be dealt with in a special study for the furnishings phase of the project. At that time, and especially in adding to or remodeling an existing building, the disposition of the existing furniture should be established. If it is to be kept, is the new furniture to be sympathetic to it or can the existing furniture be used in isolated areas? Most designers would, of course, prefer the freedom of using all new furniture. Without that freedom, it is usually desirable to incorporate the existing furniture, perhaps refinished, in as compatible a fashion as possible. The question of who is to undertake the inventory of existing furniture should be addressed. It is suggested that the persons responsible for the interior design should at least share in this effort, even if they do not undertake full responsibility.

Details such as these will affect both the design fees and the final cost, and, to avoid false expectations, they should be spelled out. All that may influence the design should be in the building program; the rest can be included in the specifications document or in furniture specifications. As with other aspects of the program, attention to detail will increase the likelihood of a satisfactory product. Further, it conveys to the architect a good understanding of actual operational conditions and of the institutional expectations with respect to design detailing. Yet the advice of the design team should not be discouraged. The program presents the facility goals of the library, which, with a suitable degree of communication and understanding between designer and client, can be refined as more is learned of the project as it proceeds through the design phases.

NOTES

1. Paul J. Korshin, "The New British Library: Some Facts and Problems," *Newsletter,* American Council of Learned Societies 3, no. 4 (fall 1992): 13.
2. Letter to authors from Professor David Kaser, July 17, 1991.
3. Although Marquis Associates no longer exists, the patent is considered as being to the benefit of the Robert Marquis Estate; office papers are held by Mrs. Ellen Marquis, also of San Francisco.
4. Harold L. Dahnke, Dennis P. Jones, Thomas R. Mason, and Leonard Romney, *Academic Support Facilities,* Higher Education Facilities Planning and Management Manual no. 4 (Boulder, Colo.: Western Interstate Commission for Higher Education, 1971), pp. 64ff.
5. One brief introduction is *A Guide for Planning Library Integration into Distance Education Programs* (Pub. No. 2A237, 32 pp., 1993, Western Cooperative.) Key planning and management issues related to library collections, costs, personnel, and services are presented in an easy-to-use checklist for distance educators and library directors. Includes brief case studies from California State University at Chico, Colorado State University, the University of Alaska Southeast, the University of Maine at Augusta, the University of Nebraska-Lincoln, and the University of Wyoming.
6. Julie M. Hurd, "ARL Academic Science and Technology Libraries: Report of a Survey," *College & Research Libraries* 57, no. 2 (March 1996): 151.

8

Programming: Space for Staff and General Purposes

First we design our buildings, then our buildings design us.

—Sir Winston Churchill

Adequate accommodations for the library staff are essential for effective service. In academic institutions the space required does not loom large in proportion to space for readers and books. However, with few exceptions, accommodations for library staff historically have tended to become inadequate before those for books or for readers. This situation may result from modesty or timidity on the part of the librarians or from a failure to realize how much the staff may have to grow in order to process new material and provide public service. Some would argue that the advent of automation has reduced the need for staff accommodations, particularly in the technical processing areas, and in some cases this is no doubt true. However, library staff quarters are all too often congested, and such activities as information systems support, technology maintenance, programming (of hypertext Web pages, etc.), gift processing, indexing projects, administrative studies, cooperative programs, conservation, bibliographic instruction, or interlibrary loan seem to grow to overfill the space. The resultant crowding hinders, even if it does not prevent, effective work.

Every several decades it seems that national or worldwide economic conditions force local budget cuts, staff reductions, retrenchments by various euphemisms. Then the pressures of population growth and constant publication of more books worldwide constitute forces that soon require growth of educational institutions and attendant library staff growth, no matter how much library program redesign and automation help at the margin. Therefore, where there is limited flexibility for future reallocation of space to provide for staff, either as the result of a natural pattern of growth or as the result of one or more special projects, then some surge space or a slight excess of staff space in terms of absolute predictable need is generally prudent, even where it is anticipated that staff space needs will shrink as a result of outsourcing or further automation.

The only staff reduction that could be considered real and permanent is based upon the notion of moving entire functions out of the building; outsourcing or operating separate staff facilities represent the key possibilities here. In either case, the reduction of staff is really a relocation of staff such that space requirements are met elsewhere. Although the authors would be pleased to be wrong, it is likely that over the long term, automation will not dramatically reduce total staff, although the increase in staff numbers may be less dramatic in the future, and relocation of some staff will be typical.

With microcomputers, printers, disk drives, monitors, and so on, the space required for an automated workstation will be somewhat larger than that for its manual predecessor. It is suggested, for example, that at least 20 ft^2 (1.858 m^2) should be added to a secretary's workstation where use of a microcomputer or word-processing terminal is involved in addition to typewriting and other space needs. Use of a PC to replace a typewriter also requires some additional space because of the need for one or more manuals, equipment deeper and a keyboard wider than that of the typewriter, an easily accessible file of floppy disks, and, frequently, the need for an attached printer or the CPU of a workstation.

Two general points should be added. Today a strong argument can be made for sufficient and convenient computer workstations for library staff. Because of the annual expense for salaries, appropriate equipment can greatly aid the efficiency of library staff who need to use computers in all work areas. In major university libraries, it is now increasingly common for nearly all staff to need computer connections. And nearly all have computers accessible at their work area. Even though it has become much more difficult to reach a human by phone in this age of recording messages, the result can be somewhat fewer clerical positions with budget savings. Thus, the library office with four or eight professionals with different responsibilities may be aided by one or two secretarial positions instead of as many as four or eight before the age of the computer and modern telephone answering and switching systems. The provision of adequate communication devices—terminals, printers, fax machines, telephones—can be an investment that results in efficient use of staff, and it leads to different space allocation in design of library quarters.

As the second general point, it should be noted that although the number of support staff relative to administrators and managers has decreased, the space required per person has increased. As a rule of thumb, in the past a secretarial position was allocated approximately 80 to 85 ft^2 (7.432 to 7.897 m^2); today the same position with files, fax, computer, and so on will require 100 to 120 ft^2 (9.290 to 11.148 m^2), depending on the actual equipment and furnishing anticipated.

Personal space is important for library staff. The ability to add their own distinctive touches to their desk areas, with the tacit assent of management, provides staff members an opportunity for individual expression within a seemingly impersonal institutional structure. These "touches" may be postcards sent by former colleagues during their travels, posters of artwork, or pictures of a sports hero or of a famous academic, such as Albert Einstein. The variety is limitless, so long as the items do not intrude into efficient work processes, do not pose any safety hazard, or do not seem inflammatory from an ethnic, a religious, a gender, or a political point of view, thereby creating what some would consider a hostile work environment. Some libraries allow discreet decoration or adornment in public areas, and most libraries do not object to behind-the-scenes personalization.

Programming of staff quarters should acknowledge that such decorating will or by policy will not occur, in public areas or in private quarters or in both, so that wall surfaces and partitions will not become unsightly and require refurbishing because of the use of thumbtacks, tape, or other adhesives. (See also Section 14.2.5, Durable Surfaces.) The official use of framed posters or art prints, or perhaps of decorative maps or other broadsides that have no academic value, can possibly take the place of some of the "personal touches" if library staff are asked to select the wall decorations. This topic may seem trivial, yet its acknowledgment and treatment can con-

tribute to a pleasant library building in which staff are happy to work and library users feel welcomed by sensitive human beings.

Space is needed for four major staff groups—administrative personnel, public service staff, processing staff, and maintenance staff—as well as for rest rooms and lounges. (The program writer is urged to review the discussion on general relationships of major functions found in Section 5.3.3.)

8.1
Administrative Personnel

The size of the administrative staff depends, of course, very largely on the size of the total library operation. The chief librarian should have adequate quarters for office work and also for meeting with members of the staff and public. The space assigned to the chief librarian will depend on the work required and on whether the office is to serve as a conference room. The office may require as little as 125 to 150 ft² (11.613 to 13.935 m²) in a small library or as much as 400 ft² (37.161 m²) or even more in a very large library if small group meetings will be held there. An office of 240 to 260 ft² (22.297 to 24.155 m²) is not uncommon. For political reasons, the size of this office is often affected by the size of offices provided for deans and other academic officers in the institution. (See figs. 8.1 and 8.2.)

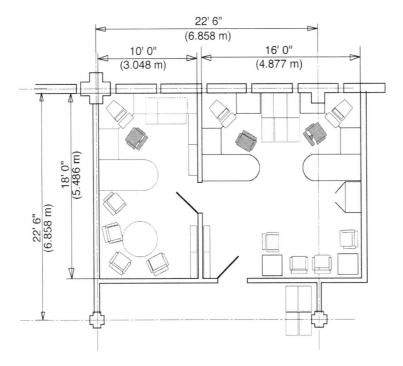

FIGURE 8.1 Library director's office as proposed for the University of California, San Diego, Biomedical Library showing how it might work with that particular module. The inner office is 180 ft² (16.723 m²); the outer office for two with waiting area is 299 ft² (26.756 m²). Storage was a concern when this sketch was developed; it was thought that space outside the office proper might accommodate a storage cabinet. Note that some administrators would wish to have eye contact with their support staff, which would suggest a different arrangement of furniture.

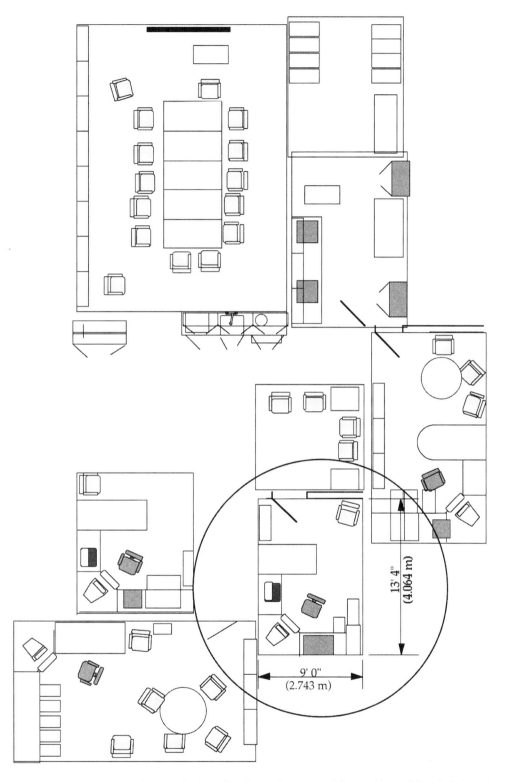

FIGURE 8.2 From a programming study done for the Delaware Public Archives, this administrative suite includes a large conference room, file room, production and storage room, and four offices. The high-lighted office (within the circle) is 120 ft² (11.148 m²). (As this was a plotting of office spaces drawn separately, some of the door locations are less than ideal.) Illustrations and text for space program for Delaware Public Archives, produced by Philip D. Leighton for Moeckel Carbonell Associates, Inc., Architects, Wilmington, Del.

For all offices, the program should outline the nature of the furnishings. This is, of course, a local decision. Is there to be a seating group in lounge chairs or at a small table? Are bookshelves required? personal computers with printers? files? sink? coat closet? What kind of work surfaces are desired? Is there any special furniture or artwork that belongs in this office? Are there to be drapes or blinds at the windows? In a branch or other small library, does this office require a secured file or space for keys and personnel records? Does the shelving of a sampling of rare books require special security or environmental consideration? Should there be extra outlets for such things as a clock, dictation equipment, a fan, a radio, a calculator, a copier, a fax, a scanner, an Internet terminal, desk or side lamps, and the like? In general, each workstation should be provided with at least four outlets, which is double that normally provided. If the office is to be used as a conference room, is there need for an easel? projection screen? tackboard? chalkboard or marker board? Should these be worked into the design of the space so that they are hidden when not in use?

If the chief librarian's office is not to be used for conferences of various kinds, a room for that purpose elsewhere in the administration suite is desirable. It may also serve as a board room or for meetings of the faculty library committee, for staff conferences, and for other small groups. The size, of course, will depend upon the maximum typical meeting size; 20 ft^2 (1.858 m^2) per seat is usually adequate. A small college library may require sufficient space for a group of 8 to 10 persons, while a large library may find accommodation for double this number or even more is appropriate. In addition to the items mentioned above, should there be space for folding or stacking chairs? a tea and coffee or bar service area? a sink or small refrigerator? phone? Should the table be sectional? Should this room have access separate from that of the administration suite? As this room may be occupied at near capacity for long periods of time, excellent ventilation is required. If projectors will be used for slides, films, or other media, the ability to dim the lighting will be essential.

In larger libraries there will be one or more associate or assistant librarians. For flexibility it is suggested that where several offices are provided for this group, they should all be the same size, although they may not be furnished the same.

An assistant librarian for collection development, for example, will need relatively more shelving, while a business manager may need secure storage for keys or financial files. These offices ordinarily will be smaller than the chief librarian's office, typically within the range of 125 to 250 ft^2 (11.613 to 23.226 m^2), with 160 to 180 ft^2 (14.864 to 16.723 m^2) being common. As with the librarian's office, the size of the assistant or associate librarian's offices may be influenced by the size of faculty offices provided by the institution. Unlike many faculty members, however, these administrative officers often have a number of departments or managers reporting to them, and it is convenient and desirable to be able to meet with most if not all of their immediate staff at a small table within their office. The urge to personalize these offices beyond a certain degree of uniformity should be resisted, because personnel changes are inevitable. For example, the desks should probably all be similar, although there may be several options in each office for desk placement. Shelving and other built-in features should also be of the same quality and otherwise similar, with the exceptions noted above. Personalization, of course, can easily be provided for in artwork and other items of a less permanent nature. (See fig. 8.3.)

Secretarial space is normally required in all but the very smallest libraries. The secretary's office may also serve as a waiting area. If there are a number of administrative officers—that is, associate or assistant librarians—more than one secretary quite likely will be required. A space of 125 ft^2 (11.613 m^2) is suitable for each secretary, with additional space provided for a reception area and perhaps a microcomputer, as noted earlier. The secretary usually needs a very large desk for paperwork, a typewriter or a word processor or both, a small file, and a side chair. Space for filing cabinets and supply cupboards is essential; in a larger office, it may be desirable to have a fairly large separate file room, perhaps with a sink, an office coffee service, supply storage, a photocopy machine, a fax machine, a table for sorting, a high-speed computer printer, an umbrella stand, and a coat closet. Space needs should be worked out based on local circumstances, and the degree of reliance on computer technology by all the library officers can somewhat reduce the administrative office requirement for secretarial support.

Accommodation for a business manager or administrative assistant librarian must also be pro-

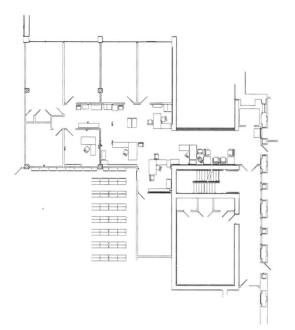

FIGURE 8.3 Stanford's Cecil H. Green Library. The administrative suite is shown with the proposed addition of a new office carved out of what was open office space. The largest office, that of the director, is approximately 315 ft² (29.264 m²). Adjacent to the director's office are four assistant/associate director's offices, each 250 ft² (23.226 m²). The new office is approximately 150 ft² (13.935 m²), though it is not proportioned for ideal arrangement.

The large space to the lower right is a conference room of about 480 ft² (44.593 m²) that seats about 16 around a table, and another 16 along the walls. The small room to the lower left of the office suite is used for files, supplies, beverages, etc. (Courtesy of Stanford University Libraries)

vided in a large library. As already suggested, this office should probably be the same size as that of the associate or assistant librarian because it can be expected that the business officer will have numerous visitors. Business support staff, including accountants, perhaps a building manager, a security officer, and a procurement officer, will require an open office landscape system or fully partitioned office space as well, which should be near the administration suite, if not part of it. At least 100 ft² and preferably 125 ft² (9.290 to 11.613 m²) per support staff member should be provided, in addition to space for a flat file of library plans, a safe, and perhaps a coin-counting room, which will need careful acoustic isolation as well as reasonable security. The business man-

ager may be responsible for a word-processing service, which also needs acoustic isolation.

Many libraries have other functions that are closely associated with the administration. There may be one or several assistants to the senior administration who typically are junior librarians doing special tasks of all kinds. Ideally, they should have individual spaces of 125 ft² (11.613 m²); the nature of some projects will require extra space with a large table. There may be a graphics technician who will need more studio space. A larger library may have, for example, a space planner, a public relations officer, a publications editor, a systems officer and staff, a research office, and a library intern or visiting fellow working with the librarian as part of a training experience. There may be a development officer responsible for donor-related matters, grant applications, and coordination of a "friends" group. The extent to which such professional staff need private offices is a local matter. The size requirements will vary. A system of movable panels creating low-partitioned, "landscaped" offices is initially cheaper and provides flexibility, but the authors favor full partitions in most cases for administrative offices because privacy and sound control are much improved thereby. Remember that serious planning discussions, hard private thought, job applicant interviews, performance discussion sessions, and occasional emotional meetings all deserve complete privacy.

A personnel office, perhaps with a separate entrance to encourage interaction with the library staff, is common in larger libraries. This office will probably need larger and more secure file space than most offices. There is always a quantity of handouts describing a variety of staff benefits, educational programs, and the like that will need special housing. A library with a large number of student employees will require space for reviewing job requisitions as well as filling out forms. A large tackboard for displaying a variety of notices for staff and potential staff will be required. The offices of the personnel managers will need careful acoustic isolation, because of the need to conduct confidential business, although they need not be larger than the 125 ft² (11.613 m²) provided for other support staff and managers. The space needs for files and a reception area should be calculated in addition to that for the staff positions.

In each group, if there is a person who is the equivalent to a department chief, he or she should be provided with an extra 25 to 50 ft² (2.323 to 4.645 m²) for guests and small group meetings. Clerical staff in the administrative support areas can be accommodated in 100 ft² (9.290 m²) per staff position unless each is using a microcomputer, which will require an additional 20 ft² (1.858 m²). To this should be added 10 ft² (0.929 m²) for each file cabinet plus similar space for general storage and supply cabinets or shelving units in a closet.

Although it need not be next to, or even on the same floor as, the administrative suite, another administrative support function (sometimes part of the technical processing or business function) is the library mail and supply room. The mail room, often referred to as shipping and receiving, is where outgoing books and other library materials are wrapped, letters and packages are franked, incoming mail is sorted, and incoming supplies and equipment are received and inventoried. In a large library, a fairly significant area will need to be devoted to the sorting of incoming mail, particularly serials. An extra-deep counter, perhaps 3 ft (0.914 m) from front to back and 10 or 12 ft (3.048 or 3.658 m) long with a portion at one end provided with a solid edge rail serves well. This counter should be about 36 in. (0.914 m) high. Mailbags are easily emptied onto the counter, and the serials may be sorted toward the end with the edge rail. Mail other than serials (which are assumed to be destined for the serials check-in division or sent directly to branch libraries) may be sorted onto open shelves or boxes on racks that should be placed nearby. If incoming materials will be unwrapped in this area, extra-large trash containers should be provided.

The letter mail, or first-class mail, generally is delivered separately from other mail, and may be sorted in another area at a 39-in. (0.991-m) high counter, which need not be deeper than 30 in. (0.762 m) from front to back. A lower counter here will cause back problems. It is a convenience if first-class mail can be sorted directly into post office–type bins, which have locking access doors, in a staff corridor. Ideally, the bins should be large enough to hold easily the largest commonly used envelope flat on its side. The access doors may be provided with a slot that permits staff to do minor sorting of their own, but if this is specified, ensure that the slot is wide enough for the widest envelope. Even though the door will certainly be wide enough, a slot cut into the door may be limited in size by the lock mecha-

nism or structural requirements, which suggests either that the bins should be 2 or 3 in. (50 or 76 mm) wider than the largest envelope or that the sorting slot should be above and separate from the access door. Some departments (for example, the public documents department) may require either a larger bin or several bins to accommodate their heavy mail receipts. It is suggested that the bins should all be of the same size, but that there should be perhaps 50 percent more bins than addressees. Labeling the bin doors in alphabetical order will aid staff in their sorting procedures. In addition to the bins, there should be a pass-through window to accommodate large items and mail slots for outgoing mail, perhaps designated for branch libraries, campus mail, the national postal system, and foreign mail.

Most mail rooms will have a franking machine, which can simply be placed on an extension of the first-class sorting counter. Provision should also be made for a large stapler, paper rolls, paper-tape machines, and generous storage for wrapping supplies, including boxes, mailing bags, stuffing material, and the like. An open area of floor space should be available for the receipt and processing of large shipments of equipment, furniture, supplies, or books returning from a bindery. Storage of first-aid and emergency supplies for coping with the early hours of a flood or other disaster may also be in the mail room. At least 250 ft² (23.226 m²) per mail room staff member should be provided, with 300 ft² (27.871 m²) preferred. If there is a supervisor, an office of 120 ft² (11.148 m²) should suffice. In a small library, of course, this operation can be scaled down dramatically.

The supply room should house the major supplies used in the everyday operations of the library. A small branch library may get by with a supply cabinet or closet, but a major library will need a substantial supply room unless this function is provided by the university or the process of managing supplies is distributed to each of the library departments. Local circumstance will suggest the amount of storage space needed, which generally can be fitted with commercial or industrial shelving, perhaps with one or two sections of bins for small items. If the room cannot be secured, then small items should be stored in a locked cabinet; otherwise, certain of these supplies will tend to disappear too rapidly. A Dutch door opening onto a staff corridor works well for serving the supply room. Some open floor area should be provided for bulk storage of such materials as pamphlet boxes or photocopy paper on pallets. A book truck or two will be handy for stocking shelves, and there should be a workstation for a clerk. It is suggested that 12 ft² (1.115 m²) per single-faced shelving or bin section plus at least 250 ft² (23.226 m²) for the supply clerk should be sufficient.

Surplus equipment, including an occasionally used lectern, a spare exhibit case, special holiday decorations, replaced typewriters and computers, extra desks, old catalog cabinets, extra carpet, damaged chairs, and similar items, almost always is a problem in a library, and at today's cost of construction, it probably should remain a problem to a large degree. Even so, some space should be allocated for such items. If the space is not in the supply room, it may be what architects sometimes call "sloip" (space left over in planning). It is almost certain that any space provided for such storage will be used, and it is suggested that the programmer should require a modest amount of general storage space that can be located nearly anywhere in the library, although elevator access is a convenience. Many library planners have erred in not providing adequately for this need. Without sufficient storage space, mechanical rooms, attics, hidden corridors, and under-floor crawl spaces usually fill the purpose, much to the displeasure of the fire marshal and maintenance personnel who from time to time will require the removal of stored materials. Storage in these areas is often against the law.

The loading dock itself should not be forgotten. Deliveries from all types of vehicles can be anticipated, including giant trucks, vans, and private cars, and from a branch library by a book truck or electric golf cart. It is suggested that provision be made in all but the smallest libraries for a dock area, ideally with a device that accommodates trucks with beds of different heights. For best results the loading dock should have a height of 48 in. (1.219 m), thereby accommodating most delivery trucks but not vans, for which a lower height is preferable. There should also be a lift or ramp to the ground to facilitate the movement of book trucks or hand dollies. The dock area should have some degree of protection from rain. A rain canopy or overhang high enough to avoid collision with the tops of delivery trucks can provide protection from rain and snow. In cold climates the dock area is often inside the building, which of course adds significantly to the cost. The library van or delivery cart may be garaged here in some cases. At some point, and it can just as well be in the program, the library will need to establish the size of delivery truck that can be accommodated. Where there is a campus receiving point, large trucks can make deliveries there, but transfer of the items to the library will need to be made, at added cost. Ideally, the length of the dock should permit receiving at least two trucks at the same time, other space permitting. The needs here clearly require local discussion.

Provision for removal of trash from the library is often a requirement for the area near the loading dock. This may involve a large trash receptacle that should be arranged so smaller containers can easily be dumped into it. A fumigation room, chamber, or blast freezer may be another feature ideally located near the loading dock so materials that are infested need not be brought inside the library proper until it is safe to do so.

8.2
Public Service Staff

Public service staff as treated here includes those responsible for library access and use privileges, reference and instructional services, circulation work, supervision of the stacks, paging from and reshelving of the collections, interlibrary borrowing and lending (interloans), and sometimes a staffed photocopy service. Most of this work is done from desks or service counters or in classrooms, all of which take space, as do those working at each desk and those who are served by it.

In a large library, private offices will be needed for the heads of the various public service departments or divisions, including circulation, reference, public documents, the rare book room, and perhaps interlibrary loan, newspapers and periodicals, microtexts, and the archives. A space of 125 to 150 ft² (11.613 to 13.935 m²) for each department head should suffice, with the rare book librarian sometimes being an exception if the library intends to court potential donors. Curators, reference librarians, and assistant heads often need an office as well, particularly as they may need to confer frequently with visitors. These offices can be somewhat smaller, but anything less than 100 ft² (9.290 m²) is likely to be inadequate, especially when equipped with a workstation and related equipment. (See fig. 8.4.)

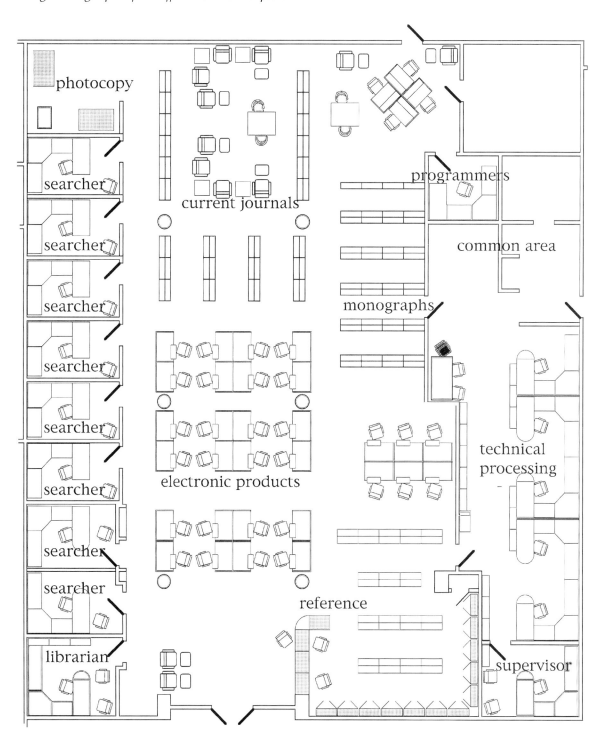

FIGURE 8.4   From a proposed alteration for the Genentech Corporation Library, one can see several different-sized offices. The smaller searcher office is approximately 106 ft² (9.848 m²), and an even smaller office would require the desk to face a wall. The librarian's office at the lower left corner is 140 ft² (13.006 m²). The larger size permits more work space, added visitor seating, and shelving on the wall opposite the desk. Note also the proposed arrangement for technical processing workstations. The major collections are held in a nearby space. The modular reference desk assumes that the uppermost modules are desk height.

For the other members of the staff, the space required will depend largely on the amount of equipment, but a rough estimate of 100 ft² (9.290 m²) per person on duty at one time is not extravagant. Indeed, unless the sharing of a desk is planned (which is not recommended except perhaps for student assistants), this allocation of space will be exceedingly difficult. Rather than determining space just for persons on duty, a far safer factor is 100 ft² for each regular staff member, including those who are not full-time. Even so, this allowance does not include space for book-sorting rooms, the ready-reference collection behind a desk, reserves or "hold" shelves behind a desk, or conference rooms or space for the public in front of the desk. It should be emphasized that demands for service, and consequently for a larger service staff, tend to increase year by year and certainly in the early years after remodeling or occupancy of a new wing or new building.

We stress one point that comes up several times below and relates to technical processing areas almost as often as the public services. Perhaps the most important aspect of book trucks at the programming stage is to ensure that adequate floor area is provided where quantities of trucks are to be stored. Areas where this may need to be considered include circulation discharge areas, sort rooms, technical processing areas, and perhaps the receiving room. At some book truck parking sites, especially in processing and sorting areas, sufficient space needs to be provided so that staff can see and access materials on each truck without moving the entire fleet.

The programmer should address the following typical subjects.

1. The specific needs of each office:

    At least four outlets? Is there a need for a phone?
    Full extent of expected computer use?
    Shelving?
    One side chair or several?
    Any work space beyond a normal desk?
    Typing stand or typing return on the desk?
    Special concern for acoustic isolation?
    Provision for book trucks?
    Sun control?
    Carpet?
    Tackboard? Chalkboard?
    Any task lighting or unusual lighting requirements?

    Any special concern about location beyond the obvious library organizational requirements, e.g., ease of access by library users?

2. Library privileges authorization desk or area:

    Number of staff? Specific staff requirements?
    Should it be visually closed during any periods when the library is open?
    Should it be accessible outside the portal control?
    Will there be a workstation here?
    Is there special provision for a cash register for fees? Will photo IDs be created or issued here?
    What kind of patron files are there?
    Should there be a public place for printed informational handouts?
    Should there be a display space for library regulations, a campus map, or other information?
    Does this area serve a dual function, such as collecting overdue fines? Is this where lockers, studies, or carrels are assigned?
    Is there need for a secure key cabinet?

3. Circulation or loan desk:

    How many service points should there be? How long is the anticipated queue? Is there need for special traffic control similar to that found in banks?
    Is the circulation system manual? If so, is it going to be automated at a future date, each service point equipped with a workstation? Is it self-service for some materials?
    Will there be nearby or remote (or both) self-service charging and discharging machines, and will these reduce over time the number of service points required?
    Should there be a bell, buzzer, or other signal to summon an assistant?
    If a book paging service is provided, is there to be some form of numerical annunciator to advise users when their book is found or question answered? If yes, how many numbers? Where should the numbers be seen? In any remote locations, such as the reference room or other reading areas?
    Will there be typing, discharging, cash handling, creation of ID cards perhaps with

a photograph, or other activities at the loan desk?

Is there to be a public address system?

Is there need for one or more book returns? If yes, is there a requirement for special features? What is the maximum size of book the return(s) should accommodate? What quantity must be accommodated in the receptacle?

Is there shelving nearby for reserved materials? For equipment to be signed out? For "hold" or "will-call" books being paged from the stacks or auxiliary collections? If so, how much shelving is required?

Are overdue notices prepared here? Computer generated?

Will books being returned to the shelves be sorted here?

4. Behind the circulation or loan desk:

How many staff? Need for computer workstations? Printers? File tubs? What are the requirements for the workstations?

Is the circulation department responsible for closing the library? Should there be a control or annunciator panel for various security alarms and lighting systems?

Should the outside book return deliver books to this area or to a sort room? Where are the books discharged?

Is there need to store extra books in bins?

Are there to be staff lockers? If so, how many? What size? What kind of lock is preferred? Should there be a coatrack? Is there need for a sink?

Is there need for a conference/training room?

Are other functions, such as bindery preparations; minor repairs of damaged books; culling for delivery to a conservation unit; or the attachment of identification marks, spine labels, bar coding, or book pockets, to be provided for here?

What is the maximum number of book trucks likely to be parked in the area?

Is some form of office partition system required?

5. Course reserves:

How many staff, including student assistants? What are their specific requirements? Might this function be consolidated with another function?

Is a rest break area required?

Are electronic reserves anticipated? Scanning stations? Copyright/royalty coordinator?

Shelving for the reserve collections? What is the security required for these materials?

Lockers? Photocopy machines? Preparation area for reserve materials? Special supplies?

Service desk? How many stations?

Will media reserves be handled here? Preview room for media reserves?

Will a catalog of reserved materials be nearby? If yes, in what form and how many stations?

6. Building or stack entrance portal control:

Is this to be part of the circulation desk function or a separate booth?

Is there to be more than one control point? How many lanes in and out? The maximum number of staff here?

Are there to be separate "in" and "out" controls, with one entry being by magnetic or bar coded card? Will identification be required for those entering the library?

What kind of control system is in use or anticipated? How will staff enter the controlled area?

Should there be options for the location of the point of control or the method of control?

Is the control point to include other functions, such as building security (e.g., monitoring video surveillance), charging out books, holding items for patrons, or providing general information?

If the control point is in a lobby, should there be special consideration for extra lighting or protection from drafts? Should there be a heater?

Should there be a computer terminal? Phone? Intercom? Emergency signal?

7. Stack sorting rooms or areas:

Are staff workstations needed? If so, how many?

Is the stack supervisor responsible for stack security? Should there be a door alarm annunciator panel here?

Is there need for a secure key cabinet?

How much shelving is needed? Will sorting be by floor? Is there book material to be returned to a locked stack area, and should this be under lock and key?

What is the maximum number of book trucks anticipated in this area? How many book trucks are to be provided in the project?

Are there to be lockers for staff? Coatracks?

Is there need for a tackboard or chalkboard?

How is the information required to page a book handled: hand carried, telephone, terminal, vacuum tube, radio?

8. Reference and information desk:

How many service points are there to be at peak times? Will an information desk be separate from reference service?

Is this to be a desk, counter, or both? Where handicapped-access standards are applied, some of any service desk must be at table or desk height.

How many computer workstations are required? How many printers? Should each workstation have a monitor for patrons to watch as searches are conducted?

Are special features required in the desk or counter, such as: Provision for handouts, and how many of what sizes? A phone placed off the top surface? Intercom? Catalog trays? A glass-covered display in the counter surface for a campus map, building plan, or arrangement of the collections in the reference room? Typing?

Is there a ready-reference collection? If so, how much shelving is required? Are a few of the volumes oversized?

What special considerations should be made in regard to the location of the desk besides the obvious? In sight of circulation or documents?

Is public access to some of the reference collections controlled? If so, how?

Should there be chairs or stools for the patrons? Is this where a lengthy computer search would occur? Is space needed for the librarian to map out a search strategy with the patron?

Are there to be nearby card catalog cabinets, CD-ROM equipment, or computer terminals for public searching of databases so as to facilitate library staff assistance where required? If so, how many? Or a nearby classroom or in-structional area, equipped for full use of computers?

9. Reference staff office area:

How many staff members are to be provided for (both professional and assistants)? Are the librarians to have private offices?

Are collection curators and their support staff also to be housed here?

Is this area to be accessible to the library user? If so, during all hours of operation?

What are the specific requirements for shelving, computer workstations, printers, photocopy and fax machines, book trucks, office landscape systems, and the like?

Would a separate workstation room with a small desk and two chairs be useful for conducting interviews with patrons and online database searching, or will this be conducted in the librarians' offices?

10. Interlibrary loan and borrowing:

How many staff members are there? What are their specific requirements?

Is there need for workstations? Fax? Ariel™ station? Scanner?

Are there likely to be cash transactions?

Are photocopies made here?

Is there need for a service counter? Book trucks? Special files?

Are incoming books and other materials held here or elsewhere for the patron?

11. Current journals and newspapers:

How many staff members are to be provided for? What are their specific needs? Book trucks?

Are materials to be paged? Is there need for an annunciator? Intercom? Can a patron charge out a journal issue?

Is there to be a public catalog terminal? How is the serials record or file handled? Is CD-ROM equipment needed?

Is there to be a desk or counter? Will it have a place to return journals?

Is there to be a photocopy machine nearby? How many?

Does bindery preparation occur here? Journal check-in?

Is there a "morgue"? Some series kept on microtext?

Does the library provide any form of clipping service?

Is there need for any special display?

Newspapers are dirty; is a sink required in this area?

12. Microtext areas:

How many staff are to be provided for? What are their specific needs? Computer workstations?

Is there to be a service desk or counter? What is the need for the special storage of supplies? Is there need for a bell or other device to summon an assistant?

How are the microtexts controlled? Are they charged out? Are they paged from a closed stack? Is an annunciator panel or intercom needed? How should the microtexts be returned after use? (Alternatively, are some or all of the microtexts and readers distributed throughout the general collections?)

Is there a card catalog? OPAC terminal? A handy reference book collection?

Is there special equipment for cleaning films, making microtext or full-size copies, or maintaining the microtext readers?

Is there need for the storage of portable readers that may be signed out?

Will this be the area that maintains the central optical disk equipment?

Are microtexts produced here? If yes, what kind and how many camera stations, scanning stations, reviewing stations, developing stations, and the like are required? Is a darkroom required? Special equipment for chemical and film storage and handling? Preparation area for materials being microfilmed? Shelving for a backlog? Provision for conversion to high-speed digital scanning stations?

13. Map room:

How many staff members are there? What are their specific requirements?

Are there special requirements for processing of maps in a staff area, such as large sorting bins, or an extra-large table?

Is there to be a service desk or counter? If so, should it have an extra-large surface for viewing maps? Need for a light table?

How are the maps controlled? Are they charged out? Is there a special place to return maps?

Is a card catalog nearby? If so, how many cabinets or drawers? Or will a public terminal be required?

Is there need for storage of special supplies, such as acid-free map folders?

Is encapsulation of brittle maps done here?

14. Media areas:

How many staff? What are their specific requirements? Ability to darken office space?

Special security requirements? Special equipment for cleaning media? Will catalogers use this area to catalog media?

Will service be centralized, or will media be handed out or provided for users to be viewed at stand-alone stations?

Is a language laboratory part of this function? Media classroom(s)? Computer cluster(s)? Interactive video? Do any of these have special staffing requirements?

What shelving or other accommodation for the collections is required? Is special environmental control required?

Is there a special catalog of media materials? If yes, how many computer workstations or cabinets?

Is there a ready-reference collection? If yes, how large?

What acoustic, communication signals, and light control requirements are there?

Is there need for classroom equipment storage, service, and distribution? Is there need for a special service counter for equipment?

Is there a studio of any kind for the production of media or television or radio? If yes, what are the requirements?

Service desks and counters are of three basic types, and some details will be provided here, though many of the specifics are developed during contract document preparation (covered in Chapter 14). These types are:

1. Circulation or charging desks from which books are borrowed for use within or outside the library and to which they are later returned. Such desks are also called delivery desks. (*Desk* is the common term, though

they are most often counters and almost never furniture similar to an office desk.)

2. Reference desks, sometimes called information or inquiry desks, from which readers are helped in the use of library collections. A library access privileges desk might be considered in this category.
3. Control or supervisory or oversight desks for reading areas or entrances and exits.

These service points can be counters or desks and, though the two terms are here used almost interchangeably, the choice of a desk or a taller and longer counter is usually based on both the local custom or philosophy of public service and the volume of traffic. Many librarians believe the desk is less formal, more approachable, even more flexible, and especially favored for information/reference service points. The desk with a chair in front brings the staff and customer to the same convenient level for conversation if the inquirer will take the time to sit down, and a desk "return" or side table(s) can provide for needed work space. (Further, where full access for handicapped persons is a requirement, all service points must have at least some part of the transaction surface at desk or table height. This includes circulation desks where the Americans with Disabilities Act is satisfied.) Others believe the counter facilitates faster service, brings the staff person to the same height as a customer walking up to the counter, and provides more working space for needed computer equipment, books, phones, papers, and so on.

A combination is feasible, though awkward if only one service staff member is on duty. Service furniture formed as a "bifurcated doughnut" about 20 ft (6.096 m) in diameter is used at Brandon University Library, one-half being counter high and the other desk height. If several staff members work with questioners at the same time, those needing consultation of several minutes can sit down, and this lower segment is felt at Brandon to work best for networked computers.

Given that either can serve well, a great volume of anticipated traffic argues for a counter, and the variety of materials and equipment needed today for service in most college and research libraries strengthens the case for counters, with added desk-height stations as required by law. Some fine university libraries still use desks exclusively for some service areas, though the need there for one or more computer worksta-

tions, printers, and attendant cables and wires creates more of an unattractive jumble than does the usual counter.

The counters can properly be of many shapes and sizes. In small branches one desk or short counter serves for authorizing library use; handling general circulation, course reserves, and current periodicals; providing reference and quick information; receiving interlibrary loan requests; conducting computer searches; perhaps servicing a clipping or pamphlet file; and offering research advisory conferences. In college libraries these functions are divided between two or three locations, and in very large libraries there may reasonably be separate service points for each function because of the amount of traffic and the staff specialization at each service point or the distance between the above functions. Treatment in this volume assumes the separate service locations; all the same functions and theory of layout pertain and need consideration in small libraries. Each type will be discussed separately.

1. *Circulation desks.* The six basic essentials for a circulation desk or counter are:

a. Enough length for the staff to provide good service at the time of peak load and to work comfortably together. The area should accommodate simultaneous transactions, perhaps in each of several functions, such as borrowing, asking for a recall, or paying a fine. Beyond the space required to charge out a volume, the counter surface should allow a small amount of extra space for the borrower to place an armload of books or a purse while transacting business. As in a supermarket, one position might be designated for lending single volumes only, or, conversely, for lending more than, say, 10 at one time.

In most libraries, queues for checking out materials will occur. A library cannot afford to have staff always available to immediately handle peak loads. On the other hand, thefts and other abuses of the library are certain to occur if the readers do not have relatively prompt service. Programming of desks or counters for lending materials must therefore be sized to handle most transactions without delays of several minutes. Automated systems thus have a great advantage, and the counter in these cases may be one-quarter or even one-third shorter than with a manual system. Self-service circulation stations are becoming more common and can diminish the problem of queues at the circulation desk, particularly for "standard" transactions; a growing number of libraries are incorporating this technology into their circulation services. However, it is predicted that for most major libraries, staffed circulation stations will be needed well into the future to handle "nonstandard" transactions, patrons who are challenged by new technology, and other factors.

Remember that all peak use will result in a multitude of library users waiting to have books charged out and to use all other services of that desk area. Especially for undergraduate libraries, careful thought needs to be given to the number of people who may be assembled in front of the desk or counter and the beneficial effect of self-service circulation.

Any circulation process will raise complaints and unusual problems that need attention by a supervisor or other senior staff member. The problems may involve materials kept beyond the due date, a request to excuse a penalty fine, harassment by another library user, a rude staff member, a library regulation that seems absurd to the complainer, a self-charge station that will not read the book bar code, and so on. Because these problems will commonly come right to the service desk, it is usually desirable to provide a semiprivate area, perhaps at one end of the circulation counter, removed from the bustle of normal services, to permit discussion with the person complaining.

b. A place where the reader may return books and other materials after use. If the lending desk is a busy one, the book-return area should be separated from the charge-out area to prevent unnecessary crossing of traffic lines. In some cases several return points may be needed, with perhaps one for general circulation books, another for reserve books, and possibly a third for some other category, such as returned headphones, microfiche, journals, and the like. The space should be large enough so that confusion will not result, but not so large that the books will be ignored until they pile up, become unsightly, and give the impression of poor housekeeping. A large pile of returned books within sight of the public will result in their challenging the accuracy of the library's records, particularly when the book has not been discharged and could easily be picked up by another reader.

The returned materials can be placed on top of the desk, handed to staff, placed in a "book drop" into a depressible-floored bin, or sent down a chute to a secure area. In most libraries

with a high volume of transactions, a fairly secure book-return chute is a preferred solution and, in smaller libraries, a protected drop is desirable. In some cases, the concern for conservation will suggest that all materials be returned to an attendant in order to avoid the possibility of damage from a book-return drop, especially during the crush at the end of college semesters.

Return slots, slides, and boxes should be carefully designed to prevent damage to the books by rapid movement, too great a fall, and one volume knifing another. Another book-return slide or box can be placed next to a slot in an outside wall for use after library hours. Because any slot into the building may be an invitation to vandalism, special precautions should be considered, including placing this unit in a separate fire-rated room. Any outside receptacle as well as outside return slots into the building should be under an overhang, in an open vestibule, or otherwise protected from foul weather, and any outside box should be of light color because dark colors in very hot weather will make the box very hot.

Harvard's Lamont Library had a book-return bin equipped with an electric eye. When the eye sensed a book, a motor started and dropped the false bottom just far enough so that the next volume would not fall too far but would not jam into the preceding ones. This bin was taken out decades ago. Another novel return is found at the Delft Technological Institute in Holland, where a spiral slide delivers books to a discharge room in a lower floor. The University of Minnesota years ago had a similar system with a straight chute leading down to a sorting table, though the books backed up all the way to conveyors above when no staff was at work on long weekends. Systems of rollers to accomplish the same thing have been used in a number of libraries, but these often are noisy and, in some cases, tend to catch small pamphlets. When the return slot is designed to coordinate with a depressible book bin, care should be taken to ensure that the slot is high enough to feed above the edge of the bin. The design of the slot also should prevent the surreptitious removal of books by a library patron. Several libraries have adopted a contrived return delivery system only to replace it with a simpler process after experiencing years of malfunctioning, the library at California State University, Long Beach, being an example.

c. A place for the temporary storage of books returned from use. This may require considerable open space for trucks onto which returned material is sorted or a bank of shelves to handle maximum loads in the same process. This feature may be near the loan desk or beside a separate discharging and sorting area. In any online circulation system, wands or reading devices on stands are required for discharging in this area, as well as a workstation for resolving problems or placing a temporary lending "hold" if materials are returned damaged. Sort and reshelving operations in a very large library may also require distribution centers or shelving on each major stack level, and these may be unlocked rooms or alcoves.

d. A place in the desk or adjacent to it for the equipment in constant use and for circulation records. The nature of this requirement will depend upon the specifics of the circulation system, but where it is currently manual, thought should be given to the possible future needs of an automated system. This may involve little more than the provision of a sectional counter that can easily be altered to accept the necessary terminals or other equipment, plus the provision of access to power and signal services. Specific requirements will need to be developed with representatives of the system's manufacturer, though electricity is certain to be required. Remember that periodic modification and alterations can be expected, perhaps every few years, as operational systems and workload change.

e. Working space adjacent or conveniently close to the desk for staff performing record work and, in a large library, for an office for the unit head and possibly an assistant or two. Special space for computer equipment is generally no longer a requirement other than to ensure that there is sufficient accommodation for terminals and their associated equipment; when a library expects to have a minicomputer, a separate large, office-sized space (say, 200 ft^2 or 18.581 m^2) should suffice. (Most people who have minicomputers in the library, as opposed to microcomputers or PCs, feel that they need extra security—the minicomputer may be supporting the library bibliographic database and the online circulation system—because of their fundamental operation with perhaps only daily backup. A library that does not feel the need for security certainly could reject this statement of requirement.) Raised floors and special air conditioning are seldom required for a library computer, although it is urged that the planner review specific requirements with a

representative of the supplier. (If there are to be impact printers, here or elsewhere, a separate space with acoustic isolation should be provided.) Where the current records system is manual, future addition of an automated system will more than likely save some net amount of space. This clearly is an area where thought should be given to the future growth of power and signal services.

f. If the desk is to serve reserved books, adequate shelving for them and extra staff work space should be provided as close by as possible. (See fig. 8.5.) This is covered in Section 7.6.

Library equipment firms have available stock units of various sizes and designs for circulation desks and counters that can be combined to suit the customer. They are expensive, but are usually well made and designed for the average library by experts who understand library needs. Among other things, they may include space sunk in the surface to house circulation-card file trays or a computer with bar code scanner, as well as cubbyholes, drawers, shelves, book returns, locked cabinets, and so forth. It is often possible to have a desk specially designed to the librarian's specifications and custom-built by the library-equipment house. Sometimes a local cabinetmaker can build one to specifications at a lower price. A good cabinetmaker should be able to build a suitable desk successfully. However, the librarian should keep in mind that for desks with specialized and unique designs, future adjustments or alterations often are more difficult.

Special care should be taken in the design. Toe space at the bottom, both in front of the desk and behind it, will make its use more comfortable for the readers and staff members who work at the desk while standing. A staff member who is expected to sit at least part of the time should be provided with a kneehole at least 2-ft (0.610-m) wide at the proper spot, and if the "desk" is counter height, a built-in footrest should be provided, although it may be wise to make it adjustable.

Five other points in the design should be considered: the length, the shape, the width, the height, and the built-in flexibility. As already noted, the counter should not be so long that staff members must walk great distances, but it should be long enough for peak use. Some counters, particularly in large university libraries, have been too long.

Many counters turn one or two corners of 45° or 90°, making them the shape of an L or two or

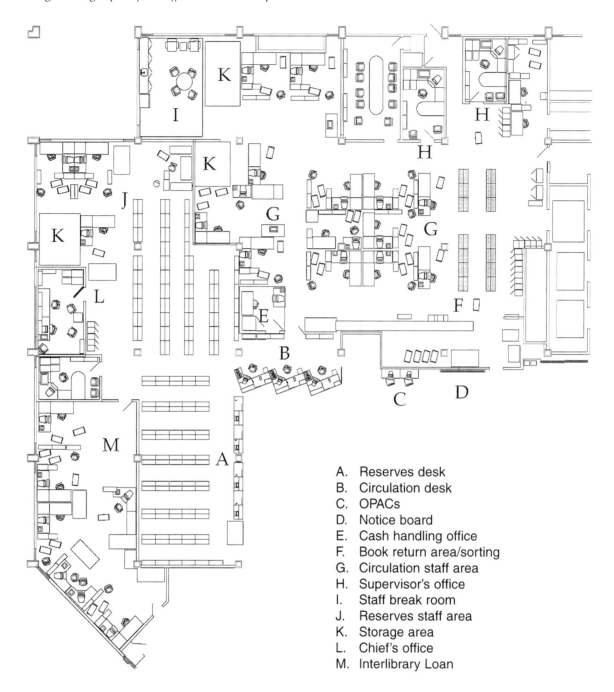

A. Reserves desk
B. Circulation desk
C. OPACs
D. Notice board
E. Cash handling office
F. Book return area/sorting
G. Circulation staff area
H. Supervisor's office
I. Staff break room
J. Reserves staff area
K. Storage area
L. Chief's office
M. Interlibrary Loan

FIGURE 8.5   From a proposed remodeling of the entry level for the California State University, Sacramento, main library. In this scheme, the reserve desk and circulation desk (A and B) have been juxtaposed (from an existing arrangement where they are totally separate). The reserve staff area has a scanning station (to the right of the J); as the reserve function moves toward digital access, its shelving need will diminish. In the future, it can be anticipated that there will be growing interest in fully combining these service desks.

three sides of an octagon, or may be curved to form part of a circle or a flat-bottom U. The curve presents a greater length to the reader than to the staff. A curved desk costs more than a straight one of the same length; file drawers placed side by side can only be used one at a time; and the staff, being on the shorter side of the curve, may not have the necessary space. On the other hand, with only one or two staff members on duty at a time, the curved desk may be useful and in some cases have an advantage aesthetically.

If the counter is more than one bay long and in the column line of a modular library, the column in it may prove inconvenient by cutting off the view between readers and staff. It is almost never good to have a column in the middle of the counter, or the middle of the staff area, or in the midst of the service area in front. To make the best of a poor situation, a column in the center of the desk may make a division between charging and return. Given a counter that bends, the non-lending side of the desk beyond the corner may make possible, by careful planning, a satisfactory, easily controlled, narrow lane leading to the bookstack or other restricted areas.

A desk can be monolithic or made up of modules of a uniform size. Modules of, say, 3 ft or 0.914 m offer the flexibility of reshaping the counter and thus facilitating rather than inhibiting beneficial rearrangement. Power and signal (phone, computer, public address system, or annunciator control panel, for example) may limit the extent of real flexibility. Having a countertop that is equally modularized is important in this regard. Such modular construction will add slightly to the cost as each module side or upright support must be duplicated, whereas they can be shared in monolithic construction. It may also be desirable to require finished sides so that each module could become an end of the counter in the future.

The width of the top of the desk can be a controversial matter. If it is too far from front to back, the staff member and reader are too far apart and passing books back and forth may seem awkward. A few desks are as much as 3 ft (0.914 m) wide, which may be desirable in a map room, and many are 2 ft 6 in. (0.762 m) or more. The wider they are, the greater the storage space on top and below, although if the shelves are too deep, the shelved books are likely to be piled up like cordwood two or more deep and be inconvenient to remove. A width of 22 to 24 in. (0.559

to 0.610 m) is generally enough, although if a computer workstation or two are to be incorporated within this desk, the depth requirement of the equipment, which may be as much as 24 to 30 in. (0.610 to 0.762 m) can be a controlling factor, depending on the design of the desk. Also, some cash registers can be fairly deep; where they are to be installed in the service counter, their depth will control.

The standard height for desks or counters—once as low as 33 or 36 in. (0.838 to 0.914 m), today considered too low—has been 39 in. (0.991 m), and 40 to 42 in. (1.016 to 1.067 m) is not uncommon. The latter is a good height, particularly where the typical height of the user is average or above. In countries where the average height of readers is less than that in the United States, 39 in. (0.991 m) may be enough. But keep in mind that if the staff member behind the desk is to sit much of the time, a high stool will be necessary for comfort, and the sitting height of the stool should bring the attendant's eye level to approximately that of the reader for the comfort of each. The stool, if it is to be used for long hours, should have a back, and a footrest should be built into the knee space of the counter so that the seated posture can simulate that of a normal chair. Accommodation of staff and users in wheelchairs will mandate some portion of the counter at approximately desk height, or 30 in. (0.762 m). Most new service desks seen in the United States now have both counter- and desk-height stations for this reason.

One other warning about circulation desks, or any desk for that matter, where the reader may have to stand for a few minutes or more. These desks are often paneled for the sake of appearance. Panels are expensive and apt to be damaged and hard to repair. One solution is the use of half rounds on the front of the desk (see fig. 8.6), where the damaged portion can easily be removed and replaced by a new one. Projection of the top beyond the paneled surface an inch or so can also help protect it from damage caused by belt buckles, purses, and the like. Of course, a more durable material could be substituted to solve the problem.

2. Reference, information, inquiry, and reader's advisory desks. The reference assistance function may include brief directional guidance, simple informational help, in-depth reference/research work, computer-aided database informational searches (sometimes of a very time-consuming

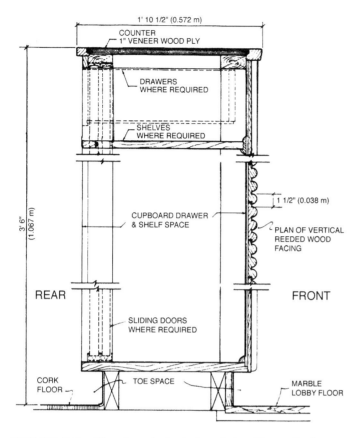

FIGURE 8.6 Charging desk designed for Harvard's Lamont Library uses half rounds instead of panels. Note top projecting beyond vertical surface and toe space on each side, both important features. This circulation counter is higher and narrower than many, but it has proved adequate.

nature), and extensive term paper or dissertation advisory conferences. In a classroom or on tour, groups may be given course assignment lectures or explanations or more extensive forms of group bibliographic instruction. The reference staff may also need to oversee the reference and bibliographical collections; UCLA's Research Library uses an electronic book-sensing portal gate (similar to those commonly used at the building exit) as a control device so books do not leave the defined reference room area.

The reference or information desk will be serviced at times by one staff member, sometimes in large libraries by as many as three or four, and at times it will be closed. Consequently, the counter or desk needs space for the maximum staff, and yet must be convenient when one person is alone to handle in-person queries, take notes, hand out leaflets, answer telephone ques-

tions, search on the terminal, and check the desk collection of ready-reference volumes. The desk needs to be inviting, uncluttered, easy to find, near reference staff offices, and not so monumental as to be intimidating. This is not a simple design task. Size and design will, of course, be determined largely by the way the space is to be used and the amount of use it will have.

Very large libraries may have an inquiry desk in an entrance lobby to enable the reader who is overwhelmed by the magnitude of the building to get started in the right direction. At any reference or inquiry desk immediately adjacent to the entrance or elsewhere, there should be a limited number of what might be called ready-reference books and a computer workstation that will allow a good many readers to obtain the answers to their questions without going farther into the library. This is also a suitable place for the display and perhaps the distribution of library publications of one kind or another.

The primary reference desk will ordinarily have in or adjacent to it a number of quick-reference books, which are those few most heavily and constantly used by the staff. This desk should, of course, be placed close to the main reference and bibliography collections and also to the public catalog, which may be used by reference librarians as much as the reference books. Access to a computer-based catalog (OPAC), provided it is relatively complete, will eliminate the need to be close to the catalog, except for staff assistance for the OPAC catalog user at a terminal cluster. Ideally, the desk should be clearly visible to the patron from the entrance lobby as well.

As with the circulation desk, the question of size comes up. The reference desk need never be as long as the circulation desk. Many librarians like to have a regular office desk, 30 in. (0.762 m) in height, with a chair adjacent for the reader to sit down and talk over problems with the librarian. This arrangement can be very satisfactory, particularly if what has come to be known as readers' advisory service is given, and, as noted above, some portion of the counter will need to be this height for accommodation of handicapped persons. With the introduction of automated bibliographic services with a huge array of networked data available at workstations, the sit-down desk makes sense in some situations. To facilitate ease of typing on a terminal keyboard, a separate typing-height surface or articulated keyboard holder at 27 or 28 in. (0.686 or 0.711 m) may be provided.

The desk-height reference counter produces some problems, however. The average librarian can serve satisfactorily twice as many readers if the reader is standing. Also, as mentioned above, both persons will find it undesirable for the reader to stand while the librarian is sitting down, a factor that leads some to feel that this configuration may inhibit certain readers from asking questions. On this account it is suggested that in most cases, particularly in large libraries, much of the reference desk should be a counter rather than a desk, and that, for staff member and patron to look over a book together, it be between 39 in. (0.991 m) and 42 in. (1.067 m) high with seating as described earlier. Even a short librarian with a stool adjusted to proper height can sit comfortably with eye level approximately that of the reader. Everyone concerned will be happier, and more business will be transacted.

If it is the policy of the library to have the attendants do a great deal of reference work for the readers, the staff must, of course, be larger than would otherwise be the case. Office space, or at least desk space, in addition to and behind the reference counter should generally be provided where the librarian can work on difficult problems, answer reference letters, and consult with inquirers who can then sit down and be dealt with on a basis different from that at what might be called the "front" desk. In many libraries, these librarians are also subject experts carrying responsibility for collection development in one or more fields; this arrangement will require somewhat larger offices than those just for reference staff because of the specific publication lists, catalogs, and directories that will be required. And in all cases, heavy reliance on networked databases—for editorial work, developing library home sites for the World Wide Web, conducting correspondence with publishers or agents, preparing lectures, and so on—will entail workstations with printers and in some cases scanners and other equipment.

The spatial relationship of the reference desk and these offices for the reference librarians deserves thought. Several universities have solved this effectively, the Wilson Library of the University of Minnesota being one. The need for, size, and location of these offices are a matter for local decision, but they do have a good deal to do with the area required for the reference staff and

incidentally with the cost of the service. Almost any large library should provide one group office and sometimes a number of individual offices for reference workers, and a very large library may use 1,000 ft² (92.903 m²) or more for this purpose.

3. *Control desks.* Control desks to supervise, oversee, or maintain discipline or to prevent unauthorized removal of books are not a recent innovation. In earlier days in academic libraries, each reading room had a control desk or at least a desk from which supervision was provided and from which, if need be, both circulation and reference service might be given. Reading-area supervision has now fairly universally been given up, except, of course, for the proctored reading of especially rare and fragile materials. With the wide use of carrels and the reduction in use of huge reading tables, the need for supervision has been reduced or altered in nature. Breaking public space into different, smaller units eases one type of problem, though it can lead at times to other disciplinary concerns.

In many academic libraries the only real control point is at the entrance, or perhaps it is better to say the exit lobby or lobbies. There, specially designed desks should be provided. A key decision is whether the library is to control or monitor both entering and exiting. If overseeing both is required by the chosen local operating routines, it is feasible to combine those operations if the traffic is sparse, especially because heavy traffic in the two directions usually comes at different times. Yet, during peak traffic conditions, it may be necessary to have separate controls from different desks. If there is any question whether one control can suffice, it is best to program separate in and out desks even if one serves as a spare and is seldom used.

Unless there are exceptional local traffic patterns, there should be a minimum of one entrance control lane (or two, if one is card-activated), if the entrance is where the library chooses to locate this control function. If there is more than one exit control desk in the same lobby, lanes, defined either by cords or dividing lines of one kind or another, can lead past the desks to the exit door or doors. These aisles should be sufficiently wide to accommodate a wheelchair or motorized carts, or they should have a bypass route.

If the traffic load is so great that more than one person has to be assigned to the control task at one time, it may be better to have two or even up to four or five separate desks in a very large library, rather than one long desk with a number of attendants working at it. There will be less chance for confusion. The introduction of electronic book security systems and automated lending greatly speeds up the checkout process and, where such systems are to be used, the number of exit control portal positions can be reduced.

Where electronic book detection systems are specified, there may be a need for a gate or turnstile, both of which have their problems, but they do provide regulated traffic control, at least for the honest. (Note that turnstiles are forbidden by fire laws in some states.) Although some would argue that such devices should be avoided because they are perceived as offensive, many students welcome them because the check is impersonal compared to a personal staff check of bags and cases. Because of the belief that the collections are thereby under better supervision, the casual removal of library materials is reduced; thus, the desired books are more likely to be found. (The Leyburn Library of Washington and Lee University has no exit monitoring or detection system, given its strong century-old honor code.)

There is increasing experience with book-detection systems where no gates or turnstiles are installed; security in this case involves an audible alarm combined with staff in close proximity. The UCLA Powell Undergraduate Library, the Alderman Library of the University of Virginia, and Brigham Young University's Lee Library are examples of libraries with significant traffic that use book detection, but no gates or turnstiles. In these examples, there is a staffed desk in the area, but inspections are only done when an alarm goes off.

As with circulation desks, the problem of the preferable length, depth, and height comes up. The desk itself typically is counter height, perhaps with a raised floor so that the attendant may be seated in a normal chair. The length and depth of the counter should accommodate a pile of books, an open briefcase, and a purse at the same time, and in general be narrow enough so the desk attendant does not have to reach to see all materials in any container brought for inspection. (See fig. 8.7.) This aids the inspection of briefcases, backpacks, and the like where routine inspections are planned. A further feature that

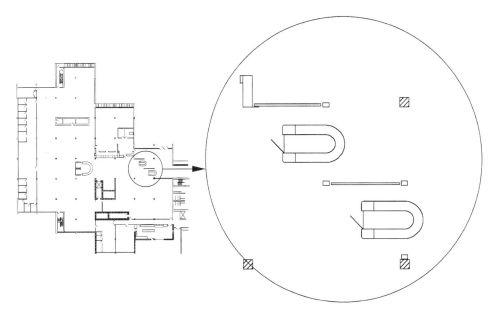

FIGURE 8.7 Stanford University's Green Library portal booth, with each booth used for monitoring both entrances and exits. Although the portal area has gone through one major design change, the original two-level portal booth remains in use today. The floor of the booth is raised so the seated portal monitor is at eye level with a standing patron. The small area of the counter to either side of the booth gate is at desk height for aiding the inspection of backpacks, shopping bags, and the like.

Today, this library does not employ a book-detection system. However, card key access (via scanning university identification cards) is in place, using an electrically controlled turnstile. (Courtesy of Stanford University Libraries)

aids inspection of containers is to set the approached section of the counter lower than the rest, where the top of a shopping bag or other container can be looked into without the attendant having to stand up.

Other features at the control portal, both exit and entrance, may include storage for first-aid equipment, a panic alert button, television monitors if television surveillance is part of the library security system, a phone or an intercom, supplementary task lighting, a heater in some climates, and perhaps an inset in the countertop covered with glass for schedules, campus maps, or other information. The library needs to consider carefully whether a computer terminal should be placed at these desks, since this equipment may or may not be needed for the function and its presence may create distractions and prompt unwanted requests.

The other public service areas, including government documents, music, art, and branch libraries in general, should prompt similar questions and design issues to be addressed by the programmer. Many of the topics are discussed in other parts of this book; the balance will require local consideration.

8.3
Processing Staff

Areas frequently considered as library technical processing (sometimes called "behind-the-scenes work") include order and acquisition work of various kinds, the handling of gifts and exchanges, descriptive and subject cataloging, classification, work with serials and documents, preparation for the shelves and for the bindery, conservation or preservation work, often automation or systems design and maintenance, and the clerical support that goes with these activities. Processing staff in some libraries include shipping and receiving, which were dealt with earlier.

For all these groups that can be lumped under the heading "processing," 100 ft^2 (9.290 m^2) per person as an absolute minimum can properly be provided for a work desk, equipment, shelves for material in process, and a book truck, plus another 25 ft^2 (2.323 m^2) for the head of each section with as many as five to ten persons. In a research library, 125 ft^2 (11.613 m^2) rather than 100 should be the absolute minimum. If 150 ft^2

(13.935 m^2) instead of 100 or 125 ft^2 can be made available, there will be that much more margin if the staff increases in size more than programmed, if special projects are funded, or if there are unanticipated receipts or backlogs. Undue congestion prevents or at least hampers effective work while flexibility for future adjustments is all but lost. To these figures should be added the space required for significant other elements, particularly large worktables for sorting receipts or repairing books, shelving for bibliographic volumes, and space for terminals, photocopy machines, or other specialized equipment. Space for staff lockers and coatracks, where they are appropriate, should not be forgotten. With all elements included, the space required will be on the order of 175 ft^2 (16.258 m^2) per staff member.

Movable office partition systems can save space by using more economically vertical space and wall-mounted equipment. However, caution is urged in this regard. Crowding staff to the maximum degree should be a last resort, not a planned condition for a new facility. The cost of landscaped maximum space use will include some or all of the following: loss of flexibility, frequent acoustic problems, a more mazelike layout of the quarters, more difficult air circulation, and difficult lighting conditions. This is not to say that landscaped panel systems are bad, but rather to urge that they be used to supplement more traditional office arrangements in terms of the program statement.

Because of changes in processing practice, a degree of flexibility, discussed in Chapter 5, should be a requirement. This suggests large, open work areas where the allocation of space to different functions can be easily adjusted or assigned to a public service function in the event the need for technical processing space diminishes. However, even with complete flexibility, staff often resist an open office pool with exposed rows of desks. If nothing is done to break up open areas, processing staff are likely to use books to create partitions and their own sense of place. To avoid this, the planner should arrange to separate workstations with shelving, movable panels, and other equipment, while striving to provide a cheerful, uncluttered work area. This is no simple task, as the concepts of semiprivacy and pleasant outlook tend to fight against each other.

For any processing staff of five to ten or more, at least one office should always be available where the unit manager can talk without interruption with a subordinate. This requirement refers to the department as a whole, but not necessarily to individual sections. In a large processing area a conference room usually will be heavily used. Also, mini-conference rooms for perhaps four people may serve as quiet areas for supervisory consultations, training sessions, committee work, and the like.

Part-time student assistants are used by most academic libraries on a large scale in both public service and processing departments. They may require locker space for wraps and at least a desk drawer in addition to work space. The total amount of floor area that should be allotted to them is difficult to determine, and the decision should be based on local conditions. It is suggested that not less than 50 ft² (4.645 m²) should suffice for each assistant who can be expected to be on duty at one time.

The general relationships of major functions in the library are discussed in Section 5.3.3, yet a few points are added here. Because the technical processing areas are staff-intensive, their functional relationships to each other and to the mail room or receiving area are a very important matter deserving careful attention. And because of the influence of computer technologies at the end of the twentieth century, work-flow organization and indeed the size and location of these operations are changing quite dramatically over conditions even one or two decades ago. As a result, we treat the processing staff space as of the late 1990s—often a picture in transition—and intersperse comments about the direction and nature of further change.

However, before turning to space needs of individual processing units, we comment on two potential strong influences for change: about the physical area and character of a computer-reliant work space, and about the influence of potential outsourcing on the location and size of the processing function.

> The application of computer technologies has influenced many technical processing units since the mid-1960s. The changes continue, facilitated by computer workstation capacities and having readily available online authority files, classification guides and manuals, standards, local and distant OPACs, the shelflist, and a range of full-text reference sources. The implementation of automation will increase the space per staff member, rather than reduce it; any savings gained from automation will only accrue from a somewhat reduced staff, and caution is advised where such a staff reduction is proposed as a space-saving measure. (Some work might even be done at home computers.) Considerable decentralization of processing steps may occur to branch libraries. In short, technology continues to change the way in which libraries operate. Each institution must know its present conditions and needs and project the future spatial requirements—always with a healthy dose of technological skepticism and financial reality.

Many of the technical processing elements are or will be sharply affected by a degree of "outsourcing," defined as contracting with a commercial firm for a specific set of services performed off-site. This academic and research library management option has existed and been used throughout this century for binding, journal indexing, microfilming, and, recently, for selection of scholarly titles to be acquired within a specific profile of collection desiderata. In the past few decades commercial processing services have increasingly been offered. These additional vendor service options include acquisitioning, online financial transactions, full cataloging, conversion of card catalog data to digital form, book conservation treatments, and shelf preparation (finishing, or end processing) with electronic security targets, classification labels, circulation forms or pockets, and ownership marks.

There are, of course, trade-offs in such outsourcing—savings of space, expense of hiring and training of staff, staff salaries and benefits, and, on the other side of the scale, some lack of control, limited options, contractual costs, issues of material security, concerns of timeliness, and so forth. The point here is not to advocate one modus operandi or another, but merely to point out the obvious influence on technical processing space. Each institution must here also determine the direction it is going and, on that basis, project space needs into the future.

All academic and research libraries will retain much traditional technical processing work; in most of the world, the changes brought on by computer technologies will come slowly. Planners therefore must build toward the future on a full understanding of the traditional past and a grasp of current circumstances.

The functional relationship of most processing units is important to the public catalog (unless the card records are fully online in an OPAC) and the major bibliographies usually housed in the vicinity of the reference collection. These close relationships are essential for the efficient operation of processing staff. Most libraries try to place processing on the main floor, but others have provided highly satisfactory space on the floor above, such as at Indiana University. It is almost certain that compromise from the ideal arrangement for any single group will be required.

In contrast with this traditional pattern, use of linked computer files today enables significant changes. The close relationship of units may no longer be necessary; major investment here can free much of processing from the traditional relationship locations needed in the past. Indeed, with full retrospective conversion of card catalog data to computer files, much of the technical processing area could be located in a separate building.

When the central library building cannot comfortably be enlarged and the need for space for books and readers and public service staff grows to require all available space, and where the funds for capital construction or renovation make it feasible, and where there is an advanced degree of automation, the relocation of all the technical services functions to a distant building may be reasonable. Rutgers University, New York Public Library Research Libraries, and the University of British Columbia are examples of this condition (though British Columbia is planning on bringing its cataloging back into the main library), and location to a remote building is projected for the University of Southern California and Stanford University. Such relocation may bring with it easier mail delivery, much easier staff parking and public commuting connections, more efficient process layouts, less cramped staff quarters, and so forth. Each situation will need special study.

For most libraries, placement of processing at a distance is not justified; in any case, it should not be a goal of the planner to isolate these activities unless there are substantial reasons to do so. Furthermore, outsourcing may result in reduction in staff so that the remaining unit can fit

into a preferred location within the library, rather than being forced to a remote site. Note, however, that the concept of outsourcing, while being tried by a number of institutions in the late 1990s, remains to be proven, particularly the effect of vendors wishing to make more money once libraries get rid of a critical mass of expertise. This business could go in cycles, and a wise library will hedge its bets.

Another basic point can be made about physical relationships. Place the mail and shipping room close to and on the same level as the acquisition, serials, and other departments with large receipts or shipments; this will be a major convenience. If other considerations make it preferable to place them on different floors, a service elevator should be at hand, but do not upset more important relationships to accomplish this proximity. Remember that the cost of using an elevator and pushing a book truck 200 ft (60.960 m) is much less than the cost of professional staff time that could be lost because of poor spatial relationships between the major bibliographic tools and their working quarters.

Now we treat the individual functional units. Understand that in different libraries, these operations may be small or large, can be combined or further divided, so that the names used here are typical but not standard. In a major branch or small library, all these functions are generally carried out with a few people, often in a single room, while a large library system may have decentralized processing and a number of separate work areas divided by function. The application of computer technologies will vary markedly, though the trend is strong in all developed countries and comments are here given as seem useful for the long term.

8.3.1 Order and Acquisitions Work

This work in small institutions may be carried out primarily by the chief librarian with perhaps some secretarial or clerical help. In large institutions with traditional order and acquisition units, processing departments may be divided into as many as six groups: selection, ordering, checking in acquisitions, billing, sometimes copy cataloging (where the cataloging process is made straightforward by use of national databases to which the local copy is added), and gift and exchange works. At least 100 and preferably 125 ft² (9.290 to 11.613 m²) for each person expected to be employed as regular staff members should be provided, with an extra 25 to 50 ft² (2.323 to 4.645 m²) for the person in charge. If unwrapping occurs here, provision for one or more extra-large trash containers plus a large worktable will also be required. Raise the question of whether a separate room for dust control may be desirable for the unwrapping function. Or, this activity may occur in the shipping room.

Shelving will be needed for recent purchase receipts, for books received on approval, and for newly purchased large collections and large gifts, and exchange materials. Security in this area is often a necessity; until books receive ownership marks, they represent attractive items for the light-fingered to "borrow." Rare books usually receive special treatment in this regard, either with a decentralized processing unit in the rare book area or with special secure cabinets in the main processing area. Files for vendors, order forms, invoices, and the like will need to be provided for.

Acquisition work is greatly altered by computers. The files mentioned above can all be online. Every staff person will have a computer workstation. A terminal or computer workstation work space will require from 50 to 75 ft² (4.645 to 6.968 m²). Books received on approval may be reviewed by various faculty and staff in an area that should be convenient but supervised to avoid theft. Remember to account for space for all the book trucks and their movements. And outsourcing may affect the number of staff positions and thus the space for this function, as will be discussed further under the cataloging function.

Gifts are welcome and valued in any academic and research library. An area or arrangement that allows book sales in the gift department without extra trucking is highly desirable in most large library systems. Such an area should be sized for people to collect and sort duplicate copies no longer needed, other titles withdrawn from the collections, and gifts to the library that are judged outside its collecting scope. Once sorted, the materials will need shelf space for holding until the campus community or secondhand dealers are given the opportunity to inspect, browse, and buy. Sometimes this entire operation is staffed by volunteers from a group of library "friends," and, because the sales will occur periodically and the need for workers will similarly vary sharply, the holding area needs to be generous, perhaps sufficient to handle the expected quantity that may accrue between sales. No recommendation of space can be made, though this need should not be overlooked in programming.

8.3.2 Cataloging

A catalog department traditionally includes professional members for subject-heading work, classification, and descriptive cataloging, and also clerical assistants, filers, and typists. Members of this department are often responsible for the shelflist of collection holdings and sometimes for preparing material for the shelves, work that is carried on chiefly by clerical workers but requires space for equipment and storage of material in process. Because preparation-for-the-shelves work and typing tend to be noisy, a separate acoustically treated area will be useful. The catalog department also will have various files, including an authority file, a shelflist, and sometimes a duplicate of portions of the main catalog. Certain of the more heavily used bibliographic sources may be shelved in this area, typically on shelves fitted with consultation counters, although some staff may prefer index tables, which consume considerably more space. Carpet for the entire technical service area is not amiss, considering the high level of work required and the need for quiet. (See fig. 8.8.)

The cataloging process using the best of computer support today will have no typists or clerical assistants, and the files mentioned above will all be online. The incoming materials arrive from the acquisition unit and are distributed to the appropriate subject or language expert cataloger who needs a large, efficient work area. Cataloger work positions for libraries with extensive computer systems can have many variations of arrangements. Some like cubicles, others landscape furniture areas (but note the comment earlier about such movable office partition systems), and some prefer open vistas across all cataloging positions. Various university libraries have studied and designed highly satisfactory workstations with ergonomic furniture, good computer workstation equipment, small book trucks right at hand for materials moving through, and adequate working surface for the book or other item being worked on, and for manuals, files, and so on used in that process. The University of Central Florida in Orlando in the late 1990s undertook such a study. (See fig. 8.9.)

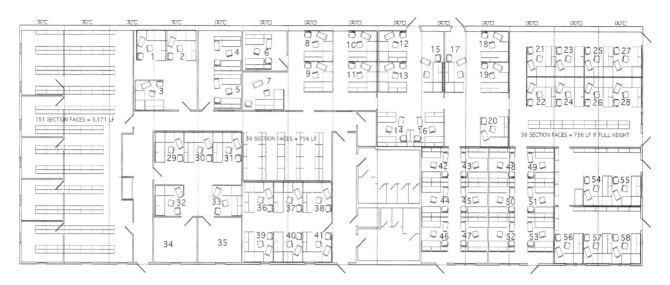

FIGURE 8.8   Stanford University, Catalog Department as planned for installation in temporary quarters (trailers) following the Loma Prieta earthquake. Note that with fully automated cataloging at the time of this plan, there are no cabinets for shelflists and the like. Most of the shelving in the left half of the plan is for the working backlog. This plan was later revised to include an end-processing unit centrally located. It has since been revised a second time reflecting a general shrinkage of the Catalog Department together with new space needs for another library office. (Courtesy of Stanford University Libraries)

For each cataloger, a few book shelves are necessary because there are always problem materials for which the cataloging can't be completed at once. Remember that those handling atlases, art volumes, or conductors' scores or cataloging microtexts or audiovisual materials will need extra space. Some may need a side chair, if consultations are expected from time to time. Depending on the computer arrangement, the type of materials being cataloged, and other variables, a cataloger may need to be assigned from 100 to 150 ft² (9.290 to 13.935 m²).

Outsourcing would reduce the space needs for the processes of cataloging and finishing. Some purchasing/receiving and cataloging steps that traditionally have been done in the library can now be handled by contract with vendors or a processing company. This management option may be used more often in the future. In small libraries and for some acquisitions in very large libraries, outsourcing may become common.

If a library could rely completely on outsourcing, space need probably would be no more than that to open, unwrap, and possibly check incoming stock against invoices. The materials then are moved directly to the shelves; the bibliographic

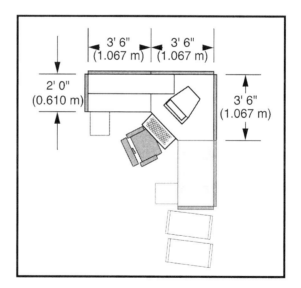

FIGURE 8.9   Cataloging workstation from the University of Central Florida Libraries. The longer rectangle to the left of the computer monitor is a separate desktop organizer. The extension to the lower right and the panels around the station are optional. The height of the work surface is 29 in. (0.737 m) with an articulated keyboard holder for the computer.

information should already be in the online catalog. Such an arrangement all but eliminates the need for staff quarters for ordering, acquisition, and copy cataloging. Even original cataloging is available through commercial firms; therefore, the bulk of on-site technical processing could eventually consist of a few offices for coordinators with the balance of the operations being offsite.

Yet sound programming should be based on firm plans before reducing library processing quarters. Far better to be cautious in the space savings resulting from such a management strategy when it is in transition. When there are no firm tested plans, at least plan flexible and contiguous space for materials handling. Keep receiving, copy cataloging, and finishing/end processing near each other and near the building loading dock. If processing must be divided between two floors, keep materials going through the mainstream in the more efficient work-flow position. The other floor could house staff for data handling (payments, ordering, database maintenance) and handling of nonmainstream materials (catalog maintenance, transfers, conversions, and authorities processing).

Processing work flow follows a rather ideal pattern. Close by the loading dock of the building, all materials are unpacked, sorted into types of processing need, and routed to the appropriate unit. Such units in a large university library might handle the main flow of monographic volumes, serials, Slavic or Hebrew units, cartographic and media items, computer data set acquisitions, gift materials, transfers, pre- and postbinding shipments, and bibliographic file maintenance, depending on how the library is organized. Some incoming material may not need to pass through the finishing process, where an assembly line types (or a computer prints out) and affixes call-number labels, stamps ownership marks, and applies bookplates, book jackets, date due slips, and security targets.

To speculate about the extent of outsourcing, materials that might come in through that route could be those acquired through major vendors. However, in contrast with most academic libraries, research libraries will retain a larger percentage of processing in-house because they do more acquiring from boutique vendors not likely to be able to support "fast-track" processing, in which the vendor may do cataloging and finishing and related processes. Local processing will

always be done for rare books, manuscript and archival collections, and many materials where the entry forms and subject heading assignments are problematic, such as prints, sheet maps, realia, and foreign government documents. Experience during the period right after the year 2000 may determine how this resolves itself among academic libraries.

8.3.3 Serials Receipt and Processing
Periodicals and other serial publications are often handled in a separate unit. The trend for at least 25 years has been for serial acquisitions to represent a larger and larger percentage of the library budget. Although it seems unlikely that there will be a reversal in this trend in the near future, one can expect CD-ROM and full-text online databases to grow as the medium for some serials—perhaps for the most popular and the least—and for the World Wide Web to have runs of back files as they are digitized over the coming years. The trends are not yet clear, though it is evident that the growth of fully digitized journal titles is astonishing. At issue is the ease with which a scholar can access a journal of choice from anyplace, as opposed to the easier reading and archival qualities of the paper version. Some libraries will likely be forced to provide both paper and digital versions of the same journal for this and other reasons; the pressure on library budgets for journals has not yet subsided.

Staff for serials may handle in some cases ordering, checking receipts, collating and preparing files for the bindery or a commercial microfilming agency, and perhaps the service to the public of this important category of material. Serials cataloging can also be part of this separate unit. Shelf and table space for materials and equipment are essential. Special shelving with bins or cubicles for sorting journals may be required, together with various cabinets for the necessary records that must be maintained. The processing of thousands of titles means tens of thousands of pieces to handle—very space consuming.

With the development of online serials check-in, the process of checking receipts for incoming materials may be decentralized to the branches in many large university library systems. This distribution may carry with it bindery preparation and other activities, though probably not cataloging except where the branch has its own catalog unit. As with acquisition work and cataloging, this also may be subject to a degree of outsourcing.

8.3.4 Physical Treatment and Preservation/Conservation

Preparation work may be in a separate department, in branches and units of central libraries, or as part of the public service or acquisitions department, or the serials section. If centralized, sufficient sorting and collating counters or benches, and shelving for temporary storage space are essential. A certain amount of mending, repair, and simple binding is done by all libraries within their own walls; larger ones, when possible, will do well to employ a hand binder or conservator to repair books in great demand and those so valuable that one hesitates to let them leave the building. If any provision for binding and repair work beyond the preparation for binding is to be made, space must be assigned, and the floor area required cannot be determined until the extent of the work to be undertaken has been decided. Floor loads must not be forgotten because heavy equipment may be involved.

With the exception of these fairly simple binding procedures and, in some cases, fine binding, the bulk of binding and rebinding work will be performed outside under contract. Thus, at least in North America, there is little economic justification for such equipment within the individual library. Yet, in some countries a bindery is still fairly common, perhaps because large-scale commercial binderies are not as readily available and advantages result from keeping material to be bound always under the library roof where it can be obtained without delay in emergencies.

Preservation and conservation work may be part of a processing department, though increasingly this function in any university or research library is itself a library department with an officer in charge. There typically are paper cutters, joggers, book presses, drying racks, a fume hood, an oversized sink for large sheets of paper, a deep sink, glue pots, irons, dry-mount machines, paper creasers, and the like, which will require unique space and power service. As is obvious, the space required is not related to the number of staff, but rather to the variety of processes supported and the equipment and work space needed for each. Bins, cabinets, and shelving are essential for supplies, some types of tools, and materials in process. The location of outlets for hand tools and other equipment becomes crucial where

extension cords are to be avoided. Worktables with accessible outlets above the work surface are needed. Glare-free lighting is perhaps a bit more important here, particularly if sophisticated repair work is being done. A computer workstation is now a basic need.

The layout for a conservation laboratory can be an exacting task. There will be conditions that differ markedly depending on the type of materials being treated, the quantities processed and being held before or after treatment, the specific equipment required, the type and quantities of supplies to be stocked, special security provisions, and the desirable efficient work-flow pattern. Most museums and archives will have an emphasis on processing flat items, such as posters, prints, broadsides, maps, drawings, and single manuscript leaves or documents. For such materials the paper conservation lab will generally require 300 ft^2 (27.871 m^2) per person. Most research libraries will have an emphasis on processing bound items, such as books and pamphlets, as well as single leaves. In such a case the typical book conservation lab will generally require 200 ft^2 (18.581 m^2) per person. (Fig. 8.10 shows a practical layout for a conservation lab.)

It should be noted that the field of book preservation is developing quite rapidly as new studies and proven applications of different techniques provide new opportunities. An efficient layout in the future will probably require changes in space and equipment. Proximity to main supply feeds for electricity, clean water, and waste disposal, exhaust air from a fume hood, and for the delivery and handling of chemicals as well as occasional infested material are important considerations. There is advantage in having the book conservation and the book repair operations part of one space and operation, though local conditions will obtain.

When a research library has a program for reformatting and replacement as part of the preservation and conservation unit, there will need to be space for microfilm inspection (with readers, densitometers, light boxes, etc.), for collation (a large worktable), and for scanning and quality control. Lighting must be lower in the microfilm inspection area. The guillotine used for disbinding books requires adequate space and can make a lot of noise, so it should be kept nearby but where noise will not disturb other work. Shelving and usually a computer workstation are essential. And a climate-controlled storage space

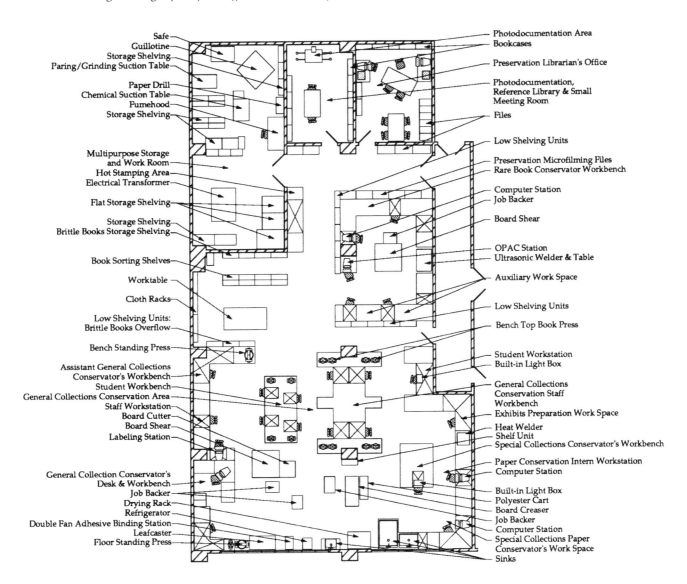

FIGURE 8.10 Princeton University Library's Preservation Office. This lab facility was created within existing space (as evidenced by the building's transformer on the left as well as the building's structure). Windows exist across the bottom of the space; note the relative size of the three sinks along this lower wall. The Xs are knee spaces. (Courtesy of Princeton University Libraries)

should hold microfilm masters before they are shipped to permanent storage.

8.3.5 Other Processing Functions

The finishing or end-process unit prepares materials for public shelving. As mentioned earlier, this operation involves spine labels, book pockets or circulation slips, bookplates, targets for book security systems, pamphlet bindings, binding tapes, and other miscellaneous supplies; all these will need to be stored here in cabinets and

in boxes on shelves. A nearby sink is almost essential. As fixatives and glues often are malodorous, excellent ventilation will be required. For some acquisitions, these procedures could be under contract to a vendor.

Conservation of the collections will sometimes involve treating infested materials, drying those items that sadly are soaked from time to time, or in the future applying techniques of mass deacidification. Any of these activities may involve the use of a blast freezer or vacuum chamber, special chemicals, water, and special ventilation. If it is anticipated that this activity will occur in-house, it is suggested that a space of at least 200 ft² (18.581 m²) might be set aside for a future blast freezer or chamber, even if one is not to be provided as part of the project. (See fig. 8.11.) If full-time ventilation with direct 100 percent exhaust to the outside is provided for this space, it can be used as a staging area for those materials arriving from hot, humid climates where infestation may be suspected. The room should have fairly easy access from an exterior delivery point so that potentially infested materials need not expose unduly the balance of the library collections. Doors will, of course, need to be wide and high enough for the delivery of a blast freezer, if it is not to be built in. Utility requirements should be discussed with a blast freezer manufacturer to ensure that reasonable future requirements may be met. The exhaust may have to be carried up to the roof level if toxic material is to be used in a fumigation chamber. In some facilities this function is adjacent to or actually part of the receiving room.

In the rare event that the library project includes a deacidification plant, a substantial space will need to be set aside for this function. It is urged that in this circumstance, the best advice can be obtained from an engineer who specializes in deacidification processes. It is probable that such plants would only appear in facilities that support very large library systems, and at this time only one such plant is known to be in operation (run by the Canadian National Archives and serving only the Canadian National Library). Part of the problem is with the chemicals involved; few if any libraries will find it compelling to have such systems within their building for this and other reasons.

Most larger libraries will have a computer systems office, particularly those libraries moving to local integrated systems, even turnkey systems. There may be a requirement for a computer room, a file server, equipment storage sufficient to accommodate incoming shipments of equipment that can be substantial and valuable, an area for making simple repairs and for setting up and testing new equipment, a training and demonstration room, and space for several staff members. For a small library with a systems office, often one enclosed office is sufficient. Larger libraries will require significantly more space for this function; the Stanford University systems

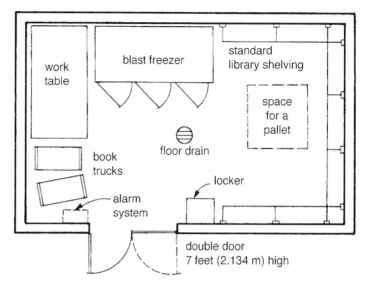

FIGURE 8.11   Fumigation room. Current technology suggests the use of a blast freezer for fumigation purposes. A room for this purpose should have ample power, excellent ventilation (preferably with negative pressure), and clear access. Flexibility for the future would be improved by providing access to water and a drain. The space illustrated is approximately 11 by 18 ft (3.353 by 5.486 m). The alarm system is intended to be used to monitor the blast freezer in operation.

office, for example, was about 3,000 ft² (278.709 m²) in 1996, and it suffered from inadequate storage and training space. The space requirements for the staff should be similar to the rest of technical processing except for the shop area, storage area, and any need envisioned as a training room or area. The training room can be thought of as a conference room (20 ft², or 1.858 m², per occupant) fitted with the appropriate computer terminals and perhaps display monitors, microcomputers, and other equipment. If each occupant is to be provided with a microcomputer or terminal, then 30 to 50 ft² (2.787 to 4.645 m²) per occupant is needed.

As noted elsewhere, the computer room can, in most cases, be a space like any other, perhaps with better security and with air conditioning at least equal to other spaces. Access to data signal ducts or conduit or both is important. The size will be determined by the actual equipment; unless it is supporting a significant user group beyond the normal automation needs of the library, it is likely to be modest in size, say, 200 to 500 ft² (18.581 to 46.452 m²). Many minicomputers are smaller than a desk, and thus the larger size suggested would be excessive in most cases. Some computer experts recommend "clean" power for small computers, but with improved filters, even this requirement is diminishing.

8.4
Building Maintenance Staff

It should not be forgotten that almost any library requires janitorial and building caretaking personnel who must have their own quarters. This is especially the case for independent research libraries. This staff function is to maintain the rest rooms or toilet facilities, to take care of the floors throughout the building, empty wastepaper baskets, replace burned-out light bulbs and tubes, and so forth.

Even on a campus where janitorial staff may cover several buildings, each building will need a place that they can use as a base and where they can keep brooms, mops, vacuum cleaners, and other equipment as well as supplies, such as toilet paper, soap, and towels. A janitor's closet with running water and a mop sink for cleaning the equipment may be a requisite on each floor unless that floor is entirely carpeted. Adequate supply and equipment rooms for material required for staff and public use are of great importance and in the long run will be an economy. A space of 100 to 125 ft^2 (9.290 to 11.613 m^2) for each full-time member of the maintenance staff or the equivalent should be enough to cover all these items.

Another maintenance need is for space to store the inevitable ladders, replacement light bulbs and tubes, touch-up paint, extra ceiling tiles, broken chairs waiting for repair, tools, carpet remnants, and the like associated with the physical maintenance of the building and its equipment. It must be acknowledged that in any large library building, particularly a central library with many functions, there will frequently be maintenance projects, with skilled laborers bringing in tools and supplies for the job. Michael McCahill has written of the University of Toronto Robarts Library: If you must have a very large library, "remember in your planning that the library will never be free of construction workers. From the moment it opened, one part or another of the Robarts Library has always been under construction, or reconstruction, or alteration, or renovation.... Technological change, changes in priority

at university or higher levels of authority, will ensure that no matter how well you plan, your building will become a permanent construction site."[1] Our experience with the main library at Stanford and reports from other universities echo this truism.

For this space requirement, an area might be set aside of up to 500 ft^2 (46.452 m^2) in a large library as a combination shop and service storage area. If repair work is anticipated, the room should not be fitted with a fire detection system based upon the products of combustion, as the first use of a power saw will set it off. Where fire detection is desired, a rate-of-heat-rise device will be required. The room should be provided with a workbench, and lockers for tools and flammable materials. Ideally, such a room will be well isolated in terms of dust control and acoustics from the rest of the building.

8.5
Staff Emergency Room and Lounge

There should be a "quiet room" with a cot or two to be used as an emergency room by the library as a whole, and adequate toilet facilities for both sexes, preferably separate from those for the public (the numbers required are generally spelled out in the building codes). This emergency room should also be available when needed to help library users, so its location should not be difficult to reach from various parts of the building. This room most days can be used by women needing to rest; thus, it serves a dual purpose when there is an emergency requiring medical attention. The room as a minimum should have a first-aid kit, pillows, and blankets. Having ceiling lights on a rheostat will be useful.

The staff should be provided with rest rooms, lounge space, and a kitchenette. (The University of Glasgow Library even provides staff showers.) For use during meals and other work breaks, the staff lounge is usually combined with the kitchenette, though with some visual separation, and the food storage and preparation area should be complete with a large refrigerator or two, depending on the size of staff and meal customs. Freestanding refrigerators and stoves are preferable to built-ins. A toaster oven and microwave oven are particularly important if there are no suitable lunch facilities in a nearby campus building or in a business neighborhood. It is essential that such food supplies as sugar be kept in tight containers to discourage invasions by insects, and disposal of waste must be frequent and convenient. Running hot and cold water and a disposal in the sink are basic for cleanliness. Collection barrels for empty glass, aluminum cans, and paper goods are frequently provided. Details need not be spelled out in the building program, but they will need attention when design development advances, for example, to assure that fire protection and detection are appropriate in the cooking area.

The lounge should accommodate a percentage of staff to be determined by local custom, perhaps a quarter to a third but not more than half at eating or lounge positions. (Student and other part-time employees and any building caretaking crew need to be taken into account.) This area may also be used for staff lectures, receptions, retirement parties, and the like when chairs can be added or removed to an adjacent storage closet. From 10 to 15 ft^2 (0.929 to 1.394 m^2) per the determined percent of staff would seem to be adequate for these combined facilities, if they are available to the library staff and janitorial crew only.

It is generally unwise to allow the public to use these food facilities, and few libraries feel that it is necessary to provide public lunchrooms. They cannot be said to serve an essential function of the library, and, where they are provided, they usually represent a maintenance headache. Libraries with public food vending areas usually find that food travels to all parts of the building.

The University of Chicago Regenstein Library has a student-run canteen called "Ex Libris" with monitors stationed just outside in the Regenstein to control wandering food at all hours. Until the mid-1990s, the Northwestern University Main Library used monitors just outside the student lounge with its vending machines, but the monitors were eliminated as not being effective. The Odegaard Undergraduate Library of the University of Washington opened in 1972 with three library floors, above a ground floor devoted to the student food service; a mature person working daytime weekday hours since 1980 plus a uniformed guard evenings and some weekend hours have been successful at controlling incoming food. The Odegaard situation has worked rather well in part because of the separate entrances to the two functions, and because it is obviously convenient to inform people that if they want to study and drink coffee or eat their lunch, they can check out books and go downstairs to the food service without going out in the rain. Even so, any academic library with nearby food service faces a constant battle to keep food out of the library.

The Huntington Library has nearby a "Footnote" snack and coffee machine service for its scholars and researchers. It should be remembered that any kitchen facility must be carefully controlled to make sure that vermin of one kind or another are not attracted and that noise and food odors do not spread to other areas. Programming any food service must be done with special thought to these problems.

The greatest problem in connection with staff accommodations is to know how many staff positions to prepare for in the years ahead. With modern modular buildings it is, fortunately, easier to provide for the shifting required by future growth, either within the present building or in an addition, than it was in buildings with fixed interior bearing walls; but, as already stated, staff quarters almost invariably become inadequate before those for books or readers.

8.6
The Catalog

The library catalog of its collection holdings is crucial to the function of all libraries. Libraries have used card catalogs, book catalogs (which are expensive to keep up to date), microtext catalogs, and computer catalogs accessed through terminals, or a combination of these. At the current rate of computerization, few academic libraries will still be using public card catalogs or card shelflists through the end of this century. However, there may in some library units be card files for some specialized lists or indexes not yet converted. Examples might be the provenance, press, and chronological files in Special Collections, an index to the campus newspaper or other in-house publication, a specialized map listing, local history or name files, a portrait file, or a card file given by a professor or donor many years ago to index a particular collection. Quite a few academic and research libraries have inherited the incomplete and unpublished results of research in progress, such as a specialized dictionary. And many such catalogs will have continuing utility, will never be converted into a database, and must be accommodated when planning space for a library department.

Computer catalogs are dealt with in Sections 7.3 and 13.4.4; libraries still relying on the card catalog and needing to design such space are referred to the detailed description of card catalog case size and layout in the second edition of this book, pages 242–46.

However, even with a complete reliance upon OPACs, there may be need for a bibliographic display. To aid new students in learning the means by which the holdings of the library may be accessed, libraries use various techniques ranging from handouts, which may require little more than a bin or series of bins at some convenient location, to a staffed information desk, which may be part of the reference area or operated as a totally separate function. In between these options there are posted instructions or a detailed display showing the various components of information that may be found in any catalog, and how this information can be used to find the material needed for research. There may be tabulations of what may or may not be found in the catalog—for example, manuscripts, maps, some microtext analytics, or prints—together with directions giving alternative places to search for materials. The anticipated needs of the library being programmed will require discussion and detailing. Note that this is an important provision in any library, fully automated or not.

Sheaf catalogs, which are in loose-leaf binders, have for many decades been used in many other countries but rarely in the United States. They have the advantage of taking less space and can be used with regular library shelving. It is probable that those libraries will in the course of time go to online computer terminals or computer-output microfiche to supplement or in some cases replace catalogs. When microfiche or computer terminals are used, a considerable number of access points should be made available, as is discussed elsewhere in this volume.

8.7
Exhibit Area

Public display of library materials is an accepted method of supporting particular educational or research activities on campus, publicizing new or unusual collections, thanking donors, cultivating a prospective donor, or providing context for a public lecture or other event on campus. Such exhibitions are often, but not always, related to or making use of materials in special collections—that is, rare books, manuscripts, valuable prints, historic maps, and so forth. Some of these displays are semipermanent; most are mounted just for weeks or months. The display of such materials for some extended time requires a very carefully planned exhibit area, and the programming of this area requires special effort if its use is to be effective.

A practice that eventually can lead to problems of space, security, and annual operational cost is the dedication of an entire room to a collection of books by and about one author or to a collection formed by one individual. Instances exist in college and university libraries in most parts of the country from east to west. Sometimes fundraising has prompted this arrangement. Sometimes it was sentiment for an exceptional, beloved local person or regional author. Where such a room exists, the program for a new building or an addition must take this into consideration. The authors recommend that no space be allocated for the eventuality unless there already is a specific plan in agreement and, hopefully, the financial aspects have been arranged and documented.

We leave aside in this chapter the issue of dedicated rooms. For the common display arrangement, the exhibition or display cases may be freestanding or built in; they may be fairly simple, resembling little more than a glass box on a table, or they may be quite complex, with built-in lighting, air conditioning, humidity control, alarms, and special devices for the display of books. The area itself may be a room, a lobby to the special collections area, or the building entrance hall, or it may be spread along a corridor. As an example of effective use of a small space, in 1971 the New York Historical Society furnished a small room with a mixture of built-in exhibition cases and grille-fronted shelves displaying highlighted collections.

In establishing the requirements for the display of library materials, several factors will need to be considered: size of each individual display unit, lighting of each case, security, environmental control, and design details.

1. *Size.* The nature of the materials being displayed and the method of display are of course critical to the size of the case. If the case is to be

principally used for maps or broadsides, the case probably should be vertical, perhaps as much as 4 ft high × 5 or 6 ft wide (1.219 × 1.524 or 1.829 m). Remember that, for short people or for those using bifocal glasses, a case that extends above 6 ft (1.829 m) will be a problem. This broadside type of format clearly would not require a case of great depth. But if at a future date there may be a need to display books, a depth that permits the installation of shelves would be welcome. For that, a depth of about 15 in. (381 mm) is generally adequate.

For the display of rare books, the ideal case is flat or slightly sloped. The size of the case may be determined from the overall space required for the largest volume likely to be placed on display plus sufficient space for a card containing a brief written description of this item, its provenance, and its importance. A case of about 3 ft × 5 ft (0.914 × 1.524 m) is generally adequate, though other dimensions may be equally satisfactory. The depth of the case should be sufficient to permit placing items on low stands; 8 to 10 in. (203 to 254 mm) will probably be minimal for this, and a greater depth will be desired by many librarians. In fact, most research libraries, especially independent research libraries, have museum objects of great interest, as is the Bancroft Library's Plate of Brass, once ascribed to Sir Francis Drake. Just outside its Special Collections, the Meriam Library of Chico State University exhibits a collection of antique oil and kerosene lamps. Some objects may require even deeper cases for effective display. The two dioramas in Harvard's Widener Library sit in very large, deep cases. The size of built-in display cases will often be influenced by the building module or the space available, which should not present a problem if the specific requirements of the materials to be exhibited are provided for. Extra space is nearly always welcome, up to a point, and it will allow spreading out the materials so that viewing them is more pleasant.

2. *Lighting.* Perhaps the most difficult design problem for the exhibition of library materials is proper lighting. Ideal lighting conditions occur only when the sole function of the area containing the display cases is dedicated to exhibitions and the designer has complete control of lighting conditions. However, in libraries these conditions are rare, and must be given far more emphasis than is usual. Even where there is a special exhibit area, the lighting conditions have often

been influenced by juxtaposed areas or exterior windows. As a result, lighting is almost always a compromise, though the Perkins Library Prothro Gallery at Southern Methodist University and the main exhibition gallery of the Huntington Library are exemplary exceptions to this dismal pattern of neglect. Another excellent example can be seen at the University of Texas at Austin, Ransom Humanities Research Center and the nearby Lyndon B. Johnson Library. Museums often offer excellent examples of proper lighting for exhibits as well.

There are four key problems in display case lighting: heat, intensity, color, and glare. To a certain extent, these factors are interrelated. The ideal condition is one in which the space has no windows and is dimly lit, to a degree that might be thought of as dark, so that the displayed materials can easily be seen with a minimum of light within the case. As the ambient light level is increased, the light on the displayed materials must be increased as well to maintain clear visibility. With increased light, there is reason to have greater concern about its effect on the materials. Certainly the ultraviolet spectrum should be minimized, either by filtration or through the use of a light source that produces minimal amounts of this damaging light component. Heat is also a concern as the intensity increases, suggesting in some circumstances that the light source should be outside the case or that the case should be well ventilated or air conditioned.

With light sources outside the case, glare is almost always a problem. Careful attention to the angle of the light in relation to the eyes of the viewer can greatly reduce the problem of glare, but it is rarely avoided altogether. Visitors to libraries will unfortunately find many a dreadful example. It is wise to use a mock-up to determine if reflection exists when a short person looks at an item on the top display shelf.

The use of black grillwork rather than glass will solve the glare problem, but then the books may be subject to damage by some person poking the spine, unless the depth of the case is such that books stand 4 in. (102 mm) or more behind the grille. The physical environment for the collections will be that of the exhibit area, which will make the mechanical design straightforward. Of course, the grille reduces the clear vision of the displayed materials, and books recessed several inches, or several centimeters, on their shelves make overhead lighting more difficult.

(The University of Glasgow Library is an example.) Even so, the use of a black grille can be very effective for shelving lining the walls of a rare book reading room (Scripps College Library is but one of many examples), and reasonable security can be maintained.

Shadows are another problem with display case lighting, particularly with vertical cases. Vertical light sources, often filtered fluorescent or cold cathode bulbs, may be placed within the case at the sides and toward the front. With this system of lighting, shadows will still occur, though they can be greatly minimized depending on the depth and width of the case as well as arrangement of the display. Glass shelves are also used to reduce shadows, and they are essential where the light source is in the top of the case. Here again, bright surfaces or edges can detract from the display. Although there are distinct aesthetic considerations, a light fixture suspended about 2 to 3 ft (610 to 914 mm) in front of the case at a level of the top of the case can provide good light, and glare, heat, and shadows can be minimized.

3. *Security.* Often the most valuable items the library owns will be placed on display, which generally means that security is a concern. There is no such thing as absolute security, and an item on display is at greater risk than one in a vault. Every year there are thefts from exhibits, attributable in part to a wide range of defective conditions. Yet display of rare materials is essential, as mentioned above. Conditions at outstanding art museums can be helpful if studied when planning the security and other details of library exhibit spaces.

The need for security will of course vary in degree with the item. A Gutenberg Bible on permanent display may have a case especially designed with bulletproof glass, an alarm mechanism within the case, and a television monitor or guard to maintain constant observation of the case while the exhibit area is open. After hours the entire case may drop into a vault, or the display area itself may be constructed like a vault with various alarms and safety features. This precaution is of course extreme.

In between the Gutenberg Bible and the latest acquisition of books hot off the press are many volumes that, although of significant value, are not multimillion-dollar items. The degree of security to be provided for these materials is of course for local discussion. However, the following might be considered:

a. Place the display cases in an area that will have a staffed position, such as an information desk, within the same space. In lieu of this, consider hidden television cameras or, depending upon the desired psychology of the situation, provide obvious television cameras with blinking lights.

b. Close the display area when the person supervising the area is off duty. This may mean that, for example, the display area is open for viewing only during the hours maintained by the rare book department.

c. Provide intrusion detection devices in the display area to be activated after hours. And test these devices every few months.

d. Provide a silent panic alarm for the supervising staff that alerts staff at another location in the library and perhaps the local police.

e. Use laminated safety glass in the cases. Tempered safety glass may be considered in combination with lamination, but used alone, it adds little to the security of the materials over the use of normal plate glass. Lexan is an excellent material, but its optical quality is difficult to maintain.

f. Have alarms in the case that detect both the motion of an item being moved and the sound of breaking glass. These alarms should be active at all times, except when the display is being installed.

g. Consider having a number of smaller cases rather than one large one, to make accessibility to a large quantity of materials more difficult.

h. Avoid case designs that encourage tampering or vandalism. For instance, where security is a concern, avoid external hinge pins, light-gauge wooden door frames, gaps in the doors, the use of a grillwork-type closure, or movable cases near the exterior door.

i. If a particularly valuable item is to be displayed, consider the possibility of removing it after hours to a more secure location. In this regard, it is well to consider the route that must be traveled from the display area to the vault or more secure area.

j. The display of exceedingly valuable items should be reviewed with the institution's insurance and security representatives.

4. *Environmental control.* Mechanically controlling the environment within the case is a difficult engineering problem, particularly the control of

humidity. Part of the difficulty derives from the fact that the volume of a display case is significantly smaller than the volume of architectural spaces that are normally air conditioned. A common method of increasing humidity involves the introduction of steam into the air supply, but the jets typically used are of such a size that a light release of steam will dramatically increase the humidity in the case. In a large space the volume of air acts as a buffer, yet in a display case what normally would be a minor adjustment becomes a major change in the environment. Most designers feel that the use of steam is too risky for display cases, and thus they choose an evaporative humidifying system. The removal of humidity, done by a process of refrigeration or desiccation, may be basically similar to that used for a larger space. Heating, cooling, and filtration of the air may also be similar; however, the engineer will need to take special care of the control mechanism.

For cases without air conditioning, there are two schools of thought. The first suggests that the case should be well ventilated, so that the environmental conditions within the case are essentially similar to those within the larger display room. When there are light fixtures within the case, a means of removing the heat from them must be found in order to avoid undue exposure of the materials to high temperatures. More than a few small holes at top and bottom of the case will be required. The second school of thought argues that a constant, average environment is maintained when the case is sealed and provided with a tray, out of sight, in which silica gel can be placed to control the humidity. This type of case of course requires external illumination, which, ideally, is not too intense. In a flat case the bottom can be constructed from a fabric-wrapped sheet of perforated metal under which alarm devices and a tray for silica gel may be placed. The fabric should of course be acid-free. In a sealed case any wood used should be well sealed to avoid acid migration. In fact, everything placed in a case that is sealed should be as free of acids as possible. Vertical cases can be constructed in a similar fashion with a tray for silica gel in the base or behind a false back.

5. *Design details.* In terms of the general arrangement, the sequence of cases should be clear so a viewer can grasp the beginning and direction of the exhibition. At times, it may be useful to number the cases in a consistent location on each case. In other situations, it may be clear that the sequence begins at the entrance to the gallery. A counterclockwise circuit can be an evident route, one that should not end a great distance from the natural exit of the gallery.

The means of access to the case and the ease of preparing the display are important concerns. Vertical cases may be constructed with sliding or swing-open doors. Both types can provide poor or excellent results. If the case is to be sealed, the swing-open doors are probably easier to detail in an airtight fashion. They also offer the advantage of full access to the case, and normally the lock mechanism is easier to install unobtrusively. The doors can be in frames, or they can be like storefront doors of solid glass, which offer the least obstruction to viewing the contents. An astragal will be required on double doors when an airtight seal is desired or where there is concern of vandalism with a long implement, but the astragal can be designed of a clear material that, although it can be seen, is not terribly objectionable. It should be kept in mind though that solid glass doors are expensive and that they are usually constructed with tempered glass, which can be shattered with relative ease.

Sliding doors also may be framed or made of solid glass. Unless considerable care is taken in the design of the case, the locking mechanism frequently ends up being a strap lock that hangs directly on the glass. Although this type of lock works well, it is not attractive. Where appearance is a concern, locks at the top or bottom of the case (sometimes used both top and bottom), perhaps concealed from view, should be carefully detailed; experience tells us that it may not be enough to simply specify that this is the type of lock to be provided.

Flat cases may be actually flat or slightly sloping, as noted earlier. A major reason for sloping the case is to try to avoid reflective glare while providing a better angle of view of the displayed materials. Both designs can be quite satisfactory. Access to a flat case may be by tilting up or removing the entire top or by opening up one side, or by creating what amounts to a drawer. Each has its problems. The top of the tilt-up case is typically quite heavy, and care must be taken to ensure the safety of the attendant dressing the case by having prop rods on both ends. This type of access is probably the easiest for preparing the case, and the inside glass of the case is easily cleaned. Cases with side or back openings are the most difficult and time consuming to mount, but the opening mechanism is probably the simplest and least expensive. The drawer case is easy to dress, provided the drawer opens fully, but the inside of the case may be difficult to clean. Often the drawer can be removed to make cleaning somewhat easier. Keep in mind that the weight of the drawer itself plus that of the items being placed on it may make it necessary to bolt the cases to the floor, which in some small measure adds to the security but reduces the flexibility of arranging the cases. Flat cases are a little more difficult to ventilate, particularly if there is a small frame around the glass. On the other hand, they are probably easier to seal than vertical cases.

One exhibition case design at the Virginia Polytechnic Institute and State University Newman Library combines several desirable attributes. Eight cases form part of a long wall of Special Collections facing the large building lobby. These vertical cases are flush fronted in the wall, are formed of plywood boxlike cubicles set side by side about chest high, easy to open at the back for mounting, and illuminated and ventilated from overhead because there is no top to each display case. Although not impressive furniture, they are inexpensive, secure, well ventilated, and well lighted, and it is even easy to place a front cover from the inside to reduce the number of cases for an exhibit smaller than the total capacity.

A concept discussed for the Delaware Public Archives is an exhibition case that would in effect be a vault with windows opening onto a passageway that itself is secured and with excellent light control. In this concept, the vault would be very carefully controlled environmentally, and of a large enough space to make the controls effective. The vault would accommodate internally some ease of changing or dressing exhibits. In this way, it was thought that maximum control could be provided for the materials while allowing a large group to see them. A similar concept was undertaken for the exhibit of the Book of Kells that traveled around the United States a few years ago.

A considerable range of possibilities exists in regard to the devices or furniture used to hold and display books and other materials, details that will be left to the designer. The librarian, however, should be concerned about how to mount manuscripts or broadsides without dam-

aging them. Any tackable surface should be acid-free and sharp edges should be avoided.

Finally, when the case is to be naturally ventilated, the slots and holes should be generous, especially when there are enclosed light sources, and a means of ensuring thorough ventilation, with openings both at the top and bottom of the case, should be provided. Too often the means of ventilation is inadequate or left out.

8.8
Other Space Uses

Several other types of public facilities are sometimes included in libraries. These include space used for auditoriums, a learning assistance center, quarters for the local historical society or friends-of-the-library group, a journal editorial office or office for publishing an online journal, a college museum, a special faculty reading room, a visiting scholars room, photographic laboratories, and perhaps some other areas used for what are generally not direct library activities but which may be related strongly to the library. Libraries house such activities as academic offices or headquarters for other departments of the institution, and classrooms may be included as well. Roanoke College's Fintel Library houses the Trustees' Board Room. Wake Forest University's Reynolds Library is host to the North Carolina Baptist History Library and Archive.

In a rapidly growing library, in order to provide adequate space for a reasonably long period, it is often desirable and even necessary to house nonlibrary activities at first. These activities should be selected from among those that will not interfere with library service and that will be reasonably easy to relocate when the space they occupy is needed for library purposes. Remember the occasional need for a social reception space for a few hundred who may attend an exhibition opening, a staff retirement party, or a memorial or dedicatory event. (For treatment of shared facilities, see Section 2.3.)

A separate media service is a common guest within the library building. Because of the similar nature of a library and a media center, they frequently are found under the same roof. Some media services are an outgrowth of a library activity. Sometimes the two are under the same administration. Both have equipment to handle and security issues of major importance; both are supportive of a wide range of instructional activities and may offer some instruction themselves. So the relationship is usually congenial. Fig. 7.26 provides a floor plan for the considerable computer and media services of the California State University, Bakersfield, Stiern Library, on a floor shared with Instructional Television, which is a separate management area.

8.8.1 Hand Printing Presses

Such historic artifacts for artistic creations provide a natural symbiosis of printing equipment with the chief cultural repository of printed products. Hand presses are a feature in quite a few academic libraries, examples being the University of Glasgow, Occidental College, Wellesley College (Book Arts Laboratory's "Annis Press" with both a Vandercook proof press and a Washington Press), Harvard University's Houghton Library, the University of California at Berkeley, the University of San Francisco, Stanford University (Improved Albion Press and a nineteenth-century German hand press), and Washington and Lee University. (A few others, such as Mills College and Scripps College, have fine printing programs now separate from the libraries.)

Some are artifacts of an earlier age; others are functional equipment for use by classes or clubs or for demonstration; some are in a very public display space and some in a printing workroom. Such a press may be an antique, a signature item of special collections, symbolic of rarity and the history of the printed word.

If it is intended as an active hand-operated printing press within the library to demonstrate the art of fine printing, it is recommended that a local hand-printing expert be consulted to develop an appropriate program. If it is to be used for that purpose, consideration must be given to the support equipment, such as a supply cabinet, storage for flammable solvents and inks and rags, a composing stone, cases for the trays of type fonts, and the like. The operation of the press can be messy and noisy; the floor should readily resist ink stains if its appearance is important. If the press is to be used for display, a public area is desirable, perhaps with a dramatic placement. If the press will be used for instructional purposes, sufficient space will be required for observers and students, with ample counters and wall space for displays, and an area appropriate for the mess

that goes with a printing process with inks. With the above in mind, the library must decide its priorities and operations with care before programming this function.

8.8.2 Outdoor Space

Outdoor features deserve programming if they are to serve a special function and be part of the library project. One possibility would be to have certain features needed by the institution in a very visible outdoor location. Just as commercial buildings sometimes have a large thermometer as a service to citizens, and several campuses have a bell tower, so have large clocks been found popular. The British Library building at St. Pancras features a large clock high on its towerlike column by the entrance court.

A different example would be an outdoor snack facility, designed to meet needs of library users in a setting outside the entrance area. The programming may include the type of vending service, the decision on lighting and power service, the nature of tables and benches or other seating, and trash and recycling barrels. Concerns for delivery and pick up as well as safety and vandalism must be thought through. The University of Florida has a good arrangement between its two central library buildings. The UCLA Research Library has another good arrangement, though this is at a distance of a half-minute walk with no special association with the library building.

Another example would be the outdoor seating (sometimes designed as a fund-raising opportunity) for those who at times enjoy reading outside in the sun or under trees or umbrellas. An attractive example is the "fragrance garden" of herbs and flowers amidst seating beside the California State Library Annex. The libraries at the University of Florida and the University of Oregon are particularly good instances, and naturally libraries in temperate zones have more examples of this than do those in harsher climates. (Note that at Columbia University's Low Library, many wide steps facing south remain a particularly popular place to sit and talk, read, and watch the world; Harvard's Widener Library steps facing north are relatively unused. Washington State's Holland Library boasts a grassy slope just outside the library facing southwest, which locals refer to as the beach; in many ways it functions as named.) Such space may be located just outside the building lobby, on a side protected from weather, in a nearby grove of trees, or in a courtyard within the building as at Scripps College's Denison Library. Smoking may be permitted in such an area; suitable ash cans will be required.

Bicycle parking is another topic that very often deserves programming. On many campuses a large number of students ride bikes from their dorms to the library, and some staff may commute to work by bikes. (Such programming may be led by another office on campus and at times is part of a separate landscaping program.) Physical security, lighting, and protection from the weather are important issues. Thought needs to be given to whether location of the racks and group corrals is sufficiently natural and convenient to the flow of traffic that bicyclists will use the provision rather than park the bikes closer to the building, under an overhanging roof, chained to railings or fences or trees. Planning to successfully encourage bike users to leave open lanes for pedestrians and those in wheelchairs can be a challenge. Virginia Polytechnic Institute, the University of Oregon, the University of California at Los Angeles and at Berkeley, and other large institutions have had to plan bicycle parking and traffic by the library locations with care, and as many have failed to anticipate the practical result as have succeeded.

8.8.3 Architectural Space

More properly called nonassignable space, this space is the difference between gross and net floor areas. Net area is the space used for the various program requirements of the library; the architectural space consists primarily of areas or volumes occupied by walls, structural elements, duct and utility shafts, stairwells and vestibules, corridors, rest rooms, elevators, mechanical rooms, and the like. A percentage (25 percent is often so used) of the exterior space of arcades, courtyards, porticos, and the like is also sometimes figured into the gross.

This is space required to enclose, support, and service the net usable areas. It is the architect's responsibility to see that the amount of unassignable space does not become disproportionate to that of the assigned net. A ratio of the net space divided by the gross space, expressed as a percentage, is said to represent the assignable efficiency of a building. This ratio typically will range from 65 percent to 75 percent and higher, depending on the size and nature of the facility. Larger facilities usually tend to have a higher efficiency, but other factors are often involved. For example, a one-room storage warehouse may be, by the definition, nearly 95 percent efficient while the efficiency of a bookmobile is probably no more than 50 percent (if such a machine could be considered an architectural space).

Conclusion

Four chapters have been devoted to the issues that should be addressed in a program; clearly the formulation of the program is exceedingly important to the success of the facility project. While many of the issues have been discussed in detail well beyond the program, it is well for the author of the program to have a clear understanding of the broader aspects of the specific issues. Samples of program documentation are provided in appendix A.

On the other hand, these four chapters should not be regarded as exhaustive. Some specific issues, such as the wiring for use of computers, the protection of exposed wall or column corners, and concerns with vandalism, will be discussed in the chapters on design and design development. In many cases it will be appropriate to cover issues such as these in the program; selected specifics can assure that librarians, institutional officers, and the architectural firm have a common understanding of quality issues, operational subtleties, safety concerns, educational goals, and financial matters of the short or long term.

The program writer should not lose sight of the fact that the program can be no more than a snapshot of a continually changing environment of facility need. Many detailed and subtle aspects of the building should evolve through the design process, with the program serving as a point of departure.

NOTE

1. Michael McCahill, "The Impact of the '80s on Academic Library Design" (paper delivered at a workshop of the International Federation of Library Associations and Institutions, Toronto, 1982), pp. 5–6.

9

Budgeting and Expense Control

Whatever is received is received according to the nature of the recipient.
      —Saint Thomas Aquinas, *On Being and Essence*

Clear justification is required from the very beginning of the library project. Gaining agreement involves an understanding not only of programmatic needs but also of three especially critical factors that require financial attention and on which a brief preliminary word is here given. One is the general quality of the building and its furnishings. This is dealt with in Section 9.2.1 of this chapter, and especially in points 2 through 6 therein. It includes consideration of the materials used in the structure, its regular or highly irregular shape, and the question of monumentality.

Second is the extent of technological integration, an issue discussed in Sections 13.2 and 13.4. It may be noted that in such a building as the University of Michigan Media Union (fig. 9.1), opened in 1996, the cost for wiring and equipment came to one-quarter of the total $50 million spent on the building; the cost of telecommunications, instructional computer labs, networked hardware, interactive and multimedia workstations, and television studios can be very large. Third is the timing of the project. In this case, the closeness to or inclusion in an institutional fund-raising campaign

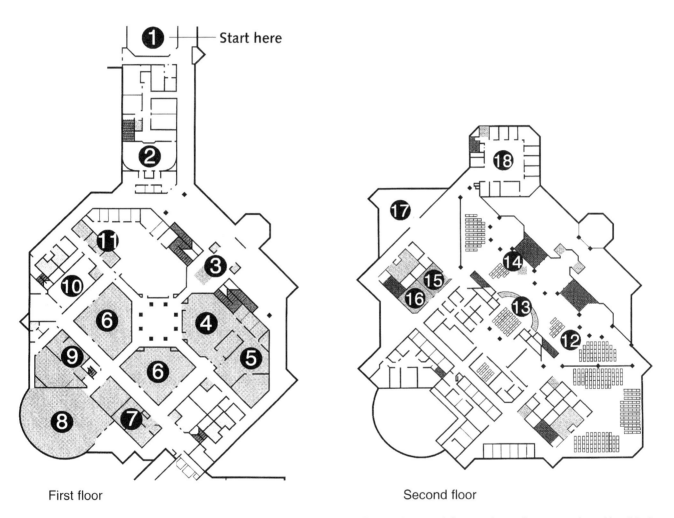

First floor   Second floor

FIGURE 9.1   University of Michigan Media Union, first and second floors. These diagrams of a self-guided tour beginning at (1) take the visitor to a video conference room (2), an information desk (3), an advanced visualization and animation lab (4), a virtual reality lab (5), design labs (6), an electronic music studio (7), a video/performance studio (8), an audio studio (9), a machine room and center for parallel computing (10), multimedia project rooms (11), the Media Union library (12), reserves desk (13), reference desk (14), media conversion room (15), computer consultation (16), the Millennium Project, which explores the future of the American university (17), and administrative offices (18). The PC and Mac training rooms, an image bank, monographic holdings, and rare books are found on upper floors. (Courtesy of University of Michigan Media Union)

and the bid climate when construction documents are ready as well as the urgency of the library need are all factors that can have a huge influence on the cost of the structure and the availability of funding. These three are emphasized because of the special financial implications.

On the costs of a library building project and execution of the program, there certainly should be no fundamental conflict between the institution's administration, the librarians, and the architect if they agree with the programmatic objectives and have goodwill, a true sense of educational values, an understanding of library priorities, and a desire to make sound financial judgments in planning a new library or undertaking major renovation.

9.1
Provision of Funds Required

Although discussions of funding a project may be found in Section 3.4, it is of such importance that it warrants extended discussion here. Ordinarily an institution does not go far with planning until funds are in sight, or until it is believed that they will be readily available. The actual realization of funding, however, particularly on a large project, may require a fairly well developed program and perhaps even the completion of schematic drawings in order that the scope of the project may be clearly understood. To reach this level of planning, some initial funding will be required, and before the initial funding, preliminary planning by the library and other administrative offices will have been completed.

Projects normally begin with a statement of need that, except perhaps for the very smallest projects, will take the form of a written document, which must receive the support of the institution's administration, if not the trustees. There is nearly always a continuing give-and-take between the scope of the project and the funding realities that begins at the earliest phase of most projects. The statement of need can establish priorities and approximate the scope of the project and the level of funding that may be required.

Once the project is given administrative encouragement, the statement of need is translated into an outline program statement (if one is not already part of the statement of need), including a breakdown of floor area requirements that can be used to establish a rough order of magnitude

for the project cost. This is easily determined by applying a cost per unit area as determined from buildings of the same type recently constructed under similar circumstances. Local experience of the added costs that typically make up the total project cost (more on this later), including a factor for inflation, can then be applied to establish an initial idea of the funding need. At this point decisions will be required to adjust the program scope or funding forecast so that the two conform.

One question that frequently must be addressed is whether the facility will be built at one time or in stages. This decision is a matter of primary importance. Building in stages is seldom desirable from a construction cost point of view and is usually not the most economical in the long run. To explain, much of the unbudgeted staff time and much of the budgeted project management costs in later stages can be saved if the total foreseeable needs are met in one project. Yet funding limitations or work on an existing facility may force acceptance of stages.

In many cases the next step involves partial funding, to permit the design process to proceed at least through the first design phase, the product of which may be used as part of the preparation for a campaign to establish funds. For small projects the statement of need is often sufficient to establish funding, but a large project usually requires much more information.

If the funds are to come from a government, various requests, justifications, and studies are generally needed; often special requirements are imposed on the project, which can add to the cost. Ordinarily the president of the institution, with the authorization of the governing board, originates the request to the governmental authorities, although the library and other administrative offices may prepare the actual application and supporting documents. The question of priority will arise between the library and other needs of the institution, and the decision will probably be made by the president or the governing board; but the librarians must be prepared to present the case clearly and succinctly. Answers to the policy decisions discussed in Chapter 3 should be clearly detailed, and the justifications of need should be well established.

Often, in fund-raising, an arbitrary value is put on the space occupied by a stack section, carrel, table, dissertation room, faculty study, or reading area. This value may properly be based on the project cost, including nonassignable space, rather than the cost of the equipment or the construction cost of specific rooms; that is, the cost of unsalable areas of the building, such as stairs, mechanical rooms, and corridors, can be prorated among the salable areas. For example, assuming that 40 percent of the project cost applies to areas that are not attractive as gift packages and assuming project cost of $150 per ft^2 (or about $1,600 per m^2), a tabulation of potential gifts may be as follows:

> Double stack section @ 10 ft^2/
>   0.929 m^2 .... $2,500
> Open carrel @ 35 ft^2/3.252 m^2 9,000
> Dissertation room @ 50 ft^2/4.645 m^2 ... 12,500
> Faculty study @ 80 ft^2/7.432 m^2 20,000
> Seminar room @ 200 ft^2/18.581 m^2 50,000
> Reading area @ 900 ft^2/83.613 m^2 225,000
> Computer lab @ 600 ft^2/55.742 m^2 .... 225,000[1]
>   (assuming that technology-equipped space costs, say, a 50% premium)

Of course, the funding strategy of a given institution may well shape the thinking for such a list of gift opportunities. A few major gifts, for example, may reduce the established cost of individual gift packages, while an expected decline in giving may argue for increasing their value. Furthermore, while $225,000 may seem reasonable for a reading area of considerable prominence, $20,000 may be excessive for a faculty study hidden in the basement stacks. It may be appropriate to introduce other factors in establishing such a list, thereby increasing somewhat some popular or more attractive gift opportunities and decreasing others. Employing professional fund-raisers who know different methods of presentation and appeal may be useful.

The long-term financing strategy needs consideration. If a new library or an addition to an old one is inadequate for space requirements for the next 20 to 25 years, obvious disadvantages will result. It may be more difficult to obtain funds for new space if the recent additional space has proved to be inadequate more quickly than many expected. If the present or about-to-be-built structure is named for the donor or in honor of a benefactor of the institution, an early necessity to obtain replacement space can cause great dissatisfaction and make future money raising a problem. The financing of a large addition is sometimes, but not always, more difficult than that of the original structure.

Financing arrangements can put together a wide variety of sources. Sometimes the full funding comes from a governmental source, though this seems to be less and less the case in the United States. Other donations from foundations and individuals can provide a significant proportion of the total. For instance, major expansion and renovation of the Knight Library at the University of Oregon was funded in the 1990s with $17.9 million of Oregon state funds and $9.7 million in gifts and grants raised as the top priority by the university fund-raising campaign. Fortunate was Pennsylvania State University to have its successful, popular head football coach chair the volunteer committee in the 1990s to raise $10 million in private funds for the library addition, matching $14.8 million in state funds for the project.

The desirability of obtaining an endowment for a new building, as well as the funds for its construction, should not be forgotten. The enthusiasm for a new central facility, desperately needed, can provide momentum for further donations. It may be that a class of alumni or an Alumni Fund Council may agree to accept responsibility for raising the endowment for the operating costs of the library, thereby relieving the college or university of a large part of the additional operating expenditures resulting from the new building. The Regenstein Library at the University of Chicago is an endowed library building. The question of endowment can be a matter of long-term importance.

9.2
Costs Involved in Construction

Costs will be affected by the geographical location of the building, and most of them by the economic climate prevailing when bids are taken and the contract is let. Is it a high-cost area? What are the local wage rates for the various construction trades? Are the demands great for new construction in the particular locality? Construction costs may be low in some parts of the country, such as the rural Southeast, and as much as 50 percent higher in such places as New York City, Hawaii, or Alaska. The architectural style selected and the quality of construction can have a great effect, as these may represent a considerable percentage of the total cost. The result of factors such as these is that any rule-of-thumb cost-per-unit area applied to the program or various design stages can represent only an educated guess. When budgets are prepared, suitable contingency moneys should be built in.

On a large project it is not uncommon to have an estimate prepared by the architect at each phase of the project. When there is great concern for the best accuracy possible, an independent estimate (sometimes called a confirming estimate) will be prepared by a separate estimating firm or construction consultant, for which of course there will be a fee.

9.2.1 Project Cost Model

To track a large project and readily be able to compare estimates, a more detailed breakdown of the costs, sometimes called a "project cost model," is a useful tool. The elements in the cost model may include 16 or more items:

1. Site preparation, including perhaps demolition, grading, and the relocation of utilities
2. Special foundations, including underpinning and basement excavations
3. Substructure, typically the structure required up to the first floor
4. Superstructure
5. Exterior walls, including windows and perhaps exterior sun-control devices
6. Roofing systems, including roof insulation, decks, flashing, gutters, waterproof membranes under floors in bathrooms or basements and, where they occur, custom shower stalls
7. Interior construction, including partitions, paneling, and sometimes carpet
8. Conveying and vertical transportation, including stairs, lifts, and elevators
9. Fixed equipment, such as toilet partitions and accessories, shelving, cabinets, chalkboards, and built-in equipment
10. Plumbing and fire protection, including rest room fixtures, roof and court drains, standpipes, sprinkler systems, and gaseous fire suppression systems for restricted areas, such as rare book stacks
11. Heating, ventilating, and air conditioning, commonly referred to as HVAC
12. Electrical systems, which include power, lighting, signal systems, and alarms as well as conduit for future systems. The HVAC controls are usually included in the preceding section.
13. Miscellaneous, which could include special protection for an adjacent structure, work in a joining building necessary for the addition, and trash disposal, which may be

substantial on a renovation or building addition project
14. Site development or landscape work, including irrigation systems, area drains, plantings, paths, site furniture and lighting, and separate parking areas for bicycles and motor vehicles
15. Utility connections, which may not be within the defined building site
16. General and special conditions applied to those portions of the work under the general contractor. This includes the cost to the contractor for bonds, insurance, and any other special costs incurred by the contractual conditions.

A final item might well be the contractor's overhead and profit. As this is usually a straight percentage of the total of the elements in the contract, it can be omitted from the cost model for comparative analysis, but it must not be forgotten in the total budget. A factor for inflation and contingencies can also be included and will be a straight percentage applied to the total of elements above.

When the cost model is used, tabulate the total cost for each category together with the cost per standard unit of area and the percentage of the total cost represented by each category. With this information, changes in cost or disagreement between estimators is easily identified and, when necessary, corrective action can be taken. The tabulation should have appropriate subtotals, particularly for those items that are not part of the general contract and thus to which the general and special conditions would not apply. Once the format for the cost model is established, each estimator should be required to prepare an estimate to fit the cost model in order to assure reasonable comparison.

In each of the estimates following a design phase, the architect and confirming estimator will clearly need to prepare costs based on an actual quantity survey, rather than on a cubic or square unit of area approximation. The latter is appropriate for the initial budgetary review, and it should be based on the program, including a factor for unassigned space. Quantity surveys are usually required under architectural agreements for government projects, and they are essential when careful control of the budget is required. In the early design phases, the architect will need to establish criteria for assumptions that are not yet fully developed in the plans so that a reasonable cost factor can be applied to cover those missing elements that are certain to emerge in later phases. Estimating is at best an informed forecast; although it is far from an exact science, the detailed estimate tends to be much more accurate.

In some cases it is desirable to tabulate other cost breakdowns. For example, in a project that involves insurance, such as reconstruction of a building after a fire, it may be necessary to separate those elements that are not covered by the insurance policy. Consultation with the institution's risk management officer and perhaps an insurance adjuster will be necessary. Another example is where there is need to tabulate the cost of energy-saving features in order to analyze their appropriateness or to seek separate funding or tax advantage. Or, major computer and other information technology costs may be aggregated if separate funding is available and exact cost accounting is desired. Such tabulations, although they may be required, can probably be best treated separately from the cost model.

In the creation of a project budget, the cost model represents only the basic construction cost. Figure 9.2 is an example of a project budget summary. It is not suitable for all institutions, but it can serve as an illustration. At the heading of the budget is some general information, including an entry for the Engineering News Record (ENR) Cost Index, which is available for various regions in the United States. This index is useful for comparing the costs on your project with costs of a similar project completed within the last few years. However, comparing current costs with costs more than five years ago is fairly difficult; it may be risky to rely on comparisons spanning many years as a means of measuring recent economies. The Engineering News Record Cost Index is also useful as a guide to future costs, but again, cost comparison is risky business in a changing economy, and it should be approached with care.

The first construction cost entries are expressed in terms of current costs. This figure may be the basis for the architect's fees, which are discussed later. Some architects wish to include the design/construction contingency in their fee calculations; to do so is appropriate only if the initial estimate of construction cost upon which the fees are established did not include such a contingency. This contingency is intended to cover the cost of minor changes in the design and changes required because of unknown field conditions. At the ear-

lier phases of a project, it should be as much as 12 to 15 percent. As the project progresses, it typically is reduced to 7 to 10 percent at the beginning of construction. Much less than 7 percent at the time of construction is generally regarded as risky unless there are other clearly established mechanisms to deal with construction surprises.

The practice in the United Kingdom with respect to contingencies is to include from the time of first estimate an amount not less than 3 percent as a design reserve, the figure varying depending on the complexity of the problem. This reserve is generally reduced to nil by the time the job goes to bid. An additional 3 percent maximum is a contingency for unforeseen site problems.

It is necessary to project the cost rise to the midpoint of construction for large projects that will take one or several years to construct, because the contractor will bid the job taking into account anticipated labor and material cost rises for the term of the project. For smaller projects a cost rise projected to the anticipated start of construction may be adequate. Probably the best guide to establishing the cost-rise factor involves taking an educated guess after consultation with various cost indexes, a contractor or two, and perhaps an architect or construction consultant. In some countries with adverse economic conditions, this factor can be major, 50 percent or even more. It should be applied to the preceding subtotal.

"Other construction" generally applies to construction that is properly charged to the project yet is not part of the architect's scope of work. Examples include a replacement parking lot if the project site takes an existing parking lot, work done earlier to stabilize a damaged building, or temporary quarters to house functions during a remodeling project. This item also should include separate contracts for prepurchased items (for example, the institution may purchase a major piece of equipment or structural component at a favorable price and assign it to the contractor once the contract is let) and the cost for utility connections that are outside the basic contract. Care must be taken to consider the need to include factors for contingency or cost rise on this line item.

"Equipment and furnishings" generally includes all the facility-related elements that are to be purchased outside the construction contract. This figure commonly ranges from 6 to 20 percent of construction cost, depending on such factors as the amount of computer and audiovisual

CITY UNIVERSITY
Facilities Project Management   PROJECT COST AND TIME SUMMARY
Project: <u>6789 Roberts House Library</u>   Pjt Mgr: <u>   Mitchell   </u> GSF: <u> 7,000</u>
Phase: <u>Schematics   </u>   Date: <u>January 18, 1995</u>   ENR Cost Index <u>3513.73</u> At: <u>San Francisco</u>

	Amount	Pct	$/SF
1A. Basic Construction (Prime Consultant's Scope)			
1. Building	$ 1,123,000	47.2%	160.43
2. Equipment in Contract	0	0.0%	0
SUBTOTAL (1A1 thru 1A2)	$ 1,123,000	47.2%	$ 160.43
3. Site Work	32,500	1.4%	4.64
SUBTOTAL (1A1 thru 1A3)	$ 1,155,500	48.5%	$ 165.07
4. Construction Escalation <u>24</u> months @ <u>0.75%</u>/month	208,000	8.7%	29.71
BASIC CONSTRUCTION BUDGET (1A)	$ 1,363,500	57.3%	$ 194.78
1B. Other Construction	26,500	1.1%	3.79
TOTAL CONSTRUCTION BUDGET (1)	$ 1,390,000	58.4%	$ 198.57
2. Fixtures, Furniture & Equipment (FF&E)			
(Not in Construction Contract)	100,000	4.2%	14.29
3. Professional Services	383,000	16.1%	54.71
4. Administrative Costs	172,300	7.2%	24.61
5. Activation	4,000	0.2%	0.57
PROJECT SUBTOTAL (1 thru 5)	$ 2,049,300	86.1%	292.76
6. Project Contingency <u>15.0%</u> of Construction Budget	208,500	8.8%	29.79
7. General Plant Improvement			
Campus plan & facility improvements			
<u>5.0%</u> × Construction Budget (1A)	68,200	2.9%	9.74
Parking / transportation system			
<u>4.0%</u> × Construction Budget (1A)	54,500	2.3%	7.79
8. Replacement Parking <u> 0</u> spaces @ <u> </u>/ space	0	0.0%	0.00
9. Other Project Costs <u> </u>	0	0.0%	0.00
<u> </u>	0	0.0%	0.00
TOTAL PROJECT BUDGET	$ 2,380,500	100%	$ 340.07

Prepared by: _____   Date: _____

Reviewed by: _____   Date: _____

Approved by: _____   Date: _____

FIGURE 9.2 **Example of the project budget summary. This particular project suggests a complex remodeling where the design fees are subsequently higher than normal. Such a form is frequently attached to numerous other pages elaborating each of the cost components.**

equipment. Movable furniture, discussed later, is usually budgeted here. Artwork may come here, though in some states, such as Florida and Oregon, a percentage of the project cost must go to art and may therefore be placed in a separate line by itself. Interior horticultural plants, building graphics, security alarm systems, pencil sharpeners, coat hooks, wastebaskets, carpet protectors, and the like would normally be budgeted here. On some projects, chalkboards, tackboards, shelving, carpet, interior sun-control devices, and other elements may be in this budget category. In establishing the budget figure, do not forget mockups, shipping, tax, storage, and installation costs as well as the cost of inflation.

"Professional services" of course includes the architect's fees. Other fees would include an acoustics consultant, soils testing, survey work, a library consultant, interior design, a construction consultant, a security consultant, and cost consultants. If there is to be an exercise of "value engineering," or a review of the energy effectiveness of the design, the fees for this work should be budgeted here as well.

Budgeting for "administrative costs" will, to a certain degree, be shaped by the policy of the particular institution. If the facility project management offices charge their time to the project, then this can be a significant budget element. In fact, if all internal administrative costs are charged to the project, it could total as much as the architect's fee. Included here may be other costs for insurance, plan check fees, and perhaps the cost of travel to other similar facilities during the design stages of the project. The cost for printing extra sets of the various documents prepared during the course of the project should be included here as well. If a special model or rendered drawings of the project are required, their cost should be here unless budgeted under professional services.

"Activation" of a new facility normally includes the installation of phones, the moving of books, staff desks, and equipment, and a thorough cleaning of the building. Institutional policy may require a factor for the first-year plant operation and maintenance cost unless it is covered in the physical plant annual operations budget. It is prudent to budget for the services of an activation coordinator, which, on a large project, could require a full-time staff position for a year or more to plan the activation strategy and supervise the installation of furniture and the actual move into the new facility.

A project contingency (to be distinguished from the construction contingency) is sometimes included and can be as much as 10 to 15 percent of the construction budget at the early stages of the project. The sum budgeted as a contingency can be reduced as the project nears completion. It is intended as a reserve for possible scope changes and it typically cannot be spent without going through a special approval process. If institution policy permits, and if there is an unexpended balance at the end of the project, it would be prudent to authorize some maximum figure, such as one-tenth of one percent of construction cost, for changes after the building is occupied. There is almost always some condition that was not anticipated—perhaps a missing door, an increase needed in the security control system, some additional carpeting, extra signs, or a few plants.

"General plant improvement" in this example is a self-imposed tax used to pay for improvements in the central steam and chilled water plants, utility distribution systems, campus streets, general parking areas, and the like. Clearly the use of this infrastructure line item will vary from institution to institution. At Stanford University this item amounts to 9 percent of the basic construction cost on interior remodeling projects in excess of $750,000, and a similar pro rata charge is applied to any new structure regardless of cost. "Replacement parking" is treated separately.

It should be noted that the illustrated budget structure suggests a cost advantage by removing as much as reasonably possible from the basic construction and placing it in the equipment and furnishings category or another appropriate line item. Such an allocation avoids the self-imposed tax as well as the money set aside as a project contingency. The prudent project manager must be aware of the budget structure in order to decide the wisest management of the project.

The entry for "other," while seldom used, might be the appropriate category to charge the professional services incurred by an earlier design that may have been shelved pending funding and later scrapped because it was found to be unconvincing. The decision to include such an expense in the current project or write it off elsewhere must come from the institution's financial administrators. The construction financing allowance is another expense that can be treated optionally. This latter item assumes that gifts or other receipts intended to pay for construction will not be in hand before the start of construction and that interest will be paid on borrowed money. If the loan is later advantageously refinanced, or gifts come in faster or slower, the financing allowance can accordingly be reduced or may be increased by reducing one of the contingency line items.

From this discussion, it can be inferred that the creation of a project budget is fairly complex and that there are a number of different ways to put it together, each having somewhat different results. Because of this, it is not useful to compare total project costs between different institutions without a complete understanding of how the total project cost was arrived at and what it includes. The example shown here probably includes more expense items than many, particularly the items for general plant improvements, construction financing, and perhaps administrative costs and "others."

The following discussion elaborates six expense categories:

1. The basic structure itself, including finishes and fixed equipment
2. Electrical and mechanical installations, including elevators, fire protection, security systems, and plumbing (the air-handling system is by far the most costly in this category)
3. Furniture and movable equipment, which may or may not include shelving, carpet, and sun control (drapes or blinds). If these items are not included here, they frequently are found in the first category
4. Site development, including utility connections, parking lots, and landscape work
5. Architectural and other fees of consultants
6. Administrative costs, including the cost of activation, insurance, plan check fees, phone installation, final cleaning costs, and perhaps an increment for the first year of plant operation and maintenance plus any institutional surcharge or local taxes applied to new projects

Taken together, these expense categories form the basis for creating the total project budget, perhaps in the format suggested earlier.

9.2.2 The Basic Structure

The largest single factor in the cost of a new building is the structure itself, which typically would include categories 2 through 7 and part of 8 in the cost model described above. Factors in other areas of the cost model may of course have an effect on the structural costs. In general in the United States, the structure will be less expensive in the South than in the North; on the average, southern labor rates are lower, and heating requirements tend to be lower, although cost of air-conditioning equipment may be greater, as may be the cost of transporting to the site material fabricated at a distance. Although the midsummer temperature is little if any hotter in the South than in many other parts of the United States, cooling equipment, if available, will be used there for longer periods of time, and so the charges for energy and maintenance may be greater, and the cost of components, which include such energy-saving factors as insulation or double glazing, may be higher where ambient temperatures require long periods of heating or cooling. In earthquake country there is added cost in the basic structure required to provide suitable seismic resistance. Living standards in the area, as well as the mechanical or structural details, are factors, both in terms of initial construction cost and of the ongoing costs of plant operations and maintenance.

In general, costs are reduced by distance from large cities, where the labor rates tend to be higher; but it is sometimes found that, because there is a shortage of local labor, the workers must be imported from a nearby city day by day or for the duration of the construction period and that city rates prevail and sometimes "portal-to-portal" charges are involved. Some rural areas, therefore, may be more expensive than urban locations.

If plans happen to be submitted for bids at a time of great or prospective shortage of labor or materials or both, quotations are likely to be high. An uncertain economic environment can be an equally troubling influence on the final bid. If the work must be rushed for one reason or another and overtime or weekend work is expected, the effect must be considered. In some places where there is a labor shortage, unions may insist on overtime with its increased costs.

An important factor in determining costs may be the need of the bidding contractors for work to hold a labor force together in slack periods. Under some circumstances they are ready to submit bids that produce a comparatively small profit or none at all. In a few cases institutions are able to take advantage of the fact that a contractor is available who for one reason or another is prepared to make little or no profit on the job—perhaps because of a philanthropic interest as an alumnus, because of religious affiliation, or because of an interest in obtaining other work at the institution. Such a reduction in price is difficult to establish as a gift for tax purposes, and it should be realized that a contractor who for any reason bids too low and is in danger of losing money may skimp and require special supervision if quality work is to be expected.

Beware of the inexperienced or inadequately financed contractor who may not be able to produce and so may involve the institution in a complicated, expensive, and embarrassing situation. Contractors (and architects, as Stanford University has found out) have gone bankrupt, resulting in delays and extra costs for the project and possibly requiring legal action with consequent expense. These problems apply to both the general contractor and subcontractors, which may suggest the institution should prequalify or reserve the right to reject any bidder, which is commonly the case.

The clarity and completeness of the plans and specifications will have a considerable influence on bids. On the one hand, an unethical contractor may submit a bid on exactly what is shown in the contract documents with minimal or no profit, expecting to make ample profit on the change orders required to complete the project. Negligence and fraud are always a possibility. On the other hand, if the bidders cannot be absolutely sure of just what will be expected of them, they may quite properly add a significant contingency to their bids or make their own interpretation of the details—a proceeding that is generally inadvisable. Both approaches result in extra costs, and the final budget cost may be 5 percent or more higher than it would have been with better-prepared working drawings and specifications.

The effect of soil conditions on the cost of excavations and foundations must not be forgotten. The excavation of basement space was expensive for the Cornell University Olin Library, placed where rock was close to the surface, and on that account the basement extent was limited. In the more recent design of the nearby Kroch Library, it was decided that the preservation of open site was more important than the cost of rock removal; the new library is basically an underground library largely excavated from rock. To avoid budgetary surprises from circumstances such as these, it is essential that soil tests and a site survey be completed in the early phases of the design effort, perhaps even before the first feasibility study is completed. The cost for this kind of survey is always in addition to normal architectural services, and it is usually contracted for by the institution directly with a soils engineer or survey firm. In completing the site survey it is important to accurately identify existing utilities as well as building elevations where two buildings are to be joined. Although this may be obvious advice, all too often the recorded information is inaccurate or incomplete, which ultimately will add to the total cost.

When rebuilding on previously used land, as occurs frequently in urban areas, old foundations unless excavated can cause serious problems, even forcing the relocation of new footings at some expense. This happened during construction of the Tompkins-McCaw Library of Virginia Commonwealth University in 1971. Poorly placed footings for an adjacent building can cause similar problems when the new building abuts the older one. Furthermore, in known rock areas, ample test borings should be made and checked carefully, because occasional large cracks in subterranean rocks cause false impressions when a test drill encounters soil. This was the experience during the 1966 construction of the University of Arkansas library. Estimated excavation costs rise rapidly when unexpected rock is encountered.

Several factors, then, result in different costs under different conditions—location, time, and the contractor's need for work or interest in getting a particular job at the time when the contract is bid, a factor referred to as the bid climate.

It has already been indicated that construction costs vary widely in different locations. They may be 15 percent higher or more in Washington, D.C., Boston, or San Francisco than in southern Virginia or central Maine. In 1996, construction cost in New York City was 36 percent higher than in Calgary, Alberta; 40 percent higher than in Washington, D.C.; and 73 percent higher than in Charlotte, North Carolina. In any location, stone exterior walls for a Gothic building will cost perhaps 75 percent more than brick in regions where brick is common or 100 percent more than concrete. Of course, the walls may involve only 10 percent of the total construction cost. Likewise, air conditioning may add to the total as much as 10 percent over the cost of a ventilation system or 15 percent over a heating system alone because of space used by ducts and the price of the mechanical equipment. Lighting installations, though they may vary widely in cost, represent only a comparatively small percentage of the total. The floor covering costs may vary tremendously. The same holds true for computer-based systems and for furniture. However, decisions to reduce the total costs in these areas are difficult or the options limited by other factors.

You get what you pay for if proper care is used, and you must decide what is worthwhile under your particular circumstances. You can pay for beauty, for utility, for comfort, for spaciousness, and for long life. You can pay for monumentality that gives little in the way of function or capacity for books and readers but that may be desirable for other reasons. The institution should select what it wants and be aware of what it can afford, always remembering that in the long run, floor area is the primary factor of costs. If the functional capacity can be increased 25 percent by careful planning without interfering with function or creating a congested effect, it should be done. The cost of the time spent in careful planning will be well rewarded in the final cost of the facility.

Construction costs can be examined from another point of view and divided into eight categories, each of which will be discussed.

1. *The cost of flexibility.* Although it is prudent to provide flexibility in the internal arrangements of a new building, the degree of flexibility must be balanced against the cost. There is no such thing as absolute flexibility, and maximum flexibility is expensive. Zones of greater flexibility may be properly established. For example, the capacity to install movable or compact shelving may be limited to the basement, or the capacity to install sophisticated electronic systems may be intentionally provided only in reading and staff areas. A required ability to put an electrical outlet anyplace in the building may suggest a ducted or raised floor system, which is expensive but justified in some cases, or an open trough above a suspended ceiling, or it may suggest that a future outlet will be installed by drilling a hole through the floor and installing conduit in the ceiling space below, which, though resulting in a greater cost later, may be an appropriate compromise. Most of the space allocated to nonstorage functions at the U.S. National Archives II is outfitted with a raised floor as a means of accommodating change.

Keep in mind that virtually every partition, even those thought of as easily moved, will require patching and changes in electrical services, if not

mechanical and other services, when the space is changed in the future. The flexibility provided by so-called movable partitions may not be worth the added initial cost. Open office movable panel systems are costly too; yet, of the flexible means of dividing space, these systems probably offer the greatest options for flexibility but often at the expense of acoustic privacy. As in the other areas of cost consideration, there must be a clear understanding of the alternatives with which cogent decisions can be made.

2. *The costs resulting from monumentality.* There is sometimes a place for monumentality, by which is meant a structure of imposing shape and expensive if somewhat lavish finishes. The question is, does the institution want it, or is the institution ready to pay for it if the architect proposes it? The new University of California, San Diego, began in 1970 with a dramatic library building of unique geometric shape, which was expanded in 1992. Shortly thereafter, the widow of Theodor Seuss Geisel, the creator of the Dr. Seuss books for children, made a gift to the university of a huge sum, explaining that the first time her husband saw that library he said, "If I had turned my thoughts toward designing a building, it might have looked strangely similar to this," for the architectural landmark was a favorite of his. The world would be poorer if it had no monuments, no buildings of a striking or dramatic design. However, much if not most aesthetic satisfaction comes from beauty and distinction, not from monumental spaciousness or grandeur that adds little else.

The 1932 Doheny Library of the University of Southern California is brick, limestone, and marble in a northern Italian Romanesque style, with the main hall 38 ft (11.582 m) high and the main reading room 131 ft (39.929 m) long. The Doe Library at Berkeley has one space 45½ ft (13.868 m) high. Both buildings are functionally difficult. The Low Library at Columbia University has been termed the perfect example of the victory of architect over librarian. The Goddard Library at Clark University has been called "a riveting assembly of architectural elements juxtaposed, cantilevered, tiled, and angled . . . a tour de force of volumes and cavities." Yet the price paid is a mix of problems of function, air handling, light, and acoustics. Particularly if funds are scarce, monumentality may be seriously questioned, unless its value for the overall objectives of the building is clearly shown.

3. *Costs arising from nonfunctional but aesthetic architecture.* This is a difficult problem and the returns, while still a matter of choice, may be so clear and evident that they are often more defensible and desirable than those for monumentality. One may ponder this question: Is true beauty ever nonfunctional? The costs should be known and understood and weighed against what could be accomplished by using the funds in another way. If one has to choose between marble walls and space for the storage of 50,000 more volumes or air conditioning, a decision must be made.

Those responsible should listen to the architect's proposal, be sure that they understand what is involved, and then act as they balance the pros and cons. If an extra $100,000 for architectural distinction will result in students using the library more, or provide stimulation and foster a love for the finer things of life, these benefits may be more important than the space for additional books that are not yet at hand. This line of thinking may well be applied to other aspects of the project, including furnishings, lighting, and those elements that make up the total environment of the library. The answers are not easily found, but the decisions should not go by default.

4. *Costs for additional comfort.* These expenditures can go for comfortable chairs, for instance; for quieter rooms, through the use of acoustic materials that will enable the reader to forget about the surroundings; for lighting as satisfactory as possible; or for better air conditioning, heating, and ventilation. All these help users to forget about physical surroundings that too often interfere with concentration. Temperature and humidity in all libraries until the last half-century were certainly secondary in design emphasis to a place to sit. Nevertheless, with the technical capacities and knowledge of psychology we now have, there is general agreement that comfort obtained at reasonable cost is worthwhile. Furthermore, control of the temperature and humidity will increase use of the library as well as add to the expected life of the books.

5. *Costs for operational convenience.* Functional convenience, as it might be called, is a lot more tangible than comfort. Anything within reasonable limits that will provide arrangements so that books can be found more easily seems unquestionably worthwhile. Convenient methods of transportation for books from one floor to another save time for the staff and therefore operating costs for the institution. Moving large

numbers of people upward by escalators may improve the desirability value of the second or third level, perhaps increasing fund-raising opportunities on those floors. Individual tables that encourage study may be included in this category as well as an underground tunnel to an adjacent building, which will help solve the space problem and aid operations of a branch located therein.

6. *Costs for sturdiness, long life, and lower plant operations and maintenance.* These costs are often not fully considered, and they prompt two sharply conflicting points of view. One may say that if, by spending $100,000 more on construction, the annual upkeep and maintenance cost will be reduced by $10,000 or more, then the expenditure will be desirable. (Some would say that a payback of less than 10 years makes an investment attractive. At a 10-year payback, the return would need to be about $1,180 per month at an interest rate of 7.25 percent to pay off a $100,000 loan.) One might also say that if at the end of 25 years the building is physically as good as it is now, so much the better. The other philosophy is that within 25 years the building will be outmoded and no longer totally functional because of changing educational methods and demands, and that the common business practice of counting on a depreciating asset and inevitable obsolescence should be followed with the initial investment minimized in terms of provision for extended utility.

When potential savings in maintenance or operational costs can be identified and quantified, it is often useful to analyze these savings in relation to the projected initial cost, using present value formulas. To do this, a number of assumptions must be made, including the rate of inflation, interest rates, the life expectancy, and the anticipated annual savings, all of which can be little more than educated guesses. The technique, however, does provide interesting data in terms of an annual rate of return or a comparison of future savings in relation to current expense. The analysis, though complex, is greatly facilitated with modern computer software. A good book on business economics will explain the procedures in detail.

Some would argue that academic institutions should reject the concept of minimal initial investment, which may well be the case where design flexibility and remodeling can prolong life value. However, in those areas where savings in cost can be established without affecting the academic program, the business philosophy may be appropriate. Clearly, the definition of the academic or operational program must be well established in order to avoid losing important elements of it for economic reasons without realizing it.

At Harvard, the philosophy of long-term utility even at added initial expense has been the accepted norm. In addition, the university typically has set up a maintenance reserve against each building with the funds always available for repair and emergency, and there is no limit to a building's length of life. It is not the function of this volume to tell the reader which is the preferable philosophy but to point out the problem and suggest that each administration make its own conscious decision.

7. *Costs resulting from technical errors.* These costs are perhaps easier to see by hindsight than foresight. Sometimes the waste and unfortunate expenditures result from ignorance with no one really to blame. For instance, Halon gas has for years been used in rare book or special collection stack vaults; now it is banned because of the effect of Halon on ozone depletion. Maintaining existing Halon systems will soon be problematic, and their replacement costly. Or the building design is about finished when an earthquake at great distance prompts the local building code to be made more rigorous. Thus, the width of the building columns is increased a very small amount, which throws the stack spacing off and much book capacity is lost. The new British Library building was found, late in construction, to have 2,000 miles (3,200 km) of electrical cabling that could have ignited, and thus had to be replaced. Or sometimes a floor covering proves to be of poor quality because of a change of formula or materials available to the manufacturer. Perhaps research simply had not gone far enough.

Keyes Metcalf identified one of his major blunders as a recommendation he made for cork tile in the sub-subbasement of the Lamont Library, which is 36 ft (10.973 m) below the entrance level and well underground. Although he knew that it was not customary to lay cork in such a place, he also knew that it had been used successfully in the Houghton Library, almost as far beneath the ground and only a few yards away, and his technical advisor did not discourage him. It proved to be a bad gamble, with resulting large expenditures for replacement. The best planning efforts will usually result in several similar stories, even if they are not of the same scale.

8. *Costs of special planning that more than pay for themselves.* To give proper consideration to each category will take time and will cost money that should be well worth the effort. A few thousand dollars of time and study is a bargain if it results in chairs that remain strong for decades, or a module size that gains usable space. Time used preparing layouts for seating accommodations is money well spent if it makes available 50 more seats without reducing aisle widths or table space per reader or causing a feeling of congestion. This list could be lengthened almost indefinitely, but the desired results will not be forthcoming without the availability of knowledge, experience, time, and patience. It is hoped that the information presented in this volume will help.

If these eight points are kept in mind and if there is a reasonable meeting of minds between the architect and the administration in regard to the needs of the institution, misunderstanding or complications need not arise. Each of the expense categories may involve disagreements, until the problems have been talked out thoroughly.

9.2.3 Electrical and Mechanical Installations

Electrical and mechanical installations would include categories 10, 11, 12, and part of 8 in the project cost model suggested earlier in Section 9.2.1. Together they may range from 20 percent to as much as 35 percent of the total cost, excluding any substantial investment in electronic equipment. The chief factors are lighting, plumbing, heating, air conditioning or ventilating, mechanical transportation, security, and control systems. In each case there is a question of the initial cost of installation as well as costs for maintenance, replacement, and operation.

Though electronic equipment, such as computers and servers, may be treated as equipment and budgeted separately, the infrastructure to support information technology is very important and can cause the electrical costs to vary greatly as suggested above. Primary factors affecting that fluctuation include the amount of floor ducts and conduit and the type and amount of cabling used—whether bandwidth needs to be 1 or 10 or 100 or 1,500 megahertz. If only unshielded twisted pair (UTP) wiring is used, the expense will be modest. However, shielded twisted pair (STP) wiring is desirable for fax, modem, ISDN, and medium to fast network connection. And coaxial high-quality video cable (RG-59, or RG-6, which has better shielding from interference) is desirable for video, cable TV, and modem or satellite TV. Then, if shielded twisted pair (called CAT-3, or level 3 UTP) or high-quality video coaxial cable (such as RG-6) is used extensively, the cable/wire cost can be tripled or quintupled. To keep down later costs of pulling or replacing wires and cables, the specification of color-coded wires and cables is necessary. Oversized conduit and raceway (at added cost) are also highly recommended to accommodate future change and increased support of wire-based information technologies.

Increased lighting intensity will, in many cases, mean a higher original cost and greater cost for replacement tubes or bulbs; the increased cost of energy may be even greater over time. A 10-foot-candle (107.6-lux) difference may gain nothing, yet 30 or 40 will. On the other hand, individual range aisle switching and task lighting are not inexpensive, yet the energy savings may be substantial. (Some codes may mandate stack lighting control devices for energy savings.) Furthermore, light originating in high ceilings is in general much more wasteful than a source closer to the working level, though the need for aesthetic ambient light is acknowledged.

Even in the South Temperate Zone, heating of some kind is at times necessary; this is true in most parts of the world outside the Tropics, although in the past many libraries in Australia, New Zealand, South Africa, India, and even the British Isles had little in the way of satisfactory provision for heating. With an increasing concern for preserving library materials, air conditioning has become common in the United States, even in the relatively cool and dry climates found along parts of the West Coast. Air conditioning may add 10 percent or even more to the total cost of the building, although it may make possible certain savings through making practical lower ceilings, more fixed windows (with improved security), less exterior wall, and more regular exterior wall shapes. Moreover, even if the need for human comfort does not convince one of the necessity for cooling, its usefulness in significantly prolonging the life of the book, manuscript, microtext, and other collections should at least be considered. This issue is discussed in greater detail in Chapter 5.

Plumbing is another expensive item, particularly where the library is fitted with a fire suppression system. Although controversy exists over the use of such a system, the authors feel that in most cases the risk and cost are well worth the protective benefit of it.

One way to reduce the risk of loss by fire while reducing the risk of water damage is to divide the library into relatively small fireproof compartments that minimize loss potential or may be small enough to avoid the requirement for sprinklers. In secure private stacks, such as those that house manuscripts and archives, a carbon dioxide or other gas-based system may be used, thus eliminating water hazard. Of the gaseous systems, gas selected for human occupation of the space is preferred because of the considerable risk to human life with a carbon dioxide system. (Yale's Beinecke Library below-ground stack is compartmentalized and carbon dioxide protected.) Of course, compartmentalization will add to the structural costs, and it may be contrary to the intended function of the library.

The costs for rest rooms and drains may be reduced if the building is planned so that the pipes are limited in number and shortened by being stacked vertically. Consideration can be given in some countries to not providing hot water in rest rooms, though this saving is not recommended, and it may not be permitted by some codes.

Mechanical transportation by means of elevators, booklifts, conveyors, escalators, and pneumatic tubes is another large item included in the mechanical group. In this connection it should be noted that air conditioning or heating and ventilating systems, as well as vertical transportation, are usually operated by automatic equipment of considerable complexity, which in turn means that specially trained personnel need to be readily available either through a maintenance contract or through the institution's plant maintenance group.

Dumbwaiter-type booklifts involve staff members at both ends to be fully effective. There are automatic booklifts, but these often are problematic and tend to be noisy. Endless belt conveyors tend to present similar difficulties unless they are kept to the simplest possible terms. Escalators are in use in a few libraries, such as at the University of Connecticut, California State University at Sacramento, the University of Miami's Richter Library, and the University of Michigan's Media Union. However, they are expensive to construct and operate, can be noisy (as the University of Miami has found out), and use more space than does a flight of stairs with landings. They are justified only where there is a large flow of people; even then an elevator will be required for handicapped access and book truck movement. Pneumatic tubes are not without their difficulties; frequently, simpler means of transporting materials and information result in a more satisfactory and cheaper solution. It should be noted that a great many library buildings that had booklifts, conveyers, and intercoms ceased using them after a few years.

Signal transmission includes phones, intercom systems, public address systems, security alarms, fire detection systems, audio and television distribution, and all forms of electronic or computer-related information systems. This area where there is frequently the greatest concern for flexibility, as suggested earlier, will need careful planning in order to avoid excessive capacity that will never be used, and yet it needs to anticipate expanding future needs.

Each of these items is complicated and may involve a not negligible percentage of the total cost of the building. A fuller discussion of these problems will be found as follows: in Section 13.2.1 on concepts of mechanical systems; Section 13.2.2 on concepts of lighting and sun control; Section 12.4.3 on vertical transportation; and Sections 13.2 and 13.4.4 on signal transmission and computer installations.

9.2.4 Furniture, Movable Equipment, and Bookstacks

Movable equipment and furniture are normally not considered part of the basic construction cost, and thus they are budgeted and tracked separately. The cost of movable equipment is no minor matter; it may represent 15 percent of the project cost of the new facility and may exceed that considerably if bookstacks, carpet, and sun control are included.

It is striking that in the late 1990s the equipment proportion of a library project budget, both for colleges and universities, finds many a project spending 10 to 20 percent on this category partly because of the costs of electronic equipment on top of the usual bookstacks and tables and chairs. Of course, what movable materials are included in the "equipment" will vary from project to project, so this project cost range for equipment is merely to illustrate the financial significance of this category. It may be indicative of the future, into the early decades of the twenty-first century, that the University of Michigan Media Union (two major branch libraries associated with a large array of information technologies) spent 25 percent to equip this new instructional library complex. This may become a more common proportion for library equipment as the Electronic Age develops, particularly where new technology is fully funded within the facility budget rather than in operating budgets.

Bookstacks may be treated as built-in equipment in the basic contract, or they can be contracted for separately and handled as furniture. Where there is coordination of electrical, structural, or other work in the installation of the bookstacks, it is recommended that shelving should be made part of the basic construction contract so the contractor can coordinate the various trades and assume the responsibility for the completed facility.

Other important and expensive equipment includes special shelving (often of wood), tables and carrels with chairs for readers (generally the largest single item after the bookstack), service desks (when they are not built in for the circulation department, reference area, the exit control desk, and so on), office equipment, index tables, and, in some cases, catalog cases. The last of these is very expensive and is rapidly being superseded by online catalogs. Carpet, in some cases, is included in the furnishings budget as it is often specified by the interior designer; it can be contracted for outside the general construction contract, generally at a savings to the project resulting from the avoidance of the general contractor's overhead and profit. Movable furnishings and carpet in 1996 could cost as much as $16 per gross ft^2 (or about $172 per gross m^2), although this can vary dramatically. Stacks would be added to this cost, though the proportionate cost to be added for the overall gross area will vary substantially depending upon the ratio of shelving to non-shelving in the library. As a rough rule of thumb, shelving will add about $15 to $20 per ft^2 (roughly $150 to $200 per m^2) for the space occupied by standard fixed shelving, or up to $100 per ft^2 ($1,000 per m^2) of stack space for motorized compact shelving, if used. Assuming 50 percent of the library is shelving, then the cost of stacks will add from $7.50 to $10 per gross ft^2 (roughly $75 to $100 per gross m^2). Other ratios of stack to nonstack space can easily be calculated.

Artwork can make a house a home. It is generally included in the budget for furnishings, though sometimes it is separately tracked or is part of the base construction where it can be treated as an "allowance." Occasionally artwork is handled separately from the building project and treated in the category for special gifts. Choices can include paintings, sculpture, murals, flags, graphic prints, photographs, banners, stained glass, and even plants. Although allowing one-tenth of 1 percent of the budget for art is usually quite reasonable, especially if a sculptural fountain or large specimen of a rare tree is desired, selecting at least some items from existing library or museum collections can keep costs down. A few states (Florida, Oregon, and Utah among them) require that a full 1 percent of construction cost be spent on artwork. An interesting example is the Trinity University Library stairwell mural, *Man's Evolving Images, Printing and Writing,* a collage measuring 15 ft × 80 ft (4.572 × 24.384 m), which took over six years for research and execution. At Bowling Green University, the University of Notre Dame, and the University of Mexico, the exterior library murals provide dominating visual images, a signature of each institution.

Certain equipment may be treated separately for various reasons and may not be part of the basic facility budget. This type of equipment often includes microtext readers, photocopy machines, special equipment for the blind or partially sighted, typewriters, audio equipment (unless it is built in), television equipment, computer terminals and workstations, and perhaps security equipment. This last item is occasionally treated separately to limit the publication of specifications for security reasons.

The balance of the equipment may be thought of as capital equipment, properly financed through the annual operating budget or through other special programs with separate financing sources. It seldom fits the definition of movable furniture or facility-related equipment. On the other hand, if it is useful and persuasive for building fundraising to make a sizable and appealing component package of audiovisual equipment or computers, then inclusion is appropriate.

Equipment as a category tends to require a larger percentage of the total cost in a low-wage area; unless equipment can be locally designed and fabricated, it may be more expensive there than in otherwise high-cost areas. A library in India might be taken as an example because steel shelving and other items have in the past had to be imported.

It should be expected that as the size of the equipment or furnishings purchase of any kind increases, the cost per piece will go down. In many small libraries the number of chairs, tables, and other items required in each group is so small that they will probably be too expensive to justify custom design. This means that the library must depend on standard equipment houses, a procedure with real advantages. The quality and design, though not always aesthetically pleasing to those belonging to the avant-garde, will be sound and sturdy. You can generally count on the equipment's long life, but you can expect that the cost will be fairly high, partly because of the large overhead costs of the companies. Fortunately, there is generally enough competition among companies to maintain costs at a reasonable level. And in some state institutions and with some purchasing cooperative organizations, the purchasing power generated by increased numbers of buying institutions can result in actual purchase costs substantially below list.

Basic decisions—such as whether to use custom-designed furniture or standard library equipment, or what materials, particularly metal or wood, carpet or vinyl tile floors, or marble or plastic laminate countertops—will greatly affect the ultimate cost of the furnishings. As already suggested, the definition of what is to be included in this budget item will have its effect as well. There may be trade-offs between what is included in the basic construction and what is included in equipment costs—especially with respect to carpet, stack shelving, standard modular counters rather than built-in units, wall hangings as opposed to stained glass for artwork, task lighting as opposed to overhead lighting, furniture-type partitions in place of built-in walls, individual clocks in lieu of a master clock system, or, to take an extreme, portable fans with windows that open instead of a ventilation system.

Although the general contractor's overhead and profit may be saved by treating the furnishings separately, the responsibility for error can become clouded and the institution assumes additional labor when these elements are separately contracted. Furthermore, as this part of the project generally comes late on the project schedule, unwise as this practice is, the funds may be viewed as a form of contingency for the basic construction effort; as a result, expectations for the furnishings are necessarily reduced. Care should be taken to avoid a first-class structure housing second- or third-class furnishings. Probably the furnishings create a stronger impression on the reader than any other aspect of the facility. They should fit the facility in a complementary manner and satisfy the programmatic need just as completely as the basic structure. Even so, it remains a fact that this area is often looked upon as a resource for budget savings. Such savings in the long term may be shortsighted, and any decisions to make budget cuts here should be challenged.

Union rules may not permit the installation of movable equipment during construction. Carrels that are attached to walls or floors and bookstacks, even if called freestanding, can sometimes be considered part of the building, thus avoiding complications. If they are considered part of the building, they may become part of the general contract, or a separate contract can be arranged. The difference between the two procedures may be important.

By making movable equipment part of the general contract, the institution can often avoid trouble because the primary responsibility for the complete installation is that of the general contractor. On the other hand, by placing it under a separate contract, the institution can make its own purchases and, unless it is under governmental regulations forbidding this procedure, can select the manufacturer and weigh the quality and functional requirements against cost, rather than depend on the contractor's purchase of a specified quality. (No matter how carefully described, quality is open to varied interpretations when manufactured items such as bookstacks are to be acquired.) This problem can sometimes be solved by specifying a single manufacturer, but the cost advantage of competition is lost. It should also be remembered that a separate contract might lead to union trouble if either the general contractor or the manufacturer is nonunion, just as there are always likely to be difficulties when responsibilities are divided and two prime contractors are working in the same building at once.

In any case, if the institution decides to enter into separate contracts, this decision should be stated in the specifications or in the agreement with the general contractor, because coordination of two or more contracts may impose certain hardships and entail added work and cost for the contractor and perhaps for the architect and the institution.

Sometimes the advantages of both plans can be realized by carrying the equipment in the general contract documents as an allowance. This means that the contractor is required to include in the contract bid an amount previously determined, a specified sum to be set aside for the purchase of the equipment or material desired, and that the final selection of the manufacturer or supplier and the cost will remain in the control of the architect or the institution. When a final decision has been reached, the contractor assumes the contractual obligations negotiated by the institution; the total contract amount is then adjusted up or down, in accordance with the difference between the final cost of the equipment or material and the specified sum previously set aside as an allowance.

Allowances are frequently carried for such items as bookstacks, hardware, elevators, special built-in equipment, artwork, and landscape planting. They are sometimes, but less frequently, used to purchase movable equipment, such as furniture and drapes.

Allowances are generally not permitted in public work for municipal, state, or federal governments, which usually require that the lowest responsible bidder be awarded a contract. Governments often consider allowances as a means of avoiding the competitive method of selecting a manufacturer; the open-bidding procedure is a safeguard against political favoritism in the selection of a successful bidder. Separate contracts are generally permitted, however, and U.S. federal agencies will often accept allowances, providing the final award is made to the lowest responsible bidder.

9.2.5 Site Preparations: Utilities and Landscaping

In most colleges and universities today the energy sources for heating and cooling (steam, hot water, and chilled water) will be generated in the institution's central heating plant rather than in the library. (A major independent research library may require an internal plant.) Of course heating or cooling coils, fans, ducts, filters, and controls must still be provided in the library. Funding of the central plant may be part of the project in the form of a pro rata tax on the construction cost or as a direct cost of any expansion required by the new facility. A new library can make expansion of the central plant necessary or even require the construction of a new one. Wherever the building is located, it must receive electric power and phone and other signal systems, usually but not always placed underground. It also must receive water, storm and sanitary sewers, steam if provided from outside, and sometimes chilled water for air conditioning. If the distance is great or if there are special problems in connection with the new installations, these costs may be considerable. The means of funding the utilities can dramatically alter the total library budget.

Construction of any kind is bound to require more or less extensive landscaping, unless it is a full city block, as is the Bobst Library of New York University. The total cost ordinarily is not large in proportion to that of the building as a whole. In some cases the institution may do the landscaping with special funds allocated for this purpose and with its own grounds-maintenance force, but ordinarily the cost is assigned to the building budget. Depending upon how these elements are treated, they may be included in the project cost model as discussed earlier.

9.2.6 Architectural and Other Fees

A major part of the fees are those for architectural and engineering services, although fees for consultants and other professional services should not be forgotten. There are three common approaches to establishing the fees: (1) as a fixed lump sum, (2) as a percentage of the construction cost, and (3) as an hourly charge plus a factor for overhead and profit. A combination of these fee structures is common when, for example, the basic work established in a contract with the architect is performed for a percentage of the construction cost as established by the first cost estimate, and any extra services outside of the scope of the contract are paid for on a cost plus overhead and profit, which may total two and a half times the wage rate of the personnel working on the project. Some years ago guides were published recommending compensation levels for architectural services, but to avoid accusation of price fixing, they are not generally used in the United States. Such a guide, however, may be useful for the client or the academic institution to have a feeling for the level of expense that may be expected for the design effort. It should be cautioned that the rates differ from state to state and even from firm to firm and that they vary with the project construction cost and with the complexity of its architectural and mechanical character.

Typically the architect's fee will fall between 6 and 10 percent of this construction cost for a significant new building. A renovation project can run as high as 12 to 15 percent, and even higher if the project is small or exceedingly difficult.

When the compensation for usual services, as described in Section 4.4, is a percentage of construction cost, it may by agreement be based on an early estimate of the construction cost. In this case, any increase in the scope of work can rightfully be claimed by the architect to require additional fees. Or the total fee is initially based on a reasonable construction cost projection, refined later as determined from construction cost estimates based on the completed drawings and specifications, and, if bids have been received, then adjusted to the lowest bona fide bid or bids for construction including fixed equipment and bookstacks. Even better in terms of firm control of the budget is to agree on a flat fee for services regardless of final cost, thereby eliminating an incentive for the architect to "gold plate" (the greater the cost, the more the fee). Compensation for supplementary services is added to the fee. Interior design work may, for example, be based on a percentage of the movable furniture and equipment budget (more on this later). Other services may be cost plus overhead and profit or a flat, lump-sum fee.

A building of a simple architectural character may involve complex mechanical services and a variety of technical problems, such as are involved with extensive electronic installations. The extent of these complications and the study required in their solution will be considered by the architect in selecting the appropriate rate. Although a few architects may still use a schedule similar to the one issued through 1952 by the Massachusetts State Association of Architects (see page 37 in the first edition of this book), it is no longer promulgated by the American Institute of Architects; thus, it could only be used for a rough idea of the fees that can be expected. Even when it was common to use such a chart, considerable variation occurred among firms. Section 4.4 provides further information on the determination of fees for architectural services.

Payment of the design fee may be made based upon a specific schedule. One such schedule follows:

1. Of the total estimated fee, 10 percent is due as a retainer for services to be rendered in connection with initial conferences and schematic studies at the time the architect is

engaged. In some cases no retainer is paid, but the first invoice from the architect covering these services may be 10 percent of the estimated fee.

2. An additional 15 percent of the estimated fee is due at the completion of the design development phase. On a large project there may be monthly invoices based on the percentage of the work completed, or based on a schedule of costs incurred by the architect.

3. The total of 50 percent of the estimated fee, in monthly payments based on the percentage of the work completed and with this 50 percent entirely paid by the conclusion of contract documents.

4. Of the remaining 25 percent, proportionate payments are due from time to time during the execution of the work, and in proportion to the amount of service rendered by the architect, until the aggregate of all payments equals 98 percent of the amount of the final fee computed on the basis of the actual total cost of the work, including all change orders. The final installment of this portion of the fee becomes due when the work is substantially completed.

5. The final 2 percent of the fee is due upon receipt of a record set of drawings, usually called "as-builts," together with any operations manuals or other documentation or staff training as required by the institution. No portion of any compensation should be withheld or reduced on account of penalties, liquidated damages, or other sums withheld from payments to the general contractor.

One large university has followed a standard architect's payment schedule: 15 to 20 percent at completion of schematics, another 15 percent at completion of design development, 45 percent at end of construction documents, 18 percent at end of construction, and then the final 2 percent as above. The payments are billed monthly by the architect during all stages.

Reimbursements for incidental expenses and extra compensation for supplementary services become due when the expenses are incurred or the extra work is performed. These are generally considered to include expenses incurred for transportation and living, long-distance telephone calls, reproductions of drawings and specifications in excess of five copies, and other disbursements on the architect's account approved by the institution. Much of this portion of the expense can be covered by the basic architectural agreement, but it may be expected that, if this is done, the basic fees may be somewhat higher.

When the institution or the nature of the project requires them, the architect offers certain additional services, such as the following, for which increased fees may be expected in proportion to the value of the services rendered.

1. Site development, including unusual or complex engineering design for underground and overhead utilities, grading, streets, walks, planting, water supply, and sewage disposal.
2. General surveys of existing conditions to aid in establishing the building program.
3. Detailed surveys and preparation of measured drawings of existing structures preparatory to alterations.
4. Special analysis or design in connection with exceptional foundation conditions or with unusual structural or mechanical problems.
5. Study of special or complex acoustical or electronic problems and their solutions.
6. Research reports, cost and income analyses, expert testimony, preparation of special drawings or developed scale models.

The most costly extra services are generally those for programming, interior design, signage programs, and redesign of elements that have previously been approved. Some would argue that many of these elements should be identified and made part of the architectural agreement, but a higher fee than would normally be expected may result.

This long statement on the architect's fees is provided to give the librarian or other academic professional some comprehension of the financial and other problems involved in an architect's contract for professional services. It should not be considered definitive in scale or scope.

As already suggested, there may be other professional fees. For example, it may be desirable to budget for the services of a library consultant. In this case there is no accepted schedule of payments for library consultants, although, as is the case with architects, there are three fairly definite methods used in establishing the charges. One is on a percentage basis, the percentage varying according to what the consultant is expected to do. Is the consultant to follow the procedures through from beginning to end, as the architect does, being on call during the construction as well as during preliminary planning and the working drawings and specifications stage, or will the assignment be completed when the working drawings are authorized? The answer of course makes a difference in the percentage.

The second method is an agreement that the work will be done for a definite sum, or at least an amount not exceeding that figure, with consideration given as the plans develop to the amount of time spent. In 1960 Ralph Ellsworth suggested that one-tenth of 1 percent of the estimated building cost may be budgeted for the consultant. This is probably still a reasonable measure today, provided the size of the project, experience of the consultant, and the degree of use of a consultant are accounted for.

The third method is for the consultant simply to say that the charges will be so much a day plus expenses. The per diem may vary from $500 up to double this amount, and probably in some cases, more according to the experience and, one might say, the prestige of the consultant and the job at hand. A small college library or a branch library costing $1 million might need a consultant, but one-tenth of 1 percent of the total, or $1,000, may not be adequate, even if only a few days are involved, especially if the expense of transportation, food, and lodging is considered.

A consultant with a great deal of experience may feel that, in a situation where there are likely to be complications of one kind or another, $500 a day is not adequate and that $750 or more is not unreasonable. A team of consultants, working together and contributing among them expert knowledge in various fields, may require altogether a larger percentage of the total cost but perhaps less per day per person, and so on. This work is not sufficiently well organized or set in its ways at present so that a definite scale for any of these methods can or should be proposed. Some consultants, particularly those working with institutions in which they are personally interested for one reason or another, do a great deal without charge except for expenses.

The authors make two definite suggestions in connection with charges. The institution should not base its selection primarily on the cost but on the person it wants. The consultant should not try to bargain and charge as much as traffic will bear but should set the rate for a particular job and let the institution take it or leave it.

Interior design often suggests yet another consultant for whom funds must be budgeted. Although interior design is certainly within the accepted province of an architect, it generally is not part of the basic services of the architect. Often this aspect of the work is taken out of the architect's hands and, unfortunately, turned over to the purchasing agent of the institution to save the architect's commission, which may run, for this particular type of work, up to 10 percent of the total furniture budget. If the furniture does not fit the structure, however, the effects will be unfortunate.

The library building consultant has primary responsibility for the functional arrangements and can rarely, if ever, be counted on to give satisfactory advice in connection with the aesthetic side of the problem. Because library furniture and equipment is a special field in itself, it is sometimes thought best to contract for the services of an interior designer who specializes in library work, although a good designer who has never done a library often will produce superior results. A fee scale for interior design services is difficult to state; it is unwise to propose a definite formula. In the first edition of this volume, Metcalf included a statement prepared by one of the foremost interior planning consultants and designers specializing in library work. It is still valid, and is included here.

> This work may entail critique of architect's preliminaries to equipment layouts, color schemes, furniture selection, the writing of detailed construction specifications, including "instructions to bidders," aid in assessing alternate proposals—this is most important—and final inspection of the installation. There are several different methods of charging.
>
> One is a percentage of the overall cost of furnishing and equipment; normally this is ten per cent, although the size of the project can affect this. Another is a percentage of the overall building and furnishing budget, with one per cent being a common base. Again, the one per cent figure can be unfair. On one project recently the budget was approximately two million, yet a survey of the program made it clear that a twenty thousand dollar fee was considerably too high.
>
> Of the two methods stated above, the percentage of overall budget has the advantage of immediately clarifying the approximate amount the fee

will come to, since this budget is normally a known factor. On the other hand, a percentage of furniture cost alone can be greatly altered as the job proceeds:

1. The original furnishing budget might prove to be entirely unrealistic and require revision.
2. The cost of the building itself might force a drastic cut in final furniture allowances—not a happy thought, but it does happen. In such an event, I have found a reverse ratio occurring: my fee is thereby cut, but my required time and energy to cope with a greatly reduced budget is expanded.
3. Steel stacks are sometimes included in the furnishing budget, sometimes in that of the architectural work. Since the cost of stacks is high, this matter must be clarified before arriving at a fair percentage fee.
4. In some instances a library will require a time-consuming survey of existing furniture to determine what might be re-used in non-public areas. This, too, must be determined since the use of existing furniture reduces expenditure and thus the fee.

In brief, I have had some clients question a percentage of furniture costs by saying: "But we must have some idea what we will actually pay you." (In one case which I won't mention by name, I contracted with a Board on a percentage of furniture basis, and only after my contract was signed did they inform me of anticipated reductions, additional surveys and studies that were necessary, and planned use of considerable existing furniture. That job was a source of loss as well bitterness, I must admit.)

A third method of charging is of course a flat fee, in which a study of the program is made and a definite dollars-and-cents amount is quoted.

Rather than complicate matters I usually work out a fee arrangement to include travel, with a stipulated number of trips this is to include. Six seems to be an average in my case.

There are two additional points which might require comment: sometimes it is necessary or advantageous for one reason or another to place the interior designer's contract under the architect's. Often when this is done it is because the Authority refuses to hire such a consultant—who perhaps is wanted by the librarian—but is agreeable to extending that of the architect to include interior matters. The second point has to do with consolidating consultants into a single contract—that of the library buildings consultant and the interior planner. I have started doing this in some cases. Under this method I will accept an entire contract to cover the entire scope of consultation with the agreement that I will in turn retain a competent library consultant, paid from my fee, to round the "Team." This is done because some Boards resist the hiring of one consultant after another, becoming confused by the multiple advisory "needs" requested.

Finally, there may be special consultants for acoustics, graphics, security, electronic systems, other special systems, energy design auditing, soils testing, and site survey work. As with the consultants already discussed, each of these will have a practical fee structure.

Probably the best method of establishing the budget for services such as these is to rely on the experience of the institution on other projects. Furthermore, discussions with the various consultants may provide the necessary budget information, short of asking for a complete proposal, which of course would be the basis of a contract. Although the proportionate project costs for these consultants may be small, their value is often very great indeed.

9.2.7 Administrative Costs

There are other expenditures that, although often representing a comparatively small percentage of the total, may have to be provided for. Most larger institutions maintain an office for facilities project management that is staffed with architects and various engineers. Some project management offices may include experts in contracts or purchasing agreements, urban or campus planners, plant accountants, construction administrators, and construction inspectors or coordinators. The intent and function of this office are to assist the "client" in obtaining the best possible building for the least cost and to ensure that institutional standards, legal requirements, program needs, and contractual obligations are met within budget and on schedule. When these services are charged against the project, the expenses can be substantial, and in some cases they may be as much as the architect's fee, although these are exceptions and would be likely only on small projects.

Administrative costs may include the expense of writing and publishing the program, preparing a master plan, selecting an architect and other consultants, preparing a budget and schedule, writing contracts of all types, coordinating design reviews with the various offices that must be involved, coordinating information gathered for the trustees or others who may need to make key decisions, and, in general, managing the project from start to finish, including day-to-day inspection during construction. There may be a similar and somewhat parallel effort within the library administration that may be charged to the project as well, though it is usual for the library staff to take on this additional work with little or no budget increment. In some institutions the costs of raising funds might appear in this category.

It is imperative that the owner have on duty during all phases of construction an independent, qualified inspector whose responsibility it is to avoid errors, oversights, or omissions. The employment of an independent construction inspector may be necessary as part of administrative costs unless it is covered by regulating government agencies or by the institution itself. The larger the project, the more important this becomes. Large institutions will always have inspectors on staff.

The institution may require that a significant project be insured to cover institutional liabilities beyond those covered by the contractor's insurance as spelled out in the general conditions. Some institutions are self-insured, which means that the budgeted sum for insurance is transferred to an insurance reserve account. Although the proportionate cost of insurance and, for that matter, many of the other budgeted elements is small, these are expenses that always must be accounted for.

Other costs that may appear under the title of administrative costs include county or city plan check fees, architectural review board fees, printers' costs, travel costs, and the like. The cost for an environmental impact report may appear here or within the professional services of the architect. Several thousand dollars may be required to print extra sets of the plans and specifications for bidders and internal reviews. Most architectural contracts specify a limited number of prints beyond which copies must be financed separately. Building permits are generally the responsibility of the construction contractor, although many code jurisdictions have a separate review process referred to as the plan check for which fees similar to the permit fees may be charged. There may be special fees for required code review by local health departments, the fire marshal, and other state, county, or city offices.

The total of these six groups plus the other costs discussed earlier (see the sample budget) represents the project cost, as contrasted with the construction cost. The latter is usually the major part and, therefore, the one that should be determined with the greater accuracy; yet all costs should be estimated as closely as possible. The project cost must at best be a very carefully informed forecast; estimating is a technical skill, not an exact science. Unless a satisfactory estimate can be made, the institution may find when the bids are opened that the cost is greater than anticipated and consequently that it is impossible to go ahead with the building or that its size or quality must be reduced. The latter happens all too frequently, as Stanford University and others can attest, and the results can sometimes be disastrous.

9.3
Estimating Procedures

Estimating procedures, mentioned earlier, are of such importance that they warrant further discussion here. A good estimating procedure in a library project might include the following:

1. A first order of magnitude estimate can be prepared based on the facility program, usually expressed in terms of net floor area. An efficiency factor can be applied to project an estimated gross floor area for the project. For a large project it is suggested that multiplying the net area by a factor of 1.43, which represents 70 percent efficiency, is reasonable. Smaller projects might be more appropriately multiplied by a factor of 1.50, while a warehouse storage facility might be best projected with a factor of 1.33, which represent efficiencies of 67 percent and 75 percent. For major new academic library space, 75 percent efficiency is frequently achieved, and 80 to 90 percent is occasionally possible though unlikely, particularly with significant and typically increased space (that is, increased during the 1990s) allocated to telephone and data rooms, mechanical facilities, ramps, and the like.

The unit area construction estimate is based on buildings of similar size, complexity, quality, and location together with an appropriate adjustment for inflation, which can be obtained from, for example, the Engineering News Record Cost Index. With the sample project budget outlined earlier, the estimated construction cost is usually about two-thirds of the total project cost, although this is little more than a rough rule of thumb and will vary greatly depending upon contingencies, the amount of electronic furnishings, and costs of special conditions.

2. At the time of completing the schematic phase, the architect should prepare an outline specification that establishes basic assumptions about all building systems that have not yet been detailed. With this information the architect prepares a cost estimate that, with a large project, should be confirmed by a separate estimate prepared by a professional estimator or a responsible general contractor who is paid for this work. Even if the contractor bids on the job, the cost estimate can be valid because the bid will be competitive. The contractor has gained advance time to know the plans and determine the best means of construction; the institution can invite helpful advice from the contractor about where design details or particular specifications may inadvertently push up costs because of current construction methods or materials known to the contractor and perhaps not to the architect. This estimate should result from an actual quantity survey that should conform to a project cost model, such as that outlined earlier. For instance, using information from a current university library project, the contractor can, for comparison, determine such figures as the following: $15 per cubic yard to excavate and remove unsuitable soil, $20 per cubic yard to obtain off-site structural fill, $200 per cubic yard for rock excavation, $250 per cubic yard where trenching rock is required, and $600 per cubic yard where caissons are required. Similar methodology is used to generate cost for each of the cost model categories; with this system, the estimated cost for each aspect of the project can easily be compared between estimators, and, where major differences occur, the reasons can be discussed and identified.

3. This process should be repeated at the end of the design development phase and when the working drawings or contract documents are essentially complete. Adjustments, as appropriate, can be instituted at any of these phases, although major changes late in the project will result in delay and perhaps additional architectural fees, depending on the details of the design contract.

In all these estimates, the total project cost should be projected with as much detail as practical, including factors for cost rise and contingency. It is believed that if this estimating is done conscientiously by competent persons, a project will rarely be unable to proceed because of the need for additional funds.

It is wise in all cases, however, to have plans so prepared that some part of the building or finish or equipment may be omitted if estimates run somewhat higher than anticipated. These are called "deduct alternates." Having a means to pull the construction cost within budget is highly prudent and strongly advised. Similarly, one can have "add alternates" in anticipation that the bid may be lower than expected. Alternates are frequently included in the bidding (in limited numbers, e.g., three to six) that will indicate accurately the monetary value of constructing or finishing some specified part or parts of the proposed building, and these can be added or dropped from the contract, as will be detailed in Chapter 14. It should be added that renovation projects may well have more than a handful of alternates, given the unknown conditions and therefore the wide range of bids that are sometimes received. A very large, complex library renovation has been known to have as alternates: 2 for plumbing, 2 for HVAC, 6 electrical, and 11 general contracting, the last of which included storm sash, a refrigeration room, and casework in several rooms for special collections and photographic services.

Here is one example. When renovating and greatly expanding its Atkins Library, the University of North Carolina at Charlotte was careful to keep open its options for financing the project by including seven alternates under the general contracting bid, two under plumbing, four under mechanical, and six under electrical. The general contract alternates included construction and landscaping of a "rondel," "upfitting" the original third floor, third-floor shelving, sound isolation of the fourth-floor slab, compact shelving tracks, and specialized exit devices. The university judged that it might have to cut as much as 12 percent to bring in the project within budget. In fact, local circumstances resulted in bids sufficiently low that a majority of the alternates could be accepted. Although the general construction bid was within 7 percent of the estimate, the mechanical and plumbing bids were off (one high and one low) by larger amounts and the electrical was right on the estimate, a not unusual pattern and one that demonstrates the very real advantages of using add and deduct alternates in the bid process. The decisions made in this case left the library still needing a million dollars each for selected furniture, renovation of the third floor, compact shelving, and building communication technology. The bid results usually require administrative decision in a matter of a few weeks, and the decision can be difficult to reach when the library operating budget provides no flexibility and fund-raising is already stretched to the limit.

In any case, a careful and accurate estimate must be made at some time, based on a quantity survey rather than on unit area costs, to ensure the institution as far as possible against finding that the construction cost is greater than anticipated and that it is difficult or impossible to go ahead with the project.

To give here any precise construction cost figures is extremely dangerous, because it is practically impossible to avoid misunderstanding and misinterpretation. Wishful thinking too often leads those involved to believe that costs can just as well be less than should be expected. But beyond this human failing are three cogent and concrete reasons for misunderstanding.

1. Anything that is true and accurate today may not and probably will not be true tomorrow. Whether we like it or not, we are living in an inflationary age; costs have tended to go up several percentage points almost every year, and for some years the cost increase has been 1 percent or more each month. There is a good likelihood that this pattern will continue and, in some countries, it may be a truly staggering figure. Any cost figures mentioned in this book are only illustrative and might well be doubled geometrically each decade to come.

2. Costs vary considerably from place to place because of materials cost, local labor conditions, and building codes, to say nothing of building practices.

3. Each institution decides for itself, with the aid of course of the architect, what type of construction, architecture, and materials it is prepared to use; these have a great influence on costs. A rare book library, planned as an architectural gem to attract gifts, will cost much more per unit area than a remote book-storage facility or a one-story library structure for a poor rural college that will have few if any irreplaceable volumes in its collection and may be able to use non-fire-resistant construction without building-code restrictions.

It has been suggested that a calculated cost per reader and volume housed satisfactorily may be a more meaningful measure of facility costs, but even this breakdown has factors that will lead to misunderstanding. In addition to those mentioned, the program will have a significant effect on such a cost figure. For example, a large library system with centralized technical processing will have quite a different cost per reader and volume in a branch library than would an institution with decentralized processing. The word *satisfactorily* must come under scrutiny as well. A building that has accommodations for 200 readers but can seat comfortably only 150 is not recommended any more than one that claims to be able to house 200,000 volumes when it will actually be uncomfortably full with 150,000, because its stack capacity has been exaggerated by overestimating the number of volumes that can be shelved in a standard section. Self-deception about items like these seldom helps anyone.

Wishful thinking is a natural tendency for many persons. Too often many costs are underestimated even by professionals, either because of a desire to encompass the total program within a predetermined budget or because of an unwillingness to face facts. On the other hand, to overestimate and not use all available funds sometimes results in leaving out a much needed security system, air conditioning, or such an essential facility as a service elevator and in providing a booklift instead. As suggested above, this situation can be largely avoided by including a few bid alternates as part of the final design. Every effort should be made to strike a happy medium in estimating. A librarian should never be even indirectly involved in construction estimating; however, aspects of activation and specialized equipment may require information from the librarian to assure a reasonable cost projection—both of these examples generally fall outside the construction cost estimate. The architect should realize that good estimating will raise the client's ability to properly plan for funding the project.

Library building costs have been tabulated from time to time. Those for individual libraries are often recorded in library periodicals. Although these may be helpful, it should be remembered that they may not include each of the six categories of expenditure discussed in this chapter and on that account are too often not comparable to each other. Do not forget the three basic cost factors: (1) time of construction and the economic climate when bids are submitted; (2) the geographic location of the building and the site problems; and

(3) the type of architecture and the quality of materials used. In other words, only a fool would compare apples with oranges!

9.4
Value Engineering

A number of institutions and states have developed systems of what is called "value engineering" as a means of assuring the taxpayers or trustees that the best possible solution meeting the stated requirements of the project has been obtained in terms of the best ultimate value. Also known as function analysis and value analysis, this exercise can bring forth valuable possibilities that may accrue from the project process; the process of value engineering, therefore, not only is designed to cut cost, it also can improve the results of the project.

The point that the project can be improved cannot be stressed enough. Most architects, planners, and library staff who have by now spent a substantial amount of energy and time may view the prospect of value engineering with trepidation. Properly handled, it can be a positive experience, and, if the homework has been well done, there should be no major surprises. On the other hand, if the design team has overlooked some vital point, it should be found through this process, thereby saving money or achieving improvement, either of which can hardly be criticized.

The process of value engineering can be applied at almost any stage of a project, though the most cost-effective point is at or near the conclusion of the schematic design phase. At this point, enough information should be available to have a good sense of the total project scope, and the cost of various components of the project can usually be easily estimated.

The value engineering team is made up of interdisciplinary personnel not associated with the project being reviewed. Indeed, they typically are from altogether different institutions, brought in for this specific process. The team should have, as a minimum, a value engineering consultant, an experienced contractor who is familiar with construction techniques and cost, a mature librarian from another institution, and often a few others who may have expertise in mechanical systems, structure, architecture, or other aspects of the design process. For the sake of credibility, it is important that the team be unassociated with the project and free of agendas that could influence their findings.

The process has five phases: the information phase, the value cycle phase, the development phase, the presentation phase, and the decision and implementation phase.[2] Some of the phases of this process (especially the first two) will involve the design team, including representation of the library, the architect, the campus project management office, and the library consultant if there is one. In this model, the design team serves as staff to the value engineering team, which guides the entire process through to the final presentation phase but not the implementation phase.

The information phase begins with a period of data gathering for the value engineering team, a key document being a clear and concise statement of the goals of the project, in as few words as possible. This statement is then used as a test for all aspects of the project as the process progresses. Working with the design team, lists of decision criteria, issues and concerns of the design team, and two- or three-word statements as to why the project is being put forward may also be generated during the information phase; examples of inclusions in these lists and statements are the following:

Decision criteria might include consideration of: achievement of program objectives, effect upon public image, operations efficiency, life cycle cost, preservation of assets, instructional effectiveness, adaptability, ergonomics, future effect of facility, campus culture, the degree of risk, and the effect on the schedule.

Issues and concerns might include such items as: maintaining preservation environment, assuring adequacy of equipment budget, achieving project goals, identifying bottom line, identifying the decision process, and keeping an open mind.

Reasons why a project is being put forward might include such items as: reduce service points, avoid cost, focus resources, reduce duplication, simplify access, improve adjacencies, orient users, improve personnel coverage, utilize an existing facility, capture opportunity, improve access, consolidate service, accommodate growth, balance resources, implement master plan, improve pedagogy, consolidate staff. Some of these elements may be further detailed. For example, "simplify access" might include: up-grade technology, orient user, facilitate self-instruction, focus entry, protect collections, develop supermarket, and unify system.

Information gathering generally will include a site visit as well as receipt and organization of documents, including preplanning documents, the space program, current drawings and specifications, and the most recent cost estimates. Each member of the design team is asked to present in fairly substantial detail the basis of the project, the direction the project is taking, and why. Each aspect of the project is discussed to a level necessary for the value engineering team to grasp its importance, particularly the project goal, and to have a feel for possible alternatives. Virtually anything is fair game at this point. During the discussion, areas offering potentially significant improvement to cost-benefit performance are identified and prioritized for further study.

During the value cycle phase, each area identified as having potential cost-benefit improvement is analyzed for its functional requirements and best functional alternatives. The costs driven by functional requirements are considered, and the functional requirements themselves may be considered. During a brainstorming session with facilitation by the value engineering consultant, all wild, crazy, and sometimes effective ideas are raised and discussed. At this point, judgment about any idea is withheld; the point is to expose the value engineering team to every possible alternative to each of the functions and each of the proposed solutions. After every idea is recorded, all the ideas are evaluated and screened to identify those that warrant further development and comparison to the design scheme and to the goals of the project.

The development phase is used to clarify the concept and cost of the most attractive alternatives. The cost is based upon the approximate type, size, and location of design elements. Advantages and disadvantages are tabulated for each of the concepts, and simple side-by-side comparisons are prepared. During the presentation phase, the alternatives are documented, and a report is presented to the decision-making authorities. Often the institution for which the project is being designed is offered the opportunity to comment upon the findings of the value engineering team. Comments in this context would be from the major stakeholders, including possibly the chief librarian, the project manager, the campus architect, the provost, or even the president. Once final decisions are made, the accepted alternatives are incorporated into the project plans and the project budget is adjusted as appropriate.

Clearly, this is not an inexpensive process. Quite a large number of very expert people are involved for up to a week, sometimes more. Yet there are experts who claim that the return on the investment consistently exceeds 20 to 1. Value engineering has been around for many years in manufacturing; it is a more recent application for construction. Such a process should be viewed positively; it can be absolutely worth doing, though it is still relatively unusual among major academic library projects. The U.S. government (since 1996) and at least one U.S. state now require value engineering, and this may well become a trend.

When value engineering is to be undertaken, the costs of the process can be budgeted as a separate line item or included in the line for professional services. The process should be guided by proficient personnel; there are firms that specialize in value engineering. (The value engineering consultant to facilitate the process often is certified as a value specialist by the U.S. Society of American Value Engineers; an international association also performs a similar accreditation function.) The institution should be aware of the process and progress of value engineering throughout, though there may be meetings of the value engineering team or the decision body that are closed. Copies of the report will be given to the institution at the same time they are given to the financing authority; the institution will likely give copies to active members of the design team.

The results can range from a fundamental change in the program to a fundamental change in the building project, and anything between. Cost savings frequently are in the range of 3 to 5 percent. In one recent report on a university library project, the recommendations were:

1. Consolidate the library on floors two and three of the existing library and the converted neighbor building, and add a second-level connector bridge, for a cost reduction of $1,022,000, which was accepted;
2. Program the total library rather than just the building addition (include design for renovation of the existing library) at an added cost of $25,000, which was not done;

3. Use ground floor of the neighbor building as transition surge space for main library renovation for a life cycle reduction of $750,000, which was not done;

4. Provide access flooring in computer labs, and retain concrete floors in other general university and utility areas for a cost savings of $34,000, which probably will be done;

5. Simplify HVAC approach to improve reliability and reduce maintenance cost, saving $399,000, which probably will be done; and

6. Pull wiring for data network infrastructure now rather than later at an added cost of $67,000, final action unknown.

Value engineering only makes sense for substantial projects. Even then, the strongest reason in the mind of some participants for undertaking such a process may be more political than practical. However, the results can be quite beneficial, both to the project and to the budget. Real improvement is often possible.

9.5
Special Factors That Affect Building Costs

With one exception this section will refer to but not discuss in detail special factors affecting building costs that are discussed elsewhere. It will, however, list a limited number of factors with just enough comment to explain their importance. They all cost money, and under some conditions they can be avoided or omitted. The point to be emphasized is that an institution should understand what it is spending its always inadequate funds for and should choose intelligently if any choice is available.

Institutional buildings cost 15 to 30 percent more than noninstitutional buildings, a fact explained by analysis of building components. The weight of library bookstacks is very significant in explaining this difference. Furthermore, academic program requirements have a dramatic effect on this cost differential. To explain: Bare minimum commercial buildings generally have a shell costing 37 percent of construction; aesthetic costs are 17 percent, and program costs are 46 percent. In contrast, a university building shell cost will perhaps be only 16 percent, aesthetic costs 10 per-cent, and the programmatic costs 74 percent. The special program requirements for a current academic or research library are a good case in point, with large collections of books, manuscripts, and other materials, and a great investment in electronic and other informational technology.

Data on construction costs are published annually. For instance, construction materials in 1996 in the city of San Jose cost 110.6 percent and installation labor cost 132.7 percent of the national average. Further, of the total costs of library construction that same year, equipment accounted for 2.8 percent, plumbing 4.9 percent, masonry 9.5 percent, and electrical and HVAC both were 11.0 percent (taken from R. S. Means, *Building Construction Cost Data—1997*).

Any cost estimate in this book should be considered to be for illustrative purposes only. The estimates are at best rough, they are certain to change, and in all cases costs should be obtained locally. The authors do not oppose the use of funds for the elements discussed below; any of them may be desirable, and under some circumstances essential.

The first point has to do with the construction methods and materials used. The higher the quality of each, the better the results and the greater the construction cost. On the average, outside-wall costs may amount to about 10 percent of the construction as a whole, but, according to the type of wall used, there can be tremendous variations, not all of which directly affect the prospective length of life or operational and maintenance costs of the building. For example, in California, a reinforced brick wall is more than twice the expense of a tilt-up concrete wall or a wall constructed of concrete masonry units. In other areas of the country, where brick is a common material, its cost may well be competitive with concrete. A precast wall-panel system with a granite finish may be nearly four times the cost of a simple concrete wall. Of course the insulation and interior finish, typically required of all exterior walls, will tend to reduce the proportionate difference of cost, but these cost variations should be realized as decisions are made in regard to the materials and techniques of construction.

There is another cost factor for exterior walls based primarily on the ratio of the length of the exterior wall to the inside area. Curved walls and walls with many corners are somewhat more expensive than straight walls. A square building might be said to make the most efficient use of the exterior wall per square foot of floor space enclosed, although it will be about 12 percent longer than a curved wall. For each corner that is turned, a distance of approximately 2 ft (610 mm) should be added to the length of the wall used to calculate its cost in order to record comparable relative costs. The shape of the building will therefore affect the total cost of construction.

To use a specific example, a building with 20,000 ft^2 (1,858 m^2), if square, would be just under 141½ ft (43.129 m) long on each of the four sides (fig. 9.3). Adding an allowance for the four corners, the total outside measurement would be some 574 ft (174.555 m) long. A rectangular building measuring 200 × 100 ft (60.960 × 30.480 m) would have the same 20,000 ft^2 (1,858 m^2) of floor area, but its walls, adjusted for the corners, would be 603 ft (183.794 m) long, for an increase of about 6 percent. If the wall cost for the square building is 10 percent of the construction cost, then the increase in total construction cost for the rectangular building is about three-fifths of 1 percent.

If the building were E-shaped, with overall dimensions of 100 × 250 ft (30.480 × 76.200 m) and with two partially enclosed courts each 50 × 50 ft (15.240 × 15.240 m), the area would be the same; but with 12 corners, the adjusted length of the outside wall is 924 lineal ft (281.635 m), or just over 60 percent greater than that required for a square building. All other elements being equal, this shape would add 6 percent to the construction cost. At $150 per ft^2, these calculations suggest an added cost of some $18,000 per floor for the rectangular building and $180,000 per floor for the E-shape. For a building 5 or 10 stories high, this added cost can result in a very considerable sum. It should not be forgotten, however, that changes in the type of wall construction might make an equal or greater difference; that is, the cost of a fine stone building, even if square, might be greater than that of the E-shaped building faced with brick or with one of the other less-expensive methods of wall construction.

This statement is not presented in order to argue that the building should be square in order to save $18,000 per floor or that it should not be E-shaped to save $180,000. The point to be made is simply that, as this example illustrates, costs mount up. A square building provides more square footage in contents than buildings of other shapes. On the other hand, in an E-shaped building, no space is more than 25 ft (7.620 m) from an exterior wall, assuming each leg is only 50 ft (15.240 m) wide. This fact may serve to advantage in moderate climates for natural lighting and ventilation. However, in climates with temperature extremes, the heat gain and loss through the longer exterior wall will result in increased energy consumption. The E-shape will also increase somewhat the cost of floor and roof construction. The same cost factor applies to a building with straight vertical walls instead of overhangs or setbacks. A simple shape in plan and elevation will always cost less than a more complicated one. Those responsible must decide, given all the factors, which they prefer to select.

Interior light wells, which used to be common in large libraries for ventilation and light, go back to the days when electrically monitored mechanical environmental control was in its infancy. Such courts are often proposed today, not so much for light and ventilation as for aesthetic, or what might be called humanistic, purposes, affording a spatial relief to the library as a structure and an intimate attractive outlook for the reader. This consideration may be of special importance in an unattractive urban environment even though the wells reduce the available floor area, increase expensive wall areas, and interfere with traffic patterns.

When an old library with courts is relighted and air conditioned, there is a natural temptation, if more space is needed, to fill in the courts, as doing so provides assignable space where it is greatly appreciated and seems a natural development. It has been done in a number of libraries, including the Library of Congress, but it turns out that filling in the space is typically more expensive for a unit of net floor area gained than a new wing would be. The excuse for filling in courts is that the location may make the added space worth the difference because there may be no other land available, the space in the heart of the existing building may be more valuable and usable, or the balance of the building may be enhanced by improved internal circulation and juxtaposition of functions.

The following paragraphs discuss more briefly other items to watch for and show where money can be saved.

An inexpensive flooring material may cost more than $.50 a ft^2 less throughout the whole building than another that might be chosen. If the building has 100,000 ft^2 (9,290 m^2), the difference could be $50,000 or more. Remember, however, that the less-expensive flooring may be unsatisfactory from the acoustic point of view. It may also be unsatisfactory because of the cost of maintenance, because it lacks static control properties needed in computer areas, or because it will wear out and have to be replaced in a comparatively few years. The cost of replacement at more frequent intervals may exceed the cost savings of the original installation. The use of present value analysis, discussed earlier, may be appropriate here, although it cannot be used to analyze the value of acoustic benefits.

When it comes to other acoustical material, the question may be a little more difficult to decide. A cheaper variety may last just as long and require no more upkeep; but the question is whether it satisfactorily performs its other functions and is fireproof and looks acceptable.

The cost of monumental stairs may be in the stair construction itself; however, a more important consideration is likely to be the amount of floor area involved, which might be used for other purposes. Because the area is the same for every floor reached by those stairs (excluding the effect of a lobby area), an unnecessary 20 ft² (1.858 m²) of stair area in a five-story building means the loss of space to house, for example, 1,500 volumes.

The cost of an entrance lobby with 2,000 ft² of space where 1,000 would be sufficient (185.806 m² rather than 92.903 m²) would be an additional $150,000 if figured at the rate of $150 per ft². On the other hand, if the lobby houses the checkout, entrance control, circulation, and reserved-book desks, for instance, and it is too small to handle the peak loads without congestion, the insufficient space is a serious fault and often one that cannot be corrected later. The lobby should be large enough to provide a satisfactory distribution point from which emanate the circulation traffic patterns for the building as a whole.

Complete air conditioning can be expected to add as much as 15 percent to the net construction cost, even taking into consideration the savings in cubage that it may make possible by reducing ceiling heights. Even so, it probably is of vital importance in connection with the preservation of books (see appendix D) and in making the library an inviting place for students and faculty.

Each additional elevator or booklift has a price attached. Although you can build the shaft and leave out the equipment for years, it is cheaper to install one at the time of construction than it

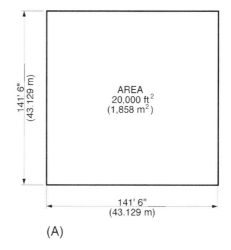

(A)

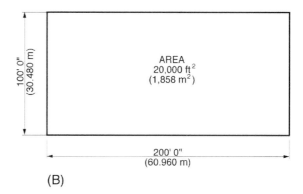

(B)

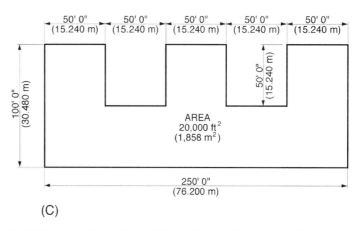

(C)

FIGURE 9.3   The effect of irregular walls on costs. For three floor plates of the same area, (A) requires 566 ft (172.517 m), (B) 600 ft (182.880 m), and (C) 900 ft (274.320 m) of exterior wall. If the cost of the outside wall for (A) is estimated at 10% of the total for the construction, that for (B) will be increased by 6% of 10%, or 0.6%. The increased cost of (C) over (B), excluding the added cost of extra corners, will be 50% of 10%, or 5% of the construction cost. That of (C) over (A), including a factor for the corners, will be 60% of 10%, or 6% of the total.

will be later. Remember that a shortage of service elevators may be very expensive in staff time.

The cost of shelving can be reduced up to 30 percent by stripping it of finished bases, end panels, and canopy tops, and by limiting shelf depths to a minimum, but in many cases economies of this kind are not desirable. The cost of the floor area occupied by the equipment is, however, much more important than the cost of the equipment itself. The fact that less-expensive shelving is possible does not mean that industrial or commercial shelving should be used in regular bookstacks; it is far more difficult to adjust and its appearance generally is much less satisfactory. In most cases, the decision can be based on utility and appearance rather than on cost.

The above discussion relates to only one of at least five aspects of the whole story. The second one deals with the utilization of the space. If only 60 percent of the total gross area is what is known as assignable, or net usable, space, you will have more use from a 100,000 ft^2 (9,290 m^2) building than from one with 80,000 ft^2 (7,432 m^2) where 75 percent is net usable. In this case, the differences in construction costs alone could come to $3 million or more, which is probably greater than any possible difference in costs between the various types of outside walls, floor coverings, shelving, and so on. A rough estimate would place the maximum difference between the best interior and exterior finishes and the most economical but feasible ones at only 15 percent; much more than that is often expended on what could be an unnecessarily low percent of net to gross floor area.

Extra floor area can be saved if planning is done carefully with costs in mind. The amount of floor area should be considerable if used for a monumental stair, a circular stair, an entrance lobby or a corridor larger than required to take care of peak loads (unless it is used also for exhibition purposes, making a separate exhibition room unnecessary), extra cross aisles in the stacks, unnecessary walls, and other assignments of space that perhaps are not functionally essential or aesthetically justified.

A third important factor is the use of the floor area available for library purposes. For example, if reading areas are so arranged that one reader can be housed in 25 ft^2 (2.323 m^2) of floor space instead of 30 (2.787 m^2), and 1,000 readers are to be seated in the building, the difference of 5,000 ft^2 (464.50 m^2) could, at current cost, result in a savings of $750,000 or more. If allowing only 25

ft^2 (2.323 m^2) per reader results in unsatisfactory accommodations and if many seats will not be filled because they are inconvenient or are perceived to be occupied or preempted by other readers, it makes no sense to crowd them in. However, if you are convinced that by careful planning, readers can be seated just as satisfactorily as in the larger amount of space, you should make the change. Do not be overly influenced by wishful thinking. It is not uncommon to find a well-arranged seating area with minimal spacing to be never more than 50 percent occupied, while a similar seating area with larger carrels and fewer chairs at the tables may have 100 percent use in what may be regarded a more extravagant assignment of space. Absolute frugality is not recommended here. An increase or a decrease in the size of a reading area without changing the number of seating accommodations does not affect proportionately the other facilities of the building; they will still require the same amount of furniture and equipment, the same number of doors, janitor's closets, stairs, toilets, and similar added costs, which prorate themselves over the total area of the building.

The same thinking holds true for book storage. If, by careful planning and without causing any inconvenience, 15 volumes can be stored per ft^2 instead of 12 (or 160 versus 130 volumes per m^2), and 900,000 volumes are to be provided for, the difference will be 15,000 ft^2 (about 1,400 m^2), which, of course, could result in a substantial cost savings. Again, watch out for wishful thinking!

Sometimes space can be utilized to better advantage by using it for different purposes at different times—that is, making it multipurpose space. For instance, a small auditorium, if properly designed, can be used as a reading area during the examination period when pressure for reading space will be at its peak. Collapsible tables can be stored in a very small area and be made available quickly, but it should be cautioned that these do not make ideal reading tables; this approach should only be used where there are no better alternatives. Main corridors can serve as relatively satisfactory exhibit areas or, if they are made a little wider, can house open-access reserved books, but the degree of control over these materials may be compromised. Excessive restrictions of space in any regard may significantly reduce long-term flexibility, and thus should only be undertaken with careful thought and planning.

A fourth cost factor deals with cubic space rather than floor area and relates to the height of rooms. This issue is discussed elsewhere, but it should be noted here that if, in order to place reading areas, book storage, and staff anywhere in a building, greater total height is required, then it will cost money. If the bookstacks are all on certain floors with low ceilings and all the areas requiring higher ceilings are on other floors, height and money will be saved. This does not mean that a building should be planned inconveniently for use by readers and staff in order to save cubage, but the difference in cost should be kept in mind in making the decisions. At the least, all floors do not have to have the same height as the entrance level, which for psychological reasons may at times be somewhat higher than absolutely necessary.

A closely related factor is that if the services to readers are concentrated in one part of a building and heavy book and other storage in another, floors with a lower load-bearing capacity can be used for the former group, thereby saving a considerable sum of money in a large building. On the whole, however, it is better to make all space available for any library purpose, in order to obtain more complete flexibility. Those who have tried to economize by limiting the structural capacity of the building to the currently planned need have too often lived to regret it.

The effect on costs of the column spacing that is selected should not be forgotten. Generally, the closer the column spacing, the cheaper the floor construction. The columns themselves are expensive though, and a building 110 ft (33.500 m) square with 27-ft (8.230-m) bays will have just over one-half as many columns (assuming interior columns and an exterior bearing wall) as one of the same size with bays 18 ft (5.486 m) square. It is not easy to choose the most economical size of bay. As shown elsewhere, the column spacing can have a great effect on the capacity of the building for housing readers and books, particularly the latter. The economic factors to be reckoned with here are thus (1) the maximum use of the resulting net space (a library factor) and (2) the cost of the columns and footings versus the cost of the floor slabs and beam spans (a structural factor).

Closely related to the column-spacing problem is that of the coordination of sizes of building materials and equipment on a basic standard module of 4 in.(102 mm), which is common in construction work. It can result in considerable savings in field-labor costs by making it possible to use materials produced on a production line in a factory without alteration.

It is suggested then that the following five factors in construction and equipment costs should be kept in mind:

1. Those that deal with the construction itself and thus are affected by the type and cost of materials used, the amount of outside wall required to enclose the desired area, and the size selected for column spacing.
2. The percentage of architectural, or non-assignable, space that cannot be used for library purposes; this space includes that occupied by walls, columns, ducts, and pipes, as well as by lobbies, corridors, stairs, elevators and lifts, mechanical rooms, and rest rooms.
3. The utilization of the space that is available for library purposes.
4. Ceiling heights.
5. Load-bearing capacity throughout the building.

Each member of the building team should be on the lookout for other factors that should be weighed and discussed so that all concerned will know and understand just what is involved.

Renovation projects are often more difficult to estimate than are those for new structures. Additional problems may be faced—for example, when a wall is penetrated, a ceiling exposed, or a utility run traced, or when logistical or access issues arise in a building that is partially occupied by staff and users. Project contingencies therefore need to be slightly higher, often 1 to 2 percent higher. Large renovation projects range widely in cost per unit of floor area, generally comparing with the lower half of the typical range of floor area costs for new library construction. It will naturally vary greatly, depending on the amount of structural work, new utilities, waterproofing, furniture to be replaced, and a host of other factors. When a project combines an addition with renovation of the existing structure, the economy of renovation can be somewhat assured through the protection given in the contractor's bid when the contract covers the completely new work on the addition as well as the renovation. Note, however, that some contractors specialize in renovation, and renovation work sometimes is best handled by a different contractor. Contract bid add and deduct alternates are especially important for renovation projects.

9.6
Financial Implications of New Construction

An institution can at times become involved in planning new library quarters without considering all the financial implications of the undertaking. Sections 9.1 through 9.5 have dealt with the obvious considerations: Funds must be provided for the project; an estimate of construction and equipment costs must be made; and ways should be considered by which construction costs can be reduced.

There are two other groups of expenditures that may result from a new building and that, in the long view, are often as great or greater than those already discussed and as difficult to finance. The first of these depends directly on how well the building has been planned as a structure. The second results from the increased use of and demands on the library, which are apparently the inevitable and indeed exceedingly desirable results of an attractive, convenient, and comfortable building. Too often, unfortunately, sufficient attention is paid to neither.

9.6.1 Future Financial Effects of the Design Itself

A building can be well planned from most functional points of view, but overnight become problematic, even a white elephant. These concerns come from two directions: one, the changes in the academic process and environment, and two, the deterioration of the new structure or mode of maintenance.

Challenges to the librarian in planning a building are the anticipation of instructional practices as well as student ethics and social behavior for decades to come:

- Will there be a sharp shift to programmed learning?
- Will there be heavy use of courses available online or via television?
- Will there be widespread online tutorials? More use of course readers?
- Will there be much more of the basic instruction in use of online resources and other in-

formation technology provided in the high schools before students move on to college?
- And—the other unknown—will there be respect for the honor code and the library building, or further disdain for public property? Greater or lesser marking of library books and graffiti on desks and walls? The desire for more privacy or a stronger trend toward group study? More or less rebelliousness or conformity to rules?

These trends or fluctuations are rather impossible to forecast with any certainty, though they greatly influence how well the new building will function in years to come and what operational expenses there may need to be. Some conditions seem to ebb and flow over the generations. Also, as secondary schools have gone through cyclical periods of one philosophy or another, so undergraduate education has varied in methodology and expectations: for example, mass courses in Western civilization or undergraduate seminars, a January project period between semesters, or heavier reading assignments during terms of the school year. The extent of necessary supervision has changed over recent decades. As scarce scholarly books become dearer, should the library segregate an ever larger proportion in a supervised rare book room, close the bookstacks to all except faculty and graduate students, use closed-circuit television or student proctors or staff employees for supervision? Will texts be used much more widely and the competition of students in the stacks be reduced? Will the "wired campus" prompt much heavier dorm use of online instruction and less use of the library, or will computerizing the library study accommodations with widespread networked outlets and in-house, in-person help and tutorials result in much greater use of the library building? It is necessary to monitor the trends, prepare for some flexibility in use of the building, manage wisely and economically at the present, and recognize that there will be surprising changes in the decades ahead.

Some librarians feel it necessary to plan the building so that there will be, if needed, a large number of service points that could be staffed during all hours of opening. (This is particularly the case with public libraries.) They may conclude that full-time staff members must be kept at the circulation desk, the periodical room, the rare book room, and in a large library at a number of other areas assigned for special subjects, such as public documents, fine arts, music, micro-texts, audiovisual facilities, and perhaps divisional reading rooms for humanities, social sciences, and sciences. However, each desk requiring full hours of service results in an addition to the payroll that may approach or equal the salary of a full professor. This is more likely to be the case today with the very long hours of opening that prevail in the average academic library than it was several decades ago when many libraries closed by 9 or 10 o'clock on weekday evenings. The many forms of budget-reduction programs that have been common over the past decade have resulted in shorter hours in some libraries, yet 90 to 100 or more hours a week is not unusual, and some have 106 hours a week or more during the academic term.

Careful planning should hold the number of service points to the minimum that will permit the desired type of service to be given. It does not mean that students can serve themselves completely or that there is no such thing as a disciplinary problem today. It suggests that a considerable amount can be saved if the new library or addition or the remodeled space can be planned to minimize service points that require staffing, and this will challenge the skill of the librarian as a new facility is planned.

If today one service desk instead of two will suffice, so much the better. For instance, when the reference load is comparatively light, perhaps all types of guidance and service can be provided from one desk instead of two, or from two instead of four. Seating may be so arranged that reading rooms do not require supervision; individual seating, which is used so much today, is a great help in this connection. A building exit check may suffice and may be electronic, without staff ever at an exit-control desk. Microtexts and current periodicals can possibly be served from a desk used for other purposes, at least evenings and weekends.

A building plan that requires service staff to travel unnecessarily long distances naturally increases the size of the staff that is needed. Going up and down stairs frequently is a matter of particular importance; it takes time, which is always costly. Where an automated catalog is not planned, efforts should always be made to house members of the processing staff close to the card catalog, without upsetting other features of the plan that might be even more important. If a library is not a large and very busy one, and the reference,

reserved-book, and circulation desks can be fairly close together, one or two assistants may be able to serve all three during meal hours and other slack times of day, between semesters, or during long holiday or summer breaks.

The second type of expenditure that can be limited by proper planning comes in connection with maintenance, operations, and repair costs. There are many detailed arrangements that can contribute to operating savings. Many of them are mentioned elsewhere in this volume; they are only briefly noted here.

1. Items that may reduce building maintenance and operations cost:
   a. Janitor's closets with water connections and sufficient storage space for cleaning equipment and supplies on each level; placement should allow them to be used without entering reading areas.
   b. Furniture that can be cleaned under and around easily; lighting fixtures that can be easily cleaned and bulbs or tubes easily replaced.
   c. Windows that can be cleaned without the use of exotic equipment.
   d. Floors that can be kept in order easily without constant buffing and waxing.
   e. Window shades, blinds, and draperies that do not constantly require repair or replacement or staff attention for opening or closing.
   f. Maintenance operations planned so that as large a share as possible of the cleaning can be done during daytime or evening, rather than during night hours when wages may be higher and security and work supervision less satisfactory.
   g. The avoidance of too much glass, inadequate insulation, and unsatisfactory protection from the sun through lack of shades, blinds, draperies, awnings, overhangs, or tinted or mirror glass, each of which affects heating, ventilating, and air-conditioning costs.
   h. Lighting that avoids unnecessarily high intensities, inefficient light sources, and too few light switches (which make it difficult to cut off light when it is not needed).
   i. Mechanical installations that are not so complex that an engineer must be on duty all the time, and mechanical rooms that

are so well planned and lit that access for routine maintenance procedures is not excessively difficult.

j. A proper number of telephones, because too many add to current operating expenses and too few frustrate staff and use more time.

k. Fire extinguisher tanks in wall receptacles rather than on brackets protruding from walls.

l. Avoidance of decorative water fountains or pools within the building, a frequent source of problems.

m. Location of water pipes so that mains are not over or within bookstacks, and never in rare book, archive, or manuscript areas.

2. Items that affect repair and replacement costs:

a. Furniture that will not withstand wear, such as chairs, tables, and catalog trays with joints that weaken or with finish so poor that it must constantly be renewed.

b. Poorly designed rest rooms; they should be as vandal resistant as possible.

c. Exposed, unprotected corners in corridors or columns that may be damaged if hit by a loaded book truck. They should be specially treated with hard edges at least three feet up from the floor.

d. Vulnerable surfaces. Walls near public phones, elevators (including the inside thereof), lobbies, rest rooms, and perhaps certain major corridors as well as the vertical face of all service desks or counters should be extra durable or easily refinished.

e. Electronic and audiovisual equipment that is not bolted or tethered or kept in a locked inventory storeroom.

f. Inadequate heating and ventilation installations that make necessary constant repairs, to say nothing of opening and closing windows.

g. Leaking roofs, skylights, and windows and inadequate gutters, downspouts, and exterior surface drains.

h. Floor or floor coverings that require frequent replacement, expensive repairs, or refinishing, such as carpeting in lobbies and in front of major service desks.

i. Signs that require difficult or expensive processes to accommodate change.

j. Elevator ceilings so low that their panels can be easily lifted and light fixtures reached, a target for pranksters or vandals.

k. Electrical wiring and cabling that is not color coded in floor distribution, so that replacement or tracing problems become much more expensive.

It is recommended that during the building design development phase, senior maintenance staff of the institution should be asked to consult with the architect and the planning team to consider these and similar ongoing cost-saving conditions. Note that the cost of servicing the building and keeping it in good condition may be double in one library what it is in another with the same area. At Stanford, the average cost of library maintenance over four years ending in 1997 ranged from $0.18 (for a storage facility) to $0.54 (for the undergraduate/technology library) per gross ft^2 ($1.99 to $5.83 per m^2) per year. The highest plant maintenance cost (excluding custodial service) in any one year was $0.61 per gross ft^2 or $6.60 per m^2. Because any one major system replacement could seriously inflate figures while differed maintenance could deflate them, the figures presented should be viewed with caution; local information should be sought.

One theoretical estimate of the cost for monitoring a building (exclusive of energy and custodial service) suggests a figure of 1.5 percent of the construction cost. From the recent Stanford experience, this rule of thumb appears to be on the high side. However, custodial costs currently range from $0.50 to $1.00 per net ft^2 ($4.65 to $9.30 per m^2) per year, and energy cost (again drawing upon the Stanford experience and keeping in mind that this cost will vary from place to place) is as high as $1.50 per gross ft^2 ($16.15 per m^2) per year; the cost of building maintenance, including energy and custodial service, will easily exceed a 1.5 percent rule of thumb. In a building of 100,000 ft^2 (9,290 m^2), which might cost $15 million to construct, using the 1.5 percent rule of thumb, at least $225,000 per year will be spent to fully maintain it. In the most expensive Stanford example, including custodial maintenance, plant maintenance, and energy, the cost would be much closer to $250,000 per year for a 100,000-ft^2 (9,290-m^2) building. Clearly, a savings of as little as 10 percent over the years could be substantial.

Let us take another example. Because utility charges are so high, special attention needs to be given to this aspect. At some institutions, all plans for HVAC and lighting must be approved by energy consultants before design documents are approved. Lights in washrooms, stacks, and storerooms can be placed on motion-sensitive switches, devices that can also be used in faucets in the washrooms. Water conservation is another concern in many arid areas. A study of energy costs is also important as part of any renovation project, and some colleges and universities have funded special projects just to address what are considered excessive energy costs in certain parts of a library building, such as bookstacks, corridors, lobbies, and exterior lighting. The costs of paper towels (together with the need to replace and dispose of used towels) versus electric hand dryers are studied in some institutions. Efforts to assure operating and maintenance economy of HVAC and lighting systems will have long-term financial benefits.

Better planning and quality of construction, although it may increase the original cost considerably, may reduce the total capital expenditures if the long-term view is taken. Remember that if a 100,000-ft² (9,290-m²) building has no more useful space than a 75,000-ft² (6.910-m²) building, it is better to choose the latter and to improve the quality of the construction and reduce the maintenance cost.

Colleges and universities typically face large basic upgrading of their buildings. In 1990 the Association of Physical Plant Administrators of Universities and Colleges found staggering total national needs, and the breakdown is suggestive of where campus buildings are in need of maintenance: $21 billion for life and fire safety (which would include the dangerous unreinforced masonry structures), $21 billion for HVAC systems, $7 billion for exterior structures (especially roof repair or replacement), another $7 billion for electrical upgrades (to meet greatly increased campus needs, including telecommunications), $5.6 billion for plumbing, and another $5.6 billion for interior treatment. Operational and maintenance costs for a building during a 30-year period can approach one and a half times the initial cost of construction. Life cycle considerations should be made during the design of buildings so this type of unmet cost does not accumulate.

In connection with this consideration of maintenance and repair expenditures, it is strongly recommended that whenever possible an additional sum of money amounting to 20 percent of the cost of the building be set aside as endowment to be invested, and the income be used periodically to maintain and repair the structure. If there is a single donor who can be persuaded to add endowment to the basic donation, so much the better. For older buildings, an amount equal to a certain percentage of annual operating cost for heat, light, and power could be budgeted as a building repair fund, and it could logically vary according to the age and nature of the building. Such a growing repair allotment might even be placed by the institution into a conservative investment fund, so that the accumulated sum can earn interest or dividends until needed for periodic expenditure on the building.

9.6.2 Results of Increased Use

A fine new building almost inevitably increases the demands made on the facilities, perhaps to such an extent that the staff must be increased. Many institutions have found that use of a new library by students more than doubled immediately. Such experiences have been observed at Cornell, Louisiana State, the University of Michigan, Northwestern, Stanford, and elsewhere, regardless of whether the campus is largely commuting or residential. This can and probably will happen in your institution, even to a surprising degree after a major remodeling or renovation. The librarian should be prepared for the additional demands and for the possible incremental cost of the additional service that is required.

Forecasting increased use is a matter of judgment. One method would be to collect use data for very good libraries in a selection of peer institutions. The local institution can expect a greatly improved library to result in use that may be near the mean and at least within the range of use in its peers, and a rough percentage increase can be estimated. Another method would be to look for a comparable institution that had a recent comparable improvement in its library facility and find out how the use increased in each of the first few years after occupying the new space. This growth pattern can then be adjusted somewhat to reflect any different characteristics between the two situations. No matter what method is used, change should be expected and some estimate of the consequence to staff anticipated.

At Stanford University, in anticipation of the opening of the much enlarged and improved Cecil H. Green Library, designed as the main research library, there was concern that the nearby

J. Henry Meyer (undergraduate) Library would fall into disuse. It turned out that this was not the case, as the Meyer Library continues to be well used. It has its devotees, social attractions, reserved-book collections, and, from the early 1990s, a primary emphasis on the use of media and online networked instructional technologies. However, the much-enlarged Green Library of 1980 attracted many more users, at times being virtually 100 percent occupied, while the undergraduate library for many years seldom had more than 50 percent occupancy. In the 1990s, with the introduction of new technologies in support of information access (video, audio, digital, interactive video, etc.), the use of the two libraries has equalized. To initially reduce the adverse influence on graduate research by undergraduates needlessly moving into Green, a costly effort was undertaken to make improvements to the Meyer Library so that its reader accommodations would be perceived as being equal to those of the newer Green Library. Where an adverse reaction can be predicted, the expense of this kind of effort may well be warranted.

We might go farther and add that as the library use increases, there is also inevitably a demand for a larger collection, which again adds to the costs. This demand is usually marginal. However, demand for longer hours of the new facility can be more substantial and persuasive. And greater-than-expected use of computer-based systems will put pressure on the annual operating budget, especially when use of these informational technologies is already growing at a vigorous rate. This condition is like riding a tidal wave! Above all else, the library and its use will change; flexibility to cope with this change is essential.

NOTES

1. Except for this last figure, these figures are determined by a simple algebraic formula: Gift Value equals $150 times the Area of Gift divided by 0.60. The last figure, because of the technology-equipped space costs, has been calculated at a premium based upon $150 times the Area divided by 0.40. Clearly the cost and percentage will need to be established for each unique project.
2. From a description of value engineering methodology prepared for Western Washington University, October 29, 1992, by Hill Architectural Planning VE Consulting, Kirkland, Wash. See also: Theodore C. Fowler's 1993 paper "Value Engineering," available on the Internet addressed as http://akao.larc.nasa.gov/dfc/va.html; Fowler was Vice President for Education of the Society of American Value Engineers.

10

Building Additions
and Renovations

*I, the new owner of this ancient house, take over more than
walls and hearths and stairs; there has been sorrow here and
human pride, and I am taking over things like prayers.*

—Robert Peter Tristram Coffin, "Taking Over an Old House"

The better-designed academic and research library buildings of post–World War II can continue to serve effectively, which was not the case for many before that watershed. This condition will prompt many more renovations of and additions to existing library space than separate new library buildings. Other reasons for the preponderance of renovations and additions are less space on a developed campus for new structures; a greater emphasis than 50 years ago on sharing collections instead of financing larger independent collections; sharply increased reliance on computer-based databases, which creates some caution about the long-term growth rate of book collections; the tight economic conditions forecast for the future; and greater appreciation for older structures even if not of top quality.

This chapter examines some of the special conditions encountered during a building addition project and some of the problems when renovation is part of that project. The chapter addresses both additions and renovations because the former often involves the latter, or at least raises questions about renovations. Building examples will be cited as illustrating how different conditions led to unique solutions.

Furthermore, the remodeled structure with or without the enlarged building is the unified expression of a new space need. To put it another way, the eventual building expresses the whole of a projected program need, a need that may be attained by substantial renovation with no addition or with an addition and no remodeling. Both renovating and adding on create several significant planning, design, and construction problems that do not exist in work on a separate new structure.

There is more variety in building addition projects when compared to construction of new and separate structures. This comes about because of the variety of preexisting conditions that must be accommodated when working with an existing structure, whether or not that structure is currently occupied and in use. A building project that is concerned with a new structure, one that is separate from other structures, is simpler than one involving a building addition in which the original structure is to undergo substantial renovation. Providing for future flexibility is an especially important point in any addition, just as it is in a new separate structure. The academic justification for a building addition or major remodeling is essentially similar to that for a new and separate structure. However, it will need to take one of several possible courses in the presentation.

First, it can assume that the existing building will be retained; the program would then explicitly deal with the functional use of that structure as part of the total program document, and the design team must begin with that assumption.

Second, it can begin with the assumption that the program will be written without any reference to the current structure. The design team would thus be presented with a program pure of any bias about the current structure, and the architect would be free to resolve the question of whether all or some of the present structure should be used to meet part of the program.

Third, the program can be written merely to state in very broad terms the academic needs and functions to be covered and to provide the basis for an engineering and architectural study of feasibility. This latter course may be very wise when there are serious doubts about the structural and mechanical conditions of the existing building, when its quality may be marginal, and when its site is less than the ideal. Otherwise it is usually best to use the second option; the solution to the problem will then be applicable to existing conditions yet not be restrained by them.

Whatever the nature of the program document, a similar thought process must take place in analyzing the current library building for its academic purposes, but it is complicated by the existence of a structure that one way or the other must be taken into account. College or university officers as well as the librarian and the chosen architect will need to decide exactly what steps to take when dealing with an existing structure. In most cases at least cursory architectural and engineering review of the present structure would be advisable. For any building that is to have an addition twice as large as the original structure, such a review would be very wise indeed. An original structure more than 40 years old will have been designed and built under conditions that differ substantially from today's code requirements or standards, and so an engineering and architectural review is essential. Even a 20-year-old building could require substantial improvements to make it structurally and functionally sound.

10.1
Basic Questions before Deciding on a Building Addition

On what basis can an institution decide to settle on an addition to an existing structure rather than a replacement of that structure? Furthermore, if there is to be an addition, should it be with no renovation or considerable or extensive renovation of the original structure? These crucial questions may take months or even a year of thorough study to decide. Seven basic questions need answering before making this decision.

1. *Is the location of the existing structure a good one?* Consideration must be given to campus plans for building changes and functional use over several decades to come. If the library is in an ideal location, then there is a strong argument to work with the existing structure or to consider a replacement on the same general site. Hollins College is a case where the 1985 flood of Carvin's Creek into the Fishburn Library convinced the college that the new library should be on a different site—the other side of the campus entrance.

Architects should remember that the surest thing about a general academic library is that its space needs are almost certain to grow over time. In due course and long before the building is worn out or outmoded, new space will be required, and the need for a new wing or additional areas provided in some other way will be a matter of future importance. Thus, two prerequisites to an addition must be kept in mind: the amount of space on the site and a building design without serious aesthetic, construction, or functional complications.

2. *Is the original structure sound?* All buildings sooner or later need renovation or extensive refurbishing, such as repainting, new flooring, or new light fixtures. Over some decades the ventilation system may become difficult to maintain, electrical and telecommunications capacities may be exceeded, heating pipes may become corroded, foundations may crack and roofs wear out, window sashes may develop problems, and safety requirements may be more exacting than when the structure was built. A special study may be needed to determine whether the building can handle digital, video, and audio data transmission through existing conduits or cable trays. Whether the existing structure was designed for a library or not, a special engineering study of floor loads may be essential because book collections are far heavier than almost any other academic activity except certain scientific or engineering equipment. Microtexts housed efficiently will weigh twice as much as books, and phonograph discs are even heavier.

As one example, the Harvard Yard includes Boylston Hall, an 1857 structure of handsome stonework and with a mansard roof. It has been remodeled four times. In the 1960 remodeling the Harvard Yenching Library moved out, and a small modern language branch library was assigned part of the first floor and a new mezzanine. Insertion of a new complete floor between the second and third levels was also possible. Reconstruction was $800,000 for new space of 14,000 ft^2 (1,300 m^2) and extensively renovated old space—some $500,000 less than was estimated to construct a new building on the site.

A decision on the feasibility for renovation may relate to a judgment about the value of the existing facility. In this context, it may help to realize that the exterior envelope and structural skeleton typically represent about 33 to 40 percent of the total value; interior construction represents 20 to 25 percent; and the mechanical and electrical systems 35 to 40 percent. Unless all systems and structure are in need of replacement, a potential for cost savings is often realized even though renovation work is generally more expensive than new work when the same components are compared.[1]

Renovating a building of rather mediocre quality may be sending good money after bad. One will not wish to dress up a poor building with superficial improvements. A thorough engineering evaluation to assess the structural, code, energy, access, programmatic, and other aspects of the existing structure may be a very wise expenditure of time and money.

3. *Is flexibility in the original structure acceptable and can the existing floor heights work satisfactorily with an addition?* In adding on to a small original building with fixed interior walls, there will always be significant problems. It is thus necessary to weigh the amount of limitation that is caused by those fixed elements. Consideration can be given to breaking out an occasional wall if there is enough headroom to put in a new beam, and almost always one can break through to install a passageway or a new door unless a mechanical or plumbing shaft is within that wall. As a rule, limited flexibility is easier to accept if the original structure was of fairly good size and, particularly, if the addition is to be much larger than the original structure. In this case, the original structure may be used for certain administrative offices, for small functionally discrete sections or units of the library that can be separated from larger units (such as a learning resources center or instructional services), or for such specialized collections as rare books, manuscripts, oral his-

tory archives, or maps where the size of the spaces may be suitable and the feeling of the older space or its nostalgic character may be suited to the housing of cherished rarities.

Floor heights of the original structure are an important aspect of flexibility. Modern developments in lighting, heating, and ventilation have changed the required distances from floor to floor, and great distances in old construction are often inconsistent with today's requirements. To match the heights used in the original construction might result in increasing the cost of an addition so much that little would be left of a savings that otherwise might result from the use of an old building. Always remember that height greater than is necessary or desirable functionally and aesthetically costs money, both initially and in annual operation, and should be questioned. Fitting two levels of bookstack into a high reading room may, of course, gain assignable footage. If floor heights between the existing structure and the addition do not match exactly, that may be entirely satisfactory, although steps or a ramp will be required on one or more levels to go from the old to the new. Wheelchair movement may be a problem. Considerable difference in floor height between one or more levels may require a very long ramp or several ramps, with resultant inconvenience, accidents, and extra effort in transporting books back and forth.

4. *Is the original structure of sentimental importance or controlled by a state or federal historic building regulation?* Because a library is frequently a central building on campus, may be prominently situated, and have an imposing facade, graduates and friends of the college or university may feel very strongly about retaining the building and perhaps maintaining it as a central library. As one case in point, the University of Tulsa in 1928 adopted a campus development program that firmly established the library as the central campus building. That structure of 1930 was a very pleasant space with a very large park in front of it. In 1965 the university built an addition on the back with some renovation of the original structure. Within 10 years it became necessary to plan another addition, and, in this case, given the location of the library and the importance of its facade, a very large underground addition in front toward the park was added. An addition of 66,000 ft² (6.130 m²) was made to the existing 61,000 ft² (5.670 m²).

Another example is the Sacramento City College Library, a historic building constructed in 1937 with Public Works Administration (WPA) funds in the once-popular Streamline Moderne style. A 1985 proposal to rehabilitate the structure turned into a plan to tear it down to free a site but came up against the California Environmental Quality Act and the objections of the California Office of Historic Preservation. An Environmental Impact Report was prepared and $40,000 had to be spent documenting the historic building before the plan was approved, the old building demolished in 1996, and a three-story Learning Resources Center was under way. That same year the State of California took a much-disputed position by deciding not to rehabilitate or restore any old buildings anymore. The tension between valuing past designs and wanting modern efficiencies often logically leads to thoughtful cost analysis and value engineering studies. Yet the symbolic or sentimental importance of an existing structure should not be underestimated.

5. *Are the costs of the alternatives a trade-off over a 10- or 20-year period?* Although costs are not the only determinant of whether to add on or build anew, the financial conditions may well weigh very heavily indeed. The costs of the new structure can rather easily be estimated, and a thorough analysis should result in rather accurate estimates for dealing with the existing structure.

In figuring the expense of remodeling, the institution will need to decide whether it wishes to attach a new structure to a building that will have nothing done to modernize it. Alternatively, there will need to be a decision about the extent of renovation, which can vary greatly. In the simplest condition there may be some repainting, some new carpeting, perhaps replacing some weakened furniture, and providing new signs. The remodeling can be carried farther, to replace chairs with ones of a new style, replace unfunctional shelving, provide new light fixtures, even add a contemporary entrance door. Or it can be even more extensive, to alter some partitions, improve or replace mechanical systems and lights, deal with acoustical problems, correct fire hazards, add air conditioning, and improve the condition of the exterior shell of the building.

After 50 years or so of snow, ice, rain, wind, and very hot weather, the building shell must often be repaired so as not to let faults increase and costs of repair compound. Roofs of slate, copper, tile, and built-up tar and gravel will all deteriorate. Brick and stone walls need to be scrubbed down and repointed. The beloved ivy holds moisture to rot windowsills, crawls into crevices and forces gaps, gets behind downspouts and gutters, and causes hidden havoc. Ground settling can crack foundations, and lack of suitable ground-water drainage can undermine exterior walkways just as roots can cause upheaval. How far to go in such projects needs careful study. Planners should consider the nature of problems they will be leaving their successors.

Decisions of this sort require a determination of whether this is the best time in the history of the institution to bring the old structure up to date, whether fund-raising for remodeling costs is feasible, and whether the resultant building will have the old and the new parts work well together. This last point is of great importance and is dealt with later in this chapter.

6. *Is there another institutional facility need that can be best met by the use of an existing library facility?* Although many older libraries have significant features, such as tiered stacks and monumental reading rooms, that would not be easily adapted to an academic department or other functions, it may be practical to consider reassignment of portions of an existing library to capitalize on the potential opportunity to create a better library facility. Even when tiered stacks are a problem, they might serve as a practical auxiliary storage site should the new library site be separated by some distance. More recent libraries generally can be readily adapted to other functions, a possibility that may be particularly attractive where the existing library really does not provide for adequate future expansion. The two former campus libraries of the University of South Carolina (dated 1840 and 1940) are examples of reuse that was very well done. Columbia University's Low Library is a case of awkward space reused but of very high sentimental value.

7. *Is fund-raising possible just for the addition or for renovations as well?* If raising funds for a library building is difficult, funding major renovations is more difficult and especially so in privately supported institutions. Just as the estimate of costs for various options must be in hand, so it is necessary to estimate the capacity to raise the funds for the addition, or for modest or substantial renovations in the existing structure, and to compare the fund-raising capacity if the present structure were to be replaced altogether. Not an easy task, though highly desirable.

A few talented financial minds, usually outside the library, should be asked to make this kind of study. If the institution does not have experience at funding major renovation projects or with tearing down an original structure, inquiring about the experience of similar or neighboring institutions may provide insight into the nature of the problems and prospects for success. These financial matters, of course, are critical for the success of the project, even though they are but one of the seven basic questions in deciding whether to plan an addition or a replacement to the building.

It has been common experience that raising funds for a separate structure is difficult enough, even though there is a possibility of putting the major donor's name on the building and giving important rooms within the building the names of other significant contributors. However, if the building addition is small, if it is merely a book-stack wing or storage facility for lesser-used books, if it is all underground, or if much of the money goes into renovating an old structure, there will be increased difficulties in attracting large donors. It takes a very understanding and devoted friend of an institution to be willing to contribute to providing rather utilitarian space, or space that is rather invisible, or certainly to renovation of space that already bears another's name. Most institutions are nevertheless likely to find the fund-raising for an addition to be easier than for a new and separate structure, and for considerable renovations to be more difficult.

Although not as fundamental as the above seven, there are at least eight additional questions that need to be answered before plans are made for an addition.

8. *When the present building was planned, was an addition contemplated?* If so, were drawings for it prepared? Are they available and still suitable? One good example is the Miller Library building of the Stanford University Hopkins Marine Station in Pacific Grove, which had a wing included in the initial construction—first used for storage of laboratory materials and furniture, and then available for compact shelving to meet growing library needs. Many architects fortunately have realized that an addition would eventually be needed and have proceeded accordingly by at least schematically establishing the possible character of a future addition.

The plan of the 1926 main library building of the University of Illinois at Urbana-Champaign may be regarded as an example in this connection. Six additions have been made in space originally set aside at the rear of the library. The most recent expansion of 1984 was virtually all compact shelving, which filled much of the remaining expansion space on the block. The limitations of the Illinois plan were that additional cubicles in the stack are in places where there is no outside light, though this really is not a problem for stacks. There was concern that new space for readers and stacks may not be in a satisfactory proportion in each addition and that the additions do not easily provide for new staff housing, yet the capacity to add collections in the central main library has been well managed.

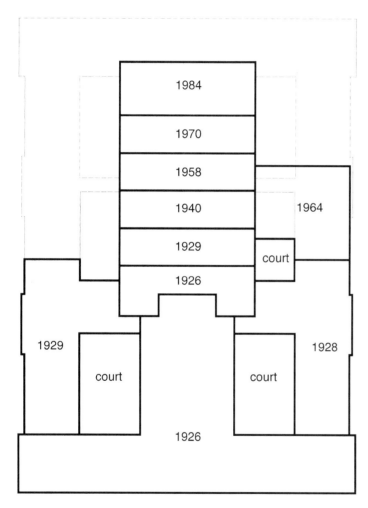

FIGURE 10.1   University of Illinois phases. The dotted outline represents the originally conceived maximum library footprint created in the 1920s. The building has been expanded through the years as indicated. The ultimate expansion is currently being considered, which would result in a total building very close to that originally plotted, with overall dimensions of 440 ft × 300 ft (134.112 × 91.440 m) and at least 700,000 gross ft² (65,032 m²). (Courtesy of University of Illinois at Urbana-Champaign)

The famous Illinois expansion plan is coming to an end, challenged by a new university chancellor and provost who wondered when there would be a final stack addition. The library returned to the original plan of architect Charles A. Platt, of New York City, namely to finish the building on the block site with a gross area of about 700,000 ft² (65,030 m²). Thus the current plan completes the building, 80 years after its opening, with three elements: a major public services structure, a seventh stack addition, and a large Special Collections Wing occupying the full width of the western end with its own separate entrance on Sixth Street. Clearly, the library master plan of the 1920s has served the state of Illinois well! (See fig. 10.1.)

9. *Is it possible when adding to a library building to obtain an easy and satisfactory circulation pattern with direct access to the new part of the structure?* It was not unusual during the past century to plan a library in which it was impossible on any level, even the main one, to go from one end of the building to the other without ascending or descending a few stairs along the way. American technology has not yet devised a satisfactory and inexpensive method of taking a loaded book truck up and down short flights of stairs, though adaptation of the now common electrically run stair lifts could solve this. Additional elevators may help, but they are expensive, particularly if the mechanism must be capable of making frequent stops a few feet apart.

The Cornell University Uris Library, dating to the 1890s, was and still is a good example of what ought not to be done. Shifting books from one part of the building to another was seriously complicated by the numerous short flights of stairs, many of them without elevator connection.

The University of Florida Library at Gainesville, dating from 1929, has already had two additions, one of them being a totally separate building. It is an example of a library that is still in good physical condition many decades later but is hard to enlarge because difficult circulation patterns would result and would require the sacrifice of valuable space. Sufficient additional space to provide for a considerable period ahead is not available on the site in any direction. Further, the original building is now on the Historical Register, so the renovations done in the late 1990s are entirely internal.

Libraries with excellent circulation after a major addition are the University of Northern Iowa,

Clemson University, and Brigham Young University. However, circulation is poor at the University of California at Santa Barbara, exceedingly bad at Walla Walla College, and still problematic at the University of California at Davis, Furman University, and the University of Virginia's Alderman Library.

10. *Is it possible to accommodate greatly expanded needs for electrical power and signal runs?* Libraries in the last third of the twentieth century needed far more wiring and cabling than before. Not only are there requirements for telephone lines, vacuum cleaners, microtext readers, copying and fax machines, and a variety of traditional pieces of equipment, but also for computer terminals, word-processing machines, personal computers and servers, videotext display facilities, optical disk playback machines, and technological devices still to come.

Older buildings (especially those nonmodular ones before 1970) can create significant problems for pulling coaxial cable for hard-wiring of local area networks: for example, penetrating walls that may be two or even three feet thick or surfaces that may be marble, and locating room in underground conduits. Without suspended ceilings it may be nearly impossible to guard against unsightly installations. All such conditions will push the cost up significantly.

11. *Is it possible to achieve air conditioning for the preservation of the collections?* Even in benign climates, it is desirable to maintain collections of long-term research value. Thus all university and independent research libraries and most college libraries have achieved or are striving to achieve controlled temperature and humidity. This is today a basic question when considering whether to add on to an existing structure or seek a replacement. Engineering studies will be needed to determine whether ceiling heights are sufficient to accommodate ductwork, or whether existing ducts can be resized to meet current airflow requirements and adequate distribution. The question of effectively sealing the shell of an older building must be considered as well, especially where humidity control is a goal (for complete humidity control at minimal operational expense, the space must be surrounded on all sides with what amounts to a vapor barrier membrane). At Cornell and the University of California at Los Angeles, the old university structure was recast into a collegiate library, on the basis that the materials there were not of research nature over time.

12. *Will the addition overwhelm the existing structure?* It is one thing to add a small stack or small wing for reading areas, increasing the size of an old building by 20 to 25 percent. It is quite a different matter to build an addition that is larger than the original building, something that often seemed required during the 1950s and 1960s. The small addition, if it will provide satisfactory space and will not crowd other buildings or encounter other complications, is often desirable.

The Waterloo Lutheran University in Ontario added two floors on top of the library. A large addition is likely to be more cost efficient, though it tends to perpetuate any unfortunate features of the old building. Eventually the additions become so massive that the scale used in the original exterior treatment may be wrong aesthetically. Facing that circumstance, the University of South Carolina in 1976 added 260,000 ft^2 (24.154 m^2) to the 1959 Undergraduate Library of 30,000 ft^2 (2,787 m^2), forming the Thomas Cooper Library, with four of the new seven levels being underground. The University of California, Davis, solved the question of mass by placing the addition on the open side of a large **U** with the new public entrance in the addition, thus letting the library face two directions—one toward the older campus green and the other to the larger, current campus scene and traffic patterns.

13. *Are there serious aesthetic obstacles to an addition?* Following the style of an older structure may be prohibitively expensive, but building a contemporary wing on a collegiate Gothic, Classical, or Georgian building may be very difficult. Even if it is done to the satisfaction of many persons with good taste, it may arouse violent alumni criticism.

It has been done successfully—the 1958 addition at Wellesley College is an example and Duke University's library addition is at least externally another—but there have been many failures. Consider what might have been if Columbia University had built the Butler as an addition to Low!

14. *Is there a very strong commitment to retain the Georgian style or another predominant style?* If so, special consideration should be given to retaining the same firm that designed the original structure, if it is still in business. Some institutions have a long-standing relation with an individual or a firm. If the firm has within the past decade continued to do well-regarded work for the institution, that also might argue for the commission being given to that firm. However, most institu-

tions feel that a major building, even a major addition, is a project for which various architectural firms should be considered.

15. *How long can the proposed addition, plus the present building, be expected to provide adequate space, and what can be done at the end of this period?* Some librarians have found that poorly planned and hastily constructed additions have exhausted the possibilities for later expansion. Will still another addition then be practical, or will this one be the last? Does the original have flexibility? Will the addition provide sufficient collection and reader space for decades to come? Cornell, Harvard, Indiana University, the University of Kansas, and Yale moved the special collections to new structures (now an objective of the Universities of Illinois and Virginia), thus simplifying the main library building function and gaining time.

For a rapidly growing institution, are the space needs of its library increasing so quickly that a much larger building will be needed within 20 years? If so, it may well be uneconomical to enlarge now instead of starting over. In a privately endowed, liberal arts college, an addition may be desirable, even if the existing building is 50 years old, so long as the college does not expect to increase its student body to any considerable extent. This is especially so if its library collections are mature enough to be growing not more than 3 percent a year.

Many if not most projects aim to utilize many arguments and solve a variety of problems. For instance, the Harvard Law School's major 1996–1997 renovation of famous Langdell Hall (built 1905) used the above points 2, 4, 5, and 9–11. Despite an "unpleasant" experience for the entire school, closing the building and dispersing the library for some 15 months seemed a more tolerable schedule than incurring four years of piecemeal construction. So "in one fell swoop" a new power substation was built; air conditioning was added; each of the 700 library seats were wired for access to legal databases and the Internet; and new stairs, elevators, wheelchair ramps, and a first-floor entrance were provided, as were more carrels and seats in the stacks and more stacks in the grand reading room as part of an open-stack policy.

Because building additions are common, and becoming more so, an institution ought to ask the architect to provide a site utilization study that will show how one or more further additions could be accommodated if and when they

are needed. Important issues for the architect to keep in mind are the following:

The location for connections should be anticipated. This issue is dealt with later in this chapter in Section 10.3.

The traffic routes to and around the building should be planned with forethought. The traffic lanes inside the building should be planned so that they can work with one or more additions. This consideration is particularly important to avoid a maze. (As successful as it is, Stanford University's Green Library offers a challenge to students needing to find collections in the original West Wing building or in the collection space beneath the Meyer Library. The route at Harvard from the Widener Library Reference Room to the Widener-level collections under the Lamont building also is quite circuitous.)

Placement of utility cores, stairs, and elevators is critical, in terms of horizontal layouts as well as vertical. The horizontal will, of course, more deeply affect the potential addition, but the mechanical space is especially important and needs consideration as much as the architectural arrangements. (The 1975 Sacramento State University Library has stairwells that project outside the initial structure, which conceptually should make for a particularly easy accommodation to an addition. Indeed, a substantial 1990 addition to the south has been achieved; it is interesting to note that no particular advantage of such an arrangement is evident with the addition except for the fact that the stairs, which once were at the edge of the building, are now nearly at the center of the building.)

Knockout walls may be useful if you can project exactly where the addition will connect. If so, floor-to-ceiling window walls may be placed in that location so that masonry does not have to be removed and so that sentimental or financial objections will not be raised against a wide and fully effective connection.

Consideration of areas to be placed next to the potential addition is important. Consideration needs to be given to which rooms or functions will need expansion so that they might be placed next to the junction. This is particularly the case for mechanical space in order that heating or ventilating equipment can be added without the problems incurred by an additional and separate equipment room.

Remodeling is more common than it was 50 or 100 years ago. Significant reasons for recent college library remodeling have included: reducing noise and future energy costs, increasing handicapped access and comfort of users, preventing loss of book materials, upgrading the building structure to approximate current earthquake code, removing asbestos, and enhancing the building's attractiveness. Data from a study by Michael S. Freeman also reveal that 63 percent of American college library buildings built in 1967 received interior relocations or adjustments by 1981, and over one-third had three or more such changes.[2] The nature of these changes were, in decreasing order of frequency: audiovisual services, microtexts, current and bound periodicals, government documents, maps, reference department, special collections, acquisitions, staff lounge, public card catalog, interlibrary loan, and serial processing. In more recent years with such rapid information technology and telecommunication changes, it sometimes seems as if renovation in a university library building is constant.

Because so many variations exist in the handling of additions, it is particularly desirable to visit and study several and see whether some of them have conditions similar to those faced at your own institution.

10.2
Historical Lessons and Trends

The study of building additions and renovations is especially rewarding. Looking at library building projects of recent decades, one can find quite a number of examples where an existing building was given up and a completely new structure provided at a site a great many yards or even some blocks away. Examples include Bowdoin, Hollins, and Rollins Colleges, and the Universities of Glasgow, Indiana, Minnesota, North Carolina at Chapel Hill, South Carolina, South Florida at St. Petersburg, Texas, Toronto, and California at Los Angeles.

Also in recent decades there have been a much larger number of additions, sometimes a second

or third addition. Some representative college examples are Colby, Goucher, Occidental, Roanoke, Vassar, Wellesley, Whitworth, and Trinity in Dublin. Universities that have built additions include: Birmingham; Brigham Young; California at Davis, San Diego, Berkeley, and Los Angeles; Colorado; Cornell; Fresno State; North Wales; Duke; Georgia; Georgia Tech; Illinois; Michigan; Newcastle upon Tyne; Northwestern; Oregon; Pennsylvania; Princeton; Stanford; Vanderbilt; Virginia Polytechnic; Utah; Wake Forest; Washington State; and Washington. These examples merely suggest the frequency of additions.

Given the financial conditions of colleges and universities, it seems probable that over the next several decades there will continue to be a heavy emphasis on additions. Particularly, because buildings constructed over the past 40 years have far greater flexibility than those built earlier, retaining the original structure is far more reasonable.

Some conclusions can be drawn from the recent history of library construction. First, there will be a great many more examples of additions than of completely new and separate buildings, at least in terms of central facilities. Second, there will be much more use of underground space, partly as buildings in the central part of a campus become more crowded and planners need to retain planted area and open space for air and pleasantness. Third, additions will sometimes be larger than the original and can work very well. Fourth, the older structure may be used for such functions as an undergraduate collection, one or more branch libraries, special collections, audiovisual services, administrative and processing offices, and, sometimes, nonlibrary activities. Fifth, the old building will very seldom be razed. Generally, an old library building continues to serve, often in some typically library-related function. (One of the last notable libraries razed was Gore Hall at Harvard in 1913, though later, university library buildings were razed at Denison, Drew, and Rochester and college library buildings at Benedict, Kenyon, Knoxville, Oberlin, and Talladega. During renovation in the mid-1990s of the Powell Library at UCLA, an older bookstack addition was removed.) Sixth, there will be a constant increase in the number of library storage facilities located away from the campus center.

Although each campus presents a special set of circumstances, one university library may be taken as an example. This is meant merely to suggest some of the prevailing effects of timing, university priorities, fund-raising, philosophy of library service, and traffic patterns. Stanford's Main Library was a 1919 structure with fixed functions, meaning that the tiered bookstack, light courts, monumental reading room, and monumental main stairs together with a relatively fixed pattern of corridors considerably limited moving many functions. There had been no modification to the building when a distinguished consultant was brought from Chicago to California in March 1948 to survey the space problems. The report included the following:

> Functions and concepts of functions are fluid and change with time, while a physical structure is more static in character. Thus a building that structurally closely matches its functions at the time of its erection, may fail more quickly than a building which originally was a poorer "fit" in relation to function. . . . The Main Library at Stanford is one which gives the impression of having been very carefully fitted to its functions at the time of construction, but in which very little consideration was given to the possibility of future changes in needs. . . . The monumental features, together with the light courts, not only take a high proportion of the available cubage, but interfere most seriously with the internal communication in the building. There are areas of the building, particularly on the mezzanine and top floors, which would be extremely useful if they were more accessible.

The four major light wells, the 30-ft (9.144-m) ceiling in the main reading rooms and the monumental stairway, and the domed ceiling delivery hall on the second floor—all typical early in the twentieth century—presented formidable problems. The recommendation included removing the monumental stairway, building new stairs in the larger two light wells, bridging over monumental space on the second and at least some of the third floor, adding forced-air ventilation, and providing an underground passageway to the Hoover Institution library tower next door.

It is interesting to note that the university solved its central library problems with a feeling of considerable satisfaction even though none of the above recommendations were followed. Financial limitations and university priorities played a major role. In the late 1950s, the upper two unfinished main library stack levels were completed. In the mid-1960s, a new basement floor was constructed beneath about three-quarters of the building because the footings were not deep

enough for more. Also in the mid-1960s, an undergraduate library was opened some 40 yards (37 m) away, with a two-level basement to handle the overflow of the main library book collections. In the 1960s, the Hoover Institution tower received a major building addition and, in the late 1970s, a second major building addition. In 1980–81, a first large addition to the back of the main library was provided, which connected with the undergraduate library basement, and a considerable renovation was then accomplished in the original 1919 structure. But even that was not the end, for the 1989 Loma Prieta earthquake wreaked havoc in the 1919 structure. After six years, the financing was found to reconstruct, with several of the 1948 recommendations and many other changes incorporated, and rebuilding and reoccupancy followed in the late 1990s. The future will likely include, at some point, further expansion and refinement of the central library facility at Stanford, while at the same time an increasing amount of material will be accommodated in a nearby storage facility.

Thus, 50 years passed while the problems were solved piecemeal, decade by decade. Very little money was expended in altering the original structure until its modest 1981 renovation, and that renovation was largely an expense for the air conditioning and security of quarters for rare books, manuscripts, archives, and rare government documents. Indeed, the monumental spaces were deliberately retained and became considerable assets. The 1989 earthquake forced the hand of the university, leading to the major rebuilding between 1996 and 1999.

It is, of course, unknown what might have been the course of history if other options had been followed. The building development was based on acceptance of the site, the assessment that the quality of the original structure was good, and a tolerance of the degree of flexibility provided by the original structure, combined with financial considerations that were major determinants. Diligent work was required over a great many years to solve a complex space problem that seemed never to go away; nevertheless, the operating condition at any time was reasonable, and options were left open in nearly all instances. This history is recounted only to underscore the necessity of very careful thought as well as persistence, the usefulness of engineering and architectural studies, and the strong effect of financing on a library building project.

10.3
Special Planning Issues

An addition can be an economical and entirely satisfactory solution from the standpoint of the library. There are, however, a number of issues that need additional consideration or a different approach from that of a new separate building. The following will be of special concern to anyone faced with such a project, and many examples are mentioned to illustrate points and show how various may be the solutions to local space problems.

10.3.1 Site Issues

Site studies are exceedingly important in considering any addition. When considering an addition, or before attempting extensive and expensive renovation of an existing structure, make sure that the site permits a later addition that will still be satisfactory functionally and aesthetically when space gives out, as it probably will if past experience is a guide. Alternatively, the institution can commit to future decentralization (branches or off-site storage or both), a decision with significant risks but one that validates an addition, though probably exhausting further expansion of the building.

If the site of the original building has sufficient area, an addition or at least an underground extension can increase the assignable floor area. Underground extension of the Fogg Art Museum at Harvard provided the library needed growth space, as did the underground addition for the Avery Architectural Library at Columbia University. If the immediate site has no spare land, then a connection to an adjacent building may permit easy growth, such as the tunnel between the Houghton and Lamont buildings at Harvard. The underground Pusey Library later provided further Houghton expansion. The Law Library of the University of Georgia uses a bridge between two buildings to join two large portions of the library, a situation aided by the fact that the ground level or the original library structure is a floor above grade of the addition, so a service road on grade is beneath the bridge.

The University of Glasgow Library presents a case of a very confined sloping site. The original building of 1968 has 13 levels, including 3 levels below grade. A temporary north wall constituted a "decaying eyesore" until the large 1986 addition, but this third and final stage of construction

(reaching 195,132 ft², or 18,135 m²) was frustrated by uncharted old mine workings beneath the site, a situation that required strengthening the 54-in. (1.380 m) deep concrete slab by pumping liquid concrete into existing and new foundations for four months! The site was no small problem.

Particularly important in site studies are traffic patterns, both internal and external. If the original building has an imposing entrance, as is very often the case when compared with more recent buildings, the addition may need to be to one side or the other or in back of the original building. However, the University of Alberta Rutherford Library and the University of Kentucky King Library have additions in front and neither is underground. In the 1979 addition to the University of Tulsa McFarlin Library, the addition is in front and underground. The Brigham Young University Lee Library in the late 1990s was given an addition of 234,000 ft² (21,739 m²) by expansion into three floors in front underground. This addition is being landscaped over with 18 in. (0.457 m) of topsoil for grass and shrubs; a new main entry has a large glass atrium to bring considerable light in two levels, the highest level has a north window along the entire width and height of the floor, and four skylights also bring light to two levels.

If the library is near the center of campus, doubling the ground area of the library will require outside traffic to go that much farther in bypassing the building. Eventually that can become quite a trek. The Harvard central complex of library buildings solved the problem by having walkways around each of the three principal structures and over the top of the fourth. The Stanford University Hoover Institution's three buildings permit walking over the top of connecting basements; however, the combination of stairs and a ramp makes for an awkward situation whenever someone outside wishes to go north and south through that building complex.

A particularly challenging architectural project in the early 1990s was expanding the University of Washington Suzzallo Library, which in 1915 was placed in the exact center of the campus. Space existed on the west and north, precisely where there was a major and favorite pedestrian traffic path. This expansion site was complicated with utility structures, abandoned building foundations, a small building remaining from the 1909 Alaska-Yukon-Pacific Exposition, and severe water drainage problems. The widely admired architect solved these problems with a six-story addition, the Kenneth S. Allen Library, with a ground-level arcade to accommodate the traffic path. The scheme successfully obscured an unpopular 1963 addition, used an updated Tudor Collegiate Gothic (rather than the architect's usual contemporary designs for corporate clients), and required four building entrances, which made for user convenience despite an obvious operational disadvantage—a problematic site reasonably overcome.

Vistas favored by the board of trustees and alumni as well as campus planners can control the site, as can trees. In the case of Vassar College, the Lockwood addition took an awkward L-shaped configuration because of a 150-year-old Norway maple tree to the north of the original structure and a line of trees serving as a buffer between the library and a major avenue to the west.

Underground utility lines can also block some sites because of relocation costs. As examples, the desired connection between the Stanford University Green Library and Art Library was not realized because of a utility corridor, one that also would frustrate any underground connection between the Hoover Institution and the Green Library. The Braun Music Center at Stanford constitutes a building addition to a music auditorium, with a site made exceptionally awkward by underground utilities and a pedestrian route through the middle, which university planners concluded was sacrosanct. The design that evolved has a ground-level tunnel for people and is a somewhat expensive result.

10.3.2 Mass and Articulation of the Addition

Architectural studies need to be done with great care for the height and visual mass of the addition when seen next to the original structure. The older architectural styles, such as Gothic, Renaissance, Classical, and, to a lesser extent, Georgian (particularly if it has a pitched roof), are often too costly to duplicate, though Duke and Princeton have done so. An addition can depart radically from the style of the original building, but the design has to be accomplished with consummate taste. Some solutions may be good on the outside and problematic on the inside, such as at Colby College, Virginia Polytechnic Institute, and Wake Forest University. A glass-sheathed link may

successfully provide for visual distinction between two styles; glass lets the eye separate the two, whereas metal or masonry are not so effective. Remember that even a skilled architect cannot have one style gradually make a transition into another when an addition is joined. One tries not to have a formal entrance and a banal rear. Such anomalies have been created and certainly they create a degree of dissatisfaction for the entire institution.

If a distinctive link—such as one bay of glass—is the method of joining old and new, the size of the link is a matter of aesthetic importance. The equivalent of one bay is typical, and more may be useful but less is seldom if ever satisfactory. Further, it is important to consider whether to keep the two facades in line, or have the building addition project farther outward or be slightly inset. If the architect prepares schematic models of large scale, these can be very helpful in making the best decision.

Alternatively, the addition can be placed at least a little distance away, as at the Delaware Public Archives (current plans will change this condition), the University of Florida, Queen's University in Kingston, Ontario, and the University of North Carolina at Chapel Hill. Such a solution must be compelling for reasons outside the library; it is never an approach one would choose where there is a choice. It is well to remember that close buildings of sharply contrasting styles are not necessarily bad. If each building seems to respect the other, the eye may well enjoy the difference, the variety. The Beinecke Library at Yale sits nicely amidst Gothic structures. Some, however, seem to jar or crowd, like the 1962 Carpenter Art Center by Le Corbusier at Harvard, crowded and discordant between the Fogg Art Museum and the Faculty Club. Indeed, the architect was shocked when he saw it for the first time. Placing the new structure well away from the facade of the original building can help. In the case of the Vassar addition, the study of mass and site resulted in the contemporary and the earlier Tudor-Gothic stating their own stylistic identity yet being compatible because the architect used a similar scale, continuation of horizontal window and roof lines, comparability of columns to the turrets on the earlier structure, and a narrow, glazed connecting space between old and new. The limestone exterior also matched the stone trim on the earlier building.

Studies of mass at the University of Michigan led to an eight-floor addition connected to the General Library, towering fully four stories above the earlier structure. In this case the original stack building of 1898 had been wrapped in the early 1920s by additional space. The possibility of wrapping a third building around the second was considered in the middle of the century, but the Shapiro Undergraduate Library was built instead. Still later the General Library eventually had to have another addition, even though the Undergraduate Library, a special storage library, and numerous branches had postponed the day of reckoning. The new Hatcher addition in the 1970s is but the first unit of what could be several units, and there still is the question of whether the pre–World War I portion may be eventually replaced. Studies of massing also had to provide for pedestrian traffic along and through the complex, to avoid impinging on part of the president's residence property, and to maintain an underground tunnel housing the existing heating and utility loop system.

10.3.3 The Nature of the Connection

Should all levels be connected? Will there need to be ramps to go from one level to another on certain upper floors if the first floor and the basement can be kept at the same elevation? Can the connection be broad throughout the depth or width of the building or will it have to be a passageway only? Generally, all floors should connect and at least the main floor be level. A very broad connection between the two is usually desirable to achieve operational flexibility.

The site may have a great deal to do with the nature of the connection, and the configuration and degree of ornate original exterior will also have a bearing. The classic New York Public Library building has an underground addition under Bryant Park, because no architect could disturb the famous facade. This addition has two levels, the upper now outfitted with electrical compact shelving and accessed from the original building via a very long ramp. (One oddity is that at least one of the emergency exits involves a stair that opens on the park above, but only after an explosive charge blasts away the lawn!) Clearly the site left little option for the addition, though the nature of the connection was not problematic beyond the obvious disadvantage of level change.

Those libraries with a full-width connection of old and new include Roanoke College and the Universities of Durham, Maryland Eastern Shore, North Alabama, Northern Iowa, Pennsylvania, Reading, and California at Los Angeles and Santa Barbara. These are operationally highly satisfactory. Internal flexibility is not impinged upon by any inset of the connecting structure.

Examples of buildings that have a moderate connection are those at Brigham Young University, Duke, Occidental College, Stanford, and the University of Tulsa, where the site, traffic, and the nature of spaces in the existing buildings constitute a restraint. Others with very narrow connections (including sometimes a bridge or tunnel) are East Carolina University, Georgia Institute of Technology, the University of Michigan, and Northwestern University, as well as Vassar and a planned expansion to Western Washington University. In these cases there were even more rigid site conditions that led to the corridor-like connections, even though, from a point of view of internal library operations, the configuration limits flexibility in spatial assignments and is usually undesirable. A connection of any kind, however, represents substantial improvement over two separate buildings, especially if an entrance/exit control can be saved, collections flow accommodated, and reasonable functional relationships maintained.

To see a difficult example of two building additions, one need only study the University of California at Davis. The current connections are substantial, but the room division, passageways, and unaligned floor levels create problems. The third addition in the early 1990s was not able to fully resolve the historic problem. Examples of difficult additions include California State University at San Francisco, Western Washington University, the old main library at the University of British Columbia, and many others. The nature of the planned connection between the old and new requires special study for the two parts to work well together to provide required flexibility over decades to come. It can be one of the more difficult parts of a building addition project.

10.3.4 Functional Distribution between Old and New

From the comments above it can be seen that there can be considerable variations in deciding which functions go into the new structure and which remain in the original, whether it is remodeled or not. This determination must be based on consideration of floor area requirements in the building program and the degree of flexibility in accommodating them. One useful approach is to work from both ends: Thus, if the addition is large and flexible, determine those functions that require the largest space, have the greatest growth potential, and should, therefore, be in a large addition; at the same time determine those functions that are small, that can be operationally separated from other functions, and for which the prospect for growth is minimal and put those in the older structure. If the old structure cannot receive much renovation and is in mediocre condition, consider which reader services or staff processes can be accommodated and operate well in such quarters.

Librarians must not leave that basic layout entirely to the architect. The librarians who worked at writing the building program should have the best feel for what future growth may be required, what interaction among functions is common, and what operational and political conditions may affect placement in the old or new. It is well to work up a number of variations of functional deployment and to test each of the possibilities against a set of basic criteria.

Furthermore, university and college officers should understand that fitting a library into a completely new building is one thing, but requiring that the library fit into an old and inflexible and awkwardly shaped structure is quite another. In the latter case it is hoped that officials will be understanding if the match is not perfect and if the floor area requirements do not work out to ideal efficiency. Almost always in dealing with an old original structure, there is much less efficiency in assigning floor area than in a more modern and flexible building.

Not to be overlooked are potential fund-raising advantages in giving one function a more prominent location. Experience shows that named areas in the old wing, if it is being nicely renovated, may be as attractive for fund-raising as are areas in the new wing. This is especially the case if the old wing has some spaces of special character, has discrete rooms in contrast to open unpartitioned modular regions, and has some sentiment attached to either the room or the function going into that room. Cornell's Uris Undergraduate Library is an example. A room that was uniquely paneled and will now house, for example, the col-

lege archive may be appealing to a prospective donor. If the rooms are already named, double names, such as the Rockefeller-Smith Room, may be possible. In most cases, however, the funding advantages should not be the dominant reason for functional assignments.

At the time the layout is being considered, there may be further discussion of whether a branch should be brought into the enlarged structure or whether one or more functions could be moved out to a different building altogether. Yale University presents an interesting example. A new music library was needed since the 1970s, yet fund-raising stymied several efforts. A Sterling Library light court (originally planned for a second stack tower but now far too expensive) is being utilized, with half the necessary total area found in remodeled Sterling bookstack space. This three-level addition is under a roof supported by six arches, with clerestory windows around the entire courtyard just under the roof, all the design resonating the Gothic idiom of Sterling. Although this is one example of branch centralization, utilizing both old and new space, note that decentralization is far more common in universities (see Section 2.6).

10.3.5 Code Problems

The requirements in different states and countries for meeting building codes vary. Frequently after a notorious hotel, restaurant, or dormitory fire or severe earthquake damage, local codes are reviewed and made more stringent. At the least, variance from current codes may become more difficult to achieve for a given project. The result is that over decades, codes are more demanding. Whenever a building is to have substantial renovation or an addition, there are questions regarding the requirement to bring the original building up to code. This requirement is generally not made for a very small renovation. Whenever the work to be done is equal to one-half the value of the original building, authorities in the United States will usually require that the old building be brought fully up to the current code. Of course, all new work must meet current codes.

There is some leeway at times for negotiation with local authorities. For example, if existing basement areas have inadequate exiting capacities, the requirement may be waived if the institution agrees to install a sprinkler system throughout the entire building. Likewise, there may be an authorized variance given on exiting from quarters that house rare books or manuscripts, particularly if the code has a museum or bank type of category that can be broadly defined to encompass the enclosed storage quarters for rarities—where only staff are permitted access to the shelf areas. A strict interpretation of the Uniform Building Code requires stack aisles to be 42 in. (1.067 m) wide; in California and elsewhere, the state fire marshal has allowed stack aisles of 36 in. (0.914 m) in libraries in compliance with the requirements of the Americans with Disabilities Act. Those who apply the building codes may be more or less strict in their interpretation, and the interpretation and authorization in one county or state may vary between public and private institutions. This review and authorization sometimes seem motivated by ego or political purpose. A knowledgeable officer of the institution, the local construction chief or fire department captain, or a skilled architect may be able to negotiate reasonable terms for conditions that otherwise might prevent any renovation or addition whatsoever to the building if a very strict interpretation were applied.

Particular attention needs to be given to access and exiting routes, fire protection, and seismic conditions. Problems may be found in almost any building that is several decades old. The width of corridors and stairs may be inadequate by current standards, particularly if the seating in the library has been increased by adding spaces in nooks and crannies. Any use of wide corridors for shelving, seating, or offices may make the route too narrow to be legal. Corridors or stack aisles that exceed 20 ft (6.096 m) in length and that dead-end, frequently found in older fixed-function buildings, may be illegal. Conditions may be illegal in meeting access by those with physical mobility or visual limitations. The seismic bracing in elevator shafts may be less than currently required. Entrance requirements for fire department staff will also have to be reviewed, and the location of sprinkler systems and standpipes may need to be extended. In many cases the new and old buildings may be treated differently by code and may require a legal fire separation between the two.

This list could go on at considerable length. The point is that institutions should be alert to the possible issues raised by design of additions and renovations. In any estimate of the project cost, an architect and engineer as well as a repre-sentative of the local fire department should review the building in order that cost estimates can include those changes that may be mandated.

10.3.6 Engineering Improvements to Consider

Because the new addition will look fresh, clean, and contemporary and will have modern hardware and fixtures, consideration needs to be given to the extent to which the old and the new should be brought to more nearly equal quality. If the original structure is not to be retained after the next 10 or 20 years, it will, of course, be wise to spend as little for cosmetic improvements as possible. Where the building is regarded as a long-term investment, study should be made and costs determined for such improvements as fire protection and safety, water drainage, heating, ventilation and air conditioning, lighting, power and signal wiring and electrical capacity, building underpinnings, floor alignment, earthquake seismic protection, and waterproof joints. One could, of course, add to this list. It would be well to list all the present deficiencies—those things that do not operate well, where there have been leaks, cracks, or breaks, where appearance is shabby, where discoloration is evident, where severe storms or wind conditions have periodically caused problems—as well as those that are more superficial but will provide an obvious difference when a new building is sparkling and the old building is dreary.

Priorities can be assigned once the possible improvements have been defined and costs estimated. First priority attention might very well be given to those elements of fundamental importance. For example, the integrity of the foundation and the waterproof condition of the roof as well as seismic bracing will be most basic. Second, attention might well be given to personal safety issues, such as fire and smoke-detection devices, sprinklers, hose cabinets, extinguishers, and annunciation systems. Third, water and fire protection for the book collections is of obvious importance. Fourth, support for extensive use of computer technology may have educational urgency. One can go on down the list considering the value of various potential expenditures.

Consider adding air conditioning in an old building if it does not already exist, for it is universally recognized that cool air and stable temperature and humidity night and day as well as summer and winter are best for preserving book collections, particularly if they include difficult-to-replace books or manuscripts and archives. It is, of course, more expensive to install air conditioning in an old building than in a new construction, and sometimes it is practically impossible, yet it may be one of the best investments.

The question of replacing lighting systems is not only a question of aesthetics, but also one of operating costs. Fluorescent tubes provide up to three times as much intensity with less heat from the same amount of wattage required for incandescent lighting. Conduit may not have to be changed for the conversion from incandescent to fluorescent lighting at satisfactory light levels, even though the building may have been previously underlighted.

A review of the existing structure by an engineer and architect will bring out the range of possibilities to supplement those identified by the library staff. The cost judgments will have to be made about putting a lot of money into the older structure, and many officials in the institution will have what may be competing priorities among the various options. Each institution will need to make these trade-offs for itself.

10.3.7 Design Issues within the Original Structure

Besides the usual architectural and engineering issues that are mentioned above and treated elsewhere in this volume, a few questions about maximizing use of the older structure should be considered whenever a building addition is projected.

Academic objectives properly should be a primary design goal. An example is the Columbia University renovation of the Butler Library in the late 1990s. In addition to improving electrical and mechanical systems, adding data and telecommunications wiring, reclaiming the basement level for technical staff, and completely renovating the first floor, an interesting plan was the creation of seven thematic reading rooms for graduate students and faculty. To test this proposal, a pilot reading room for Ancient and Medieval Studies was established. Students reported that the new facility transformed the whole experience of study and research in beneficial ways. The result may be a major educational improvement. Columbia's other proposed reading areas are American/Latin American and African History, English and American Literature, European History,

Modern European Languages and Literatures, Middle East and South Asia History and Literature, and Philosophy and Religion.

One question may be whether one or two floors could be added in the original structure in order to gain more assignable floor area. Depending upon the ceiling heights, structural requirements, and the feasibility of adequate ventilation if additional floors were inserted, the cost could be well worth it. The main floor ceiling height of the Furman University Library raises this question. Even if new forced-air ventilation has to be added, the additional area may be in such important places in the building and be so helpful in providing flexibility and growth in key functions that it is a wise expenditure. There must be structural studies to see if the footings and load-bearing elements would tolerate extra loads. Disruption created by noise, fumes, and dust may be a factor, though it can be overcome. Further, there is the aesthetic question whether it is desirable to lose some or all of the higher-volume spaces that cannot be afforded in most modern library buildings.

Another issue is floor alignment. Ramps may need to be strategically placed in the original structure so that book trucks can be moved from one to another level without having to navigate two, three, or more steps. Elevator modification may be a concern to address. Stairs may deserve reconsideration, especially if there is danger that the users of the building will fall on unexpected steps. For instance, in Harvard's Widener Library, where there were two steps and then a landing just before the main stairway to the reading room began, someone fell on the average of every week for 30 years. The two steps were finally replaced by an unattractive ramp, which has saved countless sprains and breaks and bruises. It is highly recommended that short flights of stairs, primarily for architectural purposes, be avoided wherever possible.

Another consideration is filling in light wells, courts, or an atrium. This may be relatively easy space to claim so long as it does not present ventilation or structural problems. (Yet, aesthetics must be considered; note comments in Section 10.5 about removing stacks in such central halls.) Light wells and most courts built before 1950 were put in primarily to bring natural light into interior space. If that was the original justification, then filling them in may represent space well gained; if they were designed for ventilation purposes, however, capture of this space may require adding a mechanical system to compensate for the loss of exterior exposure. The main floor filling of a light court at the Virginia Polytechnic Institute was exactly where more space was needed, though the sky-lit space gained in this case is very awkward. Another type of study might be of lobbies, corridors, and arcades. These may be claimed for assignable space if exit requirements permit. Basement or attic spaces might be considered, provided problems with groundwater, drains, and other utilities or heat buildup in the attic are addressed.

Renovating or converting space can require special engineering. One example is Rutgers University, which, in 1991, decided to convert shelled top floor library space into a "scholarly communication center." With the existing mechanical room directly over a new 100-seat auditorium with audiovisual and videoconferencing capability, major acoustical treatment required double suspended gypsum board ceiling, walls with double layers of gypsum board on both sides, alternating acoustic panels of reflective and absorbent materials, and lined ducts of maximum size. Further, a column center to the auditorium had to be eliminated, functionally replaced by a beam two bays long placed horizontally on the roof, from which the roof is now suspended.

These and other issues certainly need consideration when planning an addition. Many libraries built before World War II have presented opportunities for improved use and may still offer possibilities. As in so many instances, local circumstances will dictate the best choices.

As an example, architectural studies of Stanford's original west wing (1919) of the Green Library have repeatedly advised against adding a floor in two very high reading room spaces. Floor connections in the upper part of the original building were not resolved in the reconstruction of the mid-1990s and probably never could be justified in cost or from the perspective of historic preservation. The lowest part of two large light wells was in 1964 filled in, resulting in useful gain of shelving space. Until the major renovation following the Loma Prieta earthquake, earlier work did not fill in more of the light wells for ventilation and aesthetic reasons and because that area was not where the press for space existed. For numerous reasons, the renovation in the late 1990s filled in the light wells, and air conditioning will be provided to much but not all of the building. The major front lobby of the old structure was

reduced in size so that over half its floor area was made useful for staff quarters. Basement space was also gained in an early renovation.

10.4
Construction Problems

Renovation of a busy, full library building can be a challenge. No specific guidance can be offered, though considering options and being alert to problems are obvious necessities. Consider the renovation of the UCLA Powell Library, done while the building was essentially emptied. This undergraduate library moved into a temporary, new, tent-like structure fabricated on vacant land less than a block away. Contrast that with the Butler Library at Columbia, renovated in stages over several years, while the library was kept in full operation. The Columbia approach took extra time with difficult logistics, yet there was no space nearby for a temporary structure, no surge or swing space existed, and insoluble was the relocation of over 2.5 million volumes, a Rare Book and Manuscript Library, numerous service points, and over 200 staff. Columbia accepted extra inflationary costs of carrying the project for additional time and the extra "general conditions" costs applied to work in an occupied space (for example, increased security, temporary enclosures, overtime for some labor, and the method required for asbestos abatement). Each institution faced with such a complete renovation must consider options, think through the logistics, and conduct a complicated financial analysis of the best feasible approaches.

In any library building project that includes remodeling or major additions, a great deal will go smoothly. However, just as certainly, a few things are bound to go wrong. These are not exactly predictable, although one or more environmental conditions will surely go awry for any number of reasons. One should expect some problems from reduced security, increased dust and noise, temperature and ventilation extremes, and possibly major water problems and fire. A satisfying project will have the contractor respond to surprising problems in sympathetic and timely fashion with such actions as placement of temporary walls, temporary ventilation duct feeds, Visqueen seals, and noise abatement to reduce headaches and irritation of library staff and users, safety risks, and potential damage to library materials. Consideration of construction site neighbors should be regarded as just as important.

Even with very conscientious contractors, security, dust, and noise problems are certain to occur. The contract documents can help minimize difficulties by careful specification of conditions. However, one must not draw the specifications so tight that the contractors will bid high accordingly. It may or may not, for example, be better to tolerate a bit of dust and expect to have to clean thousands of books after the construction is finished—and budget accordingly—than to have the contractor take extreme precautions to control dust at the origin. It is possible for water sprinkling to be done periodically during excavation work. One can also require polyethylene sheeting to be put over openings with all edges taped to be dustproof, and yet dust can be carried out one window and in the next, sheeting can become damaged, and some work requires going between the old and the new structures. Special keys may need to be issued for access to various areas within the existing facility, and special precautions will likely be required to ensure that the building is secured at the end of the day. Although most contractors are honest, they are human; they do sometimes forget to lock doors or supervise an entry while they are bringing materials in. Smoking in work areas may also be a problem. With work scheduled within an existing building, it is prudent to plan on having some library staff time devoted to supervising these areas of concern. Even when the contract documents indicate the possibility of litigation, construction specifications generally do relatively little to control problems without constant institutional supervision.

This is also true of noise, because there is no way that pavement breakers, jackhammers, powder-activated fasteners (also known as shot-in fasteners), compactors, and hammers will not create noise that can be transmitted through the air or through the structure itself. Although limiting hours for certain jobs with particularly bad noise can be required, the convenience of library staff and readers can come at great financial penalty to the project if the contractor is not enabled to do the job in an efficient way. It can, in fact, cost two and a half times the normal charge for work that is done outside regular hours. However, special consideration for end-of-semester exam periods is reasonable and can be specified. It is important to alert staff and readers to disruptive work in advance—certainly several days or a week or more in advance rather than just one day. Reporting what may be called a "rolling schedule" can be useful, based upon a total project schedule updated weekly to describe what is to follow the next week and the week thereafter.

Sharp variations in temperature and ventilation may occur, depending on the nature of the construction. Here again, good advance notice to staff and readers can lead to some acceptance of the discomfort. Most people will be able to find alternative reading spaces or put up with the temporary environmental problems as they look forward to much better conditions in the near future. Realizing that mechanical engineering is often more art than science, one needs to be prepared for what may be months or several years of HVAC maladjustments from almost any new system. Balancing the controls should start early and often requires at least a year under various climatic conditions before good adjustment is achieved.

It is fortunate that problems due to water and fire are somewhat less common than are the preceding. Yet it seems that more problems of water and fire are caused during construction or renovation than at other times. The danger goes up sharply whenever workmen are altering water lines, welding, using temporary electrical connections, and using water for some aspects of the construction job. One accident afflicted the 1996–1997 renovation of the Harvard Law School Library in Langdell Hall. A large crane beside the building crushed chilled water lines supplying air conditioning to neighboring buildings. Because Langdell Hall sits astride an underground stream, at times 128,000 gallons (485,120 liters) of water a day were pumped out of the new electrical power substation hole over a five-month period before the lines were restored.

Although construction activities should be insured under builder's risk coverage by the contractor, specific instructions on the degree of protection to be provided may, in fact, be limiting in such a way that the institution becomes partially liable in the event of a fire loss. Because of this, careful consideration must be given to what is specified. In other instances, where the institution keeps the responsibility for builder's risk insurance, it is quite appropriate to specify the exact protection that is required. For example, this specification can require a contractor to provide one 10-lb ABC fire extinguisher for every 3,000 ft² (278.70 m²) under construction; welding safety procedures can require a second person present with at least one fire extinguisher in hand; and all welding can be done before noon in order to ensure an absence of lingering hot spots after the day's work ends.

As one example, 1978 work on Stanford's Green Library addition brought two instances of severe water problems. In one case holes were cut in an adjacent basement wall for connecting pipes between the old and new buildings; by chance, an old pipe in the ground outside the actual construction area gave way in the middle of the night (probably caused by galvanic corrosion when a copper, a steel, and a cement-lined cast-iron pipe were laid too close to one another without a sand bed to give some protection from corrosion produced by adverse soil conditions). The result was that water accumulated in a trench that fed to the open core holes. Obviously, the holes should not have been left open even for one night; yet such oversight occurs and accidents happen.

In a second case the contractor was worried about fire and activated the sprinkler system before the waterflow alarm was hooked up to a campus monitoring center. A sprinkler head under a new skylight was by accident rated at 160° F. (61° C.) instead of 220° F. (104° C.). As a result, the sprinkler blew on a hot summer weekend, and it was Monday morning before staff found that wood paneling and some uninstalled carpeting had been flooded. Eternal vigilance and monitoring of remodeling projects as well as additions are required.

Other difficulties may arise. Security of the old building can be breached as exterior door keys are handed around. Entire rolls of carpet have been known to disappear, not to mention books. Interruption in utility service to the existing occupied building can be anticipated when an addition is under construction, and this can, of course, affect several buildings in the vicinity. When excavations occur, there may be disturbance to existing utility lines (as in the Harvard Law Library example above). Older materials may have become fragile; for example, a fiberglass material called Techite was once thought to be sound and reasonably priced, but a much sturdier material, such as Transite, which is a cement and asbestos substance, or an even different material without asbestos, may now be specified. Telephone, elec-tricity, drinking water, sprinklers, and plumbing lines may all inadvertently break down with service interrupted for hours or several days.

The best advice is that any construction costing as little as $500,000 today may require a full-time and full-scope inspector, not an occasional technical inspection by someone who oversees several projects. You can also try to anticipate as much as possible—know a dependable source of emergency pumps, provide cover for books and selected equipment, have staff on hand when testing occurs, train key library staff so they may take immediate action if called upon, and anticipate that significant problems will frequently come evenings and weekends when workers are not present to see the consequences of some condition they have left.

These problems are especially troublesome to a job of remodeling or adding on to an existing building. The impact on library staff and those who need to use the library makes the events upsetting. A special word of advice: Prequalify contractors for remodeling jobs. In any instance where construction is going on under the same roof as an operating library, make special effort to communicate frequently and explicitly in clear language with construction management as well as with library staff and library users. This point needs emphasis, as any library staff can attest if they have gone through a major remodeling or addition.

Finally, no library staff should remain in the construction area if at all possible. This advice is easy to give but in many cases is impossible to follow; the process of construction access and phasing together with the necessity to continue operations all too often results in staff being in or virtually in the construction zone. For example, the technical processing area in Stanford's main library was completely refurbished in 1986. However, it was physically impossible to relocate all 100-plus staff from the processing area; some part of the staff continued to work with no more than a thin sheet of plastic separating them from fairly substantial construction activities. The results are difficult, to say the least. At Western Washington University, a major asbestos abatement project in the early 1990s was done in the occupied Wilson Library; even though operations were moved out of the immediate area of the project, the proximity to such a serious project within the same building forced many difficult situations. The presence of staff during construction will compound difficulties several fold.

It is always best to build the addition, move in and free areas in the older space to be remodeled, and then make the final deployment. Really major reconstruction requires it; in modest renovation it is desirable, though circumstances will alter what is best practice.

10.5
Making Old and New Work Well Together

The environmental psychology of working in and using both old and new space is important. Serious attention needs to be given to the effect on staff and on library readers of spaces that are contiguous. Though architects will pay attention to this, the library staff who will live their working hours in the building should also give consideration to this condition. It is by no means automatic for the old space to work well or feel comfortable next to the new, or in some cases the reverse.

In some instances there have been staff who feel they have been left in second-class areas. Their morale may drop. There may be many more complaints about workloads, backlogs, the visual appearance of the area, and the lack of fresh paint or new carpeting or modern lighting. Some conditions that were accepted before the new addition may now be the cause of persistent complaints. It is true that staff newly hired after the addition may feel less put upon because they tend to take it as a given; however, other staff may well convince them that their area has been neglected.

Similarly, students will neglect or may abuse the older, unimproved areas. This psychology is natural and should be expected. It is, in fact, desirable for the building to feel as if its parts work well together. Some attention must be given to detail, wall color, carpeting, artwork, and directional and informational signs. Such relatively inexpensive improvements, which are sometimes called "cosmetic," can help a great deal. It may be possible to go farther in improving an old facility by modernizing an elevator, rest rooms, the principal entrance from the new to the old, and selected furniture.

A good example of achieving harmony is the 1970 addition to the American Antiquarian Society. The original classic structure of 1910 had additions in 1924 and 1950, but the 1970 work added more space and excellently related the four parts. Only the original bookstack looks its age, and nearly all staff quarters feel as if they were part of the new construction. Even better harmony was achieved at Roanoke College's Fintel Library in its major 1991 addition to the 1962 original, a structure that was gutted for total integration with fine results. Other good examples are the Research Library at UCLA and the University of Maryland Eastern Shore. The exteriors of the University of Georgia Little Library and its expansion do not match, and the 1980 addition to the 1955 Newman Library of the Virginia Polytechnic Institute leaves users feeling as though they are walking around a doughnut hole.

As a building project begins, it is desirable to reach agreement on the general quality and "feel" of the old as well as the new. Consider the thought that needs to be given before removing a large amount of good-quality shelving. It was the feeling a few decades ago that a tall stack in the midst of the Wheaton College Library (Norton, Massachusetts) had been a most unfortunate expedient years before when the college was desperate to add more shelving. The tiered stack was thus removed as part of a major rebuilding, leaving everyone happy with the change and enabling the new and the old to "feel" a harmonious whole. The same thinking occurred at Mount Holyoke College early in the 1990s when the seven-level tiered bookstack was removed from the tall grand lobby of the Williston Library. And the UCLA Powell Library in the mid-1990s had a large stack block removed from between wings in the back of the building, what an architectural award jury called the "brilliant creation of a new [garden courtyard] achieved by the removal of less desirable elements." There are few times in the course of the life of a building when engineering or architectural travesties can be rectified, and a major renovation or addition provides a rare opportunity to correct problems and establish a sympathetic treatment for the total structure.

It is relatively easy to determine local costs for bringing old space to reasonably match the new. The project budget should be constructed with both aspects in mind, though phasing may be very desirable and in most cases is essential. Institutions are urged to view the enlarged building as one, yet it too often is the case that funding is so difficult that paying adequate attention to modernizing the old wing is left for separate attention at some later date. It is not possible to give general advice in such a circumstance, for each situation needs analysis of various circumstances and local opinions.

When building construction budgets are under financial pressure, it may be quite easy to postpone treatment of the old wing because so much emphasis is being placed on the new wing. Realistic budget expectations for improvements in the next few years may lead to some phasing in of the improvements, but all too often the problem is merely ignored. Do not concentrate just on the rare book department or a faculty reading lounge; consider technical processing staff and other "behind-the-scenes" areas and try to preserve the warmth and comfort of older spaces, while blending those qualities with the freshness of newer spaces. No responsible person would wish to discard sound furniture. No one should dress up old space merely to be able to say that it has been redone. Change merely for the sake of change is almost never warranted.

However, attention to how the new space and the old space feel next to each other and some attention to the psychology of those who will use the old and the new is an important part of any addition and renovation project. As has been said, although form may follow function, human needs go beyond function and beyond mere style. No specific advice can be given because the local conditions will be unique; but the point is made that this concern needs conscious attention in order that the effect of the total space available can be regarded as satisfactory.

10.6
Conversions

Another aspect of building renovation is that of converting a building or part thereof into library space (see fig. 10.2). In most large universities that date back a century, there will be a number of small branches and maybe a few larger branches that are now in space that was not originally designed for library purposes. St. John's College in Annapolis has used two conversions for its library, one the 1899 Woodward Hall structure as its home before 1996 and the former Maryland Hall of Records building of 1934 as its home thereafter. Across the country, the famous Art Deco five-story Bullocks Wilshire store in Los Angeles was converted to house the Southwest-

ern University School of Law, including a state-of-the-art computerized library to house 370,000 volumes. As high-density book shelving facilities, Ohio University recently opened a storage library in a converted car dealership, and the University of Pennsylvania is creating one in a former newspaper warehouse near campus.

Given the cost of construction, the scarcity of good building sites on older campuses, and greater attention to preserving well-designed or historic buildings, it seems probable that more conversions will take place in future decades. These are not likely to be for very large units, although, even there, some conversion of adjacent space may help solve, at least temporarily, the space problems in a large or central library facility.

As an example from the 1980s, one can cite Stanford. None of the professional schools has a library in converted quarters. Yet, of the departmental branch libraries, conversions provided the current quarters for chemistry, communication, philosophy, mathematics, and the food research institute. Space had been converted from warehouses, an office loft, wet laboratories, a student snack facility, and general teaching spaces. In some instances the building was completely gutted before the library and other quarters were built; in other instances nothing structural was changed and the costs were kept down to those for removing laboratory plumbing, a new door between the old and the new sections of the library, and some superficial improvements in appearance.

Such conversions can be very tasteful in treatment of small spaces, as in the Ticknor Modern Language Library in Boylston Hall at Harvard, or of extensive projects, such as the Harvard-Yenching Library, which included addition of a modern stack structure and very extensive remodeling for reading room and staff quarters in the original building. In Berkeley, the University of California used a former Ford assembly plant as its storage library for lesser-used materials on double-deep industrial shelving for some two decades before a larger, new structure was designed. The University of Michigan did the same with a vacant plant being converted to auxiliary storage, though the storage technology differs (tiered shelving). The storage facility at Stanford is yet another technology (two levels of compact shelving) placed in a converted food warehouse. At Oxford University, All Saints Church was converted into the library for Lincoln College. Strath-

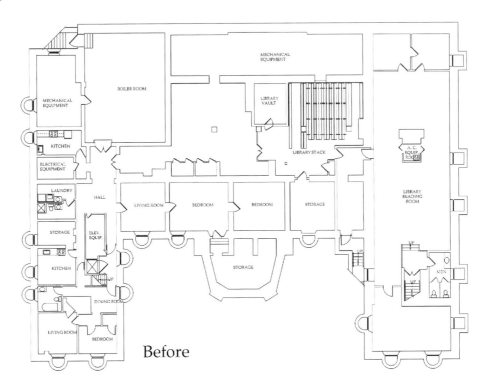

Before

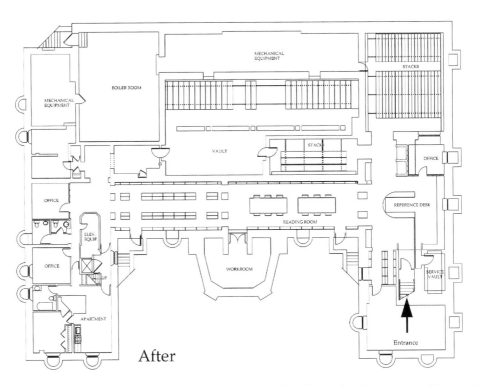

After

FIGURE 10.2   Society of the Cincinnati, Washington, D.C. The library has been created in the basement of a former residence, in at least two conversion steps. The flow of functions in the "after" diagram relative to the entrance, service point, and offices works quite well, especially considering the structural walls that had to be respected. Access by elevator is not so gracious, driven largely by the existing building. The "workroom" off the reading room serves as the photocopy room. Note the extensive use of compact shelving. (Courtesy of Archetype, Architects, 1841 Columbia Rd., NW, Suite 202, Washington, DC 20009)

clyde University converted a publisher's warehouse into a 10,000-m² (107,640-ft²) unified library on four floors. Indeed, the first home of the British Library Document Supply Centre (DSC) was a wartime factory.

Laws will very often govern the changes possible in historic buildings and will always do so if the structure is on a Register for Historic Buildings. Even where such laws do not exist, good architectural practice will urge saving and reusing well-designed spaces and limiting the nature of external changes that may be made. City ordinances may lead to scrutiny by governmental agencies whenever a significant change of use is contemplated. Different countries as well as different states and cities deal with the issue in varying ways, though a prime motive is the desire for sensitive treatment of those buildings, courtyards, and vistas that have aesthetic and cultural values, qualities that may be as important as the monetary value of the structure itself.

The possibility of a conversion raises some of the same issues that come up in any remodeling. There usually will be a requirement to bring the existing space up to current building codes in order to protect personal safety and health. The architects and planning team will need to have firm principles to apply in making such a conversion so that the original building does not constitute an unreasonable constraint on the library program—making the foot fit the shoe instead of the shoe fit the foot. There will need to be a decision whether the conversion is temporary, and, thus, the effort much more modest than a complete change.

A conversion is not necessarily a cheaper alternative to a new building, though some administrators may jump to such a conclusion. When the Stanford Quadrangle buildings have been rebuilt they have almost always cost more than a new structure; however, an additional floor was fitted within the older structure in most cases. The historic, visual, and aesthetic factors made conversion worth the expense. One must remember that evaluation of design and functional effectiveness is made more difficult in any conversion because of the number of constraints imposed. These may be constraints of floor-to-floor height, probably the base size or footprint at ground level, the fenestration most certainly, vertical shafts to a considerable extent, perhaps on roof elevation and design, and limitations on future flexibility depending on the extent of interior bearing walls

and other similar elements. The facade may be the last part that an architect can change. Even then, new glass doors, new signs, and lighting can create a new effect.

Vertical expansion may be all but impossible because of weight. Carrying new columns through an old building in order to support additional superstructure is usually exceedingly expensive, even though it may occasionally be justified in one portion where the floor loads require or perhaps for only the lower floor. One major example of vertical expansion is the Florida International University, University Park Campus, which, during 1996 and 1997, wrapped its original "Athenaeum" library within a 14-floor addition, boring right through the older three stories to create the required new footings so the 280,000 ft² net (26,012 m²) can surround and tower over the old. Remember that, without taking mechanical HVAC space in the building being converted, a basement connection to an adjacent building may provide the solution to a major problem.

Although every remodeling project will differ from others, one excellent example at Brown University will be briefly described. Listed in the U.S. National Park Service "National Register of Historic Places" as part of the College Hill Historic District, the John Hay Library dates from 1910; since 1971 it has been devoted to archives and special collections. A decade of study and fundraising was required before the antiquated building was turned into proper quarters to protect rare materials for scholars. A 1977 program documented requirements to bring the structure into code compliance, including replacement of plumbing and sewer lines, addition of air conditioning and humidity and security equipment, and control of ultraviolet light. After work by a planning consultant, a study concluded that equivalent new library space would cost more than renovating John Hay and that renovating it for purposes other than a library would be more costly. With funds from the federal government, foundations, and alumni, Brown then retained an architectural firm to prepare plans—including phases of work so that the library could function during the renovation.

Although John Hay already had a new roof, the white marble exterior walls had suffered from industrial pollution. On advice of a stone consultant, the marble was not cleaned or sealed for fear of trapping moisture; however, the mortar joints were raked and repointed. New light-filtering, sealed windows were installed in new mahogany frames, the glass a three-layer sandwich with a vacuum between two layers. Many fluorescent lights were replaced with incandescent fixtures, and those fluorescent fixtures that were retained were equipped with ultraviolet filters. A major cost was the new air conditioning, with temperatures controlled within two degrees of 68° F. (20° C.) and relative humidity within 2 percent of 50 percent, with 90 percent recycled air and particulate filtration. Humidity heads and reheat coils were widely distributed to assure constant environment in stacks, exhibition cases, and reading rooms. (Areas not used for storage or exhibition were given only standard air conditioning.) To meet fire protection codes, all electrical wiring was replaced, new corridors and fire stairs were equipped with dry-pipe sprinklers, and a 47-zone products-of-combustion smoke-detection system was installed with city and university alerts. It was possible for Brown to receive a code variance from the fire marshal so no sprinklers in collection areas were required. (Halon had been rejected due to the cost of purchasing and maintaining the extinguishing system, and is now not legal.) Finally, a combination 87-zone security alert system was installed, including ultrasonic and infrared devices, window and door contacts, and vibration sensors; all stack windows were sealed as well.

From the above you can begin to see the range of technical issues involved, each one deserving careful professional resolution for concerns of historic integrity, cost, durability, aesthetics, legality, and operational convenience and dependability.

10.7
Design Issues of Separate Subject Libraries

Major subject libraries may have their own physically separate building (for example, law, medicine, business, and sometimes the unified science library). In these instances, the problems of design, expansion, and renovation are fundamentally similar to those of a central research library in a college or university. This section deals with those academic disciplinary or departmental or branch libraries that share quarters with the department. Such libraries sometimes have one entire floor, part of one or more floors, or a several-story wing of a building—the alternatives are many. For such libraries the expansion is less often into a new

addition than it is into an adjacent section of the building already occupied. Law library additions at the University of Georgia and at Harvard University present good and not-so-good examples of how space expansion was handled.

Addition of space brings special problems. Even though the options may be very few, some issues that should be considered will be enumerated. It would be well for such an expansion to be regarded as a very serious matter, even though it may seem like a small amount of floor area and cost compared to those for a new building. Remember that for the one or several academic departments which regard that unit as their "main library" for teaching or research purposes, it is an exceedingly important matter—just as important as the main library may be to those in the humanities.

If the expansion of the branch library was anticipated and provided for at the time it was originally designed, which is sometimes the case, the growth may be accommodated with some ease. (The library of the University of Central Florida, in Orlando, took over the rest of a large building with much nonlibrary occupancy, and a significant floor-level problem remained.) Offices or large, flat-floored lecture halls or dry laboratories may provide feasible room for expansion. Wet laboratories are more difficult. Museum space may be so open and have such a high ceiling that expansion is a bit difficult.

Subject or disciplinary libraries that often have the greatest rate of growth are those, such as art, biology, geology, law, and music, that have a strong historical base that requires cumulative collections rather than the much more prevalent weeding that takes place in the engineering and physical sciences. This important point suggests that expansion potential for some subject departmental libraries is much more significant than in other disciplines.

Need an architect be used for such an addition of space? Not always, especially if the expansion was anticipated, if the addition is modest, and if an institutional planner is available to take care of such important details as location of light switches, installation of security devices, and emergency exiting. In general, one should use an architect if the job entails extensive spatial studies, new walls and different surfaces, structural review, and mechanical equipment and lighting. One may rely merely on an engineer if the project almost exclusively deals with the installation of air conditioning, plumbing, computer power and signal provisions, or fire protection systems. Qualified experts are needed, and the staff in the university planning office or in the office of the university or college architect may be quite sufficient for such a task.

Remember that a very large library building may well have enough flexibility so that the results of a planner's oversight and omission may be a few mistakes in any one area, whereas in a branch library an oversight can rarely be afforded, because the flexibility within a branch is less and the competition for extra space within the total building may be severe.

If there are several options for expansion, then consideration should be given to whether horizontal or vertical access is preferred. Generally, the first floor for major public service areas and staff quarters, with a commodious basement for book shelving and associated reading spaces, may be ideal. This arrangement is based on the fact that future expansion in a basement may be much easier than on the first or second floor. A second preference might be for the first floor alone or for having the entire library in a basement. Where water hazards are extreme, the second floor would be far preferable to any basement space whatsoever. Least convenient may be a top floor of a building. However, there are advantages and disadvantages to each of these locations.

Long-term growth possibilities may often be the controlling factor. Remember that if access is exceedingly convenient, the library may well become a student lounge or social center for that part of campus. The restlessness of a student who is passing time between classes can be extremely disturbing. If the library is hidden that also is unfortunate yet may be entirely satisfactory.

Points to consider in the nature of expansion should include the following. How easy is access to this library found? How direct a route would there be evenings and weekends if the rest of the building is closed? How can books be most conveniently brought from a central library receipt and processing center or bindery to the branch? How can the heavy traffic to and from classes be kept away from open windows or the front door of the library so that such conditions are not noisy and visually disturbing? Is safety a consideration in the expansion? How safe from human harassment will the library be for readers or staff, including routes away from the library during evening hours or at closing, especially if that part of the building is rather lonely? Can the addition provide expansion for book and reading spaces so that the flow of the collection classification can be natural and the spaces contiguous? Can computer power and signal cabling be added in a fashion that is not unattractive and does not create any hazard to foot traffic?

Up to a point, a horizontal expansion is usually the best. It eliminates the elevator issue, at least until further expansion is considered. Such an expansion should not cross a public corridor unless that corridor can be taken over and incorporated in the library layout or unless the corridor can terminate at the library entrance. However, an elevator can be within the library and access to it from other parts of the building can be controlled by a library key, although careful analysis will be required to ensure that security of the branch is not compromised. Last but not least, try to consider what will happen to this library in 10 or 20 years when the question of adding space once again must be faced. This issue should be given serious thought and the conclusions documented for use in the future.

Another point needs consideration. A branch library project is complicated by the special nature of the planning team. Campus politics can be compounded in such a project, and all involved should make particular efforts to work as an effective team. In addition to those who may be involved in a main library project, there will usually be one or more representatives of the academic department that "owns" the building, probably the departmental library committee, and perhaps a representative of the appropriate dean's office. Few of them will be as knowledgeable about libraries as those who deal with the main library. Few in the department will believe they are less than experts. Almost certainly none will have library building experience. Few if any will take the time to learn and study library planning. Some may feel those from the main library are outsiders who do not understand their departmental culture and educational goals and practices.

Expansion of a branch library can be made particularly difficult when the current library is in a good location within the building but is "landlocked" by such other spaces as classrooms, faculty offices, and labs. Departmental "turf" becomes an issue if, for example, favored offices are considered as part of the library expansion. The departmental regard for the branch librarian and feelings of quasi-independence from the main library administration also affect the weight given to various opinions. There is one real advantage, however. In contrast to a project for a new departmental building where the library is a minor consideration in the arguments, all participants in an expansion project for the branch library are primarily focusing on how best to resolve the library space needs.

As library expansion examples to study, you can look at how the same subject library was handled at other comparable or larger institutions. Alternatively, you may look at how a variety of subject libraries have been handled in institutions with many such units, for example, Yale University, the University of Michigan, and the University of California, Berkeley. One notable example of an expansion is the University of Michigan Law Library (an effective underground solution). Other branch library expansions that can be informative are the Music Library at MIT, the Marquand Art Library at Princeton, and the Psychology Library at the University of Virginia. The Bioscience and Natural Resources Library of the University of California, Berkeley, is not strictly an expansion, though in the 1990s the Biology Library was given different and larger space within the same renovated building and formed into this new library by merger with the previously different library collections of Natural Resources, Forestry, Entomology, and the paleontology portion of the Earth Sciences library.

Conclusion

Projects that entail an addition and remodeling can be particularly difficult. There are usually unique and often awkward conditions with which the architect and engineers must deal. There will be uncertainties, and surprises will turn up during construction. The budgeting is a more complicated matter. The fund-raising may be more difficult than for a completely new building costing the same as an addition and a renovation.

Be alert to these aspects of such a project. This type of project is becoming increasingly common. It certainly constitutes a significant challenge to the planning team. It is therefore especially unfortunate that in the past many a building was planned as a complete architectural unit by an architect who did not want to have his or her "gem" modified or damaged aesthetically by future generations. Although this basis for the design may have been inadvertent on the part of the architect, it was most unwise and caused problems for administrators in following decades.

This last point calls for further comment. More than one architect has said that a commission would be refused if the instructions from the institution included a requirement that the building be planned in such a way that additions would be readily practical without impairing it functionally.

It would be rash to propose a universal rule that no library building should be planned without a suitable addition or two in mind. However, the presidents and governing boards of colleges and universities ought to realize that most academic and research libraries, unless they are much more mature than most of those in this country, still grow at a rate that doubles their space requirements every 20 years or less—every 10 years in some cases. Unless the institution is prepared to provide completely new housing for its library at frequent intervals, it ought to anticipate expansion at a later time. The economic conditions in higher education will make it all the more important that building additions and extensive remodeling of existing quarters must be accommodated in the coming decades. A wise planning team will always leave options open for its successors.

Notes

1. Harvey H. Kaiser, *Crumbling Academe* (Washington, D.C.: Association of Governing Boards of Universities and Colleges, 1984), p. 23.
2. "College Library Buildings in Transition: A Study of 36 Libraries Built in 1967–68," *College & Research Libraries* 43 (November 1982): 478–80.

11

Master Planning
and Siting

*No building is an isolated object, sufficient unto itself. It belongs
in a large setting, within a bit of nature or a neighborhood of
other buildings, or both, and derives much of its character from
this natural or manufactured environment that embraces it.*

—Spiro Kostof, *A History of Architecture: Settings and Rituals*

In some degree, selecting the site is the most important step in planning a library. A campus will change and usually grow. Interiors will be altered, spaces redefined, facades sometimes modified as structures are expanded. However, the location of any particular major building will never change. All concerned with finding the best solution for library needs must give this the most serious thought. The principles are discussed, assuming there is considerable flexibility so one may apply theory. A penultimate section here discusses the more complex situation on a mature campus, illustrating the range of options in these circumstances.

11.1
The Campus as City

Each institution has a unique physical character. A college or a university may be part of a city; some institutions are more integrated into the city than others. If set apart from a city, the institution takes on many of the characteristics of a city, though it is more homogeneous. In all instances, the interaction of town or city and state or province with the educational institution has been and always will be substantial, even if the institution is in unincorporated territory. A rural setting will in due course become suburban and probably urban as the activities of the institution draw supporting services and related occupations. Employees of a college have families, and homes will be built. Food, clothing stores, automotive stores, and recreational facilities are needed, and eventually inns or motels for visitors to campus will be necessary. So even the rural settings of Hampshire College, Valencia Community College in Orlando, Furman University, Washington State University, the University of California at Davis, and the University of Connecticut are affected by these entrepreneurial enterprises. Few are for long as truly rural as is Sweet Briar College.

A campus is, therefore, substantially involved with urban planning concerns and pressures. They may involve zoning studies, environmental impact statements, spheres-of-influence studies, and hearings as well as pressures from various groups for or against open space, concern for traffic, or other causes. Furthermore, the campus uses the same design elements and the same architectural options and engenders the same human reactions to space, color, and form as those in other communities with hundreds of years of trial and error. (Richard P. Dober and Paul Turner, cited in the Bibliography, provide useful treatments of campus planning issues.)

To understand planning, one should know some design concepts, which each campus applies in different ways. For some, Gothic architecture was best suited for conveying a sense of history and permanence. For others, Colonial seemed more indigenous and nostalgic. Romanesque was elsewhere favored. "This desire that college architecture be 'venerable' and 'substantial,' be laden with 'associations,' and testify to an 'old and honored' institution, became common in the mid- and late-nineteenth century."[1] Thus a special image, or "feel," may be created by an institution, developing its own physical expression of the academic needs and philosophies of successive generations. Some images are, of course, more distinctive than others. Some plans succeed fairly well, others brilliantly; most do well in some respects and fall short in others.

Seven qualities in the design vocabulary will be mentioned as suggestive of the many elements that affect campus planning. Those chosen are accretion, balance, linkage, open space, sculptural form, surprise, and thigmotropism. The idiom of the planner may be as abstruse as the acronyms of the information scientist!

Accretion is the incremental physical growth, the additions of wings, the occupation of new acreage. Each growth should be so placed, in balance or contrast, to maintain spatial harmony and coherence. Consider how the Harvard, University of Illinois, and Princeton libraries were enlarged.

Balance may mean symmetry, such as the four towers of the Bibliothèque nationale de France, or relations of mass, such as the Low Library and Butler Library at Columbia University, or the rhythmic repetitions of form, shape, and definition that relate one space to another. The axial pattern planning of the French Ecole des Beaux Arts extends this concept and was followed at the University of California, Berkeley, in the Doe Library.

Linkage may be expressed as traffic requirements for bicycles, pedestrians, and vehicles, and for delivery and removal of goods, equipment, and refuse or trash. Yet it may connote a positioning of paths and building lines to provide desirable relationships, or the contemporary use of classical architectural vocabulary, such as a frieze. Continuities in a college are of special importance, the arcades in the Stanford University Quadrangle serving that purpose.

Open space emphasizes the advantages of nature, whether it be playing fields, a picnic grove, an outdoor bench for reading, or a bower for post-class lecture discussion. The green before Dartmouth College's Baker Library is a noted example, as is the drill field at Virginia Polytechnic Institute and the horseshoe at the University of South Carolina.

Sculptural form denotes the sharpness or the softness or relief from rigid shapes that comes from a rounded arch, a dome, a knoll, and careful landscaping. The texture of the facade of library buildings can help provide this treatment. Consider the form at the University of California at San Diego.

Surprise refers to the interest that humans experience in an unexpected building form or vista, which may be a spire, an outdoor sculpture, a high void inside a building, a changing shadow, or the glimpse of a lake between distant buildings. A university example is the Beinecke Library at Yale University.

Thigmotropism is the extent to which people find comfort or pleasure in walls, nooks, cubbyholes, carrels, courtyards. For many this closeness is comforting, a psychological security blanket, an environment conducive to serious study in a library.

The planner uses a catalog of concepts that has historic validity and that conveys from expert to expert a precise and useful design meaning. The artistry and skill of the individual designer come into play; taste can be educated but it cannot often be created where none existed before. So the planner is expected to create functional and pleasant spaces with a feeling of comfort, awe, surprise, strength, and liveliness. No one building may achieve all that; however, the academic institution as a whole should strive to satisfy those human yearnings. The campus plan and its architecture should inspire and educate while young people are still in their formative years, often living away from home, sometimes fearful of being on their own, under pressure, and trying to live mature lives while hardly beyond adolescence. Campus planning needs to fulfill a significant social value.

11.2
Planning Concepts and Influences

The history of community planning has many lessons for colleges and universities. When campus planning permits great latitude in library site selection, and particularly when the campus is new or relatively young, experiences in community planning can provide instructive lessons. Without providing a detailed discussion of this topic, six concepts will be treated.

11.2.1 Privacy and Protection

From the earliest times, students have needed both privacy and protection. The life of the student and the life of the church required quiet and privacy (thigmotropic space) for study and contemplation. Campus walls and gates used to be common. Oxford University's private residential halls and colleges, founded in 1264 and later, provide a protective environment; the interconnecting quadrangles, containing farms, gardens, or greens, look inward. Because so many colleges were founded for the study of theology, it is no wonder monastic designs had an influence.

Considerations of privacy for study and reflection and protection from assault or physical or sexual harassment still exist, though the campus is no longer a walled city. Further, many institutions are strongly influenced by the high cost of land or even the limited availability of sites; their buildings are often closely placed and they take on the character of cities. Yet, where buildings are closely placed, it is now considered undesirable to have one window directly face another closer than 75 feet (22.860 m) away, and paths are often laid out so that there are not nearby hiding places.

11.2.2 The Square

A parklike square in a residential neighborhood became common in the seventeenth century. Town squares used for markets, proclamations, plays, hangings, and parades existed for centuries. The campus makes good use of such plazas, courtyards, and greens. The Dartmouth College Green and the Harvard Yard are sentimental places, with the library dominating. Where no such formal area exists, as at the University of California, Berkeley, students will find its counterpart by Sather Gate at the head of Telegraph Avenue. To serve pageantry and provide a setting for people to meet, play, talk, protest, advocate, Columbia University's common acreage in front of Alma Mater and between the Low and Butler libraries is exemplary.

Clearly, one major concern about placing a library on "the square" is noise and disruption—concern for the cacophony of amplified street oratory and music. Where a campus has multiple squares, it may be desirable to site the library on a secondary square to remove it from what could be the negative influence of some activities. Such a secondary square can be designed to discourage loud musical concerts, speeches, and other activities that can disrupt library activities. For example, through the use of plantings, benches, walks, steps, and other landscape elements, small groupings of people may be encouraged rather than the large gatherings that can occur in a main square. The introduction of a fountain that produces pleasant noise can further reduce disruptive activities. Bicycle parking, where bicycles are common, should also be part of the design of the square.

11.2.3 Axis and Connections

Students have only a few years to adjust to the campus. Its symbolism in those years can be profound and replete with idealism and memories. The church, the library, and the stadium can have great importance; and those buildings are important for what goes on, as well as for what they represent. Many students have considered the physical setting and structure of the campus to be as important as academics in deciding which college to attend. The physical image, or at least the key scenes, can evoke all the past and present glories of the halls of academe with which one wishes to identify.

The frequent view of the church and the library reminds one of the intellectual and spiritual purpose of higher education. So the physical setting becomes important, such as the central axis that can provide a view from many places of the symbolic structure, the frequent glimpse of which is a reminder of purpose.

Campus planning or site planning for the library in terms of axis and connections is important for how on- and off-campus library users find the entrance. It is generally not terribly controversial as far as the operation of the library is concerned. It can be important to a prospective donor. It can clarify exterior circulation patterns, and it may suggest axial views that might be an asset worth developing as the design of the library proceeds. College offices of admissions, development, and community relations will see this as quite important. But perhaps the greatest concern for the librarian is the notion that designing around an axis may imply a rigid symmetry that can lead to problems later when it is necessary to add to the building. Care should be taken where the site may be too prominent or precious.

11.2.4 Clusters and Superblocks

The grouping of academic buildings or student residences can follow several options. The alignment around a square or on either side of a street offers easy orientation, though it may be visually monotonous. Buildings massed around courts or cul-de-sacs can eliminate through traffic. The access may be only for pedestrians with service access from the periphery. The approach may be formalized by a gate and fences. Experience with residential development shows that cul-de-sacs should not extend downhill, because of surface drainage and utility waste-flow problems as well as to the feeling at the end of the circle. The same applies to the library site.

Clusters form an alternative used for both academic and residential purposes as well as a large module for planned campus accretion. The University of California, Santa Cruz, is described as a clustered campus (see fig. 11.1). Clustered buildings provide proximity and visual interest, offer great variety for massing, engender social rela-

tions, and save open space; yet they may make orientation and access more difficult.

Where the main body of the campus is in effect a superblock with limited vehicular access, care must be taken in considering the needs of the library. Recognizing use patterns during class hours, access to the library should be influenced by the location of significant groupings of classrooms, lecture halls, laboratories, and other teaching facilities. At other times the library orientation

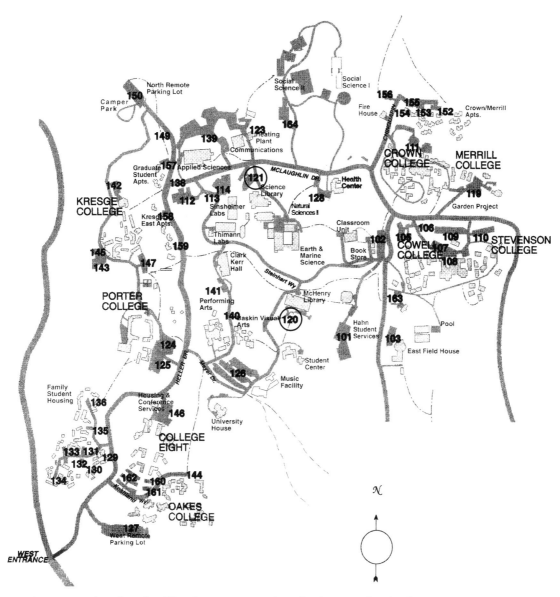

FIGURE 11.1   **University of California, Santa Cruz, is a classic example of a cluster campus. The main and science libraries (located in the circles) are surrounded by eight colleges. The site of this campus is particularly beautiful; the colleges and shared facilities are located in a redwood forest to the north of the campus site; the grounds sloping down to the south toward the main entrance are mostly open grasslands.**

should recognize relations to living quarters or to external public transportation, and personal bicycles, motorcycles, and automobiles.

11.2.5 Renovation and Symbolism

Some of the meaning of campus life, or urban life, comes from the juxtaposition of old and new. This visible association of episodes of institutional development is enriching to the sensitive eye and mind. Furthermore, the reuse of good, old structures can provide the new functions with a charming patina. St. Johns College, in Annapolis, and the University of South Carolina have excelled in this.

Campus development is sometimes an important component of an urban renewal plan, such as was the University of Illinois at Chicago, though most commonly the campus deals with one building at a time. One building may be judged too wasteful of space to retain and the construction of another too poor, while others may have qualities that argue for retention and renewal.

Cities now do better jobs of selecting good older structures for renewal, some of them for sentimental or symbolic reasons. The campus can do likewise. Even in the 1970s one aged and wasteful academic building in the treasured Harvard Yard was demolished to provide a new student residential site. In other cases, such as the Stanford Quadrangle, renewal within the original shell was the architectural choice, and the use of old wrought iron stair balustrades in Stanford's History Corner of the Quad is an instance of the tasteful detail that can provide special pleasures.

11.2.6 Terrain and Climate

A planner using the concepts mentioned above, as well as others, will be influenced by natural conditions. Each piece of land is composed of a set of interrelated factors—some above ground (atmosphere, wind, precipitation), some on the ground (drainage, plant and animal life), and some below (soil characteristics, seasonal water table, bedrock). Each condition in some degree affects the land use, or at least the economics of overcoming limiting conditions. As Rome and San Francisco worked with their hills, so does Simon Fraser University (fig. 11.2) blanket and dominate its elevation. As Venice has water and soil problems, so Simmons College, the University of Bremen, Clemson University, and Tulane

University have had to cope with adverse soil and water table. Earthquakes test library structures, as was experienced in 1906 and again in 1989 at Stanford University, and 1994 at California State University, Northridge.

Climate is also a constant influence on plans, partly for site density and partly to protect against occasional storm conditions (e.g., hurricane areas by the shore, tornado stresses, spring tide, or tsunami). A hurricane can severely batter a building, and the University of Miami Library is only one of many library buildings whose designs have fortunately been significantly and beneficially influenced by this prospect. Prevailing winds, snow depths, humidity, solar angle, even the length of daylight—from Arizona to Alaska or even Quebec to coastal Maine—may be striking.

Soil conditions may change markedly over just a few feet of terrain. Careful studies are needed to detect problems, the greatest deriving from a high water table, evidence of subsidence or floods, silt or water-bearing sand, mud or muck, clay or adobe, or filled and uncompacted land. Such sites may tremendously increase normal foundation costs, while rocky sites will cost only slightly more than normal depending on the nature of the rock and the necessity of blasting for a basement, utility lines, or surface drainage. Tulane University's Tilton Library is a case in point. The foundation, on muck soil only two feet above sea level, supports four floors with the footings sufficient for four more levels, because there is said to be no land for horizontal expansion.

Hurricane regions should have library buildings with no glass or strongly protected glass to windward, especially on the top floor, which may bear the brunt of high winds over lower adjacent buildings, and on the ground level, where branches and outdoor furniture or bicycles may be blown against the building, causing damage. Florida Atlantic University's Wimberly Library of 1964 with a 1987 addition is a case in point. One enters an attractive link between the old and new; however, this link is a three-level, full-height glass facade that faces the south, a situation to be avoided in a hurricane region.

To conclude, the above concepts and factors have much more effect on campus planning than is often imagined. The design precepts that have succeeded in urban development over the past four millennia will in all probability have similar success today. Nevertheless, the subtleties can escape even very good planners and designers.

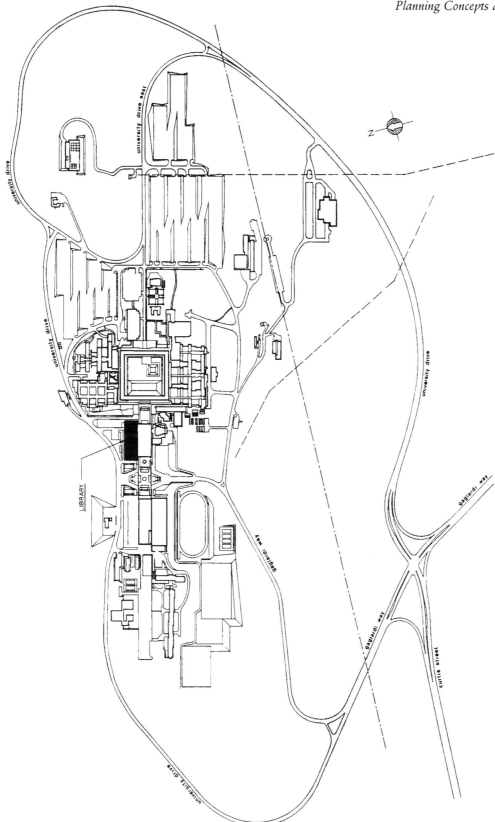

FIGURE 11.2   Simon Fraser University, Burnaby, British Columbia, campus plan. The library, shown as a black rectangle, is on the side of Burnaby Mountain, which slopes upward toward the major academic center, shown to the right of the library.

Stanford's Meyer Memorial Library of 1966 uses Greek temple elements: a classical columnar style mounted on a historic three-step platform base. The roof to column proportions, however, fail in comparison to the Greek. To many it seems that the lesson was not adequately learned!

11.3
Long-Term Campus Planning

Site selection should be derivative of master planning, either for the library specifically or for the institution as a whole. (A notable very early master campus plan was that for Union College in Schenectady in 1813, still governing the site development.) It might be supposed that the logical order of procedure would be to decide that a new library is needed, then to decide the sort of building it ought to be and the architectural style to be used, and finally to decide where it should be placed. The situation is practically never so simple as this.

The availability of a satisfactory site is one factor that affects the decision whether to build. One can hardly determine how much space is necessary for an adequate site unless one has studied the objectives of the library and projected its space needs and its future growth. One can hardly judge whether a particular location will be reasonably convenient for those who use the library unless one can predict the extent and direction of future physical growth of the institution served by the library. If the institution is in its infancy and there is ample room, it may be wise to select the library site first and to plan the future building program for the whole college or university around it. More often, however, the problem is one of fitting a large building or addition into an existing pattern that may have made no provision for it. Section 11.5 comments on this latter condition.

It should be emphasized also that one cannot design a satisfactory building and then look about for a vacant space that is large and convenient enough for its placement. Instead, many features of a good building are determined by its site. To compare the advantages of two sites, one must compare the two somewhat different buildings that could be erected on them.

The problems that have been alluded to above indicate that the selection of a library site is so important for an institution as a whole that it should be preceded by the preparation of a master plan for physical development of the campus. Master planning of this sort is a problem for the institution as a whole, not just for the library. Even neighboring communities or the host city will be a major influence on the master plan. This master plan should consider, among other things, the following:

1. The objectives of the institution. (Included here might be a directive to joint venture with other organizations for library support, in which case many of the points that follow must be applied to a broader audience.)
2. The estimated prospective size of the student body and faculty, including separate figures for graduate and undergraduate students and professional schools, if there are or are to be any.
3. Intellectual affinities among disciplines and the nature of experimental laboratories, which may suggest physical clusterings of academic departments and library sites.
4. The proportion of student and faculty housing to be on campus, if any.
5. The size of the physical plant that will be required in the next 25 years and, if possible, longer. Therefore, density studies are needed.
6. The nature, timing, and frequency of events designed to attract off-campus attendees—for example, concerts, games, plays.
7. The parking facilities required for faculty, staff, and students, and means of transportation used by commuters.
8. The general landscaping and servicing plan for the campus.
9. The degree to which police and fire protection, security, medical aid, and facility maintenance are provided from campus quarters or from off-campus.
10. Policy decisions regarding the type and architectural style of the buildings to be erected.

To view how a master plan may be conceptualized, interesting examples can be drawn from the statements of guiding philosophy that gave shape to six new English universities.[2]

Bath (est. 1966): The interaction of academic, social, and residential life underlies all the plans. Because only a minority of the students can be housed there, the 12 schools are the focus for social life, with each "entrance" providing a nucleus of common rooms, coffee bars, and meeting places. In turn this entrance leads to a "central pedestrian parade," the linear center of the university beside which will develop clubs, societies, a student union, a sports center, a theater, shops, restaurants, and bars.

Bradford (est. 1966): This undeniably urban technological university has firm links to industry. Thus a structure must present few barriers to the mixing of disciplines. "Individual buildings are out—installments of a continuous structure are in!" Yet the library is a separate central structure.

Essex (est. 1965): On 200 acres (80.940 ha) in an eighteenth-century park, the university is expected to be large. The scheme, therefore, aims at concentration of people so one should not walk more than five minutes on the ground. To make a continuous teaching building, the structure has "the beginnings of a snake with rather square bends in it." The library is at the arts and administration end.

Kent (est. 1965): The university's stated goal is not merely to train but to educate, to get away from the "9–5" university, from the limited collegiate commitment. Thus the teaching and residential functions are mixed in college buildings. The large structures of the colleges are spaced on a ridge, the campus being half in the city of Canterbury. Near the colleges are the library and a considerable site on which to develop "the ganglion of sciences."

Sussex (est. 1961): Three and one-half miles (5.632 km) from Brighton is a site rich in trees and lovely landscape. The architect believed the architecture should be low and the trees should break the skyline. Growth will be handled by adding courtyard to courtyard. The architect has said, "I feel strongly that a rigid axial plan will fall by the wayside." The architectural unity comes from the internal rhythm of materials and arched forms, a sensitive use of site, a consistent feeling of enclosure, and an attempt to leave a lasting visual memory.

Warwick (est. 1965): The site is 420 acres (169.96 ha) in open country over two miles (3.219 km) from Coventry. Over 15,000 students could be accommodated, a maximum of two-thirds to be given lodgings. The plan is compact to achieve economies in roads and services and to preserve open spaces for sports and general amenities beyond buildings aligned on each side of a central spine. The library is at the center, with other general use buildings (assembly hall, chapel, senior common room, shops, arts center, and coffee house) important in establishing the community of the university.

Without a master plan for development of the institution's physical plant, the difficulties of selecting a satisfactory site for a new library will be greatly increased. It should be noted that certain architects and landscape architects make a specialty of preparing master plans for the development of colleges and universities. Indeed, in 1953 Furman University was moved from downtown Greenville to a new campus, designed by just such an architectural firm, with the library placed at the very center of the academic buildings. And in 1961 the entire campus for the new State University of New York at Albany was also given just such a total plan by a noted architect, with the library and other essential functions placed centrally on an academic podium around a pool.

If a master plan exists or if the governing board has approved a building site, the selected architect may for some good reason feel that a better site could be found and may properly recommend it. If such a suggestion is made, the institution should give it serious consideration, and the librarian should certainly be given an opportunity to study the suggestion and express an opinion to the campus planning group, to the architect, and to the regular supervising architect of the campus, if one exists, because that architect's approval may be required for all new construction.

11.3.1 The Process

Master planning involves a skillful blending of analysis, quantification, and synthesis. As is mentioned above, the analysis includes data on the nature, size, and trends of each component of the institution. This covers students, subdivided by undergraduate, graduate, and special (such as post-doctoral) and by major field; teaching faculty and research staff similarly broken down; business, maintenance, and administrative staff; and numbers, types, peak loads, and timing for campus visitors: parents, entertainment audience, delivery and service personnel, construction and other contractual staff, and visitors for academic purposes (public lectures or library use) or official purposes (accreditation, governmental review, foreign delegations, etc.). The analysis also requires that the current philosophy of educational processes and trends be thoroughly understood—including developments in intellectual or departmental affinities, the effect of joint ventures and affiliations with other institutions, the nature of experimental research, the attitude toward housing students on campus and using student residences as a setting for informal teaching, and the extent and type of extracurricular activities, such as club sports or dormitory theatricals.

The quantification process is a numeric and topographical formulation of the analysis data. It results in tables of campus population and of land and buildings, even noise levels, as well as plans detailing land use, building sites, roads and paths, hydrants, outdoor lighting, and underground conditions. It may include contingent and conjectural data for projections 10 or 20 years ahead. The result may constitute several volumes of organized planning data and dozens of land maps, aerial photos, survey sheets, zone and building plans, and so forth. It may well include a physical model of the entire campus.

The synthesis process is iterative and, to a considerable extent, subjective. It takes the data and the trends, the philosophies underlying the institution, the external forces of a social, political, and economic nature, and blends them into an assessment of current suitability and a forecast of changes needed in the years ahead. As the intellectual modeling process alters one factor (for example, a plan for increased adult education, less intercollegiate athletics, or more microlaboratory–based courses), the quantified data of needs are revised and tested against constraints. The revised synthesis results in a new model or master plan.

As an example of this iterative process, a "Facilities Plan" is annually submitted to Stanford's trustees to report renovations and new construction over the past two years, estimate and seek approval of such work for the year ahead, list projects seriously considered for the following two years, and present funding strategies and a report on current debt financing. Some projects are described as growing from university objectives, some are stimulated by donor interests, others reflect governmental mandates and prior-

ities, and many are "the result of the march of time and the demands of progress."

The process of facility development is presented in figure 11.3 and one representative table (fig. 11.4) summarizing all the projects at one university in what is called the Capital Plan.

11.3.2 Major Considerations

As the planning process advances and shapes the library options, five factors bear heavily on the viability of the master plan, which in turn expresses the physical goals toward which the institution and its library need to move to satisfy the scholarly goals.

1. *The financial capacity* is paramount in every country and in any age. No matter what the source, and no matter how persuasive the other influences, available funds will unyieldingly constrain the capacity.

2. *Academic factors* should in the course of time hold sway. This is what has led many institutions to place the library close by the campus center or on a principal axis, or to place the library in an especially imposing structure as symbolic of scholarship and education.

3. *Utility and other nonacademic factors* at times can dominate some of the planning. Rather like the economic influence, these should be subordinate to the academic. However, there are times when some service function in the college or university will have substantial influence on the exact site.

An example would be utility lines that usually follow trunk routes on campus and streets in a city. A good separation is necessary between incompatible systems. Relocating utilities can be extremely expensive, and closing a street does not solve the below-ground problems. Having the library bridge the utilities may finesse the problem, as was done at Brooklyn College and the University of Pennsylvania.

The University of Michigan Hatcher Library site was rigidly controlled by utility lines underground and pedestrian traffic right through the plot, as well as a political constraint. The librarian, planner, and architect should try either to dodge such factors or to use them to advantage.

On most campuses the surface drainage is a critical issue. Studies of rain and meltwater will include research on flow accumulations of the entire site as well as adjacent sites and capacities of ditches, swales, ponds, and storm drains. The historic experience with a particular site may be

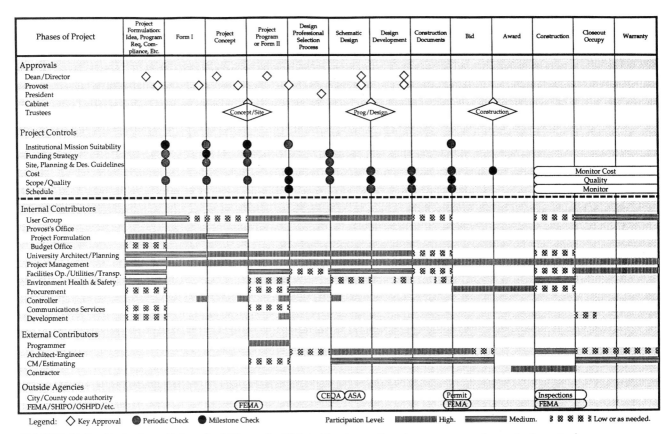

FIGURE 11.3 **Typical capital project life cycle. This table shows the phases, approvals, project controls, and contributors for projects at one university.**

a warning to stay away or build high, as Hawaiians are well aware. Areaways constitute a threat to any library when exceptional storms or burst water mains can flood them and break into the building.

Parking in an urban center was a key factor in planning the Ruhr University of Bochum, an institution of 25,000 students that opened in 1965. The library and a broad open forum behind it are located above a large parking garage. A few large urban public libraries have below-ground patron parking. The 1994 addition to the Holland Library at Washington State University has not only parking, but a loading dock under the library. The site, being on a hillside, helped make this solution possible. When one remembers that nearby parking is impossible at Columbia, Berkeley, and Harvard, such a utilitarian service requirement can at times be a boon, especially for visiting scholars and others making brief use of the library. One wonders about the campus parking solutions of the future—parking structures, underground parking, or remote parking with shuttle transportation?

An intriguing problem existed at Lyndon State College in Vermont. With buildings sitting on two slight hills beside a meandering stream, the campus was bisected by a county road and overhead power utilities. This division was overcome in the early 1970s when the road was rerouted, utilities were put underground, and a library was built between the hills. The roof of the structure is a pedestrian causeway, capable of supporting a future additional floor on the two-level library. The stream was piped beneath the library, creating three ponds great for winter skating and key elements in the unified campus master plan. And in 1996 the building received two additional floors, after structural engineers determined that the new third floor could only have stacks on the end thirds and the half-sized fourth floor could never have books on it.

4. *Aesthetic factors* frequently dominate the siting. The prominence of a building like the

Capital Plan—1995/1996—1999/2000

(in millions)	Project Schedule FY(S)	Target Project Cost	Amount of Work in Progress as of FY95	Sources of Funding								
				Identified					To Be Raised			
									Gifts To Be Raised	Debt		University
				University Reserves on Hand	School Reserves on Hand	Gifts in Hand/ Pledges	Govnt	Unrestr. Revenue		Schools	Auxiliaries/ Service Ctrs.	
I. EARTHQUAKE REPAIR AND SEISMIC RISK MITIGATION												
Planning Goal: To complete earthquake damage repair and to strengthen buildings identified as possible risks in future earthquakes												
Loma Prieta Recovery		$97.6	$31.9		$1.2	$39.6	$38.5		$6.3			$12.2
Unreinforced Masonry		$56.0	$4.3	$16.0	$0.5				$2.4	$4.0		$33.1
Other Seismic Risk Mitigation		$39.7			$3.0	$4.2					$14.4	$22.3
Fundraising Goal									$10.0			($14.2)
Subtotal		$193.3	$36.2	$16.0	$4.7	$43.8	$38.5		$18.7	$4.0	$14.4	$53.4
II. ACADEMIC PROGRAM DEVELOPMENT												
Planning Goal: To support the highest priority initiatives across the University through the construction of new buildings or major renovations												
Science and Engineering		$175.7	$51.4	$1.4	$5.1	$137.6	$2.0		$19.0	$2.2		$27.4
School of Medicine		$56.2			$5.0	$33.3			$10.8	$7.1		$7.6
Other New Building Projects		$60.8	$1.6	$1.0		$14.0			$7.7	$18.0	$16.2	
Athletics Projects		$22.7	$0.4						$4.7			
Facilities Renovation		$35.3			$11.8			$16.8				$2.0
Subtotal		$350.7	$53.4	$2.4	$21.9	$184.9	$2.0	$16.8	$42.2	$27.3	$16.2	$37.0
III. DEFERRED MAINTENANCE												
Planning Goal: To address costs associated with the deferred maintenance problem												
Deferred Maintenance		$76.3	$10.0		$4.3			$42.0				$30.0
Student Housing		$46.4									$46.4	
Subtotal		$122.7	$10.0		$4.3			$42.0			$46.4	$30.0
IV. PHYSICAL INFRASTRUCTURE												
Planning Goal: To develop and maintain the physical infrastructure necessary for the academic mission												
Utilities		$37.3									$37.3	
Campus Infrastructure		$11.2							$5.0			$6.2
Subtotal		$48.5							$5.0		$37.3	$6.2
V. COMPLIANCE												
Planning Goal: To address required code compliance work												
Americans with Disabilities Act		$10.0									$6.0	$4.0
Fire and Life Safety		$5.0						$5.0				
Utilities Regulatory Compliance		$0.3									$0.3	
Subtotal		$15.3						$5.0			$6.3	$4.0
GRAND TOTAL		$730.5	$99.6	$18.4	$30.9	$228.7	$40.5	$63.8	$65.9	$31.3	$120.6	$130.6

Total Debt: $282.5

FIGURE 11.4 A university capital plan and list of projects. This table is abbreviated to show the totals of projects divided into the listed categories. A list of individual projects would be substantially longer. Libraries could be part of any of the groups other than IV, Physical Infrastructure.

Baker Library at Dartmouth controls planning within its visual domain. There is no question that the 42-story University of Pittsburgh Cathedral of Learning created an aesthetic impression, as did the new University of Glasgow Library with its intent to be recognized in the skyline.

The first decade of the twentieth century saw the beginning of highly professional city planning, in part for the purpose of enhancing living and working conditions. In 1909, the first British Housing and Town Planning Act was passed and the Chicago Burnham Plan was published. In 1916, New York City passed the first zoning law regulating land use and the height and coverage of buildings. Such laws are now almost universal and, together with the national or local control of historic buildings and districts, serve to restrain the worst excesses.

These governmental controls exist for good reason, yet resolution of conflicts can take years. The problems faced by Concordia University in Montreal in planning a new library serve as an example. First, zoning bylaws for the library site restricted height to four floors whereas eight were desired. Second, an existing building on the site had a rare, glazed terra-cotta facing, which the Save Montreal Architectural Protection Society wished preserved. And third, immediately across the road from the site was a building on the list of historic buildings, and design of buildings within 150 feet (45.720 m) is subject to provincial approval. When the building opened in 1992, it was constructed around the terra-cotta building, at great additional expense. Further, the historic neighbor forced the new construction to be a few stories lower on that one side of the building.

In California, to discourage urban sprawl, local commissions since 1971 have responsibility for shaping orderly environmental development in their sphere of influence, including social and economic interdependence and interaction with the area that surrounds it. Thus, even if a private college is in another jurisdiction, such as unincorporated land, its plans for housing, roads, utilities, and so forth are subject to external review and approval, or "no objection." The environmental evaluation covers substantial atmospheric emissions, changes in drainage patterns, increased noise, new light or glare, increased density of humans, additional traffic and traffic hazards, substantial use of energy, need for new utilities, impact on quality of existing recrea-

tional opportunities, and any proposal that obstructs a scenic vista. A community can set high aesthetic environmental expectations, and an institution may need support from its neighbors.

Trees may take on significance. Certain mature specimens may be untouchable for a particular shade pattern, a prominent vista with an appealing silhouette, or historic or sentimental meaning. Many a campus has altered a building site to spare such a tree, sometimes at great expense. As one example, a marvelous old copper beech tree by the north side of the Williston Library at Mount Holyoke College shaped the footprint of its 1992 Miles-Smith Science Library addition.

5. *Politics* can all too often influence in major degree the siting of a building. Within a city it is natural that real political issues control a site. Urban renewal priorities or civic conscience can be influential. (How many Martin Luther King Jr. or John F. Kennedy libraries are there?) The civic political ramifications of choosing a campus site for the Kennedy presidential library—first at Harvard and then at the University of Massachusetts in Boston—or the state and campus rumpus over the Richard M. Nixon and Ronald Reagan libraries are only the best-known cases in the United States.

On most campuses there is what one distinguished university librarian has accurately called:

> an inordinate amount of local political machinations which often have nothing to do with a rational and logical approach to library space planning. I could cite several examples where planning documents have been prepared and never considered or implemented because of political and financial problems peculiar to venerable private institutions.
>
> Our efforts to consolidate the eight departmental science libraries is a good example. That effort was initially thwarted by the contribution of $2,000,000 by a foundation to complete a floor in the Life Sciences building, a floor which the foundation stipulated had to include a Biology library in space far too small by any rational standards. We were able to fit into the space by including in the plans a substantial sum for conversion of back-files to microfiche. We then lost the proposed space for a consolidated science library to the School of Engineering which won the political battle for space for the new Department of Computing. The third event in this historic struggle is the University's commitment to the Chemistry Department to assist in raising funds for a new Chemistry building on the condition that it contain a joint Chemistry/Physics Library.

Such factors can, regrettably, override the most logical master planning and the best library arguments.

11.4
Library Site Determination

Although the choice of site is irrevocable once construction begins, the choice should not be changed once design is begun; if it is, added cost will result.

The most limited choice is usually for expansion of a branch library within a host building, described in Chapter 10. The project with somewhat more options is a building addition, also treated in Chapter 10. The greatest leeway is for a new building, especially on a new or young campus, the focus of this section. One should recognize that site selection gets rapidly more complex when the campus is full of existing buildings. Solutions to the problem may even include acquisition of off-campus property or demolition of outmoded structures as the only options. Although it is an extreme case, consider the site of the New York State Library, which was assigned within the Cultural Education Center building all of floors 6 through 8 and parts of 10, 11, and the basement, which houses a three-tier stack! This library retained some 50 linear miles of shelving in its former 1911 home, and, in the 1990s, was expanding onto floor 5 to obtain its 75,000 ft^2 (6,967 m^2) for stacks. Yet its location works well, the Cultural Education Center being a focus of attention as it forms a commanding presence at the end of a spectacular plaza from the state capitol.

Five major factors should be taken into account in evaluating a site for a library. (This section assumes ownership of the land. If this is not the case, cost of acquisition may be a primary factor.) First, is the location suitable and is its size adequate? Second, what is its relation to neighboring buildings and to the whole population distribution and traffic flow of the institution? Third, what orientation is possible for a library building erected on it? Fourth, are there advantages or disadvantages in the slope of the land or other natural features? Finally, what complications will arise from the nature of the ground beneath the building?

It may be, of course, that only one site will be available that is large enough and in an acceptable location. Even so, the other factors should be examined to determine how they will affect the proposed building. How, in other words, can it be designed to make the most of favorable circumstances and to overcome the difficulties presented by this site?

11.4.1 Location and Size

A new building ought, if possible, to provide for present collections, staff, and readers, plus anticipated growth and, preferably, with capacity for later additions. There may be cases where for one reason or another it is impossible to build a new library large enough to meet foreseeable needs, and a significant fraction of incremental growth can wisely be accommodated by other options, including auxiliary shelving facilities. The size of an addition to an old building or of the first stage of a new building may be determined more by available funding than by precisely determined prospective needs during a specified number of years. This question of total space needs is dealt with elsewhere, but one point should be emphasized here: The site selected, wherever it is, should be large enough for additions that will extend the useful life of the building until it is outmoded functionally or in other ways.

A building on a campus with typically separate buildings does not look good if it fills a plot too full. Spacing of buildings is an aesthetic problem and is affected by what has been done already on a campus or is planned for the future. Another point is that fire vehicles must be able to approach all exposed sides of a building. Proper landscaping can often help to make space go farther than might be expected, and its possible usefulness in this connection should not be neglected.

The size of the plot also depends on the height of the building, which involves functional as well as aesthetic considerations. Rest assured that even when the desirable floor area has been determined for a building and its prospective additions, there is, alas, no definite formula that will translate it into the minimum dimensions for the site. The number of floors that will be satisfactory from the functional standpoint cannot be determined without taking account of the total floor area, the type of library, its collections, the extent of information technology, and use. As explained in Section 12.3.4, Problems Relating to Height, a library requiring 10,000 ft^2 (929 m^2) or less will usually be more satisfactory functionally if it is all on one floor, and very large buildings may have as much as 50,000 ft^2 (4,645 m^2) on one floor.

Sometimes a site will prove to be large enough for the library if expansion takes the form of additional floors. This solution is expensive and inconvenient, but, even so, it may be preferable to any other alternative. At Louisiana State University in Baton Rouge, the Middleton Library has a central location in the heart of the campus, and fills the available plot almost completely. In the mid-1980s, two additional floors were added to Middleton, giving the maximum feasible of a ground-floor level with four floors above. This site for the library seems to many a tragedy, for when it was constructed in the 1950s, this building was placed by the president at the apex of the north-south and east-west cross, destroying the balance and blocking the open views of the original 1922 campus plan—yet the president wanted the students to have "to trip over the damned thing."

The total height of a building above ground is determined by four factors: the percentage of the building that is below ground level, the number of levels above ground and their floor-to-ceiling height, the height of the spaces between finished ceilings and finished floors above, and the type of roof used. If a large part of a building can go below the main entrance level, as at the Princeton University Firestone Library, the Holland Library at Washington State University, and the Green Library East Wing at Stanford (which, in some ways, resemble icebergs, with the major portion of their floor area in the lower levels), the total apparent height can be correspondingly reduced. It should be noted that the percentage of space required for stairs and elevators generally, although not necessarily, increases with each level that is added. Also, three levels with 8-ft (2.438-m) ceiling heights require no more height than two with 12-ft (3.658-m) ceilings, except for the thickness of one additional floor.

In buildings with as many as five floors above ground, the space between the ceiling in one room to the floor level above is an important factor in the total height. If each one, for instance, is 5 ft (1.524 m) thick instead of 2 ft (0.610 m), the five would take 5 × 5, or 25 ft (7.620 m), instead of 5 × 2, or 10 ft (3.048 m), making a difference of 15 ft (4.572 m), or almost enough space to provide two additional stack levels unless one

chooses to reduce the height of the building for aesthetic reasons.

Although this section comments on exterior mass and site issues, detailed treatment can be found in Chapter 12, Schematic Considerations.

11.4.2 Central or Eccentric Location?

The library has often been called the heart of the university; it is visited frequently by nearly everyone in the institution and, if a good library, will be used at least as much as any other building on the campus. Obviously, its location ought to be convenient. Does this mean near the dormitories, the classroom buildings, the laboratories, the student union, or the athletic field?

No one answer is correct for all institutions. If most students commute to the campus, it may be best to place the main library near the transportation center, enabling students to return books on the way to classes and borrow others when leaving for home. The location of lockers for commuting students may also be an important consideration.

A location near the classroom center is usually preferable to one near the dormitory center; to lengthen the walk to the library between classes by two minutes is more disadvantageous than to lengthen by five minutes the time required to reach the library in the evenings from dormitories. If there are dormitories on opposite sides of the campus, as was once the case in many coeducational institutions, a location near classroom buildings can be best and may be approximately equidistant from the dormitories, as at Furman University.

If a choice must be made, such as for a college that may have only one library, it is preferable in some instances to place the general library near classrooms for the humanities and social sciences rather than near those for the physical sciences, because the former disciplines usually generate heavier use than do the latter. Increasing access to digitized information currently is of greater general benefit to the physical sciences, thereby lending support for a bias toward the humanities and social sciences, though in time this trend should equalize. On the other hand, use by the sciences is often more episodic and may be tied closely to experiments in progress, and in some instances this relationship may justify a bias closer to the sciences. Individual local circumstances should lead to the best solution for a particular case. A heavy component of computer systems can also be a significant factor, not that the cost of cabling should be controlling but rather that the pattern of heavy usage as students move from classrooms to libraries to computer labs may be a valid influence.

In the larger institutions, the location of a general library relative to various buildings housing academic disciplines raises questions of intellectual affinities. On a particular campus, for instance, do the departments of classics and art have strong connections, perhaps sharing faculty, considerable use of museum objects, and course assignments requiring heavy library use? Are the language departments offering service courses with heavy reliance on a language laboratory? If the answers are affirmative, the affinities argue that the main library be at least as convenient to art and classics as to language departments. Are one or more computer clusters located in campus libraries a dominant campus feature, or are clusters distributed in several places around the campus? The academic patterns on each particular campus must be studied to sort out these intellectual determinants.

The same approach can be followed in placing branch libraries. Yet one should recognize that, especially in the laboratory disciplines, faculty will opt for an in-building branch rather than a multidisciplinary branch over 50 meters from their laboratory and office. Except where tight economy is controlling, this 50-meter rule may be a major determinant of branch library composition and site selection. In this connection, see Section 11.5 in its treatment of the UCLA library master planning.

Convenience implies a central location, but it is possible for a site to be too central. Some campuses will have a large, unoccupied space in the central square, and this might at first glance seem to be an ideal site for a new main library. In fact, however, there are usually serious drawbacks. (See figs. 11.5 and 11.6.)

First, because the space is so centrally located and conspicuous, the donor and, less frequently, the officers of the college and even the architect may be tempted to decide that it is the place for the single most imposing building on the campus. To be sure, it is possible for a good library to be impressive, but it is less likely to be a good functional library if it is planned primarily for grandeur. The successful combination is rare. Moreover, a monumental building usually costs much more than one that is primarily functional.

If funds available for library construction are limited, it may be impossible to pay for the space that is needed if this space has to be housed in a building that is to be the showpiece of the campus.

Second, if a library is in the center of the campus, with students approaching it from all directions, there will be inevitable demands for public entrances on all sides. The University of Connecticut 1978 library is a case in point. One objection to multiple entrances is that each entrance, with the lobby attached to it and the corridors leading from it to the circulation desk and other central services, takes valuable space. If, for example, an extra entrance requires a vestibule of only 100 ft^2 (9.29 m^2), plus a small inside lobby of 500 ft^2 (46.45 m^2), plus a corridor (otherwise unnecessary) 100 ft (30.480 m) long and 10 ft (3.048 m) wide, there is a total of 1,600 ft^2 (148.64 m^2) that adds nothing to the building's seating or shelf capacity, may interfere seriously with its functional properties, and costs perhaps $250,000. This is some 5 percent of the total in a $5,000,000 building (which is not a huge library by any means), but it would provide space for shelving 25,000 volumes or, used as endowment, might bring in an income of $15,000 per year for books or services. The extra entrance will involve costs for staff or for electronic exit monitoring unless the separate entrances all lead to a single control point (as at the San Francisco Public Library). It will be hard to resist the demand for one or more additional entrances and exits if the building is too centrally located; students and professors do not like to walk around a building and then have to return part of the way as soon as they enter.

Third, traffic patterns around a central building can be so heavily used and important as to urge the architect to seek an entrance above or below the main pedestrian level. An example is the well-regarded 1992 Tilburg University Library building. (See fig. 11.7.) In this case a dominant philosophy was that knowledge is central in the sciences, so "the source of knowledge" was allocated the most central point of the university grounds, making it "equally easy to reach and accessible from all faculties and institutes [and] easily accessible for visitors from outside the University." Yet this campus junction of the north-south axis and the urban promenade on the east-west axis resulted in a three-story building with the entrance gained awkwardly by a flight of outside steps and then the crossing of a bridge.

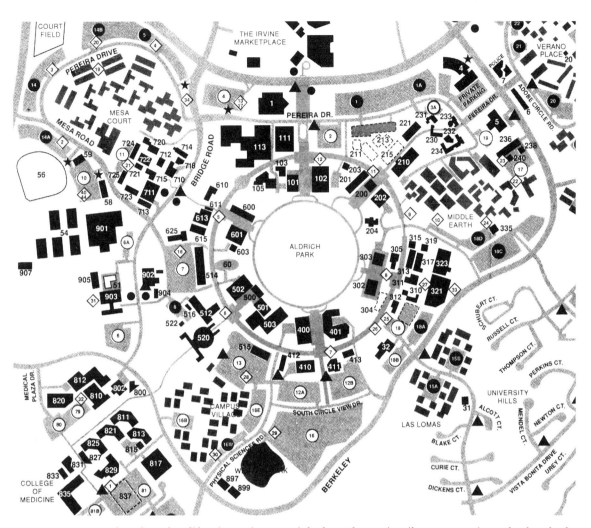

FIGURE 11.5 University of California, Irvine, partial plan. The Main Library (102) is at the head of a large, open park. Six building clusters of academic disciplines run clockwise from this building: Social Sciences, Computer Science and Engineering, Physical Sciences, Biological Sciences, Humanities, and—to complete the circle—a region with student services and campus administration. The Fine Arts are farther out to the northwest, the Medical Sciences farther to the upper left, and the College of Medicine is to the extreme lower left. Note the relatively new unified Science Library building (520) just to the lower left of the Biological Sciences zone. Note that the Main Library is juxtaposed between a major parking area and the academic center. (Used by permission of the Communications Offices at University of California, Irvine.)

Fourth, and the most serious objection of all to a location at the center of the campus, is that it increases the difficulties of making an addition to the building that will be aesthetically and functionally satisfactory. Often, indeed, it makes an appropriate addition almost impossible. A centrally placed building tends to be symmetrical, and an addition usually threatens to destroy this symmetry. If it is also monumental, the cost of an addition will be greatly increased. It should be emphasized once more that most library buildings, if they continue to serve the purpose for which they were designed, have to be enlarged sooner or later, and ought to be planned with this in mind, even with underground expansion if in no other fashion.

A final and not unimportant objection to a too central location is that it may occupy space that is very precious, particularly in an urban area, and should be retained as an attractive lawn and planting. Such a central green serves various important functions and may become sacrosanct

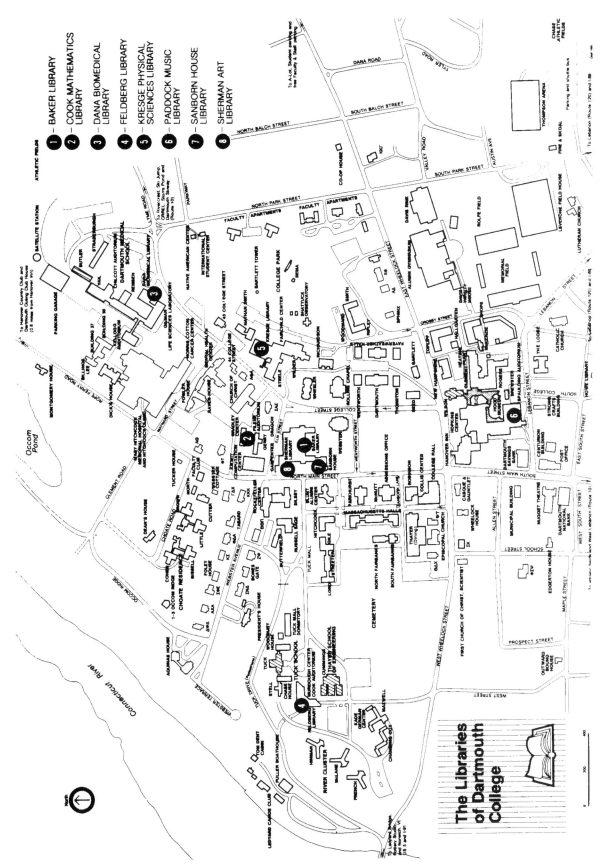

FIGURE 11.6 Dartmouth College. In many respects, the main library (Baker) is at the heart of the campus.

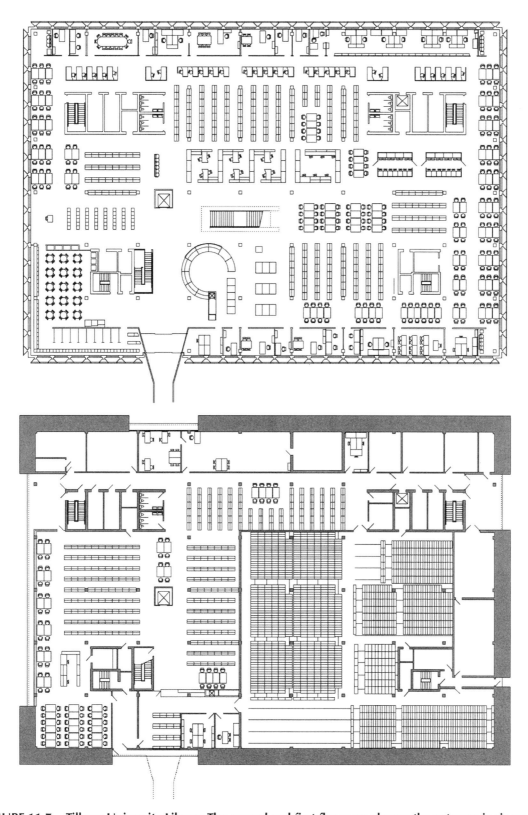

FIGURE 11.7 Tilburg University Library. The ground and first floors are shown; the entrance is via a separate stair and bridge to the middle of three levels (shown with a dashed line on the lower level to indicate that the bridge is overhead). The lower level has a substantial installation of compact shelving. The upper level is stacks and reading. (Courtesy of Tilburg University)

space in the eyes of alumni. This circumstance can lead to underground libraries that, if skillfully done, can be very effective and tasteful—witness structures at Hendrix College and the following universities: Brigham Young (the planned expansion of the Harold B. Lee Library, their main library), British Columbia (Sedgwick—for undergraduates initially, now part of the Walter C. Koerner Library, which is their main library), Columbia (Avery—architecture), Cornell (Kroch—special collections), Harvard (Pusey—university archives), Illinois (undergraduate), Michigan (law), Oregon (science), and Yale (Cross Campus—for intensive-use collections).

What is wanted, then, is a convenient location for the main library, close to the center of academic classroom and laboratory buildings, and, in large institutions, it is hoped not more than one long block from the farthest of these buildings, but not one so central that it calls for an unreasonably expensive, monumental, and unfunctional structure. The University of California at Irvine and Simon Fraser University are examples of very satisfactory locations somewhat off-center. Figures 11.8 and 11.9 illustrate some of the points that have been made. Figures 11.1, 11.2, 11.5, and 11.6 illustrate the library site among other campus buildings at several institutions.

11.4.3 Orientation

No single orientation is ideal for all seasons, climates, and other conditions. Orientation is nevertheless a factor to be considered, particularly in areas where extremes of heat or cold, strong winds, or intense sunlight may be expected. Near the Tropics the sun shines in east and west windows more than in south. As one goes farther north, the southern sun becomes more and more of a problem; the situation is reversed, of course, south of the equator. Although architectural design can handle such problems, they can be significantly ameliorated by a site that permits a beneficial orientation of the building. Comments in this section are applicable for the North Temperate Zone, and they must be interpreted in other geographical locations.

Orientation can provide a psychological encouragement to go to the library. Designers should make it easy for the user to find and approach the entrance, as through a clear, ground-level entry. California State University, Bakersfield, is an example of a fine building oriented with its front door to the south and with this entry raised

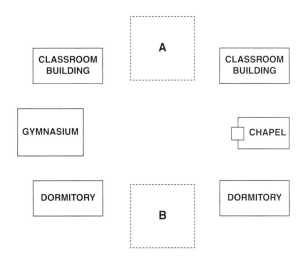

FIGURE 11.8   Library site selection. (A) Suitable site for library because of nearness to classroom buildings, but limited in expansion possibilities (unless the site can be larger). (B) Possible site for library, but one closer to classroom buildings is preferable, other things being equal.

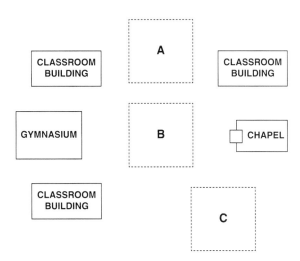

FIGURE 11.9   Library site selection. (A) Site too small, and there may be limited possibilities for an addition (unless the site can be larger). (B) Site difficult if not impossible to expand and would encourage demand for entrances on several sides, which would reduce assignable areas on the critical entrance level. A shipping entrance would present problems. Its central location would increase the temptation to erect a monumental structure. (C) Apparently the most desirable location for the library—expansion possibilities are substantial and problems presented by (B) are lacking.

some 12 feet (3.658 m) above grade, an approach via long ramps and flights of stairs, often in temperatures over 100° F. (38° C.), for which a different solution might have been found. The Bakersfield planning rationale ostensibly was to enable users of the computer labs, multimedia services, and so forth on the lower level to enter on grade when the library is closed. This may be contrasted with the Leavey Library of the University of Southern California, which also has an entire lower level, below grade, devoted to computer-related use, and approached from the first-level entrance, with a convenient orientation on grade to the central campus.

The extent to which the sun penetrates rooms at the hottest time of day is a matter of some importance in most areas. The problem is minimized if it is usually cloudy. In a country where central heating is not customary, the winter sun may be a useful source of heat. More commonly, however, when direct sunlight streams into a building, it creates glare and overheating and is bad for the books; the need for air conditioning will add to costs. An architect should be able to provide drawings showing the penetration of the sun into a room at any latitude during any month of the year for any proposed orientation of a building.

The amount of direct sunlight, as well as heat and cold, that enters a room depends also on the height of windows, the percentage of wall space that they occupy, the depth of the window inset from the outside face of the building, the presence of exterior shading features, and the depth of the room from windows to inner walls. Double windows and certain special kinds of glass may help to counteract unfavorable conditions, but they are expensive and, if broken, are sometimes difficult to replace. Prevailing winds and extremes of heat and cold should also be taken into account.

In most parts of the United States, the western sun is the most difficult to control. The eastern sun generally presents much less of a problem because it is rarely as hot, and the sun is ordinarily higher above the horizon and penetrates a room a shorter distance by the time the library is open or heavily used. The southern sun becomes more of a problem as distance north from the equator increases. Sunlight rarely causes trouble in northern windows in this hemisphere, as it occurs only in early mornings and late afternoons in midsummer. The sunshine and its glare can be kept out during these periods by trees because the sun is low in the sky.

Outside screens of concrete, tile, brick, wood, or metal have been developed to reduce the problems resulting from excess sunlight. Solar energy collectors can be designed to serve in the same fashion. These screens may be placed a few feet beyond the outside wall and protect windows from direct sunlight except, possibly, for a few minutes at the end of the day on a western exposure. Examples of such screens can be found in the University of Miami, the undergraduate library of the University of South Carolina, the University of South Florida in both Saint Petersburg (the new building of 1996) and Tampa, California State University at Bakersfield, and Oregon State University. In place of screens, awnings or wide shelves projecting horizontally from the building above windows, or metal vertical venetian blinds outside the building can be used. A variety of treatments can be found in libraries in the state of Florida. Inside the windows, venetian blinds (vertical or horizontal), curtains, or drapes will help. (See also comments in Section 13.2.2.)

The inside and outside installations sometimes tend to interfere with the circulation of air in an unexpected fashion if there is no air conditioning. Each is an expense, often a good deal to construct or install and replace when required. An engineer should be asked to supply estimates for the specific locality.

Considering the negative aspects of the sun, it follows that a rectangular building with long north and south sides and short east and west sides is to be preferred if practical in other respects. A building placed at a 45-degree angle to the major coordinates may be found to suffer even more. If a building needs to align with its neighbors, windows can be slanted (not parallel with the face of the building), as is sometimes done to good advantage.

However, with an increased interest in energy conservation and the general desire to utilize the energy of the sun for heating loads, it may be found that orientation earlier thought to be a problem is now an asset. Numerous technologies may be employed to capture the sun's heat, and not all of them are contingent upon the orientation of the building. The building orientation only becomes critical where solar collectors are made part of the exterior wall, in which case the collector wall must obviously face the most intense sun, especially in the winter when the heating demand will be at its peak.

If the north side of a building is the best area for reading, it will be preferable, other things being equal, to have the main entrance on the south, leaving the entire north side free for reading space. Furthermore, if the stronger winds and storms usually come from the north and west, an entrance on the south or east is preferable and may require a smaller entrance vestibule than would otherwise be needed.

The ideal orientation may be impractical in many cases because of other considerations. A convenient location may be more important than an ideal orientation; but orientation is a factor to be considered, and its effects on building costs and energy consumption should not be overlooked. If other factors dictate a particularly undesirable orientation, special attention should be given to avoiding the complications that would arise from large areas of unprotected glass.

11.4.4 The Slope of the Land

If a campus is not flat, the extent to which the ground slopes and the direction of the incline may warrant consideration. In the following comments it must be remembered that the overriding consideration should be ease of access for readers, staff, and those who are physically challenged. However, other concerns being equal, the use of the land slope may help solve a number of other problems.

A low site is always suspect because of drainage concerns. A high site usually solves this problem, and it can be useful as long as the elevation gain is moderate. Hollins College Fishburn Library experienced the 1985 consequences of an exceptional rain that swelled the nearby creek, inundating the lowest level of bookstack and leaving 15 percent of the total collection a loss. Therefore, when a library expansion was needed over 10 years later, the college decided to begin anew, about 300 yards (0.274 km) on the opposite and higher side of the campus, a plan that also met the consultant's recommendation to strengthen the east-west axis and provide the first building that visitors see when coming to campus—signifying the academic importance of the library.

So is a flat site on a slight elevation the ideal? A flat site for the library is not always ideal; it has distinct disadvantages. If the main entrance is to be at ground level or only one step up, it will probably be difficult, but not impossible, to have windows in the basement. This point may not be of too great importance, but even with the best of air conditioning and lighting, some persons are inclined to think that reading and staff accommodations without any outside light are substandard. This is particularly likely to be true if the rooms also have low ceilings, as they often do in basements. A basement is not essential, and may be impractical because of ground and soil conditions; but a basement can always provide a large amount of useful library space comparatively inexpensively. Assuming the basement is in fact the lowest floor, it is the most easily adapted to the weight of compact shelving technologies; this suggests that the ceiling should be at least high enough to accommodate standard shelving on carriages, possibly with the height of the track added, and with any required clearance for fire protection. With central heating and air-conditioning plants for whole campuses, basement space may not be needed for mechanical rooms, and as much floor area may be assigned to readers, staff, or books in the basement as on any other floor—more, usually, than on the main floor, where a large entrance lobby is almost always required. If the basement has windows, this space may be highly attractive, and it has the great advantage of being only a short flight of steps from the entrance level. It may also make possible an additional separate entrance and, if so, can house facilities that are open at times when the rest of the building is closed.

A short flight of steps leading to the entrance on the main floor may make it possible to have a basement with windows all around. However, a building without such steps, entered directly from the grade level, has a much more inviting entrance and facilitates access for all. Areaway windows can sometimes provide nearly as much light as those completely above ground, but they entail problems of landscaping and drainage and can be a serious weakness in the most severe rainstorms. If the first floor is approximately 30 in. (762 mm) above ground level on a flat site, a loading platform at the rear is automatically available. Although not essential, it is a convenience when sending or receiving crates, furniture, large mail sacks, binding shipments, large supply orders, or other material on pallets.

One further observation on flat sites may be made. If soil conditions permit, modern earth-moving machinery can change ground levels a few feet at small expense, and, with adequate landscaping, the results may be excellent. It may thus be possible to have a front entrance at ground level and a loading platform at the rear.

A considerable slope may be a distinct advantage or disadvantage, depending on its relationship to the main entrance. At a given site there is usually one side where the main entrance ought obviously to be, a point at which traffic to the library naturally converges. If there is a fairly steep downward slope from this entrance to the rear of the building, as at the University of California, San Diego, it should be possible to have windows in the basement, possibly on as many as three sides and even part or all of the fourth. Indeed, if the slope is sharp enough, there may also be windows in a subbasement or, as it is sometimes called, the minus-2 level. At the Princeton and University of Cincinnati libraries, even the minus-3 levels have windows on one or more sides. A slope of this kind offers the further possible advantage of reducing the height of the building above the entrance level on the most prominent facade. One may enter a building with three to five floors at or near the middle of its levels.

In order to get a minus-1 level with windows, some libraries have an entrance set back from the top of a hill and approached by a bridge, as at the Carleton College Library in Northfield, Minnesota; Clemson University's Cooper Library; Douglass College of Rutgers University; Trinity University in San Antonio; and Washington and Lee University's Leyburn Library. Construction of a short ramp up to the front entrance can serve the same purpose. A long ramp, such as at the Bakersfield and Sacramento campuses of California State University, is undesirable. At the Grinnell College Library there is a ramp and then a bridge to the entrance; the result is that, though the campus is relatively flat, windows can be provided wherever wanted in the basement. Tilburg University presents a similar case with stairs (or elevator) and bridge to enter the main (second) floor of the library, yet enabling windows around the lower level. (See fig. 11.7.)

On the other hand, if there is a sharp upward slope toward the rear of a building, the back of the first floor may have to be sunk into the ground; windows may not be possible on one or more of its sides and there will be none at all in the basement. This may be a disadvantage if natural lighting is desired and may also involve difficult drainage problems.

If the ground falls off to one side of an entrance and rises on the other side, the slope may facilitate basement fenestration on one side but make it impossible to provide windows on the other side of the main floor. It may complicate the landscaping and make architectural planning of the building more difficult. There are successes, such as the UCLA Research Library, Emory University, and the Moffitt Library at the University of California, Berkeley. It is necessary, however, to consider whether the slope could seriously complicate plans for a subsequent addition.

In general, then, a site is to be avoided if the ground slopes upward from the entrance or if it slopes from one side of the entrance to the other. A flat site is preferred to one that slopes objectionably; but it is better yet if the ground slopes from the entrance downward toward the back of the building. No one of these factors is of overriding importance. Nevertheless, they may prove to be the deciding considerations in site selection.

11.4.5 Soil and Ground Conditions

A site for a library should never be selected without knowledge of ground conditions. When information on this subject is not available, at least one or two and in some cases a considerably larger number of test borings should be made. The tests may cost hundreds of dollars for each hole, but they will be well worth the total of several thousand dollars if they prevent great unanticipated expenses for excavation and foundations—misfortunes that have been too common in library building. The cost for a boring report will vary dramatically depending upon the depth and difficulty of the soil. Local advice is the best source of information. One university library had spent more than $60,000 on its plans before it was determined that foundations alone would cost approximately $500,000 extra because of ground conditions.

Because this volume is not an engineering treatise, it should suffice to give a brief summary of the points that ought to be considered.

If the foundation runs into ledge or boulders over ½ cubic yard (0.382 m^3) in size, there may be substantial additional costs for removing this material. The extra costs that would result from placing a building in this type of soil should be carefully estimated by a qualified professional estimator or a contractor familiar with this kind of work. On the other hand, keep in mind that solid rock makes a fine foundation for a library;

books are heavy, and stack areas in particular need a firm foundation. In an excavation for one library, shale was reached before the foundation was excavated to the proper depth, but practically all of it was friable enough to be handled by a power shovel, and, as it was removed, an excellent foundation of harder rock was exposed for the footings.

If loose, fine sand, soft clay, silt, or peaty materials are encountered, piles or caissons may have to be driven down great distances in order to provide an adequate foundation. Along the Charles River in Cambridge and in the Back Bay section of Boston, Massachusetts (areas that once were tidal swamps), it may be necessary to go 200 ft (60.960 m) or more below the surface to reach a solid bottom, and the cost of driving piles or sinking caissons to this depth is great. Clemson University's Cooper Library building of 1966 was built over a stream site, requiring giant pilings to support the building.

Under certain conditions it is possible to pour a concrete mat on which the building will "float." The Charles Hayden Library of the Massachusetts Institute of Technology is built in this way. But adoption of this method dictated the construction of the building around a large court in order to spread the weight, and this resulted in a disadvantageous traffic pattern. The Yale University Library is built over quicksand on which a concrete slab was poured; however, conditions were such that it was possible to build a tower stack, despite the great weight of such a structure.

There are problems in connection with floating a building on a concrete slab or mat. It may sink quite a number of inches. This may not be too serious in itself, though if the sinking is greater on one side than another, it will be a serious matter! Also, if an addition is to be constructed later, the problem may occur again.

In many sections of the country there are numerous springs, subsurface groundwater flow, or other water conditions to complicate the construction of foundations. It is possible to excavate for a foundation, keep the water pumped out, and waterproof the building either outside or in; but these undertakings are expensive, and unless the construction is of highest quality, difficulties will arise sooner or later. During flash floods the water table around the Widener Library at Harvard occasionally rises above the subbasement floor; twice during nearly 50 years, water

has come up through the concrete slab in small sections of the floor.

The Louisiana State University Library in Baton Rouge is built on Mississippi River delta land that can carry only a limited weight per unit area of surface. It was necessary to reduce the pressure on the bearing strata by removing the overburden. This made it necessary to include a basement in the building, and consequently a drainage problem was involved. The basement and the drainage difficulties could have been avoided if the site had not been so small that it was necessary to plan for what in the 1980s became the present five-level building.

A summary of ground and soil concerns includes bearing capacity of the soil, site drainage, frost and water table levels, and seismic shake potential. Poor conditions can always be overcome, but doing so can have very significant cost implications.

A specific example illustrating some of the considerations involved in the selection of a site may be provided by the Lamont Library at Harvard. This site was selected from four possibilities after some weeks of discussion and the preparation of rough sketches of a suitable building in each location. Its position in the southeast corner of the Harvard Yard was chosen because:

1. It was the only remaining available site in the Yard large enough for a building of the desired size. Its location in the Yard close to the two other central library buildings, Widener and Houghton, to which it could be connected by tunnel, was an important factor.
2. It was so placed that (for its first 45 years) the freshmen passed its front entrance six times a day going to and from their meals in the Freshmen Union. It was near a main walk between the houses where the upperclassmen lived and the classrooms, and closer to the latter.
3. It had a long east-west axis, giving the desirable long north and south exposures for the reading areas.
4. The ground slope was such that two levels with windows below the main entrance, which was only one short step up, were possible, with two more without windows below them. It was possible to have above the entrance level a mezzanine, a full second floor, and a penthouse with a good

deal of useful space in it, and still have the latter closer to the ground than the main reading room in Widener.

5. Policy decisions by the university administration, limiting the number of undergraduates (until Radcliffe College's women students were given access several decades later), and by the library authorities, limiting the size of the undergraduate book collection, indicated that provision did not have to be made for a future extension.

One other chance condition may provide a concern about the site and especially about the time required for excavation. Colleges and universities may occupy sites with important archeological artifacts or fossils that can come to light during excavation, if they were not in fact previously known. As an example of the planning consequences, the following is from the Facilities Planning Manual of Stanford University (about 1980).

> Stanford lands contain archeological sites which are known to have yielded evidence of historic or prehistoric human occupation. These sites should be avoided in planning and construction activities. If they can *not* be avoided, they must be monitored scrupulously, with sufficient archeological surveying to ensure the protection of artifacts suspected or found.
>
> Current practice is for the Project Manager to determine from appropriate University sources whether the proposed site of a new facility or project of any kind involves *any* work which may be significant from an archeological viewpoint. If so, an archeological consultant will be engaged to study the site, and perhaps to monitor the excavation. Should any artifacts be found on site, the Office of Design and Construction is obligated to halt construction until their presence can be verified and the items removed. If construction on or near any known archeological site is anticipated, California environmental regulations may require full-time monitoring during excavation or re-siting of the facility or bar the work completely. Interruptions to contractor's construction resulting in monetary loss will be handled by an appropriate change order.

To recapitulate, the site should be large enough to provide for the building and for projected additions, and it should be in as convenient a location as possible. This does not mean that it ought to be in the exact center of the campus; but a general library ought to be readily accessible from classroom buildings and laboratories.

The orientation, ideally, should be on a long axis running directly east and west, with the entrance on the south. A site that slopes downward from the entrance to the rear may be advantageous. Costs of construction may be greatly increased if ground conditions are unsatisfactory. Parking and delivery problems should not be forgotten. Because a site will rarely be found that is ideal in every respect, careful assessment of the advantages and disadvantages of each possible site is called for before a decision is made.

11.5
Master Planning on a Mature Campus

The preceding comments in this chapter are appropriate given freedom of planning, as on a new campus or for a new independent research library. Conditions, however, are seldom so simple. Most efforts to design library buildings are required to cope with a dense clustering of structures, with constraining administrative and political realities, with limited options for expansion or new construction sites, and with the challenge of implementing what often nowadays are dramatic new academic imperatives, such as the major integration of information technologies.

In old institutions just as much as in newer ones, the master planning process can be and usually is a valuable step. This process may require years of collaborative work. It will delay the time of occupancy for new space and thus will exacerbate the situation when space is already inadequate. There may be some expense in this part of the planning process. It may seem frustrating to librarians and others who already feel they face an urgent situation and "know" the solution. Yet experience shows that in many instances, but not all, this step can be the most useful in reaching a satisfactory early solution.

There are two types of master plans. One is a physical plant program, prepared by an architect or a planning office in a study of the physical development of a campus, or part thereof. It will study the various options for site commitments, traffic patterns, and so on. This type of master planning may come either before or after the library space needs have been written in a formal program document. It may come before as part of an ongoing plan for campus development. It would reasonably come after when there is more than one obvious solution to the library spatial requirements.

The second type of master plan is an academic program expressed primarily in terms of the physical plant requirements to meet educational and research objectives. This programming effort may strive to take a fresh look at the overall picture of support for instruction and research, may consider new combinations or divisions of functions, and may relate its reasoning to the required infrastructure and administrative issues. This study is often conducted by a faculty committee, though others on campus will usually be involved and may even provide the leadership in such planning. This section of this chapter speaks only of this second type of master planning. Such planning may give primary focus to solving building problems, or it may provide an academic framework within which the building solution can be suggested, and in this latter case the team effort may phase into building programming. However, there almost always would be approvals between these two phases and we therefore treat master planning as a distinct, separable step.

Each institution will need to determine the proper auspices, appropriate timing, desirable person or group to lead and conduct the master planning, and the suitable charge to this planning group. Although the process and certainly the results will vary widely, four examples of the result of university master planning are here summarized to suggest the breadth of approaches.

One example deals only with the need for and nature of libraries on campus. As mentioned elsewhere in this text, Cornell University years ago began study of whether computers might obviate the need for new library space, or at least reduce the quantity needed. By the 1990s the momentum was under way to expand or rehouse several parts of the library system. A major, experienced architectural firm was hired to develop plans. The resulting plan in the late 1990s accomplished or put in process six library additions, each including major electronic information connections (for agriculture and life sciences, fine arts, industrial and labor relations, management, music, and law) and a new facility to house part of the overcrowded central John M. Olin Library (of 1961). The planning process included critiques and recommendations by the Campus Planning Committee, the Ithaca Landmarks Commission, the Capital Funding and Planning Committee,

the university administration, and the Building and Properties Subcommittee of the board of trustees—not an unusual number of approvals needed for new facilities in any major institution.

Cornell's 1992 facility is a three-story underground structure, the Carl A. Kroch Library, housing the collections of rare books, manuscripts, South and Southeast Asia and East Asia collections, university archives, history of science collection, human sexuality archives, and the Icelandic collection. Recognizing that the adjacent Olin Library was severely overcrowded and that 100,000 ft^2 (9,290 m^2) would be needed before the twenty-first century, the master planning process needed to cope with the historic Arts Quadrangle, which was cherished green space with stone buildings dating to the university's founding. Some opposed any building on this quad and saw no appropriate central-campus areas. The planning eventually concluded that space could be used next to Olin as long as it was below ground. And the Kroch building of 97,000 ft^2 (9,011 m^2) was designed, sized, and detailed to meet this planning criterion and come within the project budget, thus matching aspirations and available funding.

A second example looks at the total campus pattern of library needs in the context of new budgetary realities and administrative processes. In 1991, the UCLA Library Physical Master Planning Committee was formed, headed by the professor who was chair of the Geography Department, and including five other members of the faculty (from the Arts, Civil and Environmental Engineering, Earth and Space Sciences, English, and Physics Departments), the assistant director of capital planning, the associate university librarian for sciences, and the university librarian. (It is paradoxical that this planning committee was slanted toward the physical sciences, which probably are more nearly suited to intensive use of digital access to information than are the humanities and social sciences.) Their October 1993 report gave penetrating attention to the changing conception of a research library, the "rather archaic structure" of UCLA's library, the sharply constraining financial conditions, and a deteriorating library physical plant deficient both qualitatively and quantitatively.

The principal UCLA Library Physical Master Planning Committee recommendations, which soon received the chancellor's endorsement, were better to integrate the library into the process of academic and capital planning, to expand the central Research Library into a new third increment, to expand and renovate the Biomedical Library, and to merge six branches into two new library buildings, each with appropriate electronic capabilities. The mergers would reduce the number of campus libraries from 14 in 1993 (18 in 1990) to 7; Music and Arts would be combined, and four others would become a consolidated Physical Sciences/Engineering Library. Each of the present libraries is moving to include plug-and-play wiring throughout, computing and multimedia commons, interactive electronic classrooms, and compact shelving in public areas.

Note that administration integration was a major recommendation at UCLA, while site selection for library expansions and new buildings was not part of this particular master plan. In discussing administrative relationships, the report includes one important paragraph concerning capital planning and outside fund-raising:

> All capital planning deliberations that include academic buildings should involve the University Librarian at the very earliest stages. This recommendation refers to both discussions of new buildings as well as renovation of existing structures. Also, the Development Office should work more directly with the University Librarian in planning for future fund-raising campaigns. Use figures demonstrate that the Library plays an important role as an information resource for the Los Angeles community. This role combined with its function as an essential academic resource should allow the Library to be accorded a high priority in future development campaigns.

Another example deals with libraries along with the burgeoning demand for computer-based technologies, to shape a new student learning culture. The University of Michigan is this example. After some years of thought, the university in 1996 opened its Media Union building, a new facility housing the Art Library, Architecture Library, Engineering Library, and, in their own words, "a virtual reality laboratory and computer animation library, interactive multi-media classrooms, high-tech theater and performance spaces, and cutting-edge design and innovation studios." The Michigan objective is that the Media Union serve "as a crystalline catalyst, seven days a week, twenty-four hours a day, growing a new community without walls. The Union will provide flexibility and break down barriers—both of distance and of discipline. It will help scholars, artists,

engineers, and others reach out to each other across intellectual boundaries, recreating our ideas of art, engineering, and the humanities. Many participants will join international collaborative teams, pursuing research and design projects face-to-face through video across thousands of miles."

If this language sounds like jargon, a use of currently popular words and phrases that in the past would have seemed meaningless, be assured that the statement is reflective of current collegiate concepts in the late 1990s, and these represent an effort to convey some idea of the aspirations of higher education applied to a new instructional facility as the academic institution adapts to the innovative and educationally advantageous uses of printed information with information technology.

Many other collegiate institutions have created facilities somewhat in this same mold, in some instances modifying one or more existing buildings or parts thereof, and in other instances creating a new amalgam of functions and spaces to provide the teaching faculty with new tools. The technologies and library functions are here so integrated into a collaborative environment that one cannot state what percent of the 250,000 gross ft^2 (23,225 m^2) forms the library. In this new North Campus facility it calls its Media Union, the University of Michigan has created one of the most ambitious of this new genre of library-cum-teaching facilities.

The site chosen for the Media Union is a mile (well over a kilometer) from the Central Campus, clustered in downtown Ann Arbor. The College of Engineering outgrew its Central Campus buildings and started fresh on the North Campus, now joined by the School of Music, School of Art and Design, College of Architecture and Urban Planning, and many student dorms. The library in this integrated facility provides multiple catalogs to full-text resources from 500 workstations anywhere in the building. The integration is also suggested by the administrative structure: three directors for Information Services (a librarian by training and experience), Information Technology, and Academic Programming all reporting to the vice provost for Information Technology/ dean of Academic Outreach and to an executive committee of deans from around the campus.

The fourth example is an institution that dealt with the major student services, including library and technology issues. George Mason University (GMU) is this example. The 1995 Johnson Learning Center is the result of GMU's academic master plan for the "learning center concept." The task force, made up of faculty, staff, administrators, and students, looked at melding curriculum support and student culture in a large, rather recent (1957) commuting institution. In this instance, the university "center" includes a learning library occupying about one-quarter of the very large building (320,000 ft², or 29,728 m²), currently the largest academic building in any of the state-financed institutions in the state of Virginia.

The site was chosen because the academic activities as a whole were moving south (to much higher profile structures), leaving the older northern end (low-profile) buildings to become business offices: admissions, computing, financial aid, health, registrar, and so on. Further, the Johnson Center is on the highest spot of campus land, described as being in the center of the new campus. The long-term plan is to expand the main Fenwick Library, possibly in the direction of the Johnson Center.

The GMU Johnson Learning Center library has a book and media collection aimed at primary undergraduate needs (though the earlier Fenwick Library a block away is full of books and computer support) and many well-designed carrels for networked use of laptop computers plus a 35-seat computerized bibliographic instruction room, so the combination might be a state-of-the-art electronic teaching library.

However, as one enters this library/student center building, one has the impression of being in an enclosed large shopping mall; there is a bank, a credit union, food services (currently pizza, Chinese, Mexican, etc.), a bookstore, a bistro (in which to hang out and enjoy music), a movie theater, assembly rooms, a computer store, a convenience store, more than 1,000 lockers, student government offices, plus four computer labs and the library located in the back of the ground floor and much of the second level. This is literally a place where students can freely move among food and other auxiliary services and the library books and seating—aimed to be a model of gathering all the components of college experience under one roof, a microcosm of student life at GMU.

One can see from these examples that the academic emphasis in some institutions is focused primarily on the library needs with reasonable incorporation of computer-based technology. In other efforts the technology has been given a more dominant role, perhaps exercising a signif-

icant influence on the total instructional support in which the library shares. In this connection, almost all institutions share the view, as expressed at UCLA, that "the move toward greater electronic access to materials will alleviate this [library book collection space] pressure somewhat, but the continuing demand for printed materials, the explosion in the volume of such materials being produced each year, the costs of converting materials to electronic formats, and continued limitations of access to electronic hardware, especially among students, will mean that computerization alone will not solve the problems of collection space shortages."

Still other results of the master planning effort involve administrative adjustments and financial imperatives along with the direction to be taken to meet library physical requirements. Each institution has its educational priorities with current physical needs to support these objectives. The process of academic planning, once the recommendations receive the highest administrative support, can result in a strong commitment to the solution of library needs. Thus this process becomes one of great importance in creating an adequate library for the future.

11.6
The Review Process and Refinement

As can be surmised from some of the above, the process of site selection is one of the most significant decisions in the planning of a building. It is a principal influence on success or weakness of the library building. Even when the architect and librarian may be left alone to decide on the interior arrangement, many individuals are involved in exterior appearance and in site selection. Boards of trustees should always be involved, as should the president and the chief librarian.

This stage of a building project may also have the greatest duration, except for funding, and can have a changing cast of participants if it extends over 10 years, which is sometimes the case. The master campus plan may have designated precincts or zones for sciences, for humanities, for open space, and so on. Thus the library expansion site (or sites) on older campuses has been a matter for preliminary discussion or tentative decision long before the institution is ready to make a final precise determination for a new library building or building addition.

Over the years various deans or officers may have eyed desirable plots, the sizable piece of land adjacent to the existing library, or a poor building nicely located that has been discussed for possible razing. The librarian or other officers must guard against inappropriate assignments of land. The librarian may need to muster all the supportive help possible—individuals, committees, officials, and even trustees—to protect what in the long run may be the best library site. This may occur even when a new facility is not an immediate prospect but is anticipated years in the future.

As the final site selection process takes its course, it may require quick actions. As implied above, a beloved tree or utility corridor or a dean's academic goal may suddenly alter or reduce the site. The librarian may never hear some of the arguments—maybe a trustee's private talk with the president argued some change—and in the last days before the trustees are to make a final determination, the unseen maneuver may surface. The University of Alberta is a case in

point where the site for the library addition was usurped for another purpose. Most campus decisions about site involve compromises. The skills of the librarian, help by the faculty library committee, and counsel by a consultant should assure a wise outcome.

Beyond that, once the building program records the selected site, the architect has the final say. The architect may have good reason to suggest some change or minor shift. The whole nature of the building, its height, exterior configuration, orientation—the refinement goes on as a steady process, which is part of the architect's discipline. Once schematic plans are produced, debated, and accepted, the refinement of site has ceased. The structure begins to assume its final design form.

NOTES

1. Paul Venable Turner, *Campus: An American Planning Tradition* (Cambridge, Mass.: MIT Press, 1984), p. 117.
2. Statements adapted from *University Planning and Design: A Symposium,* ed. Michael Brawne. Architectural Association Paper no. 3 (London: Lund Humphries, 1967).

12

Schematic Considerations

Form ever follows function.

    —Louis Henri Sullivan, *Lippincott's Magazine*

It is a bad plan that admits of no modification.

    —Publilius Syrus, *Sententiae*

The schematic design phase is the portion of the design process that translates the written facilities program into a graphic representation of an architectural concept. It provides a tentative, feasible design solution involving site usage and building spaces, rooms, and relationships, both horizontal and vertical, to meet the program. It leaves for the design development phase the changes, alterations, refinements, and details to reach a final plan.

By the time the first phase of the design process is reached, a great deal of work will have been completed by the institution in terms of the academic and facilities program, selection of the architect, funding strategy, and often the site selection. This chapter will address those concerns that typically are part of the schematic phase.

Almost always there will be some overlap of the various phases; much of the information discussed in the chapters on programming, budgeting and expense control, additions and renovations, and siting and master planning (Chapters 5 through 11) may in many projects be developed as part of the schematic phase.

In this and other chapters, the word *room* is used when *area* can often be substituted. It was formerly routine to have rooms with doors, for acoustic, heating, and security reasons. Heating and ventilation practices have changed, and most security is now commonly at the building exits. Thus more open spaces are favored. "Rooms" appear more often as "areas" with greater or lesser demarcation by use of shelving, carpet color, furniture, or architectural treatment. The concept of rooms as areas should therefore be kept in mind.

12.1
The Scope of the Schematic Design Phase

The schematic phase should be a period of intense communication between the architect and the other members of the design team. Written information will include the facilities program, soils test reports, a site survey (including utility locations, adjacent buildings, and other significant features), and, in many cases, a copy of the institutional facility standards. Supplementary information may include existing building plans, existing furniture and equipment inventories (although this often comes later), an academic pro-

gram statement, library statistical reports, an organization chart and staff list, and perhaps a booklet describing the history and nature of the institution. Most if not all of this documentation should be given to the architect at or before the first meeting.

Following the initial transmittal of what may be a considerable volume of written material, there generally is a "getting-to-know-you" period during which site visits to other similar libraries are conducted, with the project architect responsible for design and the chief librarian as essential participants. The establishment of a solid rapport during this early period of the design effort is essential. A mutual vocabulary will develop so that both the librarian and architect will understand what is meant by such words as *circulation, section, range, scale, mass, space,* and *volume.* Each profession is likely to have a completely different understanding of these and other concepts; thus, clear communication must be established at the start.

Site visits usually are extra beneficial if the buildings visited require overnight travel, because the discussion that often develops in the less-formal atmosphere during the evening can be exceedingly useful. Such topics as the philosophy of architecture and librarianship, the discussion of architectural or library arrangements that were observed during the day, or even a discussion of other projects in which the participants are currently involved will lead to a fuller understanding of the desires for and scope of the project at hand. The importance of these early meetings cannot be overstated. They establish the communication linkage that will be necessary during the balance of the project to ensure that the product fully meets the goals of the library and the institution.

The first design efforts of the architect will generally involve working with the facilities program to develop space or function relationships. This will be directly related to the site requirements as well as to any larger master planning effort that may be required as part of the project. Early studies will be fairly crude with rough floor areas blocked out for each major function so that the form and mass of the proposed building can be studied. Meetings during this phase of the design may include the chief academic officer or provost, a member of the development office (fund-raising), the university architect, the university project manager, and one or more members of the library administration. Issues of siting, height, number of floors, and the general footprint of the building will be fairly well worked out during this period, although they may be adjusted later as more details are added.

The question of aesthetics will be apparent nearly from the beginning, and there is always a give and take between the client and the architect. It is often said that the design of a building, good or bad, is half the client's and half the architect's. It is often difficult to draw the line in making decisions that affect the aesthetics, but it is suggested that issues in this area should be left to the design professionals and a representative of the institution, providing anticipated funding and academic or operational programs are not adversely affected. Few librarians, if any, are qualified to decide on aesthetic issues. Unfortunately, it is often the experience that others, directly or indirectly involved in planning, who are no better equipped in this respect than librarians, have decided opinions on these matters and do not hesitate to express them. The struggle to deal with these opinions too often results in more confusion, complaints, and emotional unhappiness than almost any other phase of planning library buildings.

A statement by Nikolaus Pevsner, the British author and critic, is pertinent: "Architectural quality is of course aesthetic quality but it is not aesthetic quality alone. The work of architecture is the product of function and art. If it fails in either, it fails in quality."[1] At the convention of the American Institute of Architects in May 1963, Pevsner said that the great ages of architecture have depended "as much on knowledgeable clients as on the flowering of architectural genius," and added that today "clients tend to be too timid." They "take the architect's vision with rather less checking of the fulfillment of the brief than they ought to do."

On the other hand, Donald Canty, editor of the *AIA Journal,* wrote what is every bit as valid today:

> For every architect who follows his "vision" to the disadvantage of the building's function, there are others who are pushed by the client into doing things which they know are mistakes.
>
> The client must strike a rather delicate balance. On the one hand, he cannot let himself be "controlled" on this point where the building becomes no longer his, but solely the architect's. On the other hand, presuming that he has chosen an archi-

tect of some talent, he should not hamstring that talent to the point where he is no longer getting his money's worth in terms of design quality. . . .

> Most architects stand . . . somewhere in the midst of a diamond. The four corners of the diamond are aesthetics (what the building should look and feel like), technology (how it can be built and its interior environment controlled), economics (the limitations of the budget), and function (what the building is to do). Each corner exerts a magnetic force on the architect, and his outlook depends largely on his response to the tugs of one over the others.
>
> There is nothing in the rules to say that the client can't do a little tugging too, provided he knows what he is about.[2]

The role of various members of the design team is further discussed in Chapter 4.

12.2
In Response to the Site

A first consideration should be whether the site chosen has been explored sufficiently to reveal historic relics, archeological remains, ancient burials, toxic waste remains, or other conditions that can be important in their own right and may delay the project schedule by months. These surprises can occur in any country in the world and in urban as well as rural locations. This is important regardless of whether a building has previously been on the exact site because new, larger buildings will usually have deeper foundations and because many countries and states now take a much stronger stand than previously to be sure the important historic, social, and cultural values are respected and such conditions as toxic waste are cleaned up. Besides sample diggings, new techniques may be employed to facilitate this inspection, including magnetometry, flux-grade gradiometer equipment, and ground penetrating radar. The issue of ground cleanliness—the legal right to use the land to build—should be resolved now before it causes escalated problems.

If the building planning can start from the inside, the result will be a better building functionally. It is a serious mistake for the architect to plan the building with the facade uppermost in the design priorities before knowing something about the functional requirements. Nevertheless, unless the library is intended to form the basis for a new campus situated on a flat site with little or no environmental influence, there will be factors from outside the building envelope that should affect the interior arrangements. The orientation of the building will nearly always be determined by the site, including existing nearby buildings, rather than internal requirements. Site factors should be identified and utilized in the development of the functional facility. It is not suggested that a perfect building envelope should be designed, and then the functional aspects squeezed in. Rather it should be a balanced process with cogent recognition of both the functional internal factors and the external influences as the design process proceeds. Compromises may have to be made between dealing with external and internal factors, but they should be reached only after the persons directly involved have given full consideration to the consequences.

Major foot traffic routes may well suggest the best location for an entrance, but care must always be taken to avoid the temptation for multiple entrances unless they can be arranged to feed into one control point. Through traffic for a building located in the middle of a major pedestrian route can be a problem too, particularly in climates where considerable energy is required to maintain the environment. Vehicle access will likely be limited to only one or a few points on the parameter of the building. Seldom is vehicle access appropriate to more than one side of the building. If the building is a major addition, will an existing delivery point suffice, or will a new one be constructed to serve both the old building and the new addition? From what distances and approaches should the entrance be seen?

Other factors may be important in determining the entrance location. Is there another library next door? Are there negative influences, such as a busy street, a railroad track, or a prevailing wind, that could influence the entry location? Is there a bus route or subway system that will serve the library? Are bicycles heavily used, and will there need to be some allocation of the site for bike parking? Will there be provision for returning books from an automobile? These factors and others must be considered in dealing with the entrance location.

The location of major utilities often will influence the shape of a building. This can present a very serious limitation, as was indicated in the previous chapter. Few would welcome the expense of relocating utility corridors, although this has been done. The machine room, transformer vault, phone room, and other supporting services may well be located near the utility services.

The topography and soils condition of the site can influence the building configuration in a number of ways. There may be practical height limitations or basement depth limitations caused by local soils and the water table. The height of the building and its mass may also be influenced by nearby buildings or even local codes and ordinances. Natural features, such as a floodplain, a rock outcropping, a forest, or views, may influence the shape of buildings. Colors, scale, and materials often are suggested by the local architectural fabric.

These factors and others are discussed in detail in Chapter 11. It should be clear, however, that the arrangement of internal functions must reflect such essential elements as where traffic will be, how books are returned, how the building will relate to other buildings, where library materials are delivered, and the like. This arrangement can be achieved in the early design phases as the design team reviews and critiques various options and possibilities presented by the architect. Of course, the architect should be well aware of the assets and limitations of the site before any design effort is begun.

12.2.1 Soil Mechanics and Foundations

A firm foundation is essential for any building. Because of the weight of books, if nothing else, libraries place a heavier load on their foundations than do many other structures. These loads must be carried with a reasonable margin of safety. To oversimplify, the static, or "dead," load is the weight of the structure itself and fixed elements; "live" load is the weight added to the structure by its contents. In libraries the latter consist primarily of the movable furniture and equipment, the book collections, and persons using them. There is no need here to discuss what are known as repeated loads, impact loads, and a number of other kinds of loads, including those that come from wind, earthquakes, and weight of snow on the roof. With the general exception of concern for proper support of the library and its contents (for example, seismic bracing for library shelving), these are of importance to the architect and engineer and must be provided for in the structure, but are outside the field of this volume.

Except for bookstacks, shelving for phonograph discs, map cases, and a few other pieces of heavy equipment, it is fair to say that 60 pounds per ft^2

(2.873 kN/m²) for reading areas is sufficient as far as live load is concerned. But 100 pounds (4.788 kN/m²) should ordinarily be provided for corridors, 150 (7.182 kN/m²) is standard for stack rooms, and up to 175 (8.379 kN/m²) may be required for rather dense book-storage areas and map cases. As much as 200 pounds (9.576 kN/m²) may be required for garages with heavy trucks, and 250 pounds per ft² (11.970 kN/m²) for vaults. And 300 pounds per ft² (14.364 kN/m²) is recommended for areas where compact movable shelving is anticipated, although some may argue that this is excessive. The floor loading at the University of Edinburgh was designed for 11.200 kN/m² (233.9 lb/ft²), which should be adequate for many compact shelving systems provided they do not house phonograph records or other exceedingly heavy collections.

Today it has become customary, and on the whole wisely so, to construct all library floors strong enough to carry a live load of 150 pounds per ft² (7.182 kN/m²). Such strength will make it safe to install bookstacks anywhere, to change internal arrangements freely, and to place practically any equipment wherever it is wanted. In many older libraries, which were not so constructed, it has often been found unsafe to place bookstacks in reading areas. This limitation has complicated matters when additions were being planned or changes were made in space assignments.

It may be argued that structure sufficient to house compact shelving adds about 10 percent to the construction cost while doubling the potential storage capacity. On this basis it may make sense to require that extensive portions of the building be of sufficient capacity to house movable compact shelving, and the basement is frequently so engineered. Even upper floors can be suitably and justifiably structured to accommodate movable compact shelving, and this is becoming increasingly common.

Buildings are supported by columns or bearing walls or a combination of the two. Bearing outside walls do not present a problem, except that they may be very much in the way if an addition is made to an old building, because they may restrict connections between the old and new anywhere except where there has been a door, window, or other opening. This is important if an addition is anticipated later in a building now being planned, or if plans are now being made for an addition to an old building. Internal bearing walls present more of a problem, as they complicate any alteration within a structure. If a flex-

ible building is desired, they should be avoided, except perhaps around fixed features, such as stairwells, elevators, and toilet rooms. Of course, bearing walls are a fact of life where the structure must withstand earthquakes, but with careful planning they can be designed with minimum negative functional impact. Remember that interior bearing walls are not the same as nonbearing wet walls. The latter are inflexible only in that they are difficult and messy to remove, but removal of a bearing wall requires a structural change in what might be called the building's skeleton.

Adequate footings under both columns and bearing walls must be provided so that no part of the building will sink. Chapter 11, on site selection, discusses this issue. Sometimes deep piles are required and may prove to be very expensive. If the piles are of wood, they must not be allowed to dry out, or they will rapidly deteriorate. It often is desirable to sink caissons because of soft soil conditions. Sometimes the whole building must be supported by or floated on a concrete slab, to spread the weight and avoid the possible shifting of the soil beneath if there is quicksand or slippery clay. Sometimes soil must be removed to a considerable depth to lessen the ground load before the new building is constructed. Sometimes the problem is expensive excavation of solid rock by blasting, which can be costly and dangerous.

Always be sure that soil conditions are known before a site is irrevocably selected. If a later addition is anticipated, remember that it should be arranged without interfering with the footings in the original structure. This can sometimes be managed through cantilevering out beyond supporting columns or load-bearing walls in the new part of the structure. If the addition or the old structure is floated on a concrete slab, very careful calculation will be necessary to avoid having the addition sink too far or not far enough, and so leave a step up or down between the two. There can be danger that a floating building or one with unstable foundations may tip slightly to one side or the other, as happened to the Leaning Tower of Pisa.

12.2.2 Roofs

Roofs may be flat or they may be sloped, or pitched, as the inclination is sometimes called. The silhouette of facades and roofs of structures bordering the site will influence though not govern the choice of roof shape and perhaps materials. For persons going to or around the planned building, sight lines will be a concern if the site is either very low or very high.

A sloped roof has the advantage of letting water run off and consequently is easier to keep waterproofed. Heavy snow will tend to slide off, but the live load from wind will be increased. It may also provide inexpensive mechanical space in the attic, if that is desired. But the greater its slope, the larger its area and cost.

A flat roof is always difficult to make watertight. It must be custom-built and seamless if possible. Where seams are required, they should be minimized, as leaks are more likely to occur at seams than elsewhere. Certain types of roofs, particularly single-ply roofing, which can be of excellent quality, require seams unless the area involved is quite small. Roof drainage systems are important, especially with flat roofs. Downspouts are either mounted externally or are run in pipes within the exterior wall. Some codes require the provision of a backup or overflow drain. Scuppers are a common technique for handling the occasional overflow. However, beware the runoff that can soil the face of a building, as many libraries can demonstrate. The 1983 addition at the University of Central Florida has an attractive reading room on the first floor, north side; however, the roof drains over the reading room skylight, leaving heavy stains. Also, consider the runoff over horizontal portions of sunscreens, for they can cause this same problem. The overflow drain designed for the Cecil H. Green Library at Stanford emerges below the roof from a soffit. When activated, it drains over a window area, leaving water marks that are removed only during the rare window washings. This detail could have been picked up during the working drawing phase, but it was overlooked.

A flat roof will be walked upon at one time or another, and if access to mechanical equipment is through the roof, walking on it will be frequent. This may suggest special treatment for the access route that will increase the life expectancy of the roof. A slightly elevated boardwalk is sometimes used for this reason. If it is necessary to use the roof to service equipment, guardrails may also be required by code.

12.3
Early Structural Concepts

Except in a few quite small libraries, construction above the foundations, whether supported by columns or bearing walls, is ordinarily of masonry, concrete, or steel. In some locations local sand for use in concrete may be unsuitable and present a problem, as in certain parts of upstate New York. Careful estimates of the comparative costs of concrete and steel should be made. The latter may amount to considerably more than the former, but if it makes possible smaller columns, particularly in the bookstack, the saving in space may make up for the additional cost.

It is important for the architect to keep up-to-date with innovations in construction, which continue to develop rapidly throughout the world. A new type of steel beam may be introduced that is claimed to be cheaper and stronger than beams used in the past. Can it be used to advantage in your building? Will prestressed or precast concrete make possible the effects desired and still save funds for other purposes? Can reinforced concrete-block construction be economical for a subsidiary or ancillary library? Can plastic panels satisfactorily serve as exterior walls? Will lift-slab construction be useful or are there advantages from the long spans that can be provided by prestressed beams? Some of these techniques may be functional but not particularly satisfactory aesthetically.

It is not easy, perhaps not possible, for anyone but an expert in the particular branch of the construction field to decide on the suitability of new methods or units for incorporation in a building. A great danger in the use of new materials and methods is their lack of time testing. This can sometimes be provided only by experiments that require considerable technical equipment and involve considerable expense. Unfortunately, changes in the quality of products, both new and old, occur frequently with what may be unfortunate results. For example, metal stud walls backing up face-brick skins have become accepted building practice for economic reasons, though this method has on occasion been found to permit moisture penetration and foster material deterioration. Indeed, the effects of environmental pollutants, sunlight, and water on some new building materials used for exteriors remain untested.

Another example, though not of a new technology, is the concept of using steel rather than reinforced concrete for major spans in the library (which is commonly done when steel structures are economically favorable). A steel frame designed for a particular load tends to deflect more than reinforced concrete designed for the same load. This can be a serious problem if not accounted for, particularly for compact shelving. If, however, the maximum deflection allowable is accounted for, then deflection should not be a problem. Compact shelving vendors recommend from ¼ in. over a 10-ft span (1/480 of the span) to ⅜ in. over a 20-ft span (1/640 of the span). Deflection specified at no more than 1/600 of the span with the shelving loaded will be workable. Even where the deflection is somewhat greater, remedies exist to prevent the carriages from rolling to the low point, although they add friction to the system; the ideal is to avoid deflection. Sometimes new materials and new methods are difficult to make use of because of labor restrictions of one kind or another, and even traditional technologies often need care in their application to ensure proper results.

12.3.1 Modular Construction

The most important structural concept that must be settled early in the design process is the module. To control construction costs, nearly every building is made of units of a multiple of a specific dimension. This basic dimension is the standard used repetitively for many construction components. The module is especially important for interior finishings, such as windows, hung ceilings, nonbearing walls, and interior columns. The word *module* is used in this section only with reference to the spacing of interior columns and structural elements, which is a basic result of modular construction.

Under the modular system, as the term is used here, a building is supported by columns placed at regular intervals. With the exception of shear walls in earthquake country and in a few cases exterior walls and walls at stairs and core elements, nothing within the building is weight-bearing except the columns. Columns in this case include the shelving uprights in a tiered stack. It follows in theory that nothing within the building is fixed and immovable except the columns, though in fact it is generally impractical if not impossible to shift the location of stairways, elevators, air ducts, plumbing, and utility risers.

Programmatic aspects of the module are discussed in Chapter 5, the details of shelving dimensions and aisle widths are covered in Chapter 6, and reader requirements will be found in Chapter 7.

If the modular system is to be used, what should be the column spacing? No one has been able to find an ideal size for all libraries or, indeed, for all parts of even one library, and it is

doubtful if anyone ever will. Spacing depends on the library and the use to which it is to be put and to some extent on the current construction technology. If the library is to be primarily for undergraduates, with a very large seating capacity and a small book collection that can be shelved chiefly in the reading areas, spacing is quite a different problem from that which exists in the library that is primarily for advanced research work, with a tremendous stock of books and comparatively few accommodations for readers. Therefore, if a primarily undergraduate college becomes a research institution, what was once a suitable module size may then no longer be entirely satisfactory. This fact is somewhat reduced in the United States by the effect of current codes and the Americans with Disabilities Act, which requires typically wider stack aisles than in the past.

An examination of the module sizes selected in libraries shows a tremendous variation from as low as 13 ft (3.962 m) in the short dimension to as high as 33 ft (10.058 m) or more in the other. On top floors in those instances where only the roof needs to be supported, a much wider space, of course, is practical. This was the case in the Rutgers University Library main reading room, where there are spans of 83 ft (25.298 m). Recent developments in trusses and concrete have made available very large spans, which are not unduly expensive under some circumstances. In the Illinois Institute of Technology Library in Chicago, much of the weight of the building is hung from tremendous steel roof beams that make possible bays of over 2,000 ft² (186 m²) and an area without columns on the first floor of some 20,000 ft² (1,858 m²).

The Lafayette College Library, with the aid of special construction methods, was able to provide spaces as large as 45 × 99 ft (13.716 × 30.176 m) separated by smaller areas. Larger module sizes may be possible, but there are trade-offs. Structural codes are becoming more conservative; with the higher than normal library loading of 150 pounds per ft² (7.182 kN/m²), longer spans will require greater structural depth, which increases the volume and height of the building, all other things being equal. Of course, as the columns must carry more weight, they themselves become more significant elements.

If the modules are square, with standard construction, they may vary from 16 ft 6 in. to 27 ft (5.029 to 8.230 m) where 3-ft (914-mm) shelving is used, or, in a limited number of cases, even more than that. Almost every imaginable combination between 18 and 27 ft (5.486 and 8.230 m) in one or both directions can be found. Some dimensions selected seem to have been accidents rather than the result of deliberate decisions. Some were chosen for reasons that are now obscure and may have been based primarily on the fact that the architects, because they wanted the building to be so many feet long by so many feet deep, adopted a module size to fit those dimensions. The size in more than one library has been determined by the size in adjacent buildings, because this may affect facade designs.

Dimensions of the module need not be determined by the total length and breadth of the building; it is possible to cantilever out beyond the outside columns up to at least one-third of the distance between columns and thus increase the overall building size up to two-thirds of a bay by the cantilever in both directions. This creates no serious engineering problems, but aesthetic involvements should not be forgotten, and careful planning is required to make sure all the cantilevered space will be useful. (See fig. 12.1.)

Perhaps because of the difficulty of deciding on the optimum module size, some architects and librarians have reached the conclusion that almost any size can be adapted to library use and have selected one arbitrarily, failing to realize that the one chosen may reduce bookstack or reading accommodations by as much as 10 percent or in some cases even more. If this loss is only 3 percent in a $4,000,000 building, the $120,000 involved could be used to better advantage, and if, for instance, it took even 10 percent of this saving to figure out a better size, it would be money well spent.

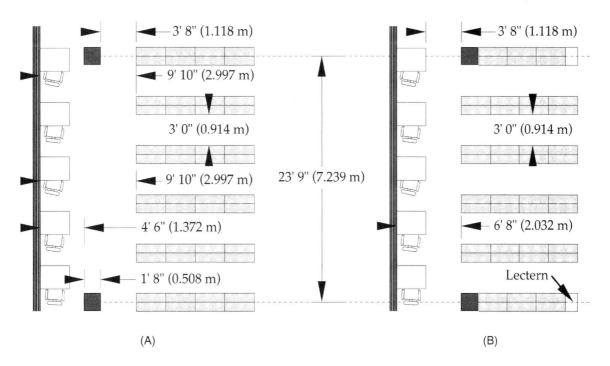

(A)   (B)

FIGURE 12.1 Cantilevered construction in a bookstack. (A) Cantilevered construction providing 4½ ft (1.372 m) beyond the outside columns. This is not wide enough for even a minimal carrel and aisle. (B) The cantilever provides 6 ft 8 in. (2.032 m) in the clear beyond the columns, which is sufficient for a minimal carrel and an aisle that should meet the local building code in most areas, with the shelving reaching to the outside face of the column. Depending upon the column size, this arrangement saves floor area equal to over 3 ft (0.914 m) times the length of the area, which easily makes up for the slight reduction in shelving capacity as illustrated caused by the use of lecterns or return areas for books ready for reshelving in the column ranges to the right.

To sum up, in the words of Nancy McAdams:

> For at least three decades, the accepted practice in library planning has been to arrange the stacks on 54″ centers, (4′6″, from center to center), and to design the building structural system on a module that is a multiple of that 54″ dimension. [It is probable that the Tilburg Library, fig. 11.7, is based upon a close approximation of this dimension of 1.372 meters.] It works out to 18′, or 22′6″, or 27′, and so forth, so that you get efficient bookstack layouts.
>
> This plan worked extremely well until state and federal regulations for access by the handicapped began to require 36″ aisles between the bookstack ranges, as a minimum. The old 54″ spacing, with the 20″ wide stack base, produced only a 34″ aisle. So the structural module for new buildings now needs to be a multiple of at least 56″ (4′8″) [which assumes the shelving is no more than 20 inches from face to face], and that changes the bay size from 18′ to 18′8″, from 22′6″ to 23′4″, and from 27′ to 28′.
>
> Some planners, to play it safe, are increasing the range spacing a little further, to 4′9″ or even 5′, and enlarging the bay even more. The end result is a slightly less efficient building, in terms of net growth ratio.
>
> The real problem occurs with additions and renovations when the stacks in the existing building have to be re-spaced to meet the current handicapped access code. The end result is a really inefficient stack layout and a significant loss of storage capacity.[3]

The balance of this section will deal with the problems involved and attempt to state as clearly as possible the points on which the decision should be based. A choice must be made for each library with its specific requirements in mind.

12.3.2 Selection of the Module for Bookstack Areas

Today in the United States, the critical dimension in the stacks is the open-stack aisle. The Americans with Disabilities Act currently requires minimum clear stack aisles of 36 in. (0.914 m). Based upon this requirement, ranges with 10-in. (254-mm) base and adjustable shelves together with an inch (25 mm) allowed for growth and error (most shelving is slightly deeper than the combined nominal shelf dimension, though at least one manufacturer is virtually exact in face-to-face dimensions provided no end panels are planned) will require a minimum range spacing of 57 in. (1.448 m) on center. With nominally 12-in. (305-mm) base shelves, and allowance for "growth" (defined in the fifth of the 10 points below) and error, 61 in. (1.549 m) minimum on center is required. For standard library shelving of these dimensions, the most efficient module accommodating range aisles as described is thus going to be typically a multiple of 57 or 61 in. (1.448 or 1.549 m). Some code authorities may require range aisles of as much as 44 in. (1.118 m). Layouts can be generated based upon these modules (see table 12.1 and fig. 12.2).

First, a few comments. The examples of module analysis illustrated and the table demonstrate the area required per section in a somewhat idealistic circumstance. In all cases, the arrangement of the shelving is fixed with 10 section ranges and 6-ft (1.829-m) cross aisles, with one cross aisle at the edge (to the left of the illustrations) of 44 in. (1.118 m). Also, in all examples, the best arrangement in terms of lost sections of shelving for a given module was found, and only full sections are used. A number of factors could alter the areas as determined in these illustrations; they are meant only to demonstrate the general differences between modules, shelf depth, and aisle width. Finally, nothing is factored in for required oversized shelving.

Given the caveats, it is clear that as the number of range aisles per column bay increases, the efficiency of the space also increases. With 10-in. (0.254-m) shelving, a seven-range bay is 5.62 percent more efficient than a four-range bay. It is also clear that as the standard shelving depth increases, the efficiency of deployment for standard shelving goes down. With five-range bays, 10 in. (0.254 m) is 7.1 percent more efficient than 12-in. (0.305-m) shelving. Finally, going from 36-in. (0.914-m) to 44-in. (1.118-m) range aisles, using the example for 12-in. shelving and six ranges per bay, results in an efficiency loss of 13.69 percent. For a large stack area, these differences can be significant, and they can be seriously aggravated by a module that wastes space.

To calculate the exact ideal module, the planner must know the exact dimension of the shelving (or an allowance to be accepted) and the required clear width of the range aisle. Shelving dimensions can vary by an inch or more from one manufacturer to another, and range aisle width may be established by code. Narrower shelving is possible and used in many libraries, the most common being 9-in. shelving, but where ranges are bolted to the floor for seismic bracing,

TABLE 12.1 **Modules based on range aisle widths meeting access and some code requirements, and allowing for modest growth in the range size from face to face. Note that this table is based upon a series of sketches similar to those shown in fig. 12.2. This table differs from past module discussions because it is based upon range aisles and shelf depth, rather than the length of sections, which has traditionally been used to establish modules.**

Number of Ranges	Range Aisle Width		Nominal Shelving Depth		Square Module Size		Area of Plot		Number of Single-faced Sections	Area per Section	
	inches	m	inches	mm	ft	m	ft²	m²		ft²	m²
4	44	1.118	9	229	21.00	6.401	2,660	247.1	268	9.93	0.922
5	44	1.118	9	229	26.25	8.001	3,325	308.9	336	9.90	0.919
6	44	1.118	9	229	31.50	9.601	3,990	370.7	408	9.78	0.909
7	44	1.118	9	229	36.75	11.201	4,655	432.5	478	9.74	0.905
4	44	1.118	10	254	21.67	6.604	2,744	255.0	266	10.32	0.959
5	44	1.118	10	254	27.08	8.255	3,431	318.7	340	10.09	0.937
6	44	1.118	10	254	32.50	9.906	4,117	382.5	410	10.04	0.933
7	44	1.118	10	254	37.92	11.557	4,803	446.2	480	10.01	0.930
4	44	1.118	12	305	23.00	7.010	2,913	270.7	264	11.04	1.025
5	44	1.118	12	305	28.75	8.763	3,642	338.3	338	10.77	1.001
6	44	1.118	12	305	34.50	10.516	4,370	406.0	408	10.71	0.995
7	44	1.118	12	305	40.25	12.268	5,098	473.7	482	10.58	0.983
4	36	0.914	9	229	18.33	5.588	2,322	215.7	260	8.93	0.830
5	36	0.914	9	229	22.92	6.985	2,903	269.7	334	8.69	0.807
6	36	0.914	9	229	27.50	8.382	3,483	323.6	406	8.58	0.797
7	36	0.914	9	229	32.08	9.779	4,064	377.5	480	8.47	0.787
4	36	0.914	10	254	19.00	5.791	2,407	223.6	262	9.19	0.853
5	36	0.914	10	254	23.75	7.239	3,008	279.5	338	8.90	0.827
6	36	0.914	10	254	28.50	8.687	3,610	335.4	410	8.80	0.818
7	36	0.914	10	254	33.25	10.135	4,212	391.3	482	8.74	0.812
4	36	0.914	12	305	20.33	6.198	2,576	239.3	264	9.76	0.906
5	36	0.914	12	305	25.42	7.747	3,219	299.1	336	9.58	0.890
6	36	0.914	12	305	30.50	9.296	3,863	358.9	410	9.42	0.875
7	36	0.914	12	305	35.58	10.846	4,507	418.7	482	9.35	0.869

10-in. base shelves are generally considered minimum. Much deeper shelving is desired for archival and manuscript storage; 15-in. (381-mm) by 42-in. (1.067-m) shelves are common. Other shelving dimensions may be appropriate for a particular collection.

Where range aisle width is not established by code, narrower range aisles can be considered. In the discussion that follows, the square structural modules are determined by the length of the section rather than by the combination of the aisle space and depth of the section; greater efficiency than illustrated can be achieved with this approach, but for the most part, this is only possible outside the United States or in circumstances where code authorities are willing to accept a variance (which will be rare).

Perhaps the most common module used in libraries based upon the standard 3-ft (914-mm) length of library shelving has been 22 ft 6 in. × 22 ft 6 in. (6.858 × 6.858 m), with columns preferably no more than 14 in. (356 mm) in diameter or square. This allows five stack ranges in a bay if they are placed 4 ft 6 in. (1.372 m) on center and room for seven 3-ft (914-mm) sections in each range between columns. In this configuration, the range aisle will be about 35 in. (0.889 m) with 9-in. (0.229-m) nominal shelving or 33 in. (0.838 m) with 10-in. (0.254-m) shelving. Narrower shelving is possible and has been used, but, for most collections, the results will be a measurable increase in the number of items that are either shelved on oversized shelving, or the number of items projecting into the aisle. Of course, if the

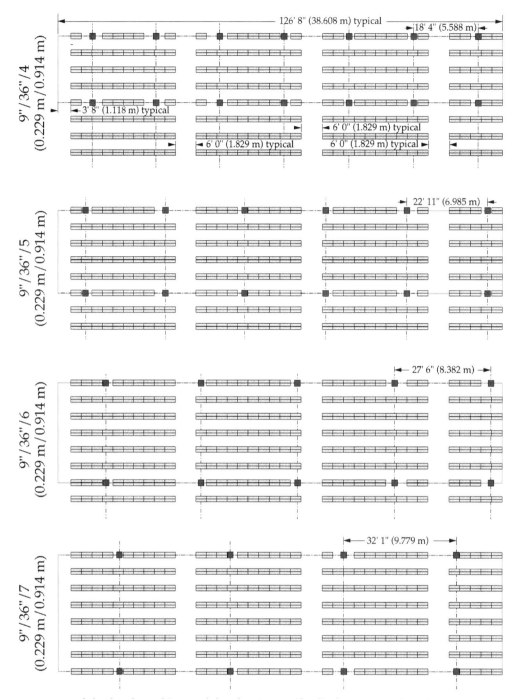

FIGURE 12.2   **Module sketches. This set of sketches is specifically for range aisles of 36 in. (0.914 m) and shelves nominally 9 in. (0.229 m) in depth. The shelving arrangement, except for columns, is the same in each model; the columns have been moved to account for the cross aisles and to minimize the required removal of shelving. Increased efficiency is possible with the addition of shelving of different dimensions or, in a few cases, by moving some shelving. An inch (25 mm) has been added to the overall range thickness to account for error and minor differences in manufactured dimensions; if the planner is certain exact dimensions can be maintained, or that the code authority will not be a stickler for precise dimensional clearance, then that added inch might be saved. However, if there is doubt, it will be safer to include the added inch.**

Similar sketches can easily be prepared for other dimensions and assumptions; some additional dimensional possibilities are included in table 12.1.

standard stack section is 1.00 m in length, the bay size would be more like 7.40 m, which would give a range spacing of 4 ft 10 in. (1.473 m) on centers, which would be wasteful in some libraries.

Similar logic suggests that a bay size accommodating eight sections between columns up to 21 in. (533 mm) square requires spacing of 26 ft (7.925 m), while a similar bay with 14-in. (356-mm) columns requires only 25 ft 6 in. (7.772 m). Here the range spacing would be 4 ft 4 in. or 4 ft 3 in. (1.321 or 1.295 m), depending on the column size, and the resulting range aisle will be proportionately narrower. This is good spacing where allowed for a middle-sized university with a collection of over 500,000 volumes and a relatively small number of students, not more than 5,000 for instance, or for a larger university with access to the stack limited to faculty and graduate students.

If the shelves are 39 in. (1 m) in length and the space required for the column and range ends is limited to 19.5 in. (5.918 m), the bay size for a similar number of sections would obviously be 27 ft 11 in. (8.509 m), which is sufficient to handle six ranges at 4 ft 8 in. (1.423 m) on center, or seven ranges at about 4 ft (1.219 m) on center. The latter would only be suitable in a closed stack or a storage facility with light use.

It can be seen that as the section length increases from 3 ft to 1 m, the aisle space also increases, all other things being equal, which may suggest somewhat different modules in terms of the numbers of standard sections held between columns for the two measuring systems given similar anticipated use.

The decision in regard to bay sizes for bookstacks might seem to be easier and simpler to make than that for reading areas, because, in general, one part of the bookstack differs from another less than one reading area from another. Taken as a whole, however, it is the most complicated of the module-size problems, because of the possibility, and often the desirability, of different depths of shelving and widths of aisle in different parts of the stack. If these variations do not exist, multitier fixed stacks, discussed in Chapter 6, are an option and might be preferable.

The following 10 points should be kept in mind, and it is desirable to delay the final decision until the effect of each on the whole has been considered. This does not mean that the architect must wait for the best solution of all 10 to be reached before work is begun. The process of making rough sketches will be started early in the design to show the possible effect of the decisions made later on the different points and on other areas of the building. It is hoped that this section will help both the architect and the librarian decide what to do. Here, as elsewhere, compromises will inevitably have to be made.

The 10 points are:

1. The size and shape of the supporting columns
2. Arrangements for housing ventilating, mechanical, and wiring services
3. The length of each stack section
4. The length of the stack ranges between cross aisles
5. The design of the shelving upright or columns, and providing for error in the layout
6. The depth of shelves and ranges, and width of the stack aisles between ranges
7. The width of the main and cross aisles
8. The direction in which the stacks run, now or later
9. The clear ceiling heights
10. The type of lighting

Because these conditions are strongly interrelated, we emphasize that column spacing should be decided with all 10 points in mind.

1. *Column sizes.* The size of the columns in a library building depends on: (a) technical requirements based on the loads to be carried and their height; (b) the type of construction; (c) whether they enclose heating and ventilation services; and (d) their shape. The larger the bay size and the greater the overall height of the building, the larger the columns will be.

Older library buildings were supported not by columns but by load-bearing walls, both external and internal, except for the concentrated book storage area in multitier stacks, where the section uprights supported all the stack levels above, and sometimes, in addition, the top floor, which was used for other than book-storage purposes, as in the Widener Library at Harvard and the New York Public Library central building. The section uprights may support the roof also if stacks go up to it. Multitier stacks are still used and, in most but not all cases, will be somewhat less expensive than freestanding stacks. The latter are recommended in most cases because of the flexibility they provide.

It should be noted that the size of the columns is of importance anywhere in a library, because the larger they are the more they tend to get in the way of activities, services, and equipment. The effect on seating arrangements and other facilities is dealt with in Section 12.5. It is obvious that the columns in a bookstack should always come in the line of the stack ranges, not in between where they would partly or completely block the aisles. It is also evident that if the column is thicker through than the book range, it will partially block an aisle and get into the way of the readers, staff, and book trucks passing through the ranges. This means that the first requirement, if it can be managed, is to keep the columns no wider than the ranges. (See fig. 12.3.)

a. *Weight-bearing requirements.* The heavier the weight to be carried by the columns, other things being equal, the larger the column must be. The weight to be carried includes the dead load (the floors themselves) and the live load (the equipment, books, and persons that the floors may support). In earthquake country the lateral loads caused by the horizontal movement of the ground are sometimes partially carried by the columns, although a specially designed wall, called a shear wall, usually does most of the work of handling this type of load. The vertical weight and the amount of lateral force that must be resisted, of course, depend largely on the size of the bay.

The architect and engineers should understand the weight requirements and provide for them. Building codes always require a safety margin. If construction provides for 150 pounds live load per square foot (7.182 kN/m^2) throughout all parts of the library, the floors will hold anything required of them with few exceptions. If bay sizes get much beyond 25 to 27 ft (7.620 to 8.230 m) in each direction, the column dimensions and floor thickness may have to be increased and the cost of construction tends to rise correspondingly. If flexibility is desired—and in most cases it should be—it is suggested that the whole building be designed for 150-pound (7.182 kN/m^2) live loads. The extra cost will rarely be as much as 1 percent of the total cost of the finished building and its equipment.

b. *Type of column construction.* Columns are generally of reinforced concrete or of steel cov-

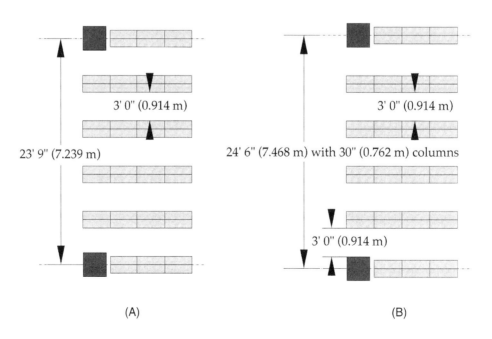

(A)   (B)

FIGURE 12.3   Columns wider than the ranges. Columns in a bookstack should always be in line with the ranges and not so large as to project into a stack or cross aisle as they do here. Where the range aisle width is the minimum acceptable, either the condition as illustrated simply does not work (A), or the module must be increased to account for wider columns (B), resulting in less-efficient space use. Even without dimensional problems, they present a fixed obstacle in a traffic artery that sooner or later will be bumped.

ered with concrete or vermiculite for fire protection. Occasionally heavy timber or pipe columns may be used, although they are rare in institutional buildings. Building codes generally forbid the use of steel alone unless protected by concrete because fire can cause steel to buckle. It may be impossible to hold a reinforced-concrete column to the desired size of 14 in. (356 mm) in diameter or square if a large bay size is selected or if there is a multistory stack. A reinforced-concrete column takes more space than a steel column protected by concrete, but almost always costs less. Types of column construction and arrangements for services in them are shown in figure 12.4.

Where the dimension between column faces is critical, it is best to use 14-in. and 32-in. (356-mm and 813-mm) columns instead of 18- and 36-in. (457-mm and 914-mm) because they leave a margin of 2 full in. (51 mm) on each side to provide for irregularities that occasionally appear in column sizes and for the end upright and a finished end panel of the bookstacks if one is used. It should be noted, however, that 14 in. (356 mm) is not critical; 16 or 18—even 20 in.—(406

mm or 457 mm, even 508 mm) is suitable where 10-in. (254-mm) shelving is used. But these larger dimensions will affect column spacing, and they may require odd-sized shelving, which, after all, is a workable though slightly less convenient solution.

c. *The shape of the column.* Should the columns be square (or perhaps round) so that the ranges can be turned in either direction? Or should they be rectangular, longer in the direction of the ranges so that they can be large enough to carry the required weight (and, if desired, other building services) and yet not interfere with the aisles? The question of range direction will be discussed under point 8 below. The columns, with occasional exceptions, should be square or round if the ranges are to run in different directions in different parts of the bookstack now or later, because, as already shown in fig. 12.3, they must be no wider than the ranges.

A rectangular column occupying the space of a standard section of shelves has the advantage of making all ranges, whether they contain columns or not, end at the same line without the use of odd-length sections. With rectangular columns,

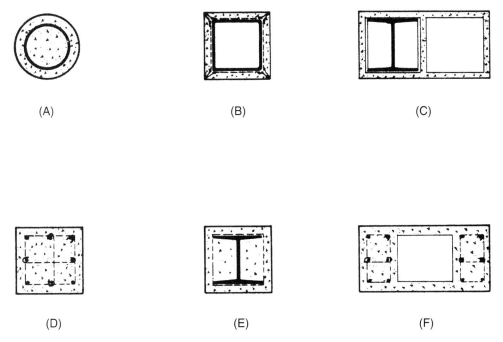

(A)   (B)   (C)

(D)   (E)   (F)

FIGURE 12.4   Types of column construction. (A) Lally column; (B) hollow steel column protected by concrete with services in center; (C) divided column with left-hand section of reinforced concrete or steel protected by concrete, and the right-hand section enclosing a duct for services protected by reinforced concrete; (D) reinforced concrete column; (E) steel column protected by concrete; (F) column similar to D with duct in center. Because of the way beams come into columns at the structural floor, it may be a bit of a trick actually to use the column for services, though it has been done.

it may also be possible to have cross aisles at the end of any section instead of only after two 14-to-16-in. (356-to-406-mm) columns are included in a range. (Because it takes two such columns to occupy the space of one section, there must be two of them in a range if the measurements are to come out even.)

One other comment about the shape of columns is pertinent. Often a circular column is cheaper than a rectangular one, and in some places it will look better. In a bookstack either shape will leave spaces that are difficult to keep clean unless fillers are used to cover the gaps.

Corners of rectangular columns are particularly vulnerable to bumping and disfiguration. Any column covered by plaster, whether it be round, square, or rectangular, is impractical in an exposed position, adjacent to a traffic artery of any kind, unless it is protected in some way. It can be covered with plastic cloth, sheet rubber, or even noncorrosive metal protecting surfaces up to the height of a book truck, if not higher. A wide base, which may protect it from most collisions, may be a hazard in other ways. Columns may be unfinished amidst bookstacks and be specially covered in public areas for improved appearance. For instance, the Cooper Library of the University of South Carolina has columns in public areas faced with wood and the vertical corners protected with bronze-colored metal protection. Such treatment can add as much as an inch (25 mm) to the width of a column, and this may be important in detailing layouts of furniture in public spaces.

The problem of column sizes might be summed up by saying that they can be square, rectangular, or round. A square or round column will not get in the way of stack ranges if it is no greater in dimension than the depth of the ranges, and it results in greater flexibility than a rectangular column displacing single- or double-faced sections. In practice, each rectangular column will probably take the space of a double-faced stack section in each bay, whereas a square or a round one may well occupy only one-half that amount of floor space and can thereby make available the equivalent of one additional single-faced section of shelving in many bays. If rectangular columns are used, the direction of the stack ranges cannot be changed later without loss of space. The bay sizes also are affected because in this case, as shown in fig. 12.5, they should be multiples of a standard stack section—not of a standard section

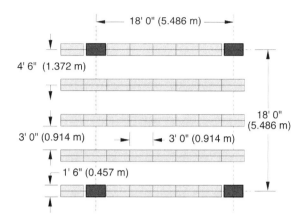

FIGURE 12.5   Effect of long rectangular columns on bay sizes. The capacity is reduced by two sections instead of one in each bay. The ranges all come out even. The dimensions between column centers should be a multiple of the shelving length, not the shelving length plus a half section (in this case, a multiple of 3 ft, not 3 ft plus 1½ ft).

plus a half section (as shown in figs. 12.6, 12.7, and elsewhere).

It is sometimes possible to reduce the size of most of a column by making it expand near the ceiling. This will not cause trouble except in a bookstack with shelving going all the way to the ceiling. It is not completely impossible to have columns that project into aisles, particularly if codes do not require a larger width, if the stack is little used by the public, and if the aisles beside them are wide enough to permit passing; but, as will be shown in point 6 below, every inch (25 mm) added to a typical stack aisle reduces stack capacity by approximately 2 percent. The additional cost of a steel column protected by concrete (beyond the cost of reinforced concrete) may be less than the value of the space lost by widening stack shelving, so that the columns will not project into the aisles, or by widening the aisles, to make the projecting columns less dangerous to the users and the equipment.

A further statement relating to column sizes and their effect on column spacing is presented after the other factors that determine module sizes have been discussed.

2. Arrangement for housing services. Another factor closely related to column sizes deals with whether they are to include heating and ventilating ducts. Angus Snead Macdonald recommended

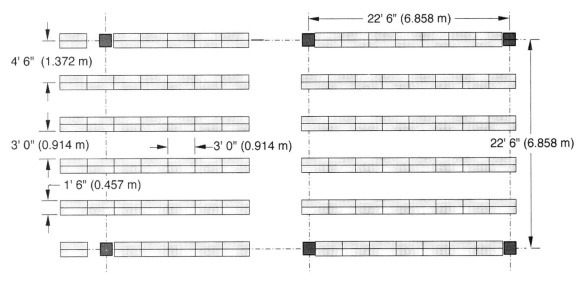

FIGURE 12.6 Column spacing 22 ft 6 in. × 22 ft 6 in. (6.858 × 6.858 m) with 15-in. (0.381-m) columns and standard shelving provides a very efficient arrangement (especially as shown to the right of this illustration). However, the next bay of shelving to the left (or right) is somewhat less efficient, depending upon the particulars of the layout. To be clear about the efficiency of any module for anything but a small library, more than one structural bay must be considered.

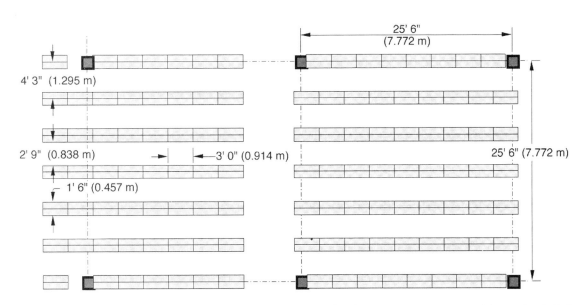

FIGURE 12.7 A column spacing module 25 ft 6 in. × 25 ft 6 in. (7.772 × 7.772 m) with standard shelving provides a very efficient arrangement as illustrated. Although this module has been used in many libraries, it does not meet the minimal ADA requirement of a 36-in. (0.914-m) range aisle. This module works better where 10-in. (254-mm) shelving is required, and with one less range between the columns. As in fig. 12.6, the true efficiency requires consideration of more than one bay.

that these services be placed in the center of hollow steel columns, thereby taking little or no space that could be used for other purposes and making the services available in each bay or even in each corner of each bay. Most building codes forbid this use of columns because of the fire hazard it would present.

Types C and F in figure 12.4 require more space than do A, B, D, and E and will necessitate more than 14 in. (356 mm) in at least one direction. Type D may also if the number of levels is more than four. In many cases 32 in. (813 mm) overall the long way should be sufficient for C and F, although at least one library has columns that include ducts and have a long dimension of almost 6 ft (1.829 m). If 15 in. (381 mm) or, better still, 14 in. (356 mm) proves impossible, 32 to 34 in. (813 to 864 mm) is a convenient length in the direction of the book ranges, because the column then takes the place of one 3-ft (914-mm) stack section, and irregular-length shelf sections are avoided.

Remember that if ducts are largely vertical, whether in the columns or elsewhere, they take only a comparatively small amount of square footage; whereas if they are horizontal, they require deeper spaces between a ceiling and the floor above, which, in some libraries, have been up to 5 ft. (1.524 m) thick overall. These very deep interstitial spaces enable the engineer to run the ducts any place desired without careful planning, but they take a tremendous amount of expensive cubage and, in addition, may make a multistory building considerably taller than is necessary. This result will be good or bad architecturally as the case may be. Of course, where the new facility is an addition, a key factor will be the floor levels of the existing structure and minimizing the number of ramps. The best method of dealing with ducts may therefore be determined without much further thought.

3. *The length of each stack section.* In many parts of the world, the standard section will be 3 ft, or 914 mm, nominally on centers; in other areas shelving of 1 m (about 3¼ ft) on centers may be the standard. The actual length of the shelf will be about ¾ in. (19 mm) less than the center-to-center measure, although this dimension loss will vary from 2 in. (51 mm) to as little as ½ in. (13 mm) depending on the manufacturer and the type of shelving. The amount is a key factor if it is anticipated that there will be a mix of existing and new shelves, as the shelves themselves may

not be interchangeable between manufacturers. It should also be noted that the difference between a 2-in. and a ½-in. space loss for a 3-ft nominal shelf can represent more than a 4 percent difference in shelving capacity, which is not insignificant. As discussed in Chapter 6, other shelf lengths are possible. With a structural column size selected to be about 2 in. (50 mm) less than one-half of the standard section, two columns take the space of one section, and, with the clear space between the columns being a multiple of the standard section plus "growth" space discussed in point 5 below, there will be practically no waste space. The ranges will come out even with those where there are no columns, as shown in figs. 12.6 and 12.7.

There is one difficulty with this proposal, however. The main cross aisles tend to be limited to a few widths, and no one of them may be just right. This problem will be discussed under point 7 below.

These problems can be simplified if the library is ready to accept odd-length sections when they are required by the column spacing. A 14-in. (356-mm) column may require an 18-in. (457-mm) shelf section to fill out the range. There is nothing impossible about this arrangement. However, an 18-in. (457-mm) section may cost about as much as a 36-in. (914-mm) one, and it complicates planning for shifts of books. It is sometimes advisable to fill out the range, which is 18 in. (457 mm) or less too short because of one square or round column, by hanging a lectern from the end of the last stack section and thus providing a convenient stand-up reading accommodation for persons examining books at the nearby shelves. (See fig. 12.8.) Alternatively, a set of low shelves or a bin of appropriate size can be placed there to receive books used in the stack that are ready for reshelving. This should generally be done in the column ranges only, as a lectern is rarely worthwhile at the end of more than one range in a bay. But the important point to note here is that, if possible, the distance between columns should be an exact multiple of the shelf section length plus extra space for stack uprights.

4. *The length of the ranges.* There are several problems in connection with range lengths. The first is a question of what length ranges can be permitted without undue inconvenience to the reader and staff. This matter is discussed in Chapter 6. It is sufficient here to say that: (a) range

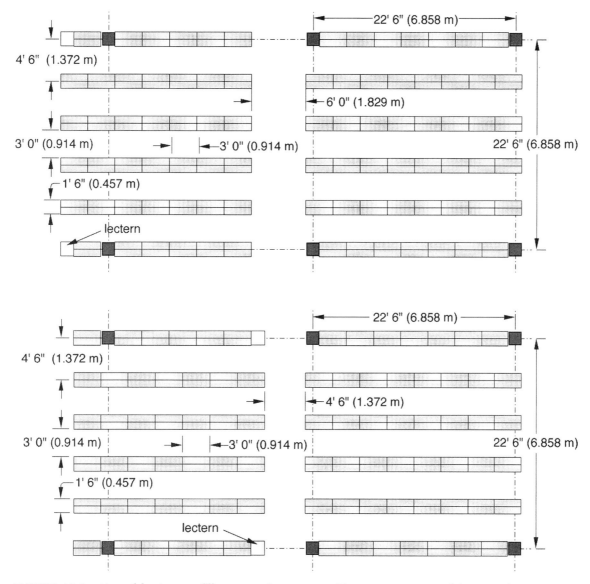

FIGURE 12.8 Use of lectern to fill out a column range. Two arrangements of lectern placement are shown with their effect upon the main cross aisle. While 1 ft 6 in. (0.457 m) is reserved for columns here, the column itself should not be more than 15 in. (0.381 m) in order to provide space for stack uprights, shelving growth, and a margin for irregularities.

lengths should vary with circumstances; (b) ranges longer than those that have been considered standard are possible, particularly in large installations where the use is light; (c) long ranges may increase total stack capacity up to 10 percent or more; and (d) other things being equal, the longer the range or the heavier the use, the wider the stack aisle should be.

A second problem, which deals with column sizes, was discussed under point 1 above, where it was stated that if column size in the direction of the range is 14 to 16 in. (356 to 406 mm) and the range, before a cross aisle is reached, includes two columns, it will not interfere with the cross aisle.

The third problem is that if the module size is based on the distance between columns and hence is a multiple of the standard section, the width of cross aisles will also normally be a similar multiple, that is 3, 6, or 9 ft for 3-ft (914-mm) shelving, or 1, 2, or 3 m for shelving 1 m long. This is dealt with in point 7 below.

5. *The design of the shelving upright or columns, and providing for error in the layout.* Though this has been discussed earlier, it is of such importance as to warrant further mention. Certain manufacturers construct standard library shelving units with a structural frame that is the exact measure of the shelving module. With this type of construction, the exact length of a range should be an exact multiple of the shelving unit, and the clear space provided between the columns needs to be only slightly more than this exact dimension. However, if there is any gap between adjoining sections, such as might occur where gusset plates are installed between the sections, there will be "growth" in the length of the range. For a range of eight sections, this could easily amount to an inch (25 mm) or more, a factor which, if not provided for, can result in considerable frustration when it is time to install the shelving.

The so-called growth is also a factor with commercial or industrial shelving, discussed in Chapter 6 in detail. With this shelving, the growth factor is considerably larger. Even where shelving units are made up of "starters" and "adders," as is the case with much standard library shelving, the projection of the shelf uprights at the ends of the range must be accounted for. In this case, 2 in. (51 mm) is not an uncommon dimension that must be added to the multiple of standard units.

Finally, construction techniques are never absolutely exact, and where a standard manufactured product must fit between structural members, it is only prudent to allow a small dimension for error. For standard library shelving, it is suggested that the clear space between columns ideally should be 4 in. (102 mm) greater than the multiple of standard shelving units, and that for commercial or industrial shelving, this dimensional requirement should be greater, depending upon the range length.

6. *The depth of shelving and width of stack aisles.* On first thought one might fail to see why the bay sizes are affected by the shelf depth or, for that matter, the stack-aisle width. But they are, and affected greatly, especially where minimum range aisles are specified by law. This occurs because if space is to be used to advantage, the distance between columns should be an exact multiple of the distance from the center of one range to the center of the next, and this distance should be determined by two things: the optimum depth from front to back of each range and the optimum width of the aisles. Figure 12.9 shows the results when this rule is not followed. Many stack layouts have been unsatisfactory and uneconomical because this necessity has not been kept in mind in deciding on the column spacing. The question of range depth and aisle widths is considered further in Chapter 6.

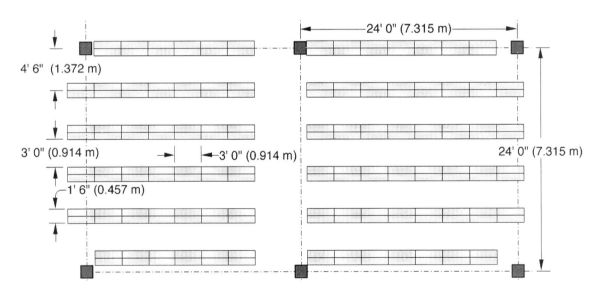

FIGURE 12.9   Columns and minimal range spacing fail to mesh. Clearly this module could accommodate wider shelving (10 in. or 254 mm deep) or wider range aisles and work better, though gaps would remain in the ranges along the column lines. Where minimal spacing and 9-in. (229-mm) shelving is the goal, this module does not work.

In libraries with comparatively small collections but with large numbers of students and faculty using open-access shelves, 3-ft. (914-mm) wide stack aisles are indicated, and ranges 4 ft 6 in. (1.372 m) on centers might be called standard. It should be noted that these dimensions assume an exact 18-in. (457-mm) dimension from face to face of the shelving; many shelving manufacturers do not provide this exact dimension. This becomes a problem only where code-mandated minimum aisle width is sought. Any aisle width of up to 5 or even 6 ft (1.524 or 1.829 m) may be desirable in locations where reference books or other very heavily used collections are stored. Note that if range aisles are to be finished with precut carpet tiles, it may be desirable to choose an aisle width between base plates that is an exact multiple of dimensions for squares on the market. The dimensions of such tiles will vary from time to time and with manufacturers, but in the United States, 18 in. (457 mm) is common today.

In a stack designed around 3-ft (914-mm) standard sections and ranges 4 ft 3 in. (1.295 m) on centers (with a range 16 or 18 in., 406 mm or 457 mm) deep and with a 35- or 33-in. (889- or 838-mm) stack-aisle width, the bay sizes can be 25 ft 6 in. (7.772 m), with six ranges installed in each bay and, in the other direction, eight standard sections between columns. (See fig. 12.7.) A bay of this size has a further advantage. If more compact storage is required later, seven ranges can be placed in a bay instead of six, giving 3 ft 7⅝ in. (1.108 m) from center to center, which is fairly comfortable and certainly possible in the case of little-used material with closed access. On the other hand, with this same bay, it is possible to use only five ranges 5 ft 1 in. (1.550 m) on centers, a useful arrangement in a heavily used section or for oversized books on deeper than standard shelves, or where the law requires a 36-in. (0.914-m) range aisle and 12-in. (305-mm) shelving is planned. In the case of reference books in a reading room or of a newspaper stack, four ranges can be installed, giving 6 ft 4 in. (1.930 m) on centers with this column spacing.

A smaller size bay that fits many stack situations with 3-ft (914-mm) sections and one that has probably been used more than any other in libraries constructed in recent years is 22 ft 6 in. (6.858 m) in each direction. (See fig. 12.6.) This is the next possible square bay that is smaller than 25 ft 6 in. (7.772 m) and is a multiple of 3 ft plus

1½ ft. It gives approximately 6 percent less capacity per square foot because the ranges will be 4 ft 6 in. (1.372 m) on centers, instead of 4 ft 3 in. (1.295 m). It will make possible an increase from five to six ranges, which will be 3 ft 9 in. (1.143 m) on centers, if at a later time more compact storage is desired, or a decrease to four ranges 5 ft 7 in. (1.702 m) on centers for reference books or in other heavily used sections. Other possible bay sizes will be considered later in this chapter.

It should be repeated here that unless the range spacing is changed correspondingly, an increase of 1 in. (25 mm) in double-faced range depth decreases the aisle width a similar amount or decreases the stack capacity, provided one assumes that the ranges would be placed on closer centers if the shelving was narrower. In this case, the difference of 1 in. results in a potential savings of 2 percent in the construction cost for the stack area. However, it may not be desirable or, in many cases, legal to save the 2 percent and have crowded conditions.

7. *The width of the main and subsidiary cross aisles.* Here a problem arises in a modular stack that can be avoided in a multitier stack. In a multitier stack it is possible to arrange for aisles of any width desired, so long as those above and below use the same layout. They can be found from as narrow as 2 ft 6 in. (762 mm) or even less for a subsidiary or side cross aisle up to 6 or even 7 ft (1.829 or 2.134 m) for the main central aisle. But in a modular stack, if the plan is based on 3-ft stack sections and a multiple of 3 ft between columns, these aisles apparently must be 3, 6, or 9 ft (0.914, 1.829, or 2.743 m) wide or sections of a nonstandard length will be required. It seems obvious that 3 ft (0.914 m) minus the extra inches occupied by the adjacent uprights, although wide enough for a subsidiary aisle, will not be satisfactory for the main aisle of a heavily used stack. The current minimum typically in the United States is an aisle of 44 in. (1.118 m) clear. Six feet (1.829 m) may be wider than necessary, although in a very large, heavily used stack it may be ideal. Needless aisle width will decrease capacity of adjacent bays. In other words, a 4 ft 6 in. (1.372 m) cross aisle in place of a 6 ft (1.829 m) one will, if the ranges are 30 ft (9.144 m) long, increase capacity by 2.5 percent. A 3-ft (914-mm) aisle would save another 2.5 percent, but, as already noted, it is not wide enough for a main cross aisle, although it will do very well for a secondary one that is comparatively little used

where legal minimum width is not a constraint. A width of one and one-half standard sections is entirely adequate, but ordinarily will not work out if the distance between columns is a multiple of a standard section. There are two possible remedies to this situation.

a. Make the distance between columns in the direction of the ranges multiples of standard sections plus one-half section in every other bay, and place the cross aisles in those bays as shown in fig. 12.10, but make no change in the column spacing in the other direction. Doing so does away with the advantageous square bay and flexibility suffers.

b. Use a lectern, or a book return shelf or bin, to fill out any column range that includes only one column. This will permit a main aisle a section and one-half wide, as shown in fig. 12.8.

8. *The direction in which stacks run.* If the column spacing is so designed that the stacks must always run in one direction, a certain amount of flexibility is lost. Is this serious? It may well be, particularly when portions of the stack are used for reading areas, and shelving meeting at right angles would be useful. If the bay is square, there is no reason why all the shelving in any bay should not be turned at will at right angles to that in other bays, except that it may affect both

the natural and artificial lighting and will probably necessitate replacement of the floor covering. (See point 10 below in connection with the lighting arrangements.) Also, in earthquake country, as well as elsewhere, there may be overhead bracing that must be changed. The architect and the librarian must decide whether the extra flexibility, made available by a square bay with its other advantages in economy, is worthwhile. In practice, shelving is almost never reoriented, and with code-established minimum aisle widths, the probability of reorientation is very small.

A stack with shelving all running in the same direction tends to make the traffic patterns simpler. Many librarians therefore prefer to have all main-stack shelving run in the same direction and find that, if a comparatively small amount of shelving is wanted in other areas with a different orientation, it can well have different range spacing and that at worst the book capacity lost is negligible.

It should be noted that a stack range parallel and adjacent to an outside wall is undesirable if that wall has windows and is so oriented that the ultraviolet rays of the sun reach books. And book ranges should not extend at right angles from a wall next to windows; if ranges extend to any wall, they should do so only to a wall with-

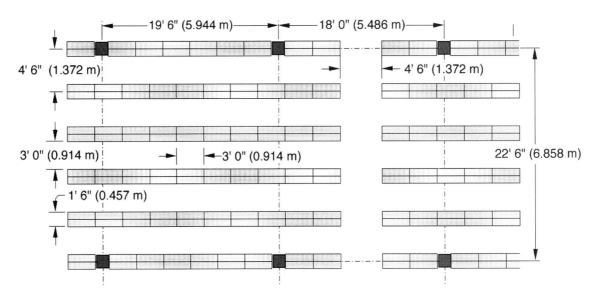

FIGURE 12.10 Mixed column modules can be used to control the width of the cross aisle. This figure shows that if the distance between columns is changed or staggered in the direction of the ranges, with every other row of columns one-half section farther apart or closer together than the next bay, main aisles equal to one and one-half sections become possible instead of an aisle equal to one or two sections, but all bays will not be square or equal. If the ranges to the right stop before the next column line, the ends of the ranges can be filled out with one-half-width sections or lecterns, as shown in fig. 12.8.

out windows. Even bright natural light coming to book spines, with never any direct sunlight on the books, will rapidly fade bindings. This problem can be solved by changing the direction of stack ranges on that side of the building. But such a change may turn out to be a complicated affair, because it also changes the direction of the cross aisles and the traffic lanes. A row of carrels along the window wall and then an aisle may help to solve the problem without changing the range direction.

9. *Ceiling height.* The clear height of a stack level between the finished floor and the finished ceiling is a bay-size problem only indirectly, but it may be a matter of importance in connection with cubic footage in the building. The lowest ceiling that will permit seven shelves 12 in. (305 mm) apart on centers is just under 7 ft 6 in. (2.286 m). (See Section 6.1.9 for a full discussion.) But any space for shelving above 7 ft 6 in. (2.286 m) in the clear is useless for collections, except for semidead storage, because the top shelf will be 6 ft 4 in. (1.930 m) above the floor, and only a very tall person can reach it. Of course, where the code requires a full sprinkler system for the library, there may also be a requirement for at least 18 in. (0.457 m) clear vertical space between the sprinkler head and the storage of combustible materials.

A number of libraries have stack rooms 8 ft 4 in. or 8 ft 6 in. (2.540 or 2.590 m) in clear height, with room for inserting an extra shelf for storage or for shelving books in an auxiliary collection or in a superseded classification. Portable one-step stools would need to be within a short distance. This arrangement will, of course, increase the gross capacity by nearly 15 percent, but it may be confusing to the reader if it is in an open-access stack unless different-colored shelves and adequate signs inform readers. The extra height can also be useful for two purposes other than increasing book capacity. The first is discussed in the next paragraph. The second is that the additional height makes the space convertible for multiple-seating accommodations with pleasant room proportions.

10. *Lighting.* The effect of lighting in the determination of the size of a stack bay relates to ceiling heights and also to the number of fixtures to a bay and their spacing. In a modern bookstack, artificial light must be available in every stack aisle. Normally, the lighting is installed down the center of each aisle in lines parallel to the

ranges. If this practice is followed and if, at a later time, capacity is increased by providing an additional range in each bay, the wiring and fixtures must be changed. Or, if it is decided to turn the shelves at right angles for one reason or another, the lighting must also be changed if the ceiling height is only 7 ft 6 in. (2.286 m), which is an unusual circumstance.

If the clear height of the ceiling is 8 ft 4 in. or 8 ft 6 in. (2.540 or 2.590 m) or more and fluorescent lighting in long strips is used, it can be placed at right angles to the ranges, and the shelves will still be illuminated even if the range spacing changes. The library at John Carroll University in Cleveland and the Wellesley College Library are examples of this arrangement. However, such an arrangement removes the possibility of range aisle switching, which has become important as an energy conservation measure.

One rule: Never have ceiling fixtures in any part of a library located in line with the structural columns, where the stacks will run. That is an obvious error in stacks; it is also an error in public areas where stacks may someday need to be installed. A demonstration of that is in the 1980 Carpenter Library of the University of North Florida, a lesson to all.

In summation, the points above suggest the large number of variables in selecting a module. And the cost significance of small dimensions becomes clear when multiplied many times in a large bookstack. The Yale University Seeley G. Mudd Library of 1982 provides one example of attention to detail resulting in very high density in a traditional stack. In this instance octavos are on eight shelves per section with 23-in. (584-mm) aisles, 16 sections per range, and quartos on six shelves per section and a 25-in. (635-mm) aisle. The octavo shelves are 7 in. (178 mm) nominal depth, the quartos are 9 in. (229 mm). Under these arrangements studies showed that squatting to use bottom shelves and using a one-step stool for top shelves were reasonable, though the limits of convenience were strained. The Mudd Library basement provides higher ceilings so that octavos can in most places be nine shelves high, with 11 in. (279 mm) clear between the shelves. Because the sprinkler placement is less than the fire code requires, the stack has been classed "limited access."

This discussion of the 10 points that affect module sizes in a bookstack has brought out the interrelated problems involved, and shown that final decision on structural column spacing should be made after serious consideration. No one column spacing is suitable for all library stacks. The module selection can be even more of a problem in major renovation projects. This can be seen in the University of California, Berkeley, Bioscience and Natural Resources Library, a large and very efficient layout with shelving well matched to column spacing—except for four columns that are right in the middle of stack aisles.

12.3.3 The Module Size for Other Areas

Space for purposes other than concentrated book storage is seldom seriously affected by column spacing though it requires consideration. There may be some inconvenience if the areas required are larger in both directions than the bay size selected, as columns will be required in those areas instead of around the periphery. Likewise, bay sizes should be taken into account if there are numerous identical small units, such as enclosed carrels, dissertation rooms, faculty studies, or offices, that ought to fit evenly into the module if space is not to be wasted.

If the wrong bay size is selected, the areas so large that they may be affected by columns might include the following:

1. Large reading areas for any use, such as for reference collections, current periodicals, reserve books, public documents, divisional reading, maps, large special-subject rooms, and night-study areas
2. Public areas around service desks and the card catalog room
3. The processing room or rooms
4. Classrooms and auditoria; audiovisual rooms and library-school areas
5. Nonassignable space for lobbies, mechanical areas, and stairwells

Small areas that might cause difficulty because two or more of them should fit in between columns should not be forgotten. Faculty studies are a case in point.

Spacing problems in most of these areas can be resolved without difficulty. In open-stack libraries the tendency is away from large reading rooms; yet with the tremendous seating capacity still required in a large library, some problems may be unavoidable and deserve discussion. This will be particularly true in a closed-stack library, such as the independent research library or many university libraries found in Europe and elsewhere.

A reading room 18 ft (5.486 m) the short way (this is generally the smallest bay recommended) can be extended to 72 ft (21.946 m) in length through four bays without seeming to be completely out of proportion. With the larger bays—22½, 25½, and 27 ft (6.858, 7.772, and 8.230 m)—rooms 90, 102, and 108 ft (27.432, 31.090, and 32.918 m) in length, respectively, can be available without columns. If the room is next to the outside wall and additional width is wanted without a row of columns down the center, it can be obtained by cantilevering out beyond the last row of columns for 6 to 9 ft (say, 1.829 to 2.743 m) and widening the room in that way. Of course, the result will be a row of columns down one side of the room unless unusual structural tricks are contemplated (see below). On the other side, space for an aisle required under any circumstances can be included, making a room up to 30 ft (9.144 m) wide the narrow way with an 18-ft (5.486-m) column spacing and perhaps 42 (12.802 m) or more feet wide with a 27-ft. (8.230-m) column spacing.

There are at least five other methods of providing larger areas unbroken by columns:

1. Place the room on the top floor with no weight overhead except the roof, supported by special trusses. Interior columns can then be left out, as was done in the very large reference room at the Rutgers University Library.
2. Make the room high enough so that heavier beams can be used in the ceiling. As noted below (in Section 12.3.4, Problems Relating to Height, which discusses mezzanines), this decision will not necessarily require high rooms elsewhere on the same floor.
3. Make the column spacing narrower in one direction and so make possible a wider spacing in the other direction, as in the three large reading areas in the Lamont Library, which has 13 × 33 ft (3.962 × 10.058 m) column spacing.
4. Hang the upper part of the building from heavy roof beams, as was done at the Illinois Institute of Technology Library in Chicago.
5. Use one of the precast-concrete methods, which permit larger spans.

If a small bay size is used in a reading area and columns protrude into it, they may interfere with seating arrangements, particularly if long tables are used. Table sizes are discussed in Section 12.5, but remember that if tables are 4 ft wide and 12 ft long (1.219 × 3.658 m) or more, there should be an aisle at least 5 ft (1.524 m) wide between and parallel to them, in order to give comfortable access. It is important too that aisles adjacent to tables and at right angles to them should not be obstructed by columns. Ingenuity in preparing layouts ordinarily can overcome most difficulties without undue loss of valuable floor space.

Many university libraries and some colleges have circulation desks longer than the distance between columns. The size may be inconvenient if the column comes just in front of or behind the desk, as vision may be obstructed. A column dividing a desk into two is rarely satisfactory. Four comments may be useful and can also be applied to reference and information desk operations:

1. If possible, place the desk far enough in front of or behind the column line so that neither staff nor readers are bothered by it. A desk should have free space behind and in front of it without column interference.
2. Try to plan the service so that the space between the columns will be long enough for any desk required. Many desks, if the staff is effective and makes use of good housekeeping procedures, do not need as much space as is provided between columns in a 22½-ft (6.858-m) or larger bay. This should be even more evident as automated circulation systems are installed, provided they reduce the transaction time at the service point or permit distributed self-charging.
3. Plan a curved or L-shaped desk, which will be in one bay, not in two, but will thus provide the required extra length.
4. If no one of these methods is possible and work is so heavy that a longer desk is necessary, break the desk-work assignment into two. Use one part for the return of books and the other for charging, each in a different bay. Or use part for ready-reference or online catalog questions and the other for research queries. If the desks are adjacent, one person may be able to service both during quiet hours.

In a very large library it may be desirable to have an entrance lobby so large that a column will fall into it, but this ordinarily should not create a problem. The same is true in large staff areas, such as the catalog department.

Finally, stairwells should be considered. With the low ceiling heights now in use and with reasonably large bays, stairwells should not create a problem, unless they are monumental. Although this seldom occurs, if capacity requirements demand very wide stairs, one option is to wrap the stairs around the columns. If this solves the fitting of stairwell to bay, be careful not to have solid walls near a corner where people will turn and bump into one another.

Certain small areas should be given attention: walled-in areas for offices, studies, and enclosed carrels; reading alcoves combining shelving and reader accommodations; and individual seating, both for staff and readers. Reading alcoves present the most difficulty, but again, a little ingenuity should solve the problems. (See fig. 12.11.) Accessing the collections in alcoves is distracting to the readers, and the distribution of the collection becomes strung out and difficult to follow; some argue that this is not a good arrangement in most cases.

With any of the bay sizes recommended, such as 18, 22½, or 27 ft (5.486, 6.858, or 8.230 m, although these dimensions may vary with metric shelving or where the aisle space is critical), the chief librarian's office can be fitted in easily without column troubles. Two small offices can be placed in any of these sizes. They do not need to be square; for instance, a 9 × 12 ft (2.743 × 3.658 m) office has just about as much space as one 10 ft 5 in. × 10 ft 5 in. (3.175 × 3.175 m). But another problem arises. If these areas are adjacent to outside walls and the walls have windows, sizes must to a greater or lesser extent conform with the fenestration pattern. Window space for offices is at a premium. Consequently, in most cases, an office or a study or a closed carrel should use as little outside wall space as possible and reach back into the building far enough to provide the desired area.

If the column, particularly one on an outside wall, juts into a room, it may complicate matters for an office or study, and even more for a carrel, because the column size is a greater percentage of the area under consideration.

An 18-ft (5.486-m) bay will take care of one large office, two small ones, two adequate studies or three small ones, three good-sized closed carrels, or four open ones.

A 22½-ft (6.858-m) bay will provide outside wall space for two fine small offices or large

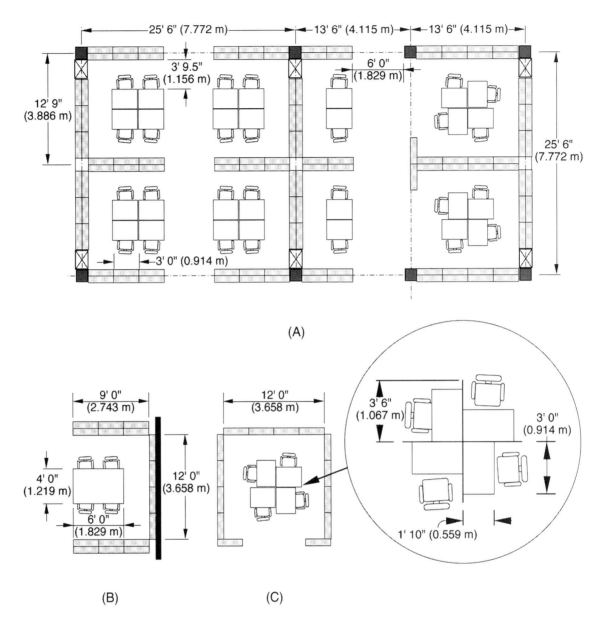

FIGURE 12.11   Tables in book alcoves: (A) tables for two to four persons, with partitions fitted in different column spacing; (B) standard table with no partitions; (C) nest of tables in pinwheel formation with partitions to give added privacy. Note that accommodation of ADA requirements will generally require greater space.

studies, three adequate studies, four good-sized closed carrels, or five open ones.

A 25½-ft (7.772-m) bay will provide for two fine offices, three minimum ones, three good-sized or four small studies, five closed carrels, or six open ones.

The extra 1½ ft (457 mm) provided by a 27-ft (8.230-m) bay will not provide any more offices, studies, or carrels than one 25½ ft (7.772 m).

Appendix B lists in tabular form recommended sizes for offices, studies, and carrels, both open and closed, and for reading alcoves.

12.3.4 Problems Relating to Height

The height selected directly affects construction costs. At least seven general factors influence the height of a building, which will in turn affect the structural system and arrangements considered in the early design phases of the project. These factors are:

1. Is the building project an addition that must relate to an existing facility?
2. How much clear height from floor to ceiling is desirable functionally and aesthetically in a library? How much is required to meet code, especially with fire sprinklers?
3. How thick should the floors be (from ceiling to floor level above)?
4. Are mezzanines desirable?
5. What considerations should be kept in mind when determining the preferable size and number of floor levels?
6. Do mechanical and electrical equipment affect height problems?
7. Do geologic conditions influence the height?

Each factor will be discussed, and the compounding effect of most of these factors should be recognized.

1. *Is the building project an addition that must relate to an existing facility?* The question of additions is discussed generally in Chapter 10. It should be noted that the floor-to-floor height in an older building, particularly one that depends upon natural ventilation for air circulation, often will be significantly higher than that required for a modern building. Matching the height of an original building, where the dimensions are inconsistent with modern construction techniques, might result in increasing the cost of an addition so much that little would be left of the savings that otherwise might result from the use of an old building.

Height greater than is necessary or desirable functionally and aesthetically costs money and should be questioned. On the other hand, the floor heights in old multitier stacks are often so low that a modern freestanding stack with thicker floors and more flexibility cannot be installed in the same vertical space. If floor heights do not match, the few steps up or down that must be added to allow passage between the old and new areas are inconvenient, and the constant transportation of books will present serious problems if not resolved without stairs.

Elevators that stop at half or partial levels can be considered, but their design is complex and their use awkward because they require two doors in the cab. Ramps may offer a better solution and they do have several advantages, yet they require a considerable amount of space. A typical ramp will be at a slope of 1 in 12 (this is the maximum slope allowed by the Americans with Disabilities Act for new construction); it takes little calculation to realize how quickly a large space may become devoted to such devices. A compromise may be considered where the main and second floors are designed to align with the existing structure while remaining floors are accommodated with some combination of ramps, stairs, elevators, and escalators.

2. *How much clear height from floor to ceiling is desirable functionally and aesthetically in a library?* Questions relating to the clear height of library areas are complex. It may be functionally desirable to use one level for many different purposes or for a single purpose, such as reading accommodations, as well as for rooms that differ in size. A height that is functional and economical may not be aesthetically satisfactory. Plans that make a library building satisfactory from the operational point of view are likely to call for areas on the same floor level that aesthetically as well as functionally differ widely in optimum height requirements.

An added complication arises from the fact that library needs may change as time goes on. Every effort should be made to provide a building in which practically all the space can be used to advantage for book storage, or for reader accommodations, or for staff. Ideally, the building should have heights throughout that are usable for all these purposes, without involving expensive building alterations when shifts are made from one function to another.

The problem of flexible space has always been difficult. To fully understand the influence on ceiling heights, noting a few twentieth-century historical conditions can help. Early in the century when one feature of a library was a monumental reading room, that room was at least 22½ ft (6.858 m) high in the clear. One of the first requisites in a reading room was natural light. To provide it in an area 35 to 40 ft (10.668 to 12.192 m) or more across required a room approximately two-thirds as high as it was wide, with large windows going practically to the ceiling. Skylights were also often thought to be necessary, and the main reading room was therefore sometimes placed on an upper floor. Its height went a long way toward providing more or less satisfactory ventilation, at least at standing and sitting height, because hot and polluted air tends to rise without the aid of forced ventilation, which was not generally available. A height of 22½ ft (6.858 m) or more made it possible to place in other parts of the same floor three levels of a multitier stack and thus avoid short flights of stairs.

Over 50 years ago, with better artificial light and forced ventilation available, it was found that the 22½-ft (6.858-m) ceiling height could be cut to 15 ft (4.572 m). This was done successfully in a large reading room at the University of Virginia Library in Charlottesville and was a surprise to many who had come to believe that the need for greater height went back primarily to a sense of proportion and not just light and ventilation.

But as time went on and building costs increased, as architects and interior designers learned how to effect changes in impressions of height, and as lower ceilings become customary in private homes, apartments, and office buildings, even lower heights were experimented with for reading areas of various sizes. More recently the cost of heating, cooling, and lighting a large space with expansive windows and perhaps a skylight have further argued for lower ceilings. Of course, skylights have their own special problems of heat, glare, leaks, and sunlight damage to the library materials.

The reading room on the fifth level of the Lamont Library is 131 × 31½ ft (40.000 × 9.600 m) in dimension. Because nothing but the roof is overhead, it was possible, without floor-level complications, to place the ceiling at any height that appeared aesthetically suitable. Requested to make the ceiling as low as he thought would be aesthetically desirable, the architect decided that 9½ ft (2.896 m) in the clear would be satisfactory if the room was partially divided into three equal areas, each nearly 44 × 32 ft (13.411 × 9.754 m), by open-slatted screens that were some 7 ft (2.134 m) high and 15 ft (4.572 m) long. This room has generally been regarded as a success, and though there are certain positions in it from which, looking down the full length, the ceiling seems rather low, little or no criticism has been heard.

At about the same time, the Firestone Library at Princeton was being planned, and it had been decided that a large part of its total area was to consist of three levels below the entrance floor to be used primarily for a bookstack. It was important to keep down the height of these levels if they were to have outside light. This was accomplished and made easier by the downward slope of the ground to the rear of the building and the construction of a waterless moat. The desirable height was complicated by the requirement of making, on the same levels, seminar and reading areas of at least two bays, making them 25 × 36 ft (7.620 × 10.973 m) in size. A mock-up was erected with an adjustable ceiling that could be cranked up and down. "Guinea pigs," including professors, administrators, students, and architects, as well as librarians, were assembled and asked to complain when the ceiling was lowered too far for comfort and appearance. The conclusion was reached that 8 ft 4 in. (2.540 m) in the clear would be adequate for reading and general-purpose areas as large as 25 × 36 ft (7.620 × 10.973 m). The decision made at Princeton has been accepted generally throughout the United States, and a minimum of 8 ft 4 in. (2.540 m) has been considered standard for small reading areas, if for other reasons no greater height seems desirable or necessary.

The University of Michigan Shapiro (Undergraduate) Library and the McKeldrin Library at Louisiana State University have very large reading areas with ceilings approximately 9 ft (2.743 m) in the clear. The planners have found that this height is satisfactory with the use of divider screens, recessed lighting, light-colored ceilings, and, when desired, space broken up by bookcases. It is suggested that librarians and architects perplexed by this problem visit libraries with low reading-area ceilings and talk with librarians and students about the results.

For large reading rooms, the above applies to the theoretical minimum satisfactory heights of fairly sizable areas. For smaller groups of individuals, ceilings of even less than 8 ft 4 in. (2.540 m) have been found to be possible and satisfactory. One mezzanine in the Lamont Library, which measures 91 × 45 ft (27.737 × 13.716 m), proved adequate for shelving 30,000 volumes and for seating 75 readers at individual tables and tables for four. It has a ceiling height of 8 ft (2.438 m). Another mezzanine of the same size has a ceiling height of 7 ft 9 in. (2.362 m). The latter height has proved adequate and satisfactory in a large mezzanine in the Georgia Institute of Technology Library. In the University of Iowa Library in Iowa City even larger areas have an 8-ft (2.438-m) ceiling. A height lower than 7 ft 9 in. (2.362 m) has been widely used for many years for individual seating in carrels and faculty studies adjacent to bookstacks.

Very low ceilings have been used in study space for a single person. The ceiling height of the

Widener stack area at Harvard is just over 7 ft 2 in. (2.184 m) in the clear, and some 400 open carrels—called "stalls," which is perhaps a better name for them—are in use, with no complication from the lack of height because the three-dimensional scale is comfortable and most have a window. A number of carrels are placed among the Amherst College bookstacks, but any fixture suspended from the 6 ft 9 in. (2.057-m) ceiling will become a problem for basketball players. This is true of 7 ft 2 in. (2.184-m) ceilings as well. Lower ceilings can be found, but they are not recommended. Indeed, they would not be allowed by many current codes.

Where the height is determined by stacks with fire sprinklers, the common requirement is that there be 18 in. (457 mm) clear between the books and the sprinkler heads. Assuming that books will not be above the height of the shelving (which can be questioned, especially if there are no canopy tops), then with standard library shelving at 7 ft 6 in. (2.286 m) high, the minimum ceiling height is thus 9 ft (2.743 m). Added height will be required where it is expected that the books will project above the top of the shelving or where compact shelving, commercial-type shelving sometimes used for music collections, or archival shelving is anticipated together with fire protection sprinklers.

To summarize: From the point of view of the comfort of the reader, aesthetics, and proportion, the above seems to indicate that a large reading room need not be more than 9 ft 6 in. (2.896 m), although this would be a minimum height if high-intensity, kiosk-type lighting fixtures are proposed to provide ambient light. With lighting in the ceiling and air conditioning, a 9-ft (2.743-m) height is possible if the room is broken up by bookcases or in other ways. A room 25 × 36 ft (7.620 × 10.973 m), which is large enough for up to 36 readers and 75 to 100 persons sitting in a conference is not unpleasant with an 8 ft 4 in. (2.540-m) ceiling if ventilation and lighting are adequate. With a smaller concentration of readers, 8 ft (2.438 m) or even 7 ft 9 in. (2.362 m) is enough for individual seating. To go below that to the figures that have been used in some libraries is to go below the height needed for economical book storage. It is suggested that the minimum height, except perhaps for storage spaces and doorways, should not be less than the height of standard shelving plus an inch or two (25 mm or 50 mm). In this regard, music libraries or archives that may use commercial- or industrial-type shelving to advantage may need somewhat higher ceilings.

What is the maximum desirable height for bookstacks? First, remember that any additional height increases cost without materially adding to capacity. The following figures cannot be considered definitive because conditions will vary, but it might be helpful to estimate that a 6-in. (152-mm) increase over a 7 ft 6 in. (2.286-m) height, while increasing cubage between the floor and ceiling by nearly 7 percent, will probably increase the square footage cost by less than 1.5 percent. So small an increase in height will not change the cost figures for equipment, ceilings, floors, doors, and furniture, or for lighting, although the last would be affected if there were any considerable increase in height. The extra cubage, of course, adds to the cost of both exterior and interior walls, of stairs, and of heating and ventilating, although it may also be helpful by facilitating the horizontal distribution of sprinkler lines and ventilation ducts where they are suspended below the ceiling.

The question then is whether or not the additional height is worth what it will cost. If 8 ft 6 in. (2.590 m) in the clear increases square-foot costs of the building by less than 3 percent, 9 ft (2.743 m) by 4 percent, 10 ft (3.048 m) by something like 6 or 7 percent, and so forth, the answer will depend upon what the extra height contributes aesthetically, or in capacity, comfort, and flexibility. As far as books are concerned, nothing is gained in capacity, unless an eighth shelf or compact shelving is installed. When it comes to flexibility, there are certain advantages resulting from the additional height. As has already been seen, a very few inches over 7 ft 6 in. (2.286 m) makes it possible to use space for multiple occupancy by readers.

What about height in areas used by the staff? Staff members are likely to be in the library longer hours than readers and should have more, rather than less, comfort, but in general the same rules apply to both. With good light and ventilation, a ceiling height of 7 ft 6 in. (2.286 m) will do in small areas if divided up by shelving or movable partitions. In the 1960s the Pennsylvania State University Library located processing staff on one of the stack levels where an additional 10 in. (254 mm) beyond its standard of 6 ft 8 in. (2.032 m) is provided. This is a multitier stack with the uprights every 9 ft (2.743 m) in each direction, instead of the more common 3 ft × 4 ft 6 in. (0.914 × 1.372 m). Of necessity, staff worked there for some years without serious complaint, but the arrangement is not recommended.

The greatest problem in connection with height comes when large reading areas are required on the same floor level with extensive book-storage areas. If the reading room is large enough to require a 10-ft (3.048-m) ceiling, and the ceiling adds 7 percent to the square-footage cost of the stack portion (or, let us say in order to be specific, $10 a square foot), it may increase the cost of the construction of 10,000 ft² (929 m²) of stack space by $100,000. This figure will, of course, vary according to local construction costs. The dilemma can sometimes be avoided to a large extent by deciding to keep large reading areas off levels with large book-storage areas, or by using mezzanine stacks where a greater height is required for the readers. The alternatives will be discussed later in this section.

One other point in connection with ceiling heights is a special concern in multitier stacks. If they are under 7 ft (2.134 m), tall persons going down staircases placed one above the other will bump their heads on the steps above. As heights increase, stairwells take more floor space.

Advantage can sometimes be taken of different requirements for different uses on the same floor. Ventilation ducts can sometimes run under the ceiling in a bookstack and leave greater heights in adjacent reading areas.

3. *How thick should the floor be from ceiling to floor level above?* The answer will depend on bay and module sizes, which are discussed in Section 12.3.1; on the weight to be carried and the type of construction, which is dealt with in Chapter 13; on what mechanical services a floor is to contain between the finished ceiling below and the finished floor above; and, last but not least, on the ingenuity of the mechanical and structural engineers and the care with which they work. These last·two points are discussed briefly here.

Other things being equal, the larger the bay size, the heavier the floor beams or flat slabs required, and the greater the thickness of the floors. If the plans provide for floors everywhere in the building on which bookstacks can be placed, something that should be required in most libraries, any bay size over 27 ft (8.230 m) square will tend to require more steel and extra thickness, which in turn takes additional cubage. Library floors that will hold bookstacks anywhere have been made with flat-slab construction no more than 8 in. (203 mm) thick and with bays 18

ft (5.486 m) square. With reinforced concrete slabs, the floors need be no more than 12 or 13 in. (305 mm or 330 mm) thick and with bays up to 27 ft (8.230 m) square if they do not have to provide space for ducts and pipes. These thicknesses are structural and do not include the finished floor or ceiling. Additional thickness will likely be required in earthquake country to resist lateral forces.

Space required for the utility services varies greatly. Pipes for steam and hot water without air-handling ducts and the main supply and drainpipes take little space. Some, but not all, wiring requires little in the way of additional thickness for floors. Telecommunications cabling will not in itself add height to a building, although microwave dishes placed on top of the building are another matter, as is discussed below. When an entire floor is devoted to media and computer use, the design may include extra inner-floor space for cabling distribution and this may increase the overall building height by up to 10 in. (254 mm). More commonly in libraries, where raised floors are required for ease of altering cable distribution, this is accomplished by inserting the false floor, thereby reducing the floor-to-ceiling distance, but not by raising the building height by that amount. (See also comments in Section 13.4.4.)

On the other hand, air ducts for heating, ventilation, and air conditioning involve much more required space. Complications always arise when air ducts have to cross each other. If the mechanical engineer is careless or lacks ingenuity, a floor thickness of 5 ft (1.524 m) or even more may be required to include the structural floor itself as well as space for ducts, for plumbing, and for recessing the lighting fixtures into the ceiling, something that is often desirable. It seems absurd, however, to use floors 5 ft (1.524 m) thick, and then reduce clear ceiling heights to perhaps as little as 8 ft (2.438 m). Too large a proportion goes into space, most of which is not used. Vertical runs and distribution of the ventilation take more floor space but often reduce total costs, if you take into account the additional height in the underfloor space required by horizontal runs for ventilation ducts. Clearly, this subject requires careful analysis by the architect and engineers.

4. *Are mezzanines desirable?* The answer to this question, like many, involves aesthetics, function, and cost. The excessively high ceilings of the past are no longer required functionally, and yet one should hesitate to plan a large library

building today with no room in it higher than strictly functional needs demand. A mezzanine over part of a level (typically no more than 33 percent to qualify for the code definition of a mezzanine) might make up for all or a large share of the extra cost of providing an area that would give the desired effect of greater spaciousness. As long as the added level is classified in the building code as a mezzanine, most codes will allow emergency exiting via the main floor.

If the formula suggested earlier (in the summary of factor 2 above) is assumed to be correct for comparative purposes, a floor 17 ft (5.182 m) high may cost some 20 percent more than one of a minimum height. If 75 percent of this floor has a mezzanine over it and only 25 percent of it is full height, the construction would add something like 5 percent to the construction cost of the floor as a whole. It should be noted, however, that many codes would regard a mezzanine of this size as a separate floor; exiting requirements thus are different than for a mezzanine as defined by the code. If the floor is not a mezzanine, there must be at least two protected routes of egress directly from that floor. If it is a mezzanine, egress may be via the floor below. Even so, in order to obtain one spacious room, this 5 percent addition might well be worthwhile. The cost comparisons are at best approximations and will differ, of course, in different places under different conditions; the architect should be asked to check them.

Let us see now what would happen if, instead of using a mezzanine over part of the floor, the whole floor were made 12 ft (3.658 m) high in the clear, one-fourth of it for a large reading area and the remainder for services that in the earlier plan were placed on or under the mezzanine. The increase in the cost of the whole area—using the same formula for cost approximation for increased height as before—would be about 10 percent, or 5 percent more than with the mezzanine arrangement. (The cost of the furniture and equipment on the mezzanines must not be forgotten.)

These percentages are simply rough estimates to illustrate the problem, but they indicate that if a mezzanine covers the major portion of a floor level and a clear height of 12 ft (3.658 m) or more is wanted for aesthetic reasons in at least one large reading area, it is not a luxury to go up to 16 or 17 ft (4.876 or 5.182 m) for the part without a mezzanine, if the area concerned is not too large. Angus Snead Macdonald once said that a

mezzanine, to be practical from the cost point of view, must occupy at least 60 percent of the floor area. The code implications mentioned above must not be forgotten. The general principles underlying these observations are confirmed by talks with architects and contractors.

It is of course possible to plan for a future expansion by adding a mezzanine at a later date. Where this is done, provisions for structural support, ventilation, booklifts, elevators, stairs, and utilities must be made in the initial construction. It should be noted that, when the mezzanine is added on anything but the lowest level of the library, even though the structure is designed for the additional weight, doubling of the load will cause some deflection, which can produce cracks in plaster ceilings or cause doors to stick on the floor below. Even so, such a plan can provide excellent expansion possibilities, particularly in a branch library where adding space in the future may be particularly difficult given the location of the library in the host department.

Though it should not affect building heights, mezzanine ceiling heights need consideration. Low ceilings will feel oppressive if a reader can view mostly the ceiling of the mezzanine extending into the large adjacent room. However, such a ceiling feels fine if users normally look down to activity below or across the space to an interesting or attractive scene. Further, if the ceilings of the mezzanine and adjacent area are not at the same elevation because of some design element, such as ventilation ducts requiring a hung ceiling, it will feel worse for the mezzanine ceiling to be the higher of the two. As people use more subways, tunnels between buildings, and tight airplane seating, human acceptance of lower ceilings has increased—so long as ventilation and light are very well managed.

Another problem to be considered in the planning of a mezzanine is noise, if the spaces created are open to each other. It is especially a problem where the mezzanine creates a natural theater, a situation that should be avoided in a library. A central, open light well can create similar problems, as was the case in the Meyer Library at Stanford University before the well was glazed a decade later.

5. *What considerations should be kept in mind when determining the preferable size and number of floor levels?* No set formula can be recommended for size and number of levels. Until the advent of mechanical systems and improved lighting

techniques, the dimensions and shape of library buildings were determined to a considerable extent by lighting and ventilating requirements. Often the extreme limit in the depth of a building was placed at 80 ft (24.384 m) so that no part of it would be more than 40 ft (12.192 m) from windows. Skylights over the center, with a great hall below and galleries on the outside, made somewhat deeper buildings possible. The situation has now changed. Artificial light and ventilation can be relied on, and windows can be reduced to a minimum if desired. Indeed, where environmental conditions are designed to promote collections preservation, exterior windows must be sealed; all fresh air must be provided with proper conditioning through the mechanical system.

Some persons with considerable knowledge of the problems involved have suggested that a library of up to 10,000 ft^2 (929 m^2) should be kept on one floor if possible, and there should not be three levels unless 20,000 ft^2 (1,858 m^2) is exceeded. However, a library with 50,000 ft^2 (4,645 m^2) on a single floor can work perfectly well if properly arranged. Where there are three levels, there is advantage in making the entry level the middle of the three so that few persons will regularly have to go up or down more than one floor at a time, especially if the middle level can be accessed without exterior ramps, lifts, and stairs. Total areas of the exterior walls and roof will have considerable effect on costs, both in terms of construction and ongoing operating costs. In general, the nearer the building is to a square and the fewer the floor levels, the less the exterior walls cost; the more levels, the less the roof costs.

How many levels can a library building have relative to function and cost? Four factors should be taken into consideration.

a. In general, the larger the square footage on each floor, the smaller the percentage of the total gross square footage that is required for stairwells, elevators, and booklifts, and the smaller the proportion of outside wall to total square footage. Thus, the layout of larger floors is generally more efficient.

b. If all parts of the building used regularly by readers are no more than two flights of stairs above or below the entrance, passenger elevator service can be minimized and funds saved for other purposes. A site on a hillside with windows on one or more basement levels is advantageous in this connection.

c. If the librarian expects to provide service and supervision on each level, the number of levels should be held to a minimum in order to reduce the number of posts to be covered by the staff.

d. It is important in many if not most libraries to have the entrance level—whether it is called the main, first, or ground floor—large enough to house the central services of the library.

What are the essential entrance-level functions? While exceptions can be found for almost any library function that might be on the entrance level, good library design principles suggest that these include the main information and circulation desks, the reference and bibliographical collections and services, the public catalog (especially if still in card form), and, in many libraries, the current periodicals and the closed reserved-book collections. It is also desirable to have as many reader seats as possible on this floor, or easily accessible, particularly in a library with closed stacks. In a small research or academic library these services may require more than one-half of the total net floor area. Even in a library with 100,000 volumes and seating 300 readers, this figure should probably not be reduced to under one-third. But in a university or research library with large book collections that occupy up to one-half the total floor area, and particularly where a considerable percentage of the seating is scattered in one way or another through the stacks, additional floors are not so serious, although the effect on elevators should not be forgotten.

Tower stacks, such as those at the University of Massachusetts Amherst campus (of 28 levels!), at the California Institute of Technology, and at the University of North Carolina, Charlotte, have not been found satisfactory. The floor capacities are so small that the frequent need to use elevators is quite troublesome. The floors at Yale's Sterling Library, the University of Notre Dame, the University of Maryland in Baltimore County, and Columbia University's Butler Library are large enough in area so that they are not troublesome. The Sterling Library has five elevators for 16 stack tower floors, the smallest of which is 9,425 ft^2 net (875.6 m^2) and houses 160,000 volumes (6 percent of the total) and an average of 25 carrels. The University of Miami Richter Library with two elevators also works well, the tower floors four through seven each being a little over

8,000 ft² net (743 m²) and housing about 140,000 volumes and about 50 carrels. The University of North Carolina, Charlotte, Dalton Library Tower (of 1971) has two elevators serving 10 floors, each being about 3,750 ft² (348 m²) and housing about 55,000 volumes and about 40 carrels. These two Dalton Tower elevators are about 4 ft × 6 ft (1.219 × 1.829 m) to hold six to eight persons each, and access is too limited for convenient use, a situation exacerbated by the pressure to house collections, which resulted in reduction of seating. One might conclude that a smaller, younger collection in stack towers with relatively few study seats and few or very small elevators is likely to present difficulty for users. Tower conditions

need special design study with use of the building projected well into the future.

Harvard's Widener Library has a large enough area per floor so that its 10 stack levels are not a serious inconvenience, although a user concerned with material in widely different fields will encounter a tiresome amount of walking and stair climbing because each stack floor is a huge **C** shape. Some would suggest that stack floors as large as the A level in Princeton's Firestone Library (fig. 12.12) and the National Library of Medicine (fig. 12.13) are too large for convenient use, because the traffic patterns tend to become too complicated. However, the lowest level of Stanford's Green Library is quite convenient to

FIGURE 12.12 Princeton University's Firestone Library, level A before 1970. Note the very large stack area, which has tremendous book capacity but a more complicated circulation pattern than that in fig. 12.13. Only two of the nine main aisles run from one end of the area to the other. However, students probably enjoyed the possibility of a unique hideaway. Note seven empty areas of one-half bay each in the stacks, designed as small, convenient reading "oases." (This library was expanded in 1970 and 1988; though the general size of this floor remains largely the same, the character has changed with increased seating and reduced open-stack shelving. The sense of complexity still exists, though in a reduced state.)

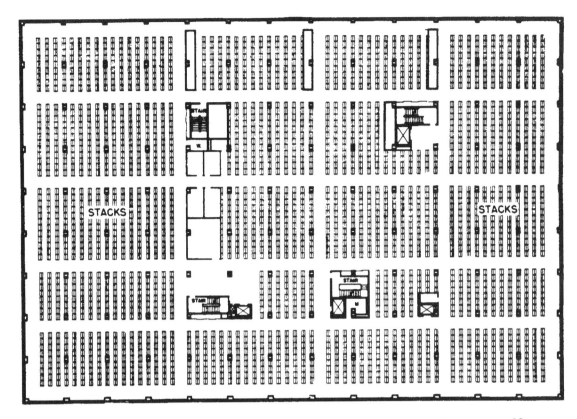

FIGURE 12.13   National Library of Medicine, B level. A very large stack area (about 50,000 ft² or 4,600 m²) designed with a simple circulation pattern. No one of the four cores intrudes on a main aisle. Each of the 11 main aisles goes through from one side of the building to the other.

use once the configuration is learned, though it extends 643 ft (195.830 m) from north to south and has 75,000 ft² (6,970 m²).

If the total required floor area in a library is as large as 80,000 ft² (say, 7,430 m²), three or four or even five floors can properly be considered. Even if extra elevator service is required, the increased number of floors will not be unduly expensive and inconvenient. The value of the available ground space, the desirability of limited ground coverage, and the aesthetic effect should also be considered relative to local conditions.

The total floor area that can satisfactorily be included in a library building before it becomes so unwieldy as to be avoided is a problem that, with the rapid increase in collections and the number of seating accommodations called for, will have to be faced in our larger libraries in the years directly ahead. Several library buildings in the 500,000-ft² (46,440-m²) range exist, and, though they may require some getting used to, they are manageable. And the University of Toronto Robarts Library has 16 floors, each one of

which averages 65,000 ft² gross (6,000 m²) and it works well.

6. Do electrical and mechanical equipment affect height problems? Generally electrical and mechanical equipment do not limit the height of a building, but added height may be required. Elevator machinery may need to be on the roof, though able engineers can solve that problem in nearly all cases so as not to require a rooftop eyesore.

Microwave dishes are another matter. Too many have been placed exposed on roofs where they do not add to the actual building height but are nonetheless a blight on the campus skyline. In some cases these are installed long after the library was built, with sometimes as many as three per rooftop. They can be particularly visible, such as at the University of Alaska at Fairbanks, Goucher College, Hollins College, and Sweet Briar College. Yet even when placed behind the library on the ground, as at the University of Central Florida in Orlando, a berm may not be sufficient to achieve an aesthetic placement. Older bar-type antennas do not have the mass of a dish, but also can disfigure a roof line, as at Stanford's J. Henry Meyer Memorial Library. Better solutions need to be found for this evidence of the age of technology. The current generation of small dishes may be part of a better solution. Other options include recessing the antenna in a part of the top floor or erecting a screen to mask the device, as is often done with exposed cooling towers. Placement far from the library is a possibility for particularly large dishes and microwave ground links, with cabling to all needed reception and input facilities; this expense may not differ much from the cost of screening or hiding equipment within the library roof area.

Chilled water and steam usually reach the library from a central plant, but where chilled water is manufactured within the library, there may be a local cooling tower. Where chilled water is produced, there must be a way of removing heat from the plant. Heat removal can be done with a fountain or running water or other systems. Cooling towers with or without water evaporation represent the most common method of heat removal.

Mechanical space can be a problem if an air-conditioning cooling tower must go on the roof. If a machine room requires headroom higher than the library requires, and if geologic conditions prevent a lowered mechanical room in the basement, the building height will probably be increased.

7. Do geologic conditions influence the height? A site with rock or limited bearing capacity or a very high water table or floodplain will need special study to determine if the building needs to sit higher as a result, or whether engineering solutions can keep construction cost down to a point where the adverse geologic conditions can be overcome without influencing building height. Coping with such conditions can be very expensive. On the other hand, geologic conditions have frequently had a positive influence by enabling the building to be lower, perhaps to sprawl down a hill or into a gully, to real advantage. The addition to the University of California at San Diego flows down a ravine, thereby not disturbing the geometric form of the dramatic original above-ground structure. The 1994 addition to the Holland Library at Washington State University is entered at the top level, a design made possible by the slope of the land. And the Leyburn Library of Washington and Lee University is pleasantly approached from the old central part of campus, and appears to be a one-story building since

three of its four levels are set down into the hillside. Elsewhere mentioned in this book, the several underground library buildings represent cases where geologic conditions enabled the library to have no height above grade. Thus, geologic conditions can either be a plus or a minus influence.

The preceding comments relative to building height and module illustrate the problems involved. Their solutions may differ in a closed-access independent research library, such as the American Antiquarian Society, the Huntington Library, or the Linda Hall Library, from those for an open-access academic library. Modules in storage facilities will reflect the storage technology, and almost certainly will differ from the modules discussed here. The early structural concepts must respond to the facility program, the site, the selected module, the economies of various structural systems, the distribution of the mechanical systems, the number of floors, and other factors. It is clear that the selection and application of a structural system must be carefully planned, for, once decided upon, it is usually difficult to change.

12.4
Internal Configuration of Major Elements

Chapter 5 and, to a lesser degree, the other chapters on programming discuss in some detail the interrelationships of various functions of the library. One essential characteristic of a functional building is the accessibility of all parts with a minimum of disturbance. If planning is to produce satisfactory traffic patterns, it must take into account four particular aspects: the entrance area, spatial relationships, communication and vertical transportation, and the problems of supervision and control of the building and its exits. Each of these is discussed here.

12.4.1 The Entrance Area

Although the position of the front door may seem like a simple matter, several points must be given consideration beyond the mere location. The visibility of the door is an advantage when strangers are seeking the entrance. A repetitive inset architectural form, as at the University of California at Irvine, leaves one wondering where the front door is, especially if there is no "Library" sign over or beside the entrance that is visible from a building away. The door or doors should be clear, heavy plate glass or otherwise have a major clear portion, so that people can see approaching traffic. Clear doors psychologically invite people inside. The solid library entrance doors of the Ladd Library at Bates College, Hofheimer Library at Virginia Wesleyan University, and the Douglass Library at the University of Maryland Eastern Shore provide a blind invitation to enter.

Many people would not wish to have to climb stairs or ramps to get to the entrance, though some recent buildings still force this on the library user. For those who must use crutches or a wheelchair, the building should present a direct and generally level approach. Once at the front door, users generally appreciate some form of an overhang under which they can shake an umbrella or dust off snow before entering, or perhaps deposit returning books in a slot under cover of the weather. This inset is quite universally preferred to having the entrance, or its vestibule, project outward from the face of the building, though some libraries provide a theater-type marquee.

A vestibule should be considered. Many buildings in temperate climates do not have two sets of entrance doors even when the building is air conditioned. However, where the winters are severe or summer heat is excessive, especially where preservation of collections through environmental control is a goal, the vestibule is a proven way of helping control the inside environment. The original library building at the University of South Florida in St. Petersburg is a case in point, allowing heat and humidity constantly to creep through the single doors. Where occasional storms are prevalent from the direction to which the library door faces, a vestibule is always desirable. The library of Louisiana State University, New Orleans, faces north to Lake Ponchartrain, over which winds howl and buffet the library entrance. Note that the relatively small vestibule differs from the much larger lobby, which frequently is a major center of traffic distribution and several library functions. Generally speaking, the greater the distance between the inner and outer set of doors, the better the environmental separation. Of course, where heavy traffic results in the doors being open for extended periods, even this distance will mean little.

For the best environmental separation from the outside, a revolving door should be considered. The new Bibliothèque nationale de France in the Tolbiac region of east Paris was planned with oversized revolving doors for this purpose. Passage of a wheelchair or a person on crutches should not be a problem.

Once through the entrance, users should be inside the library or find it right at hand. The library of Regent University in Virginia Beach, for example, is hidden behind a monumental stair centered in a ceremonial hall of flags. Directory information should be readily seen. Sometimes a staff attendant has a post, perhaps to provide information or to check books leaving the building. At the University of Georgia Little Library, there is a staffed "Security Office" at this point.

Narrow exit lanes will facilitate checking everyone who leaves the building. Turnstiles are sometimes used in order to assure a relatively slow flow of such traffic, but these may also require bypass exits in the event of fire or for handicapped persons. Still, many individuals object to turnstiles or to any personal inspection of their materials. Electronic circulation and security systems are becoming increasingly common in all sizes and types of libraries; even though they are not without their problems, it is reasonable to consider these systems as the standard method of monitoring book security.

Three other aspects of the entrance are the provision of exterior seating, bicycle corral areas, and one or more places for posting student notices, campus advertisements, and the like. A nearby source of coffee and tea and possibly food is always welcome. The University of Florida Smathers Libraries have many convenient benches, arranged in conversational clusters amid trees and other plantings, creating a popular area for people to meet, take a break from their library work, or have refreshments from a nearby vending service. Valencia Community College's 1991 Learning Resource Center was designed with 16-in. (406-mm) deep, ground-level window sills, under cover of the sun, which provide such convenient casual seating that staff in offices inside have to post requests in the windows asking that they not be so used. UCLA offers an attractive food service area with outdoor seating near the main library with excellent results.

If bicycle parking areas are not obvious and equipped with suitable racks, people will find their own space and locking posts, be they trees, railings of stairs, bench frames, or so on. Generally a suitable rack is one that is easily found, is convenient to the destination of the bike rider, has space for the arriving bike, offers an easy ability to lock bikes to the rack while providing adequate support so that the wheels will not be damaged and the bike will not fall over, and is large or secure enough so that the rack with bike attached will not be removed. Such parking of bikes can be chaotic if not unattractive and often can be dangerous for some handicapped persons.

Handling posted signs or discouraging their random placement should be thought through, as campus organizations will seek places to publicize their events and offerings. Too many institutions have not adequately provided for this need, and library entrances have suffered as a result.

One other aspect of the entrance should be given attention: the use of flowing water. Architects sometimes like to use water outside or inside the building for its sound, motion, and interest. For some people, water and architecture provide a charming contrast, a balance, a constant theater. With all its attractiveness, there are pitfalls when it comes to the library. The University of Miami Richter Library was built with a shallow square pool under the main stair, which added humidity into the building while the air conditioning tried to pull the humidity out! Water frequently will lead to leaks, and water and books never go well together.

Outside the building, water certainly has charm, as noted at Lyndon State College Library. Clemson University's Cooper Library faces a delightful 2½-acre (1-ha) pool that serves as the chiller for the library and four other buildings. (This is an example of a chilled water plant without a cooling tower!) However, campus newspapers and other loose debris blow into the pool, as they do at the Cooper Library of the University of South Carolina. Such pools should be very shallow so as to pose no danger for youngsters and should have at least a low surrounding wall to keep debris from blowing in. If there are a few terraces leading down to the pool, people will sit facing it, rather than facing away if the steplike risers slope away from the pool. Thought must be given to whether the pool will reflect sunlight in unwanted directions at any time of the day or the year, and the architect can be expected to provide satisfactory answers on this score.

These particulars deserve wide attention during review of schematics, though some may be studied as part of landscape design. The treatment of the entrance is a particularly critical element, as it gives people the first impression of the library. Although the design development phase will refine this feature, the schematic review is the best time to study all aspects of the entrance and its surround.

12.4.2 Spatial Relationships

The schematic design effort will begin to express the program statement in three dimensions and, to a significant extent, establish the basic relationships of major components of the library. Because of the importance of this aspect of the design, it is discussed further here, although Section 5.3.3 discusses spatial relationships from a programmatic point of view. Appendix A gives examples in the section on Program Divisions covering spatial relationships.

Ease and convenience of use are matters of prime importance. This is certainly true of a college library, where some of the students may never have used anything but a small public or high school library and are quite awed by what may seem to them to be a tremendous collection of 100,000 or more volumes, particularly if they are given stack access. Convenience is equally important in a great university library where the necessarily large and complex areas for reading, public service, and book storage may seem maze-like. A large public building of any kind with many rooms may be difficult to navigate, and an academic or research library, with 1,000,000 volumes and 30 linear miles (48.280 km) of shelves and with reading accommodations for 1,500 persons, can well present a formidable puzzle to even an experienced scholar, particularly during the first few visits to the library. On the other hand, a large library is often highly regarded by students once they master the system, as they can find a "sense of place" or their own niche that is convenient for their studies.

The architect may use several concepts, usually deriving from the program document and the master plan statement, which guide the schematic design. "Sense of place" is one of these principles, as at Duke University during a major library building programming effort in the mid-1990s. The University of Southern California Leavey Library and the University of Michigan Media Center would have resulted from the architect's application of other concepts. A prominent Japanese architect of libraries believes in the concept of "transparency," open spatial relationships that lead to social connections, more opportunities for communication among people. This is the time when the architect applies all the professional knowledge of the firm to provide a building concept that fully meets the program and is economical, attractive, and a fine addition to the institutional setting.

Taking the major relationships outlined in the program, the architect must piece together a plan that works within the context of the module, the size of a given floor, and external influences. The scheme will show placement on the site, massing of major elements, and probably a rough shape for the envelope of the structure. This is an effort that should command the involvement of the librarian and others in the decision process, as some degree of compromise is almost certain to develop. It is during this stage of the design that such key elements as the entrance, stair and elevator cores, shear walls, the service delivery area, and rest rooms must be located. Care must be taken to ensure that no element precludes needed flexibility in another element. As has been suggested several times elsewhere in this volume, it is certain that the library operations will change with the passage of time.

As the layout of the library emerges and compromises are made, remember that vertical movement is normally more difficult and time consuming than horizontal movement, and stairs are not preferred. Elevators are expensive and may cause delays. As a result, a strong and desirable tendency has emerged in recent decades to plan the "central services" on the entrance level of the library. Space on that level is properly considered the most valuable area in the building. Entrance lobbies are important and must be fairly large in a busy academic library, because of the movement of users in large groups between classes. Therefore, less space on the entrance floor can be left for books, readers, and services than on the other floors, and choices must be made.

One solution is to restrict the use of this floor largely to the central or key services, even if this means that less reading space and less shelving for main collections are available than would have been preferred on this level. To overcome the difficulty at least in part, the Olin Library at Cornell University has a first floor more than twice the size of the levels above, which has made it possible to put all these services, as well as processing staff quarters and several special collections, on the main floor (see fig. 12.14). In spite of this, the library's processing department space is already congested, a fact that is all too common in library design, though the condition may be resolved by automation.

But the particular points to be made are that these central services should be placed as close to each other as possible and that their relationships to each other are a matter of importance. The whole area should be planned carefully so as to leave available as much space as possible for reading accommodations and heavily used parts of the collection, but the areas assigned for lobby space and the central services should not be reduced to an extent that will cause congestion. Library staff should carefully study the probable traffic patterns in and around the lobby and advise the architect on the effectiveness of the scheme. The lobby should be especially attractive and give a feeling of spaciousness that can carry through the whole building, but an extravagant amount of space should not be assigned to it for monumental rather than functional purposes. There is no room here for space that will not be heavily used.

In a number of new libraries, a great deal of space that would otherwise have been available on entrance levels has been sacrificed by having a setback of the outside wall on one, two, or even four sides for the sake of an architectural effect. Such a setback can be very attractive. In certain circumstances there may be special reasons that make it desirable in spite of the obvious disadvantages. A good example of this situation would be a library designed for an urban university where, because of the limited ground space available, a skyscraper building may be a necessity. In this case, it may be determined that even if it used all the possible area the site afforded, the library could not have an entrance lobby and what might be called the main distribution points (exit control, elevators, stairwells, and escalators to the basement and the second floor, which may be desirable to relieve the load on the elevators) in addition to the central services. Such a circumstance may suggest transfer of all or most central services to the second floor, where these services could have the whole level and would require less space because the undergraduate use of course reserves, which does not require these services, could be funneled off to a lower level or made to be wholly electronic.

At this point it may become evident that all the primary functions desired on the entrance floor cannot be accommodated there. The architect may see and pose this as a problem. The librarian may see it as plans are laid out. So this would be the time to reconsider the desired functional relationships stated in the program. Some

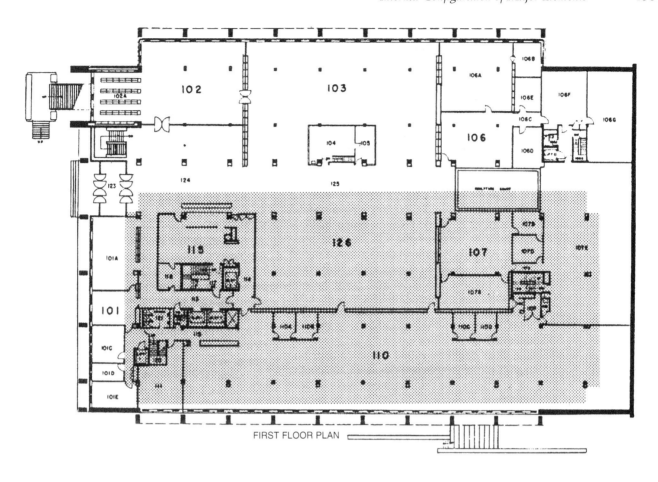

FIRST FLOOR PLAN

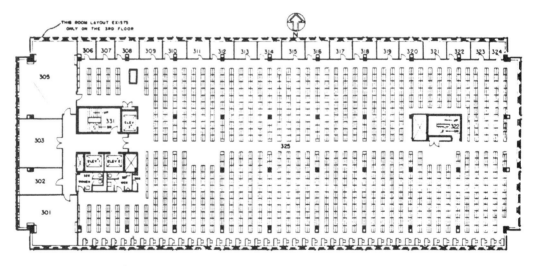

TYPICAL FLOOR PLAN
3rd, 4th, 5th, and 6th FLOOR

FIGURE 12.14 Cornell University, Olin Library, entrance level and a typical upper floor. The shaded area on the entrance level indicates the location and outline of the upper floors. The first floor is larger than those above it in order to house the central services and three important special collections. Key to significant functions: 102 = current periodicals; 103 = reference; 110 = technical services; 115 = circulation; 126 = catalog and bibliography; 101, 106, 107 = special collections; 301 to 305 = seminar and study rooms; 306 to 324 = faculty studies; and 325 = stacks.

functions may need to move upward or downward to another floor. Examples of what can be reconsidered are current periodicals, a computer lab, an instructional classroom, a food or snack facility, a special collections service area and offices, the library director's office suite, mail and supply and service quarters, and the like.

One essential spatial-relationship issue, which is too often neglected, is shelving for the main bookstack collections. It has already been noted that a large bookstack—there are some today and there will be many more in the years to come—with 500,000 volumes shelved on one level may become a maze. Equally serious is the question of a logical arrangement of the books on the shelves, a concern that has become more complicated with the great efforts made in recent years to house readers and books in juxtaposition. Anything that breaks up a logical arrangement of the books should be avoided if at all possible. The situation is complicated by fixed areas for stairs, elevators, toilets, or special rooms of any kind, and by reading "oases" or irregularities of any kind in walls or aisles; careful study and planning, however, can generally prevent many of the difficulties, even in a very large library.

The very large A stack level at Princeton, with nine main aisles (see fig. 12.12) at right angles to the ranges and with several elevators and stairwells, many special rooms, carrels, and oases, illustrates the problem. The B level at the National Library of Medicine in Bethesda, Maryland, which was planned by the same competent architectural firm, represents a simpler pattern (see fig. 12.13), and the still simpler pattern at Cornell's Olin Library (see fig. 12.15) shows what can be done.

The plans of the Widener stack (fig. 4.1), the Widener level in the Lamont building at Harvard (fig. 12.16), the main stack at Columbia's Butler Library (fig. 12.17), and the New York Public Library main stack (fig. 12.18) show other simple layouts. That of the first and second phases for the University of California at Los Angeles (see fig. 12.19) shows in the heavy black lines the problems created by special building requirements (shear walls) to prevent earthquake damage and the great effort made to prevent complications that could easily have arisen. However, even with an addition, the building works well.

It should be stressed that these plans probably do not reflect ideal solutions for any proposed library. Indeed, the academic program and goals of the library staff may suggest quite different solutions. While complexity for its own sake may not be desirable, not all librarians are opposed to more complex arrangements. There are even some who find the three short towers of the Northwestern University main research library an agreeable solution, although many would argue this point because of the radial shelving and inflexible layout.

Similar understanding and review of schematics must be undertaken for other public and staff

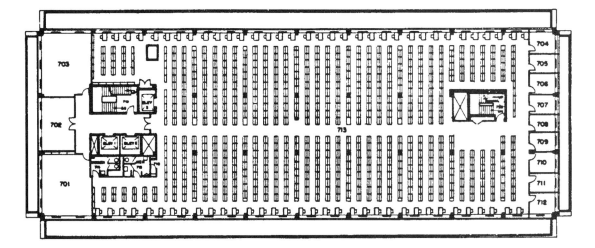

FIGURE 12.15   Cornell University, Olin Library, floor 7. Note the clear circulation pattern with the main stairs and elevators at the main entrance end of the building (see fig. 12.14). Note also the fairly wide center aisle and the narrower side aisles with open carrels, departmental rooms at the end adjacent to the main stairs, and faculty studies at the other.

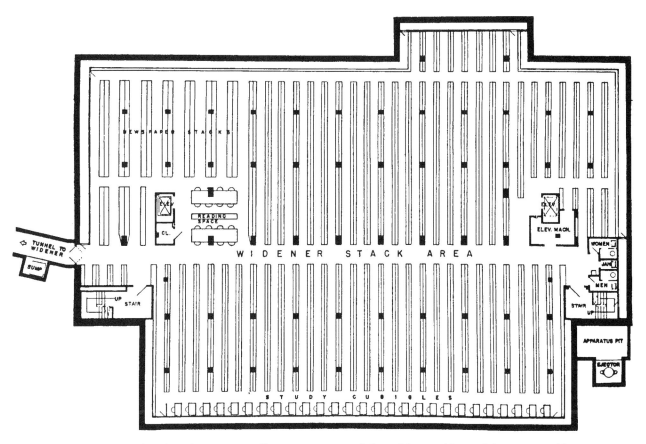

FIGURE 12.16 Harvard University, Lamont Library, storage stack for Widener. This stack is connected by a tunnel with the Widener building. The circulation pattern is simple, with a range 51 ft (15.545 m) long on one side and a 42-ft (12.802-m) range on the other side of a wide center aisle. The alcove at the upper right and the shelving to the right of the machine room near the rest rooms will be awkward to use in a natural sequential order. The double exterior walls are necessary to control groundwater.

areas and their spatial relationships. Section 12.5 on the schematic phase of interior design treats these from a different point of view.

12.4.3 Vertical Transportation and Communication

Unless a library is very small or on a single level, mechanical or electronic devices or both will probably be needed when people and books move from one floor to another and where service points, collections, and staff areas are widely distributed. These considerations will need initial work during schematics, though detailing them will be part of later design phases. A discussion of communication and vertical transportation must consider stairs, ramps, escalators, booklifts, elevators, conveyor belts, and pneumatic tubes. (Other communication devices are dealt with in Section 3.2.) The needs of tele-

phones, public-address systems, television, and computer networks may affect the schematic planning and are important in the specifications document, but they are commonly detailed in design development or construction documents.

Stairways. The desirable number of stairways will depend, of course, on the amount of traffic, the number and size of floor levels, and, to some extent, the total floor area of the building. Local building regulations and fire codes may also impose specific requirements. The Uniform Building Code states the maximum distance from any point in the building to an enclosed exit stair shall not exceed 150 ft (45 m) for a building without a fire sprinkler system, and 200 ft (60 m) with sprinklers. Enclosed fire-protected corridors can be used to increase these dimensions by up to an additional 100 ft (30 m). Codes often permit only one open stairway—that is, only one

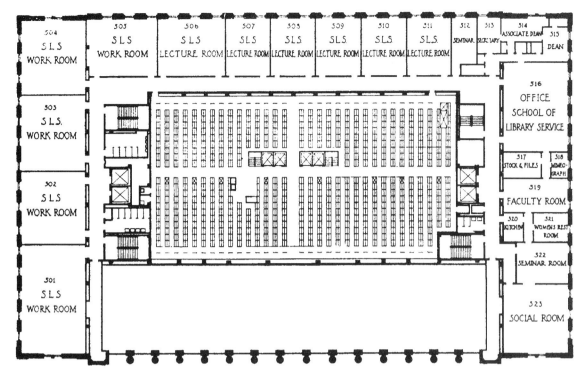

FIGURE 12.17 Columbia University, Butler Library. Shown is one of 14 levels that, though varying in size, are in the center of the building with rooms on each of the four sides. There is only one public stack entrance, that through the circulation area. This was one of the first modern stacks without ventilation slits between levels and with stairways and elevators closed off so as not to form a chimney effect.

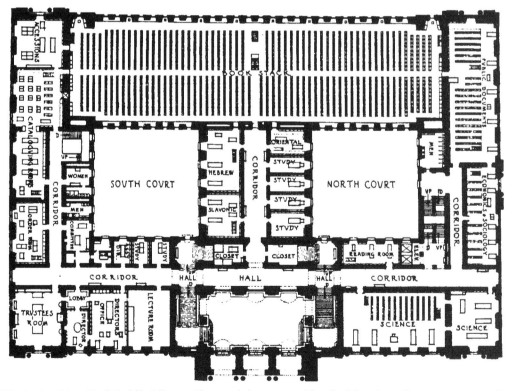

FIGURE 12.18 New York Public Library. The stack has seven identical levels under a monumental reading room and has an exceptionally clear traffic pattern for a large area. A more recent underground addition with two levels of compact shelving extends to the west off the basement level (top of figure).

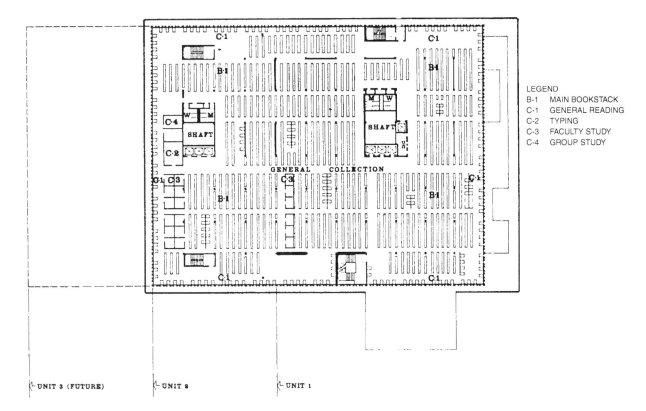

LEGEND
B-1   MAIN BOOKSTACK
C-1   GENERAL READING
C-2   TYPING
C-3   FACULTY STUDY
C-4   GROUP STUDY

FIGURE 12.19   University of California at Los Angeles, Research Library. This floor plan is typical of the upper floors of the first two phases of the Research Library. The heavy lines represent earthquake reinforcements, which can complicate shelving arrangements. The main stair is placed next to the main entrance to encourage use.

outside a fireproof enclosure with closed doors at each level. They may permit the open stairway on only one level; if it is open on the first floor, it must be enclosed at the second or the basement level. They may also determine the stair widths according to a formula or formulas based on occupancy (discussed later) of the floor or floors that are served.

Some buildings do not come under code restrictions, either because there is no applicable state law or local regulation or because the institution is exempt for one reason or another. Sometimes a limited exemption can be obtained if sprinkler systems are installed. Fire risks are discussed in Chapters 5 and 13. No building should be planned without checking the codes and regulations to which it must conform.

The location of both main and subsidiary stairways is important; indeed, it is usually a primary factor in determining floor layouts. Stairways should be convenient for use and reasonably conspicuous if people are to find them readily and use them instead of looking for mechanical

transportation. The City University of New York Baruch College's 1994 Newman Library and Technology Center has a generous semicircular stair directly opposite the entrance, with the bank of six elevators visible but set off two bays to the side. This is one of the better examples of stair placement. On the other hand, stairways should not be allowed to obstruct the major traffic arteries on each floor. Architects may recommend that open stairways, often monumental ones, rise from the main floor as an architectural and aesthetic feature. A monumental stairway in a small library may be out of proportion, but it can be attractive and also functional in a large building.

Stairways are often placed in one or more building cores, together with elevator shafts, shear walls, duct shafts, toilets, and other vertical services, leaving the remainder of the building as flexible and adaptable as possible. The original part of the main library at California State University, Sacramento, and Towson State's Cook Library have the stairwells outside the rectangular floor area to gain such flexibility and construction economy. Such a core will extend in a stack from the basement through the top floor. This plan also reduces the extent of the interior walls that will be required. Another common solution is to place the main stairway immediately adjacent to the main entrance and next to an outside wall as at the Wilson Library at Western Washington University, leaving the rest of the building unobstructed by a permanent installation. As has been noted, however, the fire laws and also the amount of use usually necessitate at least one secondary stairway, and large buildings require more than one; in some cases a stairway in each corner may be desirable in addition to the central stairway.

Decisions on the steepness of stairs involve questions of design, comfort, and the use of space. If a stairway ascends too gradually, space will be wasted and many people will find it awkward to climb. If stairs are too steep, many people will find them dangerous to descend. In general, the most acceptable height for risers is no more than 7½ in. (190 mm), and risers of less than 6½ in. (165 mm) should be avoided. Treads should vary from 10½ to 12 in. (266 mm to 305 mm), though some building codes allow 10 in. (254 mm) or less. Bookstack stairs may be steeper, particularly if the number of levels is limited, and some building codes conform to the ancient standard of about 8½ in. (216 mm) for the riser and a tread depth of 9½ in. (241 mm). The Uniform Building Code allows risers of not less than 4 in. (102 mm), and not more than 7 in. (178 mm). And the run shall not be less than 11 in. measured horizontally between the vertical planes of the furthermost projection of adjacent treads, the only exceptions being the minimum tread in a circular stair, which is 10 in., and stairs to unoccupied roofs, which may have an 8-in. maximum riser and a 9-in. minimum tread.

The following simple formulas are often used:

1. The product of multiplying the riser by the tread should be between 70 and 77 in.[2] (or about 0.045 m² to 0.050 m²). For example, one comfortable product comes from a 7-in. riser and an 11-in. tread (178 × 279 mm).
2. The riser plus the tread should be from 17 to 17½ in. (432 to 444 mm).
3. The sum of the tread plus twice the riser should be between 20 and 25 in. (508 mm to 635 mm), preferably between 24 and 25 in. (610 mm and 635 mm).

Stair width for two-way traffic should be at least 56 in. (1.422 m), though 69 in. (1.753 m) is more comfortable. However, decisions on stair widths depend primarily on the occupancy of the building or the traffic expected at times of peak load. Indeed, many decisions in library planning must be based on anticipated peak loads, which often are established by the code or negotiated with code authorities. For main stairs in academic institutions, these peaks normally occur when classes change. However, the minimum width of the stairs and exit routes will be established for emergencies, such as fire; at such times traffic can be expected to move in a single direction making the full width available, and alternate routes of egress may be used.

The Uniform Building Code, for example, specifies a minimum width for an exit route or stair of 44 in. (1.118 m), including the handrails, for an occupancy of 50 or more people. Where the occupancy is less than 50, a stair 36 in. (914 mm) wide is permitted. The handrails may project into the required space no more than 3½ in. (89 mm) from each side. The total width of all exits from a given floor must provide at least 12 in. (305 mm) for each 50 people served on that floor. For the first adjacent floor that must exit through the same passage, 6 in. (152 mm) for each 50 people is added, and for each subsequent floor 3 in. (76 mm) is added for each group of 50 occupants. The maximum width of a stair between handrails is 88 in. (2.234 m) in this particular code.

The top of the handrail, again based upon the Uniform Building Code, must be placed from 34 to 38 in. (864 to 965 mm) above the nosing of the tread, though some say that 35.6 in. (904 mm) is the ideal. There must be a landing for every 12 ft (3.658 m) of vertical rise. Where a landing requires a guardrail, it must be 42 in. (1.066 m) high, and the space below the rail must be protected so that a 6-in. (152-mm) sphere cannot be passed through. This also applies to stair rails where there is an exposed edge.

Numerous other details are typically specified in the code, including dimensions of the handrail and construction of the stair. It should be remembered that local authorities may apply different code requirements, and, of course, these will be controlling.

Two other characteristics of stairs must be considered: tread surface and color. Any slippery surface must be avoided, particularly where rainwater may fall or run onto the stair. Some abrasive quality is highly desirable as one approaches and descends a flight. Carpet provides some degree of abrasion and noise control, and it also is a major protection to any person who falls on the stair. Color is especially important for the beginning and ending of the flight, so that a person will subconsciously feel the start or ending even if talking with another person and not actually looking at the flight. A color change in the stairwell wall and different lighting can also help alert one to stairs.

Concerning handrails, where a code does not specify diameter or configuration, it is wise to make them of modest diameter (a golf ball is better than a tennis ball) and configuration so that a falling person can immediately get a good grip from the top. Be sure they extend smoothly around turns, are of material so hard that cracks or splintering will not occur and so constituted that it will not get uncomfortably hot if it stands in a baking sun, are free of sharp edges, are very firmly anchored, and begin and end in a way that rings, buttons, and clothing can never get caught. All library stairways should have handrailings. A railing that goes a short distance beyond the bottom step will help those who are handicapped, but it must be so installed that it is not a hazard for persons rounding the corner to go up the stairs. Architects must not make handrails major design features, even if the stair is monumental, for they quickly can lose their utility if overscaled. When stairs turn a corner at a landing, particularly if they are heavily used, try to arrange the landing width on the down side a full stair tread wider, as shown in fig. 12.21.

The occupancy is generally established by a formula that, in a large library, can result in an unrealistic number. However, if the building is being designed with flexibility for future use— for example, as an office building—this factor should be considered in establishing the occupancy. Occupancy levels in some cases can be negotiated, but care must be taken to be realistic in evaluating maximum potential occupancy loads if the proscribed formula is not used, as it is difficult and expensive to add stairs later.

A recent code specifies that for assembly areas, such as an auditorium, planners should calculate 7 ft^2 (0.65 m^2) for each occupant; for conference rooms, one occupant for each 15 ft^2 (1.39 m^2); for classrooms, computer labs, and lounges, one for 20 ft^2 (1.86 m^2); for library reading rooms, one for 50 ft^2 (4.65 m^2); for offices,

one for 100 ft^2 (9.29 m^2); and for warehouses, which may be regarded as stack areas, one occupant for each 300 ft^2 (27.87 m^2). Although this information may be used to estimate the occupant load, the local governing codes should be used to establish the final design.

If a stairway is to be a fire exit, it must lead as directly as possible to an outside door, and this door must always be made to open without a key from the inside during periods when the building is open to the public. If the library is fully sprinklered and outfitted with smoke detectors, the code authorities may permit a delayed-action locking system, which can give staff up to 15 seconds to respond to an exit alarm before the door can be opened. This type of delay lock will open immediately in the event a fire alarm is activated.

When the stair continues below ground level, there must be a one-way gate that forces persons coming down from upper floors to take the exit, for otherwise they would continue on down and be trapped below grade. (A low stair gate at the University of Maryland, Baltimore County, is properly painted a bright red.) Remember that, in emergencies, groups of people will be hastening to go outside and will seldom if ever take time to read signs.

Clearly, the code requirements apply primarily to the emergency exiting requirements of the building, and a main central stair often does not serve this purpose. The width of the main stair becomes a design question. In most libraries a width of 5 ft (1.524 m) is a typical minimum for a main stair; 8 ft (2.438 m) might be considered generous. Some code authorities might require an intermediate handrail if the stair exceeds 88 in. (2.234 m) in width, although it can often be argued that if this stair is not a required exit, the intermediate rail is not required. The center handrail is a nuisance when large furniture or equipment needs to be moved on these stairs, and young adults will use it as a transportation device. Monumental stairs 15 or 20 ft (4.572 or 6.096 m) wide sometimes do not have an intermediate handrail, although this type of stair is not encouraged.

Apropos of stairways and safety, one further warning may be offered: Always avoid a flight of only two steps; a single step is even worse. In some places it is illegal to create a hazard in this way, but the infraction cannot be excused whether it is an offense against the law or only against common sense. And even a single step prohibits use of a book truck. Yet architects of earlier days sometimes placed short flights of steps at a variety of points in a building. The old library at Cornell, now completely rehabilitated as the Uris Undergraduate Library, was an example of this style. If a library is afflicted with such stairs, they should be properly marked and lighted. In some cases it may be possible to replace them with ramps.

The Leyburn Library of Washington and Lee University has a situation with three steps leading from one level to a small, windowed lounge located behind a floating stair. This becomes an attractive and popular seating area, with a Washington Hoe hand printing press beneath the stair; yet, if the architect could have resolved the condition, the steps should have been avoided for the sake of those in wheelchairs if for no other reason.

Another danger is the underside of stairs, which should be protected or blocked to prevent people from walking below the rising stair and butting their heads, a condition especially prevalent in circular stairs. Architects sometimes propose circular stairs because of their aesthetic advantages, but many people believe that they are to be avoided in most cases. Here is one case of a minimum condition: Clemson University's Cooper Library uses two circular stairways for travel between level 5 and the smaller level 6. These stairs have a radius of 3 ft (0.914 m), and rise 10.5 ft (3.200 m) in 18 steps. Each step is 4 in. (102 mm), growing at the outer edge to 17.5 in. (445 mm). To some people these stairs are pretty to look at, but a bit scary to use because they seem insubstantial, they revolve in a rather tight circle, and the treads seem narrow, which adds to the perception of instability of the stair itself. As one can imagine, if the narrow edge of the circular stair tread is wide enough to seem reasonably safe, considerable space must be left in the center. Legal requirements often set a minimum diameter for the well.

Other people reject the old assumption that circular stairs are more dangerous, claiming that statistics show they are actually safer because they are more difficult to walk on, so users are more cautious, and because a fall brings the person into the railing instead of down an entire flight. Very few students will sit on and block traffic on a circular stair, whereas they do at times enjoy conversations while sitting on straight flights, especially if carpeted.

The total floor area required by a reasonably generous circular stairwell is greater than that needed for a direct stairway or for one going around one, two, or even three corners. This is particularly apparent if you realize that the space immediately outside the circle is ordinarily useless for library purposes because of its shape. This same commitment of space results if the square is placed within the circle. Roanoke College's Fintel Library addition of 1991 has a square stair within a glass-walled circular shell 40 ft (12.192 m) in diameter, with exhibit displays in the glass wall. Though the stair leads to the College Trustees' Board Room on the top floor, this design feature takes 6,400 ft^2 (594.56 m^2) for the main stairs among the four levels, for a cost no doubt exceeding $640,000. Sometimes a stair can be an attractive visual feature in a building that otherwise seems quite utilitarian.

If a circular stairway is to be installed in spite of these disadvantages, it should be designed, in countries where pedestrians normally keep to the right, so that the person going downstairs on the right uses the wide end instead of the narrow end of the tread; this will reduce to some extent the dangers presented by any nonrectangular stair tread. Of course, where pedestrians keep to the left, a stairway rising counterclockwise is indicated. It appears that in too few instances this principle has been taken into account. (See figs. 12.20 and 12.21 for circular and rectangular stairs.)

Ramps. A ramp is better than a step or two or three, and is the lesser evil when an addition is made to an old library and it is impossible to make floor levels match. An interesting example is outside the Perkins Library at Duke University where a lengthy paved path includes six steps midway, and beside these steps a beaten path has been formed in the grass because people preferred the sloping ramp provided by nature! Steep ramps are to be avoided if book trucks must traverse them, and any slope greater than 5 percent will be difficult for a person on crutches. A 5 percent incline entails 80 ft of ramp for only 4 ft in altitude (20 m of ramp for 1 m of altitude); a 10 percent gradient takes only half this space for the same rise, and 10 percent should be the limit even for short ramps. A typical code maximum slope is 1 in 12, or about 8 percent. This is the maximum steepness allowed by the Americans with Disabilities Act. A nonskid surface is essential on all ramps, and handrails should be provided (see comments above for stairs, though the height requirements are somewhat different). If a change in level is required at the approach to a staff elevator, a ramp is preferable to stairs, but the change in level should be avoided altogether if possible.

Escalators. Escalators, which can handle a large volume of traffic and use relatively little power, are very useful in some cases. They can be designed to function only when a person approaches, or to function continually. In the very large Robarts Library, University of Toronto, escalators have served between the first and fifth floors and work very well, though they require maintenance. Few libraries, however, can afford to install them between as many as four levels, and it is generally out of the question to go beyond three. For heavy traffic between only two levels, they may be both useful and economical, as in the University of Connecticut Library and in the Columbia University Law School Library where every reader must go up one high-ceiling level to reach the library from the floor below. Yet, at the University of Minnesota, the escalator was removed in the late 1970s at considerable cost because it monopolized some of the most desirable space on the main floor (as is the case at California State University, Sacramento, where planning efforts have been undertaken to improve arrangements) and the lower level entrance-exit had been closed except in the winter. Energy costs were thereby significantly reduced.

In the 1962 University of Miami Richter Library in Coral Gables, escalators go from the first to the third floor, with three lifts in all, as two are used between the first and second floors. These escalators go up only, although they can be reversed at closing time. Service in both directions at the same time would cost twice as much and would require twice as much space. It was estimated at Coral Gables that, though only of medium width, these escalators have a greater capacity than four elevators, and cost less for space, installation, and operation; it is exceedingly doubtful that four elevators would have been necessary to handle the traffic in question. Because of their expense, escalators can be justified only where there are exceptionally heavy flows of traffic.

The location of escalators calls for careful consideration, and each end should be located where it will not obstruct traffic. Particular care is necessary if more than two levels are involved. It is

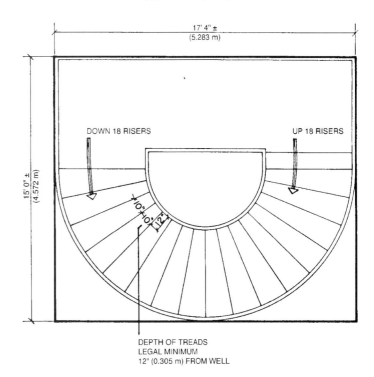

AREA USED: 17' 4" x 15' 0" = 260 ft²
(5.283 m x 4.572 m = 24.154 m²)

FIGURE 12.20 Circular stairway. The total area required for circular stairs exceeds that for rectangular stairs with landings. The space around the stairway on each floor is less usable because of its shape. It is more expensive to construct, particularly if enclosed by walls. It is dangerous because of the varying depth of each tread. If circular stairs are used, persons going downstairs should go counterclockwise, as shown in the drawing, so that when walking to the right, they are on the wider part of the treads. (Persons should go down clockwise in countries were people walk to the left and drive cars on the left.)

also essential that escalators be very carefully installed; they must be tailor-made for the building if they are not to be unduly noisy. Unfortunately, the Richter Library escalators are in the middle of floors and the mechanism has become disturbingly noisy. Special fire-protection devices may also be required.

Booklifts. Booklifts, sometimes called dumb waiters, vary widely in size; some are only large enough to hold a folio volume; others opening at floor level will take a loaded book truck. One disadvantage of any booklift is that, if no staff member is stationed at the level to which the lift

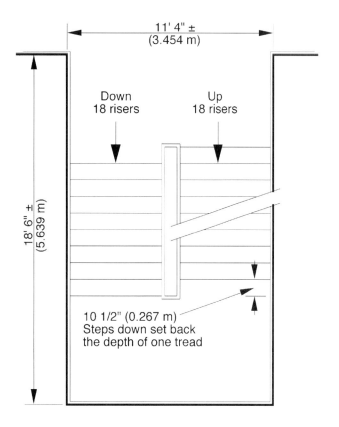

11' 4" ±
(3.454 m)

Down
18 risers

Up
18 risers

18' 6" ±
(5.639 m)

10 1/2" (0.267 m)
Steps down set back
the depth of one tread

FIGURE 12.21   Normal stairway. At 210 ft² (19.5 m²), it takes less space and is safer, but in some ways is less attractive aesthetically than a circular stairway. Rails on both sides are often required by code.

is sent, the person who loads the lift must climb up or down stairs to unload it; even in a large library, where an attendant is stationed at each level, confusion may result if the attendant is temporarily absent. Also, if the lift is too small to handle a truck, its use almost inevitably involves at least one or two extra handlings of each book transported. Many booklifts in libraries are rarely used. However, in a branch library, with no elevator conveniently located in or next to the library, a book truck lift is usually essential. A booklift, particularly if large enough to carry a truck, is better than nothing. In this type of installation, building codes may require fire-resistant shafts, and insurance rates may be affected.

Elevators. Elevators are clearly preferable to booklifts in every respect but one: They are more expensive. The cost, in a small library, may represent a substantial fraction of the total expenditure for construction. It will be affected by several factors. Is the elevator propelled by cables or water or oil-driven pistons? What is the size of the cab? What is the maximum weight to be carried? What is the total length of the rise? What speed is stipulated? How complex are the controls required to provide service without an operator? Is there to be an accurate leveling device?

Electrically powered elevators using cables are always used in high buildings, and often in others. Elevators propelled by water or oil-driven pistons are sometimes used in lower buildings, and they are considerably less expensive to install. They are recommended where economies force this choice, and, in fact, they have in recent years been used in most new libraries in the United Kingdom.

The machinery for electrically operated cable elevators is usually located in a penthouse rather than in the basement; this saves in cost of installation and operation, reduces wear and tear on the machinery, and minimizes noise enough to obviate special acoustic treatment. Where there is a desire to reduce the height of the penthouse for architectural reasons, the machinery can be placed in the basement. If the basement machine room is near reading or staff areas, it will need heavy internal sound absorbent treatment, including an excellent door gasket. When heavy loads are to be handled and speed is not important, what is known as two-to-one roping is used instead of one-to-one.

The number of passenger-elevator cabs that will be needed depends on the volume of traffic, the waiting period that will be tolerated, the capacity of the cabs, and their speed. Traffic customarily is measured by the number of persons to be transported in a five-minute peak-load period, and certain standard formulas can be used. These take into account the time required for a full-speed round trip without stops, plus time for accelerating and slowing down at each stop, time for leveling at each stop, time for opening and closing gates and doors, time for passengers to move in and out, lost time resulting from false stops, standing time at top and bottom floors, and reaction time of the operator if there is one. The wider the doors, the more rapidly passengers can move in and out; doors that open at the center of the wide side of the cab speed up operation to a considerable extent. It should be obvious that the number of elevators is influenced by whether stairs are in sight. The Cooper Library of the University of South Carolina has four grouped elevators, and finding stairs is not at all easy except to the administrative office and to special collections.

Nearly all new elevators are automatic, and, if wages are to be saved by eliminating operators, automatic elevators must be installed. These are of three principal types. The simplest responds to the first button pushed and does not "remember" any other calls. The selective-collective type answers only calls in the direction in which the car is moving. Finally, a fully automatic system can be adjusted to operate in a variety of ways designed to suit traffic demands of different levels and of different times of day. For instance, it can automatically proceed to a "home" floor when not in use. The more complicated the controls, the more the elevator costs. Small libraries are rarely justified in installing anything but the simplest type. Safety devices, however, should always be used to prevent the car from moving when doors are open. Automatic leveling devices appropriate for heavy loads are essential for the movement of book trucks. Car speed should be increased in high buildings.

Two elevators in one bank will carry more traffic without undue delay than three widely separated ones, and three together in a large building will probably be as satisfactory as five or six that are widely separated. In the Widener Library, where there are four automatic elevators averaging something like 125 ft (37.850 m) from each other, a passenger often has to wait five minutes or more for a car; three elevators in a single bank would have given better service, though passengers on the average would have had to walk greater distances to reach them.

Special attention needs to be given to the number of elevators; it is too simple to say that the smaller the floors the more elevators are needed. However, consider that the traffic among the floors increases as a smaller fraction of the local collection is shelved on any one floor. Persons looking for four books located on four stack floors will naturally use the elevator four times more often than if the books were located on one floor. Although there is no guiding formula, bookstack towers seem to work well with only two elevators so long as each floor has at least 10 to 14 percent of the total collection, or at least holds the entire collection on a fairly broad subject. Library staff should give this careful consideration based on the local library collection at the current time.

A major question in locating elevators is whether to place them in a part of the building not open to the general public or to restrict their use in other ways. Traffic may be unduly heavy if they are used unnecessarily by undergraduates going up or down only one or two floors. Use can be restricted by having elevator doors and call buttons operate only by key, and distributing keys only to members of the staff and to physically handicapped readers. Another possibility is to locate elevators behind desks where an attendant is always on duty. Control has been facilitated in several new buildings where the bank of elevators is at the rear of the circulation desk lobby or in the central core of the building. (The location of stairways leading to restricted levels in similar space is an advantage.) Control may be needed, for example, to restrict stack access to professors, librarians, and graduate students.

The gravity of the problem will be recognized by anyone who has waited 15 minutes for an elevator in the University of Pittsburgh's Cathedral of Learning, as well as by anyone who has helped to plan an 18-story library building in which six elevators for passengers and one for freight, including space for them and for their lobbies, would cost at least $1 million today. A single elevator in a five-story building will cost at least $100,000 (probably much more) in addition to the cost of the space occupied by its shaft and by the lobbies in front of it. It should be added that when an automatic elevator is pushed too hard by heavy traffic, its electrical control system is likely to break down, and repair is costly.

One means of reducing the load on elevators is to confine the library's most heavily used facilities to the entrance level and the levels immediately above and below, which most readers can be expected or required to reach by stairways. If this can be done, it will be much easier to provide satisfactory elevator service for those who must use the elevator or who will use the further reaches of the building but do not rush in and out in such large numbers between classes.

Finally, the details of interior surfaces, ceiling height, a phone, bells, Braille or audible annunciation of floor levels, and signs need consideration, though consideration of these aspects will often be left for a later design phase. Examples of concerns about these features include the following: The phone should be low enough so that a person who has collapsed on the floor can reach it; the interior surfaces should be exceptionally durable or easily repaired; the ceiling should be high enough to discourage tampering and permit the movement of library shelving components; graffiti should be discouraged by avoiding surfaces inviting defacement both inside the elevator and in the vicinity of the elevator lobby; and, in terms of signs, although the elevator user should know the desired floor before entering the elevator, decisions are needed as to the information to be displayed inside the elevator.

Conveyors. Conveyors should be considered if there is a fairly continuous flow of books or other library materials through a multilevel building with closed stacks; they occasionally provide a more satisfactory solution to book transportation problems than either booklifts or a second service elevator. An endless-belt conveyor or a conveyor that transports totes is similar mechanically to an escalator. Like elevators, conveyors moving materials vertically through the building must be enclosed in fire-resistant shafts. Carrier prongs are attached, usually at approximately 9-ft (2.743-m) intervals, to the chains that go up and down. Books can be placed on the prongs as they go past, or they may be placed in totes that are picked up by the conveyor. The books, or totes laden with books, can be placed on the conveyor at any level; they then go to the level that has been indicated by pushing a button when they were loaded. If this level is below their starting point, they first go to the top, swing around, and then come down.

A central location for conveyors is highly desirable, of course; installation by a stairwell is advantageous because it may facilitate access for servicing and repair. Precautions should be taken to make conveyors as quiet as possible; many have caused trouble by creaking and groaning or banging when making a delivery. It should be noted that the simplest conveyor installations have proved to be the most satisfactory; those that pick up material at any level but deposit it at only one—for example, the reading-room level—are the least likely to get out of order. Two conveyors of this sort have been in operation at the New York Public Library for well over 60 years with very few difficulties, though an extension serving the new underground storage stack has been problematic. More complicated installations are to be found at Yale, at the Bibliothèque nationale de France, and in the Library of Congress where, because the stack is not directly above, below, or adjacent to the charging desk or reading room, the conveyors have to travel horizontally for a considerable distance. The California State University at Long Beach Library once had a complex system of conveyors and sorting areas used to facilitate the return of large quantities of books to the shelves. Replacement parts soon could not be obtained, maintenance became a problem, and the entire equipment was abandoned within a dozen years and later removed as part of a renovation project.

An example of conveyor advantages and problems exists at the Robarts Library, University of Toronto. In this huge building, two vertical conveyors serve all 16 floors. One is for paged books and is connected on each of the stack floors, 9 to 13, to horizontal conveyors that encircle the stacks. The other is for internal mail, returning empty totes and books for reshelving, but it can also be used for paged books if the first is shut down. All floors have short horizontal runs off the second conveyor. At each entrance to the conveyors, the opening is guarded by a photoelectric cell; if the beam is broken by an overloaded tote, the conveyor automatically shuts down, and can only be restarted by the building engineer after the blockage has been cleared. Both conveyors accept two containers 6 × 12 in. (152 × 305 mm)—a tote tray 4 in. (102 mm) deep and a tote box 10 in. (254 mm) deep. These are made of molded fiberglass, and both sizes can be nested for easy storage. To load, totes are placed on a slide, manually or automatically depending on location, and addressed to a specific floor at a single control panel. The slide moves forward into the conveyor shaft, and the tote is lifted by the next pair of arms ascending on the continuous chain. To unload at the designated floor, the slide moves forward into the shaft on the descending side and catches the tote, moves back out of the shaft, and ejects the tote onto the horizontal run.

As reported in 1983, the system has had problems:

1. During the first year or so there was a good deal of misuse of the system by library staff unfamiliar with conveyors. This caused some damage, and far too many shutdowns. It is essential that a system be used by staff who have been thoroughly trained.
2. The horizontal ring conveyors on the five stack floors are no longer used. If the Robarts had been designated as an open stack library during the planning stage, the horizontal conveyors would

probably not have been built. Most patrons prefer to go up to the stacks and find books for themselves, so the horizontal conveyors were never much used. Then, after a few years of operation they began to get rather noisy, which led to complaints from people studying in the stacks, so use of them was discontinued.

3. The vertical continuous chain conveyors are in operation for 94.5 hours a week, and have been subject to considerable wear and tear; more than was anticipated. In the ten years that Robarts has been open, there have been several extended shutdowns for major maintenance and repair. And despite the continued existence of the company that made and installed the conveyors, some replacement parts have proved difficult to get. The design is now rather out of date; if it were being installed today, the loading and unloading mechanisms would be quite different.

As reported in 1996, even the vertical conveyor has been used less and less, as it has been judged more cost effective to sort the returning books directly onto trucks for reshelving and wheel them directly to the appropriate floor by elevator, rather than load and unload the conveyor. Parts and maintenance became even more of an issue, and it is "difficult to justify the high costs" associated with such specialized equipment.

On the other hand, the conveyor system at the Library of Congress made up of several discrete systems serving the Madison, Jefferson, and Adams buildings continues to be used with satisfaction after many years. The systems transport boxes or trays, and they are reported (in late 1997) to be free of experienced damage to books.

Pneumatic tubes. Pneumatic tubes have been used for many years to transfer call slips from circulation desks to attendants in the stacks. Propulsion is by compressed air or vacuum, and slips can be delivered much more rapidly than by elevator or conveyor. For very large closed-stack libraries, use of a rapid message system and conveyor for book delivery can be very efficient.

Much larger pneumatic tubes have been used for transporting books over considerable distances when vertical or horizontal endless-belt conveyors did not seem practical. The connection between the Library of Congress Jefferson building and its Capitol building (approximately ⅓ mile or ½ kilometer) is an example that continues in use with no experience of damaged books. Another is the pneumatic connection between the undergraduate and main research libraries at the University of California, Los Angeles, where the

containers used were approximately 1 ft (305 mm) in diameter and 18 in. (457 mm) in length. Unfortunately, they stopped at their destination with an abrupt jar, the containers got stuck in the tube, maintenance was expensive, and the system did not cut down on staff time for pickup and delivery between the Powell Library and the Research Library buildings because the tubes were not big enough for many books. UCLA would not consider installing such a system today.

Air tubes have also been used to transfer loan request slips. Such tubes are found at the Library of Congress with service between the control rooms and various stack decks. The Robarts Library at the University of Toronto no longer uses those as a result of two conditions: (1) virtually every member of the university who has stack access prefers to browse the stacks, and (2) retrieval slips are taken by staff from the circulation desk to the shelves because there are now few stack staff on all levels to whom the slips could be transmitted. Thus, in 1996 the tube ducts were removed as part of a remodeling for a new Teaching and Learning facility.

Other communication systems. Other forms of communication should be considered, either for their own merits or as supplemental to those already discussed. These, of course, include computers for in-house messages, telephones, and television. Their detailed requirements will be discussed in Chapter 13 as their use, other than possibly reducing the need for the mechanical systems discussed here, will have less of an impact on the schematic phase of the design effort. Their potential advantages should be considered as the design team thinks through the various possibilities of spatial relationships, and the internal configuration of the major elements.

One caution: Many library buildings have installed elaborate intercoms or book conveyors as part of initial construction and ceased using them in a very few years. Though it is obviously more expensive to add them at a later time, consider carefully whether inclusion of such devices is justified.

12.4.4 Supervision and Control

Librarians would rather help than supervise those who use their buildings; they have no desire to act as police officers and are eager to make controls as inconspicuous as possible if they cannot be eliminated. Fortunately, less supervision is required now than was thought necessary early in the twentieth century, when closed-access libraries were the accepted standard. Today students, both graduates and undergraduates, seem to be more serious than their predecessors and most come to the library for study rather than for social purposes. There will always be exceptions, and, in some cases, the design of the library can regrettably promote unwanted social activities. Most libraries in the United States and Canada now admit students to the stacks, where close supervision is impossible; consequently, it is illogical to supervise most reading rooms. At least three out of four students prefer individual seating; and seating of this kind, which is being provided generously, discourages conversation in reading areas and hence reduces the need for supervision. Improved acoustics, better traffic patterns, variety in seating options, better designed carrels, and improved seating layouts help to reduce noise and confusion, and create an atmosphere conducive to orderly behavior. Finally, there is management realization that the most economical, and in many ways the most satisfactory, location for control is at the building's exit or exits.

It should be emphasized that no one advocates supervision anywhere in a library if it can be eliminated without serious consequences. Unfortunately, students seem to be tempted to appropriate library materials for themselves; the problem is particularly serious in the case of traditional reserved books (electronic reserves will correct this condition). Attendants at the exits cannot search everyone who leaves the building; books can be concealed in clothing, particularly during the winter; and electronic systems can be circumvented. If it is known that repeated unauthorized borrowing is a serious offense punishable by dismissal or suspension, inspection at the exits can be more effective than the former method of reading-room supervision. Given the now common use of electronic book-detection systems, most new buildings provide for limited control at the exits without directly inspecting for library books.

Several types of electronic detection systems are suitable for use in libraries; each has its own set of facility requirements. Library staff should review the literature, perhaps visit several different installations, and select a specific system for which the control area should be designed. In determining the ideal facility arrangements, it is essential to consult an expert engineering representative of the firm selected, as sales representatives frequently are not aware of some of the details of an ideal installation. Besides the obvious requirements for power, the more subtle requirements of spacing and layout may be derived from such a consultation. Failure to follow this procedure can result in considerable frustration resulting from false alarms, interference with computer systems, interference caused by photocopy machines, ineffective detection, or inadequate response to an alarm when it occurs.

It should always be recognized that any system can be circumvented by the intentional thief. Control at the exits is no safeguard against theft of rare books by professional thieves; the only satisfactory procedure is to keep very valuable materials in closed stacks, make them available only to persons who have signed for them, supervise their use, and check them in immediately on their return and before the reader leaves, in order to make sure that they have not been mutilated. Exit controls can be expected, however, to prevent unauthorized borrowing by forgetful or impatient professors and students, and to deter deliberate theft. If individuals must conceal a book or mutilate its binding to get it past the controls, they can hardly pretend that it has been taken thoughtlessly rather than deliberately.

It may be suggested also that, though controls may not seem necessary at the time a building is planned, conditions do change. The building should be planned, therefore, so that staffed exit controls, with or without an electronic book-detection system, can be provided at some later date without expensive alterations and without harming the appearance of the lobbies.

Various methods of entrance control are possible. Turnstiles, with or without a staff member to monitor the traffic, are commonly used where entrances are controlled, though they mandate an alternative route for handicapped persons and book trucks. A typical turnstile has only a 16-in. (406-mm) space for a person to squeeze through. Use of magnetic card-reading devices to permit turnstile action is becoming increasingly popular. Where the turnstile is a full-height revolving door or cage, as was used in the Woodruff Library of Emory University and as some subway train exits, there is no need for staff oversight. Each institution will need to decide the nature of access to the library.

Electric eyes, pressure-sensitive pads, or turnstiles can be used to count those who enter, though neither can be relied upon for a completely accurate count because there are service and staff doors. Generally, though, turnstiles provide a means of traffic control in or out or both, which is regarded by many librarians as being more effective than relying solely on an attendant or on signs.

Velour-covered ropes or fixed railings on stanchions of some kind can be used to channel readers through a narrow exit lane past a desk. At the Lamont Library as many as four exit lanes can be opened at one time in the main entrance (see fig. 12.22), but only half of these have proved to be necessary in order to handle the traffic without forcing students to line up. In this regard, it may be prudent to provide for excess capacity, for it would be very difficult to add it later if it is found to be needed, and the cost initially is small in relation to the total project.

Another exiting method, used in the Widener Library when the unattractive turnstiles were removed, is to leave a passage more than 4 ft (1.220 m) wide with a counter on the right-hand side behind which an attendant sits on a high stool (see fig. 12.23). This arrangement proved to be reasonably satisfactory at Widener, which is used most by professors and graduate students. In an undergraduate library, where there is very heavy traffic just before each class period begins, and in a research library at times of peak loads, narrow passages would be preferable if not as pleasant.

Entrance monitors may also serve as information staff where the stranger can obtain directions, which are often needed in any large library. Counters at exits are preferable to desks, because it is not convenient for readers to show books on a low surface; a height of 39 in. (990 mm) is suggested because some persons feel that this is high enough to lift a heavy briefcase. A portion of the control booth or counter may be constructed with a lower, table-height surface, so that the attendant can easily inspect shopping bags or backpacks. For comfort when not standing, the attendant should be provided with a high stool having a back and footrest or a platform in the

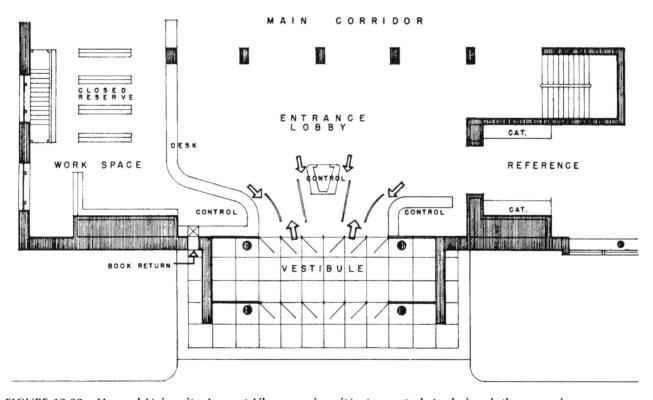

FIGURE 12.22   Harvard University, Lamont Library, main exit/entry control. As designed, there are six doors between the vestibule and lobby. Handles are on the vestibule side of only the second and fifth doors, counting from left to right. On the inside these doors are labeled No Exit. Door 1 is always in use when the building is open. Doors 3, 4, and 6 can be used whenever necessary, as each has a control station available. When not in use, they are blocked by bars.

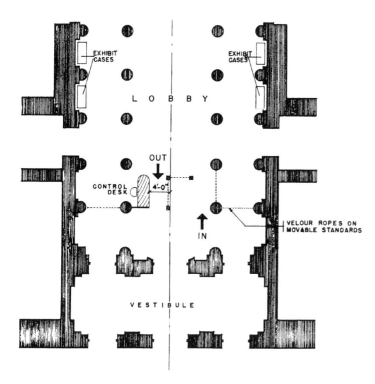

FIGURE 12.23 Harvard University, Widener Library, main exit/entry control. Incoming traffic automatically keeps to the right. Persons leaving the building automatically keep to the right past the control desk. This arrangement can easily be adapted for any of the several book-detection systems, although the remote location will always require a staffed position. Being near a service point can be an advantage in this regard.

kneehole of the counter. A slightly raised floor can aid the inspection process, and, with a raised floor, a standard secretarial chair should be adequate. The booth should be provided with a phone. Other features may include a panic alert button, first-aid supplies, and a covered display area in the counter for a campus map, library diagrams, or other information that may aid the visitor. It should be possible for the attendant to reach the outside door quickly if necessary.

A long control desk at the exit can in some cases serve also as the main circulation desk and even as the desk for service of books on closed reserve, as at Harvard's Lamont Library. If this is possible, there are advantages. The noise and

confusion that circulation services always create are confined to the entrance lobby; the number of staff members who must be on duty during quiet periods is reduced, a fact that may be an important financial consideration; and the reader may avoid having books checked twice, once when they are charged out and again upon leaving the building. On the other hand, staff may not juggle effectively the task of exit checking with circulation service. The former is likely to suffer. Electronic exit review can help solve this quandary.

Nothing has been said thus far of how many entrances and exits may be needed. Most libraries, of course, must have a separate shipping and receiving entrance, which may be available for use by members of the staff. Such entrances are now frequently monitored electronically, with the door controlled by use of a magnetic personalized card issued to some or all staff. For external and internal doors with access to rare books, computer installations, and other selected areas, doors monitored electronically customarily provide a computer readout giving the name and exact time when the door was opened. Each public entrance and exit is expensive; attendants must be paid and floor space must be provided in the building plans. Moreover, the whole traffic and security problem within the building can be simplified if there is a single entrance and exit. In a large library, however, traffic is often so heavy and distances so great that a second controlled entrance and exit is essential. Fire laws may require it; if they do not, emergency exits with crash locks or panic hardware and an alarm system with a loud local alarm and perhaps a remote signal should be available.

Control of an additional staffed exit will require payment of two or three salaries in a library that is open for 75 to 100 or more hours a week; moreover, a secondary exit will normally be used considerably less than the main one and may not be a suitable place for circulation or reserved-book services; there may be a problem in keeping the attendant profitably occupied. In the Lamont Library at Harvard, a portion of the reserved-book collection was once kept behind the desk at the now-closed secondary entrance (see fig. 12.24), which is on a floor level different from the main entrance. In the Widener Library, the second entrance is also on a different level from the front door and controls a secondary entrance to the bookstack, which is a great convenience in a 10-

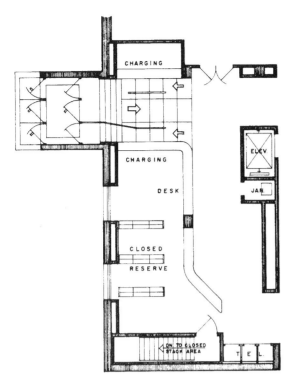

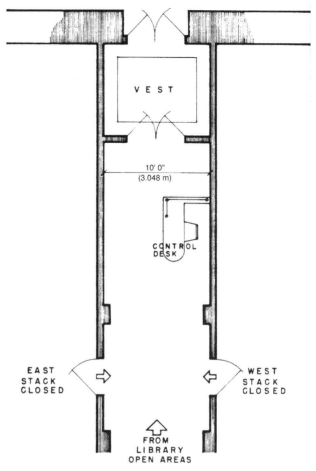

FIGURE 12.24 Harvard University, Lamont Library, secondary exit control (no longer in use). At this entrance, only the middle door is provided with a handle on the outside. The reader goes down five steps immediately after entering, which almost automatically restricts the use of this entrance. It does not meet ADA requirements.

FIGURE 12.25 Harvard University, Widener Library, secondary exit control at ground level. Checking counter is on the right as one leaves. Secondary stack entrances a few feet from the door are controlled by push button from the desk; thus, stacks are available only on request to the holders of permits. Because this type of entrance must be staffed, it may not be justified in times of operating budget restraint.

level stack (see fig. 12.25). Fire regulations require that two exits be provided in both Widener and Lamont at all times they are open.

Elsewhere, however, there are equally large buildings operating under regulations that call for one regular exit, supplemented by emergency exits guarded by electrical or mechanical alarms that operate automatically if the door is opened. This type of exit control is fairly effective if it is very obvious that use of the exit will sound an alarm. A clearly visible sign stating "Emergency exit only—Exit sounds alarm" will help. A crash lock can be broken, of course, and a thief or errant student can escape even though there is an effective alarm system. The Von Duprin emergency exit device has door monitoring as well as a programmed delay in its action, so an alarm is given but the door cannot immediately be opened.

This device will often need approval from a local building inspector and safety officials, but approval is typically given when the library is fully sprinklered and smoke detection is in place. Where a serious problem is expected, the alarm system can be augmented with television surveillance, such as that at the Perry-Castañeda Library at the University of Texas, Austin. Proliferation of entrances should be discouraged in almost all instances.

A discussion of problems of control and supervision would be incomplete if it did not mention the difficulties that sometimes occur when there are outdoor reading terraces, sometimes at ground level and other times at higher floors. These can be attractive, and some architects delight in them, but their disadvantages ought not to be overlooked. Unless they are carefully designed so that external access is at least difficult, books can be dropped from them to a waiting confederate or to the ground if a secluded spot is available. An open reading terrace placed far within the roof areas of the building can solve the security issue, though such a location would of course lose any scenic views that placement around the exterior could achieve. Dust and air pollution may make them unsatisfactory places for reading, and, in most sections of this country, the number of dry and warm days when they can be used is discouragingly small. Operable windows create similar problems as well as seriously compromise environmental control for preservation of the collections.

Entrances and exits are where traffic patterns begin and end; the decisions made regarding them also affect the security of the library's collections and its operating costs. It is important, therefore, that entrance lobbies be designed with a view to installation of control desks in the future if not at once, with space for channeling past a desk those who are leaving, and with the capacity to handle rush-hour traffic.

In summary, this section has dealt with basic spatial relationships and a variety of traffic problems, the solution of which plays a large part in the planning of a successful library building. Among them, directly or indirectly, these traffic issues affect all the basic elements of planning. A successful library must have its public service, its reading accommodations, and its housing for collections and staff conveniently related to each other, and must enable the desired degree of supervision and control and must facilitate the vertical transportation. Nothing in the design should be "frozen" until each of those primary traffic aspects and their relations to one another have been given adequate thought and study. Furthermore, audible and visual distraction must be minimized so that a quiet, comfortable place for study and work will be provided.

Unless these requisites are fulfilled, aesthetically pleasing exteriors and interiors and the other important features of a library will not make up for its defects. Each of them should be studied and analyzed from the beginning. The traffic patterns in all their aspects should be diagrammed

and tested in their relationship to other problems as the location of each area is considered. The simple and successful traffic patterns in the Olin Library at Cornell are noteworthy. Stephen A. McCarthy, the director of libraries, reported: "The continuous study of traffic patterns in the Olin Library moved the entrance from the middle of the north side of the building to the west side; it moved the elevators from the center toward the west end; and this in turn dictated the location of the graduate study rooms and the conference rooms at the west end. The disposition of many of the facilities in the building flows naturally from the traffic patterns."[4]

12.5
The Schematic Phase of Interior Design

In the ideal design process the interior design effort will parallel that of the architectural design. All too often in the past the interior design was left to the librarian or a purchasing agent. In any significant project it is recommended that the services of an interior designer should be part of the design effort and that involvement should begin during schematics. Assuming such is the case, the schematic phase of interior design will involve the preparation of layouts and a preliminary presentation of types of materials, including fabrics and carpets, colors, and other features.

Layouts carefully prepared during the architectural schematic phase are essential for testing the adequacy of the program and the space arrangements presented by the architect. If an interior designer is not used, this testing must be done by the architect, librarian, building projects manager, or consultant. Tentative layouts are also essential for the librarian, trustees, university administrators, donors, and others to visualize the nature of the space and the scale of the project. A plan of a single rectangular room without furniture could be an immense barn or a small closet to the individual who is not familiar with the use of scale, unless furniture or other elements to which the viewer can relate are placed upon the drawing.

Figures 12.26 through 12.38 are intended to help the librarian visualize the kind of space needed for people in libraries.

As with the architectural design, the design process for the interiors should require numerous meetings with the designer and library representative and perhaps the institution's project manager. A tour of nearby libraries and an overview of the program are useful to start meaningful discussion. In some cases, particularly where an existing building is being remodeled for library purposes, the entire design effort may be under the guidance of an interior designer rather than an architect. In a few cases, the architect will design a building with large empty spaces, leaving the interior arrangements and assignment of space entirely up to the interior designer; however, this approach is not recommended unless the architect and the interior designer are working closely together in the same design phase at the same time. Without such coordination, problems are certain to result.

Concerns about module and bay size, traffic routes, the relationships of major functions, durability of surfaces, flexibility for future change, a philosophy of what the library should be like, and many other aspects of the building program will be just as important for the interior designer as they are for the architect.

The ability to change the interior design, particularly furniture layouts, will remain somewhat easier for a longer period of time during the design process than is the case with major architectural elements. The schematic phase of interior design is thus a testing of the space arrangements rather than a final arrangement of furniture patterns. Once the configuration of the structure and major components is established, it should only be changed with great care. However, furniture can, to a larger degree, be moved around even after the building is occupied.

What then is the importance of the testing? Basically, the testing is to determine answers to the following, so any inadequacy can be addressed during the next design phase:

1. Is the amount of space provided sufficient for the number of elements that are to be placed in it? This is essentially a test of the program statement.
2. Is the configuration of the space suitable? Can the elements within the space be arranged in a logical order? This should take into consideration not only the shape of the space, but also other features, such as doors, stairs, windows, skylights, lighting, and so on.
3. Are there important conditions that must relate to the interior design? These would

(A)

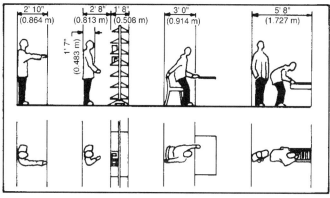

(B)

FIGURE 12.26   Human dimension. Note that the seated figure in A requires additional space to get into the seated position as shown in B. These dimensions are suitable for planning purposes in many cases, but there will be exceptions, notably for meeting ADA where greater space is typically required (see figs. 12.34–12.38 for ADA dimensions).

include the need for power outlets, communication systems, special lighting, and other details that are closely related to the layout but that may be reflected in the architectural design.
4. Are there architectural qualities that will influence the interior design? These might include materials, colors, style, and other aspects for which the design of the interior arrangements should complement the architecture.

These questions will be discussed in order in the following paragraphs.

1. *Is the architectural space adequate?* For any programmed function or area, there should, of course, be a tabulation of requirements, including

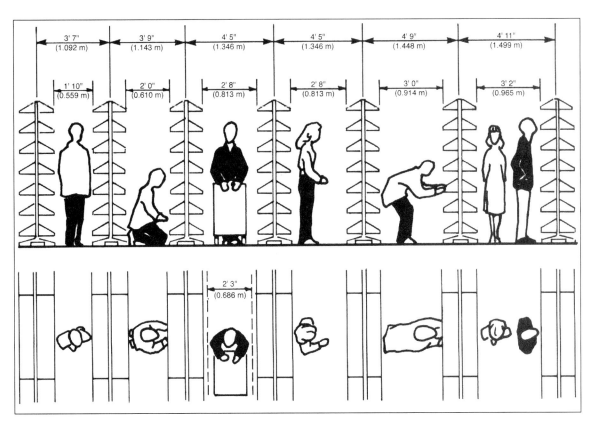

FIGURE 12.27 **Human dimensions in stack aisles. The kneeling position, second from left, would be difficult for many users. It is more likely that the reader would squat in alignment with the shelves in a minimum-width aisle rather than face the shelves. This illustration is based upon a range that is 21 in. (0.533 m) from front to front, which suggests 10-in. (0.254-m) nominal shelves plus 1-in. (25-mm) growth space.**

the number and type of furniture, acoustical concerns, telecommunications needs, special lighting requirements, and other specific needs that will, at least in part, be reflected in the interior design.

One of the first steps then is to prepare drawings, using the architectural design as a background and showing each of the significant furniture elements, including shelving, chairs, desks, side tables, floor lamps, lockers, carrels, typing stands, service counters, stools, and anything else that occupies floor space. Using the program as a basis, the interior designer or other responsible member of the design team will create a first draft or design, plotting out major functions with circulation routes, space for book truck parking, or a queue waiting at a service point, and, of course, the specified furnishings together with adequate space for the user.

The interior design process is similar to that of the architectural effort, only on a smaller scale.

Individual units within a major function will be grouped together and organized with consideration given to the concepts of communication, materials flow, privacy or group activity, acoustic need, window conditions, and outlook. While the architect may provide a single large area for technical processing, the interior designer will divide up the space, perhaps only in terms of furniture groupings, into the smaller elements of binding preparation, finishing, gift and exchange, acquisitions, cataloging, serials processing, and perhaps an area for the supporting bibliographic tools.

Although at this stage it is not critical that all the functions within a space are properly arranged, it will be the beginning of the study of those crucial aspects of the design detail that will make the facility function smoothly. It may also illustrate that the configurations of the space could be improved by altering the architectural

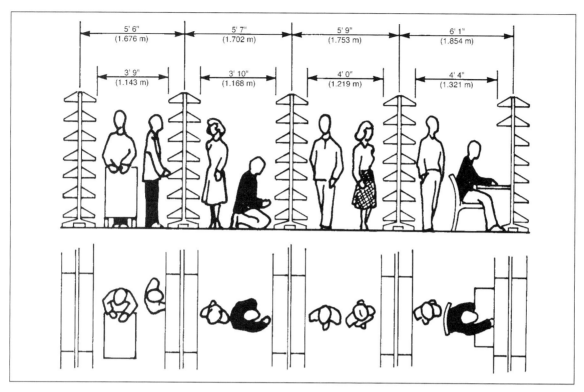

FIGURE 12.28 Human dimensions in larger stack aisles. Again, this figure is based upon 10-in. (254-mm) shelving and 1-in. (25-mm) growth space through the range. These aisle widths are best suited for access by the handicapped and for heavy use. In some cases the width of the aisle in the far right illustration is excessive, although having a continuous row of reading positions as suggested may substitute for an index table. At an index table, stools may be better than chairs.

envelope, which should still be possible at this stage of the design.

2. *Is the configuration of the space suitable?* The interior designer may well be influential in the decisions about the shape of a given space and its proportions and lines. In general, most rooms should be rectangular, usually not square, and the height of rooms should ideally be related to the other dimensions.

Round or triangular or, for that matter, octagonal rooms are wasteful of space, as furniture and equipment—this includes accommodations for readers, services to readers, and shelving—do not fit into them economically. In spite of the unfortunate historic experiences at the British Museum, the Library of Congress, the Brotherton Library at the University of Leeds, the State Library in Melbourne, Australia, and many others, each generation of architects again tries out areas that are not rectangular, and the interior designer must deal with the problems or assets that result.

Noise and other distractions are fundamental problems in the planning of traffic and circulation

patterns that are part of the interior design. Sound-absorbing materials can do much to minimize noise, but, whenever possible, prevention is better than absorption. And some degree of background sound is essential. Visual distractions constitute a related and equally important subject. Window glare, garish color, and heavy traffic in one's field of vision can produce unwanted distractions.

Certain fortunate individuals find noise and motion no problem; those who have grown up amidst large families or have worked from an early age in open offices or have lived with amplified music may be nearly immune to visual and auditory distractions. Many undergraduates, however, even those who prefer to study with the radio on, are not immune; and undergraduates, as well as more advanced students, may deserve consideration in this respect. The professor can usually find a secluded corner at home even if there is no private study in the library. The graduate student in many institutions is now provided with a reasonably quiet and secluded cubicle or carrel. But for the less advanced student,

FIGURE 12.29   Human dimensions in very large aisles are clearly intended for very heavy use. The figure at the far right assumes a file cabinet that is 17½ in. (0.445 m) deep, which is shallower than most. Even the typical card catalog cabinet is about 20 in. (0.508 m) deep, including the handles.

the only alternative to a library reading room may be the dormitory, where a roommate may operate on a different timetable and gregarious friends may be plentiful. The reading room is likely to be crowded with contemporaries, and table space available there may be no more than 30 in. wide × 18 in. deep (762 mm × 457 mm), which is not enough for spreading out books or, indeed, for opening more than one if space for taking notes is also required.

Fully as serious as any of the handicaps that have been suggested is the fact that the reading room or area may be in almost constant turmoil; it may settle down 20 minutes after a class period begins, only to be disrupted again 10 minutes before the period ends as students begin to leave. Afternoons and evenings may be disturbed by more continual though less concentrated coming and going.

In many ways contemporary undergraduates may be worse off than their predecessors; the great monumental reading rooms of earlier days tended to engulf the reader in the constant mix

of sounds, just as a large stadium filled with a cheering crowd may leave the athletes oblivious of everything but their immediate surroundings. The newer, more intimate reading areas are too often still surrounded by shelves that attract traffic. The clicking and chirping of computers, unless isolated in acoustically separate areas, is an everyday intrusion. Entrance to the room is often through a single passageway in the center of the long side or, worse still, at one end; few readers can enter or leave without going past many tables at which others are attempting to study.

The foregoing account of the undergraduate's woes may be enough to indicate why the following basic principles need to be emphasized:

Noise and confusion should be kept out of reading areas or controlled insofar as possible. Consider designated areas where computers can or cannot be used. Design material into the accommodations for computer use to absorb and isolate sound. Circulation and reference desks should be elsewhere,

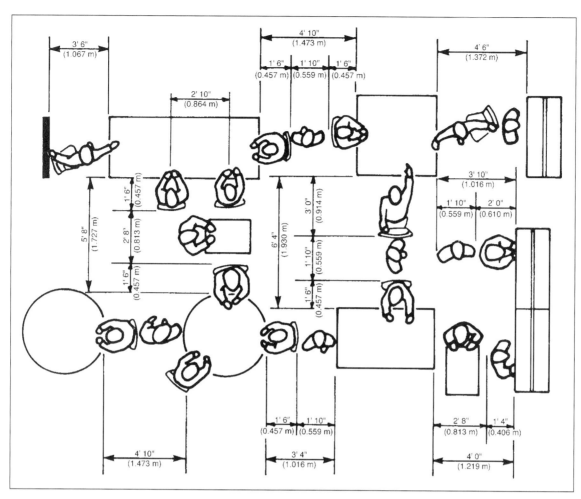

FIGURE 12.30 Human dimensions between tables. Note that round tables are not normally recommended for research purposes, but they may be desired in a staff room or in an area for light reading.

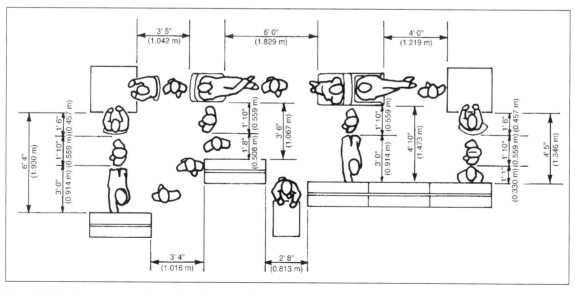

FIGURE 12.31 Human dimensions between lounge chairs, tables, and shelving.

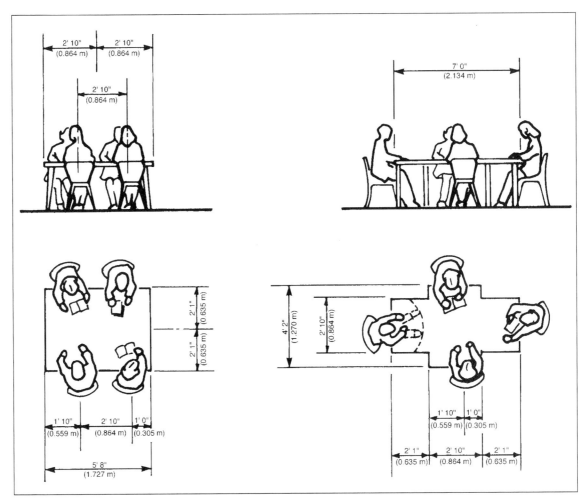

FIGURE 12.32   Human dimensions at tables. The unusual shape of the table at the right is intended more to illustrate minimum dimensions than to suggest an ideal table. The suggested width is not sufficient for the student doing serious research, although it is more likely that four students would sit at the table to the right because of the greater separation.

with books, walls, distance, or acoustic materials—perhaps more than one of these barriers—to separate them from readers. The public catalogs and, to a lesser extent, shelves holding reference collections are also areas of relatively heavy traffic. Use of current periodicals involves a good deal of movement. If periodicals or reference books must be in the reading area, used also for general reading, they should at least be placed at one side or one end, with adequate acoustic insulation that can be provided by walls, acoustic floors and ceilings, and books.

*Access to reading areas should be provided through as many well-distributed entrances as possi-*ble. If students can usually find a seat near the point at which they enter the room, they can be expected to leave the same way, and both visual and auditory disturbance can be kept to a minimum.

Individual seating accommodations are highly desirable. They will be most satisfactory if a barrier at the back of each individual table can be built up to a height of 52 to 54 in. (1.320 to 1.371 m), which is enough to prevent the reader from seeing the head of the person in the opposite carrel. In a seat of this kind, a reader should be able to turn slightly away from the rest of the room and obtain visual privacy if desired.

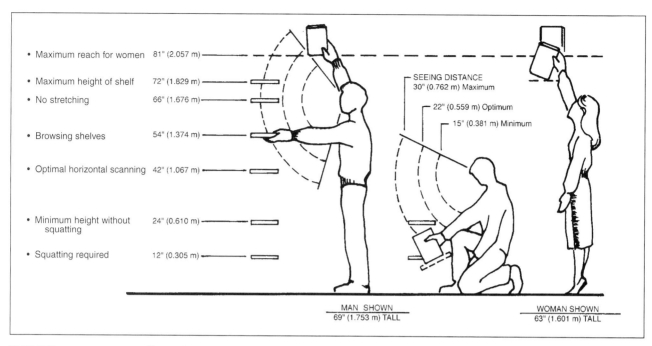

• Maximum reach for women 81" (2.057 m)

• Maximum height of shelf 72" (1.829 m)

• No stretching 66" (1.676 m)

• Browsing shelves 54" (1.374 m)

• Optimal horizontal scanning 42" (1.067 m)

• Minimum height without squatting 24" (0.610 m)

• Squatting required 12" (0.305 m)

SEEING DISTANCE
30" (0.762 m) Maximum

22" (0.559 m) Optimum

15" (0.381 m) Minimum

MAN SHOWN
69" (1.753 m) TALL

WOMAN SHOWN
63" (1.601 m) TALL

FIGURE 12.33   Human dimensions at shelving.

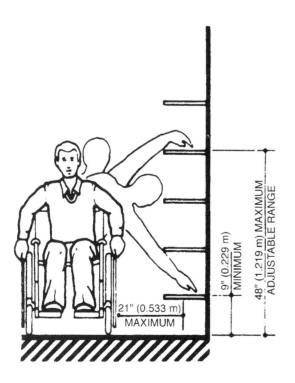

9" (0.229 m) MINIMUM

48" (1.219 m) MAXIMUM
ADJUSTABLE RANGE

21" (0.533 m)
MAXIMUM

FIGURE 12.34   Dimensions of vertical and horizontal reach from a wheelchair and the ADA range for display shelving. Note that these requirements are only for shelving that is described as "display" shelving; the height of standard library stacks is not currently limited by the ADA. If a library is designed to meet the dimensions shown here, the added space required will be substantial unless the collection accommodated is very small. Some authorities will limit the height of what is called "journal display shelving" to these dimensions because of the display function of that shelving. (Department of Justice, "Nondiscrimination on the Basis of Disability by Public Accommodations and Commercial Facilities, Final Rule," *Federal Register* 56, no. 144 [July 26, 1991]: 35656.)

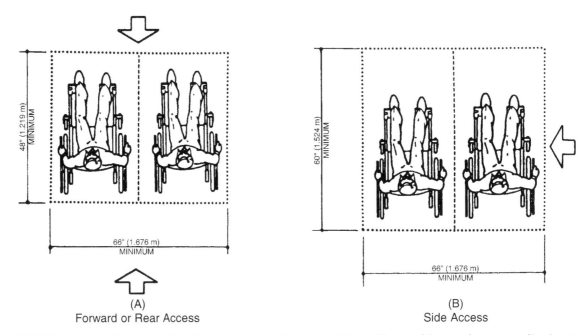

FIGURE 12.35   Minimum ADA clearance for seating in a setting without tables (such as an auditorium). Where there is a choice in seating of "line of sight" or admission price (which could be the case if the library provides a presentation hall with the capacity to offer movies or lectures for a fee that differentiates favored seating), that seating choice must be provided for wheelchairs as well. Where wheelchair seating is provided in a room with fixed seating, at least one fixed companion seat must be provided with each group of wheelchairs.   (Department of Justice, "Nondiscrimination on the Basis of Disability by Public Accommodations and Commercial Facilities, Final Rule," *Federal Register* 56, no. 144 [July 26, 1991]: 35663.)

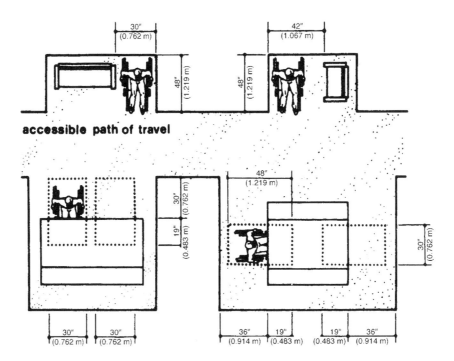

FIGURE 12.36   Dimensions at tables and seating meeting ADA requirements. A minimum of one seat or 5 percent of the seating (whichever is greater) in any area of the library must be provided with clearances meeting those in this figure. (Department of Justice, "Nondiscrimination on the Basis of Disability by Public Accommodations and Commercial Facilities, Final Rule," *Federal Register* 56, no. 144 [July 26, 1991]: 35663.)

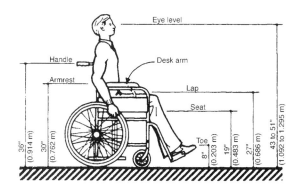

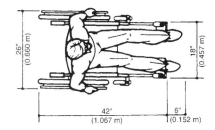

Note: Footrests may extend farther for tall people.

FIGURE 12.37 **Dimensions of wheelchairs. Note the height of the wheelchair arm for table clearance. (Department of Justice, "Nondiscrimination on the Basis of Disability by Public Accommodations and Commercial Facilities, Final Rule,"** *Federal Register* **56, no. 144 [July 26, 1991]: 35676.)**

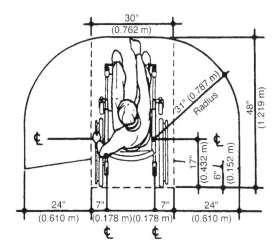

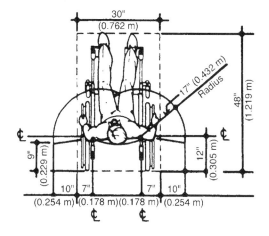

FIGURE 12.38 **Dimensions of horizontal reach from a wheelchair. (₵ stands for center line.) (Department of Justice, "Nondiscrimination on the Basis of Disability by Public Accommodations and Commercial Facilities, Final Rule,"** *Federal Register* **56, no. 144 [July 26, 1991]: 35676.)**

Table surfaces should be large enough to permit the student to spread out materials. Space on an individual table goes farther than space on a large shared table; a surface measuring 22 × 33 in. (559 × 838 mm) is as useful on an individual table as a segment measuring 24 × 36 in. (610 × 914 mm) on a table that must be shared.

A plan designed to avoid disturbing readers should not make a maze of the library. Devious and complicated traffic lanes will discourage use of the building and cause frustration and wasted time. Some librarians would not agree with this point, but the fact is that the more difficult it is to find an empty seat, the more noise will be created.

Traffic patterns in bookstacks also vitally affect the welfare of readers. The tendency is to locate a larger and larger percentage of total reading accommodations in the stacks. It is important to keep heavily used traffic arteries away from open carrels.

Noise and other distractions should be kept in mind when planning traffic lanes throughout the building. Stairs in the vicinity of reading areas should be acoustically isolated and treated. The main stair at the University of Victoria Library in British Columbia is a concrete construction with openings through operable windows to adjacent reading areas. Aside from the obvious fire risk, the windows constantly stand open for air circulation, creating a serious acoustic problem. Elevator lobbies should be separated from reading areas.

Background sound from the ventilation system or from another "white sound" source is essential. Although this goes beyond the scope of normal interior design, it is a crucial factor. Even with excellent acoustic materials provided on all the surfaces, minor sounds, such as the clicking of computers or even the turning of pages, become a distraction when there is no background sound. Everything can be heard clearly if there is nothing to mask it.

These are obvious principles; yet most libraries have disregarded one or more of them. Good traffic patterns, plus adequate lighting and ventilation, are essential if the library is to be a satisfactory place for work or study. For the most part, these are factors that can be greatly influenced by the interior designer at this stage of the project.

The flow of the classification sequence for the open-access collections is another important area influenced by interior design. In this case there is little argument that simplicity is an asset. The librarians should think through the arrangement of the collections, including the obvious but often overlooked sequence of call numbers from the end of one range to its continuation in another. These should flow without great gaps of space. Where there are parallel blocks of ranges, the sequential line will likely double back on itself. However, where the blocks of ranges are interrupted or displaced by building elements, there can be considerable distance between the end of the call number sequence in one shelving area and the resumption of that sequence in the next. This problem is often aggravated in a tower library where a natural sequence is broken up by a separation of vertical as well as horizontal distance. Furthermore, it is virtually impossible to break the collections into discrete packages, each with its properly proportioned amount of growth space so that all the stack areas run out of space at the same time.

In the staff areas, internal circulation, lighting, outlook, air flow, safety, and other aspects must be considered in terms of architectural space. Noise here can also be a problem. The provision of an exterior book return in the circulation department staff area, for example, will produce noise that may suggest that staff positions should be located some distance away, or that the return should be in a separate room, or should be kept outside the building. The acoustics in the technical processing areas will be important too; thus, it is necessary to decide whether to place in separate rooms the high-speed computer printer, typists, photocopy and fax machines,

and conference accommodations, and to decide on their configuration during this schematic phase. Furthermore, the relationship of technical services to other functions, such as the catalog, reference collections, or even rest rooms, may influence the thinking about the shape of the space.

3. *What facility features are influenced by the interior design?* As the layouts are developed and approved, such items as the location and swing of doors, the need for electrical and signal outlets and their exact location, and many other facility features will obviously require refinement. Because much of this effort can most conveniently be done during the design development phase, it is certainly one reason for an early start on the interior designs. The following list represents the types of questions to be considered:

a. Is there to be wall-mounted shelving that will require special structure? A common structure for walls involves sheet metal studs and framing. Where the walls may support shelving, the spacing of the studs and the gauge of the metal may be affected, or a special horizontal member may be added to carry the shelving brackets. Plaster or gypsum board alone is not a good material to which to fasten shelves.

b. Are carrels to be provided with task lighting or computer support or both? If so, the required access to power and signal sources can be achieved in a number of ways. The three key approaches involve bringing power and signal to the point needed either from the ceiling, through a system of walls, or through the floor. Future needs for flexibility are a major consideration as well.

c. Are there spaces, such as faculty studies or enclosed carrels, where the small amount of space requires a built-in work surface in order to achieve a furniture arrangement that fits and is most effective? If this is the case, there may be components of the interiors that should be included in the architectural design documents and thus constructed by the general contractor. This may be true of service counters and desks as well; but where this is done, it may be wise for the custom or built-in counter units to be modular and of similar construction to standard units manufactured by library supply houses to ensure flexibility for future change. Care must be taken to ensure that movable equipment fits the custom or built-in features. For example, if a two-drawer file unit is required to fit under a work surface, the clear height must anticipate the installation of carpet. The measurements made by the contractor will be from the concrete slab, not the top of the carpet.

d. Are there to be low partitions or office landscape systems that may affect the circulation of air? If so, the mechanical engineers should be informed.

e. Is there to be a special wall where a portrait or a major donor plaque is to be placed? If there is, such things as fire pull boxes, hose cabinets, or clocks should be avoided. It can be quite a surprise at the time of occupancy to discover that a special wall has been usurped by safety or security devices.

f. Is there the possibility of a concentration of loads that may require special structural considerations? This type of problem will be most common in the conversion of an office space to library functions; it can be a problem if the interior layouts suggest compact storage on an upper floor.

g. Is the delivery route sufficiently wide to receive the furniture being planned? Some conference tables and oversized carrels are quite large. Without double doors it may be necessary to assemble the furniture in the space. To avoid this expense, the delivery routes to each major area should be considered.

h. Is the ceiling height adequate to accommodate a 100-in.-high (2.538-m) grandfather's clock in the library director's suite or special collections reading room? Or, is there a particular room of sufficient size to take an oriental carpet intended as a special furnishing?

i. Are there outside windows in the computer lab, where strong light would always need to be controlled? Traditional CRT monitors can be seriously affected by sunlight. The development of LCD monitors may change this circumstance; active matrix monitors, such as found on laptop computers, can actually be seen quite well in direct sunlight, provided the source of light is behind the viewer. However, CRT-type monitors will likely remain the standard for desktop computers for some time.

This list is by no means a complete tabulation of the influences of the interior design on the arrangements of the physical facility. Much of the thinking on these issues will occur as the design process progresses, but it should be accomplished early in the design process for the resolution of emerging problems to be reasonably easy.

4. *Should interior design reflect architectural features?* Any good interior designer will try to make the interiors and the architecture work well to-gether so that each will complement the other. This effort will influence the designer's palette of form, light, scale, texture, and color. Clearly, successful interior design will require close communication between the interior designer and the architect.

Although it is not the intention of this volume to influence the aesthetic design, it is recommended that the librarian generally be supportive of the designer's recommendations in this area, provided they work in functional and management terms and provided they fall within reasonable economic constraints.

The need for architect and interior designer to work especially closely is most acute if the building is, for example, to include features from a grand private home, such as glass-fronted bookcases, an ornate double door, or stained-glass windows. The schematic design phase is the time when such reuse must be fixed as to exact dimensions of wall and ceiling; and the lighting requirements must be understood as the solutions may affect the architectural treatment. The seventeenth-century Sir Walter Raleigh rooms and the Early Carolina rooms with mid-eighteenth-century house paneling are examples, fitted within the Wilson Library of the University of North Carolina.

12.6
The Review Process

The schematic design phase is perhaps the most exhaustively reviewed phase of any project, as it is basically the only phase where the drawings represent the program in a graphic form to which nearly every reviewer can relate. Furthermore, it is a crucial phase for review in that it represents the larger and extremely important aspects of the relationships of major elements and the general feeling of the proposed building as a whole. A refined bubble diagram or other visual depiction may now help in the understanding of spatial relationships. The building mass and scale may be conveyed by a perspective and a small working model. It is not uncommon for faculty, students, staff, administration, donors, and trustees all to participate in some degree.

As the architect presents the design concept, the project team representing the institution should be open to what is presented, withholding judgment until they fully grasp the plan and its rationale. Be sure the team understands the principles driving the concept and being used in the schematic. And remember, a schematic is only that—an approximate vision to be followed, after critique and modifications, as the total design process advances. The following two issues are of interest in the schematic review process:

1. *How are the plans reviewed, and by whom?* There are three common approaches, and it would not be unusual for each to be used on a major project.

The first is simply to display the drawings in an exhibit area and ask for comments. This might be supplemented by articles in the student newspaper, a staff bulletin, and a quarterly publication prepared for the friends of the library. Although this technique is valuable in terms of a broad exposure to the institutional community, there usually will be very little if any useful input to the design team. It serves as a form of community education, is good public relations, and is encouraged, yet it will do little to improve the product.

The second review technique involves making group presentations. The groups may be a faculty library committee, perhaps with student representation; a student group, perhaps made up of students who have, in response to a questionnaire, expressed interest in the design of the library; a special committee of faculty, staff, and students who review all facility projects for the institution; a donor or perhaps a group of potential donors or friends of the library; the trustees; and the library staff. The presentations may be made by the library administrator who is the library representative in the design team. For special groups, such as the trustees, the presentation may include or be made by the architect or the institution's planning officer, but this type of presentation should be limited because of the time involved. A representative of the development or fund-raising office may make presentations to donors. The project architect may be particularly interested in a presentation to a student group as its representatives would reflect the views of the ultimate library user.

Presentations to all but very large groups will result in some interesting comments. Each group will have special interests. Students, for example, will be especially concerned about where the nearest snack facility is or the location of bike parking. Certain staff will wonder about safety conditions, or the staff lounge. Other staff will have a keen interest in where they will sit, how far they must go to service desks, and what is the working environment. Potential donors will be interested in how prominent "their" space will be. Faculty will be concerned about adequate research space near the books and, perhaps, how they may obtain a computer connection in their study. The trustees will be especially interested in the budget, the general aspects of the design, such as exterior facade and roof, and how the proposed facility fits into the campus. Operations and maintenance personnel will look at access, energy efficiency, and whether the facility meets the institutional standards. All the comments should be responded to where possible, if not during the actual presentation, then in a follow-up.

The third technique is for individuals carefully to review the plans by themselves or as part of a small group—thinking over every room, every space, every function, even every occasional event. This should be done by most members of the design team, at least key department heads, the chief librarian, the institutional project manager, and those who are concerned about special aspects of security, safety, access, operations, and maintenance. This process may well include a library consultant. In this process the comments should be written and forwarded to the institution's project manager. Then a review meeting with the architect may be used to discuss each of the comments. For a major project such a review may be broken up into the various interest groups; otherwise, there will be considerable discussion of aspects that hold little interest for many of those in the meeting. It would not be uncommon for such a session to last a half day. At least one member of the library staff may spend parts of several days on the review and write-up.

2. *What kinds of things should reviewers look for?*

The first aspect that will catch the eye is certain to be any dramatic part of the building plan, exterior or interior. A huge void in the middle of or above the main floor, a deeply cantilevered upper floor, acute angles of walls, a vast glass facade, a monster skylight, huge exposed beams (though this last is not likely to be in evidence in a schematic)—these capture attention: the unusual and surprising handling of spaces that are not cognitive images of an academic or an independent research library building.

Many academic libraries and public city libraries have these striking architectural features, especially the very large buildings. Just consider several built in the mid-1990s. One wonders how the librarians reacted to the rather traditional large atrium that rises in the middle of the library of Purdue University at Indianapolis, a size void that many have faulted for decades in case after case. In the Newman Library and Technology Center of Baruch College of CUNY, the well takes six bays right up through the middle of the structure; however, this is an inward-looking building in the heart of a crowded city of high-rises and the atrium takes but 8 percent of the floor area and is screened of noise intruding reading areas, and the librarians might well have regarded the design as a desirable solution. Then there is the hollow, geometric, dysfunctional 1994 Science Library of the University of California, Irvine, which was designed by a famous architect and must have shocked the librarians, not least because of the difficulty of finding the entrance. On the other hand, there is the strength and visual impact of the neo-Gothic facade of the new main library of Queen's University in Ontario, which the librarians must have soon realized picks up on and provides a modern exterior idiom based on its best neighbors.

This book does not take a stand on the desirability of such building characteristics, because the publicity gained, the public visibility, the "signature" nature for the institution, and the aesthetic excitement generated can all be positive, so long as the library program is met and the building functions well now and into the future. One needs to be open to the architectural schematic. Yet one should, after careful reflection, voice judgment as to whether its more striking internal or external features will serve the institution well over the years to come. Unfortunately, many of the more dramatic buildings with their large spatial voids or innovative engineered spaces are before long seen as having functional flaws. (It may be useful at this point to review Professor David Kaser's eighth chapter of *The Evolution of the American Academic Library Building* on irregular shapes, interior and exterior courts, monumentality, too much or too little glass, and below-grade buildings; see the Bibliography.)

Be that as it may, this feature of the schematic will be the first topic for discussion. The team should consider the pros and cons, state their opinion, and then move on to consideration of the host of practical issues that must be considered

in the schematic. Meanwhile, if the flamboyance or exuberance of the design impairs the functioning, the librarian and other officers of the owner should at once enter into discussions within the institution and then with the architect so that the best features can be retained and reinforced and the problem aspects eliminated or altered or modified satisfactorily. Consider the words of Donald Canty, quoted at the beginning of this chapter. Function should be the top priority.

While each interest group will be looking at other, different aspects of the project, the following list is merely indicative of the types of questions that the librarian or the library representative should think through and might raise at this stage of the design.

Has the site been explored for toxic waste conditions and for archeological remains?

Does the schematic presentation meet the operational intent of the program? Is there sufficient capacity for the collections, readers, staff, and building services? Is flexibility for growth and future change adequately provided?

Are the major elements in proper relation to each other? Where compromise has been made, is it reasonable?

Imagine yourself walking through the building as a staff member, then as a student, a faculty member, a visiting scholar, and a first-time visitor. Is the sequence required to find a book logical? What is the sequence of processing new book materials, or of a book being returned to shelving? Think through a wide variety of conditions regarding personal safety.

Are the fixed structural, mechanical, communication, and circulation elements situated properly? Are the stairs easily found? Are lavatories convenient but not obtrusive? Is there sufficient flexibility to allow for internal reallocations of space? Is future expansion provided for? How will staff cope with routines and emergencies at all hours of the day and evening, and on weekends?

Do the seating arrangements meet the philosophy of the library? Are the carrels large enough? Is there sufficient visual privacy? What will create noise, and be a problem? Where are the lockers, phones, computer clusters, classrooms and group study rooms, and the like? Are the lounge chairs grouped to encourage or discourage conversation? Similar questions can be applied to staff areas.

Are there areas where the layout can be improved to save space? Has space saving been taken too far to the detriment of the function or flexibility of the library?

Has the concept of preservation-based environmental control been included in the schematic design? What is the basic concept for environmental control? Does the budget reflect preservation criteria? Is there a first concept of heating? Cooling? Humidification? Dehumidification? Lighting?

Have local environmental conditions been accounted for (soil drainage or subgrade water, wind, pollution, humidity and temperature extremes, and the like)? Have functions producing pollution been isolated sufficiently from collections?

Are the books protected from direct sunlight? How is the outside book return dealt with? Where are books kept awaiting reshelving? How suitable is the route of new collection materials from incoming mail receipt to processing to binding to public shelving? (Often many of these aspects have not been worked out with care at this stage of the design, but it is important that they be on the agenda if they are part of the program requirement.)

How will deliveries be made, not only of books, but of furniture and equipment? Where will delivery vehicles park? How will physically limited persons enter the library? How will bicycles be kept clear of the main entrance?

Will there be serious maintenance problems created by the scheme? Is a high ceiling or an unusual stairwell justified if it will result in frequent extra costs to change lights? Is there sufficient attention at this stage to energy concerns?

What might be conditions in a heavy snow, or heavy rain, or wind? Is the strongest heat of the sun controlled, and are any sunscreens going to do the job? How will the outside of exterior windows be cleaned, and will birds roosting on flat window ledges create a problem?

Is the overall design agreeable? Are there places to sit outside? Is the interior system of corridors clear? Is a snack area reasonably located, and are there areas for smoking? Does a suitable location exist for bulletin boards? Can a book detection system be installed? Are there space and connections for adding more computers?

Are there elements that were inadvertently left out of the program that clearly will need to be added at this point?

Will the budget estimates require phasing of the project? Will it be likely that additive alternates will be required?

Such questions could go on and on. Clearly, the review process is a time-consuming activity, but errors and problems caught here will be much more easily dealt with than those discovered later. If a project delay results from the review process, it should be viewed as a sound investment; corrections made at this stage will almost always be far less expensive than corrections to a completed building, even if the process adds to the project schedule. And, the earlier such corrections are made, the less design time they will require. Even though an excellent and detailed program may have been prepared, there will be many details to resolve and surprising problems to work out.

NOTES

1. Nikolaus Pevsner, "News: Quote . . . Unquote," *Architectural Forum* 120 (January 1964): 13.
2. Donald Canty, "What It Takes to Be a Client: 3. How to Turn a Problem into a Set of Plans," *Architectural Forum* 119 (December 1963): 94–95. See also Andy Pressman, *The Fountainheadache: The Politics of Architect-Client Relations* (New York: Wiley, 1995), especially p. 106 where Kent Larson states: "We know that architects do their best work when the client is a strong, open-minded individual with vision."
3. Nancy McAdams, "The Changing Axioms of Library Planning," in *Minutes of the 118th Meeting* (May 15–17, 1991, Montreal, Quebec) (Washington, D.C.: Association of Research Libraries), p. 21.
4. Personal communication to Keyes Metcalf for the first edition of this book.

13

Design
Development

In the architectural structure, man's pride, man's triumph over gravitation, man's will to power, assume a visible form. Architecture is a sort of oratory of power by means of forms.

—Friedrich Wilhelm Nietzsche, *The Twilight of the Idols*

There is a close relationship between the material in this chapter and that in the chapters on programming and schematic design. Readers having a role in the design development and contract documents phases should be familiar with the earlier phases of the project, and if they have not been involved from the beginning, a review should be undertaken.

13.1
The Scope of the Design Development Phase

The schematic phase, as stated in Chapter 12, is the process of analyzing the major factors of the site, program, and budget and of developing a conceptual approach to the building project. In the event a value engineering exercise is planned, it should be completed at the end of schematics and prior to the start of design development. Once approved by the institution, the project designer moves into design development, or what is sometimes called the preliminary phase, which is a period of refinement and development of the schematic plans. The purpose of the design development phase is to establish the final shape, relationships, sizes, scope, and appearance of the project, including major dimensions, materials, and finishes.

The exact services to be performed in this phase by the architect and consulting engineers will have been spelled out in their contract for services. Typically, the services include the preparation of drawings, including plans, sections, elevations, typical construction details, and perhaps one or more three-dimensional sketches. These may be accompanied with one or several study models, final architectural and structural materials selection, and equipment layouts. The structural system together with its basic dimensions will be established, as will the approximate sizes and capacities of the mechanical and electrical equipment.

The aspects of energy conservation, preservation-based environmental criteria, lighting criteria, requirements for telecommunications and communications systems and acoustics, floor loading capacity, and any other major element affecting the design of the facility should now be finalized, if this has not already been done. Although criteria for these aspects should be established as part of the program, it is during design development that the adopted concepts are tested, their influence on other elements analyzed, and more detailed budget information prepared. This is the time when final decisions should be made on major design criteria; a later decision will likely add significantly to the design cost.

Involvement of a number of people with diverse backgrounds will be required during the design development phase. Besides the architect, structural engineer, mechanical engineer, electrical engineer, cost consultant, library representative, and the institution's facility project manager, this is the time for detailed involvement, if wanted, of an energy consultant, a conservation environment consultant, a value engineer, a code consultant, an interior designer, a library consultant, and others who may be influential in shaping the final product. Unless the selected mechanical engineer is expert on the type of HVAC problems in research libraries, it is usually wise and cost-effective to hire an expert consultant with significant experience in the requirements of libraries, archives, or museums to work with the engineer on this aspect. Indeed, it is good to have such a consultant as part of the team from the programming stage on.

Numerous meetings should occur, but their emphasis will typically be more technical than those in the earlier phase. Even so, it is important for the library representative to continue to be involved, as many proposals and considerations can affect the operation of the library.

It would be wrong to conclude from the above that a set of concepts is adopted in schematic work and that only refinements are made later. Perhaps half the schematics first presented by architects will be rejected in some degree before and, once in a while, even during the preliminary or design development phase. As examples, fenestration, energy economy, roof profile, entrance, and connection to an existing structure have each in different projects caused disagreement that led to repeated concepts being developed—sometimes over many months—before a consensus was reached in favor of one treatment.

13.2
Refine Schematics

The following seven topics are important in this phase of design development.

13.2.1 Concepts of Mechanical Systems

Mechanical systems normally include the design aspects of heating, ventilating, and air conditioning. In addition, plumbing, fire suppression systems, elevators, and other mechanical devices are sometimes included, and thus these elements are briefly discussed in this section from the mechanical point of view.

Each of the basic mechanical issues—heating, ventilating, and air conditioning—presents complicated and highly technical engineering problems. They are dealt with in detail in the *Handbook* issued frequently in updated editions (in both an Inch-Pound edition and an International System of Units or SI edition) by the American Society of Heating, Refrigerating, and Air-Conditioning Engineers. See especially the *ASHRAE Handbook: Applications* (Atlanta, 1995), Chapter 3, Part 8, which deals with libraries and museums. A competent mechanical engineer, working closely with the architect, should design the systems and select the equipment. Tables and formulas for use are readily available.

This section is not for engineers, but for administrative authorities of the institution, the building-planning committees, the business manager, and the librarian. (See also appendix D, Environmental Guidelines for Collection Preservation.) It will attempt to present the problems that the architects and engineers must solve and also to indicate the types of installation from which the institution can select. Simplified comments on desirable requirements and costs will be given, with only enough detail to explain and outline the various facets of the problem and make it possible to guide the architect in regard to the library's requirements. The basic direction should be part of the basic program; however, the exact final requirements should be reached no later than the design development phase of the project.

In some parts of the world, climatic conditions make heating of any kind unnecessary; in other parts the need for heat is so slight that it is uneconomical to provide a central heating system, and it is customary to get along with local units of one kind or another. In other areas the cost of central heating can be large enough to make it impossible to consider. As a result, various emergency devices have been used, from electric heaters to kerosene stoves. None of these methods will address humidity requirements without additional equipment.

In libraries in the United States, with the possible exception of Hawaii, the need for heating of some kind for temperature control is taken for granted. Even where heat is not required for temperature control, it is required to dehumidify, even when the temperature is hot outside. The same is now true for most Western European countries and in many other parts of the world, although in the Tropics, where the outside temperature rarely falls much below 60° F. (16° C.), the problem can be ignored without any great consequent discomfort unless humidity control for preservation reasons is to govern.

Heating is expensive to install, operate, and keep up, and the lack of it does not harm books provided the humidity is maintained within reasonable limits. The paper in books stored in unheated or poorly heated rooms is generally in better condition than that in many American libraries where the custom for many years was to overheat. However, with increasing concern for energy and the preservation of library materials, overheating is less of a problem. In general, provided that humidity is controlled, the lower the temperature, the longer the books will last (see the discussion of isoperms in appendix D).

If exceedingly cold bookstacks are found to be desirable, book-storage arrangements may have to be replanned and books and readers housed in separate quarters; this solution seems doubtful at present except in closed stacks, such as is often the case for rare book libraries, storage facilities, and in some great libraries of Europe.

In one example, the University of Toronto Robarts Library aimed at 60° F. (16° C.) for the two basement floors, which were designed for compact shelving with the air supply introduced at 66.2° F. (19° C.) and extracted air measured at an average of 70.3° F. (21.3° C.).

The University of Chicago Regenstein Library was planned with stacks, reading rooms, and staff work areas all separately zoned and controlled with thermostats. A computer monitors return air temperature and controls fan systems, the specified temperature differential being consistently maintained. Original technical specifications for Regenstein called for equipment that could maintain a mean of 68° F. (20° C.) year-round in stack areas and a mean of 72° F. (22° C.) year-round in reading areas. The equipment installed was designed to maintain these temperatures and did so for many years. However, for a short time under the university's austere energy conservation program of the 1980s, no attempt was made to maintain differential temperatures in Regenstein stack and reading areas, and mean service hour temperatures were roughly 68° F. (20° C.) in the winter and 72°–74° F. (22°–23.4° C.) in the summer building-wide. Currently public and staff areas are kept at 71° F. (21.6° C.).

If a library is to be heated, how and how much? A warehouse-type book-storage facility might require heat only for the control of humidity. Many Americans believe that comfort requires a temperature in cold weather of not less than 70° F. (21° C.), although most of them and a considerably larger percentage of persons in other English-speaking countries would be content with 65° F. (18° C.) in a draft-free room.

It is generally agreed that there is no exact ideal temperature for comfort or productivity. It is also widely accepted that so long as the temperature remains in the comfort zone, productivity will not be affected. The range of the comfort zone will vary with the customs of clothing, the degree of acclimatization of the individual to the prevalent atmospheric conditions, the radiant temperatures of surrounding surfaces, the relative humidity, the velocity of air movement, the color of surroundings, and the health, age, and weight of the individual. It is almost certain that at any given temperature, individuals can be found who would not be happy. It also appears clear that most people are relatively comfortable in a library with the temperature maintained between 68° and 72° F. (20° and 22° C.), and many people can be comfortable within a range of 65° to 78° F. (18° to 26° C.), although the factors of acclimatization, customs, and airflow will be more important at the extremes. It is interesting to note that, provided the temperature is not high enough to induce perspiration, relative humidity plays a fairly minor role in the comfort level.

The atmospheric conditions for human comfort and book preservation conditions can be broken down into seven topics: heating, cooling, humidifying, dehumidifying, filtering, insulating, and ventilating. For more information on preservation-based environmental conditions, appendix D should be reviewed.

Heating. In parts of the world where the average temperature day and night may be below 55° or 60° F. (13° or 16° C.) for weeks at a time, central heating is certainly indicated and can generally be found. A library in such a climate should be heated along the outside walls, particularly near windows and doors, to prevent drafts that can easily make the space uncomfortable and too often uninhabitable by a reader. Methods of providing the heat as well as the fuel to be used—gas, oil, coal, electricity, or solar energy—will vary according to locality.

Heating arrangements should not interfere with library activities and usable space. These facilities may occupy floor space and reduce the area available for other purposes. Vertical heating ducts take the most floor area and hydronic (hot water) and radiant sources of heat the least. Horizontal ducts use cubage, sometimes on a large scale. It must be realized that the space used by the heating plant and the total cost of installation and operation will vary also. Some form of a ducted system will almost always be required where humidity control is part of the design.

As to general design criteria, make sure that rooms are provided with reasonably uniform temperature and that they are not 60° F. (16° C.) beside the windows with a strong draft, while 70° to 75° F. (21° to 24° C.) elsewhere; that they do not have cold floors; and that the heating does not provide a blast that is unpleasant to feel and noisy to hear unless it is the intention of the design to provide white sound by this means. A good installation can avoid variations from one part of the building to another by the use of thermostats, proper insulation, and adequate zoning of ducts and piping. Thermostats, except those in private offices, should be designed so that they cannot be adjusted by anyone other than an authorized member of the staff.

Make sure that the mechanical engineers and architects have considered the heat loss through floors, walls, windows, and unheated attics; that each room is a unit that has been figured separately; and that the pressure coming from heated air in a duct installation is sufficient to prevent cold air infiltrating through windows and door cracks.

The heating-plant capacity should be equal to its task in severe weather—that is, the heat load it provides for should be capable of equaling the heat loss through conduction, radiation, and infiltration. Careful calculation of the heat load is required because if the plant is too small and pushed beyond capacity, results will be unsatisfactory, but if it is too large, the installation cost will be unnecessarily high. Normally a heating system is designed to meet a specific theoretical "low" temperature, and when this low is exceeded, the designed room temperature will drop. In Boston, for instance, the design is quite generally for 0° F. (−18° C.). In Nashville, Tennessee, it is for 3° F. (−16° C.).

Operating difficulties frequently come in reducing the quantity of heat provided on a warm day or in increasing it on a cold one. To do so requires monitoring instruments, a signal system, and flow-activation control mechanisms. The person responsible for the design should know the possibilities and costs involved, should understand what different heating methods will do, and should know their flexibility under different conditions in providing the desired temperature. These are technical areas, and the librarian need not perform an in-depth review of the mechanical design. Rather, the librarian should reach a general level of confidence in and understanding of the mechanical system in consultation with the design engineer so that there is reasonable expectation that the design issues have been properly addressed.

Heating is ordinarily by one or more of three methods or combinations of them:

1. Warm air, with heat supplied by bringing in air above room temperature to a degree sufficient to counteract the heat losses. Warm-air systems today generally have fans to propel the air, instead of depending on gravity. Air is ordinarily discharged at a temperature of 90° to 100° F. or, with certain types of installation, up to 135° F. (32° to 38° or up to 57° C.), because at lower temperatures the room will feel drafty as the air comes into a cooler space. It should be so arranged as to blow a curtain of warm air across cold or exposed walls and windows. A certain amount of fresh outside air is included, and the controls may vary the percentage during different hours of night and day. The velocity of the air is important. If too low, the ducts must be very large and there is risk of stratification within the space, resulting in a sense of stagnation or a lack of air movement. If too high, the system will be noisy and the rooms drafty. As has been indicated, the mechanical engineers will use detailed formulas that involve all the pertinent factors. With proper system design and thermostatic controls, it is not difficult to provide a satisfactory range of temperature.

With the added requirements of cooling, filtration, and humidity control, forced-air systems make the most sense and are the most common in library design.

2. Hot water or steam, with the heat coming to the rooms through pipes and radiators or convectors. Hot water is ordinarily pushed along by a circulation pump just as warm air is pushed by a fan. Gravity systems have been used for both in the past, and may even have limited uses today.

The pump in hot-water systems provides greater flexibility in design and speeds response to changed requirements. The forced circulation makes possible smaller pipes and more sensitive control. Expansion tanks are a necessary adjunct, as well as properly located vents. The librarian and the officers of the institution should remember that these take space for housing, as does the other mechanical equipment. Enough area must be provided for this functional necessity, which all too frequently is crowded into too small a space for efficient operation by the seemingly more demanding needs of the library. Always remember that a properly planned and organized mechanical plant requires space for operation, maintenance, and possible later replacement of units by new ones that may differ in some dimensions.

Hot-water or steam systems that are properly designed require less space than forced-air systems, but they do not address humidity control or the requirement for fresh air. Unless the fresh air is ducted, filtration will be a problem, and filtration of internal air will be nonexistent (which can be desired where interior pollutants are expected). Steam systems can be noisy; water systems are generally very quiet. Certain hot-water systems (also called hydronic systems) can serve cooling needs as well. Perhaps the best application of hot-water systems in a library is as a retrofit in a stack space with very limited space for ductwork supplemented with a minimal forced-air system for fresh air and a modest amount of humidity control.

3. Panel or radiant heating, consisting of warm coils in the floor, ceiling, or walls, provided with warm air, warm water, or electric-resistant heating elements. Like the steam and hot-water systems above, humidity and filtration of the air are not addressed with radiant systems. There are also limitations to the extremes such systems can deal with, though a warm floor can be very nice to sit on!

The amount of heat—British Thermal Units, or BTUs as they are called—required to keep the temperature at the desired level can be determined by standard formulas. The formulas are based not only on the number of cubic feet of space to be heated but also on the heat loss and gain resulting from three sources:

The number of persons occupying the space. People produce heat, the amount depending on whether they are active or sedentary.

The heat provided by the lighting, photocopy machines, computers, and other typically electrical equipment. In the past this was a significant source of heat, amounting to enough to warm almost the entire building. With more energy-efficient computers and lower light levels resulting from steps to conserve energy, heat from light and electrical equipment today is less than in the past. Even so, the heat coming from lighting, electrical equipment, and people should not be left out of consideration when selecting equipment for cooling.

The heat loss or gain through floors, walls, doors, windows, skylights, and ceilings. In a library this comes chiefly from outside walls and windows, from the roof to some extent if there is no attic, and more and more often from the floors (because of a cold, unheated basement) or from an overhang, resulting from a floor cantilevered out over the great outdoors.

In cases of overhanging floors, unless heat is provided in the floor, or unless at least proper insulation is applied to the underside of the slab, the area around the periphery of the building may become almost uninhabitable in severe weather. The amount of the heat gained or lost through the ceiling will depend partly on the type of roof insulation, particularly in the ceiling of the top floor of the building. But the great problem is the outside walls. There the heat loss or gain depends on the construction of the walls, the insulation used, and the amount of window space, together with the kind of windows and the kind of glass used.

Some will remember the metal frame casement windows in older libraries where the cold air tended to come in around the frames because they were not quite tight. Metal sash loses heat more readily than wood sash through the frame itself. Casement windows present a problem, particularly those with poor-fitting metal sashes. Weather stripping can be useful in solving the problem. Leaky windows present a condensation problem also.

Fixed sash is often used today in air-conditioned buildings and eliminates the leakage problem as well as a security problem. With fixed windows the operation of the building is at the mercy of the air-conditioning system; if the unit breaks down in hot summer weather, the building can become unusable, with no relief available from open windows. However, fixed windows can have key-controlled opening panels for such emergencies and for exterior window washing. If the system relied upon is prone to break down, and particularly if a good repair mechanic is not always available—something that is not unusual in rural areas and sometimes even in large cities—the use of absolutely fixed windows may be questionable, or consideration of an alternative backup system may be warranted. Still, the improved security and environmental control of fixed sash are very important benefits for research libraries.

Buildings whose walls are made largely of single-thickness glass lose more heat than those with masonry walls. Glass is made today that, it is claimed, will reduce heat loss from the cold, or heat gain from the sun for that matter, but it is rarely if ever completely satisfactory. Double- and triple-pane glass provides an air space between the layers and is the most effective method of insulating the outside from the inside with glass. Quiet air is perhaps the best of all insulation materials, and double- or triple-pane glass reduces condensation of water on windows if the room is humidified in cold weather.

The architectural program should indicate the temperature to be maintained in the building as a whole and in the different parts if there is to be variation within. The institution's representatives should keep in mind the effect of different types of walls on the cost of heating and should certainly talk the problem over with the architect before plans are approved in order to avoid misunderstanding.

The desirability of installing heating pipes or an electric radiant heating system to melt snow on sidewalks at the entrance or on roofs and gutters should be considered in planning heat installation. Roof pipes circulating hot water must be planned with care so that freezing temperatures will not burst the pipes if the system is inactive.

Cooling. High temperature can be combated by a design that takes advantage of cooling breezes or night air, though such an approach will not control the humidity. Most academic and research libraries in India, for example, where construction costs are low, are planned on this basis, with the floor area used for readers and books being much larger than would be required in the United States. Natural ventilation is a basic requirement, because the apparatus for artificial cooling is more expensive than in the United

States and often, because of governmental regulations, cannot be considered. In an industrially underdeveloped country where cooling apparatus has to be imported, it costs more than in the United States and Western Europe and very much more in relation to other construction costs. Where it can be afforded, air conditioning can be especially beneficial for preservation of collection materials on paper.

Cooling consists of reducing or removing unwanted heat by supplying cool air. An excess of heat results from heat transmitted to the space through its shell, directly or indirectly, from radiation from the sun; from the heat generated in the library from lights, people, and electrical and gas appliances; and from outside air brought in for ventilation purposes. Artificial lighting, especially that with high intensity, complicates matters considerably, varying with the type of the light source. Incandescent lights use more current to produce the same amount of light than fluorescent and therefore generate much more heat for the same lighting intensity, perhaps two and one-half times as much. Photocopy machines, visual projectors, computers, and other electrically powered equipment add heat as well.

The total heat load—that is, the load imposed by transmitted plus internally generated heat—must be determined so as to decide on the size of the cooling plant required. The temperature to be obtained by the cooling must be agreed upon. Formulas are available for use by the engineers. A total cooling load is divided into two parts—sensible heat, which shows on a dry-bulb thermometer and comes from the sources listed in the preceding paragraph, and the latent load, which is the cooling required to remove unwanted moisture from the air-conditioned space.

For comfort, cooling a room to 80° F. (27° C.) dry-bulb and 50 percent relative humidity is, under some circumstances, acceptable. If the outside temperature is 95° F. (35° C.), to cool to 70° F. (21° C.) would be unduly expensive and actually would provide too great a contrast for comfort, although this may be a desired level of cooling for the preservation of the books. Some quite satisfactory installations are made with a capacity to keep the temperature no more than 10° F. (−12° C.) lower than it is outside. If people are to remain in a room for long periods during hot weather, a lower temperature may be more desirable than it would be if they are coming and going at short intervals.

It is suggested, at least for comfort, that in hot weather there never be more than 15° F. (8° C.) difference between inside and outside temperature in the shade and that 72° F. (22° C.) be considered satisfactory until outside temperature gets above 82° F. (28° C.). When the temperature goes above 82° F. outside, the inside temperature can reasonably go up at least 2° for each 3-degree increase outside. It is suggested that from 72° to 75° F. (22° to 24° C.) for inside temperature is a good criterion to be planned for where comfort is the controlling value, and in very hot weather that it be permitted to rise higher.

Specifications will vary among countries and institutions depending on local circumstances. For instance, Australia's government moved away from specific standards for the university library buildings to which it contributes funds; the Building Code of Australia and Australian Standards cover ventilation, but none is specific about temperature and RH. In Great Britain the norms have been determined by the government, and its grants for a university library building cover the cost needed to achieve the following: The conditions for open-access stacks and areas designed for human occupancy should have a steady controlled temperature range of 18° C. (65° F.) in winter to 21° C. (70° F.) in summer, and a relative humidity range of 50 to 60 percent, never to exceed 65 percent RH, though this humidity limit may not now be valid. It is expected that close control of temperature will not be necessary, and that from time to time, when the external climate is extreme, a substantial drift (of say 5°–6° F.) can be tolerated over a short period. When a university library holds a special collection of rare books, an air-conditioning system providing more precise conditions can be provided.

As already noted, it may be found that lower temperatures are desirable for book storage. These temperatures are not too difficult to maintain in many places if the stacks are in well-insulated locations, such as below-surface basements, where the ground temperature is between 45° and 60° F. (7° and 16° C.) year-round, as it is in most of the United States. Where book preservation is the major concern, other criteria must be used. Again, see appendix D.

Humidification and dehumidification. The third and fourth factors are humidification and dehumidification. Many people fail to understand that heating systems in places where there is severe winter weather, where the outside temperature can be 20° to 30° F. below zero (–29° to –34° C.), will reduce the relative humidity in a room heated to 70° F. (21° C.) or more to a point where it is no more than 10 percent.

What are the results? Most people will become accustomed to it; the skin and the mucous membranes dry out and may feel unpleasant, and respiratory ailments may increase. Alas, bindings and paper under these conditions dry out also. Old pigskin bindings, after surviving for hundreds of years undamaged in English manor houses without central heat, warp in a short time under American library conditions, so that the cover leather actually pulls off the boards. Dryness does tend to make poor-quality paper more brittle, and heat causes a more rapid chemical deterioration, which is even greater with high humidity. The larger the amount of acid in the paper, the more rapid this action. Almost all newspapers dating to the beginning of the wood-pulp era in the 1870s have a short life at best, and in a well-heated library that life will be greatly reduced, often to less than 25 years.

The useful life span of printed and manuscript material might well be doubled if the relative humidity in the rooms where they are stored is kept to between 30 and 40 percent year-round and if the temperatures are maintained at the lowest reasonable level. Fortunately, in the winter this is not too difficult from the perspective of temperature, although it may be expensive to accomplish satisfactorily in terms of humidity. With warm-air heating installations, moisture can be added to the air as it leaves the heating system. Five problems must be dealt with, however. See illustration of mechanical system and text on humidity control in appendix D.

1. The moisture must be controlled and the ductwork properly designed, for otherwise the process of adding humidity may rust out the ducts.

2. The water must be filtered; otherwise, when it evaporates it may leave a residue of solids that settles in the form of dust on books and elsewhere. Dust is an enemy to books, not only because of the dirt but also because, however fine it may be, it is an abrasive. In no case should steam generated in a central plant be used directly as the source of humidity because of the additives typically used.

3. In severe winter weather, when air with a relative humidity that is satisfactory strikes the cold surface of a glass window or any other cold substance, the moisture tends to condense and will run down the window or the wall with possibly serious results. Excellent insulation design is required. And, if the building is to be humidified, the walls should have a vapor barrier.

4. The introduction of moisture, which may be by a steam jet, presents certain risks, particularly if a valve is stuck or a control device fails. Where there is water, it seems to always find its way to the books eventually. Means of early detection of such an event together with a fail-safe shutoff system and perhaps a remote alarm are suggested. Design of a system such that all humidification is achieved within the mechanical room rather than within the stacks can help with this area of concern.

5. In spaces containing a small volume of air, such as display cases, humidity control is particularly difficult, especially when one wishes to add humidity. Careful analysis of the problem will be required to avoid dramatic shifts in the humidity where a small area requires minute additions of moisture to maintain the desired level. It should be constantly monitored.

For exhibit display cases that must have a separate carefully controlled environment, one technique is to design a sealed case with no internal heat source and to provide space for a tray of silica gel or other material to control the humidity within the case. Such an approach assumes that the ambient room temperature is satisfactory for the materials being displayed. Air conditioning, especially humidity control, is a particularly difficult problem in display cases, although it has been done with mixed success. Part of the problem is that most of the components of an air-conditioning system are designed to handle large volumes of air. Because of this, dramatic changes in the temperature and humidity within the case often result. Steam as a source of humidity in an air-conditioned display case is probably not a good choice unless a means of throttling the steam to very small levels can be found. A carefully designed evaporation system is likely to be a safer solution, although the maintenance problems typically will be greater.

The authors have had some unpleasant experiences in trying to humidify rooms that were constructed years ago with no thought of later winter humidification. Double-pane glass—Thermopane, for instance—will prevent condensation, but it is, of course, expensive, particularly in modern "glass-box" buildings. Satisfactory insulation of walls and inclusion of a vapor barrier will help solve the problem if there is not too much glass. But beware the five traps noted above.

If severe winter weather is of short duration, the condensation problem can sometimes be avoided without double glass by permitting the percentage of relative humidity to drop for a few hours. The 5 to 7 percent of their weight in moisture that is usually held in the books and bindings will help temporarily, but the period must not be prolonged more than perhaps 48 hours at the most or damage will result. Conservation experts are likely to balk at this concept. This is not a concept we recommend, except maybe for materials that do not have preservation-based criteria, as might be the case in a "public" library function or possibly an undergraduate library.

A rapid drop in outside temperature will bring condensation on walls and particularly windows and ductwork. Because all building materials are porous, condensation of moisture in the walls may freeze in severe weather conditions; the expansion that comes from freezing may then cause structural cracks and severe damage in concrete or cinder blocks. As previously mentioned, a vapor barrier is required.

Commercial-quality controls for humidity can be used both for the controlling mechanism and for an alarm system. They generally are accurate to a tolerance of ±5 percent or less, but the control set points tend to drift. In an installation requiring careful control, the use of commercial controls may require a maintenance adjustment and perhaps cleaning on a monthly basis. Industrial controls are generally more accurate, and maintenance should be reduced to perhaps an annual adjustment and cleaning, but industrial-quality controls are significantly more expensive than commercial-quality controls. When an alarm system is employed, it is suggested that it be separate from the control system except for a shut-off feature. Further, if commercial controls are used in the general system, the alarm system should be of industrial or equal quality.

Dehumidification is in most ways and in many locations as serious a problem as humidification. This is particularly true in coastal areas in climates where there are prolonged hot and humid spells. Where the normal summer temperature stands in the eighties (27°–32° C.) with long periods of high humidity, mold spores, which are always present, begin to grow. This even happens frequently in New England and through the northern and central states, particu-

larly if wet basements result from rains and floods during a humid hot spell.

It is difficult and expensive to remove moisture from the air. Four methods are used:

1. Condensing machinery in connection with the ventilation installation. The process involves cooling the air until moisture condenses on the surface of cooling coils, fins, or tubes followed by heating the air to a temperature appropriate to the air-conditioning need. Such systems, like air conditioning, require energy. They are expensive to install and maintain and, like most apparatus with moving parts, can be expected to wear out in due course. Actual life expectancy can be substantially affected by the quality of the materials and design; a range of 20 to more than 50 years can be expected with proper maintenance. Mechanical condensing is the most common method of removing humidity in air-conditioned buildings.

2. Chemical moisture absorbers. With these the air is passed through or over moisture-absorbing chemicals, such as silica gel, which is then dried by heating and discharging of the heated air. One approach, sometimes called a desiccant wheel, cycles the moisture-absorbing material between treating room air and being heated to dispel moisture. Another approach is to place trays of the material within the space to be dehumidified. In this rather crude approach, the trays are then hand carried to ovens for extracting moisture. The capacity of this manual technique is fairly limited, although it may be well suited for properly designed display cases. To be effective in a display case, the case must be sealed airtight.

Where extremely low temperatures are to be maintained, as might be the case in an archive storage vault, the desiccant wheel solution may be the only effective way of reducing humidity, in part because the process of condensing moisture out of the air becomes less effective as temperature approaches the freezing point.

3. Local portable unit dehumidifiers. These are sometimes installed in damp basements. They may resemble an old-fashioned oil heater. No expensive ducts are required, but the moisture they remove must either be carried out of the building by hand at comparatively short intervals during very humid weather or the unit must be provided with a drain connection that will run the condensed water outside. Although portable unit dehumidifiers may aid a difficult situation where a well-controlled and balanced system does not

exist, they typically are put into service as a stop-gap measure.

4. A fourth method is to exhaust the hot, humid air with fans during the hours when the outside air is cooler than that inside but not too humid. The library is kept closed in the daytime (in terms of ventilation) with window shades lowered to prevent overheating from solar radiation, and then late at night, when the outside temperature is at its lowest point (and no doubt the RH is at its highest point), an exhaust fan is set in motion, and the day's hot air is removed and replaced by the cool night air. Unfortunately, in very humid weather, it sometimes happens that the night air brought in is very close to the dew point, and, if the daytime temperature does not go up, condensation inside may result and mold spores may grow. If a humidistat is placed in the intake and adjusted to stop the change in air when the relative humidity outside is too high, this difficulty can be largely obviated. The general thinking of library preservation experts is that the humidity and temperature should not only be kept relatively low, but they should be maintained at a relatively constant set point, which is virtually impossible with this last approach. Still, where energy or equipment is simply not available, a design along the lines suggested here may be better than doing nothing to try to control temperature and humidity.

Filtering. All ventilation installations should, if possible, include filtering units. Removal of dust, pollen, and other airborne particles results in a healthier atmosphere and lower maintenance costs for cleaning. It also prevents cooling and heating coils and ducts from becoming blocked, and, perhaps of even greater importance, prevents damage to books. Evidence that air passing through a library can be dirty is available with a good look at a used filter or at the accumulations of dust and dirt near air intakes. Filters may be of either a throwaway or a cleanable type, and they are manufactured to block particles of a certain size. A dual or even triple mechanical filtration, each successive filter of a greater efficiency rating, can improve the effectiveness.

One factor of great importance in filtering is the removal of industrial chemical pollution, which, particularly in our large cities, tends to include a considerable amount of sulfur dioxide. Pollution can occur naturally, too; even libraries in rural areas should consider pollution as a potential problem to be dealt with. This, combined with the chemical residues left in a large proportion of modern paper, hastens the deterioration of the paper and, in fact, gradually permits it to burn up, with the distressing results that we have all seen in an extreme form in late-nineteenth- and twentieth-century newspapers. Activated charcoal or some form of dry chemical filter medium is the best way to eliminate sulfur dioxide and other noxious gases that are harmful to paper. These are expensive filters that require special maintenance routines; they may only be justified in special-collection areas of research libraries or where gaseous pollution is at excessive levels.

In earlier days air was passed through a water spray to remove the dust, and oil filters were sometimes used. There was at least one significant library that used an electronic precipitator to remove pollutants. However, concern has been expressed regarding volatile solvents that may be produced by an oil filtration process, and the moisture produced by such a spray must be removed and any remaining dust dealt with. And, electronic filtration, though effective for particulates, contributes ozone to the air (ozone is an active oxidant and something not wanted in the library). The more common approach today is to use a dry filter medium to remove gaseous pollutants and particulates.

The location of the air intake is important. If it is close to the ground, chemical and exhaust pollutants, which unfortunately abound in urban areas, may enter the air-supply system. Be sure the intake is not near the truck delivery area of the building. In most cases an intake near the eaves or roofline, rather than on ground level, is the best option, provided it is well separated from the building exhaust. However, where the design places the main fan room in the basement, a roof-level air supply will require moving the air down to the basement; thus, the engineers may seek another solution to save space and cost.

Insulation. Both heating and cooling are provided to limit the inside environmental temperature changes. This maintenance of a desirable inside condition is greatly aided by insulation. Good insulation greatly decreases the demands on the heating and cooling systems, as has been suggested above. More money can be put into heating and cooling to make insulation unnecessary, or the reverse emphasis can be chosen. Engineers need to calculate the comparative costs to attain the specified design conditions.

As one example, the Davis Library built in 1983 at the University of North Carolina, Chapel Hill, was determined to require insulation with an "R" value of 7.04 because the design goal of 10 was only in part met by an inside surface providing 0.61; a 3-in. (76 mm) average tapered roof-deck fill giving 0.84; a 5-in. (127 mm) structural concrete deck, 0.41; vapor barrier worth 0.15; a built-up roof with slag providing 0.78; and an outside factor of 0.17.

Although roofs are of prime concern, other exterior faces are important, especially the south and west exposures. The inert nature of insulation makes it an excellent investment for the long term, and it deserves more attention for the economy of the life cycle of a library building.

Ventilation. Heating, cooling, humidification, dehumidification, and filtering by themselves will not provide completely satisfactory atmospheric conditions. Full air conditioning also requires ventilation to change air rapidly enough to counteract odors and interior pollution of any kind. Building codes and local rules establish minimum standards. In most places with limited occupancy, ventilation is provided through the heating system in cold weather, or through leakage of air or open windows in hot weather, or by "gravity" circulation caused by the weight difference of hot and cold air. A slight positive pressure should be maintained so leakage is cleaned air going out, not polluted air coming in.

A ventilation system may be called a dilution process, by which odor or heat removed is equal to that generated on the premises. It is particularly useful in windowless or below-grade areas, where, without a change in air, a stale or musty odor may result. It is very important in photocopy alcoves or rooms, critical for audio-equipment areas, any kind of film processing area, preservation labs where noxious chemicals may be in use, projection booths, and computer mainframes if air conditioning is not provided.

The amount of fresh air that should be brought in will depend on the total cubic footage of the area and the amount of heat, moisture, and pollution generated in it, which in turn will be largely affected by the number of persons occupying the premises and their activities. Many ventilation systems are unsatisfactory primarily because they do not provide adequate changes of air. One code requires a minimum of 5 cubic feet of fresh air per minute (CFM) for each occupant, but it does not specify the number of air changes per hour.

With 10 percent outside air used as a standard for recirculating systems, the amount of fresh air usually exceeds 5 CFM per person. The ventilation norm in the United States is 12 air changes per hour in toilets and 3 to 10 elsewhere, depending on the extent of smoking. The British norm is 10 in toilets and 6 elsewhere.

Where greater energy efficiency has been a driving force, reduced air changes may be mandated. In this case, building pollution can be a problem, especially where attention has not been paid to the materials used in the building from a pollution point of view. Interior pollution, in addition to leading to what have been called "sick" buildings (where occupants complain of physical maladies resulting from poor air quality), can affect the well-being of the collections. In some cases, the design of air filtration systems may be as important for internally generated pollutants as for exterior contamination. Yet, for a design to result in a "healthy" building, contaminants from paints, glues, carpets, and other finishes must also be considered. Indeed, where buildings are designed based upon conservation-generated environmental criteria, the building will be healthy even though the introduction of outside air is minimized. See appendix D regarding building products as sources of pollution.

HVAC summary. Air-conditioning and ventilation systems in libraries today are generally part of what are known as central-heating, ventilation, and air-conditioning (HVAC) systems that cover the building as a whole. To be satisfactory, even with a perfect installation, there must be local thermostats or controls in all areas and most rooms within the building. The demands on the system will vary with the number of occupants, the direction of the wind, the amount of sunshine, and the amount and type of glass in the building shell. No installation without local controls can be completely satisfactory, though local controls, of course, add to the cost.

In some buildings the whole system is based on unit conditioners, one for each room or section of the building, as is fairly common in single rooms in private houses, apartments, and offices. The Grinnell College Library has used this method. It is sometimes useful in small areas with special problematic conditions, where a major reworking of a central system would be very expensive. The use of local units to this extent is generally frowned on by mechanical engineers and maintenance personnel. Decentralized maintenance arrangements present complications, and the provision of satisfactory "comfort" cooling or heating within a reasonable degree of engineering standards is lost. On the other hand, there is less likelihood of the building becoming completely uninhabitable because of mechanical breakdown.

Air conditioning requires not only machinery, electric current, and the availability of an expert mechanic, but also an adequate water supply. If an adequate water supply is not available at a reasonable cost from local governmental or private agencies or perhaps from a well driven for the purpose, a cooling tower or, in small installations, an evaporative condenser will help. Note that there may be local restrictions against "waste water" used in air-conditioning systems and that wells have been known to run dry.

Whether or not a new library should provide for full air conditioning will depend on local conditions and funds available. The decision may be difficult to make because the costs involved are considerable. Furthermore, sizable and valuable space is required for the mechanical equipment and ducts, and cubage and floor area are the basic costs in a new building.

Space for the mechanical room and perhaps for a water tower can, however, sometimes be found in an unused basement area or on the roof of an adjacent building, thereby saving valuable floor area in the new structure. Space was found in the Widener Library at Harvard for the mechanical equipment and cooling towers for the Houghton and Lamont libraries.

Except as driven by a need for preservation-based environmental criteria, complete air conditioning is unnecessary in many institutions. If an institution is located in a section of the country where the number of days with the temperature rising above 85° F. (29° C.) is limited, exhaust fans for use at night in all but very humid weather may solve the problem with reasonable satisfaction. The deciding factor may not be the comfort of the readers and the staff but the value of the collections. If so, a solution may possibly be found by segregating rare and irreplaceable books and manuscripts and providing superior temperature control as well as humidification and dehumidification for them but not for the building as a whole.

Three generations ago comparatively few libraries were air conditioned; indeed, satisfactory air conditioning had not been developed. Theoretically, the Widener Library, built in 1915, was air conditioned, but the system was so expensive and the results were so unsatisfactory that within a few months after the opening of the building it was given up and never used again. In the winter of 1941–1942, the Houghton Rare Book Library at Harvard opened with a complete air-conditioning installation that was very satisfactory until 20 years later, when the refrigerant condensing apparatus wore out and it became difficult to maintain the desired relative humidity. This condensing-equipment installation has been replaced.

The inexperienced librarian expects to walk into a newly completed building and have the air-conditioning system operate in accordance with the design criteria set up for the architects and engineers. Unfortunately, all air-conditioning systems are fairly complicated and require a "shakedown cruise" of at least one year and often more during which (1) the controls, airflow, fan speed, valves, and so on are adjusted and balanced for accurate operation and maximum results, and (2) the best method of operation is learned by the personnel who are responsible, a method that often is quite different from those with which they have previously been acquainted.

Most new libraries throughout North America are now using air conditioning. In some cases, in order to save funds, unsatisfactory installations have been made. In others the air-conditioning ducts have been installed with the hope that the mechanisms involved would be acquired at a later time. Unfortunately, when this has been done, the ducts have not always been adequate in size, and when the air-conditioning system has been finally installed, its distribution has proved to be inadequate.

Complete air conditioning is not recommended for all new library buildings. Undoubtedly there are libraries where, because of climatic conditions, comparatively small summer use, relatively limited collections, or a lack of funds to provide for other equally or more important requirements, air conditioning is deemed to be not essential. But it might not be an exaggeration to say that in a majority of cases in the United States, a new library without air conditioning is obsolete at the time its doors are opened. This is certainly the case where research collections are involved.

From time to time the question of air conditioning an old library building comes up. Often it is feasible, though the installation tends to be more expensive than in a new building because holes for the ducts must be opened up in walls and floors; it may be difficult to conceal the ducts satisfactorily; and too often the results have not been up to standard. An example of a good installation of this kind is at the Newberry Library in Chicago.

Sometimes it is possible and less expensive in an old building to provide local air conditioning for parts of the structure or to use small, high-velocity ducts with sound absorbers, as was done at the Harvard-Yenching Library of Harvard. Top-floor rooms, where the attic can be used for the apparatus, or first-floor rooms adjacent to basements, where there is space unusable for other purposes, are possibilities. Window air conditioners are another, but they do not add to the attractiveness of a facade and are not satisfactory in other ways. Freestanding unit air conditioners are a possibility, but they will require a means of removing the heat, which in turn requires either a water source or an exterior cooling device.

Before commenting on a few related aspects, we summarize the air-conditioning and ventilation problem. There are at least five alternatives:

1. *Heating only:* This is not recommended in most libraries.
2. *Minimum recommended installation:* Heating and ventilating with air filtration and controls that allow the use of nighttime air for cooling.
3. *Comfort installation:* Heating, ventilation, air filtration, good insulation, and cooling. This is recommended if the library is open to the public during long hot and humid periods or has a modest concern for the preservation of the books.
4. *Conditioned installation:* Heating, ventilation, air filtration, good insulation, cooling, and humidity control. This is the minimum recommended for situations noted in 3 (above) if the collections have rare and irreplaceable books and manuscripts.
5. *The ideal installation:* Heating, ventilation, air filtration, cooling, and humidity control, all within certain specified narrow limits in order to maintain ideal conditions of temperature and humidity year-round, regardless of outside conditions. Excellent insulation. This is recommended for all research libraries with valuable collections.

One word of warning about air conditioning. Because of the multitude of variables, it is less than an exact science. Some would even claim it

is an art. Any installation should be designed by a reliable and competent architect and engineer, and consulting services of an expert in preservation environments from an engineering point of view should be considered.

If a library adopts the minimum environmental control system, it may be desirable to size the ductwork and equipment space to specifications based upon a more rigorous system so that the comfort and conditioning installations can be added in the future without undue cost. In some cases, the size of ductwork required for a heating/ventilation system is actually greater than that required for a heating/cooling/ventilation system; in this case, ductwork sized for the ultimate system will be inadequate for the interim less-complete system. Some caution is required here. Filtering is desirable in any system that brings outside air into the library and is necessary in any area with considerable air pollution.

If air cooling for the building as a whole is not possible because of the cost and if use of the library during the unpleasantly hot months is limited, it may be desirable to install local room units in working areas and possibly in one reading area. These typically will not deal with humidity unless they are specifically designed to do so, in which case they will be fairly sophisticated units requiring a drain and a water source, access to a means of removing heat (usually outside air), and power. Such a unit system is really not portable. It will also represent a risk from water and possibly steam.

The cost of heating, ventilation, and air conditioning depends primarily on the availability and the cost of three factors: (1) the heating agent, generally coal, oil or gas, solar energy, or exhaust steam from an electric generating plant; (2) the cooling agent, generally water; and (3) electric current to provide the power required. These costs vary considerably in different parts of the United States and in other countries and even from year to year in the same place. Many institutional heating plants today are so designed that a shift from coal to gas or oil can be made fairly readily and inexpensively.

There is a tremendous variation in water costs. Occasionally enough water at a desirable temperature can be provided by a well on the premises, yet an institution must be wary of well water for wells are notoriously unreliable. Often water costs are high enough so that a water-cooling tower will pay for itself, or it may be required by law.

It is desirable and economical to recirculate the water used for condensing the refrigerant.

The cost of electric current varies also. In figuring costs, the intensity of artificial light and the heat gain and loss resulting from too much natural light or poor insulation in walls and roofs may be a large factor. On the other hand, satisfactory physical conditions are bound to promote the use of the library and are well worth paying for. Add to this the extended life for the collections, and the return is even greater.

It is important for the institution to know whether the capacity of existing utilities is sufficient. An engineering study may be essential to determine this, even for major remodeling if heavier requirements are involved in support of audiovisual or computer installations and for air conditioning. A major addition or an entirely new structure often requires enlarged utilities for electrical power distribution, steam and chilled water generation and distribution, sanitary and storm sewer systems, and perhaps even telecommunications. Libraries with precise environmental conditions are very demanding of utilities.

Acoustic problems are created by air conditioning. A satisfactory solution may require the use of an acoustic engineer. Problems are created by vibration if equipment is not adequately isolated from the structure as well as from air movement. Acoustic problems arise from:

1. Compressors or transformers immediately above, below, or beside a reading or workroom area.
2. Fan and motor noise, transmitted as vibrations felt through the structure and walls or heard through ductwork.
3. Air movement at too rapid a pace through supply or exhaust ductwork.
4. Cooling-tower fans, a noise usually more disturbing outside than inside the building and a serious matter when the building is near dormitories or residences, particularly at night when noise is amplified by the quiet prevailing elsewhere. This problem has been too often neglected.

To indicate how an environmental concept involves various mechanical systems, the 1986 Harvard Depository in Southborough, Massachusetts, is described. It is protected by security guards and provided with smoke, heat, and intrusion alarms. The detection system is connected to the local fire department through a direct, dedicated telephone line. A pre-action sprinkler system was installed in the administrative area and the stall used for night storage of the electronic lift, areas separated from the stack by fire walls. The storage building itself meets fire code regulations without requiring a sprinkler system. Air quality is aided by the building's vapor barrier insulation. The interior environment is controlled for harmful particles, oxides of nitrogen, ozone, sulfur dioxide, and formaldehyde by carbon filters, and the quality of internal air improved constantly by the facility's heating and cooling process. The facility is constructed of materials that do not emit gases, and the closed stack also protects air quality. To control against infestation, the Harvard Depository will fumigate when necessary before shelving materials. Materials are also protected by a sophisticated air filtration and rotation system. This environmental control system is designed to limit the rate of change in both temperature and humidity levels, rather than to maintain a single level of temperature and humidity. The design criteria for temperature is to ±3° F. (±2° C.) daily variation, and for humidity, to ±3 percent daily variation. The operating plan allows for gradual changes in temperature and humidity as the seasons change, with the rate of change strictly limited to 9° F. (−13° C.) and 5 percent relative humidity per month. The maximum summer and minimum winter relative humidity indexes are 60 percent and 40 percent. To maintain climate control standards, there is unobstructed air rotation space around each 30-ft stack and between the stacks and the outer walls. Each aisle is served individually by multiple intakes (set low) and supply ducts (set high), and, as a further protection against the formation of microclimates, temperature and humidity sensors identify any stratification between the top and bottom of the stack. Air in the stack rotates a maximum of six times per hour.

13.2.2 Concepts of Lighting and Sun Control

Lighting is perhaps the most important and, at the same time, the most controversial aspect of library design. It is both an art and a science. Some aspects of lighting are easily specified and measured; others may be easy to describe, but measurement is difficult if not impossible.

For a library to function at all, it must have light that works; the librarian should therefore be keenly interested. What are the factors? One must consider reflective glare, direct glare, contrast, reflective qualities, the nature of the task, flicker, hum (from ballasts and, where it is very quiet as can be the case in parts of a music library, the light source itself), aesthetics, scale, shape, intensity, energy consumption, life expectancy, the ease of cleaning, the distribution or diffusion of the light, color, and cost of replacement. To add to the complexity, the designer has natural light as well as incandescent, fluorescent, and high-intensity discharge light sources. Furthermore, the design of lighting fixtures is almost limitless.

Lighting is treated both here and in appendix D in fairly substantial detail—the emphasis here is on the human relationship to light; in appendix D it is to the conservation concerns. This section will discuss a number of the aspects that should be considered during the decision process. The critical factors to be considered, not necessarily in their order of importance, include the type of light source, glare, contrast, intensity, aesthetics, flexibility, and cost. These factors will be discussed in the order listed. Together, these elements determine the quality of the light.

Light sources. Until about 1900 the sun was the chief source of light in most libraries, and the need for making full use of sunlight was a more important consideration in library architecture than almost any other single factor. The Furness Library at the University of Pennsylvania is an interesting example of a library designed for the maximum use of natural light. However, natural light does present a number of problems.

Even what is considered good north light on a bright winter's day may prove to be a source of discomfort if fresh snow is on the ground, unless the windows are protected from the snow glare. South light with a low winter sun can be very troublesome in northern latitudes. Western windows, late in the day, make shielding of some kind essential in all parts of the world. In spite of wide overhangs and glare-protecting glass, a set of drapes or screening of one kind or another is desirable.

Perhaps the greatest concern about natural light in libraries is the damage it does to library materials if they are exposed to direct sunlight day in and day out. Of course, the sunlight can be filtered, and devices can be used to remove all direct sunlight. But the best control is to avoid natural light altogether in the collections area of the building. Even north light is damaging to library materials and should be filtered or avoided

where preservation is a serious concern. On the other hand, natural light is said by many to be important for psychological reasons. Yet, in many libraries, large areas used for reading, as well as for book storage, have no natural light today, and few people complain.

Today most libraries have windows—some claim that many have too many windows. Nevertheless, in the United States, and to a lesser extent elsewhere, there is comparatively little dependence on natural light. Artificial illumination might be said to be required during approximately one-half the hours that the average library is open for public use, and it is used, in fact, during a very much larger percentage of that period. However, concern for energy conservation and for preservation suggests that even the use of artificial illumination needs to be controlled. In large areas of the building, the lighting may be turned off except when it is needed, provided the capability to do this is built into the design and the nature of the occupancy permits.

The Brigham Young University Library in Provo, Utah, in 1962 had two large underground floors with some 45,000 ft^2 (4,181 m^2) each, seating for 1,000, and no windows, but it was so well arranged and lighted that the reader soon forgot that windows were lacking. A major addition was completed in 1977 that also has two windowless underground floors so well lit that readers do not feel closed in or shut off. Brigham Young moved in the late 1990s toward a large underground expansion of their main library that will be windowless. The Louisiana State University Library in Baton Rouge has a windowless lower floor with 66,000 ft^2 (6,130 m^2) of floor space and accommodations for many readers. And the early 1990s expansion of the Doe Library at the University of California, Berkeley, is totally underground and, except for the entry area, without windows with little ill effect.

Large window areas also have the serious disadvantage of permitting cold to enter in the winter and heat in the summer. Natural light, particularly if the sun shines directly into the room, almost inevitably brings unpleasant glare and shadows in its train. Yet it can be very pleasant. Natural light, as has been said, may be "for readers, not for reading," but its use is more successful if controlled. Windows are discussed later in this chapter.

Electric lamps today come in four main types: high-intensity discharge (HID), incandescent, quartz halogen (a form of incandescent light), and fluorescent. Because of their color, low-pressure sodium and some mercury vapor light sources are not common in libraries. However, color-corrected mercury and metal-halide lamps are found in standing kiosk "up" light fixtures as well as in occasional "down" light fixtures in rooms with very high ceilings. High-pressure sodium fixtures may be found in a few institutions. HID lamps provide greater intensity than incandescent bulbs using an equal amount of current. They are slow in reaching their full intensity after being switched on, but the length of the delay has now been reduced, and there is a prospect of their increased use in the years ahead, often in combination with one of the other types of lamps. The fixture for mercury and other HID lamps may have a lens that is very important to maintain as it serves the function of an ultraviolet filter. Without this lens, there is risk of a health hazard created by potential excessive UV radiation. The HID bulb itself has a protective outer shell, yet in some cases, if this shell is broken, the lamp will continue to function while producing excessive amounts of UV radiation.

Metal-halide (HID) and quartz (incandescent) light sources are very intense; their use is typically for accent lighting or indirect or long-range (high-ceiling) lights. It should be realized that a fair amount of radiant heat is generated by this type of fixture, which can lead to some discomfort if it shines on people. This type of light source is not very suitable for general reading.

Incandescent tungsten bulbs and fluorescent tubes are by far the most common source of light in libraries. It is commonly recognized that incandescent bulbs produce an excellent quality of light. They are relatively expensive in terms of replacement and energy costs, but for special effects or circumstances, these should not be concerns. For general illumination, however, these costs are significant. An incandescent bulb, or any other high-intensity bulb, concentrates the source of light into a small space, which makes it easier to remove dust and dirt but creates more filament brightness; this must be shielded to prevent glare. Any unshielded light source, however much it is dispersed, should be avoided because it causes discomfort if one looks directly at it or if it reflects off the task into the reader's eye.

For many years it was felt that the fluorescent tube was a poor second choice in many areas of the library. However, with its many advantages and improvements over the years, the pendulum has swung in favor of fluorescent, in spite of the slight flickering and ballast noise that are still common faults. It should be added that all the HID lights require a ballast, which often will produce a hum. Careful design and the selection of the correct ballast can reduce the hum. At a considerable increase in installation costs, modern remote ballasts can completely eliminate the humming, with the minor exception of humming bulbs, which can only be heard in very quiet space. The practice of using two parallel fluorescent tubes in each fixture or two tubes end to end on the same ballast will largely overcome the stroboscopic effect. The use of indirect or shielded lighting will also help, as will the replacement of the tubes before they fully burn out.

Some authorities still believe that a few people for some physiological reason are allergic to fluorescent lighting, and in a large library it may be desirable to provide for their use a limited number of seating accommodations with incandescent bulbs, though such people may simply prefer the earlier lighting pattern because it is less visually distracting and gives the feel of a home rather than a factory. There have been attempts to improve the color effects by going back to incandescent or to a combination of the two. Incandescent bulbs have by nature a warm color, and fluorescent and mercury tubes are visually cold. Both mercury and fluorescent tubes, however, are obtainable "color-corrected" to various degrees of warmth and can be further corrected by the use of colored reflectors. Where high-pressure sodium is used, it is sometimes combined with metal-halide lamps for color correction. Examples of this combination may be found in large department stores.

Fluorescent lamps project light satisfactorily at right angles to the tubes, but their reduced efficiency beyond the ends of the tubes makes it difficult, when using direct lighting, to light shelves or individual tables along a wall at right angles to the light source without the installation of additional tubes parallel to the wall and fairly close to it. If the fixtures installed provide primarily indirect light, this problem may be solved, provided the fixtures are not too far from the wall.

Although light from unprotected fluorescent tubes will fade bindings, special sleeves are available that will provide the required protection to a large extent, but this form of protection will not reduce glare. A better solution is to control the unwanted light spectrum with a lens designed to filter ultraviolet light, such as UFII or III Plexiglas. The Verd-a-ray Fadex light tube is a third solution. Even with relatively standard fluorescent tubes, careful selection can result in reduced deterioration of library materials. However, be aware that the name of the tube may have little to do with the most damaging ultraviolet range of light output. Specifications obtained from the tube supplier or manufacturer should be compared with other tubes, and only those with minimal output in the ultraviolet spectrum should be selected. Fluorescent lamps can provide a good overall illumination with great flexibility, and, with a carefully selected fixture, they may make it easier than it is with incandescent bulbs to shift furniture and bookstacks around without relocating lighting fixtures.

One can choose from a number of fluorescent tubes having a variety of diameters, and each is effective for specific applications. There are many types of them: rapid-start, instant-start, jumbo, slimline, HO (high output), VHO (very high output), Watt Mizer, Fadex, circular, and square. Many of these and other varieties are or have been available in a wide variety of colors. By using a "lower light output ballast," 8-ft-long (2.438-m) tubes using only 40 watts of current can be provided, thereby distributing the light obtained over a larger area than is the case with a 4-ft (1.219-m) tube using the same wattage. These tubes are used in the bookstacks, as well as in the reading areas, in the Lamont Library at Harvard.

The advantages of fluorescent lamps can be summed up as follows: They use less than one-half the current required by incandescent lights to obtain the same intensity and result in less than one-half the heat, a very important consideration if high-intensity lighting and air conditioning are to be used. Fluorescent tubes have a long life, up to 10 times that of common incandescent lamps, particularly if not turned on and off frequently. They give greater flexibility. They have the disadvantage of higher installation and tube-replacement costs, and fixture cleaning may take more time. Long-lasting incandescent lamps are available, though their cost is high, and heat and energy are still a potential problem.

If lights are required for a large percentage of the hours the library is open, fluorescent light is cheaper, if the long view is taken, particularly if the cost of current is high. It should be remembered in this connection that many modern libraries rely almost altogether on artificial light because of the depth of the rooms from the outside walls combined with comparatively low ceilings and often with small window areas. Lights in reading areas are commonly left on during full opening hours in the United States, in spite of efforts of thrifty administrators to prevent it.

Glare. Two general types of glare concern the designer—direct and reflected glare. Both represent serious problems requiring attention. Direct glare results from the presence of areas of high brightness that can be seen in the periphery of one's vision. Direct glare can be produced by the brightness of a luminous ceiling, exposure to a window, or a brightly illuminated wall or other surface. Indirect glare results from the reflection of light off the surface of the task. Of all the qualities that can be discussed for light, the control of glare is probably the most important.

Glare can be controlled by locating the light fixture so that the reflection of light off the task is away from the reader's eyes and so that the brightness of the light source itself is not within the range of the reader's peripheral vision. This is most easily done where the task location is relatively fixed or when the reader can adjust the light source or reading position so as to avoid glare. A second alternative is to identify a fixture for general illumination that has qualities of low glare. Several possibilities exist, with varying degrees of success.

Indirect light results in improved quality but reduced intensity derived from the same wattage. The amount of reduction depends on the distance the light must travel from the source to the task, the reflecting surfaces of the fixtures and ceilings and walls, and also the amount of dirt and dust on the fixtures and elsewhere. Even if the intensity is reduced, the quality may be so improved as to provide a higher degree of visual efficiency. Indirect light is generally regarded as the best possible lighting system where computers are used.

No individual fixtures are universally satisfactory, as most "systems" are more suitable for a specific lighting requirement than for general illumination throughout. The lighting requirements for the lobby, circulation desk, display area, general reading areas, rest rooms, studies, and closets are all different; each will require a different approach or a certain degree of compromise. In reading rooms fluorescent lamps with troffers and reflectors are sometimes recessed into the ceiling, with acoustic tiles or plaster filling the space between the fixtures. The distance between the troffers depends on the intensity desired, on whether the tubes are single or multiple, and on their wattage. The fixtures and tubes do not need to be in rows. Different patterns can be used, but one must be careful to avoid what might be called a disorderly appearance, which too often causes distraction. Fixtures and tubes set in a hollow square pattern seem especially unpleasant.

In the early 1960s, H. Richard Blackwell determined that a lens designed to polarize the light in the vertical axis would significantly reduce the problem of reflected glare for general illumination. He was able to demonstrate also that as the distribution of the light sources increased (again for general illumination), the ability to read the task improved until the ultimate configuration of a fully luminous ceiling with polarizing lenses was reached. Several libraries installed polarized light fixtures, including the Meyer Memorial Library at Stanford, and it is generally accepted that this type of light is an improvement over other lens systems. However, the light source is still fairly bright, and, therefore, some glare from fixtures does occur some distance away in front of the reader or as a reflection off a computer screen from behind the reader.

Another fixture that has been popular recently is constructed of a specially anodized aluminum in the form of a parabolic reflector or series of reflectors. The key advantage of this system is that the light is cut off at an angle that dramatically limits direct glare. However, if one looks up into the fixture, the fluorescent tube is fully visible, which means that reflective glare can be a problem. This type of fixture is particularly well suited for range aisle lighting or lighting where the location of the fixture in relation to the task can be determined to minimize reflected glare. However, the fixtures probably are not ideal for general illumination, even though they have been thus used in many libraries.

A combination of the key principles of the two systems just described probably would produce the best possible general illumination—that is, a fixture that produces well-diffused light (even if not polarized) while cutting off the light at an angle (about 45°) so as to eliminate direct glare. Such a system was designed for a conference room, the Ida Green Room at Stanford, but the light level is so reduced by the introduction of the light-diffusing lens that the room has a darkened feel. Such an approach would require added

fixtures or tubes to produce the same light level as a direct-light fixture.

A quick test of a lighting fixture is to place a mirror in the position of the task. Then, if from a normal reading position you can see a bare tube or a very bright light source in the mirror, you will be looking at a fixture that produces enough reflected glare to be a problem.

Well-done indirect light is similar in quality to a luminous ceiling, and probably superior to separate fixtures with common translucent lenses. With the advent of improved HID light sources, the standing kiosk or suspended up-light fixture has been available as an excellent source of indirect light. However, the kiosk fixture consumes floor space; and in order to avoid excessive brightness, the ceiling must be fairly high, about 11 ft (3.353 m) being ideal. This type of lighting is attractive in part because of the efficiency of the HID light source, but the replacement of an HID bulb is not particularly cheap.

There has been some concern about fire and indirect kiosk light fixtures. These fixtures are typically within reach of a person standing on the floor; it is conceivable that paper will be placed on top of the fixture. The heat produced by the light source could ignite the paper. The authors are not aware of this actually happening in libraries, but we are aware of this concern.

The next generation of lighting is described as electrodeless lighting, which should produce excellent quality light with long life and low energy requirements. Further, it has a short turn-on time, very low ultraviolet radiation, superior lumen maintenance, and unequaled color rendition. And, there is no mercury to worry about at disposal time. In electrodeless lighting, sulfur is stimulated by microwave energy, which produces very bright (equal to 250 standard 100-watt incandescent bulbs), near-sunlight-quality light. The light thus produced is focused down a tube whose surface allows light to leak out, thereby giving the tube a distributed glowing appearance. The design of the tube also focuses the light downward (or upward as the choice might be). Although not yet found frequently in libraries, it is predicted that this lighting type will become common; it has been installed in the U.S. National Air and Space Museum (NASM) where the light tubes are over 27 m long and 266 mm in diameter (over 88 ft long and 10½ inches in diameter). The system as installed in 1994 at the NASM is a Sulfur Lighting System (SLS).

With indirect lighting, ceiling reflection is important. In small rooms the value of wall reflection should not be forgotten, and in larger ones the same holds for floor coverings. Light colors give better reflection, but glossy surfaces should be avoided. Paint containing titanium dioxide pigment is said to be superior for absorption of the ultraviolet spectrum of light.

One more comment about glare. It is important to avoid it anywhere both in its reflected and in its direct form, particularly in places where older persons are reading. The deleterious effects of glare increase considerably in middle life and later as a result of a physiological sclerosis of the lens.

Contrast. Eyestrain is reduced if the surroundings provide comparatively little contrast with pages of the book that is being read. It is recommended that tabletops be fairly light in color, floors not too dark, and the walls, ceilings, and woodwork on the light side. Then when the eye wanders from book to tabletop or to the floor or walls, the pupil of the eye does not have to shift in size, an adaptation that may cause temporary discomfort. A glossy white table, used with direct lighting, tends to produce an excessive brightness in relation to the other surroundings. Glossy surfaces and finishes result in glare and must be avoided. In spite of what has been said, some architects and librarians feel that, even if dark surfaces in the reading room are less comfortable for the eyes and more light must be provided, they make the whole room so much more attractive that they should be used. A room without any color tone contrast can itself be tiring on eyes and aesthetically may seem to lack "character."

Intensity. The topic of intensity was briefly treated in Section 5.3.8. Intensity is always a controversial subject, and it directly relates to several of the other lighting issues, especially glare, contrast, and the nature of the task being performed. This problem is confounded by the fact that intensity is relatively easy to measure while the other factors are not. Because of this, there has been a historic tendency to specify the exact intensity desired while little was said about anything else. The fallacy of this approach has been well documented; the fact that quality is more important than quantity is generally accepted.

Ophthalmological specialists recommend levels well below those proposed by the engineers and fixture manufacturers. Dr. David G. Cogan, chief of neuro-ophthalmology, National Eye Institute, Bethesda, Maryland, has clearly voiced his view: "The beliefs that relatively intense illumination is necessary for visual efficiency and that weak illumination induces organic disease of the eyes are probably the most widely held misconceptions pertaining to ophthalmology."[1] Dr. Cogan goes on to say that the recommendations of this science have come as a considerable surprise to those familiar with the human ability to adapt to dark and to those who are acquainted with previous reports that 10 footcandles (107.6 lux) were adequate for ordinary purposes and that not more than 20 footcandles (215.2 lux) were required for exceptionally fine work. He also says that intensities greater than 20 footcandles (215.2 lux) have no practical significance.

The eye can adjust to a wide range of intensity. Further, there seems to be no evidence that, when lower light intensities were customary many decades ago, there was more defective vision than at present or that reading speed and comprehension were less than they are now.

It may be well to note in this connection that H. Richard Blackwell, whose 1958 studies on the effect of the quantity of illumination were so extensively quoted by the advocates of high intensity, clarified his position in a series of articles in which he insists that quality, which is largely based on contrast, is more important than intensity. In a contribution entitled "Lighting the Library—Standards for Illumination," he says:

> The light intensity we require depends drastically upon the task we are to perform. . . . The data certainly suggest that more light is needed for many tasks than for well-printed books. . . . Illumination quality, as measured by the task contrast a lighting system provides, is much more important than illumination quantity. . . . With the best quality light, considerably lower footcandles can be used. . . . Thus we can say categorically that the best lighting installation can provide the visibility criterion with less than one fourth of the light level required with the worst lighting installation.[2]

Under these circumstances what does a library planner do? One possibility is the course that was followed in the Lamont Library. Lighting there was installed to provide from 20 to 25 footcandles (215.2 to 270 lux) maintained, but it was so wired that, with comparatively little expense for alterations, the intensity can be doubled. There seems to have been no need for a subsequent increase. In this connection it should be borne in mind that fluorescent lamps have gradually increased in light efficiency since then, and, as a consequence, the intensities available in the Lamont Library have increased 25 percent rather than decreased, as they might be expected to do in some installations. Newer-style ballasts could maintain the intensity at between 30 and 40 footcandles (322 and 430 lux) and simultaneously reduce by about 50 percent the electrical consumption.

Because desirable lighting levels are relative, when they are high in one building in an institution, the levels in other buildings that had previously seemed satisfactory will begin to appear inadequate, and there may be a tendency to push up levels in one area or another.

In any consideration of intensity of light, it should again be noted that it is "maintained" light—the intensity provided when the light source has had some months of use—that is the concern.

The authors suggest several general guidelines regarding intensity:

1. It should always be remembered that high-intensity light of poor quality is less desirable than low-intensity light of good quality.
2. Every effort within reason should be made to improve the quality of the internal visual environment. The comfort of the readers and the aesthetic results are of first importance.
3. For persons with normal or close to normal vision, an intensity of 50 footcandles (540 lux) on the reading surface should be satisfactory for all but the most exacting reading tasks in a library.
4. Twenty-five to 30 footcandles (270 to 322 lux) should be sufficient in most library reading areas so long as 50 (540 lux) are readily available in some areas and 75 (800 lux) in a very few places for those who have impaired or defective vision or who are using difficult-to-read manuscripts or other material. Fifty footcandles might be provided in large sections of processing rooms where staff members are working long hours, frequently with difficult material, and in a small percentage, perhaps 25 percent, of the public reading areas. It is suggested that these reading areas should not be too readily accessible or viewed from the rest of the building, as the higher intensity, when seen, will reduce pupil size, and one's own table with lower intensity will tend to appear as though it has inadequate light.

5. Different persons prefer different types of seating accommodations, different temperatures, and also different light intensities. In a large library it should be possible to provide what each one prefers, instead of making everything uniform, representing a compromise with mediocre results.
6. Light intensities in lobbies, corridors, smoking and lounge areas, stairwells, and toilets can be kept down to between 10 and 20 footcandles (107.6 and 215.2 lux), which is entirely adequate, except for concentrated reading and study. Then, when the reading and work areas are entered, they will seem bright.

The wiring throughout the building should be of a gauge heavy enough so that future changes made in fixtures in order to improve the quality, which may necessitate the use of higher-wattage light sources, will be possible without expensive rewiring.

Aesthetics. The problems of aesthetics in lighting are fully as challenging as the selection of the light source, fixture, and arrangement. If one were willing to disregard aesthetics and accept a factory or grocery store atmosphere, satisfactory lighting from a strictly functional point of view is probably possible at lower cost. Fortunately, no institutions are satisfied with this.

The difficulty of resolving this to everyone's satisfaction stems from the different wishes of different people, some using bifocal glasses, some wanting the lively interior of a popular student union, some seeking the quiet, even somber, tone of a lounge, some with weakening vision, and some even claiming to be allergic to a particular kind of light. These desires and physiological and psychological factors need to be balanced against the physical conditions of the building where there can be harsh sunlight coming through windows, bad reflections off glass, the direct glare of lighting tubes all too visible, and the dark corners in bookstacks where insufficient light makes it difficult to read spine labels on the top or bottom shelves. This all is made still more complex because of activities that produce many variant lighting situations within one library—for example, entering via a lobby to find a person at a service desk, reading materials some of which are on glossy paper and some printed in very small type, looking for classification numbers on shelves amid bookstack ranges, viewing text on a microfilm reading machine, studying a display of rare manuscripts, or attending an illustrated lecture in an instructional room. Satisfactory aesthetics requires careful distinction among library functions, subtlety and skill in introducing artificial light, and, of course, the professional knowledge and experience of an electrical or illuminating engineer. The topic deserves special attention during design development.

In a library it may be desirable to provide a lighting environment in which the light sources are unobtrusive, even invisible. This suggests the luminous ceiling, though that approach provides such a monotonous condition that it is not aesthetically pleasing to most people. Indirect lighting can be a close substitute with the advantage of superior UV filtration, easier access for relamping, greater flexibility in creating lighting environments, and lower cost. The alternative is to carefully and specifically design the lighting environment, including the exact location of each lighting fixture in relation to the anticipated task. This, of course, does not maintain flexibility for furniture placement, though it can result in satisfaction for years and may not frustrate functional relocations to too great an extent. Is it better to have a high degree of satisfaction for a decade, and face modest expense during future modifications, or to provide an average compromising solution? This is a functional question as well as an aesthetic one for the local team to resolve.

The importance of the relation between the intensity in different locations in the same building is great. At the Air Force Academy Library near Colorado Springs, some of the rooms used by the processing staff have no windows. Although theoretically the rooms are adequately lighted, the staff is unhappy because they enter their quarters from parts of the building where the Colorado sunlight coming through the glass outside walls has intensified the light far beyond any normal artificial illumination.

A brightly lighted supermarket has been found to attract customers. The same may hold true for the lobby of an academic library in an urban institution with brightly lighted stores on all sides. On the other hand, some argue that the real reason for bright lights in stores is to make the merchandise look bright and sparkling and spiffy and create high turnover. Some parts of some libraries (especially public libraries) will benefit from this special brightness, but only selectively.

Furthermore, the same amount of brightness is not useful or desirable throughout an academic library. An occasional room with greater or less brightness than the rest of the building can be visually interesting, if the areas are carefully selected—for example, exhibit quarters with case lighting but subdued ambient room lighting, or a brightly lit below-grade periodical reading area.

The aesthetics of two conditions deserve further comment. The first is the exhibition gallery, because very few academic and research libraries have done well with exhibit lighting and its aesthetics. One has to look at many such libraries to find one good instance. In general, the goal is to highlight the displayed objects with minimum light levels (for preservation reasons), facilitate reading of all explanatory text, sharpen the observer's visual acuity of the objects, and dramatize the event by substantially reducing the ambient light in the gallery. Visits to outstanding art museums can be instructive, because they often do far better than libraries, given museum staff experts in the art of mounting displays.

The other condition is the aesthetic pros and cons of skylights. The light coming from skylights can sometimes help with aesthetics; it brings a warm tone and implies a relationship with the natural attractiveness of the outdoors. Yet sunlight through any high-level window may glare directly or reflectingly, may provide too great a contrast of intensity, will fade many fabrics as well as book spines, and can cause problems when it comes to illuminating reading areas beneath the skylight after sunset. Light coming from a skylight on the north slope of a pitched roof will normally be far more pleasing aesthetically than the light from a skylight on other slopes, but circumstances will vary the local result.

Although the functional and quality aspects are generally considered first, the total aesthetic effects of lighting are important. They should relate to the architect's basic concept for the building and thus their design and specification generally are considered to be part of the architect's scope of work. This responsibility may be delegated to an electrical or illuminating engineer or to an interior designer selected by the architect or the institution. The building program should have given the owner's general guidance; the design development phase is the time for the specific aesthetic execution to be critiqued.

Ralph Galbraith Hopkinson's *Architectural Physics: Lighting,* contains objective studies of lighting problems. A chapter entitled "For the Future" lists the following principles of good lighting:

1. We see better the more light we have, up to a point, but this light must be free from glare.
2. We see better if the main visual task is distinguished from its surroundings by being brighter, or more contrasting, or more colorful, or all three. It is therefore important to identify the main focal points and build up the lighting from their requirements.
3. We see better if the things we have to look at are seen in an unobtrusive and unconfusing setting, neither so bright nor so colorful that it attracts the attention away, nor so dark that work appears excessively bright with the result that the eyes are riveted on to the visual task. Good lighting therefore provides a moderate and comfortable level of general lighting, with preferential lighting on the work. This can be called "focal lighting."
4. The surroundings should be moderately bright, and this should be achieved by combination of lighting and decoration.
5. No source of light should be a source of glare discomfort. Excessively bright areas should never be visible. Windows should be provided with curtains, blinds, or louvers, to be brought into use when the sky is very bright.
6. In order to dispel any feeling of gloom, and to reduce glare, plenty of light should reach the ceiling.
7. Sources of light should be chosen to ensure that the color rendering they give is satisfactory for the situation in which they will be found.
8. Care should be taken to eliminate any discomfort from flickering light sources.
9. A dull uniformity should at all costs be avoided. Small brilliant points of light can give sparkle to a scene without causing glare.
10. The lighting of a building should be considered always in relation to its design and in particular to the scheme of decoration to be installed. On no account should lighting be considered to be merely a matter of windows or fittings. The whole environment enters into a good lighting installation.[3]

Flexibility. Complete flexibility in lighting, as is the case in other areas, is expensive. It would require the best reasonable system of general illumination throughout the library, the exception being only those areas that will not change, such as rest rooms, closets, lobbies, and perhaps some offices. In most libraries this approach will require that all the lights will be on during all hours of operation, although there could be zones where by separate circuits the lighting level might be controlled in perhaps two or three steps. Although this form of lighting may be appropriate for a heavily used undergraduate library with limited separate shelving areas, it makes little sense today in any library where there are discrete shelving and reading areas, particularly in view of concerns for energy consumption.

In most cases, therefore, the best lighting for each major area of the library should be selected, which will mean that there will be either additional cost or compromise when the distribution of the functional areas changes. Sufficient capacity should be provided, perhaps only with conduit and junction boxes, so that the function of any area can be changed reasonably. In this regard, open reading areas probably are more likely to change than stack areas.

The concept of providing a fairly low level of ambient lighting combined with task lighting in reading areas satisfies both energy conservation and the need for flexibility. If the lighting is properly done, the problems of glare and contrast can be minimized, and the psychological "feel" of the space enhanced. Individual range aisle switching is not flexible, but the potential energy savings may outweigh the advantages of flexibility by a considerable margin. At Stanford and elsewhere there have been cases where it paid to install, retrospectively, separate switching for range aisles. If this can be justified economically, then certainly it warrants serious consideration at the time of construction.

To help flexibility, selected areas may have fixture installations where half or all the tubes in one fixture can be turned on by switches under staff control—for example, using 25 footcandles (270 lux) in microtext or computer use areas with the ability to turn on twice as many tubes in the fixtures to double the ambient light for a change to general reading of books and journals. Some energy-driven codes require switching systems such as this in rooms with general illumination. Clearly factors of aesthetics, function, long-range planning, and cost must be considered before adopting a program of complete flexibility.

Cost. Lighting expenditures fall into three groups.

1. Installation costs, which include wiring, switches, fixtures, lamps, and the construction costs of the structure that derive from lighting and also those required to dispose of the heat generated by lighting. This last may be very considerable and should not be forgotten if high-intensity light is to be used.

2. The cost of maintenance and upkeep, which includes the repair and cleaning of the fixtures, and the replacement of lamps. Careful planning will help lessen the expense.

3. The cost of electric current, which depends, after the installation has been made, on cost of current per kilowatt-hour (kWh) and the number of hours in a year that the lights are on. The amount of kWh required is set by the intensity provided, the efficiency of the lights, the type of fixtures used, and the number of fixtures required. Costs vary a great deal from place to place. Large users generally pay a lower rate. For many institutions, a figure of about 10 cents per kWh will include the cost of current, plus the maintenance and repair of the installation and lamp replacement. The figures used in the following paragraphs are based on that rate; they are included for illustrative purposes only. Local experience should be relied on in reaching any final decision.

Costs should not be overemphasized, because the library cannot set the cost per kWh or choose the electrical source, but disagreement over the desirable quality and intensity complicates the problem. Too often librarians and other administrative officers have given little thought to lighting costs because these have not been included in the library budget but have been paid directly by the institution.

In the early 1960s Keyes Metcalf talked with a librarian in a fine new library with attractive lighting, giving unusually high intensity even for that time—over 100 footcandles (1,100 lux)—and asked what the lighting bill came to. The reply was, "We don't know yet, but it has been suggested that it would come to some $400 a month." A little figuring—multiplying the wattage used in each bay by the number of bays, the hours of opening a week, and the cost per kWh of current used—indicated that $4,000 a month would be closer to the mark. Whether or not this amount would be serious expense for the university, which was endowed, is another matter; but because the building was almost a glass box, this intensity might be said to be necessary or at least desirable, in order to avoid too great a contrast with the excessive natural light available through the glass walls.

In 1995 the average collection held by 108 ARL libraries was 3,300,000 volumes. If we assume the average student body was 20,000, and the libraries are of traditional design and in single buildings, and that there is no provision for growth, then the average library would need to be about 460,000 ft^2 (43,000 m^2) based upon 15 volumes per ft^2 (161 per m^2), 25 ft^2 (2.323 m^2) per seat, seating one-quarter of the students, and adding 25 percent to the sum of these figures for all other functions. Illuminating engineers report that 1½ watts of light per ft^2 of floor space (16 watts per m^2) should provide 25 footcandles (270 lux) in a typical installation today. With energy-efficient light fixtures in an office setting, light levels in excess of 50 footcandles (540 lux) are possible with 1½ watts per ft^2. With task lighting and individual range aisle switching, the actual energy use will be a great deal less. Based on 1½ watts per ft^2, the 460,000 ft^2 (43,000 m^2) in the average ARL university library would use 690,000 watts, or 690 kWh, to obtain uniform lighting throughout the building, and this, at 10 cents a kWh, would cost $69 an hour. If the average university library is open for public use 4,000 hours a year, this would mean $276,000. This cost estimate can be reduced, however, to perhaps $250,000 because hallways, which can appropriately have a lower intensity, and processing quarters, which are used for shorter hours, more than cancel out the cleaning time. Stack-lighting intensities are generally less but require nearly as much wattage per square foot, and, in most libraries with open-access stacks, lights are kept on all day long. If the library uses 100 footcandles (which is the level frequently recommended) with an inefficient system, and if the above calculation is correct, lighting will cost $500,000 a year. If, on the other hand, half the lighting is turned off at any given time, the savings would, of course, equal $250,000 a year based upon a design for 100 footcandles, or more if the designed light levels are higher. One can pay off a loan in excess of $1,700,000 at 7½ percent interest in 10 years with this kind of annual payment, a fact that may well justify a lighting design with local switching capability. These figures are presented simply to give some indication of the amount of money involved.

Conclusions. The question that administrative officers must answer is whether it is more important to spend the money for better quality, greater control, or increased intensity of light or for something else—books and service, for instance. What is reasonable? The authors suggest the following 10 guidelines:

1. Institutions should always watch for opportunities to improve the physical conditions provided for their students and staff, just as they should seek to improve the quality of the education that they provide. They should not be content with the present on the basis that what was good enough for the preceding generation is good enough for the generations to come.

2. Whatever the cost, the lighting should be of a quality that will attract, not discourage, use, and that will not be tiring to the reader. The quality of the light and the efficiency of the illuminant and fixture should be a carefully considered trade-off. A low-efficiency fixture may require double the wattage to attain a specified light intensity but, at the same time, may improve the quality of the light made available.

3. It is suggested, as noted in the section on intensity, that a new library be wired so that at least 50 footcandles (540 lux) of light intensity on reading surfaces can be made available anywhere without complete rewiring; that extra intensity be provided in at least a few public rooms and in selected staff work areas; and that in the rest of the building where reading is carried on, including the bookstack, from 25 to 30 footcandles (270 to 322 lux) be installed. It should be noted that the bookstack intensity refers to reading surfaces 30 inches (762 mm) above the floor and not to the backs of the books on lower shelves.

4. The high-intensity reading areas should include those for manuscripts, archives, and rare books and the space set aside for use by persons with defective vision. Some supplementary local task lighting will be useful. It should be noted that very small "egg-crate" fixtures and those with polarizing lenses can reduce intensity by perhaps 50 percent, but they may improve quality and give better aesthetic effects.

5. It is evident that, if as much as 100-footcandle illumination is used, the heat generated, even with fluorescent tubes, will become so great as to place additional loads on air-conditioning equipment or to make buildings almost impossibly hot in summer months if air conditioning is not available. The costs involved here are difficult to predict but will be considerable.

6. If higher-intensity light sources are deemed desirable, ways and means should be worked out so that during the winter the buildings can be heated as far as possible with the heat resulting from the lighting. It does not, however, relieve the overheating during the summer.

7. If high-intensity lighting has been installed, particularly with tubes in pairs, it is possible to arrange light switches so that the right-hand tubes can be used one week and the left-hand ones the next, or some similar arrangement. (This practice is in vogue in the Lamont Library main-entrance lobby. There the use of one-half the tubes at a time practically doubles their life, a matter of some importance because, regrettably, a scaffolding is required when they are changed.) Some codes will require switching of this nature as an energy-conservation technique.

8. Good reflecting surfaces can help, such as light-color ceilings, walls, and floors, particularly in bookstacks where lower shelves are a problem. Avoid glare, and do not neglect the importance of the aesthetic effect of light.

9. If the lights are to be left on all day in the reading areas and throughout the bookstacks, the wiring and switches can be greatly simplified and installation costs reduced. Switches should be controlled by the staff and should be inaccessible to readers where general illumination requires that all the lights should be on. Ideally, the switches should be centrally located to simplify the opening and closing process. However, local switching is recommended in most cases, perhaps with a low-voltage master control, as discussed in Chapter 5.

10. Talk the problem over with the architect and the illuminating engineer, and make sure that everyone involved understands the situation and the financial implications.

In all significant projects the librarian should insist on seeing either an example or a mock-up of the general or typical lighting fixtures with the fixtures specified installed at the same point in relation to the task and provided with the same light source and similar surfaces as proposed for the building project. Only in this way can one be convinced that all the factors come together— intensity, lack of direct and reflective glare, ease of servicing, color, appearance, hum, flickering, and so on—that contribute to the total lighting system.

There will be fixtures for which a mock-up is simply not practical. For example, a few display cases or a portrait may require special lighting techniques. (Display cases present a special problem for proper lighting to avoid reflective glare and heat buildup within the case. Display case lighting is discussed briefly in appendix D.) Or, there may be an unusual architectural feature that calls for a unique fixture. In these cases the librarian can only ask for answers to the questions of glare, heat, intensity, serviceability, cost, and the like which will be of concern.

13.2.3 Fixed Elements

During the design development phase, it is important that the final decision be made on shear walls, duct and elevator shafts, stairs, rest rooms, mechanical rooms, and telephone closets. The planning for functional relationships and flexibility will certainly have an influence, as will the size and configuration of the building scheme. Local codes often require certain considerations for stairs and their location in regard to providing emergency egress. No building should be planned without checking the applicable codes and regulations, and it is urged that the designers consult code authorities during the design phases. Several points are listed here to consider in making the final decision on fixed elements.

1. Do the fixed elements work within the module? Structural or bearing walls, for example, can take the place of a range of shelving and have relatively little impact.
2. Looking toward the future, is it possible to anticipate a potential for a changed circulation pattern? What if one area of the library shrinks and another increases in size? How might a future addition affect the proposed arrangements? Will moving the core or a structural wall one bay away provide greater flexibility for future change? Is the orientation of the major elements correct?
3. Should other provisions be made for the future? Should a retaining or perimeter wall have knockout panels or other features to allow for future expansion? Should openings be provided in structural walls, which can be relatively thick and difficult if not impossible to alter in the future? Openings for corridors and conveyors as well as ducts and conduits should be considered.
4. Will the corridor and aisle circulation system resulting from the location of the fixed elements be clear and easy to use? Will it permit a reasonable arrangement for the stacks? Are there clues (needed especially

in a large building) that will lead the reader back to the main stair, or will an abundance of signs be required?
5. Are the routes to other major library elements made as simple as possible? Are exiting routes simple and evident?
6. Is the width of the stairs adequate for the anticipated traffic (see Section 12.4)? Will the elevator accommodate the furniture and equipment, or is it planned that this material will be moved by the stairs? Has handicapped access been provided for?
7. Will the provision of utilities or mechanical services conflict with other aspects of the library? Remember that elevators and machine rooms make noise and that plumbing eventually will leak. A reading area next to the elevator machine room will be a problem, as will rest rooms located over a rare book stack.
8. How is exit security handled? Are internal doors with alarms in the right places?

Because of special concerns for four fixed elements, extra comments are here provided concerning walls, windows, doors, and plumbing.

Walls. Interior walls may present other problems. Efforts have been made in recent years in many libraries to avoid wet walls—those that cannot be removed without breaking them up. In their place it is possible to use bookshelving or dry walls, which in nontechnical terms are simply movable partitions, often of steel. It should be understood that there is a range of flexibility in the nature of walls. On the one hand, shear walls cannot be moved. At the other extreme are office panel systems that are essentially furniture; their movement and reuse are fairly simple matters. In between are masonry walls and stud partitions typically faced with gypsum or plaster wallboards. These can be moved, but surfaces will require patching, and mechanical, electrical, and lighting systems may be affected.

Shelving with solid back panels in each section used as a partition or divider can often be satisfactory and, if freestanding, is more flexible than anything except the low office panel partition. But such shelving may create acoustical problems as noise is carried over from one area to another.

Metal and glass partitions, as well as folding partitions, are also too often unsatisfactory acoustically. They must be fitted tightly to floor and ceiling with no gaps through which noise can penetrate. Filling gaps with plastic or fiber strips is never sufficient to limit sound transmission. Any partition must extend through a hung ceiling for a tight fit to the underfloor for the same reason. Movable steel partitions for offices and faculty studies are often considerably more expensive than wet walls. However, if moving is necessary as often as twice in 10 years, it will probably be less expensive to provide steel partitions than to demolish and reerect wet walls.

Dry partitions of Transite or of plaster or gypsum board with metal studs are being used extensively in all types of structures and can well be considered for library interior walls, as they are comparable in price to unplastered cinder or concrete block walls. Keep in mind the method by which shelving might be installed. Plaster or gypsum board is not strong enough to support shelving fully loaded with books; proper anchorage must be provided within the wall.

Cinder and concrete block walls, particularly for inside walls, have been used much more in recent years than earlier. When used for outside walls, they may present a difficult problem because of cracking, and therefore waterproofing and insulation may be necessary if they are exposed to the elements. Another block used today is pumice. It is often left unpainted, as in the Harvard Divinity School Library, because of its pleasant natural color. No doubt in other parts of the world other types of blocks are available.

Windows. Windows represent another form of fixed element that should be settled in the design development phase. Windows are of many varieties. They may have wood or metal frames, be unopenable or double-hung or casement or have other arrangements for opening; they may be of different shapes and sizes and may be made of large or small panes of clear, opaque, or colored glass, to say nothing of glass blocks. Skylights are windows, and comments about their use have been provided in Section 13.2.2. The window pattern can take innumerable forms, and the resulting facade is of first importance aesthetically.

The librarian should give particular attention to the effect of windows on library functions. Where windows exist, no shelving can later be located. On the other hand, windows provide light and they can provide ventilation; and human reactions are aroused by their presence or absence because the exterior view can provide visual relief, can enable one to judge the weather or degree of darkness, and may reveal the beauty of a tree or other vista.

Unless the building overhangs or there are sunscreen controls, the closer the windows are placed to the ceiling, the higher the intensity of light admitted. But if the windows are above eye level, nothing can be seen out of them, except possibly sky, tall trees, other buildings, or another part of the same building. Any window through which anything can be seen may be a distraction for some people and will interfere with reading; on this basis one could advocate a completely windowless library. Many people today spend much of their working lives in windowless areas. On the other hand, few people are ready to recommend that a library be completely windowless, particularly in its reading areas and especially in areas occupied by the staff. Windows bring visual relief and interest.

Halls, corridors, and stairwells do not need to rely on outside light and probably should be provided with at least low-intensity artificial lighting during all hours the library is open. In all other areas, even if they are well supplied with windows, artificial light is required in most libraries today for approximately half the hours of opening. Library users, at least in the United States, seldom depend on only natural light, and reading areas are artificially lighted throughout the day even when this interior source is functionally superfluous. If natural light is not depended upon, it is possible to plan a building with large sections far away from natural light. Remember that books are harmed by direct sunlight because ultraviolet rays and any bright light fade bindings and hasten paper deterioration.

One important decision in connection with windows concerns the percentage of the outside wall that should be of glass. In some states there are regulations for schools and some other public buildings specifying at least 20 percent glass, but these regulations are falling more and more into disuse with the improvements in artificial lighting and ventilation and sometimes for security and vandalism reasons.

For over 35 years the "all-glass box" style of building has been a popular design solution, but one that can present physiological, psychological, and also functional problems. If any area in a library has an all-glass facade, it will be practically impossible to store books near the outside walls without harming them, unless, of course, the glass is completely covered up and protected.

If the windows go down to the floor, there are several concerns: the possibility of a leak or flood from outside, the need to protect the glass from book trucks, a hesitancy by women with short skirts to sit by them as there is no modesty screening, and greater expense, because codes usually require tempered glass when glass is below 18 in. (457 mm) from the floor. If the windows are on the west or south, much of the space, if it is not shaded in some way, will be practically unusable for reading during parts of bright days because of unpleasant intensity, unless suitable protection of some kind is available. Windows can also let in so much light that they make higher intensities of artificial light desirable. Ignoring the sun's effect on heating and ventilation, which can be an asset in a system utilizing solar heat, it is easy to overdo the use of glass as far as reading is concerned because of the resulting glare.

On the other hand, it would be a shame in many locations to prevent the users of a library from looking out on a handsome lawn, trees, and distant hills. Keyes Metcalf remembered some years ago recommending large windows in every bay on one side of the Bennington College Library where a fine mountain view was available, and architect Pietro Belluschi saying, "This view will be appreciated more if there isn't too much glass."

Windows can also be protected from the outside in three ways:

1. *Movable sunscreens.* One design involves large, vertical metal fins a foot or so (say, 305 mm) wide, which can be adjusted by a crank operated from inside the building or by automatic equipment that turns them with the sun. Because they are outdoors and have movable parts, they tend to get out of order and to become noisy in a high wind. It is suggested that persons who have had experience with them be consulted before they are adopted.

2. *Fixed sunscreens.* Screens of one kind or another can be placed parallel to the walls and windows, and a few feet away from them. Screens have been used for hundreds of years in India and were introduced on a large scale some 40 years ago in the United States by Edward Stone, Marcel Breuer, and other architects. They may be of metal or concrete, or they may be of hollow tiles of various depths, shapes, and sizes, through which comes comparatively little direct sunlight except for a few minutes a few days in the year. They can be decorative and pleasing aestheti-cally. They are not inexpensive, and they may present a serious cleaning problem and become a nesting place for birds. See also comments on such screens in Section 11.4.3, treating the orientation of the building.

3. *Horizontal projections* reaching out from the building at the level of the floor above or by overhanging the higher floor. Roof eaves frequently are designed with this in mind. The projections can extend out 10 or 12 ft (3.048 or 3.658 m) or even more. On the south and west sides, where the sun may be a particularly difficult problem, they will almost completely shut out the direct sunlight. This concept, utilizing cantilevered floors, is an important part of the system of sun control in the Cecil H. Green Library at Stanford. The lower western sun in late afternoon may be troublesome, but on lower floors at least, trees and shrubs should prevent any difficulty. If the soffits project too far, they shut out a good deal of light and may make the use of artificial light necessary throughout the day except during periods of bright sunlight.

There may be a temptation to use these projections as porches for strolling, or as outdoor reading areas, but such use involves various hazards; readers inside may be distracted, and books may be passed from porches to the ground without proper authorization. On the whole, because of the limited number of days during the academic year when the weather and the sun make them satisfactory for use, outdoor reading areas in most of the temperate zones are seldom worth what they cost. This evaluation may change where summer schools become common, and outdoor reading areas may prove very useful in the Tropics and in the parts of the temperate zones nearby.

One difficulty with screening from the outside is that any extra cost for the treatment, added to that of the glass itself, tends to be greater per square foot than a good masonry or concrete wall. This certainly can be the case if the cost of inside sun control is added. Further, outside screening can look very heavy and mechanical and soil easily unless the design is by a very skilled architect. Still, exterior sunscreens can help the appearance of what otherwise may be a plain drab box. And, for heat gain, exterior solar screening of one kind or another is much more effective than drapes, blinds, tints, films, and other treatments at or just inside the windows. Florida offers many examples worth study.

As has been stated, windows contribute considerably to the aesthetic design of the building. Covering large window areas with a few folds of cloth—light-colored glass-fiber curtains, for instance—is functional in preventing glare and also has aesthetic advantages both day and night, but especially at night for the reader, when curtains cover the hard, unpleasant, reflective, and typically dark surface of glass; they also might be said to humanize the space enclosed. Lighting the area outside to a low intensity will also help create that effect.

Windows, particularly very large windows, make it more difficult to heat and cool the building properly. Single-pane glass does not keep out the cold or the heat as well as a masonry wall, particularly if the latter is satisfactorily insulated. Closely related to this objection are several other facts. If the building has winter humidification, water will condense and run down the windows when the outside temperature is low enough to reach the dew point at the glass. If windows are sealed shut and the air conditioning breaks down, a serious situation develops; yet, unless the windows are locked or sealed shut, someone sooner or later will open them, and the effectiveness of the air conditioning will be ruined along with the control of security for the collections.

On the other hand, it might be added that with air conditioning in an area where the electricity is likely to break down and where repair personnel are difficult to reach, it may be unwise to seal the windows. In a large city where such mishaps are less likely and where competent mechanics may be readily available, windows can be sealed without fear of serious consequences. A limited number of them should be openable by a key. Remember that sealed windows must be cleaned from the outside, which will present a problem on upper floors unless some means of access is provided. Double-glazed windows are nearly always sealed, and, as already indicated, they are practically necessary if the humidity in the winter is to be kept above the middle thirties when the outside temperature falls below the freezing mark. With increased concern about the cost of energy, the benefit of double-glazed windows is far more attractive and their use is becoming common.

There is one other point about windows as a fixed element. If seating can be adjacent to a window, even a small one, it is attractive, although this arrangement is not necessary for an open carrel. A small, closed carrel, without a window, will rarely be popular. The same holds true even for a larger faculty study. Any room with much less than 60 ft² (5.57 m²) that is completely closed and has no windows will be objectionable to many people. Glass in or next to the door through which the occupant can look down a stack aisle or into an area with outside light will help, as will a clerestory window near the ceiling. The use of bright colors will also be helpful. With even a small window, 40 ft² to 50 ft² (3.72 m² to 4.65 m²) may be adequate for a completely closed room. If the area is completely open, except for a front and back partition high enough so that the top of the head of the person in front cannot be seen, a carrel 3 ft (0.914 m) wide and 5 ft (1.524 m) on centers may be entirely satisfactory without windows. (In a research library, larger carrels are recommended, which will affect both the width and possibly the space on centers.) It is worth repeating here that with the use of color, and with seating arranged so that the reader does not face blank walls on two or three sides, most people will very soon forget about the lack of windows. This has been proved in many recently built university libraries.

Doors. Still another element that should have fixed location during this phase of the design process, doors serve to bar or permit entrance and exit to a building and to secure interior spaces. They are also useful for acoustic purposes and to prevent the spread of fire. Each of these functions should be kept in mind, as well as the cost of doors, their psychological effect, and their effect on architectural harmony and ornamentation. They may slide horizontally or vertically, fold or revolve, but note that revolving doors should not be the only passage because wheelchairs cannot pass through them unless they are quite large; there are revolving doors designed to accommodate wheelchairs.

If doors are hinged, remember that they can swing a full 180° only when the hinge is on the side of the opening where the full swing is expected and where wall space is available. Door closers may also prevent a full swing. If the door is hinged so that it can go in both directions, it can with difficulty be made tight enough to avoid drafts and the transfer of sounds to the other side.

Double, or French, doors, one opening to the right and the other to the left, with no upright molding (an astragal) between, are unfortunate, unless at least one door is normally to stand open. This is a poor choice of doors if there is much traffic and if the doors are heavy, because a person coming from the outside and pulling the right-hand door tends to stand partially in front of the left-hand door; a person coming out at the same time can cause an accident. Where there are pairs of doors swinging in only one direction at a busy entrance, both should be hinged on either the right or the left. (See fig. 13.1.) A pair of doors swinging both ways, in and out (variant B of fig. 13.1) is a good option where traffic is heavy, and traffic conflicts will be minimal because people can push on one door without standing in front of the other door panel.

Do not use double doors for emergency exits. Securing single doors is much easier than double. (The exception to this is the use of dead bolts into the floor, as was done for the front doors of Stanford's Green Library East Wing. This is not often legal, however, and may be questionable even for Green, except that the front doors technically were not an emergency exit.) Normal panic

hardware will not work on double doors where there is no astragal, for it can be opened from the outside in a few seconds with a simple tool. The provision of an astragal with double doors is always a problem, though it can be arranged for the panels to close in the required order with an overhead door coordinator. Yet coordinators seldom work well, and they are noisy. The route for delivery of large furniture should be considered, usually through a service entrance. It may require some double or oversized doors, perhaps with one leaf fixed.

Ellison doors, which are hinged some 6 in. (152 mm) from the side of the door, may be useful for doorways 4 ft (1.220 m) wide or more, as they are easier to open. (See fig. 13.2.) They may be dangerous when used by children; they are more expensive and are not desirable for narrow openings. (A type of Ellison door was used to good effect on a number of the Washington State ferries serving the greater Seattle area.)

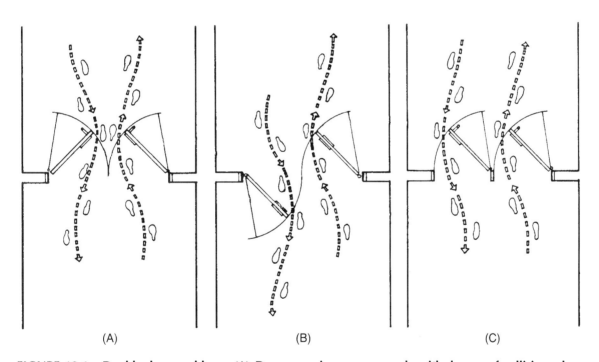

FIGURE 13.1   Double-door problems. (A) Doors opening one way only with danger of collision when used from opposite directions at the same time. Not recommended. (B) Doors opening both ways and used from opposite directions at the same time present less danger of collision, but if they are outside doors with uneven air pressure, they may be difficult to keep closed when not in use. Possible. (C) Doors opening in one way only, but each hinged on right-hand upright (if moving up on diagram). No danger of collisions. Recommended. Note that only B (as illustrated) allows a user to push any door open from either direction if both hands are full.

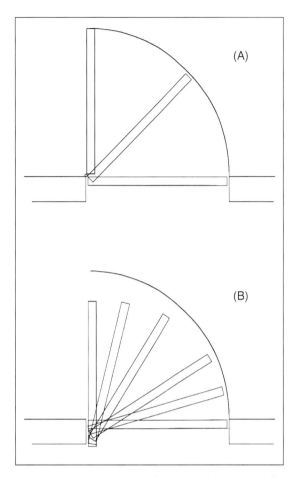

FIGURE 13.2 Door swing. **(A) is a normally hinged door; when opened against air pressure or a wind, the full face of the door offers resistance to opening. (B) has Ellison hinges (or a variation thereof), which effectively rotates the door about a point well away from the hinged side of the door (toward the latch side of the door), and slides the door back into the opening. This type of door is easier to open against air pressure or wind. Both doors, when open at 90°, occupy some of the door opening. Only when the standard door is open at 180° (which is not commonly done) does it fall totally outside the door opening.**

Frequently, doors in a library should have a glass panel large enough for both tall people and those in wheelchairs to see through it to prevent accidents, as well as to make supervision possible. Eye level for an adult in a wheelchair ranges from 3 ft 7 in. to 4 ft 3 in. (1.090 to 1.295 m). Every double-swinging (in and out) door with rather frequent traffic must have such a vision panel.

Some buildings will require fire separation, using doors that are normally open. These doors may be held open by a fusible link or a magnetic device controlled by the fire alarm system. The use of a fusible link in this case is generally not recommended, as the heat required to activate the door will place the protected part of the building at risk. On the other hand, magnetic hold-open devices are fairly expensive. It is a fairly simple matter to design doors that are normally open so that they are contained in a pocket and thus have the appearance of a continuation of the wall surface. This concept is of course somewhat compromised if the door must also have panic hardware.

Folding doors are sometimes used to divide areas temporarily, for instance, to make a small classroom into two seminar rooms or to break up the staff lounge so that part of it can be used for other purposes. These doors may be wide enough so that they become partitions, in fact if not in name. They may be collapsible or of the hinged type. Unfortunately, they are seldom sufficiently soundproof. The door itself may have all the required attributes, but the sliding mechanism at both top and bottom has gaps through which the sound is carried. If this is a serious matter, two folding doors parallel to each other can be installed with an air space in between. The great virtue of the folding door is the flexible division of space that it provides and the fact that it is easier to operate and install than is a sliding door panel.

Roll-down doors may be desirable to secure a service point or wide entrance during certain hours of operation or, if solid, to provide a fire separation. These doors can be of open mesh construction or of visually solid construction similar to a rolltop desk. Their operation tends to be noisy; thus, their use is suitable only for infrequent closure, such as once a day.

Although the exact location and swing of a door can be refined at later stages of the design, such changes frustrate the architect who will no doubt be under pressure to complete a complex set of contract documents. Later changes are not welcome. Figure 13.3 shows a door placed improperly and seriously complicating the use of a small area.

There are several things to look for in terms of door location and configuration.

1. Can a person on crutches or in a wheelchair open the door, enter the space, and close the

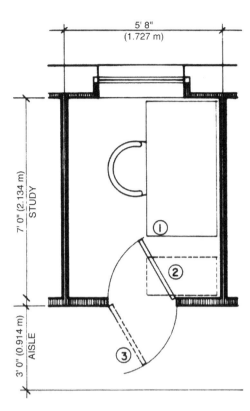

FIGURE 13.3   Poorly placed door. This door interferes seriously with the use of the room. The door swing (1) is obstructed by furniture, (2) displaces furniture, and (3) obstructs the aisle. If the door had been placed farther to the left and hinged on the left, it could swing inward without difficulty. This illustration is of a fairly minimal study; where the study is slightly wider, shelving may be possible on the wall to the left; in this case the hinged side of the door would ideally be about 13 in. (330 mm) from the left wall. See also fig. 4.6 for door swing problems.

door? (See figs. 13.4 and 13.5.) Most wheelchairs can fit through a 27-in. (0.686-m) space though the requirement as stipulated by the ADA is a minimum of 32 in. (0.813 m) from the face of the door standing open to the opposite frame, resulting in a door larger than 32 in. (See fig. 13.6.) Doors of 36 in. (0.914 m) meet this requirement, are standard, and are commonly used in the United States. Aside from the width requirement for wheelchairs, the way the door swings and the pressure required to open the door may be critical. For fire doors, the ADA states that the minimum allowable opening force is required; for all other interior sliding and swing doors a

maximum force of 5 lbf (22.2 N) is stipulated, though this limitation does not apply to the force required to retract latch bolts or other devices that may hold the door closed. The ability to enter the building by pushing the door will help those with an armload of books. Devices to assist door opening and automatic openers should be considered. Yet, consider the consequences of rain, ice, and snow before using a floor-located automatic pressure opener outside the front door.

2. Will the door stand open during part of its use? If this is expected, it should be able to swing out of the way of traffic and avoid blocking regular access to files, shelves, or other equipment. In an office or a faculty study, it is often best to locate the door at least 12 in. (305 mm) from an adjacent and perpendicular wall so that shelving can be installed on the perpendicular wall even though the door will have to be closed to access the shelving. Again, see fig. 13.3.

3. Are some doors needed for future flexibility? One technique for providing this kind of flexibility is to construct within the wall a door frame that can rather easily be activated at a future date. If it is a metal frame, consider the hinge and latch locations for future need.

4. Will provision of a door affect air circulation? In small, enclosed carrels it may be appropriate to install a louver or to undercut the door an inch or two (25 to 50 mm). (Remember the allowance for carpet.) However, this space or a louver will remove any acoustical quality that may be desired of the door.

5. Will the door require other special features, such as a door closer, a kick plate, panic hardware, acoustic insulation or weather stripping, an alarm, or special locking devices? Although this level of detail is not critical at this stage, it is well to be thinking of it, especially in any case that may require conduit for an alarm or electrically actuated lock.

6. Is each door needed and correctly placed? Most important in design development is to think through and test the need for doors and the routes and flow of expected traffic. It is often tempting to have more than one door to a supervisor's office; some offices have been designed with three doors. Such an arrangement makes the office space very limited. Multiple doors into an office should be avoided if at all possible.

Place each door with traffic patterns definitely in mind. Figure 13.7 shows how the door at the main entrance of the Widener bookstack, until a

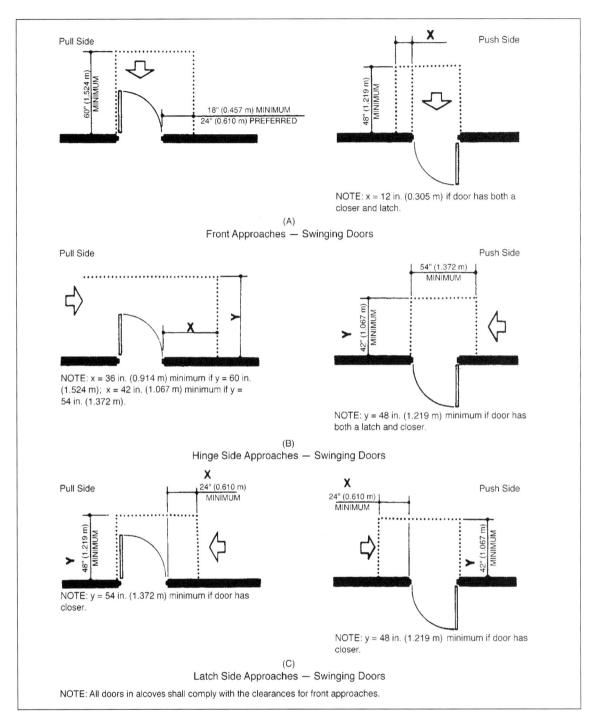

FIGURE 13.4 Minimum maneuvering clearances at doors for a wheelchair. Note that for most doors, both sides of the door must be considered in this context, including conditions within offices and studies that are ADA accessible. A "closer" is a device that automatically closes the door. As illustrated, the extra space to the side of a number of doors allows a person in a wheelchair to more nearly approach the latching device straight on, and, in the case of a door swinging toward the wheelchair, gives space for the wheelchair to clear the door swing. (Department of Justice, "Nondiscrimination on the Basis of Disability by Public Accommodations and Commercial Facilities, Final Rule," *Federal Register* 56, no. 144 [July 26, 1991]: 35644.)

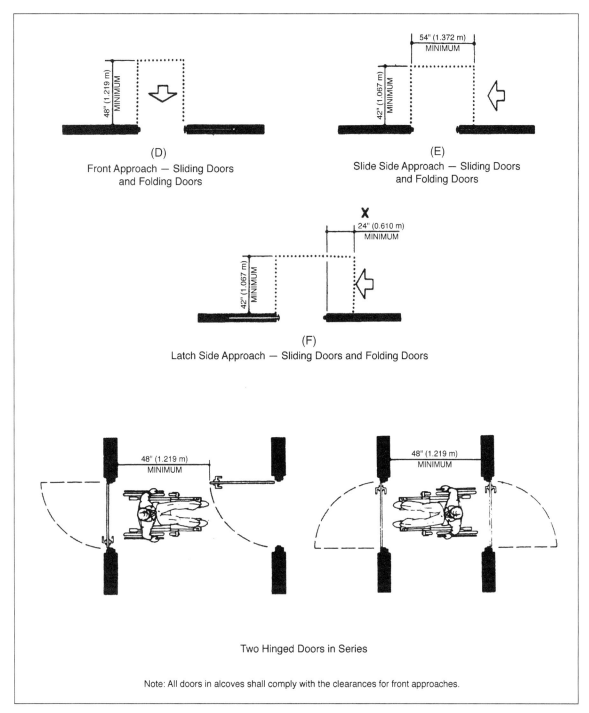

(D)
Front Approach — Sliding Doors
and Folding Doors

(E)
Slide Side Approach — Sliding Doors
and Folding Doors

(F)
Latch Side Approach — Sliding Doors and Folding Doors

Two Hinged Doors in Series

Note: All doors in alcoves shall comply with the clearances for front approaches.

FIGURE 13.5   Minimum maneuvering clearances for sliding doors and doors in series. (Department of Justice, "Nondiscrimination on the Basis of Disability by Public Accommodations and Commercial Facilities, Final Rule," *Federal Register* 56, no. 144 [July 26, 1991]: 35645.)

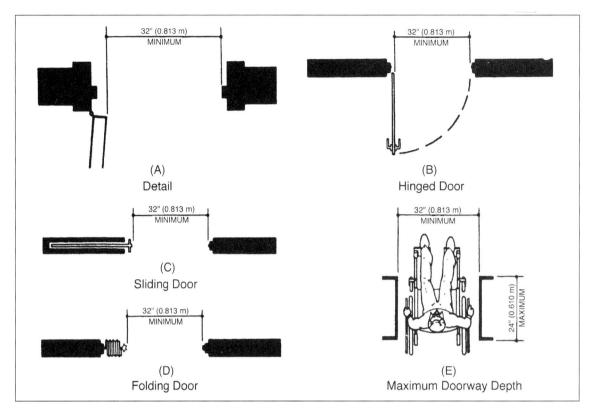

FIGURE 13.6   Minimum doorway width and depth. Note that the minimum width and depth indicated may be acceptable to some authorities for column clearance in the stacks (which can help make a layout work in some cases). (Department of Justice, "Nondiscrimination on the Basis of Disability by Public Accommodations and Commercial Facilities, Final Rule," *Federal Register* 56, no. 144 [July 26, 1991]: 35643.)

change was made, led everyone directly past the stack reading areas when it would have been possible to have the entrance adjacent to the main aisle, 30 ft (9.144 m) away from the carrels.

Plumbing. A fixed element frequently regarded as part of the mechanical system, plumbing will be treated here as it relates to the location of the rest rooms, which in turn relate to the core elements.

The problems of plumbing are many and specialized. To solve the mechanical ones, it is usual to employ a sanitary or mechanical engineer to be responsible for the layout, the operations, and the code requirements of the installation. However, a number of questions ought to come to the attention of the planning team. They are concerned mainly with the problems of (1) location, (2) noise, and (3) maintenance.

1. *Location.* Toilet and lavatory facilities should be located in the library so that they are adjacent and convenient to the main traffic arteries and also so that both the visual and audible distur-

bances attendant upon their use will be isolated from the reading and other public areas. Plumbing code regulations have not yet been standardized and vary considerably from place to place, but all of them require each fixture to be equipped with a "soil" and a "vent," the first a pipe that leads down to the basement and the sewer, the second a pipe that leads up to the roof and the atmosphere. Fixtures are arranged in batteries, either horizontally or vertically among floors, and their respective soils and vents are thereby combined. Naturally the more this combined piping principle is applied, the less expensive is the installation. Thus, grouping toilets and other plumbing facilities adjacent to one another in plan and above one another in section is economical and desirable.

Sometimes the bottom floors of a library are below the level of the sewer to which the plumbing fixtures are to connect. In this case, fixtures on these levels should be reduced to a minimum, as they will have to be drained through

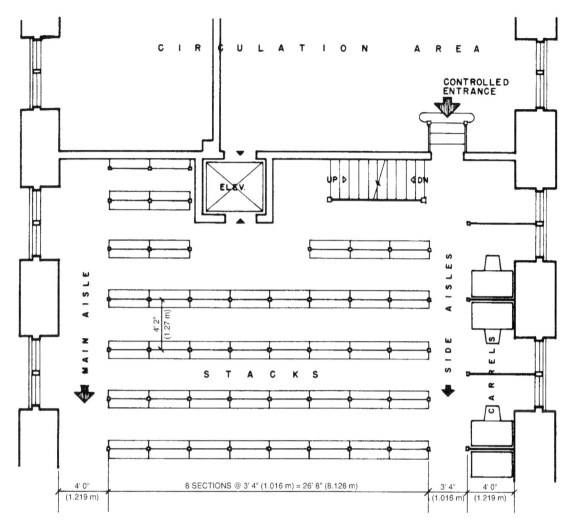

FIGURE 13.7 Main entrance to the Widener Library stack area (before renovations). The entrance leads directly to a secondary aisle that passes carrels. If the entrance had been placed at the upper left of the drawing, it would have saved 60 ft (18.188 m) of walking for most users and made the carrel area quieter and less restless. In 1963, it was in fact moved to the midpoint (between elevator and stairs), thereby retaining an office on the left and accommodating circulation staff functions to the right.

an ejector, which will pump their sewage up to the sewer above. A large installation of this sort is expensive to install, occupies space, and must be maintained. Its use should be avoided wherever practical.

The piping connections, the toilet stalls, the fixtures, and the steel or marble and tile finishes generally used in connection with fixtures all combine to make these elements almost as permanent as stair and elevator wells. They are expensive to change and difficult, though not impossible, to move. For these reasons, toilets are often grouped with the stairs and elevators and vent shafts in a core cluster so they interfere

as little as possible with the flexibility of the spaces for readers and books, which form the bulk of the library.

The number of toilet fixtures required in any library varies with the number of reader accommodations provided. Often this number is regulated by law. Where no code requirement controls, the quantity may be influenced by the proximity or remoteness of the dormitory, student union, or other similar facilities open also on evenings and weekends. The number of seats provided in the library exceeds, except under unusual circumstances, the number of readers present at any time. For this reason it is acceptable and usual library practice to provide at least one plumbing fixture for each 35 seating accommodations, in anticipation that this fixture normally can be expected to serve 25 readers. In tabulating fixtures in proportion to reader seats, urinals and water closets but not lavatories are counted. The total number of fixtures required should then be distributed in one or more toilet rooms for each sex so that they are as convenient as practical to the readers. Extended-hour or 24-hour reading rooms need to have access to toilet facilities. Sometimes separate facilities are provided for both staff and building help.

The arrangement of fixtures within the toilet room is important, for both appearance and privacy. An open space immediately inside the entrance to the lavatory area makes a better impression, and the use of screens beside the urinals, as well as stalls around the water closets, contributes to privacy. It is always desirable to enter large toilet rooms through vestibules, or to arrange the entry such that the sight line from the access point to the toilet room is blocked. The rooms themselves should allow space for anticipated traffic.

In all toilet rooms in a library, it is wise to install shelves for holding books and other papers while the facility is used. This is not only a convenience for readers but also a protection for the library materials. Each toilet stall should have a shelf large enough to hold at least an octavo book or a binder and, if a fold-down type, able to stay down if holding only a few papers. Similarly, in the vicinity of the lavatories, a shelf should be provided. There are many details about toilets, lavatories, urinals, and drinking fountains that concern persons with impaired eyesight or crippled hands, and those confined to wheelchairs. Consult published accessibility standards; for examples, see the Bibliography, Section F.4.bb.

Other plumbing fixtures are required, such as janitor's and work sinks, washbasins in work areas, kitchenettes, and drinking fountains. All of these, except the last, should be inaccessible to the public. Drinking fountains present a hazard if they are located in the vicinity of bookshelves. These other plumbing fixtures should also be grouped with the toilets if the maximum economy of installation is to be realized.

2. *Noise.* The problem most frequently neglected in connection with plumbing fixtures is the noise resulting from their use. This consideration is important in a modern library if the toilet facility is adjacent to reader areas. Unfortunately, the most efficient and easily maintained fixtures seem to be the noisiest. When this is coupled with the fact that the hard, washable finishes used in toilet rooms are anything but sound absorbing, the noise of a flushed water closet can easily penetrate beyond the walls of the toilet, unless special precautions are taken.

Use an acoustic ceiling. Be sure that the sanitary engineer has selected the quietest fixtures consistent with ease of maintenance and efficiency of operation. This statement applies to water closets and also to urinals and lavatories.

Although excellent ventilation is very important, do not accede to a ventilation air supply through the doorways to the facility. This is an economical solution, but it leaves openings through which the sounds can escape into adjacent areas. It is better to soundproof the doors by weatherstripping and to provide a self-contained ventilation system. In any case, all openings through the toilet-room walls should be protected with sound-absorbing boxes, and the walls themselves should be built to provide a reasonable amount of sound isolation.

3. *Maintenance.* The best-quality plumbing fixtures and accessories are the most economical in the end, because the cost of their maintenance will be considerably reduced. In any public facility the abuse given to both fixtures and accessories is considerable and must be offset by a first-class installation of the best and strongest available.

Toilet and lavatory fixtures that are mounted off the floor will make cleaning easier. Modern water closets are made for wall mounting, as are lavatories and urinals. When fixtures are wall-mounted, the fastenings must be strong enough to resist the pressures imposed by a person's leaning his or her entire weight on the front edge. This caution is particularly true of lavatories. Usually they are installed with large metal brackets embedded in the wall and floor. These brackets, called chair carriers, receive and resist pressures imposed on the fixtures. Though ceiling- and wall-mounted stall division panels would facilitate floor cleaning and can still be useful, the base (floor) support of panels is necessary for the same concern as with fixtures. And stall panels should be of marble or a metal laminate to withstand abuse.

Often a floor drain is installed in the toilet room in order to help the cleaning-up or hosing-out process. It is recommended. If one is installed, mopping or hosing must be done regularly; otherwise the trap, or the water seal that prevents the escape of sewer gases through the fixture, will dry out.

The floors and walls of a toilet room should be of hard solid materials easily cleaned and waterproof. Marble, tile, and terrazzo are usually used. Setting these materials on the floor generally requires a "bed," and the structural floor must be recessed in order to accommodate it and a waterproof membrane; otherwise the floor of the toilet room would be higher than the surrounding areas. This recessing adds to the cost of construction, as it interferes with the rapidity of execution desired during the rough construction period. Today, fortunately, adhesives are made that successfully fasten tile to a concrete floor without the use of a bed, but there may be some risk of leakage in the event of a spill.

The type of plumbing that has been discussed above is termed "sanitary." The soil piping from the fixtures leads to a sanitary sewer and a disposal plant. Frequently, plumbing must be installed also to drain off the "storm" water both from the roofs and the grounds around the building. Because the introduction of storm water into the sanitary sewer is likely to overtax the disposal facilities and piping, the storm-water piping is generally connected to a storm sewer with independent and less elaborate methods of dispersal. Interior cold-water pipes and roof or storm-water conductors should be insulated where they run horizontally through the building. Otherwise the cold water in the pipes will cause condensation, which is often mistaken for a leak.

Finally, remember that eventually nearly any pipe will leak. Leaking will require access for repair or replacement, but, more important, it may place the books at risk. In many ways the worst kind of water damage in a library results from a slow leak that goes undetected for an extended period. By the time it is discovered, the damage results in the total loss of the affected materials. The plumbing can often be routed to avoid crossing bookstacks, which, of course, will reduce the risk of water damage.

13.2.4 Structural Systems

The basic structural system of any building is made up of a combination of materials. Wood framing, for example, can be lightweight, as is common in residential construction, or heavy as might be found in a warehouse. Steel can be exposed or encased, it can take the form of a truss or a beam, and it can be welded, bolted, or riveted. Concrete can be precast, cast in place, reinforced, prestressed, and so on. To the librarian all these options may create considerable confusion about his or her role in selecting a structural system. There are two roles, both of which should be performed. The first is to ask questions to assure oneself about soundness, cost, quality, and appearance. The second is to learn enough to understand the structural engineering and the required space and shapes of the structure as they affect the architectural plan.

Foundations. If a good, solid foundation base is not available, should the building be floated on a concrete slab, or should it rest on caissons or piles? Should the foundation go down to solid rock, or is there sand, clay, or gravel that will provide a satisfactory base without going so deep? How deep below the surface will it be safe and economical to go for the lowest floor level of the building? Have arrangements been made for trial borings or test pits? One or the other is almost always desirable well before this stage is reached. The cost will generally be a separately budgeted item for which the institution is responsible. The answers to these questions are the engineer's province. The structural engineer can properly suggest alternatives and their financial and other implications. Some institutions retain a soil-mechanics consultant to work with the structural engineer.

The depth of the lowest level will, of course, be influenced by the soil and the slope of the ground and by the institution's desire or willingness to have one or more basements without any windows or with windows on only one, two, or three sides. A properly insulated basement with or without windows may often provide floor area that is cheaper to construct, maintain, and operate than space above ground because walls can be less expensive, and heating and cooling may be simplified. However, underground space may not be very attractive to potential donors. Toronto's Robarts Library, built in 1973, is an instance of building height being dictated in part by the soil. Bedrock was down 70 ft (21.336 m), below sand filled with water to within 20 ft (6.096 m) of the surface. The building sits on heavily reinforced concrete 7 ft (2.134 m) thick, and the lowest level is only 12 in. (305 mm) above high-water level.

Framing. Should the building framing be of wood, steel, steel protected by concrete, reinforced concrete, or precast or prestressed concrete? Should the floors be flat concrete slabs or of beam construction? Should the walls be of the bearing type? Wood is often the cheapest framing material, but because it may be a fire hazard, it is seldom used except in a very small library. Steel, unless covered with concrete, succumbs readily to fire. Reinforced concrete brings with it fire resistance. Steel covered with concrete may be more or less expensive than reinforced concrete at any particular time and it is equally fire resistant. It may make smaller columns possible and may be therefore not only desirable but necessary if columns are to be kept to no more than the width of the stack ranges so as not to interfere with stack aisles. Deflection must be taken into consideration where compact shelving is contemplated. If precast concrete is used, care must be taken to make sure that joints are tight. Exterior walls must not leak around the windows or anywhere else. They should be well insulated. They have much to do with obtaining a satisfactory aesthetic effect, and care in the selection of brick or stone or other wall materials is required.

It may be well to obtain cost estimates for several different types of framing. Even if there is an expert on the planning team, decisions on these matters should certainly be left to the architect and structural engineers. If bearing walls are used, remember that they may limit flexibility for future stack and furniture layouts and for openings required later on when an extension is added to the building.

Ceilings and roofs. Whether the roof is flat or sloping or gabled may be of importance to the institution if it is trying to provide architectural unity on its campus. Whether it is covered with slate or some other roofing material should certainly be considered from the point of view of maintenance, fire protection, and aesthetics. Remember that if a flat roof is recommended for a low building, it cannot hide a microwave dish and provide a visually obscured place for the elevator penthouse and for ventilation apparatus that might cost less and be more efficient if it were placed there. There have been libraries constructed in which elevators do not reach the two upper stack levels to prevent a penthouse showing on the roof; such a solution should not be allowed. One can easily understand the inconvenience that results. A flat roof, particularly if the building is low and large, may present aesthetic problems.

Climatic conditions must be considered in connection with roof design. If skylights are used, see that special precautions are taken against leaking. Plastic domes may be preferred, as they are generally easier to keep tight. Valleys resulting from gables or irregular construction can be a special hazard, as are gutters in an area with heavy snow and frequent freezing and melting. Roof insulation may be important to prevent overheating of the top floor and thereby adding to the ventilation problem.

Desirable ceiling qualities resemble those for roofs in most ways. Heat and cold and noise must not penetrate unduly from floor to floor. Well-designed ceilings should have satisfactory acoustic properties. Areas where quiet is a functional requirement should be specified in the program, but the design development phase is a good time to review this kind of requirement. Where acoustic isolation is required, the walls should fully enclose the space even above a suspended acoustic ceiling. This is too frequently overlooked, and sound then carries between offices or other rooms where people want privacy.

The decision whether or not ceilings should be furred and hung affects the decor and will determine whether there is hidden space for horizontal mechanical air distribution below the floor construction. (Ducts, cable trays, and pipes can be and often are exposed, as was attractively done in the library of Washington University in St. Louis.) Today most libraries are lighted from ceiling fixtures, either flush with the ceiling or hung from it. Consideration should be given to the possible difficulties in changing lighting sources—bulbs and tubes—when they are in or near the ceilings. Radiant heating is sometimes successfully placed in the ceiling.

The planning team should study the architect's proposals for walls, ceilings, and roofs. The architect should initiate them, but should be informed of the institution's previous experience and its wishes.

It is suggested that the library should have three concerns:

1. The structural system should be fire resistant. This pretty much rules out light timber and exposed steel construction, although with proper fire protection, these systems might be considered in certain circumstances. Indeed, there could easily be a requirement to renovate an existing structure for library use that is not of fire-resistant construction. For example, the structure of a tiered stack is not fire resistant; in the event of an intense

fire, the possibility of collapse is real. Where there may be a choice of systems that might offer improved fire protection, the advice of the architect or a fire protection consultant would be of particular benefit.

2. The structural system should be flexible. On this subject the librarian should have a special interest in the module, the size of columns, the floor loading capacity, and the ability to alter internal arrangements, including nonstructural partitions and utilities, especially power and signal, as the need may require. In this regard, load-bearing walls and tiered stacks may be a problem as would a floor system that would not permit the future drilling of a hole for conduit or plumbing. Beyond this, most structural systems can be designed for reasonable flexibility.

3. Cost is the final area of concern. The construction cost estimator is the best source of information for making a decision on cost. At any given time, in different regions or countries, the cost advantage of one system over another can change, but at some point in the design process, this decision must be made. The time to decide is during the design development phase in order to avoid significant duplication of design effort.

The best advice is to listen to your consultants, ask questions, and contribute to the decision as may be appropriate from the point of view of the function of the library.

Buildings are still known to collapse because of faulty construction, faulty engineering techniques, faulty materials, or sometimes earthquakes, unprecedented floods, and hurricanes. In most areas building codes are in force to minimize such hazards. They should, of course, be observed. It should also be noted that building codes may be out of date and require what are obviously unnecessary precautions and expense. This problem may be outside the province of the librarian, but certainly the administration of the institution should be in a position to speak up and try to obtain suitable changes.

13.2.5 Hazards of Fire, Water, Insects, Vandalism, and Injury

This section will deal with hazards of various kinds. Proper attention to them and to their causes during the planning process can reduce their occurrence and may avoid them altogether. They may be grouped as follows: (1) fire, (2) water, (3) acts of nature, (4) insects and mold, (5) theft, vandalism, and mutilation, and (6) injury to physically limited persons.

Consideration of the design requirements in response to fire and other hazards will be part of each of the design phases, and Chapter 5 contains some discussion about treating these risks in the program. Much of the detailing of systems and devices will occur during the working drawing or construction documents phase of the design. However, the preparation of the budget estimate at the completion of the design development phase must include a sufficient budget increment to ensure that the response to fire and other hazards can be adequate. Therefore, preliminary design consideration of hazards will show up in many cases as part of the outline specifications rather than on the drawings.

A general cautionary point can be made: Consider every conceivable threat to the library. Internal design factors that may endanger the collections or personnel can come from steam pipes, electrical transformers, pressured water mains, toilet drains, and the like. External design conditions that are potentially dangerous can derive from surface water drains, exterior doors, large trees near windows, and other circumstances. A good example of precautionary action: Librarians at the University of Chicago required that several high-pressure steam lines be routed all the way around the Regenstein bookstacks in a service corridor, rather than, at less cost, straight across the ceiling of the stack; and electrical transformers for the building were placed in a vault, below grade, structurally separated from the building, but directly accessible from the shipping dock and truck driveway.

The above six hazards overlap to some extent. Water damage, for instance, may and frequently does result indirectly from fire and from external storm conditions. Earthquakes, which here come under the heading "acts of nature," can bring destructive fires and floods in their train. Insect infestation and mold may stem from humid conditions that, in turn, are the result of dampness.

Fire hazards. Guarding against fire is covered in much greater detail in a volume entitled *Managing the Library Fire Risk,* by John Morris, a volume that should be examined with care by one or more members of any library building planning team.[4] Fire hazards in a library stem in almost all cases from one of four sources:

1. The heating plant, where there may be defective or overheated chimneys or equipment, hot ashes and coals, or escaping gas.
2. Wiring used for lighting, heating, electrical devices, and appliances.

3. Careless housekeeping and smoking habits and use of matches, the storage of combustibles near heaters, and spontaneous combustion.

4. What might be called outside intervention, such as lightning, earthquakes, arson or fire originating elsewhere, or fires resulting from the use of welding and cutting torches by maintenance and other workers.

Each of these sources has been responsible for a considerable number of library fires, and the danger is likely to continue. The third and fourth sources might be said to fall outside the scope of this volume, except as good construction can prevent the spread of fire, if careless housekeeping or smoking habits have started it, and lessen the risks from lightning or earthquakes by providing a structure and equipment that will minimize the hazards.

Because approximately one-fourth of library fires have their source in defects in the heating plant, it is evident that all parts of the heating installation should be designed and installed so as to prevent the possibility of fire. The same holds true for the electrical services. The engineers designing them must pay proper attention to the related building codes, which have been prepared to reduce risks and hazards of all kinds. The workers who install the heating plants should, of course, be competent also, and their work should be checked by experienced and knowledgeable inspectors. In the United States, the national codes of both the Electrical and the Heating, Ventilating, and Air Conditioning Societies should be used as a minimum standard.

But with the best of care, even if the construction itself is satisfactory, accidents happen, although the better the quality of construction, the less chance there will be of fire starting. There are five major types of construction. They are listed below in order of cost, from the least expensive to the most expensive. The fire risks decrease as the more expensive types are used.

1. Wood-frame construction, in which the structural members are wood.

2. Ordinary construction, in which the supporting walls are masonry, the floors are wooden joists, the interior finish too often conceals space in which fire can spread, and there is little protection for the stair shafts. This was a common type of construction in older libraries.

It can be used, however, with protection for the stair shafts by isolating them with masonry walls and self-closing fire doors. The wooden floor and roof joists can be, and often are, protected with fireproof plaster or gypsum board, and the concealed spaces can be fire-stopped. (*Fire-stopped* means that enclosed spaces are broken up, or made into small compartments, so that fire cannot easily spread inside the wall or under the floor.) If these three steps are taken, the risks are greatly diminished. If they are not, this construction is little better than the wood-frame type.

Consequently, construction of this kind is of three grades: (a) where no attempt to protect from fire is made; (b) partially fire protected with fireproof floors but with a roof with wooden rafters; and (c) fire protected.

3. Noncombustible construction of steel or steel and masonry with exposed structural members. Exposed structural members do not necessarily mean exposed to view, but exposed to fire—that is, not protected from contact with a fire if it should start.

4. Mill construction, which is sometimes called "slow-burning," or heavy timber construction, with thick brick or masonry walls, floors of 3-in. or 4-in. (76-mm or 102-mm) planks, or 8-in. to 12-in. (203-mm to 305-mm) posts and girders of wood, and no concealed places behind interior finish. This construction is desirable for many buildings and is used especially in factories and warehouses.

To the layperson, the exposed steel and masonry construction in type 3 might seem safer and more fire resistant than the wooden mill type. But remember that steel exposed to fire will quickly buckle and collapse. Mill construction uses structural members of wood at least 3 in. (76 mm) in thickness. When exposed to fire, such members will, of course, burn, but, because of size, they will burn so slowly that they will remain intact through a serious blaze, usually until the fire can be controlled.

5. Fire-resistive construction, more commonly called fireproof construction. It is usually of reinforced concrete or steel and masonry with steel structural members encased in concrete or other fire-resistant material. This type is strongly recommended for academic and research libraries whenever possible.

The removal or lessening of hazards will not stop fires altogether. The question of fire detection, alarm, and extinguishing must be considered.

Insurance companies and code authorities usually insist that the solution of the problem in libraries is the installation of a sprinkler system. An examination of the Morris volume referred to above shows that there are various types of sprinklers available that should be considered.

Historically, there has been a firmly held belief among librarians (including Metcalf in the first edition of this volume) that the risk of water damage exceeds the risk of fire in a properly constructed and maintained facility. However, if one considers that only the sprinkler heads affected by the fire are activated and that modern techniques of restoring water-damaged materials can be quite effective, then it can be argued that the risk of fire in a building without a sprinkler system is greater than the risk of loss from water. The Morris volume is quite enlightening in this regard.

Fire risk with or without sprinklers can be reduced if the eight following conditions prevail:

1. A building of fire-resistive or fireproof construction in a location with good public fire protection.
2. Division of the building into fire areas by the use of fire walls and fire doors. These areas may be as large as 15,000 ft² (1,400 m²) and in some cases even more. Fire codes may specify the size allowed, in order to limit the spread of fire to a predetermined area. The smaller the area, the smaller the spread of fire. This problem may have to be taken up with the fire authorities or the insurance companies. Many large areas without fire walls have been built and approved in recent years.
3. Elimination of vertical draft conditions and prevention of propagation of fire upward by means of horizontal barriers, such as fire-resistive continuous floors, enclosure of stairways and elevator shafts, and "fire-stopping" vertical mechanical shafts.
4. A minimum use of easily combustible materials in interior finish and furnishings, through which fire spreads rapidly and poisonous gases may be generated.
5. The installation of a good detection and alarm system, regularly inspected and maintained in good working order.
6. Careful supervision of library operations, including good housekeeping practices and also control of smoking.
7. An effective system of periodic inspection of the entire premises for unsafe fire conditions, such as defective electrical wiring,

or deficiencies in the air-conditioning or heating systems.
8. Installation of protective devices, such as automatic closing of fire doors, or the use of self-closing fire doors, cutoff of air-circulation ducts, and first-aid and fire-fighting equipment kept in good working order.

A poorly designed configuration of automatic fire doors may lead to disaster by leaving personnel on the wrong side. The self-closing doors may not be quite so satisfactory in preventing the spread of fire, but they can be opened from either side and might be said to be more considerate of human life if not of property. Some experts in the field suggest that fire walls and fire doors are old-fashioned and out of date, going back to 1890 building codes and insurance company standards, adopted when construction methods resulted in much greater hazards than are involved in good contemporary buildings. But always remember that, unless modern construction is used, special protection, such as a sprinkler system, should be installed, and that, even with modern construction, areas containing materials or use conducive to the incidence of fire should be isolated and sprinklers should be used.

Although the authors currently recommend the use of sprinklers in most libraries, it should be added that the following circumstances require sprinkler protection:

1. Library buildings of wood-frame construction or located close to or beside such a building.
2. Libraries in areas not protected by an organized fire department or more than five miles (about 8k) from the nearest fire department station. In the few cases that fall in this category, the use of walls to prevent the spread of flames and smoke damage might be considered in addition to sprinklers.
3. Library buildings with highly combustible interior finishes and equipment. These hazards should not be permitted, and if finishes or equipment of this kind have been installed, they should be replaced.
4. Libraries located in basements or other building areas to which access for effective fire fighting is difficult.
5. Library buildings of combustible construction in areas subject to high incidence of arson.

6. Those rooms or areas in libraries presenting greater than ordinary hazards, such as storage and work areas, carpenter shops, paint shops, printing and binding shops, garages, and so forth. Egress routes, though they may not present additional risk of fire, will provide greater safety for the building occupants if they are sprinklered. This is particularly true in buildings with transoms over the doors or with panels of glass along corridor walls.

It is well to consider the advantages of sprinkler systems. These include proved capability on a 24-hour basis to detect, control, and, in many cases, extinguish fires before they have caused extensive damage. In addition, sprinkler systems may discharge less water in extinguishing a fire than might otherwise be used. Because the particular sprinkler heads that open are immediately above the fire, they discharge water only into the actual combustion zone. The 15 to 20 gallons (57 to 76 liters) of water per minute normally discharged from a single sprinkler head can often do a far more effective extinguishing job than 250 gallons (946 liters) per minute discharged in a hit-and-miss manner from fire hoses.

Disadvantages include the chance of a broken pipe with water under pressure, a head accidentally or maliciously hit to weaken the keeper or knock off the plug, a "cold flow" in which part of the fusible keeper actually creeps (generally taking 18 years), a defective head that shows up without warning, or the installation of a head rated at too low a temperature for the particular location under extreme conditions. A glass bulb sprinkler head can be specified to avoid all possibility of "cold flow."

Sprinkler systems are not generally required in space occupied by offices, even though there may be furniture of wood, combustible floor coverings, and wooden wall paneling, as well as much paper in the open or stored in steel or wooden files. The fire hazard in ordinary offices is considered to be low. It would appear that sprinklers should not be required in those areas of libraries with comparable fire risks. However, if the building is to be fully protected, and if offices may be converted to other purposes, these areas must have sprinklers as well.

If the sprinkler system is not to be used, other types of fire detection and arrangements for fire extinguishing should be considered. These are described in detail in Chapter 5, as well as the Morris book, and only methods of fire extinguishing with portable equipment will be discussed here. To be useful, fire extinguishers should meet four fundamental requirements:

1. They must be located properly; at least one not more than 100 ft (30.480 m) from most if not all staffed positions; one for every 2,500 ft^2 (232.25 m^2) in most library areas, according to the hazards in that particular area; and at least one on each floor and one at the approach to each exit.
2. They must be in good mechanical condition, which means inspection at least annually by a competent person.
3. All staff members should be acquainted with their location and the way to use them.
4. Extinguishers must be appropriate for library use and not too large for use by staff members. ABC-type extinguishers are recommended, as they can be used on any kind of fire.

The problem of fire extinguishers is complicated by the fact that there are different classes of fire—wood and paper, inflammable liquids, and those with the hazard of electrical shock. The various types of extinguishers include soda acid, water under high pressure, dry chemicals, FE-36 (a Halon substitute specifically for handheld extinguishers), and carbon dioxide. The soda-acid type is very effective with wood and paper fires, but it may damage the books. High-pressure water is easily controlled and generally preferred to soda acid. Carbon dioxide is useful for small fires and often recommended, but it is extremely dangerous to people if used in large quantities; it is recommended especially for compartmentalized rare book collections as being less damaging to books. Water under pressure under complete control to avoid unnecessary water damage should be considered. New types of dry chemicals, including FE-36, may prove satisfactory, but Halon is illegal in most countries and should never be used. (See Section 5.3.6 for extended comments on Halon.) Always remember that re-ignition, after a fire is apparently suppressed, is a serious danger.

Special problems and their possible solution should be considered. Danger may come from interior finishes and from open spaces with vertical drafts. Hazardous areas should be segregated and protected with sprinklers or possibly with fire walls. These may include garage areas for library vehicles; storage for gasoline-powered lawn mowers and for flammable fuels, lubricants, and paints; shipping and receiving areas; miscellaneous storage areas for recent gifts; binderies; carpenter, electrical, and print shops; heating plant; and a kitchen or kitchenette. The risk of fire in connection with burning grease in a kitchenette should be kept in mind, and a different type of extinguisher considered (an ABC or CO_2 or FE-36, not water).

There is danger that air-circulating ducts can permit the spread of fire as well as smoke. Dampers with fusible links should be required at points at which the ducts pass through fire walls and floors. These ducts should have shutoff valves that will close automatically when smoke appears, or, if they must be closed manually, the valves should be readily accessible. Where the fire damping system is automatic, the function of the dampers should not be compromised by the fire itself. The dampers must be accessible for inspection and resetting, a detail too often overlooked. However, dampers are not a safe substitute for fan cutoff devices because they do not operate rapidly enough. Fan motors should be connected to a fire-detection system. The shutdown action is then immediate and automatic. The use of a smoke-detection device in the air-circulation system will help. Thermostats are sometimes installed in the circulating ducts to shut off the motors, but this is not recommended because damage can occur before the ducts are hot enough to activate the thermostats.

Whether or not automatic protection is provided, there should always be a conveniently located station from which the circulating system may be manually shut down by the librarian or members of the staff. Many libraries lack such manual trip stations. Others have all such controls located in the building utility areas where they are readily accessible only to the maintenance personnel. Smoke spreading throughout a building makes evacuation of personnel more difficult. Smoke also makes it difficult to determine the exact location of the fire itself. Air-circulating systems should therefore be capable of being shut down quickly in an emergency.

Electrical services should have ample capacity for the addition of new circuits and other safety factors. When fluorescent lighting is used, each ballast should be individually fused. Protection against circuit overloading should be provided by circuit breakers as opposed to simple fuses. Special emergency circuits supplied directly from the electrical service entrance points should be used for fire detection, alarm purposes, exit lights, and emergency lighting. If it appears, as is very often the case, that additional lighting is needed for exits, emergency power arrangements supplied by batteries or a standby generator might be considered.

Although not strictly a hazard issue, telecommunications circuits also need attention. They need to have "clean" service, and Ethernet will often and increasingly be the preferred service. This field continues to change rapidly, with trends toward faster transmissions, broader bandwidth, greater standardization, and service reaching far more outlets on campus. It is necessary to use local talent or consultants to advise the electrical engineers on requirements of cabling, modems, signal distribution panels, and so on for a particular institution. In some institutions, a local team manages some or all of this distribution because of peculiarities on campus and the need to coordinate service interruptions with academic schedules.

Although one mezzanine stack tier produces no special hazards, a series of one above another, often used in the nineteenth century, does. In spite of fire safety precautions, too many new libraries are being constructed with open stairways running between more than two floors, often for purely aesthetic rather than functional reasons. From the standpoint of safety, proper enclosures provide safer methods of exit and also prevent the open spaces from serving as flues for fire, smoke, and toxic gases.

A building planned with few or no windows means that emergency access in case of fire may be a matter of special significance. If the design of a new building calls for large open areas without fire walls, the overall fire safety measures taken must compensate for the increase in the single fire risk thus presented. Noncombustible acoustical materials should always be used.

Fire-risk consultants are sometimes recommended, but the institution must be careful not to choose one who is primarily a sales representative for some special piece of equipment. The right person will be hard to find. To some candidates, a remote possibility becomes an immediate hazard, and neither the laws of probability nor the value, or lack of it, of the material protected has any place in their analysis. Some large institutions that are self-insured and thus particularly anxious to avoid losses employ fire-prevention experts who may well give sounder advice than those with a different motivation.

Water hazards. Many librarians are much more worried, and properly so, about damage from water than from fire. Besides risks from sprinklers, other obvious and common sources are floods from heavy rains or melting snow, water from broken pipes, clogged drains, inadequate waterproofing, and leaky roofs. If there are drains under or in the basement floor, they should be designed with backwater valves that automatically cut off floods when the water level rises to a point where it could back up into the building.

Broken or defective water, steam, and drain pipes present special problems in libraries because of the possibility of water damage to books. In planning a new library, the architect should locate the joints of all water pipes so that in case of failure they can be reached easily and also so that books will not be exposed to damage. Several rare book libraries have a protective apron under all water pipes, which will collect water from a leak, carry it to a safe place, and set off an alarm. The Newberry Library stack addition is even safer in that it has no water pipes within the stack spaces.

Rooftop mechanical rooms should have a waterproof floor with drains and provision for future vertical penetration through protected shafts, with waterproof curbs.

In addition to attention given to the location of pipes and waterproofing, water alarms can be considered. A sump pump should have a high-water alarm that is remotely annunciated to ensure a proper response. Simple detectors designed to sound an alarm if there is water on the floor can be specified as well. Furthermore, a humidity alarm, which activates a shutoff valve for the steam source in the building, can reduce the risk of a steam leak.

Acts of nature. Acts of nature include primarily lightning, earthquakes, and wind. Modern library buildings have rarely been struck by lightning, and unless the building construction creates a higher than average susceptibility, this should not present a problem today.

Earthquakes are another matter. Local building codes in regions where earthquakes are prevalent have introduced design and construction requirements that greatly reduce the probability of damage from earthquakes. If your library is in an earthquake zone, be sure that proper precautions for extra strength are used, following the provi-

sions in the appropriate building codes. These sometimes present a functional problem, as they frequently result in solid structural walls in places where a main traffic artery would be placed under normal conditions, and special care in planning circulation patterns must be taken to avoid complications, which were discussed earlier. The design and attachment of shelving and major furniture, equipment, or art elements must also have special attention.

Wind damage should not be a problem with a properly designed structure, though if the panes of glass are too large and the wind is very strong, glass breakage and its results may be serious. Wind damage is an especially important concern in hurricane and tornado areas or other locales subject occasionally to very high winds. Hurricane-force winds will drive water through even well-designed window casings. The continuing tendency toward the construction of "glass boxes" causes concern, particularly if the glass used is too thin and set too tight. (In this connection, it should be noted that operable vertical fins that are used for sun protection tend to become noisy in a high wind and, after exposure to weather, may become immovable. Their design should be carefully considered.)

Furthermore, libraries within a mile of seacoasts or tidal bays may need to guard against wave action on the elevated sea level that can result from severe storms, when the surge may range from 5 ft (1.524 m) in small storms to as much as 25 ft (7.620 m) in the most powerful hurricanes.

Insects and other animal life. Damage from insects, bookworms, silverfish, cockroaches, and the like has not been a significant problem in American libraries in recent years, but it has been very serious in tropical countries. Most insects dislike light, general cleanliness, and ventilation and temperature control within the limits of human comfort. In spite of this, various precautions should be taken. Termites in northern parts of the United States, and more frequently in the South, can be a problem in any wooden structure or in any part of a building where wood comes in direct or fairly close contact with the earth. They have done considerable damage in some libraries, eating out floor framing so that equipment and furniture drop to the floor below.

Bookworms cause trouble in much of the world, including major libraries in which books are acquired from tropical countries. A small fumigation chamber or blast freezer for the treatment of book shipments is desirable in research libraries, unless a nearby facility can provide adequate service when needed. The advent of the blast freezing technique of killing infestations shows great promise and is generally the method of choice in the United States as it avoids the use of toxic chemicals. Where the use of toxic chemicals is not regarded as a problem, a vacuum chamber designed for the use of Vikane has wide acceptance as being both effective and relatively benign to library materials. Vikane fumigation is still used by the University of Florida. Ethylene oxide has been widely used as well, but has fallen into disuse in the United States because of the toxicity of the gas.

Provision of a room with negative air pressure and exhaust to the outside, together with reasonably airtight construction, may serve as a staging area for infested materials. It should be remembered that bookworms and other insects may be very fond of leather, wood, parchment, and glue as well as paper, and that great damage may result from their depredations.

If food is to be served in the library, the greatest care must be taken to provide for proper housekeeping, as cockroaches and mice tend to appear wherever there are food operations. This is the greatest objection to the installation of snack bars and food-dispensing operations in a library. The best advice to minimize exposure to damaging infestations is: Do not have food service within any part of the library structure.

Mold will develop whenever and wherever high humidity is present at the same time as high temperature. The mold spores seem to be ever present, waiting for suitable conditions to arise. Air conditioning with humidity control will solve the problem, but without it mold may grow almost anywhere in the Temperate Zone and still more prevalently in the Tropics. If humidity control is not possible, keep the air moving and avoid dead air pockets in basements and elsewhere, particularly during sultry summer days and after heavy rains when basements may have taken in some water.

Just like some bell towers, some libraries have problems with bats. Bats especially like to live under Spanish tile roofs, and, on occasion, they have moved into the library building. The best protection is a tightly sealed or fully screened outer envelope. Once inside the building, a bat is especially hard to capture, and it can be a real health hazard. Tiles, on the other hand, can be "bat proofed" by simply stuffing crevices in the open ends with a wad of fiberglass. If it is expected that bats may be a problem, and a tile roof is selected, the open ends should be sealed in this way. Any other openings to the outside should be screened with a mesh fine enough to keep a small mouse out. A coarse form of hardware cloth may not be fine enough in all cases. The openings should not exceed ¼ in. (6.4 mm).

Theft, vandalism, and mutilation. The problems of theft, vandalism, and mutilation can be reduced but not completely avoided by proper exit controls, supervision, and design. The latter is especially important, as will be explained.

Libraries in colleges and universities have had their share of vandalism and there is every reason to expect that it will continue in the future. Although it will seldom include the mass "trashing" of windows that many American universities experienced in the late 1960s, there will be constant actions resulting in graffiti on walls, the "ripping off" of signs, and a wide variety of other activities that create undesirable conditions.

It is a worldwide problem in greater or lesser degree. A wide variety of experiences exists in terms of the damage to libraries in different parts of the world. A college in a rural setting in Maine will not have the problems of a large commuter college located in a tough neighborhood of an inner city. One would expect even fewer problems in academic libraries located in Japan, Sweden, or Switzerland. Furthermore, branch libraries will have nowhere near the degree of vandalism that exists in a large general library building. Yet no library is immune from some of the more innocuous outlets for human emotions. The design team for the library can learn from the experiences of schools and other types of institutions. The building design and its details, both exterior and interior, must minimize the opportunities for vandalism.

The design development phase of planning is not the only time to consider these matters, but it is perhaps the principal time during the design process. The schematic phase will be important in terms of general placement on the site and configuration of the building. In the design development phase, the great majority of conditions that are conducive to vandalism can be averted by refinement of the plans.

Throughout this century there has been a constant trend toward a philosophy of openness, of access to collections. Although this approach provides more opportunities for unsociable behavior (and more need for education), instances of maliciousness can be expected. Security conditions even in the most distinguished private research libraries are vulnerable, as we are reminded by the removal of the Gutenberg Bible from the especially secure Widener Memorial Room at Harvard. Library buildings can and should be designed to minimize these opportunities. At the same time one must not create an impression of siege conditions.

It is well to understand what prompts vandalism, to the extent that is possible, and then to see what approaches may ameliorate the possibilities. Eight conditions may be identified as a convenient way of understanding the damage to buildings:

1. *Wear and tear*—for example, poor-quality carpet will, with heavy use, look shabby, soiled, and damaged and perhaps will be hazardous within a few years.
2. *Accidents*—a door where the restraining bar or bumper stop has come loose may slam into a wall and break the plaster or the glass in the door.
3. *Vindictiveness*—hostility may be directed against a library staff member or teacher because of a grudge.
4. *Maliciousness*—rough play may be the result of sheer deviltry.
5. *Ideological expression*—an attempt to dramatize a cause by a major public statement written on a building, fence, or wall.
6. *Acquisitiveness*—petty theft, such as the removal of building or street signs. The more serious acquisitive vandal may rationalize theft for financial reasons, which can include taking material or equipment with the intention of resale.
7. *Boredom*—where there is no constructive outlet for energy, the imagination may find opportunities.
8. *Frustration*—the reaction to impersonal conditions, the callous indifference of an institution, or the pressures of growing up and perhaps living for the first time away from home and under an increased academic pressure. These feelings can lead some people to feel "boxed in" and make them want to lash out at something, to vent their feelings of inability to deal with the situation.

It seems to be part of the natural development of young people to explore and manipulate their environment. This need sometimes results in their testing their strength on buildings, dismantling things, throwing objects. Although much damage may stem from a relatively opportunistic and casual form of behavior, if breakage or markings are not rather quickly repaired, the damage will spread like an epidemic.

To some psychologists, geneticists, sociologists, and anthropologists, the more extreme of the above activities are the result of a deep vein of violence or aggression in humankind. Some would claim that excessive permissiveness engenders such antisocial behavior. Others accept it as part of growing up and accommodating to society. Where secondary schools have a huge problem with vandalism, one cannot expect college-age people to suddenly mature and adjust to a larger and more challenging social situation. Throughout history, rebelliousness has been focused on buildings and property. Feeling powerless, or perhaps dehumanized by a very impersonal physical environment, some individuals will take it upon themselves to alter that environment and create their own personal statement. Conditions vary greatly from time to time and from place to place.

There are five fundamental approaches to dealing with the undesirable potential. First, library management's rules, and penalties for breaking them, can be established. Second, clientele can be educated by informing them of the cost of damage to property and the effect it has on their education or on their tuition payments or tax dollars. Third, flattery, which can take the form of greatly improving the quality of the furnishings, often results in people living up to the implied expectations. Fourth, "target-hardening"—that is, making space and its furnishings indestructible—may be called for. This is a regrettable but often necessary treatment, frequently in secondary schools and occasionally in institutions of higher education. And fifth, diversion, or eliminating obvious opportunities for damaging actions, may help. The last three of these approaches should be carefully considered and choices made in the design of the library and its interiors. The key to successful design responses to vandalism is in the thoughtful planning of space, finishes, furnishings, and their details.

Before indicating some of the particular actions that can be taken in regard to architecture, landscaping, and furniture, it is well to point out the desirability of reviewing plans by attempting to guess what library users may do or try. It is useful to walk mentally through each room in the plans, to walk around the building, to try each reading space or common area, and, in particular, to consider the details. Will shoes mark the stair risers? Is there a column where patrons turning the corner will quickly soil a painted surface? Will the seams in upholstered chairs be located where it is easy to unconsciously pick at them or poke at them with a pencil?

Still, there will be limits. If an exceedingly heavy person stands on a lower shelf to reach a top shelf, a steel shelf is likely to bend. If several people yank on a handrail simultaneously as a game, it may well pull out of the wall. Consequently, the evaluation of areas should deal with the more common opportunities and not with the rare or unique case, since protecting against all such abuse would mean an uncomfortable, cold, hard, and unfriendly library and is certain to push up the cost of the building considerably. Remember that wise library management and some modest changes in architectural programs can markedly reduce damage and vandalism. Libraries should be able with careful planning to channel activities into the most acceptable locations.

As a general design approach, some principles can be applied. First, select the design and quality of materials so that the natural effects of age and wear do not provide an opportunity for idle abuse. Second, repair damage promptly to minimize any enjoyment by the perpetrator and to eliminate the visible reminder to others of what can be done. Third, utilize small modules or units so that the effect of damage is minimized and the cost of repair is reduced. Fourth, alter designs where an area might seem to have its aesthetic value improved by marking, such as a long and prominently located smooth wall. Fifth, lessen the rewarding feedback to the vandal. Sixth, provide visual or physical diversions to steer the individual away from potentially damaging activities.

A sample of actions that can be taken in the landscape, architectural, or interior design will suggest some applications of the above principles. Elsewhere in this volume other suggestions have been provided in order that buildings stand up well in use. These suggestions in part derive from a 1974 survey conducted by the National Association of School Security Directors. (See other comments on security in Section 5.3.6.)

1. *Site selection.* A building is more vulnerable if it is located by a main highway or if it is adjacent to a playing field or public grade school. A building may have more damage if it is on the periphery of the campus site, if it is immediately adjacent to or in the chosen center of campus student demonstrations, and if it is on a site to which many off-campus persons are attracted.

2. *Exterior surrounds.* Parking for bicycles and motor vehicles should be visible from the building windows and from major adjacent paths. Facilitate foot and bicycle traffic around the building, including police patrols, but do not have the paths within arm's length of the building itself. Place emergency phones or alarms on walkways to parking lots.

    Lights around the exterior can be argued pro and con, but it is generally felt that the grounds but not the building should be illuminated. Although lights will, during evening hours, serve as a deterrent, break-resistant lenses are desirable and the luminaire itself should be a minimum of 14 ft (4.267 m) high. The lights may be on a time clock so as to turn off at, for example, midnight or 1:00 A.M. Light poles must be of substantial material and set back at least a foot (305 mm) from the curb of any road. Bolts used to secure poles should be tack-welded. Light fixtures on buildings should preferably be recessed flush with the walls, especially if they are not very high.

    Trash receptacles should be sufficient in number and be quite heavy, while at the same time being easy to empty. Flat, light-colored surfaces at ground level may be protected from graffiti by placing them behind landscaping and using a heavily textured or dark surface. Treat any surface inviting of graffiti with one of the new protective surfaces that can be cleaned readily. Consider using glass instead of a convenient writing wall.

3. *Landscaping.* Paths must provide logical access and direct routes and yet should generally keep people away from the sides of the building. Bicycle and footpaths through landscaping and lawns are the result of faulty landscape design that fails to recognize the human tendency to take the shortest route between two points. Grade changes can

help keep pedestrians and cyclists on walk-ways. Keep grounds free of rocks and loose bricks or pavers. Anchor tables and benches unless they are exceedingly heavy. Keep plants quite low and well away from any basement or ground-level windows. Thorny plants are not a good protection because groundskeepers will be loathe to collect lit-ter blown into them.

4. *Building shell.* Minimize niches, recesses, courtyards, and other hiding places created by the exterior configuration. Avoid ornate, nonfunctional building materials and pro-tuberances, such as brackets, low overhangs, grilles—anything that can be climbed on or swung from. Furthermore, be attentive to this point regarding special signs on build-ings. A flower bed planted around a sign in front of a building will sometimes protect it as the flowers seem to convey the idea that somebody cares. Above all, provide a cheerful and humanistic environment rather than one that could seem repressive, impersonal, cold, and uncomfortable.

   There should be no mail slots in the ex-terior, if at all possible. An exterior book return that delivers books inside the build-ing may be a special problem; it should ter-minate within a fully enclosed room with a fire suppression system. An alternative is the freestanding book return, which cre-ates other problems, including the risk of damage from rain.

5. *Windows.* Most windows should be of moderate-sized panes and of standard sizes. Avoid any exterior transom and be wary of skylights and roof hatches. Any window facing an alley or a service area may need break-resistant glazing. Laminated glass, acrylic, or polycarbonate glazing must be properly installed, perhaps using pop rivets and reverse installation (from the inside so that putty is not on the outside). Note that tempered glass is fairly easy to break un-less it is also laminated.

6. *Doors.* Use heavyweight hardware. Leave no hinge pins exposed and removable on doors to any secure area. Consider door pivots rather than hinges. Always use a cen-ter column or an astragal for double doors unless panic hardware is not required and dead bolts can be used. In any room with free exterior access, such as rest rooms,

never have an inside locked door leading into the rest of the building. Use delayed-egress alarms on emergency doors. Do not have rest room doors that can be locked from the inside. Have a doorbell at the ser-vice entrance. Use interchangeable core key locking systems with multilevel master keys or a fully programmable card key sys-tem (which can take multiple forms).

7. *Utilities.* Hide or recess and protect the lo-cation of utilities. Avoid utility tunnels con-necting into any high-security area, such as the rare book stack. Provide a drain slot in any book return chute to reduce damage from flammable material being poured in and ignited, and a floor drain in case water is dumped in; or use a book return with a "snuffing-out device." Use flame retardant paint in vulnerable areas. To curb vandal-ism, interior roof drains or use of scuppers is preferable to downspouts where such spouts are accessible to the public. (But be aware that interior roof drains can leak.) Exterior drinking fountains and display fountains should be easily cleared of debris. Large display fountains or pools need low surrounding walls or another arrangement to keep newspapers, leaves, and other debris from being blown into them. Tamper-proof electric hand dryers might be considered if paper towels lead to littering.

8. *Interiors.* Elevator cars should have the op-erating panel provided with tamper-proof fasteners so that buttons cannot be crea-tively rewired. Car walls should be of a hard surface or perhaps carpeted. (Plastic lami-nate will chip at the edges. Woven metal mesh can be clogged with crayon unless the texture is in low relief and not mesh. Stainless steel is quite durable but, once de-faced, cannot be retouched. Baked enamel can be scratched.) The ceiling of the car should be at least 8 ft (2.438 m) high to safely accommodate standard library shelv-ing components or a sheet of plywood. Solid-metal nonprotruding buttons will avoid the breakage of plastic protruding ones. Study carrel surfaces should be hard and washable, such as plastic laminate. Do not provide soft ceilings below 8 ft (2.438 m) in study areas, and 10 ft (3.048 m) in cor-ridors and rest rooms. Use washable epoxy paint in vulnerable areas (a good choice for

preservation concerns as well). Recessed soap dispensers and shelves are desirable, but do not recess trash and paper receptacles as they jam once bent. Base supports for all rest room facilities should be provided, yet with access for persons in wheelchairs. Use the most minimal grouting in enameled tile walls in rest rooms. Reinforced doors are needed wherever computer, audiovisual, or business equipment is to be stored, and consider having no explanatory sign of the contents of such rooms. Use plastic lenses for all wall clocks. Consider porcelainized marker boards in seminar rooms and in after-hour study rooms. Consider walls where murals may discourage marking.

9. *Security.* Any intrusion detection system should be zoned to allow for partial building use. Where codes permit, fire alarms might be placed in the rooms that are occupied rather than in hallways, and consider providing a 10-second delay on alarms to allow false ones to be verified by closed-circuit television and canceled to reduce the results of pranks. And use motion-activation of surveillance cameras so staff review time is not wasted when nothing is going on. Consider where a dish mirror might be useful or closed-circuit television, though there can be a psychological downside. Use surface-mounted alarm system contacts or, even better, use hidden, recessed magnetic switches on doors and operable windows. Thought may also be given to magnetic coded card-entry systems that can record who enters a room (but not how many at one time), and when and where the room was entered and left. Such systems will control the door opening by authorization.

Be particularly careful of the vulnerability of the mail room or staff entrance. More major security lapses are likely to occur here than elsewhere in the building. Cash management is another particularly vulnerable aspect of library procedures. An inset floor money safe with a slot for after-hour deposits may be useful in certain locations that collect cash in the late afternoon or evenings. Although it is regrettable, experience in commercial as well as not-for-profit organizations shows that approximately two-thirds of all thefts are by staff. Install prop-door alarms on doors that staff should never prop open. The librarians will need to think all this through carefully so that the building does not become like a bank in its operation, and yet does not provide opportunities that can foster theft.

From the above, it can be seen that details make a great deal of difference. There are frequently new materials and new ideas that the planners may know about and use when they seem advantageous. Similarly, the librarians may know about techniques and practices that make a great difference, such as in the treatment of books.

Very valuable books should ordinarily be kept under lock and key, although unique material and volumes with the greatest value can be difficult to sell at their true value, particularly if they have concealed library ownership marks. The best method to prevent theft of irreplaceable materials is to place them on closed-access shelves. If the materials must be shelved in a reading area open to the public, they should be protected by locked doors on the bookcases. These books should be made available only on signature, and the call slip records should be kept in a safe place until the books have been returned and have been examined to determine that they have not been damaged. For less important books that are kept on open shelves, the best protection is examination of the holdings of all readers as they leave the building.

The question of book mutilation is a much more serious one, as there is no way to prevent it when students and others have free access to bookstacks and are not supervised. Little can be done in library planning to minimize this problem short of moving toward closed-access stacks and proctored reading. Where students cut pages so their use can be more convenient or where phrases of special interest are highlighted or underlined for later reference, library education can help counter these selfish actions. Such actions have sometimes been encouraged unwittingly by professors who give assignments beyond the capacity of the library and who mark their own books, thereby setting an example that students are likely to follow with library books. Book mutilation has been found to be reduced if convenient photocopy machines are available at a reasonable cost.

Injury to physically challenged persons. It is necessary to take into account persons who are limited by being confined to wheelchairs, who require crutches, who are blind or have other sight impairment, who have hearing disabilities, who have faulty coordination caused by brain, spinal, or other nerve injury, or who, because of age, have reduced mobility, flexibility, coordination, and perception.

Special consideration to such conditions must be given in planning a building. Help for these individuals should begin outside the building, with a parking area so designed that it will not be too difficult for a person on crutches or in a wheelchair to leave the car. Curbs must have appropriately placed ramps at least 3 ft (0.914 m) wide. The bottom of any sign projecting over a path must be at least 7 ft 6 in. (2.285 m) high. There should be no nearby trees that drop nuts or large seedpods or have limbs that break under ice or snow loads. Walks to the library should be at least 4 ft (1.219 m) wide, should have a grade no greater than 5 percent, and should follow a route uninterrupted by steps. Steps can be an important deterrent to the clumping of bicycles in front of the main entry; where this is a goal, the ramped approach should be subtle or otherwise limited to nonbicycle use.

At least one building main entrance should be reached without going up steps, and a ramp should be available if necessary. The ramp should have a slope not greater than a 1-ft (305-mm) rise in 12 ft (3.658 m), or approximately 8 percent. On at least one side, and preferably on both sides (as required by the ADA), a ramp longer than 6 ft (1.829 m) should have handrails between 34 and 38 in. (864 and 965 mm) in height and extending 1 ft (305 mm) beyond the top and the bottom. The ends of the handrail should not become a hazard; they will not if they terminate on the side of a wall. In addition, curved rather than sharp ends will help. The rail diameter should be between 1¼ in. and 1½ in. (31.7 mm and 38.1 mm) and permit continuous sliding of the hand. Ramps must have a level platform before a door is reached. Any ramp must have 5-ft-long (1.524-m) landings at the top and bottom as well as with every 30-in. (0.762-m) vertical segment or where there is a change of direction. Where bicycle parking is a problem, special emphasis will be required to provide ample bicycle and moped parking to avoid blocking the access route.

Doors should have a clear opening of not less than 32 in. (813 mm). The door itself will have to be 34 in. (864 mm) wide. This dimension applies to both exterior and interior doors. Use of automatic doors should be considered, at least for the main entrance. Doors with two leaves should be avoided, unless each provides a 32-in. (812-mm) clear opening. This amount is required for wheelchairs as well as for persons using crutches. Typical length for occupied wheelchairs ranges from 4 ft to 4 ft 6 in. (1.219 to 1.372 m), and an average diameter of 5 ft 3 in. (1.600 m) is required to turn around (though the ADA requires a diameter of 5 ft or 1.524 m for turning around; see fig. 13.8). Motorized chairs for quadriplegics require more area, so generous spacing is needed.

For the sake of occupants of wheelchairs, there must be an elevator if the building has more than one level, with a door of at least 32 in. (812 mm) in the clear (the ADA requires a 36-in. or 0.914-m minimum door width) so that a wheelchair can enter it. The ADA-specified minimal clear dimensions of the cab interior are either 80 in. (for a central door) or 68 in. (for a door to one side) in width by 51 in. with 54 in. to the face of the cab door (2.032 or 1.727 m by 1.295 m with 1.372 m to the door). (See fig. 13.9.) Stairs required to be accessible should have handrails between 34 and 38 in. (0.864 and 0.965 m) above the tread at the face of the riser. Stairs with overhanging or square nosings should be avoided, as they present a hazard for persons with restriction in knee, ankle, or hip movements. Main stairs should have risers that do not exceed 7 in. (178 mm) unless an elevator is available, and tread size will be determined by formula. (Codes usually allow risers to be a maximum of 7½ in., or 190.5 mm, high for general usage.)

Slippery floors are dangerous and should be avoided throughout the library. There should be a common level throughout each floor of a building. A step up or down going from a corridor to a toilet room, for instance, should be avoided, as should door sills or thresholds. Carpet laid on floors, stairs, and ramps should have a tight weave, low pile, and firm underlayment. No underlayment and uncut pile is preferable.

Every library should provide at least a few chairs with arms, as some people can get up from a chair only by using the arms for support. U.S. accessibility standards specify at least 5 percent or a minimum of one of each element of fixed seating, tables, or study carrels to be accessible to people in wheelchairs. They also specify the knee space to be at least 27 in. high, 30 in. wide, and 19 in. deep (0.686, 0.762, and 0.483 m). They

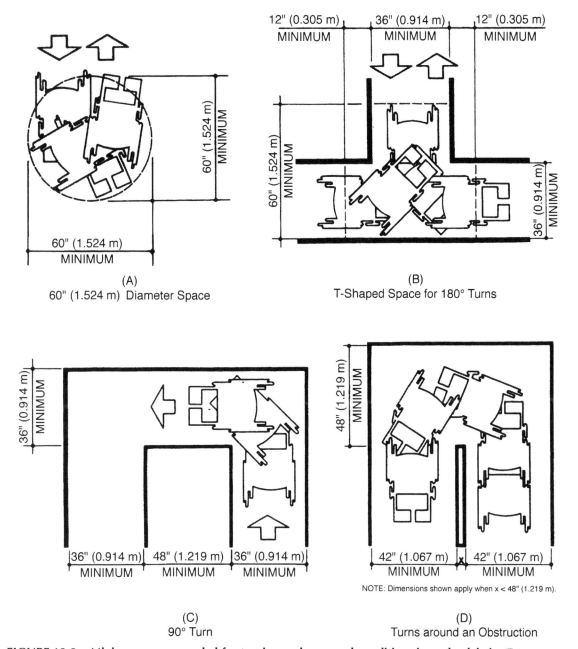

12" (0.305 m) MINIMUM | 36" (0.914 m) MINIMUM | 12" (0.305 m) MINIMUM

60" (1.524 m) MINIMUM

60" (1.524 m) MINIMUM

36" (0.914 m) MINIMUM

60" (1.524 m) MINIMUM

(A)
60" (1.524 m) Diameter Space

(B)
T-Shaped Space for 180° Turns

36" (0.914 m) MINIMUM

36" (0.914 m) MINIMUM | 48" (1.219 m) MINIMUM | 36" (0.914 m) MINIMUM

48" (1.219 m) MINIMUM

42" (1.067 m) MINIMUM | 42" (1.067 m) MINIMUM

NOTE: Dimensions shown apply when x < 48" (1.219 m).

(C)
90° Turn

(D)
Turns around an Obstruction

FIGURE 13.8   Minimum space needed for turning under several conditions in a wheelchair. (Department of Justice, "Nondiscrimination on the Basis of Disability by Public Accommodations and Commercial Facilities, Final Rule," *Federal Register* **56, no. 144 [July 26, 1991]: 35622, 35626.)**

specify a clear width between bookstacks of 36 in. (0.914 m) and they prefer 42 in. (1.067 m) where possible.

Other facilities that should be considered to make them accessible to the physically limited include drinking fountains and a public telephone with a shelf low enough so that a person in a wheelchair can roll up to it and reach the dial.

Thresholds should be avoided even at the main entrance. Easily approached elevators and electrical switches of all kinds are also of importance.

Regarding signs, consider that red-green is the most common color-blind deficiency. Raised letters are needed for tactile sign reading at a standard height of no more than 4 ft 6 in. (1.372 m) for complete access. Such hazards as low-hanging

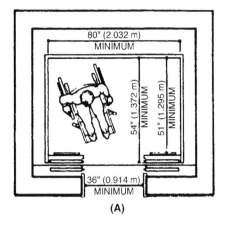

(A)

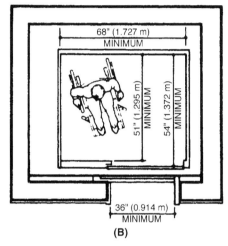

(B)

FIGURE 13.9   Minimum dimensions of elevator cars. (Department of Justice, "Nondiscrimination on the Basis of Disability by Public Accommodations and Commercial Facilities, Final Rule," *Federal Register* 56, no. 144 [July 26, 1991]: 35640.)

signs and ceiling lights must be avoided; a minimum height of 6 ft 6 in. to 7 ft (1.980 to 2.134 m) from the floor is recommended for interiors. Some recent codes require the use of fire alarm horns that include a flashing light.

Detailed specifications can be found in documentation from the American National Standards Institute, located at 1430 Broadway, New York, New York 10018. These specifications or those promulgated by the U.S. Architectural and Transportation Barriers Compliance Board (ATBCB) may govern the design when federal money is involved. Three documents issued by the ATBCB are listed here in the Bibliography, including the "Technical Paper on Accessibility Codes and Standards, a Comparison of Domestic and Selected Foreign Standards and Codes," which gives sources in each U.S. state and in 11 other countries. The requirements of the Americans with Disabilities Act are available in the *Federal Register* of July 26, 1991. Guidance can also be obtained from, among others, the American Foundation for the Blind in New York City, the Disabled Living Foundation in London, and the Research Office of the Syracuse University School of Architecture.

13.2.6 Outline Specifications

At the completion of the design development phase, the specifications will not yet be fully developed. The general and special conditions, for example, will typically be omitted, and the specifications for each of the building trades will consist of a general description of the design intent. It is unlikely that specific products will be selected, although it is possible in a few cases. A more detailed description of the complete construction specifications will be found in Chapter 14.

Although there is no fixed rule regarding the contents of the outline specifications, the following might be considered reasonable:

1. A project statement giving a general architectural description of the building. This would include the selection of basic exterior materials, such as the stone or other facing material, a description of the roof type and material, and other major visual features of the building.
2. An area analysis with the figures developed showing the gross and net floor area for each floor, together with the area assigned to mechanical functions, walls, circulation, and other features that contribute to the nonassignable space.
3. A program area analysis showing the area assigned to each program element, together with the excess or shortage in relation to the written program. Where the new facility is an addition, the analysis might include the breakdown of space assigned in the new and existing structures.
4. A structural statement describing the soil conditions and the proposed materials and technique. The codes that apply to the design may also be cited. The structural system will cover the footings, columns, bearing walls, and the floor and roof systems.
5. A mechanical statement giving a general description of the proposed system and

the criteria against which the system is designed.

6. A general description of the electrical systems and any special computer accommodation.

7. A series of sections covering each of the building trades, including statements of the materials that are to be used, the finish, the scope of work within the trade, and, in some cases, the method of installation. In the outline specifications these descriptions will be fairly general, except perhaps when the institution requires a particular product for maintenance or operational purposes.

The librarian should pay special attention to those aspects that may adversely affect the operation of the library. Those would include shelving and special equipment, alarm systems, lighting, hardware, and perhaps the mechanical, general electrical, elevator, flooring, and painting sections. Others may be important as well. One should review the requirements for samples, mock-ups, construction operations information (such as limitations for exceptional noise and the requirements for security, water, power, smoking, and sound and dust control during construction, which may be covered in the general or special conditions remaining to be written), and the operational aspects (quality, durability, flexibility, etc.) needed to ensure that the "owner" will receive what is wanted. It is important at this phase to ensure that there is sufficient information to generate a sound budget estimate, which often is essential before approval can be given to proceed to the next phase.

Although the building program should have stated the most important library operating requirements, the engineering conditions affecting mechanical systems, lighting, plumbing, safety, and security must now be specified. The result is dependent on following through on these points.

The Newberry Library in Chicago is a good example of involvement. First of all, the library's conservation officer was an early and a most important member of the planning team. He had great and consequential influence on the specifications for the building, with the important backing of the library so the conservation needs would be foremost. The basic design of the 1982 Bookstack Building was itself a result of this planning approach. Besides being off-limits to readers, the building is windowless, is of double-shell con-

struction, and has no vertical penetrations between floors, no cooling tower on the top of the building, and no mechanical equipment within the structure. Treatment of air, humidity, and access security is stringent. Special sheathing is provided to waterproof the basement level. The exterior double-shell wall is composed first of a layer of brick, then 1½ in. (38 mm) of air (an insulation layer), then an 8-in. (203-mm) concrete-block wall, another air cavity, and finally plaster board as the interior wall surface. The air-cleaning system uses three high-efficiency filters to remove atmospheric particles and gaseous impurities. Environmental constraints are 60° ±5° F. (16° C. ±3° C.) and 50 percent ±3 percent RH diurnally and 50 percent ±6 percent RH seasonally. (The master microfilm copies are, however, controlled at 35 percent RH.) All air mixing and humidity adjustments are done outside the Bookstack Building, in a structure linking the original building and the addition, before being fed horizontally by duct to each floor for distribution. Regarding access security, there is motion detection in some areas. Each staff member has a magnetic card that enables entrance to controlled parts of the building and into areas within the stack, and any use of the card makes a record of that person's entrance and departure. The fire protection system includes ionization smoke detectors and rate-of-rise temperature detectors, plus a Halon fire-extinguishing system in the vault, which has walls with a four-hour rating. Physical intrusion, smoke, fire, and environmental conditions are monitored through local reading devices, the results of which are fed through a field processing panel to a central computer. In addition to a printout record, the computer terminal provides precise display of current conditions in color, keyed to the plan of mechanical features and security points and the sensing of those local conditions. Staff attend the monitoring station within the building on a 24-hour basis.

It is interesting to note that the Newberry Library had to obtain a variance from local building codes to permit the library to be designed so that stack aisle and emergency lighting could be switched off whenever there was no staff person on that particular stack floor. It also required a variance in order that the single emergency stair turret, which was required by code, could have a 30-second time delay on the exit door before it could be opened. With staff alerted by a signal from the exit door, and with closed-circuit television to record and display at the central staff monitoring station that a person was in the stairwell, staff could then take protective action. However, a variance was not allowed for a single security-card-activated pair of doors into each stack level; the county insisted on extra vestibule doors that automatically close when magnetic holds release upon sensing a fire—a requirement that added to the cost of the structure.

Computer installations. Specifications must be quite rigorous and cover many aspects. Special building requirements for a minicomputer or larger computer may be needed for security, backup and clean power, electromagnetic interference protection, fire suppression, floor loading capacity, and air conditioning. Many of these issues are becoming increasingly less critical as computers become smaller, more powerful, cooler, more stable, and, in general, more sympathetic to varied environments and conditions. Power requirements should be met with a voltage range of ±8 percent. There must be a power line analyzer, lightning protection, and all lines in metallic conduit. Carpeting should be of a nonstatic type. Space must be sufficient for all doors on all equipment to be wide open at the same time. Other specifications will be provided by the manufacturer, and a computer consultant is advisable on any sizable installation. Section 13.4.4, Computer Terminals and the Catalog, provides other comments applicable for any computer installation.

It is perhaps worth noting how difficult it is to judge what the computer requirements may be 10 years hence. Some university general library buildings included a computer room in the design. The University of Minnesota Wilson Library is an instance, yet it is not used for that purpose and is not expected later to be. Other buildings had no such designed space and were able to install small mainframe computers with no great difficulty. Many have minicomputers and file servers with no problem of accommodation. Distributed processing, relatively universal Internet port access, and use of minicomputers and microcomputers have changed the picture from that of a decade ago.

The University of Toronto Robarts Library, which was programmed in the mid-1960s and occupied in 1972–1973, is a building that, as one of its planners has said, "was planned for the computer age [but] considering the way things have gone, it might almost just as well not have been." Even so, in the 1960s, the university rejected use of very large cable ducts in every floor slab, which would have added 10 percent to the total construction cost. Instead it chose ordinary modular three-cell ductwork in floors in the reading rooms, workrooms, and a few other areas, and assumed that extra future cabling would be carried in troughs or trays at ceiling level. The Green Library addition at Stanford, seven years later than Robarts, used only vertical power and signal chases and a main artery trough (cable tray) run above the suspended ceiling. Extra power capacity was provided.

It may be worth noting that power requirements vary greatly. Some color monitors and letter-quality printers use about three times as much energy as monochrome monitors and printers. Hard-disc storage generally uses more energy than floppy disc. Maximum electricity wattage required by devices will vary greatly; as typical examples, today keyboards range from fewer than 40 watts for a laptop to over 400 watts for a server. Monitors vary depending upon size, and color versus monochrome; one brand ranges from 70 watts for a 14-in. (356-mm) color monitor to 160 watts for a 21-in. (534-mm) color monitor. Printers range from very-low-current portable units to a maximum of 1,200 watts for a high-speed, networked printer. Typical printers are in the range of 150 to 300 watts. Scanners require about 50 watts. And, of course, there is a vast array of other equipment requiring power; for an accurate assessment of current power requirements, a survey may be needed, the results of which must be projected into the future. Libraries may have three to four times as many devices 15 years from now, though the average wattage per device may decrease. Responsible institutional officers must assure the capacity to adapt to changing technology and yet not overdesign, which can with hindsight prove to be a waste of funds.

13.2.7 Maintaining Flexibility

Much attention has already been given to the topic of flexibility; little more needs to be said here except to underscore the importance of clear thinking and analysis of and reasonable solutions to library needs. Decisions will be made during the design development phase that will largely establish the nature of flexibility in the final product. By the time this phase is completed, the librarian and institution should feel that these decisions are correct, as they ought not be changed at a later date except as they may apply to the development of project details. The needs of flexibility must be kept in mind during all the design process, including change orders during construction. And constant checking for this flexibility is the responsibility primarily of the librarian, the library planner, and any experienced library building consultant. It is not a responsibility that can be handed off.

13.3
Testing the Budget

With the completion of the design development drawings and outline specifications, a budget estimate should be prepared. The process of budget estimates and budget control was discussed in Chapter 9. If the design team has done its work well, no surprises should result from the budget estimate; unfortunately, this is often not the case.

However, it seems to be the rule, rather than the exception, that each time there is a cost estimate, the projected cost increases. This occurs as a result of an increased understanding of the design and site, material supply, or other factors that come to light as the design progresses. It also results from program improvements, which are often related to the learning experience of the design process, or they may be related to newly developed technologies in library operations, energy control, maintenance processes, and the like. On a large project several years may pass between the first writing of the program and the completion of the design development phase, and things do change.

When the design team learns that its project no longer fits within the budget, the first reaction may be to obtain a confirming estimate. Although another estimate may be lower, remember that any estimate can be off by as much as 10 percent; even though the estimator may not agree, this is probably a reasonable range, especially at this phase. Assuming that the design team has confidence in the abilities of the estimator, and assuming that there is sufficient breakdown (see the discussion of the cost model in Chapter 9) so that obvious errors or misunderstandings can be identified, one might reasonably question the merit of expending additional project money for a confirming estimate. It is, however, prudent to deal promptly with the problem if the costs will exceed the capacity of budget contingencies.

The choices are simple to identify but usually difficult to implement. For the design team, the most pleasant solution would be to increase the budget. To do this, a fair amount of homework must be completed. There must be a clear understanding of why the budget estimate has increased. And, there must be sound justification for the need that leads to the increase. It is in this circumstance where, under certain political pressures, a confirming estimate may be warranted. The homework should include an analysis of the alternatives. Answers to such questions as the following should be in mind:

> Can deduct alternates be identified? Can the project scope be reduced, such as by eliminating a parking lot that had been tacked onto the project scope?
>
> Can the quality be reduced? Care will be required here!
>
> Can special alternative sources of funding be obtained? For example, are there different funding sources that might deal with energy conservation, with providing handicapped access, with code problems in existing facilities, or with providing landscaping outside the building?
>
> Are there construction techniques that could reduce the cost without adversely influencing the project? In an era of high inflation, the fast-track construction system has sometimes been found to reduce costs, but there are risks, and the end of design development is a late date to begin a fast-track program. (The concept of fast-track is discussed in Chapter 15.)
>
> Is there another part of the budget that can be reduced? Here, the only budget item that should be reduced, assuming the original budget was properly done, is the design contingency. This is justified because more is known about the project at this phase than when the budget was originally formulated.

If any of the above is possible with negligible impact on the project, and this process does not close the gap, some hard decisions will be required. The best advice that can be given is that the librarian should have a clear view of the priorities to ensure that the facility will work well for future generations. In general, the authors tend to prefer add or deduct alternates over a reduction of the quality, reasonable flexibility, or the general arrangements established to this point.

There is one other option: Can the project be phased over a decade or so? This can be a problem in the design development stage. Few projects would offer an easy division into phases, and any such change in the design will involve extra costs for architectural and engineering work and, of course, will result in some extra costs to the institution in obtaining the full program as, for example, building connections will need to be opened and additional shifts of collections and functions will be required. This option actually divides the original program into two projects— one now and another to be faced later. This is costly and disappointing, though it may at times be required if the original budget was poorly constructed and the options above have not resolved the discrepancy.

It should be recognized that the design of alternates or significant changes in the project scope will affect the architect's fee. This knowledge should be clear at the start of any analysis resulting from budgetary problems. In Great Britain, where architects and quantity surveyors are expected to estimate building costs accurately, a bid (or tender) in excess of the agreed expenditure limit is modified by compensating savings determined by the design team and prepared by the architect at no cost to the institution.

13.4
Design Development of Interiors

The schematic phase of design is intended to test the assumptions made about space assignment and to aid both the designer and the owner in the analysis of the space arrangements. In the design development phase, greater attention is paid to the dimensions of the furniture and equipment and their layout as they affect space utilization. Concerns about vandalism are discussed in Section 13.2.5, and concerns about details, durability, and color are covered in Chapter 14. This section discusses a number of issues in terms of layouts, mock-ups, and space utilization, which should be at the heart of the design development phase of interiors.

Equipment layouts cannot be completed until there has been agreement upon the large-scale spatial relationships and the quantitative requirements for seating accommodations, volumes to be stored, and other space uses. Aesthetics and physical comfort are important. Equipment layouts should look good. A satisfactory layout must

be based on properly designed, comfortable furniture of the right size for the task at hand, so arranged that it is easily accessible and provides the desired work space without undue interference from or to others.

The designer, with the program submitted by the institution as a guide, will in due course prepare schematic drawings or preliminary sketch plans that will be shown to the library's representatives. The first ones will probably do little more than indicate spatial relationships. Later, the floor areas of the different functions will be included, but in rough terms. Later still, proposed equipment layouts should be shown. These can sometimes be arranged by drawing in the equipment with the sizes that have been agreed upon. It can be done to advantage by using templates of paper, cardboard, or metal drawn to scale. These have the advantage of making it possible without erasure to shift the templates and find the most suitable arrangements. The use of a computer with CAD software can greatly facilitate this process. With a laptop and a computer-driven projection system, the process of moving furniture and equipment around can even become a group exercise involving interested staff. Making the drawing on a grid, with each square representing one foot or one-quarter of a meter, may ease the task. If grid paper is not used, it is particularly desirable to have a large-scale drawing, so that it will be easier to move the templates around. A scale of 1 in. to 4 ft (or 1:50 in the metric system) is suggested, unless a very large area is to be covered. Special boards fitted with magnets that hold a metal template in place are sometimes used. With the computer-based approach, the scale can be quickly changed in order to see details, and the size or dimensions of a particular area can be quickly determined using the power of the CAD software. A paper copy can be created by simply connecting to a printer in the library or by faxing a copy to the library.

Many laypersons find it difficult to picture from a drawing just what the finished results will look like and to decide whether a 3-ft (914-mm) aisle between tables, for instance, is adequate, whether a 3-x-5-ft or a 4-x-6-ft (0.914-x-1.524-m or 1.219-x-1.829-m) reading-room table is preferable for four persons, or whether a shelf 7 in. (178 mm) deep will give space enough for books. The architect, or interior designer, who is more experienced and adept with tasks of this kind, may be able to give satisfactory answers to questions, but in some cases a visual demonstration is desirable.

One method is to go to a library where tables, shelving, catalog cases, computer terminals, and other equipment of different sizes can be seen in their proper setting. A demonstration with furniture is useful in a library with rooms approximately the size planned in the new building. An experienced library consultant can suggest libraries to visit. In almost any large city or metropolitan area, it is possible to find examples of arrangements that would be useful.

If new types of equipment or methods of construction are to be used, there may be occasions when a mock-up on a larger or smaller scale will be advisable. When Princeton's Firestone Library was being planned, soon after the Second World War, the architects arranged for construction of a four-bay mock-up. In two of the bays, sample bookstacks of various types were installed. The other two were used for layout of other accommodations. A false adjustable ceiling that could be cranked up and down was installed to test ceiling heights. Sample lighting and other equipment was made available. Those interested had an almost ideal visual demonstration of problems for which solutions were desired. Although this is an example of a fairly ambitious mock-up, smaller-scale mock-ups using existing space and proposed lighting and furnishings can be useful. Remember that the window areas and the intensity of the light coming from the outside at different times of day have an effect on the desired and required intensity of the light within the building as well as on its quality.

When the Lamont Library at Harvard University was under construction and plans were made for a larger number of open carrels than had ever been used before in a library, sample carrels with tables of different sizes, with and without shelves, with backs of different heights, and with other variations were built and carefully studied.

Appendix B gives sizes of furniture of various types, aisle widths, the resulting capacity for books and readers, and other items of interest. The optimum size of the proposed equipment should be agreed upon. Should a table for four be 3 × 5 ft, or would 4 × 6 ft (0.914 × 1.524 m or 1.219 × 1.829 m) be more satisfactory, although it takes more space? If these sizes are used in combination with library visits and suitable drawings, the results should be satisfactory. Consider that the interior design scheme may help to make a room look larger and more spacious, just as it may make it look more crowded and congested.

Satisfactory layouts may be products of an exact science, but often they are achieved only by reasoned judgment mixed with trial and error. The following 10 general principles are suggested:

1. Aisles consume more space than equipment, and, to be economical in space utilization, every aisle should be used on both sides.
2. An aisle that has chairs backing into it should be wider than one without seating used even more heavily as a main traffic artery.
3. Visual and auditory distractions should be minimized, and these design conditions should be studied with care.
4. Main traffic arteries in a straight line are preferable, unless they are at least 100 ft (30.480 m) or more long. If they have to turn corners and pass obstructions that are above eye level in height, a hemmed-in feeling and confusion may result.
5. A great reading room with row after row of tables parallel to each other gives an unpleasantly regimented effect, which shelving or screens 6 ft (1.829 m) high or more placed at intervals may help to eliminate.
6. A long row of open carrels along a wall on one or more sides of a room with table backs 4 ft 6 in. (1.372 m) high will not be nearly so monotonous as an equally long row of carrels placed between two ranges in a bookstack. In a long row of carrels or tables, a break used for lounge chairs or other seating arrangements may relieve the monotony. (See fig. 13.10.)
7. Wall shelves in a large reading area are seldom desirable from the space assignment point of view, as they require wide aisles in front of them. Shelving can be placed more economically on ranges with shelving on both sides, as the aisle then receives full use.
8. Shelves along a reading room wall have the additional disadvantage of increasing the distances involved in using the collections and of creating visual and auditory distraction. Reference and other heavily used materials should be concentrated as far as possible, with accommodations for readers who will be using them adjacent on one or all sides.
9. A wall on one side and, to a greater extent, walls on both sides of an aisle or corridor

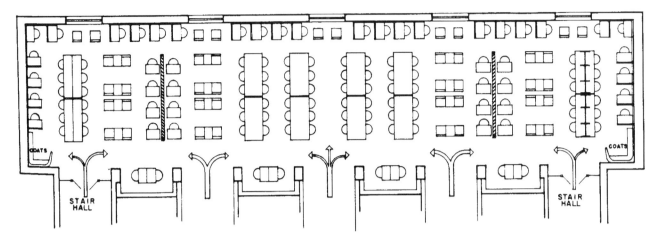

FIGURE 13.10   A variety of seating accommodations used in a large reading area. Students do not all want the same kind of accommodations. The use of a variety relieves monotony. There are too many large tables here, but comfortable semilounge chairs diminish the rigidity. Slanting-top tables, partitions on long tables, individual tables separated by screens, and double carrels facing each other in shallow alcoves all help. Note also the five entrances that reduce distances to be traveled to reach the seats, and the coat-racks in two corners in sight of many readers. This plan is adapted from an original design for the Lamont Library. See also figs. 7.2 and 7.9.

make it seem narrower. A 3-ft (914-mm) corridor with walls on both sides reaching above eye level appears very narrow. A 3-ft (914-mm) corridor with an open carrel on one side and the ends of book ranges on the other will seem quite adequate visually and, when two persons pass in it, one of them can, if necessary, slip into the stack aisle or the space in front of an unoccupied carrel table while the other goes by. A room seems open with no obstructions above table height, that is, 30 in. (762 mm), plus or minus. Partitions 4 ft 6 in. (1.372 m) in height on three sides of carrels do not take much away from a feeling of openness for a person who is standing; and one sitting and studying is generally not interested in openness and enjoys being partially shut off from neighbors so long as light and ventilation are good, and the person can look out in at least one direction. Most people in a reading room will feel that floor cases up to 5 ft 6 in. (1.676 m) high, which permit five shelves of books, will give a surprisingly open feeling going down a 4- or 4½-ft.-wide (1.219- or 1.372-m) aisle at right angles to the ranges, particularly if the ceiling is 8 ft (2.438 m) high or more.

10. The use of curved walls or those with angles that are not 90° should always be questioned, especially in small buildings, as good space utilization will be difficult and never completely successful. Curved bay windows in their proper place can be attractive aesthetically, but they are expensive to construct, and furniture and equipment are seldom designed to fit them. Radial stacks planned on the basis that they permit better supervision may be useful under some conditions, but floor area of 10 percent or more is lost, and some congestion inevitably results when ranges approach each other near the center where traffic is heaviest; it is invariably difficult to use the periphery to advantage. See, however, the radial catalog, which can be satisfactory and take no more space than a more regular layout (fig. 13.11). If radial stacks are used in very large areas, somewhat better space utilization becomes possible, but most readers will find it difficult to keep properly oriented and will often have to come back to the center and take extra steps before going to another section. Circular arrangements for shelving and seating have been tried again and again in the past (for exam-

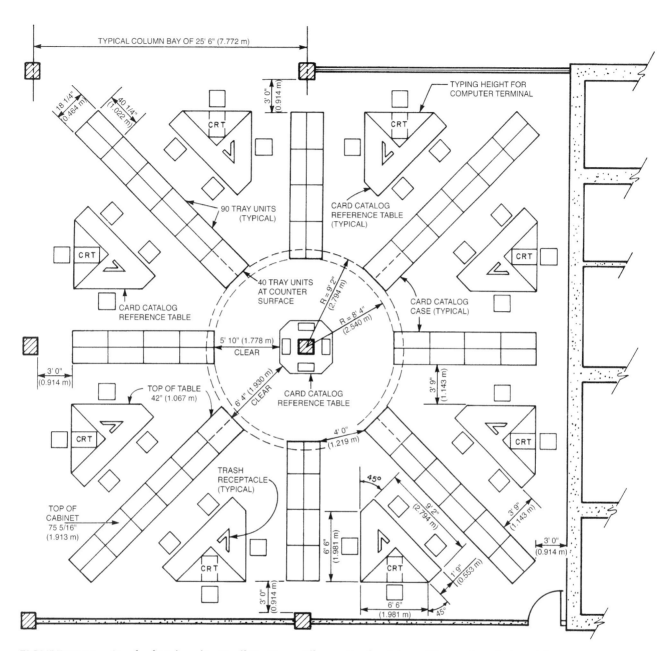

FIGURE 13.11   Stanford University, Cecil H. Green Library. Card catalog with counters designed for consultation of card trays and for computer terminals supporting the online catalog as originally set up. Note that each card case section nearest the center in each diagonal row is counter height for tray consultation and for traffic visibility. This configuration of cases uses little more floor space than traditional arrangements (housing about 3,000 cards per ft², or 32,000 per m²), and it considerably shortens the distance traveled by a person checking references that are not in alphabetical sequence. (Layout by interior designer Phyllis Martin-Vegue.)

ple, at Leeds, Manchester, and Northwestern University), and, as far as the authors have been able to learn, have never proved to be completely satisfactory.

13.4.1 Influence of Specialized Needs of Equipment

Although the effect of equipment is of great importance to the design development process, the design team is urged to review the programming chapters (5, 6, 7, and 8), which cover in detail the issues of shelving, reader tables, acoustic control, and the like. It will also be desirable at this point to scan appendix C. This brief section is included here to emphasize the importance of a thorough understanding of equipment requirements, including floor loading, space, lighting, temperature, and other requirements.

Two policy decisions are discussed here as they may affect the layouts. Shall the furnishings and fixtures be stock or custom-built? Should they be contemporary or traditional in style?

Stock or custom-built. A small library can rarely afford to consider the purchase of anything except stock furniture, lighting fixtures, or other building components. To have them specially designed and built to order would be too expensive in all but exceptional cases. This situation may well be different for a very large building. If the number of chairs to be purchased runs into four figures, it may well be that a special design can be afforded. In many cases the custom-made chairs can be less expensive than those from a standard library-equipment house with its necessarily large overhead for selling and service. The danger arises from the fact that specially designed furniture does not always stand the test of time and is less likely to be well designed structurally.

Major weaknesses in chairs and tables are joints that loosen after heavy use. A number of academic institutions have recently used the patented Eustis Designs chair and book truck with their permanently rigid I-beam joinery, and academic and research libraries may wish to consider such construction for its life-cycle economic advantage.

A compromise between stock and custom-built furniture was used in connection with the selection of the chairs for the Lamont Library building at Harvard. The time was 1947, soon after the war, when furniture stocks were depleted and the types of chairs available were limited. However, some 40 samples were found. The architect and the librarian, with advice from many others, selected the three that seemed closest to what they wanted. They then called in the manufacturers and asked whether they would make certain changes in the design and what the cost would be. One of the three was chosen. The manufacturer made the alterations requested after a number of different samples were submitted. The chairs have been satisfactory in every respect except for the finish. (The finishes available at that time were not as good as they are today.) Only one chair in 1,100 broke in the first dozen years, despite the use and the abuse that are inevitable in a busy undergraduate library. But this procedure could not have been carried out without the aid of an architect who was interested and knowledgeable and a manufacturer who was ready to make use of its wide experience and also to work closely with the institution. Given these conditions, custom-built furniture may be a money saver, but a risk is involved.

Another potential advantage the planner may realize from custom furniture is the possibility of unique or special configurations. Carrels, for example, might be designed to fit the space or the special needs of the library. This is especially useful where computer workstations have extra space needs, or where audio or microtext carrels are to be provided, as improvements over a stock item may be realized. Stanford's Green Library has custom-made carrels of extra size and unique shape, which have proven to be very satisfactory over the first 15 years. Circulation counters also can be stock or custom-made; the difference may be little in cost, but a great deal in terms of meeting the program specifics or the aesthetic coherency of the furniture in the space.

Any one of the standard library-equipment houses has the knowledge and experience to produce first-class library furniture, and its better lines will generally fulfill the library requirements, at least for community and many four-year colleges. Competition is keen enough to keep prices within reason. The manufacturer's special knowledge of library problems can also be used to good effect, particularly if a library consultant is not on the planning team. A library in a city where library equipment and furniture are manufactured can sometimes obtain considerable discounts from regular prices. A cabinet-making firm, if controlled by persons belonging to the same religious group that sponsors the institution seeking equipment, may make special discounts. Much can be said for the use of furniture from manufacturers other than those who specialize in library equipment, as the furniture, especially the lounge chairs, may have aesthetic advantages. But make sure that it is sturdy and will stand the wear and tear of library use. The local situation may well affect the choice made.

Light fixtures are items for which a custom design may be considered. As with the example of chairs, a fixture for a carrel of special design may be excessively expensive in small quantities; however, the price may be worthwhile in larger quantities. In the Cecil H. Green Library at Stanford, a custom light fixture was designed for the over 200 faculty studies and dissertation rooms. The goal was to provide excellent, glare-free light in an exceedingly energy-efficient fixture. In a later project, when only four fixtures were needed, the manufacturer could not reasonably produce such a small quantity.

Custom versus stock is a decision that might be applied to other elements as well, including carpet, signs, book returns, book trucks, tables for reading folios, atlas and wall map cases, and even shelving for some rare or special collections. Each case must be considered in the context of what is to be achieved and how much it will cost.

Contemporary or traditional. The question of contemporary or traditional design is another perplexing one. Simple lines, good proportions, and carefully selected, properly cured, and well-finished wood or other materials of similar quality are the primary essentials; unfortunately, they are likely to be expensive and may be difficult to obtain. Keep these four points in mind:

1. The functional aspects in the broad meaning of the term must be satisfactory. Sturdiness, comfort, appearance, and a reasonable cost are all possible with both traditional and contemporary furniture. They should come first.

2. Furniture should not be so extreme in its design that it will be dated, so that in the year 2020 it will be referred to, perhaps contemptuously, as "obviously 1990s." Only in a special area or room, one that is meant to be a "period piece" in terms of design, would an extreme design be suitable if it fits the character of the space. A reception area outside the administrative offices could be an instance.

3. The design of furniture should "fit" the building. This is a way of conveying a subtle issue of taste, and it is of critical aesthetic importance for the success of the building. Furniture should usually be of the same style as the building—contemporary or one of the classic period styles. Yet a tasteful blend can be harmonious, and a

contrasting accent can be very effective in carefully chosen locations. The Alvar Aalto tables and chairs in two rooms of Harvard's Lamont Library are liked by some and disliked by others. A Gothic or Renaissance piece in a contemporary rare book reading room may be found tasteful. An Italianate cabinet or Spanish chest can provide an item of interest. Such accents can add a richness and an interesting variation. However, furniture that is obviously left over from a tired building will look like a "hand-me-down" or army surplus and will not suit the building even if it may work functionally.

4. Consider also the economic aspect of quality, upkeep, and finishes, which are closely related. Quality is not good if upkeep is high or if frequent refinishing is necessary. The cost should have a definite relationship to quality and should generally be considered in connection with the expected length of useful life.

In addition to fulfilling the functions assigned to it, furniture and equipment should be attractive, sturdy, and comfortable or practical. Sturdiness depends to a large extent on unseen structural aspects of design and materials used. Good engineering involves a practical knowledge of factory procedures and also ingenuity. The problems of vandalism, discussed in Section 13.2.5, must also be considered. A study chair and table and other pieces of furniture and equipment can be said almost to pay for themselves in a relatively few years if no repairs are required. It is sometimes said, "the quality is built in." If that is indeed the case, the more expensive furnishings may well be the more economical.

13.4.2 Seating Accommodations

As an aid in planning layouts, suggestions are presented below for 13 arrangements for seating in reading areas and bookstacks. They are based on the theoretical discussion of seating arrangements in Chapter 7. Remember that academic and research (not public) libraries are under consideration and that the sizes and arrangements suggested are for academic and research use.

The physically challenged and the left-handed require a suitable proportion of specialized reading accommodations in most of these 13 examples. Accommodating left-handed users, for instance, applies to typing returns, tablet arms, and microtext reading arrangements. The working surface should be at a typing height of about 24 to 27 in. (610 to 685 mm) for computer terminals and microtext readers, except for those carrels high enough to clear the arms of a wheelchair, which are typically 30 in. (762 mm). It is also important to avoid obstructions under the carrel or table that could be hit by the wheelchair arms or the knees of the seated reader. (Note: Do not use counters for typing, because a second typist will create surface jiggle and increase sound reverberation for the other. Stand-alone desks, carrels, or stands are best.) Although the higher typing height represents the generally accepted standard, the lower height of 24 to 25 in. (610 to 635 mm) is more ideally suited to the requirements of machines that involve long sessions in a fairly rigid posture. Where a mouse is used to a large degree,

a slightly higher return or bread board to the side of the keyboard support can be an advantage.

1. *Single open carrels with the long axis of the tabletops at right angles to a wall.* (Figs. 13.12 to 13.15.) These may be in reading areas, in bookstacks with walls on one side and a subsidiary cross aisle on the other, or at the end of stack ranges beyond the aisle, or they may take the place of the last stack section in a range. Unless they are quite heavy, single carrels should be fastened to the wall or floor in some way so as not to get out of position and to help maintain connections for power and signal in support of task lighting and computers.

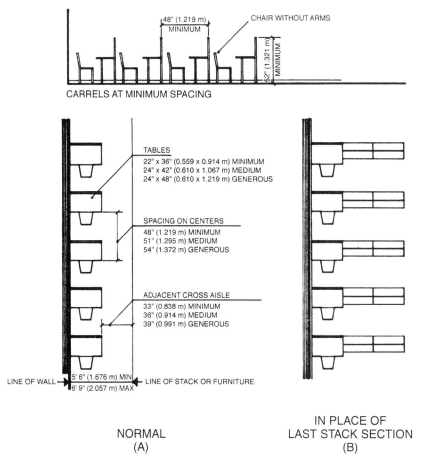

FIGURE 13.12   Carrels at right angles to a wall. (A) Suggests sizes and spacing and shows elevations. (B) Carrel in place of last stack section next to a wall. The working surface of the carrel must be in line with the stack range instead of the aisle, in order to make it easier to get into the chair. In other words, the 6-in. (0.152-m) recesses at the front support, as shown in the elevation, together with armless chairs are required to make these dimensions work. Omitting a carrel at one range would make the next carrel accessible for wheelchairs provided no chair is there (see fig. 13.8 for turning requirements). More generous spacing will allow armchairs and a carrel without the recessed front support. Note that application of code and ADA criteria will almost certainly result in wider aisles, particularly the one across the ends of the carrels. Handicapped access will be difficult with all but the most generous dimensions.

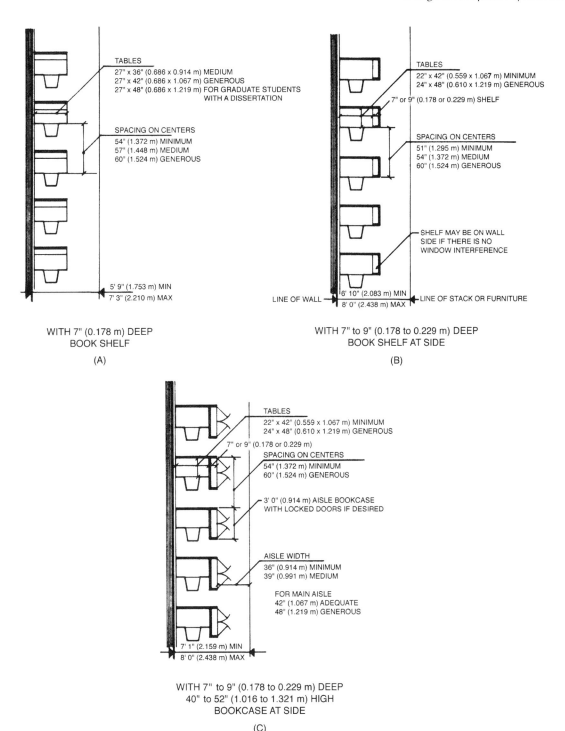

FIGURE 13.13 Carrels with shelves. (A) Shelf in front of reader. The table should be 5 in. (0.127 m) deeper than one without a shelf, and adequate spacing between carrels may be difficult to arrange where it is desired to align the carrels with stack ranges. (B) Shelf at one side instead of in front. (It can be at either side.) This arrangement requires more width but less depth. (C) Shelf at one side facing the aisle. This arrangement can provide more shelf capacity and greater privacy; it also demands greater total width. Also, at some stations, the open space between shelving units will need to be at least 3 ft (0.914 m) to accommodate a wheelchair—although it is not dimensioned, the sketch suggests about 2 ft (0.610 m) clear at this location. Note that application of code and ADA criteria will almost certainly result in wider aisles across the ends of the carrels than suggested by the minimum dimensions.

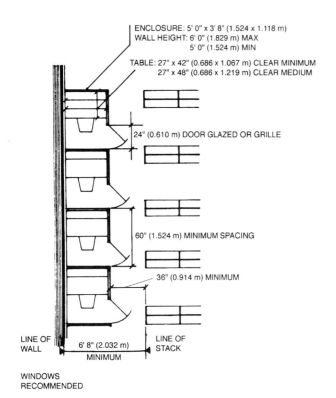

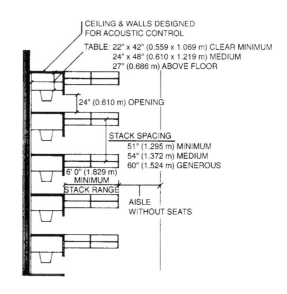

FIGURE 13.15   Partly open typing carrel in place of last stack section with acoustically treated walls and ceiling. These may be useful for dealing with the clicking of computers in some cases. Adjacent books also help to muffle sound. Absence of other seating close at hand makes doors unnecessary for acoustic separation. If two units are omitted, the next unit would be wheelchair accessible and allow a T-type turnaround, provided the absence of a chair. One would expect power and data access at these and most of the other carrels illustrated.

FIGURE 13.14   Closed carrels with door and shelf. The doors can be hinged as shown or pocket doors. If there is no window, wider spacing is desirable to prevent claustrophobia. Ventilation and lighting will present problems. The suggested wall height is more for privacy than security; where security is required, full-height (or nearly so) walls will be required together with provision for ventilation and a locking door. A few will need to be larger to accommodate wheelchairs, and the aisle between the range ends will almost certainly be larger than suggested where ADA criteria are met; the Uniform Building Code requires a minimum of 44 in. (1.118 m) for such aisles.

The suggested minimum size for the tabletops, without bookshelf or shelves above, is 22 × 36 in. (559 × 914 mm); medium size, 24 × 42 in. (610 × 1,067 mm); and generous, 24 × 48 in. (610 × 1,219 mm). Shelves are rarely recommended for undergraduate work or for carrels in the reference area. If they are used, 5 in. (127 mm) should be added to the depth of the tabletop. A preferable size is 27 × 42 in. (686 × 1,067 mm). A still better carrel for a graduate student writing a dissertation has a tabletop 27 × up to 48 in. (686 × 1,219 mm). Anything larger might be called extravagant, except where special equipment or large volumes will be used (for example, in art and music libraries and archival and manuscript reading rooms). For microtext readers or for a computer station with a large monitor, peripheral equipment, and space to have an open book or to

take notes, a carrel up to 60 in. (1,524 mm) wide and 36 in. (914 mm) deep is not too large. Most computers, and especially laptop computers, will require less space, but many will argue that a standard minimal carrel is inadequate. And, a few computer stations with potentially multiple monitors, a printer, possibly a separate disc drive or two, a scanner, a graphic input device, and maybe a camera of some kind will require even more space.

If the table in the bookstack can be placed in a line with the stack ranges, the reader is in a better position to look out for visual relief. If the stack ranges are only 4 ft (1.219 m) on centers and the tables are to have the same spacing, a table that is more than 22 in. (559 mm) deep will leave the student less than 26 in. (660 mm) to get in and out of a seat. This will be totally inadequate for the ADA. An armchair becomes questionable, and the table leg under the corner where one enters should be set back at least 6 in. (152 mm). Stack ranges 4 ft 6 in. (1.372 m) on centers will be possible on the same terms for a 27-in.-deep (686-mm) table, with a shelf provided above. Ranges 4 ft 3 in. (1.295 m) on centers with a 23-in. (584-mm) table give 28 in. (711 mm) behind the table, minus the thickness of the back of the table.

The carrels, of course, do not have to match the stack ranges in spacing. For graduate carrels and their access requirements, it may be desirable to provide greater distances on centers in spite of the resulting irregularity. Here the question of windows and the facade should be considered.

Single carrels similar to those just described, but with shelves to one side, are sometimes used. If space between carrel centers is at a premium, these may be useful. If the shelving faces or backs to the aisle, it can at the same time provide additional privacy. (See fig. 13.13, parts B and C.)

2. *Single closed carrels along a bookstack wall and opening into a subsidiary stack aisle.* (Fig. 13.14.) Sometimes called study cubicles or dissertation rooms, these are similar to the open carrels described above, but with partitions and a door. Unless considerably larger, they may be difficult to ventilate and to light and tend to cause claustrophobia. Partitions to the ceiling are not recommended for undergraduates; but, because security for scholars' papers is a prime rationale for this type of carrel, the walls should be high enough to prevent unauthorized access. If the area, including the adjacent aisle, is at least as much as 5 ft × 6 ft 8 in. (1.524 × 2.032 m), it can be used for graduate students if there is glass in the door. Light from an outside window will help.

An enclosed area of approximately 6 × 6 ft (1.829 × 1.829 m) provides adequate space for a generous work surface, a full section of shelving, and a two-drawer letter file, which many graduate students would welcome. With proper design, the space could easily be used by a person in a wheelchair.

3. *Single carrels in place of a stack section at the end of a book range.* (Fig. 13.12, part B.) As far as space use is concerned, this is the most economical way to provide seating. It gives a great deal of seclusion, which many readers want. It presents four problems, however:

a. The space from front to back is limited to the distance between range centers, which in some cases is minimal.

b. Unless the tabletop is specially designed to occupy the full depth of the double-faced range, as shown, it may be difficult to get into the chair because the tabletop will jut out into the aisle.

c. Some readers, particularly if there is no adjacent outside window, will feel too shut in for comfort.

d. Because the seat is at the end of a blind aisle, the length of the range should not be more than half that of a range with cross aisles at both ends. Many codes will limit the length to 20 ft (6.096 m) as the maximum for a dead-end aisle.

If acoustic walls are installed on all sides except at the stack aisle, such a carrel will be fine for computer typing and satisfactory for traditional typing and no door will be required. (See fig. 13.15.) The tabletop for typing should be at least 3 ft 6 in. (1.067 m) wide by at least 20 in. (508 mm) deep and 27 in. (686 mm) above the floor, instead of a standard 29 in. to 30 in. (736 mm to 762 mm). A work surface with adjustable height would be better. If used in this way as a typing carrel, with no door provided, the insertion of Celotex or other similar material between the front and back of the adjacent double-faced stack section will help acoustically, and the books themselves have good acoustical properties. However, this addition will reduce the flexibility for shelving the occasional oversized volume.

4. *Single seats facing a reading room or stack wall or a high partition down the center of a regular reading room table.* (Fig. 13.16.) These are

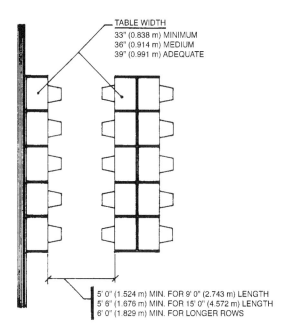

FIGURE 13.16 Reading-room table with divided partitions. Not very satisfactory if the table seats more than four and the reader is hemmed in on both sides. If light is hung from the partition, it tends to cause an unpleasant glare. If partitions between readers sitting side by side are extended on both sides to provide more privacy, they become too confining.

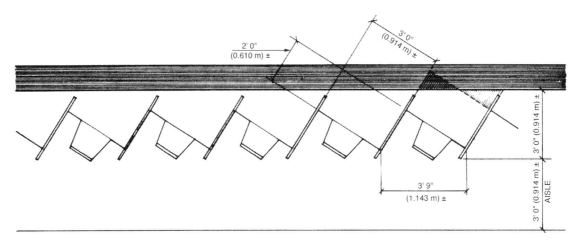

FIGURE 13.17   A dogleg carrel, though disliked by many, is a compromise for one facing a wall. The partition on one side is extended enough to provide seclusion; the carrel is open on the other. As elsewhere, the cross aisle will be wider under many codes; with a wider aisle, these carrels are easily wheelchair accessible.

sometimes provided with a high partition at the sides, projecting 6 in. (152 mm) beyond the table-top into the aisle, to cut the reader off from the neighbors. There is no place to look out when leaning back in the chair, except directly at the neighbor to the right or left. (These seats have been used in long rows at Bryn Mawr College, M.I.T., Cornell University, the library on the undergraduate campus at the University of Tokyo, and elsewhere.) They are not recommended, except in an open area in groups of four, where the reader can look out in at least one direction, because few students enjoy facing a blank wall, unless they can look out at least a few feet on one side without seeing a neighbor close at hand.

Single carrels in a sawtooth or dogleg arrangement is another variant. (Fig. 13.17.) This style was used at the University of Notre Dame Library and is popular in Sweden and elsewhere. This arrangement is preferable to those directly facing a wall, as the reader can look out on one side and still is protected from the neighbors. It requires more space than carrels facing a wall, but less than the typical arrangement of carrels perpendicular to a wall, and results in an unequal-sided table surface. Left-handed persons would prefer carrels facing toward the left instead of right, because that gives the full depth on the writing side.

Any carrel and nearby building wall can (and most will) suffer marking, so the choice of wall surface is especially important. This is particularly true where the wall presents an inviting tablet, as may be the case in this as well as other examples.

5. *Double carrels in rows in a reading room.* (Figs. 7.5 and 13.18.) Working-surface sizes pro-

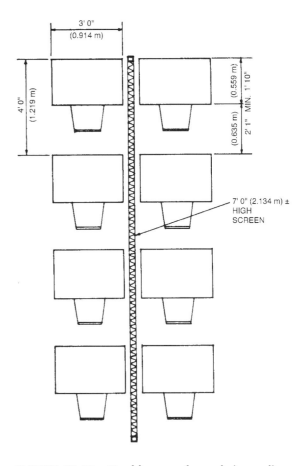

FIGURE 13.18   Double row of carrels in reading area separated by a screen. Carrels can be used with or without backs. A few will need more area for seating where ADA criteria are met (see fig. 12.36).

posed for type 1 above are adequate. Separating partitions should be at least 52 in. (1.320 m) in height in the front and on one side of the working area. Or, partitions in front can be held down to 3 in. to 10 in. (76 mm to 254 mm) above the tabletop, because a full view of one's neighbor all the time is less distracting than a head bobbing up and down occasionally; but 52 in. (1.320 m) above the floor is preferable. In some places two rows of individual tables separated by a screen (as in fig. 13.18) may be useful.

6. *Double carrels in rows in place of two stack ranges.* (Figs. 13.19 and 13.20.) A carrel size of 33 × 22 in. (838 × 558 mm) can be used in place of

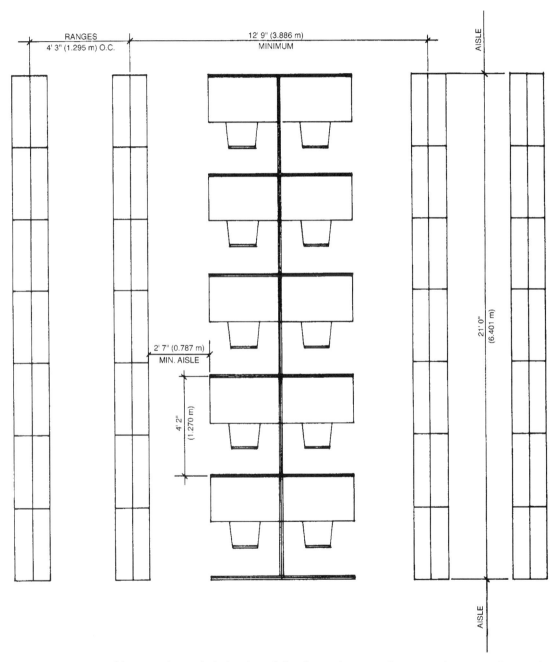

FIGURE 13.19 Double row of carrels in bookstack in place of two stack ranges. The currently mandated wider range aisles in the United States will improve this configuration, which, as illustrated, is minimal (the dimensions suggested require 7-in. (0.178-m) nominal shelving to achieve a 36-in. (0.914-m) range aisle). The minimum aisle illustrated does not meet most current codes in the United States. A few carrels should have larger seat space for the ADA, or the horizontal panels at the lower edge could be omitted.

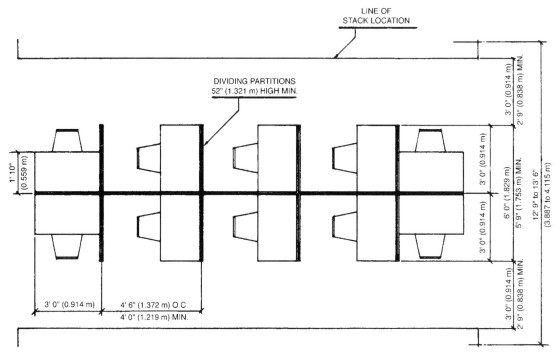

FIGURE 13.20   Double row of carrels in bookstack in place of two stack ranges, with end pairs turned at right angles to provide adjustment to length of ranges. As elsewhere, the access or range aisle will need to be wider in most cases; this will help the configuration.

two stack ranges, when ranges are 4 ft 3 in. (1.295 m) on centers, leaving an aisle of about 31 in. (787 mm) if 12-in. (305-mm) base shelves are used. A size of 36 × 22 in. (914 × 558 mm) can be used comfortably with ranges 4 ft 6 in. (1.372 m) on centers. By placing one or both end pairs at right angles to the others, the carrel range and the stack range length can be made to match with tabletops and distances between centers of standard size.

7. *Double carrels at right angles to a wall.* (Figs. 13.21 and 13.22.) This style can have partitions on two sides and with two readers facing in opposite directions or the same way. (This style has been used at Brandeis, in Cornell's Uris Library, and in the Douglass College Library at Rutgers.) The partitions should be at least 52 in. (1.321 m) above the floor to prevent visual distraction. Tabletops of the same sizes as in type 1 above are recommended. A distance of 4½ ft (1.372 m) on centers represents a minimum, with 5 ft (1.524 m) on centers preferred. These two variations are possible but not recommended, because the readers are sitting side by side. The arrangements described in the next three paragraphs are preferred.

8. *Double-staggered carrels with the adjacent tabletops overlapping by one-half their depth.* (Figs. 13.23 and 13.24.) Sizes are the same as in type 1

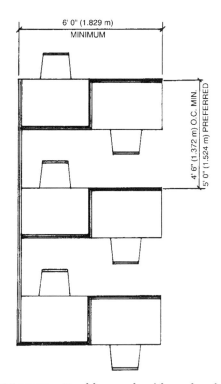

FIGURE 13.21   Double carrels with readers facing in different directions. Used at Douglass College at Rutgers and Uris Undergraduate Library at Cornell. This arrangement is quite reasonable, but the arrangement shown in fig. 13.23 is recommended.

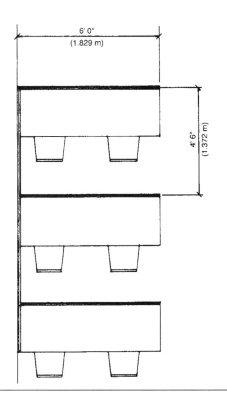

FIGURE 13.22   Double carrels facing in the same direction. This arrangement is an adaptation of that used at Brandeis. It encourages conversation and thus is not generally recommended. However, with increasing group work in academic settings, this kind of carrel combined with some acoustic treatment may make sense. With slightly more space between the carrels, perhaps three seats rather than two, and slightly deeper carrels, this arrangement works reasonably well for small-group video viewing.

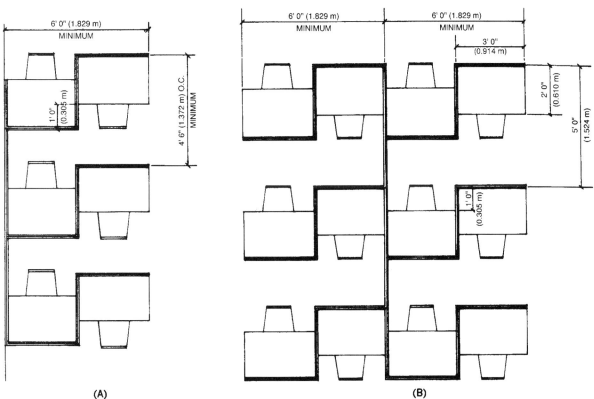

(A)

(B)

FIGURE 13.23   Double-staggered carrels. (A) Double-staggered carrel adjacent to a wall. The carrel by the wall will be helped by a window. Partitions should be 52 in. (1.321 m) high or higher (recommended). (B) Double-staggered carrels on each side of a screen or partition. A space saver, but recommended only when necessary to provide required seating capacity. The backs of the inside carrels should be no more than 40 in. (1.016 m) high to ease claustrophobia.

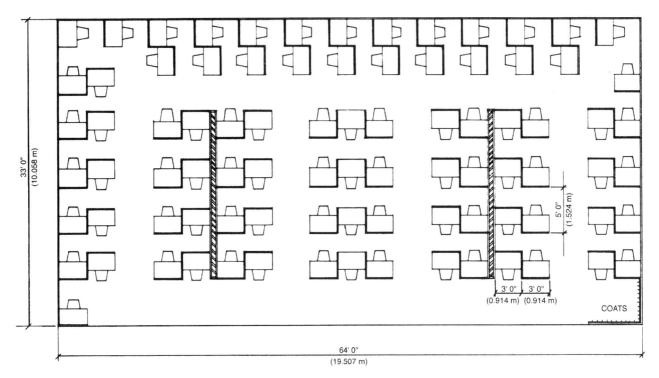

33' × 64' (10.058 × 19.507 m) Study Hall of 2,112 ft² (196.211 m²)
with 88 Seats

FIGURE 13.24   Triple-staggered carrels. This arrangement can be used in a large reading area in conjunction with double-staggered or other arrangements, or in place of three stack ranges that are 4 ft (1.219 m) or more (in most cases) on centers. If the top of the back of the center carrel is held to no more than 40 in. (1.016 m), the occupant will feel less hemmed in.

above placed along walls, with 4½ ft (1.372 m) minimum on centers and 5 ft (1.524 m) preferred. Placing pairs of them on each side of a screen or low partition is quite possible, if the back of the inside carrel is kept low.

9. *Triple-staggered carrels in a reading area.* (Fig. 13.24.) These are preferably 5 ft (1.524 m) on centers with tabletops of the sizes proposed for others. If the center carrel in each group of three is thought to be too confined, the partition at the back of the table can be left out altogether or, preferably, held down in height to from 3 in. to 10 in. (76 mm to 254 mm) above the tabletop to give some privacy. Or, if the lateral distance permits, the middle carrel can be wider, making it attractive for some student study needs and offsetting the disadvantage of being in the middle.

One set can be separated from another set of three by an aisle at least 3 ft (0.914 m) wide; preferably one 3½ to 4 ft (1.067 to 1.219 m) wide should be used. A series of them, or of double-staggered carrels as proposed in the preceding arrangement, on each side of a partition might be considered in some cases, if a very large seating capacity is required with a small collection of books. Such an arrangement might be set up in a city university in a large study hall in order to increase capacity or be used in place of three stack ranges. (See fig. 13.24.)

10. *"Pinwheel" groups of four carrels.* (Fig. 13.25.) These pinwheel groups have been successful in large reading areas, but they tend to give an impression of disorderliness when not in an alcove. However, this impression may not be altogether bad, depending on one's philosophy, as it reduces the feeling of regimentation. If the alcove is 12 ft × 12 ft (3.658 m × 3.658 m) in the clear, tabletops 22 in. × 36 in. (558 mm × 914 mm) are recommended, with partitions at least 52 in. (1.320 m) in height, which extend 6 in. (152 mm) beyond the end of each table. Shelves are ordinarily not recommended, particularly if the tabletop is less

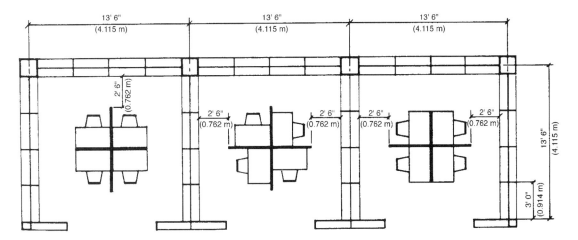

FIGURE 13.25   Carrels in alcoves. The pinwheel arrangement as illustrated is suitable if ADA access is not required and if the alcove is at least 12 × 12 ft (3.658 × 3.658 m) inside measurement. Not recommended for heavily used collections.

than 27 in. (686 mm) deep. Carrels with shelves or with a larger work surface will require somewhat more space.

This arrangement fits perfectly in a 27-ft (8.230-m) column spacing with two alcoves to a bay. If the module size is 25 ft 6 in. (7.772 m), the space in each alcove will be reduced a total of 9 in. (229 mm), and one of the shelf sections will be only 27 in. (686 mm). It can be used for shorter shelves or set up as wall space for a bulletin board or for a picture or other decoration.

If ventilation is adequate, alcoves can be partially closed in on the fourth side by a single-faced or double-faced book section, which may help to use the space to advantage and make possible the best utilization of the available bay size. The main aisle between double rows of alcoves can be as narrow as 4½ ft (1.372 m). (See also fig. 12.11, part C.)

11. *Carrels in alcoves with two-directional tables for four.* (Fig. 13.25.) These carrels can be installed with 52-in.-high (1.321-m) partitions in each direction. These alcoves may be as little as 9 ft (2.742 m) deep and 11 ft 3 in. to 12 ft (3.430 to 3.658 m) wide in the clear. With a bay 25 ft 6 in. (7.772 m) and a main aisle 4 ft 6 in. (1.372 m), an unusually large capacity is possible. (See also fig. 12.11, parts A and B.) With a 27-ft (8.230-m) bay, the space utilization is still good, and the main aisle can be widened to 6 ft (1.829 m), or the size of the carrels can be increased. The question of shelving books in alcoves such as these should be considered as, if frequent access is required, their use will be an annoyance for the readers.

12. *Individual lounge chairs.* (Fig. 13.26.) This style takes somewhat more space per seat than does a chair at a table, as is clear from the figure. Besides providing the preferred seating of some students at some times, the arrangement also can

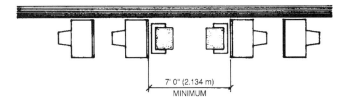

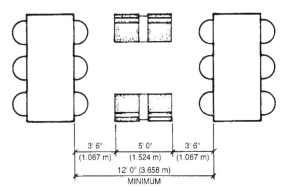

FIGURE 13.26   Lounge chairs replacing carrels along a wall or between tables for six in a reading area to relieve monotony. Conversation may be encouraged by this arrangement. Footrests are recommended.

break the monotony of a long row of carrels or tables. Facing lounge chairs must not be closer than 7 ft (2.134 m), otherwise one of the two chairs merely becomes a footstool. Placing two lounge chairs beside each other will invite sleeping if there are no armrests.

This style requires consideration of anchoring the chairs, and possible provision of side tables or coffee tables and footstools, each of which affects the space needed per seat. Also, remember that different light fixtures are needed to serve table-based and lounge-based work. With possible use of table or floor lamps, the difference in lighting can be one of the several attractions of lounge seating and will provide visual variation and interest also for those who work near the lounge area.

13. *Pairs or groups of lounge or semilounge chairs.* (Figs. 13.26 and 13.27.) The configuration options are many. One common arrangement is paired seats attached on opposite sides of a low table, which is at least 1 ft (305 mm) wide, preferably 1½ ft to 2 ft (457 mm to 610 mm), and of seat height. These may be preferable to single chairs, which are more likely to be pushed out of position. They can be used in place of two single carrels if they take less than 9 ft (2.743 m) in length or in pairs or trios between rows of carrels or tables in a large reading area. However, as a single unit, some flexibility is lost.

In reading areas, lounge chairs should be arranged so as to discourage sizable groups from taking over the area for conversation. Such groups should go to a group-study room or outside the building. Yet, it is natural and common for two people to wish to study together. In this case, a coffee table can hold the books and papers not in their laps, and eliminating the side table will bring the two lounge chairs closer together, with the result that the two will talk more softly than if they needed to talk over the table.

Many of these 13 arrangements for individual seating accommodations in lounge chairs or at carrels can be placed between rows of standard library tables in a large reading area. They can also be placed, preferably in bay-sized groups interspersed with carrels, in a large bookstack. Small groups, sometimes called oases, as used at Princeton, may not be desirable because they tend to complicate shelving arrangements and to become noisy, although many librarians like this arrangement and conversations buried in a stack should not disturb others. (See fig. 13.28.) The larger

groups can be made quite attractive by changes in the lighting and floor covering; these breaks in the monotony of a very large stack are often a relief.

13.4.3 Bookstack Arrangements

The following eight principles should be kept in mind in connection with bookstack layouts.

1. Traffic patterns should be kept as simple as possible, particularly if open access is provided, so that the uninitiated or infrequent user can easily find the material wanted.

2. If there is more than one main aisle in a stack, finding books becomes more of a problem unless the aisle pattern is easy to perceive.

3. Blind corners or pockets, which result from stairwells and elevators, should be avoided if possible. If for any reason they seem necessary, it is suggested that they be used for purposes other than housing parts of the main collection, where there should be a simple and logical sequence of classes. (See fig. 13.29.)

4. Review the flow of the book classification sequence to eliminate complexities. Ideally, there will be no leaps from one part to another on any one floor in following the classification flow. Simplicity in layout is desirable.

5. Every aisle should be useful to the space on both sides of it, not as in the upper right corner of fig. 13.29. This can sometimes be accomplished by placing carrels, studies, small conference rooms, or other rooms, such as seminars, on one side of an aisle, with book ranges on the other. (See fig. 12.15.) Book ranges can run to a wall with no cross aisle beyond, or to a carrel at the wall end in place of the last section or sections of stacks, as shown in fig. 13.12, part B.

A blind or dead-end aisle between stack ranges (as at the top of fig. 13.29) should not be more than one-half the length agreed upon as the maximum suitable for a range with aisles at each end and, where the building code applies, no longer than the length of a dead-end corridor.

6. A bookstack arrangement that is a simple rectangle with no more than one center and two side aisles is desirable, other things being equal, but it is not always practical, particularly in a very large stack area. If more aisles are required, be sure to keep the traffic pattern as simple as possible. (See fig. 12.18.)

7. All stacks should have prominently displayed on each level in at least one place, and preferably in more than one, a chart or plan

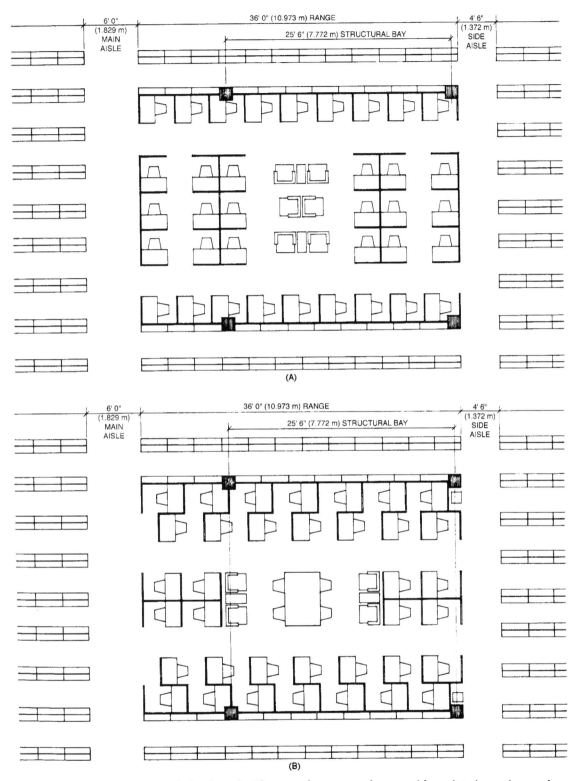

FIGURE 13.27 **Large "oases" in bookstacks. These are large enough to provide variety in seating, and special lighting can help to overcome the monotony of a large bookstack. Less than 25 ft² (2.323 m²) per person is required in these layouts. A special carrel will be required where it is notched around a column. If desired, either oasis shown can be reduced to one full bay in size without causing complications. For a research library, this arrangement provides very restricted work space for the individual reader.**

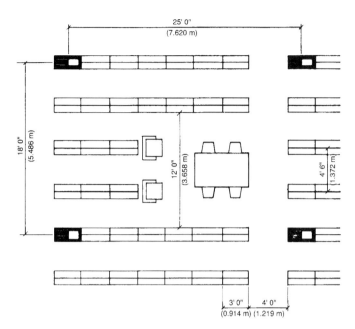

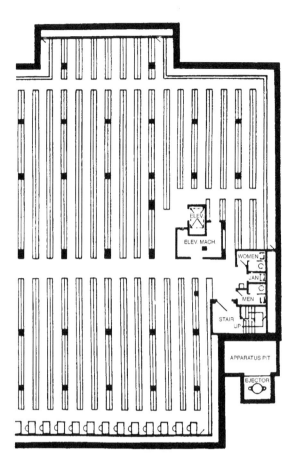

FIGURE 13.28 Small oasis in bookstacks. This tends to disrupt shelving arrangements. If done as suggested here, it may promote undesirable sociability. Such oases may become noisy unless occupied completely by individual seating with readers well protected from one another.

FIGURE 13.29 Blind corners and pockets in a bookstack. The shelving above the long, secondary cross aisle at the top and that to the right of the elevator can represent pockets unsuitable for the main collection, which should be arranged in a simple and logical sequence.

showing the stack layout, the deployment of books on the range sections, and exit routes. The chart should always be oriented with the top of the chart in the direction the reader is facing. Too often this orientation has been neglected, with confusing results. Emergency telephones and perhaps OPACs and public computers should also be widely and obviously placed.

8. Stairs and elevators should be enclosed to reduce fire risks. There should be adequate lobby space by any elevator door so that passengers (staff or public, including wheelchair users) and book trucks can get in and out without difficulty, and the same is even more necessary for the stairs if they have doors that open into stack aisles. This area attracts graffiti; thus, the selection of surface treatment is important. Three types of stack stairs are shown with dimensions in fig. 6.19.

The total stack capacity depends primarily on the number of equivalent full-height stack sections, double-faced plus any that are single-faced, that are installed in the area available, minus a small percentage of total shelving if there are book-return shelves in every range, or if shelf spaces at

counter height are left for brief consultation of books. Space needed for such items as phones, OPACs, pencil sharpeners, stack directories, drinking fountains, and the like is negligible and can be ignored, though the locations will need to be determined as the design progresses. If the problems stemming from column sizes and column spacing are left out of consideration, capacity will be based on: (a) the width and number of main and subsidiary cross aisles, (b) the length of ranges, and (c) range spacing on centers, which in turn must be affected by stack aisle widths and shelf depths. This economy of stack layout was discussed in detail in Chapter 6.

The above stresses clarity of aisle patterns, simplicity of bookshelf layouts, elimination of pockets and dead ends, and good stack charts or plans and emergency telephones. These plus good lighting are the essential criteria against which to test the design development of bookstack arrangements for a feeling of safety and utility. With large student populations using large open stacks, this design for the physical and psychological safety of people must be of the greatest importance. Without personal safety, an open bookstack is not feasible in any college or university, and the ability to fulfill the objectives of higher education is severely crippled.

Security personnel concerns treated above in Section 13.2.5 also pertain to bookstack arrangements, as do those mentioned in Section 5.3.6. As one example, the upper underground stack level of the 1990s addition to the New York Public Library Research Library building is fully outfitted with electrical compact shelving integrated with a security system for rare books. Each staff person must swipe a card and enter a PIN to access the shelving, which automatically returns to a closed position once the staff member exits the system.

13.4.4 Computer Terminals and the Catalog

This section discusses briefly the requirements of the automated catalog and other machine-related equipment, supplementing the treatment in Section 7.3.

Computer terminals need not be centrally located, as are card catalogs, or reference collections in book format, and, usually, manual lending charge systems. However, a certain amount of skill is required to use any but the most straightforward computer system. Because of this problem of learning the inquiry process, it is common to locate a few terminals near a staffed information or reference desk so that user assistance can be readily provided.

For bibliographic access, if a main library is planning to have, for example, 18 public terminals, perhaps ten would be placed by the card catalog (where such still exist) or near the entry and near an information desk; three might be located in the reference department near the main service point; three or four might be spread out in the major stack or reading areas; and one or two might be located in the periodicals reading area. Peer assistance is facilitated by some clustering. This distribution is, of course, a matter for local decision as many factors can bear on the distribution pattern.

At a service point where the online catalog is provided by terminal access, most of the terminals should be on a counter where they can be used by a standing person. The counter should be some 3 in. (76 mm) below normal counter height to put the keyboard at a convenient elbow level for most people. A few terminals should be provided at tables with seats, for those who prefer not to stand or who need to do extensive searching, and in this case the table surface should be at 25 in. (635 mm). At least one of these positions should be at a height where 30-in. (762-mm) arms of a wheelchair can fit easily under the table.

The proportion of terminals at stand-up and sitting positions is also a matter for local consideration. If a library needs to encourage brief use to minimize queuing and to keep costs down, such use is encouraged by terminals arranged for standing. It may be desirable to arrange terminal positions so they could be raised or lowered if custom changes and as experience dictates. For example, keyboards mounted flush in the counter or screens partially inset and tilted as one might read a book might become the preferred style, served by a higher counter.

Although there is no exact formula for the appropriate number of terminals, the quantities of catalog access stations are discussed in Section 7.3, where it is suggested that as many as one OPAC per 30 average daily library visitors may be appropriate, and more may be required depending on such factors as the amount of data on the OPAC (such as course reserves), the paucity of computers elsewhere, and the diurnal pattern of reader visitations. The fact that catalog information can be obtained from nearly any computer connected to a phone line or to the network suggests that the number might be pushed down in some cases, but the convenience of easily accessed, quick, dedicated OPAC stations located with some staff assistance available still will have merit. Even where the numbers projected do become excessive for strictly the catalog-access need, other needs can be met at these computers; the rate of use will likely not diminish with increased availability of laptops. The appropriate number for a particular library is influenced by several factors:

1. How decentralized is the library system, and how many service points are provided per building? Centralization will require fewer terminals without undue queuing.

2. How extensive are the data files available on the terminal? Use will be more limited if only the last five years of monograph holdings are accessible; use will be more extensive if full retrospective holdings and if journal indexing and abstracting are available, or if some items have full-text display. Increasingly, any connected computer can access not only the catalog, but an ever-increasing array of data throughout the world.

3. How easy is the computer system to use? If basic instruction is off-line, or if online prompts are clear and simple, the terminal time is reduced.

4. Is an online public catalog linked to a circulation system, campus bookstore holdings, or a statewide database? And is local printout provided from the display? The convenience of such an arrangement will likely increase its use by library clientele, especially if comparable printing service is not provided elsewhere.

5. Is there heavy use by visiting scholars and others from outside the institution? Access by the general public can have a considerable influence, especially in an urban setting. Although many library catalogs are accessible from any computer through the World Wide Web, in many cases the access protocol limits general public access to computers in the library.

6. What is provided in campus computer labs? If these labs have the local OPAC database, printing, 24-hour unlimited access, and workstations in sufficient numbers, pressure on the library bibliographic center will be greatly relieved.

The best guide is the local experience with online catalogs. As with the provision of such other equipment as microtext readers, tape players, or calculators, the number provided can be equal to or a bit short of the anticipated demand, depending on available funds and educational goals. The demand may well grow rapidly and then level off. Only time, enrollment, data accessibility, changing technology, and financial aspects will shape the actual future. Until use levels become more consistent, it is probably best to provide for the electrical capacity and space, and then build up terminal numbers as observation of use suggests and funds permit.

The numbers and distribution of terminals designed to support a videodisk system or other systems providing complete text may be somewhat different. A compact disc (CD) system intended to supplement the reference collection, for example, would likely require that most of the terminals should be in the reference area at the start. As the system grows in use and in capacity, it might in time replace the bulk of the reference collection in book format. When this occurs, it could make sense to distribute most of the terminals in appropriate subject reading areas of the library, though the cost and vulnerability to damage or misuse of the machines, difficulty of system use, and need for servicing all argue for centralization at first. However, mounting this reference information on the campus network, accessed by PCs and laptops via file servers, can reduce the central load and greatly improve accessibility. This is another case where rapid changes in technology and system economics will prompt local changes, for example, as digital videodisk (DVD) technology supersedes the compact disc.

As the proportion of information in reference books shifts to digital formats, the number of public access computers should increase, depending on factors similar to the above six for online catalog terminals. For example, when it is anticipated that 50 percent of reference information will be accessed by a computer, and the program provides for 30 seats in the reference area and a peak of 10 users at one time, then it is likely that five reference terminals would be about the right number. When indexes, abstracts, directories, and full texts on file servers can be accessed campuswide from workstations, PCs, and laptop computers, some believe there might be a reduction in the need for reference terminals.

It is obvious that library staff use reference books as heavily as do other library users. Thus, videotext terminals will need to be at the reference desk as well as terminals for accessing library catalogs and indexing-abstracting services. Desk or counter configuration may today need to accommodate two terminals as a minimum. Printers for hard copy will be attached, or wired to a nearby location.

At the reference desk, it is very helpful to have two linked monitors back to back, so there can be staff discussion with the patron about the search strategy being pursued. Such an arrangement, allowing both parties to watch the search, is fast and convenient, and is preferable to a "lazy Susan" turntable for the monitor as wire twisting can result if the turntable can turn through the full circle. Simultaneous viewing of one monitor is possible if the screen is placed at the end of a counter so the patron can watch over the shoulder of the searcher, though that obviously is a less desirable alternative.

Even though the above argues for a somewhat larger service desk or counter than historically has been the case, remember that a staff member can do only so much at the desk and the library can afford only a limited staff. Thus, the planner should accommodate networked computers at the service desk, but the image of future technological use must not lead to an excessive provision of equipment space at this site. Similar judgment may be applied to the use of computers for access to journals, government documents, manuscripts, and other areas of the collection as this technology develops.

The lending of materials is almost totally self-service, using "smart cards," at such libraries as the Kanazawa Institute of Technology in Japan and Tilburg University Library in The Netherlands. For example, at Tilburg all students, members of the faculty, and university employees carry an electronic identification and account card, in which there is a computer chip. This card enables patrons to check out and return books themselves at two different machines, one of which takes the book away on a conveyor belt after changing the computer record to show that the book has been returned. Any overdue charge is automatically deducted from the card. This system does not entirely do away with the need for a traditional circulation desk, yet it does permit decentralization of the borrowing process. Similar systems of self-charge are becoming more common in the United States, though experience suggests that they do not yet remove much in the way of staffed circulation stations. They do, however, provide a means for students to avoid queues during peak traffic, and they may, over time, become as accepted as an automated teller at the bank.

At work, study, and reading positions throughout the library, the space per reader is different because of technology. Computers used in association with printed texts or taking notes will require a work surface somewhat larger than that of a standard carrel. Though the work process will vary, it always requires a larger table surface, a telecommunications data port, and electricity. Such a work surface of 30 × 60 in. (762 × 1,524 mm) is not excessive for many installations. Even space for laptop use will have the same work area and connectivity. There should be space on one or both sides of the computer for the user to place books, papers, notebooks, a purse, and so on, and for the library in central locations to mount a briefing flip chart or post simple instructions for entry into the catalog search process. There should be space for a printer if that capability is to be provided. For each of these computers, connection to the network by a small coaxial cable or a cable similar to a telephone line and two heavy-duty electrical outlets are required; four are recommended as a minimum so that one might be available for test equipment. In most cases, some degree of wire management is also useful. IBM's *A Building Planning Guide for Communication Wiring* (2d ed., 1984, though current in 1996) listed in the Bibliography (Section 4w) is useful for the full range of aspects for planning cable routing.

Staff access computers should not be forgotten for collection development, processing, communications, and other functions. Where staff or patrons are expected to sit at a computer for many hours, there should be special concern for ergonomic comfort. Unlike reading a book, using a computer often requires a relatively fixed posture over long periods, which, in turn, suggests that superior seating and other work area features should be considered. Until the day when each staff member has a computer (which is already the case in many institutions), the height of the chair for a shared workstation must be adjustable, and the work surface should perhaps initially be placed somewhat lower than the standard typing height of 27 in. (686 mm). A height of 24 in. to 25 in. (610 mm to 635 mm) has been suggested. Some staff will benefit from a footrest, and the back as well as the seat of a chair for a shared workstation should be easily adjustable.

Computers and most printers still make some noise, though much less than a decade ago. Where noise is a concern, machines should be isolated acoustically. The best acoustic isolation includes providing partitions that fully enclose the space, running from the floor to the underside of the floor above. The treatment of ductwork may require attention, and the door may require insulation, especially for a high-speed impact printer. Laser printers and quieter keyboard action eliminate the problem in nearly all cases.

Screen reflective glare can be a problem, as it is with television and microtext readers. If the screen is nearly vertical, the source of glare for the computer will be quite different than it is for books. The image of a bright window behind the reader will be reflected in the screen, thereby making its use unpleasant if not impossible. The dimming of lights is generally not required for computer terminals, although an exception might be in an area of excessive illumination. Bright light sources that fall within peripheral vision will be a problem even more than they are for reading a book. Because of the angle of the screen, the computer user can be very sensitive to this kind of problem. As with laptops, desktop computers with adjustable screens ameliorate this problem.

Computer machine rooms go beyond the scope of this volume, except to note that, should one be part of the library program, expert advice must be obtained. Concerns about security, access, power, fire protection, mechanical systems, radio frequency disturbance, floor loading, and the like should be addressed. Workstations, minicomputers, and file servers are, however, now common in libraries. They require modest space and current installation and operational conditions, which change with each generation of technology. Space layouts and specifications for today are probably roughly sufficient in planning building spaces for tomorrow. Yet any plans for construction must meet the then-current technical requirements for the chosen system of equipment.

A few general comments can be made at this time, while IBM's *A Building Planning Guide for Communication Wiring* is detailed. Power and data receptacles can be reached by cabling in at least four different methods, each of which has its costs and advantages. Cable can be laid under a raised floor, as is common in major computer mainframe rooms or in a sophisticated language laboratory. Cable can be pulled through plenum spaces between or under floor beams, sometimes running it beside mechanical ducts and sprinkler pipes. Cable can be pulled through prefabricated channels within steel decking, using a cross grid spaced for anticipated access needs and incorporating covered hollow-access boxes. Or, conduit can be laid within off-the-shelf cable trays attached to the underside of a floor slab. In each of these, it is necessary to continue the conduit through walls, floors, or electronic chases built into custom casework. This is necessary in order

to reach from the central electrical and data room or closet of the building (where the telephone company cable and campus fiber-optic, Ethernet, or other data network reach the building) to local LAN servers or other distribution points on floors and to rooms and areas.

Design development review would include study of the power and data distribution to serve each part of the building. Questions to be asked are of the following type, some of which will not be answered until the design process continues into the contract document or working drawing phase. Is the current philosophy of access to digital resources and the teaching of digital search strategy for the institution met? Is there sufficient anticipation of future changes and needs, as much as can be foreseen? Is it understood how your successors will get wire to any table or carrel or service counter in the library? Will it be simple to replace all classroom technology to utilize new capacities? Are the infrastructure components (the phone closets, the distribution of cables, the main building service entry) logically arranged to minimize the problems of future developments? Does the basis of the budget accommodate the level of technology anticipated in several years when the building will be activated? Are the desktop outlets conceptually coordinated with the proposed furniture layout? Can the library staff with installation responsibilities manage equipment and cabling changes with the proposed raceway access method? Have furniture layouts been done skillfully to minimize the need for unattractive power poles, sometimes called energy pillars? Although resolution of the details can come in review of final working drawings, it is wise to do as much critique of these technical plans as possible at this stage as revisions will be easier and less costly.

Card catalog use will diminish as online catalogs are increasingly adopted. It seems probable that the computer-based OPAC will be the common form used throughout the world in academic and research libraries. Any library that today relies on card catalogs is referred to the second edition of this book, where pages 449–55 provide detailed layout guidance for catalog cases and seven illustrations that would still be helpful for small and large libraries. Note that fig. 13.11 in this third edition gives a plan for a large card catalog layout that, in 1980, included eight seated work positions designed for use of OPAC CRTs, a transitional plan that worked well until this card catalog was removed in 1995 (the catalog records having by then been entirely online for several years) and the space considerably redeployed.

13.5
The Review Process

Three techniques may be used in the design development review process: (1) A general display and widely distributed description of the project, such as to the faculty; (2) presentations of the project to appropriate groups, such as to several committees or groups with special interest and responsibility; and (3) detailed review by individuals and small groups, such as library working units. The latter two techniques are most appropriate, as the documents will have become more detailed and are less suitable for general display, except perhaps the floor plans. Donors, trustees, friends of the library, and others will be interested in any significant changes that may have occurred since the schematics. People concerned with energy, maintenance, access, safety, and the like will take a greater interest as the building systems are designed in greater detail. Of course, the librarian should undertake a thorough review.

Although a series of formal steps can be followed in reviewing schematic designs and design development plans, the most creative work is usually done through solitary efforts or in the discussions and exchange of ideas when members of the planning team interact with one another. It is in response to those questions and probing challenges, which sometimes back the architect or librarian figuratively to the wall, that a previously held concept is dropped, a new thought emerges, a variation is proposed, and an improvement in the design solution begins to take shape.

Some of these sessions can be difficult and some topics may be discussed for weeks or months. As an example, the Newberry Library in Chicago worked with a superior architect and had good internal planning specialists and good help from consultants. Three major areas of contention arose between the architects and the client with respect to the 10-story bookstack facility, which was occupied in early 1982. The architect wanted to have windows at least in the four corners of this bookstack building, and it was only after considerable debate that the library succeeded in eliminating all windows for reasons

of security to the collections. A second point was the question of structural floors. The architect wished to have a poured floor for every second level and to have tiered stacks for the two levels resting on each structural floor. Here again, the discussion of functional advantages and costs was finally resolved to the satisfaction of the library staff when they were able to prove that the cost of the alternative designs was a toss-up and that flexibility and protection against fire and water were improved if each floor was a poured structure. A third issue was the location of the addition on the site. This was a hotly debated matter, with the architect wanting it to be centered at the rear of the original building, which was itself a very symmetrical structure. The library administration was able after months of debate to locate the addition at the extreme west end of the site on the basis that it leaves far better space on the block for a still later addition, provides more useful space for delivery and parking in the interim, anticipates a more economical construction whenever another addition is built, and presents an appearance that many regard as equal if not superior to the plan that had it centered on the back of the original building.

From the preceding example, it can be seen that, for the librarian who has been directly involved in the design effort, the review process at the end of the design development phase should be fairly straightforward, assuming the major arguments have earlier been settled. The program requirements for specific space allocations and arrangements should have been essentially completed during the schematic review, except where there have been major changes, which, of course, can happen. Even so, the outline specifications often will contain a space analysis that may warrant review.

The librarian or the library representative or both must be current with the development of the plans in detail. Because of this closeness to the project, it may be useful to involve fresh personnel in the review process. The design development phase will be the last time that it will be fairly easy to involve a larger representation of the staff and others in a fairly thorough review, as the construction documents are fairly difficult for the novice to read and understand, and their bulk generally limits easy distribution.

The design development review process may be similar to the schematic review process except that, by this stage, major changes of space configuration cannot generally be tolerated. Before the institution signs off on the design development phase for the mechanical system, the programming sections, particularly those in Chapter 5 dealing with the control of the environment, should be reviewed. Engineering decisions made at this phase should be considered as fairly fixed; changes later will be costly.

Be sure the library representatives and others from the institution fully understand where the architect has made changes from the schematic designs, and why. These changes and the outline construction specifications require particular consideration as part of the review process. Warranting careful attention also are those design aspects that are now in greater detail, including perhaps the following, several of which have previously been mentioned but deserve emphasis (the institutional planning office, safety offices, and others sharing in the review will have their own and different aspects that will be checked or rechecked at this stage):

Is adequate access provided for those who are physically limited or challenged?

Is there a need for heating devices under the entry walk for eliminating slippery conditions from ice and snow?

Have door saddles or sills been avoided except where absolutely necessary for weather control? (Door sills, though a problem for book truck traffic, can serve as a critical weather stop eliminating penetration of water and drafts.)

Are selected doors wide enough to move in major equipment?

May extreme narrowness and height of entrance doors cause warping and other maintenance problems?

Is the arrangement of the collections clear, simple, and workable?

Is there appropriate environmental isolation for those areas of the building that warrant special criteria?

Are the spaces dimensioned adequately so as to permit reasonable furniture and equipment layouts? Test every item of furniture.

Has reasonable flexibility been provided among rooms and areas? Does the location of key elements permit expansion of the building? Will the structural system permit cutting openings in the floor for new cabling?

Is adaptability for new technologies and functions adequate? Can power and signal be added anyplace in the building in ways that you understand and accept?

Are computer cable tray runs adequate in number and routing path?

Are wire and cable connections kept off the floor where student feet can damage them?

Is a microwave dish needed and located (hidden if possible) with good judgment?

Is the anticipated degree of security sufficient? Have emergency phones, including perhaps exterior emergency kiosks, been provided? Will exterior lighting be adequate?

Has the method of clearing the building at closing and dealing with emergency announcements been dealt with? Is there need for a paging or other communication system?

Is the system of artificial lighting suitable, and will sun control be adequate? Has appropriate consideration for collections preservation been applied in the lighting concepts?

Are you comfortable with the mechanical systems? Is there reason to include a service tunnel instead of placing lines in the soil? Have humidification, dehumidification, filtration, control, alarms, and the like been accounted for in the concept and budget? (Be aware of potential mechanical budget cutting in order to bring the building into budget; such cutting must be done with open eyes and a view to the longer term.)

Are there floor drains where water could be anticipated (by accident or otherwise)? This might include mechanical rooms, rest rooms, exterior stairs, and basement areas where water could otherwise accumulate in a flood.

Does the roof slope encourage water to run off, or is it relatively flat? Is there an architectural option that permits sloped roofing over the collection areas?

Does the building envelope include a vapor barrier? Has the methodology of dealing with condensation at windows, exterior walls, skylights, and the like been adequately explained?

In those areas where maintenance and durability of products or surfaces is especially needed, are they adequate? Is a trash chute provided? If yes, is the fire risk low enough or addressed?

Has the prospect of off-gassing from various building and furnishings components been considered and dealt with?

Have the operational requirements been provided for? annunciator panels? book returns? public address systems? acoustic control? requirements of automation? buzzers or bells or both to summon help at critical service points?

Are there sufficient janitorial facilities? public telephones? public lockers and those needed for staff? photocopying and fax locations?

Is the proposed use of built-in equipment (as opposed to freestanding furniture) appropriate? Will a great amount of custom furniture be required? Is this a problem?

Is every office and workroom door properly located? Can shelving be installed conveniently on the adjacent wall?

Will an isometric perspective be helpful in understanding roof lines, and will it be useful to have selected renderings of important ground-level vistas?

Are any full-scale mock-ups needed to test an interior space, or is a small-scale model needed for exterior review?

It would often be worthwhile to again use the questions at the end of Chapter 12 dealing with the schematic review. Points once seemingly resolved may have to be reopened by subsequent changes in the plans. Looking again after a lapse of several months may reveal problems not seen before. And a more intense review of selected aspects is useful because at each stage of the design some kinds of changes will result in extra cost, time delays, and difficulty in resolution.

Where there are special technical consultants, including perhaps experts in energy, lighting, environmental control, security, cost control, or other areas, it is during the design development stage that their advice may be crucial. Although later reviews can also be beneficial as the more detailed design and specifications evolve, the direction will be set by the end of design development, and the testing of this direction at a later stage by the use of consultants will serve little beneficial purpose. The special consultants must be part of the design development review process.

Part of the review process will include a testing of the budget. This aspect was discussed in Chapter 9 and in Section 13.3 above. Should there be budget problems, this is the time to identify possible reductions or, even more appropriate at this phase, possibly add or deduct alternatives. In sorting out the budget, the project manager should keep in mind the architect's fee, which may change with alternatives or other aspects that add to the design effort.

The last aspect of the review will be the sign-off, which may involve a considerable number of people on a large project. Technically, the next design phase should not begin until the sign-off is complete; but when there is concern about the schedule and there is a high degree of confidence in the design, it may be appropriate to have the architect continue to work on the project even though there is some risk. On a large project the review process can take up to a month to complete, and, with inflation, the loss of a month can result in a substantial extra expense. However, when there are serious budget problems or other difficult issues requiring resolution, work must not continue until the sign-off is complete.

NOTES

1. Quoted by Metcalf in the first edition, 1965.
2. Reprinted in *Reader on the Library Building,* ed. Hal B. Schell (Englewood, Colo.: Microcard Editions Books, 1975), pp. 215–20.
3. Ralph Galbraith Hopkinson, *Architectural Physics: Lighting* (London: HMSO, 1963), p. 125.
4. John Morris, *Managing the Library Fire Risk,* 2d ed. (Berkeley: Univ. of California, 1979).

14

Construction
Documents

It is far more difficult to be simple than to be complicated.
—John Ruskin, *Modern Painters*

14.1
The Scope of Construction Documents

The end of design development establishes the final scope and appearance of the project, including relationships and sizes of the spaces, dimensions, architectural materials, and finishes. The construction document phase, sometimes called the working drawings or contract documents phase, creates the definitive plans, elevations, sections, details, schedules, and specifications that will give sufficient description to the project so that a contractor can proceed to construction. (The design process is not yet complete even at the end of the construction documents phase; there will be field orders, change orders, and clarifications, during the course of construction, as discussed in the next chapter.)

The architect's scope is spelled out in the contract for design services. The work includes project administration and coordination between the architectural work and the efforts of other professions, including structural, mechanical, and electrical engineers, the landscape architect, and the interior designer. The architect's scope of work should also include representing the owner in presentations that may be required by various governmental agencies. The preparation of an environmental impact report, the application for a variance, or simply the process of plan approval by code authorities or architectural review boards are part of the process of dealing with agencies.

The architect may be required to assist the owner in the preparation of bid documents, special conditions to be made part of the specifications, research on special materials or techniques, and the compilation of a project manual. Presentations of the project to various interest groups may involve the architect.

The owner will be responsible for continued assistance in establishing design criteria and providing data, as necessary, in the review process, including the reporting of comments resulting from the various reviews. The owner also will inform the architect and coordinate as necessary construction that is not part of the agreement for architectural services. Instances may be security systems, or some parts of information technology when unique conditions and skills of institutional personnel warrant keeping that in-house.

Finally, the architect will be responsible for the preparation of the documents, including those of the associated consultants. These will include, typically at the 90 percent complete stage, an analysis of the anticipated construction cost, along with identification of factors leading to change in this budget estimate from earlier estimates.

The product of this work, which is by far the largest single segment of the architect's effort, will consist of sheets of drawings divided by their content (plans, sections, elevations, details, structural plans, and so on) and a book containing the written specifications. To the uninitiated these are often difficult to read and understand, because the drawings are diagrams drawn to scale, the writing is technical, and both are replete with conventions and abbreviations—a language understood by both architect and contractor but hard for the layperson to comprehend. Only a brief explanation of these documents is attempted here in the hope of doing little more than acquaint the reader with their appearance and purpose. No library planning team should be considered complete if it does not include at least one member representing the institution who has had previous experience with and a full understanding of contract documents.

A more detailed discussion of the contract and legal documents themselves will be found in Chapter 15.

14.2
The Development of Working Drawing Details

The completeness and clarity of the plans and specifications may have a considerable effect on bids. If the bidders cannot be absolutely sure of just what is expected of them, they may quite properly add a contingency to their bids or make their own interpretation of the details, which is generally inadvisable. This lack of precision results in extras, and the final construction cost may be 5 percent or more higher than it would have been with better prepared working drawings and specifications.

Although the construction documents—that is, the working drawings—tend to be very technical in nature, there are certain to be issues that may arise during this phase that must include the library representative in the process of resolution. For these technical issues not already discussed, we will list the problems, define a few terms with which the librarian should be acquainted, and state some of the requirements that the building should meet to be functionally satisfactory.

Most of the issues dealt with in this chapter should have been resolved well before review of the final, or even some of the preliminary, plans and documents. The essential nature of all these matters should be fixed before this phase. Yet final review and refinements must come now if they are ever to be done; change orders should be used only as a means of correcting matters that could not be known before the job was let.

The librarian must leave the highly technical problems to the specialists, although there should be a general understanding of the problems and the solutions that are selected. As an example of such technical work, HVAC performance specifications will be understandable to librarians, yet the construction document specifications will not. The language is totally different, the latter being the engineered version of the performance that is required. A competent architect will understand the problems, although the expert advice of the consulting engineers may be required for resolving various details.

Construction details on which a final decision must be made during the preparation of working drawings include the following:

1. Building materials of all kinds
2. Window details
3. Door hardware
4. Wall construction and floor details
5. Carpets
6. Durable surfaces
7. Ceiling plans
8. Lighting controls
9. Built-ins
10. Information technology
11. Plumbing

14.2.1 Building Materials of All Kinds

The contract documents will spell out in very precise terms exactly the materials that the contractor can use. Included will be specifications for structural steel or reinforcing steel, the color and finish of the concrete as well as its design strength and other details, the kind of wire that will be used for power and signal, the finish of the rest room hardware, the construction of the roof, and so forth. The finish of built-in furnishings, shelving in the construction contract, wall surfaces, and other treatments of particular inter-

est to the librarian will also be included. There is no definitive checklist of what to look for. The best advice can only be to try to have a good understanding of those materials that will most directly affect the operation and maintenance of the library, and, where there is concern or lack of understanding, ask questions.

In looking for the best selection of materials, choices can often be made to use materials or methodologies that perform better from a preservation point of view (that is, they exude less material that can be damaging over time to the collections). See appendix D for more on this point. There may also be choices of materials that have longer (often more expensive initially) or shorter (perhaps less expensive initially) life spans; in some cases a life-cycle cost analysis may be needed to decide between different roofing systems or flashing systems or lighting types or floor coverings or other treatments where durability is a potentially substantial factor. Other materials will provide a major part of the look or feel of the building. Changes here can be difficult to justify unless the look and feel result in serious problems of aesthetics, maintenance, or operation for the institution.

Another factor that can be of interest is the notion of fast tracking, and especially the concept of prepurchasing certain materials. For example, it may be concluded that, because steel prices are going up or because of a favorable purchasing arrangement, it might make sense to purchase the shelving early in the project and store it until it is needed. This in fact has been done to good effect; the problem of course is the storage of this material in a condition that will not cause unwanted deterioration or "spillage." A decision to treat a class of material in this way will need to be developed as part of the construction documents.

14.2.2 Window Details

There can be three types of problems with windows. First is the window material itself. The pane can be glass or plastic (both of which can be scratched), tinted, of single or double thickness with or without air space in between, tempered, laminated, fritted (fritted glass has scribed lines and is sometimes used for decorative reasons, or for reducing glare—it has a very high-tech look), frosted, floated, plate, opaque spandrel glass, and so on. There are many different kinds of glazing, and not all of it is what you might think of as a window. And there can be too little or too much window exposure, windows can be in the wrong or a sympathetic relationship to interior space and furnishings, cleaning can be made difficult or relatively easy by the design of the glazing system, and panes can be relatively easy to replace and use standard sizes or can be a problem in both cases. We have in Sections 11.4.3 (Orientation) and 13.2.2 dealt with external sunscreens, internal curtains, and other adjustable controls of sunlight.

There are many instances where the choices of window materials have not been well thought through. Visits to academic libraries may not reveal the problems, though inquiry will turn up difficulties in one or another feature of the material. The most common problem is too much window area, a condition that is an architectural decision and must be subject to review and approval by the owner. This is a major concern in any research library or archive, and review of working drawing details in this respect should include north-facing windows just as much as windows on other sides.

The glazing may be selected with the intent of filtering ultraviolet light, thereby reducing fading and other damaging aspects of sunlight. Be aware that any light is damaging to library materials, and direct sunlight, even at 50 percent filtration, is still very bright. Heat is a related problem that is not totally eliminated even with the most up-to-date glazing designs.

The second problem is the enclosure for the window and its seal. Long-term maintenance will be an issue to consider; should you accept aluminum or wood or some other material? On this point, seek the best advice of your architect or other consultants. The transmission of heat can be an issue if the material does not have some insulation value; this point should be taken into consideration as part of the design detail. Avoidance of condensation where humidity is added in cold environments is a related concern with any window design, including both the frame and the glazing.

Naturally a major concern is the seal that forms a storm-tight and vapor-proof window, one that must withstand the occasional exceptional storm driven with gale force, or with hurricane or tornado force in regions subject to those types of storms. That is an engineered condition, one that most librarians can merely inquire about. However, a common problem stems from the window framing, and particularly the sill.

The concern with the sill is its depth, which may encourage birds to perch there. Many public buildings in urban areas have fought these intruders because of the unsightly mess they leave. Fake owls located nearby have at times been found successful. (One device is an inflatable owl-patterned ball with holographic eyes that seem to track the view!) Netting or thin taut wires set in various configurations can be effective; the Butler Library at Columbia University is one example of the application of these control methods. Nixalite is one company using the wire technique. And eliminating such sills is also effective, though there may be compelling reasons for the architect to use sills conducive to birds. Look carefully at the detailing of windows and their enclosures.

Acoustic isolation for the library, particularly from potentially noisy exterior activity, is also part of the design of the window frame and the glazing. Double and triple glazing is sometimes used for this purpose, but with significantly more space between the glazed surfaces than is the case for purely thermal isolation; as much as six inches or more is sometimes used for spacing of the glass sheets in an acoustic application such as a music library, where the design philosophy dictates complete sound isolation. The reviewer should question how the interior space is cleaned; do not assume that it will be perfectly sealed against dust and spiders.

Another issue, one that all too often is not carefully considered, is how is the exterior of the window to be cleaned? This is especially a problem for any sloped glass, which will certainly collect dust and need to be cleaned with some frequency. Libraries simply do not have budgets (with very rare exceptions) to do cleaning. Is the notion of sloped glass going to be acceptable after a year or two?

And the third problematic aspect is the opening and security situation. The building program may properly have spoken of securing windows in the library. However, the architect may have thought of the need for window washing and provided for it by making the windows operable. The review of working drawings must include a careful look at which windows open, how they open, and how they are locked. Correcting an oversight here will be expensive once the building is under construction or occupied. At the same time, the security conditions of all other exterior openings should be checked so the library managers know exactly why each condition exists.

14.2.3 Door Hardware

The selection of the hardware to be used in a library is important enough to require the attention of both the librarian and the building maintenance department, as well as that of the architect. The importance of quality in hardware cannot be overstressed. Too many recent library buildings have exterior doors that bang, scrape the floor, or do not close properly. The building program will say nothing on this topic. The institution may have a standard or specification for some hardware types. Yet this will be the first opportunity to see the architect's choice, though it will be expressed only in terms of a manufacturer's model "or equal."

The better the quality, the lower the maintenance and replacement needs in the future. Door hardware that contains moving parts, such as a latch, if it is installed where it will be continuously turned and operated by the general public, will require considerable upkeep no matter how good the quality. Thus, it is advisable to have most, if not all, of the heavily used doors operate on the "push-and-pull" principle and confine the use of latches and similar hardware to the staff areas of the library.

The pressure required to open a door may also be stipulated by local code; the Americans with Disabilities Act as published in 1991 stipulates the pressure for interior doors only as 5 lbf (22.2 N). Push-and-pull doors require mechanical closing devices. These may be installed at the top of the door, incorporated in the hinges of the door itself, or recessed in the floor. (See fig. 14.1.) The third method results in the best appearance but needs considerable maintenance and is more expensive than either of the other two. The self-closing device located at the top of the door has generally proved to be the most satisfactory method overall. In addition, modern designers have considerably improved the appearance of hardware and, with only a small sacrifice in durability and some increase in cost, have produced devices that may be concealed either within the door or in the frame above.

In this use of self-closing devices, take care to avoid designing a gate or door that is too heavy for the closing device to handle, particularly where the gate swings both ways. In a double swinging configuration, the closing device must also center the gate, and if the mass of the gate is too great, it will typically stand ajar. A librarian reviewing this can only ask if the closer is adequate, or ask to see one in operation.

Self-closing doors are usually required for public safety at the entrances to stairs and other fire-protected shafts and spaces. They are necessary, in any case, on outside and vestibule entries if the air pressure, temperature, or humidity conditions within the library are to be maintained at levels different from those outside. (See fig. 14.1, parts C and D.)

Sometimes, because of pressure difference, if outside doors are large and heavy, they become difficult to open and the pressure required may exceed the planned criteria. Automatic opening devices by means of "magic carpets" or "electric eyes" are useful, but they are expensive to install and require continuous maintenance. "Assist" hardware is also available to provide much of the effort for opening the door once a person has pushed or pulled against the device, and the cost of maintenance is less than that for automatic opening devices. Automatic doors are becoming much more common in libraries where accommodation of physically challenged people is a goal.

The Ellison hinge is another device that decreases the area of the door that one pulls open without decreasing the usable width of the opening. It is considerably more expensive than the normal hardware. Its action is peculiar and feels strange until the user becomes accustomed to it. Although helpful on wide doors, it definitely seems to interfere with comfortable passage through a narrow door and may be dangerous when used by children.

Double doors should be avoided or at least seriously questioned, especially if they need to be locked. It is usually better to install two single doors side by side with a center post, rather than a double door, because there will be a slight gap between double doors. This gap leaks the controlled, filtered air from inside, which can be an energy waste. It may create a draft, a discomfort for staff stationed nearby. It could permit rain or snow to get in under severe conditions. Furthermore, it destroys after-hour security if persons can insert a wire hook between the doors and pull down on an exit panic bar. An astragal (fig. 14.1, parts A and B) covers that gap but has its own problems, the most difficult being the coordination of the doors so that they always fully close after use. Various hardware designs are intended to solve this problem, but they often are less than satisfactory. Use of an astragal also tends to be noisy, and, if it bangs, the door probably will be standing ajar.

If turning knobs and latches are used, it is wise, from a maintenance point of view, to have the hardware devices incorporated into a large escutcheon plate rather than individually mounted in or on the door. This placement strengthens the entire assembly and enables it to take more abuse from the users. Where handicapped access is a concern, knobs should be avoided. In their place lever-actuated latches may be used.

Locks are most important hardware items, and most large institutions have standardized the locking system they use in all their buildings. This standardization frequently restricts the choice of hardware and limits the price advantage of competitive bidding for the supply. This need no longer be so, because of the invention of removable "key-way" devices that enable any type of keying to be inserted easily into any lock. In the end, the decision on this matter of locks is determined by the policy of the institution rather than by the librarian, the architect, or the planning team.

The method of keying, on the other hand, is in the province of the librarian, who should determine which areas are to be locked and who should have keys for them. From this determination a system of master and submaster keys will be developed to suit the needs of the library. (See fig. 14.2.) A locksmith can, without too much difficulty, change the keying of any particular lock after it has been installed. This change is made even more rapidly and easily if the removable key-way device referred to above is installed. However, changing the keying after the fact is not without cost. In a large library there can be several hundred locks that should be keyed properly when they are installed. To avoid distribution of keys to the contractor, a special construction insert can be provided that will allow the use of a construction master key. Once the building is ready for activation, it is a simple matter to remove the insert, which voids the construction master key and activates the building keying system.

The locking of exit doors is usually a special problem, as public safety requires that in any emergency these doors should be capable of be-

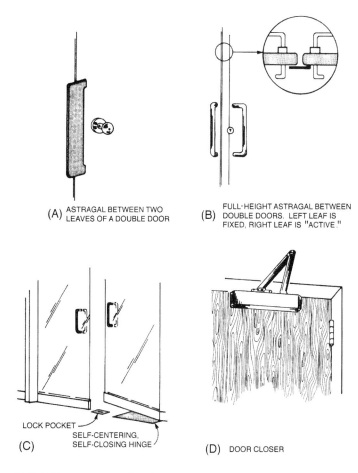

(A) ASTRAGAL BETWEEN TWO LEAVES OF A DOUBLE DOOR

(B) FULL-HEIGHT ASTRAGAL BETWEEN DOUBLE DOORS. LEFT LEAF IS FIXED, RIGHT LEAF IS "ACTIVE."

(C) LOCK POCKET — SELF-CENTERING, SELF-CLOSING HINGE

(D) DOOR CLOSER

FIGURE 14.1   Door hardware.

ing opened from the inside without the use of a key. This requirement introduces two difficulties.

First, if the exit door is in an unsupervised area, it may be used by a reader to leave the library without passing a control point. This defect can be largely overcome by installing on the door a mechanical or an electric alarm, which goes off if the door is opened, and perhaps also by requiring glass or other breakable material to be broken to open the door. In many cases it will be necessary to annunciate the door alarm remotely to ensure that the lock is reactivated.

Second, if the operation of the exit door is push-and-pull and it is to be locked from outside use, some method of releasing the lock from the inside must be installed. The device usually employed is a panic bar or handle, which releases the locking mechanism when pushed. However, public safety laws frequently allow the use of small knob turns on the locking device if no

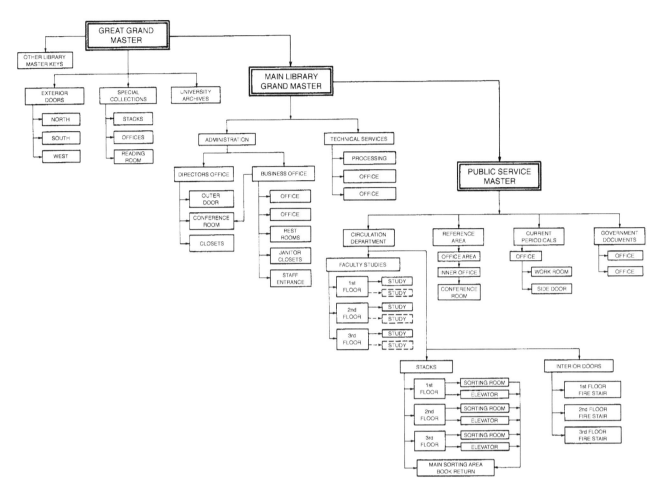

FIGURE 14.2   Key tree. In preparing a key tree, the assignment of space and the means of access must be fully understood. In this example some spaces, such as the studies and the reference area conference room, are at the seventh level in the key hierarchy, which implies reduced security. Those areas that require greater security, such as the university archives and special collections, are at a much higher level. In this diagram each rectangle represents a unique key that will also open any door described by a subsequent lower rectangle in the hierarchical progression (determined by the lines and arrows).

considerable number of people will be in the building when it is locked.

Other aspects of doors to be considered during review of working drawings would be the location and operation of smart card access, or security keypads; the recording of smart building passings in and out for selected doors (including such interior areas as a business office, a conservation lab, and special collections); and the vault door if one is used for certain materials. In addition, the entire list of doors should be checked to determine which are to have a glazed panel and, if so, the size of the panel and the safety strength of the glazing.

14.2.4 Wall Construction and Floor Details

Materials used in walls and floors can affect the long-term preservation of the collections. Concrete needs sealing as does wood and other materials that can exude volatile solvents, dust, or acids. Or, materials need to be selected that are benign in terms of collections preservation. Other issues of wall construction needing review are the ability of the wall to support shelving, the extent of provisions for effective acoustic isolation, the provisions for future changes in wall configuration, and the measure of environmental isolation for the more carefully treated environment.

The construction of the wall as well as the nature of the materials can contribute to most of these factors.

For preservation-related issues, consult appendix D. The structural engineer should be asked about the ability of the wall to support shelving, especially where such a condition is anticipated; it may require thicker than normal studs or other structural treatment. The alternative is to require that no shelving ever be mounted on the wall, a condition that can be limiting in a library.

Acoustic issues are generally treated with mass, completeness of closure, separation of surfaces, and the introduction of sound-absorbing materials, along with a constant background sound. The best acoustic separation is a heavy wall without holes through it of any kind, and with full closure between the floor surface and the structural deck above, where the exposed surfaces are not structurally connected to each other, and where the space between the surfaces is filled with sound-absorbing material. Such a wall would be an unusual construction, and it represents an extreme. Between this extreme and a typical residential partition is a considerable array of treatments that can help the acoustic value of the wall; the librarian must ask questions about the choice of the wall as designed.

The base for library floors may be of concrete, terrazzo, marble, ceramic tile, brick, or wood; in the past, glass was used in bookstacks, although it is not recommended, and steel decking is common in tiered stacks. Concrete is often left uncovered in basements, but it should be sealed to prevent dust from becoming troublesome. Terrazzo is often used in entrance lobbies and sometimes in washrooms; it is very hard and can be handsome, though it can be dangerously slippery when wet. Marble floors are expensive, and any but very hard marble, particularly if used on stairs and in heavily traveled areas, will wear down; marble stairs will also eventually become dangerous.

Ceramic tile is long-wearing and can be considered in heavily used corridors where noise is not a problem. Brick pavers can be used in place of tile. They are less likely to be slippery when wet (if the brick finish is left relatively natural), and they wear well. The janitorial staff will claim that they are difficult to keep clean, and book truck traffic will be especially noisy, because of joints in the brick pattern. Wooden floors, particularly of hardwood, can be handsome and long-

wearing, but they require considerable care to keep them in good condition. They have the advantage of permitting refinishing. Softwood floors do not wear so long but can be suitable in certain areas. Glass floors produce static electricity in cold, dry winter weather, and in time they lose strength and can be broken by a sharp blow, with disastrous results. Steel decks in a tiered stack with limited use may simply be painted. The decking may be given a nonslip epoxy coating, with a slight or more granular texture. Both degrees of texture are used in the Southern Regional Library Facility on the UCLA campus. An open steel grate has been used at the Northern Regional Library Facility in Richmond, California, where the entire structure was considered as one space for environmental control; serious concerns can be easily imagined with such an approach from fire, dust, water control, and other points of view. Where noise is a concern, the steel deck should be carpeted. Heavy traffic will require at least a layer of some kind of flooring to protect the steel because paint alone, even of excellent quality, will quickly wear out, exposing the raw steel surface.

Most concrete library floors today, except those mentioned above, have a covering of one kind or another. These coverings are often tiles made of rubber, cork, asphalt, linoleum, vinyl, and other similar products that are commonly called resilient flooring, generally 9 or 12 in. square, or even 12 by 24 in. (Metric dimensions are similar.) They may come in different patterns. Many resilient flooring products are also available in sheet form. Each product has its advantages and disadvantages.

Cork, for instance, has high sound absorption and resilience, qualities that make it suitable for libraries, but it is difficult to maintain. The wear and the maintenance costs can be reduced by coating the tiles with a penetrating sealer and wax or some other recommended coating, such as varnish or lacquer. However, where there is heavy traffic, the protective sealer will soon wear, and the cork will deteriorate. Cork should not be used for on- or below-grade concrete floors that have not been adequately waterproofed. It is particularly important to have it laid on a dry, level, rigid, and clean subfloor. The quality of cork available in the American market has fallen off in recent years. In some older libraries, cork can still be found that has not had particularly good care and is in good condition after 50 years, but much of the cork that has been installed more recently has not lasted. Some institutions have found that Spanish cork is more satisfactory and long-wearing than the cork tile manufactured in the United States.

Rubber floor coverings in general have good resistance to wear and residual indentation, and they are resilient and make a comfortable floor. They are generally not satisfactory on concrete floors in direct contact with the ground, unless the concrete slab has been waterproofed.

Linoleum, either in tile or sheet form, is less expensive than rubber tile. It has been on the market for many years and has had a good record. Its resistance to wear is satisfactory. It should not be installed on floors in direct contact with the ground. Heavy battleship linoleum has in the past made a particularly satisfactory library floor, but it is difficult or impossible today to find a good quality linoleum without importing it. The color selection is limited.

Vinyl floor coverings are the most commonly used material other than carpet. They tend to be less expensive than cork, rubber, and linoleum. Their surface is generally somewhat harder and, as a result, noisier, although the noise can be reduced by the use of a felt base. Vinyl asbestos has some advantages over regular vinyl but as asbestos is being phased out of the construction industry, vinyl asbestos tile is no longer used, at least in the United States. Vinyl tile floors do reflect glare as do other forms of tile, and they tend to project an "institutional look," which may or may not be desired.

Asphalt tile is one of the least expensive floor coverings. It is one of the few types that can be satisfactorily installed on a below-grade concrete floor subjected to appreciable moisture from the ground, but it is not as resistant to wear and indentation as the other floors. In heavily used areas it will not last many years, but it has often been found satisfactory in restricted stack areas. It is considerably noisier than other coverings.

An advantage of the last four types of floor covering, and of carpet tile, is the ability to cover a floor trench system when that is the means of bringing electric and telecommunications cables to workstations. Lift-out floor panels are standard in major computer facilities. They are expensive in other locations, generally costing three times as much as installing the power system in the plenum above the acoustic tile ceiling. However, for a computer cluster, high-technology classroom, language laboratory, or video viewing area, a raised floor with lift-out panels can make a lot of sense.

14.2.5 Carpets

For several decades, carpets have been installed on a large scale in a constantly growing number of libraries throughout the United States and elsewhere. The areas chosen for carpeting have varied considerably. In some libraries it has been installed in reading rooms only; in others, throughout the building, except perhaps in little-used bookstacks. Sometimes carpet is installed in open stairs and stairwells, for acoustic and safety purposes. Some libraries have used it in the entrance lobby, on the basis that it was a first-class shoe cleaner and reduced maintenance requirements throughout the rest of the building; others have left it out of the lobby because it would wear out so quickly there.

In earthquake country some engineers recommend against putting carpet under shelving because of the reduced bearing rigidity or soft footing that results. Also, bolts that would normally be stressed in shear under earthquake loading become cantilevers structurally with a carpet spacer between the structural floor and the shelving unit, and cantilever forces may be more difficult to resist than shear forces.

There are eight basic issues to consider:

1. *What type and quality of carpeting should be purchased?* The generally agreed-upon conclusion is that a carpet of first-class quality is justified because it will wear so much longer. There may be some dispute about which type is the best in this respect. In general a dense, closely packed pile will keep its looks and texture. Tightly twisted yarns can be expected to wear better than loosely twisted ones. A looped pile usually stands up better than a cut pile.

Carpet is available in roll or tile form, the tiles being approximately 20 to 24 in. (0.508 to 0.610 m) square; one major brand is exactly 0.5 meter square. With careful choice of pattern, as at the University of Miami's Richter Library, these can hardly be seen as tiles. Carpet tile has several advantages that have now met the test of time, the most important of which is that it permits easy access to underfloor electrical or signal ductwork. Carpet tile is frequently used on top of a raised floor or with flat wiring, which permits considerable flexibility for electrical and signal services without the normal requirement for conduit. A raised floor with between three and four inches of space (76 to 102 mm) can be installed with a modest ramp over an existing floor for a computer cluster, classroom, or language lab. Excellent wiring flexibility is achieved in this way, and the penalties of a more traditional raised floor with a foot or more of space are avoided (the penalties including substantial cost, frequently a requirement for sprinklering of the space, and a difficult transition to the raised floor surface). Although use is limited by local code and custom, a grid of flat wiring can be placed directly on a concrete floor, glued or taped in place, and then covered by carpet tiles. Flat wire can be especially helpful in solving difficult access problems in an existing building where even a modest raised floor must be avoided.

Some manufacturers of carpet tile claim that the tile does not need to be glued down; however, it is recommended that a release adhesive be used on at least frequent rows of tiles to control their movement. A good quality of carpet tile is more expensive than a good grade of normal carpet (up to 100 percent more depending on what is being compared, because of the more expensive PVC backing typical to carpet tile). At least one carpet tile manufacturer makes a carpet with animal fibers (horse hair?), which, it is claimed, results in a very durable product though of a drab color. If a single tile is damaged, it can be easily replaced. But do not expect the color to match exactly after the passage of time.

Any carpet that becomes heavily soiled will mat and be difficult to clean. Wool has always made a fine carpet, having natural resiliency and ability to recover from crushing, but good nylons and acrylics do well in this respect also. The way the carpet is made is as important as the type of fiber used. However, nylon with static control is perhaps the most practical commercial grade of carpet.

Durability of colors is also a matter of importance. Expect fading, which may make it difficult to patch or match the carpet at a later time. Some shades, blue for example, tend to fade more rapidly than others. Some have superior qualities in concealing soiling. Light colors quite naturally show soil most, and speckled or other combinations of color least.

2. *How does the original cost of installation compare with that of other possible floor coverings?* It does not pay to order any but high-quality carpet, and the cost of any quality carpet is without doubt greater than that of the most expensive

cork, rubber, or vinyl tile or sheet covering that might be used as an alternative. A life-cycle cost analysis can be done to guide a decision. The resultant preferred material will vary depending on the local competitive market, building area use, aesthetics desired, possible changes in use, maintenance frequency, and ability to make patches or small replacements as well as initial installed cost.

3. *How do the wearing qualities compare with other possible coverings?* Although the best modern carpet has first-class wearing qualities, the carpet manufacturers do not claim that it will wear as long as the best-quality vinyl, rubber, and cork tile.

The Meyer Memorial Library at Stanford, which opened in 1966, was provided with a combination of vinyl asbestos flooring and excellent quality wool carpet. Over the years more carpet was added for acoustic control; very little of the vinyl asbestos flooring remains exposed. The added carpet is all nylon, and the color does not quite match. By 1983, the carpet was still serviceable, but it looked tired. On the other hand, the vinyl asbestos tile, even where there is considerable traffic, still looked quite good after more than 15 years. In both cases the levels of maintenance are less than would be recommended by the manufacturer, which is probably a more serious detriment to carpet than to tile. Over the past decade, the original carpet has been replaced with a commercial grade nylon carpet, which is not holding up as well as the original installation.

4. *What about the upkeep?* This question of maintenance is debatable. The carpet manufacturers claim that vacuum cleaning at frequent intervals will cost considerably less than the cleaning, buffing, and waxing that is advisable for other coverings, and that this factor will more than make up for the extra cost of the original installation and also for the cost of replacement if it is found that the carpet will not wear as long as another covering that might have been selected. This claim is based on the experience of hotels and, to some extent, on schools that have used carpet. The decision on this point may well turn to the question of the level of maintenance that the institution is accustomed to providing for its floor coverings. A first-class hotel vacuums its carpets every day; is this true in the library? How often are floors buffed and waxed, procedures that are time-consuming and expensive? Many libraries economize on maintenance, and many buff floors infrequently and wax them per-

haps once or twice a year. Check with your maintenance department on this point before making your decision. Be sure you are comparing like with like.

5. *Leaving initial cost aside, does carpet have other advantages in addition to a possible saving in maintenance cost?* Here there can be no question. Carpets have first-class acoustical properties, good enough so that costs for other acoustical installations may be reduced. In some places acoustical tile in the ceilings will be unnecessary with carpets on the floor. Sometimes, where there is a special acoustical problem, carpets will save money. In recent years, with low ceilings and intensive space utilization, libraries have too often presented very unsatisfactory acoustic conditions. Carpets are pleasant to stand on, as well as quiet to walk on. They can also be used on vertical surfaces, such as the walls of an elevator or the front of a service counter, for both acoustical purposes and durability. There is no other floor covering, not even the best quality of rubber tile or cork, that will be as comfortable as a good carpet for a library attendant to stand on for hours at a time.

A less definite but significant advantage of carpets is the effect on the behavior of the users of the library. In schools it has been found that children seem almost automatically to behave better with carpets. Rooms are quieter; the whole aspect and atmosphere change; all are more likely to conduct themselves as they should. If carpeting becomes the norm instead of occurring in a minority of public places, it will be hard to say how long the improved social behavior in carpeted libraries can be expected to last.

Another aesthetic virtue of carpet over other floor coverings is that it is available in a broad range of colors, textures, and patterns. Even custom colors are reasonable for any large installation, and the pattern of colors can be arranged so that those areas likely to receive the greatest wear can be replaced without need for an exact color match. See also Section 14.3.2, Color.

6. *What about patching or repairing when the covering is damaged?* Here carpet has its pros and cons. In such areas as stairs and main traffic arteries, it will wear to show paths, though a pattern or system can be devised so that sections can be replaced without disturbing the aesthetics. Seams will part where they fall in areas of heavy traffic, especially those areas where people's tread turns or where chairs are used. Red wine used in library receptions, such as an exhi-

bit opening, will stain carpet. Gum and ink stains, if treated promptly, can be cleaned or patched. The great advantage of carpet tile in terms of patching has already been noted.

One problem with the maintenance of all floors comes from the danger of scorching from cigarettes. The carpet manufacturers insist that although a live cigarette may damage a carpet just as it will other floor coverings, or tabletops for that matter, it is possible to cut out a small section and patch it just as easily as or more easily than tile, and certainly more easily than sheet material of one kind or another.

7. *What about the padding or underlay on which the carpet is placed?* A good base will lengthen the life of the carpet and improve its acoustical qualities, but it will also make travel somewhat more difficult for wheelchairs and for book trucks. It is recommended that for most of the library, the carpet should be a direct glue-down installation without a pad. Where a pad is desired, a fairly dense pad with minimal "cush" should be selected. The book truck problem can be reduced by providing larger wheels on the trucks to reduce rolling resistance, but pads under the carpet are still a problem.

Do not forget that, in a remodeling project in which carpet is added, the doors will need to be undercut unless carpet was there before. This is generally true even without padding where there was no carpet.

8. *What about dust and vapors that carpet is known to contribute to the atmosphere?* Carpet holds dust, which can be a particular problem for individuals with allergy problems. Short of frequent steam cleaning, there probably is little that can be done for dust elimination with carpet. There are also people who are very allergic to materials exuded by the carpet or related materials, including the glues and padding used with carpet. Some of these materials are also said to be damaging to library collections over time. See appendix D for details on preservation concerns about carpet. Some types of backing and glue should be avoided in the research library, and recirculated air may need to be treated to remove these harmful substances.

14.2.6 Durable Surfaces

Although carpet can provide a durable surface, thought should also be given to the durability of other surfaces. Walls in high-traffic areas may be constructed with a vinyl surface rather than painted. Although vinyl is durable, it is often more difficult to repair than a painted surface. Elevator lobbies and main corridors may be candidates for vinyl wall coverings.

Bumpers of various kinds may be designed to improve durability. A bumper low enough to prevent a book truck from touching a glass wall makes sense. The front edge of a service counter may have a projecting edge serving as a bumper to minimize scratching from belt buckles. Exposed corners of plaster or gypsum-board walls may be protected with angle iron or a sheet metal bumper. (See Section 13.2.5 for a treatment of vandalism and mutilation.)

Concrete, though it is very durable, tends to absorb stains from oils on people's hands, particularly on columns, beside elevator doors, or along stair rails. Also, at the base, floor cleaning operations add their own patina over time, so baseboards may be considered. Light woods, particularly for such items as stair rails, will be difficult to keep looking clean. Countertops should be made of a durable material, such as high-pressure plastic laminate, granite, or marble. Other materials may be equally good, but a wood surface will look bad in a fairly short time. Wood trim is somewhat less of a problem, but it too will require maintenance from time to time.

Consideration should be given to wall surfaces in staff quarters for decorative purposes. In a private office, posters, family pictures of one sort or another, or artwork may provide attractive items to soften or liven or personalize the space. In this case, wallboard can serve to support the items, and sometimes a track for hanging framed material is provided. In other staff quarters, the walls or office landscape partitions may be used for posting signs, schedules, or operational reminders, for postcards or posters or prints, or for any of a wide variety of decorative materials, even perhaps a small vine or plant holder. Therefore, where personalizing the work area is permitted, wall surfaces need to be strong enough to support such items and should be of a material that, if at all possible, does not show stains or hanger marks when items are removed. It can be useful to have permanent walls with a more formal surface, while landscape partitions subdivide the area. Office landscape partitions typically have somewhat coarse fabric- or cloth-covered panels that can continue to look attractive even after many changes of decor.

Ceilings are not normally thought of as problem areas from the standpoint of durability. However, where a concealed spline acoustic ceiling is specified, it eventually will be damaged because of the problems of access to the hidden space above. An exposed grid for an acoustic ceiling is recommended for suspended ceilings where long-term durability is desired.

The selection of colors is important in terms of the durability of surfaces. Light colors in general show dirt rapidly, but they are better for reflecting light. Dark colors, particularly on horizontal surfaces, tend to show dust. Something between light and dark is probably the best in most cases, but aesthetic concerns may override this logic. In areas of frequent soiling, a glossy finish will facilitate periodic washing. The designer should be sensitive to the maintenance problems in the library.

14.2.7 Ceiling Plans

The contract documents phase may be the first time the librarian sees reflected ceiling plans. Shown on the ceiling plans are the locations and general dimensions of light fixtures, air registers, fire sprinkler heads, smoke detectors, skylights, and other visible features of the ceiling along with a layout of the ceiling itself. This plan can be viewed effectively only by having a thorough understanding of what is going on below the ceiling; the ceiling plan must be compared, ideally, with a floor plan that has at least the shelving shown. The reviewer should also check the electrical drawings for an indication of smoke detector locations and other features, as well as the plumbing and mechanical plans for their related features. A well-coordinated set of plans should all agree with each other, a point that often is a problem.

Things to look for include coordination of lighting with the shelving and furnishings plan (including the location of motion detecting switches, if used); locations where a concealed spline acoustic tile or Sheetrock or hardwood ceiling may be specified (which may be perfectly fine, but this fact should be understood); points where structural elements may project down from the ceiling, thereby limiting (possibly) shelving flexibility; and the like. Coordinating the features of the ceiling with those of the shelving is particularly important in cases where the installation of shelving is not part of the general contract. An error or oversight can be very difficult to correct later!

14.2.8 Lighting Controls

It is worth the time to check the switch location for every room relative to the door. Also consider how easy it will be to locate the switch when entering each room. Consider when two-way switches are desirable in a room with two entrances, consider dimmer switches in any media room or microtext reading area, review with special care the lighting and switching for exhibition areas, consider whether certain lights outside should be tied to daylight sensors, and determine whether motion sensors are to be used in lavatories and certain corridors or other areas. The list can go on. It is obvious that once light controls are built into wall surfaces, they are seldom changed because of the cost.

See also Section 14.2.10 regarding electrical drawings.

14.2.9 Built-ins

The decision about what is to be included as a built-in (versus movable furnishings) should have been made long before the working drawing phase. Arguments can favor stock versus custom items, and modular versus unitary, but either can be built-in or affixed to the building, which is our focus here. During this phase the librarian will have the opportunity to be involved in the detail design consideration of components, dimensions, flexibility, hardware, special details, and shop drawings. Each of these will here be briefly discussed, followed by a discussion of exhibition cases.

Components. Does the unit have the appropriate drawers, adjustable shelves, footrest, cabinets, and the like? Is there space under the counter or work surface for a wastepaper basket, stool, chair, depressable book bin, or other equipment that should be out of the way except when used? Is the front surface of the counter durable enough or set back sufficiently from the top to avoid damage from belt buckles or rings? Is there a toe space? Is there any part of the design that will catch fingers or clothing? Certain units might include pencil drawers, box drawers for minor supplies, cash drawers, file drawers, card file drawers, and sliding shelves. Shelves might include some extra-deep shelving for a few heavily used folios at a reference desk, or for books on hold or being returned at a circulation desk. Has a service counter suitable for service to a seated person been provided (as required by the ADA)? Have the needs

for scanners, bar code readers, desensitizing and sensitizing equipment, slave terminals, and other equipment planned at the counter or desk been accommodated? Computer terminals, laptop ports, typewriters, and cash registers are likely to be situated on lower work surfaces, and they all may require some handy supplies.

Dimensions. The dimensions have been discussed elsewhere, but this is the time to review the drawings. Counter height can range from 36 in. to 41 in. (0.914 to 1.041 m). The authors prefer a higher counter for most library transactions, although the lower counter is superior where packages must be handled (as in the mail room), and the lower counter will be necessary where ideal conditions are desired for those in wheelchairs. The Americans with Disabilities Act stipulates that at any circulation counter, at least one station must not be higher than 36 in. (0.914 m); table-height counters (about 30 in. or 0.762 m) for this purpose are often designed. This requirement is generally applied to any service point in the library. Computer and typing heights should be adjustable or, if fixed, probably somewhat lower than what is normally accepted as standard except, of course, for those stations meeting the requirements of wheelchairs. (Standard typing height is 27 in. or 0.686 m; a height of 25 in. or 0.635 m will probably be found to be more comfortable for more people.) To serve the physically limited, check the washrooms, lockers, public phones, and other facilities in this regard. Finally, check that the dimensions of lockers, built-in trash receptacles, book returns, and the like will provide the desired capacity.

Flexibility. Once you have decided to have a built-in unit, the concept of flexibility applies principally to service counters. The unit can be constructed on a module that provides the capacity to remove an individual unit and have it altered or to rearrange the units in a new counter configuration. This kind of flexibility will require unit construction where each part could be structurally freestanding, rather than a construction that shares vertical support from one unit to the next. There will be some increase in cost, but the modest added expense may be acceptable when consideration is given to the problems of future change.

The top surface should be modular as well, which can be done with minimal inconvenience from seams in the surface. This, too, will add slightly to the expense, but it is recommended. For example, computer charging machines may be added at a later time, necessitating the lowering of the counter. Or self-service charging and discharging may be instituted, resulting in raising the counter.

Wire management is another aspect of flexibility and can result in an unsightly mess unless it is thought through all the way from the communications head end to each port or outlet, and especially around the PC or workstation itself. A good handling of this condition at the built-in unit can be in the form of an easily accessible chase running from unit to unit. Access from this wire chase to the building power and signal system will be required. Do not forget to keep power and signal separated, or unwanted "noise" may be evident in the signal lines until the day when ISDN or fiber-optic cabling is in place. Unshielded twisted-pair and coaxial (RG-59) video cable are rather poor for noise protection; "high-quality" video coaxial cable and shielded twisted-pair are far better.

Hardware. In publicly accessible built-in equipment, the key concern about hardware is its vandal resistance. Exposed screws, for example, will be taken out over time, and attractive attachments removed. At the service point, drawers that are expected to be fairly heavy when loaded might be provided with track-type glides. The doors on a cabinet can slide laterally or swing open. The latter are preferred for total access to the interior except where the door will get in the way because of limited space arrangements.

Locks should be considered not only on the drawers and cabinets and perhaps on gates but also on major features, such as a roll-down screen at a service point that may be closed during part of the day. Often, this type of lock should be included as part of the building keying system, but it is overlooked because it is not on a door schedule.

Lockers seldom are built in, but when they are, the construction is another point and the design always is a concern. Should the locker be large enough to house a laptop, portable typewriter, or briefcase? Should one be able to see into the locker? Are the lockers located where noise will be a problem? (Most steel lockers are quite noisy.) The locks provided (or hasps without locks) will need review. Are the lockers located where they must be routinely inspected? Will they be assigned? Are combination (recommended) or key-type locks desired? Can the combinations be changed? Is there need for a master key?

Special details. Are there display panels, devices for holding graphics, or bins for handouts? Is there a niche for charge cards or scratch paper at a built-in consultation counter? Is there to be an annunciation panel designed as part of a service desk? How are the phones dealt with? Is there a special place for the phone or a phone jack? Is there a panic button, and, if so, is it located where it will not accidentally be activated? These and many other questions should go through the mind of anyone involved in the design and review of built-ins.

Shop drawings. Although the construction drawing phase is the best time to incorporate this type of thinking, there should be one other chance for input, and that is during construction when the detailed shop drawings are submitted for approval. The librarian is advised not to count on the shop drawings for this type of review for two reasons. First, because of the fact that time costs money, the review process during construction is always under pressure from the contractor. As a result, it is difficult for the library representative to be involved in the review process. Generally, the librarian will not see the shop drawings at all unless a special effort is made to do so.

The second reason not to put off a detailed review of the built-ins is that any change of scope—such as adding locks, making fixed shelves adjustable, or adding a cable chase—will result in an extra cost from the contractor that will not be competitively bid. Late changes will add to the cost; they should be avoided except where they are obviously necessary. The intent of the shop drawings is really to check the more detailed aspects of construction and materials technique. The design concepts should have already been well established in the construction drawings. Review of the shop drawings is important, however, to ensure that no concept is compromised or lost because of misinterpretation, omission, or conflict of construction technique.

Exhibition cases. In any research library or archive where a number of treasures are to be on long-term display, the cases need to be considered part of the permanent storage facility. Such a facility requires conditioned air to preservation standards; therefore, exhibition cases in research libraries are likely to be built-ins so ducts can feed all the cases with air of narrowly controlled temperature and humidity. Or, the cases must be within space that is well controlled and designed to assure the same conditions within the case. Use of ambient room air, even of relatively well-controlled conditions, is quite likely to be less satisfactory unless the room itself is also the display case, with its contents viewed through glazed panels from outside. Display cases require careful consideration of dimensions, materials and hardware, and lighting and light control. Review and approval of the construction drawings and specifications are essential, though the basic criteria will have been set much earlier.

Dimensions and flexibility of display cases need special consideration as to what and how the displays will be mounted, an oversight in all too many large libraries, especially when flat cases have shallow (vertical) and deep (front to back) display access. Will there be occasional need to display folios, or elephant folios? Will the volume position be inclined at perhaps 45° above horizontal for ease of viewing? Should each vertical case have two or more shelves to exhibit more material than one shelf can hold, or so several shelves can be positioned closer together when smaller books are displayed? Is a solid back desired, and should it be capable of having prints, broadsides, and posters mounted on it? How many items must the largest exhibit accommodate, and how will capacity be reduced when smaller exhibits are scheduled? Flexibility is obviously needed, as is the ability for staff to reach in and clean the glass on the inside of the case, mount fragile materials on stands or cradles, position descriptive cards, or include an artifact of related interest, such as a vase or pocket watch. Although opening and mounting the case from the back can assure the best security, staff will find it much easier to see the positioning and attractive adjustment of items from the front. All this needs thinking through for the result to be satisfactory.

Materials and hardware for the cases are another concern. Heavy metal has been used, though wood is most common. There must be no odor or other effusions that might pollute the atmosphere (see appendix D for preservation concerns; wood, glues, and finishes are of special concern in this context). Materials must be suitable for extreme security so door frames cannot be forced. The door locks should be in a location hidden from view and will sometimes be underneath or in back. Locks for exhibition cases should be set uniquely—that is, one key per case—and always separate from the building schedule. The interior case backing or lining materials may need to be easily replaceable so color can be changed, and must accommodate pins as well as heavier hangers to meet a variety of needs.

Lighting and light control are crucial for successful display because the cumulative damaging effect of light is well known. Can the light in the exhibition area be dimmed, or should it be kept to a very low ambient level? Would it be desirable to completely eliminate outside light so the case contents are the sole focus of attention, as in the Prothro Gallery of the Bridwell Library of Southern Methodist University? Should illumination of the displayed items be from outside or inside the case? Light from outside frequently leads to reflections off the glass fronts, regardless of whether vertical or horizontal, and can produce shadows on one item cast from another above. On the other hand, light inside produces unwanted extra heat, though with the current availability of low-intensity directed light from small lamps, this is much less a problem than heretofore with bulbs the size of a hotdog. There are a variety of places for these small lights within the cases; one common technique is to place them behind the vertical mullion. Yet there is much more flexibility today and a good interior designer can explain the options. There are experts just in the field of exhibit mounting and lighting.

Environmental control is a special concern in case design, as discussed elsewhere. To monitor the temperature and humidity, each case will probably have a small portable thermometer and humidistat in a corner for ease in checking the current conditions.

See Section 8.7 for other comments about programming of exhibition areas, the advantages of different cases, and their security. This is the last time for a detailed critique of the plans for this area and any built-in equipment.

14.2.10 Information Technology

This section covers various electrical systems that deserve special attention when reviewing construction documents. Computer-related technologies are changing so rapidly that this topic requires very careful thought and invites discussions with experts to project the direction of these changes. Some planning in advance may save headaches and costs later; it may also turn out to have been a waste. As a few examples, there can be speculation as to whether distance learning will be a major cost-effective part of a university program and should be built into the library building if that facility is to be the major high-technology, computer-intensive center. The programming will have been done long ago; design development efforts will have refined the size and character of the facility; the present phase must now lead to agreement on such topics as the size of cable trays, the need for a satellite dish, and the quality of sound-proofing between broadcast rooms. Should cabling be ISDN? Will the prospect of cordless and cellular transmission eliminate the tendency to add cable capacity? Will improvements in flat-screen displays and short-distance radio transmissions of "unwired" network connections lead to frequent changes in the desk or counter provisions for PCs and workstations? Perhaps the screen will be separate from the keyboard and with voice-activation, and therefore in a flexible plane for reading as one would a book.

The point here is that this is the last time to detail construction provisions for the range of information technologies. Once the contractor signs the contract, only change orders with added expense can alter the design. An alternative, of course, is to leave spaces in what are thought to be appropriate places throughout the building so that the needs of this technology can be put in place after the finished building is turned over. However, that will delay by months the full availability of the facility for instruction and research. So educated "guesses" are almost always the chosen way of determining the exact arrangements for information technologies.

Points to be looked at carefully during this phase of review are the location and size of head-end quarters, floor wiring closets, vertical and horizontal runs of electrical and signal lines, the extra capacity in selected places, the need for power poles or alternatives, the sight lines in computer labs and especially in any instructional room equipped with PCs or workstations, the adequacy and specific provisions in any equipment storage and maintenance quarters in the building, and the separation of sensitive electronic equipment from such machines as elevator motors or any generator. The list could go on at length. It is wise to have several experts within the library and institution, in both telecommunications and computer and media equipment, go over selected aspects of their particular interest.

Some other electric equipment also requires thoughtful review. PA systems (discussed some in Chapter 5) and "white sound" are two on which comments may be worthwhile. The public address system is very useful in informing readers of the closing of the library or, in the case of an emergency evacuation or practice drill, giving instructions to readers. The equipment is probably best located near the main circulation desk. The installation should be designed to avoid interference from other sources of electronic "noise," including separation of speaker lines from phone lines. Where conduit is required, separate conduit should be provided for the public address system. Consideration must be given to whether each study room and all faculty studies are to be covered, whether all staff areas should be included, and how the system will actually serve in emergencies. Where the project is an addition, coverage of existing spaces must also be considered.

White sound may be desired in some cases, and the speakers of the public address system may serve this function. However, to do so would tend to reduce the flexibility needed to tailor a white sound system to the specific requirements of each space. Because of this, it is likely that the designer of a white sound system will recommend a totally separate system, with which the authors would agree. This approach also serves the important objective of disguising the source of the white sound.

The matter of the distribution of the public address system and white sound system may differ as well. The public address system should be heard throughout the stacks and in most enclosed spaces, although speakers would be outside a bank of enclosed studies rather than inside each. White sound, on the other hand, is intended for the open reading areas. It is not necessary in the general stacks or corridors except as it may be required to mask the transition into the reading area; there should not be an abrupt change in the acoustic environment that draws attention to the white sound system. Of course, this problem becomes more difficult as the volume of the white sound system is increased.

Music libraries should not have white sound in listening areas, and selected zones of the system must be easy to turn off in any area, such as an exhibition hall where a public talk and reception may occasionally be held. Noted earlier is the point that the authors feel that many white sound systems are too loud and that, with a reduction in volume, they would still represent an acoustic improvement while being far less obtrusive.

14.2.11 Plumbing

Selective review of the working drawings for the plumbing is also desirable. If a fountain is anywhere in the project, look for the overflow path of water if the drain gets clogged and consider its adequacy. See how rainwater and melting snow and ice will run off the building and its surrounds, and think of flood conditions, which are certain to occur every decade or so. It is also worth remembering that some joints in pipes carrying liquid or steam will leak at some time in the life of the building; thus, consider whether the routing of such pipes can go around rather than over bookstacks or other sensitive areas, especially when the area does not have staff present most hours of the working day to notice when slow leaks begin.

This is the time to review lavatories. Consider whether the counters around washbowls will collect water or permit it to run onto the floor, look for where library users and staff will place books and papers and bags while using the room, and consider the capacity of paper towel receptacles unless electric hand dryers are included. Also, go through the plumbing notes included in Section 14.5 below.

Conclusion. There are many aspects of the construction documents (or working drawings phase) that will require detailed involvement. Aspects discussed elsewhere in this volume, including specifications, arrangement of the stacks, graphics, clocks, security systems, and computer terminal locations, will receive careful attention during this phase. The project, when the final documents are about 90 percent complete, will be tested one final time with a cost estimate, which is discussed in Chapter 9 and elsewhere for the other phases. With careful attention to the financial aspects of the decision and a little luck, there should be no problems. Section 14.4 discusses alternatives, some of which may be necessary where there are budgetary problems.

14.3
Construction Documents for Interior Design

Depending upon the nature of the design contract for interior design services, the construction documents phase for interiors may or may not be separate from the architectural design. Where the architect also provides interior design services, much of the interior work, especially built-ins, will probably be designed by the architect's interior design staff. Where there is a separate interior designer contracted by the institution, the construction documents for interior design generally do not include the built-ins. They may, however, deal with signage (discussed in Chapter 16), carpet (found earlier in this chapter), and furniture. Clearly, the interior designer should also be involved with interior materials, color, and finish decisions as well as some aspects of the built-ins, though these will be treated in the architectural rather than the interiors construction documents.

This section will briefly discuss the construction document design process for interiors as well as aspects of color and furnishings. They clearly are and must be closely related to the architectural work.

14.3.1 The Process

Furniture, equipment, built-ins, colors, finishes, and other surfaces are an integral part of the library design. If the results are to be satisfactory aesthetically, they must be sympathetic and complimentary to the architecture of the building. This does not mean that the same person must be responsible for all aspects of the design. Nor does it mean that in a modern building, all the furniture or other features must be modern as well. It is, for example, possible to design a more traditional rare book room in a facility of contemporary style. It is equally possible to translate those positive aspects of more traditional design into a more modern design solution. The direction one takes in the rare book room, or, for that matter, in any part of the interior design, depends a great deal upon the philosophy of the designer and the institution. Any good architect or interior designer, working together or under separate contracts, can bring about good results. And the remodeling of an old library by a different architect and a separate interior designer can also be highly satisfactory—for example, UCLA's Lombardian Romanesque/Moorish 1929 Powell Library, remodeled in 1996.

Because most users and staff will be more aware of the building interior than any other aspect, the interior design has a strong effect on how the building is perceived. Because much of the interior design must follow the architectural, this design process will usually continue well after the construction phase has begun. Movable furniture, of course, does not need to be ordered until perhaps nine months before the activation is anticipated, although a year might be prudent when there are quantities of custom-designed furniture. Likewise, the carpet does not need to be selected until late in the project. When it is to be installed as part of the general construction contract, only the type of carpet needs to be specified, with the color to be selected later. Or, an "allowance" can be provided for the carpet, which fixes the dollar amount contained in the contract for carpet. An allowance may also be used for major built-in elements when it is desired that the furnishings and built-ins should be closely coordinated and the furniture remains to be specified as the architectural construction documents are completed.

Even under the best of circumstances, the interior design process usually will overlap the construction phase. Ideally, the interior design would be completed at the same time as the rest of the design phase, but this is in fact seldom the case, and there should be much concern if the interior design process is not well along by the midpoint of the architectural construction document phase, if not earlier. What are the reasons for this concern?

A substantial overlap is desirable because so much of the interior design effort will relate to the exact locations of the power outlets, door swings, lighting, signal ducts, and the like. Where carrels will be provided with task lights or computer terminal capability, their arrangement will be greatly affected by the arrangement of the required supporting utilities. Conversely, the exact location of the supporting services should only be established after the precise arrangements for the furniture have been determined. Adjustments in outlet locations can be made after the construction contract is signed, but this is not the ideal way to fine-tune the design. An allowance for outlets can also be provided, yet the decisions about location must be made early in the project, certainly before conduits are poured in concrete.

As already stated, interior walls, columns, ceilings, floors, and finishes will be contained in the documentation prepared as the architectural contract documents. The colors for equipment, paint, vinyl wall coverings, and the like are often specified "color as selected by the architect," and samples are often required before the final decision is made. There may well be, however, separate contract documents for furnishings, carpet, and graphics, as each of these elements may be supplied and installed under a separate purchase contract. Of course, when the interior designer is working for the institution rather than for the architect, the interior design contract documents will be separate as well. The actual documents will be similar to the architectural documents, in that there will be plans showing furniture, carpet, or other arrangements together with plans, elevations, sections, details, and specifications for the custom furniture. Furniture that is only slightly altered or is selected directly from the manufacturer's stock will be treated in a schedule with cross-reference by furniture type and individual building areas or space. This schedule will indicate special features, such as the type of upholstery for a given chair or the configuration of a desk. The drawings will indicate where each item is to be placed. These documents will enable the institution to place orders and ultimately locate the furniture during the activation phase of the project.

14.3.2 Color

Color is but one of the several elements with which the designer must work. In addition to color, there is texture, scale, rhythm, symmetry, form, and light. It is color, however, that seems to generate the greatest controversy; it is color that most dramatically is identified as an element one likes or dislikes.

The reaction to color seems to be constantly changing, and different societies have different ideas about color. In the United States the favored color scheme seems to change every decade or so. At the turn of the century, a decor of pastel shades together with light-colored inlaid and enameled woods was the popular treatment. The teen years featured mustards, yellows, blues, and violets. By the 1920s, silver, black, and white rooms were fashionable, although probably not in libraries. Glitter and white satin, as well as overstuffed furniture, came in the 1930s. The colors of the 1940s, affected by the war and the difficulty of obtaining dyes, tended to be subdued—greens and tans. The 1950s were the jukebox gaudy decade; hot pink was popular. Indeed, Stanford still had one branch library in 1970 that sported a pink color, or perhaps it was called salmon. The 1960s were the electric era with brilliant primaries—red, blue, green. The 1970s tended to be somewhat more subdued, leaning toward the earthen tones. Blues were used much more in the 1980s, and eclecticism seems the trend of the 1990s.

What will the future bring? We may be in an era in libraries in which the colors of book bindings are about right, perhaps with a little toning down. Oak is today's popular wood, although other woods are certainly being used. The solid oak furniture from the 1920s is generally felt to be attractive again. It is interesting to note that oak is one of the less desirable woods from the point of view of preservation concerns. The use of "natural" materials, popular for some time, continues to have merit. Brick, for example, has been nearly timeless, as have bronze, copper, marble, and other materials that have their own color. Lavender, purple, and plum were recently popular (and all three tend to fade badly!), while yellow, orange, and turquoise, unless severely toned down, are not so popular. Dark green accents are common today. Gray may replace beige as the most common "neutral" color other than off-white. Chrome is more widely used for sparkle.

What can one learn from this? It is very difficult to create something today that will not look dated in 10 years. Natural materials are usually safe, and everything else is going to change. It is well to recognize that although bright colors may be an attraction at first, they often become over-stimulating and even repulsive over time. On the other hand, dull colors may not be so attractive, but they are less likely to be repulsive. Too much color is probably just as wrong for the typical library as too little color. Darker colors often connote the club or board room and are frequently found in public parts of special collections and the librarian's office. The eye needs elements to delight and stimulate, but they must not be overwhelming. Variety may be an important concept here. Finally, a fine-quality job may well transcend the changing fads, and so the superior design treatment is judged over time to become classic.

It is the authors' philosophy that, provided there are no glaring diversions from common sense, this is an area best left to the design consultants. The library representative should be concerned, however, about maintenance, the effect of light on the colors or the colors on the quality of light, fading, and reflection. In the exceptional case of the art library, the effect of color on the ability to view plates faithfully may be a concern.

The interior designer will prepare a color and texture board for review and approval by the institution. It will include actual samples of the building materials, shelving color, upholstery fabrics, paint chips, hardware finish, carpet, wood finish, and the like. When looking at the color samples, it is very important to be in a lighting situation similar to that anticipated in the proposed new library. Colors selected when viewed under one light source may simply look terrible in another light. This applies to exterior color as well; colors for exterior elements should be viewed in sunlight or some surprises can be expected! The color selection for the Shumway Fountain at Stanford is an excellent example; the intended color was a deep, rich red, which was selected under mercury vapor/flourescent light. The result in sunlight is a somewhat garish lipstick red that was indeed a surprise to those involved with the selection process.

Where the colored surface is intended to reflect light, remember that considerable differences exist in the amount of light reflected by different colors. For this reason lighter colors should be considered where the light levels will be low.

Texture will also play a role in terms of how color is perceived. The texture of a surface will reflect light in different ways depending upon the angle of observation. Carpet, for example, will look quite different when observed at 90° or 30°, a fact that is often overlooked when samples are viewed. It is best to have a large enough sample so that it can be placed for observation in a position similar to the plan. Remember that surrounding colors will affect the color sample as well. Paint applied to a wall will always look different from the small chip, especially if it is a strong color. On a large surface it will tend to become more intense.

Carpet color is an important decision. Although a very light carpet will show soil from dirt or mud that is tracked in and will show stains from any spilled coffee, colored soft drinks, and red wine, a very dark monochromatic carpet will show such items as paper fragments, paper clips, and even staples. Heavy matting of light, monochromatic carpet will be particularly evident where people turn (examples are doorways, corridor angles, by a drinking fountain, stair landings, and in front of a service desk or counter). Still, a coarse or grainy mix of colors can be unattractive when viewed close at hand. A "salt-and-pepper" pattern may indeed make wear, soiling, and dropped material relatively unseen, yet it is often unappealing. Bands of colors can be even less suitable because of the dizzying or confusing impression. Viewing large installations is the best way to avoid error.

Clearly, there are many tricks and pitfalls to selecting colors and textures. For this and other reasons, interior design is best left to a professional expert. Good results are seldom obtained from a democratic process as each individual will have different ideas and taste. The best advice is to be careful about distracting colors, avoid large expanses of high-gloss surfaces, and shun the most recent fad. Super graphics (remember the immensely overscaled graphics used as decoration?), for example, became old fast and are seldom seen today. Consider that if an error may occur, it is probably better to err toward the subtle than toward the bold. This is especially the case because most library use is quiet, solitary intellectual activity.

For safety reasons, be certain to change floor color, both indoors and out, to call attention to small differences in levels, such as one to three steps. Color may also highlight the first and last step in a flight of stairs, but remember that it is safer to have the distinctive color just *before* the first step up or down rather than *on* that step. Landings are another place to consider a change of color, especially when the flights before and after the landing are in a straight line so that a person may not be aware of the beginning or end of the landing as would be the case if the stair turns onto or from the landing. Some have even advocated the use of contrasting colors for doors (particularly in a large space) so that persons with limited vision can more easily see them.

Finally, consider applying the concept of variety. Different reading areas, floors, or wings of the building can readily have different color treatments, which will provide relief for the individual who dislikes a particular color. Variety can also be used as an aid for orientation and major traffic routes, which may be of importance in a large library. Because people differ in their tastes, it is well to provide some degree of variety, though not so much nor in such a distribution that the interior lacks coherence.

14.3.3 Furnishings

Much has already been discussed in regard to furnishings. Carpet was treated earlier in this chapter. Signage is covered in Chapter 16. Details of most library furniture are covered in the chapters on programming. This section, because of the importance of the topic, will discuss window treatment (sun control) and book trucks, and review the more critical concerns about tables, carrels, and chairs.

Window treatment. Although the architect generally is responsible for inside shielding of exterior windows, interior design will be affected. Consideration must be given to direct and indirect sun control as well as to visual privacy and aesthetics for interior windows.

On the outside overhangs, grilles and trees are used to shield windows from direct sunlight. Yet there are disadvantages to these. Overhangs provide no shade when the sun is low in the sky. Trees grow slowly and the deciduous type are bare half the year. And outside grilles (including sunscreens and fins of various types) are often unattractive, are conducive to birds and dirt, and provide very broken glimpses of what may be a grand view from the library. So there is heavy reliance on internal control of excessive sunlight.

On the inside, old-fashioned window shades, which shut out the light almost totally, are one option. If they are made so that they can be drawn down from the top and up from the bottom, they can take care of the light under different conditions at different times of day, but, of course, constant adjustment is necessary. Shades are now made that are semitransparent and provide a silk-screened type of view of the outside. These are good-looking and effective, and can be drawn up easily when full view is desirable.

Both horizontal and vertical venetian blinds are also possibilities. The horizontal ones have been used for many years. Their cords tend to wear out, and they may present a cleaning problem. But if they are used carefully, if they are not so large as to be difficult to manipulate, and if the outside air that comes in is filtered, they will last many years with little cleaning or repair. Vertical blinds are in some ways more effective, but they present the same problems, and, in addition, if the room is high and the blinds are long, they tend to get out of order quickly.

Drapes of various materials are also used extensively. They can be very decorative and add texture to interiors. The Georgia Institute of Technology had a tremendous quantity of specially designed, made-to-order draperies, which add a great deal to the decor of the library. Unfortunately, because the bright Georgia sunlight fades them rapidly and because it is expensive to replace them, the librarian, who had been enthusiastic about them, later issued a warning about their use. At the Massachusetts Institute of Technology, where the large windows on the south wall of the reading rooms look out over a very handsome view of the Charles River and the Boston skyline beyond, the draperies have presented similar difficulties. They burn out rapidly and are so large and heavy that they are difficult to move. At the Air Force Academy a tremendous expanse of glass has been covered by draperies so extensive in size that it has been found necessary to operate them with motors, and, if the motors break down while the drapes are drawn, they cannot be opened, or, if open, they cannot be drawn and a good part of the reading area becomes uninhabitable.

A number of coatings are available that can be applied to windows to reduce heat gain. A polyester plastic sheeting coated on one side with microscopic metal particles and fixed with an adhesive to the inside of the window will reflect up to 80 to 85 percent of solar energy and make it impossible for the glass to become hot enough to produce excessive radiation. It is recommended for use in overheated rooms designed with huge expanses of glass, though the appearance from the outside should be considered (the most effective films reflect heat in a mirrorlike fashion). In some installations the glass has become hot enough to break. Clearly, some analysis is required before jumping to this solution. Glass can also be produced with various tints to filter and reduce the effect of the sun. This technique, combined with double glazing, can provide an excellent solution to most of the heat problems, although it is not without cost.

Book trucks. Book trucks, which in other parts of the English-speaking world are called book trolleys, are essential in a library of any size. They are expensive pieces of equipment, whether they are custom-made or purchased from a library equipment firm. The wheels are the most expensive and one of the most critical parts. They must be so arranged that the trucks can easily be swung around corners within a short radius, because stack aisles where they are used are frequently narrow. The trucks can be made with only three wheels, two at one end and one at the other, but this configuration is likely to be unstable unless the trucks are very low slung.

Four-wheel trucks can have two wheels at one end and two at the other with one or both pairs on pivots (fig. 14.3). Unless the wheels are widely spaced, perhaps even projecting beyond the sides, the truck may be none too stable. Four pivot wheels may help to make trucks easier to turn in tight quarters, but when one pair of wheels swings in one direction and the other in a different one, they are balky to steer. A truck with two fixed wheels is easier for one person to steer, especially in a straight line.

Some four-wheel trucks are built with two wheels in the center and one at each end, the end ones being on pivots and, for the sake of stability, well out toward the end or even beyond it. This configuration allows the truck to negotiate tight corners while maintaining an ease of control for straight travel, but it can be quite unstable where there are floor-level changes, such as at a ramp or upon entering an elevator. The six-wheeled truck is similar in concept except that each end has two pivot wheels. The center pair of wheels may project slightly lower than the others so that by bearing down on the rear end of the truck and pushing, the front wheels are freed from the floor and the truck is easy to turn.

Be sure that the wheels, whether pivot or stationary, are first-class quality so that they will not bind. If possible, they should be made with ball bearings, should not have to be oiled, and should not squeak. The larger the wheels are in diameter, the more easily they will push, but the large wheels raise the center of gravity and affect stability. Even so, larger wheels are generally rec-

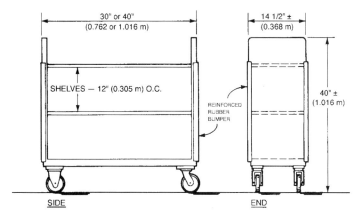

FIGURE 14.3 **Book truck. Length depends on aisle widths (for ease of maneuvering and turning around) and type of use. Width of 14 in. (0.356 m) is the minimum desirable to make possible shelving on each side. Width of 18 in. (0.457 m) is safer but may present difficulty in narrow aisles. Note rubber bumpers on the corners.**

ommended, particularly where carpet is used. They should be made with a hard rubber or plastic rolling surface to minimize rolling resistance while assuring a reasonably quiet ride. For a book truck carrying a 200-lb. (90-kg) load, a 5-in. (127-mm) wheel with a 1- to 1½-in. (25- to 38-mm) tread width should be selected. For larger trucks carrying a 400- to 500-lb. (181- to 227-kg) load, a 6-in. (152-mm) wheel with a tread width of 1½ in. (38 mm) is significantly better.

The body of the truck may be metal or wood. Trucks have been designed as a frame to accept standard library shelves. The critical aspect of the upper construction is the strength of the joints. As the book truck is pushed about the library, considerable lateral force is transferred through the frame of the truck to the wheels. If there is any weakness in the joints, they will eventually fail.

New trucks should not be acquired without bearing in mind the "bottlenecks" that they must go through in the building being planned—that is, the narrow aisles and sharp corners. Even where there is ample space, there is always danger of a book truck body bumping stacks and books if they protrude. The corner uprights and perhaps the sides of the book truck shelves should be fitted with bumper strips of leather, soft plastic, or rubber. An end-loading book truck, as illustrated in fig. 14.4, may be desirable in stacks with long, narrow aisles.

Watch for the vertical distance between shelves when selecting trucks, so that books will seldom have to be turned down on their spines, which weakens their bindings. A distance of 12 in. (305 mm) on centers is suitable, providing for books 11 in. (279 mm) high. The truck shelves should ordinarily be wide enough so that two rows of good-sized books can be carried on each shelf without danger of their falling off, although a wide truck in a narrow aisle can make it impossible for a person to pass or for a staff member to withdraw books for shelving. (A compromise may be that the book truck will need to stay out of the narrow range aisle, which often is not a serious problem except during major shifts or in areas of high use where the aisles should be wider.) A truck shelf width of at least 14 in. (356 mm) is advisable, and 16 in. or even 18 in. (406 or 457 mm) is better if aisles are wide. Trucks come all the way from 22 in. (0.559 m) to 48 in. (1.219 m) long. They are generally from 39 in. to 45 in. (0.991 to 1.143 m) in overall height.

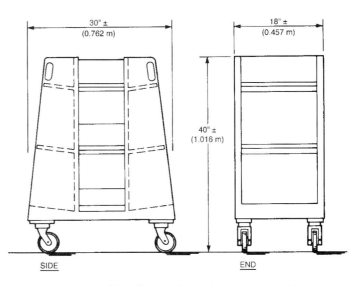

FIGURE 14.4   End-loading book truck for narrow aisles.

If materials are to be moved over rough surfaces or long distances, the provision of heavy rubber cords, commonly used to strap packages on a bicycle rack, are helpful to keep books from falling off. The means of hooking these cords onto the book truck should be considered, as projecting screw eyes can be somewhat of a hazard. No doubt a clever designer could solve this problem, but one idea may be to inset the screw eye or to place the eye on the end instead of the side.

The programmer might wish to specify special book trucks adapted for use as mobile lockers, which can replace a need for standard lockers and provide greater flexibility for the student to maintain secured materials near a favored seating position. This has been done at the University of California at Los Angeles with good effect. The sides were enclosed with transparent panels, with one side fitted with hinges and a lock.

Other special trucks are possible, such as trucks designed for maps or for giant folios. Similar to the trucks described, these tend to be wider. Trucks have been designed with a concave curved top shelf to help keep flat materials (maps or prints slightly bent to match the curve) on the truck. Such trucks have been designed for the National Archives II.

Carts designed for computers and audiovisual equipment tend to be higher and in some cases larger. In cases where such carts are rolled about the campus in support of classroom activities, the wheels may be considerably larger than described earlier. Even pneumatic wheels have been used for such carts. Where such carts are planned, the routes they travel will also need consideration to avoid hazards of elevation changes, pedestrian traffic (these carts can be heavy and difficult to see around), and floor or street grates.

Furnishings concerns. As a form of review, it is urged that the following issues be considered as furniture is being selected.

1. Tables, Carrels
   a. Ensure that where more than one seated position is provided at a single unit, it does not wiggle when one user is writing.
   b. Avoid fasteners that attract tampering. They should either be out of view or designed so that a simple tool cannot remove them.
   c. The work surface should not be glossy, exceedingly dark, or very light because of problems of glare.
   d. Where task lighting is to be provided, have a mock-up prepared to check for glare.
   e. Provide for the installation of electrical and signal ports for computers or other similar equipment where appropriate. Check on wire management above and below the surface.
   f. Consider the process of refinishing, which may be needed at a later date. A wood trim that is slightly below the main work surface will be easier to sand and refinish without damage to the main surface than one that is exactly flush. Review the process for removing fabric or acoustic panels for refinishing or replacement.
   g. Avoid bold colors on any back panel facing the reader.
   h. A desk of standard typing height of 25 in. (635 mm) is probably better for more people than the normally accepted 27 in. (686 mm). The best solution is a typing surface with adjustable height.
   i. Provide some work surfaces high enough for wheelchair access, that is, 30 in. (762 mm) clear from the floor to the underside of the work surface. Some 5 percent of the seating in this configuration is probably more than enough, though the ADA stipulates at least 5 percent or a minimum of one in every reading area.
   j. Where a unit is superior for a right-handed person, such as space for note-taking at a microtext reading station, provide a number (for example, 6 to 10 percent) for those who are left-handed.
   k. Select furniture that is adaptable for changed configurations. In this regard, individual units are superior to ganged units that cannot be taken apart.
   l. Consider clear plastic carrel dividers in some locations, such as those used in the language laboratory at Osaka Gakuin University Library.
   m. Consider exactly which tables and carrels need anchoring so they cannot be moved.
   n. Consider using rolled or eased edges for carrels and tables to reduce carpal-tunnel syndrome, as used in the USC Leavey Library.

2. Chairs
   a. Avoid detail elements that can be picked at.
   b. Consider using a densely woven fabric rather than vinyl—the library patron will favor it.
   c. Review the process of reupholstery or refinishing.
   d. Consider sled-base chairs without glides for standard reader chairs in carpeted areas. Adjustable office chairs with wheels are probably even better, but their cost and mobility may limit their selection to faculty studies and staff areas.
   e. Where lounge chairs are planned, provide a footrest. Consider a carpet-covered box large enough so two to six people can use it as a footrest, as is done at Dartmouth College.
   f. Provide a mix of armless and arm chairs. No more than 85 to 90 percent of the reader chairs should have arms if the preference of some people for armless chairs is to be satisfied.
   g. Where high stools are provided at a counter, ensure that there is a footrest.
   h. Anchor all outside chairs and benches so they will not be removed.
   i. Above all else, select a reader chair that will withstand tipping, heavy use, and

abuse. Durability will save considerable headaches in the future. On the other hand, many like a chair that will tip, thus providing variety to the sitting position, which can be a comfortable change.

3. Special Equipment

   Review the sections in this volume on carpet, service points, shelving, mail room equipment, and the like when these are part of the interior design. Go over appendix E as a memory prompt for equipment items that some libraries use to advantage.

14.4
Establishing the Bid Alternatives and NIC Items

This section deals with one of the key means of budget control: the provision of construction alternatives that can be selected once the bid is received, and the removal of certain project elements from the construction contract so that decisions can be made at a later date or so that more economical methods of providing the product may be achieved. The NIC (Not In Contract) items are representative of the latter approach. Although this topic has been discussed elsewhere in this volume, most notably in Chapter 9, it is of particular importance to the final stages of the design process when a financial problem is expected.

It should be stressed that the process of budget control should have been part of the design process right from the start. Major decisions about the project scope should have been made well before the final plans are nearing completion, and major construction alternatives, such as an additional floor, a basement, or an added wing, should already be part of the plans. But one needs to know what can be done at this stage if it is likely that the project exceeds the funding available. There are at least five ways to look at the problem, each of which will be discussed.

The first obvious option is to put the project on the shelf and seek additional funding. This is never a very happy solution, although it may be the only practical approach when the funding gap is exceptionally large. Two contradictory problems are involved. On the one hand, one may argue that with the cost of inflation, the funding possibilities may never catch up. This was the case at Stanford University for the proposed new main library when the contract documents phase of the design was completed in early 1970 and the project was ready to go to bid. By 1974 it was clear that there was no realistic expectation that the project could ever be funded; thus, it was started over from scratch. The cost of the shelved and eventually discarded design, exceeding $500,000 even in 1970, became a form of tax on the revised project. On the other hand, once construction is begun on a building, many would argue that a gift or grant is much more difficult to obtain as the potential donor perceives that other, unrealized projects may currently have a higher urgency. Of course, this is not always the case, though it is a real concern. In the case of Stanford, a fine new facility was ultimately realized, although it is considerably smaller than the original plan. Examples abound of institutions that have pressed ahead under equally difficult circumstances. The authors cannot recommend the appropriate action, as each institution and project will have its own unique set of financial constraints. One would hope, however, that with careful budget control and reasonable estimating procedures, this type of decision will not be faced.

The second option is to identify aspects of the project that could be removed without serious impact on the operational or academic program. As already stressed, major elements of this nature should have been identified at the end of the design development phase, if not earlier. At the end of the construction document phase, alternatives should be limited to those aspects that will not involve more than minor revisions to the documents. In selecting possible alternatives to add or deduct, great care must be exercised to avoid seriously affecting other aspects of the project.

The following list of possible alternatives should be viewed with considerable caution. None of them may be appropriate for a given institution; they are presented only as an illustration of the kind of elements that the design team should consider when there is a budget problem. Consideration should be given to elements that can be removed totally and still allow the project to proceed. These might include, for example, some specialized mechanical devices, such as an electronic book-detection system, a trash compactor or incinerator, an elaborate annunciator panel, a first-rate book return system, or perhaps even an elevator. Other possibilities might include a fume hood, a fumigation chamber, a special display area, or a fountain. Shelving and perhaps other equipment and finishes might be reduced or eliminated from an entire floor. The installation of a movable-shelving system might be put off to a future date. These last two are common alternatives, used either as an add alternate or as a deduct alternate.

Many of these possibilities will result in other costs. The removal of the book-detection system may add staff cost to the process of exit control. Loss of the fumigation chamber may require contracting for the services of an outside vendor for the treatment of infested materials (which may be beneficial). The loss of an elevator, unless other elevators remain, could have a significant effect on staff costs. On the other hand, all the elements suggested can be added at a later date as funding permits.

The increase in cost to add elements later will probably exceed the cost of inflation, as it is always more costly to alter or add elements to an existing facility than to include them in the first place. This is caused by problems of quantity, access, and working with an existing structure, which requires extra coordination to ensure that everything fits.

The advantage of making such elements alternatives in the contract documents is that a clear picture of their cost can be obtained, and a rational decision reached. It is suggested, however, that the number of alternatives be limited to no more than four to six items, as a lengthy list will likely result in other bidding problems. (One eastern state university library in 1985 went to bid with 21 alternates, including four for special casework, one for storm sash, two for HVAC, two for plumbing, six for electrical, and one for a refrigeration room.)

A third area that warrants review is restrictive specifications. Demanding that a particular brand be used for virtually any aspect of the project removes the possibility of competitive bidding and usually increases the cost for that element. Aspects that may be in this category include shelving, hardware, mechanical systems and controls, and perhaps even unique or unusual architectural materials or finishes. When this is the approach taken, it is important to develop a carefully worded performance specification so that those features that are truly required are included.

An alternative is to prequalify several vendors so that at least limited competition is assured.

Stanford recently rejected a sole source bid for library shelving for a particular project. The result, after opening the bidding process up to competition, was a low bid at less than half the original bid. This is not meant to imply that the original vendor was being dishonest, but rather that an error in interpretation by the sole source bidder may later have been identified because the competitive bidding process requires a sharp pencil. Clearly, there must be a very sound basis for electing to specify any product as a sole source item.

The fourth possibility for dealing with budget problems involves quality. Here the authors are reluctant to urge cost cutting as, in the long run, the institution will almost always end up spending more. Still, the budget may require a review of the quality levels established in the project. Are there materials that could be substituted to achieve the same effect? Is a fancy hardwood specified for a ceiling treatment where a less expensive material might suffice? Might the amount of vinyl wall covering be reduced and replaced with paint? Other areas where quality might be reviewed include light fixtures, hardware, mechanical controls, surface treatments, carpet, furnishings, and the like. None of these is easily upgraded later, and all of them will have a long-term effect on the utility of the facility. Of all the cost-cutting possibilities, this is generally the least satisfactory, although the review is warranted.

The fifth possibility to achieve a balanced budget is to identify elements that can be provided in less expensive ways. Often, for example, there are features in the contract documents that could be installed by other than the general contractor with a savings of the general contractor's contingency, profit, and overhead. These elements might include shelving, carpet, certain built-in equipment, drapes or blinds, chalkboards, tackboards, lockers, clocks, intrusion alarm systems, and the like. These elements then become NIC items. They are shown on the drawings for the general contractor's information, but they are installed under separate contract.

It is difficult to identify the exact savings that result from this technique, and it adds some element of risk that there will be budget problems later in the project. Further, where coordination of several trades may be involved, as is the case where light switches are incorporated in the shelving or the shelving supports the light fixtures, it may not be prudent to make the product an NIC item. Other than the issue of coordination, though, it is probably reasonable for the institution to assume the risk of cost rise, the problems of contracting, and the issues of coordination for such products as those listed above rather than include them as part of the general contract. Although the savings may be modest, they probably are real.

Another similar area is the identification of aspects of the project that can be managed "in-house" by the library or institutional staff. The move into the new facility is a good example, when student labor and staff supervision can probably save as much as 50 percent of the cost that a professional moving company might charge. The installation of furniture, signage, and such items as pencil sharpeners and tackboards can easily be done in-house at considerable savings. These elements are part of the activation process, which is dealt with in detail in Chapter 16.

14.5
The Review Process

The review of construction documents will differ in several respects from the review of earlier phases. First, it is a time when detailed review by the institution's engineers and maintenance personnel will ensure that the institution's facility design standards are met. The operations and maintenance people will be particularly interested in the access provided for mechanical equipment or other systems for maintenance procedures. They will want to learn and understand the mechanical system and its controls. The insurance and fire protection representatives will wish to review in detail the fire protection systems, where the control valves are, how the alarms are interfaced with the campus system, and the like. The affirmative action officer may wish to review the contractual requirements for encouraging the use of minorities as subcontractors and as staff of the general contractor. An administrator responsible for handicapped access will have special interest in the elevator controls, the height of public phones, the features of the rest rooms, aisle and door widths, and a number of other details. In essence, the review of the contract documents is the only time when many of the concerns of the institution can really be checked.

The second unique aspect of the contract document phase is that, because of the number of documents, the only practical way to undertake a review in any depth is on an individual basis. It will do little good to present the working drawings to a group. Unless you have been involved in the design process or are familiar with reading contract documents, little will be gained by reviewing the entire set. As a courtesy, it may well be useful to offer the opportunity to review the documents to a fairly wide audience, but it is suggested that for any project of significant size, this general review should occur at a specified office rather than circulating sets to a large number of people. The exception to this recommendation is, of course, those administrators who have specific need to review aspects in the area of their responsibility. Furthermore, each member of the design team should have a chance to pour over the documents.

Third, the contract document review phase is the period in which various governmental agencies must conclude their approvals. These may include the fire marshal's office, the government building inspector's office, and perhaps an architectural review board (although it may wish to see drawings resembling schematics rather than working drawings), the health authorities, and perhaps others, such as those concerned with historic preservation, urban planning, and energy conservation. Further, an environmental impact study and report may be required at this phase if not before. The government plan-checking process is necessary before a permit will be issued, and, on a large project, this process can take a month or more. In order to avoid a delay in the start of construction, it is reasonable to have the government plan checking begin at the 90 percent complete stage, along with the institution's review. Any changes that occur as a result of the review process can easily be passed on to the government agency, and the plan-check process can thereby be accelerated. Once the review is complete, any final corrections or changes will be made on the documents, and the project will be ready to go out to bid.

What should the librarians or library representative look for? Hopefully, nearly all the concerns of the library will have been incorporated into the documents long before this stage is reached, although there may well be numerous details that have been discussed but never seen on the drawings or in the specifications. These are the key elements to check, as well as points that were brought up in design development to see if the changes made meet the earlier library requests. It is also well to read everything, and, when something is not clear or seems out of order, ask a question. Remember, too, that these drawings are not yet 100 percent complete; there will be some minor things missing. But if you are concerned about a detail or what is missing, ask about it. It certainly does not hurt to be thorough; it will be too late if an error or omission is not caught now.

All the points raised now—as in previous stages of review—should be documented in a memorandum in the form of clear, precise references to specific drawing sheets or specifications so the architect can understand each point without need to seek clarification.

What kinds of things might the librarian wish to review? The following tabulation lists examples. Others have been mentioned earlier in this chapter and in previous chapters. The key to any review is to keep an open mind and think about what you see. This is always more easily said than done. Have your library building consultant also look over the plans. Often a fresh eye with similar interest and concern can turn up unseen issues to great benefit.

1. Landscape Drawings

    a. Check the grading plan. Make sure the exterior surfaces slope away from doors and areaways. Where would groundwater collect? Does it look like there are enough drains? Can snow be plowed wherever necessary?

    b. Do retaining walls have drainage apertures? Do they lead water into a swale or onto a pedestrian walkway?

    c. Review the planting. Are there trees that will block windows? Are there deciduous trees whose leaves will clog drains? Will shrubs block egress from an emergency exit?

    d. Have a look at the arrangements for exterior lighting, especially at stairs. Will there be dark areas that seem dangerous? Is it easy to replace the bulbs in the neat little light fixtures that are concealed in the steps? Will low light fixtures present a problem of glare? Are the light fixtures relatively vandal resistant?

    e. Watch for fences and other elements that provide natural bike racks, especially near the main entry. Can bicycles be sheltered in the rain? Are there con-

ditions to be eliminated because they are especially conducive to use of in-line skates or skateboards?

    f. Have a look at the arrangements for an exterior book return. Is it well lighted? easily accessible? under cover?

    g. Is exterior seating appropriate or desired? Is it movable, shaded from the sun, and will rain drain off? Will people sit on walls? Will they take shortcuts and cross garden beds?

    h. Have trash containers and ash urns been included? Are they conveniently located? Where will the wind blow debris?

    i. How is the main trash removal from the building handled? Is there a Dumpster that needs landscape treatment?

    j. Are there plantings that will create a security problem because they offer hiding places?

    k. Have security and safety issues been addressed? Lighting? Emergency kiosks (with direct lines to the police station)? Fire access?

    Others as well as library representatives will be interested in the switching for the light fixtures, the irrigation system, access for fire trucks, paving details, lawn-edging details, plants and how they are placed, preparation of the soil for planting, and many other aspects.

2. Architectural Drawings

    Most of this volume has been devoted to the design problems in libraries. The following is only a representative listing.

    a. Review the requirements of handicapped access to all areas, staff as well as public.

    b. Security issues warrant review. Which doors are locked, and how? Where are alarm devices? How will alarms be responded to? Will emergency exit routes compromise security, and is this dealt with?

    c. Are walls appropriately designed to receive wall-mounted shelving?

    d. How will the outside windows be cleaned? Do sills offer bird perching sites?

    e. Are the details for the built-ins appropriate?

    f. Are the items that are "not in contract" properly labeled?

g. Will one be able to move large carrels, tables, or other equipment where needed?

h. If phasing is part of the project, is it clearly detailed?

i. Is there provision in the drawings for controlling security, dust, water, or sound in an existing building during construction?

j. Check the details. Are display cases with internal lights well ventilated? How are they locked? Is built-in shelving adjustable?

k. Is access to and from the roof secured? How will roof utility areas be serviced?

l. Do you understand the roofing system? Is it acceptable quality? What about the flashing and rain gutters?

m. Check for thresholds. If they are not absolutely required, they should be avoided.

n. Where acoustic control is a problem, do the walls extend through the suspended ceiling to the underside of the floor above? (See fig. 14.5.)

o. Is the ceiling an exposed grid or a concealed spline? Or plaster or gypsum board? Or other material? Will access for maintenance be a problem?

p. Are entry mats included in the design? Will they creep? How easily can they be replaced? Has drainage been provided below mats where climate requires?

q. Are the paper towel dispensers in the washrooms separate from the sinks so paper bits will not fall in the drain? Are adequate shelves provided in the washrooms? Is the floor waterproof? Has moisture-resistant gypsum board been specified? If desired, is there a trash chute?

r. Is there enough room where the photocopy machine is to be placed to open all equipment doors to service the machine?

s. If carpet is part of the contract documents, review the seaming plan in conjunction with furniture layouts. Are the seams located so as to minimize wear?

t. Review the provisions for sun control. Where will drapes collect if pulled open? Is light control as needed for

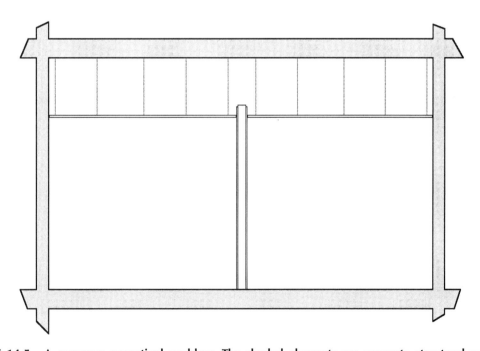

FIGURE 14.5 A common acoustical problem. The shaded elements are concrete structural walls and floors; they are normally excellent acoustical separators (provided there are no holes). In the middle is a typical interior wall; it does not go to the structure above, but only penetrates the suspended ceiling and stops. Sound easily travels over this wall and into the adjacent space. The correct installation for acoustic separation is to have the wall, including the surface material, extend entirely to the concrete above.

comfortable reading of computer and microtext screens?

u. Are the doors undercut as necessary for ventilation and carpet installation?

v. Do the dimensions for the height of built-in work surfaces take into account the thickness of the carpet? This may be critical where file cabinets or other standard units must relate to the built-in unit. Do the built-in work surfaces have sufficient underside bracing?

w. Are there adequate coat hooks or racks?

x. Is floor-to-ceiling glass protected from book truck traffic, and vertical protection provided for vulnerable corners?

y. Check the footing drains and other drain systems. Are they higher than the drain system serving the site? If not, is there a sump pump with redundancy and a system for capturing silt? Are the sump pumps on backup power?

z. Check for preservation-related issues. Is the roof sloped (for positive drainage)? Have materials been selected with preservation in mind? Has light been dealt with adequately? Is there a ceiling in the stack areas that could be eliminated to positive effect (making mechanical problems more easy to find, and reducing the probability of dust problems and other problems)? In an archive setting, has carpet been used in the stacks? Is the color of the floor in the stacks as light as possible so as to minimize the required lighting levels? Are pollution-producing functions isolated from zones that must be kept "clean"?

3. Structural Drawings

a. Have the columns or other structural elements changed size? Are there any obvious structural surprises, such as a flared base or capital of a column? Is the final column size as expected in earlier design phases?

b. Is headroom impaired at any point?

c. Has reasonable provision for future expansion been made? If a knockout panel has been agreed on, for a later building addition, is it shown in the right place? Can compact shelving be added in the future? Will the added weight of loaded compact shelving cause deflection in the floor sufficient to create problems?

d. Look at freestanding walls and retaining walls. Is the foundation sufficiently deep and with reinforcing steel bars so the walls will withstand waterlogged conditions and not tend in time to lean?

4. Mechanical Drawings

a. Try to gain an understanding of how the mechanical system works and how it is controlled. Are preservation issues dealt with? Is there a constant source of heat for humidity control? Is the filtration adequate? Is the arrangement of the components appropriate?

b. Review access to duct shafts and mechanical equipment rooms. Are they secure? Will access require an altered furniture arrangement? Will service personnel be required to carry all their tools, ladders, cleaning materials, spare parts, and the like through the library to gain access to the equipment? Will this weaken book security?

c. Have the acoustical concerns been reasonably attended to? Which pieces of building equipment or operations are most likely to create disturbing noises?

d. Is the building divided into zones to allow shutting down the systems to those areas that close earlier than the major part of the library? Is the stack area planned to be treated environmentally 24 hours a day?

e. Look at the elevator cab design. Is there sufficient space for the floor indicator graphics? Are the surfaces durable?

f. Is the sump pump on standby emergency power? What about exhaust fans?

g. Is the floor of the mechanical room (if it is on the roof) waterproof and sloped so as to drain? How will future pipes or changes be added without compromising the waterproof membrane?

h. Are there mechanical devices—such as reheat coils, duct vane actuator motors, and humidifiers—above the ceiling of the library that will require servicing from time to time? Is a hatch needed? Is any form of steam or water protection reasonable or appropriate?

i. Are all the fire dampers accessible?

j. What kind of filters are shown?

k. Are there street-level air intakes that might invite a stink bomb? Are they well separated from sources of exhaust fumes?

l. Do the air-delivery registers seem adequate or are there dead pockets? Check the bookstacks for any such apparent pockets. Will there be drafts where students or staff sit?

m. Is there some kind of heating device for dealing with ice at the entry? (It may be electrical, and shown in the electrical plans.)

5. Plumbing Drawings

a. Try to follow the routes of pipes to see where water hazards may occur. Keep in mind that these drawings are somewhat diagrammatic, but if water hazards are a concern, they can be dealt with by requiring specific routing.

b. Check the location of sprinkler main controls.

c. Check the nature of the sprinkler system. See if higher heat-range sprinkler heads are to be provided any place near a heat source. This includes under skylights! Is there a desire for on/off-type sprinkler heads, and have they been specified? Is it a dry system (not recommended in most cases)? Is it a pre-action system? Has a fire-cycle system been specified? Is there also a smoke detection system?

d. In a tunnel connection, are there utilities that should be encased in a protective pipe or insulating cover? Are there any pipes or ducts where heads can be bumped?

e. Ensure that the mechanical rooms, rest rooms, stairs with outside exposure, and janitor's closets have floor drains. Is a floor drain desired in the basement? Where are sewer clean-outs, and can they be kept outside of bookstack areas?

f. Note the capacity of the sump pumps. What happens if one fails?

g. Review the drinking fountains, both in terms of their fixture design and their location, particularly for handicapped access.

h. Look at the plumbing under the washroom sinks. Will it be covered with sponge rubber to protect the knees of a person in a wheelchair?

i. Follow the route of storm runoff and consider its implications for pedestrians, and for building doors, windows, and areaways.

6. Electrical Drawings

a. Review the arrangement of light fixtures, particularly in relation to the furniture layouts. Are preservation concerns addressed?

b. Check the switching arrangements. If this aspect is not clear, ask about it. Are any light switches or thermostats on columns where they project and could be broken or hurt someone passing by?

c. If there are light fixtures shown that you are not familiar with, ask for a photocopy of the manufacturer's catalog description.

d. How will bulbs and tubes in difficult-to-reach light fixtures be relamped? Are there any fixtures where heat buildup will result in short life of the lamp?

e. Check power outlet locations. Ensure that, even in the stacks, outlets are provided for maintenance purposes. Where the outlet is to be above the work surface, review the height shown.

f. Does each workstation have sufficient outlets? Four are recommended.

g. Note the indicated phone locations. Is there sufficient flexibility for alternative furniture arrangements? Are emergency phones needed and dealt with?

h. Look at the arrangements for flexibility, including floor duct systems, cable trays in the ceiling, core voids in the floor, empty conduit runs, and the like. Do they work with possible furniture arrangements? Do the horizontal runs tie into vertical shafts?

i. Are data ports and electrical outlets paired and located where needed in a convenient part of tables, carrels, and desks? Is it clear that there will be sufficient capacity for both future flexibility and the installation of those aspects that are not part of the general contract, such as phones, computers, or an intrusion alarm system? If this is not clear, ask questions.

j. Are the floor outlets coordinated with the furniture arrangements? Are they flush or the monument type, and will any of the latter be hazardous?

k. Can different areas of the building have the lights turned off while other areas remain open and active?

l. If bookstack aisle lighting turns on for a limited number of minutes by motion-detection devices, are there cutoff switches for staff who may need to work in aisles for longer periods? Are the motion detectors hidden from people using the stack by the shelving such that people using the shelving may need to enter a particular aisle to make the lights go on?

m. Is there a master clock system? If so, review the location of clocks. Do not overlook staff areas.

n. Is there a signal distribution closet on each floor? How will computer terminals in other public and staff areas be added in the future?

o. Does the products-of-combustion detection system reasonably cover the building?

p. How is emergency lighting dealt with? Will such lighting enable users to see exit lanes from every room in the building?

q. Are conduits shown for the security system? How about the electronic book-detection system? Is there a conduit to each exterior door for the alarm system? Is the exterior book return protected in any way against malicious behavior?

r. What is the distribution of the white sound system, if provided? Is there indication of individual area control?

s. If low-voltage switching is provided, is there any special provision for access to the solenoid switches? When they are hidden above the ceiling, they can be hard to find.

t. Have the needs for public address systems, paging systems, panic alarms, bells at service desks to summon help, transaction annunciators, and the like been covered?

7. Specifications

a. Look at the general and special conditions. Is there reasonable protection for ongoing operations? Are security, temporary fire protection, water protection, noise, and dust adequately dealt with?

b. You may wish to review a number of sections, but be sure to read the section on library shelving. Are the book supports correct? Are range indicators or finders included? Are the numbers of shelves per section and their dimensions correct? Is it clear that the dimensions are nominal or actual? Is the base closed or open? Is fastening of the shelving to the structure specified? All shelving details must be reviewed in these specifications.

c. Review the hardware schedule with the architectural plans. This is an area where errors can be easily made.

d. Look at the fixture schedules, such as for lavatories and lighting. Are some unfamiliar? If so, ask for manufacturer's information. For example, can a person with arthritic hands operate water faucet knobs?

Clearly, this list could go on and on. A similar review will also be needed for furnishings. There is no substitute for simply spending a substantial block of time with the plans. As has been noted before, it is less expensive to make corrections at this stage than later. The time spent will be worthwhile.

15

Bidding,
Business Concerns,
and Construction

When we mean to build, we first survey the plot, then draw the model, and when we see the figure of the house, then must we rate the cost of the erection which if we find outweighs ability, what do we then but draw anew. . . .

—William Shakespeare, *Henry IV,* Part 2, I.iii

The whole difference between construction and creation is exactly this: that a thing constructed can only be loved after it is constructed, but a thing created is loved before it exists.

—G. K. Chesterton, *Criticisms & Appreciations of the Works of Charles Dickens*

This chapter deals with the bidding and construction phase of the project, which, on a small project, may span a period of only six to eight weeks but may require two years or more for a large project. It is a time of considerable satisfaction for the design team as the project finally takes form, yet there is also anxiety about bids coming in within the budget.

During the course of bidding and construction, there will be a continuing need for involvement by the library representative and others as there will frequently be a need for decisions and actions that may affect library operations. However, the intensity of involvement will generally be reduced until it is time to start planning for activation, although it is not uncommon for some design activity, particularly the interior design, to overlap the construction period.

15.1
The Management Team

In dealing with contractors, the architect is almost always the representative of the owner or institution. Technically, all approvals, directions, clarifications—virtually all communications—are to go through the architect to the general contractor, who then is responsible for passing information on to the various subcontractors. The only exceptions are when the project is very small or when a special arrangement is made, as might be the case in the renovation of an occupied building where close coordination is required with the occupants. In these cases, discussions about scheduling, for example, may occur through the institution's project manager or through a representative of the library. The architect, though, will still have primary responsibility for the project.

From the start of the bid period, because of the changed role of the architect, there will usually be other changes as well. Some institutions, for example, have an office specializing in construction. Even where the institutional project manager retains primary responsibility for the project, the key role for the institution may be assigned to a construction manager. In many cases, the construction manager will be assisted by one or several construction inspectors who are responsible for ensuring daily that the execution of the construction effort meets the full intent of the contract documents. Depending upon

the circumstances, the architect may provide the detailed inspection services, which would, of course, be reflected in the architect's contract and fees.

Once the contract is signed, the contractor takes on full responsibility for the construction site, including liability for injury or damages. Visits to the site must be arranged with the contractor's approval, although usually a few named individuals, such as the architect, inspectors, the project manager, and the construction manager, are granted free access by the construction contract document.

Besides inspections by representatives of the owner and the architect, there will be inspections by others. For example, a soils engineer may be hired by the contractor, owner, or architect (depending on the contractual specifications) during the period of excavation. An archeological expert may make periodic inspections or be called in when any unnatural evidence turns up during ground excavation. A materials-testing laboratory often will inspect the concrete placement and take samples for testing. During the course of construction, the code authorities will be involved in routine inspections. These on-site reviews will involve principally the building inspection, but occasionally they may include specialists in fire protection, elevators, health, and other fields.

The architect's consulting engineers will visit the site, although less frequently, to undertake an inspection. They include the structural, mechanical, electrical, and perhaps acoustical engineers as well as the landscape architect and other specialized consultants. Of course, it can be expected that the librarian will, from time to time, inspect the project.

The reports from all these inspections should eventually be sent to the architect, who is responsible for coordinating any corrective action. The governmental inspectors will generally deal directly with the contractor, as it is the contractor who holds the building permit. The institutional representatives should, of course, report problems observed during an inspection through the project manager to the architect. The architect's consultants will deal directly with the architect.

As already suggested, most projects of any size will have a full-time inspector, or a clerk of works, representing the institution, whose duties are to see that the construction matches the working drawings and specifications, to keep track of the innumerable details, and to call the contractor's and architect's attention to discrepancies. The architect, as part of the contract, must supervise construction along the same lines. The differences between the supervision provided by the architect and the clerk of works are two:

1. The clerk's supervision is continuous and the architect's periodic, generally no more than once a week, unless at critical times and on a very large enterprise.
2. The architect can interpret and direct procedures and initiate required changes in structure or design, while the clerk's duty is to see that the requirements of the contract drawings and specifications are fulfilled by the contractor and crew.

Careless workers may seriously lower standards. Too often a contractor may hope to save money and increase profit by skimping on the concrete mix or finishings of all kinds, or by providing slightly inferior quality material that could escape detection if not watched. It is to be hoped that a reliable and honest contractor has the assignment and can be trusted; but, particularly in government jobs, where the "lowest responsible bidder" must be assigned the contract, if the bid has been figured too closely and there is danger of financial loss, very careful supervision must be provided. It is very difficult to prove that a bidder able to be bonded by an insurance company is irresponsible; not all insurance companies have as high standards for contractors' qualifications as might be desired. Consequently, a first-class clerk of works representing the institution, and sometimes the architect, is of great value. The clerk of works must, of course, be acceptable to both the institution and the architect and can be employed by either but is not part of the usual architectural services.

From the preceding, it can be seen that technically, at least, the lines of communication are fairly rigid. It suggests that the librarian should not have direct contact with the contractor, except in response to a request through the architect, as confusion will result if the builder and foreman have more than one source of information and direction. If there are two sources, conflicting directions inevitably result. The librarian should, of course, be interested and also watchful, but all dealings must be through the architect, or, if this has been agreed upon, through the representative of the institution or architect at the construction site.

Any library questions or afterthoughts should be directed only through the owner's planner or inspector to the architect. In practice, some of these questions will come up properly in the job review meetings and may be answered and acted upon at once, yet it is necessary to remember the correct channels and who has what legal authority. When job meetings become touchy or heated, it is especially necessary to remember what legal role each plays. The library representative usually has the least authority during construction. Documenting these meetings is customary, and can be useful and reduce later problems.

15.2 The Bid Package

A typical bid package for a large project will include an invitation to bid, instructions for bidders, the proposal, the agreement, general conditions, supplementary general conditions, affirmative action/equal employment opportunity special conditions, the drawings, the technical specifications, and any addendum or clarification issued before the bid date. Most of this material is very technical in nature, and it is not the intent of this volume to go into great detail. However, for the information of those who may be interested, a brief description of the most important elements is presented here. For small projects, parts of the bid package are abbreviated or combined to reduce the volume.

15.2.1 Invitation to Bid

The invitation to bid solicits contractors to bid on the project. Although each project may have a different document format, it is not unusual for the invitation to include a brief description of the project, an outline of the nature of the bid, the time and place for the bid opening, and perhaps a statement reserving the right to reject bids. Other important aspects may be pointed out in the invitation, such as a requirement for a corporate surety bond for payment and performance to be provided by the successful bidder, or the requirement that the bid must be accompanied by a bid bond.

15.2.2 Legal Documents and Bidding

Normally, written specifications are accompanied by a preface or introduction, which describes in detail (a) the "general conditions," or the legal contract terms under which the construction or remodeling of the building is undertaken; (b) "supplementary general conditions," which alter and amplify the "general conditions"; and (c) the "instructions to bidders," or the methods that will be used to arrive at and ensure the performance of these contract terms.

Because the first part of this preface, "general conditions," is basically a legal document, standard forms are available that incorporate into them the past experience of actual court or arbitration proceedings in connection with construction contracts. In the United States, standard contract forms of the general conditions for the construction of buildings are prepared and distributed by the American Institute of Architects and are regularly revised to incorporate or recognize the most up-to-date procedures. The architectural organizations of other countries have similar forms. Public authorities and governments responsible for directing a large amount of construction frequently have prepared their own standard form of general conditions. Sometimes a lawyer may be engaged to draw up one for an individual project.

The general conditions define the rights, duties, and responsibilities in the mutual undertaking of the institution, the architect, the contractor, and subcontractors, and they determine or direct ownership, protection, inspection, changes, claims, termination, payments, insurance, bonds, liens, and other general procedures.

Most frequently, the standard form is used for the general conditions, and its terms or procedures are adjusted to the local custom and law by means of the "supplementary general conditions." This supplement describes the modifications and additions to the standard form that may be desired or required on the particular project for which it is written. It is tailored to the specific project, to local conditions, and, perhaps, as the result of recent litigation, to the experience of the architect or institution.

The third part of the preface, "instructions to bidders," as its title implies, instructs all prospective contractors, who are planning to bid or present proposals to the institution for constructing or remodeling the building, on the methods they must follow and the obligations they must assume in their submission. These instructions are often accompanied by forms that are prescribed for the contractor's use (a) in submitting the proposal, or tender, (b) in providing for any required

bonds or guarantees, and (c) in signing an agreement with the institution.

The instructions to bidders should document for the contractor the intentions of the institution and the architect relative to the scope of the work, the bidding procedures, and the method of contract award.

The "scope of the work" presents a general description of the work to be done by the contractor, the premises upon which this work is to be constructed, and the contract documents in which it is specifically defined. It should point out any difficulties the contractor might be expected to encounter during the conduct of the job because of the requirements and operations of the library or any other department of the institution. If it is planned to have the general contractor work with other contractors engaged by the institution under separate contracts or if the contractor will operate in the same building jointly with the library, the full implications of required cooperation and coordination should be expressed. Together with a drawing describing the construction site, this section might elaborate upon temporary storage sites, worker parking, utility hookups, access routes for the site, and reuse by the contractor of surplus stone or marble or dirt held by the institution. Some of this descriptive information may appear in the section called "supplemental general conditions."

In the "supplemental general conditions" one should find requirements established by the institution to avoid excess noise during final exams, special coordination with campus experts on telecommunications and computer installations, provision of adequate protection for adjacent facilities and landscaping, and other special requirements.

"Bidding procedures" need to be defined so that the bidder may know the proper channels to follow to obtain bidding documents, to request and receive interpretations and clarifications of them, and to submit the bid in proper form.

Bids may be received in several forms, the most common of which is the "lump sum." This term is used to indicate a proposal on the part of the contractor agreeing to provide all labor and materials required for completion of the project as specified and drawn for a stated sum of money. On occasion the contractor may be requested to submit only an estimate of the construction cost and the amount of the proposed fee for conducting and directing the process of construction.

Sometimes, in this instance, the contractor is expected to guarantee that the final construction cost will not exceed the total amount of his or her estimated cost. Various types of contractual possibilities are discussed in Section 15.3.

The bidder is frequently required to state alternate prices, which may be added to or deducted from the base price, either lump sum or estimated cost, for increasing the scope of the work or for omitting or changing some part of the specified scope or quality.

15.2.3 Plans

In contrast to the schematic or design development phases, there will now be included no perspectives, isometric, or axonometric drawings. Although these were useful for understanding the way the building will look from campus approaches, and are frequently used during fundraising or presentations to trustees, they are of no help to the contractor.

There should be an architectural plan drawing showing each floor level of the building. It will illustrate this floor diagrammatically as if the roof or floor above had been removed, exposing the shape and size of all rooms and spaces and the location of all the doors, windows, columns, walls, stairs, elevators, and vertical shafts for distribution of utility and mechanical services. In addition, all fixtures and furnishings built into or attached to the building, such as washroom fixtures and bookstacks, will be shown. (See figs. 15.1 and 15.2.)

The locations of loose furniture may also be indicated, as these will help materially to clarify the objectives of the plan. Such locations are usually indicated with dotted lines or on a separate plan, as movable equipment is rarely the responsibility of the building contractor, who uses the drawing in estimating and constructing the library. Dotted lines contrasting with the solid lines of the main parts of the plan indicate that the object or space so presented is not part of the work expected from the contractor. They are frequently marked with the initials NIC (Not in Contract).

The dimensions must be given on the plans in feet and inches, or meters, and drawn to scale. In other words, the plans must be exact and proportionately reduced from the actual "full" size desired in the completed building so that any desired dimension can be determined by measuring it on the drawing and multiplying that measurement by the amount of reduction employed. Architects and engineers use rulers that have this multiplication factor incorporated in their markings and that can then be read directly in feet and inches or meters. These rulers are called architect's, or engineer's, scales, and the act of using them is "scaling." The scale, or the amount of proportional reduction used, should clearly be stated on each plan.

In the United States the term *architectural scale* is usually given to one expressing a foot by ⅟₁₆, ⅛, ¼, ⅜, ½, ¾, or 1 in.; the term *engineer's scale* to one expressing a foot by ⅟₂₀₀, ⅟₁₀₀, ⅟₅₀, ⅟₄₀, ⅟₂₀, or ⅟₁₀ in. The usual architectural scales employed on plans are ⅟₁₆ in. = 1 ft or ⅛ in. = 1 ft or ¼ in. = 1 ft. If a more detailed plan explanation is required, larger scales (⅜ in., ½ in., ¾ in., and 1 in. to 1 ft) are used, but these are more frequently employed for sections.

Metric scales, on the other hand, are referred to as 1:20, 1:25, 1:50, 1:75, or 1:125, where 1 mm equals 20 mm (1:20), 1 mm equals 25 mm (1:25), or 1,000 mm equals 50 meters (1:50), and so on. Because a scale of ¼ in. = 1 ft represents a scale of about one-fiftieth of full size, it would roughly be equal to a scale where 20 mm equals 1 meter, or 1:50. Likewise, ⅛-in. scale would be similar to 1:100, and ½-in. scale is close to 1:25. It is interesting to note that the proportionate scales of the drawings between the two systems of measurement are very close to the same, being off by 4 percent.

Plans of the roof and the plot are also included. These are sometimes combined on one drawing and usually use an engineer's scale, particularly if the building is a large one. However, architectural scales of ⅟₁₆ in., ⅟₃₂ in., or even ⅟₆₄ in. are sometimes employed. These would be equivalent to 1:200, 1:400, or 1:800 in metric terms. The roof plan is required to show the pitch, or direction of slope; the method of drainage on the roofs; and the location, housing, and size of mechanical services that project above the roof levels. Usually, safety regulations require door access or window access from the building to all flat roofs, a provision that is also an aid to maintenance and that should be shown on the roof plan. (See figs. 15.3 and 15.4.)

If a great deal of mechanical equipment is on the roof, rather than within the building, a roof plan at an architectural scale may be required in order to illustrate properly the sizes and locations.

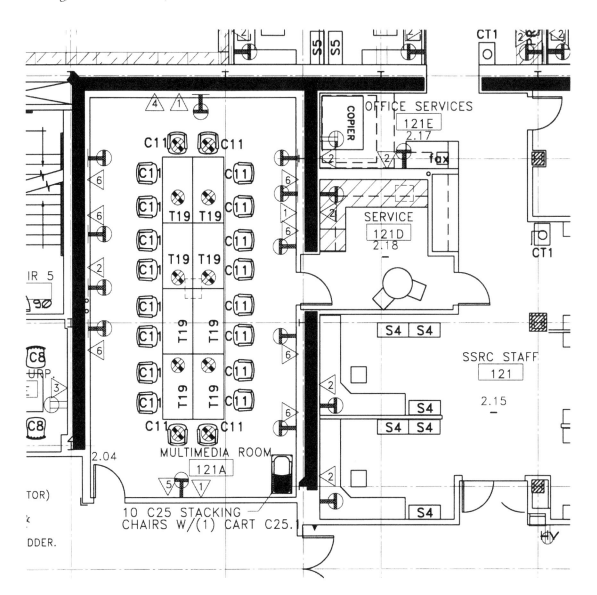

FIGURE 15.1   Furniture plan for a multimedia room. The style of tables and chairs was selected to provide flexibility in furniture arrangement, depending upon the size of the group and type of presentation. The symbols along the walls represent power and telephone/data outlets. The 10 symbols within the tables (four are under chairs) represent flush, floor-mounted combination power and telephone/data outlets. The dashed rectangle in the center of the room represents a ceiling-mounted data/video projector. The room also has marker boards on two walls, and a ceiling-mounted, motorized projection screen. (Fields Devereaux Architects & Engineers)

The increasing importance and amount of mechanical work in modern buildings has led to such an extensive use of the roof for elevator equipment, fans, cooling towers, and related ductwork and piping that there is a tendency to enclose all of it on a separate floor or roof-house of its own or to contain it within a barrier or fence built on the roof so as to screen the usually untidy appearance of this heterogeneous assembly of mechanical equipment. Radio and television

antennae and microwave dish receivers are also increasingly included in such plans.

The plot plan illustrates the location of the building relative to adjacent structures and the ground. It shows the source and direction of all services that must be brought into the building from outside and locates all walks, roads, parking areas, and planting beds and grass required as part of the completed building. If the site has existing trees, planting beds, ponds, streams, walks,

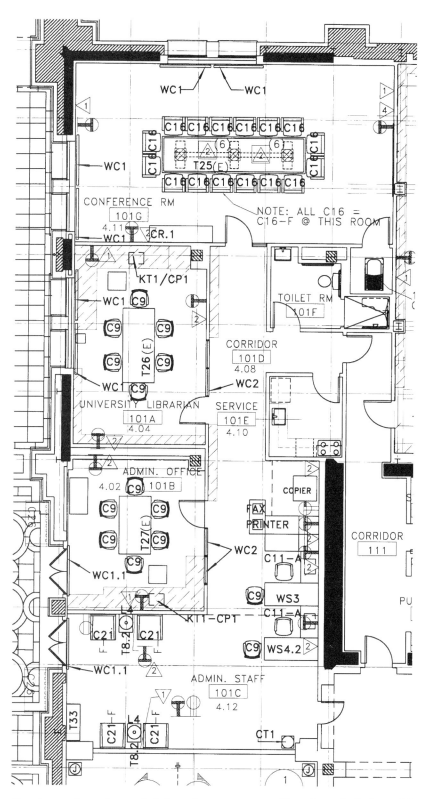

FIGURE 15.2 Furniture plan of an administrative area. Two offices have built-in (cabinetwork) work counters in addition to conference tables and chairs. The conference room has a marker board; a ceiling-mounted, motorized projection screen; flush, floor-mounted combination power and telephone/data outlets under the table; and a small closet for the storage of stacking chairs. The tables in two offices and the conference room are existing tables as indicated by the symbol (E). (Fields Devereaux Architects & Engineers)

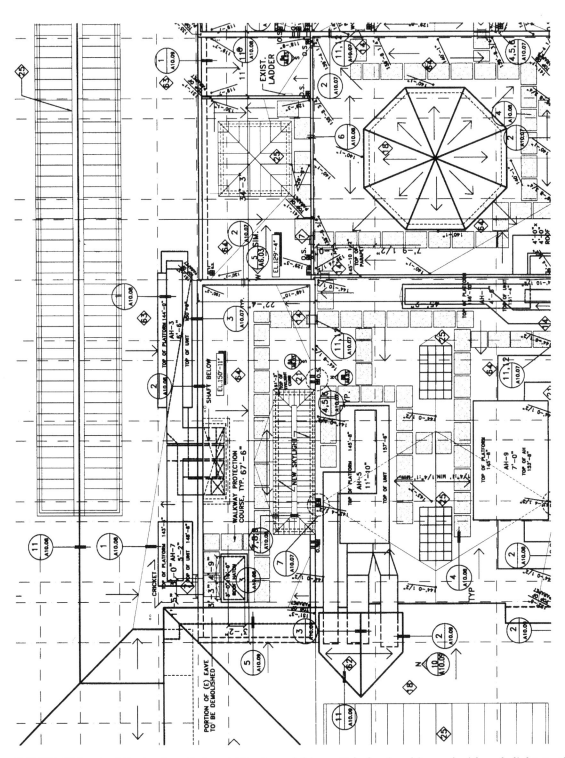

FIGURE 15.3 Architectural roof plan. At the top of this partial plan is a hip roof with a skylight; to the left is a portion of a hip roof; and at the lower right is a cupola. The remaining roof area consists of flat surfaces at different levels (note the height of two of the levels can be seen). This plan also shows the location of a roof hatch and protected traffic paths. Note the many arrows, all of which show the direction of drainage flow. (Fields Devereaux Architects & Engineers)

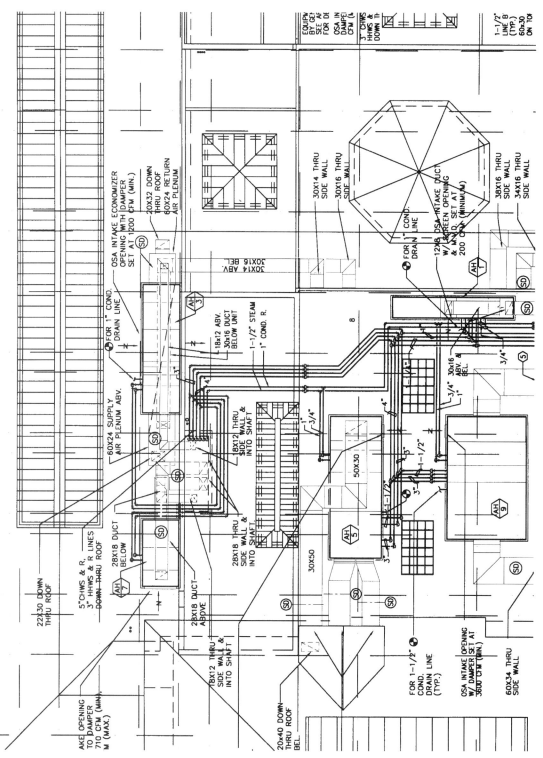

FIGURE 15.4   Mechanical roof plan. Note the differences between this plan and that of fig. 15.3. This plan shows piping and ductwork related to the building's mechanical systems. (Fields Devereaux Architects & Engineers)

roads, or buildings, the plan should show them so that they may be properly protected during construction or removed as part of the contract. Frequently, the land made available for the use of the contractor during the construction period must be restricted and protected so that the operations of both the institution and the contractors may be conducted without undue interference with each other. The limitation of the areas assigned to and to be protected by the contractor should be shown on the plot plan. In determining their size and locations, the architect must remember that space is required not only for storing and receiving equipment and building materials, but also for construction shanties, worker's facilities, and parking. Difficult access to the site will increase the building costs and the hardships placed on the contractor, and will be reflected in the construction cost.

The plot plan shows the relationship of the building to the ground by elevations or grades, which indicate the number of feet, or meters, any particular spot is above sea level or some other predetermined point that will remain undisturbed during construction. These grades are based upon a survey of the site, usually made by a professional surveyor. The main floor of the building should be given a grade, and elevations of the new grounds and walks should be indicated either by spot grades or by grade lines, which represent the cut that would result if all the ground above any particular elevation were removed.

In the United States, grade elevations are usually indicated in feet and tenths of a foot (261.25), rather than in feet and inches (261′ 3″), just as plot plans are usually in engineers' rather than architects' scales.

Elevations. The plans of the architect are supplemented by elevations. Whereas the plan is a horizontal graphic representation of the library to a scale, the elevation is its vertical external representation to a scale. Drawings of interior walls of a particular room are also called elevations; these are commonly prepared for rest rooms and for walls with special features of nearly any kind. Like the building plans, the scale is almost always an architectural one.

The elevations show building heights and the location in the vertical planes of doors, windows, and columns or supports on the various facades, and the materials from which they and the walls are built. Interior elevations will show mirrors,

paper towel dispensers, and other rest room fixtures, and other special features, such as counters, book return slots, special panels or moldings, counters, built-in shelving, and the like.

Thus, elevations also illustrate the appearance of the building or interior wall. (Because it is a graphic representation, there is no attempt at perspective, and the most distant facade or element is drawn to the same scale as the closest.) For each elevation a "picture" plane is chosen, usually parallel to the facade or wall that is represented, and nothing is illustrated on that elevation that is not reached by a line drawn perpendicular to that chosen plane. Thus, a rectangular building or room can be fully illustrated by four direct elevations, one taken parallel to each of its four sides. The elevation of one of these sides shows no part of any other.

This would not be true of another building shape; at least one of its facades would be shown foreshortened on one of the picture planes parallel to the other sides, because it can be reached by lines drawn perpendicular to that plane. A circular or curved shape results in a gradual increase in this foreshortening in proportion as the curve recedes away from the picture plane.

The foreshortened part of an elevation always shows the actual scale of the vertical dimensions, but the horizontal scale is reduced in accordance with the degree at which the plan slopes away from the picture plane.

An elevation is drawn to give information necessary in the construction of a building. The locations of floors, roofs, and other objects hidden by the facade that is being illustrated are shown by dotted lines. The design of features, such as windows and doors, can be drawn carefully once and repeated elsewhere only in outline. The indication of materials is stylized and usually confined to one end of the elevation.

It can be seen, as a result, that an elevation drawing frequently gives a very inadequate idea of the aesthetic appearance of the building. Such drawings are often used, however, as the basis for an elevation "rendering," which represents in different colors or values the materials and openings of the building and which often ranks among the most interesting and artistic products from an architect's office. These, of course, are usually products of an earlier design phase and can be especially useful during fund-raising.

To the layperson, however, the stylization required in an elevation and its lack of perspective make this type of rendering somewhat difficult to visualize. As a result, during schematics many architects furnish their clients with rendered perspective drawings or models, both of which illustrate the aesthetic appearance of the building with more realism and are generally better understood.

Sections. To illustrate a building completely, the plans and elevations are supplemented by one or more "sections." A section is a vertical cut through a chosen part of the building that exposes the elevations and vertical relationships of the spaces. It shows ceiling heights, interstitial space (between the ceiling and the floor above), construction methods, stair details, and interior design, and furnishes an excellent visual picture of the spatial relationships in the building, which can only be deduced from a combination of the plans and elevations. Sections are usually drawn at a cut through the building at column lines where there are distinctive details to be explained. Sections taken 90° from each other are useful, and some are needed to depict, for example, all four distinctive walls of certain rooms.

Illustrative sections are usually drawn to the architectural scale used for the plans or elevations. However, one of the most frequent uses of sections is to detail specific objects or features in the building, in which case they are drawn to a much larger architectural scale, usually ¾ in. or 3 in. (which would be 1:16 or 1:4 in metric scale), but sometimes as large as one-half or actual full size. Detail sections of this nature may be cut either vertically or horizontally and are used to explain the construction details and shapes of walls, windows, toilets, stairs, and any other architectural feature that needs such careful illustration in order to ensure that the required soundness and appearance will be incorporated into the building.

A plan, elevation, or section is said to be "reflected" when the surfaces it illustrates are behind or above, rather than before or below, the chosen plane or cut being used on the particular drawing in question. (A reflected electrical ceiling plan as shown in fig. 15.5 is a common example.)

Because plans, elevations, sections, and details for a building are drawings to a scale, a desired size or dimension can be ascertained from the drawings by the use of a rule or scale. In addition, important dimensions that cannot be left subject to the small inaccuracies attendant upon

scaling are written on these drawings. Notes explaining the construction or specifying the finish or materials that are being illustrated supplement the drafted information. The extent of the written dimensions and the items noted are indicated with arrows or dots at the end of light connecting lines.

Schedules. Drawings contain insufficient information to enable a contractor to estimate time and costs and build a satisfactory building. They must be supplemented with written directions. Most of these are incorporated into schedules, which may either be included on the drawings or bound in the specifications. Such schedules are usually keyed by symbols, numbers, or letters to those parts of the drawings to which they apply.

Schedules are most frequently used in the following ways:

1. *Room or finish schedules.* These schedules tabulate the materials that will form the finished surfaces of the walls, floors, ceilings, base, and dado, and verbally point out any special feature that may be required in a particular room. In order to key a room or finish schedule to the plans, each room is given a name, area designation, or number on both the plan and schedule. The finish schedule then tabulates the finishes after each space designation.

2. *Door schedules.* The doors or openings inside the building may be of different widths, heights, design, and material. (See fig. 15.6.) They may be solid or may contain glass panels. They may be flush wood or paneled metal. They may be hung in wood frames or metal bucks, which in turn may have sidelights or transoms. Ventilation requirements may call for the use of louvers in the doors or for leaving a specified amount of clear space between the bottom and the floor. Sound or temperature insulation may require soundproofing or weather stripping.

The individual requirements for doors may be, and usually are, many and varied. As a result, each door or opening in the building is given a symbol that refers directly to the schedule, where the size and other characteristics can immediately be determined. This schedule is usually accompanied by scale elevations showing the main type of door designs that are being described.

3. *Hardware schedules, painting schedules, furniture schedules, and stack schedules.* These schedules relate to or supplement the finish and door schedules. Supplementary schedules such as these are often compiled during, rather than before,

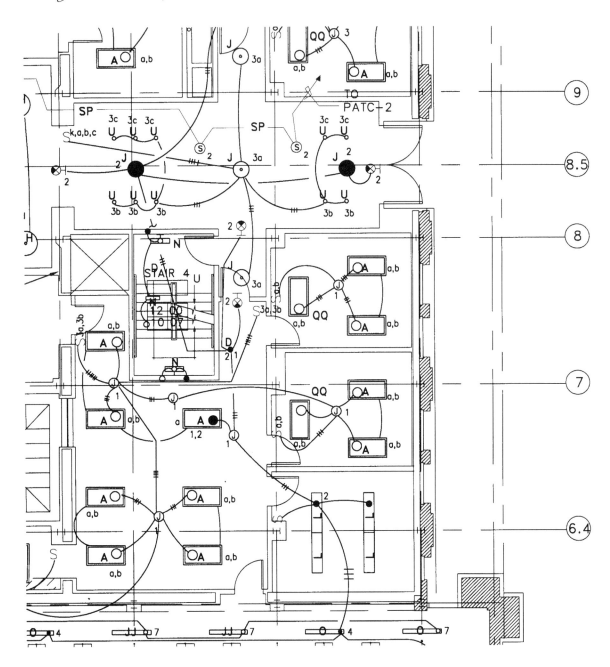

FIGURE 15.5 Electrical lighting plan. Although similar to the architectural reflected ceiling plan, this plan shows especially the light fixtures and lighting circuits (generally curved lines with hatches across them indicating the number of wires represented), junction box locations (small circles with Js in them), switch locations (a big S at the wall, usually to one side of a door), speakers (circles with Ss in them), and other electrical features that relate to the ceiling. The type "J" light fixtures (along column line 8.5) happen to be custom fixtures with incandescent lamps designed in a style compatible with the original fixtures in this 1918 building. Other fixtures in nonpublic areas (including type "A") are contemporary fluorescent fixtures, recessed in a suspended T-bar and acoustic panel ceiling. (Fields Devereaux Architects & Engineers)

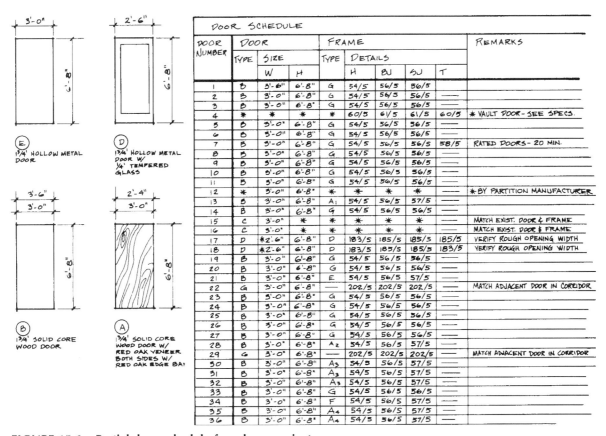

DOOR NUMBER	DOOR TYPE	SIZE W	SIZE H	FRAME TYPE	DETAILS H	BU	SU	T	REMARKS
1	B	3'-6"	6'-8"	G	54/5	56/5	56/5	—	
2	B	3'-0"	6'-8"	G	54/5	56/5	56/5		
3	B	3'-0"	6'-8"	G	54/5	56/5	56/5		
4	*	*	*	*	60/5	61/5	61/5	60/5	* VAULT DOOR - SEE SPECS.
5	B	3'-0"	6'-8"	G	54/5	56/5	56/5		
6	B	3'-0"	6'-8"	G	54/5	56/5	56/5		
7	B	3'-0"	6'-8"	G	54/5	56/5	56/5	58/5	RATED DOORS - 20 MIN.
8	B	3'-0"	6'-8"	G	54/5	56/5	56/5	—	
9	B	3'-0"	6'-8"	G	54/5	56/5	56/5	—	
10	B	3'-0"	6'-8"	G	54/5	56/5	56/5	—	
11	B	3'-0"	6'-8"	G	54/5	56/5	56/5	—	
12	*	3'-0"	6'-8"	*	*	*	*	—	* BY PARTITION MANUFACTURER
13	B	3'-0"	6'-8"	A1	54/5	56/5	57/5	—	
14	B	3'-0"	6'-8"	G	54/5	56/5	56/5	—	
15	C	3'-0"	*	*	*	*	*	—	MATCH EXIST. DOOR & FRAME
16	C	3'-0"	*	*	*	*	*	—	MATCH EXIST. DOOR & FRAME
17	D	*2'-6"	6'-8"	D	183/5	185/5	185/5	185/5	VERIFY ROUGH OPENING WIDTH
18	D	*2'-6"	6'-8"	D	183/5	185/5	185/5	183/5	VERIFY ROUGH OPENING WIDTH
19	B	3'-0"	6'-8"	G	54/5	56/5	56/5	—	
20	B	3'-0"	6'-8"	G	54/5	56/5	56/5	—	
21	B	3'-0"	6'-8"	E	54/5	56/5	57/5	—	
22	G	3'-0"	6'-8"	—	202/5	202/5	202/5	—	MATCH ADJACENT DOOR IN CORRIDOR
23	B	3'-0"	6'-8"	G	54/5	56/5	56/5	—	
24	B	3'-0"	6'-8"	G	54/5	56/5	56/5	—	
25	B	3'-0"	6'-8"	G	54/5	56/5	56/5	—	
26	B	3'-0"	6'-8"	G	54/5	56/5	56/5	—	
27	B	3'-0"	6'-8"	G	54/5	56/5	56/5	—	
28	B	3'-0"	6'-8"	A2	54/5	56/5	57/5	—	
29	G	3'-0"	6'-8"	—	202/5	202/5	202/5	—	MATCH ADJACENT DOOR IN CORRIDOR
30	B	3'-0"	6'-8"	A3	54/5	56/5	57/5	—	
31	B	3'-0"	6'-8"	A3	54/5	56/5	57/5	—	
32	B	3'-0"	6'-8"	A3	54/5	56/5	57/5	—	
33	B	3'-0"	6'-8"	G	54/5	56/5	56/5	—	
34	B	3'-0"	6'-8"	F	54/5	56/5	57/5	—	
35	B	3'-0"	6'-8"	A4	54/5	56/5	57/5	—	
36	B	3'-0"	6'-8"	A4	54/5	56/5	57/5	—	

FIGURE 15.6   Partial door schedule for a large project.

the construction of the building, but they should be completed in time to have the materials and work based on them ready for installation and performance without delaying the progress of the job.

4. *Mechanical schedules.* Schedules for the finished materials required for the mechanical trades are important items in the appearance of the building. Electrical, plumbing, and heating fixtures have a functional purpose, and also a conspicuous and extensive aesthetic effect. Their location and use are generally keyed into the mechanical plans by schedules, and an adequate understanding of the completed library cannot be reached without carefully consulting these schedules.

5. *Structural engineering schedules.* The structural engineering also needs to be supplemented by schedules that indicate to the builder the size and strength of columns, beams, and floor slabs. If they are of steel, the size and weight must be given; if of concrete, the dimensions, the amount of reinforcing, and the strength of the mix are given.

6. *Fixture schedules.* The electrical engineer will supply information sufficient to identify each light fixture in a schedule. (See fig. 15.7.) It is often surprising how many different light fixtures there will be in a new building.

7. *Wiring schedule.* There may be a schedule of site-specific electrical services, including telephone, fiber-optic, ISDN, various forms of coaxial cable, and twisted pair with each service box and the nature of the service listed. Other kinds of wiring schedules apply to the listing of circuits for a circuit panel, the listing of wire types for power service, and the listing of various other electrical components. As with all schedules, these will supplement the drawings and be used in part as a form of check to ensure that each unique condition is accounted for.

15.2.4 Specifications

The drawings and the schedules explain and illustrate the size, shape, finish, and relationship of all the spaces, walls, and materials contained in the building. They do not specify the quality of the materials or the level of the workmanship. These are described and enumerated in a written specification that accompanies and complements the drawings. In the United States, specifications group under the various trades or suppliers all the work in the building that each will perform or furnish. The required quality is carefully explained and the expected performance of all materials is specified. The method of workmanship

---

LIGHTING FIXTURE SCHEDULE

TYPE	DESCRIPTION
A	Recessed fluorescent fixture with oneway deep cell parabolic louver containing one F35T12 lamp and one single lamp ballast. See spec. Section 16500/2.03C for additional requirements. Columbia #4551G-43-141-SU/A Lightolier #CD1791R-1
AA	Same description as fixture Type A except fixture contains a two lamp ballast. Columbia #4551G-43-141/SU/AA Lightolier #CD1791R-1
AB	Same description as fixture Type A except the fixture does not contain a ballast, i.e., the lamp in this fixture is served from the two lamp ballast located in fixture Type AA.
B	Same description as fixture Type A except fixture contains two F35T12 lamps and one two lamp ballast. Columbia #4551G-43-142-SU/B Lightolier #CD1791R1-3
C	Recessed two lamp fluorescent fixture with one-way deep cell, parabolic louver assembly of semi-specular anodized aluminum sheet secured to housing with concealed latches. Die-formed steel housing with louvered or slotted back for plenum air return through the fixture, "quick connect" plate to permit wiring without opening fixture wire way, and perimeter slots with adjustable blade dampers for return air capability directly into the plenum. Provide snap-on shrouds for installation of fixtures in concealed spline ceiling in continuous rows as shown. Perimeter air slot finished in matte black; trim frame matte white baked-on enamel. Two F35T12 lamps. Columbia #451G-43-142-HE-S Lightolier #68574-HE-MOD
D	Surface mounted 4'-0" fluorescent fixture with extruded prismatic acrylic wrap-around diffuser and injection molded end caps. Two F35T12 lamps per fixture. Fixture rated for installation on low density ceilings. Lightolier #10321-LD Sylvania #ND-2404-LD
EA	Ceiling recessed mounted "edge-lit" exit sign with 277 volt ballast for F8T6 fluorescent lamps. Housing and trim shall be diecast aluminum. 6" high x 3/4" stroke engraved green letters on white background. Provide two F8T6 lamps (2 circuit) per housing. Ceiling trim plate to be painted matte white. Provide directional arrows as shown on drawings. Prescolite #ER7 Series McPhilben #45AR-6-F Series

FIGURE 15.7 Lighting fixture schedule. This example is one of nine pages of the fixture schedule for a large project in which some 57 different fixtures are described. In this case, they are part of the specifications.

is described and procedures explained sufficient to achieve a desired level of quality. The control of materials and workmanship explained in a carefully written specification can aid materially in accomplishing a satisfactory result, both aesthetically and functionally.

Often the desired result or quality can best be attained by specifying one particular material or manufacturer. The architect may have decided that the granite or limestone from a predetermined quarry is necessary for the proper appearance of the building, or that a particular bookstack or elevator manufacturer can best satisfy the functional requirements of the library. If so, only that material or, if legal, the particular manufacturer should be specified.

In buildings for private institutions, this can be done directly by name or carried in the contract documents as an "allowance" of the amount of money determined as necessary for purchase or installation. The specification may name a firm producing the required quality and add "or equal," thereby allowing others to bid but placing on them the requirement for proof of equivalency in every respect. If, however, other materials or manufacturers are considered as equals, the specifications will also name them.

For public institutions or those projects funded by government agencies, the general requirement is that at least three manufacturers or suppliers be named, and naming of only one is not allowed, except under unusual circumstances. If allowances are permitted in public projects, work covered by such a budget line must also be let competitively.

Specifications often describe in detail the material or manufactured items desired and allow any supplier or manufacturer who is able to satisfy the specifications to furnish the required items. It is common to treat metal bookshelving in this fashion. Several pages may be devoted to important details, from bookends to cantilevered shelf brackets and from the quality of paint finish to the acceptable forms of interior cross bracing. If one or more names "or equal" are specified, the architect is responsible for deciding if a particular product is actually equal, although the owner often is a key contributor to this decision.

Specifications of shelving may need to be very detailed. The Harvard Depository, for example, required paint on the 6-ft-deep (1.829-m) shelving to be nonacidic. The book trays 18 in. (457 mm) long, stored at right angles to the shelving, were specified to meet tests of strength, durability, ease of assembly, and potential acidity. Trays were sealed with a coating that gives a pH of 9.9, resists abrasion, and prevents absorption of acid, other gases, and moisture. Should the sealant wear away, each run of the paper composing the trays was tested to ensure nonacidity; paper pH was held between 7.2 and 8.5 and the pH of the glues between 10 and 10.5.

In the specifications document, the sectional division into trades and suppliers most frequently used today is as follows: general requirements; site work; excavation and grading; concrete work; masonry; waterproofing; roofing; structural steel; miscellaneous metalwork; doors, windows, and frames; carpentry; lathing and plastering; tile work; flooring; painting; glass and glazing; and the "mechanical trades"—that is, plumbing; heating, ventilating, and air conditioning; and electrical and telecommunications work.

The last three sectional divisions of the specifications listed immediately above, the "mechanical trades," cover work that has become more important in recent years. For instance, in 1900, in a good many library buildings still in use today, the cost of the work assigned to the mechanical trades was no more than 15 percent of the total construction cost of the job. Today, it is rarely less than 35 percent and, if the library is air conditioned, may run as high as 45 percent or even somewhat more depending on the extensiveness of the computer technologies.

As the importance of the mechanical trades in building construction has increased, so has the complexity of the installations. Electrical and pneumatic controls, computers, head ends, servers, transformers, motors, fans, pumps, switchboards, valves, and contactors, to name the more usual devices hidden from view in panels, closets, and mechanical rooms, multiply with every added mechanical comfort; space is required to house them, and new building laws or regulations must be satisfied to ensure that any possible faulty operation will not create a hazard to the occupants or contents of the building.

An electrical specification, for instance, may cover raceways, cable trays, conductors, outlets and junction boxes, interior pull boxes and wire ways, cabinets, wiring devices, nameplates and warning signs, disconnect and safety switches, vibration isolation, restraining devices, main and distribution switchboards, grounding system, panel boards, and so forth. Here is a sample of the specification for cable trays:

> Cable tray shall consist of galvanized sheet metal side rails, galvanized ladder type metal bottom parts, straight sections, connectors, tees and elbows. Cable tray shall be 12″ wide, 6″ high and 18″ wide, 6″ high (305 by 152 and 457 by 152 mm). Tray shall be capable of supporting 125 pounds of cable per lineal foot (186 kg per m). Provide all associated components for a complete installation. [Then follow details of the supports and supplementary framing, and then names of acceptable manufacturers: three for cable trays, two for beam clamps and steel channels, and two for fire barriers.]

Just as the structural engineer prepares structural drawings and specifications and assures the architect that the strength of the floors, walls, and columns will be adequate to support the loads expected to be imposed on them by the building, its contents, and its occupants, similarly the architect also engages mechanical engineers who are responsible for assuring the proper installation and operation of the mechanical systems. To accomplish this, these engineers prepare special plans devoted entirely to illustrating the work of the mechanical trades, write their sections of the specifications, and compile any schedules pertaining to these specifications and drawings.

The architect may employ one engineer to prepare drawings and specifications for all the mechanical work or one or more separate specialists in the engineering work required for each of the three trades—that is, a heating, ventilating, and air-conditioning engineer; an electrical and lighting engineer; and a sanitary and plumbing engineer.

These engineers are responsible to the architect for the preparation of drawings illustrating the installation and operation of work assigned to their respective trades. These installations will occupy space and affect the appearance of the building, and their operation will be accompanied by a certain amount of noise and will affect the comfort of the occupants. To ensure that the satisfactory operation of the mechanical plant will not adversely affect either the aesthetics or the function of the library, the engineering drawings and specifications prepared to illustrate the mechanical trades must be coordinated with the architectural drawings and specifications prepared to illustrate the space relationships, sizes, finishes, and structure.

This coordination among the mechanical trades and the structure, architecture, and furnishings is difficult at best and can be accomplished only if the drawings ensure space enough in plan and elevation for the equipment, ductwork, piping, and conduit, and if they assign proper locations in the library areas for the visible parts of the installations. Every detail must be consonant with comfort and aesthetics and must not allow the work of one trade to conflict with that of another.

In addition to this coordination on drawings, the specifications require coordination during construction between trades. They state which trade will have precedence in the choice of the space available; and they indicate that the mechanical drawings are, of necessity, largely diagrammatic, so that the actual job installation must be made to fit precisely into the space assigned to it on the drawing or available for it on the job. Librarians should note that, due to field conditions, the horizontal routing of ducts and conduit frequently varies somewhat from the drawings, so special comment on routing may need to be in the specifications if that is crucial over or around bookstacks, computer facilities, preservation labs, and the like.

15.2.5 Addenda, Clarifications, and Shop Drawings

The architect has three other written instruments that are employed during the bidding and construction periods to ensure the completeness and proper interpretation of the working drawings and specifications.

The first of these is the addendum, which is a written amplification of the contract documents distributed after they have been issued to the bidders just before the bids have been received. It is the result of a careful review of the drawings and specifications by the architect, engineers, and the institution, a review that is often conducted during the bidding period and that should correct any discrepancies, conflicts, errors, omissions, or misunderstandings that may have crept into these documents during their preparation. Because addenda are prepared and issued before bid opening, they become part of the contract documents and are just as binding on the building contractor as the basic drawings and specifications.

The second and third of these instruments are produced during the construction period. The architect, during this period, may issue explanatory detail drawings, sometimes called "clarifications," which will enlarge and clarify sections of the original drawings so that the parts in question may be manufactured and installed in exact accordance with the functional and aesthetic requirements. This may be necessary, for example, if it is found that an unanticipated condition of a duct run crossing a sprinkler pipe below a beam in the ceiling requires the replacement and realignment of a specified metal frame supporting the ceiling, and this condition was not previously depicted.

Much the same objective is also attained by shop drawings. The difference between a detail clarification drawing and a shop drawing is that, whereas the former is produced by the architect and permitted by the specifications, the latter is required by the specifications and produced by the contractor and approved by the architect, often very close to the time when that drawing condition must be fabricated.

Both are valuable tools, and both may make as important a contribution to the success of the work as do the supervision of construction and the written directives of the architect. Details can be very important to review. Concerning carpet installations, for example, a seaming diagram may be required, at least for critical traffic areas, to guard against maintenance problems at seams that could appear much earlier than should be expected given normal wear.

15.3
The Type of Contract

A contract can be established in several different ways. The decision as to how the contract will be set up may be made quite early in the project, but certainly no later than the end of the contract document phase. Most discussion in the preceding section assumed that the contract was based upon a competitive bid.

Other contract methods include construction management (sometimes called CM), fee contract, turnkey, design-build, fast track, negotiated based on cost plus overhead, negotiated as a lump sum, or a combination. Each of these will be discussed briefly.

Competitive bid. Competitive bidding is probably the most common form of establishing a contract in the United States. For obvious reasons, it should assure the best possible price, provided the contract documents are clear and complete, and provided several reputable contractors bid the job, sometimes as many as six or eight, occasionally more, especially on public works. There are risks and consequent steps that can be taken to reduce those risks. To minimize the prospect of contractors who lack experience, who bid for change orders, or who may be in financial difficulty, bidders are sometimes prequalified. Bid bonds and performance bonds are aimed at reducing certain risks of the bidding process. Retention of a right to reject a bid for any reason can help in dealing with unanticipated problems. The best protection from contractual risk may be provided by architectural and construction experts; their advice should be sought and considered. Where there are unusual conditions, such as working in an existing occupied building, and if the project is to be competitively bid, great care must be taken to ensure a smooth operation. In the case of the occupied building, probably some form of a negotiated contract is the safest; unfortunately, this is not always possible.

Competitive bids are the norm for projects in publicly financed institutions and are often required by governmental regulation. The lowest qualified bid must ordinarily be taken, for equipment as well as for construction and landscaping. Such a policy, which requires contracting with the low bidder under competition, is regarded as a protection against political pressures, thus reducing the chances of favoritism deals and kickbacks.

Construction management. One technique of cost control is to hire a construction manager early in the design process to work with the design team to achieve the best product for the least cost. The construction manager in this case is usually a contractor who provides a form of "value engineering," though this value engineering is typically less formal and perhaps less effective than the value engineering process described in Chapter 9.

In the pure construction management project, the construction manager will provide cost estimates through the design process with a guarantee that the project can be constructed for the estimated price. At the completion of design, assuming everyone finds the estimated cost within reason, the construction manager takes over as the general contractor as agreed upon under the last estimate. The weakness of this method is that it is nearly impossible to know if the price is really realistic. The advantage, of course, is that the general contractor is very much part of the project virtually from the beginning, which can be very beneficial when the project involves unknown conditions, such as in a complicated building reconstruction, or when the working drawings or specifications are incomplete for whatever reason.

A construction management contract can easily be segmented so that at the end of the contract documents phase, should the institution wish, the arrangement can be terminated and the project put out for competitive bid. But, if this is likely, the construction manager should know from the start. It should be noted that the construction management process involves fees.

Fee contract. A fee contract is basically another name for construction management. Such an approach is ideal when the time of completion is a factor, if the quality of construction desired is unusually high, if the project requires an extraordinary approach to the design and methods of erection, or if the proper determination of the full scope of the work by means of drawings and specifications is difficult.

A fee contract is usually negotiated directly with a chosen contractor of predetermined competence and ability, but the selection is sometimes the result of competitive bidding between two or more contractors. The final choice between them can be based either on the fee requested, the amount of the estimated cost, the time required for completion, or any combination of the three. This type of contract has every advantage except that of predetermined minimal cost. Because of the careful selection of bidders, choice of a contractor may be made and construction begun before the drawings and specifications are fully finished. Thus months may be cut from the schedule for completion of construction. The contractor is selected on the basis of ability rather than of minimal cost, and the institution and architect have much greater control over construction procedures and purchases. The advice, experience, and cooperation of the contractor are made available during the determination of building procedures and costs rather than afterward.

Turnkey. A turnkey project is one in which the architect, the construction manager, or both are handed the program, schedule, and budget (or request for proposal, the RFP) at the beginning, and it is agreed that the project will be produced within the schedule and budget for a fixed price. This technique is particularly well suited for a tight schedule. It is not very responsive to the evolution of the design in response to a changing environment as the review process may be very limited. It has been used in academic institutions, and it has merit under certain circumstances. However, the authors would be reluctant to recommend this technique in most cases. An exception might be a warehouse storage facility, though even then the program must be exceptionally thorough if the product is to meet fully the needs of the institution.

Design-build. A variation of the turnkey project is the design-build concept, which may take several forms. The following outlines three phases of the general procedure.

First, a very complete program is developed, including the detailing of basic design and planning requirements. Established with considerable care are the building module, size, and shape; the size and location of wall openings, stairs, rooms, and other building and site elements; design criteria for the structural, electrical, and mechanical systems, including the testing requirements; and the bottom line budget figure. The detail necessary in the program phase is such that a person well established in architectural construction must be involved, and, unless this expertise is available in-house, fees will be added to the established budget figure.

The second step takes the form of a competition. Again the program must spell out the exact details. One project allows the prequalified participants three weeks to review the program (in this case referred to as a request for proposal, or RFP), after which eight weeks are provided for the development of each participant's proposal. All drawings and other documentation are to be carefully prepared so as to hide the identity of the participant during the judging process. The process, for example, involves specifying exactly the paper to be used for the drawings, as well as the use of a separate auditing firm, which receives the documentation and assigns numbers to each item. The judging process is also detailed. It may involve a system of quality points that are assigned to the proposal. The winning entry is thus the one with the lowest price per quality point. Any entry that exceeds the basic budget is rejected.

In the example referred to, the winner receives the contract, and the five runners-up receive a stipend of $5,000 each. This cost, as well as the cost of administration for the competition, must be added to the base budget to determine the total project cost.

The third phase establishes a firm contract for the preparation of the construction documents and the construction itself for a fixed fee. The construction may be either conventional or fast track as discussed below. Alternatives are not allowed, and change orders are strictly the responsibility of the contractor.

As with the turnkey process, the evolution of the design in concert with the librarian and evolving library needs is limited. It is an interesting concept that warrants consideration, but it may not be ideal for exceedingly complex projects. As with any approach, there are risks. The benefits over more traditional methods, though difficult to fully substantiate as real, include accelerated turnaround time, minimal involvement on the part of the institution once the process is in the hands of the contractor (which may be an attraction for smaller institutions), realization of a product for a fixed budget, and exposure to a field of solutions. Some may argue that this approach gets the most for the least cost, but this point is difficult to prove in most cases.

Fast track. The fast track approach to a project breaks the project up into several sequential projects, such as site preparation and mass excavation, footings and foundations, the structural shell, the exterior envelope and interior partitions, and interior finishes and equipment. The concept holds that while construction is under way on one phase, the design work can continue on the next phase, resulting in an accelerated schedule and presumably cost savings, especially in an era of high inflation.

There are substantial risks with the fast track method, and it probably should only be considered for a fairly straightforward project that might have extended over one or more years. Among the risks are changing code requirements, a lack of firm commitment to a final budgeted cost for much of the project, and the possibility that a design change at a later date will render earlier work obsolete. Except under special circumstances of unusual urgency, the authors are reluctant to recommend the fast track method as a general approach.

Negotiated contract. Just as the name implies, a negotiated contract exists when a single contractor is asked to submit a proposal for a project. Design contracts are usually, in effect, negotiated contracts. They can be based on cost plus overhead, with perhaps an agreed-upon maximum, or they can be a fixed price contract, often called a lump-sum contract. Contractors welcome negotiated contracts as the risk of losing money is almost zero. By the same token, negotiated contracts usually will cost more, although this is difficult to prove unless there is also a competitive bid. However, it is unlikely that a contractor will provide a proposal for a negotiated contract when there is also going to be a competitive bid. One or the other technique must be chosen.

The major advantage of the negotiated contract is that there is greater flexibility to work with the contractor in refining schedules, construction techniques, or even design details during the course of the project. The negotiated contract is especially suitable in difficult renovation work when the scheduling may be very complex or where there is a great deal of unknown work in an existing structure. Most publicly funded institutions can only use a negotiated contract under very unusual conditions; and on most large projects it is probably not an appropriate approach even in geographically very remote or difficult locations.

Combination. For a given circumstance, a combination of the above techniques may be used. For example, a negotiated contract may be formulated with a construction manager to oversee the work, but the subcontractors may be required to submit competitive bids with final acceptance by the institution. Or, the excavation might be contracted as a negotiated bid, and the balance of the work as a competitive bid. The concept of the fast track method might involve the prepurchase by the institution of major items, such as the structural steel or the mechanical equipment, which is then assigned to the contractor once construction begins.

Nearly all the techniques have good and bad points; the final decision will be in the hands of the institution's business offices, with the advice of the architect and perhaps the institution's project or construction experts. For the librarian the area of greatest concern will likely be in renovation projects in an occupied facility where the ongoing operational needs of the library must be accommodated. The nature of the contract will dramatically affect the specifications and drawings in this case, as the more competitive the bid, the more carefully one must describe the requirements of the project to ensure expected results. Another way of looking at this is to expect that with greater competition, more change orders will be required as surprises are found and room for negotiation is limited.

In most cases, but not all, the type of bid received determines the method of contract award. Thus a lump-sum bid usually results in a lump-sum contract, an estimated cost-plus-fee bid in a cost-plus-fee contract, and a guaranteed-maximum estimate in a guaranteed-maximum-cost contract.

Public authorities are usually required to let all building contracts on a lump-sum basis. The advantages of this type of contract are several. In theory, the cost of construction can be budgeted at a specific amount, and all risks of actual costs greater than those estimated are assumed by the contractor. However, the fact is that there will be change orders, which are discussed later. On the open and highly competitive construction market, lower bids are apt to be realized than by any other method. Frequently, on private work, the bidders are limited to an invited, previously approved group of contractors whose former work has been satisfactory to the institution and the architect. In this case, also, the award is usually made to the lowest bidder. The institution, however, in both public and private work, retains the right to reject any and all bids, if it is in its or the public's interest legally to do so.

In any case, when the plans and specifications have been prepared, bids have been received, and the contract has been let, a new member of the planning team has been chosen. The contractor enters the picture, and actual construction begins. Obviously, the contractor is essential to the success of the project, perhaps at this stage the most important member of the team, for upon the contractor rests the responsibility to construct what has earlier been only a concept drawn from the minds of architects, librarians, and engineers and set down in diagrams and words on paper.

15.4
The Review Process and Negotiations

This section will discuss the review process and, to some extent, the planning process that occurs following bidding and during construction.

Once the bids are opened, they are good for a fixed period of time as specified in the contract documents. Sixty days is typical. During this period, the successful contractor is selected and a period of review or negotiation or both takes place. The bid review rarely will involve the librarian. Yet the librarian may have some interest in assuring that certain aspects are carefully considered.

In a competitive bid, if the bids are all within 10 percent of each other, there is reasonable assurance that a good bid has been received. A "good" bid means that bidders did a thorough job, did material "takeoffs" carefully, and prepared estimates with a minimum of padding over their necessary margin of profit. A set of bids that range much more than 10 percent may indicate a booming construction business climate, which is not favorable to the institution, or that the drawings and specifications have omissions or ambiguities that the contractor covers by bidding higher than would otherwise have been necessary, or that the institution's reputation suggests extra meetings or time delays that can push up costs to the contractor. Where there is one exceptionally low bid, there is always the possibility of an error on the part of the contractor. Unless there are human errors or other problems, such as an incomplete bid, the lowest bidder should be awarded the contract provided the bid is within the established budget. In this instance, the review process will likely be limited to checking that all the bid requirements have been met and that the contractor's firm is financially sound.

In many cases, bids vary a good deal from the estimates. Table 15.1 is from a project in 1996, and the point to be noted is that the total project cost was 4 percent below the estimate, while the general construction bid was 8 percent below, mechanical 19 percent, and electrical 2 percent below, while the plumbing was 14 percent over. Although the total cost represented in this recent bid appears low for library construction, variations of this degree one way or the other are not unusual.

In another instance, a major reconstruction job of an academic library building was bid under a "construction management" Not-to-Exceed-Price (NTEP) contract. Bidding was conducted after considerable "soft demolition," which included asbestos abatement. This example shows the role of "value engineering" as applied by the construction management company that analyzed the bids and recommended contract awards, and the consequence of time urgency for certain work, the results of an inadequate number of bids, the results of incomplete bid documents, and reasons to inquire about the basis or scope of the bid received.

- Demolition (3 bids): "Choose low bidder. Their work on the preliminary phases of the project and their knowledge of the drawings indicate that they have the demolition scope of work covered in their bid. They have excluded the removal of lead paint from existing structural steel as this scope cannot be determined until the removal of concrete fireproofing is complete. An allowance has been included for lead paint abatement."
- Underground utilities (1 bid): "The bid documents did not include any information for tying the new building storm and sanitary sewer into the existing site utilities. Re-bid once design is complete. Relocation of chilled water and steam is critical to the progress of the structural upgrade work to prevent delays to the project and minimize disruption to adjacent building."
- Concrete (3 bids): Owner needs to provide approval because the contract management construction firm was the low bidder. "Familiarity with the existing conditions will insure that there will be no changes due to undefined scope of work, and will provide greater level of control for the overall progress of the construction schedule."
- Masonry and sandstone (2 bids): "Due to incomplete design documents, it is difficult to determine if both bidders included all work that is required. The specs required subs to be responsible for surveying field conditions and providing a bid based upon their interpretation of what needs to be done. To correct this, the construction management firm directed subs to provide unit pricing for each detail. Once drawings are complete, owner should work with low bidder to finalize the scope and pricing, since re-bidding could cause an increase in the overall cost not currently carried in the NTEP."
- Structural steel and misc. iron (4 bids): "Low apparent bidder is missing scope. The price from the next highest bidder has been included in the NTEP. We shall interview low bidder to verify scope; if this sub's price needs to increase to cover missed scope and is still below the next bid, we shall recommend this sub."

TABLE 15.1 Bidding range on various construction components. A table such as this contributes to the process of bid analysis. Where figures differ widely, there is reason to suspect an error of some kind; it is generally considered that if the figures are within 10% of each other, it is a good bid. The project manager on this project probably will have a conversation with the estimator about plumbing cost.

	Low Bid	Unit Cost
General Construction		
Low bid	$10,399,000	$43.14/SF
Average of 3 lowest bids	$10,682,741	44.33/SF
Estimated bid	$11,231,352	46.60/SF
Mechanical		
Low bid	$ 2,825,000	11.72/SF
Average of 3 lowest bids	$ 3,384,000	14.04/SF
Estimated bid	$ 3,372,293	13.99/SF
Electrical		
Low bid	$ 2,326,730	9.65/SF
Average of 3 lowest bids	$ 2,679,287	11.18/SF
Estimated bid	$ 2,374,957	9.85/SF
Plumbing		
Low bid	$ 859,500	3.57/SF
Average of 3 lowest bids	$ 937,062	3.89/SF
Estimated bid	$ 741,167	3.06/SF
Total (Single Prime)		
Low bid	$16,990,000	70.50/SF
Average of 3 lowest bids	$17,552,855	72.83/SF
Estimated bid	$17,719,769	73.53/SF

- Roofing and waterproofing (3 bids): "The apparent low bidder did not bid the specified 'Suprema' roofing system. Award to the lowest bidder using the specified roof system."
- Resilient flooring and carpet (6 bids): "The apparent low bidder bid carpet quality less than the second bidder, who appears to have a more complete scope of work for their bid price. Interview the three low bidders to review the scope and quality of work prior to award of the work. The NTEP includes the bid price of the second bidder and an allowance for carpet upgrade."
- Fire protection (5 bids): "The apparent low bidder did not include any work in the bookstack area, as did the others. Only two bidders included complete replacement of the stack system. Addendum #9 changed the pre-action sprinkler system to an interlock

system, requiring an increase in pipe size and therefore rendering the existing sprinkler system in the stack obsolete. Award bid to the one meeting this requirement with the complete scope of work."

The use of additive or deductive alternates is the common way of dealing with the spread between the low base bid and the project construction budget. The advantage of alternates is that each is quoted or bid before the fact, which should result in better prices. Table 15.2 is an example of bid add or deduct alternates, which suggests the range of costs involved as the owner makes decisions to keep or bring the project within budget.

Should a bigger budget problem exist, a period of negotiation will follow. In contracts that involve public funds, it is generally required, and in all competitive bidding it is wise, to limit any change in contract scope after receipt of bids to a small percentage of the total proposed construction cost, generally 5 percent. Thus, a proposed construction bid of $1,000,000 can be legally and properly negotiated up to $1,050,000 or down to $950,000, by changing the scope of the work after consultation with the contractor.

If, however, the desired change in proposed construction cost is greater than 5 percent, some amount of competitive rebidding is generally advisable from the point of view of the institution and is more considerate of the bidders. This rebidding may be confined to the three or four lowest original general contract bidders, and even to certain subcontract bidders, such as those for heating and ventilating, electrical, or plumbing work, if the increase or decrease in the scope of work is to be confined to one or more of these trades.

The problem becomes a bit more difficult if the low bidder is substantially below the next lowest bidder. As mentioned above, the concern here is that an error has been made or there was a misinterpretation of the contract documents. The owner may wish to review the bid with the low bidder and perhaps the second lowest bidder to try to understand the reason for the discrepancy. The review process may follow the format of the cost model as discussed in Chapter 9. If an error is found in the low bid, it should be rejected, or the bidder should be allowed to withdraw, and the next lowest bid taken. Negotiations with the low competitive bidder to compensate

TABLE 15.2   Bid alternatives. This is a particularly long list of bid alternatives for a typical project, though such a list can help the project team fit the project into the budget. With such a list, the low bidder on the main part of the project may not be the low bidder when selected alternatives are added. A list of a half-dozen alternatives is more common. A major issue for the project team is to establish a sense of priority for such a list unless all items can be afforded. It would be quite unfortunate to omit a number of these items should that be necessary.

Bid Alternate Item	Bid Value
Landscaping	$ 25,000
Sound isolate 4th floor slab	$ 47,500
Von Duprin exit devices	$ 18,725
Plumbing sprinkler tower	$134,996
Mechanical var. speed fan	$ 29,160
Mechan. var. speed pumps	$ 20,162
Elect. sprinkler tower	$ 8,200
Compact shelving	$513,900
3rd floor bookshelving	$114,400
3rd floor upfitting	$198,700
Compact shelving tracks	$ 60,000
Plumbing 3rd floor upfit	$ 69,596
Mechan. 3rd floor upfit	$166,562
Archit. roof feature	$125,000
Elect. 3rd floor upfit	$128,000
Telecommun. cable	$199,500

for an error would normally be regarded as unethical. Furthermore, entering a contract with a contractor who has already made a mistake will result in later problems; to do so is not good business practice.

With a negotiated contract the review process is limited to a comparison of the contractor's quote with earlier estimates prepared by the architect or a separate cost estimator. The comparison might be along the lines of the cost model approach. The negotiation might include altering the requirements of the contract so as to keep the cost within the budget, or identifying errors or misunderstandings and taking corrective action. Here, negotiation in regard to an error is completely ethical as there is no competition involved.

A second area of review and perhaps negotiation is for a change in proposed subcontractors who are, for one reason or another, more acceptable to the institution or the architect. In any case, a list of the principal subcontractors that the general contractor proposes to use should be reviewed and agreed upon. Sometimes a change in subcontractors may be negotiated without change in the proposed cost, but more frequently a small increase is required in order to effect such changes. Any such change should be negotiated with the contractor for clear, objective reasons—for example, the contractor may have had fine service from the sub chosen, while the institution in previous jobs had significant performance problems of a continuing nature.

In public bidding for states and cities in the United States, the principal subcontractors may be required by law to submit "filed" bids—that is, bids the amounts of which are public knowledge—or even to submit the separate bids directly to the awarding authorities.

In private work in the United States, the general contractors are usually required to name the principal subcontractors and their respective costs in the bid proposal, but separate bids are rarely taken on any subcontract. If closer control of the subcontractor selection is desired, the "allowance" method is usually employed.

In work requiring funds from the U.S. federal government, the naming of subcontractors or the filing of their bids is usually omitted and sometimes forbidden under present construction procedures. The omission of this requirement from the bidding rules generally results in a lower total construction bid.

When the subcontractors' bids are filed, or recorded, a change from one subcontractor to another may be made by adding or, rarely, deducting the recorded difference in bids to or from the total proposed cost. Under most public bidding laws the contractor is not restricted in the choice of subbidders, but the institution is required to accept the lowest responsible subbidder. In private institutional work, no such restriction exists, and a discreet review of the subcontractors who will be employed on the work may be advantageous and a change for cause is not unethical.

Another step that may occur before signing the contract takes the form of an interview with the contractor and the proposed construction superintendent. Such an interview would be outlined in the bid package, including a description of the nature of the concerns to be addressed in the interview, such as the care with which water is handled, dust is controlled, security is provided, and welding is achieved in and around the existing library, or there may be a discussion of a special area of coordination between the work specified for the contractor and work being done or provided by others. The bid will typically give the contractor's estimate of the number of days to completion, and this may lead to discussion for a mutual understanding. (Contract treatment of the completion is discussed in Section 15.5.) Although the interview process probably is not a very effective means of assuring a certain quality level, it does serve to introduce the key players and to emphasize particular concerns about the project. Of course, this can also occur at the construction kickoff meeting discussed later.

After any negotiations have been completed, or even during the negotiation period, general contractors may be willing to commence construction upon receipt of a "letter of intent." Such a letter, sent to the contractor by an authorized officer of the institution or by the architect, states the conditions under which it is the intent to award the contract. Work may then legally be commenced, pending the preparation, approval, and signing of the formal contractual documents, and pending the receipt of the building permit, which is usually obtained by the contractor.

Once the contract is signed, there may be a construction kickoff meeting, including the library representative and other members of the design team, the contractor, perhaps several major subcontractors, and others, such as the institution's risk manager, fire marshal, and construction manager. This meeting has three purposes. First, it serves as an introduction of key officers for the project. Second, it offers a forum for such questions as: Where do you want the excavated dirt? How are parking permits obtained for the construction crew? and Is there any preference about where the job shack is to be placed? Third, it is an opportunity for various persons to underscore special concerns. For example, the fire marshal may be concerned about maintaining emergency access to nearby buildings. The architect may have a concern about the finish quality of exposed concrete. The project manager may have concerns about employment of minority personnel. The librarians may have special concerns about water, dust, noise, and power outages.

15.5
Special Concerns

During a task that will occupy many people on highly skilled and unskilled jobs over many months, with constantly changing conditions and many hazardous situations, the library staff will need to be alert to a few matters.

Construction zone. This area is specified in the contract documents. The owner or client may specify another area for the parking of cars, although construction workers will not walk very far, and they usually arrive well before the library staff in the morning. Routes for hauling heavy loads may be approved so as to keep from interfering unduly with other activities, to minimize hazards to students walking or bicycling, or to protect a secondary campus road with inadequate roadbed that cannot handle very heavy vehicles.

The designated contractor's yard is off limits to all others without special permission, and there are legal liability reasons to be scrupulous in observing the limits. Job review meetings will usually be held in the general contractor's office on the site. However, visits to the project, usually with hard hats, must be approved by the clerk of works and, until the very last stages, are usually escorted because of the many hazards that can exist.

Arrangements for workers to pass through or work in a connecting building outside the construction zone should be a matter of agreement at a job review meeting. These intrusions, however, are difficult to control; library staff can expect some surprises no matter how much planning and discussion have occurred.

Schedule. The contract may deal with the question of when the finished building will be turned over to the institution and made available for installing the movable furniture and equipment that is not included in the basic contract. This may be handled in one of four ways, as follows:

1. The contract may make no mention of time (a procedure that is not recommended).
2. It may state an estimated time for completion (usually based on calendar days).
3. It may state an agreed-upon time for completion.
4. It may state an agreed-upon time for completion with penalty and benefit payments if time is delayed or bettered.

If either option 3 or 4 is to be used, it should be included in the bid form and discussed during the negotiations; option 4 is rarely used in institutional work, because its chief application is to commercial business that can make or lose money through early or late completion dates. In other words, it may be argued that an actual monetary loss must be demonstrated before a contractor will be required to pay a penalty. However, this does not prevent the inclusion of a penalty clause in the contract with a predetermined fee to be charged for each day (specified as a working or calendar day) that beneficial occupancy is delayed. One should realize, though, that this penalty is very rarely applied. The contractor has other incentives, including receipt of the final payment, to ensure that the project is completed in a timely manner.

Although an agreed-upon completion date is a little more forceful than an estimated date, it is impossible to enforce if the agreement is not met, and means little more than an estimated date. Either the estimated or agreed-upon construction period is quite common in institutional work, but both generally represent optimistic estimates on the part of the contractor, and inevitable and usually excusable delays sometimes postpone completion quite seriously.

The following factors may affect the dates for bidding as well as building construction and, therefore, the completion date.

1. The start of construction may be delayed. There are a variety of possible causes.
   a. The contract documents may be delayed because the architect fails to complete the task on schedule. The firm may have been delayed by the institution's constantly holding up decisions on vital points, by a shortage of help, or by the inability to get the details from the engineers who are doing the mechanical services or other planning. Any of these, in turn, could hold up approval by a governmental authority and delay issuance of the building permit.
   b. The time when the plans and specifications are ready may not be propitious for taking bids. An economic boom with great building activity may result in bids 10 percent higher than if they could have been taken earlier, and perhaps a delay may result in lower bids, though that is always a risk.
   c. Plans and specifications may be ready for the taking of bids during a strike. An increase in wages may result in higher prices, and contractors are cautious about making

close bids. Frequently there is an anticipated and sometimes a previously agreed-upon wage-rate increase, which affects bidding as the bidders are well aware that the increase is due to come. It does not necessarily have to be accompanied by a strike. A strike itself is no more likely to affect bidding than the anticipation of one. A strike during construction will delay completion but may not materially affect the cost to the institution, unless the contract contains some form of negotiated cost-plus-fee agreements.

    d. Weather conditions may be unfavorable. In many areas a late spring, for instance, may delay the start of work for two or three weeks. Frozen ground, a late heavy snow, an early beginning of the rainy period, and so on are all possible delaying factors.

2. Local labor conditions may affect the completion. Labor may not be available at the required time. Strikes may interfere, or a building boom in a nearby city may attract labor away from the job. The contractor is anxious to carry on the work at a pace that will provide the largest possible profit. The construction company does not want to have to import labor from outside the area at extra cost. On the other hand, the longer it has to keep its team in operation, the lower the profit tends to be.

3. The nature of change orders can have a major effect. A poor foreman may be unable to get the work properly coordinated, and considerable delay in finishing the task can result, or the contractor may become engrossed in more profitable work elsewhere and not push the library project. The effectiveness of the owner's or architect's job inspector is another factor; if omissions and poor workmanship are reported week by week, there should be less corrective action on the punch list at the end, and mop-up tasks can be done far more expeditiously.

4. Soil, weather, and supply of materials or heavy equipment may slow down construction. Faulty or unfortunate test borings that have failed to discover ledge rock, pockets of quicksand or peat, unknown archeological remains, or other soil conditions affecting the foundation can cause considerable delays. Unexpected wet spells or a very severe winter may also bring about loss of progress before the roof is on and the exterior walls closed in. If much of the material for use within the structure is brought in from a distance, there is always a possibility of delay, first at the point where it is fabricated and second in transportation to the site.

5. Construction surprises or oversight can also delay completion. As one example, upon completion in 1976 of the major Cooper Library addition at the University of South Carolina, one of the contractor's workforce left an air vent open at the end of the workday. There were 900 lockable research carrels with walls salt-impregnated to retard fire, and the moisture coming in through the vent that night led the salt to bleed through. All the woodwork and doors had to be scraped and repainted, causing an eight-month delay in opening the building.

It can be seen from the above that "there is many a slip 'twixt the cup and the lip." At any rate, the time schedule should be given careful consideration, and the contractor should be requested to notify the institution as promptly as possible if any delay is anticipated in the completion date so that the institution can alter its plans. These may be of very great importance to accommodate to a new semester, to meet a schedule for the old building to be used for other purposes, or to receive furniture deliveries and plan book collection moves that require careful scheduling, hiring of special crews, or other preparations. The simple matter of scheduling a dedication or other social or program events can become a major issue if the schedule is not clear.

The contractor is usually required to prepare a project schedule showing the time frame for each of the major segments of work. This schedule may be a critical path chart, a bar chart, or some other technique (see fig. 15.8), though the method used is not of prime importance. What is important is that the schedule should be maintained and updated. As delays occur or are anticipated, for whatever reason, they should be noted on the schedule. This sounds very reasonable and simple, but in fact it is a problem to achieve. The job superintendent, who is the key manager of the construction effort, is likely to be so wrapped up in day-to-day activities that scheduling anything more than a week in advance is unlikely.

Typically, where a master schedule is required, it is prepared on a computer by a scheduling specialist who is only vaguely familiar with the plans, who probably knows nothing about the site conditions, and who may know little about the mode of operation of a particular contractor. Without information from the manager in the field, this schedule has little value. To be useful,

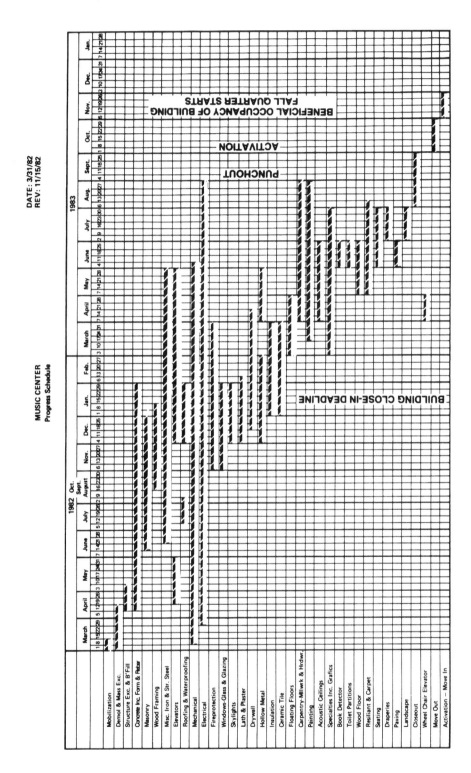

FIGURE 15.8 Construction schedule. The schedule was prepared early in the construction phase of the project: Activation actually occurred in late 1983 and early 1984, with the dedication in March 1984. The schedule reflects construction of a complex building with substantial attention to acoustics. The building is approximately 55,000 ft² (5,100 m²) gross, of which the library represents nearly 45% of the space.

it must be maintained on a weekly basis. This activity should thus be a basic requirement to be undertaken as part of the site meeting process.

One final point about the schedule. The schedule logistics for the dedication were mentioned above. Because the dedication usually involves a number of busy people, it may need to be scheduled as much as a year in advance. Because of the uncertainties of construction, the prudent planner should allow ample time between the anticipated completion of construction and the dedication date. On a major project six months may not be too much, and, even with this much time, there will likely be a rush to make the final preparations for the dedication.

Security and hazards. With dozens of workers temporarily working on the library job, the chance for accidents is great. Heavy equipment is less the cause than the more mundane: just taking chances, cutting corners, or being careless or tired. The result can be an injured back, a cut, occasionally a broken bone, or a fire or flood. Furthermore, theft of materials or tools can be a temptation. Thus safety rules and security are major concerns of contractors and of the institution.

The authorized construction zone is a principal worry. Yet from the institution's point of view, properties next to the project and traffic routes can be the chief concern. Utility trenches need proper barriers and flashing lights for nighttime warning. People on campus are so familiar with their customary routes that a small temporary digging may cause an accident. On most campuses, bicycles are ridden on seemingly random routes, sometimes at high speed, and major accidents, even deaths, have occurred. Motorbike riders sometimes act as if they have the right-of-way, even in pedestrian malls. So construction barriers and signs must be prominent and properly located to assure reasonable safety when construction is under way.

The institution has the right to expect reasonable cleanliness near and on the construction site. Lengths of lumber should not be left around. Broken glass, loose nails, flammable material, and other hazards need to be disposed of promptly. It is sad that nearly every major library construction has its accidents. If one worked with the college inspector who fell over a low barrier in a dark attic, dropped 10 feet, and lay unconscious for an hour, or if one remembers the old construction trade rule of thumb "for each million dollars, one life," one has reason to require good safety precautions.

In any work on a building addition or major remodeling, the security of the original building is made far more vulnerable. Temporary holes in walls, temporary walls, extra keys being distributed, and many strangers in and around the premises—these and similar lapses in security can result in loss. It is not the casual or professional book theft, but people who have little regard for higher education or libraries who may find appealing a computer, an upholstered chair, or a large bolt of carpeting. During construction projects, opportunities do present themselves to the unethical.

Temporary heat. In cold climates, construction in winter months is complicated by the need to provide temporary heat to prevent the freezing of building materials that initially contain moisture (such as concrete, mortar, plaster, adhesives, and paint), to dry out the building so that moisture damage to the finished materials may be avoided, and to eliminate the danger of "freeze-ups" in the mechanical and plumbing installations.

Temporary heat may be provided in many ways. In the open, concrete is usually poured only at above-freezing temperatures, and it is then protected with straw covering until it has dried out, or "cured." Otherwise, this work is done under tarpaulins or similar tent coverings and kept above freezing by space heaters. Another technique is to use electric insulating blankets, although this method is expensive. A concrete mix that more rapidly reaches its working strength will help reduce the expense. Antifreeze "admixtures" have been used in the concrete mix, but, at present, most engineers object to their use because of the effect they may have on the ultimate strength and durability of the mix. In any case, the new concrete must not be allowed to freeze until it has reached its design strength.

When the building structural frame is in position, it may be completely or partially covered with a temporary skin of tarpaulins or plastic, often transparent, and the enclosed portions heated with space heaters. If the exterior walls are complete, only the window and door areas need this temporary protection in order to enclose the building.

The types of space heaters employed for temporary heat vary, depending upon whether gas, coal, oil, or electricity is used. The most commonly used types in very cold climates are charcoal braziers and oil-fired unit heaters, which are frequently equipped with electrically operated blowers.

When the heating system for the building has been installed and all window and door openings have been either permanently or temporarily closed against the weather, the contractor is frequently allowed to use the heating system of the new building for supplying temporary heat, provided always that no permanent damage to the system is allowed to result. Where this is permitted, the owner should insist on new filters before acceptance of the building.

In institutions equipped with central heating plants, the steam may be either sold to the contractor or provided free of charge if the quality of weather protection and the amount of heating requirements can be controlled.

In any case, all construction contracts for buildings in climates susceptible to subfreezing temperatures during the construction period should contain specified requirements for temporary heat, generally entirely at the expense of the contractor, who is responsible for closing in the construction and for maintaining and providing the labor, equipment, and fuel necessary to keep the closed-in space at several degrees above freezing temperatures.

When installation of finished woodwork, flooring, or painting is in progress, the required minimum temperature should be raised to simulate that of an occupied space (or about 60° to 65° F., or 16° to 18° C.).

Payments. Payments to the general contractor on account and for the work of all subcontractors are usually made monthly and cover the cost of all labor and materials incorporated in the construction and all materials on the site at the time the application for the payment is made, less any retention that may be specified in the contract. This application is itemized and prepared about 10 days before each monthly payment is due. It is submitted to the architect for approval and may be required to be supported by receipts or vouchers for material, labor, or subcontractor payments. Progress payments are basically similar for all contract types, though there may be a construction manager rather than the general contractor, and the amount paid may be a percent of the total contract based upon the amount of work done rather than a figure calculated from the labor and materials cost.

If a clerk of works or resident engineer is employed on the job, that person's approval of the contractor's application for payment is generally made a prerequisite to final approval by the architect. When the application for payment is approved, the architect issues to the institution a certificate for payment to the contractor for such amount of the application as the architect decides is properly due at the time. The requisition should then be honored by the institution.

Payments to the contractor may be withheld by direction of the architect if defective work is not remedied or if the contractor fails to make proper payments to subcontractors for material and labor, or for other actions detrimental to the interests of the institution. But payment must be made once these grounds for withholding it are removed. Payments made to the contractor by the institution do not indicate the terms of the contract.

After construction is essentially completed and before final payment, the contractor legally commits the construction company to remedy any defects caused by faulty materials or workmanship that appear within a period of one year after the date of occupancy by the owner or the date of substantial completion of the building. Before final payment, the contractor should also supply the owner with evidence and affidavits that all its obligations have been paid for material and labor entailed as a result of the contract.

To ensure such payments and to facilitate completion of the work if the contractor should default before it is completed, it is usually the custom for the institution to retain 10 percent of the funds applied for by the contractor during the progress of the work. This retained percentage is insurance that the contractor will fulfill financial obligations before it is paid. If the contractor fails to do so, the institution may then pay these obligations directly with the retained percentage.

Frequently, on large buildings that require a large sum of money and a long construction period, this 10 percent retainage becomes quite considerable by the time the building is well along, and the continued withholding by the institution creates a financial hardship on the contractor. For this reason, either through prior arrangement or in consideration of this hardship, the institution frequently rewards the contractor for acceptable execution of the contract by reducing the retained percentage in proportion to the amount of work remaining to be done.

Before final payment the architect, the institution, and the contractor should jointly prepare a check, or "punch," list that itemizes all the known defects, deficiencies, and omissions that remain to be corrected or completed on the job before contractual obligations can be considered to have been fulfilled. The library representative must be very much involved in the compilation of this list.

Renovation conditions. Construction problems are a modest concern for the librarian of a new separate building and yet they are a more serious concern during construction of an addition to an operating library building and are often a headache during a renovation project. Renovations are treated in detail in Section 10.4, which should be read for its applicability to construction of new structures and additions.

Phasing can be a special need and yet a complex problem in renovation. On the one hand, the general contractor will wish to bring in one trade to do all its work for the whole renovation project. On the other hand, the library probably will need to occupy and operate parts of certain floors while renovation goes on in other areas. These goals often are not compatible. To save money, the institution needs to make it as convenient for the contractor as is reasonable, preferably clearing one major section entirely and then relocating staff and collections to release the rest to the contractor at a later date.

In renovating the Columbia University Butler Library in the 1990s, choosing the option to phase renovation over several years was forced by two logistical conditions: (1) the cost and service inconvenience of relocating over 2.5 million books, a Rare Book and Manuscript Library, numerous service points, and over 200 staff would have been great, and (2) there was no swing space available on this dense city campus, as there was when UCLA's Powell Library was renovated. Columbia accepted the fact that phasing would increase (1) overhead costs of carrying the project for additional years, (2) the costs of increased security, (3) the expense of temporary enclosures, (4) personnel overtime costs for work when the building was closed (for example, asbestos abatement), and (5) the expense of escalation over time in the construction trades. In any such major renovation, a time-benefit-cost analysis may be useful when options exist, as was not the case at Columbia.

In renovating the Stanford Green Library old wing in the 1980s, the construction schedule was worked out so that library units and collections had only one move, except for the Government Documents Library, which had to camp out for several months on a different floor and in the staff room, which was given up for several months.

Even so, the contractor caused substantial disruptions in technical services while plumbers, electricians, and sheet metal trades worked next to the ceiling, having to move scaffolding in and around and occasionally over staff desks. Every major renovation of a large building can pose significant problems of logistics, costs, safety, security, and service inconvenience; the project team may need to give these all serious thought, and the analysis in some cases should be taken for decision to senior academic and financial officers of the institution.

No library staff members can say that they enjoyed the Green Library renovation while it progressed. Most would probably liken it to a battle zone. Yet it behooves management to work out a reasonable accommodation for the contractor, and the staff can well suffer a bit—as will the contractor in other terms—for the staff can look forward to improved conditions once the job is done.

Phasing should be worked out in writing by the librarian and planner, sometimes with the architect's guidance, and then negotiated with the contractor. Some give and take is necessary, especially by the library staff, because tough requirements will only drag out the work, cost more, result in frayed tempers, and perhaps produce some examples of inferior workmanship. It is suggested that, for a renovation, the contractor should be required to maintain a rolling schedule that anticipates the specific activities for the coming two weeks and is updated at each weekly meeting. This type of schedule will be of great help in the coordination of power shutdowns, required interruptions of the other utilities, and time for necessary relocation of computers and other library equipment. Access, noise, and delivery problems may be anticipated as well so that the project may progress as smoothly as possible.

15.6
Change Orders

The institution and its planning team will find, if they did not realize it in advance, that their tasks have not been completed when the building contract is signed, the time schedules set, and the construction begun. Every project will have problems. Even with the greatest of attention to detail in the contract documents, there will be errors, omissions, conflicts, and surprises during the construction period. These problems can be reduced with a carefully prepared set of documents; nevertheless, they are never all eliminated except on the smallest of projects. Many decisions will have to be faced as the building work proceeds.

During the course of construction, the routinely scheduled site meetings will provide a major vehicle for review. The librarian or library representative should be a member of the site meeting group. Although much of the discussion will not involve the librarian, there will be issues and discussions the results of which can affect the future operations of the library. Some of these issues result in change orders. The architect will keep and distribute minutes of the site meetings. It is helpful if the minutes indicate the status of each issue, and who is responsible for action. An unresolved issue should reappear in each set of minutes until resolved in order to avoid forgetting or losing an issue that may need attention.

Change orders reverse earlier decisions or take care of previous omissions on the part of the planning team, the architect, and possibly the engineers involved. Change orders may also, and frequently do, reinstate items or work previously omitted in the interest of economy, particularly if a more favorable bid was received than had been expected or if additional funds are made available. Use of the change order must be quite limited as will be seen below.

Where change orders or field orders deal with finishes, fixtures, or details affecting the utility or operation of the facility, the project manager should ensure that the library representative has a chance to review the issue. This assurance often will be given orally in the site meeting, but it may involve reviewing the documentation prepared by the architect.

Usually, minor conflicts or other problems will be resolved on the spot by the contractor, perhaps with the approval of the inspector. However, if there is a cost or time delay involved, the solution to the problem must go through formal channels. There may be a requirement for clarification drawings from the architect, followed by the submission of a quote from the contractor. If solution to the problem is urgent and it is clear that its cost will be minor (say, no more than $2,000 to $5,000), a field order may be written to authorize the change in work. At a later date the field orders will be incorporated into a change order, which alters the basic contract. A field order may be issued by the project inspector to

keep the work moving, but a change order always comes from the architect. It will include the current contract price and schedule; the added or deducted sum resulting from the change order; any added or deducted construction time; and signatures of the architect, owner, and contractor.

The representatives of the institution must remember that change orders have to be given sufficient lead time. Although the height of an electrical outlet can in most cases be easily changed before installation, a change in door swing, for example, may mean that door, frame, and lock set that were ordered long before must now be changed and perhaps at extra cost.

Also, while the change order process is a means of correcting design flaws or accommodating a changing program, remember that the work authorized by a change order is not competitively bid and that the process of arriving at an approved change order is expensive for all parties. Because of these factors, change orders should only be used when absolutely necessary. The librarian should be particularly aware of this point, as the temptation is to request even minor changes as new and better ideas come to mind. Extra cost is also a concern if, during construction, the institution decides it must, for example, upgrade computer signal cabling; it may be best to await beneficial occupancy and then, under separate contract, to achieve the cable replacement. (Note that in the sample change orders listed below, only C.O.12 and 17 may in part have been driven by changes in library thinking since the design development phase.)

This temptation to adopt a new product or detailing must be suppressed except where a change of great importance is identified. Most change orders should be limited to the changes that are required because of the conditions of the site and of errors and omissions in the drawings, not changes in the program. However, at times, academic urgency or donor or public relations arguments can justify the new extra expense. (See the example below of C.O.4.) Those trade-offs may often require the approval of higher college or university officers when the decision involves large noncompetitive costs.

The contractor can, of course, take advantage of change orders to increase unduly the contract cost. The librarian's view tends to be that this increase is unwarranted, but in the contractor's defense, it should be pointed out that the construction company would generally prefer that no changes be made during the progress of the work. Any change, no matter how small, may upset schedules and procedures to some extent and will cost the contractor money, just because it is a change. That is why contractors do not allow full value for work omitted and charge more than normal rates for work added.

There are, it must be admitted, legally minded contractors who comb the specifications and drawings for omissions and discrepancies on which extra charges can be based, although in general the contractor is eager for the sake of reputation, if nothing else, to present a complete and acceptable job to the institution. Reputation is an essential value because a contractor will want further business and wants the client to provide a favorable reference. The institution will almost always enjoy the services of a satisfactory contractor if it has a free hand in the selection of bidders.

If change orders add to the cost of the building and to the sum that must be made available, a problem arises unless there is a contingency line item in the original budget, part of which was left over after the contract was signed. There should always be a sum for contingencies in the budget, both before and after the signing of the contract or contracts. This figure can vary from as much as 12½ percent at preliminary stages of planning to as little as 2½ percent after the contract is awarded. The usual figure is 10 percent at the design development stage, 7½ percent after quantity survey estimates, and perhaps 5 percent after award of the contract. The economic climate at the time of planning may properly affect the percentages; in periods of inflation they may need to be made greater than at other times.

To have a good margin is always desirable because the winning bid may be higher than was expected, and also because of the possibility of the need for change orders. Even though the librarian has been cautioned against their use, it is generally cheaper and more suitable and timely to place change orders when it is compelling that they are desirable, rather than to wait and make alterations after construction is finished.

One important precaution if trouble is to be avoided: The AIA (American Institute of Architects) general conditions of the contract includes an agreement on procedures to be followed in any changes made in the working drawings and specifications. This agreement, or any similar agreement found in the supplementary general conditions, must be followed.

Change order example. Presented below are examples of change orders that may be expected on any major project. At first glance, it may appear as though most of the items will be of special interest to the librarian, and, in some respects, this may be the case. By this stage of the project, however, most of the changes should be little more than technical adjustments requiring little response from the librarian. Still, it is well that a library representative be aware of the construction progress, including change orders, to ensure against surprises or mistakes resulting from a lack of understanding by the contractor and others of the special needs of the library. The typical change order covers the results of several bulletins or field orders. In this case, it is the change order that formally adjusts the project cost and schedule.

C.O.1. Deletes two feet of construction fence, where it was decided that a six foot high fence would suffice in place of the eight foot fence specified. Also, the add alternate (completion of the third floor) is accepted as part of the construction contract.

C.O.2. Adds caissons and other footings due to unexpected soil conditions.

C.O.3. Allows payment of a unit cost for footings as established in the original bid package; makes changes in the basement electrical layout and service desk reflecting late design changes; adds electrical room door labels as required by the county inspector; approves substitution of materials from those specified for the electrical feeder, door hold devices and pipe hanger supports in order to reduce cost and expedite the project.

C.O.4. Adds fountain machine room rough-in in response to expectation that a donor has been identified who will pay for the fountain (which is not currently in the project). The work accepted here will save redoing landscape work at a later date.

C.O.5. Alters the central stair handrail in response to a design error (the rail, as designed, was too large for a normal person to grip); approves the interior transparent woodwork finish following submittal of a number of samples; changes an operable window to a fixed window to improve security in the mail room; and authorizes payment of the expense for soils testing as an added contractual element.

C.O.6. Details changes of the first floor layouts because a major wall was constructed one foot off of its designed location. (It was decided more was to be gained through minor adjustment than by requiring the contractor to rip out the wall and start over.) Adds panic hardware at several doors that was missed in the specifications, and approves a change in the exterior lighting in response to recent changes in the campus lighting plan.

C.O.7. Provides for a change in the faculty study shelving, including the shelves and the wall framing required to support the shelves, in response to continued development of detailed furniture layouts; makes changes in the elevator shaft resulting from a conflict in the drawings.

C.O.8. Removes ceiling light fixtures in the reading areas where it was decided to use task lighting with kiosk type light fixtures for ambient lighting; and establishes the exact method of fastening and supporting the Spanish tile roofing (which was not clearly specified).

C.O.9. Alters the chalk boards, tack boards, and several door swings in response to furniture layouts; makes a number of miscellaneous mechanical changes; and provides for a contract for balancing the mechanical systems.

C.O.10. Revises the fascias, soffits, wall framing and related insulation to resolve a problem discovered by the contractor; adds flashing and reglets in an area where water problems are anticipated; and establishes elevator finishes not previously specified. Deletes a portion of the site work because of an adjacent construction project which recently started. Provides for testing of the shot-in fasteners for the suspended ceiling.

C.O.11. Makes changes in the gutters, drains, and ceiling layouts including related duct and lighting work to resolve conflicts which have developed; alters furred space in the exterior walls because original space was not large enough for pipe joints and other fixtures; establishes the locker keying; and alters a retaining wall due to new grade levels as determined by the adjacent project.

C.O.12. Adds book lockers in the library shelving and deletes range finders and card holders (which are added to the separate graphics contract). Adds a ventilation fan for the sound system, and modifies the air diffusers in the lobby, as a design improvement.

C.O.13. Provides for miscellaneous electrical revisions in response to the furniture layouts; adds risers for door stops where the doors were undercut for ventilation; relocates sprinkler pipe and outlets where the old and new buildings join; and authorizes painting of the diffusers specified in the previous change order.

C.O.14. Adds filler at window wall blind pockets and paint at the exposed wall ends behind glass at certain faculty studies; revises exterior doors because of structural problems; provides for testing of the roof gutters; and adds a time extension of 42 days because of a lengthy rainy season.

C.O.15. Revises light fixtures as required to accommodate ceiling conditions; provides identification plates for the exterior stand pipes to replace those previously supplied, but lost by the owner; adds hardwood base (omitted on one wall in the original drawings); and relocates a floor outlet reflecting continued work on the furnishings.

C.O.16. Details in legal terms the various aspects of a dispute between the owner and contractor, including points of agreement in regard to payment and completion schedules.

C.O.17. Alters the cabinets in the photocopy areas to allow for a larger machine; provides tamperproof thermostat covers and mounting for humidity gauges; and adds door hardware, and phone and power outlets discovered to be needed as the planning for activation progresses.

C.O.18. Outlines miscellaneous mechanical and electrical revisions resulting largely from a walk-through by the campus physical plant personnel; adds a catch basin where there is concern about excessive run-off; adds a few door astragals; provides for repainting factory finishes on electrical raceway to match other architectural metal on the project; adds hooks for the hanging of a large art work that is to be given to the library; and adds heavy duty casters on a mobile sorting unit to replace the original casters that simply were too weak; provides for the removal and reinstallation of the floor-mounted door stops, following the carpet installation by others; alters the book return slide/conveyor where the designed slide does not work; and deletes the graphic allowance, following a decision to contract separately for the graphics.

C.O.19. Makes cost adjustments for "allowance" items; alters the final grading to reflect new conditions; and revises the entrance-exit gate control devices, to achieve wider workable gates.

The above list is not exceptional for a very large project. It can be seen from this example that the need for change orders comes from a number of sources, including:

Continuing work on furniture layouts

Changes in the library operational program that are judged to be of an essential nature

Discovered surprises, or unknown conditions previously hidden

Contractual matters dealing with testing, allowances, approval of alternatives, and disputes

Conflicts, errors, and omissions in the drawings and specifications

Outside forces, such as weather problems, strikes, and changes in the availability of materials and projects

Continued review during the construction process by numerous personnel who may, for a variety of reasons (such as code, campus standards, or operational necessity), require that changes be made

15.7
Inspections

During construction, some shop drawings should be reviewed by the librarian or responsible library representative as they come up during construction. Yet the librarian will need to be watchful, for the shop drawings all too often are approved without the librarian's involvement. Most of the shop drawings will be of little interest to the librarian, but those dealing with built-ins, special equipment, or shelving are very important. The librarian should insist upon being involved in the review of those shop drawings of special interest.

The same can be said about any mock-ups required by the architect. Samples of brickwork, a unique student carrel, lighting in faculty studies—any such mock-up is subject to review and approval by the architect, and the librarian appropriately is involved in any that concern the operations and effectiveness of the library. One may need to ask to be involved with the review, because here again the press of construction and the authority of the architect will normally move this process on rapidly, and library concerns may be overlooked unless the librarian is present. Mock-ups are often made within the construction site, but some may be created in an off-site shop in which the inspection is performed.

During the construction effort, numerous inspections will be made by highly qualified individuals who know what to look for or observe. All too frequently these individuals focus on code requirements, safety conditions, or trade specifics, such as concrete pouring. Those checks are necessary; however, they may well ignore or pay scant attention to critical library operational conditions. In particular, branch libraries and college libraries may have this problem. Finally, there will be the inspections in which the librarian will no doubt be involved from time to time. During a tour of the project, it is quite reasonable to ask questions; however, one must not tell the contractor what to do! Should there be a problem, take it up with the inspector or project manager.

Librarians are urged to make inspections at least weekly, especially when work commences on interior partitions, electrical switches and convenience outlets, door frames, and windows, and throughout the work on interior finishes and built-ins. How might the library representative make an inspection? During early stages of construction, pay attention to the result of a particular trade, such as cement work, laying of tile, wallboard, and electrical work, as the trades perform their segment of the job. If you happen to note and question a condition that was not noticed before, it is still entirely appropriate to raise the question, and better then than later. Walking around with the inspector is the common process, raising questionable conditions as they are seen. Make notes as a reminder for yourself, as a basis of checking field reports issued later by the clerk of works or change orders by the architect to see that the point was raised and resolved. Late in construction, it is necessary to do a more systematic room-by-room inspection of conditions, with or without the inspector, and again taking notes. It can be efficient to use a checklist of points to be looked over in each room, and a one- or two-page form kept on a clipboard may be convenient for checking and recording each individual room or space.

What specific conditions might the librarian look for on the occasional tour? That is not an easy question. To help answer it, the following list of things that might concern a librarian may suggest some general directions.

While the floors are exposed, are there large and deep puddles after a rain? Will these irregularities cause problems with the adjustment of the shelving, typically limited to about ½ in. (12 mm)? Adjustments even this large will leave gaps above many carpets. And, a compact shelving installation on such a floor may exhibit serious problems of stability.

As the concrete forms are being placed, note whether the outlets look right. In walls, the height of the outlet may be important. Don't forget clock and signal outlets.

Watch for sandblasting, as existing buildings should be closed while it is going on.

In a renovation, watch for fire hazards, including smoking and especially welding. Any welding operation in an existing building should require two people, one with an appropriate fire extinguisher. The welding process should be completed or stopped at least an hour before people leave the site to guard against the possible flare-up potential of a hot spot.

Where there is an addition, watch for possible water intrusion into the existing facility as the walls are opened up.

Review with the inspector the importance of accurate dimensions, particularly where shelving must be placed between columns. As the architect's representative is likely to be new to the project, details such as this may be forgotten.

Be aware of potential damage to waterproof membranes. Where waterproofing is applied to a basement wall, is it protected during the backfill operation? As the rest room floors, roofs, or other areas with waterproofing are being constructed, are they being subjected to loads that may cause damage?

Review all door, gate, and window swings. Do they work freely? Will they interfere with planned shelving or movable furniture?

As the built-ins are completed, check that the drawers and doors do not bind, that the locks work as intended, and that there are no sharp edges. Where future access may be required for power and signal, check for a removable panel or other means of access.

During the installation of a complex electronic system, ask the inspector to ensure that adequate wiring diagrams are in hand or being prepared.

As the carpet is being installed, have the inspector watch the seaming patterns to ensure that they match those shown on the plans.

As the job nears completion, try everything. Each detail in the drawing, schedules, and specifications should be checked if it has aesthetic or functional importance. Look for chipped paint, scratched finishes, missing items, binding doors, locks that stick, and so on.

During the course of construction, be aware that this kind of inspection may not be enthusiastically welcomed by the contractor or others. Requests to visit must be made, ordinarily through channels, and permission received. Tact will be required in asking for an explanation or pointing out a condition that appears to differ from drawings or specifications. The owner has a contractual right to inspect and should exercise it. For instance, Swarthmore College librarians found deviations from specifications that could be, and were, corrected during construction: unsuitable doors on offices and seminar rooms, incorrect operable windows, and shelving that would intrude into space planned for microtext readers and printers. The point must be clear that the ultimate client must be able to fully, safely, and efficiently use the facility for many years after the contractor leaves. Corrective work is always easier to achieve while the contractor is still on the job.

15.8
Wrap-up

Construction wrap-up entails preparing for beneficial occupancy (that is, moving in before the final acceptance), and, ultimately, acceptance of the building. The final inspections will result in a list of items requiring correction. There will sometimes be a need to begin moving into a portion of the building before the entire project is accepted. Once the library begins to occupy a space, it is in essence accepted, and the warrantee clock is started. If mechanical systems must be operational to allow occupancy, then they too are in essence turned over to the institution. From that point on, some types of problems newly identified become far more difficult to resolve because there is always the question of who is legally responsible. If damage to a surface has not been previously identified, it is probable that the contractor will not freely correct the problem once the space is occupied.

Before the building is finally and legally accepted, the representative of the institution should have in hand the signed-off building permits, a set of as-built drawings showing the actual constructed conditions, operations manuals outlining maintenance routines, approval from the architect for final payment, documentation relieving the institution of any responsibility for mechanics' liens or other obligations of the contractor, and a report on the balancing of the temperature and ventilation or air-conditioning systems. There may be other contractual requirements as well, such as a final cleaning, training for the institution's operations and maintenance staff, and a one-year maintenance agreement for the landscaping. These details can stretch out for some time, and the contractor will be anxious to receive the final payment.

Eventually, however, the building will fully belong to the institution. One final point was mentioned earlier in this volume. The contracts may require a meeting of the design team and the contractor one year after occupancy. The intent of this meeting is to promote a process of education for all involved. Philosophically, this is a nice idea, but in reality it seldom has significant value. Although it is not the intent of the authors to discourage such a meeting, we wonder if it is worth the time of a number of busy people, though it is something for the institution to consider if there have been recent problems with programming, designing, and constructing either new or renovated buildings.

One example shows the type of lessons that might be identified and documented during such a postoccupancy review. This summary of construction issues is just one (13E-1) of 15 aspects of the project, taken from the lengthy 1994 document *Lessons Learned from Archives II,* of the U.S. National Archives and Records Administration.

- While plastic automatic temperature control tubing is acceptable, copper tubing continues to be specified. Accordingly, every contractor submits a value engineering suggestion to change, with consequent savings.
- Standard notation on electrical drawings attempts to specify the maximum number of circuits permissible within the homerun conduit. A recent U.S. Board of Appeals decision rejected the implication of the standard notation, so the government needs to specify the maximum number and not rely on standard notation.
- Pipes requiring insulation should be provided with hanger shields with inserts for support. The use of MS Standards with fiberglass pipe wrap will result in compression of insulation and possible tearing of the vapor barrier by the pipe shield.
- Pipe valve manuals should not provide a multitude of manufacturers' model numbers, as these numbers become outdated or typographical errors occur.
- Specified motor efficiencies and power factors should indicate to what percentage of load condition these numbers apply. Contractors often look at furnishing and installation of capacitors to achieve the required power factor as an additional cost not included in their bids.
- Do not ever use metal baffle ceilings under conditions where one can sight down the length of the baffle; joints result in a wavy appearance which is aesthetically unacceptable.
- Review drawings to ensure that no utility lines run through wire closets or elevator machine rooms.
- Since most mechanical and electrical elements are concealed above ceilings or in dedicated rooms in high-visibility areas, locations need to be coordinated with interior aesthetics. Light switches, electrical outlets, and thermostats should not be placed on marble or wood paneled walls.
- Since some mechanical/electrical systems require steam vents for air handlers, and exhaust pipes for engine-driven fire pumps and emergency generators, locations of these pipe penetrations should be organized and not appear haphazard in exterior walls or even as large exterior louvers.
- The "roofscape" of a building is always important aesthetically; mechanical elements such as powered exhaust fans and smoke evacuation ducts can be sizable and bring unpleasant surprises, so their visable locations should be organized.

16

Activation

*The surest test of the civilization of a people . . . afforded
by mechanical art is to be found in their architecture, which
presents so noble a field for the display of the grand and
the beautiful, and which, at the same time, is so intimately
connected with the essential comforts of life.*

—William Hickling Prescott, *The Conquest of Peru*

*The sight of such a monument is like a continuous and
stationary music.*

—Madame de Staël, *Corinne*

Although most of the planning team is no longer involved as the construction winds down, library staff will be even more busy during the final months of construction. The activities covered in this chapter will vary markedly in the time required and the number of individuals who are involved; yet they can be surprisingly time consuming for any new building, a sizable addition, or a major branch, as well as substantially converted or rebuilt space. The work will in lesser degree continue for one or a number of years beyond occupancy of the new facility.

The decisions and tasks involved before, during, and after activation are considerable. The building occupancy and initial period of use can be a sore trial for the staff and a matter of grave disappointment to faculty and students if those final steps of occupying and operating a building are not as carefully managed as were the earlier stages in the planning process. Preparation for occupancy should therefore begin a year or two in advance. A time schedule, perhaps using the PERT (program evaluation and review technique) or critical path planning method, can help assure a timely and comprehensive staff effort.

Although the activation process does not involve the expense of construction in time or money, the reputation of the library staff will for a while rest just as much on the success of the activation as it will in the long run on the basic suitability of the building structure itself.

16.1
Preparing for Occupancy

The purchase of movable equipment should be a very early concern. Whether the furnishings have been designed by the architectural firm or an interior design consultant, or selected by the library and the institution without outside assistance, it takes a great many months or well over a year for some furniture to be selected, purchased, delivered, and, if necessary, assembled for installation. In cases where furniture needs to be custom designed, it may require a year or more to have designs drawn to scale, bids requested and evaluated, contracts signed, and fabrication completed.

Perhaps during programming or schematic design, and certainly not later than the design development effort, decisions will have been made about which items are outside the scope of the architect, the interior designer, and the general contractor. Built-in furnishings and items tied in with the electrical or mechanical systems will commonly be in the basic contract. This usually includes book shelving because of structural and electrical connections and, often, because of the relationship of floor tile or carpeting to the shelving.

However, furnishings that are stock items, are not built-ins, are not tied in with electrical or mechanical systems, and are not required to be installed before some task of the general contractor will commonly be purchased by the institution separately from the construction contract. This arrangement enables the institution to make decisions at a much later time and, most important, to save the management or overhead costs when that responsibility is assigned to the contractor. In such an arrangement, the institution's purchasing office should advise on the necessary lead time. And the library staff must do everything possible to assure that the list of needs is complete, the specifications are accurate, the budget covers at least all essential priority items, and the purchase orders are placed according to the required lead time so that all material will be delivered at or very soon before the time when the contractor plans to finish the building and turn it over to the institution. Close effective work between library staff and the institution's purchasing department is of paramount importance.

This book does not provide extensive treatment of furniture selection; however, the necessity of obtaining functional compatibility and reasonable aesthetic harmony between the furnishings and the building is an obvious goal. This criterion applies to reused and refurbished furniture as well as to new items. Such use of existing items needs as much thought and time as does the purchase of new items. Indeed, special care is needed because reused items usually have dimensions different from those of the same item newly purchased, and thus may not fit designed spaces. Frequently, a degree of repair and refurbishing must be, or should be, undertaken. And, temporary operational arrangements within the library must be planned when an item regularly used, such as a service counter, needs to be taken out of service for such refurbishing.

If early delivery is anticipated, arrangements will need to be made for equipment to be stored on campus or in a commercial storage building. Alternatively, it may be possible for the manufacturers of equipment and furniture and for the carpet installer to hold their items for a few weeks, thereby temporarily postponing delivery. If the manufacturer is a considerable distance away, it can be desirable to have all materials critical to the initial operation of the library shipped for local holding in order to minimize delivery problems when the building is ready for furnishing.

There are a number of business aspects and logistical problems in obtaining the movable furniture and equipment, some deriving from the fact that one can almost never be certain that the contractor will be able to complete the building on the stipulated date. The date for actual turnover of the building for occupancy may not be known until a very few weeks before that time is reached. Further, there may well be negotiation between the contractor and the institution about whether part or all of the building should be turned over at one time, and whether it should be turned over before all the punch-list items are completed or before landscaping is finished. If a period of "burn-in" is specified for preservation reasons or for health reasons, requirements of such a process must be factored into the occupancy schedule and process, for both the building and new furnishings.

It should therefore be evident that one or two years' lead time for the movable equipment is not too much for large quantities and especially for nonstock items.

In the year or more before occupancy, the library staff need to understand the detailed layout of the new facility and its service philosophy, develop the collection deployment, and learn security and safety arrangements. Few will be so familiar with architectural drawings as to be able to fully grasp directional problems, the best routes from place to place, what can and cannot be seen, what acoustic problems may turn up, and the general ambiance of the new space and what it may mean to their own unit.

Tours should therefore begin during the final stages of construction for small groups of the staff to be taken through the building by the project manager, with authorization from the contractor. Early in the project hard hats will be required for those going on a tour, but late in the project they may not be necessary, though normal caution is required because hazardous objects may be lying on the floor or stairs and some areas will be unfinished. These tours for selected staff should help their understanding of functional arrangements and enable them to moder-

ate criticism, improve understanding of how the whole structure will work, inform their support staff of the new possibilities, and contribute to the revision of existing regulations and practices of their unit or the preparation of new procedures and regulations, as well as help staff morale by letting them in on an exciting preview.

Such tours may be offered occasionally for the faculty library committee or senior officers of the institution. The staff who were responsible for fund-raising, the dean of instruction, and the president may welcome a tour late in the construction phase. This gesture helps those individuals see the results of their support. It can help with further fund-raising if financial needs still exist for the building or for furnishings; certainly it would enable academic officers and the faculty to talk with their colleagues and develop a general understanding of any change in habits that may be required and of the role the library plays in the teaching and research program of the institution.

Revised and additional procedures and regulations are frequently required in a new facility. The building may have included new functions and specialized quarters, each of which requires explaining to the community and clarifying for those on the library staff who will operate or manage them. Thus there may be revised staff manuals to be drafted and reviewed with staff, and printed guides or brochures that explain altered services. These take time to produce. There frequently are new audiovisual or computer facilities, different book-checking arrangements at building exits, new book-return accommodations, arrangements for use of personal computers, new service areas or combined service desks, altered arrangements for required course readings or for current periodical issues, new photographic services, and other such features. Preliminary draft documents should be prepared while construction proceeds, though published versions should be distributed only after staff are assured of final building and equipment details and room numbers. Frequently such regulations or documents need at least slight revision within months of occupancy, and so interim versions may be prudent. Occupancy of a new or extensively remodeled building is, after all, the most convenient time to make changes that previous physical conditions inhibited.

Embarrassing moments and difficulties may be avoided if the librarian determines which are new conditions and services and assigns to appropriate staff the preparation of operating and contingency plans and the drafting of the required documents. This responsibility should even involve such matters as handling cash for fines for overdue or lost books and for deposits for audio headsets, checking tags for personal computers or typewriters brought into the building, issuing keys or combination locks, and arranging building closing routines and daily staff entrance before the building opens for service.

16.2
Operating Budget Considerations

Another key step preparatory to occupancy is budgeting for additional staff positions, if any are necessary to the operation of the facility. This may require requesting increases a year or two or three in advance of occupancy and opening of the new facility. It may mean beginning even farther in advance if the opening of the facility is rather late in a fiscal year, if the institution has a biennial budget, or if the institution's budget cycle requires 12 months or more for justification, negotiation, and approval. It may be desirable to add temporary staff several years earlier if a new book collection is being formed and needs to be purchased and cataloged, or if new computer software must be obtained in support of a new procedure or service. A small cadre may need to be hired and trained two or three months in advance in order to understand a major new building and help with final plans for moving in and opening the facility.

It should be noted that in library after library, the demands on a new facility may increase only slightly for a modest building expansion but may double or even triple if the facility is a new one and constitutes a very significant improvement in quality and size from the previous quarters. The number of books circulated, the number of students and faculty who remain to study in the library, the number of reference questions, the use of specialized facilities and services, and merely the traffic within the building and in and out of the exits will usually be strikingly greater than was the case previously.

The probable growth in use should be estimated and built into budget planning for the first years of the building. The institution should recognize that this increased use is certain to come in any facility that is much improved, and the dimension of it cannot be exactly predetermined. Thus some allowance in the number of staff in the first year or two is often justified, and, in any event, some budgetary flexibility is prudent to accommodate changes within the first year.

How can one be comfortable in making such projections? Examples of increased use in a comparable new facility in several institutions may help academic budget officers realize the prospects. They no doubt hoped that the academic program would benefit when they supported the library addition or new building; and, although increased budgets may cause them problems, their predisposition for an improved institution should result in a sympathetic response to library staffing requirements in the facility. Typically, a major new facility will seem to bring unforeseen additional use; student use that was nowhere evident seems to materialize almost overnight, and reduction in use of an older, nearby library may be negligible or at least quite temporary. A major undergraduate library building and a nearby major research library, one brand new and the other old, may both grow in use quite steadily from the very beginning.

When the new library at Louisiana State University in Baton Rouge was occupied, the use of the library by students more than doubled immediately. At Cornell just after occupancy of the Uris Undergraduate Library, attendance was some 50 percent larger than when it was the Central Library of the university, while the Olin Research Library was used by approximately the same number as formerly used the old building; the net increase in use was over 150 percent. The University of Michigan found that the major addition to its main library resulted in growth that went up some 20 percent to 30 percent the first year and a similar amount the second year. Stanford's large addition to its main library resulted in a similar growth pattern, though of much greater degree, while use of the nearby undergraduate library dipped during the first two or three months and thereafter returned to its former level. Given similar experiences in a large number of buildings erected in recent decades, one should anticipate that this growth will occur, find parallel situations if possible so as to provide a basis for planning, and budget to support those conditions.

To spoil the effect of a fine new library building on the academic program of the institution because the staff is inadequate in size or quality or both would be exceedingly unfortunate.

16.3
Immediately before Occupancy

Tours of the building four to six months before occupancy will help key staff understand in three-dimensional space what they were trying to understand from architectural drawings. As examples, it may become evident that sunlight conditions are not what the staff expected, the need for directional signs is different from that anticipated, a visually troublesome condition may become apparent, or the usefulness of an art object may be evident in the building itself whereas its desirability was not seen when reviewing plans. A number of these insights may take months to clarify, have policies approved, or have brochures printed before opening day.

In the last month or so before occupancy, other tours will be helpful. Certain library staff need to review the building to plan the move of furniture and book collections. There needs to be an understanding by selected library staff about all the computer and other electronic equipment, alarm systems, emergency exits, telephone outlets, valves, electrical outlets, switches, or circuit breakers. Representatives of the fire and police departments as well as the grounds and building operations staff need to review the building from their perspective even though they have had plans in hand; these operational personnel must have explained to them any change from current conditions in the building's academic program, its security provisions and library reasons for their existence, and the importance of the performance criteria for environmental systems and critical electrical systems. There will also need to be agreement on the schedule for caretaking or janitorial service in the building, covering such matters as the issuance of master keys or access to areas with special security, the frequency of emptying paper receptacles in the rest rooms, vacuuming of carpeted areas, dusting empty shelves in the stacks, and the hours when vacuuming or other noisy operations should take place in order not unduly to disturb readers.

Preservation experts and others will insist upon a burn-in period. The intent of this activity is to run the HVAC at relatively high temperature for up to a month before actual occupancy in order to accelerate the initial and heaviest off-gassing of the materials used in the building. This process is meant to reduce the damaging effects of volatile solvents and acidic vapors upon the collections; such a procedure is recommended where collections preservation is a serious goal. This procedure will also be welcomed by those concerned about allergic reactions and "sick building" syndrome; some staff will actually become ill from workday exposure to a new building without the burn-in process.

Where the university is to undertake the wiring for networks, arrangements will be required to get this process moving well before the actual move-in date. The process just of pulling cable for computers, servers, and printers will take a considerable time. New computer equipment will need to be accumulated in secure space (which may not exist outside of the new building); it will need to be unpacked and accounted for, have software mounted, be tested, and be placed in final location and hooked up before opening day, and much of this can happen only after the building is secure. Certain systems may need to be set up early within the existing building so that staff can become familiar with them and be ready to support them when the new facility opens. Although setting up a computer is not terribly difficult, a large number of computers simply takes time. And the almost certain glitches will add to that time.

Installing telephones is another task that may require several weeks, particularly where phone instruments are rearranged in a building that received a major addition. Indeed, in the planning of the building, there may have been provision for what seemed to be the ultimate number of instruments; library managers will need to determine a few months in advance which outlets will be activated, how many lines will be provided as well as what type of instruments, and that the budget support is available.

During the last week or two before the institution takes responsibility for the building (or before the final installation of furniture, books, and computers), security systems may be installed and tested. Alternatively, the institution may have a separate contract with a security firm and wish to have that work completely apart from the contractor's responsibility. In such an arrangement, which is rather more common, the alarm-system electrical runs would be pulled in advance, but the alarm devices and monitors would be installed immediately after the contractor has turned over the building. If library security staff are needed, they should be hired, and, in any event, appropriate staff must be given necessary training on use of the system before the institution takes over the building.

The door locks will probably have had key blanks inserted to enable the construction crew to open all doors during their work in the building, and those key blanks need to be pulled at the time that the institution takes control of the building. A keying pattern must be designed, based on a hierarchical diagram tree, which can be quite complicated for a large building. (See fig. 14.2.) The library staff will need to decide who needs key access to each room, where magnetic card access is to be provided, what group of unique locks will be controlled by one master key, which grand or great-grand masters can save some staff carrying many keys, and what limits are desired on exterior and high-security door access. The issuance of keys to library staff is generally planned some months in advance; cutting the number of keys required of each type may take many weeks. Keys then need to be signed for and issued, and a key control system set up. The activation of this system is a matter of important timing in order that the construction crews who had free access to the building do not have unintended access once expensive and specialized equipment is moved in. All too often there have been instances of large rolls of carpeting, furniture, soft chairs, or electrical equipment being stolen during the activation period or immediately after the institution takes responsibility for the building. The security at this stage is a matter of great importance, especially where computers are being installed but not yet used.

Security is, of course, complicated if the institution takes partial occupancy of the building. Such occupancy may be required in order to have sufficient time to move the book collections in or to have space and time adequate to stage the installation of furniture and computers. The timing of these closing activities will need careful coordination, and the sense of urgency is likely to play a role as everybody will be anxious to begin using the new facility as soon as possible.

The final cleanup is an obligation of the contractor. However, the institution may choose to conduct an additional cleanup with its own staff, or the cleanup may be covered by part of the budgeted activation funds that allows cleaning to be performed by a commercial firm. This cleanup is not merely the normal cleaning of brick pavers, tile floors, carpeting, and windows; it should also include most, if not all, vertical surfaces where

dust will have accumulated—and this can be a significant and surprising need. The amount of dust created during construction is great; the cleaner the facility can be, particularly if it is an air-conditioned building with an excellent filtration system, the better for the book collections and the people when the building is occupied and the mechanical equipment is in use. Even the process of moving in will create dust; multiple "final" cleanings are common.

At the end of the construction period, the university or college should be given as-built architectural plans, which show the precise routes taken by wiring conduit, ducts, and pipes that were not detailed in the architect's working drawings. Instruction manuals for mechanical, electrical, and security systems need to be given to institutional authorities.

16.4
Signs

All but the smallest library buildings require posted room numbers, name signs, directional guides, public directories, and other graphics to assist users in finding their way in the building. There simply are not enough staff available during all service hours to provide basic direction to several hundred or as many as 10,000 people who may use the library building in a single day, and such use of staff would, of course, not be cost effective. Furthermore, it is well known that many students and faculty are hesitant to ask for help in using the library even when an information or a reference desk is obviously placed and staffed to provide assistance. This reticence may stem from a subconscious belief that one should know how to use something as basic as a library if one has qualified to matriculate—or teach—in an institution of higher education.

A library may have a dozen reading areas and may have huge book collections shelved in various rooms or areas or stacks. Each room or area of the library serves a different subject matter, type of material, or segment of the clientele. Computer systems both facilitate and complicate use of a library. Information desk personnel can handle only a limited number of questions, even if every patron were willing to ask and were willing to wait a few seconds or a minute to receive help. The library can be especially complex in a very large institution—individuals from off campus who are occasional users must be guided to the appropriate library service or area. Thus signs in an academic library are a matter of considerable importance. These graphics will certainly include the name on the building, its hours of opening, the location of each major library service, a list of library offices and officers frequently sought by visitors, and particular reading rooms and bookshelf areas.

Not all information that the institution wishes to convey to clientele should be displayed on signs. If that were done, the library would look like the worst main street—garish, with the profusion of signs visually clashing! In fact, if there are too many signs in view, the mind tends to ignore them all. Whenever considerable explanation is needed that may occupy a paragraph or more, it is better to have inexpensively printed flyers or other handouts available. Examples might be an explanation of lending regulations, a description of what materials are and are not represented in the card and computer catalogs, the range of specialized facilities and services to help handicapped or physically limited individuals, or the location and current hours of service in branch libraries throughout a university campus.

Computer displays in multiple locations are increasingly used to provide substantial information, including maps and plans, and may have audio information for the visually limited. Some argue that computer kiosks used as building directories have serious limitations (speed of answering a question, the need to spell accurately or even to know a name, privacy of information, capacity to display for a group of people, dealing with downtime, etc.). Until content and delivery designs are improved, it may be prudent to assume that computer-based directories and information kiosks are supplemental rather than a complete replacement of more traditional directory and handout systems. Computer-based information systems certainly do represent a service improvement for those who can view directory information even before entering the library. The time may well arrive when the computer will totally replace traditional methods, but this must only be done with clear vision.

In the design of a set of traditional graphics, some principles may be suggested for all academic libraries. In designing signs, put yourself in the position of an occasional library user and think of the questions that arise if you wish to use the library without staff assistance. Try to

have enough signs or guides to answer each of the most frequently asked questions (or have available leaflets or flyers to serve that purpose) but not so many as to present a clutter. The basic and most frequently sought services should have the largest signs, and the larger signs must be kept to a very few words, perhaps five or six at the most. Signs of more moderate size may have somewhat more information—for example, a building floor directory, list of key staff offices, and perhaps an indexed campus map. Only a few signs need to be read from quite a distance, for which super graphics are occasionally used; other signs can be much more modest in size if they need only be read from four or five paces away. (The former instance may include identification of a loan desk or photocopy service, while the latter type may include room numbers.) Certain signs should be in braille for tactile reading—for example, floor levels and room numbers and names. Meaning must be unambiguous. Signs are usually not a place to try humor or to use a specialized local meaning that is campus jargon or an "in joke." In many countries or parts thereof, bilingual signs are appropriate. With increasing frequency, use of international standard symbols can be helpful and much briefer than text signs, though commonly symbols and words are used in combination. Color coding is helpful, but it should be used only if the meaning is absolutely clear or can quickly be learned. Tracking a particularly difficult route from one functional area to another, and one that is used with frequency, may be aided by a tile or carpet color stripe that runs between the two locations. Where signs are changed rather frequently, small bulletin tackboards are useful, or hooks for hanging a temporary sign.

Signs should be tasteful and compatible with the architecture and decor. This requirement need not lessen their prominence at all. Signs of all sizes can be of one design, or of only two or three designs that bear a family resemblance. This characteristic can be particularly useful in graphics for a building addition, to relate the old and new portions. Some people prefer a classic typeface, such as Centaur or Bodoni, while others may prefer a sans serif face; some like subtle understatement, while others prefer boldness and striking color. But remember that large graphics are a form of design statement just as much as windows, lights, walls, and floor treatments. They help to create a tone, a mood, an environment, and, unless developed in the context of the architectural palette, they may seem discordant.

The minimum effective size of lettering is a function of the distance and angle from which it must be read, the lighting on the sign, the general contrasting visual field against which it will be read, the height and width of the letter strokes, and the degree of contrast between the letters and the background colors of the sign. One must consider effectiveness at night, reflections from lights, convenience for persons using bifocals, which signs need to be read from across the room, and invisibility when the space is rather full of people. Mock-ups are highly desirable, even when the design is by an expert architect, an interior designer, or a graphics designer.

Periodic changeability with an evident degree of permanence may be a final principle. It is particularly important that most signs be rather inexpensively changed, because over even a few years library functions shift in location, individual library departments are renamed, senior staff depart, and popular terminology changes. Library staff must handle such changes within the operating budget. Signs should nevertheless be tamper resistant and even theft resistant. Surprising as it may seem, the imaginative student seems to find it a challenge to add one or a few characters to make an entirely different meaning out of words in a sign. With student minds working the way they do, the theft of signs as souvenirs extends even to small signs. As in other aspects of the library building, making signs relatively impervious to mistreatment may be nearly as essential in an academic institution as it would seem to be on the streets. And yet, names set in concrete or stone are wrong except for names intended to be permanent, such as for the donor of a room. Even names on rooms occasionally change!

One technique that has been used with success at a number of institutions is a sign system in which the devices that hold the signs are carefully designed by expert consultants, but the signs themselves are paper-based and produced on computers in-house, perhaps with advice and guidance of the experts. In this approach, a frame with a room number might accommodate a business-card-sized sign created on paper, easily permitting a change of title, name, or function for the room. Stack directories, staff directories, and even building plans, which tend to change often as collections grow, staff move on, and functions change,

can easily be kept up-to-date with this technology. And, the holding device can be a striking visual element offering protection, changeability, and visibility for the paper-based sign.

The selection of signs, text, and location requires care and may consume months. To return to the first principle, one can follow a sequence moving from the general to the specific for the clientele expected to come to the building. Thus, in a highly specialized branch library, one need not have a campus map mounted in the lobby, perhaps not even floor plans for that branch, but one would treat its basic functions and shelf areas. In the main research library of a university and perhaps for many a college library, a campus map as well as the library building floor plans will save many questions. Such a map should tell north-south directions and should be oriented as is the person viewing it. Building floor plans should also be so oriented, must not be overly detailed (architectural plans never would be good), and yet should normally include bookstack ranges because the walls of the large space will only occasionally be seen. Indeed, in a very complicated building, there may need to be a building cross section. A few libraries have used such elaborate devices as push-button illuminated directories, though we never recommend this because of the expense of keeping them up-to-date. Signs sometimes can be placed and words chosen to help smooth over what may have been architectural weaknesses, such as not being able to see the principal circulation desk from a reference desk.

In numbering rooms, you need to consider whether to put the number and the name of the room on, beside, or over the door. If the door has a large glass panel, do put more than one or two rather small words on the glass; any appreciable blocking of view or distraction of those walking toward the door may result in somebody inadvertently being hit as the door swings open. An advantage of wording or decorations on unframed glass doors or floor-length windows is the safety of seeing the glass, as is provided by the Shakespeare quotations on some windows at the Sedgwick Library (now the Walter C. Koerner Library) at the University of British Columbia. Putting the sign beside the door is best for those doors that may occasionally be propped open. Placing the designation over the door may work if the architect has left room over the frame, though the designation may be more easily overlooked than if it were at eye level. Yet this higher location can accommodate a larger name for the room and would be visible at a greater distance and above the heads of a group of persons. Individual circumstances need to be considered. Compromises occasionally need to be made for specific conditions.

Another detail: Consideration may be given to putting large words on top of shelving to help locate major subjects or types of reference materials, such as to indicate the sections for dictionaries, encyclopedias, atlases, phone books, and the like, or for history, literature, and religion. If a card catalog is still in use, similar treatment on the top of catalog cases can indicate the content of each linear segment of trays when a catalog has three or four thousand trays.

Because each building is unique, those responsible for the library management must adopt a coherent plan. The detailing of the exact text of each sign may be delegated to a small staff committee, or each administrative unit may suggest needs in its area. However, one individual responsible for coordinating the public services of the library or of the project must do a precise review of the text for every single sign. This review should always include testing on a few individuals, perhaps some student employees as well as the designer. Of course, local codes will usually dictate signs for location of fire extinguishers and emergency exit routes, even the color and size of the characters in such signs. One final word of advice: When in doubt about the necessity for a sign, do not install it, and if in doubt about the wording or location, try a temporary sign.

The time needed for designing, manufacturing, and mounting signs will in part depend on the choice of design, a matter that can be handled in various ways. If a standard campus design exists, no time is expended on design. Otherwise, the choice is between commercially available standard signs, a special design, and, quite often, a combination of these two. The options in choosing the designer are reliance on the architect if the task is in the contracted scope of services, an interior designer, a specialist firm, an institutional service, or the library graphics staff if such exists. Regardless of the chosen route, it is advisable to arrange for some guidance from those responsible both for the architectural design and for selection of the interior finishes and furnishings. This may well be another case of an institution getting what it pays for; little investment of funds will result in only a modest achievement.

Signs may be prepared rather quickly if they are all bought from a library supply house or produced within the library or by a printing or graphics service of the institution. Months of advance notice, however, may be required for large or nonstandard orders to be sure that the local supplier can fill the entire order from local stock or get timely delivery, or that the in-house production unit has time available or can hire additional staff and obtain equipment needed to produce the signs. Specially designed signs may require as many as four or five months when new designs and a custom product are wanted, or when there is a large directory to be silk-screened and framed, or when special coloring or illumination is needed. Thus, for a large and relatively complex building, the graphics program design, fabrication, and mounting could well be initiated with final text in hand six to twelve months before occupancy.

Because signs will seldom be part of the general construction contract (with minor exceptions), they ordinarily cannot be installed until the building has been turned over to the institution, and so the building may be opened with few, or at least not all, of the permanent signs in place. When it appears that signs may not be ready in time for opening, or when temporary signs are needed during the activation period, computer-produced signs can be useful stand-ins. The priority for putting up signs can be designated so that the in-house studio or commercial firm produces first those that are most important for initial use and for appearance at the dedication ceremony. Certainly the clientele should be understanding if there are some temporary signs. Indeed, the classes of books to be housed in a particular range of the stacks are often not final until the deployment of books in the stack has been completed and any unanticipated crowded sections have been spread out. So temporary signs do not become permanent, a deadline for completing permanent installation should be established.

The permanent installation may be done by the library's own crew, although commercial custom products will usually be installed by the manufacturer as part of the contract. Installation will involve drilling where signs are mounted on concrete surfaces, and hangers will be used for those to be suspended from a ceiling. During installation it is desirable for one individual in the library who is fully familiar with the graphics program to be present much of the time; there may have been generalized placement instructions (such as 48 inches or 2 meters off the floor, just to the right of the door, and so forth) but the exact location will need to take into account special field conditions. A permanent sign may be impossible to move an inch or more without leaving a visible mark, and so precision in installation is important.

Estimating and budgeting for the cost of signs is referred to in Chapter 9. It usually is part of an activation allowance. Occasionally it may be left to be covered in the contingency for the project, though this is inadvisable. The cost estimate will vary greatly, depending on whether it is an in-house product or a standard commercial or specialized commercial design and whether installation labor is included. The name on the building and emergency directional and door signs may be the only signs for which the architect and the contractor are responsible. Signs generally done in-house are the range indicators for shelving of book materials and the labels for any card catalog trays. Between these extremes are many options, and the price will vary accordingly. Generally cost cannot be estimated on a square foot or meter basis as can so many other costs. Rather it is a combination of three factors: the number of rooms and the range of services in the library that must be given signs; the complexity of the building, which demands more or less; and the quality of the product. Signs for a large university main library building could easily cost as much as $35,000 to $50,000—without a computer display of customized guidance or instruction.

Illustrations in publications cited in the Bibliography indicate the wide range of possibilities and thus help the institution answer some of the questions raised.

16.5
Room Numbering

Earlier in this volume it was pointed out that, given no other direction, the architect will establish a floor, room, and area numbering or lettering system in the design process, at the latest during design development. Ideally, this system and the one used in the completed building will be the same, thus saving confusion and repeated effort as the building is activated and the graphics system completed. For example, an early room or area numbering system that is agreed to be fi-

nal can provide accuracy in fund-raising descriptions of a certain room, panel boards for security and safety alert systems, drafts of staff operating manuals, and furniture move plans. Numbering is, however, treated here because the graphics art design and installation may be part of the general signage task, although numbers for floors, in elevators, and of major areas are sometimes part of the architectural design and basic construction. Like so many other efforts, this choice of system often appears to be a simple task, while it can actually be quite complex.

An institutional policy in regard to room numbers may dictate a system and rule out certain configurations. Otherwise, although any particular building may have features that suggest special considerations, 10 principles should be considered.

1. A basic plan generally would be clockwise numbering of rooms and areas per floor, unless the floor is very large.
2. Similar numbers should, if possible, occur in the same location on each floor. For example, one would expect to find 212A directly above 112A. Clearly, this only works for those spaces that are repeated on each floor, but even if the general number group is repeated on each floor, it will be an aid to orientation.
3. Given a room number, one should find that the logical pattern of the numbering scheme should aid in finding the room. Finding the room, however, can be a problem in a large library, for, unlike a hotel or large office building, it has large areas with unstructured corridors. One technique is some form of a matrix, but be careful to avoid too many tricks that may require careful learning of the system. Let us explain. Some directionality is an advantage. As one proceeds across the floor, the numbers should change in a logical sequence, such as front to back, left to right, or another natural sequence. This demand probably rules out a spiral; it should, in most cases, rule out using odd numbers for one side of the building and even numbers for the other except where a clearly identifiable part of the building is organized on a long central corridor.
4. Try to keep the system simple. Four-digit numbers are preferable to five-digit numbers.

In a large building this may mean that a perfect solution covering every possibility is not reasonable. The "perfect" solution can simply be too complex.

5. There should be provision for adding spaces or dividing spaces. This is usually done by reserving numbers for such contingencies or by adding an alpha character. Ideally, the system can be expanded to any future building addition. This may be uncertain if the addition could go on two or more sides, yet it can be worth a try.

6. If bookstack ranges or range aisles can fit within the numbering system, it would be advantageous, provided it does not add undue complexity. Carrel numbers probably would stretch the system beyond reasonable limits, though the carrels might be lettered, such as 130G being the seventh in area 30 on the first floor.

7. Numbering rooms and areas is important for staff responsible for fire and safety protection and for building maintenance workers. Room and area names will not suffice; there should also be numbering, generally placed in the same location as for other, similar spaces.

8. Some may suggest that indication of the room function within the numbering system would be advantageous. We recommend against this. Use of space often changes, and it is doubtful that this would aid the user (or fire department) in finding a space. Separate numbering systems for carrels, ranges, lockers, and the like (such as C100, R821, and L47) may be entirely appropriate.

9. In branch libraries, if the prevalent building scheme does not suffice, the library may have one number in building terms and be subnumbered independently within the library area (such as L1-12 for the 12 library areas or zones and offices).

10. Above all, the numbering system should be easily explained to the user. Building directories should be designed to illustrate the logic of the numbering system and should, if possible, be oriented consistently as the user would view them at the head of main stairs, beside elevator doors, or in a lobby location.

Having outlined the principles of a numbering system, what is the next step? The first digit should be easy, as it will almost invariably represent the floor, with "1" being the entry level, "0" being a lower level (or, where there are multiple basements, "A, B, C . . ."), and "2, 3, 4 . . ." being the upper floors. In many countries, of course, "1" is one floor above ground. In the rare case of a library exceeding 10 floors, two digits may be required for the floor level.

The next two digits should indicate fairly closely where on a given floor the room is located. The logical sequence mentioned above enters at this point. Libraries typically have major vertical movement cores centralized in the building; the question no doubt will be, where should the sequence begin? One quickly discovers that beginning in the center leads in large buildings to a complex and difficult system to learn. It is probably best to begin at one side or to develop a simple matrix, such that the central stair is actually located in the center of the numbering system. Except for a very simple layout, clockwise numbering probably will be a problem just as is a spiral numbering system.

The final digit (preferably only one) will identify exactly the space. It is this digit that should also provide for future divisions of the space. A large room may be identified by the first three digits, while smaller rooms opening off of it are identified by the fourth character—a letter or number. In this case a clockwise pattern is appropriate.

Numbering-lettering schemes are a great expense to change. Thus it is well to test the proposed scheme on a sampling of faculty, staff, and students. Checking large or comparable buildings in the area can show problems to be avoided. Fig. 16.1 suggests three distinct approaches for numbering, each responding to the nature of the building itself.

16.6
Moving In

The actual physical move is a chore. To make the process as easy and smooth as possible, the task must be worked out in detail in advance in order to save time and confusion while the move is taking place. This section does not provide guidance for detailed planning and execution. Questions needing resolution and a few techniques are suggested, with extensive information provided in materials listed in the Bibliography.

The logistical problems of a move can be quite complex. Will the physical plant be ready when the move is scheduled to take place? Will the approach walks and driveway to the building be completed? Will the equipment and the furniture have arrived and been installed? Will the light, heat, and the elevators be operational so that the building is habitable? Have rooms been numbered? Will temporary route markers be needed?

What is to be done about library service during the move; will it continue or be shut down for a few days or even a few weeks? Can course reserves be provided at another temporary location? Can and should the move be made at a time of year when the service load is low? How will it proceed if there is rain or snow?

How can rapid relocation of computers be accomplished, and by whom, and should expensive equipment be the last installed before opening? How should fragile materials be protected? What responsibility do staff have for moving or preparing their own desk area materials? Is there money and help available for preparation for moving and the shift itself? What extra help must be employed? Is inventory protection assured throughout this period? In selected instances, a responsible staff member will accompany an item throughout its move.

The equipment to be used in connection with moving must be ready and available. There is, of course, a basic difference whether one uses a commercial firm or does it completely in-house. If it is necessary to minimize the time taken by the move and if there is a suitable budget, using an experienced commercial firm may be the wisest course, especially if the library is a large one being moved some distance. If a move is the distance of a city block or farther, quite clearly trucks or vans are going to be needed. Commercial movers or professional movers within the institution are essential, of course, for particularly heavy equipment and, generally, for office furniture. They not only have special equipment but are trained to move such items efficiently and safely. The location of each piece of equipment that is to be moved must be recorded. This includes office equipment, files, framed pictures, any card catalog, pamphlet files, cabinets, and so forth.

16.6.1 Planning the Book Collection Move

In contrast to shifting of equipment from one building to another, moving the book collection is quite a different matter. Although many academic libraries use a commercial firm for a great

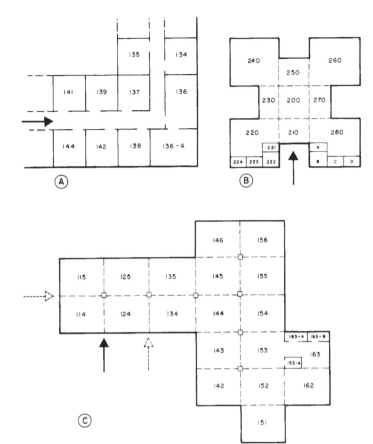

FIGURE 16.1   Room numbering. Several schemes are possible. Use of odd-even is most suitable for a linear progression of spaces, such as found in an office building or a hotel (A). (Note that 136-A is so numbered because it opens off 136; if it had a door directly off the corridor, it would be 138.) A clockwise numbering system (B) may be suitable for a symmetrical building where the numbered zones contain rooms of the particular numerical sequence. If there are more than 10 rooms in any zone, then an alpha character may designate the specific room.

In very large buildings, both the odd-even and rotational schemes will be difficult. The best arrangement may be a very simple matrix where the numbered zones become larger as one progresses across the building in two directions (C). Ideally, the numbers would increase starting from the entrance. The temptation to add the concept of odd-even in the deployment of number zones in a large building should be avoided, as simplicity seems to serve the lost patron better than sophistication.

many moves, even of relatively short distances, it is more common to use library staff and student help for short moves. In this case the library must have sufficient numbers of book trucks, and boxes or containers if required. Containers in which books are to be packed may have to be designed and constructed, which may take time, or they may be rented. However, it turns out that books are seldom moved in containers any more, the major exception being where they must be transported up stairs or over a route that is not suitable for book trucks, which should be rare. Another exception is for small collections or parts of collections, especially where there is ample time to prepare for the move and where needed access to the boxed materials is limited.

A technique used with success for fragile and rare collections is shrink-wrapping, which is superior to boxes for service and access during and shortly after the move. Shrink-wrap is less expensive than boxes, and labeling requirements are reduced. Shrink-wrapped books are then placed on carts just as normal books. Shrink-wrapping should be a superior substitute for boxes where book carts cannot be used as well.

Regardless of whether the move is to a new wing, into remodeled space, or to a distant building, ways and means must be decided for moving the material in the least expensive and most expeditious manner. Do not overlook the special types of materials that are not included in the main collection, such as the compact discs, globes, rare books, manuscripts, anything that goes into a vault if one has been provided, any separate popular and paperback collections, new-book displays, the duplicates that have not been disposed of, the uncataloged materials and those in process, the unbound periodicals, and office collections.

Keep in mind that safety of the people involved and of the material is very important. The well-planned move that is carried out successfully can be one of the most satisfying experiences that a librarian will ever have, but an ill-planned one can be a catastrophe and is to be avoided at all costs.

The largest task is the decision on the location of each book in the new quarters; the more precise the decision, the better. This means that measurements of books in each class must be made to attain the goal so that, as far as possible, material has to be moved only once. Material out on loan is almost always no complication, and growth of the collections can easily be factored in. However, the goal of providing precise location information can be complicated by the need to reintegrate stored parts of the collections, especially if the stored collections are to be heavily interfiled with the main collection as opposed to their being discrete, easily measured blocks of materials. When adjustment is necessary, moves

should not be more than a few feet, so books will not again have to go onto book trucks. It is necessary for each range and section in the new space to be numbered (for example, 127C4 for shelf 4 in section C of range 127) and labeled in some way so that it is easy to find, with a card attached to it, perhaps with temporary tape, showing just what classification block is to be placed in each section and with a duplicate of that card placed with the specific material in the old library.

Decisions are needed on whether to shelve in strict classification sequence, or whether, for example, political science should be next to history and on the largest stack floor or near the government documents library. Stack floors may or may not be uniform in size, while the spaces taken by classification segments never are the same size. In large collections it is well to precisely allocate a block of sections or ranges to a segment of the classification, and certain classifications to a floor, for otherwise seemingly careful measurement on each shelf can accumulate errors and the deployment in one area may come up with books to fill a few sections too many or many sections may be needlessly left empty. Some stack managers identify each shelf break for the moved collections so that with careful planning, there will be no problem of running out of space or ending up with empty shelves without intent. Planning to this level of detail is necessary if more than one moving team is to work on a floor or area of the stack at the same time.

As for details, decisions will have to be made about how full the shelves are to be, how much space is to be left in each section or on each shelf, and whether top and bottom shelves are initially to be left vacant.

Should the same subject in two classification schemes, for example, Dewey and L.C., be shelved on the same floor? Should a subject classification be started on one floor if it has to be concluded on another, or are there small collections that fit the remaining floor space and thus keep all of any one classification on one floor? Would certain collections be a greater loss than others if they were shelved in a basement with some vulnerability to water damage, and are certain collections in need of the best environment for book preservation? Should classifications with heaviest use be placed near the stack entrance to minimize traffic? The fullness of shelves will properly differ from one part of the collections to another. Volumes in classifications no longer used may be shelved to capacity, allowing only for books in circulation or the growth of serials that may still be in the old classification system. A journal run will fill shelves except for space at the end for future growth; and the space left for the desired number of years before stack capacity is reached can be reckoned by the current annual space required. The plan can recognize that some parts of the collection are more dynamic in growth than others, and some may deliberately be of very limited growth.

16.6.2 The Method of Moving Book Collections

The technique of the move must be determined, with costs and collection security and the time required all being key factors in deciding on the process. Questions such as the following need to be thought out. Should moving be done by hand, by handcart, by an endless chain of students or others passing the books from one to another, or by book trucks? If the last method is selected, can the trucks be pushed out of one building and into the other without difficulty? Should dollies be used with boxes piled on them, or will a motor truck or pallet lift be required? How do you get from one floor to another in the old and in the new building? A critical constraint: The speed of moving may depend on the number of elevators available in both wings or the two buildings. If elevators are inadequate, it may help to arrange shifts so that books going to a level where an elevator will not be needed can be moved concurrently with those that require an elevator. Will a temporary book chute or a ramp be useful to carry books from the older building to the ground floor or outside? Will it be worthwhile with a very large collection to rent and install one or more temporary endless-belt conveyors? Are the books to be cleaned and fumigated before or at the time of moving before going into the new location? Different methods used for book moves are explained in references given in the Bibliography.

The staff member in charge must be very good at coordinating, at getting people to work smoothly and rapidly, and at keeping everyone busy and yet not too busy. It may well be that one person can effectively plan the job and do the measuring and labeling, but that a person of different talents is best in charge of the actual shift personnel. Yet in such a case, teamwork by the two persons and immediate access by the latter to the former during the move is very important. Responsible staff should be at each end of the move, with cellular phones or walkie-talkies or ready access to phones, to coordinate the rate of flow, particularly if books from different areas are being moved simultaneously. Each team needs good instruction as to the process, sequence of the move, attention to book order, and the proper way of lifting loaded boxes (with bent knees and straight back) so as to guard against injuries. Daily briefings can update plans and means of coordination.

If the books are to be shifted with dolly trucks and transported in motor trucks, a satisfactory loading dock must be available, as it is impossible to push a loaded dolly truck from the ground up a ramp into a motor truck. A truck fitted with a lift gate can be a substitute for a loading dock. Book trucks fully loaded may receive quite a racking when loading onto and off the truck, and book trucks with the permanent I-Beam joinery of Eustis Designs may be cost effective, as several university libraries have found. The use of a fork or pallet lift can be efficient. These comments are perhaps enough to indicate the problems; a study of the literature on the subject may indicate the best solution for a particular library.

Some materials will require special security provisions during the move. Especially valuable, rare, unique, and fragile materials and any items kept in a vault may be candidates for this special treatment. Bonded movers can be considered, though such an arrangement would usually be deemed insufficient for the most rare and valuable items. Most libraries use their own staff, particularly the staff of a Department of Special Collections, to handle such materials, or at least to ride along as escorts to monitor the move from one locked area to the other. The extra out-of-pocket costs are modest because regular staff salaries are all that is involved. But keep in mind that this part of the move can take a surprising amount of time, and it must proceed in a way and at a time that does not conflict with the move of the regular collections.

The costs for a move will, of course, vary greatly and must be budgeted, as described in Chapter 9. Cost estimates need to be obtained and will depend heavily on the amount of commercial moving utilized, the employment of students, and the number and capacity of elevators, as well as the efficiency with which the smoothness of the move is planned. No examples of moving costs are given because they go out of date rapidly and because each move is a unique set of conditions. However, it can be stated that direct costs can be kept down if students and other hourly employees of the library move all the books, provided student wages are not exceptionally high. (In cases where student labor is paid at essentially the same scale as full-time staff, the savings can be negligible.) With typically lower student wages, it is not uncommon for the cost with the use of students to be half that of a commercial mover. Part of this savings results from the fact that much of the supervision is by staff who are already on the library payroll; supervision of in-house work is thus largely a soft cost that is seldom accounted for. Of course, the academic schedule can affect the availability of student labor; even where it is desired to save money, it may not make sense in some cases. Cost can also be kept down if the move can be done over many weeks and therefore have the best equipment, the most efficient use of vertical transportation, trained supervisors and an experienced crew, and a minimum of overtime and premium payments. In most cases, this means scheduling the move for as early as possible during the longest annual vacation period or most slack period of use.

The librarian in one large university, planning to move into a new building during the Christmas holidays, realized in time that the building would not be ready and relaxed the pressure on the contractor, with the result that the building was barely completed in time to move in at the end of the next summer. Some librarians have absolutely refused to attempt a major move during the regular academic school year, yet Cornell managed successfully to complete its shift in midwinter, just in time for the second semester, in spite of the upstate New York severe weather. The move was made possible because a tunnel connected the old building with the new. Comparatively few libraries will enjoy such an advantage. The major part of the move of the 75,000 volumes from Harvard's Widener Library to the Lamont Undergraduate Library took place in four hours on a Sunday morning during the Christmas holidays with the aid of 40 staff members who volunteered to help, working with four elevators in the old building, using the tunnel connecting the buildings and two elevators in the new one. This move transferred five loaded book trucks every three minutes.

Unexpected delays that make postponement of moving necessary often come from delays in arrival of equipment, rather than from slowness of construction. The trouble may stem from the supplier, but in most cases it results from delay on the part of the institution in selecting and ordering the equipment. Many librarians, and even too many business managers, fail to realize that an order for anything but stock furniture takes time to design, to produce, and to ship and, in the case of bookstacks, to install. Even stock furniture is sometimes out of stock, particularly if ordered in large quantities; it may have to be fabricated after it is ordered. It is critical to order furniture and equipment for delivery when needed, and especially so for all book shelving while remembering the "burn-in" period, as mentioned in Section 16.3 above and in Section 6.1.11 under comments on bookstack color and finish.

16.7
Settling In and the Shakedown Period

From the first day of moving in until the end of the warranty period of the construction contract, there is likely to be a certain turmoil. This will be a period for the surfacing of certain unanticipated problems, cleaning, punch-list residuals, final equipment adjustments, and usually a constant difficulty with balancing the ventilation or air-conditioning system.

Understanding and tolerance by all during this period will be beneficial as will persistence by library staff in following through on the myriad issues that may arise during the warranty period. Staff adjustment may be very rapid in some cases and difficult in others as they experience surprising acoustic conditions, direct sunlight, noises or ventilation drafts, and nonfunctioning or malfunctioning equipment. Unfamiliarity with the new quarters may be unsettling to those who very much enjoyed their niches in the previous quarters. All these complaints need to be listened to sympathetically. The staff should be encouraged to raise questions so that those responsible for the building can analyze the nature and cause of the condition and consider whether it needs immediate correction (with financing from the activation budget or, if covered by the warranty, from the contractor), whether it can be postponed and perhaps changed through the normal operating budget process, or whether it arises from a certain resistance to change and that nothing need be done. It is not uncommon to end up with a condition that is technically covered by the warranty, but that is so minor or the correction through the contractor so difficult that it is most expeditious and possibly cheapest (when staff time is factored in) simply to have the correction made on the activation budget.

In regard to some conditions, staff may be asked to live with the new situation for a few months in order to see whether the problem is persistent and major or whether it is merely the experienced difference between the old and the new. For example, some staff may feel much more claustrophobic in the new quarters or, conversely, may feel they are now living in a gold-fish bowl. Perhaps the staff can be led to realize in advance that working conditions will be different, that the ambience of the new quarters will be different by design, and that change should be expected and time allowed for people to try out and accommodate to the new circumstances.

Similarly, students and faculty may be very complimentary of the new quarters but also may be vociferous in their complaints about something they feel was overlooked and that is to them very disturbing. It is wise to listen sympathetically to each complaint, sorting out those that seem to be personal idiosyncrasies and those that are indicative of some fundamental problem.

Problems are certain to exist—some minor, some inconsequential, and a few major. Some of these may have been on the contractor's punch list, and it may be many months before each item is analyzed, diagnosed, and corrected or a solution negotiated. Some typical examples can suggest the range of conditions: incorrect wiring of switching, a blocked ventilation duct, carpet seams that gape, a door scraping the floor, settling that results in sticking doors, problems in key lock tumblers that are still new, humming in a faulty ballast, a door that was not hung correctly, hardware not heavy enough to withstand the amount of use already evident, and problems with computer connections and audio facilities that may be difficult to trace. The institutional representatives and the contractor need to continue to work on the punch-list residuals; the architect and the representative of the institution will need to consult on unanticipated conditions, determine which are covered by the bid documents, which were planning oversights, and which are of such urgency that they must be corrected whether funded or not.

The University of Guelph Library is an exceptional building, but in the published report of its creation, a handful of problems are enumerated.[1]

Furnishings: The custom designs were not adequately tested and the librarians were not insistent enough in some of their specifications; service counters and card catalog trays were particular problems.

Basement space: This was more chopped up by walls than they now wish and some areas were not sized properly for the operations, such as for binding preparation or storing bulk collections before processing.

Doors: Access to certain rooms was too narrow to admit the equipment that was to be used.

Coatrooms: Except for occasional large groups of visitors, the public coat areas in the upper and lower lobbies are seldom used nor do the students use individual coat rods throughout the stacks but instead use the back of their chairs or the corner of carrel tops.

Closing bell: An alarm for emergencies or fires was included, yet a means of alerting users to closing was overlooked.

Staff facilities: More attractive space could have been provided, perhaps at the top of the building; a democratic decision to allow individual tea and coffee making has proved time consuming and untidy in comparison to vending machines; staff lockers have been somewhat of a problem and coat hooks should have been installed in the women's washrooms.

Access by the handicapped: The entrance doors are too heavy for a person confined to a wheelchair to handle alone (the severe climate requires fast-acting heavy-duty door closers).

Sun control: The use of exterior horizontal and vertical sun fins and louvers on the second and third floors are effective except for a few weeks a year when, at certain times of the day, the sun is not screened by these exterior devices.

Glass in doors: Faculty studies have no glass panels, an inconvenience for staff who need to determine if they are occupied.

Floor covering: The only major area of the library that was not carpeted was technical services where vinyl tile was used; maintenance problems have resulted and the noise level is high; carpeting should have been provided.

Service points: There were found to be too many to staff within the operating budget.

Basic design: An architectural consultant felt the original design, with each upper floor the same size, was not sympathetic to its site. So the fourth (top) floor was redesigned into three smaller floors, extending it to six—thereby creating a bad loss of important library service objectives.

"It would be foolish to expect that any library could be planned, designed, and built without mistakes having been made or problems having occurred."[2] This statement by planners of the McLaughlin Library of the University of Guelph is representative of how almost any librarian or other member of the planning team would feel after going through the process on any large library building.

Thus, even in an exceedingly successful building, there will be a variety of matters that would have been done otherwise if planners had full hindsight while the process still allowed time. It is probably fair to say that no operational problem is so difficult that during the shakedown period a practical solution cannot be found.

This period of settling in and adjustment will go on for much of a year in a large building (and perhaps for some weeks in a branch library). Most of the problems will surface and be resolved in the first four to six months, although some may be tenacious. Problems with the ventilation system in Stanford's Meyer Memorial Library persisted from 1966 until 1979, when a completely rebuilt ventilation system had to be installed after years of complaints. Acoustical conditions remained unsatisfactory until 1982, when acoustical isolation of the three upper floors was achieved by glazing in the central open well.

Relations with an institution's plant operations department will be particularly important during this shakedown period, most particularly for the HVAC and security alarm systems. One can expect relatively few electrical problems and even fewer plumbing problems. Drainage, however, should be specially watched because of the horrendous damage that can come from faulty plumbing or inadequate storm drains. Drain problems can become apparent during the first heavy rains or the first spring thaw, creating peak conditions that should have been accommodated by the engineering design.

Cleaning up is another task of the shakedown period. If the contractor did a good job of cleaning before turning over the building, the institution is fortunate indeed. The contractors usually do a "broom clean" job. Although a commercial cleaning firm may have done a thorough job, there is a good likelihood that some areas remain that need extra cleaning. A particular question to resolve is whether to clean the book collection before moving the books from old quarters, which may not have been air conditioned, into new quarters, bringing much of the dirt with the books. It is always best to clean or at least hand-vacuum before the books are moved or as the move is begun. Time or congested conditions may not permit this, however, and in such an eventuality the cleaning of books in the new facility may be an important part of the shakedown. Cleaning books can be combined with the final specific shelf placement for the collections in their new quarters—that is, the individual adjustment of shelves within each section to accommodate quarto or folio volumes if they were temporarily shelved flat or on their spines during the rush of moving.

It is suggested that on opening day and during the weeks or few months immediately following, operations will be smoothest and a favorable impression made on the clientele if a public service staff somewhat larger than normal can be on duty. Technical service and management staff may be asked to volunteer to share in this temporary service and can find it exhilarating as well as needed and much appreciated. A special temporary information desk might be located in the lobby or foyer if the regular reference or information desks are farther into the building. It will also help if a short fact sheet about the building and small floor plans are available to hand out to students and visitors. There will be a demand for tours, and, therefore, the library staff may save time by offering a guided tour at regular intervals, perhaps each hour on the hour during the first week, tapering off to once a day for a few months. Tours may or may not be needed in new branch library facilities. Tours for institutional staff and neighboring librarians may also be in demand and can in fact be offered as part of the dedication events. All library staff should recognize that the building was provided for the students and faculty, and, if the library staff take pains to assure that it is seen in that light and that the staff are not overly concerned with their own working amenities, the relations between the staff and users can ride the crest of this exciting event.

16.8
Dedication

Recognition of those who have contributed funds for a library building is an important and sensitive matter. Without support from governmental sources, an institution is completely dependent on individuals, foundations, and a combination of fund-raising efforts to finance a library building. Even if financing is entirely governmental, as was the case for the University of California Northern Regional Library Facility, it is still desirable to thank publicly those who were instrumental in obtaining funds and approvals and were otherwise important to the project. Such recognition often includes on the plaque the names of selected governmental officials, or offices, or committee members, and sometimes includes the name of the architect, engineer, construction firm, and contracting authority. The fund-raising will occasionally be completed before the building is under construction. In most cases, however, an institution is motivated to begin construction when a majority of funds has been pledged because construction price increases warrant a gamble on the ability to put the final financing in place. Of course, this complicates preparation of the dedication plaque because the final list of contributors will not be known. In part for this reason, the dedication may take place some months after the library is open for use.

Ceremonies in connection with the start and completion of a library building are invariably helpful in donor relations, and the decisions about what to have and when need consideration by several institutional officers. Everyone likes a party, and this party can have several objectives. An event may be desirable as a way of publicly thanking donors who wish to have their name associated with a building that will be visible and long-lasting, it may be an indirect way of publicizing the institution's needs and therefore encouraging other gifts, and finally it may be an occasion to bring attention to the academic achievements of the institution and thus contribute toward its long-term reputation and encourage support from the neighboring community, governmental circles, alumni, and friends. Each institution must decide for itself what it hopes to accomplish by this ceremony.

It is customary to have a ceremony of some kind at the groundbreaking or early during the construction. This may be completely informal or may be accompanied by speeches. It may come when the excavation starts. There may be a cornerstone laying, with the insertion in the cornerstone of documents appropriate to the occasion and dealing with the institution's history and the donor's relationship to it. The stone may be placed with the aid of a senior representative of the institution as well as the donor.

Long before the new building is completed, moved into, and opened to the public, it is to be hoped that the institution and the librarian will have been making plans for a dedication or other ceremony to celebrate the completion. The cost of such programs can range from a small sum to tens of thousands of dollars, the larger sums covered perhaps by a special gift if they are not budgeted into the building project itself. This dedication can take place just before or during the occupancy, as happened at the National Library of Medicine and the Library of Congress Madison Memorial Building, but it is generally preferable to schedule it after the library is in full operation, so that those interested can observe the resultant use of, and activity in, the new building.

The budget for any such event will vary greatly depending on local circumstances and event size and quality. Examples of the wide variety of potential dedication expenses include: printing of invitations and programs, advertisement in a student paper, postage for selected mailing, banners and balloons or other decorations, flowers, music of several types, food catering for the reception(s), dinner parties, still photographer, filming or videotaping service, special campus transportation, lodging for honorees or special guests, chair and platform rental, sound system, tents or awnings, mementos for donor(s), preparation and printing of memorial booklet to document the occasion, extra police/traffic assistance, traffic barricades, portable toilets, and after-event grounds cleanup.

The planning for such ceremonies takes a good deal of time and may involve library staff, the development office, faculty, the administration of the institution, and perhaps trustees. The donor may also be involved if there is one major contributor. Where more than one or two sources of gift funds are involved, it is wise for the institution to begin at least six months in advance of the event to determine the means for recognizing donations, settle on the design of plaques, obtain approval from the donor (or trustees or descendants) to make public the name, and approve the exact form in which the name will appear. It may require even longer advance scheduling if a

Groundbreaking Ceremony
Saturday, April 16, 1983
11:00 a.m.

Presiding
Susan Brynteson
Director of Libraries

Welcome
Dr. E. A. Trabant
President

Remarks
The Honorable Pierre S. du Pont IV
Governor

Mr. J. Bruce Bredin
Chairman, Board of Trustees

The Honorable Richard S. Cordrey
President Pro-Tempore, Delaware Senate

The Honorable Robert F. Gilligan
Majority Leader, Delaware House of Representatives

Dr. Samuel Lenher
Chairman, 150th Anniversary Advisory Committee

Mr. Gordon Pfeiffer
President, University of Delaware Library Associates

Address
Dr. Carol E. Hoffecker
Richards Professor of History, University of Delaware
and President, University Faculty Senate
"The First State and Its University, A Tradition of Partnership"

Groundbreaking

Luncheon

FIGURE 16.2 Groundbreaking ceremony program, University of Delaware. (Courtesy of University of Delaware)

major political figure or other celebrity is to participate. If there is to be a formal portrait of the principal donor, it will also need to be budgeted; and if a painting is to be done, it may need to be started as much as a year before the dedication so that it can be completed and approved by the donor, framed, shipped, installed, and lighted appropriately. Figures 16.2 to 16.9 illustrate parts of brochures and programs issued on the occasion of groundbreaking and dedication ceremonies.

FIGURE 16.3 Prededication program of the University of Maryland Baltimore County. This invitation and program for a "preview" was prepared as a bookmark and promoted to the campus faculty, staff, and friends as a special event before occupancy of the building. The enticement of seeing this long-awaited building before it opened made the sneak preview a great hit. (Courtesy of University of Maryland Baltimore County)

COME TO THE HEART OF UMBC

A Special Preview of the Library Tower, for UMBC Students, Faculty, Staff, Alumni, and Friends

Monday, December 12, 1994
3 to 5 p.m.
Albin O. Kuhn Library and Gallery
The University of Maryland Baltimore County

3 p.m.
Ceremony and Ribbon Cutting

4 p.m.
"Development of the
Albin O. Kuhn Library and Gallery"
Dr. Joseph Arnold
Professor
Department of History
Seventh Floor, Regents Room

Tours

Music by the Maryland Camerata and
the Chesapeake Brass Quintet

Festive Fare

RSVP by December 9 to 410-455-2902

Order Of Ceremony
Friday, October 25, 1991
11:30 a.m.

PRELUDE
The Brass Dominion

BELL DECLARATION

PROCESSIONAL & PRESENTATION OF SELECTED LITERATURE
Accompaniment by The Brass Dominion
(Audience please stand.)

INVOCATION
Rev. Paul Henrickson, Chaplain

WELCOME AND ACKNOWLEDGMENTS
David Gring, President

"FESTIVAL JUBILATE"
Written and directed by Daniel Pinkham for the Roanoke College
Sesquicentennial Celebration
Performed by The Roanoke College Choir, with accompaniment by The
Brass Dominion

DEDICATION REMARKS
John Turbyfill '53, Chair of the Roanoke College Board of Trustees

RESPONSE FROM THE COMMUNITY
James Olin, Congressman, 6th District, U.S. Congress

RESPONSE FROM THE FACULTY
Gerald Gibson, Vice President-Dean of the College

RESPONSE FROM THE STUDENTS
Kevin Hartz '92, President of the Student Government Association

RESPONSE FROM THE LIBRARY
Stan Umberger, Director of Library

REMARKS FROM THE HONOREES
June McBroom, Honorary Chair of the Dedication
Norman Fintel, President Emeritus
Jo Fintel, First Lady Emeritus

Alma Mater Hymn
Directed by Jeffrey Sandborg, Associate Professor of Music. Performed by the
Roanoke College Choir, with accompaniment by The Brass Dominion.

Deep in our hearts a flame is softly burning.
   Deep in our thoughts the mem'ries are returning.
Bells that are ringing, choirs that are singing
   Bring back the joys that we have known.

Learning to live, and loving as we're learning.
   Seeking to find the truth for which we're yearning.
Years come and go, but we'll always know
   That Dear Old Roanoke served us well!

To live once more here in these hallowed halls!
   To know once again all the joys that we used to know!

Some day the winter of life will pass before us
   Then we'll remember the place that proudly bore us.
Then we'll remember, Alma Mater!
   Then we'll remember Thee.

-Frank Williams, Professor of Music

RIBBON CUTTING CEREMONY
Dr. Gring, officiating
Drs. Fintel, Dr. McBroom, and Mr. Turbyfill

BELL DECLARATION

PRAYER OF DEDICATION AND BENEDICTION
The Rev. Dr. Richard Bansemer, Bishop of the Virginia Synod of the Evangelical
Church in America

RECESSIONAL
The Brass Dominion
(Audience please stand.)

★ ★ ★

LIBRARY OPEN HOUSE
Noon-2 p.m.

★ ★ ★

LUNCHEON
Back Quad. Noon-2 p.m.

FIGURE 16.4 Dedication program of Roanoke College, Fintel Library. This schedule of events is found in a small keepsake brochure. Note: The "Processional" was formed of 11 in the platform party, three special guests, and 92 members of the faculty, each of whom carried a book personally or professionally significant in his or her life. All members of the procession and their books were listed in the program. (Courtesy of Roanoke College)

The institution will have to decide whether every individual is listed regardless of the size of the gift or whether the recognition will include only those who contributed above a certain amount. In each institution there can, of course, be a variety of ways of handling this, and it may be possible to list every individual "including several who requested anonymity" in a printed booklet that can be handed out as a keepsake at the dedication. The formal plaque may list only those who contributed above $1,000 or $5,000, with the text also reading "Supporting gifts were made by many other individuals." An example of the text contained on a plaque is shown in fig. 16.10.

An important decision is the extent to which individual spaces are to be labeled with signs or whether a single plaque in the lobby or by the main entrance will suffice. In some institutions it has been thought desirable to "sell" individual rooms, offices, study carrels—one can go to almost any length. Small brass plaques on chairs and other items of furniture and equipment are still occasionally offered. In deciding such matters,

THE FINTEL LIBRARY . . .

♦ contains 167,000 volumes and has the capacity to hold 300,000 volumes, an increase in stack space from the former library of 88%.

♦ is 75,944 square feet in size, an increase of 162% from the former library, and provides rooms for private or group study.

♦ houses a state-of-the-art microcomputer lab, darkroom, video production studio, and audio-visual classroom.

♦ includes a climate-controlled archival area for rare books, historical records and the Henry H. Fowler Collection.

♦ exhibits in its central stairwell 49 limited edition porcelain sculptures by artist Edward Marshall Boehm.

♦ utilizes a computerized catalog and research system.

FIGURE 16.5   Roanoke College, Fintel Library. Gift bookmarks distributed on the occasion of dedications can increase the number of people who get to know the new facility and serve as a reminder of selected key facts. (Courtesy of Roanoke College)

THOMAS COOPER LIBRARY DEDICATION

Wednesday, December 8, 1976

11:00 a.m.

PROGRAM

Presiding	Dr. William H. Patterson
	President of the University
Invocation	Dr. Lauren Brubaker
	University Chaplin

Speaking for the Construction Project

For the architects	Louis M. Wolff
	Lyles, Bissett, Carlisle & Wolff
For the builder	Archie S. Dargan
	Dargan Construction Company
For the University Administration	Harold Brunton
	Vice President for Operations

Acceptance

On behalf of the Board of Trustees	T. Eston Marchant
	Chairman
On behalf of the Faculty and Students	Dr. Keith E. Davis
	Provost
On behalf of the Library Staff	Kenneth E. Toombs
	Director of Libraries
Music	USC Student Brass Ensemble
Introduction of Speaker	President Patterson
Address	Jack Dalton
	"The Cornerstone"
Benediction	Dr. Brubaker

FIGURE 16.6   Dedication program for the Thomas Cooper Library, University of South Carolina, Columbia. (Courtesy of University of South Carolina, Columbia)

Program

Dedication of the
JOHN T. WAHLQUIST LIBRARY

October 15, 1982
2 p.m.

Processional	**University Trumpet Ensemble**
Welcome	**William Dusel**
	Executive Vice President Emeritus
Greetings	**Maureen Pastine**
	Library Director
	Tony Anderson
	Associated Student Body President
Introduction of Guests	**Gail Fullerton**
	President
Keynote speaker	**Charles Burdick**
	University Archivist and
	Professor of History
Vocal solo	**Gus Lease**
Remembrances of John T. Wahlquist	**Arthur K. Lund**
	Halsey C. Burke
	William Sweeney
Remarks	**John T. Wahlquist**
	President Emeritus
Dedication	**Gail Fullerton**
	President
Reception and Tours	**John T. Wahlquist Library**

FIGURE 16.7   Dedication program for the John T. Wahlquist Library. California State University, San Jose. (Courtesy of California State University, San Jose)

THE UNIVERSITY OF MICHIGAN MEDIA UNION

Dedication Program of Events   Friday, June 21, 1996

PRE-PROGRAM MUSIC
Mark Kirshenmann, trumpet
Stephen Rush, synthesizer

WELCOME
James J. Duderstadt
President

REMARKS
The Honorable John Engler
Governor, State of Michigan

Douglas E. Van Houweling
Vice Provost for Academic Outreach and
Information Technology
and Dean for Academic Outreach

Philip H. Power
Regent

TRUMPET & DIGITAL EFFECTS
Mark Kirshenmann
Stephen Rush

REMARKS
Allen Samuels
Dean, School of Art and Design

Erik M. Gottesman
Media Union Student Advisory Committee

RIBBON CUTTING
The Honorable John Engler
James J. Duderstadt

FIGURE 16.8   University of Michigan Media Union dedication ceremony. Dedication day activities included three performances plus tours, demonstrations, and exhibits. The building links the disciplines of Architecture and Urban Planning, Art, Engineering, and Music. It supports use of library resources, information technology, audio/video resources, teleconferencing, design visualization, and simulations, among others. (Courtesy of University of Michigan)

the institution administration will need to consider its style of fund-raising and donor recognition, whether the fund-raising requirements must call upon donations of small amounts as well as medium-sized and large gifts, what the long-term consequences are if a precedent is set with labeling parts of the building for smaller gifts, and how such signs or plaques affect the aesthetic aspects of the building.

The dedication program sometimes includes general cultural or social programs, such as a dance or a musical concert, a major address on a subject of broad importance to the institution, a

University of Maryland Baltimore County — MIND FEST
A Celebration of the Power of Ideas and Information at the Albin O. Kuhn Library & Gallery

Discover the riches of UMBC as we welcome Baltimore to our new Library Tower. We invite you to join in the excitement and energy on campus at UMBC Mind Fest. With seminars, exhibitions, performances, student events, and children's activities, there's treasure enough for everyone!

FRIDAY, NOVEMBER 10
Library Tours. Explore the Library's resources, including a behind-the-scenes look at areas not open to the public and a glimpse at how books are processed for collections.
Press Conference for Student Journalists: Get the facts about the grand opening along with student reporters from Baltimore County.
Grand Opening Ceremony. Keynote address by past president of the American Library Association. Co-sponsored by the Friends of the Library & Gallery.

Performances, Exhibits, and Activities
[N.B. Each of the following was briefly described as to time, place, and scope]
The Role of the Library at a Medium-Sized Research University. An open seminar.
Maryland Celebrities' Favorite Books.
Introduction to the Information Superhighway.
Empty Shelves: A multi-media reading of books banned from libraries.
Our Favorite Works: UMBC community members read from books which inspired them.
Undergraduate Research Presentations.
Teachers' Discoveries.
First Amendment Web Site: chat on-line with award-winning journalist.
Reception for Reopening of the Library Gallery.
Solitaire for Virtual Ensemble: A live dance/music/visual arts collaboration.
MindMania: UMBC students celebrate the Library opening with live music.
The Baltimore Sun Editor's Forum: A panel of editors addresses issues concerning the redesign of the newspaper.
Alumni Library Tour with Library Director.
Alumni Bonfire: hot drinks and dessert with festive fireworks.
Fireworks.

SATURDAY, NOVEMBER 11
Activities for Children and Parents:
Library Tours.
The Wild and Wonderful World of Editorial Cartoons: Slide show and demonstration.
Emerging Literacy: Individual Interviews with Preschoolers.
Find It! Science, The Book You Need at Lightning Speed: a CD-ROM project which assesses children's science literature.
International Culture Bazaar: international student groups host activities.
World Folklore and Storytelling Workshop.
Animals 'n Action: storytelling with the Kindersingers.
Musical Entertainment: high school steel drum band.
Food for Thought: [refreshments for sale during noontime]

Go on a Quest for Knowledge
Introduction to the Information Superhighway.
Information Scavenger Hunt by five county schools using the Library's resources.
Look Up Your Birth Date.
College Bowl Competition of UMBC student groups. Mystery celebrity host.
Research Methods for High School Students.
How to Organize a Book Group.
Encounters with Shakespeare.
Fields of Vision: Women in Photography.
Empty Shelves: a multi-media reading of books banned.
Solitaire for Virtual Ensemble.
Parent-Student Book Discussion.
Explore Catonsville's Roots.
Explore Your Roots.
International Education Panel.

FIGURE 16.9   University of Maryland Baltimore County, Albin O. Kuhn Library & Gallery. This example is unusual in terms of involvement of the greater community. In its original form, the program was printed in festive color; this clearly was an event for all to enjoy. (Courtesy of University of Maryland Baltimore County)

*On behalf of the Stanford University community in this and
generations to come, we gratefully acknowledge
the gifts of those who made possible the construction of this library building and
the renewal of the adjoining structure of 1919. Together, they are dedicated as the*

CECIL H. GREEN LIBRARY

on this 11th day of April, 1980.

Gifts were made by

Ida M. and Cecil H. Green
The James Irvine Foundation
The Kresge Foundation

Martha and Royal Robert Bush
W. B. Carnochan
Betsy B. and William A. Clebsch
Jean and Dewey Donnell

Frances K. and Charles D. Field
Charlotte J. and Richard E. Guggenhime
Gulf Oil Foundation
Elise and Walter A. Haas
Constance W. and Edde K. Hays
William R. and Flora L. Hewlett
Margaret and George D. Jagels
Lucile W. and Daniel E. Koshland
Florence Thompson Kress
Roger and Elly Lewis

Louis R. Lurie Foundation
Mrs. Eugene McDermott and Mary McDermott
The Eugene McDermott Foundation
The Charles E. Merrill Trust
PACCAR Foundation
Gaye and James C. Pigott
Alan J. and Marie Louise Schwabacher Rosenberg
Dorcas Hardison Thille
Doreen and Calvin K. Townsend
Ann Pigott Wyckoff

*Gifts were made by many others. The generosity of all those whose
philanthropy has provided this library is deeply appreciated.*

Peter S. Bing
Peter S. Bing
President of the Board of Trustees

Richard W. Lyman
Richard W. Lyman
President of the University

David C. Weber
David C. Weber
Director of University Libraries

Michael H. Jameson
Michael H. Jameson
Chairman of the Academic Council Committee on Libraries

Design of the 1980 addition to the CECIL H. GREEN LIBRARY
and of the renewed west wing was the work of
Hellmuth, Obata & Kassabaum Inc. architects;
Marquis Associates, interior designers and Interrupto Inc. graphics.
In addition, we gratefully recognize the contributions of faculty,
consultants, contractors, advisors, and members of the Stanford University staff.

FIGURE 16.10   Donor recognition. Note the varying emphasis in the presentation of the text in the donor graphic that is placed in the lobby of the Cecil H. Green Library at Stanford. The text of this donor graphic also appears in a handout that was made available at the dedication of the building. (Courtesy of Stanford University)

benediction or an offering of prayer and thanks, some formality thanking the donors, and officially turning the library building over to the board of trustees. In a publicly supported institution, the program usually gives the chief governmental official an opportunity to be seen, heard, and photographed and to gain some positive publicity by being seen as supportive of education and the future of the citizens. The program may also give recognition to the design concepts as presented by the library administration and interpreted by the architect and interior designer. The dedication ceremony generally is a reasonably brief program, though it may be accompanied by one or several luncheons or dinners for donors and a variety of other events that may extend over two or three days. Credit should be given where credit is due; generous appreciation

and gratitude for all participants, including the architectural firm and contractor, is a welcome part of such a happy occasion, although it is a matter for local decision, and a great deal of variety occurs in such events.

In the case of a major renovation, a dedication or celebration is also common, and in the case of opening new branch library quarters, there usually will be at least a reception for members and friends of the department. Depending on the need for donor recognition, there may be reason to have an elaborate event.

The occasion of the dedication of a major library building can be used to focus attention on the place of the library in the institution's educational program and its support of teaching and research, as well as note the expected effect of the new building on the institutional ability to serve students and faculty. This may be a time to conduct a major symposium presenting recognized authorities speaking on some problems of interest to libraries all over the country. This sort of program may be beneficial to the institution and its staff and to the library world in general. Such an occasion is generally accompanied by a luncheon, a reception, or perhaps a banquet to which the distinguished guests are invited.

Successful dedications require, in addition to a good program, much additional planning. Who is to be invited? What plans should be made for the housing and transportation of out-of-town guests? Who will pay for each local expense? Will there need to be attendants assigned to accompany distinguished donors and other visitors who may have physical problems getting around on campus? Must special parking be arranged, or a shuttle vehicle provided? Are name tags needed? Do chairs have to be rented? Will a lectern and special lighting and sound system be needed? Will the program be recorded or filmed? Will library staff provide guided tours of the building before or after the dedication to the friends whose interest and support are essential? Will there need to be flowers, music, photographs, a news story issued, and perhaps an awning or a tent if rain is possible or if speakers and dignitaries may be in the hot sun for some time? Then there are invitations, perhaps a map to find the parking and dedication site, programs, a keepsake, and thank-you notes to be written after the ceremony to those who contributed significantly and generously. The institution may have an internal checklist or manual giving guidance on the multitude of details that such ceremonies involve.

16.9
After the Warranty Period

If the warranty runs the customary 12 months after the contractor turns the building over to the institution, various adjustments and residual problems must be resolved during that period. It would, however, not be surprising for some significant problems to remain after the warranty period is over. The Meyer Memorial Library acoustic and HVAC problems referred to in Section 16.7 are a case in point. Some physical problems in a building may be very difficult and expensive to solve; their resolution leads one back to some fundamental considerations in the need

for building alterations, which are dealt with in Chapters 2, 3, and 4. Thus in some cases, regrettably, the next building project cycle may begin as soon as the building is completed. Yet it would be imprudent to press the case right after dedication of the new space!

An especially serious matter is planning to maintain the new or renovated space in reasonable condition. Accounting data suggest that a college or university should place in escrow at least 1 percent of the replacement value of its physical plant each year to be used later for maintenance. In fact, the Syracuse University vice president for facilities administration recently recommended that colleges and universities set aside 1.5 to 3 percent of the total replacement value of their buildings and equipment for renewal and replacements.[3] Few institutions do this. As a result, it is well known that academic institutions have a formidable backlog of building maintenance problems, the result sometimes of decades of neglect. Each institution must face this problem, and it is merely pointed out because it is shortsighted to pour money into emergency patches when a regular, sound building maintenance plan would in the long run be a more economical approach.

It may be useful, after the building has been occupied and had time to become settled, for the head librarian to lead a serious review of the project and its end result with the responsible librarians, architects, building representatives of the institution, and perhaps one or more consultants. What might be done better the next time, and thus what lessons may be learned and should be recorded to help those dealing with future projects? At least a few universities do this for major projects. A historical record of the entire building project will help those who wish to learn from the project in the near term as well as those who work on institutional history. Finally, there is the obligation of those involved in a major project to respond to requests for sharing the experience with others who may be faced with a similar challenge, just as those involved with the present one may have benefited from others.

NOTES

1. Stephen Langmead and Margaret Beckman, *New Library Design* (Toronto: Wiley, 1970), pp. 84–85.
2. Ibid., p. 84.
3. Harvey H. Kaiser, *Crumbling Academe* (Washington, D.C.: Association of Governing Boards of Universities and Colleges, 1984), pp. 33, 35–37.

APPENDIX A

Program and Other Document Examples

A map of the world that does not include Utopia is not worth even glancing at, for it leaves out the one country at which Humanity is always landing. And when Humanity lands there, it looks out, and, seeing a better country, sets sail. Progress is the realization of Utopias.

—Oscar Wilde, "The Soul of Man under Socialism"

Just as no two libraries exactly duplicate each other, so no two library building programs should be alike. No library should copy another's program. Thus, the following examples of building program statements and several other project documents are given to stimulate thought and imagination, and not to result in imitation. (A few of the program examples were prepared by architects, most by librarians or a library consultant. Documents concerning the site were prepared by architects; the technical review was by consultants.)

These excerpts should be used primarily to consider the options in style and format and to call attention to points that might be considered for inclusion in a particular program. So there are several examples of spatial relationships, often depicted in some form of diagram generically called "bubble diagrams" because they look like a grouping of clustered or overlapping bubbles.

To be most helpful to the architect, the program moves from the conceptual and general to components and specific details. Thus the 38 examples are topics in this sequence:

1. Facility character
2. Planning parameters

3. Library operational functions
4. Site planning considerations
5. Site options
6. Site analysis
7. Building orientation
8. Space planning based upon state guidelines
9. General project requirements
10. Operational goals (flexibility and building control)
11. Information technologies
12. Program summary tables (2 examples)
13. Space summary (2 examples)
14. Relationships of functional areas (7 examples)
15. Outline of program topics
16. Program components or elements (space sheets):
    a. Vestibule
    b. Administrative offices
    c. Development office
    d. Circulation
    e. Computer lab
    f. Instructional services laboratory
    g. Map room
    h. Microform reading room
    i. Interlibrary loan office (2 examples)
    j. Exhibition area
    k. Special collections vault
    l. Physical treatment quarters
    m. Mail room
    n. Receiving and shipping quarters
17. Technical review of building plan
18. Phasing of construction

1. Facility Character*

THE TEACHING LIBRARY FACILITIES

The Teaching Library will be the campus focus for the Center's support of information technologies in learning; "learning" implies both teaching and research, since new technologies encourage end-users to create or find their own information, and the tools to turn information into knowledge. As a catalyst to bring information technologies into the classroom and the library, the Center will have three roles in the Teaching Library:

---

*Courtesy of University of Southern California, Leavey Library (from the "Program for the New Teaching Library" prepared by the architect, Shepley Bulfinch Richardson and Abbott)

1. Direct support for the creation and use of instructional software by faculty and librarians;
2. Collaboration with the library in the creation of new kinds of information services;
3. Influence on the use of technology in support of traditional library services.

1. Creation of instructional software and facilities for student use

The Software Development Center [10.0] will be the campus center for supporting faculty, librarians, and staff in designing, creating, and testing instructional and information-access software.

The Computer Commons [9.0] will be the largest campus center for students to use information technologies in their individual studies [9.3], and to learn new skills through consultants [9.1] and online training materials [9.1]. The Computer Commons will also include special rooms for collaborative work using information technologies [9.2], in recognition that much creative work and learning is collaborative.

2. The creation of new kinds of library information services

The Teaching Library is a new kind of library, both in its intensive use of services as well as traditional library activities, and in the concept that it is a gateway to the library system as a whole. As a gateway, the Teaching Library will teach the USC community how to use all of the computing and library resources of the University, through Library instructional services, network data services, and Reference services.

Library Instructional Services [5.0] will include high technology training rooms for teaching the library and technical skills necessary to use any library or any computing facility on campus. When configured as an auditorium, they will be the site of Center-sponsored events focused upon the appropriate uses of technology in teaching and learning.

Network Management/Data services [12.0] will be a clearinghouse to provide Teaching Library users access to campus and national information resources, and provide campus network access to Teaching Library resources.

Reference [4.0] will be the intellectual center of the Teaching Library, offering both traditional reference information and consulting and classes about the use of information technology in finding and using information. Reference is the synthesis of the Center's high technology approach to library services, and the continuing strengths of the traditional library.

3. Using technology for traditional library services

The Teaching Library is also a library with a collection and services to support undergraduate and graduate teaching; and it is a gateway to the research collections in Doheny and the specialized subject libraries where expert research help is available. The center will extend the number and kinds of formats within which information is stored and used. Thus, Course Reserves [3.0] will include audio- and videotapes, CD-ROM, and computer based information, and Collections [7.0] will comprise software (including that developed by the Center), and video- and audiotapes as well as books.

2. Planning Parameters*

SUMMARY OF LIBRARY PLANNING COMMITTEE RECOMMENDATIONS

#1 Renovation of the Existing Facility

The Library staff in conjunction with the Library Planning Committee makes the following recommendations:

a) The future addition to the present facility must treat the entire building as an integrated whole. The exterior of the future structure should be so designed that the "old Library" and the "new addition" will not be distinguishable from each other. Rather people will see only one unified Library.

b) Because the present facility was built on a modular basis it should be regarded as an "empty shell." None of the existing services, stacks, or administrative areas should be regarded as being fixed in their present location. The Library's interior should also be designed and regarded as an integrated whole without making distinctions between the present facility and the new addition.

c) In order for the design of the future Library to function properly many aspects of the present facility should be repaired or updated. Particular emphasis should be given to the renovation of the existing Heating, Ventilating and Air Conditioning system, elevator, and roof gutter and leader system.

#2 Late Night Study Area

The Library staff and LPC recommend that we do not provide a late night study area because of the mixed responses from students. The large number of negative responses to a Library site and the number of "unsure" responses would give a late night study area in the Library a very low priority when space could well be used more constructively. In accomplishing this the staff would recommend and stress that the building be so designed that one person (normally a student assistant) would be able to open and close the facility with relative ease.

#3 Planning Assumptions

a) The LPC will assume that the Library's budget will remain relatively constant in proportion to Roanoke College's total budget.

b) Enrollment will probably not exceed a head count of 1,600 students or a Full Time Equivalent of 1,400.

c) The LPC will assume that the number of personnel will remain relatively stable and no large increase in staffing is foreseen.

d) The Library will grow at an average net rate of 4,000 volumes per year. This would bring the total holdings of the Library to 270,000–300,000 volumes.

#4 Incorporation of Media Services into the Library

As plans for Library expansion develop, so should plans for including the Media Center into the Library structure.

---

*Courtesy of Roanoke College, Fintel Library (from a document written by the Planning Committee)

The Media Center would provide adequate storage space for equipment, a graphics/drafting area, a maintenance area for audiovisual equipment, production area for other audiovisual teaching aids, photographic facilities with a darkroom space, a multimedia classroom, a video production studio, and a campuswide video distribution center.

#5 Nonprint Collections in the Library

The incorporation of the Media Center into the Library leads to the development of a nonprint collection for campus use. While most agree a film/video collection would be excellent, no assessment of need for other nonprint media was done. If it is found that this area should be expanded, an arrangement with the Fine Arts Library should be worked out to avoid collection duplication.

#6 Bibliographic Instruction Classroom

The LPC recommends a Bibliographic Instruction classroom which would accommodate 40–50 students. Because of anticipated use it seems best to plan this room in addition to but connected with the Media Center's classroom.

#7 Incorporating an Integrated Library System (ILS)

This committee recommends that automation of library systems be an integral part of the overall library improvement plan. This includes the acquisition of an Integrated Library System.

#8 Telecommunications: Connecting the Library to the Rest of the Campus

a) The Library Planning Committee recommends that a telecommunication network be utilized that will make library services available to departments across campus. The ideal system would be data-transmission lines alongside campus telephone lines, making remote library terminals as convenient as the nearest phone jack. The new College telephone system will provide this type of service by the time the Library improvement program is ready for it.

b) In selecting an integrated system, a system that would require additional terminals in offices should be avoided. Either the hardware must be compatible or software should be acquired to allow communication between systems.

#9 The Extent of Retrospective Conversion of Materials

The LPC recommends complete retrospective conversion before going online with the catalog and the implementation of an ILS.

#10 The Use of Microcomputers by Users in the Library

In recognition of the concern of the LPC to plan for the next thirty years and the positive survey results, the following recommendations for a microcomputer room are suggested:

- The micros should be in one room rather than spread throughout the building.
- The room should be staffed at all times it is being used. Student staffing would be adequate.
- The room should be arranged to allow class instruction as well as individual use.

- Printing should be available at a central location in the room.
- There should be phone jacks for each terminal.
- 22 terminals would be a sufficient number. The ratio and number of microcomputers to academic terminals will be set at a later date.
- Maintenance contracts should be purchased for each machine.
- Decisions regarding purchase and circulation of software would be needed. Purchase of either multiple copies or site licenses would work.

#11 The Use of Other Types of Automation

Assuming the acquisition of an Integrated Library System, the subcommittee and the library staff did not identify any other specific automation needs at this time.

#12 Use of Library System Terminals Outside the Library

The subcommittee and the library staff recommend that Library system terminals be made available to other parts of campus depending upon demand. Initially, terminals could be planned for each building on campus and, if demand exists, placed in each department.

#13 The Location of the Minicomputer If an ILS Is Acquired

This committee recommends that the minicomputer supporting the Integrated Library System be housed in the Computer Center if the data transmission lines are indeed available when needed. However, some attention to security and safety is needed. The location of the Computer Center directly under Chemistry Lab water pipes causes concern. Also, the vulnerability of Library files to manipulation of other than Library staff is increased. These potential problems would need resolving before the final location is made.

#14 Library Seating

The LPC recommends 532 seats distributed in the following manner:

> 60% or 320 individual carrels (open & enclosed)
> 25% or 132 group study seats (4 seats per table)
> 15% or 80 lounge seats

This distribution is consistent with Metcalf's *Planning Academic and Research Library Buildings* and other building programs examined by the staff.

#15 Lounge/Vending/Smoking Areas

The Library staff recommends that an enclosed lounge area with vending machines be included in the Library plans. The room should be so designed that noise would be contained in the lounge.

Smoking would not be permitted in the lounge but rather a separate, enclosed, and well-ventilated smoking area would be adjacent to the lounge. This smoking room would contain seating for group study seating, individual seating, and a small number of casual seats. Food and drink would be allowed in this area.

#16 Microforms

New titles will be added on microform after checking the frequency of use, cost, shelf space savings and if the periodical is indexed. New space will be utilized in a like manner.

#17 Archives and Special Collections

a) The LPC recommends that the library be the center for the storage and indexing of archive materials and special collections. Special consideration, therefore, must be given to the type of housing for both preservation and security while at the same time providing proper facilities for access and use of the materials.

b) The Subcommittee felt that the Fowler collection should be kept as a separate entity.

c) The LPC committee recommends that the following are essential to storage and preservation and should be provided: storage above ground to minimize the possibility of water damage from flooding; environmental control (i.e., humidity, temperature, etc.); a vault to provide for both security from theft and protection from fire damage for archive materials and other irreplaceable items such as rare books; a provision for sealing the entire area from the rest of the Library.

d) Provision should be made for an exhibit area.

3. Library Operational Functions*

No one will have reason to enter the stacks except the staff, and the arrangement of the research room must allow ready access to the stacks by the staff while precluding it for the researchers. All materials used by the researcher will generally be brought to him in the research room by a staff member.

Visits to the research room may vary as widely as from 500 upwards of 2,000 per year. The 150 to 700 individuals who will make these visits fall generally into the following classes:

(1) High school and undergraduate students 24%
(2) Graduate students doing research on dissertations 21%
(3) Faculty members doing research on books and articles . . . 25%
(4) Journalists/free-lance writers 12%
(5) Government researchers/writers 4%
(6) Other/unidentified 14%

The users of the research room are not casual browsers or the idly curious, but serious scholars focusing on the President and his administration. The high school and undergraduate students are usually advanced placement individuals and are often brought as a class for specialized research topics. Researchers usually make advance written application for permission to use the materials, and their application must show that they are engaged in research for which the Library has unique holdings.

The average length of stay at a Presidential library for a particular researcher is four days; however, it is not uncommon to have researchers spend several months, and biographers may spend upwards of a year. More than two-thirds of the researchers will come from distances greater than 50 miles, and will need to find inexpensive lodgings in the vicinity. Approximately 60 percent of these will arrive by car, with the rest coming to the Library on foot or by public transportation. Because the academic profession

---

*Courtesy of Gerald R. Ford Presidential Library (from the program of the Gerald Ford Library)

is attractive to physically handicapped persons, a higher than average percentage of the researchers will be incapacitated in some way, and the facilities must be planned to accommodate such persons.

Normal Activities of Researchers

In the majority of cases, the researcher will have written or telephoned the Library in advance of arriving, and the staff will be aware of the general nature of his project. When a researcher first comes to the Library, he will be oriented on the nature of the holdings as they relate to his topic and the rules and procedures to be followed. Ideally, this orientation should take place in a room adjacent to the research room. This room should be comfortably furnished to put the researcher at ease and allow the staff member to communicate with him on an informal basis. Researchers may often need to consult further with staff during their visit, and if this room is located adjacent to the research room, it will enable longer conversations to take place without disturbing others in the research room. Since eating, drinking, and smoking are not allowed in the research room, this area can also serve as a place for the researcher to relax during his stay in the Library. National Archives regulations for research rooms prohibit briefcases, pocketbooks, and other large packages which could be used to conceal documents. Therefore, an area near the research room should contain 20 to 24 lockers where researchers may deposit their belongings while in the research room. It would also be convenient to have facilities here for hats, coats, and umbrellas.

Once in the research room, the researcher will need to consult several of the finding aids which will enable him to locate the materials he wishes to see. Finding aids may be in printed form, card catalog, or computerized. Space for the card catalog should be provided in an area convenient to the working area of the staff member on duty in the research room. Space for the computer terminal should also be close to the staff member, printed finding aids may be shelved along the wall. Bookcase space (preferably with built-in shelving) should also be provided in the research room for approximately 150 linear feet of standard reference works for researcher use.

In most cases, the researcher coming to the Library will have used most printed materials pertinent to his subject before he arrives. This is not always the case, but persons coming from a distance to do research usually prefer, for financial reasons, to make their stay as short as possible. Therefore, they tend to concentrate during their visit on use of the unique archival resources of the Library, and the research room should be planned with this function in mind.

4. Site Planning Considerations*

10. Site Considerations

Landscape design and site development are important components of the total project: every opportunity should be taken to enhance existing landscape elements and to improve the pedestrian and vehicular

---

*Courtesy of University of Maryland Baltimore County. Prepared by Ingraham Planning Associates, Inc., Consultants for Facility and Long Range Planning, Fairfax, Virginia

circulation system. Walks, driveways, parking areas (with a capacity of 25 spaces, including spaces for the handicapped), landscape design, exterior lighting, security lighting and dumpster location with visual screening must be included.

The purpose of this section is to provide an outline of site problems, assets and project requirements for the A/E. Preserving and enhancing natural site amenities is an important part of the site development process. Important site characteristics or influences on the site are represented graphically (where appropriate). The A/E must be aware of the constraints imposed by the site and deal successfully with the relationship between the building and the site.

The information provided in this section is intended to supplement the A/E's own site evaluation.

The Library is bordered by a major inner campus roadway serving student apartments to the North, a student playing field which heretofore has been designated permanent green space to the East, a man-made pond and landscaped green area to the South and a heavily treed natural watershed area to the West which feeds into the pond. The area comprising the NW and SW quadrants is extremely hilly with slopes nearing a 1:1 ratio.

The immediate area of proposed construction is nestled between two existing wings of the Library situated at right angles to each other. A difference of 12 feet plus exists between the site and the existing ground floor elevation, which must be excavated. The immediate construction area is roughly 1.33 acres. (See site map.)

10.1 Landforms

Topography is an important element in the utilization of the site and critical to development decisions. Careful consideration of the site character is required in the development of the site and placement of the building. Integration of topographical features with facility orientation and function is required. Utilization of advantageous landforms and avoidance of undesirable site features should be incorporated into the design solution.

The building site area has an average elevation at approximately 238, most of which slopes 1 foot of rise in 15 feet. Within 40 feet of the existing structure, the site drops off dramatically from elevation 236 to 220 and levels off again within 20 feet of the building.

10.2 Drainage

Drainage patterns around structures should be directed away from foundations, walks, paths, roadways and turf areas so as not to interfere with the function of these site elements. Inlet, conduit, concrete flumes, drainage diverters, etc. should be designed to accommodate actual runoff and to integrate with natural and built site amenities.

Positive drainage has been maintained at the site, and existing storm drains are within the immediate proposed construction area. The A/E shall evaluate and integrate or redesign the existing stormwater drainage system, as appropriate for the building addition.

10.3 Vegetation

Existing vegetation is vital to the character, microclimate, and aesthetic quality of the site. The site development and building design solutions should respect vegetation as a potential design element. Plantings of various types and textures buffer sounds, noises, and odors as well as moderate sun, wind, and precipitation. Vegetation and landscape features should have climatic and aesthetic purpose and relate to the prescribed functions of the facility.

Vegetation shall be restricted to that which maximizes maintainability and should be coordinated with the Department of Physical Plant's Landscape Shop. Vegetation which grows in vines, such as ivy, should not be considered.

10.4   Soils

The A/E is expected to provide a soils analysis to determine the condition of existing soils and their ability to support the proposed facility.

10.5   Pedestrian Circulation

Pedestrian circulation is an important element in development of the site. The site development plan for this facility must accommodate existing and proposed pedestrian circulation in such a way that it does not conflict with on-site requirements.

Pedestrian ingress and egress to the existing Library is controlled on the main entrance level accessing the circulation and administrative spaces. The lower level currently accesses the Academic Computing Department, which is to be relocated. Presently, no traffic is permitted between these two levels.

The building addition shall also be accessible only from the library spaces. Additional means of access must be addressed to maximize convenience for departments whose offices will be housed in the space and the location of new parking for the handicapped and for visitors.

10.6   Vehicular Circulation and Parking

Vehicular access to and through the site and facilities for vehicular parking are important elements in the site design. The A/E must take into account these considerations when developing the site plan and provide for appropriate segregation to avoid conflict between vehicular and pedestrian circulation.

The site shall be developed to accommodate 25 new parking spaces.

10.7   Service and Functional Organization

Building service areas are an integral function of any facility, but they are often the source of noise and visual clutter. Therefore, the A/E must provide a design solution that reduces the impact of service functions from incompatible activities that are also a part of the site. The following criteria should govern the design of the service area(s).

a. Consolidation

Service areas should be consolidated wherever possible so that service access points can be minimized. Parking for service vehicles should be located primarily in the service area.

b. Location and Screening

Service areas are to be screened from surrounding activity centers and pathways. Service areas should be located away from incompatible activities such as pedestrian circulation and recreation.

c. Design Process

Service requirements should be designed as a unified system from the early stages of design development. Service access and egress may prescribe building location or orientation, especially in cases where adjacent compatible support functions exist.

d. Separation of Public and Private Areas

The site and structure should be designed so that public and private space is clearly defined. Parking areas located directly adjacent to service areas without visual separation can be a source of security problems and vehicular circulation conflict.

e. Fire Apparatus Accessibility

Access requirements for fire apparatus are partially dependent upon building type and internal fire protection (e.g., sprinklers). The A/E must review code requirements and coordinate with the identified University representative for environmental safety.

f. Lighting

Security lighting is an important element of the site design. The A/E is required to provide for the safety and well being of the facility users with regard to access to and from the site and the building. The A/E must coordinate this effort with the identified University representative.

10.8 Handicapped Accessibility

The purpose of this section is to outline considerations relating specifically to the use of the site by physically handicapped individuals. The following are to be incorporated into the site design.

a. Parking

Specifically designated and dimensioned parking stalls designed in accordance with current standards are to be located in close proximity of major access points to the building. These should be level and clearly marked as reserved for the handicapped.

b. Walkways

Walkways connecting accessible building entrances to handicapped parking, off-site circulation and other facilities within the building complex must meet identified design criteria for the disabled. Stairs, curbs, and excessive grades should be avoided or alternate means of movement provided. Curb cuts in accordance with current design criteria must be provided where walkways intersect roads or provide access to parking facilities. When excessive grades are encountered, ramps with level resting areas at regular intervals are to be provided.

c. Entries

Major points of entry to the building must facilitate access for the disabled. In addition, all other entry points should be accessible if physically and economically feasible. In all cases, entry points closest to designated handicapped parking areas must be designed for handicap accessibility. Ramps or other special features are to be integrated into the total design so as not to appear as a special conciliatory feature.

10.9 Utilities

New and existing demands on utilities in the building area are to be examined by the A/E. The A/E's recommendation as to alignments and new-to-existing points of connection are to be submitted at the schematic design stage of the project. Should the A/E foresee a negative impact on existing utilities and it is outside the contract limits of the project, it is the responsibility of the A/E to bring this to the attention of the University.

The A/E is responsible for the complete design of all new utility extensions from the points of the connection with existing systems to the building site and to establish the precise location of all underground utilities and/or services in the construction area. It is the responsibility of the A/E to design the extensions from existing systems to serve the new facility.

The successful completion of this project is dependent upon the completion of an electrical distribution upgrade serving the entire campus. The A/E shall conduct and provide the University with a complete analysis of electrical loads in the Library to show existing loads, loads eliminated and/or added, and resulting final loads.

10.10 Site Reforestation

As of January 1, 1988, Natural Resources Article, Section 5-103 specifies that all state construction projects let for bid which require the clearing of forest land, one acre and larger, clear only those trees necessary and replace those trees removed on an acre-for-acre basis. The replacement trees are to be planted on the same site from which they were cleared, if a suitable planting area is available. If not, then the constructing agency must find a suitable site within the watershed sub-basin.

10.11 Fire Suppression Sprinklers

Water from sprinklers or burst pipes can cause great damage to library materials and electronic equipment. If required by code, sprinklers in this project should be of the dry-pipe type, located in coordination with the stack arrangement and location of other materials.

5. Site Options*

1. General

Originally, expanding the Olin Library remote Annex was considered as a solution to library space needs. Faced with a remote facility that ultimately would be larger than Olin and require considerable duplication of staff, increased transportation requirements, and serious inconvenience to all concerned, remote storage was rejected as a long-term solution to Olin's major space problems. Consequently, only sites directly adjacent to Olin were explored.

The following site plan shows the various site options considered. Long-term library growth requires an addition with a floor area equal to

*Courtesy of Cornell University Library (two plans with 10 site options and evaluations)

approximately two-thirds of the floor area of Olin. No single adjacent location easily accommodates such a large addition. Rather, a combination of locations, with a combination of above and below ground buildings, is necessary. Utilization of more than one location facilitates phased construction, which is advantageous considering the immediate needs of Olin. Following is an evaluation of the usable sites contiguous to Olin [see figs. A.1 and A.2].

2. East of Olin (Sites 1 and 2)

   Demolition of Stimson (Site 1) was ruled out because of the quality of the building and the University's position regarding its historic significance. Building above ground north of Stimson (Site 2) was ruled out because it blocked the vista from President White's house. All of the above led to Scheme A, which includes renovation of Stimson and a major new underground facility north of Stimson.

3. South of Olin (Sites 6, 7, 8, 9, and 10)

   Building above ground directly south of Olin (Sites 6 and 7) was ruled out because this would block the view of the Uris Library tower from Tower Road. Building above ground west of Day Hall (Site 9) was ruled out because it blocked the significant vista from the Arts Quadrangle to Sage Hall.

   Sites 6, 7, and 9, even all together, are too small and too close to existing buildings for any significant amount of underground construction

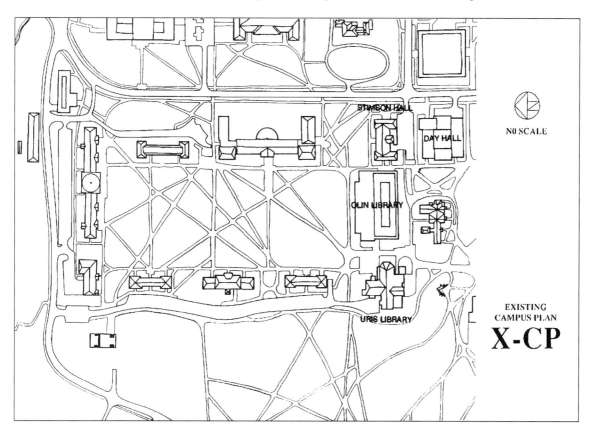

FIGURE A.1   Partial campus plan at Cornell University. Prepared by Shepley Bulfinch Richardson and Abbott Architects

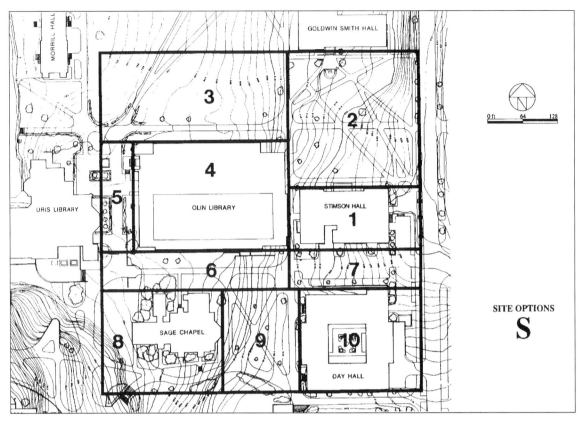

FIGURE A.2   Site study plan for the library at Cornell University. Prepared by Shepley Bulfinch Richardson and Abbott Architects

and would not accommodate the Library's needs without a large associated above-ground facility.

Demolishing Sage Chapel (Site 8) was ruled out because of its historic significance and architectural quality. Day Hall (Site 10), on the other hand, is historically less significant and of a lesser quality than its neighbors.

These factors led to the development of Scheme B, which calls for an underground building on Sites 6, 7, and 9 linking Olin to a new building on the Day Hall site (Site 10).

4. North of Olin (Sites 3 and 4)

   Building above or below ground north of Olin (Sites 3 and 4) was at first dismissed because of the assumed inviolability of the Arts Quadrangle. However, considering that this is clearly the most economical and functionally ideal location for an addition to Olin, it was felt that it could not easily be dismissed. Also, it was felt that the way Olin and its terrace terminated the Arts Quadrangle could be improved. Following from these considerations, Scheme C was developed to include a below-ground building north of Olin and an above-ground building above Olin's north terrace (Sites 3 and 4).

5. West of Olin (Site 5)

   The site directly west of Olin (Site 5) is too small for any significant addition above or below ground. It is also a significant campus space that should be preserved. Uris Library itself, as the symbolic and functional center of undergraduate study, is not available for expansion by Olin. Sites further west of Uris are too remote, both horizontally and vertically, to be able to make a reasonable connection to Olin. For these reasons, no further study was made for use of this site.

6. Site Analysis*

Although funding for subsequent phases of development has not been approved, it is nevertheless considered essential that whichever option is selected, there must be a natural, obvious, and functional direction for additional growth. Here, only three options (3, 4, and 5) rated better than poor. Because so many of the site options are tenuous with the existing Sedgewick Library structure, their additional expansion only serves to heighten the less-than-ideal relationship. In turn, these lead to strange configurations, linear (unsquare) proportions, and the need for additional major entrances in the future which result in decreased security, dilution of the concept of the "main entrance" and the notion of a "first stop" service centre for the Library. None of the site options are considered ideal for expansion, mainly due to the congestion of prospective adjacent building sites around the core of the campus. Nevertheless, the sites of the Old Administration Building, the Mathematics Building and the Mathematics Annex have been considered as acceptable growth options, given the anticipated several year lag before subsequent phases will be funded, and the aspiration within the Campus Plan to replace the old buildings in this part of the campus.

Weighted Scores

The second score sheet [see fig. A.3] displays weighted scores for the site options. Each of the criteria has been assessed a relative degree of importance. Of the 16, five (perhaps the least important) have not been given added weight. These are:

- prospective configurations with Sedgewick Library
- respect of pedestrian thoroughfares
- respect of vehicular routes
- respect of views, and
- respect of the Main Mall and Main Library axes.

Seven criteria have been weighted × 2. These are:

- proximity to the Sedgewick Library
- enhancement of/detraction from the Sedgewick Library
- functional integration with existing structure
- respect of the "Heart of the Campus"
- relationship to the users (recognizing that in its initial development, the major collection in Phase I will be Humanities/Social Sciences)
- respect of the landscaping and the Library Garden
- capital cost premiums/savings.

Four criteria are considered most important, and have been weighted × 3, as follows:

---

*Courtesy of University of British Columbia (from *Phase 1 Library Centre UBC Site Analysis Report,* prepared by Malcolm Holt, Principal, HSP Humanité Services Planning (BC) Ltd., April 1991)

| | Criteria for Consideration | | | | | | | | | | | | | | | | |
| | Sedgewick | | | | Campus Plan | | | | | Others | | | | | | | |
	Proximity to Sedgewick	Prospective Configurations with Sedgewick	Enhancement/Detraction from Existing Plan	Functional Integration with Existing Structure	Respect of Pedestrian Thoroughfares	Respect of Views	Respect of Vehicular Routes	Respect of Heart of the Campus	Respect of Axes (Main Mall/Main Library)	Relationships to Users	Respect of Landscaping Including Library Garden	Creation of New "Main Library"	Creation of a New Main Entrance	Phase II & Phase III Expansion	Capital Cost Premiums/Savings	Donor Appeal	Totals
Weighting Factor	2	1	2	2	1	1	1	2	1	2	2	3	3	3	2	3	
1. Sedgewick NE	6	3	6	6	1	0	5	0	1	10	0	3	6	3	6	9	70
2. Sedgewick SE	6	3	4	6	0	0	5	0	1	8	0	3	6	3	6	9	60
3. NW Sedgewick	6	3	4	6	1	5	5	6	4	8	10	6	9	9	0	9	91
4. Sedgewick West	10	5	8	8	5	4	5	10	5	8	8	15	15	9	8	9	132
5. Sedgewick SW	6	3	6	6	1	2	5	6	3	6	10	6	6	9	0	9	84
6. Buchanan South	4	1	10	4	5	5	0	10	5	10	8	0	3	3	6	0	74
7. Sedgewick East	10	5	8	8	4	3	5	2	1	8	2	12	15	3	4	0	90
8. North Main Mall	8	3	8	8	4	5	0	8	5	10	4	0	3	3	4	0	73
9. Lasserre South	4	1	10	4	5	5	0	10	5	8	8	0	6	3	6	0	75
10. South Main Mall	8	3	8	8	4	5	0	8	5	6	4	0	3	3	2	0	67
Library Phase I, Site Options: Weighted Scores																	

FIGURE A.3   Table of weighted scores used in decision making relative to site selection at University of British Columbia. Information prepared and developed by Malcolm Holt, Principal, HSP Humanité Services Planning (BC) Ltd.

- the creation of a new "Main Library"
- the creation of a new main entrance to the Library system
- Phase II and Phase III expansion capability
- donor appeal

The weighted scores provide evidence of the real disparity between the site options, and a means of recognizing their relative strengths and weaknesses. Scores range from a low of 60 for Site Option 2, to a high of 132 for Site Option 4.

Three sites (options 3, 4, and 7) emerge ahead of the majority. Site Option 3, paradoxically, is considered unacceptable for reasons mentioned earlier (the site of the Old Administration Building). Of these three, Site Option 4 scores a relatively exceptional 132.

7. Building Orientation*

The only public entrance will be from the mall. The central location of the building should create a natural physical and psychological sense of move-

---

*Courtesy of Leyburn Library, Washington and Lee University, Lexington, Virginia

ment for those crossing the ravine. That is, the library will be the "hub" of the campus; intellectually and in traffic orientation; however *its interior is not to be the means* for crossing the campus.

The top floor of the library, including any mechanical features should not exceed the first floor height of Washington Hall.

The building's orientation must accommodate future expansion in terms of effective library service as well as structural demands.

Natural light is of considerable importance in a library building; however, the view and the largest areas of open expanse appear to be to the South and West. We want to capture the views, but not if it is necessary to use curtains to curtail the glare or protect the library's holdings.

A parking area for the library staff and handicapped persons is to be adjacent to the library.

8. Space Planning Based upon State Guidelines*

PRIORITIES FOR ADDITIONAL SPACE

The existing conditions in the Albin O. Kuhn Library dictate the priorities for additional space. It is readily apparent from a physical tour of the facility that the most pressing needs for additional space relate to stack space; the least pressing need is for additional technical services space. On all three existing floors the reference, general circulation, serials, documents, and special collections are overflowing the available stack areas and are encroaching on designated seating/study and storage space. The problem is most apparent in the Reference Room and the Serials Department.

The space deficiencies evident from a physical survey are corroborated by statistical findings [see table A.1]. A comparison of the quantity of 1988 "justified space" with the 1988 Inventory reveals: the current collection justifies 69,647 NASF in stack space, but only 43,127 NASF is available: for reading/study (seating) space, 36,270 NASF are justified while only 25,308 NASF are located in an area with potential for such use: the library technical services justified space is 21,183 NASF, as compared with the 16,708 NASF now devoted to that function.

These comparisons indicate a *current deficit of 41,957 NASF* in the amount of space provided for library functions. When projections for 1998 are introduced [see table A.2], it is apparent that the shortage of justified space for these functions equates to the existing total of library space. The existing deficit of library space is a result of growth in student enrollments and in the basic library collection, and with the additional factor of space needed to house projected future growth, construction of an 85,000 NASF addition to the Albin O. Kuhn Library and Gallery is required to accommodate materials, students, and staff for the library/gallery functions, and to allow space for interaction of all three.

---

*Courtesy of Ingraham Planning Associates, Inc., Consultants for Facility and Long Range Planning, Fairfax, Virginia, and the University of Maryland Baltimore County, Kuhn Library

TABLE A.1   Summary of space as determined by formulae at the University of Maryland.

Summary of HEGIS 400 Space Justified by Formulae
Using Maryland Space Guidelines
Actual 1988 and Projected 1998

| | Count | | | | NASF | Guide Allow |
	1988	1998			1988	1998
HEGIS 400 Seating						
Undergrad FTDE @ 17%	1,025	1,037	@30 NASF		30,750	31,110
Graduate FTDE @ 30%	78	240	@40 NASF		3,120	9,600
Faculty FTE @ 10%	47	66	@40 NASF		1,880	2,640
Administ Staff @ 5%	13	17	@40 NASF		520	680
Subtotal, HEGIS 410 Seating				36,270	44,030	
HEGIS 420/30 Stacks						
First 150,000 PBVE	150,000	150,000	@.10 NASF		15,000	15,000
Additional PBVE	683,091	1,032,439	@.08 NASF		54,647	82,595
Subtotal, HEGIS 420/30 Stacks					69,647	97,595
HEGIS 440/45 Services						
Total 410–430	105,917	141,625	@20%		21,183	28,325
Grand Total 410/45 Stacks, Seating, and Services					127,100	169,950
		1985 Numbers			116,836	144,246
		Gain over 1985			10,264	26

TABLE A.2   Summary of existing space compared to formula-based need at the University of Maryland.

Existing Inventory and Projected 1998 Space Guidelines
Albin O. Kuhn Library and Gallery

HEGIS Codes Category	Existing Kuhn Library	1998 Guideline Allowance	1998 Surplus (Deficit)
410/15 Seating	25.308	44.03	−18.722
420/30 Stacks	43,127	97,595	−54,468
440/45 Lib Service	16,708	28.325	−11,617
400's Totals	85,143	169,950	−84,807

9. General Project Requirements*

Artificial Lighting

The lighting level shall comply with the Campus Building Standards. Lighting should be designed and fixtures selected and arranged so as to minimize

*University of Illinois Grainger Library (from *Program Statement,* Engineering Library Information Center, University of Illinois at Urbana-Champaign, compiled by the ELIC Advisory Committee, December 5, 1991, pp. 9–13). Courtesy of University of Illinois at Urbana-Champaign Grainger Engineering Library Information Center

glare on computer screens and work surfaces. Also, lighting should be planned so that the reading and shelving areas can be interchanged without revising lumenaire locations. A special provision to blink all lights momentarily is required to announce library closing times. Provision for dimming the lights is required in certain areas. There should be no individual carrel lighting nor use of table or floor lamps except where indicated in a detailed program.

Natural Lighting and Windows

It is highly desirable to take advantage of natural lighting. Windows should be tinted with multiple glazing and should be operable and securable.

Broad Band Coaxial and Signal Cabling

There should be a provision for a building entry to these special cables and for horizontal and vertical distribution of signal cables within the building. Signal cables should be isolated from power cables.

Telecommunications

All assignable areas will be provided with telecommunication outlets. The telecommunications system on campus is wholly owned by the University and managed by the Office of Telecommunications. This office is responsible for the coordination and implementation of all on-campus low voltage media installation and charges for voice and data services including emergency telephone service in all elevators. The commissioned A/E is required to comply with the telecommunications standards as outlined in the Campus Building Standards and be in contact with the telecommunications construction coordinator for planning and coordination of activities. Public telephones should be placed near the lobby of the building and on each floor, but located so that ringing and conversation will not disturb patrons in reading areas or staff members in offices. The project budget should include funds for all distribution facilities, including in-building wiring, media and underground infrastructure from the building to an appropriate node site as required.

Computer Metropolitan Area Network Cabling

Computer networking equipment and facilities will be provided. This includes: network wiring, closets, connections and repeaters, and all auxiliary equipment. The in-building design of the data system and associated infrastructure will be developed and coordinated by the Network Design Office under the direction of the Computing Services Office. Installation and cabling will be performed in cooperation with the University of Illinois Office of Telecommunications. Common horizontal "lay in" cable trays, shared with telecommunication cables, should be provided for distribution of data cabling. Sufficient conduits and jacks to permit the flexibility of connection between telecommunication B-jacks and data network systems should also be provided.

Heating Ventilation and Air Conditioning

This facility is to be completely air conditioned year-round. Pneumatic controls should be used for this building and the Operation and Maintenance Division should be consulted for requirements. Designs should incorporate energy consumption per square foot (insulation, fenestration, HVAC, lighting, motor speed controls, etc). All areas require a constant temperature in the range of 65–76° F and relative humidity of 40–60%, year-round. Humidity and temperature controls must be separate from each other.

Electrical Requirements

Only special electrical requirements beyond those of normal 110V electrical service will be indicated. The number and location of electric service outlets will be determined on a set of preliminary drawings. Each floor should have adequate reserve capacity to make it relatively easy to add electrical outlets where needed. Line voltage to the building should be chosen in consultation with the Operation and Maintenance Division.

10. Operational Goals*

Flexibility

It is not a contradiction to assert that the success of a large, research library building will be critically related to an accurate analysis of functions and a skillful translation of these into efficiently planned and related space and equipment, while at the same time one asserts, with equal conviction, that changes in library functions and requirements are absolutely inevitable, and the library must be able to adapt to them over a long period of time.

The new library building reflects the dual nature of this problem; i.e., it must be well planned to perform its tasks as these are now understood, and it must have very great capability for easy and economical change in space use and relationships in the future. The building must achieve these objectives at reasonable cost.

"Total" flexibility is in some ways a chimera and, in a building of this size, such complete flexibility in the use of space may be prohibitive in cost and, in terms of probable functions, not absolutely essential. However, a very substantial degree of flexibility is a firm requirement, and can, we believe, be provided at reasonable costs.

Apart from basic design features, e.g., floor loads, ventilation, lighting, module size, etc., long-range flexibility will be critically related to: (1) the way in which the bookstack space is distributed in relation to other facilities; (2) a design that will easily permit a variety of functions in substantial areas of the building—and especially in those areas that, initially, are located between reader or staff areas and the bookstack; (3) the use of movable partitions, furniture, and equipment; (4) a well-chosen module size; (5) the efficient location and grouping of fixed elements, e.g., stairways, elevators, toilets, air ducts, etc.; (6) adequate ducts for the later installation of a variety of communication circuits; (7) basic equipment capability and design, e.g., the book conveyor, pneumatic tube system, etc.; and (8) floor structures adequate for bookstack loads in all or most parts of the building.

This matter of flexibility, at reasonable cost, is stressed for these reasons:

(1) Some important aspects of the proposed building are relatively new and untried. It is believed that these plans are sound, but a more conventional pattern of relationships must be readily possible if they are not.

(2) Patterns of book relationships and reader needs are constantly changing in a university. Libraries have always found it difficult to adapt to these changing needs; the new building must not only minimize these difficulties, but provide easy and economical responses to changing requirements.

(3) The new library is deliberately being planned as an experimental laboratory for the investigation of better channels for the flow of information. It must be possible to rearrange some elements of the library to facilitate this work.

---

*Courtesy of University of Chicago, Regenstein Library

(4) There will be unpredictable changes in the number of students, intensity of library use, and the growth of segments of the collections.

Building Control

The architect should recognize that three interrelated control systems are involved in the structure. This may seem unduly complex, but there presently appears to be no easy alternative.

(1) All persons upon leaving the building will be asked to present books and briefcases at the building exit for inspection to determine that the books have been properly charged to an authorized borrower. The physical arrangements for this check are important and should be discussed with the owner early in the planning.

Note: It is planned that anyone may presently enter the building, and proceed at will to any of the specialized reading areas. It is not impossible that in the future, the University might find it necessary to limit those persons using the specialized reading rooms—or even the library building—to University students, faculty, and staff, except by special permission.

(2) Only authorized persons will be permitted into the bookstack. They will need to show University-issued identification cards in order to enter the stack, and will be asked to leave coats, books, and briefcases at the stack entrance (usually these will be left in lockers, carrels, reading rooms, etc.).

(3) The Library must secure as promptly as possible as complete a record as possible of books taken from reading rooms or the bookstacks. This record is essential to good library service to readers.

It is assumed that a very high proportion of the charging operations from the bookstack will take place at the specialized subject facility stack entrances, but the load on the central Circulation Desk is also likely to be substantial. It would in some instances be an economy in the reader's time and staff time to be able to combine the general circulation desk book control responsibility with the building exit control, but we anticipate that the probable traffic loads and physical relationships will make this impossible.

11. Information Technologies*

In recognition that information technologies are profoundly changing teaching and research in higher education, the Center for Scholarly Technology was created by the University Library and Academic Computing. The Center conducts research and development to support the creation of computer software for instruction and research, to support librarians in creating software for searching online information resources, and to develop and evaluate prototype programs and facilities for the Teaching Library. The Center conducts these projects in collaboration with the University Library and University Computing Services.

12. Program Summary Tables

See table A.3 and fig. A.4.

---

*Courtesy of University of Southern California, Leavey Library (from *Program for the New Teaching Library,* University of Southern California. Boston: Shepley Bulfinch Richardson and Abbott Architects, September 12, 1989, p. 8)

TABLE A.3   Central library program summary, Cornell University. Courtesy of Cornell University Library and Shepley Bulfinch Richardson and Abbott Architects

			1992 - S.F.		2010 - S.F.	
		Existing - S.F.	min	max	min	max
CENTRAL SERVICE DEPARTMENTS						
C1	Central Administration	1,950	3,225	3,225	3,225	3,225
C2	Administrative Operations					
C2a	Administration	3,208	4,550	4,550	4,550	4,550
C2b	Photocopy Operations	1,497	1,975	1,975	1,975	1,975
C2c	Shipping and Receiving	2,864	4,364	4,364	4,364	4,364
C3	Library Development	405	875	875	875	875
C4	Systems Office	501	1,250	1,250	1,250	1,250
C5	Conservation	3,418	3,700	3,700	3,700	3,700
C6	Central Technical Services					
C6a	Cataloging	2,910	6,525	6,525	6,525	6,525
C6b	Catalog Management	1,531	4,075	4,075	4,075	4,075
C6c	Serials	2,106	3,963	3,963	3,963	3,963
C6d	Acquisitions	4,501	7,126	7,126	7,126	7,126
	Subtotal Central Service	24,891	41,628	41,628	41,628	41,628
OLIN DEPARTMENTS						
O1	Olin Administration	340	1,075	1,075	1,075	1,075
O2	Collection Development	1,035	2,300	2,300	2,300	2,300
O3	Access Services	3,640	5,135	5,135	5,135	5,135
O4	New York Hist. Resources Center	790	850	850	850	850
O5	Reference	6,965	8,870	8,870	9,230	9,230
O6	Maps Microtexts and Newspapers					
O6a	Microtexts and Newspapers	5,720	6,393	6,623	7,790	8,032
O6b	Maps	3,520	5,063	5,094	7,174	7,236
O7	Manuscripts and Rare Books					
O7a	Manuscripts and Univ. Archives	9,555	9,925	9,925	16,117	16,117
O7b	Rare Books	8,310	6,777	7,259	7,354	7,919
O7c	History of Science Collections	2,380	2,181	2,278	2,563	2,714
O7d	Icelandic Collection	1,455	1,490	1,574	1,660	1,769
O8	Asian Collection					
O8a	Wason Collection	10,060	12,380	13,788	18,253	21,368
O8b	Echols Collection	6,280	8,015	8,785	11,987	13,840
	Subtotal Olin	60,050	70,454	73,556	91,488	97,585
GENERAL AREAS						
G1	Staff Meeting Rooms	270	830	830	830	830
G2	General Collection	77,030	77,151	88,173	117,723	141,267
G3	Card Catalog	3,330	3,100	3,100	300	300
G4	General Reading	—	2,500	2,500	2,500	2,500
G5	Current Periodical Room	2,370	2,370	2,370	2,370	2,370
G6	Graduate Study Rooms	6,130	6,130	6,130	6,130	6,130
G7	General Seminar Rooms	1,670	1,670	1,670	1,670	1,670
G8	Faculty Studies	7,320	11,070	11,070	11,070	11,070
G9	Graduate Study Carrels	—	—	—	—	—
	Subtotal General	98,120	104,821	115,843	142,593	166,137
	Grand Total Net	183,061	216,903	231,027	275,709	305,350
	Grand Total Gross (Net Add × 1.4)	242,000	289,378	309,152	371,705	413,203

Facility Component Summary Sheet

		Net Square Feet	Gross Square Feet Equivalent	% of Total	User Seats General/Terminal		Seat Total
1.0	Entrance Lobby	1,000	1,350	1.3%	0	0	0
2.0	Circulation Services and Stack Management	1,955	2,639	2.6%	0	0	0
3.0	Reserves / Current Periodicals	5,886	7,946	7.8%	175	24	199
4.0	Reference	5,466	7,379	7.3%	80	46	126
5.0	Library Instructional Services	6,440	8,694	8.6%	0	180	180
6.0	Library Materials Processing	1,175	1,586	1.6%	0	0	0
7.0	Collections / General Seating	30,192	40,759	40.1%	700	0	700
8.0	Photocopying and Printing	550	743	0.7%	0	0	0
9.0	Computer Commons	10,412	14,056	13.8%	0	308	308
10.0	Software Development Center	4,821	6,508	6.4%	0	94	94
11.0	Professional Offices	4,010	5,414	5.3%	0	0	0
12.0	Network Management / Data Services	1,435	1,937	1.9%	0	0	0
13.0	Receiving	1,925	2,599	2.6%	0	0	0
Total		75,267	101,610		955	652	1,607

Efficiency Assumption = 74%

Resultant NSF Multiplier = 1.35

FIGURE A.4 Leavey Library component summary, University of Southern California. Prepared by Shepley Bulfinch Richardson and Abbott Architects

13. Space Summary

See tables A.4 and A.5.

**TABLE A.4   Space summary, University of Michigan Media Union.
Courtesy of University of Michigan**

UNIVERSITY OF MICHIGAN MEDIA UNION
Space Summary and Area Estimates

LIBRARY			48,500
Collections (46,000 lineal ft.)		17,000	
Seating		28,000	
At Tables	650		
Casual	100		
Carrels	200		
In Study Rooms	100		
Administrative & Staff		3,500	
INSTRUCTIONAL COMPUTING FACILITIES			31,700
Laboratories (8@30 seats)		10,000	
Public Computer Stations (300)		12,000	
Computer User Support		3,500	
Staff Offices		700	
Support (storage, repair, etc.)		3,000	
Open Study (100 seats)		2,500	
CLASSROOMS, SEMINAR ROOMS			7,000
Lecture Hall (200 seats)		4,000	
Classrooms (3@50 seats)		3,000	
INTERDISCIPLINARY FACILITIES			31,000
Computer Aided Design Labs (3)		3,200	
Mock-up/Simulation Lab		3,000	
Building Materials Resource Center		3,000	
Video Recording Studio		4,500	
Sound Recording Studio		600	
Control Room		400	
Sound Isolated Workstations (8)		800	
Viewing Rooms (5)		500	
Small Workshops (10)		1,000	
Large Workshops (2)		1,000	
Staff Offices (10)		1,200	
Student Lounges		2,400	
Gallery		2,000	
CAREER INFORMATION AND COUNSELING CENTER			3,800
		Total Net Square Feet	118,200

TABLE A.5   Space summary, Delaware Public Archives. Text for space program for Delaware Public Archives, produced by Philip D. Leighton for Moeckel Carbonell Associates Inc., Architects, Wilmington, Delaware

DELAWARE PUBLIC ARCHIVES
20-Year Plan from 1995

Functions	Section IV Page Number	Net Area	Subtotals of Net Area
IDENTIFY—INVENTORY			
Deputy Records Administrator	2	180	
Analyst's Offices	5	600	
Analyst's Coordinator Office	8	120	
Support Staff	10	120	
Analyst Common Work Area	12	840	
Office Support (included in common area)	12	0	
Analyst Supply Closet (included in common area)	12	0	
Conference Room	15	300	2,160
IDENTIFY—SCHEDULING			
See above—no added space			
IDENTIFY—TRANSFER			
Loading Dock	17	540	
Receiving Area	20	396	
Receiving Process/Distribution	22	825	
Examination Area	24	1,000	
Dirty Room	26	300	
Treatment Room for Contaminated Material	28	200	
Destruction Staging Area	30	300	
Records Center Supervisor	32	120	
Courier	35	120	
File Room	38	120	
R C Clerical Support	40	120	
Receiving/Shipping Supervisor	43	120	
Shower & Dressing Rooms	46	240	
R C Box Storage	48	510	
Office & Microfilming Supply Storage Space	50	500	5,411
IDENTIFY—DESTROY			
Included above—no added space			
Note that dumpsters sit outside			
COLLECT—APPRAISE			
Use examination space detailed under "Identify—Transfer"			
Local Records Manager	52	180	
Local Records Staff	55	240	
Office Support	58	120	540
COLLECT—ACCESSION			
Use examination space detailed under "Identify—Transfer"			
Use office space defined elsewhere			

(continued)

TABLE A.5 Continued

Functions	Section IV Page Number	Net Area	Subtotals of Net Area
COLLECT—STORAGE (ARCHIVES ONLY; EXCLUDES RECORDS CENTER STORAGE)			
Security Vault	61	1,218	
Color Film Vault	63	1,218	
Black and White Film	65	1,218	
Security Film	67	1,218	
Microfilming Backlog	69	2,437	
General Stacks	71	53,608	60,918
PRESERVE—PROCESS			
Deputy State Archivist	73	180	
Deputy State Archivist's Support	76	180	
Accession & Processing Coordinator	79	150	
Reference Services Coordinator	82	150	
Special Projects Room	85	364	
Intern Workstations	88	600	
Archivist Workstation	91	120	
Senior Archivist Workstation	94	360	
Volunteers	97	160	
Oversize Tables	100	600	
Paper Cutter on Table	100	30	
Archival Shelving	100	100	
Library Shelving	100	40	
Photocopy (noise & light control room)	102	240	
Archival Supply Closet	105	750	
Staff Coat Closet/Lockers/Sink	108	120	4,144
PRESERVE—DESCRIPTION			
Use space described under "Preserve—Process"			
PRESERVE—IMAGING/MICROFILM			
Administration Offices	111	300	
Project Room	113	120	
Team Leader's Offices	115	240	
Support Staff Work Area	117	120	
Office Support	119	120	
Small Meeting Room	121	240	
Planetary Camera Room	123	1,080	
File Master Camera Room	126	896	
Scanning/3M5000 Room	129	1,400	
Microfilm Reading Room	132	300	
Over-Sized Machines	132	150	
Cart Parking (in File Master room)	126	0	
Splicing Room (in 3M room)	129	0	
Fiche/Roll Film Duplicators	134	180	
Silver Film Duplicator—Handling Darkroom	136	100	
Dark Room for Developing	138	150	
Photo Studio	140	300	
Cartridge Loader w/End Processing	142	100	

Functions	Section IV Page Number	Net Area	Subtotals of Net Area
Inspection Station w/End Processing	144	120	
Long Counter w/End Processing	146	200	
Film Processing	148	300	
Silver Lock Room	150	120	
Chemical Storage	152	300	
Paper/Plastic/Safety Storage (@ loading dock)	50	0	
Film Storage (in vault)	65	0	
Documents Prep Area (8 stations)	154	880	
Documents Prep Oversize (2 stations)	156	275	
Documents Processing Office	158	120	
End Processing Area	160	240	
Backlog Stacks included under collections	162	0	8,351
PRESERVE—CONSERVE			
Contamination Room—included earlier	26	0	
Conservator's Office	164	120	
Conservation Lab	166	4,000	
Exhibit Prep (in conservation lab)	166	0	
Archival Supplies—included earlier	105	0	4,120
ENSURE ACCESS—REFERENCE			
Research Room (as illustrated including seating, oversize reading, the reference desk, finding aids, the "wall paper" display, 72 drawer catalog cabinets, 5,500 volumes on library shelving, 500 oversized volumes, an atlas case, periodical shelving, and OPACs)	172	5,110	
Research Orientation Room	176	300	
Audio/Video Self Service Room	179	180	
Audio/Video Staffed Viewing	181	280	
Microfilm/Images Reading Room	184	1,400	
Confidential Reading Cubicles	187	100	
Microfilm Storage	189	400	
Microfilm Storage Shelving/Stool	189	included	
Special Projects Reading Room	191	270	
Reception Desk	194	250	
Locker Area	197	240	8,520
ENSURE ACCESS—CATALOGING—SPACE ACCOUNTED FOR ELSEWHERE			
PROMOTE—EXHIBITION			
Exhibit Vault	199	570	
Exhibit Area	202	900	
Exhibit Support	204	240	
Sales Area (included in exhibit area)	202	0	
Public Rest Rooms (unassigned space)	?	0	1,710
PROMOTE—PUBLIC PROGRAM			
Auditorium	206	1,125	
Projection Room	209	250	
Preview Room	212	250	1,625

(continued)

TABLE A.5   Continued

Functions	Section IV Page Number	Net Area	Subtotals of Net Area
ADVISE—TRAINING			
Training Room for 25 (two of them)	214	1,000	
Training Room for 75	216	1,500	
Training Support	218	750	
Caterer Kitchen/Public Vending Machine Area	219	240	3,490
ADVISE—CONSULT			
Space accounted for elsewhere			
MANAGE—ARCHIVE ADMINISTRATION			
Staff Library & Conference Room	220	440	
Kitchenette/Coats	223	120	
Staff Lounge	225	600	
Staff Kitchenette	227	150	
Meeting Room (included with analyst grp)	15	0	
State Archivist's Office	229	250	
Administrative Officer	232	120	
Public Program Office	235	180	
Support Staff	238	240	
Sitting Area	241	100	
Copy/fax/VCR/Supply Storage	244	150	
File Room	247	120	
Computer Room (one per floor)	249	360	
Telephone Rooms	251	540	3,370
MANAGE—DIVISION OF HISTORICAL AND CULTURAL AFFAIRS OFFICES			
Division Director	253	275	
Division Special Assistants	255	575	
Division Senior Secretary & Clerical	257	390	
Division Supply & File Room	259	180	
Division Meeting	261	230	1,650
	Total Net Area of Archive		106,009
	Records Center (may or may not be included)		20,000
	Net Grand Total at Hall of Records Site		126,009

14. Relationships of Functional Areas

The seven examples in this section are generally called "bubble diagrams." The circles, or bubbles, are usually drawn to scale such that their size is relative to the programmed size for the function. Figs. A.5, A.6, and A.8 are basic forms of presentation, but note that fig. A.6 has no indication of relative size of functions.

In all such depictions, the bubbles are arranged in groupings representing relative working relationships. The arrows in fig. A.5 generally suggest secondary relationships between working groups or parts of working groups (though these relationships as expressed here are not the full picture).

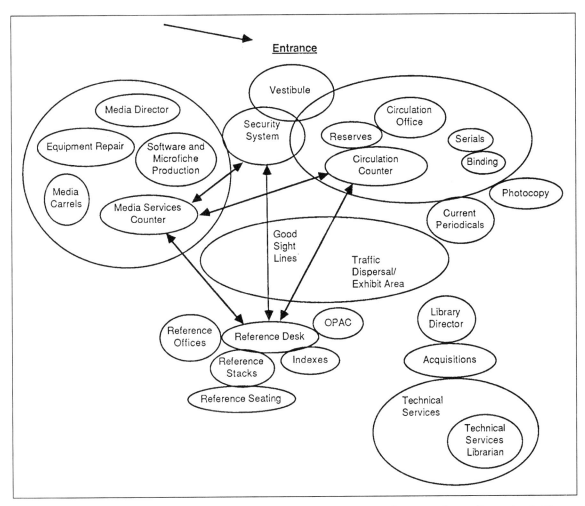

FIGURE A.5 Bubble diagram, an example used in the planning of the Roanoke College Fintel Library building. This type of diagram is merely intended to convey relationships, usually not size of space. Courtesy of Roanoke College, Fintel Library

Arrows or lines can convey material flow, staff circulation, public traffic, and the like. Fig. A.6 shows use of single and double connecting lines to convey relative importance of the relationship, and other graphic symbolism to show primary public service points, office staff, and possible remote elements.

Figs. A.7 and A.8 begin to show architectural character, not always a desirable approach unless done to clarify program intent. (In fig. A.7, the three dark, vertical rectangles are stairs. This project involved expanding from the existing library—the upper rectangle—through a new connecting element to a nearby existing building—the lower large rectangle.) Indeed, fig. A.7 is more likely to result from early spatial blocking by the library consultant or architectural firm, rather than by the owner. This is also true of figs. A.9 through A.11.

Most figures here do not take into consideration the prospect that the building design will almost certainly involve multiple floors. Fig. A.11 suggests one possible vertical distribution, assuming all cannot be on one floor. When this type of depiction is used, relationships between working groups can be seen to be improved.

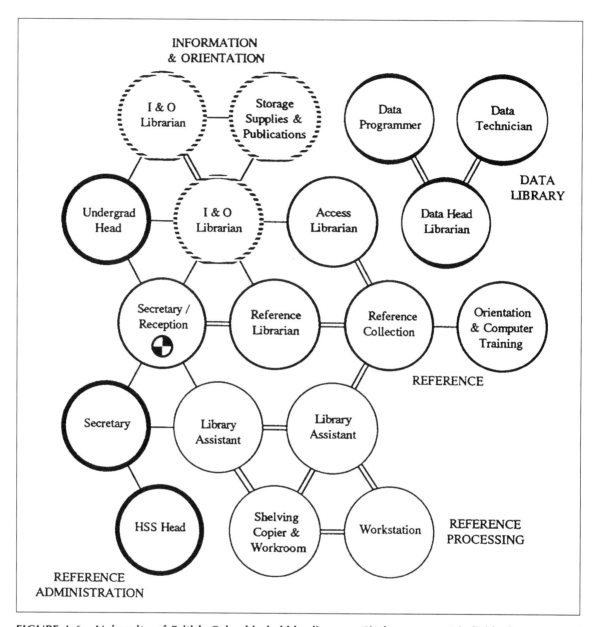

FIGURE A.6 **University of British Columbia bubble diagram. Circles represent individual spaces, and circle line differences relate them to one of the five different functional headings within the component. The small circle with two black quarters is an access control point. Single connecting lines show a relationship, and double lines a close relationship. Note that using circles of equal size, together with a regular, hexagonal grid, focuses attention upon the relationships between space pairs. Once relative areas are introduced, it is difficult to avoid "space planning." Courtesy of Process Four Design Ltd., Vancouver, British Columbia**

Figs. A.9 and A.11 are included to show how much can be conveyed on one page. Fig. A.10 is a detailed depiction of the upper right corner of fig. A.9, showing how it is feasible to move from a macro view to the various components.

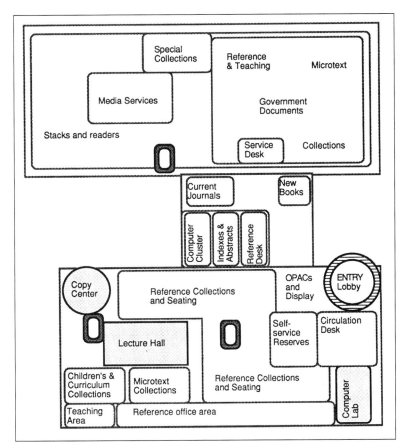

FIGURE A.7 This particular bubble diagram for Western Washington University, Wilson Library and Haggard Hall, is superimposed upon the existing library (upper rectangle) and a neighbor building proposed for an expansion (lower rectangle), together with an assumed linking element. Each functional element is a close approximation of the programmed size to the same scale as the floor plates. Courtesy of Western Washington University

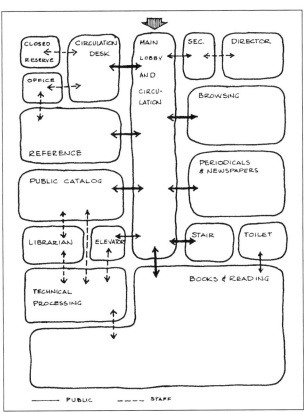

FIGURE A.8 Spatial relationships for ground-floor requirements shown in diagrammatic form for Lake Forest College Library. Courtesy of Lake Forest College Library

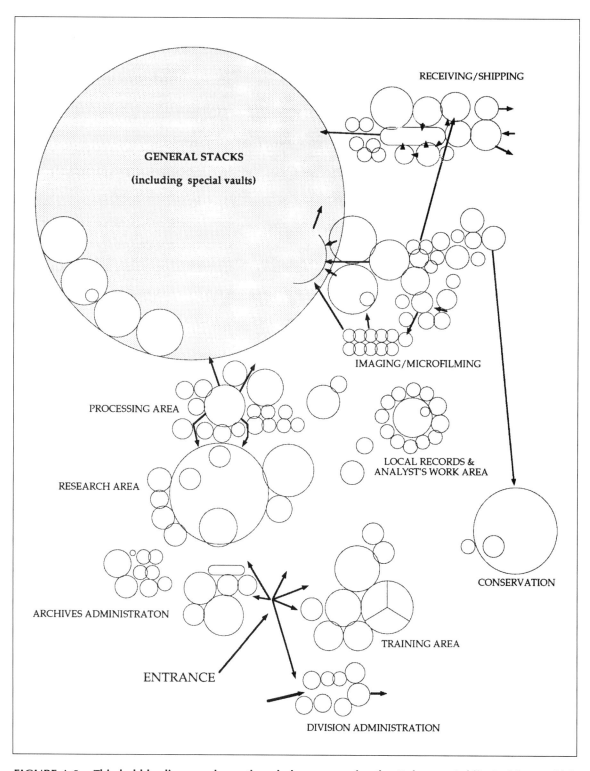

FIGURE A.9 This bubble diagram shows the whole program for the Delaware Public Archives, which makes some of it difficult to read. All the bubbles are to relative scale. Fig. A.11 is the same diagram with an idealized floor designation superimposed. Illustrations and text for space program for Delaware Public Archives, produced by Philip D. Leighton for Moeckel Carbonell Associates Inc., Architects, Wilmington, Delaware

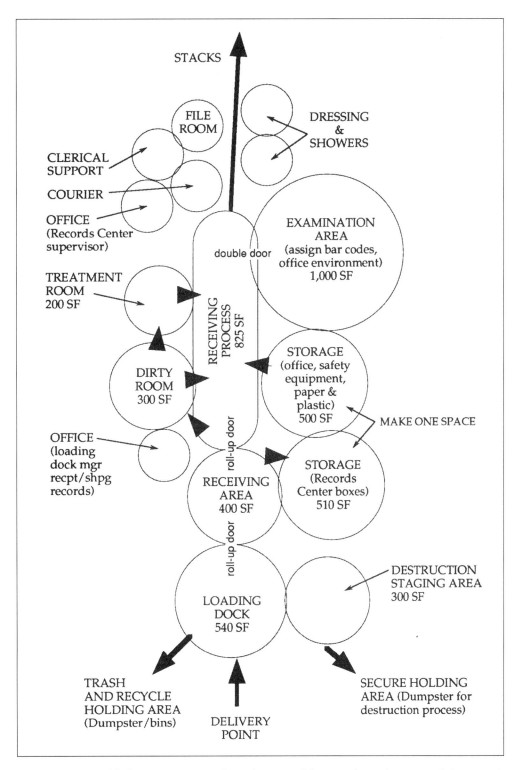

STACKS

FILE ROOM

DRESSING & SHOWERS

CLERICAL SUPPORT

COURIER

OFFICE (Records Center supervisor)

double door

RECEIVING PROCESS 825 SF

EXAMINATION AREA (assign bar codes, office environment) 1,000 SF

TREATMENT ROOM 200 SF

DIRTY ROOM 300 SF

STORAGE (office, safety equipment, paper & plastic) 500 SF

MAKE ONE SPACE

OFFICE (loading dock mgr recpt/shpg records)

roll-up door

RECEIVING AREA 400 SF

STORAGE (Records Center boxes) 510 SF

roll-up door

DESTRUCTION STAGING AREA 300 SF

LOADING DOCK 540 SF

TRASH AND RECYCLE HOLDING AREA (Dumpster/bins)

DELIVERY POINT

SECURE HOLDING AREA (Dumpster for destruction process)

FIGURE A.10   This larger representation of a part of fig. A.9 (from the upper right corner) shows more clearly the level of detail contained in the bubble diagram (Delaware Public Archives, receiving and shipping). Illustrations and text for space program for Delaware Public Archives, produced by Philip D. Leighton for Moeckel Carbonell Associates Inc., Architects, Wilmington, Delaware

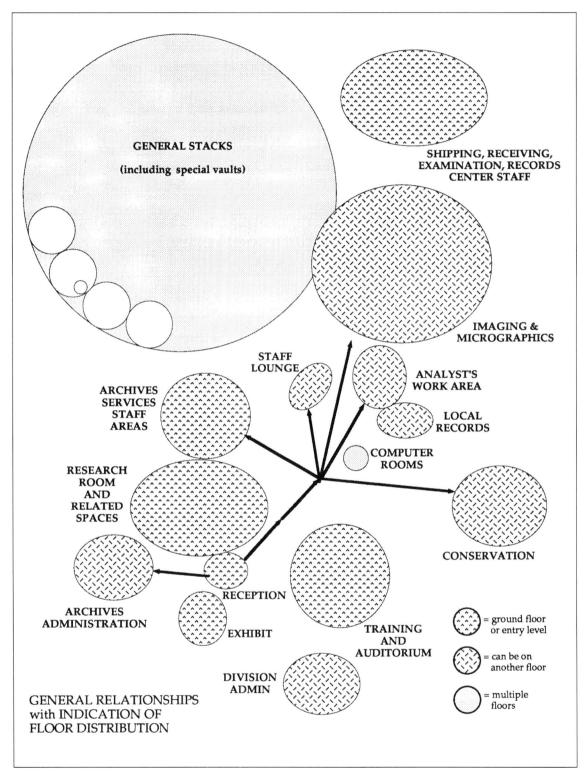

FIGURE A.11 Floor distribution diagram at Delaware Public Archives. This is the same diagram as illustrated in fig. A.9, but with the addition of floor distribution information. Illustrations and text for space program for Delaware Public Archives, produced by Philip D. Leighton for Moeckel Carbonell Associates Inc., Architects, Wilmington, Delaware

15. Outline of Program Topics*

Foreword by the President Explaining the Educational Philosophy of the University and the Purpose of the Library.

    I. Librarian's Statement
    II. General Objectives and Requirements
    III. Pattern of Library Service
    IV. Outline of Space Needs
    V. Size and Space Needs of the Library Collections
    VI. Accommodations for Readers and Description of Spaces
        A. Vestibules and Entrance Lobbies
        B. Exits and Supervision
        C. Main Desk
        D. Public Catalog
        E. Reference Collection
        F. Bibliography Collection
        G. Periodical Collection
        H. Reserve Book Room
        I. Documents Collection
        J. Map Collection
        K. General and Special Collections
        L. Crane Reading Room
        M. Exhibits
        N. Browsing Room
        O. Group Study Rooms
        P. Typing Rooms
        Q. Audio-Visual Area
        R. Microtext Reading Area
        S. Curriculum Laboratory
        T. Faculty Studies
        U. Facilities for Smoking
        V. Toilet Facilities
        W. Coat Rooms
        X. Table Sizes
        Y. Chairs
    VII. Staff Accommodations
        A. Administration and Department Heads
        B. Book Selection and Processing
            1. Acquisitions
            2. Cataloging
            3. Mechanical Preparations
            4. Bindery Preparations
        C. Supply Closet
        D. Receiving and Shipping Room
        E. Storage Room for Equipment
        F. Library Staff Room
        G. Facilities for Janitor and Maids

---

*Courtesy of Tufts University, Tisch Library

16. Program Components or Elements (Space Sheets)

a. Vestibule*

The vestibule should provide protection from the elements and a natural traffic flow into the main lobby and into the Special Collections area. As the only public entrance, it should be attractive, inviting, and utilize a permanent decorative feature—possibly the University's coat of arms. There should be an outside book return drop here if the Circulation Department can not be situated along an outside wall, near the public entrance.

As the vestibule leads into both the lobby and the Special Collections area, it should be arranged in such a manner that each area may be used and controlled either separately or together.

Located discreetly off the vestibule should be coat rooms combined with toilet facilities for ladies and men, and the public telephone booths.

Space	
Vestibule	250 sq. ft.
Coat Room & W. C.	250 sq. ft.
Total Space	500 sq. ft.

b. Administrative Offices†

Administrative Offices and Other Requirements

1. *Administrative offices.* An area on the main or an alternate floor will house the chief librarian and his supporting staff for administration. Space in this same area will be utilized for the secretarial staff, the clerical staff, the accounting staff, as a reception area, for a conference room, and for other purposes.

Library administrative office, estimated in square feet: Total 4,032.

Schematics

This section is intended to further demonstrate the relationship of one major library area to other areas and to record estimates of the square feet to be assigned to each. These estimates are based upon policies used generally for determining space allocations, the present utilization of space for these functions, and staff knowledge of the operations that will be assigned to each area.

Space for accommodating readers, for the storage of library materials, and for the staff to conduct library services is of concern. Major allocations are subject to subdivision for efficient library operation, with some overlapping of reader and staff use of many areas.

In preparing space estimates *Higher Education Facilities Planning and Management Manual Four, Academic Support Facilities,* hereafter referred to as *Manual Four,* has been relied upon. Published in 1971, it records modern space requirements based upon practice and current trends. (Reference: *Higher Education Facilities Planning and Management Manuals, Manual Four, Academic Support Facilities, Planning and Systems Division,* Western Interstate Commission for Higher Education in Cooperation with the American

---

*Courtesy of Leyburn Library, Washington and Lee University, Lexington, Virginia

†Courtesy of University of Texas, Perry-Castañeda Library

Association of Collegiate Registrars and Admissions Officers.) [U.S. Office of Education Contract Number OEG 0-9-150167-4534, May 1971.]

Schematic M: Administrative Office

This grouping of offices is planned to house the University Librarian, the Associate University Librarian, and assistants assigned to heading the major divisions of the library including technical processes, public services, systems and management, business and personnel, and branch library supervision.

The supporting administrative staff requiring space assignments include the executive assistant, secretarial staff, receptionist and clerical assistants. Library bookkeepers are assigned space in this unit in order to conserve space in the main floor assignment to acquisitions.

A conference room large enough to handle meetings of department heads is desirable. For thirty people at 20 square feet per person, about 600 square feet will be required for the conference room. (See fig. A.12.)

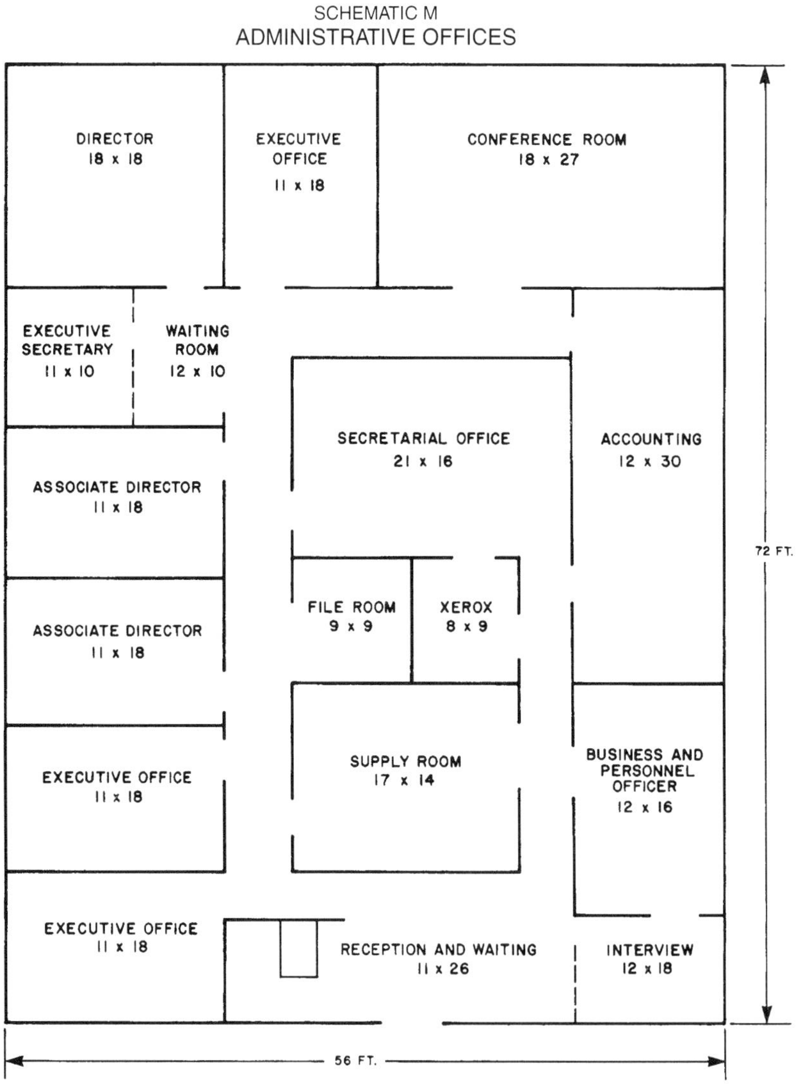

SCHEMATIC M
ADMINISTRATIVE OFFICES

FIGURE A.12 University of Texas, Perry-Castañeda Library. Administrative office layout schematic. As a schematic, it is interesting to note that the dimensions do not add up in several places, leaving room for the designer to work things out.

c. Development Office

See fig. A.13.

[Draft 4.1 — 3/88]

Olin Space Planning Program

Department: LIBRARY DEVELOPMENT

Location: 214 Olin Library

Functional Type: Office area appropriate for distinguished visitors

Space Element	Existing	Required 1992	Required 2010
Current _____ Room _____ Activity _____			
Office/Work Space As the department moves into a pre-campaign mode and takes on responsibilities for more inter-action with individual large givers and a volunteer network, it will be necessary to add another mem-ber to the Development staff. One to two more staff members will be needed to run a campaign between 1988 and 1992.			
214C Director Should include space for small meetings (3–4 chairs).	110	200	200
214B Development Assistant	80	125	125
214A Secretarial & Recep. Area Reception area should seat 2–4 people.	215	300	300
— Development Assistant	0	250/1–2FTE	250
Area Total	405	875	875

FIGURE A.13 **Space planning study for Cornell University, Olin Library. Because of tremendous space deficiencies, the University embarked on a "fast-track" project schedule to design and construct the adjacent Kroch Library. As a result, no formal program study was undertaken by the library for Kroch beyond what was done by Shepley Bulfinch Richardson and Abbott. Final programming for the building ended up being a part of schematic design, and, with a very tight budget, was "capped" at a certain square footage. Prepared by Shepley Bulfinch Richardson and Abbott Architects. Courtesy of Cornell University Library**

d. Circulation

See figs. A.14 and A.15. A.15 is a continuation of A.14.

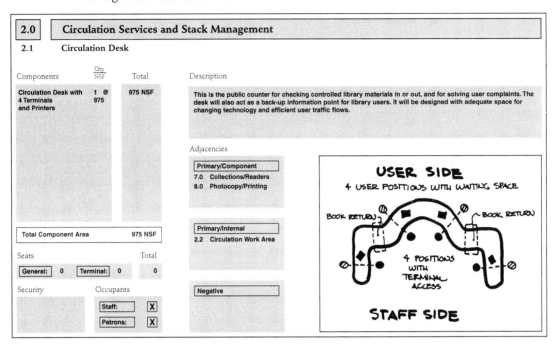

FIGURE A.14   This program space sheet is a form in which information is added as it is developed. Each page pair describing a particular function (see below) has the same design, but with different information. Prepared by Shepley Bulfinch Richardson and Abbott Architects. Courtesy of University of Southern California

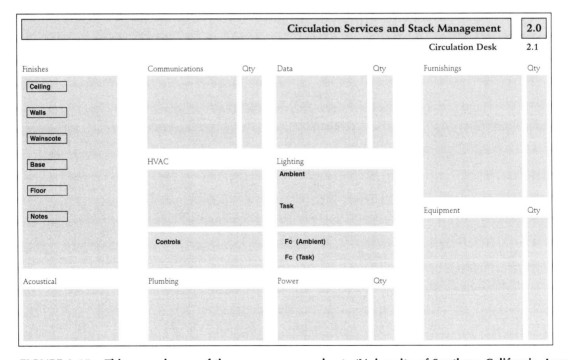

FIGURE A.15   This second page of the program space sheets (University of Southern California, Leavey Library circulation desk) has not been filled in, but the nature of the information to be shown is clear. Together with fig. A.14, these make up fairly typical program space sheets. Prepared by Shepley Bulfinch Richardson and Abbott Architects. Courtesy of University of Southern California

e. Computer Lab

See figs. A.16 and A.17. A.17 is a continuation of A.16.

Group:	University
Division:	Academic Technology & User Services
Room Name:	Computer Labs (5 of them)
Square Footage:	Five at 1,218 SF each for a total of 6,090 SF
Function:	Computer labs for general university use by students. The one lab located within library space will be used for teaching access to information via computers
Adjacencies:	Four on the main entry floor with easy 24-hour access, one within the library envelope on the same floor as General Reference
Capacity:	Each with a capacity for 30 plus instructor
Hours of Operation:	Typically 168 hours per week except for the lab within the library which will be approximately 97 hours per week
Special Finishes:	Carpet
Special Ventilation:	Air conditioning for heat gain by equipment
Plumbing:	None
Gas Services:	None
Power:	Convenience outlets for maintenance, the equivalent of one 4-plex for each computer station, duplex outlets for printers must be on circuit separate from those serving the computers
Lighting:	Fluorescent—indirect is best for computers—lab in library must be dimmable
Communications:	One TSO for each computer and printer.
Fixed Equipment:	Overhead computer driven projector and projection screen for lab within library. What is illustrated as a "table for printers" may be a built-in counter. Wire management for banks of computers within room.

FIGURE A.16   Space sheet for computer labs at Western Washington University, Wilson Library. Note the similarity of information between figs. A.16/A.17 and A.14/A.15. Courtesy of Western Washington University

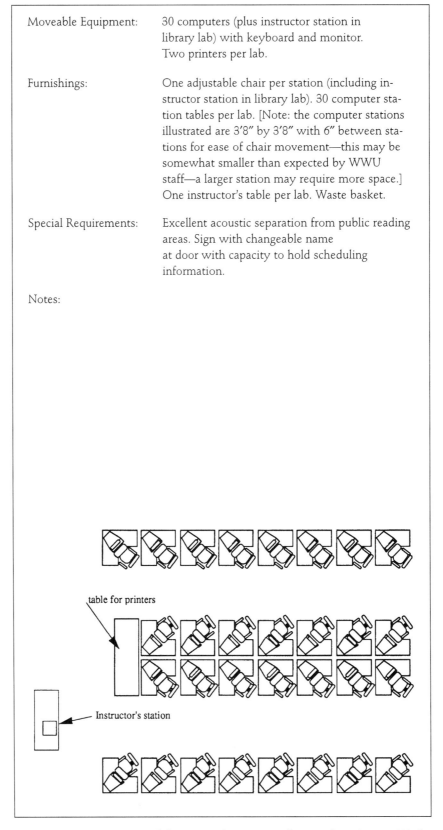

Moveable Equipment:	30 computers (plus instructor station in library lab) with keyboard and monitor. Two printers per lab.
Furnishings:	One adjustable chair per station (including instructor station in library lab). 30 computer station tables per lab. [Note: the computer stations illustrated are 3'8" by 3'8" with 6" between stations for ease of chair movement—this may be somewhat smaller than expected by WWU staff—a larger station may require more space.] One instructor's table per lab. Waste basket.
Special Requirements:	Excellent acoustic separation from public reading areas. Sign with changeable name at door with capacity to hold scheduling information.
Notes:	

table for printers

Instructor's station

FIGURE A.17   Computer labs space sheet, second page, for Western Washington University, Wilson Library. The sketch reflects staff input on how such a room should be arranged. Courtesy of Western Washington University

f. Instructional Services Laboratory

See fig. A.18.

<u>B11 Instructional Services Laboratory</u>   750 ft²
                                                                                          Floor 4

    Requires access to: B8, B9, B10, B12, D1 and D2
    Communications: telephone and computer networking
    Special Features: carpeting and must be a lockable area

This area will serve the library instructional mission by providing individuals with the framework and skills necessary to effectively access information services.

Office Furniture/Equipment:	Computer Furniture/Equipment:	Special Furniture/Equipment:
(5) study tables (36 × 36)	(8) library info workstations with video capabilities	(1) hidden projection screen
(1) small table	(4) printers	(1) overhead projector
(20) chairs		(1) LCD panel
		(1) microcomputer file server with multimedia peripherals (video and CD-ROM using Toolbox software with classroom stations hardware
		(1) LCD panel/computer cart
		(1) slide projector
		(1) lectern
		(1) white board
		(1) VCR projector
		(2) flip charts

FIGURE A.18   Space sheet for instructional services at the University of Illinois, Grainger Library. Note how brief this one is compared to those in figs. A.16 and A.17. Courtesy of the Library

g. Map Room*

A. *Purpose:* The Map Library will house and service the Library's collections of maps and aerial photographs and a substantial portion of its atlases. The special nature of this material requires special equipment and makes self-service by users undesirable or impossible. Reading and staff work space will therefore have to be provided adjacent to the map storage areas.

B. *Major Elements and Space Requirements:*

	Sq. ft.
175 map cases (4′ × 3′ plus 1/2 of 4′ aisle) @ 20	3,500
16 single-face sections shelving 12″ deep for atlases and gazetteers, @ 9	144
6 folio atlas cases (3′ × 2′) for large atlases, @ 12	72
Reading room	
12 seats, @ 40	480
2 light tables, @ 36	72
1 staff work and sorting room	400
1 office for curator	100
	4,768

---

*Courtesy of University of Chicago, Regenstein Library

Special Note: It is recognized that there may not be sufficient space for this collection in the building. A review of whether to try to include it or not shall be made by the owner early in the planning process. The space has *not* been included in space summary figures.

C. *Suggested Location:* Natural relationship will be with Economics, Business, and Geography insofar as users are concerned. However, the Map Library should not displace the bookstack space immediately adjacent to this reader facility.

D. *Arrangements:* The work area, which will inevitably present a cluttered appearance, should be separated from the public areas by partially solid or obscured partitions. It should be so located, or the doorways should be so disposed, that the Map Library's users will not be led into the work area. The partitions need not extend to the ceiling. Layout must allow for a cabinet (4′ × 3′ × 5′ in height) for the temporary storage of maps being processed, for a supply cabinet 4′ × 2′ × 6′ in height, and for 2 long work tables at least 4′ deep.

h. Microform Reading Room*

Purpose

To house, service, and provide reader stations for the bulk of the library's microform collections.

Suggested Location and Relationships

A location vertically adjacent to the two Reference Departments, with maximum ease of user access, is highly desirable.

Arrangement

Public Service Desk (400 net sq. ft.) should be immediately visible upon entering room. This Desk will house attendants, reader-printers and duplicators, a card catalog and guides, and it will be noisy. Arrangement should be such that, either by location or sound-conditioning, Reader Stations (carrels) are protected from noise as much as possible.

Microform storage (4,000 net sq. ft.) will be a mix of open shelving, 140 microfilm cabinets, and other forms, with specifications to be provided. Storage space may be in two stages: (1) approximately 20% should be immediately and horizontally adjacent to the Public Service Desk; (2) 80% can be at a greater distance, horizontally or vertically, provided there is direct access from the Public Service Desk. This 80% could be part of the Book Stacks, provided that humidity requirements can be met and that it is enclosed, or secured from the Book Stacks proper.

Special Equipment and Other Requirements

Subdued overhead lighting in Reader Station area; principal light source will be from carrels themselves.

110V outlets for each Reader Station.

In Microform Storage areas, a humidity level of 45–55% must be maintained.

---

*Courtesy of University of North Carolina, Davis Library

Reader Stations

1. The five closed carrels (200 net sq. ft.) should each have a LMM Superior Library Microfilm Reader (Model AB) or equivalent. Dimensions of this unit as follows: Height: 60 in. (152 cm), Depth: 30 in. (76 cm), Width: 48 in. (122 cm), Weight: 195 lb. (88 Kg).

In addition each carrel should be equipped with a chair, a small table or workbench, and individually controlled indirect light source. The occupant of the carrel should be able to control the direction and intensity of his light, (i.e., some sort of light on a flexible shaft, such as a goose-neck, with a rheostat control for intensity).

One of the five carrels should be easily convertible into a station for reading microfiche, although most of the concentrated lengthy uses of microfilm will involve roll microfilm.

2. The forty open carrels (1,000 net sq. ft.) should be divided as follows: roll film readers (LMM model AB as in 1 above), 15; Microfiche readers, 20; and micro-opaque readers, 5.

a. The 15 stations for roll film readers should be designed to accommodate the same machine as described in 1 above except that stations will not be enclosed and table or workbench will not be necessary. These units rest on the floor and will not need a table to hold them.

b. The twenty microfiche stations would be equipped with tabletop readers such as the Realist Vantage L with dimensions as follows: Height: 17 in., Depth: 9 inches, Width: 13 in., Weight: 26 lbs.

These machines can be lined up along a large table, two or three machines per table, with adequate chairs accompanying. Each station should have individually controlled lighting (reading lamps as in 1 above).

c. The five micro-opaque readers should be tabletop units also. A design such as the Readex Universal Micro-Viewer, Model 5, would be used. Its dimensions are as follows: Height: 23 in., Depth: 20 in., Width: 11 in., Weight: 24 lbs.

Other specifications for opaque readers should be similar to those for microfiche.

The room, as a whole, should be lighted with indirect, subdued lighting. Each station should have some control over its individual lighting conditions. THIS IS IMPORTANT! User resistance to microforms, according to latest studies, has been minimized by offering personalized lighting.

i. Interlibrary Loan Office

(1) University of Maryland Baltimore County, Kuhn Library*

Interlibrary Loan Workroom
HEGIS 440

No. units:	1	NASF/Unit:	400
Unit Capacity:	4	Total NASF:	400

Function

Office workstations for the library staff Interlibrary Loan section of the Reference department are to be provided in this space.

---

*Courtesy of Ingraham Planning Associates, Inc., Consultants for Facility and Long Range Planning, Fairfax, Virginia, and the University of Maryland Baltimore County

Characteristics

- Provide "typical" layout to include four desk zones (desk with chair, file cabinet, storage for 100 books), and layout table (30" × 60"), and a shared work zone with work table (36" × 72").
- Provide floor surface of anti-static carpet and ceiling of acoustical material.
- Equip desk station with telecommunication capability for both voice and data communication, as well as sufficient space for a microcomputer and printer, and at least two duplex 115 volt electrical outlets.
- Provide space and access within the workroom for terminals and printers linked to the LIMS, to OCLC and other bibliographic utilities with dedicated wiring as appropriate.
- Provide quality and quantity of light in accordance with Maryland DGS "Procedures for Energy Conservation."

Desired Space Relationships

Locate adjacent to and within visual and direct connection to the Reference/Documents Desk.

(2) Western Washington University (see figs. A.19 and A.20; fig. A.20 is a continuation of A.19)

Group:	Library
Division:	Access Services
Room Name:	ILL Staff Area
Square Footage:	506 SF
Function:	Receives requests for materials from service points (reference and circulation desks) in library, confirms and/or determines site for borrowing attempt, places request with lending library. Processes lending requests from other libraries and forwards them to the Document Delivery area.
Adjacencies:	This function must be in the Access Services processing area due to current staffing and oversight. Juxtaposed to supervisor's office, close or easy access to the Document Delivery staff area (where requested materials are received), the reference desks and collections (close to internal circulation pattern). Separate from, but adjacent to Technical Services.
Capacity:	5 FTE
Hours of Operation:	Normally during office work hours (7:30 to 5:00 ± Monday through Friday)
Special Finishes:	Carpet, book truck protection at walls where appropriate.
Special Ventilation:	Heat gain from five computers.
Plumbing:	None.
Gas Services:	None.
Power:	Clean power for computers on circuit separate from possible future photocopy machine. Outlets spaced for future general work area use (no more than 12' on center, and on each wall) 4-plex for each anticipated computer station.

FIGURE A.19   Area space sheet, first page, for Western Washington University, Wilson Library, Interlibrary Loan (ILL) staff.

Lighting:	Low glare for computer, indirect lighting ideal for this purpose. Direct lighting is best for sorting areas. Control of direct sunlight is required. Maintain at least 50 fc at table height throughout room.
Communications:	Provide TSOs for future use as general work area (no more than 12′ on center, and on each wall); activate five with this project (see sketch for computer locations).
Fixed Equipment:	Six single face shelving units made up from standard library shelving approximately 5′ high, each with back panels, canopy tops and end panels where appropriate—fixed because these need to be bolted to the floor or to walls. Clock. Unit (shared) tack board.
Moveable Equipment:	Five computers, five printers.
Furnishings:	Office "landscape" panel system with wire management capability, each station to have a panel mounted shelf, a panel mounted tack board, a task light, a double pedestal desk, a 2 1/2′ × 2 1/2′ printer table, a 2 1/2′ × 2 1/2′ computer table with an articulated keyboard holder, a 4-drawer legal file with lock, an adjustable desk chair with arms, and a book truck with rubber bumpers and wheels at least 5″ in diameter for use on carpet. The area also has two side chairs with arms and two coat trees, a pencil sharpener.
Special Requirements:	Control of direct sunlight. Excellent access to power and signal for future flexibility. Excellent acoustic separation from office and public reading areas, secured from public area outside normal work hours.
Notes:	The sketch below represents one possible configuration of five workstations. One of the workstations should be somewhat separate (for a lead person). Note that one section of shelving requires access from outside the space as defined—this could be relocated to avoid this problem if necessary.

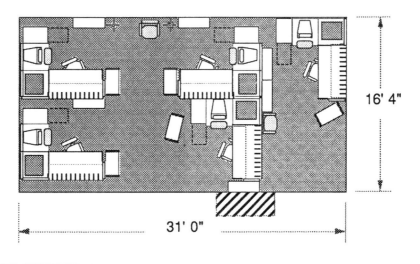

FIGURE A.20 Space sheet, second page, for the Western Washington University, Wilson Library, ILL staff area. Note: The sketch of this space assumes that it is part of a larger space in which access is provided as part of the nonassignable space; otherwise, staff could not move from one part of the work area to the other as shown. Courtesy of Western Washington University

j. Exhibition Area*

Purpose

To house and/or display permanent two- and three-dimensional fine arts collections and rotating displays of interest.

Location

In the vestibule of traffic dispersal area for display cases. At other appropriate areas throughout the library for two-dimensional collections.

Equipment and Space

Display case either built into the walls or freestanding. Seventy-two linear feet of 15″ deep × 15″ high (min.) display shelving, may be on adjustable standards. No equipment defined for two-dimensional works; however, these areas should be located where staff would have visual access to discourage vandalism.

Special Requirements

Display Cases (may house Boehm Bird Collection with value in excess of $500,000).

1) High security
2) Dustproof
3) Illuminated

k. Special Collections Vault†

In all Presidential libraries there are restrictions on the use of some of the manuscript and microform holdings. These restrictions (for purposes of this discussion) are of three types: (1) those imposed by law or Executive Order for the protection of national security; (2) those imposed by the donor to avoid unwarranted invasion of personal privacy; and (3) those imposed by the archival staff to avoid loss or destruction of rare and valuable items. Each of these requires separate handling facilities, and items of one category cannot be intermingled with items from another category.

Federal laws and various agency requirements prescribe standards for the vault necessary for storage of national security classified materials. Specifications for construction of such a vault are available from the National Archives and Records Service. This vault area should be about 1,500 square feet, with adjustable steel shelving sufficient to hold 1,500 linear feet of material. The balance of the area will be used for locking file cabinets and processing tables. This vault should have a "day door" and adequate ventilation, as staff will frequently need to work in this area.

The area used for storage of donor restricted material and rare/valuable material should be separated by a semi-movable partition. The quantity of donor restricted material will be initially high, but will decline over the years as the need to keep this material closed decreases. Conversely, the material which will be placed in the rare/valuable category will increase over the years as more time is allocated to processing and preserving the documents. This area should have the same floor space as the security classified vault (1,500 square feet), but should be entirely devoted to adjustable steel shelving.

---

*Courtesy of Roanoke College, Fintel Library

† Courtesy of Gerald R. Ford Presidential Library

l. Physical Treatment Quarters

See figs. A.21 and A.22.

Area:	Shipping/receiving.
Room Name:	Treatment room.
Square Footage:	200 sq ft.
Function:	Treatment of contaminated, and/or wet materials prior to permanent or long-term placement in stacks. Cleaning in this area is assumed to be without water—it may involve a vacuum cleaner or a brushing process, or simply unpacking and discarding dirty wrappings. More detailed preservation related cleaning will be done in the conservation lab once it is determined the materials are not contagious.
Adjacencies:	Dirty room, distribution corridor.
Capacity:	Blast freezer plus space for handling contaminated and cleaned materials.
Hours of Operation:	Normal office hours (7:30 to 4:30).
Special Finishes:	Archival quality, hard floor.
Special Ventilation:	Should prevent contamination of general stack areas.
Plumbing:	Drain, water source.
Gas Services:	None.
Power:	Access to 220 volt power on single circuit to support commercial blast freezer. Convenience outlets for maintenance purposes.
Lighting:	Direct overhead lighting.
Communications:	Ability to hear paging system and loading dock doorbell.
Fixed Equipment:	None assigned to this area.
Moveable Equipment:	Blast freezer such as Wei T'o Freezer/Fumigator (6′H × 5′W × 40″D).
Furnishings:	Small work table, kitchen counter high (30″ × 60″ shown).
Special Requirements:	Card key locks. Double door access (blast freezer is LARGE!).
Notes:	

FIGURE A.21   Treatment room, Delaware Public Archives. Illustrations and text for space program for Delaware Public Archives, produced by Philip D. Leighton for Moeckel Carbonell Associates Inc., Architects, Wilmington, Delaware

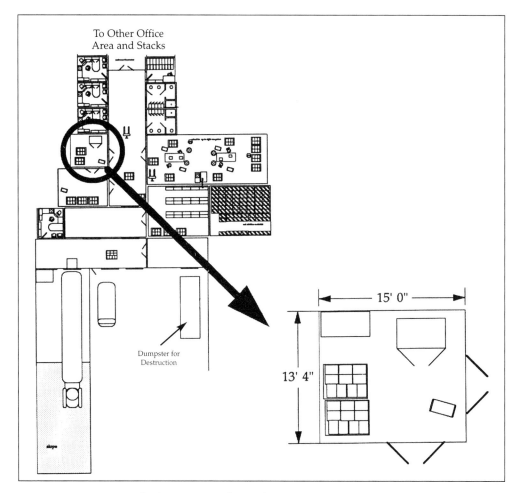

To Other Office
Area and Stacks

Dumpster for
Destruction

15' 0"

13' 4"

FIGURE A.22   Second of two space sheets for the Delaware Public Archives, treatment room. This is part of the same space represented by the bubble diagram in fig. A.10. Illustrations and text for space program for Delaware Public Archives, produced by Philip D. Leighton for Moeckel Carbonell Associates Inc., Architects, Wilmington, Delaware

m. Mail Room*

UBC Central Library Phase I

8.0 Mail Room

This component will accommodate receiving and shipping of all materials for the UBC Library system and the Central Library.

Component Summary:

Sub Component	NASM	CGSM
8.1 Mail Room	129.1	174.3
TOTAL	129.1	174.3

Description

The Mail Room will receive all incoming deliveries, including mail from Canada Post, books and other materials from branches of the UBC Library, all new books from the Library Processing Centre, and bulk supplies, equipment, and furniture for the Library system. All materials are sorted and sent

---

*University of British Columbia. Courtesy of Process Four Design Ltd., Vancouver, British Columbia

to the appropriate part of the system. Outgoing materials are moved in plastic bins, on booktrucks, or on pallets or dollies as required. Circulation receives a large volume of materials from the Mail Room, as does Periodicals. Large volumes (2 pallets) of photocopy paper are received regularly.

Space List

		Quantity	Unit NASM	Area NASM	Total NASM
Service					129.1
8.1.01	Workstation, Administrative Clerk	1	4.2	4.2	
8.1.02	Workstation, Clerk	1	3.3	3.3	
8.1.03	Staff Lockers	2	0.5	0.9	
8.1.04	Loading Dock	1	46.5	46.5	
8.1.05	Holding and Sorting Area	1	55.7	55.7	
8.1.06	Central Supplies	1	18.6	18.6	
Collections: None					0
Use and Study: None					0

n. Receiving and Shipping Quarters

See fig. A.23.

Space Description — Santa Cruz Campus   Space Number __19__

__1__ Like spaces

Project ___University Library, Unit 1___

Department _____

Use of Space

RECEIVING AND SHIPPING ROOM

Receiving and shipping room for all materials coming to or leaving the Library; temporary storage space for acquisitions; work area for minor repairs to library equipment.

Area and Occupancy
Assignable area each space in square feet: ___565___
Classroom or Seminar — number of seats: _____
Teaching Laboratory — number of student stations: _____
Teaching Laboratory — number of lockers per station: _____
Other spaces — normal number of occupants: ___1___

Architectural Requirements
Location: ___Contiguous with the Technical Processes Area; must be adjacent to and on same level as loading platform___
Dimensions: _____
Special floor loading: _____
Special acoustical: ___Sound control of noisy operations___
Other: _____

Mechanical and Electrical Requirements
Sink with utilities: ___Sink with drainboard___
Lab utilities: _____
Special environmental conditions: _____
Special electric services: _____
Special exhaust: _____
Other: _____

(Continued)

FIGURE A.23 Receiving and shipping room. University of California at Santa Cruz, library program. Courtesy of the Library

FIGURE A.23   (Continued)

Comments

_____Space for storing 8 bindery boxes (3' × 1') in 2 piles of 4 _____
_____Space for parking book trucks and moving book trucks around _____
_____Doors wide enough to take furniture and equipment. _____

Equipment — Fixed and Movable

Quantity	Description		
1	storage cabinet, 36×78×24	1	5-drawer file
1	gravity-feed conveyor to receiving	1	large paper cutter
	desk, Technical Processes area	1	small paper cutter
1	postal scales	1	wastebasket, extra large
1	gummed paper dispenser	1	wastebasket
1	postal meter		
1	custom-built work table		
1	workbench		
1	small tool cabinet		
8	bookcases, 36×90×10		
3	book trucks		
1	hand truck		
1	dolly		
1	desk, 60×30		
1	stool		
2	typist chairs		

Prepared by _____D. T. Clark_____   Date _____May 1963_____ DDP-4

17. Technical Review of Building Plan*

Value Engineering and Technical Review

The necessary reconstruction of the Powell Library Building, in order to provide adequate life safety to the occupants of the building, is extensive in scope, and consequently disruptive to the campus and programs housed within the building. In order to evaluate the cost benefit of proceeding with extensive renovation, a value engineering review has been conducted of the conceptual approach to the project. This technical review is discussed below, and the description of the proposed reconstruction follows in section V.

The architectural firm of Leidenfrost/Horowitz Associates, was commissioned to conduct a Value Engineering Study of the project as originally developed by the firm of Moore/Ruble/Yudell, Architects and Planners. The purpose of this review was:

- to investigate and evaluate the project design concept;
- to comment on the suitability of the design recommendations to appropriately and economically meet the needs of the University;
- to explore and define design options or alternative concepts that might more appropriately meet the University's needs;
- and to provide a historical evaluation including consideration of the campus urban fabric in order to assess the appropriateness of the reconstruction work.

---

*University of California at Los Angeles, Powell Library. Used by permission of UCLA Capital Programs

The value engineering team explored seven different alternatives to the originally proposed project. These seven alternatives basically fall into three general categories. The first category includes three alternatives which are modifications, in varying degrees, to the original Moore/Ruble/Yudell proposal. The second category includes two alternatives which explore the potential of lesser modifications to the central stack area of the building. The third category explores two alternatives which propose different uses for the building, including total demolition. Alternatives are discussed briefly below.

Alternative 1A is essentially the same as the Moore/Ruble/Yudell proposal, except the addition over the loading dock, on the south side of the building, has been omitted, and the new stack structure has been reduced by about 15,000 GSF. The total ASF is reduced by approximately 7,000 square feet resulting in smaller office accommodations and diminished flexibility of space assignment and building circulation.

Alternative 1B is similar to 1A, but with one significant exception: stack levels 1.5 and 3 are omitted. This reduces the floor area by about 16,000 ASF. The loss of the third floor in the Central Stack area impedes the flexibility of use and the circulation between wings at that level. Stack area could be recaptured in the future by adding one or two levels of multi-tier shelving on the second floor.

Alternative 1C is similar to the Moore/Ruble/Yudell proposal, but has only minimal floor reductions. The only substantive changes are the elimination of the infill stack floor (level 1.5), and a decrease in the ASF available in the stack structure. The total ASF is approximately 8,000 square feet less than the original proposal.

Alternative 2A maintains the same configuration of the existing building, but with new stacks. The existing metal stacks would be removed and replaced with new metal library stacks in keeping with present standards of function and safety. This process would reduce the total stack space from the current 75,000 ASF to approximately 64,500 ASF. The stack areas would have sprinklers installed throughout, and the stack areas would be separated by two-hour fire doors. The building walls and frame would be seismically reinforced, and new exit stairs and passages to the exterior would be constructed. A higher degree of safety than presently available would be realized by the widening of aisles and exit paths, and improved lighting. Access for the mobility impaired would be provided in the stack areas. The ventilating ducts and other components would be brought up to current fire protection standards. While the fire-resistive and life safety measures are superior to that of the current building it still does not provide the protection of a true fire-resistive concrete floor system at each level; and exiting paths remain difficult. In addition, this alternative does not provide for any functional programmatic improvements, or allow for the future flexibility of space assignments.

Alternative 2B is the same as presented in Alternative 2A except, in reconstructing the stack areas, the south wall would be moved outward a bay to provide additional floor areas. The additional stack area could be utilized to house other undergraduate libraries. This alternative has all of the disadvantages of Alternative 2A, but loss of space on the south side of the building is minimized compared to other alternatives.

Alternatives 3 and 3A provide for a new College Library building with the Powell Library building space being reassigned or the building demolished. If the building were not demolished the stack shelving would be removed and the seismic renovation and building systems would be upgraded. The interior space would be reassigned for other University programmatic functions. The current museum quality rooms could be utilized as exhibition space, or the building could serve as a staging arena for other projects. These alternatives, however, are significantly more costly than all others.

The value engineering team strongly recommended that the proposed project to be implemented should be either the original proposal that was submitted by Moore/Ruble/Yudell, or one of the alternative proposals presented as modifications to the original proposal as discussed earlier. The Campus is focusing on the alternatives similar to the original proposal with the exception of eliminating stack level 1.5. The proposed project . . . follows this recommendation.

18. Phasing of Construction*

Detailed List of Future Phases Areas

The following table lists the areas for the identified components of Future Phases, which are the replacement areas for the existing Sedgewick and Main functions not included in Phase One. Note that the list includes only those components currently in the existing Main and Sedgewick Libraries. Additional components have been identified for inclusion in the new Central Library, but a calculation of the areas required for these was outside the scope of this study. These include the Library Processing Centre and the Music Library, which would likely put the new Central Library in the range of 56.000 BGSM (600,000 BGSF).

	Total CGSM	Total NASM	Service NASM	Coll NASM	Study NASM
Component Gross Factors			1.35	1.20	1.35
Circulation	226	167	167		
Fine Arts	1,600	1,319	111	1,208	
Science Reference	509	399	195	204	
Wilson	147	116	51	65	
Preservation	125	93	93		
*Gifts and Exchanges	161	125	70	56	
Extension Library	143	116	23	93	
Graphics	125	93	93		
Special Collections	2,993	2,481	111	2,369	
Maps	723	585	139	446	
PATSCAN	68	51	46	5	
General Collections					
Phase I Growth to 2011	2,676	2,230		2,230	
Remaining HSS	11,183	8,919	418	5,714	2,787
Science	2,397	1,997		1,997	
Phase I Other Collections					
Growth to 2011	323	269		269	
Storage	4,537	3,781		3,781	
*School of Library, Archival,					
& Information	1,329	985	836		149
Total Areas Future Phases	29,267	23,727	2,355	18,437	2,936
Total BGSM Future Phases	33,657				

Asterisked (*) component areas are based on areas from existing UBC space inventory.

---

*Extract from *The Central Library Phase One, University of British Columbia: Predesign Report,* vol. 1, July 1992 (Vancouver: Arthur Erickson [and] Aitken Wreglesworth Associates), p. 13. Courtesy of Architectura Inc. and the University of British Columbia

Assumptions

The amount of growth which will be accommodated is used to determine the Collections areas. Study areas are the result of existing Main Library carrel counts calculated with revised carrel area allocations, except asterisked (*) components. Service Areas are based on inventory of existing furnishings at standard area allocations, except asterisked (*) components.

Future Phases are calculated for 2011 collections at 87% full, allowing for about ten years (from opening day) of internal growth at 2.9% annually (not compounded), longer if the growth rate is lower. On opening day in 2001, stacks are about 67.5% full.

Volumes stored at 158.44 per NASM at 87% full. Other items at existing areas per item, adjusted for accessible aisles.

Future Phases Component Relationships

This diagram indicates groupings of components identified for Future Phases which would allow an expanded Central Library to accommodate the required areas, and reflect the possible arrangement of spaces in the subsequent development of the Central Library. They are grouped by the degree of relationship to Phase One. A small group of components is integral with Phase One, and another group is directly related to Phase One. A third group is not directly related to Phase One [see fig. A.24].

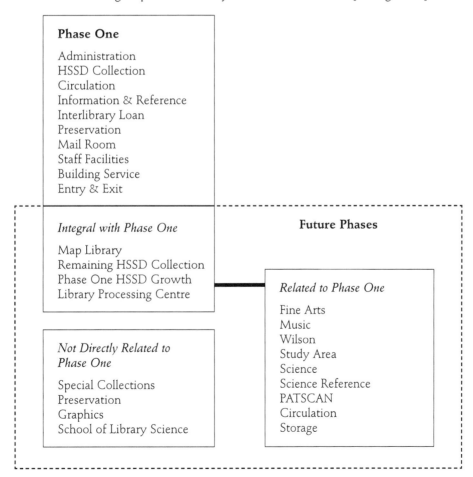

FIGURE A.24   Phasing diagram, University of British Columbia, Walter C. Koerner Library

APPENDIX B

Formulas, Guidelines, and Standards

The golden rule is that there are no golden rules.

—George Bernard Shaw,
Maxims for Revolutionists

B.1 Conversion of Measurements

To help with conversion between metric/customary measurements and formulas, a selection of common equivalencies is provided. (The U.S. Customary scale differs from the British Imperial System from which it had its origins. The metric scale is also known as the International System of Units.)

U.S. Customary to Metric Conversion

Area:

1 square inch (in.^{2})   = 6.45 square centimeters (cm^2)
1 square foot (ft^2)   = 929.0 cm^2 [0.0929 square meter (m^2)]
1 square yard (yd^2)   = 0.836 m^2
1 acre (a) [43,560 ft^2] = 0.4047 hectare (ha)
1 square mile (mi^2)   = 2.59 square kilometers (km^2)

Force (used in converting floor loading values for structural requirements):

1 pound per square inch (lb/in.^{2}) = 6.89457 kilo-Newton's per square meter (kN/m^2)
1 pound per square foot (lb/ft^2) = 0.047879 kilo-Newton's per square meter (kN/m^2)
                                      = 47.8789 Newton's per square meter (N/m^2)

Length:

    1 inch (in.)   = 2.54 centimeters (cm)
    1 foot (ft) [12 in.]   = 30.48 cm
    1 yard (yd) [3 ft]   = 91.44 cm [0.914 meter (m)]
    1 mile (mi) [5,280 ft] = 1.610 kilometers (km)

Light:

    1 footcandle = 1 lumen per ft^2
    1 footcandle = 0.0929 lux

Pressure:

    1 pound per square inch ($lb/in.^2$ or psi) = 0.0704 kilogram per square
                                          centimeter (kg/cm^2)
    1 pound per square foot (lb/ft^2)   = 4.8824 kilograms per square
                                          meter (kg/m^2)
    1 bar [1,000 millibars (mb)]   = 1.020 kg/cm^2

Temperature:

    32° Fahrenheit = 0° Celsius
    (Fahrenheit × 5/9 after subtracting 32 = Celsius)

Volume:

    1 cubic inch ($in.^3$)   = 16.4 cubic centimeters (cm^3)
    1 cubic foot (ft^3)   = 0.0283 m^3
    1 cubic yard (yd^3)   = 0.7646 cubic meter (m^3)
    1 quart (qt) [0.25 U.S. gallon (gal)] = 0.95 liter (l)
    1 gallon [4 quarts]   = 3.79 liters (l)

Weight:

    1 pound (lb) [16 ounces (oz)] = 453.6 grams (g)
    1 U.S. ton (tn) [2,000 lb]   = 907.2 kilograms (kg)
                             = 0.9072 metric ton (MT)

Metric to U.S. Customary Conversion

Area:

    1 square centimeter (cm^2) = 0.155 square inch ($in.^2$)
    1 square meter (m^2)   = 10.76 square feet (ft^2)
                            = 1.196 square yards (yd^2)
    1 hectare (ha)   = 2.4710 acres (a)

Force (used in converting floor loading values for structural requirements):

    1 Newton per square meter (N/m^2)   = 0.02089 pounds per square
                                          foot (lb/ft^2)
    1 kilo-Newton per square meter (kN/m^2) = 0.14504 pounds per square
                                          inch (lb/in^2)
                                          = 20.886 pounds per square
                                          foot (lb/ft^2)

Length:

    1 millimeter (mm)   = 0.0394 inch (in.)
    1 cm [10 mm]   = 0.3937 in.
    1 meter (m) [100 cm]   = 39.37 in. [3.28 feet (ft)]
    1 kilometer (km) [1,000 m] = 0.621 mile (mi)

Light:

> 1 lux = 1 lumen per m^2
>   = 10.76 footcandles

Pressure:

> 1 kilogram per square centimeter (kg/cm^2) = 14.20 pounds per square inch (lb/in.^{2})

Temperature:

> 0° Celsius = 32° Fahrenheit
> (Celsius × 9/5 then add 32 = Fahrenheit)

Volume:

> 1 cubic centimeter (cm^3) = 0.0610 cubic inch (in.^{3})
> 1 cubic meter (m^3)   = 35.314 cubic ft (ft^3)
>   = 1.31 cubic yards (yd^3)
> 1 liter (l)   = 1.06 quarts (qt)
>   = 0.264 gallon (gal)

Weight:

> 1 kilogram (kg) = 2.20 pounds (lb)
>   = 0.0011 ton (tn)

B.2 Column Spacing

B.2.1 Stack Areas

No one size is perfect for column sizes or column spacing.

Other things being equal, the larger the bay size, the better, so long as it does not unduly increase construction costs, floor-to-floor heights, or column sizes.

Column spacing—that is, the distance between column centers—is generally more important in concentrated stack areas than in combined stack and reading areas, because in the latter suitable adjustments are easier to make.

Clear space between columns—this is not the space between column centers—in a column range should preferably be a multiple of the shelving unit (typically 3 ft or 900 mm) plus an additional 4 in. (102 mm) to allow for irregularities in the column sizes and for the end uprights in the range. Note that some shelving types require a "growth" factor—that is, the center-to-center spacing required for each section is slightly more than the nominal section width.

Range spacing and range lengths have a greater effect on book capacity than the distance between columns in a column range. The reduction of space between range centers by 1 in. (25 mm) increases book capacity by approximately 2 percent. The reduction of space used for cross aisles at right angles to the ranges is also of importance.

If practical, columns should be no greater than 14 in. (356 mm) in the direction of a range, and the dimension in the other direction should be kept down to 18 in. (457 mm). If over 14 in. (356 mm) in the direction of the range is necessary, the column might almost as well be 32 in. (813 mm) in that direction. It could then occupy the space of a full stack section and perhaps enclose a heating duct. If a column is wider than the range, it will jut into the stack aisle. Irregular length stack sections are inconvenient, are unduly expensive, and can often be replaced to advantage by a lectern or consultation table.

Tables B.1A and B.1B deal with standard layouts in commonly used module sizes without special attention given to ADA. (A discussion of module can also be found in Section 12.3.2.)

The following comments may be useful in connection with tables B.1A and B.1B.

1. SPACING OF 3 FT 9 IN. (1.143 M) or less should be used for closed-access storage only where handicapped access is not required, with ranges not more than 30 ft (9.144 m) long and not more than 18 in. (0.457 m) deep.
2. SPACING 3 FT 9 IN. TO 4 FT 1 IN. (1.143 TO 1.245 M) can be used to advantage for large, little-used, limited-access stacks, with ranges up to 30 ft (9.1 m) long. Closed-access ranges up to 60 ft (18.3 m) long have been used successfully with 18 in. (0.457 m) or less deep, 4 ft or 4 ft 1 in. (1.219 to 1.245 m) on centers. Where conformance with wheelchair access codes is required, wider spacing will be necessary.
3. SPACING 4 FT 2 IN. TO 4 FT 6 IN. (1.270 TO 1.372 M) can be used for open-access stacks, preferably held to 18 in. (0.457 m) in depth with the range length based on the amount of use. With 18-in.-deep (0.457-m) shelving units and 4 ft 6 in. (1.372-m) spacing, most (but not all) handicapped accessibility codes will be satisfied, provided a fully clear 36-in. (0.914-m) range aisle is realized. In this context, it should be noted that many (but not all) shelving manufacturers actually require 19 in. (0.483 m) of space for what is called 18-in. (0.457-m) shelving.
4. SPACING 4 FT 6 IN. TO 5 FT (1.372 TO 1.524 M) is generous even for heavily used, open-access undergraduate stacks if ranges are five sections long and 4 ft 6 in. (1.372 m) on centers, and in some cases up to ten sections long if 5 ft (1.524 m) on centers. In most cases, handicapped accessibility requirements can be met within this spacing category.
5. SPACING 5 FT TO 5 FT 10 IN. (1.524 TO 1.778 M) is unnecessarily generous for any regular stack shelving and is often adequate for periodical display cases and for heavily used reference collections.
6. SPACING 6 FT (1.829 M) OR GREATER is adequate for newspaper shelving and generous for periodical display cases.

Square bays are more flexible than those that form a long rectangle and are generally somewhat cheaper if the ceiling height is limited. But if the latter are used, the number of suitable sizes can be greatly increased. Table B.2 shows possibilities with 22 ft 6 in. in one direction and different spacing in the other direction.

Similar tables can be prepared for a multitude of dimensions, including metric dimensions. (Other examples may be found in Chapter 12.)

If section lengths are changed from 3 ft to some other size, tables comparable to tables B.1A, B.1B, and B.2 should be prepared with those lengths as a base. In table B.2, note that the bay size is a multiple of the sections between the columns *plus* one section.

Always keep in mind the probable cost advantages available if standard sizes are used. Remember that columns so large that they interfere with aisles are seldom necessary.

TABLE B.1A Square Modules with the Column Spacing a Multiple of the Shelving Unit (plus half a shelving unit for the column itself)[a]

Bay Size	Sections between Columns Standard 3 ft	Sections between Columns Standard 900 mm	Ranges to a Bay	Range Spacing on Centers
19'6"	6		5	3'10"
×	6		4	4'10 1/2"
19'6"	6		3	6'6"
5.7 m		6	5	1.154
×		6	4	1.442
5.7 m		6	3	1.923
22'6"	7		6	3'9"
×	7		5	4'6"
22'6"	7		4	5'7 1/2"
6.8 m		7	6	1.133
×		7	5	1.360
6.8 m		7	4	1.700
25'6"	8		7	3'7 5/7"
×	8		6	4'3"
25'6"	8		5	5'1 1/5"
	8		4	6'4 1/2"
7.7 m		8	7	1.100
×		8	6	1.283
7.7 m		8	5	1.540
		8	4	1.925
28'6"	9		8	3'6 3/4"
×	9		7	4'0 6/7"
28'6"	9		6	4'9"
	9		5	5'8 2/5"
8.6 m		9	8	1.075
×		9	7	1.229
8.6 m		9	6	1.433
		9	5	1.72

[a] Column size should not be wider than the depth of the range; 14 × 14 in. up to 14 × 18 in. or, for the metric, 350 × 350 mm up to 350 × 450 mm.

TABLE B.1B Square Modules with Column Spacing a Multiple of Standard Section[a]

Bay Size	Sections between Columns Standard 3 ft	Sections between Columns Standard 900 mm	Ranges to a Bay	Range Spacing on Centers
18'	5		5	3'7 1/5"
×	5		4	4'6"
18'	5		3	6'
5.4 m		5	5	1.080
×		5	4	1.350
5.4 m		5	3	1.800
21'	6		6	3'6"
×	6		5	4'2 2/5"
21'	6		4	5'3"
6.3 m		6	6	1.050
×		6	5	1.260
6.3 m		6	4	1.575
24'	7		7	3'5 1/7"
×	7		6	4'
24'	7		5	4'9 3/5"
	7		4	6'
7.2 m		7	7	1.029
×		7	6	1.200
7.2 m		7	5	1.440
		7	4	1.800
27'	8		8	3'4 1/2"
×	8		7	3'10 2/7"
27'	8		6	4'6"
	8		5	5'4 4/5"
	8		4	6'9"
8.1 m		8	8	1.012
×		8	7	1.157
8.1 m		8	6	1.350
		8	5	1.620
		8	4	2.025

[a] Columns should not be wider than the depth of the range. Suggested is 18 × 32 in. or, for the metric, 450 × 800 mm.

TABLE B.2   Long Rectangular Modules, 22 ft 6 in. in One Direction[a]

Bay Size	Ranges to a Bay	Range Spacing on Centers
22'6" × 18'	4	4'6"
22'6" × 20'	5	4'
22'6" × 20'10"	5	4'2"
22'6" × 21'8"	5	4'4"
22'6" × 24'	6	4'
22'6" × 25'	6	4'2"
22'6" × 26'	6	4'4"
22'6" × 27'	6	4'6"

[a] A bay of this size will give seven sections 3 ft long between 14-in. columns in the direction of the column range. The column sizes suggested in table B.1A are suitable here.

B.2.2 Seating Accommodations

Column spacing is of less importance in connection with seating accommodations than with shelving. Tables B.3 and B.4 show the maximum number of carrels available on one side of standard-sized bays and the number of studies available in such bays, assuming the use of minimum-sized reading accommodations. Some would argue that by providing more space, greater utilization will be realized. Provision for wheelchairs will also have its effect. The authors urge care in using these data.

Any small room will seem less confining if it has a window, and, because window wall space is generally at a premium, a room can well have one of its short sides on the window wall.

TABLE B.3   Carrels[a]

Bay Size	Open[b]	Double- or Triple- Staggered[c]	Small Closed[d]	Large Closed[e]
18' (5.5 m)	4	4	4	3
19 1/2' (5.9 m)	4	4	4	3
21' (6.4 m)	5	4	4	4
22 1/2' (6.9 m)	5	5	5	4
24' (7.3 m)	6	5	5	4
25 1/2' (7.8 m)	6	5	5	5
27' (8.2 m)	6	6	6	5

[a] A carrel, as used here, is an area in which a reader is cut off from any neighbor who is closer than 3 ft (914 mm) on either side or front and back and one side. The minimum desirable width of an adequate carrel working surface is 2 ft 9 in. (838 mm), which is as useful as 3 ft (914 mm) for each person at a table with two or more persons sitting side by side. Minimum depth suggested is 20 in. (508 mm).

[b] Distance between centers should be not less than 4 ft 3 in. (1.295 m), unless the front table leg is set back 4 to 6 in. (102 to 152 mm) and armless chairs are used, in which case the distance on centers can be reduced to 4 ft. (1.219 m). Any distance over 4 ft

6 in. (1.372 m) is unnecessarily generous. A clear space of 27 in. (686 mm) or more between working surface and partition at the rear is recommended. A shelf above the table interferes with overhead lighting and makes a deeper table desirable.

[c] Distance between centers should seldom be less than 4 ft 6 in. (1.372 m); 5 ft (1.524 m) is preferred; anything greater is unnecessarily generous. With triple-staggered carrels, the back of the center one should be held down to no more than 10 in. (254 mm) above the tabletop if it is believed the person in the middle would feel boxed in.

[d] Distance between centers should be not less than 4 ft 6 in. (1.372 m); 5 ft (1.52 4 m) is preferred. Watch out for ventilation. A window is psychologically desirable. Closed carrels are not recommended for undergraduates or any student not actually engaged in writing a dissertation. Glass in the door or grilles can be provided for supervision.

[e] A room less than 6 ft (1.829 m) long at right angles to the desk will permit shelves above the desk or a bookcase behind the occupant, but preferably not both. One less than 6 ft (1.829 m) parallel to the desk will not permit a 4-ft-long (1.219-m) desk, and a second chair, and may make it necessary to open the door outward.

TABLE B.4   Faculty Studies and Small Multipurpose Rooms

Bay Size	Small Faculty Study[a]	Small Conference Room or Generous Faculty Study[b]
18′ (5.5 m)	3	2
19 1/2′ (5.9 m)	3	2
21′ (6.4 m)	3	2
22 1/2′ (6.9 m)	3	2
24′ (7.3 m)	4	3
25 1/2′ (7.8 m)	4	3
27′ (8.2 m)	4	3

[a] A room of this size can house a large desk, shelving, and a filing case, and permit a door to open in, except for those studies provided for handicapped persons, where additional space will be required. It is suggested that a "generous" faculty study be provided for this purpose.

[b] This will provide for conference rooms for four, an adequate small staff office, or a generous faculty study. It should be at least 8 ft (2.438 m) in the clear in one direction and have a total area of over 70 ft^2 (6.5 m^2).

B.3 Ceiling Heights and Floor Areas

Minimum and maximum ceiling heights and floor areas involve basic functional and aesthetic problems. Suggestions from the functional point of view are proposed as an aid in reaching decisions.

B.3.1 Ceiling Heights

Ceiling heights greater than functionally necessary may be desirable aesthetically but involve increased cost, unused cubage, and larger areas to allow the stairs to reach a higher level. Ceiling heights have desirable functional minimums also and, if reduced beyond these minimums, may be unpleasant to the users, may seriously affect book capacity and flexibility, and may needlessly complicate lighting and ventilation. Table B.5 suggests functional minimums and maximums.

TABLE B.5 Clear Ceiling Heights

Area	Suggested Minimum[a]	Suggested Functional Maximum[b]
Bookstack[c]	7'6" (2.286 m)	8'6" (2.590 m)
Stacks with lights at right angle to ranges[d]	8'4" (2.540 m)	8'9" (2.667 m)
Stacks with lights on range tops functioning by ceiling reflection	9'0" (2.743 m)	9'6" (2.896 m)
Stacks with fire sprinklers	9'0" (2.743 m)	10' (3.048 m)
Compact shelving with fire sprinklers	9'8" (2.946 m)	10'8" (3.251 m)
Archival shelving (4-post) with fire sprinklers	9'6" (2.896 m)	11' (3.353 m)
Compact archival shelving (4-post) with sprinklers	10'2" (3.099 m)	11'8" (3.556 m)
Reading areas under 100 ft² (9.29 m²)	7'6" (2.286 m)	8'6" (2.590 m)
Individual seating in large areas	8'4" (2.540 m)	9'6" (2.896 m)
Large reading rooms over 100 ft long (30.5 m) broken by screens or bookcases	9'6" (2.896 m)	10'6" (3.200 m)
Entrance or main level with over 20,000 ft² (1,860 m²)	9'6" (2.896 m)	10'6" (3.200 m)
Floor with mezzanine[e]	15'6" (4.724 m)	18'6" (5.639 m)
Order-picker storage	35' (10.668 m)	40' (12.192 m)

[a] Heights lower than specified have been used successfully on occasion, but ceiling lights should be recessed and good ventilation assured. Financial savings will be comparatively small. Note that the local codes may affect the minimum height.

[b] Greater heights may be useful aesthetically and provide added flexibility by making areas available for a wider range of purposes.

[c] 7 ft 6 in. (2.286 m) is the lowest height that permits an adequate protective base (equivalent of a kickplate) and seven shelves 12 in. (305 mm) on centers (standard for most academic libraries) with suitable clearance at the top. The top shelf will be 6 ft 4 in. (1.930 m) above the floor, the greatest height that can be reached without difficulty by a person 5 ft (1.524 m) tall. Space above 7 ft 6 in. is not useful for storage of open-access collections and will be confusing if used for other shelving.

[d] This height used with fluorescent tubes, at right angles to the ranges, permits stack ranges to be shifted closer together or farther apart without rewiring, and is high enough so that heat from the tubes will not damage the books on the top shelf. If the fixtures are flush or nearly flush with the ceiling, the clear height can be reduced a few inches.

[e] Mezzanines provide inexpensive space if they occupy at least 50 percent of the floor area (building codes may prohibit them unless the mezzanine is partitioned off and made a separate unit), and if the overall height of the two resulting levels is not much more than 6 ft (1.829 m) greater than would be provided if there were no mezzanine.

B.3.2 Floor Areas

Both the number of floors in a library and the area of each floor may be important functionally and aesthetically. Decisions in regard to floors may be influenced by the site surroundings, the slope of the ground, and the value of the property. It is obvious, however, that a skyscraper with only 5,000 ft^2 (465 m^2) on each floor would be undesirable, and that a 250,000-ft^2 (23,225-m^2) area on one floor would involve unnecessary and undesirable horizontal traffic.

Table B.6 makes suggestions (which at best are only approximations) as to the percentage of the gross floor area of a library building that functionally should be on the entrance or central-services level in a typical academic library.

These computations are approximations only, but figures smaller than those in the last column will often necessitate shifting part of the central services to other levels and, incidentally, may add considerably to staff payrolls.

TABLE B.6   Suggested Formulas for Percentage of Gross Floor Area Functionally Desirable on the Central-Services Level[a]

Gross Building Area in ft^2 (m^2)	Size of Collections in Volumes (in thousands)	Minimum Percentages of Gross Area on Central-Services Level
Under 20,000 (−1,860)	Under 100	40–50
20,000–45,000 (1,860–4,180)	100–250	33 1/3–40
40,000–80,000 (3,720–7,430)	250–500	25–33 1/3
75,000–150,000 (6,970–13,940)	500–1,000	20–30
135,000+ (12,540+)	1,000+	16 2/3–25

[a] Central services as used here include the main control point, circulation and reference services, reference and bibliographical collections, the public catalog, and acquisition and catalog departments. Note that automation may facilitate location of technical processing departments on a level other than that accommodating central services.

B.4 Reader Accommodations

Seating accommodations for readers and the service to readers are the largest space consumers in most libraries. The required areas depend on:

1. The number of accommodations provided
2. The types of accommodations and the percentage of each
3. The dimensions of the working surfaces for each type of accommodation
4. The average floor area required for each type of accommodation
5. Additional space required for service to readers

B.4.1 Number of Accommodations Provided

The formula used to determine the percentage of students for whom seating accommodations are required should depend on:

1. The quality of the student body and the faculty. The higher the quality, the greater the library use.
2. The library facilities provided. The more satisfactory the seating accommodations and the services provided, the greater the use.
3. The quality of the collections. Superior collections increase use.
4. The curriculum. In general, students in the humanities and social sciences use the library more than do those in the pure and applied sciences.
5. The emphasis placed on textbook instruction, which tends to reduce library use, and the emphasis placed by the faculty on the library and on nontextbook reading.
6. The percentage of graduate students and the fields in which they work.
7. Whether the student body is resident or commuting, and, if the former, whether the dormitories provide suitable study facilities. Heaviest library use in most residential institutions is in the evening; in commuter institutions, during the daytime hours.
8. Whether the location is rural, suburban, or urban. Large population centers tend to decrease evening use because of housing/transportation factors and other available activities and attractions.
9. The departmental library arrangements, which may make available other reading facilities and reduce the use of the central library.
10. The institution's policy in regard to use by persons other than those connected with it.

Table B.7 suggests formulas for determining the percentage of students for whom to provide seating.

TABLE B.7 Formulas for Percentage of Students for Whom Seating Accommodations Are Suggested

Type of Institution	Percentage
Graduate-level professional school library	50–100%
Arts and humanities research branch	50–80
Superior residential coeducational liberal arts college in rural area or small town	50–60
Superior residential liberal arts college for men or women in rural area or small town	45–50
Superior residential liberal arts college in a small city	40–45
Graduate-level science research branch	35–50
Superior residential university	35–40
Typical residential university	25–30
Typical commuting university	10–20

B.4.2 Types of Seating Accommodations and the Percentage of Each Type

1. UNDERGRADUATE STUDENT ACCOMMODATIONS

a. *Tables for four or more.* Not more than 20 percent. Should be largely restricted to those in reserved-book and reference rooms.

b. *Lounge chairs.* Not more than 15 percent. Should in general be restricted to lounge areas, smoking rooms, or current-periodical rooms, or used to break up unpleasantly long rows of other types of accommodations. In many libraries 8 to 10 percent of seating of this kind is adequate.

c. *Individual accommodations.* Up to 85 percent. In most cases, these should provide for working surfaces cut off from immediately adjacent neighbors, by aisles or partitions on one, two, or three sides. The partitions should be high enough—52 in. (1.321 m)—so that heads do not bob up or down above them and cause visual distraction. These accommodations may include:

(1) Tables for one. These can be quite satisfactory along a wall or screen if the readers all face in the same direction. When placed in a reading area, they are not recommended.
(2) Tables for two with partitions down the center. For limited use only.
(3) Tables for four or more with partitions in both directions. A great improvement over a table for four without partitions.
(4) Pinwheel arrangement for four. Satisfactory, but requires more space than 3 above.
(5) Double carrels with readers facing in different directions. Not as satisfactory as 6 below.
(6) Double-staggered carrels.
(7) Pairs of double-staggered carrels on both sides of a screen.
(8) Triple-staggered carrels in place of three stack ranges or in a large reading area.
(9) Rows of single carrels at right angles to a wall in bookstack or reading area.
(10) Single carrels in place of last stack section at the end of a blind stack aisle.
(11) Typing carrels similar to 10 above, but with special acoustic protection.
(12) Rows of double carrels in a reading area or in place of two stack ranges.

Closed carrels are rarely recommended for undergraduates. Shelves in carrels tend to encourage undesirable monopolization. A shelf outside the carrel with an open or a locked cupboard provides for books and papers to be reserved and makes possible longer hours of carrel use.

2. GRADUATE STUDENT ACCOMMODATIONS

a. *At tables for multiple seating.* Not recommended for general seating, although some tables are desirable for those who feel a need to spread out or who are using very large volumes, maps, or newspapers.

b. *Open carrels* of any of the types proposed in 1 above. Graduate carrels may have shelves over the working surface, but this will require deeper tabletops because of lighting problems, unless the shelves are installed at one side.

c. *Closed carrels.* See C and D below for working surface dimensions and requirements. Closed carrels require special care for satisfactory lighting and ventilation. Unless larger than necessary to provide adequate working surfaces, claustrophobia tends to result. A window for each carrel or an attractive grille on at least one side will help.

3. FACULTY ACCOMMODATIONS

If possible, closed studies should be provided for faculty members engaged in research projects that require the use of library materials. They should generally not be used as offices. See C and D below for working surface dimensions and floor area requirements.

B.4.3 Dimensions of Working Surface for Each Type of Seating Accommodation

Table B.8 gives suggested minimum and adequate dimensions. No attempt is made to propose maximum or generous sizes.

TABLE B.8   Suggested Working Surface Area for Each Person[a]

Type of Accommodation	Minimum Size	Adequate Size
Table for multiple seating for reserved-book use	33″ × 21″ (0.838 × 0.533 m)	36″ × 24″ (0.914 × 0.610 m)
Individual table or open carrel for undergraduates	33″ × 20″ (0.838 × 0.508 m)[b]	36″ × 22″ (0.914 × 0.559 m)
Open carrel for graduate student without bookshelf over it	36″ × 24″ (0.914 × 0.610 m)[c]	42″ × 24″ (1.067 × 0.610 m)
Carrel, open or closed, for graduate student writing dissertation, with a bookshelf	36″ × 27″ (0.914 × 0.686 m)[d]	48″ × 30″ (1.219 × 0.762 m)
Faculty study	48″ × 30″ (1.219 × 0.762 m)	60″ × 30″ (1.524 × 0.762 m) if shelving is over it

[a] Note that although surface dimensions are given, the critical issue is the amount of work area. Although some surface configurations may be inefficient, a rectangle is not the only suitable shape. In general, an undergraduate may need 6 to 8 ft² (0.557 to 0.743 m²) of surface, depending on the task and the size of materials; a graduate student 7 to 10 ft² (0.650 to 0.929 m²); and a professor or graduate student working on a thesis or dissertation 9 to 12 ft² (0.836 to 1.115 m²). Those in such fields as chemistry, engineering, and mathematics will need less surface space; those in earth sciences, systematic biology, art history, music, and most other humanities and some social sciences will need the more generous provision.

[b] A space of 33 × 20 in. (838 × 508 mm) goes farther in an individual accommodation than at a large table because others do not intrude on the space. Remember that this is a minimum size.

[c] Shelves are frequently not recommended over open carrels because they make it easier for an unauthorized student to monopolize a carrel.

[d] A shelf over a carrel table requires additional depth because it interferes with lighting. A closed carrel should preferably have a window, glass in the door, and more space around the table than an open one, or claustrophobia may result.

B.4.4 Average Floor Area Required for Different Types of Accommodation

The square-footage requirements suggested in table B.9 are at best approximations, but they may be helpful in preliminary stages of planning. (See also appendix C.)

TABLE B.9   Approximate Square-Footage Requirements for Different Types of Seating Accommodations[a]

Type of Accommodations	Requirements in ft² (m²)		
	Minimum	Adequate	Generous
Small lounge chair[b]	20 (1.86)	25 (2.32)	30 (2.79)
Large lounge chair[c]	25 (2.32)	30 (2.79)	35 (3.25)
Individual table[d]	25 (2.32)	30 (2.79)	35 (3.25)
Table for four[e]	22.5 (2.09)	25 (2.32)	27.5 (2.56)
Table for more than four[f]	20 (1.86)	22.5 (2.09)	25 (2.32)
Individual carrel[g]	20 (1.86)	22.5 (2.09)	25 (2.32)
Oversized carrel with equipment	30 (2.79)	35 (3.25)	40 (3.72)
Double carrel[h]	22.5 (2.09)	25 (2.32)	27.5 (2.56)
Double-staggered carrels[i]	22.5 (2.09)	25 (2.32)	27.5 (2.56)
Triple-staggered carrels[j]	22.5 (2.09)	25 (2.32)	27.5 (2.56)
Double row of carrels with partitions between, placed in a reading room or in place of two stack ranges[k]	22.5 (2.09)	25 (2.32)	27.5 (2.56)

[a] The figures used here include: (1) area of working surface if any; (2) area occupied by chair; (3) area used for direct access to the accommodations; and (4) reasonable share of all the assignable space used for main aisles in the room under consideration.

[b] These chairs, if in pairs, should be separated by a small table to prevent congestion and to hold books not in use.

[c] Large lounge chairs are expensive, space-consuming, and an aid to slumber, but they are highly regarded by students. They may or may not be appropriate.

[d] Individual tables are space-consuming, are generally disorderly in appearance because unless anchored they are easily moved, and result in a feeling of commotion if there is traffic on all sides. Not recommended except along a wall or screen.

[e] Tables for four are the largest ones recommended, unless pressure for additional capacity is great.

[f] Tables for more than four are space-savers, but few readers like to sit with someone on each side. They will avoid using them as far as possible.

[g] Individual carrels are economical in use of space if placed at right angles to a wall, adjacent to an aisle that must be provided under any circumstances. They reduce visual distraction if partitions 52 in. (1.320 m) or more in height are provided on at least two of the four sides.

[h] Double carrels are useful, but the staggered ones described below are preferred.

[i] Double-staggered carrels are as economical of space as tables for four and reduce visual distraction.

[j] Triple-staggered carrels are as economical of space as tables for six or more and reduce visual distraction.

[k] Double rows of carrels are economical in space use and reduce visual distraction.

B.4.5 Additional Space Required for Service to Readers

Space for direct access to seating accommodations is dealt with in table B.9 and elsewhere.

Additional space required includes:

1. Assignable Areas

    The public catalog or OPACs or both

    Space around the bibliographical and reference and current-periodical collections, which is required because of heavy use

    Public areas outside service desks

    Special accommodations for microfilm reproductions, maps, manuscripts, archives, and other collections not shelved in the main stack area. These may include audiovisual areas of various types.

    Staff working quarters

2. Nonassignable Areas

    Entrances, vestibules, and lobbies

    Corridors

    Areas used primarily as traffic arteries

    Stairwells and elevator shafts

    Toilets

    Mechanical and electrical equipment space

    Walls and columns

It is suggested that not less than 25 ft^2 (2.32 m^2) per reader in assignable or nonassignable areas will be required for the services in these groups, and that unless the special accommodations mentioned above are held to a reasonable minimum and careful planning is provided throughout, the 25 ft^2 may have to be increased to 35 ft^2. In many cases the space required for reader accommodations will appropriately be 35 ft^2 (3.25 m^2) or even larger, and it is urged that the area needed for accommodation be calculated exclusive of the nonassignable area that is generally applied as a factor to the total program requirements based upon the anticipated efficiency of the building. Note also that the requirements for providing handicapped access and the growing use of special equipment, such as computers, video equipment, and microform readers, may argue for more than the minimum space.

For these and other reasons discussed in the text, the authors recommend using 30 to 35 ft^2 (2.79 to 3.25 m^2) for typical seating, and larger figures for selected facilities in research libraries, such as microtext reading rooms.

To determine the space required for the nonassignable areas, it is suggested that an efficiency of 67 percent be assumed for small libraries, with up to an efficiency of 75 percent for large libraries. One may then divide the total assignable space for all functions by the assumed percentage to establish the total required gross area. The difference between the net assignable and the gross area is, of course, the anticipated nonassignable area.

B.5 Bookstack Capacity

Bookstack capacity is based on: (A) the number of volumes shelved in a standard stack section, and (B) the floor area requirements for a standard stack section.

B.5.1 The Number of Volumes Shelved in a Standard Stack Section

The number of volumes that can be shelved in a standard stack section depends on: (1) book heights and the number of shelves per section; (2) book thickness; and (3) the decision regarding what is considered a section usefully full of books.

1. BOOK HEIGHTS AND SHELVES PER SECTION

Stack sections in academic libraries in the United States are considered standard if they are 7 ft 6 in. (2.286 m) high and 3 ft (0.914 m) wide. Sections of this height make possible seven shelves 12 in. (0.305 m) on centers over a 4-in. (0.102-m) base. This spacing is adequate for books that are 11 in. (0.279 m) tall or less, which, as shown in table B.10, includes 90 percent of the books in a typical collection.

TABLE B.10   Book Heights[a]

8″ (203 mm) or less	25%	12″ (305 mm)	94%
9″ (229 mm) or less	54%	13″ (330 mm)	97%
10″ (254 mm) or less	79%	Over 13″ (330 mm)	3%
11″ (279 mm) or less	90%		

[a] Adapted from Rider's *Compact Storage*, p. 45, which was based to a considerable extent on research done by Van Hoesen and Kilpatrick on the height of books in academic libraries. From Fremont Rider, *Compact Book Storage: Some Suggestions toward a New Methodology for the Shelving of Less Used Research Materials* (New York: Hadham Press, 1949).

It is suggested that most of the remaining 10 percent will be concentrated in a comparatively few subjects, that 70 percent of this 10 percent will be between 11 and 13 in. (279 to 330 mm) tall, and that six shelves 14 in. (356 mm) on centers will provide for them.

Another way to look at book heights and capacity per section is by determining what percentage of large university research collections fall within certain sizes. This is illustrated by table B.11, which is derived from a breakdown of over 2,500,000 volumes in the University of California Southern Regional Library Facility. (See tables 6.1 and 6.2 on p. 179.)

TABLE B.11   Sizes of Large University Collections Sorted by Height and Depth of Books[a]

Category	Height	Volumes	%	Cumulative %
B	Under 6″ (0.152 m)	15,872	0.6	0.6
A & AA	6″ to 10″ (0.152–0.254 m)	1,573,360	60.6	61.2
D	10″ to 13″ (0.254–0.330 m)	789,224	30.4	91.6

(Continued)

[a] In this example, only items in categories C and H will not fit on shelves 9 in. (0.229 m) wide. Adapted from figures prepared by the University of California Southern Regional Library Facility.

TABLE B.11   (Continued)

E	13″ to 16″ (0.330–0.406 m)	91,136	3.5	95.1
C	Over 16″ x more than 9″ wide (0.406+ x 0.228+ m)	30,967	1.2	96.3
G[b]	6″ to 11″ (0.152–0.279 m)	82,616	3.2	99.5
H[b]	Anything larger than G	13,568	0.5	100

[b] Books from Special Collections are in these categories.

2. BOOK THICKNESS AND THE NUMBER OF VOLUMES THAT CAN BE SHELVED SATISFACTORILY ON EACH LINEAR UNIT OF SHELVING

No two libraries are alike in this regard. The average thickness will depend on: (a) the definition of a volume; (b) binding policy, particularly for pamphlets, serials, and periodicals; and (c) the collection under consideration.

A commonly used formula for thickness of books is suggested by table B.12.

TABLE B.12   Volumes per Shelf for Books in Different Subjects[a]

Subject	Volumes per Standard Shelf	Volumes per Single-faced Section
Circulating (nonfiction)	24	168
Fiction	24	168
Economics	24	168
General literature	21	147
History	21	147
Reference	18	108
Art (not including large folios)	21	126
Technical and scientific	18	126
Medical	15	105
Public documents	15	105
Bound periodicals	15	105
Law	12	84

[a] This table, or a variation of it based upon the same data, is in common use by stack manufacturers. It was used by Wheeler and Githens, who suggest that 125 volumes per single-faced section be considered practical average working capacity. The figures here represent full capacity, although as a guideline, they should be considered conservative. Actual measurements often suggest that greater quantities are possible, and thus an analysis of the existing collection as outlined elsewhere is recommended. From Joseph Lewis Wheeler and Alfred Morton Githens, *The American Public Library Building: Its Planning and Design with Special Reference to Its Administration and Service* (New York: Scribner's, 1941), pp. 414–15.

3. THE DECISION ON WHEN A SECTION IS FULL

In table B.12 a suggested number of volumes per single-faced section is proposed. It is evident that if books are shelved by subject, it is unwise to fill the shelves completely, and any estimate must be an approximation. For many libraries 125 volumes per stack section is considered safe, although Robert Henderson's "cubook" formula proposes only 100 volumes per section.

Shelving 125 volumes to a single-faced section, as suggested by Wheeler and Githens, is often done, but it is safer and preferable to estimate the number of standard sections the collection now fills completely and then add 50 percent to that number to determine the present requirements for comfortable shelving arrangements. This would make the shelves two-thirds full on the average and would leave 1 ft (305 mm) of unused space available on each shelf. If collections are growing each year by 5 percent of the collection at the end of the previous year, it will take between five and six years for the shelves to become six-sevenths full, and to leave an average of 5 in. (127 mm) vacant on each shelf. By the time this occurs, the annual cost of labor for the constant moving of books that will be necessary, plus the damage done to bindings by the moving, leaving out of consideration the resulting inconvenience, may well be greater than the interest on the capital sum required to provide for additional shelving.

Table B.13 shows the period required for a collection that now occupies two-thirds of available space to reach six-sevenths or between 85 and 86 percent of absolute capacity at different rates of growth.

Table B.14 shows the period required for a collection that now occupies one-half of the available shelving to grow to the point where it occupies six-sevenths of the shelving, with the growth at various percentage rates. In both tables the rates are figured with the annual increase estimated at a given percentage of the previous year's total and by a percentage of the total at the time the estimate is made—that is, arithmetically instead of geometrically.

TABLE B.13 Years Required for a Collection to Increase from Two-thirds to Six-sevenths of Full Capacity

Rate of Growth	Years									
	1.5%	2%	2.5%	3%	3.5%	4%	5%	6%	8%	10%
Geometric increase[a]	17	13	10+	8+	7+	6+	5+	4+	3+	2+
Arithmetic increase[b]	19+	14+	11+	9+	8+	7+	5+	4+	3+	2+

[a] A geometric increase represents an increase of a given percentage each year of the total number of volumes at the end of the previous year.

[b] An arithmetic increase represents an increase each year of a given percentage of the total number of volumes at the time used as a base and so does not become larger year by year.

TABLE B.14 Years Required for a Collection to Increase from 50 Percent to 85 Percent of Full Capacity

Rate of Growth	Years									
	1.5%	2%	2.5%	3%	3.5%	4%	5%	6%	8%	10%
Geometric increase	35+	26+	21+	17+	15+	13+	11+	9+	7+	4+
Arithmetic increase	46+	35	28	23+	20	17+	14+	11+	8+	7+

B.5.2 Floor Area Requirements for a Standard Stack Section

The floor area requirements for a standard stack section depend primarily on: (1) range spacing; (2) range lengths; (3) the number of cross aisles and their widths; (4) cross-aisle area charged against adjacent reader accommodations; and (5) nonassignable space.

1. RANGE SPACING

Range spacing should be based on column spacing, which was discussed at the beginning of this appendix; on shelf depths, which are discussed here; and on stack-aisle widths, dealt with in item 2 below.

Shelf depths as used here are based on double-faced bracket shelving with 2 in. (51 mm) between the back of the shelf on one side of the range and the back of the shelf on the other side. Shelf depths specified by stack manufacturers are 1 in. (25 mm) greater than the actual depth—that is, a 7-in. (0.178-m) "actual" shelf is called an 8-in. (0.203-m) nominal shelf, because 8 in. (0.203 m) is available if half the 2 in. (51 mm) noted above is assigned to the shelves on each side of a double-faced shelf section. Table B.15 shows depths of books. If these figures are correct (they represent the average in research and academic libraries), a shelf with 8 in. (0.203 m) actual depth, together with the space available between shelves on the two sides of a double-faced section, will provide for practically any book that does not have to be segregated because of its height, and 8-in. (0.203-m) actual-depth shelves (they are designated by the manufacturers as 9-in. or 0.229-m shelves) are recommended in place of the 7- or 9-in. (0.178- or 0.229-m) actual-depth shelves that are commonly used. In many libraries a 7-in. (0.178-m) actual-depth shelf is suitable for a large part of the collections, although deeper shelving is normally preferable. Where diagonal or other bracing occurs in the space between the backs of the shelves, a shelf 1 in. (25 mm) deeper than discussed above is recommended.

TABLE B.15   Percentage of Books in an Academic Collection Below Different Depths Measured from the Back of the Spine to the Fore-edge of the Covers[a]

5″ (127 mm) or less	25%	9″ (229 mm) or less	94%
6″ (152 mm) or less	54%	10″ (254 mm) or less	97%[b]
7″ (178 mm) or less	79%	Over 10″ (254 mm)	3%
8″ (203 mm) or less	90%		

[a] Adapted from Rider's *Compact Book Storage,* p. 45.

[b] An 8-in. actual-depth shelf (i.e., a 9-in. [203/229-mm] nominal-depth shelf) will house a 10-in. (254-mm) deep book without difficulty, unless another deep book is immediately behind it. Most books over 10 in. (254 mm) deep will be more than 11 in. (279 mm) tall and should be segregated on special shelving that is more than 9 in. (229 mm) in nominal depth.

2. STACK-AISLE WIDTHS AND STACK-RANGE LENGTHS

Stack-aisle widths should be based on the amount of use by individuals, by the need to provide for handicapped access, and by trucks and length of the range before a cross aisle is reached. Other things being equal, the longer the range, the wider the aisle should be because of increased frequency of the need for users to pass one another or a truck and to have to back out of a very narrow aisle. Although 1 in. (25 mm) makes little difference, 2 or 3 in.

(51 or 76 mm) does. Table B.16 suggests desirable stack-aisle widths in conjunction with stack-range lengths under different types and amounts of use.

Do not forget that stack-aisle widths must be based, indirectly at least, on the column spacing dealt with at the beginning of this appendix, and are affected as well by the shelf depths discussed above, if columns are not to obstruct the aisles. The distance between column centers should be an exact multiple of the distance between the center of parallel stack ranges within the stack bay, which in turn is determined by the sum of the depth of a double-faced range and the width of a stack aisle, *including growth space*.

TABLE B.16   Suggested Stack-Aisle Widths and Stack-Range Lengths[a]

Typical Use of Stack	Aisle Width[b]		Range Lengths (Sections)[c]	
	Min.	Max.	Min.	Max.
Closed-access storage stack	24″ (0.610 m)	30″ (0.762 m)	10	20
Limited-access, little-used stack for over 1,000,000 volumes	26″ (0.660 m)	31″ (0.787 m)	10	16
Heavily used open-access stack for over 1,000,000 volumes	31″ (0.787 m)	36″ (0.914 m)	8	12
Very heavily used open-access stack with less than 1,000,000 volumes	33″ (0.838 m)	40″ (1.016 m)	5	10
Stacks meeting the Americans with Disabilities Act (ADA)	36″ (0.914 m)	44″[d] (1.118 m)	5	20
Newspaper stack with 18-in. (0.457-m) deep shelves	36″ (0.914 m)	45″ (1.143 m)	5	10
Reference and current-periodical room stacks	36″ (0.914 m)	60″ (1.524 m)	4	8
Current-periodical display stacks	42″ (1.067 m)	60″ (1.524 m)	4	7

[a] These are suggestions only and not to be considered definite recommendations. Circumstances alter cases.
[b] Stack aisle widths of 24 in. (0.610 m) should be considered an absolute minimum and are rarely justifiable. Anything under 26 in. (0.660 m) is difficult with a book truck, even when the use is light. The minimum width proposed should generally be used only with the minimum range lengths suggested.
[c] Stack-range lengths are often determined by available space, rather than by their suitability. The maximum lengths shown in the table should generally be used only with the maximum aisle widths suggested. The "standard" section of 3 ft (0.914 m) is used here as the unit of measure.
[d] Although the ADA requires only 36-in. (0.914-m) clear stack aisles, in some cases interpretation of particular building codes may suggest a minimum of up to 44 in. (1.118 m).

3. WIDTHS FOR MAIN AND SUBSIDIARY CROSS-STACK AISLES

Cross-aisle widths should be based on amount of use and are inevitably affected by the column spacing. Column spacing often makes it difficult to provide any cross-aisle widths except the width of a standard section or a multiple of this width. If standard shelving width is altered or if columns equal to one-half a standard section, less about 4 in. (0.102 m) for stack uprights and error, are used and the column range is filled out with a lectern, aisles 4 ft 6 in. (1.372 m) can be made available. These would meet ADA requirements.

Table B.17 suggests desirable cross-aisle widths under different types and amounts of use.

TABLE B.17   Suggested Cross-Aisle Widths[a]

	Main Aisle		Subsidiary Cross-Aisle[b]	
Typical Use of Stack	Min.	Max.	Min.	Max.
Closed-access storage	3' (0.914 m)	4'6" (1.372 m)	2'6" (0.762 m)	3'6" (1.067 m)
Limited-access stack	3' (0.914 m)	4'6" (1.372 m)	3' (0.914 m)	3'6" (1.067 m)
Heavily used open-access stack	4' (1.219 m)	5' (1.524 m)	3' (0.914 m)	4' (1.219 m)
Heavily used open-access stack for large collection and ranges 30' (9.144 m) long	4'6" (1.372 m)	6' (1.829 m)	3'3" (0.991 m)	4'6" (1.372 m)

[a] These are suggestions only and not to be considered definite recommendations. Note that the minimum clear cross aisle established by codes in the United States and meeting the ADA is typically 3 ft. 8 in. (1.118 m). In determining minimum or maximum widths, keep in mind the length and width of the book trucks used, the need for handicapped access, and the amount of use. Minimum-width stack aisles should not be accompanied by minimum cross aisles. From the widths shown in the table, up to 4 in. (0.102 m) may have to be subtracted to provide for adjacent stack uprights and irregularities in column sizes.
[b] If open carrels adjoin a subsidiary aisle, they will make it seem wider, but traffic will tend to be disturbing to the carrel occupants.

4. CROSS-AISLE AREA CHARGED AGAINST ADJACENT READER ACCOMMODATIONS

The effect on floor area requirements per stack section and volume capacity per net unit of stack area, resulting from the provision of reader accommodations in the form of stack carrels, should be considered. The assignment of one-half of the adjacent cross-aisle area to reader space when carrels are on one side of the cross aisle and bookstack ranges are on the other may increase rather than decrease book capacity per unit of net stack area, and, in addition, provide desirable and economical seating accommodations adjacent to the books. (See table B.18.) If closed carrels open from a subsidiary aisle, they will make it seem narrower.

It is evident that many variables are involved in bookstack capacity. Table B.18 is based on the floor area required for a single-faced standard section in stack layouts, with different range spacing, range lengths, and cross-aisle widths, as well as stack carrels. A similar chart may easily be prepared for other units using proportional ratios. For example, with range

TABLE B.18   Floor Area Required for One Single-Faced Standard Section

Range Spacing	ft² (m²) with Minimum Cross Aisles[a]	ft² (m²) with Generous Cross Aisles[b]	ft² (m²) with Adequate Cross Aisles Combined with Carrels[c]
6'0"	11.00	11.10	10.32
(1.829 m)	(1.022)	(1.031)	(0.959)
5'9"	10.54	10.64	9.89
(1.753 m)	(0.979)	(0.988)	(0.919)
5'6"	10.08	10.18	9.46
(1.676 m)	(0.936)	(0.946)	(0.879)
5'3"	9.63	9.71	9.03
(1.600 m)	(0.895)	(0.902)	(0.839)
5'0"	9.17	9.25	8.60
(1.524 m)	(0.852)	(0.859)	(0.799)
4'9"	8.71	8.79	8.17
(1.448 m)	(0.809)	(0.817)	(0.759)
4'6"	8.25	8.33	7.74
(1.372 m)	(0.766)	(0.774)	(0.719)

[a] Based on a six-section blind-aisle range, each with 2 in. (51 mm) growth space to account for gusset plates, end panels, or shelving columns. The shelving is placed on each side of a 3 ft 8 in. (1.118-m) center aisle, which should satisfy the requirements of most codes and the ADA, provided the range aisles also meet the ADA and the applicable codes.
[b] Based on two 3 ft 8 in. (1.118-m) side aisles and a 6-ft center aisle separated by 10 section ranges, each including 4 in. (101 mm) growth space.
[c] Based on 3 ft 8 in. (1.118-m) side aisles between carrels and 10 section ranges (with 4 in. or 101 mm growth space), the latter separated by a 4 ft 6 in. (1.372-m) center aisle. One-half of the side aisles are charged against the carrels, but even on 5-ft (1.524-m) centers, the carrels occupy only 22 1/2 ft² (2.090 m²), and the floor area for a section is low.

spacing of 1.5 m and generous cross aisles, the area required is 1.5×836 divided by $1.524 = 0.823$ m².

Table B.19 shows stack capacity per unit of floor area if 100, 125, 150, or 160 volumes per standard stack section are used in connection with 7, 8 1/3, 9, or 10 ft² and 0.65, 0.75, 0.85, or 0.95 m² occupied by each section.

5. NONASSIGNABLE SPACE

Nonassignable space includes, as far as its effect on book capacity is concerned, the floor space occupied by columns, mechanical services, and vertical transportation of all kinds. We mention it here simply to call attention to it. In a carefully designed stack for 25,000 volumes or more on one level, nonassignable space should amount to no more than 10 percent of the gross stack area, and considerably less with a larger installation. However, it is recommended that, in most cases, nonassignable space should be calculated for the total facility using the complete program as a basis, in which case a figure of 25 to 33 percent of the gross area is reasonable.

TABLE B.19   Volume Capacity per 1,000 ft² and 100 m² of Stack Area with Different Areas and Volumes per Section

ft² per section[a]	Number of Sections in 1,000 ft²	Volumes per 1,000 ft² with Different Number of Volumes per Section[b]			
		100[g]	125[h]	150[i]	160[j]
10[c]	100	10,000	12,500	15,000	16,000
9[d]	111	11,100	13,875	16,650	17,760
8 1/3[e]	120	12,000	15,000	18,000	19,200
7[f]	143	14,300	17,875	21,450	22,880

m² per Section	Number of Sections in 100 m²	Volumes per 100 m² with Different Number of Volumes per Section			
		100	125	150	160
0.95	105	10,500	13,125	15,750	16,800
0.85	118	11,800	14,750	17,700	18,880
0.75	133	13,300	16,625	19,950	21,280
0.65	153	15,300	19,125	22,950	24,480

[a] Examination of table B.18 should help in determining area to allow for a single-faced section.

[b] Volumes per section has been covered in detail in part IV.A of this appendix.

[c] Ten square feet (0.93 m²) per section is the "cubook" formula proposed by R. W. Henderson. Where handicapped access is required, this is a satisfactory figure for a large collection with open access.

[d] See table B.18 for an approximate example. In a well-arranged stack, the ADA probably can be met within this figure.

[e] The authors suggest that this is a satisfactory and safe figure to use for a large collection accessible to graduate students and a limited number of undergraduates, but with limited handicapped access (the ADA probably will not be met).

[f] Adequate for a very large collection with limited access and without ADA compliance.

[g] One hundred volumes per section is the cubook formula.

[h] The authors suggest that this is a safe figure for comfortable working capacity in an average library. See part IV.A of this appendix for a full discussion.

[i] Allowing 150 volumes per section is too often proposed by architects and librarians. Although it is a possible figure, it often approaches full capacity and should be used with careful analysis or in cases where additional space is immediately available when capacity is reached. The time to consider what comes next will have passed.

[j] Allowing 160 volumes per section should not be considered for most academic libraries, unless the collection has an unusually high percentage of abnormally thin volumes, for example, individually bound pamphlets or Oriental collections with the traditionally slim Chinese fascicle or ts's (satsu in Japanese).

B.6   Computer Terminals

Computer terminals will vary from simple keyboards with a display screen (or simply a display screen in the case of a touch screen directory) to units that require additional space for a small computer, a printer, a mouse, perhaps a scanner, a modem, documentation, and space for notes or copy.

For workstations that will be fitted with a terminal, it is suggested that an additional 20 ft² (1.858 m²) be provided. Public terminals for the catalog or for charging out books should each be provided 25 ft² (2.323 m²). Terminal stations provided for composing a dissertation should be provided with at least 35 ft² and preferably as much as 50 ft² (3.252 to 4.645 m²).

The number of terminals to be provided will vary dramatically depending upon the academic program of the institution and the stage of computer cluster development and personal ownership of computers. The topic of quantity is discussed in Section 7.3 where it is suggested that one computer per 100 visitors may not be enough; an example of one terminal per 60 daily visitors is cited. It is probably better to err on the high side in terms of allocating available space, and to add terminals slowly until queuing is no longer a problem.

Other design guidance is provided in Section 13.4.4. No professional association or governmental standard exists either for quantity of outlets or display terminals.

B.7 Professional Association Standards and Governmental Planning Guides

It is possible, and in some cases necessary, to base space-assignment figures on standards promulgated by governmental authorities supervising the institutions concerned. These standards can be helpful but, like all formulas and tables, they should be used with caution because, as has been emphasized throughout this volume, situations differ and circumstances alter cases. Do not put yourself into a straitjacket. With this word of warning, standards for two associations and guidelines of five governmental bodies are provided for reference.

B.7.1 Standards for College Libraries

Adopted by the Association of College and Research Libraries in 1995, the standards were published in *C&RL News* (April 1995: 245–57).

In dealing with space assignment, Standard 6: Facilities notes:

> The library building shall provide well-planned, secure and adequate housing for its collections and personnel; secure space for users and staff; and space for the provision of services and programs.

The need for attention to access for disabled persons and the need for support of new technologies (including computers, flexibility, climate control, and compact shelving) is noted. The space requirement is then based on the following three-part "formula."

1. *Space for readers is based upon the FTE enrollment.* When less than one-half of the FTE students reside on campus, seating for 20 percent of the FTE enrollment should be provided. For a typical residential college, seating for 25 percent is recommended. The space is then calculated using 25 to 35 ft² (2.323 to 3.251 m²) per seat depending upon the functions of the reader station. It is not uncommon to find institutions averaging this area application as 30 ft² (2.787 m²) per seat.
2. *Space for books* is based upon the size of the collections and is calculated cumulatively as follows.

Collections	ft²/vol	m²/vol
First 150,000 volumes	0.10	0.0093
Next 150,000 volumes	0.09	0.0084
Next 300,000 volumes	0.08	0.0074
Above 600,000 volumes	0.07	0.0065

3. *Space for staff,* including the library administration, technical processing, catalogs, and files, is calculated as 1/8 of the space determined for the books and readers.

It is interesting to note that this last part of the formula has been reduced by 50 percent from earlier versions of the ACRL formula. The standard appears to not account separately for public services and alternative format collections; some caution in application of this formula for programming is advised. Its real intent is more for comparative analysis than for establishing exact need within a particular institution (though this can be said about any formula).

The resulting figure is said to represent the net area required for a college library. The standard discusses other aspects, including a caveat about decentralized libraries, the need for including the librarian in the planning process for any new facility, and a statement that local conditions will substantially shape the quality of any library.

B.7.2 Standards for Community, Junior, and Technical College Learning Resources Centers

The ACRL standards for these institutions may be found in the May 1994 issue of *C&RL News* (274–87). This standard states:

> The learning resources program should provide adequate space for housing collections in a variety of formats, for study and research, for public service activities, for staff workrooms and offices, and for basic production.

The total space required for this function can be calculated by applying a formula that reflects the enrollment, the public services provided, the size and type of collections, and the staff. Beyond that, it is stated that local conditions will determine the size of the library.

It is suggested that seating should be provided for a minimum of 10 percent of the FTE enrollment; that individual carrel and table seats be provided 25 ft^2 (2.323 m^2) per seat; that lounge chairs be provided 30 ft^2 (2.787 m^2) each; that computers and workstations be provided 40 ft^2 (3.716 m^2) each; and that microform reader stations be provided 35 ft^2 (3.252 m^2) each.

For books and other bound collections, it is suggested that the formula be based upon 10 volumes per ft^2 (108 per m^2), and that these figures be doubled for compact shelving.

For staff, it is suggested that a minimum of 175 ft^2 (16.258 m^2) per staff member be provided to accommodate new technologies, equipment, and hardware. Individual offices should be based upon 200 ft^2 (18.581 m^2) per person.

Beyond noting the need, this particular standard statement is not terribly helpful in suggesting the space required for public services and collections other than books. Other resources will be required to fill this need.

B.7.3 Higher Education Facilities Planning and Management Manuals

The Planning and Management Systems Division of the Western Interstate Commission for Higher Education, and the American Association of Collegiate Registrars and Admissions Officers published a seven-part series of manuals in 1971. Manual 4, on academic support facilities, covers libraries. It presents a very well thought out statement of planning guidelines, or standards, from which the following four tables are extracted (tables B.20–B.23).

TABLE B.20   Density of Stack Utilization by Type of Material

Type of Material	Items per Stack Unit	ft² per Stack Unit	m² per Stack Unit
Bound volumes	125	8.7	0.808
Documents and pamphlets	1,000	8.7	0.808
Microfilm reels	400	8.7	0.808
Microfilm cards	10,000	8.7	0.808
Newspaper titles unbound	7	8.7	0.808
Newspaper—bound vols.	9	8.7	0.808
Periodical titles—unbound	15	15.0	1.394
Periodical titles—boxed	30	8.7	0.808
Recordings	500	8.7	0.808
Reference volumes	75	15.0	1.394
Maps	1,000	42.0	3.902
Slides	5,000	17.0	1.579

TABLE B.21   Proportions of Projected User Populations to Be Provided with Reader Stations

Type of User	Percent Provided Seating
Lower division	20%
Upper division	
Humanities	30
Social sciences	30
Life sciences	20
Physical sciences	20
Business	30
Education	30
Graduate	
Humanities	40
Social sciences	40
Life sciences	25
Physical sciences	25
Business	30
Education	30
Faculty	25
Public users	3

TABLE B.22   Assignable Area per Reader Station

Type of Station	ft²	m²
Open tables	25	2.323
Small carrels	30	2.787
Research carrels	40	3.716
Microform & AV	40	3.716
Typing	30	2.787
Lounge	30	2.787
Small group	25	2.323
Faculty studies	50	4.645

TABLE B.23 Area to Be Provided Staff

Type of Staff	ft² per Person	m² per Person
Administration		
Director	240	22.297
Associate director	160	14.864
Assistant director	120	11.148
Director of systems	120	11.148
Secretary	100	9.290
Acquisitions		
Head	150	13.935
Area specialists	120	11.148
Clerical	100	9.290
Cataloging		
Head	150	13.935
Catalogers	120	11.148
Clerical	100	9.290
Reference		
Reference librarians	120	11.148
Clerical	100	9.290
Circulation		
Head	150	13.935
Circulation librarian	120	11.148
Clerical	100	9.290
Reserve		
Librarian	120	11.148
Clerical	100	9.290
Interlibrary Loan		
Librarian	120	11.148
Clerical	100	9.290
Binding and Mending		
Technician	250	23.226
Clerical	250	23.226
Photocopy		
Technician	250	23.226
Clerical	100	9.290
Shipping and Receiving		
Clerical	300	27.871
Office Support		
Conference room	25	2.323
Staff room	25	2.323

B.7.4 University of California Library Facility Planning Standards (11/83)*

The University's facility planning standards are used to calculate space allowances that provide indicators of the amount of space needed to house general library functions. They do not justify space requirements in themselves; proposed facility projects should be justified on the basis of project-specific analyses.

Furthermore, they are not design standards used to generate a building design program or to define the space requirement and layout of individual

---

*From Library Facility Planning Standards, University of California

activities. The planning standards are abstract measures applied at arm's length to evaluate campus library facility needs and test specific project proposals.

These standards are based on the library planning structure presented in *The University of California Libraries—A Plan for Development,* dated July 1977, prepared by the University's Office of Library Plans & Policies, and accepted by the State for university planning.

The allowance is generated by three categories of functions: collections, users, and library staff. All conventional library functions are included in these three categories. Special functions such as Multi-media Learning Center facilities are not provided for by the standards. If such special functions are included in a library building project, their space needs should be separately calculated, justified, and included in addition to the basic allowance generated by the conventional library functions.

Collection Space—is based on collection material counts as documented in the annual campus report to the Office of Library Plans & Policies. Future year counts should be projected from that base, using approved acquisition budgets minus discard and storage. Collection materials to be stored in the Regional Library facilities should be excluded.

User Space—the allowance covers all categories of users, including undergraduate and graduate students, faculty, and non-UC patrons. It is calculated on the basis of 25 asf of the three-quarter average headcount enrollment of the campus, or the approved long-range enrollment plan.

Staff Space—is based on the actual FTE staff of the library, and covers not only specific work stations but also all space for library materials being processed, work rooms, storage of supplies, equipment, public service desks, catalogs, and any other assignable areas not covered by collection and user allowances.

Category	asf/unit*	units/asf*
Collection		
Bound volumes	0.08	12.5
Other materials		
Maps	0.042	24
Microfiche	0.00087	1,150
Microfilm	0.02175	46
Pamphlets	0.0087	115
Sound recordings	0.0174	57.5
Manuscripts	0.0002014	4,965
Documents not counted as vols.	0.0087	115
Periodical subscriptions unbound-display	1.0	1.0
Periodical subscriptions boxed	0.29	3.45
Microform readers	25.0	0.04
Users		
25% of enrollment	25.0	
Staff		
Actual FTE staff	168.75	

* Derived from *The University of California Libraries—A Plan for Development,* University of California, 1977.

B.7.5 California State University System of Campuses: *Policies, Standards and Plans for CSU Campus Library Facilities* (1991)

Excerpt from the section on "Space Standards":

A. Collections Space. The space for the collections is to be comprised of "open stacks" (OS) and "movable aisle compact shelving" (MACS). The amounts of each type of collection space will change as a campus' collections grow.

1. *Open Stacks* (OS): Space for the collections contained in an "open stacks" area is to be planned at the 10:1 ratio. (Ten volumes per one assignable square foot.) Each campus library will be constructed to provide a sufficient "open stack" area to accommodate 40 volumes per FTES at the campus' approved enrollment level. . . .

2. *Movable Aisle Compact Shelving* (MACS): . . . MACS is calculated at 35 volumes to the assignable square foot of library space. Each campus library will be constructed to provide sufficient MACS in addition to the "open stack" area to accommodate the projected volumes count at the approved FTES enrollment level for the campus. [Note: MACS will apply to all campuses except CSU Northridge which has just opened a new library using the Automater Storage Retrieval (ASR) technology for high density shelving. ASR . . . will enable CSU Northridge to store over 100 volumes per ASF. While ASR has been proven in various types of warehousing, this is the first time it is being used by a library. The CSU did not feel it could adopt ASR as a standard at this time.] . . .

B. Non-Book Materials. Space for non-book library materials is to be calculated at 40% of the space allocated for "open stack" collections.

C. Reader Stations. In total, three types of reader stations are to be calculated at 20 percent of the projected full time equivalent students (FTES) enrollment ceiling. The following provides the space standards for each type of reader station.

1. *General Purpose Stations*—88 percent of the total projected reader stations are to be this type and are to be sized at 25 assignable square feet per station.
2. *Study Carrels*—10 percent of the total projected reader stations are to be of this type and are to be sized at 35 assignable square feet per station.
3. *Library Telecommunications/Computer Workstations*—2 percent of the total projected reader stations are to be this type and are to be sized at 49 assignable square feet per station. [Not student-access computing workstations, these are "to generate and enhance the transfer of bibliographic and full text information as an aid to the instructional process."]

D. Technical Processing and Public Service Space. Space for the library staff is to be provided at the rate of 225 assignable square feet per projected staff member [a projection based on the enrollment for various campus sizes; e.g., 73 staff for 10,000 enrollment; 130 staff for 20,000 enrollment].

B.7.6 Oregon State Systems of Higher Education

Chapter 3.12 in the Planning and Procedures Handbook for Campus and Building Development (1980), which deals with library space standards, includes the following recommendations.

1. Reader space should be provided for 15 percent of the full-time-equivalent (FTE) undergraduate students, and 25 percent of the FTE graduate students. Reader space is based upon 25 ft^2 (2.323 m^2) for undergraduates and 30 ft^2 (2.787 m^2) for graduate students.
2. Some space may be added for an allocation to faculty use depending upon the academic field. For example, 15 ft^2 (1.394 m^2) is added for each FTE faculty member in such fields as business, economics, philosophy, and the social sciences, while 3 ft^2 (0.279 m^2) is added for faculty in architecture, communications, music, the physical sciences, engineering, and so on.
3. The space for books is broken down and shown in table B.24.

TABLE B.24   Volumes Per Unit Area

	Health, Science & Law		All Others	
	Per ft²	Per m²	Per ft²	Per m²
100,000 volumes	9	97	10	108
Next 100,000 volumes	10	108	12	129
Next 800,000 volumes	12	129	14	51
Next 1,000,000 volumes	15	161	16	172

The space allowances shown in table B.25, which have been developed by measuring collections and the space required for storing, handling, and using nonbook materials, will be used in projecting their space needs.

4. For library staff and administration, space equal to 25 percent of the space required for the collections and readers is provided.

TABLE B.25   Formula for Nonbook Materials

Item	Items per ft² (m²) of Floor Space Suggested Standard	Space to Be Allotted in Minimum Units of ft² (m²)
Microcards	6,000 (64,580)	10 (0.93)
Microprints	1,400 (15,070)	10 (0.93)
Microfiche 4″ x 6″	2,500 (26,910)	10 (0.93)
Microfiche 3″ x 5″	6,000 (64,580)	10 (0.93)
Microfilm reels	60 (645)	10 (0.93)
Filmstrips	200 (2,150)	10 (0.93)
Slides	700 (7,530)	12 (1.11)
Transparencies	500 (5,380)	10 (0.93)
Motion picture reels	12 (130)	12 (1.11)
Videotape reels	3 (32)	10 (0.93)
Computer tape reels	9 (97)	10 (0.93)
Tape reels	30 (320)	10 (0.93)
Phonograph discs	75 (810)	10 (0.93)
Picture files	500 (5,380)	10 (0.93)
Maps	50 (540)	30 (2.79)
Pamphlets	150 (1,610)	10 (0.93)
Test files	150 (1,610)	10 (0.93)
Multimedia kits	9 (97)	10 (0.93)
Government documents	50 (540)	10 (0.93)
Unbound periodicals	15 (160) bibliographical units	10 (0.93)
Archives and Manuscripts	Space requirements for collection will be submitted by institutional librarian.	

B.7.7 The Generation of Space According to Canadian Provincial Norms

A Canadian example, published in 1978 (from the Office of Institutional Research, Concordia University, Montreal).

1. It is usual for the library to accommodate 25 percent of the university's student population.
2. Twenty-five ft² (2.32 m²) is adequate per seat.
3. On average, 15 volumes could be stored in each ft² of stack area (or 161 volumes per m²). [Note that this is difficult to achieve while meeting the ADA unless some amount of compact shelving is used.]
4. An average of 75 volumes per FTE student would satisfy the institution's students and faculty. [The authors urge extreme caution in using a figure such as this!]
5. Sufficient staff space for the library would be available on the basis of 1.25 ft² (0.116 m²) per FTE student. [Again, the authors urge caution!]
6. Equipment associated with the library can be based upon 0.75 ft² (0.070 m²) per FTE student. [Once again, caution!]

This set of directives is not a standard, but rather a planning guide. It is interesting in that the entire space program is related to the student enrollment, a measure that says little about striving for excellence or differences in academic program or subject coverage. The figures probably were never intended for use in planning a library for an institution with a significant graduate population offering doctoral degrees. It is also interesting to note the following guidelines used by Concordia University in planning its new library facility.

1. Shelving is based upon a 5 percent simple growth rate for 20 years, or double the currently occupied shelving. The space required is based upon ranges 1.5 m on center (59 in.), 1.25-m cross aisles (49-in.), and 10 double-faced section ranges of 9 m each (29 ft 6 in.), which works out to 0.769 m² (8.27 ft²) per section. [Canadian and some European libraries can have problems if metric is used for planning a building to accommodate standard stacks of U.S. manufacturers.]
2. Seating is based upon equivalent-full-time (EFT) enrollment for undergraduates and actual student count for graduate students, with the percentage assigned as shown in table B.26.
   A reduction factor of .67 is applied to the master's program seating to account for general purpose seating.
   The area assigned for seating breaks down as follows in table B.27.
3. For staff areas the Concordia guidelines provide office space as follows:

Division head, department head, staff officer	18 m²	(194 ft²)
Librarian or other professional	10 m²	(108 ft²)
Senior assistants	6 m²	(65 ft²)

In addition, for each office area, there is to be a small conference room for four people of 10.25 m² (110 ft²). It should also be noted that these space assignments do not include the space required for special equipment beyond that found in a fairly standard office.

TABLE B.26   Seating Based upon Student Population

Student Groups	Seating for Percent of Population
Undergraduates	
Lower Division (All)	20%
Upper Division	
Humanities, Social Sciences (including Fine Arts)	30%
Life Sciences	20%
Physical Sciences (including Engineering)	30%
Commerce	35%
Education	35%
Graduate Students—Master's Program	
Humanities (including Fine Arts)	45%
Social Sciences	40%
Life Sciences	25%
Physical Sciences (including Engineering)	25%
Commerce	35%
Education	35%
Graduate Students—Doctoral	100%

TABLE B.27   Seating Allocation

Seating Type	m^2	ft^2
Individual open carrels	2.325	25
Tables for four (per table)	10.25	110.3
Lounge chairs	2.5	26.9
Graduate/faculty closed carrels	4	43.1
Microform, A/V, or typing carrels	3	32.3
Catalog consultation stations	2	21.5
Seats in seminar rooms	2	21.5
Catalog card cabinets (including standing room)	2	21.5

B.7.8 *Capital Provision for University Libraries: Report of a [British] Working Party* (known as *The Atkinson Report*) and SCONUL *Space Requirements*

In Great Britain the University Grants Committee (UGC) established library norms or minimum standards relating to the funding of new facilities (London: HMSO, 1976). Although they appear to be somewhat more restrictive than the other standards outlined, it should be remembered that they were established to identify the most worthy projects needing funding rather than to propose an ideal library program. Even so, the proposed allocations were no doubt influential in Great Britain and elsewhere in the world.

Note that the UGC function is now served by separate Higher Education Funding Councils in England (including Northern Ireland), Scotland, and

Wales. Further, the 1993 "Follett Report" of the Joint Funding Councils' Libraries Review Group based its quantitative assessments and funding recommendations upon the UGC norms as being "arguably the best available."

The key emphasis of the UGC report is the creation of a system of "self-renewing" libraries limited in size. It is assumed that beyond the standard of 3.8 m (12 1/2 ft) of shelving, or 0.68 m² (7.32 ft²) per FTE student, materials will be removed for various forms of storage at nearly the same rate as incoming materials. Most of the materials are assumed to be on open-access shelves; thus, using their rule of thumb of 5.83 m² per 1,000 volumes (or nearly 16 volumes per ft²), the formula works out to about 117 volumes per FTE student.

By comparison, the statistics of the 101 universities reported in the 1981–82 ARL Statistics (Washington, D.C.: Association of Research Libraries, 1982) indicate an average of over 460 volumes per FTE student. Numerous factors can be considered in this comparison, such as the now heavy use in the United States of off-site storage stacks; it should not be taken as an absolute. The point is made simply to illustrate the restrictive nature of the UGC standards.

The following represents the UGC norms for library accommodation expressed as a feasible working scale:

1. Reader places are based upon 1:5 (20 percent) for arts students and 1:7 (14.3 percent) for science students. Where postgraduate research students are not provided space in other buildings, their needs may be added to the library requirements. The total area is determined using 2.39 m² (25.7 ft²) per reader station.
2. Materials space requirements based upon working capacity are determined by the following assumptions (table B.28):

TABLE B.28   Space Allocation for Collections

Type of Collection	m² per 1,000 Items	Items per ft²
Open-access books	4.65	20
Closed-access (fixed) books	4.03	23
Closed-access (rolling) books	2.07	45
Open-access bound journals	9.35	10
Closed-access (fixed) bound journals	8.06	11.5
Closed-access (rolling) bound journals	4.13	22.5
Typical mix	5.83	16
Periodicals—1/4 display, 3/4 storage	25.13	3.7

These figures include the necessary factor to establish working capacity based upon 85 percent of absolute capacity.
3. The administration and all other support functions can be provided in space equal to 18 percent of the sum determined in 1 and 2 above excluding any reader space added for postgraduate students.
4. Reasonable provision for growth over a 10-year period will be taken into account.

Adverse reaction to the Atkinson Report was immediate. In Great Britain, the Standing Conference of National and University Libraries (SCONUL) rejected the concept of the self-renewing library. And in 1996 SCONUL published an official paper: *Space Requirements for Academic Libraries and Learning Resource Centres,* prepared by Andrew McDonald on behalf of the SCONUL Advisory Committee on Buildings. This document is here reproduced in full because of its relevance to planning formulae or norms and its judicious presentation.

Space Requirements for Academic Libraries and Learning Resource Centres*

Background

1 Norms or guidelines for the size of a university library in the United Kingdom were last approved some twenty years ago by the then University Grants Committee when it accepted the recommendations of the Atkinson Committee Report (1976) on *Capital provision for university libraries.* According to what have become known as the Atkinson Norms, the appropriate net size of a university's central library should be assessed by the following formula:

$1.25m^2$/FTE student numbers

plus $0.2m^2$/FTE student numbers in 10 years' time

plus   assessed provision for special collections

plus   adjustment for special circumstances.

The gross size of the library can be derived by adding the balance area (for toilets and staircases etc.) to this net figure. Depending on the shape of the building, this balance area is commonly about 25%.

2 The figure of $1.25m^2$ was based on $0.40m^2$ for seating and $0.62m^2$ for bookstacks with an additional 20% allowed for administration (library staff). It was also suggested that there should be one reader place for every six students (FTE) on average, and the space required for each reader place was $2.39m^2$. It was recognised that different provision was appropriate for different academic disciplines, for example one place for every two law students was recommended.

3 These norms have been widely adopted not only in the UK but also around the world, and have been used by many universities in planning their libraries and bidding for the necessary resources. On the other hand, some universities have never achieved the level of funding necessary even to approach these minimum standards.

4 They were developed at a time when higher education was very different. The emphasis was upon formal teaching in faculties and departments, and university libraries contained predominantly print-based collections.

5 Space provision in the former polytechnics has historically been less generous than in the pre-1992 university libraries with their larger collections. Before the removal of the binary divide, the sector average for polytechnics was reported to lie toward the lower end of the range 0.8 to $1.2m^2$/SFTE (space FTE). The basic allowance recommended for polytechnic libraries by the Department of Education and Science in 1971 was only $0.8m^2$ per SFTE. However, additional space was permitted for 'non-specialised teaching accommodation,' giving a possible gross figure as high as $1.6m^2$/SFTE. One reader place was recommended for every 4 to 5 SFTE students. These minimal and now disregarded guidelines made no allowance for the growth of significant collections and were formally withdrawn in 1991. In the Republic of Ireland, a guideline of one place for every 3.75 students is used, reflecting the relatively heavy use of academic libraries.

6 The Report of the Joint Funding Councils' Libraries Review Group (The Follett Report, 1993) considered library and information service provision in

---

*Reproduced by permission of the Standing Conference of National and University Libraries, 102 Euston Street, London, NW1 2HA, England

the higher education sector and assessed, amongst other things, the space requirements resulting from the recent growth in student numbers. The Group utilised the existing UGC norms (one reader place for every six students at 2.39m² each) and concluded that, as a result of the expansion in student numbers between 1988/89 and 1992/93, an additional 49,000 reader places were required in higher education libraries in the United Kingdom at an estimated cost of £140 million.

7 Although Follett recognised that the UGC norms 'may not always be regarded as appropriate,' the Report conceded that they 'are arguably the best available' and based their quantitative assessments and funding recommendations upon them.

Current pressures on space

8 It is widely accepted that the UGC norms are now outdated and no longer reflect the real pressure for library space. A number [of] factors, in addition to the growth of student numbers, have contributed to this:

Information Technology

9 Despite predictions to the contrary, information technology has made a proportionately greater demand on library space and has also increased the cost of library buildings. Follett usefully drew attention to the potential for electronic media to reduce the requirement for library space in the long term, but took a commendably pragmatic view as to when in the next century this might happen. In the meantime and for the foreseeable future, libraries must provide access to *both* print-based and IT-based resources. They must also support innovations in technology-enhanced teaching and learning.

10 The existing space norm was based on a reader's module with a table measuring 900mm by 600mm. It has become increasingly clear that this was an absolute minimum even in print-based libraries; but as the use of equipment, especially computing equipment, has grown, this table size has become grossly inadequate. In order to provide space for books, computers and readers' papers, a table size of 1200mm by 800mm is necessary. As a result of increasing IT provision, the old space norm of 2.39m² per reader space has therefore been found to be insufficient, and in recent projects universities have found it necessary to make a more generous space allowance of between 2.5m² and 4m² per reader space.

11 Libraries have also found that, contrary to expectation, computers and peripheral devices have become larger and, for example, the current multimedia machines and interactive video facilities take proportionately more space than older machines. In addition, space must be given over to user support, printing services and essential distribution equipment. There is also the trend for readers to bring in their own portable machines and plug them into the network provided.

12 Many new libraries have been fully wired-up and have the potential to provide a PC at every reader place. The cost of trunking, flood wiring and connections, together with the cost of the equipment itself and the growing need for effective security, are by no means insignificant. Some library services have a planning ratio for the number of IT to traditional reader places. Some institutions have developed a ratio for the number of PCs per student in the institution as a whole, following the 1:5 ratio recommended in the Nelson Report (1983).

Teaching and learning methods

13 The change in emphasis from teaching to learning in higher education has intensified the pressure on libraries, and has reinforced the crucial importance of libraries and learning resources in the learning process. The move to student-centred or independent learning has shifted the balance from teaching in classrooms to learning in libraries and learning resource centres. The

curriculum may involve resource-based or group-based learning. Students are spending a much greater proportion of the learning time in libraries. This trend has been most pronounced in the newer universities, where libraries are no longer regarded solely as quiet study areas, but are also used for formal and informal teaching activities and for other learning support services. Areas for group discussion are now common. Occupancy and usage surveys reveal a much greater use of libraries in proportion to student numbers than was the case with more traditional teaching methods. The shift from lecture room to library use is reflected in university estates strategies. Institutions have recognised the need to invest in improving library and learning support services since they play a much greater part in the students' learning experience.

Access and ownership

14 Numbers of libraries and learning resource centres have developed strategies for moving towards providing *access* to information rather than *holding* large collections. This is for reasons of cost as much as space saving. Although both access services and holdings remain important, many institutions are placing an increasing emphasis on access services. In the long term, widespread digitisation may save space in libraries and networked services are increasingly delivered directly to the end user. However, for the moment, the effect of improved electronic services has often been to stimulate demand for conventional services and the printed collections held by libraries. It remains true that in some universities the quality of the campus network and the machines available on users' desks are not always capable of delivering the latest services. For multi-media applications and some electronic retrieval and delivery services, users turn to libraries, where the necessary equipment is provided and maintained, and where trained assistance is available.

15 Although there are a few experimental projects concerned with delivering student texts electronically, the bulk of core student provision remains in printed form.

Learning resource centres

16 The word library has been use[d] synonymously with learning resource centre. Many recent learning resource centres have been planned so as to provide flexible accommodation for a large number of reader places and a wide range of learning media, often placing an increased emphasis on electronic sources and computer facilities rather than traditional printed collections. In some universities the learning resource centre includes a variety of other learning facilities—information skills laboratories; computer clusters; media centres; teaching and learning development services; and curriculum innovation units. This, together with the provision of a variety of reader places, such as group study areas and drop-in facilities, has placed a heavy burden on available space.

Convergence

17 Some universities in planning converged services have recognised that greater space is required for IT-based provision and other learning support activities. Although there are no national norms for converged services, or indeed other academic services, space allocations as high as 4m² per reader place have been reported. In some cases the total space planned has been less than would have been provided for each service separately.

Semesterisation, modularisation and unitisation

18 University libraries have reported increased intensity of use and different patterns of demand as a result of changes in academic structure and course organisation and delivery.

Non-traditional students

19 Methods of calculating space entitlement based on FTEs have tended to underestimate the pressure placed on libraries by many non-traditional stu-

dents. Surveys have demonstrated that part-time students, mature students and overseas students often make proportionately greater use of learning resources because of increased motivation and dependence on libraries, and because the service is often their main academic and social focus. Courses based on open and distance learning have also been found to place surprisingly heavy demands on library space, especially where the students are reasonably close to campus. The use of space FTEs as opposed to conventional FTEs has diminished the space entitlement, and fails to take account of the heavy use made by the increasing number of individuals in higher education who are not taking conventional full-time courses.

Growth in collections

20 As a welcome outcome of the Follett Report, many universities have expanded their libraries and learning resource centres, providing much-needed additional reader places. However, there continues to be a rapid expansion in the publication rate of printed books and periodicals (and an even faster growth in electronic sources), placing additional pressure on space in those libraries committed to building and preserving comprehensive collections for research purposes. Indeed, they may be encouraged to develop an explicit collection development and access policy, as part of a national contribution to research provision. For major research libraries, the allowance in the old UGC norms for collections has become increasingly inadequate, particularly in those libraries committed to improving the number of reader places at the same time. Some libraries have followed the Atkinson recommendations and relegate material to make way for new acquisitions. Many others, who are committed to retaining their acquisitions, have come under intense pressure for space, and some have been forced to house their growing collections in high density shelving or in stores. University libraries are adding to their special collections and are developing new ones. Recent Funding Council grants for cataloguing many of these collections are designed to stimulate interest and use.

Range of services and reader places

21 The range of services provided by libraries has developed considerably since 1976. It is recognised that a wider variety of reader places is now required to support different learning patterns and styles, with provision for group study and quiet study areas.

Provision for disability

22 Much greater emphasis is now placed on providing access for users with disability, not only because of legal requirements and issues of equal opportunity, but also because good design for the disabled is generally good design for the able-bodied. Wider aisle widths and better access routes, nevertheless, absorb additional space.

Library staff

23 The old UGC norm assumed library staff would absorb something like 20% of usable space, but it quickly became clear that the development of subject librarians and distributed learning support required greater provision. Far from saving space, many recent advances in automation and electronic access require additional space for the staff concerned with planning, maintaining and supporting services. Some libraries have found that 30% of the usable space is required for staff, particularly in predominantly IT-based services.

Decentralisation

24 The old UGC norms were formulated to determine the size of the *central* university library. Some universities have decentralised library provision, and in such cases space is inevitably taken up by the essential services, such as issue counters, staff assistance and photocopiers, which must be duplicated on each site. Decentralisation means that greater space is proportionately necessary.

Quality of space

25 There are also important qualitative aspects in planning library space. The academic library is not intended as a high-density swotting shed but should be a good quality learning environment with an ambience conducive to study, access to information, and the delivery of high quality services. An investment in a high standard of internal finish and furnishings is essential to create this quality, and withstand heavy use over an extended period with the minimum of maintenance. Surveys confirm that students spend an increasing amount of their study time in libraries. The quality of learning resources provision is judged in quality assessments, and it can be an influential factor in students' choice of institution. Universities are also increasingly concerned about space efficiency, running and maintenance costs, and life-cycle costs.

Future norms and standards

26 Opinion varies about the value of space norms or guidelines. It is argued that some sort of guideline is better than none at all, and that nationally accepted norms can be useful for planning purposes and for making bids to parent institutions and funding bodies. Others regard standards as unattainable and unrealistic aspirations for which funding is unlikely ever to be made available, and point out that several institutions have never reached the recommended levels. Whatever view is taken, there is a sector average, and this is improving now that seventy or so institutions are expanding and developing their libraries, mostly as a result of the Funding Councils' initiative.

27 It has been suggested that space allocation is a matter for individual universities, and in practice it falls to each university to make decisions according to local circumstances which might include course structures, learning strategies, research profile, collection size, and funding levels. On the other hand, as Follett recognised, it is useful to have some guidance when taking a national and comparative view, and when making funding decisions.

28 Follett usefully identified an average cost for creating a square metre of library space in 1993 as £1,200, including building costs, professional fees, furniture and VAT. However, the planning of libraries should not simply be driven by the cost per square metre. The quality of the space must be appropriate for supporting the learning and research needs of the academic community.

29 The amount of space provided and the number of reader places have both been recognised as indicators for evaluating the performance of academic libraries in the recent Consultative Report by the Joint Funding Councils' Ad-hoc Group on Performance Indicators for Libraries *(The effective academic library)*.

30 The future of the library as a physical 'place' is a matter of considerable professional speculation and debate. Despite some almost reckless predictions about the end of the book and print-based libraries, there is an increasing number of new library buildings and refurbishment projects around the world, creating 'scholarly' environments in which learning and research can be pursued, often, as it happens, with growing printed collections. The library building provides a physical focus where people can come together (preferably without disturbing each other too much) to study, reflect, retrieve information, consult the collections, use serviced equipment and computers, seek professional assistance and make use of the services provided. Interestingly, many of the electronic libraries in the world are still buildings, and most often very pleasant ones.

31 Whatever the view on the absolute value of space norms, there can be little doubt that many universities and the Funding Councils have found them a useful guideline and planning tool. With the prevailing norms now sadly out of date, a revised assessment of the space requirements for academic libraries and learning resource centers is long overdue. Such a revision should reflect all the factors mentioned in this paper, but should take particular account of the effect of changes in teaching and learning and developments in informa-

tion technology on space requirements. They should not be prescriptive, but should recognise the heterogeneity of the sector, and should reflect good practice, leaving institutions to decide upon local provision and priorities within a broadly accepted nationally determined framework.

Andrew McDonald
Chair, SCONUL Advisory Committee on Buildings
Director of Information Services, University of Sunderland
February 1996

B.7.9 Variability among Countries

From the preceding eight examples from professional associations and governmental agencies, as well as others discussed in this volume, it is clear that a considerable range of guidelines and standards may be found; any given guideline must be used with care, for the circumstance of the local situation should be the controlling factor. Although hardly exhaustive, tables B.29 and B.30 serve to illustrate differences in study and stack space norms among several countries.

TABLE B.29   Study Accommodation

CountryOrigin/	Undergraduate	Postgraduate	Research	% Enrollment
U.S.A.	25 ft² (2.3 m²)	35 ft² (3.3 m²)	55 ft² (5.0 m²)	25–30
Canada	25 ft² (2.3 m²)	35 ft² (3.3 m²)	75 ft² (7.0 m²)	25–40
U.K.	26 ft² (2.39 m²)	26 ft² (2.39 m²)	—	16
France	16 ft² (1.5 m²)	16 ft² (1.5 m²)	65 ft² (6.0 m²)	10 (science) 12 (arts)
Republic of South Africa	27 ft² (2.5 m²)	37 ft² (3.5 m²)	37 ft² (3.5 m²)	25

From Heather M. Edwards, *University Library Building Planning* (Metuchen, N.J.: Scarecrow Press, 1990), p. 23.

TABLE B.30   Stack Space[a]

Country/Origin	Open Access	Storage
U.S.A.	10 vols./ft² (108 vols./m²)	15 vols./ft² (160 vols./m²)
Canada	10 vols./ft² (108 vols./m²)	12.5 vols./ft² (135 vols./m²)
U.K. (books)	20 vols./ft² (213 vols./m²)	23 vols./ft² (248 vols./m²)
U.K. (journals)	9.8 vols./ft² (106 vols./m²)	11.3 vols./ft² (122 vols./m²)
France	15.4 vols./ft² (166 vols./m²)	—
Republic of South Africa	10.3 vols./ft² (110 vols./m²)	—

[a] All standards assume fixed shelving in sections 7 ft 6 in. high × 3 ft wide × 8 in. deep (2.286 × 0.914 × 0.203 m).

From Heather M. Edwards, *University Library Building Planning* (Metuchen, N.J.: Scarecrow Press, 1990), p. 23.

APPENDIX C

Building Blocks for Library Space: Functional Guidelines 1995

A [sociology] of objects means that they must be seen within the concrete system of the society that creates them and receives them, so they must be seen as a language listened to as it is being spoken.

—Umberto Eco, *Travels in Hyperreality*

This appendix presents a methodology for putting together a table of space requirements based upon the occupancy of the building.[1] Although it includes information applicable to public libraries, it is of use for any library and represents a fundamentally sound approach to establishing space requirements. Many of the elements for which specific areas are proposed are illustrated in the original text. It is also expected that this material will be updated from time to time; there may be use in obtaining the most recent version.

Although what follows is quoted text, references to illustrations in this publication have been removed. Clarifications have been added in this appendix in footnotes 2 and 4.

Background and Intent

Experience in libraries has shown that in planning physical space requirements, the circulation space around or adjacent to an item (space for people

---

[1] Library Administration and Management Association, Buildings and Equipment Section, Functional Space Requirements Committee (Deborah Bloomfield Dancik and Emelie Jensen Shroder, editors), *Building Blocks for Library Space: Functional Guidelines 1995* (Chicago: American Library Association, 1995). Available through ALA's Order Department.

to move around, stand, or sit in front of, or to otherwise use equipment and furniture) has been greatly underestimated or frequently ignored, making the total space much less functional. This is a working paper, both in terms of the number and range of items included and of the feet/meters recommended. The areas given in this document are based on intensive discussions among practicing librarians, architects, and professional building consultants to determine the typical size of a given item, e.g., a piece of furniture or equipment.

The square feet/square meters required, as given in the Guidelines, are an aggregate figure of the actual footprint (exact amount of space occupied) of an item *plus circulation area*. The committee determined that not giving the actual footprint size would remove the preoccupation with the footprint itself and aid library planners in focusing on the total space required. Space estimates are based on typical or average-sized furniture and equipment, not specific manufacturers' specifications. If much larger- or smaller-than-typical sizes are needed, then some adjustment in the totals will be necessary.

Each library's equipment and furniture needs differ. The functions, areas, and items listed are intended as building blocks. Users of the Guidelines should, by selecting those areas and items needed, determine the *workable* space required. But the totals are not the final answer to how big any particular library should be. The figures do not presume placement; various placements of items may provide economies of space, e.g., OPAC stations that are back-to-back versus in a line versus stand-alones. Nor are placement clearances and aisle widths included. The list is not intended as a checklist of all areas that could or should be included in a typical library.

These are guidelines, not standards or specifications, and given factors of scale, are most appropriately used in the planning of small to medium-sized libraries. They should be used in conjunction with existing standards, such as the Americans with Disabilities Act. Applicable state, local, and institutional codes or laws should be consulted. Also, professional associations, such as the Association for Educational Communications and Technology, publish program standards for specific types of libraries. A checklist, such as the *Checklist of Building Design Considerations,* and the bibliography *Planning Library Buildings: A Select Bibliography* (both available through ALA) can provide assistance.

Recent Changes Affecting Planning

Library-planning literature written prior to 1994 generally does not reflect the need for considerable technological space and configurations. The heavy emphasis on terminals, visuals, and displays, services now available and promoted by most libraries, is not adequately represented in the earlier program-planning literature. Thus, space estimates are found to be inadequate when the space constructed is actually used. Books and paper collections coexist with technologies, rather than being replaced by them, and the totality does not fit into the same space, nor is the space required for one interchangeable with that required for the other. Many states still use 75% net-to-gross space estimates to address the space required for electrical and telecommunications closets. Unfortunately, in the automated environment of current libraries, this can be insufficient. The new ADA requirements for additional traffic space also affect the total space needs to be considered.

[This appendix provides] net space (assignable, usable, programmed space). For a complete building program, the unassigned (unprogrammed) space (net to gross) must be added to the program after the total programmed space ("assigned space," "usable area") is developed. Unassigned space includes the vestibule, lobby, public stairs, rest rooms, fire stairs, major corridors, elevators, janitor's closets, pipe and duct spaces, mechanical and electrical rooms, etc., and is added as a percentage of the total building square footage.

For a smaller building (under 40,000 square feet), 25% net to gross may be adequate;[2] for a medium-sized building (41,000–60,000 square feet), use 25%–30%; for a large building (100,000 square feet plus) or a renovation of any size, 30–35% net to gross may be required. With a building renovation, space is frequently lost because of inefficiencies. The actual net to gross may also vary according to architectural decisions or the size of the entrance or any grand open spaces in the architectural design, since all of these spaces are unassigned (unprogrammed) space.

Projecting Total Area Requirement

To determine the square footage required for a specific library facility, find the sum (A) of the areas for *all assigned individual items, tasks, and rooms*. Then to (A) add an additional factor (B) of 33⅓% for *unassignable areas* such as rest rooms, mechanical and electrical rooms, elevators and stairs, vestibules, life/safety appurtenances, public telephones, drinking fountains, and wall thicknesses. The total (C) is the *gross square footage* required.[3] For example:

Total of all items, assignable spaces and services	(A)	30,000 sq. ft.
Net-to-gross factor (A) × 33⅓% =	(B)	+10,000 sq. ft.
Gross square footage	(C)	40,000 sq. ft.

Why 33⅓%? It is the reciprocal of a commonly used net-to-gross factor of 75%. If it were determined that a library of 40,000 square feet was to be constructed, to find the net assignable area available for library use including aisles and corridors, one would typically use a 75% net-to-gross factor.

Gross square footage	(C)	40,000 sq. ft.
Net assignable square area (C) × 75% =	(A)	30,000 sq. ft.

Programmers, library directors and library boards, and university and municipal administrators should not be surprised if the program indicates a

---

[2] [That is, to determine the gross space requirement, you need to add 25% of the net space to the total of the net space as explained later in the text. Alternatively, multiply the net space by 1.25 (or 1 plus the percentage difference) to determine the gross space requirements.

The nature of the facility plays a very large role in determining the net-to-gross ratio as well; at one extreme is the heavily used college library, which will require proportionately a large amount of unassigned space, compared to the storage facility, which will have proportionately little unassigned space, even where the two facility types are the same size. A typical public library for a large city will have a very large difference between net and gross area requirements. The difference in library function probably has more influence upon net-to-gross ratios than does the size of the facility.]

[3] Note: If the facility is large (75,000 square feet or more) adding a factor of 15% of net (A) is advisable for the accommodation of corridors and larger main aisles.

space increase of 300%. Often doubling the existing areas only brings existing capacities for customers, staff, and collections into compliance with current codes. Doubling existing space may not provide for growth or for change in service deliveries. If further expansion is suggested but not affordable, then review the needs of customers and staff and modify the library mission and revise the program to include planning for a second phase of expansion. It is essential that everyone involved in the planning and funding is assured that the facility will meet the intended program.

The facility's program must reflect the library's changing needs and constituencies. In an electronic library, paper-based collections may not grow at the same rate as in the past, but the addition of electronic technologies may increase the need for more staff and new service centers. Limited growth in some departments may be indicated even as more services are offered outside the facility itself. And as barrier-free accessibility brings more disabled customers into the large community and the library, there may be a supporting need for community interaction and the provision of special equipment and services. As you can see, there are no facile answers to the question, How much space is enough?

How to Use This Guide

- From the "menu" of areas, functions, and items [tables C.1–C.4], select the necessary ones needed to match the size of, type of, or program for the library being planned. The Universal Building Blocks section lists items or spaces common to many library functions (e.g., queuing space needed in circulation, reference, or photocopying), and these items therefore are not repeated under the other headings [table C.1].
- Remember to include everything needed for a function and estimate the space accordingly; for example, a photocopying area might include the machine itself plus a sorting table, a paper recycling bin, and shelves for the reshelving of materials plus a debit card dispenser.
- For each item, multiply number required by the amount of space given for each.
- The number of square feet needed for any general functional area will be the total space for items of furniture and equipment assigned to that heading. Where equipment is grouped in close proximity, some reduction in the given space requirement is advisable because the circulation space may be reduced.
- A worksheet for this purpose may be useful:

EXAMPLE
General Area: Library Instruction

No. of items × square feet per item = minimum square footage
required for functional space

2 computer stations × 36 sq. ft.   = 72 sq. ft.
25 student seats × 20 sq. ft.   = 500 sq. ft.

- The square-foot designations should be considered as building blocks; taken together these make up the basic needs for assigned spaces that would be included in the plan for the library project. Under "Square Feet Required Per Area or Item," space has been incorporated for an operator or user and an equipment-specific circulation area.

[TABLE C.1]   Universal Building Blocks

Items and spaces listed here are common to many functional areas; consult this section when determining space required for specific functions.

	Required per Area or Item	
	Square Feet	Square Meters
Book truck parking	8	0.743
Computer stations		
Terminal, work surface, chair	36	3.345
Terminal, work surface, chair with printer	45.5	4.181
Printer (networked)	36	3.345
Conference/meeting room	20/person (150 min.)	1.858/person
Add 15% of total for storage, if needed.		
If lobby is adjacent, add 20% of meeting room space for lobby.		
Filing cabinet (lateral)	15	1.394
Lockers (i.e, one full-height or two half-height, etc.)	5	0.465
Materials and supplies storage		
For items that require permanent storage space include storage space/rooms as necessary.		
Gurney/bin	16	1.486
Pallet/skid	12	1.115
Storage/supply cabinet (2 doors)	20	1.858
Supply room (see Admin./Staff)		
Photocopying/fax		
Machine, standard cabinet mounted (with or without coin op)	52	4.831
Station (machine, table, shelf, supplies, recycle containers)	80	7.432
Queuing area	9/person	0.836/person
Recycling container	6	0.557
Rest rooms—for public or staff see local codes; include in non-assignable space		
Tables		
Two seat (nose-to-nose)	40/person	3.716/person
Four seat (youth or adult)	30/person	2.787/person
Workstation (includes terminal, printer, work surface, chair, file, shelving, guest chair)	84.8	7.886

Library shelving constitutes the largest single allocation of space in a conventional library. The floor space required by an individual shelving unit is determined by a combination of the width of the shelving unit, the depth of the unit, and the width of the aisle found in the bookstack. [Table C.2] provides an estimate of floor space required per shelving unit in different shelving environments. The [table] assumes a standard 36-inch shelving

[TABLE C.2]   Shelving and Media Storage Shelving Matrix

	Base Shelf			
Aisle Width	10 inches	12 inches	15 inches	18 inches
36 inches	8.75 sq. ft.	9.40 sq. ft.	10.30 sq. ft.	11.25 sq. ft.
42 inches	9.70 sq. ft.	10.30 sq. ft.	11.25 sq. ft.	12.20 sq. ft.
48 inches	10.65 sq. ft.	11.25 sq. ft.	12.20 sq. ft.	13.15 sq. ft.

width. To determine the appropriate space allocation for a given shelving environment, read across from the desired aisle width to the desired base shelf depth. For example, a collection housed on shelving 36 inches wide and 12 inches deep installed on a 42-inch aisle requires 10.30 square feet *per single-faced unit of shelving.* For double-faced shelving units, multiply the space allocation on this table by two. For metric conversion, multiply each number by .093.

Video Storage

Use matrix [table C.2] for shelving according to individual manufacturer for shelf base (average 12 inches/unit).

CD or CD-ROM Storage

See [table C.3] if using storage cabinets, or use matrix [above] for shelving according to shelf base.

Spinners for Paperbacks, CDs, CD-ROMs, Cassettes, Videos, Etc.

	Square Ft.	Square Meters
Per unit (30-inch base diameter)	42.25/unit	3.925/unit

Compact Shelving

	Square Ft.	Square Meters
Single-faced, 10-inch base	3.75/unit	0.348/unit

In closed stacks, every fifth or sixth range must be immovable (fixed); in open stacks, every third or fourth range, according to frequency of use. The more use, the more fixed ranges for ease of use. Figure these according to the shelving matrix so there will be aisle space.

Note: Compact shelving requires additional floor load—about 300 lbs./ sq. ft.; the normal floor load for a library is about 150 lbs./sq. ft. Refer to your structural engineer for floor load requirements.

[TABLE C.3]   Public and Specialized User Areas

	Required per Area or Item	
	Square Feet	Square Meters
Carrel		
Adult, youth, undergraduate	36–45.5	3.345–4.273
Faculty study (enclosed)	80	7.432
Graduate student (includes lockable storage bin, filing space, terminal, work surface)	63	5.853
Children's area		
Spaces given here accommodate the way in which children approach and use furniture, equipment, etc.		
Child's lounge seat	36	3.345
Child's table (4-place)	90	8.361
Floor activity space	20/person	1.858/person
Service desk	120/staff station	11.148/staff station
Storytelling/multipurpose area	15/child	1.394/child
Circulation checkout		
(see also Circulation under Non-Public for staff space)		
Self-checkout	45.5/station	4.227/station
Display area		
Display rack (wall mounted)	9	0.836
Handout display rack, freestanding	20	1.858
"New Book" display (freestanding, all types)	50	4.645
Faculty study (see Carrel)		
Graduate workstation (see Carrel)		
Information/reference or interlibrary loan area		
Atlas/folio case (freestanding)	36.75	3.414
Borrowing station (ILL)	40	3.716
Card catalog (60-drawer unit, single-faced freestanding)	20	1.858
CD-ROM station (includes printer)	45.5	4.227
CD-ROM storage	15	1.394
Dictionary stand	25	2.322
Index table	150	13.935
Information desk	40/staff station	3.716/staff station
Office (Head of Reference—see Non-Public Areas)		
Online search station (PC, printer, manuals, etc.: space for 2 people to confer, e.g., searcher and patron)	100/station	9.290/station
Patron access catalog		
Without printer	36	3.345
With printer	45.5	[4.227]
Reference service desk (includes interview and equipment space)	120/staff station	11.148/staff station

(Continued)

[TABLE C.3]   **continued**

	Required per Area or Item	
	Square Feet	Square Meters
Library instruction/user education area		
Equipment storage (to be stored, e.g., overhead projector with or without cart)	6/unit	0.557/unit
Instructor's space (incl. circulation area and console)	118	10.963
Podium	12.5	1.161
Projection screen (6-foot-wide freestanding)	48	4.459
Student seating (tablet arm classroom seating)	20	1.858
Light table/map viewing	56	5.203
Listening areas		
Individual	36–45.5	[3.345–4.227]
Group (good for both large and small groups)	15/person	1.394/person
Lobby (if separate)—Add 20% of meeting room space		
Lobby and entrance area		
Bench (freestanding)	36	3.345
Public or emergency telephone		
Wall-mounted	10	0.929
Freestanding	16	1.486
Guards desk	24	2.230
Security system (typically 4 feet × 6 feet per aisle)[4]		
(vestibule site specific, included in nonassignable area)	24	2.230
Lounge seat	32–68/seat	2.973–6.317/seat
Map viewing station—see Light table		
Media/Publications center		
Audio recording room	120	11.148
Audio studio	150	13.935
Classroom	30/person	2.787/person
Conference room	30/person	2.787/person
Darkroom	80	7.432
Editing	80	7.432
Equipment manuals	10/shelving unit	0.929/shelving unit
Equipment station—see Bibliographic instruction area		
Graphics (computer-generated)	50	4.645
Preview room	50	4.645
Production workstation	120	11.148
Repair/cleaning workstation	80	7.432
Reproduction (workstation)	80	7.432
Slide viewing station (includes projection screen)	56	5.203
Storage	15% of total space	15% of total space
TV studio	1,200	111.484
TV studio, small	600	55.742

---

[4][This is what some call a book-detection system with detection screens at each potential exit aisle.]

	Required per Area or Item	
	Square Feet	Square Meters
Microcomputer laboratory		
Microcomputer lab station (includes terminal, printer, work surface, manuals)	45.5	4.227
Microcomputer lab service desk	120/staff station	11.148/staff station
Microform equipment		
Microfilm/fiche reader	36	3.345
Microfilm/fiche reader/printer	36	3.345
Microfilm/fiche reader/printer with tablet arms	61.75	5.742
Film/fiche duplicator (hot processor, no drying cabinet)	80	7.432
Microform storage (multipurpose film or fiche cabinet)		
Single-faced (includes access/aisle)	18	1.672
Double-faced	36	3.345
Periodicals display—see also Display entries (Number of units required is dependent upon number of titles to be shelved and how densely titles are to be displayed.)		
Study room (for group work)	30/person	2. 787/person
Administration/Staff		
Coat storage	8/person	0.716/person
Offices		
Director (includes desk, credenza, guest seating, bookcase)	200	18.580
Other	150	13.935
Supervisor workstation	120	11.148
Kitchen	80	7.432
Kitchenette	50	4.645
Reception area	20/person	1.858/person
Rest room, executive	30	2.787
Safe (2.5 feet square)	6	0.557
Staff supply room	120 minimum	11.148 minimum
Work/sorting table	40	3.716
Bindery conservation		
Binding equipment (normally part of staff workstation)	10	0.929
Board cutter (60 in./152 cm blade)	85	[7.897]
Book press	15	1.393
Paper cutter (36 in./91 cm blade)	50	[4.645]
Roller backer	20	1.858
Shipping boxes	8/stack	0.743/stack
Tying machine	25	2.322
Stamper	20	1.858
Bookmobile and outreach area	Equipment and site specific	

[TABLE C.4] **Non-Public and Professional/Staff Work Areas**

	Required per Area or Item	
	Square Feet	Square Meters
Circulation control area		
This is staff space; for public space, see Circulation checkout [in table C.3].		
Book sensitization workstation (freestanding)	40	3.716
Book return unit		
Freestanding	16	1.486
As part of counter	12	1.115
Circ. desk, online single station (includes terminal and desensitization unit)	80	7.432
Circ. desk, manual, small	120	11.148
Patron transaction space	25/station	2.322/station
Sorting/staging area	20/unit of shelving	1.858/unit of shelving
Computer room		
Computer terminal	6	0.557
Console, operators	20	1.858
CPU	42	3.901
Disk drives, external	42	3.901
Environmental controls—see manufacturer's requirements		
Fire-suppression equipment—see manufacturer's requirements		
Power supply, uninterruptable	10	0.929
Printer	36	3.345
Storage	Equipment and site specific	
Tape drive, external	30	2.787
Telecommunications equipment	20	1.858
Copy service—see specific items		
Mail/Receiving		
Dumpster	86	7.990
Flat truck	16	1.486
Hand truck	4	0.372
Loading dock (minimum 1 truck)	110	10.219
Mail hampers	9	0.836
Scale	6	0.557
Sorting table	40	3.716
Stapler, foot operated	6	0.557
Tape dispensers	2	0.186
Bag rack	11	1.021
Wrapping table	33	3.066
Weighing/metering counter	33	3.066
Mail delivery cart	15	1.394
Maintenance office and area		
Facility manager (includes desk, plan file, drafting table, chairs, files, bookcases)	200	18.580
Repair room (includes workbench, tool and equipment storage)	150	13.935
Technical Services—see specific items elsewhere		

APPENDIX D

Environmental Guidelines for Collection Preservation

The great use of life is to spend it for something that outlasts it.

—William James, *Thought Character*

Except where noted, this appendix is largely based upon papers and publications by William P. Lull. Much comes from *Conservation Environment Guidelines for Libraries and Archives,*[1] written by Mr. Lull with the assistance of Paul N. Banks; we are appreciative of Mr. Lull's participation in the preparation of this appendix.

Introduction

Environment has a direct and continuing effect on the physical condition of all objects, influencing the rate of natural processes and often introducing elements that alter the nature and direction of those processes.[2] This is true whether the objects be living (plants or animals) or inanimate (stones, buildings, automobiles, books). The degree to which inanimate objects are susceptible to environmental pressures depends upon their physical and chemical structure. Some materials are very stable through a broad range of environmental conditions, while others can tolerate little change in their surroundings without themselves undergoing change.

Because books are relatively fragile and most are chemically unstable, conditions of shelving, use, and exhibition are of critical importance to their survival. The same can be said for other library materials, whether printed, photographic (as with motion pictures, microtexts, and normal photographs), magnetic (from floppy disks to audio- or videotape), mechanically or optically engraved (as with phonograph records, CDs, videodiscs), or manuscript records.

Given the singular importance of the library environment for the longevity of materials, this appendix is presented as a guide to preservation- or conservation-based environments designed to prolong the life of the collections. Where aspects of this appendix are adopted, it will be important to carry out the intent of the information presented here through the program, design phases, construction, start-up, and operations.

In considering the contents of this appendix, it should be obvious that some parts of the library or archive can be treated with less-restrictive criteria, including staff areas, reading rooms, and the like. This appendix is based upon preservation issues, not necessarily comfort or least-cost environments. Because of the cost implications of preservation-based environments (both initially and in terms of ongoing energy and maintenance cost), it is imperative that designers keep the institution apprised of cost implications and recommendations made here so that needed support can be obtained,

---

[1] William P. Lull, *Conservation Environment Guidelines for Libraries and Archives,* with Paul N. Banks (New York: New York State Library, 1990; Canadian Council of Archives, 1995).

[2] From the *Preservation Planning Manual* (Washington, D.C.: Association of Research Libraries, 1982), pp. 40–42.

surprises will be avoided, and budget priorities and expenditures will be kept consistent with institutional expectations. In balancing costs, the value of increased life for the collections will, in most cases, be the key component in support of the more restrictive environment.

This appendix does not address media alternatives that can also contribute to the life expectancy of certain kinds of information (insisting upon acid-free paper where possible, using polyester rather than acetate film, or the migration of information to more permanent technologies, including microfilming and digitization). Nor does it address certain design issues (such as book drops, rough surfaces, sharp components, knifing features of bookshelves and supports, and others that are treated in the main text of this volume), though there is information on construction materials that can affect interior gaseous and particulate pollution.

During the design and construction of any library/archive, those who will maintain the facility should be involved so they fully understand the operational needs and procedures for which they'll be responsible. This is especially true for the maintenance of building systems that will facilitate a preservation-based environment, for if those responsible for maintenance of all kinds do not understand the basis for the systems design, the original intent will sooner or later be compromised in the interest of expediency or cost savings. It is very important that the operating engineer and maintenance supervisors be fully aware of the full intent of the library/archive facility systems.

The discussions following are specific to this type of construction, and compliance is not something the typical HVAC engineer deals with on a regular basis. Where preservation of the collections is a serious goal, selecting and implementing environmental criteria may be critical to project success. The more-general statements by the Association of Research Libraries and the Research Libraries Group have served librarians in the past (see appendix D of the second edition of this book); the material presented here represents recent conclusions resulting from continuing research on the topic (for example, humidity requirements are generally lower than has been the case in the past). It is probable that until mass deacidification is economical and broadly available, optimization of the environment within the library/archive facility will continue to be by far the most effective tool for extending the life of collections. Because of this, meeting the criteria can be of such importance that even where the project engineer feels competent and able to address preservation-based criteria, an "outside" environmental consultant with credentials and experience in current library and archive design should often be hired, not necessarily to be the design engineer, but to provide guidance and review of the existing circumstance and to contribute to the program, design, and plans for start-up and operation of the facility. It is entirely possible that such an expert might need to be called in from another country, which would seem entirely justified where maximum preservation of the collections is imperative.

D.1 The Preservation Environment

What is a preservation environment? In simple terms, it is an environment designed, or natural, with qualities that minimize the degradation over time of library or archival materials. In this context, the environment meets criteria for humidity, temperature, light, particulate (solid or liquid particles suspended in the atmosphere) contamination, gaseous contamination, and physical accommodation of the collections and their use. For some materials, electromagnetic fields and high-voltage discharge (sparks) can be an environmental concern.

D.1.1 Relative Humidity

Absolute humidity is a measure of the amount of water contained in a given volume of air. Although this measure is of interest, the measure more commonly referred to is relative humidity (RH), which is a measure of the amount of water in air relative to how much can be held at saturation, or at the point condensation begins. Because the amount of water that air can hold is related to temperature (hot air can hold more water than cold air), the temperature of air plays an important role with relative humidity. With the same amount of water, the relative humidity goes down as temperature goes up. This is a fundamental fact that is used to dehumidify, and it is a fact that can lead to condensation problems in buildings in cold climates or where cold objects are exposed to a warmer, humid environment.

Almost all materials in the library collection change their moisture content in response to the relative humidity of the air in which they are maintained. With high humidity, the collections absorb moisture; with low humidity, they expel moisture until equilibrium is reached with the surrounding atmosphere.

High humidity can cause acute and chronic problems. Humidity much above 60 percent RH usually supports mold growth and pest infestations, and can foster oxidation or corrosion of metals. Acidification and acid-based reactions are also facilitated by high humidity; damage from particulates and gaseous contaminants can be increased under conditions of high humidity.

Low humidity can desiccate objects such that they become less supple and more brittle, leading to handling damage. Glues dry out and break down. Acute low humidity, below about 30 percent RH, can cause shrinkage and checks in wood and embrittlement of leather. Permanent embrittlement of vellum can certainly occur below 25 percent RH, and some institutions keep their vellum above 45 percent RH.

In the 1980s it was thought that the proper humidity for books and paper-based materials was 50 percent ± 5 percent. Lower relative humidity was recommended for film-based materials. This standard was promulgated by the *Preservation Planning Manual* of 1982, and, in some countries, it remains the standard applied to archive and library collections. Part of the attractiveness of this standard is that it emulates the thinking about museum requirements and was felt to be a comfortable compromise between the requirements of paper and vellum- or leather-based materials, which are better accommodated in somewhat higher humidity. A year later the *RLG Preservation Manual* stipulated that the ideal relative humidity should be 45 percent ± 5 percent.

More recently in the United States and elsewhere, the humidity goal in libraries and archives for paper-based materials has been typically expressed as 40 percent RH; 30 percent is generally regarded as ideal for film-based collections. Research at the Library of Congress has suggested that humidity as low as 30 percent may be even better for paper.[3] Lower humidity

---

[3] Donald K. Sebera, *Isoperms: An Environmental Management Tool,* Commission on Preservation and Access (June 1994); available from CLIR, 1755 Massachusetts Ave., NW, Suite 500, Washington, DC 20036 (based on "A Graphical Representation of the Relationship of Environmental Conditions to the Permanence of Hygroscopic Materials and Composites," Proceedings of Conservation in Archives, International Symposium (Ottawa, May 10–12, 1988), Paris: International Council on Archives (1989), pp. 51–75).

requirements are more easily maintained in cold climates (the problems of condensation are reduced with lower humidity), but more difficult in warm, humid environments (more energy is required to remove moisture from outside air).

The lower humidity requirements proposed are based upon indications that these levels (particularly 30 percent) are superior for preservation; they are said to reduce the rate of embrittlement caused by acid hydrolysis, to reduce the rate of absorption and damage from gaseous contaminants, and to increase the moisture stability in paper. It should be noted, however, that stress-caused mechanical damage can result from humidity variations beyond the range of 60 percent to 30 percent RH. Although lower humidity is important to extend collection life, avoiding these extremes is critical to protect from acute damage. When coming from these extreme conditions, collections may need to be brought to safer conditions gradually in order that the materials involved do not deform or become unduly stressed.

The actual level to be maintained should be based upon a study of the collection materials and the levels that can be reasonably maintained with current or improved environmental systems.

It has also been suggested that where humidity fluctuates, the effects of very nearly the highest humidity rather than the average humidity apply. One key goal is to establish a system that is as stable as reasonably possible.

Humidity Limitations and Priorities. Rather than simply specifying a constant humidity level, it may be necessary to consider the merits to the collection of the different aspects of humidity control, and how easily each aspect might be achieved. This can help set achievable intermediate goals on limited budgets for improved but less-than-ideal conditions.

For most paper collections, the major damage comes from humidities above 60 percent and below 30 percent RH in winter. Compromises may be indicated from cost or environmental system limitations, but most often are the result of a building envelope that will be damaged by high humidities in winter. In some cases it may be necessary to consider a low winter humidity of 25 percent RH. Depending on the collection, this may run the risk of embrittled handling or damage to vellum (even if the object is not handled).

A typical conflict is the case of a collection with vellum in a historic building that cannot tolerate 35 or 45 percent RH in winter. Treating the building to make it tolerant of enough humidity to protect the vellum might be entirely too expensive, and might damage its historic character. If the amount of vellum is limited, the vellum collections might be segregated and stored in special storage boxes, cabinets, or rooms that could have their humidity separately kept at the proper level for vellum, yet protecting the balance of the building from damage from the higher humidity within.

Stable conditions around 40 percent RH are usually desirable, but in compromise situations there may be considerable merit in reducing mold and insect growth by keeping the level below about 60 percent RH. Where this is not possible all the time, it should be done as much as possible in the humid seasons. Specific collateral actions, such as providing good air circulation and protecting the collections from initial insect contamination, will often determine how effective a compromise such as this will be.

D.1.2 Temperature

The speed of chemical reactions that contribute measurably to the deterioration of all materials is related to temperature, all other things being equal.

High temperatures accelerate deteriorating reactions, including those that contribute to the chemical breakdown of cellulose, the deterioration of binders in magnetic media, the fading and discoloration of photographic images, and the promotion of mold growth. When combined with high humidity, most of these reactions progress even more rapidly. Acute high temperatures can cause rapid and permanent damage to audio- and videotape, phonograph records, and other materials.

Research at the Library of Congress by Chandru Shahani has shown that variations in temperatures over a period of several hours, particularly from day to night, can induce humidity changes in books. In fact, ambient temperature changes can cause more variation in the humidity content inside books than can similar variations in ambient relative humidity.

The *Preservation Planning Manual* of 1982 stipulates that temperature in a library should be 65° F. (18° C.) plus or minus 5° F. (about 3° C.) year-round. More recent standards offer similar temperature requirements.

The key to selecting temperature goals is human occupancy and use of the collections; if the collections were not to be used, they could be much colder and thereby last considerably longer. The Lyndon Baines Johnson Library, at the University of Texas in Austin, maintains a vault that is kept below freezing for this purpose. However, with use, materials must be brought up to room temperature without risking condensation—an exercise that can take a fair amount of time and one that subjects the object to stress; frozen collections are not recommended where regular or capricious use is expected. However, generally speaking, cooler is better for the collections provided condensation upon access is not a risk, and provided the relative humidity can be controlled in the cold storage environment.

Limitations and Priorities for Temperature. For occupied stack and collections use areas, temperature goals do not usually present as much of a challenge as relative humidity goals and they are usually more of a one-way problem: The temperature is too high. Lower temperatures in winter can also allow easier and less expensive humidification.

A high temperature limit is a reasonable goal, and consistent with human comfort. Unless there are aspects to the building that cause severe thermal loads, such as large expanses of glass or roof, or extensive heat from lights, cooling to 70° or 75° F. (21° or 24° C.) is a reasonable expectation for a typical HVAC system. Where humidity levels are acceptable, lower temperatures should be sought.

Low temperature goals have the general benefits of slowed chemical reactions and longer collection life. However, temperatures below 60° or 65° F. (16° or 18° C.) can cause other problems. People become uncomfortable, even with supplemental clothing, and objects at lower temperatures can gain damaging moisture through condensation when they are quickly brought into warmer humidified spaces. Temperature goals even as high as 65° F. (18° C.) during the summer cooling season will generally require specialized HVAC systems that are an added cost and that many HVAC engineers cannot easily design. At temperatures much below 13° C. (55° F.), there can be problems with damage to the building systems, and special precautions may be required.

As described before, temperature can directly change relative humidity. One way of reducing humidity is to increase temperature; this technique is common in humid countries, such as Panama, where hot closets are used to inhibit mold growth on clothes and other valuables by heating a confined space to over 100° F. (38° C.). Libraries have been known to increase heat on cool, humid days to reduce humidity and the risk of mold growth in stacks. For example, when air is at 68° F. (20° C.) and 70 percent RH, mold growth would be better controlled if the air was warmed to 77° F. (25° C.) so that its humidity will drop to about 50 percent RH. One can imagine how this technique can serve to good purpose following a flood. However, it increases the rate of chemical deterioration. This technique should only be applied for short periods as an "emergency" measure to prevent mold growth; if used for extended periods, the rate of chemical deterioration can be increased dramatically.

D.1.3 Temperature and Humidity and Life of Collections

It has been demonstrated that temperature and humidity work together in the deterioration of library materials. Perhaps the most significant work done on this relationship is that done by Donald K. Sebera of the Library of Congress.[4] Its significance is as a tool to measure the effect of applying different criteria to the working life of collections. Sebera's work shows the theoretical relationship of temperature and humidity upon the life expectancy of materials through what he calls "Isoperm" diagrams.

Based upon Sebera's work, table D.1 may be viewed as a representation of the isoperm diagram said to simulate conditions for paper based upon 25 kcal/mole, arbitrarily using 20° C. and 50 percent RH as a permanence of "1.0."

TABLE D.1   Isoperms (25 kcal/mole)

RH	20%	30%	40%	50%	60%	70%	80%
41°F/5°C	26.00	18.00	13.00	11.00	8.90	7.60	6.70
50°F/10°C	12.00	7.90	5.90	4.70	3.90	3.40	2.90
59°F/15°C	5.40	3.60	2.70	2.10	1.80	1.50	1.30
68°F/20°C	2.50	1.70	1.30	1.00	0.83	0.71	0.60
77°F/25°C	1.20	0.80	0.60	0.48	0.40	0.34	0.30
86°F/30°C	0.59	0.39	0.29	0.23	0.20	0.17	0.15
95°F/35°C	0.29	0.20	0.15	0.12	0.10	0.08	0.07

These numbers, representing "permanence values," have been calculated from the isoperm equation. As the temperature and humidity decrease, the permanence value goes up; as they increase, the permanence goes down.

The beauty of this chart is that it can clearly demonstrate the relative effects of environmental specifications. For example, if one assumes that the life expectancy of commonly produced paper held at 68° F. (20° C.) and 50 percent RH is 50 years, then for any other value of temperature and humidity, the relative life expectancy can easily be calculated. For example, at 77° F. (25° C.) and 60 percent RH, the permanence value is 0.40. At this temperature/humidity, the life expectancy for our example material will be 0.4 × 50 years, or 20 years. On the other hand, if the temperature/humidity is 59° F. (15° C.) and 30 percent RH, the permanence value is 3.6; our life expectancy is therefore 3.6 × 50 years, or 180 years.

The 20 percent, 70 percent, and 80 percent columns are shaded because at these conditions the working life of collections is likely to be determined

---

[4] Sebera, *Isoperms.*

by other factors, such as mechanical, mold, or insect damage rather than the chemical damage predicted by the isoperms. Within the acceptable extremes shown in the table, the difference between the 30 percent RH at 41° F. (5° C.) and 60 percent at 95° F. (35° C.) in this example suggests that the cooler, drier environment (with a permanence of 18) is nearly 180 times as effective at preserving the collections as the warmer, moister environment (with a permanence of 0.10).

This calculation takes on an even more persuasive role when one considers the value of the collections. If we assume the average replacement cost per volume in the collection to be $100 (which is not far off the mark for most university paper-based collections where processing costs are included), and we assume the collection is 1,000,000 volumes (a collection size representative of many universities), then the cost to replace the collection today is $100,000,000. If the effective life of such an asset can be extended by a factor of 1.7 or 2.1, as suggested in table D.1, this means that a working life of 100 years might be extended to 170 or 210 years. This would lead to significant savings in the cost to replace embrittled volumes each year, or, at the least, a reduction in the rate of loss of volumes to embrittlement. It certainly suggests strongly that where collections are felt to have long-term value, the effects of temperature and humidity must be considered. Even where collection values are significantly less, the effect of improved environmental conditions can be compelling.

D.1.4 Acetate Film Collections

Recent investigations into film deterioration have shown that all forms of acetate film are at risk of "vinegar syndrome," where the acetate film base can buckle and delaminate from the emulsion. (In this process, acetic acid is released. Acetic acid is the primary constituent of vinegar, hence the term *vinegar syndrome*.) This chemical deterioration is primarily driven by temperature, and is facilitated by humidity. The only practical options are either to keep the film under cool conditions until it can be reformatted to a stable media, or to keep the film cold enough to serve its intended life. The cost to reformat an at-risk acetate film collection to more stable material, usually polyester, has to be weighed against the cost of maintaining conditions that would extend its life.

The projected life of acetate film collections is quantified by the *Acetate Film Guide,* published by the Image Permanence Institute.[5] Using the Guide, one can predict the remaining life of fresh and degrading film before reaching the next stage of vinegar syndrome deterioration. As with isoperms, the relative life of acetate film collections can be considered for different temperature and humidity conditions. It is particularly useful for planning reformatting of a collection at risk, by suggesting the number of years left before the next level of damage occurs. One can balance the option of improved storage for a longer life against the ultimate need to reformat to a stable format. This can allow a comparison of the cost to build or rent suitable storage against the cost to reformat.

For valuable master negatives that the institution need rarely access, consider arranging off-site storage at a special storage facility for film.

---

[5] James M. Reilly, *IPI Storage Guide for Acetate Film* (Image Permanence Institute, Rochester Institute of Technology, 70 Lomb Memorial Drive, Rochester, NY 14623-5604). Based on laboratory research at the IPI, this guide includes a circular scale for estimating the probable life of new and degrading acetate film at different temperature and humidity conditions.

Color Film Collections. Where a collection includes color slides, color prints, and color negatives, preservation of the original colors is a much greater challenge. Most of these media are chromogenic rather than dye-transfer, and are subject to "dark fading"—color loss without exposure to light. While nothing can reverse this chemical process, like vinegar syndrome, it can be slowed by a reduction in temperature. Most black-and-white acetate film collections are stored at 40° to 60° F. (4° to 16° C.) to slow deterioration to a rate that allows reformatting to polyester. Once on polyester, the black-and-white image is relatively permanent. On the other hand, color media, even on polyester base, may require storage at 32° F. (0° C.), –4° F. (–20° C.), or colder, to slow color loss to an acceptable rate. Needless to say, most color collections are at risk of color loss and will not survive in their original balance.

For further advice on storage of color photographic media, consult the Image Permanence Institute's *Storage Guide for Color Photographic Materials,* and Henry Wilhelm's *The Permanence and Care of Color Photographs: Traditional and Digital Color Prints, Color Negatives, Slides, and Motion Pictures.*[6]

D.1.5 Particulate Contamination

To be of value, HVAC filtration should remove as much of the particles suspended in the atmosphere as possible. Compromises include the use of containers and covers to protect the collection from particulates as they settle. Proper cleaning can also help, so long as it removes particulates rather than just stirring them up and spreading them around, as classically happens with a feather duster and, unfortunately, many vacuum cleaners.

Keyes Metcalf once claimed that all dust has sharp edges. This may only be partly true. Particulates can be anything from a nuisance to a clear danger to collections. The most common particulate contamination is a soft brown dust generated by the collection itself. This dust is made up of relatively large particles (usually paper fibers), is generally no more abrasive than the collection materials themselves, and is easily removed through dusting or conventional vacuuming.

The particulate contamination causing more serious problems is the fine black soot found in urban and industrial areas, and near heavy traffic areas. It is found on windowsills and as black stains on HVAC grilles and ductwork. This soot comes from combustion of organic compounds, typically from automobiles, boilers, furnaces, and fossil-fuel power plants. It is very small, usually less than 1 micron in diameter, and easily stains objects. It is not easily removed, since dusting seems to spread it, working it into the surface of objects. It is so small that it is not easily picked up by a vacuum cleaner, and passes through the filters of conventional vacuum cleaners and typical HVAC filters. The HVAC system can become contaminated by this dust and can spread it throughout a building, which is one good reason why effective HVAC filtering is desirable. Special particulate filtration is required to reduce this contamination.

---

[6]James M. Reilly, *Storage Guide for Color Photographic Materials* (Image Permanence Institute, Rochester Institute of Technology, P.O. Box 9887, Rochester, NY 14623-0887), published by the New York State Program for the Conservation and Preservation of Library Research Materials; and Henry Wilhelm with Carol Brower, *The Permanence and Care of Color Photographs: Traditional and Digital Color Prints, Color Negatives, Slides, and Motion Pictures* (Grinnell, Iowa: Preservation Publishing Co., 1993).

D.1.6 Gaseous Contamination and Air Pollution

Gaseous contamination may come from pollution in outdoor air, from contamination by off-gassing from the building's construction or cleaning materials, from building occupants and equipment, or from the collection itself. Harmful compounds include sulfur dioxide, oxides of nitrogen, hydrochloric acid, ozone, and many volatile organic compounds (VOCs), such as formaldehyde and acetic acid. Standards have been set for acceptable preservation levels for pollutants, but these are not easily measured or achieved.[7] Generally, contaminants should be limited to levels that reduce or eliminate the threat of damage to the collection. In most cases, this is removal of almost all airborne contaminants and pollutants to levels well below outdoor levels, as well as below levels deemed "safe" by environmental protection agencies.

The National Bureau of Standards' *Air Quality Criteria for Storage of Paper-Based Archival Records* (1983, NBSIR 83-2795) is the source for gaseous contamination criteria on most preservation projects. These numbers are shown in table D.2. It is important to note that these are below typical government criteria for pollution. For reference, typical United States Environmental Protection Agency criteria are shown next to the collection preservation criteria.

TABLE D.2 Gaseous Contamination Levels

| Agency | National Bureau of Standards | | United States EPA Levels[a] | | | |
| | | | Long Term | | Short Term | |
	$\mu g/m^3$	ppb	$\mu g/m^3$	period	$\mu g/m^3$	period
Sulfur Dioxide (SO$_2$)	10	3.8	80	1 yr	365	24 hrs
Oxides of Nitrogen (NO$_x$)	10	5	100	1 yr	—	—
Ozone (O$_3$)	2	1	—	—	235	8 hrs

[a] As described in ASHRAE Standard 62-1989.

The difference between preservation levels and "safe" levels as promulgated by the EPA is quite striking. Nominally "safe" levels of gaseous pollution for people, or air treatments that satisfy EPA or "odor control" goals, will usually not be safe for collections. Part of the reason the collection has a lower tolerance than human occupants of the same space is that the human body is living and can effect repairs to itself; the collection has no such self-renewing mechanism. The collection is also expected to have a longer life and exposure period, hopefully several hundred or a thousand years, which means that even a low level of gaseous pollution will have a significant cumulative effect.

Limitations and Priorities for Gaseous Contamination. VOCs should be minimized through an optimized selection of construction, furnishings, operating supplies, and cleaning materials, combined with a possible "bakeout" process following new construction to accelerate off-gassing and elimination of VOCs before occupancy. This is not easy. All interior finish materials, particularly paints, carpets, and processed wood products, as well

[7] See National Bureau of Standards, *Air Quality Criteria for Storage of Paper-Based Archival Records* (1983, NBSIR 83-2795). This work offers criteria for paper and system recommendation as developed by consensus of a select panel of consultants during intensive workshops at NBS in 1983. See also Garry Thomson, *The Museum Environment,* 2d ed. (Butterworths, 1986). Written from the museum perspective with good guidelines.

as all compounds regularly used in the building, must be considered as possible sources for control. Workshops, staff lounges, kitchen areas, loading docks, and lab processes can be sources of contamination best treated with appropriate and effective exhaust. Office equipment, particularly the ozone from laser printers and copiers, can be sources of contamination best treated with exhaust as well, or with local gas-phase filtration.

In some instances, the collection may be stored or displayed in closed containers, closed furniture, or display cases. This limits the exposure to pollutants because of reduced exchange of air with the ambient building environment. Care must be taken when a sealed environment is used, because the collection, enclosure, or display materials may release gases that can be concentrated to problematic levels in the confined space. Contained environments may be designed to include compounds that can remove some of the pollutants that enter or that are released, or can be made from materials that can serve as buffers against airborne pollutants. In most collections this type of treatment will not suit all parts of the collection; it is most commonly used on a selected basis for display, and for storage of photographic film and prints. This will work so long as the portion of the collection that needs this protection is limited, or extensive access is not needed. For open-shelved library stacks, containment is virtually impossible.

Local filtration, similar to collection containment, can establish specific areas where gaseous pollution control is added, rather than treating all the collection areas. This should generally be done for the most sensitive parts of the collection and will only be effective if the area filtered is not open to or is not on a common air system with other spaces. In situations where there is an acute source of gaseous contamination within the building, such as a lunchroom or smoking lounge, and exhaust is not practical, it may be appropriate to filter the offensive space rather than the collection space.

D.1.7 Light

Light, and associated radiations in the infrared and ultraviolet, have cumulative damaging effects, providing energy that promotes chemical reactions within materials. In some cases the radiant energy reaches energy activation levels that trigger deteriorating reactions that continue even after the original energy source is withdrawn. Most buildings, especially modern buildings, are often lit at levels well above those required for comfortable reading and personal safety. Control of light is particularly important in stack areas, to prevent fading and cracking of covers and damage to the edges of text blocks. It is crucial in exhibit areas, where ancient treasures may be quickly ruined if not adequately protected.

All light can damage objects; it is a common misconception that only the ultraviolet or infrared components of light cause damage. This is why it is important to maintain light levels in libraries and archives as low as reasonably possible, and to always avoid direct sunlight upon the collections. Although a collection may contain objects that can tolerate higher light levels, and some materials may be stored in opaque boxes, they are few and far between, and their segregation in storage or display cannot be assured.

Although light levels of 30 to 60 footcandles (300 to 600 lux) may be needed in reading or inspection areas, light-sensitive collections should generally be displayed for limited periods at levels no higher than 10 footcandles (100 lux), and stored at light levels of 2 to 4 footcandles (20 to 40 lux). Although this sounds low, a stack area lit at 2 footcandles (20 lux) of vertical illumination at the book spines is not uncommon, and is a quite effective light level for collection access. Higher light levels, often found at the top of unevenly lit stacks, will be the cause of differential fading of the collection, relative to the shelf on which the book is kept. The recommendations of the Illuminating Engineering Society of North America are for 20 to 50 footcandles (200 to 500 lux) vertical illumination in active stacks at 30 in. (0.762 m) off the floor.[8] This light level is too high where preservation concerns are to be addressed. For inactive stacks, the society's recommendation is for 5 to 10 footcandles (50 to 100 lux) vertically at 30 in. (0.762 m) off the floor, which, though still on the high side, is more in keeping with the goals of collections preservation.

Ultraviolet Exposure. The damaging effect of light can be increased if there is a large component of ultraviolet (UV) radiation, radiation just above the visible spectrum. Ultraviolet radiation does not improve the visual experience, and it is more damaging than visible light; it can readily be eliminated with filtration. Light sources can also be chosen that have little or no ultraviolet output.

In all cases of collection exposure, the amount of ultraviolet radiation should be less than 75 microwatts per lumen (µW/L), or roughly less than 2 to 4 percent of the energy emitted from the light source. The 75 µW/L limit will assure that the light will be no more damaging than light from conventional tungsten lamps, although not necessarily safe. For more sensitive materials, such as rare items on display, a criterion of less than 1 µW/L is practical and achievable.

Typical unfiltered ultraviolet components of various light sources are listed in table D.3.

Note that the north light often sought by architects is a particular problem for ultraviolet exposure; lumen for lumen, it has more ultraviolet than other daylight.

---

[8] Illuminating Engineering Society of North America, *Lighting Handbook: Reference and Application,* 8th ed. (1993), p. 462.

TABLE D.3   Summary of UV Characteristics for Various Light Sources

Light Source	Typical UV µW/L	Typical UV as % of total
Sunlight		
Direct or South	400	10%+
Overcast or North	800	20%+
Blue Sky	1,600	40%+
Incandescent		
Standard	60–80	4%
Tungsten-Halogen	130 with glass filter	8%
Low Voltage	60–120	4–8%
Fluorescent		
General	40–250	2–12%
Special Low UV	less than 10	less than 0.5%
High-Intensity Discharge		
Mercury Vapor	400+	10–20%
Metal Halide	400+	10–20%
Sodium Vapor (Low- and High-Pressure Sodium)	less than 10	less than 0.5%

Infrared Light Exposure. The damaging effect of light can be increased if there is a large component of infrared (IR) radiation, radiation just below the visible spectrum. As with ultraviolet radiation, this radiation does not improve the visual experience, and it can cause damage to the collection through radiant heating, thermal expansion, and spot desiccation.

It is important to remember that ultraviolet and IR only increase the damaging effect of light; totally removing ultraviolet and IR through a perfect filter will not prevent light from damaging light-sensitive objects.

Color Temperature. The color temperature of light can also indicate its potential damaging effect even if all ultraviolet and IR are removed. Light that has a blue or high color temperature will tend to be more damaging than light that has a red or lower color temperature. The higher energy levels (that is, higher color temperature) in blue light are more likely to activate damaging photochemical reactions. Work done by the U.S. National Bureau of Standards in 1953 (NBS Circular 538) shows that violet light (about 400 nanometers wavelength) damages low-grade paper almost 20 times as much as blue-green light (about 500 nanometers), while red light below 660 nanometers wavelength has virtually no damaging effects. This means that warmer color temperature lights, such as simple tungsten lamps, will cause less damage than daylight or cool color fluorescent lamps at the same light level.

Limitations and Priorities for Light. Although the design of sophisticated HVAC systems may require moderation in the expectations for relative humidity, particulate, or gaseous performance to meet budgets, there is little excuse for overlighting a collection. Ultraviolet filters are relatively inexpensive, and are usually easily applied to windows and lights. In general, less light improves the environment, reduces capital costs, and reduces operating costs. Light levels can be easily reduced through window shades, blockout panels, tinted glazing, dimmers, de-lamping, or replacement of lamps with lower-wattage alternatives. In the worst case, new light fixtures and windows may be needed, but these and other costs are often paid for by reduced lighting and cooling expense from the lower-level lighting.

D.1.8 Summary of Criteria

The following summarizes the primary criteria for the various aspects of a preservation environment. These are the best goals achievable for most projects.

Temperature: For limited-access paper storage, 16° C. to 18° C. (60° F. to 65° F.). For generally occupied areas, 18° C. to 21° C. (65° F. to 70° F.). Use lower temperatures as much as collection usage may allow; consider valuing the benefits with isoperms. Acetate film may require cold storage conditions to suppress vinegar syndrome; consider valuing the benefits of cold storage with the IPI Acetate Film Guide.

Relative Humidity: For paper, 30 to 40 percent RH; for film, generally 30% RH, but this can vary with material. Stability is an important goal of humidity control.

Particulates: Remove problem particulates; where soot is present, filter to remove better than 50 percent of 0.5-micron particles.

Gaseous Contaminants: Levels that do not exceed 3.8 parts-per-billion (ppb) of sulfur dioxide; 5.0 ppb of oxides of nitrogen; and 2 ppb of ozone.

The best available control technology should be used for volatile organic contaminants, such as acetic acid and formaldehyde.

Light: For storage, 2–5 footcandles (20–50 lux). For display, 2–10 footcandles (20–100 lux), the lower the better. For reading and work areas, 30–60 footcandles (300–600 lux), intended for only short exposures for paper and other light-sensitive materials. Ultraviolet content should not exceed 75 microwatts per lumen (μW/L), or less than 2 to 4 percent ultraviolet for all collections. Ultraviolet should not exceed 1 μW/L for the most sensitive objects. Infrared (IR) content should be limited with light levels and the use of dichroic reflector lamps. (If for some reason the light level is higher than specified, then the ratio of ultraviolet must be reduced; for example, if the lighting is 30 footcandles when it should be 10 footcandles, the ultraviolet of 75 μW/L must be at 25 μW/L or less.)

Compromises. Although compromises may be needed to have balanced achievable goals, any compromises should be developed with advice and evaluation from a trained conservator or preservation officer. The items mentioned in this section are only concepts; they should not be applied to any situation without further consideration of project specifics. Compromises should be avoided where a collection warrants a first-class environment—that is a project where the full criteria should be applied as described.

D.1.9 Collections Assessment and Environmental Monitoring

An important foundation to achieving a good preservation environment is the evaluation of the collection's needs, the collection's general condition, and existing environmental conditions.

To properly assess a collection's condition and environmental needs, a trained conservator should be consulted. If the institution does not have a staff conservator, or the staff conservator is not familiar with a particular type of collection, a consulting conservator may be needed. Various governmental agencies and professional conservation associations can assist in locating and securing the services of a consulting conservator familiar with a particular type of collection. The assessment should consider the typical goals as outlined in Section D.1.8, and consider their adjustment for specific collection needs.

Where an existing environment is to be evaluated for potential improvement, or as a context for justification of a new environment, then monitoring should be considered. This can be done for modest cost with the investment in the proper equipment. The temperature, humidity, particulate, gaseous, and light levels should be measured and documented, and a general assessment should be made of any other probable threats to the collection.

Generally survey the building and building systems that house and protect the collection and look for threats to collection life or safety. Look for areas without fire detection or suppression systems; subsurface water risks in basements or potential flooding from storm surges; windows that allow strong daylight to reach the collection; fluorescent lamps without ultraviolet filters, or lamps located too close to collections; particulate staining at HVAC grilles; radiators or lights that overheat parts of the collection; and water staining or other evidence of leaks or condensation.

Temperature and humidity are best measured with one or more hygrothermographs, or with similar charts generated from a central monitoring system or from data loggers. Spot readings of conditions are of very little value. The hygrothermographs should be rotated throughout the collection spaces to gather typical data for each space in each season. Particulate and gaseous contamination observations are usually made by inspecting collections for damage or contamination. Spot readings for particulates and gases can be of value, although these will require special equipment at a significant cost.

Light levels are readily measured with a modest investment in a light meter. Infrared observations can be made by placing a thermometer in the illuminated area for an extended period to see if the temperature is higher than outside the illumination. Measuring ultraviolet levels requires much more expensive equipment, usually best borrowed from another institution, regional conservation center, or consultant for a day or two once or twice a year. Blue wool reference fading cards can be used to measure long-term cumulative exposures for just a few dollars.

The sum of this information can be used to assess a particular environment's weaknesses to guide renovations. If a new space or building is to be built, this information can provide an important context for the design; good aspects can be repeated while bad aspects can be avoided.

D.2 Architecture and Planning

Several limitations and opportunities should be considered when planning and developing the architecture of a preservation environment.

Avoid structural elements that prevent future penetrations of floors for ducts. A floor made of precast structural tees can be a serious problem for future modifications. Any future expansion of the building should not be precluded by the location of major mechanical systems. Water control and storm drainage must be well done for obvious reasons, especially in libraries and archives that seem naturally to be problematic in this respect.

Structure and Finishes. A concrete structure is often preferred over steel because the typical applied fireproofing for steel can be a collection contamination source if exposed. Suspended ceilings are not desirable in preservation-quality stacks because of their potential for concealing leaks and the increased maintenance difficulty for ceiling-mounted equipment. Standard drop-in acoustic tile is also suspected as a contributor to particulate pollution because of both maintenance and sloughing problems; where a suspended ceiling is required, alternative ceiling treatments that cannot harbor or produce particulates should be considered.

Walkable Terrace. Where there is a regularly accessed rooftop terrace, special consideration must be given to making it positively waterproof. There are many examples of successful terraces, and there are many more that leak. The terraces that appear to be the most successful are those that are designed with clear drainage and service access below the structurally supported terrace pavers. And, the collection area under such a terrace should be fitted with a secondary water control system and alarms. Be aware of the fact that composite "sandwich" details for water control have not been successful in many cases. Also, even though a potential leak may never reach the collections proper, such leakage may make humidity control difficult.

Roofs. Sloped roofs are generally less prone to leakage problems than flat roofs; given a choice, sloped roofs are thus preferred for preservation environments. Drain piping from the roof and elsewhere should be minimized in stack areas for obvious reasons. Where required within the stack space, they should be designed for easy replacement or repair with minimal disruption for the collections, and potential problems with condensation in the winter or leaks anytime should be anticipated.

Skylights. Be aware that skylights introduce added risks and problems of leaks, ultraviolet exposure, overall excessive light levels, and heat gain. Even if carefully detailed and executed, they are more expensive and risky than an equivalent section of roof or wall.

Functional Organization. In the best of preservation worlds, the collections will be housed separately from the readers and staff. In all cases, processes and activities that produce pollution should be physically and mechanically separated from the collections. To prevent problems of infestations of various kinds, spaces designed for food service should be well separated as should a storage area for potentially infested incoming materials. Containment requires eliminating cracks and a general quality in the sealing of construction, both visible and concealed, and avoiding the use of construction that harbors or conceals pests.

Where there is a substantial holding of film, it ideally should be housed separately from paper-based collections in order to minimize exposure to unfiltered acid-gas as emitted by many paper products. It is thought these gaseous pollutants contribute to vinegar syndrome and the formation of redox blemishes with film collections.

The location of the mechanical room itself needs consideration. The mechanical room will be a major source of potential leaks; it ideally should not be directly above the collections without very careful consideration and water protection measures. Rooftop equipment and penetrations represent similar concerns.

Elevator shafts and open stairs within stack areas will make environmental control difficult because of their chimney effect. It is recommended that where a preservation-based environment is the goal, vertical transportation should be off of vestibules that in turn serve the stack through normally closed doors. An old-fashioned, self-supporting tiered stack is a particularly poor choice of shelving technology for space intended as a preservation environment for similar unmanaged airflow reasons.

Humidity-Tolerant Building Envelope. Winter humidification should be the first priority of a preservation environment in a heated building in temperate or cold climates, but the humidity tolerance of the building must be considered. In many instances, the building envelope—the walls, roof, and windows—will have problem condensation in winter at interior humidities as low as 25 percent RH, either condensation on single-glazed windows, on window frames, or inside the exterior wall or roof. Under certain circumstances, this condensation can cause cosmetic or structural damage to the building. In such cases three alternatives present themselves: (1) the winter humidity must be kept stable and below the point where problem condensation will occur; (2) the building envelope must be retrofitted to tolerate the higher humidity; or (3) the space temperature must be reduced.

Depending on the humidity level that can be maintained without problems, a collection may require that the envelope be modified to support a higher humidity. In most projects where modification of the building envelope is required to tolerate higher winter humidities for the benefit of collections within, there is a considerable design challenge and expense. The expense of such a buildingwide envelope retrofit can be as much as all other environmental modifications combined, and should not be undertaken lightly or without proper professional advice and evaluation by a licensed architect or a professional engineer or both.

If the collection needing a higher humidity does not dominate a building, but only a manageable minority of the spaces, separate humidified storage containers, cases, cabinets, or rooms are an alternative. These must be carefully sealed to preserve their internal environment and to protect the building from the damaging moisture.

Gaseous Control through Selection of Building Materials. Where possible, materials should be selected for minimum off-gassing. Construction materials that contribute off-gassing include: nonceramic tile, carpet, carpet padding, vinyl baseboard, and any rubber, silicone, or vinyl products; interior fabric finishes, such as paint, lacquer, shellac, varnish, plastic blinds, drapes, and fabric wall covering; concrete and cementatious grouts; adhesives, sealants, mastics, and caulking; insulation on wiring and other plastic coatings; and wood and wood products, including floors and trim. Much of the construction can contribute to off-gassing. Some of the products "cure" over time and substantially stop off-gassing (paint, joint compound, and concrete, for example); other products contribute by-products over the life of the product (vinyl tile, wood, some adhesives, and most sealants). The problem of off-gassing of those products that "cure" can be dealt with fairly quickly; it is the product of the long-term producers that is of greatest concern.

Avoid occupancy of the space until there is no longer an odor of solvents. This will be aided by a "bake-out" period where the air is purged rapidly, and the heat is turned up.

Lacking the capacity to eliminate off-gassing, consider ensuring that there is good air circulation throughout the building, and consider the installation of gaseous filtration equipment. (See Sections D.3.1 and D.3.4 for discussions on filtration.)

D.3 HVAC Systems

The purpose of the heating, ventilating, and air-conditioning (HVAC) systems for a preservation environment is to establish and maintain relative humidity (add and remove moisture), maintain temperature (add and remove heat), and filter the air (remove particulates and offending gases), and to perform these tasks evenly throughout the space with minimum risk of damage to the collections, at a cost and maintenance effort that the institution can support.

Although HVAC systems are the main determinants for actively maintaining the preservation environment, an effective preservation environment involves more than just the HVAC system. The basic architectural design (such as space segregation, windows, and vapor barriers) and building operation (24-hour operation and availability of tempering sources) must complement these purposes and not pose impractical challenges to the HVAC design.

D.3.1 Primary Functional Components
The following are the primary functional components and basic features of an HVAC system that provides a good preservation environment for a library, as suggested in fig. D.1.

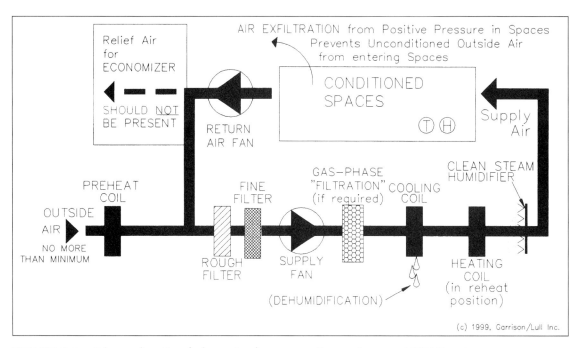

FIGURE D.1   Primary functional elements of a preservation environment HVAC system.

Constant Air Volume. Libraries rely on mechanically assisted airflow to filter the air, assure even temperature and humidity, and suppress mold growth, not just for cooling or heating. Air should be constantly circulated at full volume, regardless of space-tempering needs, and should have good circulation throughout the collections space.

Outside Air. Because a library is trying to maintain a stable indoor environment, outside air presents a potential problem. It is almost always at other-than-desirable temperature and relative humidity, and varies in this respect throughout the day. It can introduce particulate and gaseous pollution from the outside. An "air-side economizer" cycle, in which a large amount of outside air is used for "free" cooling, should be avoided because of the effect it has on humidity control and filtration requirements. Outside air should usually be at a minimum amount, to provide the necessary fresh air for occupants, and to pressurize the collection spaces. This pressurization is to cause exfiltration at doors and other leaks in the building envelope, rather than allow infiltration of untreated air. (Where an "economizer" cycle may be mandated, consider a "water-side economizer" for economical cooling of chilled water.)

Cooling and Heating. The system should provide the necessary cooling and heating, but must subordinate temperature control, particularly excessive or capricious heating, to the need for stable relative humidity.

Humidification. Humidification should be provided by clean steam introduced in the air system. "Spray" or other systems that introduce water mechanically without heating it to its vapor phase should be avoided because of their application and maintenance requirements.

Dehumidification. To dehumidify, moisture is usually removed from the air by a cooling coil, usually the same coil that also cools the supply air for space cooling.

Reheat. The air system should have "reheat" capabilities so that dehumidification can occur when space cooling is not required (which is much of the time in many environments). This means that the system must cool the air sufficiently to remove moisture, and then heat it back up to reduce the relative humidity. The reheat also prevents overcooling of the space. In many cases, reheat may be provided by having the normal heating coil in the "reheat position," downstream of the cooling coil. (For example, a portable dehumidifier combines both cooling and reheat in a single system. Cooling comes from a small cooling compressor, and the heat comes from the condenser heat produced by the compressor.)

Desiccant Dehumidifiers (not shown in fig. D.1). An alternative to dehumidification with conventional cooling is a dehumidification system using desiccants, which are usually required to maintain low humidities at low temperatures. Such systems pass the air to be dehumidified through a desiccant bed, which absorbs moisture from the air and increases the air temperature. The desiccant bed is then moved to a regenerative air stream, usually as a rotating wheel, and exposed to very hot air, which drives the moisture from the desiccant into the regenerative air that is exhausted. These systems are not common in most HVAC designs, and they almost always are in addition to conventional cooling. Because of their rarity, maintenance personnel are often not familiar with them. They should be avoided unless required to meet criteria; they are generally needed where temperatures are to be below 20° C. (68° F.) and concurrent humidities are to be at or below 40 percent RH. If required, they should be carefully selected for easy maintenance, and to prevent contamination of the collection by abrasive or chemically active particulates that might be shed by the desiccant bed.

HVAC Controls. The HVAC controls, the instruments that modulate the various active HVAC system components listed previously, are a critical aspect to a good preservation environment. Sensors, thermostats, and humidistats must be located in the collection space itself, not in the return air stream. A variation in temperature is usually preferable to a prolonged swing in humidity. This has strong implications for HVAC controls design, because conventional controls treat temperature as the primary goal and humidity as supplementary.

Particulate Filters. To avoid particulate buildup and cleaning problems, air filtration should be effective down to the typical contamination particle size. In most cases this will require two or three sets of filters. The rough or prefilter is intended to remove the large particulates, and is the type of filter used in virtually all HVAC systems. Medium and final filters are used to remove the smaller particulates. This staged filtration (rough/medium/final) allows the inexpensive upstream filter to protect the expensive downstream filters from premature loading with large particulates. In many cases only a prefilter and final filter will be used. Replacement on a regular schedule is essential, and frequency will differ among the several filters.

Gas-Phase Filtration. Where new construction materials, interior contamination, collection off-gassing, or outdoor pollution present a gaseous contamination threat to a sensitive collection, gaseous contamination control equipment should be used. Although the word *filter* is often used, this equipment does not mechanically filter the air; it chemically absorbs or physically adsorbs contaminants from the air.

D.3.2 Typical HVAC Systems

HVAC distribution systems were created to provide temperature control inside buildings. This is usually achieved by addressing discrete areas—spaces or groups of spaces within a building. These areas, or environmental control "zones," are typically tempered by delivering varying amounts of heating or cooling, through the delivery of water or air. For their application in libraries, these systems must also provide humidification and dehumidification for each collection zone, as well as other features, and in these goals they differ significantly from typical systems designed primarily for human comfort.

Most distribution systems can generally be categorized by their medium of providing tempering to each zone. The descriptions here are predicated on systems that must provide basic humidity control for each control zone.

All-Water. These systems use hot or cold water or both, through pipes, to condition the spaces served. In general, all-water systems require extensive piping, require regular maintenance activities over or in collection areas, and can rarely provide the features needed to meet preservation goals. Their greatest advantage appears to be that of a distribution system that requires significantly less space; there are cases where this was the only possible choice in an existing building because of the difficulty in routing ducts through the space. Where this is the case, compromises should be expected in collection protection and environmental performance. Careful design is required to minimize the negative effect of plumbing and maintenance activities in the collections spaces.

Air-Water. These systems deliver a combination of air and water, through ducts and pipes, to condition the spaces served. They may also require steam piping or local steam generators. In general, air-water systems require piping and maintenance activities in the collections spaces, a clear disadvantage. Although there is less piping, they share the general piping, performance, and maintenance problems of an all-water system.

All-Air. These systems deliver only air to condition the spaces served, delivering air that is warm or cool, moist or dry, to maintain space conditions. All-air systems primarily or exclusively use ducts rather than piping, which can (with proper design) eliminate the HVAC system as a water source threat in collection areas. In general, all-air systems provide the best environmental control, with little or no piping or maintenance activities required in the collections spaces.

Large Systems. Preservation needs have been best met by constant-volume all-air systems with central air-handling stations, with filtration, humidification, maintenance, and monitoring at a central location, avoiding possible leaks from water piping above collections areas. In most cases a longer system life, better performance, better reliability, and lower maintenance will come from the use of a few large systems rather than several small systems.

A typical application of such a full-feature central HVAC system is shown in fig. D.2. From a central location, it serves several spaces with individual humidity and temperature control. A boiler burns oil or natural gas and produces steam for humidification, and for use in a heat exchanger to produce hot water for heating and reheat. A chiller uses electricity to produce chilled water for cooling and dehumidification, rejecting the heat to the outside through a cooling tower. The system shown also incorporates the other primary functional components of a preservation environment system.

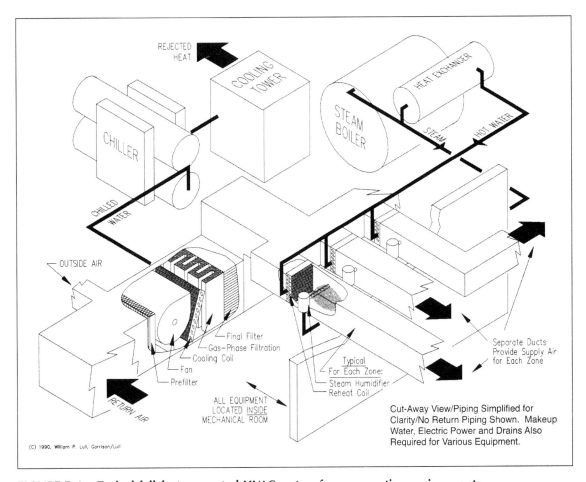

FIGURE D.2 **Typical full-feature central HVAC system for conservation environments.**

Small Systems. A large central HVAC system is not always required for effective environmental control, although it may be the best choice for larger facilities. For small, isolated areas, complete environmental systems can be found as small-package systems, combining some or all of the key preservation aspects needed for a small library or archival storage area. Typical are small-package environmental systems made for computer rooms, and for allergy and health clinics. If used, they should be located in separate spaces or closets, with any piping and maintenance activities separated from the collection space as much as possible.

A typical application of such full-feature small systems is shown in figs. D.3 and D.4. The system in fig. D.3 uses existing chilled water and hot water systems, as may be available in large buildings, along with a new steam generator for humidification. (Before considering the use of an existing chilled water/hot water system, confirm that the hot water and chilled water are available 24 hours per day throughout the year as needed, and the chilled water is sufficiently cool to dehumidify as needed. This is required to maintain relative humidity.)

The system in fig. D.4 is largely independent of any other building systems except for the most basic requirements: water for the humidifier, a drain, and electric power. An external condenser is used to reject heat for cooling. This type of system is often used where there are no existing chilled water or hot water systems, or such existing systems do not operate so as to allow effective dehumidification.

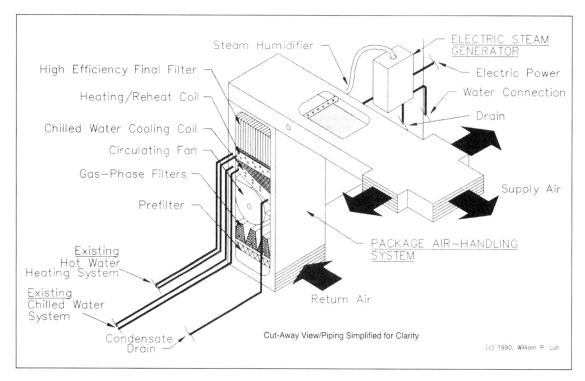

FIGURE D.3   Small chilled/hot water system.

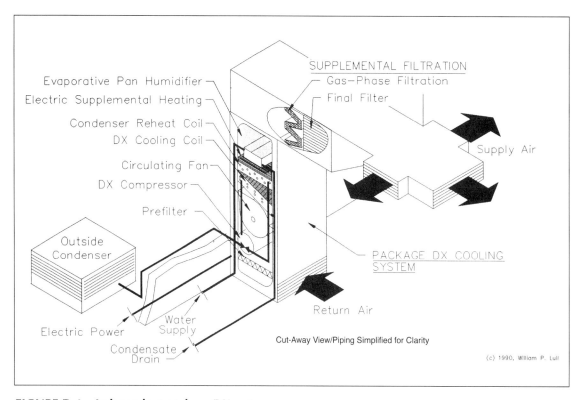

FIGURE D.4   Independent package DX system.

D.3.3 HVAC System Performance Issues

Any given system may have one or more of the primary functional components and desirable characteristics identified earlier for an HVAC system serving preservation environments. To assess the adequacy of an environment, the person concerned for the collection should ask if and how each of these components and features are provided on a proposed, a new, or an existing system. Key aspects to consider when evaluating any system are:

Heating/Cooling. Tempered air should be supplied through ducts. Baseboards, radiators, and other radiant heating can be good for human comfort, but present an environmental disaster for collection environments. They introduce dry heat with no chance of concurrent humidification, inviting spot desiccation. They provide no duct system for recirculation and destratification, general air circulation, and particulate filtration. Fan-coil or heat-pump units in the collection space present a risk of fire from motors and of water leaks from piping, and require maintenance activities in the space.

Humidification. Be sure the system has a method to effectively add moisture to the air in each zone. In many systems, without a zone humidifier, the system may be substantially compromised and may provide unstable humidity control in winter.

Humidification Steam. Humidification steam should be clean and free of additives. Well water or water described as "hard" should be softened to reduce scale buildup. The steam ideally should come from a separate boiler or steam generator with precautions to reduce corrosion. Most central steam heating systems are a poor source for the steam because they are almost always treated with compounds to protect the steam condensate piping from corrosion; however, it is perfectly safe to use central plant steam as a heat source for a local steam generator. If central steam must be used directly for humidification, the concentration of any treatment compounds must be carefully monitored and kept at minimum levels.

Dehumidification. Although many systems provide cooling that can usually perform dehumidification, without zone "reheat" for dehumidification, the system may be substantially compromised and provide inconsistent humidity control. Some chilled water systems may not be able to reliably deliver chilled water that is sufficiently cold, or may have cooling coils too shallow for dehumidification to occur.

Filtration and Fan Horsepower. Some systems have inherently limited fan horsepower and air pressure, which prevents adding good particulate and gaseous control, either initially or as a retrofit. A system should have the necessary filtration and appropriate horsepower to move the air through the filters.

Piping. Pipes carrying water or steam over and in collection areas always present the possibility of leaks. Although some systems can provide full control without running any piping to the zones, other systems require anywhere from two to six pipes to be run to each zone. To reach collection spaces these pipes must usually be run over or in collection areas and are unfortunately the pipes most likely to leak in the building.

Outside Air. This should be at a minimum amount as required for safe ventilation of the building; in addition, air economizer cycles should not be used. The outside air intake should be located away from any potential sources of outside contamination; it should be away from street level and away from any exhausts or flues.

Maintenance and Ease of Operation. A common failing in many modern system designs is poor consideration of ongoing operation and maintenance expectations. Most designs will work if properly adjusted and maintained, but many institutions find they do not have the staff, budget, or expertise to give the system the attention it needs. The regular maintenance required for any system should be matched against the institution's manpower, staff, and contract maintenance capabilities.

VAV Systems. Variable-Air Volume or "VAV" systems have become very popular since the energy crisis of the 1970s. In a VAV system, cool air is delivered to each zone, and the amount of air is varied by the amount of cooling needed in the zone. VAV systems save in capital cost of the fan and chillers, fan energy, the operating cost of reheat, or the capital cost of a multizone distribution. They are an efficient solution to the problem of conditioning office buildings and many other commercial applications where flexibility and varying internal loads are primary concerns.

However, VAV systems are not effective in maintaining stable humidities because their basic function is temperature-dependent. When VAV systems are used in archives and libraries, as a rule, they generally have problems in holding stable winter or summer humidity, they do not maintain adequate airflows for filtration and consistent space conditions, and they have a general lack of flexibility to meet more stringent environmental criteria. They pose a threat to the collection from the overhead reheat water and steam piping that must be added to make the system control humidity.

Sometimes a VAV system is recommended because of "space and budget constraints." In virtually every case, the cost and space required for the properly designed VAV system (full filtration, local humidification, local reheat, minimum air-volume settings, well-planned piping, well-planned maintenance access, and extremely well documented operating instructions) gives no observed advantage over the more conservative, less problematic, and easier to maintain multizone, dual-duct, or other constant-volume systems. Although a VAV system can be made to save energy compared to the constant-volume alternatives, it does so at the expense of the institution's collection.

D.3.4 HVAC System Component Options

Individual situations will vary, and in some cases only partial aspects of the functional HVAC system goals can be achieved or are needed in varying degrees in an existing situation. It may be helpful to consider independently the separate functional goals of environmental control systems. Each has its own range of components and component capabilities.

For each of the HVAC goals below, ranges of approaches are suggested. These are listed from lowest-cost compromises with most modest performance expectations, to the best available to meet uncompromised preservation environment goals. These may or may not be applicable to any given situation; they assume a climate that is warm and humid in the summer and cold and dry in the winter. Other options not listed may be indicated in a particular situation.

Humidification. Humidification options begin with a drain-through pad, wetted belt, or wetted drum humidifier; this type will provide only modest performance, and may require monthly maintenance and cleaning. Serious humidification begins with the use of a steam generator and some form of steam injection in a ducted supply air system. The steam can come from nonpressurized sources, such as electrode canisters or evaporative pans; these types of humidification can have problems with cycling at part-load conditions. Better control comes from the use of a pressurized clean steam source, delivered in a preheated manifold, directly modulated with a steam valve. Whenever steam is used there is the potential for overhumidification; steam systems should have a high-limit control to positively protect from runaway humidification.

Care should also be taken when humidifying buildings in cold climates. Improvements to the building envelope may be necessary to make it tolerant of the higher humidity in winter. (See Section D.2, Architecture and Planning.)

Dehumidification. Options for dehumidification begin with the use of a cooling system, operated whenever the humidity is too high; for this to work the space must have heating to reheat the air to space conditions. Where the cooling is from chilled water that water must be sufficiently cool to cause condensation on the cooling coil for the cooling to provide the dehumidification. Systems using the direct expansion (DX) of refrigerant in the cooling coil usually provide coil conditions that assure dehumidification. This can be approximated with chilled water with glycol added to allow the water to approach freezing conditions. Both chilled water and DX systems have the limitation of freezing conditions at the cooling coil. Actual freezing conditions should be avoided to prevent the problem of forming ice instead of liquid water condensate on the cooling coil. Superior dehumidification comes from the application of desiccants, because air can be dried without the risk of ice formation; cooling is still required because the desiccated air will be hot and must be cooled to room conditions.

Temperature. Cooling and heating for temperature control are like conventional institutional projects. Options relate primarily to the location and method of heat delivery to provide any necessary reheat, and to assure tempering whenever necessary—usually 24 hours a day, 12 months a year. Cooler conditions are often selected for superior preservation, and this may require more cooling capacity; most of the challenges with cooler conditions relate to the dehumidification rather than the cooling per se.

Particulate Filtration. Particulate filters are rated in their ability to remove particulates by "efficiency." More and smaller particles are removed as the particulate efficiency increases, but with higher efficiencies come higher pressures (see the pressure drop discussion following). The level of filtration required for any particular collection depends on the type of particulate contamination that must be removed.

The most common filtration found in HVAC systems is the open-weave panel or "furnace" filter. It provides virtually no value for protection of any collection situation, protecting only the air-handling equipment from gross fouling.

Better filtration comes from at least 1- or 2-inch-thick (25- or 50-mm) pleated panel filters. At the time of replacement, it is important to note that the lesser-quality open-weave filters, which cost about $1 each, are often substituted for pleated filters, which cost about $5 each, causing a major loss in filtration efficiency.

Even a good pleated filter will let most of the smaller particulates pass through, providing very little protection from typical urban black soot. Most systems need the addition of high-performance "final" filters, usually 6 or 12 inches (152 or 305 mm) deep, which can remove most of the smaller particulates that do the most damage to the collection.

"Pressure drop" is the term applied to the difference in air pressure before and after the filter. As filter efficiency increases, usually the fan pressure and motor horsepower required to move the air through the filter increase relative to the increased pressure drop. In most cases, the filter efficiency and pressure drop increase as a filter becomes loaded with particulates, until the filter essentially becomes clogged and a maximum pressure drop is realized.

Most fan systems can be adjusted or easily modified to move air through a 1- or 2-inch (25- or 51-mm) pleated filter. High-efficiency final filters can rarely be fitted to a fan system without significant modifications to the fan or motor.

Electrostatic filters remove particulates by exposing the air to a high-voltage electrostatic field, causing smaller particulates to coagulate into larger particles that are more easily filtered. Such cleaners, which consume electricity, will generally also create ozone and therefore should not be used to filter collection spaces.

Gaseous Control through HVAC. Based on the sensitivity of the collection, evidence of previous damage, pollution records or measurements, and supplemental or alternative treatments, consider the degree of gaseous pollution control needed in the HVAC system.

Several media types are available that address the needs of gaseous control. Water washes can be somewhat effective in controlling gaseous contaminants, but few institutions can give the intense maintenance they require. Most options for controlling gaseous contamination involve the use of impregnated media or granular beds. Carbon is a good general absorbent of gaseous contaminants. A problem is that it can desorb sulfur dioxide and other gases filtered in favor of other molecules. To reduce this effect it can be supplemented with special chemicals to enhance absorption of certain contaminants, although this reduces its total capacity. Potassium permanganate in alumina pellets is favored in many situations for its ability to oxidize certain contaminants, particularly sulfur dioxide and volatile organic compounds. The pollution control media must be kept relatively clean and must be changed when depleted, usually at least once a year.

The typical gaseous contamination control equipment ranges from particulate filters impregnated or coated with carbon, to panel filters filled with carbon or potassium permanganate, to "V" cells with carbon or potassium permanganate or both, to vertical chamber systems, to deep-bed scrubbers. They range from virtually no long-term protection with little pressure drop penalty, to high contaminant removal with long change intervals and large pressure drops.

The ability of a system to remove gaseous contaminants depends on how slow the air flows through the media, the amount of media in the air stream, and the amount of air that bypasses the media and is not effectively treated. These factors must be taken into account when deciding on the filtration type.

D.3.5 Energy and Operating Costs

In many cases the costs for operating a preservation environment can be a significant consideration, but for the long-term protection of a valuable collection, the annual energy costs of a good environment are a wise expenditure. On several projects, the increase in collection life expectancy, as predicted by Sebera's isoperms discussed earlier, has easily cost-justified the annual energy and operating costs to maintain improved environmental conditions.

Many aspects of a good preservation environment, including low light levels and limited window areas, can in many cases more than compensate for the additional energy used by the HVAC systems. For the institution with a small or limited operating budget that simply cannot afford a major increase in annual energy costs, some compromises might be warranted, or some initial capital investments might be made in systems to offset recurring annual costs. Most of the higher operating costs for preservation environments come from humidity control: humidification and dehumidification. The following two options are among those to be considered to control these costs.

Compromise Humidification Source. Although a considerable compromise, a drain-through, wetted pad, or wetted drum humidifier might be used for humidification. These will not give the performance or life of a steam humidification system, but will provide modest humidification at low annual operating cost. If a wetted pad or wetted drum humidifier is used, it should be carefully cleaned no less than once a month.

Dehumidification Reheat Source. A good long-term and efficient method of providing reheat for dehumidification is to use the heat rejected by the system, which provides the cooling for the dehumidification effect. This is exactly what a portable dehumidifier does. In a permanent installation, a cooling/dehumidification system can similarly use the heat generated by its condenser for reheat. This removes the need to have a boiler or an electric system provide the heating. This can be a more expensive system to install than electric or boiler reheat, but works even if the boiler is off. In some cases this is easily done by selecting the proper cooling equipment initially, and can be part of both smaller DX systems and larger chilled water systems.

D.4 Lighting Systems

Sections 5.3.8 and 13.2.2 in the main body of this book deal with lighting issues at length; they should be read along with this appendix section for guidance in developing lighting solutions.

Lighting in a preservation environment requires careful selection of the light source, the lighting treatment, and a proper design rationale.

D.4.1 Light Sources

The best method of establishing proper lighting for a preservation environment is through the proper selection of light sources. The ideal source would emit a constant level of only visible light, devoid of infrared and ultraviolet components. For display, the ideal source should additionally be able to provide point-source direct illumination as well as diffuse fill illumination.

The sources generally available as natural or electric light sources for most projects are:

Daylight. Daylight has a high content of infrared (IR) and ultraviolet (UV) radiation, and extreme variations in intensity. Because of these variations, daylighting for illumination at low light levels requires complex control schemes. Useless at night, daylighting also requires an auxiliary electric lighting system in addition to ultraviolet filtration. Rather than attempting to filter, control, and supplement daylight, it should be avoided as a significant illumination source in preservation environments.

Where daylight is required for other reasons, such as in areas of a historical building, the daylight should be attenuated to reduce its intensity and filtered to remove ultraviolet radiation.

Incandescent Lamps. Incandescent lighting, also known as tungsten lighting, provides a pleasing continuous spectrum, with little ultraviolet content. Common screw-base lamps used in homes are tungsten lamps.

Tungsten-halogen lamps, sometimes called quartz-iodine, are tungsten lamps with a special halogen gas inside and a special quartz bulb; these help allow the tungsten to burn hotter and brighter. These lamps can expose collections to significant amounts of ultraviolet because their higher temperature generates more ultraviolet, and their quartz bulbs absorb less ultraviolet than glass bulbs. These lamps can have twice the ultraviolet of regular tungsten lamps; if used to illuminate light-sensitive materials, they must usually be filtered to remove their ultraviolet component.

At high light levels, tungsten lamps may be a significant source of infrared heating, and may cause damage to lit objects. "Dichroic reflector" lamps should be used if tungsten spotlights are used to achieve high light levels and infrared damage is a suspected problem. The dichroic reflector prevents the tungsten spotlight from focusing the infrared energy from the lamp into the light beam. They must be used in fixtures with porcelain sockets, specifically rated for the use of such lamps.

When compared to other light sources, all tungsten lights are relatively inefficient, generating many times more heat for the same amount of light. This inefficiency and heat gain may cause problems in cooling and in annual energy costs if they are used extensively. Another drawback is their associated lamp costs, because of their short lamp life—they commonly last only a tenth to a thirtieth the life of other sources.

Fluorescent Lamps. Fluorescent lights use a gas excited to luminance to create a bright-line emission spectrum (only certain colors of light), usually heavy in ultraviolet. This bright-line spectrum is absorbed by the phosphor coating on the inside of the bulb, which glows or fluoresces to create light. Because they depend on ultraviolet to create their light, these lamps can have high ultraviolet output, so they must be chosen carefully. Often "energy-efficient" lamps will have more ultraviolet.

When using a special fluorescent lamp to control ultraviolet, take care in the purchasing and stocking of replacement lamps. It is easy to intentionally or unintentionally substitute a standard lamp. Before a major purchase, contact the lamp manufacturer to confirm the ultraviolet output of the selected lamp, as they may change their phosphor mixture—and change the resulting ultraviolet emission—without changing the product designation. The manufacturer is responsible for a given lamp having a specific wattage and basic light output, but not a specific ultraviolet emission. Beware that "equivalent" or "substitute" lamps from different manufacturers may have very different ultraviolet emissions. Specific and current manufacturer data must be used to select lamps; lamp types cannot be switched between manufacturers if ultraviolet output is a concern without such an analysis of the ultraviolet output from each lamp.

Sleeve filters can be used on fluorescent lamps to effectively remove ultraviolet output. Similar performance can come from adding ultraviolet-filtering film or sheets to lensed light fixtures, or replacing lenses with those that will remove ultraviolet light. Many lensed fixtures effectively remove measurable ultraviolet light, although this must be confirmed by field measurements of actual fixtures if this is to be the basis of ultraviolet control for preservation planning.

Mercury and Metal-Halide HID Lamps. The high-intensity discharge (HID) mercury and metal-halide lamps are bright-line sources using phosphors to generate much of their light (like fluorescent lamps), and are usually too intense and too strong in their ultraviolet output for anything but an indirect treatment. In fact, when the outer envelopes of some of these lamps are broken, those without an expensive self-extinguishing feature emit levels of ultraviolet that are an established health hazard to human skin. Unless used in an indirect application, the ultraviolet exposure may be too high and, with the lamp's high intensity, use of ultraviolet filters is problematic.

Sodium HID Lamps. High-pressure and low-pressure sodium HID lamps produce very little ultraviolet because of their inherent emission spectra. The most efficient of all lamps available, they are low in heat generation and operating cost. Low-pressure sodium (LPS) lamps are too orange in color, but high-pressure sodium (HPS) lamps can be used where the color rendering is not important, such as in a storage area. Because it is a high-intensity lamp, indirect lighting is suggested, usually by bouncing light off the ceiling. This ensures low illumination levels and allows large-wattage lamps to be used. This is a decided advantage in lowering initial and ongoing lamp costs. Unlike mercury and metal-halide HID lamps, which take 3 to 10 minutes to relight after being shut off, HPS lamps usually relight in less than a minute.

In general, ultraviolet filtration is needed for daylight, most fluorescent lamps, and some tungsten-halogen (or quartz-iodine) lamps. Some low-UV fluorescent lamps need no filtration, although the use of ultraviolet filters is good insurance. Tungsten lamps, when providing illumination at or below preservation levels, usually require no filtration.

D.4.2 Lighting Treatments

The lighting treatment determines the way the chosen light source is used. A treatment should try to avoid creating problems, and produce illumination at or below preservation light levels while providing an effective working environment.

Stacks and Storage. Stacks and storage spaces are usually best lit with low-UV fluorescent lamps, designed to provide 2 to 5 footcandles (20 to 50 lux) of vertical illumination at the bottom shelf. For small or confined areas, several common tungsten lamps may be a good choice. Avoid daylight, and direct mercury and metal-halide lighting treatments.

For good design of stack lighting, the lighting designer should perform "point illumination calculations" to check the maximum, typical, and minimum vertical illumination in footcandles (or lux) on the objects in storage.

To improve collection illumination under low lighting, the ceilings, walls, shelving (particularly the underside of shelves), and perhaps even the floor should be white.

Consider individual range-aisle switching in general stack areas where use is not constant; this would generally not be applicable in reference or current periodicals stacks. In addition to the energy savings, switching reduces exposure of the spines of books to light.

Indirect Lighting. Most lighting is direct, where light shines directly from the lamp or fixture to the task or illuminated object. In indirect lighting the light from the lamp or fixture first shines on a large environmental surface, such as the ceiling, and the luminosity of the ceiling provides the effective illumination within the space.

This can provide very satisfactory lighting at relatively low light levels. For economy in capital and operating costs, fluorescent or HPS lamps are usually required for indirect lighting. If possible, an indirect scheme should be used in storage areas with the ceiling or ceiling cavity painted white. While providing even illumination and improved vertical illumination and general visibility, it further reduces ultraviolet if the bounce surface is painted using a paint with titanium dioxide pigment. Bounce or indirect lighting works best with high ceilings, generally over 2.75 meters (9 feet) high, with space below for the light fixtures. In some cases the fixtures can be mounted to shelving or walls with ceilings as low as 2.13 meters (7 feet).

Large storage spaces with high ceilings might use an indirect HPS scheme. Where higher color-rendering is needed in an indirect treatment, the lighting can be a combination HPS/metal-halide light fixture.

Reading Areas. A good solution for providing illumination at the reading task area is with general illumination to a level of about 15 footcandles (150 lux), supplemented with task lights at or over the reading surfaces. This reduces the overall exposure to the collection, yet provides the high light level where needed. For the general illumination, an indirect treatment can provide a pleasing lighting environment with high task contrast and low veiling reflections, leading to a very good reading environment at light levels at a fraction of conventional direct illumination treatments.

Exhibit or Display. Display lighting should usually be based on tungsten light sources for a high degree of control, and should be based on a mix of direct and diffuse or "fill" light. Direct lighting will give color saturation and its shadows will give modeling detail to the objects on display. Fill light, either reflected from other objects, from general illumination, or from spill from adjacent lights, lessens the contrast of the direct light's shadows.

Control of Light Exposure. The recommendation for light exposure for paper-based materials in a museum setting, as promulgated by the Illuminating Engineering Society of North America, is 5,000 footcandle-hours (54,000 lux-hours) per year. For a display illuminated at 5 footcandles (50 lux) for 80 operating hours per week, this annual cumulative exposure will be exceeded in less than four months. For this reason sensitive materials should be rotated on display or shielded from regular light exposure. In the old Bibliothèque nationale in Paris, the exhibit of exceedingly rare materials in their special treasures room is done with drapes over the cases that are only removed for viewing, and viewing is done only with a staff member present to ensure that the drape is repositioned afterward. The same methodology is used in a number of college and university library exhibition halls. A similar technology is employed for the exhibit of the Star-Spangled Banner in Baltimore, Maryland, where a canvas cover is lowered at timed intervals, which limits light exposure to five minutes per hour. The notion of limiting exposure time is one effective way to minimize total display exposure to light.

Typical Solutions for Common Problems. For different reasons the same characteristics of a good lighting environment for reading rooms and stacks emerge: Shade or block off windows, use a light fixture with a large reflector or indirect lighting, and use brighter environmental finishes (lighter-colored floor, shelves, boxes, and book spines).

D.4.3 Heat Gain and Energy

A major problem, particularly for old buildings with existing cooling or duct systems, is control of heat gain from lighting. New lighting can easily cause inadvertent heating of the collection spaces, leading to heat gains in excess of the capacity of the cooling system in summer, or heating in winter leading to reduced space humidity. Where appropriate, a maximum lighting power budget, in watts, should be established, in addition to a maximum preservation light level. This should be based on a studied estimate of the capacity of the existing supply air and cooling capacity installed in the building.

Reduced lighting levels from reduced wattage has the additional benefit of reducing electric usage, cooling, and energy costs. Even in winter, the reduced heat gain will, if necessary, be made up from the main heating system; unless the main heating is electric, it will be more efficient and less costly than heat from the lights.

D.4.4 Lighting Retrofits

High light levels can be addressed through the replacement of lamps with lower wattages, installation of dimmers and removal of lamps, and blocking or shading of windows. For infrared (IR) exposure control, tungsten light sources can be chosen that have integral dichroic filters to reduce the IR exposure. For ultraviolet exposure control, ultraviolet filters can be used on windows and on fluorescent and tungsten-halogen lamps.

APPENDIX E

Equipment That Might Be Overlooked

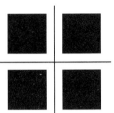

You will forget if you don't make a memorandum of it.

—Lewis Carroll, *Alice's Adventures in Wonderland*

This list supplements the 16 chapters of the text. Some of these elements are fixed to the structure and are almost always part of the basic construction contract, while many others are movable and are purchased at various times and may or may not be part of the basic contract.

No attempt is made here to include equipment for information technology or computer installations of all types, conservation laboratories, kitchens or other food or beverage service areas, media or audiovisual work, microform readers, photographic laboratory installations, and printing press rooms. Any library building will need a certain number of tools and supplies for routine machinery adjustment and minor building and equipment repairs, and these also are not detailed.

Air-conditioners, unit: If the building as a whole is not air conditioned, units can be useful in offices and perhaps workrooms or shelving areas for materials especially sensitive to extreme heat.

Artwork: Such items as framed prints, photographs, banners, flags, or posters can make a lot of difference in the aesthetics of staff quarters and public spaces. Security and lighting need to be considered.

Ashtrays and smoking urns: One or the other or both are needed wherever smoking is permitted. Should be deep enough so that a flip of a page will not scatter ashes. If too small or attractive, they will tend to disappear. Urns, if used at building entrances, should be attractive, probably partially filled with sand to prevent conflagrations, tall enough to be reached with ease, and heavy enough to discourage their removal. Trash receptacles should be next to urns so the one will not be used for the other purpose.

Atlas stands: May be provided if one or a few are very heavily used and the sloping top of atlas cases is not sufficient or in the needed location.

Benches: These may be needed outside or inside the building, in an arcade or a broad passageway, or in selected waiting areas.

Bicycle racks or stands: Should provide ability to chain both wheels to the rack. Preferably should be sheltered from rain and provide some degree of oversight to minimize vandalism.

Blackboards: see *Chalkboards*

Book bins, depressible: Provide at each site where book materials are to be returned into such a bin. Must be on wheels and of a precise height for the particular site. Sometimes provided with a backup so that an empty one can be immediately put in place as the full one is removed for book discharging.

Book rests, or cradles: Needed in rare book rooms to hold large books safely and at a convenient angle for reading. Often made of foam, with a base portion and two angled portions to hold the front and back covers open at about 120°. Should be available in at least quarto and folio and one larger size. Book stands, rests, or cradles are also needed for exhibition mounting.

Book trucks: Useful in a variety of staff locations, wherever there is frequent movement of volumes, manuscript boxes, and other library materials. Number and types of book trucks needed are usually underestimated.

Bookends: Not only needed in stacks but also in staff areas and faculty studies. Less than one per shelf will be needed.

Building directory: Should be available in the entrance lobby in all but very small libraries where almost the entire building is visible from the entrance. Should be easily changeable but quite tamperproof; a locking glass cover can serve the purpose.

Bulletin boards or tackboards: Useful in staff and public areas for temporary notices and messages. Some are made with flexible crossing bands to accommodate relatively small cards that are tucked under a band. Cork or other soft surface can be easily used with thumbtacks. A glass cover in a frame that is locked will prevent unauthorized use in public areas. Good lighting is a necessity.

Cash box or cash register: Useful where cash and checks are accepted for overdue fines, library privileges, computer search and copying charges, purchase of library publications, and so on. See also *Safe.*

Chair dolly: Used to move a large number of stacking chairs, which may be stored out of sight until needed in a meeting or lecture room. Stacking chairs are usually bought with the design of the dolly specific to the selected chair, and the number of dollies determined by the number of chairs to be stacked.

Chalkboards or blackboards or white marker boards: Can be very useful in small or large conference and bibliographic instruction rooms for readers or for staff. Smooth, light-colored boards for chemical markers are often used. All these boards may be affixed to a wall or be movable and placed on an easel. Flip-chart stands are also useful and movable.

Clocks: Should be in all but the smallest offices, workrooms, and reading areas, so placed as to be in sight of as large a percentage of the occupants as possible in order to reduce disturbing traffic that would result if they could be seen only from certain areas. They are usually part of the building construction, unless overlooked and then found needed in certain places. (In a large library, a master clock system is often justified because even a 10-minute power outage would otherwise mean manually resetting every clock in the building.)

Closed-circuit television systems: see *Television*

Coat hooks and racks: Supervised coatrooms are little used in academic libraries, as rapid change in readers makes them impractical. Unsupervised rooms are hazardous, particularly in large urban institutions, and are seldom used except in independent research libraries, archives, and rare book and manuscript quarters. Coat hooks scattered around the building within sight of the reader or staffed position are generally preferable. Coat hooks on carrel partitions or at individual workstations help to solve the problem. The hook should be large enough for a hat and perhaps an umbrella. Climatic conditions will affect the decision in regard to their use.

Compactor: see *Incinerator*

Corners: Particularly plaster- or wood-covered columns or corners in exposed places should be protected by impact-resistant materials, such as steel angles, vinyl tile, plastic strips, buckram, or high projecting bases. They are part of the construction contract, unless overlooked.

Cradles: see *Book rests*

Credenza: Small, separate, covered file cabinet placed adjacent to or behind a desk in offices when the desk-file capacity is insufficient and larger file cabinets too far away for very frequent use.

Dictionary stands: The floor or table stands can be used in various places, including secretarial quarters, where an unabridged dictionary or other large volume is frequently consulted.

Directional signs and door labels: Should be attractively designed, carefully placed, and easy to read and to change. Frequently overlooked is the sign at the entrance to the building to indicate hours of opening, and, because these hours change frequently, flexibility is essential.

Display racks: Holding library guides, campus maps, OPAC instruction pamphlets, service brochures, and flyers, racks can be wall-mounted, floor stands, or counter racks to accommodate various sizes of printed matter.

Dolly: Very useful for moving crates, book boxes, binding shipments, stocks of photocopy paper, and even some furniture. See also *Chair dolly* and *Tables.*

Doormats: This equipment is a good way to reduce maintenance costs if the items are selected and serviced to meet local conditions. Cocoa mats sunk in the floor are effective, but should be small enough so that cleaning will not shrink them so much as to result in dangerous cracks. Rubber or rubberlike mats with corrugations are sometimes useful. Some libraries use carpeting or carpet tile on the basis that, in spite of cost, it will pay for itself in lower cleaning expenditures. Also used are carpet insets in removable nonskid rubber mats with beveled edges, so that they rest on top of the finished floor. (In climates subject to snow and slush, a grating close to the main entrance doors through which the snow and slush can fall from the feet has been found to reduce the maintenance considerably and improve the appearance of the adjacent interior flooring.)

Drapes, shades, and curtains: Often needed for sun control, minimizing heat loss and gain, or aesthetic purposes. Adjustment is sometimes tied into environmental controls in a "smart" building. Their relation to furniture is important to reduce damage as they are opened or closed, raised or lowered. See also *Venetian blinds.*

Drinking fountains: These are now usually built-in, rather than separate "bubbler" or "water cooler" equipment. Should be placed where spilled water will not damage books or result in dangerously slippery floors. An exterior fountain may be prone to vandalism, even if it is in an open area some distance from the building, yet it can be much appreciated by joggers, other campus persons, and visitors.

Electric fans: Portable equipment may be needed if the building is not air conditioned or for emergencies. Wall-hung fans save floor space but must be placed very high.

Emergency power generator: As a backup power supply for sump pumps, alarm systems, emergency lights, and other critical equipment, a generator may be needed unless a campus backup or batteries or both are to be used.

Exhibit cases: Provide a place for enough of them, but do not have too many. They should be attractive and well designed, protected from theft and vandalism, and appropriately lighted. Some entrance lobbies are suitable for them, as are wide corridors. Separate rooms are expensive in their use of space and may require expensive supervision. Exhibit support today commonly requires a variety of formed plastic book stands or cradles of several types and sizes. Attention must be paid to the special lighting requirements of good exhibits.

Exit signs: Check their location with building and fire codes.

Fire extinguishers: Provide enough of them in carefully considered locations. Select them with the risks in mind (see comments in Chapter 5).

First-aid kits: Major public and staff areas would be well advised to keep a current kit.

Flashlights and lanterns: Even with building emergency lights, there will be times when lanterns will be needed, outside or inside and especially in various types of emergencies.

Flip charts: Large paper pads held on an easel, for notes and drawings produced to help meetings and planning sessions.

Floor lamps: Can be very attractive in a browsing room, but tend to be expensive and difficult to keep in repair; they may be tempting to thieves. Be sure the base is heavy enough so they do not easily fall over, and that the shade is quite durable.

Floor-plan charts: Are a must on each level of a large building. It is important to orient them so that the user is facing the same direction that is shown at the top of the plan. The architect is equipped to prepare them and will be glad to render this service, though an interior design specialist may be given the assignment. They should be produced so that they can accommodate changes inexpensively.

Fly screens: If windows are to be opened and flying insects, birds, or bats are a local nuisance, be sure that screens are provided. If in doubt, at least provide suitable construction for later screen installation.

Footstools: Placed by lounge furniture, will save chairs being pulled up to serve as footrests. They provide variety in seating options, save wear on other chairs, and for some locations can appropriately be designed of a size to accommodate two or more users.

Globes: If a large one is on hand or anticipated, a suitable space with adequate square footage should be planned for it. Consider whether electric power may be needed, as well as the best lighting arrangement and physical support.

Heater, portable: In conditions where a staff member is posted by the building entrance to check people coming or going and when the weather is very cold and there is no vestibule or other protection, there sometimes is need for a small heater to make that post tolerable.

High stools and high swivel chairs: High stools that can be pushed out of the way under card catalog consultation tables will be appreciated by the reader. High swivel chairs with suitable footrests for use by staff members serving the public at counters may prevent backaches and tired feet. They bring the eyes of a staff member more or less on the level with the reader, a matter of considerable importance and convenience to both, particularly short staff members.

Incinerator: Rarely desirable in a library. Decision in regard to its use may depend on the institution's policy on waste disposal. They represent a prospective fire hazard. All precautions for fire protection should be adopted if they are installed. A compactor or a heavy-duty shredder may be useful.

Kick stools: Located at frequent intervals throughout every bookstack area, so staff and readers can easily move the step to reach the top shelves. Made with wheels that depress and become inoperable when even a small person steps up on it.

Lanterns: see *Flashlights*

Lecterns: Needed in most classrooms, sometimes of a size to be placed on top of a counter or desk. Also useful at counter height for holding such large and frequently consulted volumes as unabridged dictionaries in reference rooms.

Letter trays: Used and sometimes stacked two or three high at office desks, perhaps for "in" and "out" and "pending" documents.

Light table: Useful for tracing of maps or other drawings. Must be near large worktable and have electrical outlet nearby.

Lockers: Should be available for staff members. For this use, they are generally full size, at least 5 ft to 6 ft (1.524 to 1.829 m) high. In areas of moderate climate, smaller lockers are suitable, and those may only be necessary for staff who do not have an office or a lockable drawer at a desk. If installed for readers, adjacent to open carrels, they can be much smaller, designed to allow space to store books, notes, and a typewriter. The noise they produce may suggest that they should be at a good distance from the carrels.

Mailboxes: A central set of boxes (either as furniture or built in) may be useful for mailroom staff to make distribution to bins from which staff can pick up letters and interdepartmental mail.

Marker boards: see *Chalkboards*

Mending equipment: A properly equipped book mending room, generally adjacent to the processing areas, is desirable, whether or not the library has a bindery or conservation laboratory. This may include a board cutter, gang punch, wire stitcher, glue pot, label pasting machine, standing press, and map edger.

Mirrors: Can be used to facilitate supervision of critical areas, though seldom used for this purpose in academic libraries. See also *Television.*

Outside lighting: Desirable at entrances, loading docks, and corners. Can be used for decorative as well as functional purposes, such as illumination of paths, bicycle parking, book-return depository, message kiosks or bulletin boards, seating benches, building name, and hours of service.

Pallet lift: A device very useful for lifting and moving a platform on which books, boxes, or cartons can be stacked.

Pedestals: Sometimes used for holding the busts of famous scholars or other notable persons, unless these are placed on shelves or other furniture.

Pencil sharpeners: Will be a convenience to readers and staff if easily seen and placed where they will not obstruct traffic or cause a disturbance. They should be permanently installed to avoid theft.

Photocopy machines: Require wide distribution in a large library and each machine must be given adequate space to service it. Photocopy machines may be supplemented by computer-driven printers. Both will require significant supplies. Acoustic control, lighting, and air return problems require careful consideration of environment. Bins or book trucks must be provided for book materials ready for reshelving.

Pictures: see *Artwork*

Plants, indoor: Some public as well as staff areas are often decorated with a major potted plant, providing an attractive color and texture. Recognize, however, they are not like a painting or sculpture, for frequent care is always required.

Print shop: Some academic institutions will have installations elsewhere on the campus, but a place in a large library where students can learn typesetting and the principles of book design can be useful and appropriate. A hand press will have considerable items of equipment necessary for its use and cleanup.

Receptions or entertainment support: Unless renting supplies is preferred, useful dishes will include punch bowls, ladles, trays, glasses, tea and coffee servers, and the like.

Recycling bins or barrels: Sometimes placed under cover in various campus locations. May be needed for paper in photocopying locations, journal and serial receiving, and also for plastic and bottles by a food service.

Repair, book: see *Mending equipment*

Safe, in lieu of a vault: Because vaults are expensive and must be adequately ventilated to prevent mold, a small safe can be very useful on occasion. In many cases, a locking closet or a screened enclosure in the regular bookstack will be sufficient, particularly if a small strongbox for cash and other valuables is available.

Screens, either acoustical or nonacoustical: Used to provide a degree of office privacy. Available as

"office landscaping" in various heights and surfaces and materials.

Screens, visual: Used to provide a degree of office privacy, in either acoustical or nonacoustical design. Available as "office landscaping" in various heights and surfaces and materials.

Shredder: see *Incinerator*

Side chairs: Useful by certain desks, such as those of a secretary and a supervisor, where a visitor may wish to sit and converse for a minute or two.

Sign-making equipment: Every library will need in-house equipment for signs (for example, for book sales, exhibits, stack range labels), unless use will be made of a campus service or outside contractor. (Temporary signs will sometimes be produced by computer or photocopy machines.)

Signs: Exterior lettering identifying the building is important, but should generally be confined to a few words. Labels at public-service desks with names and sometimes titles may save time and confusion for readers and staff. See also *Directional signs and door labels.*

Snakes: Flexible heavy belts or cords, two of which should be provided for each of the book rests or props in any area servicing rare books and similar rare or fragile codex materials.

Staff lunchroom equipment: A system for making coffee and tea, a microwave oven, a refrigerator, a sink, and cupboards can be made available in one area. Ample trash receptacles are necessary. Be very careful to avoid encouraging mice and vermin.

Staff quiet room equipment: Considered essential for a staff of as few as six. Should be equipped with a cot. Hot and cold water and a medicine chest should be available close at hand. This room can be used for the public in emergency cases. Some codes will specify the exact requirements.

Stools: Better than chairs when needed at reference counters, index and abstract tables, and similar items needing short use. See also *High stools* and *Kick stools.*

Sump pump: Be sure one is provided in the basement if there is even a remote danger of flooding, preferably a permanent installation rather than portable equipment. Complete protection can be obtained only with a duplex installation, so that maintenance repair or a breakdown will not temporarily complicate matters. Even then, it is sometimes desirable to have an adjacent overflow area, for use during flash floods, which can receive any water temporarily in excess of that which can be handled by the pump.

Supply cabinets: If adequate closets, cupboards, or enclosed shelving are not provided, a number of small cabinets will usually be needed in administrative and departmental offices and at least one large one for bulky library and building-maintenance supplies kept under lock and key. If computer, photocopy, and fax supplies are also needed, this space will increase proportionately.

Table lamps: Tend to result in glare and restrict reader's comfort unless they are adjustable. Too often subject to vandalism in an academic library, and yet, some form of the table lamp may help give a warm feeling to the environment and is quite common as a "task" light in energy-efficient design.

Tables: Although this category seems obvious, it is well to reconsider some of the specialized needs. Therefore, the following lists examples of table options: adjustable height table, coffee table, conference table, round meeting or dining table, end table, index table, OPAC table, sloped-top table, workbench. In the case of the round table used for meetings or eating, it may be folding and can be rolled into storage or moved on a table dolly.

Tackboard: see *Bulletin boards*

Telephones (public): Are desirable and will be used heavily in most libraries. Place them just off main traffic arteries for ease of locating and yet where some confidentiality of the conversation is possible and the talking involved will not disturb readers. Should be available for handicapped persons. An outdoor phone under cover will also be very useful.

Television: Closed-circuit systems can be used to facilitate supervision of critical areas. They are also sometimes used in public areas, such as a lobby, to enable people to have a glimpse into a public auditorium, stage set, rehearsal hall, and the like. A television set for reception of public broadcast or cable programs may also be useful in the staff room and occasionally is placed in a public lounge area.

Toilet-room equipment: Hooks for coats and purses, mirrors, paper towels and receptacles or drying equipment, sanitary napkin and tampon dispensers, and soap holders or soap dispensers. Also remember shelves on which to lay parcels, books, or papers in toilet stalls as well as beside the hand-drying location.

Trash containers: Useful at building entrances for small bits of paper, wrappers, and so on. See also comments under *Ashtrays and smoking urns, Incinerator,* and *Wastebaskets.*

Truck or van: Most major libraries have need for a delivery vehicle, especially if there are branch libraries to which boxes of books frequently come and go. The type of vehicle will depend of course on local need, campus traffic regulations and routes, and availability of good servicing of this equipment.

Typing stands: Where typewriters are still used, these can be useful for library users bringing portable machines to such places as a special collections reading room.

Umbrella racks: If coat racks are scattered around the building, umbrella racks may be likewise, but they involve water problems. See other comments under *Coat hooks and racks.*

Vacuum cleaners: Both portable and building-wide equipment should be considered. Installation costs and the presence of satisfactory air filtering may be factors in the decisions reached.

Van or other vehicle: see *Truck or van*

Vending machines: May have a place just outside the library or in a public lounge area, but remember that food attracts vermin, and wrappers too often do not find their way into trash containers. Vending machines also should be considered for staff lounges and lunchrooms. In all cases, distance from bookshelves and closeness to the vendor delivery access are desirable. A hard floor surface to facilitate frequent cleaning is necessary.

Venetian blinds: Horizontal and vertical blinds are available, each with certain advantages. The larger horizontal and most vertical ones can be more prone to present maintenance problems. Cleaning is difficult. See also *Drapes, shades, and curtains.*

Vertical filing cabinets: Provide suitable space for them in offices and at reference desks, for instance. Select them carefully from the different types (wood or steel) and sizes that are available on the market. Filing cases standing so that they face each other should be at least 3 ft 6 in. (1.067 m) apart to provide for easy access, even when used by only one person at a time. Lateral files can be used where the front-to-front space is limited, but even here 3 ft 6 in. clear is a comfortable minimum.

Wastebaskets: An adequate number will reduce maintenance costs, and all should be fireproof. If too light, they will be misplaced. If too attractive, they will disappear. If too heavy and too hard with sharp corners, they will be a hazard. Small ones are needed at faculty studies, selected general reading areas, all enclosed student carrels or dissertation rooms, most staff desks, and some counters. Large ones are needed for paper towels in toilet rooms, for wrappings in the shipping room and wherever book materials are received and opened, for trash in food locations (sometimes several labeled differently for specific recycling), and by copying machines.

APPENDIX F

Bibliography of Selected Useful Publications

Today ought to be the pupil of yesterday.
—Publilius Syrus, *Sententiae,* 1st c. B.C.

The clearest advantage we have today is the experience of yesterday.
—R. Buckminster Fuller

Introduction

This bibliography is a selection of the books and articles published through 1997 that have been useful in the preparation of this volume or that may be useful to its readers for further study of particular aspects of planning. A few items of continuing special interest are retained from the second edition of this book. Each is given a brief annotation.

This selection is not intended to be a list of the "best" literature on the subject, as every decade will find important new works on most aspects here treated. There are constant changes in the economics of construction, in construction methods, in the use and influence of new materials, and in the philosophies of library management (as witness the tremendous changes brought about over the past third of a century by information technologies). Similarly there is a constant flow of new and useful publications. Although there will always be new works to replace or supplement titles in this bibliography, the current list is in part intended to suggest the range and specificity of published material that can be found to help with a building project.

Quality was not the only criterion for selection; accessibility, language, and country of origin were also taken into account. All the items are in English, and most have an American frame of reference as the authors assume that readers of the volume, whatever their nationality, will want and expect to get an American approach to the subject. Relatively few publications are included under Special Topics. For example, there are many highly detailed texts, handbooks, manuals, and technical reports on each aspect and trade in the construction industry, and only a few of the more general or more useful to librarians are here included.

A long list of building programs could have been included, except for the fact that these programs are published in limited editions for local use and are not generally available. The American Library Association Headquarters Library has building packets (containing data, drawings, and photos) for winners since 1983 of the biennial building design awards, and since 1993 for all applicants (averaging 30 academic entries per year). All these may be borrowed for three weeks, and ALA can provide a list of those colleges and universities.

The best approach to recent material specifically relevant to libraries is through *Library Literature* (New York: H. W. Wilson), published bimonthly with annual cumulations, and also available in an online service. A search of other published literature in such fields as architecture, education, engineering, and interior design will find materials that pertain to an academic or a research library project but are intended primarily for practitioners in these disciplines.

Abbreviations in this bibliography are used for the American Library Association (ALA), Association of College and Research Libraries (ACRL), Library Administration and Management Association (LAMA), and International Federation of Library Associations and Institutions (IFLA). When the work has two publishers or two places for publication, only the North American is given. Only major pagination is provided.

The bibliography is arranged in alphabetical order under their headings.

F.1 General Works

N.B. Most general works contain much valuable material that could be listed under the various subheadings of Special Topics; annotations sometimes bring out coverage of special usefulness. Significant lists of bibliographic citations are found in many of the works here cited.

F.1.1 Bibliographies

Council for Advancement and Support of Education (CASE). *CASE RESOURCES, 1995–96.* Washington, D.C.: The Council. An annual publications list, including the following among over four dozen on aspects of fund-raising:

> *The Capital Campaign in Higher Education.* 1995. Includes CASE Campaign Standards.
>
> *Developing an Effective Major Gift Program.* 1993. 134p.
>
> *The Ethics of Asking.* 1995. 236p.
>
> *Major Gifts: Solicitation Strategies.* 1994. 167p.

Dahlgren, Anders C., and Erla P. Heyns. *Planning Library Buildings: A Select Bibliography.* 4th ed. Chicago: ALA LAMA, 1995. 63p., author index.

> Covers the "most useful" publications "for anyone undertaking a building project" for all types of libraries. Entries are organized usefully in two dozen categories, including one on selected building reviews and case studies.

Swartzburg, Susan Garretson, and Holly Bussey with Frank Garretson. *Libraries and Archives: Design and Renovation with a Preservation Perspective.* Metuchen, N.J.: Scarecrow Press, 1991. 235p.

> Preservation and environmental appropriateness for housing of library and archival collections; a literature guide organized into six broad aspects of buildings.

F.1.2 Standards and Guidelines

Note that each of the following ACRL documents are also available online at http://www.ala.org/acrl/guides/index.html

ACRL. "Guidelines for Branch Libraries in Colleges and Universities." *C&RL News* 52 (March 1991): 171–174.

> Very brief and general comment on facilities.

ACRL. "Guidelines for University Undergraduate Libraries." *C&RL News* 58 (May 1997): 330–333, 341.

> Scant comment on the environmental conditions for effective learning.

ACRL. "Standards for College Libraries, 1995 edition." *C&RL News* 56 (April 1995): 245–257.

> Standard 6 on Facilities has three parts, the first referring to Formula C, which gives the size of the building while taking into account the size of enrollment and staff and the extent and nature of the college collections.

ACRL. "Standards for Community, Junior, and Technical College Learning Resources Programs." *C&RL News* 55 (May 1994): 274–287.

> Standard 7 on Facilities has five parts. Its appendix C gives library facilities space standards of the California Community Colleges, from Title 5, *California Code of Regulations,* Section 57030.

ACRL. "Standards for University Libraries: Evaluation of Performance." *C&RL News* 50 (September 1989): 679–691.

> Sections B(4) and D(5) concern the "building resources" and the amount, distribution, and location of space as well as planning needs.

ALA LAMA. *Building Blocks for Library Space: Functional Guidelines, 1995.* Chicago: 1995. 25p.

> An eight-page list of component library spaces (for example, book truck parking, lockers, queuing area, tables, workstation) with footprint areas for each in square feet and meters, with 15 illustrative drawings appended. A "working paper" to which many library building experts contributed. (The text is appendix C here.)

American National Standards Institute. *Catalog of American National Standards.* New York: ANSI, 1996. 286p.

> Also available online. Among ANSI standards, see its standard of building code requirements for minimum design loads in buildings and other structures (1972).

National Information Standards Organization (NISO). *Catalog of Publications.* Bethesda, Md.

> Currently included are five shelving standards—for example, on bracing, multilevel shelving, and safety matters. Standard Z39.73-1994 for Single-Tier Steel Bracket Library Shelving is the most relevant. (See also the general industrial standards promoted by the Shelving Manufacturers Association, a Division of the Material Handling Institute, based in Charlotte, North Carolina; its Standard 28.1 of 1982 on Industrial Grade Steel Shelving

was being upgraded and cleared with ANSI in 1997.)

F.1.3 Building Institutes and Conferences

ALA ACRL. Library Building Plans Institutes. *Proceedings.* Chicago: ALA, 1952 and later.

The 1992 publication is *Libraries for the Future: Planning Buildings That Work,* edited by Ron G. Martin, 98 pages, with 12 fine papers given at a LAMA 1991 conference. This slender volume is useful for its inclusion of many specimen items: a program document, floor plans, space inventory, matrix of functional relationships, schematic map of spatial relationships, RFP for hiring an architect, and a sheet for rating prospective architects.

The historical information of earlier volumes is still useful. This series of institutes followed the precedent established by the Cooperative Committee on Library Building Plans. The purpose of the institutes was to provide a clearinghouse for the exchange of ideas on the planning of new library buildings and to make it possible for preliminary plans of libraries of colleges and universities to be critically reviewed. In earlier proceedings, the plans of seven libraries are presented and discussed; floor plans are included. Subsequent institutes devoted to building plans or equipment were held in 1953–1955, 1959, 1961–1966, 1975, and later, with proceedings published under various titles. The institute papers and building critiques with plans have been published by ACRL or ALA or LAMA.

IFLA. [Proceedings of the Building Seminars, held each few years.] New York: Saur. (Issued as numbered IFLA Publications.)

Saur has published the papers presented at the 1980 IFLA Building Seminar (on interior layout and design) held in Denmark, also that of 1985 held in Budapest (on adaptation of buildings), and that of 1987 held at Aberystwyth (on preparations for planning, published by Saur in 1989). Of note are the 1980 papers on security, fire protection, energy saving, HVAC, graphic design, and lighting. See also, as one product stemming from the IFLA series of library building seminars and study tours, the paper by Michael Dewe, "Buildings for Library and Information Services: Some International Concerns and Comparisons, 1980–

1991." In *International Information & Library Review* 25 (1993): 109–122.

F.1.4 Statistics

North American research universities and major independent research libraries (U.S. and Canada): A range of data for 1908 to date is available via the ARL at http://www.arl.org/stats/Statistics/stat.html.

United Kingdom (university libraries): Data are available for 1993 to date as the paper publication *Annual Library Statistics* by the Standing Conference of National and University Libraries (SCONUL). This publication is among services listed on the SCONUL Web site at: http://www.sconul.ac.uk.

U.S. academic library survey data for 1988 to date are compiled by the Department of Education, National Center for Education Statistics, with data for some library categories published on CD-ROM and diskette, and with some available online in compressed form at http://nces.ed.gov/surveys/datasurv.html.

U.S. university libraries: A range of operating data has been published by ALA since 1988 as *ACRL University Library Statistics,* compiled by the Library Research Center, Graduate School of Library & Information Science, University of Illinois at Urbana-Champaign.

This biennial booklet includes over 105 libraries in the Carnegie Classifications Research I and II and Doctoral Granting I and II, excluding the ARL institutions. Categories of data reported: collection information, staffing levels, expenditures, and interlibrary loan traffic. Institutional categories include degrees offered, enrollment size, and faculty size.

Worldwide basic data of national libraries are available in published form in the annual *UNESCO Statistical Yearbook,* and some UNESCO information is available online at http://www.unesco.org.

F.1.5 Other General Works

ALA. *Library Technology Reports.* Chicago: 1961 to date.

Detailed booklets are frequently issued on a wide range of topics, examples in recent years being: library chairs and tables, bracket shelving, circulation systems, photocopying, record players, facilities planning for technology, handling of microforms and magnetic media, local area networks and wide area networks, and disaster planning and recovery of resources. Future LTR publications are to be watched.

Association of Research Libraries, Systems and Procedures Exchange Center. *Spec Kit.* Washington, DC: 1973 to date, 10 issues per year.

Among this useful continuing series of practical documents submitted by ARL members, occasional topics treat academic and research library building issues—for example, Remote storage (#164, May 1990), Insuring library collections and buildings (#178, October 1991), Strategies for obtaining funding for new library space (#200, March 1994), and Technical services workstations (#213, February 1996). (Spec Flyers since 1994 are also available online at www.arl.org/speclist.html)

Brawne, Michael. *Libraries: Architecture and Equipment.* New York: Praeger, 1970. 187p., photos., with floor plans and sections.

Interior and exterior photographs of European and American libraries, a good number of them academic, with explanatory text.

Cohen, Aaron, and Elaine Cohen. *Designing and Space Planning for Libraries: A Behavioral Guide.* New York: Bowker, 1979. 250p., illus., bibl.

Treats planning of new or remodeled libraries, including layout of space, furniture and equipment, color, energy use, lighting, decoration, acoustics, and moving.

Dober, Richard P. *Campus Architecture: Building in the Groves of Academe.* New York: McGraw-Hill, 1996. 258p., illus. Also: *Campus Design.* New York: Wiley, 1992. Also: *Campus Planning.* New York: Reinhold, 1963 (reprinted 1996). 314p.

A trilogy on campus planning and design, with many anecdotes, illuminating quotes, and illustrations. Presents broad view of how campuses develop, extensive comment on plans and buildings of dozens of colleges and universities in North America, and insights into building types, courtyards, atriums, quadrangles, lawns, and plazas.

Edwards, Heather M. *University Library Building Planning.* Metuchen, N.J.: Scarecrow Press, 1990. 137p., plans, photos.

The third chapter presents selected space standards for reading stations, staff and book storage for the United Kingdom (as of 1978), South Africa ("review editions" of 1979), and a few from the United States. Much of this book is case studies with floor plans for the universities of Edinburgh, Nottingham, Loughborough, Orange Free State, Stellenbosch, Northern Iowa, Denver, and Bielefeld.

Ellsworth, Ralph E. *Academic Library Buildings: A Guide to Architectural Issues and Solutions.* Boulder, Colo.: Colorado Associated University Press, 1973. 530p.

A useful picture book, classified and indexed, of exteriors and interior details of dozens of libraries from coast to coast, including several in Europe. Also 27 floor plans with accompanying comments by the author.

Harrison, Dean, ed. *Library Buildings in the United Kingdom 1990–1994.* London: Library Services Ltd., 1995. 270p., photos., plans.

Lists dozens of academic library buildings that were new or conversions or were given additions, and provides building data and floor plans of 17 university libraries.

Hawthorne, Pat, and Ron G. Martin, eds. *Planning Additions to Academic Library Buildings: A Seamless Approach.* Chicago: ALA, 1995. 64p.

Using three case studies (Hope College Van Wylen Library, Western Maryland College Hoover Library, and University of Washington Allen Library), this aims to explain how to match old and new structures for functional efficiency and aesthetic appeal.

IFLA Section on Library Buildings and Equipment. *Library Building Planning Leaflets.*

A continuing series, the first leaflets being: No. 1: "Preparing the Building Program Document," by David Kaser, 1991. No. 2: "Security in Library Buildings" by Robert Klaus Jopp, 1992. No. 3: "Information Technology and Library Buildings," by David C. Weber, 1993. No. 4: "The Initial Brief," by Harry Faulkner-Brown, 1993. Concise statements on topics selected by IFLA as of worldwide importance and interest.

Kaser, David. *The Evolution of the American Academic Library Building.* Lanham, Md.: Scarecrow Press, 1997. 206p., illus., bibl.

A concise survey from 1840 through 1994 of new buildings, especially strong on college libraries in the eastern half of the United States and on problem areas of contemporary modular buildings.

Langmead, Stephen, and Margaret Beckman. *New Library Design: Guide Lines to Planning Academic Library Buildings.* Toronto: Wiley, 1970. 117p.

An exemplary comprehensive treatment of the rationale and process of designing the McLaughlin Library, University of Guelph. Included are plans, photographs, tables, a bibliography, and a detailed decision chart.

Lucker, Jay K. "The Library as Place." In *Research Libraries Yesterday, Today, and Tomorrow,* 3–17. Kanazawa, Japan: Kanazawa Institute of Technology, 1993.

Historical review of research library building design, shortcomings and problems, and changes in academic library buildings in the twenty-first century as projected by the emeritus director of libraries, MIT.

McDonald, John P. "Adapting Libraries to New Responsibilities." In *Research Libraries Yesterday, Today, and Tomorrow,* 204–218. Kanazawa, Japan: Kanazawa Institute of Technology, 1993.

Thoughtful review of the literature of adaptation, preservation of collections, compact storage, views of the future, and adjusting to change.

Mason, Ellsworth. *Mason on Library Buildings.* Metuchen, N.J.: Scarecrow Press, 1980. 333p.

A compilation of Mason's trenchant comments on planning, writing the building program, lighting, air-handling systems, and interior design. Includes on pp. 263–321 a detailed illustrative model program. Gives extensive critiques of three general libraries, an undergraduate library, a rare book library, and a medical library, with floor plans and exterior and interior photographs: Brown, Dalhousie, and Toronto, Sedgewick Undergraduate at British Columbia, Beinecke at Yale, and Countway Library of Medicine at Harvard. Well indexed.

Novak, Gloria, ed. "The Forgiving Building: A Library Building Consultants' Symposium on the Design, Construction and Remodeling of Libraries to Support a High-Tech Future." *Library Hi Tech* 5 (winter 1987): 77–99.

Flexibility required of building systems is cogently described in some detail by experts: Margaret Beckman, Anders C. Dahlgren, David L. Kapp, David Kaser, Donald G. Kelsey, Jay K. Lucker, and Gloria Novak.

Sannwald, William W. *Checklist of Building Design Considerations.* 3d ed. Chicago: ALA, 1996. 169p.

A long, useful set of questions in workbook checklist form.

Taylor, Sue, ed. *Building Libraries for the Information Age: Based on the Proceedings of a Symposium on the Future of Higher Education Libraries, at the King's Manor, York, 11–12 April 1994.* York, England: Institute of Advanced Architectural Studies, University of York, 1995. 94p., photos., plans.

Collection of 16 stimulating papers by U.K. architects, technology experts, and administrators, in the context of the 1993 report of Sir Brian Follett.

Thompson, Anthony. *Library Buildings of Britain and Europe.* London: Butterworth, 1963. 326p., illus., bibl.

A useful historical reference work. Part I summarizes the problems of creating a library building; Part II traces in outline the history of library buildings and gives detailed analyses of a large number of buildings erected since 1930. Examples are mostly from Britain, with some from Europe and elsewhere; includes photographs and plans on uniform scales; numerous bibliographical references at the ends of chapters and accompanying descriptions of particular buildings.

Thompson, Godfrey. *Planning and Design of Library Buildings.* 3d ed. Oxford: Butterworth Architecture, 1989. 224p., charts, drawings, photos., extensive bibl., index.

"This book is meant for beginners." A superior authoritative and comprehensive text on planning libraries of all types, it is particularly useful on space standards (Chapter 19), equipment and furnishings, the planning process, and schedule of decisions. Excellently illustrated.

Turner, Paul Venable. *Campus: An American Planning Tradition.* Cambridge, Mass.: MIT Press, 1984. 337p., illus., plans, index.

An excellent history from Colonial times to the present.

Western Interstate Commission for Higher Education. *Higher Education Facilities Planning and Management Manuals.* Boulder, Colo.: The Commission, 1971. 7 pamphlets, bibl. (Technical Report no. 17)

This national effort presents detailed discussion of program planning, evaluation of existing facilities, analysis techniques, and facilities planning and management methodologies. Primarily prepared for community colleges and four-year institutions, both public and private, yet it was expected to be useful in larger institutions. Covers graduate work through the master's and some professional degrees, and treatment of seating for different fields of study is particularly useful. No. 4 treats libraries extensively with some data on audiovisual facilities, museums, and data processing and computing facilities.

F.2 Online Resources

Various publications and useful information can be found on the World Wide Web, a resource for recent as well as historic information. Content is constantly in flux. Because Internet resources are so many and changing all the time, only a suggestion is here provided of the type of information that can be found through networked computers. It is emphasized that addresses change, especially personal ones, though institutional and organizational ones should be relatively stable. (Telnet addresses can also be used to gain access.)

F.2.1 Organizations

American Institute of Architects can be reached at http://www.aiaonline.com

American Library Association at http://www.ala.org

American Society of Interior Designers at http://www.asid.org

Association of College and Research Libraries at http://www.ala.org/acrl

Association of Research Libraries at http://www.arl.org

International Interior Design Association at http://www.iida.org

Research Libraries Group at http://www.rlg.org

Society of Architectural Historians at http://www.upenn.edu/sah

"University Links" (easy access to U.S. colleges and universities) at http://www-net.com/univ/alpha/index.html

F.2.2 Library OPACs with Fine Collections on Architecture

British Library at http://portico.bl.uk

Cornell University, Fine Arts Library at http://www.library.cornell.edu/library/finelib.html

Harvard University, Loeb Library at http://www.gsd.harvard.edu/library

International Catalogs/Databases available via Melvyl at "Online Catalog Systems" at http://www.lib.berkeley.edu

Massachusetts Institute of Technology, Rotch Library at http://libraries.mit.edu/rotch/

RLIN (union library catalog of books, serials, archives, etc.; the Avery Architectural and Fine Arts periodical article index since 1980; and Art and Architecture Thesaurus authority file of the J. Paul Getty Trust) with access information at http://www.rlg.org/rlin.html

University of California, unified campus OPAC at http://www.melvyl.ucop.edu

University of Pennsylvania, Fisher Fine Arts Library at http://www.library.upenn.edu/finearts/finearts.html

WebCat (listing of worldwide library catalogs on the Web, with addresses, and useful finding aids, such as vendor homepages and publishers' catalogs, at http://www.lights.com/webcats

F.2.3 Architectural Internet Resource Directories

Architecture Article Indexes (selective list of, but no remote access to, periodical indexes for all aspects of "architecture," UC Berkeley Environmental Design Library) at http://www.lib.berkeley.edu/ENVI/archper.html

ArtSource (networked resources on art and architecture, with pointers to resources; managed at the University of Kentucky Library) at http://www.uky.edu/Artsource

Buildings OnLine (since 1995, articles and information on institutes, products, etc.) at http://www.buildingsmag.com/index.html

Cyburbia (the Planning and Architecture Internet Resource Center, a directory of resources relevant to planning, architecture, and other topics related to the built environment, including Usenet newsgroups; sponsored by the State University of New York at Buffalo, School of Architecture and Planning; it also hosts several interactive message areas) at http://www.ap.buffalo.edu/pairc

F.3   Special Subject Libraries

A great many individual special libraries have been briefly described in periodicals, especially in the *Library Journal* and *Special Libraries*. Excluding those two helpful journals, the following are some of the most useful or extensive.

F.3.1   General Works

Dahlgren, Anders C. *Planning the Small Library Facility.* 2d ed. Chicago: ALA, 1996. 27p.

Covers all types, from school to hospital libraries, including constraints when a library is housed as one component of a larger facility.

Freifeld, Roberta, and Caryl Masyr. *Space Planning in the Special Library.* Washington, D.C.: Special Libraries Association, 1991. 150p., index.

General guide of particular help with specialized furniture, with many photographic illustrations.

Lewis, Myron, and Mark Nelson. "How to Work with an Architect." *Wilson Library Bulletin* 57 (September 1982): 44–46.

Good treatment, and especially useful with respect to branch libraries.

Mount, Ellis, ed. *Creative Planning of Special Library Facilities.* New York: Haworth Press, 1988. 197p., illus.

Five chapters by Professor Mount on basics of planning facilities; six chapters by contributors on "advanced aspects"; and four case studies with floor plans. See also "Planning Facilities for Sci-Tech Libraries," ed. Ellis Mount, *Science & Technology Libraries* 3 (summer 1983): 1–104, plans and photos, which includes chapters on science-engineering libraries at the University of California, Berkeley; Northwestern University; and Swarthmore College.

F.3.2   Archives and Rare Books

Baynes-Cope, A. D. "Creating Buildings for Rare Books and Archival Documents." *Restaurator* 17 (1996): 22–24.

Ritzenthaler, Mary Lynn. *Preserving Archives and Manuscripts.* Chicago: Society of American Archivists, 1993. 205p., illus., bibl., index.

Authoritative treatment with chapters on a "sympathetic environment," and storing and housing various formats, and an appendix on setting up a work space.

F.3.3   Art

Irvine, Betty Jo, ed. Art Libraries Society of North America. *Facilities Standards for Art Libraries and Visual Resources Collections.* Englewood, Colo.: Libraries Unlimited, 1991. 216p., charts.

Superior presentation of standards, with useful commentary on each. Includes survey of art book and art exhibition catalog measurements. Also gives planning documents for libraries of the Art Institute of Chicago, Indiana University, Purdue University at Indianapolis, and the University of Southern California.

F.3.4   Law

Grossman, George S. "Programming for the New Library: An Overview." In *The Spirit of Law Librarianship: A Reader,* compiled by Roy M. Mersky and Richard A. Leiter, 253–262. Littleton, Colo.: Rothman, 1991.

Excellent concise treatment.

Kehoe, Patrick, et al., eds. *Law Librarianship: A Handbook for the Electronic Age.* Littleton, Colo.: Rothman, 1995. 649p.

Marke, Julius J. "Library Planning." In *Law Librarianship: A Handbook,* edited by Heinz Peter Mueller et al., 1:103–143. Littleton, Colo.: Rothman, 1983. (American Association of Law Libraries Publications Series, 19)

Expert advice on preliminary steps to planning and space allocations.

Stone, Dennis J., comp. *Law Library Design and Planning.* Hartford, Conn.: University of Connecticut School of Law Library, 1994. 270p.

A case study of one law library planning and design from 1986 to 1994. Includes the long-range plan, case statement, 27 pages of U.S. university law library statistical comparisons, full building program, documents on detailed aspects of information technology and environmental controls, and six floor plan drawings.

F.3.5 Maps

Bahn, Catherine I. "Map Libraries: Space and Equipment." *Bulletin,* Special Libraries Association Geography and Map Division 46 (December 1961): 3–17. Reprinted in *Map Librarianship: Readings,* compiled by Roman Drazniowsky, 364–384. Metuchen, N.J.: Scarecrow Press, 1975.

Old but useful, including table giving weight and capacity of filled cases.

Drazniowsky, Roman, comp. *Map Librarianship: Readings.* Metuchen, N.J.: Scarecrow Press, 1975.

Reprints authoritative articles: Catherine I. Bahn's "Map Libraries: Space and Equipment" (see above), Mary Galneder's "Equipment for Map Libraries," Mai Treude's "Location and Administration of a Map and Atlas Collection," and the section on storage equipment in Walter W. Ristow's "The Emergence of Maps in Libraries."

LeGear, C. E. *Maps: Their Care, Repair and Preservation in Libraries.* Rev. ed. Washington, D.C.: Library of Congress, 1956. 75p.

Old but a classic. Includes discussion of map storage equipment, drawer dimensions, capacities, and room layouts.

Special Libraries Association, Geography and Map Division. *Standards for University Map Collections.* Washington, D.C.: 1987. 13p.

F.3.6 Media

Kaser, John, and David Kaser. "Estimating Space Needs for Media Services." *College & Research Libraries* 53 (1992): 352–358, charts.

Presents data to suggest that academic libraries in the 1980s included 3 to 4 percent of building space for media when providing basic service excluding microtexts, 8 percent if a graphics or curriculum lab or mediated classroom were added, and 10 percent if space was included for audio or video production, closed-circuit television, or radio transmission.

F.3.7 Medicine

Hitt, Samuel. "Space Planning for Health Science Libraries." In *Handbook of Medical Library Practice,* 4th ed., vol. 3: 387–467. Chicago: Medical Library Association, 1988.

An authoritative treatment of all aspects, with a few illustrations.

Ludwig, L. T. "Health Sciences Library Building Projects: 1994 Survey." *Bulletin* of the Medical Libraries Association 83 (1995): 202–208. (Survey also published other years.)

F.3.8 Microtexts

American National Standards Institute. New York.

See its current standards, e.g., "Practice for Storage of Processed Safety Photographic Film," ANSI PH1.43-19 (1983), and "Requirements for Photographic Filing Enclosures for Storing Processed Photographic Films, Plates, and Paper," ANSI PH1.53-19 (1982).

Boss, Richard W., with Deborah Raikes. *Developing Microform Reading Facilities.* Westport, Conn.: Microform Review, 1982. 198p., illus., bibl., glossary, index.

Chapters 3 and 5 give detailed advice on space design, layouts, storage areas, and equipment.

F.3.9 Music

Cassaro, James P., comp. *Space Utilization in Music Libraries.* Canton, Mass.: Music Library Association, 1991. 140p., illus. (MLA Technical Reports, 20)

Fine coverage of planning, with attention to the special needs of recordings and scores, and compact shelving, with chapters on planning for undergraduates, graduate students, and scholars.

Fling, Robert Michael. *Shelving Capacity in the Music Library.* Philadelphia: Music Library Assn., 1981. 36p., illus. (MLA Technical Reports, 7)

Pickett, A. G., and M. M. Lemcoe. *Preservation and Storage of Sound Recordings.* Washington, D.C.: Library of Congress, 1959. 74p.

A classic treatment. Chapters 2.B, "Handling and Storage," 2.G, "Predicting Shelf Life," and 3.E, "Summary of Conclusions and Recommendations for Storage of Phonograph Discs," are concerned with architectural problems, selections of shelving, air conditioning, etc.

F.3.10 Science and Technology

Lucker, Jay L., issue ed. "Contributed Papers on the Theme Library Buildings." *IATUL Quarterly: A Journal of Library Management and Technology* 4, no. 3 (September 1990): 113–191.

Descriptive illustrated articles about Arizona State University's Noble Science and Engineering Library, Central Library of the Technical University of Budapest, Chalmers University of Technology Library, Iowa State University Library, and the libraries of Finland's universities of technology at Helsinki, Lappeenranta, and Tampere.

Mount, Ellis. *University Science and Engineering Libraries.* 2d ed. Westport, Conn.: Greenwood Press, 1985. 303p. (Contributions to Librarianship and Information Science, no. 49)

Chapters 17 and 18 cover planning facilities, and furnishings and equipment.

Wells, Marianna S., and Richard A. Spohn. "Planning, Implementation, and Benefits of Merging the Geology and Physics Libraries into a Combined Renovated Facility at the University of Cincinnati." In *Proceedings of 25th Meeting of the Geoscience Information Society, 1990.* Vol. 21 (1991): 173–183. 2 floor plans.

F.3.11 Special Collections (See also Section F.3.2, Archives and Rare Books, above)

Byrd, Cecil K. "Quarters for Special Collections and University Libraries." *Library Trends* 18 (October 1969): 223–234.

F.4 Special Topics

F.4.1 Acoustics and Sound Control

Beranek, Leo L., ed. *Noise and Vibration Control.* New York: McGraw-Hill, 1971. 650p.

Includes technical chapters on sound in small spaces and large rooms, isolation of vibrations, and criteria for noise and vibration in buildings.

Eagen, Ann. "Noise in the Library: Effects and Control." *Wilson Library Bulletin* 65 (February 1991): 44–47, illus., bibl.

Comments on physiological and psychological effects, with suggestions for control of disturbing sounds.

Parkin, Peter H., H. R. Humphreys, and J. R. Cowell. *Acoustics, Noise and Buildings.* 4th ed. London: Faber & Faber, 1979. 297p., index.

A more technical book and especially helpful for audio facilities is *Acoustic Design and Noise Control,* by Michael Rettinger (New York: Chemical Publishing Co., 1973).

F.4.2 Architects and Architectural Practice

American Institute of Architects (Washington, D.C.). The AIA compiles or sponsors or both various professional works. For example: the *AIA Metric Building and Construction Guide,* Susan Braybrooke, ed. (Wiley, 1980), and *Architectural Graphic Standards* (now in 9th ed., 1994, plus supplements, edited by John Ray Hoke Jr., yet known as Ramsey and Sleeper).

AIA also publishes pamphlets and flyers on specific topics, such as adaptive reuse of old buildings, contractor's qualifications, energy conservation, handbook of architectural design competitions, instructions to bidders, owner-architect agreement, public art in architecture, and use of solar energy.

De Chiara, Joseph, and John Hancock Callender, eds. *Time-Saver Standards for Building Types.* 3d ed. New York: McGraw-Hill, 1990. 1413p., illus.

A standard manual. Academic libraries are treated on pages 297–321, partly with the Metcalf formulas and tables and partly with drawings from a report on study carrels issued by Educational Facilities Laboratories.

De Chiara, Joseph, Julius Panero, and Martin Zelnik, eds. *Time-Saver Standards for Interior Design and Space Planning.* New York: McGraw-Hill, 1991. 1160p.

Companion volume to the preceding.

F.4.3 Bookstacks

Boll, John J. *To Grow or Not to Grow? A Review of Alternatives to New Academic Library Buildings.* New York: Bowker, 1980. 32p., illus., references, index. (LJ Special Report, 15)

Includes considerable review of various book storage alternatives.

Bright, Franklyn F. *Planning for a Movable Compact Shelving System.* Chicago: ALA, 1991. 69p. (LAMA Occasional Papers, #1)

Basic information on what is movable shelving, how does it work, and its maintenance.

Shelton, John A. *Seismic Safety Standards for Library Shelving.* Sacramento, Calif.: California State Library Foundation, 1990. 45p.

Describes practices to be followed for the installation or modification or both of shelving to withstand earthquakes. Includes detail drawings and specifications.

F.4.4 Building Control Systems

Cherry, Don T. *Total Facility Control.* Toronto: Butterworths, 1986. 406p.

Broad expert treatment of integrated building monitoring and control, for economy and security.

F.4.5 Classrooms

Ring, D. M., and P. F. V. Meer. "Designing a Computerized Instructional Training Room for the Library." *Special Libraries* 85 (1994): 154–161, plan, bibl.

Practical aspects of classroom design for multiple purposes.

F.4.6 Climate and Conservation of Collections

Banks, Paul. "Environmental Standards for Books and Manuscripts." *Library Journal* 99 (February 1, 1974): 339–343.

Recommends book storage area temperature be set at 60° F., ±5°, and gives recommendations on humidity, air cleanliness, ventilation, and light. Provides extensive comments on exhibition quarters; shelving and book supports; book trucks; storage of microfilm; and systems for protection, detection, and continual monitoring of the design conditions.

Fry, Maxwell, and Jane Drew. *Tropical Architecture in the Dry and Humid Zones.* New York: Reinhold, 1964. 264p., illus., index.

Practical guidance with extensive appendixes on such aspects as sun path data; water supply; building materials; thermal movements in buildings; special glass; building costs; plant material; and protection against earthquakes, fungus, hurricanes, lightning, and termites.

Kadoya, Takashi. "On the Degradation of Paper and Printed Matter." *Research Libraries Yesterday, Today, and Tomorrow,* 334–353. Kanazawa, Japan: Kanazawa Institute of Technology, 1993.

A paper on Western and Japanese papers, with graphs and tables, by the president of the Institute for Paper Making Science.

Lull, William P., with Paul N. Banks. *Conservation Environment: Guidelines for Libraries and Archives.* Ottawa: Canadian Council of Archives, 1995. 102p., illus., lexicon of terms, index.

Discusses authoritatively collection environmental criteria, assessment, monitoring, compromises, and the achievement of practical solutions, both low-cost and interim. Updated from the 1995 (88p.) version published by the New York State Library.

Plumbe, Wilfred J. *The Preservation of Books in Tropical and Subtropical Countries.* Kuala Lumpur, Malaysia: Oxford University Press, 1964. 72p., illus., bibl.

Contains practical advice on anti-termite measures, dust storms, and wood preservation.

Wilson, William K. *Environmental Guidelines for the Storage of Paper Records.* Bethesda, Md.: NISO Press, 1995. 21p., bibl. (NISO Technical Report Series, 1)

Superior report by the former chief of the Paper Section, U.S. National Bureau of Standards. Covers temperature, relative humidity, light, air contaminants, and energy considerations in northern climates, arid regions, and tropical climates. "Not a national standard and its material is not normative in nature."

F.4.7 Construction

Cushman, Robert F., and John P. Bigda, eds. *The McGraw-Hill Construction Business Handbook: A*

Practical Guide to Accounting, Credit, Finance, Insurance, and Law for the Construction Industry. 2d ed. New York: McGraw-Hill, 1985. 1079p.

Includes treatment of contracts, OSHA compliance, bid errors, changes and extras, time extensions, compensation for delay, liability, bonds, and handling of disputes.

Mills, Edward D., ed. *Building Maintenance and Preservation: A Guide for Design and Management.* London: Butterworths, 1980. 203p., illus., index.

Contains chapters on design, materials, structure, economics, safety, security, and management of interiors and exteriors.

F.4.8 Consultants

Leighton, Philip D. "The Facilities Consultant." In *Space Utilization in Music Libraries,* edited by James P. Cassaro, 53–67. Canton, Mass.: Music Library Association, 1991.

Expert outline of where and how a consultant benefits the project, with an outline of challenging characteristics of one specialized type of library.

F.4.9 Costs

Beckman, Margaret. "Cost 'Avoidance' in Library Building Planning: What, Where, When, Why, Who?" *Canadian Library Journal* 47 (1990): 405–409.

Very thoughtful expert consideration of ways to control project cost and later operational costs.

Glazner, Steve, ed. *Capital Renewal and Deferred Maintenance.* Alexandria, Va.: Association of Physical Plant Administrators of Universities and Colleges, 1989. 192p. (Critical Issues in Facilities Management, 4)

A collection of articles on financial aspects of university buildings, and six case studies of major universities. Of special note is the second chapter: "Before the Roof Caves In: A Predictive Model for Physical Plant Renewal."

Kershner, Earl Gene. "Why Do University Buildings Cost So Much?" *Business Officer* 21 (April 1987): 29–35.

Compares costs to other buildings. Presents reasons for disparity and ways to reduce the cost of new buildings.

Rush, Sean C., and Sandra L. Johnson. *The Decaying American Campus: A Ticking Time Bomb.* Alexandria, Va.: Association of Physical Plant Administrators of Universities and Colleges, 1989. 136p.

A thoughtful warning that deferred maintenance and poor construction results in major later expenses.

F.4.10 Decoration

Brolin, Brent C., and Jean Richards. *Sourcebook of Architectural Ornament: Designers, Craftsmen, Manufacturers and Distributors of Custom and Ready-Made Exterior Ornament.* New York: Van Nostrand Reinhold, 1982. 288p., illus.

With a historical introduction, sections illustrate options of awnings, brick and terracotta, cast stone, ceramics, fiber art, glass, metals, murals, plastics, sculpture, signs, stucco and plaster, and wood.

Masson, André. *The Pictorial Catalogue: Mural Decoration in Libraries.* Oxford: At the Clarendon Press, 1981. 81p., photos.

Analysis of ornamental graphic representation in selected European libraries from classical times through the nineteenth century.

White, Antony, and Bruce Robertson. *Architecture and Ornament: A Visual Guide.* New York: Design Press, 1990. 111p.

Pictures and diagrams of decorative motifs, emblems, and heraldic devices used in Western architecture.

F.4.11 Dictionaries

Harris, Cyril M., ed. *Dictionary of Architecture and Construction.* 2d ed. New York: McGraw-Hill, 1993. 924p., illus.

Terms used in the everyday practice of architecture, landscape architecture, construction, and related fields, such as urban planning. Uses both U.S. Customary and Standard International units of measurement.

Traister, John E. *Illustrated Dictionary for Building Construction.* Lilburn, Ga.: Fairmont Press, 1993. 465p., drawings, charts.

Definitions of terms, ranging from the technical ("co-efficient of friction") to the commonplace ("glass").

F.4.12 Electrical Systems (see also Sections F.4.23, Information Technology, and F.4.26, Lighting)

Qayoumi, Mohammad H. *Electrical Distribution and Maintenance.* Alexandria, Va.: Association of Physical Plant Administrators of Universities and Colleges, 1989. 270p.

Comprehensive coverage of electrical distribution systems, including cables, switches, circuit breakers, instrumentation, and metering.

F.4.13 Energy Conservation

Meckler, Milton, ed. *Retrofitting of Buildings for Energy Conservation.* 2d ed. Lilburn, Ga.: Fairmont Press, 1994. 489p.

Covers energy audits, design and installation techniques, practical strategies for energy management and lighting, and case studies, of which one comes from East Texas State University.

U.S. Department of Energy, Federal Programs Office [for] Conservation and Solar Energy. *Architects and Engineers Guide to Energy Conservation in Existing Buildings.* Washington, D.C.: U.S. Department of Energy, 1980. 455p., illus.

Thorough technical report for engineers.

F.4.14 Ergonomics

Kroemer, K. H. E., et al. *Ergonomics: How to Design for Ease and Efficiency.* Englewood Cliffs, N.J.: Prentice-Hall, 1994. 766p., illus.

A detailed textbook with tables, charts, and drawings. The first half is devoted to understanding the dimensions, capabilities, and limitations of the human body and mind; the second half covers design applications. Metric dimensions only.

Noro, Kageyu, and Andrew Imada, eds. *Participatory Ergonomics.* New York: Taylor & Francis, 1991. 220p.

Ten papers, two on concepts and methods, and eight of case studies. Notable is J. R. Wilson's chapter, "Design Decision Groups: A Participative Process for Developing Workplaces."

Pheasant, Stephen. *Bodyspace: Anthropometry, Ergonomics, and the Design of Work.* 2d ed. Bristol, Pa.: Taylor & Francis, [1996]. 244p., illus.

Comprehensive, practical, and very well written, with many drawings to illuminate. Metric dimensions only.

F.4.15 Evaluation of Facilities

Kusack, James M. "Facility Evaluation in Libraries: A Strategy and Methodology for Library Managers." *Library Administration & Management* 7 (spring 1993): 107–111, bibl.

Summarizes the variety of methodologies for post-occupancy evaluation.

Preiser, Wolfgang F. E., ed. *Building Evaluation.* New York: Plenum Press, 1989. 354p., illus.

The 25 chapters (mostly by U.S. experts) cover post-occupancy building evaluation and recent advances in methods and applications, altogether an outgrowth of a symposium at the Technical University of Delft, The Netherlands, July 1988.

F.4.16 Exhibition Areas

Casterline, Gail Farr. *Archives and Manuscripts: Exhibits.* Chicago: Society of American Archivists, 1980. 70p., illus.

A manual covering all aspects of exhibitions; chapters on conservation and exhibit design include comments on physical space and display areas.

Witteborg, Lothar P. *Good Show! A Practical Guide for Temporary Exhibitions.* Washington, D.C.: Smithsonian Institution Traveling Exhibition Service, 1981. 172p., illus., bibl.

Expert information about design and fabrication of display areas, illumination, security, and handicapped access.

F.4.17 Expansions and Additions

Hawthorne, Pat, and Ron G. Martin, eds. *Planning Additions to Academic Library Buildings: A Seamless Approach.* Chicago: ALA, 1995. 64p., plans, layouts, photos.

A description of expansion projects achieved without sacrificing design aesthetics.

F.4.18 Floor Coverings

Berkeley, Bernard. *Floors: Selection and Maintenance.* Chicago: ALA, 1969. 316p. (LTP Publications, no. 13)

Five chapters detailing properties of the major categories of floors and floor coverings: resilient, carpeting, masonry, wood, and formed-in-place. Two chapters on selection criteria and maintenance practices and equipment.

Minick, Evelyn, J. Thomas Becker, and Stacia Brokaw. "Carpeting Your Library." *College & Research Libraries News* 55 (1994): 410–412, illus.

Practical advice from the Philadelphia College of Textiles and Science.

F.4.19 Furniture and Equipment (see also Section F.4.24, Interior Design)

Brown, Carol. "Interiors and Furniture: Questions and Answers." *Community & Junior College Libraries* 8, no. 1 (1995): 19–25.

A consultant's comments on changes brought about by electronic resources, necessity for selection of chairs of proven durability, and other issues of library interiors.

Sayers, R. "Development of a Policy for the Refurbishment and Replacement of Furnishings in Public Areas of the James Cook University Library." *Australian Academic and Research Libraries* 27, no. 1 (March 1996): 15–20, charts.

States the need for clear records of purchase, use, and repair on which to base future decisions that are fiscally sound.

F.4.20 Graphics and Signs

Ballinger, Louise Bowen, and R. A. Ballinger. *Sign, Symbol and Form.* New York: Van Nostrand Reinhold, 1972. 191p., illus.

Examples of a great variety of signs in Europe and North America.

Beck, Susan Gilbert. "Wayfinding in Libraries." *Library Hi Tech* 14 (1996): 27–36, illus.

Planning navigable libraries for persons with physical and cognitive limitations, including user comfort in wayfinding. Provides 10 sound recommendations for highly usable library buildings.

Pollet, Dorothy, and Peter C. Haskell, comps. *Sign Systems for Libraries: Solving the Wayfinding Problem.* New York: Bowker, 1979. 271p., illus.

Chapters cover the theory of signage, architectural techniques for wayfinding, sign language and materials and methods, coordinating graphics and architecture, and particular solutions for special and university and research libraries. Appended: "Technical and Psychological Considerations for Sign Systems in Libraries."

Ragsdale, Kate W., and Donald J. Kenney. *Effective Library Signage.* Washington, D.C.: Association of Research Libraries, 1996. 170p., illus.

A kit with various sample documents; and a flyer summarizing design, construction, installation, vandalism, and temporary signs (the flyer is also available online at www.arl.org/spec/208fly.html).

F.4.21 Heating, Ventilating, and Air Conditioning (see also Section F.4.6, Climate and Conservation of Collections)

Bush, Carmel C., and Halcyon R. Enssle. "Indoor Air Quality: Planning and Managing Library Buildings." *Advances in Librarianship* 18 (1994): 215–236.

A quality article, incorporating the results of recent studies. Discusses planning for new and existing buildings.

Butti, Ken, and John Perlin. *A Golden Thread: 2,500 Years of Solar Architecture and Technology.* New York: Van Nostrand Reinhold, 1980. 289p., illus., index.

A history with a minimum of engineering data.

Martin, P. L., and D. R. Oughton. *Faber and Kell's Heating and Air-Conditioning of Buildings: With Some Notes on Combined Heat and Power.* 8th ed. Oxford: Butterworth-Heinemann, 1995. 701p., illus.

Fundamentals, winter and summer conditions, systems, equipment, and operating costs are treated in this basic work.

F.4.22 Human Dimensions

Panero, Julius, and Martin Zelnik. *Human Dimension and Interior Space: A Source Book of Design Reference Standards.* New York: Whitney Library of Design, 1979. 320p., illus., index.

A reference work of anthropometric data in both inches and centimeters, based primarily on measurements at the Universities of Paris,

Newcastle, and Michigan and three studies by or for the U.S. government. Includes chapters on seating, individual spaces, offices, and elderly and physically disabled people.

F.4.23 Information Technology

Bazillion, Richard J., and Constance Braun. *Academic Libraries as High-Tech Gateways: A Guide to Design and Space Decisions.* Chicago: ALA, 1995. 180p., drawings, photos., index.

Explains technical design features to support access to online information systems and "intelligent" buildings for services of electronic study centers.

Beckman, Margaret. "Implications of Technology for New Library Facilities." In *[Proceedings]*, International Symposium on New Techniques and Applications in Libraries, 17–26. Xian, China: Xian Jiaotong University Press, 1988.

Wise comments by one of the most respected academic library building planners and consultants.

Boss, Richard W. *Information Technologies and Space Planning for Libraries and Information Centers.* Boston, Mass.: G. K. Hall, 1987. 121p.

Useful information on spatial needs for compact storage, computer systems, microtext, optical media, and telefacsimile.

IBM Corporation. *A Building Planning Guide for Communication Wiring.* 2d ed. Research Triangle Park, N.C.: IBM Corp., 1994. 91p., illus., glossary, index.

A manual to help plan space for data and voice communication wiring systems in a new or an existing building. Covers wiring from work areas to wiring closets and from closet to closet; also types of raceways for cable distribution, riser systems, grounding and lightning protection, and security for cable and equipment.

Rupp, Bruce. *Human Factors of Workstations with Visual Displays.* 3d ed. San Jose, Calif.: IBM Corp., 1984. 64p., graphs, bibl.

Latter sections briefly treat the configuration of workstations, including seated work position, work surfaces, and display location, as well as environmental considerations of lighting and acoustic noise.

Willis, Norman. *New Technology and Its Impact on Educational Buildings.* Paris: Organization for Economic Co-operation and Development, 1992. 43p.

A summation of trends and forecasts, based on proceedings of an international seminar.

F.4.24 Interior Design

Brown, Carol R. *Planning Library Interiors: The Selection of Furnishings for the 21st Century.* [2d ed.] Phoenix, Ariz.: Oryx Press, 1995. 162p., photos.

Especially useful chapters on furniture construction quality and on chairs.

Cohen, Elaine, and Aaron Cohen. *Planning the Electronic Office.* New York: McGraw-Hill, 1983. 241p., illus.

Good treatment, excellently illustrated, of space planning, systems furniture, carpeting, noise, lighting, and power.

Kuhner, Robert A. "Library Interior Design and Furniture Selection." In *Operations Handbook for the Small Academic Library,* edited by Gerard B. McCabe, 279–299. Westport, Conn.: Greenwood Press, 1989.

A superior concise illustrated discussion by an experienced planner.

Lewis, Susan A. *Interior Design Sourcebook: A Guide to Resources on the History and Practice of Interior Design.* Detroit: Omnigraphics, 1997. 307p. (Design Reference Series, no. 3)

With brief annotations, lists publications on such aspects as codes and standards, design theory, furniture, finishes and textiles, lighting, visual communication methods, and much more. Similar in scope to the *Landscape Architecture Sourcebook* by Diana Vogelsong, 1997, no. 1 in the same Omnigraphics series.

Pierce, William S. *Furnishing the Library Interior.* New York: Dekker, 1980. 288p., illus., index. (Books in Library and Information Science, no. 29)

Good coverage of furnishings in particular library areas, the selection and evaluation of furniture and equipment, and business pointers. Sample specifications are included, pp. 253–274.

Pile, John F. *Interior Design.* 2d ed. New York: Abrams, 1995. 584p., with 748 illus.

A standard work, including attention to building systems and the human issues of interior design. Covers form, scale, proportion, color, materials, lighting, furniture, and art.

F.4.25 Joint-Use Facilities

LaBrake, Lynn B. "Planning a Joint-Use Library." In [*Proceedings* of the 5th Off-Campus Library Services Conference], Central Michigan University Press (1991), 147–154.

A case study of planning for three Florida institutions.

F.4.26 Lighting

Carmichael, Leonard, and Walter F. Dearborn. *Reading and Visual Fatigue.* Boston, Mass.: Houghton Mifflin, 1947. 443p.

The classic comprehensive study of the subject.

Gordon, Gary, and James L. Nuckolls. *Interior Lighting for Designers.* 3d ed. New York: Wiley, 1995. 280p., illus.

Describes and illustrates in clear logical fashion the tools and techniques for design of light in building interiors. Presents the steps of the lighting design process: perception and psychology, luminance, color and daylight, incandescent lamps, discharge lamps, auxiliary controls, electricity, light control, photometrics, luminaires, and design.

Lam, William M. C. *Perception and Lighting as Formgivers for Architecture.* New York: McGraw-Hill, 1977. 310p., illus., bibl., glossary, index.

Clear and comprehensive treatment of visual perception, lighting, ceiling systems, and other aspects of designing the luminous environment. Pages 97–99 provide 22 rules of thumb for good design.

Mason, Ellsworth. "The Development of Library Lighting: The Evolution of the Lighting Problems We Are Facing Today." *Advances in Library Administration and Organization* 10 (1992): 129–144.

A stimulating discourse, clear, observant, and incisive.

Metcalf, Keyes D. *Library Lighting.* Washington, D.C.: Association of Research Libraries, 1970. 99p., short bibl.

This extensive treatment details lighting problems, provides advice from distinguished professionals (architects, illuminating engineers, interior designers, ophthalmologists, university financial and physical plant officers, and scholars), and makes specific recommendations.

F.4.27 Moving

Fraley, Ruth A., and Carol Lee Anderson. *Library Space Planning: A How-to-Do-It Manual for Assessing, Allocating and Reorganizing Collections, Resources and Facilities.* 2d ed. New York: Neal-Schuman, 1990. 194p., drawings, index. (How-to-Do-It Manuals for Libraries, no. 5)

Designed "to provide a systematic method and practical guide for successful re-use of library space within existing facilities." Includes special treatment (pp. 129–174) of planning and executing the physical move.

Habich, Elizabeth Chamberlain. *Moving Library Collections: A Management Handbook.* Westport, Conn.: Greenwood Press, 1998. 344p. (Greenwood Library Management Collection)

This how-to book has five major topics: planning collection space, planning the collection move, using a moving company, doing the move yourself, and special topics, e.g., pest management control issues, cleaning collections, and "moving from disorganized conditions."

Kurkul, Donna Lee. "The Planning, Implementation, and Movement of an Academic Library Collection." *College & Research Libraries* 44 (July 1983): 220–234.

Gives methodology, including planning formulas, for the series of book moves necessitated by the additions to and renovation of the Smith College Neilson Library.

F.4.28 Physically Limited Accommodations

Cirillo, Susan E., and Robert E. Danford, eds. *Library Buildings, Equipment, and the ADA: Compliance Issues and Solutions.* Chicago: ALA, 1996. 105p.

Architects offer ideas about compliance in new and historic buildings, and designers comment on furnishings and signage.

Steinfeld, Edward. *Hands-On Architecture.* Washington, D.C.: U.S. Architectural and Transportation Barriers Compliance Board, 1986. 36p.

Coverage of designs to handle knobs, handles, and rails, as well as the ability to reach and the spacing of electronic controls.

U.S. Architectural and Transportation Barriers Compliance Board (Access Board). *Americans with Disabilities Act: Accessibility Guidelines for Buildings and Facilities* [Part One]. Washington, D.C.: 1994. 71, A17p., illus.

Covers a wide range of conditions, including exteriors and interiors, floor surfaces, protruding objects, and historic buildings.

U.S. Architectural and Transportation Barriers Compliance Board. *Technical Paper on Accessibility Codes and Standards: A Comparison of Domestic and Selected Foreign Standards and Codes.* Washington, D.C.: 1994. 146p.

Compares U.S. state prescriptions with those of 11 foreign countries.

F.4.29 Remodeling

Falkner, Ann. *Without Our Past? A Handbook for the Preservation of Canada's Architectural Heritage.* Toronto: Toronto University Press, 1977. 242p., illus., bibl.

Excellent report on how one country created preservation policy, and inventories, evaluates and selects, reuses, and enhances older structures.

McAdams, Nancy R. "Enlarging the Academic Library." In *Research Libraries Yesterday, Today, and Tomorrow,* 219–227. Kanazawa, Japan: Kanazawa Institute of Technology, 1993.

Reviews the feasible types of physical options and programmatic options for the partially new university library.

Milner, Margaret. *Adapting Historic Campus Structures for Accessibility.* Washington, D.C.: GPO, for the Association of Physical Plant Administrators of Universities and Colleges, 1981. 90p., illus., bibl., index.

Recommendations and six design studies for overcoming architectural barriers to handicapped persons in older buildings. Supplements *Creating an Accessible Campus* published by APPA in 1978.

F.4.30 Security, Fire Protection, and Life Safety

Atlas, Randall L. "Designing Crime-Free Environments." *Library Administration & Management* 11 (1997): 88–93.

A concise summary of desirable external and internal conditions, including such "natural surveillance" as low landscaping, raised entrances, and windows.

Bahr, Alice Harrison. *Book Theft and Library Security Systems, 1981–82.* White Plains, N.Y.: Knowledge Industry Publications, 1981. 156p., illus., bibl.

Electromechanical exit control arrangements are detailed.

Cumming, Neil. *Security: A Guide to Security System Design and Equipment Selection and Installation.* 2d ed. Stoneham, Mass.: Butterworth-Heinemann, 1992. 338p., illus.

This "primer" for the layperson, well illustrated and clearly written, covers the wide variety of systems suitable for indoor and outdoor sensing, closed-circuit television, door and window locking, access control, and security lighting.

Fennelly, Lawrence J., ed. *Museum, Archive and Library Security.* Boston: Butterworths, 1983. 891p., illus.

Major treatment of the subject. Note especially Chapters 6, "Common Sense Security for Museum Libraries," 13, "Intrusion Detection Systems," and 18, "The Security Survey," which cover locks, keys, files, safes, vaults, etc.

Hopf, Peter E., ed. *Handbook of Building Security Planning and Design.* New York: McGraw-Hill, 1979. 31 chapters individually paged.

Detailed illustrated guide on earthquake, hurricane, tornado, and flood protection, as well as on security components, including camera surveillance, doors, electronic security, fire detection, glass, lighting, locks, safes and vaults, and sprinkler systems.

Morris, John. *The Library Disaster Preparedness Handbook.* Chicago: ALA, 1986. 129p., illus.

Authoritative treatment of building problems and solutions: fire, theft, water, and safety and security of people and property.

Robles, Patricia A. "Security upon Moving into a New Library Building." *C&RL News* 57 (July/August 1996): 427–430.

Protection against loss or theft is explained based on practical experience.

Strassberg, Richard. *Conservation, Safety, Security, and Disaster Considerations in Designing New or Renovated Library Facilities at Cornell University Libraries.* Ithaca, N.Y.: Cornell University Libraries, 1984. 10p.

Practical guidelines "based upon a detailed review of the history of fourteen libraries at Cornell University and the human, book and manuscript threatening emergencies that have occurred in them."

Wise, James. "A Gentle Deterrent to Vandalism." *Psychology Today* 16 (October 1981): 31–38.

A good way of thinking about what causes damage to buildings and property.

F.4.31 Sick Buildings

Bernheim, Anthony. "San Francisco Main Library: A Healthy Building." *Booklet 6, Division of Management and Technology,* 59th IFLA Council and Conference, Barcelona, Spain (August, 1993): 7–13, bibl.

Discussion of the actions taken to assure a healthy building, including HVAC systems, carpet, paint, particle board, adhesives, furniture, and factors considered in the construction of the library. Includes an estimation of the cost for air-quality strategies.

F.4.32 Site Selection

Lynch, Kevin, and Gary Hack. *Site Planning.* 3d ed. Cambridge, Mass.: MIT Press, 1984. 499p., illus., index.

Thorough treatment of building placement—the art, its principles, and general comments on its technicalities. Little specifically on academic institutions, but an excellent presentation on the full range of issues that affect site planning.

F.4.33 Staff Quarters and Service Points

Epple, Margie, Ann Montanaro, and Melinda Reagor. "Designing Buildings Specifically for Technical Services Functions: The Rutgers University Libraries Experience." *Technical Services Quarterly* 9, no. 4 (1992): 7–17.

Benefits and drawbacks of quarters remote from the university libraries.

Miller, Jeannie P., Julia M. Rholes, and Karen Wielhorski. "Planning Reference Service Points: A Decision-Making Model." *Reference Librarian* 39 (1993): 53–64.

Comments and a set of questions used in reference desk planning at Texas A&M University.

Rowley, Gordon, and Ivan Hanthorn. "Designing a Conservation Treatment Facility: Charting a Course into a Less Familiar Region of Planning for Libraries." *Journal of Academic Librarianship* 22 (1996): 97–104, plan.

Practical coverage of site, floor plan, workbench design, utilities, ventilation and safety, with Iowa State University as a case study.

F.4.34 Stairs

Templer, John A. *The Staircase: Studies of Hazards, Falls, and Safer Design.* Cambridge, Mass.: MIT Press, 1992. 200p., illus.

Comprehensive treatment of stair and ramp use, accidents thereon, and design desiderata. Includes treatment of handrails and balustrades.

F.4.35 Study Facilities

Liben, Lynn S., Arthur H. Patterson, and Nora Newcombe, eds. *Spatial Representation and Behavior across the Life Span: Theory and Application.* New York: Academic Press, 1981. 404p.

Psychologists treat how space is used by persons of different ages and sexes.

Lueder, Rani, and Kageyu Noro, eds. *Hard Facts about Soft Machines: The Ergonomics of Seating.* Bristol, Pa.: Taylor & Francis, 1994. 457p.

Over 30 papers on the mechanics, dynamics, and effects of seating on the sitter. Covers adjustability (including computer displays), biomechanics, posture, and users with special needs.

Rath, Gustave J., and John Ittleson. "Human Factors Design for Educational Facilities." In *Designing Learning Environments,* 142–159. New York: Longman, 1981.

Scholars at Northwestern University discuss lighting, auditory levels, heating and ventilating, layout of furniture and apparatus position, and interface with instructional media equipment.

Redefining the Place to Learn. Paris: Organization for Economic Co-operation and Development, 1995. 169p., illus., bibl., glossary.

Provides 21 case studies from 13 countries, a compilation of "important concepts for integration of technology, building organization and requirements to meet changing teaching and learning methods." Studies include Tilburg University Library, The Netherlands, and Tea Tree Gully Campus of Torrens Valley Institute of Tafe, Adelaide, Australia.

Silverstone, David M. "Considerations for Listening and Noise Distractions." In *Designing Learning Environments,* 75–86. New York: Longman, 1981.

Treats of unwanted sound, acoustics, and sound control, with recommendations, by a professor of educational administration.

Sommer, Robert. *Personal Space: The Behavioral Basis for Design.* Englewood Cliffs, N.J.: Prentice-Hall, 1969. 177p.

A classic study of spatial behavior and settings, including one chapter called "Designed for Learning" on classroom layout and student participation.

University of Cambridge Library Management Research Unit. "Factors Affecting the Use of Seats in Academic Libraries." *Journal of Librarianship* 7 (October 1975): 262–287, tables, graphs.

Superior research conducted at 11 U.K. academic institutions.

F.4.36 Underground Buildings

Fuhlrott, Rolf. "Underground Libraries." *College & Research Libraries* 47 (May 1986): 238–262.

Advantages and disadvantages are pointed out, well illustrated with photographs and floor plans.

F.4.37 Value Engineering

Brown, James. *Value Engineering: A Blueprint.* New York: Industrial Press, 1992. 251p.

The basics, with tools for an organized approach.

Fowler, Theodore C. *Value Analysis in Design.* New York: Van Nostrand Reinhold, 1990. 302p., illus.

Thorough coverage of all phases; well illustrated, and with a collection of forms and checklists.

F.4.38 Water

Moore, Charles W. *Water and Architecture.* New York: Abrams, 1994. 224p., illus.

A professor of architecture and practicing architect waxes eloquent about water flowing and still, interior and exterior, with copious photographs.

F.4.39 Weathering

Mostafavi, Mohsen, and David Leatherbarrow. *On Weathering: The Life of Buildings in Time.* Cambridge, Mass.: MIT Press, 1993. 139p.

Demonstrates how buildings stand up under the pounding of natural forces over time and how exteriors will look decades hence. Sprinkled with maxims and aphorisms: "Buildings are less durable than books." "Weathering adds as well as subtracts." "There is nothing necessarily impure about dirt."

The meaning of a word is not as exact as the meaning of a color. Colors and shapes make a more definite statement than words.

—Georgia O'Keefe, *Portrait of an Artist: A Biography*

No attempt has been made to make this a complete glossary of library or building construction terms. The inclusions are rather broad so as to help nonlibrarians, architects, planners, readers outside of North America, and those in a variety of administrative offices. The definitions provided are relevant to library buildings. Obviously, many words and phrases have other definitions in other walks of life. See also the definitions in the two dictionaries cited in Appendix F.4.11.

Absolute capacity: The theoretical maximum number of volumes that can fit on shelves, in contrast to *working capacity,* q.v.

Academic program: The institution's design of courses of instruction with requirements of distribution, departmental concentration, and credits for degree qualification.

Access flooring: Access panels or other devices to service equipment, ductwork, conduit, or other devices under the floor. See also *Raised floor system.*

Accession number: A serial or other number designed strictly as an inventory control over library materials acquired and to be added to the useful collections.

Accordion door or partition: A set of hinged panels, folding compactly as an accordion when not in use, moved on ceiling or floor tracks or both to form a solid barrier. See also *Movable partition.*

Acoustic material: Porous material for treating interior room surfaces so as to absorb sound, reduce its reverberation, and thus minimize undesirable qualities of the sound.

Acquisitions department: The technical services unit responsible for ordering, purchasing, claiming, invoice approval, and account management for all book materials being added to the collections. May include gift receiving, exchange programs, and approval arrangements.

Activation: The steps required to bring a completed physical structure to operational functioning. It includes such aspects as checking out the HVAC system, activating the intrusion system, installing necessary signs, placing furniture in final location, installing phones, and moving staff and collections. Also known as start-up, commissioning, or occupancy.

Actual dimension: In shelving, the measured dimensions of the shelf as opposed to *nominal dimension,* q.v. Applies as well to structural elements, bricks, doors, etc., where the actual dimension is somewhat less (typically) than the nominal dimension.

Add alternate: see *Bid alternate*

Addendum (contract): A written amplification of the contract documents after they have been issued to the bidders but before the bids have been received.

Adders: Bookstack range components that have only one column or end section because they attach to a full "starter" unit.

Air conditioning: The mechanical control of humidity, temperature, purity, and motion of air within buildings. In libraries the objective may be to secure either human comfort or the proper environment for the preservation of library materials. Sometimes called climatization.

Aisle: A passageway between furniture or equipment; for instance, between ranges of shelving in a bookstack, between rows of reading accommodations (chairs or chairs and tables), or between tables and shelving in a reading area. As used in this volume, an aisle at right angles to stack ranges is called a cross aisle. A main cross aisle is the main street of a bookstack and generally will have book ranges on both sides and will be wider than a subsidiary or secondary cross aisle, which may have ranges on one side and carrels or faculty studies on the other. An aisle between two parallel ranges is called a range or stack aisle.

Alcove: An area enclosed on three sides by walls, partitions, or bookcases, or a combination of these, normally large enough to accommodate a table and from one to four readers.

Allowance: A sum budgeted, identified in the contract documents, and made part of a larger contract on the basis of an estimated range of final cost rather than by contractual bid. Thus,

a sum may be held by the general contractor for carpeting, and the final cost set by bidding or negotiation within the maximum set by the allowance.

Alternate: An item or items set apart in the contractor's bid, each such item being specified as either an addition to or a deduction from the base construction bid figure.

Ambient light: see *Light sources*

Ambient sound: The constant general background sound produced by air currents, rain, electrical ballasts, white sound systems, etc. This background is in contrast to brief higher-volume sounds, such as footsteps, coughs, voiced sounds, music, bird and animal sounds, thunder, door and intermittent machine sounds, etc.

Americans with Disabilities Act (ADA): A U.S. law establishing requirements for providing physical access to work and publicly used space.

Annunciator: A device giving an audible or a visual signal.

Annunciator panel: A display board with signals, usually lights and sound, that indicate a change in condition in an exact location or area. Annunciation commonly informs staff of a smoke or fire condition, a security break or incursion, a water sump condition, or humidity variation beyond engineered limits. Also a numeric panel used to notify a patron upon the completion of a transaction. Such a panel is frequently used where books are paged from a closed stack.

Arcade: A roofed passageway, often with freestanding columns or pillars on at least one side.

Architectural space: Enclosed, built space or defined by built space, generally designed by an architect. Can also be used to refer to nonassignable space, depending upon context. See also *Nonassignable space*

Areaway: A sunken space in front of a basement or cellar window, designed to allow in light when the window is somewhat below grade.

Arrears: A backlog of work, frequently used with reference to any materials waiting for cataloging. A "working arrearage" is the material housed in or adjacent to work quarters and that is needed to keep all catalogers efficiently busy with materials in their fields of subject and linguistic expertise. It is distinct from an excess to the working arrearage, which becomes operationally inefficient and may need to be remotely housed.

Artifacts: Research libraries always have some collections other than media and book materials. These may include coins, stamps, busts, student memorabilia, or selected institutional realia, such as a groundbreaking shovel.

As builts: The working drawings with contractors' refinements, giving precise location of wire runs, ducts, etc., to enable, for example, maintenance workers years later to know exactly where to find intermediate portions of a cable or other utility run.

Assignable space: see *Net space*

Astragal: A flange fixed to one of a pair of doors to cover the gap and provide a tighter fitting against passage of air, smoke, water, etc.

Audiovisual materials: see *Media*

Auxiliary collection: see *Storage libraries*

Axonometric: A drafting perspective by which a three-dimensional structure is drawn to exact scale, resulting in the optical distortion of diagonals and curves. An axonometric projection of a cube views the cube from one edge showing two sides and the top; each of the edges is to exact measurement and, thus, for a cube, each edge is the same length in the drawing. Unlike an *isometric drawing,* q.v., the axonometric drawing looks directly at an edge.

Backfill: The compacted earth fill beside a foundation wall, added to replace soil excavation that was necessary for the construction.

Bake-out period: A period at the end of construction, prior to occupancy, during which a building is put through a cycle of heating to the highest temperature possible while exhausting and replacing the air with frequency in order to remove (as much as possible) noxious and potentially damaging vapors produced by construction materials.

Balancing: The adjustment of HVAC air outlets and control systems to provide uniform or specified airflow, temperature, and humidity among various zones or rooms in a building.

Ballast: An electrical device to provide increased voltage for fluorescent tubes and HID (high-intensity discharge) light sources.

Bar chart: A graph of parallel broad lines indicating the length of time, quantity, or personnel for a specific task.

Bar code: Coded "zebra" lines to be read by computer devices, often placed on labels on books for inventory control and circulation. Also used with *smart cards,* q.v., for building or room access control.

Baseboard: A wood, plastic, or other hard strip or finish piece to cover the joint between wall and floor and protect the lower wall surface from damage, as from shoes, chair legs, mops, vacuum cleaners, etc. Sometimes called a "skirting."

Bay: With compact shelving, a shelving bay is made up of the shelving between fixed ranges plus the shelving of the fixed range facing the movable shelving, which can be more or less than a structural bay or building module, depending upon the layout. See also *Module.*

Bearing wall: A wall that supports a structure above. Masonry and concrete walls are often (but not always) bearing walls. A wood or steel stud wall can also be a bearing wall. Generally, bearing walls cannot be removed. See also *Shear walls.*

Beneficial occupancy: A legal term referring to the use of the facility before final acceptance. The warranty period on those portions of the facility in use by the owner begins with the date of beneficial occupancy.

Berm: The shoulder of a road or a narrow earth ledge at the top of an embankment. In landscape or site design, refers to the building up of dirt to form a mound. "Berming down" is sometimes used to refer to a slope of the site down to a lower level of the building.

Bib table: see *Index table*

Bibliographic tool: Lists and indexes of publications or other materials, either with or without inclusion of which libraries own the items.

Bid alternate: An amount to be added to or deducted from the base bid if the owner chooses to add or delete the work covered by the alternate.

Bid bond: A legal financial obligation serving to guarantee the contractor's seriousness in submitting a construction bid.

Bid package: The set of documents issued to contractors invited to bid on construction. Includes working drawings, material and performance specifications, general conditions, the bid form, and other related instructions.

Black Friday: The extra paid day off acknowledged in labor contracts in the United States that occurs on alternate Fridays in many of the construction trades.

BM: The common reference to the British Library (formerly British Museum). One of its divisions is the BLLD, the British Library Lending Division, located at Boston Spa in Yorkshire.

Boilerplate: The standard legal and procedural requirements that can be added without substantial change to the specifications as part of the bid package.

Book-detection system: The equipment for electronically determining if library books are going out an exit. All processes require a "target" of magnetized material or electronic circuitry affixed in the volume. Some systems alter the sensitivity of the target when the book is charged out and discharged. Other systems do not alter the sensitivity, thus requiring the volume to be handed to staff for inspection of charging and thereby bypassing the sensing equipment so as to prevent the turnstiles from locking or an alarm from sounding. Smart targets are currently being developed and marketed that contain chips allowing radio frequency reading of unique information for each item targeted, which can facilitate self-charge and inventory processes.

Book return: An arrangement to receive materials being returned. Among various options, this may include a slide or chute onto a counter, a slot in a service desk leading to a depressible-floor bin on wheels, or a stand-alone covered box similar to an outdoor postal box.

Book-return shelf: One or more shelves on which materials returning from circulation are held for charge records to be canceled or, thereafter, for sorting preparatory to returning the materials to their proper location. Also, shelves distributed throughout the stacks, typically of a contrasting color, where patrons are encouraged to place books they have removed from the shelves.

Book sizes: Technically derives from the number of folds of standard sizes of book papers. One fold giving four pages is "folio." Two folds giving eight pages is "quarto." Three folds giving sixteen pages is "octavo." A folio book typically measures 12–19 in. (300–480 mm) in height. A quarto book typically measures 10–12 in. (250–300 mm) in height. An octavo book typically measures 8–10 in. (200–250 mm) in height. A duodecimo book typically measures 7–8 in. (180–200 mm) in height. An elephant folio book typically measures over 20 in. (over 500 mm) in height.

Book truck: A small cart consisting of a set of shelves on wheels used for transporting books within the library. Called a "book trolley" in many countries.

Booth: see *Carrel*

Boring report: The soils test report resulting from analysis of the soil core removed from a drilled hole in the ground.

Bracing: see *Diagonal bracing, Hat channel, Overhead bracing, Spreader, Strut bracing, Sway bracing,* and *Unitizing*

Bracket shelving: Also known as cantilevered shelving. Developed very early in the twentieth century, it is formed of structural columns with holes or slots on one vertical face. Shelves are supported at the two ends by brackets that, in turn, hook into the holes or slots. The brackets hold the shelf from above and form bookends, though a movable bookend is commonly added to support the right-hand-most volume when the shelf is not full. Where the bracket supports the shelf from below, it is frequently called "flush-bracket," or newspaper shelving.

Breadboard: A desk or catalog cabinet adjunct that can be pulled out to hold a mouse or notepad or catalog tray for inspection, similar in operation to the sliding board in some kitchens on which bread is sliced. A similar device in shelving systems is called a *pull-out reference shelf,* q.v.

Breezeway: That part of a building that constitutes a roofed, usually ground-level opening, usually a passageway, through which the outside air currents can move.

Brief: Used as a noun to refer to a building *program,* q.v.

Brittle books: Volumes with paper that has so deteriorated in strength that pages break when folded.

Broadside: An unfolded sheet printed on only one side.

Browsing collection: Popular fiction and nonfiction works of current interest that may be shelved in a prominent location to encourage cultural and recreational reading.

Bubble diagram: A set of library units or functions, each enclosed in a rough circle sized to simulate the floor area required and drawn on paper to depict the physical two-dimensional relation of the elements.

Building code: The civil regulations governing the construction and alterations of buildings in a given locality, setting forth requirements and restrictions as to the use, safety, size, and type of building in certain zones and areas.

Building monitoring system (BMS): see *Smart building*

Building permit: A permit issued by the building department of the governing body having jurisdiction, required before any construction can begin.

Built-in: Those furnishings that are attached to or an integral part of the building and thus included in the construction contract.

Cable, coaxial: A heavy central wire, encased by an insulator and protective membrane, to carry communication signals.

Cable, flat: Power or signal lines that are formed into very thin and broad ribbons so they can run under carpet without creating a ridge.

Cable trays: Long metal racks placed along the wall or overhead to carry electrical conduit and data networking cable.

Cable TV: Television transmitted over coaxial cable instead of over phone lines.

Cables, plugs, and sockets: Devices needed to tie together information technology equipment. Lack of standardization requires buildings to be specifically wired or cabled, because as many as 22 different types of cable are available for telecommunications.

CAD: see *Computer-Aided Design*

Caisson: A watertight metal or concrete compartment open at the bottom, used for the construction of foundation piers, particularly when the subsoil conditions require these piers to be extended below the groundwater level.

Call number: The set of symbols identifying a particular item in a library collection, indicating its location and used to request that a specific physical item be brought from the stack, shelves, or other storage location. The call number is also vital for inventory control, especially the checkout process.

Canopy top: Slightly projecting rooflike cover over sections of shelving.

Cantilever: A beam or slab projecting beyond the vertical column or wall construction so

that it is supported on one end or side only and is capable of carrying weight throughout its projection. The cantilever structure can also be oriented vertically as is the case of shelving that is bolted to the floor.

Cantilever-type bracket shelving: Shelving where the brackets holding the shelves are cantilevered off a central supporting system or upright. See also *Bracket shelving.*

Card, debit or password: see *Smart card*

Carpet tile: Carpet material in fairly stiff, small modular units designed to facilitate replacement or removal of small segments where heavy traffic wear or connections for information technology so require. Carpet tile is generally required with *flat wire,* q.v.

Carrel: A small partitioned desk or one-person alcove with writing surface at which the reader may be permitted to retain books. Open carrels often consist of desks with visual barriers formed by open bookshelves or low partitions. Closed carrels have doors and often soundproof, semipermanent walls and are also called study or dissertation rooms, or, in some European countries, "study cabins." See also *Wet carrel.*

Case shelving: A type of shelving that is only open in front and finished to have more of a cabinetlike look than standard metal library shelving. It may or may not have doors: solid, glazed, or wire grilled.

Case work: Cabinets of custom fabrication, often attached to the building and therefore part of the general construction contract.

Casement windows: Window units hinged vertically so that they open outward or inward. They can be operated either manually or by means of a mechanical crank attachment.

Catalog: A list of materials held in a particular collection or library. Library catalogs exist in the form of (1) book-format catalogs, (2) computer-accessed catalogs on terminals, (3) microfiche catalogs often produced by computers, and (4) card catalogs. See also *Official catalog.*

Catalog department: The administrative unit of a library where books are cataloged and classified. See also *Technical services.*

Catalog tray: A drawer in which cards or slips are filed, several drawers being enclosed in a catalog cabinet.

Caulking: Pliable material used to make a joint watertight or airtight.

CD-ROM: A common acronym for Compact Disc—Read Only Memory, a form of optical storage widely used to enable rapid searching of major library reference books.

Centers, or "on centers": The distance between the centers of two pieces of similar equipment or construction placed parallel to each other. Generally used in connection with wall studs, stack ranges, carrels in a reading area, tables in a reading room, desks in a workroom, parallel rows of catalog cases for the library's catalog, or with columns or windows.

Chair rail: A hard horizontal molding affixed to the wall at a height to offer protection from chair backs.

Chamfer: A bevel or rounding of sharp furniture or architectural edges to make its use more durable or comfortable, or to provide a transition between two surfaces—for example, the 45-degree edge of a concrete beam or column.

Change order: A refinement during construction approved by the owner and issued by the project architect to the contractor to alter some particular condition or specification in the contract documents.

Charge cards: The slip used to record the borrowing of a particular item. Also termed a circulation card or, if it is maintained in the item, a book card.

Charrette: The period of frenzied activity on the part of the architect during which the design is completed by a deadline. A charrette usually implies working extra hours, often all night, right up to the last moment. The term comes from an old French practice of requiring architects (probably students or participants in a competition) to have drawings prepared in time to get them on the cart *(la charrette)* as it passes the studio.

Chase: An enclosed passage usually formed for pipes or ducts.

Chute: A term used to refer to the *book return,* q.v.

Circulation department: Service department for loan transactions, often also responsible for the supervision of the bookstacks. See also *Readers' services.*

Circulation space: The floor area required for traffic within a building, usually (but not al-ways) treated as the space defined as the difference between gross and net floor area. Typically this includes lobbies, corridors, main and side aisles, passageways, stairs, ramps, and halls, but not the space in which a reading chair may be adjusted and not space for people to move about amidst furniture if the area assigned for the furniture or for the operation as a whole includes space for people to move (e.g., the floor area immediately behind a counter). Although stack aisles and stack cross aisles are technically circulation space, the space allocation is usually made with the shelving allocation and is thus part of the net space rather than a separate space allocation within the net/gross difference.

Classification: The numerical or alphanumerical notation by which library materials may be given an ordered subject arrangement on the shelving and that accommodates additions in their logical place within the scheme.

Clean out: The access to plumbing systems that enables a rather easy reaming or flushing of segments that may become clogged.

Clean power: An electrical circuit dedicated to computer usage where the simultaneous use of other equipment that could produce interference, if serviced by the same circuit, is avoided.

Clerestory window: An outside view set above head height and so placed to let in natural light over the top of a wall, shelving, etc.

Client: A computer that relies on the resources of another computer called a *server,* q.v. A workstation requesting the contents of a file from a file server is a client of the file server.

Climatization: see *Air conditioning*

Closed-access stacks or closed stacks: Stacks to which only members of the library staff normally are admitted.

Closed card catalog: A card catalog to which cards are no longer being added.

Closed-circuit television: A type of television in which the signal is not broadcast as in ordinary television but is transmitted by cable or wire to one or more receivers. Existing telephone lines have been used in experimental installations. Possible applications of closed-circuit television in libraries include transmission of educational programs to auditoriums and classrooms; and transmission of documents—pages of books or manuscripts—and of bibliographical information from a central service point to distant monitoring stations. It can also be used as an aid to supervision.

Closet, wiring: Small, secure rooms, usually one per floor and stacked in all floors, specially designed for wiring terminal systems and telephone communication equipment, such as line circuits, power supplies, and special control devices. Each wiring closet provides a concentration point for routing data cables between the controller and terminals on the floor.

Coaxial cable: see *Cable, coaxial*

Code: Building code, electrical code, fire code, etc.

Code authority: The governmental offices given legal responsibility for the administration of the governing codes and ordinances as they affect the building and its occupants during its lifetime. Besides safety, the codes and ordinances may apply to access, zoning requirements, energy usage, and other aspects established by law.

Coffered ceiling: A ceiling with a pattern of indentations created from formwork in the case of concrete construction or from a system of beams in other construction. Portions of a coffered ceiling may serve no structural purpose and may be purely decorative and formed in plaster or acoustic material, although the concept is based on a structural solution to spanning a space with minimal materials.

Collateral reading: Suggested or recommended reading designated by the teaching faculty to supplement required reading. See also *Reserved books.*

COM upholstery: "Customer's own material." Refers to furniture for which the upholstery fabric is provided separately.

Commercial HVAC controls: Standard thermostats, humidistats, and control systems as found in most buildings, as opposed to *industrial HVAC controls,* q.v.

Commercial shelving: Inexpensive metal shelving, also known as industrial shelving, that is supported by uprights at each corner of the shelving unit or section. Adjustable with the use of nuts and bolts or clips.

Commissioning: see *Activation*

Commons: see *Staff commons*

Compact shelving: Commonly used to describe movable shelving where entire ranges are

mounted on carriages that ride on tracks. In a compact shelving bay, there is one access range aisle for a number of ranges, thereby saving considerable space. Also called *movable shelving,* q.v.

Compact storage: A bookstack, usually for lesser-used materials, that has much greater capacity than is usual, either by taller sections and exceptionally narrow aisles, an *order-picker system,* q.v., *double shelving,* q.v., or a form of *movable shelving,* q.v.

Compartment: Sometimes used to refer to two sections of shelving back-to-back. Also called a "double-faced section."

Computer-Aided Design (CAD): A software program enabling architects and engineers to create plans, perspectives, and details, derive materials lists, etc.

Computer lab: A cluster of terminals for student use when learning computer data searching and manipulation, or for class assignments, independent study, or other personal use. The workstations may be set up in a classroom style, may use open counters or partitioned carrels, etc., and will commonly have some local printing capacity, an area for helpful documents, and an area for counseling or peer or expert consultation.

Concealed spline: A ceiling tile system employing a linear supporting device made of a strip of metal hung from the structure above by wire such that the metal strip, or spline, engages adjacent tiles. With this type of installation, the only visible elements other than the tiles themselves are small cracks between the tiles; the supporting spline is hidden by the edges of the tiles.

Conduit: The pipe or tube through which is pulled electrical wire or cable.

Confirming estimate: A second estimate prepared by a separate estimating firm used to verify the estimate prepared by the architect.

Conservation department: The total quarters required for the workshop, *atelier,* laboratory, or studio in which preservation treatment is given to selected library materials. It includes needed office space, but may or may not include ancillary areas for exhibits, instruction, microfilming, film processing, etc.

Construction documents: see *Contract documents*

Construction zone: The precise area specified in the bid package that can be fenced in and is legally under control of the contractor during the entire period of construction. It may or may not include parking for crews. It will include area for field offices, materials stockpiling, portable toilets, trash or waste collection, and vehicle access from one or more roads as necessary.

Consultation counter: A counter-high table or similar surface in the card catalog if a particular tray is to be taken from the cabinet for use. It is sometimes provided with built-in receptacles for charge cards, scratch slips for notes, and catalog explanatory handouts. A stool may be provided for extended use. Consultation counters are also common in reference rooms in association with the shelving where a quick use of reference materials is facilitated, and occasionally in the general stacks to be used for short consultation of materials shelved there.

Contingency figure: A safety factor included in cost estimates, schedules, or design criteria to cover any anticipated inflation or unanticipated demands and to provide for expenses that may occur at a later date, the amount of which is unknown at the time of estimating.

Contour: The outline of a figure or form, or a line drawn to join points of similar elevation on a site or landscape plan.

Contract documents: The agreement, general conditions, special conditions, addenda, change orders, etc., including the set of working drawings necessary for contractors to bid upon and build the project. Also applies to contractual documents for professional services in which the nature and scope of the services are defined. See also *Working drawings.*

Contractor, general: The firm that has the general construction contract with the institution, which may or may not include mechanical, electrical, and other work according to the construction documents. See also *Subcontractor.*

Conveyor: Occasionally used in libraries for continuous horizontal or vertical movement of sizable numbers of books.

Core voids: Holes through a floor slab made by placing tubes in the formwork on a predetermined module before pouring the concrete. Core voids may be useful in providing flexibility for signal and power installation at a future date from the ceiling area of the floor below.

Cost model: A financial formula or format applicable to estimating construction cost that facilitates the process of comparative analysis both with other projects and earlier or *confirming estimates,* q.v., on the same project.

Counter height: The working surface distance from the finished floor level, so as to provide a height that is convenient for persons who are standing. The convenient height (typically from 39 to 42 in. or 990 to 1,066 mm) will vary depending on function and the typical elbow height of the persons for whom it is designed. A counter used for handling larger objects (such as a mail room sorting counter) may be as low as 36 in. or 914 mm, as is typically the case with a kitchen counter.

Course reserves: Books, outlines, example tests, syllabi, and other materials—both library collection items and personal materials from faculty—segregated for short-term circulation as needed for class assignments. In some countries called "short loan collection." See also *E-reserves.*

Crawl space: A subfloor volume, usually found under the ground floor and with unfinished floor, which has headroom so low as to force ducking or crawling to move therein.

Critical path method (CPM): Developed in 1956, CPM uses a graphic flowchart of multiple interdependent tasks to show the shortest time possible to complete construction and occupy a building. By determining which operations are most demanding of time, including off-site fabrication and procurement of materials, and which are prerequisite to one or several subsequent operations, the minimum total elapsed time is demonstrated. See also *Milestone chart.*

Cross aisle: The bookstack aisle that passes through the midst of the stack, perpendicular to the range aisles, which are the narrow passageways between two ranges. See also *Aisle.*

CRT: An acronym for cathode ray tube, also called a video display or monitor, which creates textual images on a fluorescent screen.

Crunch point: A term sometimes used to indicate the year in which the library expects its book collection to reach the shelving *working capacity,* q.v.

Cubage: The volume of space as defined by the building envelope or outer shell. Net cubage applies to the volume of space between walls and below the visible ceiling. Gross cubage usually applies to the total space occupied by a building.

Cubicle: see *Carrel*

Cubook: A term devised by Robert Henderson of the New York Public Library for a book of average size. He estimated that 100 cubooks could be housed in a standard single-faced stack section 3 ft wide and 7 ft 6 in. high (0.914 × 1.186 m).

Curtain wall: A nonload-bearing, thin exterior wall system that envelops a structure, located between or often in front of the main peripheral structural members of steel or reinforced concrete.

Cush: Sometimes used to describe the resiliency of carpet.

Dado: see *Wainscot*

Data center: The traditional "computer room" housing the mainframe computer, with banks of disk and tape drives and connected printers, and managing connections into off-campus networks.

Dead load: The weight of all fixed items in a building. It includes the structure, lighting, partitions, and permanently fixed elements, such as equipment in a penthouse. It contrasts with *live load,* q.v.

Debit card: A plastic "smart" card with digital record of its monetary value, reduced or debited with each use, such as of a photocopy machine. Also applies to bank-issued cards that, in combination with a *PIN,* q.v., deduct directly from one's account via the network (rather than deducting from the value encoded on the card). Such cards are occasionally (and probably increasingly) seen in the form of student identification cards.

Decanting: The process of removing functions or materials from a building in order to make space for other activities.

Deck: Area occupied by one level of a bookstack, referred to in this volume as a stack level. Also applies to a tape recorder (as in tape deck).

Dedicated circuit: An electrical circuit used for a specific purpose either because of the power requirements of the equipment being serviced or in order to provide *clean power,* q.v.

Dedicated line: A connection serving information needs, such as a full-time direct phone line

connection set aside for support of a security system.

Deduct alternate: see *Bid alternate*

Depository library: A library legally designated to receive and house and make available government publications without charge.

Design development plans: Drawings developed in much greater detail following the schematic plans. Also known as preliminary plans. These drawings show not only structural building elements but also location and space requirements for everything to be contained in the building. Together with outline specifications, design development plans serve as the basis for preliminary cost estimates.

Desk height: Similar to *counter height,* q.v.; however, determined for seating with one's feet on the floor and knees bent at right angles (typically 29 to 30 in. or 736 to 762 mm).

Desktop computer: A microcomputer, less portable than a laptop and more powerful or adaptable or both to support other systems or devices than a "dumb" terminal and most laptops.

Detail drawings: Produced by the architect to explain, enlarge, and clarify sections of the construction documents.

Detection system: see *Book-detection system*

Development office: The fund-raising office.

Diagonal bracing: In shelving, this refers to what is called "X" bracing formed of cordlike members connected to the corners of a shelving section in the form of an X. Also called *sway bracing,* q.v.

Dictionary stand: A slightly sloping support large enough to hold an unabridged dictionary. It usually has a front lip to prevent the volume from falling, and it may rest so as to hold the book at counter height above a table or counter, or stand on its own legs or pedestal. Also sometimes called a *lectern,* q.v.

Directory: A public listing of offices, departments, special rooms, officials, and specialists. It is often prominently mounted in the building lobby or by the elevator. There may also be local directories and stack directories (showing the layout of the collections) on individual floors. See also *Signs.*

Disaster bins: Mobile plastic trash barrels containing salvage material, such as plastic sheeting, paper towels, clean newsprint, and sometimes a lantern, stout cord, rolls of yellow tape, large garbage bags, and markers.

Dissertation room: A one- or two-person enclosed study with locking door, providing private, secure space in which an advanced student may work and leave personal notes, papers, books, a computer, and other materials.

Distance learning: A term commonly used to describe various arrangements for educational courses to be taken far from a campus by reception of satellite broadcast, cable television, e-mail, and telephone.

Divider-type shelving: A type of metal shelving using shelves that have turned-up backs and slots designed to hold plates called dividers (sometimes called slotted shelving). This type of shelving is commonly used for technical reports and other pamphletlike material.

Divisional plan: see *Subject-divisional plan*

Donor graphic: The one or several plaques, wall lettering, or other signs acknowledging those who helped finance the building.

Double-acting (door): A door with the leaf able to swing both inward and outward, rather than being prevented from swinging in one direction by the frame or jamb.

Double-faced section: Two single-faced stack sections back-to-back, generally attached to the same upright. Also called a "compartment."

Double-hung (window): A two-paneled window in which one panel slides up and the other down. To work well, the window panels are counterbalanced with a system of pulleys and weights hidden in the window frame.

Double shelving: A space-saving technique of shelving materials in double rows on the shelf, with the back row hidden from view by the front row.

Downspout: A roof drainpipe, usually attached to the exterior wall, carrying rainwater from gutters under the edge of a roof to a lower level or to the ground.

Draw-out shelves: A type of compact shelving in which the shelf height is fixed and each shelf is actually a drawer, enabling full occupancy of space behind the front visible volumes.

Drop: see *Book return*

Dry bulb temperature: The temperature determined by any accurate thermometer without the influence of evaporating water. A combination of the dry bulb and wet bulb temperatures is used to determine the relative humidity.

Drywall construction: The use of plywood or gypsum board (also called plasterboard, sheetrock, or wallboard) for the construction of walls or, in some cases, ceilings. It excludes any wet process, such as plaster, masonry, or concrete, whether or not it is structural.

Duct: The pipe or other tubular passage through which air is carried. See also *Main.*

Duct bank: A construction consisting of multiple conduits containing wire, often servicing the entire building for power or signal or both.

Duct shaft: The vertical building void between floors that constitutes a clear route for ducts or conduits and can facilitate their servicing as required.

Dummy: A block of wood or other material used to replace a book in its normal shelf location, usually its proper classified location. The block has the book identification with note indicating its actual location. Commonly used for folio volumes when the catalog and stack directory do not alert the user to a special location for oversized materials.

Dumpster: A very large metal trash receptacle for outdoor lifting and dumping by refuse trucks. A proprietary term.

Duplex outlet: A standard electrical receptacle with the capacity to receive two plugs. Can also be doubled into a fourplex or double duplex outlet.

Economizer cycle: A mode of operation for the HVAC system where the air being returned from the building is compared with outside air, and the air source that requires the least energy to condition is selected. Economizer cycles are very seldom, if ever, practical where humidity control is mandated.

Efficiency (energy): The extent to which a building is designed to operate on comparatively low levels of energy through the use of various technologies, including insulation, solar devices, special controls, and other devices.

Efficiency (space): A factor derived by dividing the net assignable area by the gross area of the building, commonly used for comparative purposes and as a measure of the planning effectiveness.

Egress route: The legal exit required for emergency, such as fire, smoke, or earthquake.

Electronic mail: see *E-mail*

Electronic reserves: see *E-reserves*

Elephant folio: see *Book sizes*

Elevation (drawing): A vertical representation of a building—interior or exterior or both—drawn to a scale. *(see all others)*

Elevator: A platform for the mechanical vertical transportation of passengers, books, or freight, from one level of a building to the others. When used for passengers, the platform should be completely enclosed by walls and roof. Called a *lift,* q.v., in many countries. See also *Two-to-one roping.*

Ell: An extension at one end or side of a building, usually at a right angle.

Ellison doors: Trade name for heavy, balanced swing doors with pivots placed about 6 in. from the side frame at top and bottom. Doors swing both in and out at the same time because part of the swinging action goes in the reverse direction. They use less space than ordinary doors with hinges directly on the side frame. Their use is especially applicable to wide outside doors where wind problems exist and for interior parts of the building where the suction between air-conditioned and non-air-conditioned rooms makes the operation of usual door hardware difficult.

E-mail: Electronic mail, a form of communication using networked computers.

Embankment: A steep slope often forming the edge of a building site where there is an elevation change.

Emergency exit: A legal exit designed exclusively for egress during fire or other emergency conditions.

Emergency lighting and power: An auxiliary system powered by backup generators or batteries or both to provide minimally adequate light for exiting and power for emergency horns or other systems.

End panel: The finished vertical surface of steel or wood at the end of a section or range of bookshelves. For steel shelving formed of structural columns and cantilevered shelves, these panels are nonstructural. In case-type or slotted shelving, they are usually structural.

Energy column, or pillar: see *Power pole*

ENR Index: A monthly record of average building construction prices published in the *Engineering News Record* and used to establish cost trends.

Envelope of a building: The total exterior surfaces of a structure.

Ephemera: Library collections of cards, clippings, offprints, posters, programs, and other such slight and fugitive material.

E-reserves: Electronic reserves that provide access to reserve materials stored digitally through networked computers.

Ergonomics: The applied science of "human engineering," which designs physical working conditions to meet specific needs of people doing a particular task in a particular setting.

Escutcheon: A protective or decorative plate around a pipe, keyhole, door handle, light switch, or drawer pull.

Fabric of architecture: The palette of materials, colors, textures, and shapes that is characteristic of an architectural style or is chosen for a particular building. Also called "architectural character."

Facsimile: (1) A reproduction of a manuscript or printed document made by lithographic or photographic processes; not a reprint. (2) Transmission of images of documents over telephone wires or other telecommunication systems. See also *Closed-circuit television, TelAutograph,* and *Telefacsimile.*

False floor: see *Access flooring*

Fast track: The process of bidding successive portions of a building construction project so that work can begin before the full set of bid documents is finished. The bidding may be in two or more stages. The intent is to speed the date of completion and to save some cost of price rises during construction.

Fax: see *Telefacsimile*

Fenestration: The window systems, including fixed and operable sashes and integral screening, if any.

Fiber optics: A thin filament of glass or other transparent material through which signal-encoded light beams are transmitted carrying voice, data, and video. Fiber optics have high capacity, low power consumption, and insensitivity to electromagnetic interference. Fiber optics are also used to transmit usable light (as opposed to information) in display cases, artworks, and signs.

Fiche: A transparent sheet film containing reproductions of a number of pages greatly reduced in size. They are one form of *microreproduction*, q.v.

Field order: A temporary document requiring an immediate change of plan of work during construction, issued by the project architect and to be followed up by a formal *change order*, q.v.

File server: see *Server*

File tub: A bin (becoming increasingly rare) holding circulation charge cards for all outstanding loans. It is usually at table or counter height and has legs and wheels for rolling around the work area.

Fire damper: An adjustable plate or louver in ventilation ducts that automatically closes to prevent smoke or fire passage when a fire alarm is activated.

Fire rated: Walls, doors, dampers, and other devices that are used to separate parts of a building are fire rated based upon the construction of the device meeting code requirements of specific fire separations. Fire ratings are expressed in terms of minutes or hours; the code requirements for fire separation can go as high as four hours.

Fire stopped: In wall construction, a horizontal element between the floor and ceiling that conceptually stops vertical migration of a fire within the wall.

Fire tower: A vertical emergency egress stair that is separately vented so that smoke and heat from within the building cannot contaminate the exit route. It may be at the exterior wall where it can be vented to the atmosphere.

Flashing: A material (copper, galvanized steel, lead, aluminum, stainless steel, titanium alloy, zinc, or impregnated fabric) used as a protective covering to prevent water penetration into the building at joints between horizontal and vertical building surfaces, such as roofs, floors, and walls; at the head of sills or exterior wall openings; and on all sides of roof openings for gables, dormers, skylights, domes, pipes, drains, etc.

Flat wire: A system of wire that is broad and very thin such that it can be used under carpet. Substitutes for standard wire of this type are available for both power and signal. See also *Cable, flat.*

Fluorescent light: see *Light sources*

Flush-bracket shelving: see *Bracket shelving*

Flushing the building: The staff process of checking all public parts of the library to be sure every visitor has left at closing time.

Folio: The size of a volume formed by folding a sheet once. See also *Book sizes.*

Follower block: The adjustable support for cards, fiche, or file contents to the rear of a tray or file drawer.

Footcandle: Unit of illumination equal to one lumen per square foot, which is the amount provided by a light source of one candle at a distance of one foot: equals 10.76 lux. Full sunlight with the sun at the zenith is of the order of 10,000 footcandles on a horizontal surface. This term is often replaced by the use of "lumen per square foot."

Footing: see *Foundations*

Footing drain: A system of perforated pipe that is installed at the perimeter of the building foundations designed to remove groundwater before it leaks into a basement or an underground space. A footing drain may connect to the storm sewer or to a sump pump, which, in turn, is connected to the storm sewer.

Footprint of building: The outside configuration of a building at grade level, usually determined as it relates to finished grading but ignoring berms, swales, dry moats, and similar sculpturing for drainage, light, air, or aesthetic purposes.

Fore-edge: The edge of a book, opposite the binding edge or spine, i.e., the front edge.

Foundations: The supporting members of a building or structure at the ground or its underpinning if it is supported by columns; the footings at the bottom of each column or pier are its foundations. The type of foundation required for a building depends on its structural system and on the ground and climate. In soft soils, piles may have to be driven down 100 ft (30.480 m) or more. On rocks, little more than dowels may be necessary to anchor the building. If a building has no basement but is erected directly on a concrete slab, that is the foundation. If a building has bearing walls supporting the roof, the foundations are the lowest divisions of these walls.

Foyer: see *Lobby*

Freestanding stacks: Library stacks whose principal support is the floor of the story they occupy. Stack manufacturers do not regard a stack as freestanding unless its base is so broad that the stack does not require strut bracing running from one range to another or other methods to provide stabilization, such as fastening to the floor. See also *Multitier stack.*

French drain: A drain that is simply a trench in the ground, often filled with gravel so as to absorb more water.

Front matter: Similar to *boilerplate,* q.v., dealing with the general aspects of a program or specification.

Fugitive material: see *Ephemera*

Fumigation chamber: A small, enclosed area that can temporarily house book materials on racks or trucks or shelves, can be sealed, perhaps evacuated of air, and filled with gas to kill insects or their larvae.

Furring (walls, ceilings): The application of a layer of thin wood or metal to provide a level surface to receive the final surface, such as for lathing, plastering, etc., or to make an air space.

General contractor: see *Contractor, general*

Glare: Light reflectance or imbalance of brightness that is sufficiently severe so as to impair reading. Glare is a particular problem when external light, such as from a window, skylight or clerestory, or other light is visible on a CRT screen or bounces into the reader's eyes from the table surface or the pages of the item being read.

Government documents: Publications issued by governmental agencies, departments, offices, etc. The term usually is not inclusive of those issued by quasi-governmental organizations, such as a joint exercise of power agreement, nor of reports issued as part of a research or study contract for work performed by a nongovernmental agency. Also known as public documents.

Grade: The elevation above sea level, or the ground level around a finished building. A sloping grade has an incline or a pitch described as so many degrees, or as, for example, rising one foot over a horizontal distance of five feet, or expressed as a percent. To grade a site would be to shape the topography of the site to meet the design criteria.

Graphics: see *Signs*

Gross space: The total area enclosed by a building, expressed in terms of cubic footage or square footage or square meters of floor area, including walls. Gross space generally includes rooftop machine rooms, projections, and mechanical spaces and also one-half of all spaces not enclosed with walls but provided with a roof and a floor. To the floor-to-floor heights used in computing gross volume, 1½ ft (450 mm) are generally added below the lowest floor to allow for foundations.

Group study room: An enclosed room designed primarily to enable a small number of people (typically four to six) to talk as they study or work on a project together.

Grout: The thin mortar filling spaces usually between masonry components.

Growth factor: A factor in shelving to allow space for the shelf supports, gusset plates, and other devices that increase the actual dimension of the *range,* q.v., beyond a simple multiple of the nominal dimensions of the sections.

Growth rate: The annual percentage or fixed rate at which collections expand.

Growth space: The difference between the space needed for current occupancy and capacity. As the term is applied to the book collections, it is usually the difference between current occupancy and *working capacity,* q.v.

Gusset plate: A structural element to assure strength in bookstack shelving and structural building components where they join.

Handicapped access: The route by which persons who are physically limited can come and go within the building and its approach. It may include ramps, door-opening devices, and other means of facilitating access by those who have sight, mobility, or dexterity limitations.

Hard hat: The protective helmet worn on construction sites to guard against falling objects or areas of low head clearance.

Hardware: Physical components of a computer system, including such peripherals as disk drives, monitors, processors, and printers. Also, the parts of the building that one might think of buying in a hardware store, such as locks, hinges, doorstops, etc.

Hardwired: A direct connection, without the ability to disconnect—that is, there is no plug or socket or port.

Hat channel: A bent steel form resembling the shape of a hat in section, often used as overhead bracing to connect a bank of ranges for structural rigidity and for *furring,* q.v. Two hat channels fastened together have been used as the structural column in steel shelving, although the C shape is now more common. See also *Strut bracing.*

Head end: The location of the central communications hub for a building, or campus, containing reception and switching equipment and related equipment for management of a telecommunications network.

HID: An acronym for *High-Intensity Discharge* lighting. See also *Light sources.*

Homepage: The computer display on the World Wide Web that welcomes the user and introduces a library, an institution, or a person, often listing and pointing to related services or information.

Humidistat: A control device that measures humidity and adjusts the mechanical system in response to change in humidity.

HVAC: An abbreviation, frequently used in engineering documents, for the heating, ventilating, air filtration, cooling, and air-conditioning system for a building. An HVAC system can include some or all of the above.

Hydronic heating and cooling: A system for heating or cooling or both, based upon piped fluid (usually water) rather than ducted air or steam.

Hygrometer: An instrument to display the humidity of a room. A recording hygrometer will provide a 24-hour or one-week graphic record of humidity conditions throughout that period.

Hygrothermograph: A device to record the humidity and temperature in a room. Commonly used to monitor bookstack conditions, especially those where rarities are housed, thereby providing a means to check that the HVAC system is performing as it was engineered to do.

Incandescent light: see *Light sources*

Index: see *Bibliographic tool*

Index table: A large table with sufficient width to shelve indexes and other frequently used reference works down the middle, sometimes on a second or third tier of shelves, and still have room in front to open and use one or more volumes. Sometimes called a "bib" table, short for bibliography table.

Industrial HVAC controls: High-quality thermostats, humidistats, and controls systems, generally more expensive, accurate, durable, and maintenance-free than *commercial HVAC controls,* q.v.

Industrial shelving: see *Commercial shelving*

Information broker: A commercial firm that searches out and provides answers and hard copy to clients, using networked computing services, library collections, and a variety of other sources.

Information technology (IT): An umbrella term for the range of equipment, software, services, and supporting technologies for the entire field of information processing and storage. It includes computers, multimedia data, and telecommunications.

Infrastructure: The fundamental services available in support of a building or campus, commonly including human and vehicular transportation routes, data and telephone communication systems of various sorts, safety and waste disposal systems, and utility power plants and distribution systems for electricity, gas, and water.

Insulation: The materials used for reducing the passage of sound, heat, or cold from outside to inside a building and, at times, from one part of a building to adjacent space. Also, the part of wire that maintains isolation of the conducting element from other conducting elements.

Intelligent building: see *Smart building*

Intercom system: A telephone system providing direct communication between stations on the same premises. Local systems may be independent of or associated with the nationwide telephone network. The equipment often has such features as provision for conference calling, hands-free talking, and switching executive phones to public-address systems.

Internet: The high-speed backbone network of networks, commonly spoken of as "the Internet." Internet access is usually thought of as access to the *World Wide Web,* q.v.

Interstitial space: The space typically between the ceiling and the structure of the floor above, used for mechanical and electrical services and access to ducts, cable trays, equipment, etc. In some buildings (particularly laboratories), this space is high enough for a person to walk around in it.

Intrusion alarm system: A system to protect the building or rooms therein against unauthorized entry by giving an immediate alert to staff when the security has been breached. The local devices are wired to an *annunciator panel,* q.v., and may be linked to a campus security office, which is monitored at all hours.

ISDN: A common acronym for *i*ntegrated *s*ervices *d*igital *n*etwork, which is the simultaneous transmission through a single line of voice (analog) together with data and video (digital) signals.

Isometric drawing: A form of three-dimensional projection in which each plane is drawn in true dimension and, except for one surface facing the viewer, at an oblique angle view for clarity of presentation.

Isoperm: A system of translating conditions of temperature and relative humidity into the relative life expectancy of materials such that if an isoperm value of 1 is set at 50 percent relative humidity and 70° F., for an increase in temperature or humidity or both, the isoperm value decreases; for a decrease in temperature or humidity or both, the isoperm value increases. See appendix D for a detailed discussion relative to paper products.

Kickplate: A protective reinforcement at the bottom of a door.

Kiosk: (1) A thick, columnlike structure on which notices and temporary signs are publicly posted; (2) a column supporting an upward-directed light source in the middle of rooms, providing ambient light by indirect diffusion from a hidden light source; and (3) a small, columnlike structure open on one side, as are some news and coffee stands.

Lab: A shortened term commonly used for a laboratory. See also *Computer lab.*

Lally columns: Columns made of a cylindrical steel-pipe shell filled with concrete. Special types have additional reinforcement consisting of steel bars. "Lally" is a registered proprietary term of 1897.

LAN: see *Local Area Network*

Landscape offices: Semiprivate office space, created by arranging relatively low partitions in a large open space. The partitions may vary from just overhead height for a seated person to overhead height for a standing person. They may be acoustically treated; somewhat easily movable; provided with electricity, communications, and task lighting; and mated with desk and shelves or other office accessories.

Laptop: Term for a portable fold-up microcomputer of a size to fit a briefcase and powered from its own battery or from public power supply. Sometimes called a *notebook computer,* q.v.

Latent heat: The heat applied to or extracted from the process of converting a state of matter, such as ice to water, water to vapor or steam, or the reverse. See also *Sensible heat.*

Lateral file: Cabinet drawers that pull out from the long side rather than from the more common narrow side. In this arrangement, the file folders usually can be viewed by looking sideways instead of head on. The lateral file has the advantage in some locations of extending less than half as far into the passageway.

Lateral force: Horizontal pressures commonly produced by collisions, earthquakes, winds, etc.

Layout: The plan for distribution of furniture and equipment in a building.

LC: The frequently used abbreviation for the U.S. Library of Congress.

LCD: An acronym for *l*ight *c*onducting *d*iode, used for displays.

Lectern: Similar in function and shape to a *dictionary stand,* q.v.

LED: An acronym for *l*ight *e*mitting *d*iode, used for light sources of various kinds, commonly the red and green lights in control panels.

Legal file: A correspondence cabinet with drawers of a size to house documents used in procedures of law; the size is 8½ × 13 to 16 in. (215 × 330 to 406 mm), as opposed to that for a *letter file,* q.v.

Letter file: A correspondence cabinet with drawers of a size to house common documents, memoranda, and other papers to a maximum size of 8½ × 11 in. (215 × 279 mm).

Lexan: A plastic material (polycarbonate) manufactured by General Electric. In construction, it is usually clear and used largely for security glazing, though other applications are possible, including films used in graphics and molded plastic parts.

Life-cycle costs: The cost of service, maintenance, and replacement, including consideration of residual value, of an item, such as a computer or building or mechanical system, over an extended period. The comparison of life-cycle costs for a group of similar items may result in a considerably different ranking than would be the case for comparative initial cost (that is, the lowest initial cost for a given product may not reflect the life-cycle cost).

Lift: In American library usage, the term often denotes the book elevator, not the passenger elevator as referred to in many other countries. Lifts are operated by electric motors or by hand. In construction, a lift is the procedure for the placement of concrete, particularly in a wall or other vertical element.

Lift-slab: A construction process where concrete floors are poured in slabs at ground level, then raised to the proper floor level after suitable strength has been obtained.

Light sources:

Ambient light is the general area lighting provided by direct and indirect sunlight and by reflected artificial light. This latter artificial light excludes task lighting, which is directed solely for one individual's benefit or for one specific object, and general room lighting, which is down-directed lighting covering a general area or portion of a room.

Fluorescent light is generated by an electrical-discharge lamp in which the radiant energy from the discharge is transferred by suitable materials (usually phosphors) into wavelengths giving high luminosity.

High-intensity discharge is a new source of energy-efficient light. HID includes low- and high-pressure sodium and mercury vapor lights. All HID fixtures require some form of transformer or ballast. In the HID lamp, the transmission of current through a gas produces the light.

Incandescent light is produced by a lightbulb in which a metallic substance glows at white heat. Common bulbs are the tungsten lamp and the quartz-halogen lamp.

Polarized lighting is produced by a lens that controls the emission direction so as to reduce

visibility of the light source within normal sight lines when one is reading.

Sulfur lighting system is an experimental lighting system said to be without an electrode, and one that produces excellent color and no heat. Although it is not yet widely available, it has much promise to become a viable lighting alternative for museums and libraries.

Task lighting is local lighting produced by a device, sometimes adjustable, and concentrated on the desk surface or other specific task location.

Lintel: The horizontal structural beam at the top of a door or window.

Live load: Any weight within a building that is not fixed, such as that potentially shifting because of the movement of people, books, materials, equipment, and vehicles. It contrasts with *dead load,* q.v.

Load bearing: Used in reference to a wall that is specifically engineered to withstand all reasonable anticipated weights of all parts of the building that rest thereon.

Lobby: An entrance hall or foyer at or near the building entrance or in front of the elevators or both.

Local Area Network (LAN): Wiring or cabling to link computers and workstations within a single building or local work group. LANs can be interconnected by interface devices called bridges, routers, and gateways. The cable standard is usually either Ethernet, Token Ring, or fiber-optic wires, which use glass strands to replace copper cable.

Locked stack: That part of the bookstacks that is walled or caged off to house materials needing extra security.

Lumen: The basic unit of visible light or luminous flux of light.

Lump sum: A single, fixed-price payment, as opposed to cost-plus or time and materials.

Lux: The International System unit of illumination equal to one lumen per square meter.

Machine readable: Text, identification, or other information that can be read and used by a computer, and, in some cases, changed by the computer. The machine-readable device may be a text that is formed to be optically read, a bar code also optically read, a magnetic strip, a radio frequency microchip, or other technology that can be relatively secure and serve as input to a computer through an appropriate reading device.

Mail room: Quarters used for processing packages and other mail for internal and external delivery. Also called receiving room or shipping room, and sometimes functionally broadened to include supply stock and issuance, building security, caretaking or janitorial service, and the superintendent function.

Main: A conduit, pipe, or duct for channeling electricity (power, signal), fluid, or gas. The main carries service to a building and is distinguished from branch runs, which carry service to individual rooms and areas.

Main library: A building that is the administrative center of a system, where the principal collections are housed, and various business services and technical processing procedures are usually located.

Mainframe: The largest computers, usually located in a "data center," with more capacity than the smaller minicomputer and much more capacity than the even smaller microcomputer.

Master clock system: A group of clocks in a building or area of campus, where one clock can be reset and all the "slave" clocks conform.

Master plan: The general scheme under which a particular project will be developed, or the full scheme for long-term development of a building. It thus involves going beyond the immediate phase of construction.

Media: A collection of materials inclusive of cassettes, films, videotapes, filmstrips, slides, recordings, pictures, charts, kits, games, models, realia, and sometimes computer programs and maps. Formerly and sometimes still called audiovisual materials.

Mercury vapor lamps: Tubular lamps in which mercury vapor is made luminous by the passage of an electric current.

Mezzanine: A level of a building extending over only a part of the area available to it and leaving the remainder with additional height.

Microform reader: A machine for enlarging a microtext for reading at or about its original size. If it can also produce a copy of that enlargement, it is termed a reader-printer.

Microreproductions: Microphotographic copies of printed or manuscript matter. The principal forms are microfilm on reels, microfiche (sheet microfilm), microcards (opaque paper positives), and microprint (paper opaques that are duplicated in large editions by a photomechanical process). Also known as *microtexts,* q.v.

Microtext: The graphic texts and illustrations contained on microreproductions.

Milestone chart: A planning and scheduling table that plots time targets for completion of particular tasks, trades, or phases of construction. In a more elaborate form it has been developed into a detailed work-flow schema called PERT (program evaluation and review technique), which is milestone- or event-oriented. See also *Critical path method.*

Mock carrel: A semipartitioned segment of a table for several persons that gives the semblance of an individual carrel.

Mock-up: A full-sized replica or dummy of a part of a building or a particular piece of furniture or equipment, often made of a substitute material, such as wood or plaster.

Modem: A small device that controls speed and protocols of data transmission, and modulates and demodulates signals (analog to and from digital) transmitted over data communications facilities, thus serving as a telecommunications link for a computer. This device will become obsolete as full digital networks become sufficient.

Modesty panel: The skirt of a carrel, counter, desk, or table that hides from view most or all of the legs of one sitting behind it.

Modular construction: A system of building construction in which the floor area is divided into equal units defined by structural columns at the corners, instead of by arbitrarily placed load-bearing walls (though load-bearing walls can be placed on a module). This system makes it possible to provide or to extend areas for different departments as desired. A modular library is one constructed on this principle.

Module: One of the square, rectangular, or triangular units of space into which a modular construction is divided; one or more modules form a bay, the space between four columns.

Monograph: A book or separate volume or volumes of text constituting a substantial treatise on a particular subject, as distinct from *serial,* q.v.

Monumentality: The grand nature that gives a building great, significant, imposing, and enduring presence.

Morgue: A reference file of newspaper clippings.

Mouse: A computer input device controlling the movement of a cursor and permitting a series of controls at the site of the cursor through one or more microswitches, including especially a click, a double-click, and a click-and-hold. These control actions perform different functions depending upon the software in use.

Movable partition: A room divider that can be folded, collapsed, accordioned, or drawn so as to turn two separately usable spaces into one.

Movable shelving: A form of compact shelving that is denser than any other method permitting direct shelf access. See also *Compact shelving.*

Mullion: The vertical frame (structural or nonstructural) member between adjacent windows or doors.

Multimedia: A term for integrated "rich" text using a range of digitized information, such as printed words, handwriting, figures, music, pictures, and videos.

Multitier stack: A type of multistory stack construction that was by far the most popular type before the Second World War, and is still found in many large research libraries. The stack consists of vertically and horizontally interconnected sections and ranges of shelving, stacked one on top of another, which are self-supporting and support the total weight of the books stored. Its installation makes it unnecessary to have load-bearing upper floors in the building itself. The same columns that accept the shelves also support the thin stack floors. Multitier stacks ensure maximum capacity, but the stack area lacks flexibility.

Negotiated bid: A means of reaching a contract between the owner and a construction firm where the cost and terms of construction are developed as the result of conferring and responding, one to the other until agreement is reached.

Net space: The part of the gross space left after deducting the nonassignable space or balance area; the assigned or programmed space. Often called "assignable space" or "usable area."

Network: An electronic neural communication web, often connecting computers of various sizes and types. Telecommunication networks or computer networks are the combination of terminals, cabling, wires, satellites, telephones, and a variety of devices tied together to provide remote sending, receiving, and manipulation of data of all sorts. One type is a *Local Area Network (LAN),* q.v.

Newspaper rack: An open bin or frame for holding several issues of a newspaper, each one held firmly at its left margin by a rigid "stick" from which the issue is suspended horizontally in the bin.

NIC: An acronym for "*not in contract*"; used on drawings to indicate those items that are excluded from the job under contract.

Noise, electrical: The interference that can be heard in electrical sounds and that comes about when power and signal lines are not adequately separated or insulated one from the other.

Nominal dimension: Typically, a dimension based upon measurement from the center line between two closely placed units. In the case of lumber dimensions, a standard has been established based upon an accepted center line of the saw required to cut the wood to size from one side of the board to the other, measured before drying and finishing to a smooth surface. For standard library shelving, the nominal width is the dimension from the center of one shelf upright to the center of the next, while the nominal depth is measured from the center of a double-faced section to the front face of the shelf. For bricks, the nominal dimension is from the center of the grout line. For pipe, the inside diameter is the nominal diameter.

Nonassignable space: Floor area that is not available for direct library purposes. It normally includes space required for stairwells, rest rooms, mechanical equipment, janitors' closets, etc.

Nonlosable book support: A type of book support with a sufficiently thick bulk so that it cannot inadvertently "knife" the pages of a book shelved next to it or disappear from view when books are placed on both sides.

Nose: The stair-tread front edge. Also referred to as "nosing."

Notebook computer: A portable microcomputer that can be folded shut for carrying, sometimes called a *laptop,* q.v.

Oasis: A reading area in the midst of a bank of shelving.

Occupancy: see *Activation*

Occupancy permit: A formal approval of the completed construction project by the appropriate governmental agencies, including the fire marshal and the building inspection department, authorizing the occupancy of the building. In some cases the final signatures on the building permit are equivalent to the occupancy permit.

Octavo: The size of an average book, typically 8–10 in. (200 to 250 mm) in height. See also *Book sizes.*

Off-gassing: The process of materials emitting gaseous byproducts as they deteriorate or dry out.

Official catalog: A catalog maintained for the use of the library staff. The entries in this catalog often include details for the guidance of catalogers, such as added entry tracings and entry authority information.

On centers: see *Centers*

Online public-access catalog (OPAC): The catalog of library collection holdings recorded in some detail in electronic databases. An OPAC commonly is meant to refer to the catalog of the local library (the electronic version of the card catalog), yet is sometimes used to refer to union catalogs of many libraries.

OPAC: see *Online public-access catalog*

Open-access stack: Bookstack to which readers are admitted.

Optical disc: A very high density flat medium containing digitized analog of visual matter to be viewed using a laser-reading device and a display screen.

Order department: see *Acquisitions department*

Order-picker system: A compact storage system using very high shelving (in the order of 35 ft or 10.668 m high) and a computerized and mechanized system of retrieval, usually involving totes or boxes holding the materials.

OSHA: Abbreviation for Occupational Safety and Health Administration, an agency of the U.S. Department of Labor, which, since 1970, has had authority for setting minimum building conditions affecting health and safety for staff. In many states this function has been shifted to a state agency, such as Cal OSHA in California.

Outlet: see *Duplex outlet*

Outsourcing: The management action of relying on companies outside the library to provide a specific set of operations or materials that otherwise would be handled or produced within the library.

Overhead bracing: In fixed shelving, bracing that runs typically across the tops of ranges and range aisles, ideally connecting solidly to the building structure. Properly done, this type of bracing is designed to prevent a dominolike collapse of shelving ranges.

Oversized book: A volume too large to be shelved in its normal classified location, where it may be represented by a *dummy,* q.v.

PA system: A public-address system, commonly used in libraries to remind library patrons of the upcoming closing time, and for emergency announcements. See *Public-address system*

Paging system: An electronic radio device, sometimes called a "beeper," used to summon a staff member. It is distinct from the *PA* (or public-address) *system,* q.v., which directs a generally audible message to a particular part of a building.

Palette of the designer: The set of materials selected for a particular project by the interior designer and the architect. It consists of physical surfaces (metal, wood, glass, cloth, plastic) as well as colors, textures or finishes, and shapes. May be called the *fabric of architecture,* q.v.

Pam box: An abbreviated reference to a pamphlet box, usually an open-backed cardboard box that stands on shelves like a volume and houses up to a handful of pamphlets.

Panic alarm: An alarm, usually silent, that may be activated at a service desk in the event of a threat. Annunciation of the panic alarm at a central location may summon the police or a staff member, who may quietly go to the scene to assess the situation.

Panic hardware: Door-opening devices that release the catch when one pushes against a waist-high horizontal bar. A door alarm may be made part of the panic hardware or provided as a separate unit for security purposes.

Parapet: A low wall around the edge of a roof serving as a guard for those working on the roof and sometimes as a visual refinement to improve the roof line as seen from the ground.

Parging (walls): The lining of the layers in outer walls with mortar or plaster to give a smooth surface for greater insulation and to reduce fire risks and water penetration. Also lining walls that will be below grade with waterproof material to prevent leakage of groundwater.

Particulate: Small particles suspended in air.

Partition, dry and wet: Partitions may be without power and data cable (dry) and demountable, or supplied with power and signal (wet) and more difficult to remove.

Password card: see *Smart card*

PC: An abbreviation for "personal computer," commonly used to refer to any computer terminal of modest capacity (less than the capability of an engineering workstation). A *laptop,* q.v., is the portable form of PC. The term "network computer" (NC) is sometimes used for a terminal of very limited local capacity, relying on remote file servers for most of its operations.

Performance bond: A legal financial obligation serving to guarantee a contractor's execution of the contract.

Periodicals: see *Serials*

Permit: The legal document issued by a city, county, or other local authority to authorize construction of a new structure or renovation.

Personal computer: See *PC*

Perspective: The drawing that depicts a three-dimensional view of the landscape, building, or interior arrangement so as to convey the relative scale and visual relationships of objects as they would actually appear to a person standing at a particular vantage point. The lines from near to far converge to one, two, or, rarely, three distant vanishing points.

Pictogram: A visual symbol used on signs in lieu of any words. An example of such a pictogram is a stylized wheelchair picture to denote an area accessible thereby. International symbols are becoming more commonly used, though standards are limited to a few basic common sign meanings.

Piles: Poles driven or placed in the ground to support the load of a structure. Although many materials are possible, piles usually are wood, steel, or reinforced concrete; those driven by a pile driver are typically steel.

PIN: An acronym for *p*ersonal *i*dentification *n*umber, a code that can be used for controlling access to buildings, to particular rooms, to financial accounts, or to computer systems.

Pitch: The slope of a roof. See also *Grade.*

Plans: Drawings cutting horizontally through the building to show walls, doors, windows, and other arrangements of a floor. See also *Design development plans* and *Schematic plans.*

Plant room: A term for mechanical equipment space that may include areas for electrical, telephone, and security equipment. Also referred to as mechanical room.

Plenum: The contained space between a hung ceiling and the underside of the floor above that serves as an air passage. It is, in effect, a large duct space.

Plenum-rated wire: Wire that will not exude toxic vapors in a fire, usually metal clad.

Plexiglas UFII or III: A product used to filter ultraviolet light and thereby reduce light-caused damage to library materials.

Pneumatic controls: Machine or instrument control and adjustment devices that are activated by air pressure. The HVAC system is frequently controlled by a pneumatic system.

Pneumatic tubes: The pipe or conduit system used for the transportation of books or of call slips. Cartridges containing books or call slips are propelled by air pressure or by vacuum.

Pointing: The cement or mortar grout that fills and finishes the joints of brickwork.

Polarized lighting: see *Light sources*

Port: A socket or outlet from the signal transmission line to which a computer device can be connected. Also a socket or outlet on the computer itself to which other devices can be connected.

Portal: The entrance to the building or stack area through which library users are directed. A portal monitor is a staff member who supervises and may control entry by screening unauthorized visitors.

Portfolio: A case for holding the loose pages or signatures of an unbound book or other material. The case has the semblance of a book, often a very large book, and is tied or otherwise held closed when not in use. The term is improperly used in libraries to refer to any extremely large volume, bound or unbound, that must be shelved horizontally; "elephant folio" is the proper term for these volumes. See also *Book sizes.*

Poststressed construction: A structural construction technique involving concrete and typically steel whereby the steel is designed to permit the application of a stress after the concrete has set. This technique can achieve strength that is not possible with more traditional techniques. See also *Prestressed construction.*

Power pole: A thin conduit column through which power and signal lines can be pulled from the ceiling to reach desks, counters, etc. Used when floor or structural column outlets or ports are not available to bring lines to workstations.

Precast: A concrete building component that is formed off-site or within the construction zone and then moved into place.

Prefabricated: Wooden, metal, or other small (transportable) building components assembled off-site by carpenters, sheet-metal workers, or other trades. A prefabricated building is manufactured in a factory and assembled on the site.

Preliminary plans: see *Design development plans*

Preservation: Treatment to prolong the life of book materials, including actions of the *conservation department,* q.v.

Press: A publishing house, machine for printing, or device to squeeze books. See also *Range* for a different meaning.

Prestressed construction: A structural construction technique using concrete and typically reinforcing steel where stress is placed on the steel before the concrete is set. Use of this technique in beams can meet structural requirements with less material than nonstressed techniques. Another technique achieving much the same result is *poststressed construction,* q.v., though the uniformity of stress transfer between the steel and concrete is more certain with prestressed systems. In some cases, prestressed and poststressed systems are more brittle than the more traditional nonstressed placement of reinforcing steel.

Privileges desk: The counter or office where visitors may inquire of library staff regarding their authorization to use library services if they are not members of the faculty, staff, or student body. This desk may be called by such other names as visitors access, registra-

tion, or information, and the function may be handled at the reference or circulation desks or librarian's office.

Products-of-combustion system: A fire- and smoke-detection device with wiring to an *annunciator panel,* q.v., which activates an alarm if smoke (or sometimes dust) is present. Other similar devices detect a rapid increase in heat (rate-of-heat-rise), but they are not as effective in detecting a fire.

Program: (1) The academic courses of instruction; also (2) the academic plan for curriculum development; and, in this book (3) the comprehensive document describing and detailing the library building and its space requirements, its philosophy of service, functional areas and relationships, and spatial content and details as needed to communicate to the architects the desires of the owner-user. In the latter sense, called a "brief" in some countries.

Psychrometric chart: A chart showing heat content (enthalpy), specific humidity, relative humidity, and dry bulb temperature with which one can determine the effects of changing one factor upon the other factors.

Public-address system: A wired pattern of loudspeakers over which staff can make announcements to one part or various parts of a building, such as for an emergency or to forewarn of the closing time. It is distinct from an *intercom system* or a *paging system,* q.v.

Public documents: see *Government documents*

Public services: see *Readers' services*

Pull box: The fire-alarm box that can be manually activated in case of fire, smoke, or other emergencies in order to evacuate the building and notify the fire department.

Pull-out reference shelf: A shelf that can be pulled out from the face of a section of shelving, to be used for note taking in the stacks. Such shelves are generally mounted to the underside of a standard library shelf, and are no deeper than that shelf. They are sometimes used instead of *consultation counters,* q.v.

Punch list: The final inspection list prepared by the construction inspector or architect of work not meeting the construction document's specifications and which is to be completed or corrected by the contractor. Called a "schedule of defects" in some countries.

Purging: The process of removing airborne contamination by exhausting the contaminated air and replacing it with fresh air.

Purpose-built: A building designed for a specific type of function, such as a library.

Push plate: A protective hard surface, typically of metal, glass, or plastic, and located on a door where persons would routinely push, added so as to prevent soiling of the door finish.

Q-deck: A pattern of electrical signal ducts laid in a concrete floor slab to facilitate changing outlet locations as need shifts. A registered proprietary term of 1946.

Quarto: A volume larger than the average, typically 10–12 in. (250–300 mm) in height. See also *Book sizes.*

Raised floor system: A structural floor composed of modular liftout floor panels (commonly two feet square, though other dimensions are available), suspended on pedestals, with positive electrical grounding, leaving an under-floor plenum space for ducts, conduits, cables, etc. The floor panels can be surfaced with plastic laminate, vinyl tile, or carpet tile.

Range indicator: The label at the end of a range of shelving that gives the outer limits of the classification numbers for volumes shelved therein.

Range (shelving): A row of sections of bookcases, single- or double-faced, with uprights or shelf supports common to both sides. Called a "press" in British usage. See also *Aisle* and *Centers.*

Readers' services: The departments of a library that deal with the public directly, such as the circulation department, the reference department, and the interlibrary loan office. Photographic reproduction service is often included in this group. See also *Technical services.*

Ready-reference collection: Those few books used so heavily by the reference staff or needing the security of desk location that they are shelved at or right behind the service counter or desk and are not directly accessible to readers except upon a specific request.

Reference department: The department of a library that helps the reader use the library's resources and provides assistance in the search for information. The department usually supervises and maintains the collection of reference books that are not for circulation but for consultation in the library only.

Reflector: In lighting, the surface to one side of the light source that reflects light toward the task or the area illuminated.

Register: A grille through which air is delivered or removed from the space.

Reheat coil: A device used to increase the temperature of the air to the desired level for a specific area or room. A room thermostat would control the reheat coil where this system is used.

Reinforced concrete-block: Concrete-block construction (normally of walls) where steel reinforcing bars and concrete or grout have been inserted into the voids of the concrete blocks or between the concrete blocks or both. The resulting wall is substantially stronger than unreinforced concrete-block walls.

Rendering: Any drawing that is illustrated in detail, usually with shadows, texture, plants, furniture, people, and other details suitable for presentation. Typically, the term applies to the perspective illustration that is used to convey the merits of the design.

Reserved books: Books for assigned or collateral reading removed from their regular positions in the stacks and placed on open-reserve shelves or closed-reserve shelves. If the latter, they are available only by signing a call slip. They are sometimes withdrawn from the shelves by a stack attendant and given to the reader over a counter and sometimes selected from restricted shelves by the reader who then gives a signed call slip to the attendant before leaving the restricted area. Also may apply to books owned by faculty that are placed on *course reserves,* q.v. See also *E-reserves.*

Retention: The practice of withholding a predetermined percentage of the payment owed to any consultant or contractor until final approvals are obtained.

RFP: Refers to a "request for proposal," a form of business invitation for a vendor, consultant, or manufacturer to submit a specific performance proposal in response to a written specification of need.

RH: Common abbreviation for "relative humidity," indicating the amount of moisture in the air at a given temperature at a particular instant. Relative humidity is expressed as a percent of the total humidity that air can hold at that temperature.

Riser: The upright piece of a stair step, from tread to tread. See also *Tread.* Also refers to the vertical run of a duct or pipe system, or to a vertical telecommunications conduit or shaft used to run cabling from floor to floor.

Roller shelves: Deep shelves fitted with many small rollers constituting support for the horizontal shelving of very large volumes.

Sash: The usually wooden or metal framework in which panes of glass are set for installation in windows or doors. A double-hung window has upper and lower sashes; a casement window has a sash that opens on hinges fastened to the upright side of the frame. Fixed-sash windows do not open.

Satellite: A communication device in an orbit effectively stationary above the earth, used to transmit very high frequency radio signals within its broadcast range (termed its "footprint"). Such a satellite can service as many as 100 channels, broadcasting to small dish antennas placed on some library roofs or other locations to feed into local data transmission networks.

Scale: A standard basis for measurement. In the United States the most common scales for architects and engineers are the customary (imperial) and metric, respectively. The term "drawing to scale" means that all parts are drawn to the same precise reduced proportion of full size.

Schedule of defects: Used to refer to a *punch list,* q.v.

Schematic plans: Drawings for proposed floor layouts. They are developed for review and approval before the preliminary or design development plans. Sometimes several sets must be prepared before one is accepted.

Scupper: The opening in a parapet to allow water to run out when downspouts are clogged and thus to prevent roof failure.

Section (architectural): A drawing illustrating the graphic picture resulting from a theoretical cutting along a predetermined line, with a view through the building or object or a portion of it. The expressive French term for this type of drawing is "coupe."

Section (shelving): The compartment of a single set of shelves between uprights, usually, in the United States, 3 ft wide and 7 ft 6 in. high (0.914 × 2.286 m). A double-faced section is two sets back-to-back. A section is called a "tier" in British usage.

Security system: See *Book-detection system* and *Intrusion alarm system.*

Seismic force: see *Lateral force* and *Seismic load*

Seismic load: A horizontal load on the structure equal to a fraction of the vertical loading as established by code. This load is typically resisted through a heavy, rigid structural system or shear walls or both combined with floor membranes and other structural elements designed to transfer the load to the ground.

Self-charge: A system with which a person can check out material without staff involvement. Such systems rely upon a computer-based catalog, a machine-readable identification card, a means of identifying the item through the computer (using a bar code or chip technology), and, usually, a book-detection target that can be disarmed during the checkout process.

Seminar room: A small classroom for a course with library-intensive requirements. Such a room sometimes houses a core collection in a particular field for the convenience of advanced students and their teachers.

Sense of place: The architectural and design treatment that provides discussion areas, workstations, lounges, benches, and other places where people work, rest, or linger and may feel comfortable, "at home," and invited. As is sometimes stated, one may have a proprietary feeling of "turf," even as animals may stake out a domain that is theirs. At the workstation, the term often applies to the ability of staff to make arrangements suitable to their liking so that a sense of security or comfort is obtained.

Sensible heat: Heat that changes the temperature from one point to another. Differs from *latent heat,* q.v., which does not change the temperature of matter, but rather changes the state of matter.

Sequence of the collection: see *Shelving sequence*

Serials: Publications that are periodically issued in parts more or less regularly and are intended to continue indefinitely. These include magazines, journals, proceedings, transactions, weeklies, monthlies, annuals, newspapers, and the like. Weekly and monthly journals and magazines are termed periodicals. Serials contrast with *monographs,* q.v. Serials acquisition work may be the responsibility of an individual department within the technical services.

Server: A compact specialized computer that stores files and software to be used by other computers through the network. It provides rapid switching and efficient management of shared databases.

Service point: A separate staffed location where the clientele of the library can receive information, guidance, book service, photocopying, or other staff service.

Setout: see *Layout*

Shear walls: Structural bearing walls of sufficient size and nature to withstand lateral forces, such as earthquake tremors.

Shelflist: A file describing all volumes in the exact sequence as on the shelf, so as to constitute the basis for an inventory.

Shell of building: An enclosed structure with nothing more than absolutely minimal fire protection, electrical service, and lighting, no HVAC, and no finished surfaces. This is the minimum building that can be legally built and remain stable against the elements; it is a state sometimes used as a budget management tool.

Shelve through: In library use of double-faced shelving, this is the practice of letting a particularly deep book extend somewhat onto the shelf behind so as to keep the volume from overhanging its shelf in front.

Shelving: see *Bracket shelving, Case shelving, Commercial shelving, Movable shelving,* and *Stack*

Shelving by size: A method of sorting large collections of books into a few groups of about the same height so as to increase the volume capacity of the shelves.

Shelving sequence: The logical flow of arranged items from one section of shelving to the next, one range to another, and one floor to another. It is usually determined by the classification of books, which are deployed by class numbers on shelves in a ribbon pattern that is intended to facilitate location of any one item.

Shielded twisted pair: Two wires twisted together and covered with a conductive material providing any signal noise a path to the ground.

Shoe: The metal protection at the lowest end of the leg of a chair or table, a ferrule, protecting the bottom end from damage by cleaning machines or footwear or by dragging the furniture. The word is also used to refer to the outwardly directed portion at the bottom of a downspout.

Shop drawings: Drawings that are prepared by the manufacturers or the suppliers of special building equipment and are provided to the contractor for use in preparing its installation. They illustrate in detail the size, operation, and features of the special equipment and should be approved by the architect before fabrication and installation.

Shortlisted: The result of architects, engineers, or contractors having successfully passed the first screening of their qualifications for jobs, so they are on the short list of finalists still being considered.

Short-loan collection: Materials consisting of required or recommended reading for courses of instruction, separately shelved, and available only for short-term circulation, e.g., a few hours or overnight. Sometimes, very popular materials are also treated this way.

Signage: see *Signs*

Signal duct: The tubular passage for signal (computer, telephone, television, etc.) wires. See also *Duct* and *Q-deck*.

Sign-off: The formal process by which representatives of various responsible offices provide their signature approval. Sign-offs by the library and various institutional offices may be required for each phase of the design process as well as at the completion of construction.

Signs: The set of symbols or other visual messages visible from a distance that assist the user of a building to understand locations of functions and services, emergency directions, explanations of activities, donor recognition, and other matters of general necessity or aesthetic purpose.

Single-ply roofing: A roofing system consisting of a single ply of material. Several types of single-ply roofing systems are available for different applications.

Site: The assigned land area for a building, including such open spaces around the structure to accommodate any required setbacks.

Site development: The provision of infrastructure necessary to support the building including parking, grading, utilities, streets, planting, etc. Sometimes called site preparation, although in some cases site preparation is meant to be the work required to make the site ready for construction (in this case, site development is the construction including landscape work that follows site preparation).

Sling psychrometer: An instrument used to determine the relative humidity based upon the difference of the wet and dry bulb temperatures.

Sloip: An acronym formed from the words "space left over in planning," an architectural studio term for unintentional extra spaces.

Sloping shelves: Shelves with a tilting bed used to facilitate reading book titles and call numbers on low shelves. Infrequently used because books tend to move back and thus out of sight on the shelf and because the shelves are not useful in other locations.

Slotted shelving (as opposed to bracket shelving): Metal shelving designed for library use where the vertical elements defining the section are solid from front to back, are the same depth as the shelves, and have frequent slots into which the shelves slide for respacing. This type of shelving has a generally superior finished look, and is not uncommon in private law libraries. It is less common in academic and research libraries where *cantilever-type bracket shelving*, q.v., is typical.

Slotted shelving (divider-type): see *Divider-type shelving*

SLS: An acronym for *s*ulfur *l*ighting *s*ystem. See also *Light sources.*

Smart building: A facility having electronic control and information systems completely tied into its operation. Such a facility may include digital HVAC control (including high-humidity alerts); electronic security management; recording and intrusion alarms; safety systems; electronic environmental control, including periodic adjustment of sun shades and lights; white sound systems; clocks; automatic watering of plants; and elevators that talk to users. A smart building system (in some countries called a building monitoring system) may include PA systems, electronic sign systems (to guide egress in emergencies), a house phone system, and other electronics-based systems. The smart building also provides the capacity to support add-on and connected systems within the building through its well-developed electronic infrastructure.

Smart card: Plastic card embedded with a computer chip or surfaced with bar coding or a magnetic strip. One type is a nonreusable password card for entry control. Another type is a debit card of certain value that is decremented upon each use. See also *Machine readable.*

Soffit: The underside of an arch, a stair, a beam, or a cornice; commonly refers to the underside of a projecting roof overhang.

Solenoid switches: A system of electrical switching using low voltage such that the line power or high voltage is switched remotely. Advantages are that the low-voltage control wires do not need to be in conduit, and multiple switching points can easily be established.

Sort room: An area in or near the stack where staff can arrange materials before their being returned to the shelving so as to simplify the reshelving process.

Special collections department: The department caring for and serving the rare books, manuscripts, and other materials requiring special security and specialized services. Sometimes called "limited access," "reserve," or "treasure" collection. Sometimes includes the institution's archives.

Special conditions: That section of a bid document that explains any unusual condition that must be met by the contractor.

Specifications: Written documents in which an architect enumerates and describes the quality of the materials to be used and the level of the workmanship required.

Spine: The sewn or binding edge of a book; the back.

Spline: see *Concealed spline*

Spreader: A beam running between bookstack range columns to provide lateral stability, in lieu of "unitizing" or sway bracing.

Sprinkler system (fire): A network of pipes and overhead sprinklers designed to suppress a fire. The system is activated at individual sprinkler heads by the melting of a fusible link or triggering of a heat-sensitive device at a predetermined temperature.

Stack access: The point at which library users may or may not be checked for authorized entry to the bookshelves. Also called the "stack portal," "control point," or "stack entrance."

Stack (book): Space for the storage of books. See also *Compact storage, Freestanding stacks, Movable shelving,* and *Multitier stack.*

Stack directory: The public index sign describing the deployment for all materials housed in the bookstack.

Stack uprights: Columns that act as bookstack shelf supports and divide the stacks into sections or compartments. In a multitier stack, they carry the load on the levels above.

Staff commons: The lunchroom or lounge for employees of the library.

Stall: see *Carrel*

Standard conditions: That section of a bid document that explains conditions that must be met by the contractor in any work for that institution, such as an affirmative action employment requirement for all trades, including subcontractors.

Standards: The building trade conditions that have been adopted by the national association or local chapter and that are mandated for the construction job by brief reference in the bid document. Also refers to requirements that may be placed upon the design or construction of a project but not necessarily established by code. Most professional agencies develop and distribute standards for all kinds of issues, including preservation requirements, handicapped access, energy control, etc.

Starter: The complete basic unit of a bookstack range. Its columns or ends commonly have slots on the outside as well as inside so that one or more adder units may be attached to form a range of shelving.

Start-up: see *Activation*

Storage libraries: Three distinct types of storage arrangements for less frequently used books have developed among libraries in the United States: (1) local storage of auxiliary or secondary-access collections in buildings or parts of buildings owned by the parent institution; (2) cooperative storage in warehouse-type buildings owned jointly by several libraries, each of which retains ownership of the materials it is storing; and (3) cooperative-storage libraries, into which books are released from the individual contributing libraries and become jointly owned property. These storage libraries generally employ some form of compact storage system.

Stroboscopic effect: The flickering created by light periodically interrupted.

Strut bracing: The horizontal overhead beam connecting a bank of ranges and formed of metal bars or *hat channels,* q.v.

Stubbed out: The provision of utility lines to the point of service, with the final fixtures not in-

stalled. Similar to "roughed in." By this construction arrangement at a particular building spot, the possibility exists for adding utility service in the future—for example, for water, drainage, power, or signal.

Stud: The vertical wooden or metal column that frames a wall and supports the wallboard, gypsum board, paneling, or other wall material. A common stud wall is formed on 2-by-4s spaced 16 in. on center (400 mm), although 12-in. and 24-in. (305-mm and 610-mm) spacing are occasionally used.

Study: A fully enclosed private space for reading and research. The word is used to convey more generous and usually more acoustically isolated accommodation than enclosed carrels or dissertation rooms.

Study cabin: see *Carrel*

Subcontractor: Specialty firm (sometimes merely referred to as "sub") that has won a bid from the general contractor for part of the construction job.

Subject-divisional plan: Organization adopted by some U.S. academic libraries whereby resources and services are subdivided according to subject content of the collection. Subject-trained librarians are responsible for the technical and readers' services in typical areas, such as humanities and social sciences, physical sciences, and life sciences. Under the full subject-divisional plan, no centralized functional departments exist in the library. There are several variants of the plan; often it includes readers' services only, while the technical services are operated in a centralized fashion and there is a single public catalog.

Subject reading area: A portion of the building seating that specifically relates to a subject in the adjacent book collection or that is designated for use by scholars in a specific subject.

Suggestion box: A receptacle for receiving comments, action requests, book purchase recommendations, and complaints. Provides a visible encouragement to advising staff and offers an anonymous method if one so chooses.

Sump pump: An automatic pump to evacuate water from a low point in or under a building.

Support staff: The nonprofessional staff of a library. Sometimes called the "classified staff," it includes staff members with clerical, technical, and other skills, as well as those in unskilled positions.

Surge space: Extra space available for temporary demands. Such space may be needed during periods of renovation to house a library unit temporarily. It is also useful in accommodating momentary cataloging *arrears,* q.v.

Suspended ceiling: A nonstructural hung ceiling, usually a system, providing a finished appearance and covering ducts and pipes that may run above it. It may or may not have special acoustical properties, and may or may not integrate lighting fixtures and HVAC registers.

Swale: A shallow gully formed beside an inclined road or walk to control water runoff. In landscape design, a swale is roughly the opposite of a *berm,* q.v.

Sway bracing: The lengthwise stabilization of a section or range by use of heavy crossrods forming an **X**. Sway bracing ordinarily must occur every four to six sections in a long range.

Switch: A generic term for the type of small hardware that manages digital traffic routing and transmission, including multiplexing.

Take-off: The process of tabulating a detailed listing of each of the components in a building so as to create a meaningful cost estimate. The take-off is usually broken down into categories that involve unique trades or vendors.

Task lighting: see *Light sources*

Technical reports: Published research results, produced by laboratories in limited quantities and generally serving as timely reports of progress or as final reports under a contract requirement. They may in some instances be superseded by more formal journal publication.

Technical services: The materials processing departments of a library responsible for the planning and development of resources as well as their maintenance and bibliographic control, e.g., acquisitions, cataloging and classification, periodicals and other serials, conservation, and binding and preparing the book for the shelf (labeling, etc.). Photographic reproduction is sometimes included in technical services. See also *Readers' services.*

Telautograph: A facsimile telegraph for reproducing handwriting. The motions of the transmitting pencil are reproduced by a receiving pen controlled by electromagnetic impulses. A registered proprietary term.

Telecommunications: The electronic movement of information over distance by telephones, telex, satellites, cables, and the like. Computer data transmission relies upon a telecommunication system.

Telefacsimile (fax): The process of sending digitized information (of text, coded information, or illustrations) over computer telecommunication channels. Commonly now referred to simply as *fax,* q.v.

Tempered air: A ventilation system in which the air is moderated by heat but the warmed air is not intended to heat the space.

Tender: A term used in some countries for the legal contract covering construction projects.

Terminal: A device to access remote computer services via a telecommunication link. The word "terminal" generally implies "dumb" equipment, where there is no local storage but rather the equipment uses the data storage and processing software of a central mainframe or *server,* q.v.

Terminal reheat: see *Reheat coil*

Terrazzo: A hard flooring material made of marble or other stone chips set in mortar and then ground and polished.

Texture: The surface roughness and degree of shadow that can give a substance the appearance of being fibrous, grainy, patterned, or woven.

Thermopane: An insulating double- or triple-glazed pane for windows or doors. A registered proprietary term of 1931. Another trade name is *Twindow,* q.v., a registered proprietary term of 1946.

Thermostat: An instrument to control the temperature of a room by modulating the heating or cooling of air delivered to the space, or by modulating heating or cooling systems within the space. When display of the temperature only is required, a thermometer is the appropriate device.

Threshold: A doorsill, providing a slightly raised floor beneath the closed door to reduce drafts and water intrusion, provide a surface level with adjacent carpeting, and minimize some vandalism and security risks.

Tier: see *Multitier stack.* See also *Section (shelving)* for British usage.

Tilt-up: A construction technique where concrete walls are formed and poured flat on the floor, and subsequently tilted up into place once appropriate strength has been obtained.

Tote: An open box or bag for carrying or holding books or other such items.

Transfer case: A cardboard box typically used to house a large quantity of manuscripts.

Tread (stair): The upper, horizontal surface of a step or stairway.

Troffers: A relatively simple fluorescent light fixture with a reflector, but usually no lens.

Trolley: see *Book truck*

Truck: see *Book truck*

Turnkey: A contractual arrangement whereby one firm provides all services, including design and construction. The buyer must only "turn the key" to have a dependable, fully operational installation.

Twindow: see *Thermopane*

Two-to-one roping (elevators): A method for governing cab rate of movements. Electric traction elevators have either 2:1 or 1:1 roping. With 2:1 machines, the cab speed is only half the rope speed, whereas with 1:1 machines, the cab speed is the same as the rope speed.

Two-way radio: Radio communication carried on between two or more localities with portable equipment that permits receiving and transmitting of messages.

Typing height: The distance from the finished floor to the typewriter base surface, which is convenient for typing if one is seated. This is typically 25 to 27 in. (0.635 to 0.686 m).

Typing return: The wing on a desk that provides a special typewriter location at proper height for a person who otherwise must use the desk surface.

Ultraviolet light: Light in wavelengths from about 4,000 to about 40 angstroms, a natural part of mercury vapor lighting, fluorescent lighting, and daylight that causes chemical deterioration in book paper and cloth bindings unless specifically filtered out.

Undercut: The gap at the base of a door to permit it to clear carpeting when swung open or to allow some air passage for HVAC purposes.

Union catalog: The list of holdings in a group of libraries rather than in just one. The term is applied to the central catalog of a university library if it offers branch and independent library materials in a unified list.

Unitizing: The welding of corners in cantilever, case, or commercial shelving to provide stability. This technique can sometimes be used in addition to or in lieu of sway bracing, spreaders, or top horizontal hat channel bracing.

Upfitting: The furnishing or outfitting of spaces with movable furniture and other equipment to complete its functional needs.

Value engineering: A process of design review with the goal of achieving the best and least costly solution meeting an established set of criteria.

Vapor barrier: A thin sheet, usually of metallic foil and sheet plastic impenetrable by moisture, or liquid that hardens into a similarly impenetrable sheathing. Vapor barriers are designed to prevent passage of moisture through the structure (walls, floors, roofs) and to avoid condensation within (if properly placed relative to insulation and cold temperatures).

Verd-a-ray Fadex: A type of fluorescent light source that produces very little ultraviolet light and thus is favored where fading or damage to materials is a concern.

Vestibule: A small, enclosed antechamber or outer lobby at a building entrance, designed to control air drafts, help contain the climate inside the building, and provide protection against energy losses.

Videoconferencing: A method of having people in various remote locations hear and see and confer with each other in a group by relying on rooms equipped to send and receive video as well as audio, generally via satellite. A specialized room in some libraries.

Videodisk: A very high density flat disk storing an analog of information, frequently entertainment material, to be viewed on a laser-reading instrument with a low-resolution display screen.

Visqueen: A heavy-gauge plastic sheeting used for dust control and vapor barriers in construction projects. A registered proprietary name of 1946.

Von Duprin: The brand name of one type of exit-control door hardware that can be used for entrances and exits to heavily used public buildings, providing delayed egress, alarm input/output, and door monitoring.

Wainscot: The lower part of an interior wall faced with wood or colored differently from the upper part. Also known as "dado."

Warehouse library: See *Storage libraries*

Weeding: The practice of withdrawing books from the collection, either by discarding superfluous copies or transferring infrequently used books to storage or to other libraries.

Wet bulb temperature: The temperature determined by an accurate thermometer with a wick surrounding the sensing element containing water at room temperature that is allowed to evaporate. This temperature-measuring technique is used to determine relative humidity using, for example, a sling psychrometer.

Wet carrel: A carrel with electronic devices to enable use of film, video, or other media.

White sound: The acoustic background deliberately created and controlled to mask disturbing sounds. Also called "pink sound" or, as Keyes Metcalf would say, "acoustic perfume."

Will calls: Books that have been located and are being briefly held for patrons who requested them.

Wind lobby: see *Vestibule*

Wing: The ell on a building, often used to refer to an addition to the original structure.

Wire management: The design of various components of the facility, especially furnishings, so that devices requiring power or signal or both can be easily accommodated without an array of unsightly and confusing wires. Wire management involves care in the placement of conduits as well as cable trays, chases, outlets, and other devices needed to manage the wires safely and neatly.

Wiring closet: see *Closet, wiring*

Working capacity: The percentage of the total theoretical shelf capacity that can be occupied before the interfiling of new acquisitions in the classification causes such crowding on some shelves that books are damaged by careless users and shifts are rather frequently required by staff to interpolate new items.

Working drawings: The set of drawings that is part of the detailed contract documents used for the preparation of bids and for the erection of the building; they show site, architectural, structural, mechanical, electrical, landscape, and other information to illustrate construction details.

Workstation: A high-capacity computer terminal, usually part of a networked system. The term is often used to refer to powerful, specialized microcomputers of the type used in engineering and design applications. Note that when used as two words, a "work station" is a position at a counter, desk, or other post which is staffed to execute a work assignment.

World Wide Web (WWW): The graphically oriented portion of the *Internet,* q.v., having hypertext links.

Index

Page numbers followed by the letter *n* (e.g., 14n) refer to notes on that page. Notes to each chapter appear at the end of the chapter. *See also* the contents listings that appear at the head of individual chapters and appendixes, which are meant to serve as topical finding aids.

FE-36 fire protection system, 133, 528
fee contract, 616
fees, architect's, 84–86, 344–45
    and budget changes, 542, 567
    and construction costs, 332
    controlled by program, 108
    including mock-ups, 140
    payment schedule, 99
fees, contingency, 332
fees, professional
    construction management, 616
    consultants, 87, 347
    cost estimates of, 334
    interior designer, 346–47
    library building consultant,
        89–90, 345–46
fenestration, 831. *See also*
    Windows
fiber optics, 831
fiche, 832
field orders, 628, 832
file cabinets, 835
file server. *See* Server
file tub, 832
film collections, preservation of,
    770–71, 778
film reels, 173
filmstrip trays, 174
filmstrips, 214
filters, particulate, 597, 771–73,
    781, 785, 787–88
financial capacity, 398
financing for renovations, 48
financing strategy, 54–55, 67–68,
    329–30
fire alarms, 131
    vandalism prevention, 535
fire dampers, 529, 597, 832
fire-detection systems. *See also*
    Fire-suppression systems
    installation of, 527
    maintenance room, 318
    products-of-combustion
        system, 841
    review of, 598
fire exits. *See also* Alarmed exits
    ADA requirements, 517
    and fire risks, 527
    in stairways, 461
fire extinguishers, 360, 528–29, 796
fire hazards, 525–30, 632
    compact shelving, 195
    furnishings, 134
    multitier stacks, 148, 149
    stairwells, 175, 527
fire inspectors, approvals from,
    593

fire protection, 132–34
    in compact shelving, 193–94
    in design development review,
        566
    in project cost model, 331
    during renovation, 380
    in renovations, 377
    smoking, 284
    structural system, 524–25
Fire Protection Handbook, 193–94
fire ratings, 832
fire-risk consultants, hazards of,
    529–30
fire stop, 832
fire-suppression systems, 339–40.
    See also Fire-detection
    systems
    gas suppression systems,
        132–33
    water-based. *See* Sprinkler
        systems
fire tower, 832
Firecycle system, 133
fireplace, 264
first-aid and emergency supplies,
    796. *See also* Disaster
    supplies
    at control desk, 309, 470
    in emergency room, 318
    in mail room, 294
fixed elements, 21, 511–23. *See
    also* Doors; Ductwork;
    Mechanical room; Plumbing
    systems; Rest rooms;
    Telephone/data closets;
    Vertical transportation; Walls;
    Windows
fixed equipment in project cost
    model, 331
flashing, 832
flashlights, 796
flexibility, 13. *See also*
    Adaptability for new
    technologies
    in additions, 376
    of built-in units, 580–81
    in ceiling heights, 443
    costs of, 337
    and fixed elements, 511
    of lighting systems, 508
    and modules, 126–29
    planning for, 20–21, 24, 53–54,
        111
    program example, 678–79
    in renovations, 365–66
    in reviews, 485, 540–41, 566,
        597
    in space utilization, 356, 357

of structural system, 525
    in technical processing, 309
flip charts, 796
floating foundations, 412, 422,
    523
floor alignment. *See* Connections
    between buildings
floor area
    central-services level, 723(tab)
    reader stations, 739(tab), 741
    stacks, 732–36, 735(tab),
        741–42
    staff, 740(tab), 741
floor coverings, 337, 360, 577–78.
    See also Carpets
floor height. *See also* Ceiling
    height
    and height of building, 403
    in renovations, 366
    requirements, 20
floor level changes, 21. *See also*
    Connections between
    buildings
floor loading capacity. *See* Load-
    bearing capacity
floor-plan charts, 796–97
floor thickness. *See also* Plenum
    and ductwork, 434
    and height of building, 446
flooring, 354–55, 574–76
flooring, access, 821
floors
    in bookstacks, 148, 156
    for compact shelving, 194–95
    heat loss from, 492
    in inspection checklist, 632
    maintenance costs, 359
    mechanical room, 596
    in outline specifications, 539
    rest rooms, 523
    safety of, 536, 587
floors, glass, 166
floors, number of
    added in renovation, 378
    ideal number, 447–50
    in preliminary planning, 100
floors, raised, 142, 842. *See also*
    Flooring, access
    access for conduit, 62
    and floor coverings, 576
    in media center, 270
Florida Atlantic University, 5, 55,
    394
Florida International University,
    55, 385
Florida State University, 41
flow chart of building process,
    10(fig)